# Guide to
# Novell® NetWare® 6.0/6.5 Administration
## Enhanced Edition

Ted L. Simpson

Michael T. Simpson

THOMSON

COURSE TECHNOLOGY

Australia • Canada • Mexico • Singapore • Spain • United Kingdom • United States

THOMSON

COURSE TECHNOLOGY

**Guide to Novell® NetWare® 6.0/6.5 Administration, Enhanced Edition**
is published by Course Technology.

**Managing Editor**
William Pitkin III

**Product Manager**
Amy M. Lyon

**Developmental Editor**
Lisa M. Lord

**Production Editor**
Summer Hughes

**Technical Editor**
David Mansheffer

**Quality Assurance Testing**
Marianne Snow, Chris Scriver

**Product Marketing Manager**
Jason Sakos

**Senior Manufacturing Coordinator**
Trevor Kallop

**Associate Product Manager**
David Rivera

**Editorial Assistant**
Amanda Piantedosi

**Cover Design**
Abby Scholz

**Text Design**
GEX Publishing Services

**Compositor**
GEX Publishing Services

Disclaimer
Course Technology reserves the right revise this publication and make changes from time to time in its conte without notice.

ISBN 0-619-21543-7

BRIEF

# Contents

# TABLE OF
# Contents

# Preface

Since the 1980s, Novell has been a leader in the development of LAN technology. The requirement for secure access to resources and services across LANs and the Internet has created a need for more powerful and complex network systems, but the variety of computer operating systems and network protocols can make it difficult to access and manage company information and services from different locations. Novell has responded to this need with the NetWare 6.0 operating system, which includes an updated directory system and a variety of network services designed to bring diverse computer environments and networks together so that they can work as one network, or what Novell refers to as "OneNet." In addition, with the release of NetWare 6.5, Novell has enhanced OneNet administrative utilities and strengthened its support of open-source software standards, including Linux, Apache Web Server, MySQL, and PHP/Perl. Three new appendices cover new NetWare 6.5 features, improved security measures, and Linux support.

To be competitive and successful, companies and organizations need competent network professionals who can manage network environments. Novell instituted the Certified Novell Administrator (CNA) program to help establish credibility for network administrators who have the knowledge and skills needed to implement Novell networking services. We designed this book to provide the knowledge and build the skills you need to pass Novell's CNA exam for NetWare 6.0. This certification enables you to take advantage of the many job opportunities in the rapidly growing field of network administration. Appendix A lists the latest CNA exam objectives and maps them to the chapter and section of the book where they are covered. You can find more information on Novell certification options and testing at *http://education.novell.com*.

This book—*Guide to Novell NetWare 6.0/6.5 Administration*—is an in-depth study of configuring and managing networks using the Novell NetWare network operating system. Each chapter thoroughly explains concepts, tools, and techniques that build progressively from creating to administering a complete NetWare network.

## NetWare Versions

Several versions of NetWare are still in use today, including NetWare 4 and 5. This textbook focuses on the latest versions, NetWare 6.0 and NetWare 6.5. Because NetWare 6.0 is the version used for the CNA exam objectives, the main body of the textbook still focuses on that version. The latest version, NetWare 6.5, includes many enhancements, such as more powerful Web-based management tools, new user productivity software, more security options, and support for open-source software. These NetWare 6.5 features are covered in the three new appendices.

## Approach

We wrote this book to meet the NetWare 6.0 CNA exam objectives. As a result, the textbook examples are written using a NetWare 6.0 server with client workstations running Windows XP or Windows 2000 and Novell Client 4.83 (the most up-to-date configuration at the time of this writing). If you're working with a NetWare 6.5 server, you'll find that the Web-based tools look slightly different from the screen shots in Chapters 5, 9, 11, 13, and 14. To help you out, special captions have been added for screen shots that vary widely between NetWare 6.0 and 6.5. These captions refer you to updated screen shots shown in the appendices. If you're using a NetWare 6.0 server for the main textbook, you might want to install an evaluation copy of NetWare 6.5 to do the activities in the appendices. Appendix D includes a NetWare 6.5 installation example and activities using the new iManager utility and Novell's new Virtual Office software.

As networks become more powerful and pervasive, an organization's network requirements and application needs change constantly. We use a sample case—Cunningham, Burns, and Evans Laboratories (CBE Labs)—as the primary example in implementing NetWare 6.0. This example is reflected in many illustrations in the book. Each chapter also includes a set of hands-on projects and case projects for additional practice with NetWare. When you complete this book, you'll have the experience you need to actually administer a Novell network.

## Intended Audience

*Guide to Novell NetWare 6.0/6.5 Administration* is intended for people who are getting started in computer networking or want to prepare for the CNA certification exam. To understand the material in this book, you should have a background in basic computer concepts and have worked with applications in the Windows environment. This book is intended for use in a classroom or an instructor-led training environment with a NetWare 6.0 or 6.5 server installed as described in the classroom setup guide on the Instructor Resources CD.

## Chapter Descriptions

**Chapter 1**, "Networking Basics," introduces networks and network operating systems and explains the benefits of using NetWare 6.0 in the world of computer networking.

In **Chapter 2**, "Microcomputer Hardware," you examine the computer hardware components used to develop NetWare server specifications.

In **Chapter 3**, "Designing the Network," you examine the hardware and software components used to connect computers in a NetWare LAN and WAN. You also learn the different network topologies and examine the OSI model as it relates to data transmission.

In **Chapter 4**, "Planning the eDirectory Directory Tree," you learn more about directory services, including the components and functions of the industry-standard X.500 directory service system. You also learn the features, functions, and components of Novell's eDirectory system and how to design an eDirectory tree that meets the needs of your organization's network.

In **Chapter 5**, "Planning the Network File System," you learn how to design a network file system based on the new Novell Storage Services system and its components.

In **Chapter 6**, "Installing NetWare 6," you learn how to plan for and perform a NetWare 6.0 installation, how to work with common NetWare 6.0 console commands, and how to load and work with NetWare Loadable Modules and Novell Client software.

In **Chapter 7**, "Creating the eDirectory Tree Structure," you learn how to begin building your network by using Novell NetWare 6.0 utilities to implement the eDirectory tree structure and create network objects.

In **Chapter 8**, "Creating the Network File System," you learn how to begin building the network file system by creating file system objects, such as partitions, storage pools, volumes, and directories. In addition, you learn how to back up the file system and implement drive pointer mappings to ensure standardized access to data.

In **Chapter 9**, "Managing Users, Groups, and Login Security," you learn how to create groups, user accounts, and Organizational Role objects to give users secure access to the network. You also learn how to improve network security by setting up password restrictions, account restrictions, and intruder detection policies.

In **Chapter 10**, "Managing Trustee Assignments and File Attributes," you learn how to grant appropriate access rights to users and how to make trustee assignments to directories and files for users, groups, and containers. You also examine the Inherited Rights Filter and how it is used to selectively block inherited rights.

In **Chapter 11**, "Implementing and Managing Network Printing Services," you learn how to set up and maintain a network printing system that enables users to send output to network printers easily and reliably. You learn how to work with queue-based printing, Novell Distributed Print Services, iPrint, and the Internet Printing Protocol to plan and implement a network printing system. In addition, you learn basic troubleshooting techniques to identify and fix network printing problems.

**Chapter 12**, "Managing the User Desktop Environment," explains how to implement login scripts to meet users' access needs and how to provide a standard set of drive mappings and desktop functions. In addition, you learn how to use ZENworks to configure and manage desktop policies for users and workstations.

**Chapter 13**, "Accessing and Managing the Network with Novell's OneNet Utilities," delves into Novell's OneNet strategy of allowing information and services to be accessed and managed from any computer with Internet access. You learn how to set up and implement the new NetWare 6.0 utilities, such as iFolder, NetStorage, Remote Manager, and iMonitor, and how to use iManager to add user licenses and view license information.

**Chapter 14**, "Implementing and Securing Network Services," covers the NetWare 6.0 Internet delivery services, including Net Services and Web Services components. You learn how to implement these services and secure them from unauthorized access and attacks. You also learn how to use Novell Certificate Services, firewalls, and antivirus software to protect data and services when users are accessing information across a public network.

In **Chapter 15**, "Implementing Messaging Services," you learn the components of the Novell GroupWise messaging system and how to set up and configure GroupWise servers and clients so that you can implement e-mail services, create post office objects, and troubleshoot common e-mail problems.

**Appendix A**, "CNA Objectives," lists each CNA certification objective and supplies the chapter and section where the objective is covered in the book.

**Appendix B**, "Forms and Worksheets," contains copies of forms students can use to complete the end-of-chapter case projects.

**Appendix C**, "IP Addressing Basics," covers the fundamentals of the binary and hexadecimal numbering systems as it relates to subnetting your network.

**Appendix D**, "Upgrading to NetWare 6.5," covers NetWare 6.5's major new features, including installation, iManager 2.0, and the new Virtual Office. In addition, this appendix gives you an overview of eGuide, Snapshot backups, new Web development services, support for the new iSCSI standard, and the Nterprise Branch Office Appliance.

**Appendix E**, "NetWare 6.5 Security Enhancements," covers authentication security standards and how they are implemented in NetWare 6.5.

**Appendix F**, "Novell Services for Linux," discusses the growth of Linux and open-source standards and explains how Novell is providing support and services to meet these growing demands. In addition to learning about Novell's exciting new Linux direction, you learn the steps for installing iManager 2.0 on Linux and using Apache Manager to manage NetWare and Linux Web sites. This appendix also lists the objectives for the new Novell Certified Linux Engineer (CLE) certification.

## Features

To help you comprehend how Novell NetWare concepts and techniques are applied in real-world organizations, this book incorporates the following features:

- *Chapter Objectives*—Each chapter begins with a detailed list of the concepts and techniques to be mastered. This list gives you a quick reference to the chapter's contents and is a useful study aid.

- *End-of-Chapter Projects*—Concepts and techniques are explained in the context of a hypothetical company (CBE Labs) that casts you in the role of a network administrator. This case example is incorporated throughout the textbook, giving you practice in setting up, managing, and troubleshooting a network system as you follow along. The end-of-chapter projects give you a strong foundation for carrying out network administration tasks in the real world. Because of the book's progressive nature, completing these projects in each chapter is essential before moving on to projects in subsequent chapters.

- *Chapter Summary*—Each chapter summarizes its important concepts in an easy-to-browse bulleted list. These summaries are a helpful way to recap and revisit the ideas covered in each chapter.

- *Key Terms*—All terms introduced with boldfaced text are gathered into the Key Terms list at the end of the chapter, giving you a quick way to check your understanding of new terms.

- *Review Questions*—The end-of-chapter assessment begins with a set of review questions that reinforce the ideas introduced in each chapter. Answering these questions ensures that you have mastered the important concepts. The review questions can also be used to help prepare for the CNA exam.

- *Case Projects*—At the end of each chapter, you have the opportunity to reinforce and creatively apply the chapter's concepts and techniques by building a network system for another organization.

## Text and Graphic Conventions

Additional information and exercises have been added to this book to help you better understand what's being discussed in the chapter. Icons throughout the text alert you to these additional materials:

 Tips offer extra information on resources, explain how to attack problems, and describe time-saving shortcuts.

 Notes present additional helpful material related to the subject being discussed.

 The Caution icon identifies important information about potential mistakes or hazards.

 Each Hands-on Project in this book is preceded by this icon. Complete these projects to continue the process of building your own version of the CBE Labs network.

Case Project icons mark the end-of-chapter projects, which are scenario-based assignments for independently applying what you have learned in the chapter.

## Instructor's Resources

The following supplemental materials are available when this book is used in a classroom setting. All supplements available with this book are provided to the instructor on a single CD-ROM.

- *Electronic Instructor's Manual*—The Instructor's Manual that accompanies this text-book includes extra instructional material to assist in class preparation, including suggestions for classroom activities, discussion topics, and additional projects.

- *Solutions*—Answer keys provide solutions to all end-of-chapter material, including review questions and, when applicable, Hands-on and Case Projects.

- *ExamView®*—This textbook is accompanied by ExamView, a powerful testing soft-ware package that enables instructors to create and administer printed, computer (LAN-based), and Internet exams. ExamView includes hundreds of questions cor-responding to the topics covered in this book so that students can generate detailed study guides with page references for further review. The computer-based and Internet-testing components allow students to take exams at their computers, and they save the instructor time by grading each exam automatically.

- *PowerPoint presentations*—This book comes with Microsoft PowerPoint slides for each chapter. They are included as a teaching aid for classroom presentation, to make available to students on the network for chapter review, or to be printed for class-room distribution. Instructors, please feel free to add your own slides for additional topics you introduce to the class.

- *Figure files*—All figures in the book are reproduced on the Instructor's Resources CD in bitmapped format. Similar to the PowerPoint presentations, they are included as a teaching aid for classroom presentation, to make available to students for review, or to be printed for classroom distribution.

## COURSEPREP TEST PREPARATION SOFTWARE

The CD included with this book contains CoursePrep test preparation software for the Novell CNA 050-677 exam. This CoursePrep software provides 50 sample exam questions that mirror the look and feel of the CNA 050-677 exam. For more information about MeasureUp test prep products, or to order the complete version of this software, visit the Web site at *http://www.measureup.com*.

# ACKNOWLEDGEMENTS

Although we have spent many hours updating this book to NetWare 6.0/6.5 and Windows 2000/XP, it would never have been completed without the help of Course Technology management and staff, especially Amy Lyon, who directed and managed the project, and Will Pitkin, for his vision for the book and his persistence at working with Novell to obtain the latest information. We want to express our many thanks to our excellent editor, Lisa Lord, whose patient help and hard work, along with her mastery of technical jargon (also known as GeekSpeak) and the English language, brought life to the words in these chapters. We also want to thank our excellent technical editor, David Mansheffer, who contributed so much to the technical content and applicability of the chapters and appendices. Credit for identifying technical problems with the projects goes to Marianne Snow and Chris Scriver, who did an excellent job of checking each step of all projects. No book can be complete without all the work required to get it ready for printing, and we feel fortunate to have had such an excellent production editor as Summer Hughes to make sure this book was ready for publication. We take our hats off to the excellent reviewers—Dr. Marjorie Deutsch of Queensborough College, Steve Ofusu Agyei-Mensah of Clarion College, and Cynthia Mason-Posey of Prince Georges Community College—for their consistent hard work ensuring that the content and projects would meet the practical demands of teaching NetWare 6.0 concepts in the classroom environment.

**Ted Simpson:** I want to thank my wife, Mary, who made many alterations in our schedule and helped me through the sometimes daunting challenges of meeting the ever-changing schedules and requirements that go with writing a book. I would also like to say that I feel very lucky to have been part of a great Course Technology writing team. Thanks, Amy, for being such an understanding leader and excellent motivator. Thank you, Lisa, for being not only a great editor, but also a friend and partner. Last but not least, thank you, Mike, for being such a good co-author; I look forward to working with you again in the future. In addition to students who are pursuing the challenging field of computer networking, I want to dedicate my writing efforts to my mother, Rosemarie (Ode), who although she's not a technical type, has a great depth of knowledge and wisdom about life and work.

**Mike Simpson:** Special thanks to my literary agent, Neil J. Salkind; the folks at Studio B, who have kept me busy from day one; and Lisa Lord, who was much more than a great editor, but also a mentor. Thanks to Amy Lyon, who led the team of players needed to produce this book in a manner that welcomed suggestions and allowed creativity to flourish. I want to dedicate this book to my wife, Claudia, who ran MTS Consulting, Inc., while I spent hours sitting in front of NetWare servers and computer monitors writing this book.

# Read This Before You Begin

To do the end-of-chapter projects, you will be assigned to a NetWare classroom server and given a student reference number (an Admin user name preceded by your student number) and a data directory identified with your student number. Your user name will have the necessary privileges to build your own network system by creating and managing network objects, such as users, groups, printers, and files, without affecting other students' use of the server. Your assigned data directory is the work area on the classroom server where you have been given all rights to create and manage files and directories so that you can complete the projects. If you'll be doing the projects on your own computer network, you need a computer to use as the NetWare server; then install an evaluation copy of NetWare 6.0 or NetWare 6.5 on your server as described in the classroom setup instructions available in the Instructor's Resources and on the Course Technology Web site, *www.course.com*. You can also use VMWare to run the NetWare 6.0 or 6.5 server along with the client on your desktop. For more information on VMWare, visit its Web site at *www.vmware.com*.

## Minimum Lab Requirements

### Hardware:

- Each student workstation requires at least 128 MB of RAM, an Intel Pentium or compatible processor running at 166 MHz or higher, and a minimum of 512 MB of free space on the hard disk. A CD-ROM drive is also important for loading software and performing certain activities. If you're using VMWare, each student workstation needs 500 MB RAM, a Pentium II processor running at 700 MHz minimum, and 2 GB free space on the hard drive.

- To use NetWare 6.0, you need a classroom server with at least 512 MB of RAM, an Intel Pentium II or higher processor running at 500 MHz or higher (Intel Pentium III 700 MHz recommended), a minimum 8 GB hard drive (4 GB for the NetWare SYS volume and at least 500 MB for each student), a CD-ROM drive, a Super VGA or higher resolution display adapter and monitor, and a mouse.

- To use NetWare 6.5, you need a classroom server with at least 1 GB of RAM, an Intel Pentium III or higher processor running at 700 MHz or higher (Intel Pentium 4 1.2 GHz recommended), a minimum 8 GB hard drive (6 GB for the SYS volume and at least 500 MB for each student), a CD-ROM drive, a Super VGA or higher resolution display adapter and monitor, and a mouse.

## Software:

- *Windows XP Professional or Windows 2000 Professional (Windows XP recommended)* for each student workstation.

- *A copy of the Novell NetWare 6.0 or 6.5 operating system for the server.*

- *Licenses for each student account*—NetWare 6.0/6.5 uses a new licensing system called User Access Licensing (UAL) that assigns a license to each user account when the user logs in. UAL requires multiple licenses for each student because he or she will be creating multiple users. So if you're using UAL, you should plan on each student needing at least four licenses. If all licenses in the UAL are used, you can use iManager to revoke user account licenses to make more connections available. Another option is contacting Novell about obtaining an educational license. Educational licenses do not assign a license unit to each user, but allow multiple users to share a single license unit by releasing the license unit each time a user logs out. When using an educational license, only one license unit is needed for each student.

- *ZENworks for Desktops version 3.2 or higher*—You can download an evaluation version of ZENworks for Desktops by visiting *www.novell.com/products/ zenworks*.

- *Latest support pack for NetWare 6.0*—At the time of this writing, you can download the latest support pack (nw6sp3) from *http://support.novell.com*. Select the Product Updates option, and under the Product Categories section, click on the applicable NetWare product to display a list of NetWare-related products. Click NetWare 6 to see a list of products and fixes. You can then select and download the support pack. Note that support packs are quite large and should be downloaded with a high-speed Internet connection.

- *GroupWise 6*—Chapter 15 requires installing GroupWise on the classroom server. You can download a three-user GroupWise 6 evaluation version from *www.novell.com/products/groupwise*.

- (Optional) *An evaluation copy of the Novell NetWare 6.5 operating system for the appendix activities.*

- (Optional) *VMWare licenses for each student workstation (www.vmware.com).*

# 1

# NETWORKING BASICS

**After reading this chapter and completing the exercises, you will be able to:**

♦ Explain network types (including LANs, WANs, and MANs) and features

♦ Identify and describe the hardware and software components that make up a local area network

♦ Develop a recommendation for implementing a local area network system

♦ Describe the responsibilities of a Certified Novell Administrator

The 1990s brought a major change in the way organizations processed data. Traditional centralized data processing on minicomputers and mainframe computers gave way to more personalized applications and productivity tools running on desktop and notebook-sized microcomputers. Along with the rapid development of microcomputer hardware and application software has come the ability to connect these devices and applications so that resources can be communicated and shared. This rapid pace of development continues today as the Internet ties local systems into a global network. In this chapter, you learn about computer network types and how they are applied to various situations. You also learn how Novell's networking products can be used to help meet the requirements and challenges of integrating microcomputers into a network, which can facilitate communications, share resources, and exchange data locally and across the Internet. Finally, you explore the role you will play as a network administrator and learn about the Certified Novell Administrator (CNA) program.

## COMPUTER NETWORKS

A **computer network** consists of two or more connected computers that can communicate with each other. A computer network that exists in one location, such as a building, is called a **local area network (LAN)**. **Metropolitan area networks (MANs)** use fiber-optic or microwave towers to connect computers in the same geographical area, such as within a city or county. Tying together two or more LANs or MANs in different geographic locations creates a **wide area network (WAN)**. WANs use carriers such as the phone system to connect computers over long distances, including across the country or even around the world. Figure 1-1 illustrates how LANs and WANs can be interconnected to form large networks.

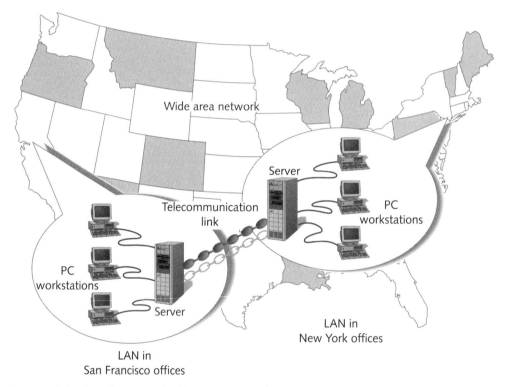

**Figure 1-1**    Local area and wide area networks

Do not confuse LANs and WANs with the global Internet or with corporate intranets. Although all are networks that link personal computers and servers, the **Internet** is a loose confederation of servers that share data among millions of users worldwide, using a common suite of protocols called TCP/IP. Protocol suites are the rules and procedures that govern sending and receiving information across networks. Because the TCP/IP protocol suite is not controlled by any one company, but is managed by committees, it is designed to allow different types of computers to exchange information across many different networks.

LANs, however, are tightly controlled, are usually limited to one company (as are private WANs), and can use protocols other than TCP/IP. **Intranets** are private networks that use the same protocol as the Internet to offer access to internal information. Intranets can be set up on both LANs and WANs, and who can access the network is usually tightly controlled. Although this book focuses on implementing NetWare on LANs, NetWare 6 offers many new network services for using the Internet to access network information and resources.

The **network administrator** is responsible for the network. The role of a network administrator is one of the most exciting, challenging, and important jobs in an organization's information systems department. However, it can also be one of the most frustrating because the field changes rapidly and the job involves many different responsibilities. These responsibilities range from hardware (computers and cables) to software (operating systems and applications) to working with people (users and vendors). Therefore, to be a successful network administrator, you need to thoroughly understand the basic components of a network system. From this foundation, you can build the skills you'll need to perform your job. In this section, you learn about the basic LAN components and some options to consider when deciding how to construct a LAN.

A LAN is more completely defined as a high-speed communication system of cables and communication devices (hardware) and instructions (software) that make it possible for different types of computers and peripherals to communicate and share resources over short distances, such as within a building or room. As illustrated in Figure 1-2, LANs differ significantly from older mainframe computers and minicomputers. In the older centralized system, the **mainframe computer** or **minicomputer** running the programs does all the processing. The users' computers are **terminals**, used simply as input and output devices for entering data and displaying results, without any computing power of their own. This setup is called **centralized processing** because all processing is done by the computer connected to the terminals.

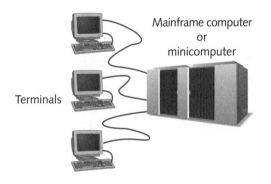
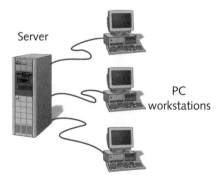

**Centralized processing**
•Terminals have no processing capability
•All processing done on mainframe computer or minicomputer

**Distributed processing**
•PC workstations have their own processing capability
•Processing done on PC workstations

**Figure 1-2**   Centralized processing and distributed processing

A LAN provides a high-speed communication system that allows **client workstations** (also called personal computers or PCs), each with its own computing ability, to work together and share resources. In LANs, processing can be done at the client workstations *and* the central computer; this setup is described as using **distributed processing**. LANs also use servers, which are specialized computers that make network resources and services available to workstations. Multiple servers providing varied services are found on many networks. Most common is a network **file server**, commonly called a "server," which provides file services for making data and application software available to users. Servers run a variety of other services, including print and application services. A print service allows users to share printers. An application service is used with **client–server applications**, such as database systems, that split the processing between the server and the workstations. In this situation, the server hosting the application service runs the server portion of the application, and the client portion runs on users' workstations. **Terminal services**, another special type of service becoming more common, perform centralized processing on a LAN by running applications on the server hosting the terminal service and using workstations as graphical input/output devices.

 The term "NetWare file server" was used in NetWare 3.x documentation. In NetWare 4.1 and later versions, the term is "NetWare server."

Since the beginning of microcomputer-based business systems in the early 1980s, Novell has been a leader in LAN technology. Earlier versions of Novell NetWare excelled at offering rapid, secure access to file and print resources to a variety of locally attached computers. Today, Novell is developing products that help make the Internet's many diverse network systems work as a single network. Novell uses the term **OneNet** to describe its strategy of developing products and services that make diverse networks separated by MANs and WANs act as a single network. Novell's OneNet strategy is to simplify the complexities of managing and accessing networks and to accelerate an organization's ability to implement Internet applications by providing the tools and solutions that work across different network environments. Although the NetWare 6 network operating system is a key part of Novell's OneNet strategy, Novell offers other products and services, such as eDirectory, ZENworks, iFolder, and iPrint, that can run on a number of network operating systems, including Windows NT, Windows 2000, and Linux. (Chapter 13 covers several of Novell's OneNet utilities, such as iFolder and Novell NetStorage.) By running on a variety of operating systems, these services and products are essential in making networks of diverse systems work together as OneNet. In this chapter and throughout the book, you learn more about the OneNet strategy and how it can be applied to an organization's network.

# Local Area Network Advantages

Although standalone computers not connected by a network can perform distributed processing, a LAN offers many advantages in sharing resources and improving communications. These advantages make distributed processing a strong competitor with centralized minicomputer and mainframe computer systems, the traditional way to share resources and communicate. As a network administrator recommending a network system, you need to be aware of the following LAN advantages.

## Cost Savings

One important benefit of a LAN is cost savings, and management is always happy to hear how network administrators can save money for the organization. By sharing and working with data in a group, a LAN offers the most direct cost savings. For example, e-mail and workflow software offer huge cost savings over distributing paper copies of information. Costs can also be saved in hardware and software; for example, several workstations can share one high-quality printer, and an application package that requires 1 GB of disk space can be run from the server rather than installed on many individual workstations. Because network systems provide a flexible backbone for a growing number of services, businesses can adapt them to meet new challenges.

## Time Savings

A less tangible but perhaps even more important advantage of networks is the time saved by giving users access to shared data and communication capabilities. Without a LAN, users must resort to a "sneaker net," in which shared files are copied onto a floppy disk and physically transferred to another user's computer workstation by being carried on foot (wearing sneakers!) and copied to another hard drive.

Another timesaving benefit of LANs is that they enable network administrators to install and maintain a software package on a server, a computer dedicated to storing commonly used program and data files, where it's accessible to all users. This setup is often preferable to installing the package on each user's workstation and spending more time configuring software or installing upgraded versions on each workstation.

## Centralized Data

Without a network, crucial and often used data files, such as customer and inventory files, might need to be duplicated on several workstations, which uses too much data storage and makes it difficult to keep all files current. By storing database files on the network server, information can be kept current yet still be available for users to access. Providing shared access to centralized database files makes LANs a competitive alternative to centralized processing.

A network server used for centralized data storage also makes regular backups of data easier, which helps establish a disaster recovery system for the organization. Data stored on users' workstations is rarely backed up, making it difficult to recover lost data if a workstation crashes or the building or equipment is physically damaged. By keeping all the critical data on the network server, you can back it up every night, if needed. Each week you can store a backup tape offsite, and use this tape to recover data if the building is damaged. If a disaster occurs, you can restore software and data onto a new server and get the organization up and running again quickly. The alternative is to back up the data on each workstation and restore each workstation's software and data after a disaster, which is more time consuming.

## Security

At first glance, centralizing company data on a network server might seem to cause more security problems than it solves because more users have potential access to the data. With NetWare servers, however, you can make data more secure on the server than on local workstations. NetWare supplies many security features, such as requiring passwords to gain access to the network and restricting user access to network files. In addition, user accounts can be limited to specific access times (such as during normal working hours) and specific workstations, making it difficult for an intruder to gain access to the system by logging in with a user name and password after normal office hours. Compare those security advantages to the alternative of storing data on a local workstation. With data on an individual workstation, anyone with a little knowledge of PC operating systems and physical access to the office can sit down at the computer and access applications and data.

## Fault Tolerance

Storing data on individual workstations increases the chance of data loss caused by operator error, software bugs, computer viruses, or hardware failure. Data stored on network servers can be placed on microcomputers that are designed and configured to protect against data loss from software or hardware problems. This capability is called fault tolerance. With a NetWare server, for example, the data stored on a disk drive can be protected by mirroring, a process that uses two identical disk drives linked to the same controller board so that all files on one disk drive are automatically duplicated on the second disk drive. If one drive fails, the data is still accessible on the second drive. A potential weakness in mirroring is the dependency on a single controller card. Should the controller card fail, both drives become inaccessible. Mirroring can also cause slightly longer disk update times because the data needs to be written twice, once to each drive. **Duplexing** also involves duplicating data on two drives, except that each drive is on a separate controller board instead of depending on only one controller board, as is the case with mirroring. Duplexing improves fault tolerance because the disk drive can still operate even if one of the controller cards fails. It also provides faster performance than mirroring because with two controller boards, data can be written to both drives simultaneously.

Many servers today use redundant arrays of independent disks (RAID) devices for hardware-based fault tolerance. RAID storage devices distribute data and control information over three or more disk drives to provide data redundancy. If one of the

1

disk drives in the RAID set fails, the RAID system can automatically reconstruct the missing information from control data stored on the remaining disks. You will learn more about RAID disk systems in Chapter 2.

## Communication

The high-speed communication between network computers in a LAN creates opportunities for major changes in office management. For example, workgroup-oriented applications, such as e-mail and scheduling, are commonly used on LANs. With **e-mail applications**, users can send messages and files directly to other users on the LAN. Many users feel that e-mail is quicker and more effective than voicemail, particularly in contrast to playing "phone tag" with hard-to-reach people. **Scheduling applications** let individuals and groups store their schedules on the server, where other users (with appropriate permissions) can access them. This saves time by allowing managers to check the schedules of people and facilities quickly and to find free time in which to schedule meetings.

A LAN can also be used to provide Internet access to all computers in the organization through a centralized router and firewall. Connecting a LAN to the Internet through a router increases security by requiring all communication to pass through a firewall, which can be programmed to filter out potential attacks. In Chapter 14, you'll learn how routers and firewalls can help secure your network from outside intruders.

 Network communication systems are rapidly incorporating support for new applications that use video and voice data. Video conferencing and computers integrated with telephone systems, which are beginning to be widely used, enable members of a conference to see data as it's being presented as well as the reactions of other members.

Additional advantages and conveniences of LANs are too numerous to include in this chapter. Examining the major advantages, however, makes it clear why the use of LANs has been growing at such a fast pace.

## NETWORK COMPONENTS

As a network administrator, you need to be familiar with the hardware and software components that make up networks so that you can select, implement, and maintain a network system that meets your organization's communication and processing needs. This section introduces the major components and services that make up a LAN and explains how they are applied in an organization's network.

As illustrated in Figure 1–3, computer networks consist of three major types of components:

- The computer hardware and cable system
- Protocol software suites to control the communication process
- Software for accessing network resources and services

In a LAN, computer hardware typically consists of client computers, servers, and shared resources, such as printers and volumes. Software consists of the network operating system and services for providing network resources that client computers can access. Communication protocols suites, such as TCP/IP, provide the rules and software that control data formatting and transmission. The following sections introduce you to these network components and explain how they are applied in an organization.

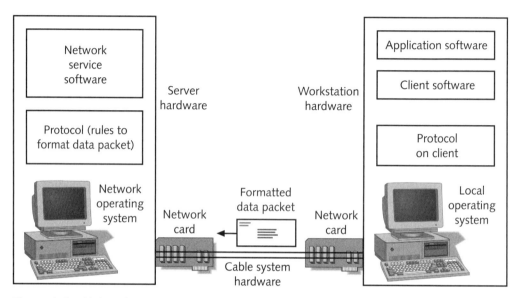

**Figure 1-3**   Network components

## Network Hardware Components

Hardware components are the most obvious parts of a network system to identify because they can be easily seen. The hardware components of a typical network are shown in Figure 1-4.

This section introduces you to a network system's hardware components; Chapters 2 and 3 give you an in-depth view of microcomputer hardware components and the network cable system as well as options for selecting and maintaining computers on the network.

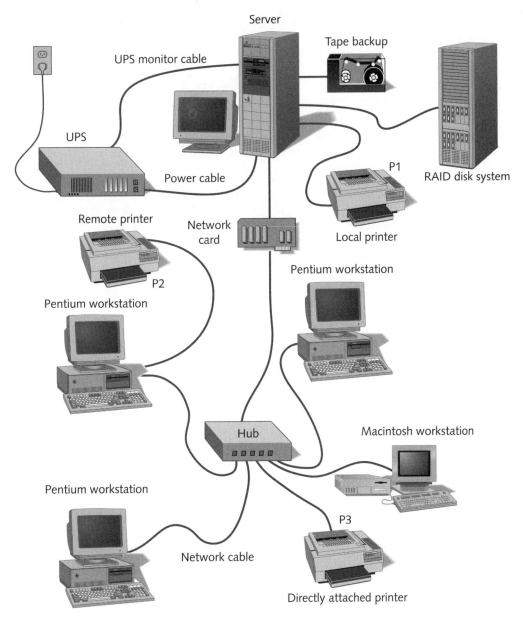

**Figure 1-4**   Sample network hardware components

## The Server

The first stop on your tour of the network hardware is the network server, called a "NetWare server" in NetWare networks. Many who are familiar with minicomputers and mainframe computers tend to think of the server in terms of network control. In a LAN, however, a server is actually a servant of the network, responding to workstations' requests for access to files and software stored on the server's disk system. With the exception of its disk system and typically large memory capacity, a server is similar to the client workstations on the network. Some servers are **nondedicated**, meaning that they can function as a user's workstation in addition to providing access to shared areas of the disk system. The server in Figure 1-4 is **dedicated**, meaning it cannot be used as a workstation. This ensures better performance and eliminates the possibility of a user shutting down or restarting the server while others are still accessing it. To prevent unauthorized access to the server's hardware and software, most network administrators keep servers in separate rooms that can be secured.

The server shown in Figure 1-4 is a PC specifically designed to be a server (many vendors offer PCs designed for use as servers); it has an Intel 1.2 GHz Pentium III processor with 1 GB of memory and a high-capacity 80 GB RAID disk storage system. The RAID storage system provides fault tolerance at the hardware level so that if one drive fails, the server can continue to provide information services by using data from the other drives until the failed drive is replaced.

## Client Workstation

Generally, each computer attached to the network for running user applications is called a client workstation, which is where the actual processing of user software applications occurs. Adding memory or a faster processor to the server does not directly increase the speed of programs run on client workstations. To increase user application performance, you must upgrade the client workstation. The client workstation's processing power often equals or exceeds the server's speed. In the sample network in Figure 1-4, the server contains a 1.2 GHz Pentium processor with lots of memory and disk space and a standard-resolution VGA monitor. The Windows workstations contain 1.5 GHz Pentium processors with 512 MB of memory, 20 GB of disk storage, and high-resolution color monitors. Because most files and software will be kept on the network server, the client workstations can focus on processing speed and graphics resolution rather than on high-capacity disk storage.

On networks requiring file and print services, the server is specialized to provide high-speed disk access, whereas the client workstations require fast processors and high-resolution graphics. On networks using client-server applications, the server needs to run the server portion of the application, so it must be specialized to handle the application processing.

## Network Interface Card

A **network interface card (NIC)** is installed in each computer attached to the network, including the servers. NICs can be wireless or attached to a cable system. As wireless standards and technology have improved, more organizations are implementing wireless NICs, especially for laptop computers or in rooms that do not have adequate cabling. The NIC, used to attach the computer to the network system, is responsible for transmitting and receiving data packets on the network. A **packet** consists of hundreds to several thousand bytes of formatted data, framed with control bits identifying its address and the address of the computer the packet is being sent to. When it's manufactured, each NIC is assigned a unique address or serial number. The NIC listens to the network and accepts any packets that contain its address. It then notifies the host computer that it has received a packet and, if no errors are detected in the packet, sends the packet to the operating system software for processing. When transmitting data, the network operating system sends a block of data to the NIC, which then waits for the network system to become available. When no other computers are using the network system, the NIC transmits the packet. In Chapter 3, you'll learn more about different types of NICs and cable systems.

## Cable System

A network's cable system is the highway through which information travels from one computer to another. A **cable system** consists of the wiring that connects the computers in the network. Just as getting onto a highway requires obeying certain traffic laws, sending information through the network requires each computer to follow a set of access rules. And in the same way that gridlock can slow down or stop traffic on a highway, a network can also experience bottlenecks when the amount of information exceeds the cable system's transmission capacity. One responsibility you'll have as a network administrator is monitoring the network cable system for errors or performance bottlenecks. The cable system in the sample network consists of twisted-pair cable, similar to the cable that connects your telephone's handset to its base unit. In Chapter 3, you'll learn about the different types of cable systems and access methods commonly used in LANs. In the sample network in Figure 1-4, twisted-pair cable runs from each computer in the network to a central connection box called a **hub** or switch, giving all computers equal access to the network system.

A switch is a special type of hub that can direct packets of data out a specific port based on its destination computer, instead of sending the packet out all ports, as with a hub. You'll learn more about hubs and switches in Chapter 3.

## Uninterruptible Power Supply

The box to the left of the server in Figure 1-4 is an uninterruptible power supply (UPS). The UPS contains batteries that supply temporary power to the server if the local power system fails. This piece of equipment is important for the server because it prevents data loss in a power outage or brownout.

Because a power outage that occurs while many users are accessing the server is likely to result in lost data, do not even consider running a server without a UPS. When a UPS unit is not attached to the server, power interruptions could require restoring data from a backup tape to restart the server.

The UPS in Figure 1-4 has an optional monitor cable that connects to a port on the server. This connection informs the server when the UPS is using battery power. This connection is also important in an extended power outage because it allows the server to close all files and take itself offline automatically before exhausting the UPS batteries.

## Tape Backup

The tape backup system shown in Figure 1-4 consists of a digital audio tape (DAT) cartridge tape drive that can use Novell's Storage Management System (SMS) software or a third-party software package, such as ArcServe, Legato, or Veritas, to back up all data on the server automatically every night. At 1 A.M. each weekday morning, the tape backup software in the sample network copies all data to the tape cartridge. The network administrator then places the tape in the organization's fireproof vault for safe storage. A rotation system using several tapes allows each backup to be kept for at least one week, and one day's backup tape (for example, the tape made on Fridays) is stored off site in case of a disaster that wipes out the entire site. In Chapter 8, you'll learn more about developing a backup and recovery system for your server environment.

## Network Printers

Sharing printers on the network is an important advantage of a LAN. Each client workstation can send output to any network printer by directing the printed output to the print server to be stored in a special directory called a print queue. After a workstation has finished printing, the server directs the printout to the selected printer with special print server software. Printers can be attached and shared on the network in three different ways: as local printers, as remote printers, and as directly attached printers.

Notice that printer P1 in Figure 1-4's network is attached to the server. This makes it a local printer because it is attached to the server's local printer port. Local printers have the advantages of working at high speeds and reducing network traffic, but have the disadvantage of limiting the locations in which they can be placed.

Printer P2, attached to a user workstation, is controlled by the print server software, which enables users on any client workstation to send output through the server to printer P2. Printer P2 is referred to as a remote printer because it's not directly attached to a printer port on the server. Remote printers can be located anywhere on the network there is a workstation. However, performance problems and software conflicts with the workstation can occur when large print jobs are processed.

Printer P3 is a directly attached printer, which has its own network card and is connected directly to the network cable system. This direct connection offers the benefit of independence from a workstation without the loss of speed associated with a remote printer. For the highest possible performance, most network administrators attach high-speed printers directly to the network cable system. You'll learn more about NetWare printing and the NDPS print system in Chapter 11.

# Network Protocols or Rules

The network system's **protocol** defines the rules for formatting packets of data transmitted on the network cable system. The software used to implement a protocol is called the **protocol stack**. Although network cards are responsible for delivering data packets throughout the network system, the functions of the protocol stack include routing packets between different networks, verifying delivery, and requesting network services. Certain protocol stacks, such as IBM's Synchronous Data Link Control (SDLC), NetBEUI, and IPX/SPX, are called proprietary protocols because they are owned and controlled by a specific company. Other protocols, such as TCP/IP, are nonproprietary and controlled by an industry organization consisting of vendors and users.

Because today's networks often need to support multiple protocol stacks for computers to communicate and access services using different operating systems, NetWare 6 is designed for multiple protocols. The NetWare 6 server shown in Figure 1-4, for example, supports TCP/IP and IPX/SPX. TCP/IP is needed to access the Internet and use Novell's OneNet services; Novell's proprietary IPX/SPX protocol stack is needed to support certain NetWare applications and older clients. In the following sections, you learn about each protocol stack and its advantages and disadvantages.

## NetWare SPX/IPX

The SPX/IPX protocol suite is the Novell proprietary system that manages routing and formatting NetWare packets on the network. To communicate, Internetwork Packet eXchange (IPX) must be loaded on each network client and server. Each client and server must also have network card driver software (described in the "Network Software Components" section later in this chapter) loaded to transmit the packets. IPX and the network card driver are brought together during client installation with a process called **binding**.

> Now that NetWare version 5 and 6 support TCP/IP as a primary protocol, most organizations are moving away from SPX/IPX to avoid supporting multiple protocols.

NetWare uses two other protocols to provide network services: Sequential Packet eXchange (SPX) and **NetWare Core Protocol (NCP)**. SPX, used by some client software to ensure successful delivery of packets, works by using special control and acknowledgement packets from the receiver that inform the sender if any data needs to be retransmitted. NCP is the language applications use to access services on NetWare servers through the client software running on the workstation. Currently, Novell provides a client designed to take advantage of all the services available by using NCP.

## The TCP/IP Protocol

The **Transmission Control Protocol/Internet Protocol (TCP/IP)** was first developed in the 1960s to support communication among mainframe computers in government agencies and educational institutions. Like SPX/IPX, TCP/IP is responsible for formatting packets and routing them between networks by using IP. IP is more sophisticated than IPX in fragmenting packets and routing them over WAN links, such as those used when connecting to the Internet. The TCP/IP specifications were developed and are still maintained by an independent agency, the Internet Access Board (IAB). Because TCP/IP was developed to connect a large number of independent organizations, it was designed to support communications between diverse computers and operating systems. TCP/IP consists of four major layers for transmitting and receiving data, as shown in Figure 1-5.

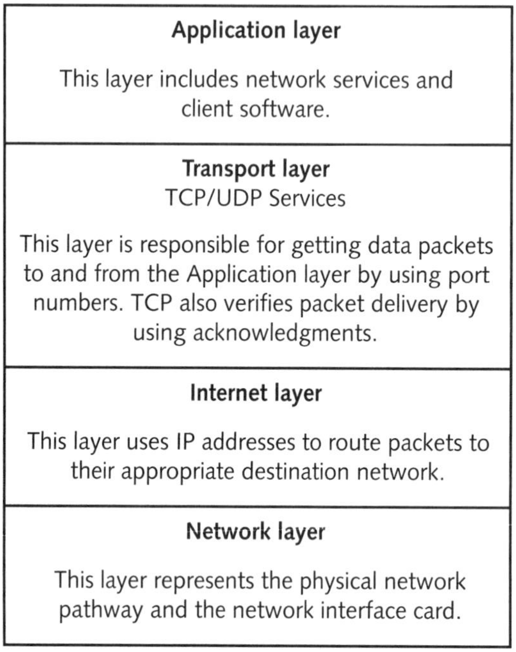

| **Application layer** |
| :---: |
| This layer includes network services and client software. |

| **Transport layer** |
| :---: |
| TCP/UDP Services |
| This layer is responsible for getting data packets to and from the Application layer by using port numbers. TCP also verifies packet delivery by using acknowledgments. |

| **Internet layer** |
| :---: |
| This layer uses IP addresses to route packets to their appropriate destination network. |

| **Network layer** |
| :---: |
| This layer represents the physical network pathway and the network interface card. |

**Figure 1-5**   TCP/IP layers

Moving from the bottom up in Figure 1-5, the Network layer provides the communication pathway consisting of network cards and drivers. The Internet layer, or IP, is responsible for routing packets between networks. The Transport layer consists of both the TCP and User Datagram Protocol (UDP) services and is used to handle packet flow between systems. Both transport services use port numbers to identify the sending and receiving applications. For example, a Web server typically uses port 80, but the FTP server defaults to port 21. UDP performs the basic service of a messenger by delivering packets to the correct application based on the port number. When using UDP, the

**1**

sender is never notified whether the packet has been successfully delivered. The TCP transport service guarantees the delivery of packets by sending and receiving acknowledgments. With this system, the sender and receiver can establish a window for the number of packets to be acknowledged. The windowing capability offers better performance than WANs do because each packet does not need to be individually acknowledged before another packet is sent. The Application layer represents a network service, such as a Web server or an FTP server, that processes client requests and returns information via the Transport and Network layers.

 Because of the popularity of the TCP/IP protocol stack for LANs and WANs, starting with NetWare 5, Novell has added the capability to use only TCP/IP for its network clients and services. Older versions of NetWare required administrators to support IPX for access to NetWare servers and TCP/IP for Internet access. By eliminating IPX, network administration and support is simplified and more efficient.

In TCP/IP, each computer attached to a network is called a **host** and is assigned a unique address. Routers connect independent networks and transfer packets from one network to another by using an IP network address, which enables packets to be sent over different routes and then reassembled in the correct sequence at the receiving station. IP addresses consist of 32-bit binary numbers, expressed in **dotted decimal notation** as 4 bytes separated by periods. Each IP address in dotted decimal notation contains network and host components, as illustrated in Figure 1-6.

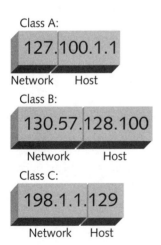

**Figure 1-6** Sample IP addresses

The network component identifies the network cable system and is the same for all computers on the same network. The host component represents a device attached to the network and must be unique for each network entity on the cable system. Notice how the dotted decimal addresses are divided into three major classes. In a Class A address, the first number represents the network cable and the last three numbers represent devices or computers attached to the network. In a Class B network, the address is split in half, with the first two numbers identifying the network and the last two numbers representing the hosts. Class C addresses are intended for smaller networks, with only one number reserved for the host computers. Setting up and working with IP addresses is an essential part of network administration. In Chapter 3, you'll learn more about IP addresses and classes as well as how to plan and implement a basic TCP/IP network.

### NetBEUI/NetBIOS

**NetBEUI** is the Microsoft protocol stack integrated into Windows products. Of the three protocols described in this section, NetBEUI is the smallest, fastest, and easiest to use. It also has the fewest features, so it's more limited in large networked environments because it does not support a Network layer needed to route packets between networks. As a result, NetBEUI is limited to communicating with other computers attached to the same network cable system. Because it does not have the overhead of routing functions, it is extremely small and fast, making it ideal for small networks of 10 to 50 devices.

**Service Message Blocks (SMB)** is the protocol that many clients use to request services from Microsoft servers. The NetBEUI protocol stack consists of NetBIOS and SMB, which provide a standard, well-defined way for servers and clients to communicate. Many peer-to-peer applications have been written to interface with NetBIOS to communicate with applications running on other computers, thus allowing an application to span multiple computers. As a result of the popularity of NetBIOS-based applications, both IPX/SPX and TCP/IP provide support for the NetBIOS protocol. An organization can use NetBIOS to allow workstations to run peer-to-peer applications and still access services from NetWare file servers.

## Network Software Components

A network's software components are perhaps the most difficult to understand because they are not physical objects. In the network configuration shown in Figure 1-7, the network software components can be divided into five major categories: network interface card drivers, protocol stacks, client software, network services, and the network operating system. Figure 1-7 shows how these software components are combined to enable workstations and servers to communicate on the network. In the following sections, you learn what role each software component plays in a LAN.

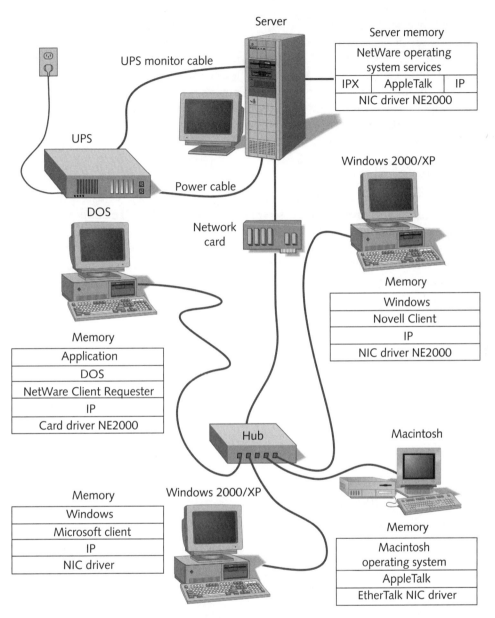

**Figure 1-7**    Network software components

## Network Interface Card Drivers

Each server and client workstation must have a NIC to attach it to the cable system and to communicate on the network. A **network interface card (NIC) driver** is software that contains instructions allowing the processor on the computer to control card functions and interface with the application software. Periodically, card manufacturers release new versions of driver software to fix bugs or offer compatibility with new applications. As a result, one responsibility of a network administrator involves updating application and system software. In Chapter 13, you'll learn how to make this task more efficient by using the automatic software update utilities built into the NetWare operating system. In the sample network configuration, the workstations use the older but reliable MicroDyne NE2000 NICs, and an NE2000 driver program controls the NICs and provides an interface with the workstation operating system software.

## Protocol Stacks

The protocol stack (also referred to as a protocol suite) consists of software layers that implement the protocol used to format requests and information packets transmitted on the network. The protocol you use depends on your server and client workstations. The default protocol for NetWare 6 is TCP/IP, commonly used with the Unix operating system and the Internet. Previously, the most common protocol on NetWare networks was IPX. NetWare networks also support other protocols, such as the AppleTalk protocol used with Macintosh computers.

NetWare 6 retains IPX as an option for those networks still using it. Although both IP and IPX can run concurrently on the same NetWare 6 server, running multiple protocols increases network traffic and can slow server performance. Because TCP/IP is necessary to access many new network services and the Internet, many organizations are switching from IPX-based networks to TCP/IP.

The IPX protocol used by NetWare was first developed by Xerox in the late 1970s and was later adopted by Novell for use in its networking products. It provided automatic addressing for network components, instead of the manual addressing used by TCP/IP.

## Client Software

Client workstations require the following components:

- Their own operating systems, such as DOS, Windows 2000/XP, or Macintosh OS X, to control local devices and run application software

- Client workstation driver software to control the NIC

- Requester and protocol software programs to format and send requests for network file and print services to the server; the requester program works closely with the workstation's operating system (OS) to examine requests and provide access to network services.

The network in Figure 1-7 shows a DOS computer using the NetWare Client Requester to send IP-formatted requests via the NE2000 driver through the cable system to the NetWare server. The Macintosh computer has an EtherTalk driver so that it can simultaneously use the same cable to send requests to the server with the AppleTalk protocol.

1

The ability to support different types of client operating systems is one of the strengths of the NetWare server.

With NetWare 6, Novell introduced the **Native File Access Protocol (NFAP)**. NFAP enables diverse clients to communicate directly with a NetWare server by using their native protocols. For example, with NFAP, Windows clients can use NetBIOS to access shared files from a NetWare 6 server. Using NFAP makes setting up clients and accessing basic NetWare file and print services simpler. However, you need Novell Client on a workstation to perform certain server-management functions or to access specialized Novell services, such as ZENworks.

## Network Services

All network services require client and server components. The **client** component runs on the user's computer and provides a connection between the application and the service running on the server. The **server** component consists of the computer hardware and NOS software necessary to run the network services and provide access to resources. Common network services include the following:

- **Security services** authenticate a user to the network with a login name and password and determine what rights and privileges the user has to the network. NetWare security services include login security, file system security, eDirectory security, print security, and server console security. These security services will be covered in later chapters.

- A directory service stores information about network objects in a hierarchical database called the directory. With Novell's eDirectory service, network objects—such as users, groups, workstations, printers, applications, and configuration information—are stored in containers. Containers are arranged in a hierarchical tree structure similar to the way folders are arranged on a disk drive.

- A **message service** is used to transfer e-mail messages and event notifications between client computers and servers.

- A **file service** enables client computers to access and save data on a shared file system.

- A **print service** allows printers to be attached to the network system and used by client workstations.

- An **application service** assists in running programs, such as spreadsheets, word processors, and database systems, by performing certain processing functions for client computers.

## The Network Operating System

The network operating system (NOS) is the software that controls network services and provides access to shared resources on the server computer. As explained previously, a major function of a server is to provide file and printer services to client workstations, so a server is often enhanced with specialized hardware and software to improve performance, security, and reliability beyond what can be expected from a desktop operating system, such as Windows 2000. The NetWare 6 NOS offers server-based software designed from the ground up to maximize the use of the server's hardware. It does this by including performance, fault-tolerance, security, and client-support features.

**Performance**   A server's performance is determined by how fast it can respond to requests for data from client workstations. Therefore, the major factors affecting a server's performance are its ability to keep frequently used information in memory, the speed of its disk system, and, if the first two are adequate, the speed of its processor unit. Some NetWare performance features are discussed in Chapter 2.

**Fault Tolerance**   Fault tolerance is the system's ability to continue operating satisfactorily when there are errors or other problems. The NetWare server environment was designed with different levels of fault tolerance in its disk system so that it can continue server operations despite physical errors on the disk drives or controller cards. NetWare's fault-tolerance system is discussed in Chapter 2.

**Security**   Security (preventing unauthorized access to information on the server) is one of the most important responsibilities of a network administrator. The NetWare server has features for meeting the security needs of your organization's users and data. Login security requires all users of the server to supply a valid user name and optional password before being given access to the network. As a network administrator, you can assign user names and passwords for each network user, thereby controlling use of the network. To further protect passwords, you can require passwords of at least five characters and force users to change their passwords within a specified time limit. In addition, the optional intruder-protection system locks out a user's account if someone exceeds the number of login attempts you have set. You'll work with user accounts and login security in Chapter 9.

**Trustee Assignments**   Trustees are objects such as users and groups that are given permission to use or manage resources. You use trustee assignments to assign privileges, called trustee rights, to NetWare users so that they have permission to perform certain functions on the network. Trustee assignments form the basis for **eDirectory security**, which controls access to objects in the eDirectory database. eDirectory is Novell's system for managing network resources, such as printers and servers. Trustee assignments are also the basis for **file system security**, which controls access to the network file system (the directory structure of the hard drive and the files in that directory structure). New users have no rights to access data stored on a NetWare server until you grant them rights to use certain parts of a file system on a NetWare server in your network. In later chapters, trustee assignments, eDirectory security, and file system security are discussed in detail.

Finally, NetWare provides **system console security** features. The **system console**, which is the keyboard and monitor connected to a NetWare server, is used for many NetWare server- and network-related tasks. NetWare enables you to set the system console so that only authorized people can use it. You'll work with the system console in Chapter 13.

**Client Support**   Because a NetWare server runs its own network operating system, it does not depend on a specific type of client environment (unlike peer-to-peer networks) and can support many types of workstations. As a result, with a NetWare server you can integrate diverse computing environments—for example, enabling Apple Macintosh users to share files with DOS- and Windows-based computers. In some organizations, NetWare has provided ways for engineering departments operating Unix-based computers with computer-aided design (CAD) software (used by engineers to draw plans and diagrams) to make design files available to DOS-based computers that control the machines that physically cut out engineered parts. Client support is discussed in Chapter 6. In the following sections, you learn the differences between network operating systems.

## Types of Network Operating Systems

Depending on their design, NOSs can be defined as peer-to-peer or client-server. **Peer-to-peer** NOSs enable workstations to communicate and share data with each other without the need for a dedicated server computer. **Client-server** NOSs use one computer as a dedicated server that acts as a central storage unit for client workstations. NetWare is a client-server operating system because its operation depends on a dedicated NetWare server. Figure 1-8 shows peer-to-peer and client-server networks. In the following sections, you learn about the features of both NOSs and how they compare to the NetWare operating system.

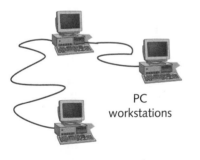
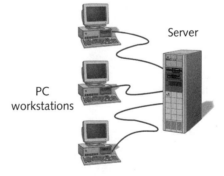

**Peer-to-peer network**
- Data stored on PC workstations
- PC workstations *can* access data on other PC workstations

**Client-server network**
- Data stored on server
- PC workstations *cannot* access data on other PC workstations

**Figure 1-8**   Peer-to-peer and client-server networks

## Peer-to-Peer Networks

In peer-to-peer networks, each computer can be both a server and a client workstation, allowing any computer to share files with other users on the network. Each computer can also function as a print server, enabling other users to share its printer. The main advantage of peer-to-peer NOSs is the ability to implement low-cost networks by saving the expense of dedicating a computer as a server. In addition, peer-to-peer systems let users in workgroups share data files and communicate easily with each other. In theory, this reduces the network administrator's burden by placing more responsibility for data sharing in the hands of users. However, large peer-to-peer networks can be difficult to administer because shared data can exist in several locations, making it more difficult to retrieve, secure, and back up. For example, if a workstation containing data other users need fails to start its system or shuts down unexpectedly, other users could lose data or might not be able to access the information they need.

Microsoft includes peer-to-peer networking capabilities in its Windows 95/98 operating systems, thus eliminating the need to obtain, learn, and integrate another NOS. Windows 2000 Professional and Windows XP represent more powerful "big brothers" of the Windows family of operating systems. Windows 2000 is a leading-edge operating system designed to support the advanced capabilities of Pentium- and multiprocessor-based computers and is a completely different operating system from previous Windows versions. Developed as a successor of the previous Windows NT software, Windows 2000 Professional was designed to take advantage of the 32-bit instruction set offered by the Intel Pentium and later processors. Windows 2000 and XP offer additional levels of reliability, protection, and security not available in the other Windows products.

Windows 2000 comes in several versions: Windows 2000 Professional, Windows 2000 Server, Advanced Server, and Enterprise Server. Windows NT Server is a full-featured NOS capable of administering large client-server networks (preferably under 200 users), although real-world experience has shown that NT cannot handle as many users per server as NetWare. Like NetWare, Windows 2000 Server is tailored to provide file and print services to a large number of users. Windows 2000 Professional and XP can be used as clients for a NetWare or Windows server or as servers for small peer-to-peer networks. Although Windows 2000 Professional software is limited to 10 simultaneous connections, Windows 2000 Server can theoretically have hundreds. When used in peer-to-peer networks, the Windows 2000 Professional system needs at least 64 MB of RAM.

 The Windows 2000 operating system is built on the previous Windows NT platform and includes enhanced capabilities and performance.

## Client-Server Networks

In a client-server network, servers running specialized software provide services to client workstations instead of the workstations sharing data among themselves. As a result, client-server networks, such as those using NetWare, provide centralized data storage, reliability, and high performance, advantages that are not currently attainable with peer-to-peer networks. One reason for their increased performance and reliability is that a server's hardware can be specialized to share files by providing multiple high-speed disk channels with a large memory for file caching. In Chapter 2, you'll learn about many hardware options for increasing your server's performance and reliability. The following sections compare several client-server NOSs you'll encounter as a network administrator.

**Windows NT/2000 Server** This client-server operating system provides client workstations with centralized and highly fault-tolerant high-speed access to data. The advantages of Windows 2000 are that it offers centralized management of multiple servers through the familiar Windows environment and supports access to TCP/IP and NetWare servers and mainframe computers. A final advantage is its usefulness as an application server (a server that runs the server portion of client-server applications). Many vendors offer client-server applications designed to run on this OS. Many network administrators use NetWare as their main network operating system for file and print services, and use Windows NT/2000 Server as application servers.

**Earlier NetWare Versions** Although NetWare 6 is now Novell's flagship NOS, earlier versions of NetWare are widely installed and highly stable network platforms that network administrators depend on for consistent and stable performance.

The primary difference between NetWare 3 and later versions is the introduction of Novell Directory Services (NDS; introduced in Netware 4), which has been upgraded in NetWare 6 as eDirectory. NetWare 3 had a flat database, called the bindery, that stored information about network files, volumes, users, and printers. A separate bindery database was stored on each NetWare 3 server, requiring users to have an account on every server containing resources they needed to access. Although the bindery system worked well in networks of one or two servers, when networks began to include a dozen or more servers and hundreds of users, maintaining user accounts on multiple servers became an administrative bottleneck. The eDirectory service, in contrast, is immensely scalable and can support more than a million objects on the network. In essence, the eDirectory database is shared among all servers, so users logging in can do so from any workstation and be recognized. With the bindery, users had to log in to each server because the bindery database was not shared among servers.

NetWare 3.x was **server-centric**, meaning each server managed the network individually. NetWare 6 is **network-centric**, meaning the network as a whole is managed through a centralized administration tool. Administration is through eDirectory, which uses a database to store information about network resources. NetWare has a set of eDirectory administration utilities for managing resources in the eDirectory database. You'll learn about eDirectory in Chapter 4 and work with it in later chapters as you add resources to the network.

**NetWare 6**    NetWare 6 is Novell's latest version of the NetWare NOS. This 32-bit dedicated NOS is highly specialized to provide a variety of services to client workstations. It is the fastest and most scalable NOS available today. NetWare 6 incorporates enhancements to earlier NetWare versions and adds previously unavailable features. Enhancements released with NetWare 6 include:

- Enhanced security

- Improved long filename support

- Increased directory entry volume capacity, from 2 million to 16 million

- NetWare Client 32 workstation client software

- NetWare Application Manager and NetWare Application Launcher network application management software

- Enhanced printer support for printers attached to workstations

- Various network operating system patches and updates

- Enhanced installation procedures, including a utility to plan the NetWare 6 network

- Major enhancements of the NetWare Administrator utility, which is the network administrator's main utility for managing the network; the enhancements include a Windows version, a configurable toolbar, and the ability to simultaneously manage multiple networks

- Support for multiple microprocessors in the NetWare server

- Software licensing management capabilities

- Integrated support for NetWare IP, Novell's version of the Internet Protocol (IP)

- Enhanced backup abilities

- Novell's network printing system, Novell Distributed Print Services (NDPS)

Features introduced with NetWare 5.0 include:

- GUI installation tool

- NDPS included in the installation process

- TCP/IP as the default protocol for communications

- Novell Storage Services (greatly enhances volume and disk management)

Features introduced with NetWare 6 include:

- The Novell NetStorage service, which allows access to network files from remote locations using a Web browser

- The ability to use and manage network printers with the iPrint service

- The iFolder service, which enables mobile computers to automatically synchronize files with a central server

- Centralized management of most network functions from the Java-based ConsoleOne utility

- The new iManager utility, which enables network administrators to perform most administrative tasks, such as creating users and groups, through a Web browser

- Remote management of the server using a standard Web browser

- Native File Access Protocol to allow non-Novell clients to access the NetWare server's shared directories and files

These features are discussed in more depth in subsequent chapters. The many added improvements, the acknowledged stability, and the increased need for Internet services in the industry will lead many organizations to upgrade their NetWare servers to NetWare 6.

# Designing a Network

Selecting a network system for an organization involves four steps:

1. Define the network needs.
2. Determine the network operating system needs.
3. Determine the cable system that will best support the needs of the network.
4. Specify any computer hardware that will be needed to implement servers and attach workstations to the network.

In the following sections, you learn about the criteria you should consider when developing a recommendation for a network operating system. In Chapters 2 and 3, you'll learn the computer hardware options and cable configurations to use when recommending and implementing a new network or maintaining an existing system.

## Defining Network Needs

Before recommending or justifying a network operating system, you need to analyze the organization's processing needs and determine how the network will support them. The processing needs affecting the selection of a network operating system include the number of users, the diversity of workstations, the type of applications to be supported, and the need for centralized data.

**Network Size**   An important consideration in determining whether to use a peer-to-peer or client-server NOS is the number of workstations to be attached to the network. As a general rule, the fewer the number of users, the more likely it is that peer-to-peer networks will meet the organization's needs. You also need to look at the organization's future growth and how it will affect the network system. If you think the organization will expand in the next few years, with more users requiring heavy-duty file and printer sharing to support such applications as desktop publishing and CAD, you might want to recommend a client-server NOS.

**Client Workstations**   Another factor to consider in selecting the type of NOS is the type of client workstations attached to the network. Peer-to-peer networks are best used when all the attached clients are running the same type of operating system. For example, if all workstations will run Windows, the Windows 2000 Professional or XP systems would be attractive alternatives, provided they meet the network's other processing needs. If the client workstations are running a combination of DOS and Windows, a client-server operating system such as NetWare 5.0 might be the best choice, depending on the organization's other processing needs.

**Network Use**   Some common uses of networks, such as printer sharing and e-mail routing, have small disk storage needs and can run nicely on peer-to-peer networks. For example, if an organization plans to use its network to support workgroup-oriented software, such as e-mail and scheduling, with some sharing of files and printers within small workgroups, a peer-to-peer operating system that supports its workstations' operating systems might be the best choice.

If an organization will be running applications requiring fast access to large network data files, such as desktop publishing, document imaging, and multimedia presentation packages, select a client-server network such as NetWare to ensure reliable, high-speed access to large disk systems consisting of gigabytes of data storage. If the network is using a client-server application, a client-server network with an application server is necessary. The Windows 2000 Server environment provides a good platform for serving applications because the operating system is designed to support application development.

Database software, such as Microsoft SQL Server and Oracle Corporation's Oracle, are designed to run on an application server performing database functions for workstations, reducing the load on the network and workstation. Database use is an increasingly important function of LANs.

**Centralized Storage**   Another important consideration in selecting an NOS is the network's need for centralized storage for files and documents. If an organization's employees use word processors and spreadsheet programs to access common documents and files, a client-server network system will give them consistent and reliable shared storage areas that can be routinely backed up to prepare for disaster recovery.

Client-server environments are also the best choice when users need access to large centralized databases containing inventory and customer information. These database files should be placed on a dedicated server or an application server to take advantage of the speed of file caching and the assurance of high reliability and fault tolerance gained by mirroring or duplexing the disk drives.

## Selecting a Network Operating System

The flowchart in Figure 1-9 shows how to analyze an organization's network processing needs to select a network operating system. As shown in the flowchart, the number of user workstations to be attached to the network is the first consideration. If there are fewer than 15 workstations, a peer-to-peer network is probably the best alternative. However, if several of these workstations will be using large files that must be shared on the network, such as those used by departments running CAD applications, a client-server network operating system, such as Windows 2000 or NetWare, is preferable.

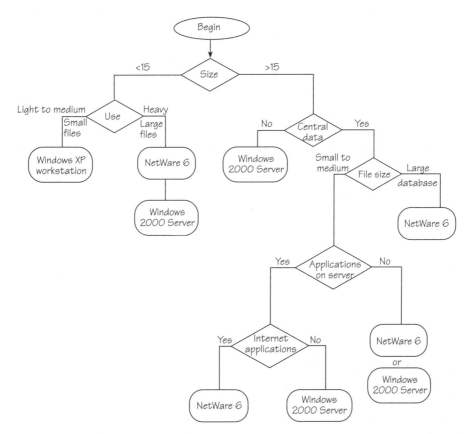

**Figure 1-9**   Selecting a network operating system

When the number of users is more than 15, the need for high-speed access to centralized data and applications that will run on the server typically becomes an important factor in choosing between a network operating system. If the network will be used mostly for sharing printers and personal communication, you need to consider the operating systems that the client workstations will run. If they will run different types of operating systems, NetWare is usually the best operating system choice because it can be configured to support communications and file sharing between different client operating environments.

When high-speed access to centralized data storage is a major function of the network, a client-server system such as NetWare 6 or Windows 2000 Server is the best choice because it provides a secure and efficient platform that helps ensure data will always be available. When different types of clients located on LANs and the Internet must access a large database or multimedia files crucial to an organization's operation, NetWare 6, with its eDirectory system and OneNet utilities, is generally the best choice. Whenever performance, security, and reliability are a must, NetWare is probably the best choice because it has been used extensively for many years and its performance and compatibility with many applications are well established. Because of the number of developers writing software for Windows, Windows 2000 Server is often the best choice for running server-based applications on the network.

Today many network administrators are gaining the best of both Windows 2000 and NetWare servers by implementing combinations of network operating systems. For example, a NetWare 6 network using eDirectory can include servers running Windows 2000, Windows NT, and Linux. In the future, network administrators will be increasingly called on to implement network systems combining compatible products to provide the services that organizations need.

# Cunningham, Burns, and Evans Laboratories

To see how what you've learned about networks can be used in selecting a new network for an organization, you'll work with a hypothetical organization called Cunningham, Burns, and Evans Laboratories (CBE Labs).

## The Organization

Located in Portland, Oregon, CBE Labs is a small, independent consulting firm specializing in testing and reporting on computer hardware and software. The firm's highly respected industry newsletter, *The C/B/E Networker*, has a reputation for impartial and detailed evaluations, and information system specialists often refer to it when deciding which hardware or software to purchase. Most Fortune 500 companies and major firms in the computer industry subscribe to *The C/B/E Networker*.

CBE Labs is organized into three departments: Administration, Laboratories, and Publications. An organizational chart for CBE Labs is shown in Figure 1-10.

President Joseph Cunningham and an administrative assistant oversee the administration of CBE. Administration includes marketing, finance, personnel, and information systems. There are three people in marketing, three in finance, one in personnel, and three in information systems.

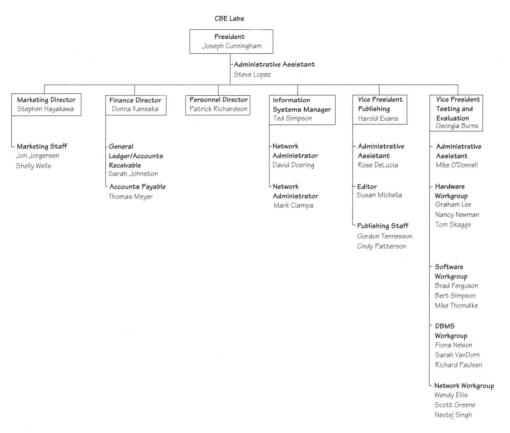

**Figure 1-10**    CBE Labs organizational chart

The CBE Labs testing labs are organized around four technology workgroups: hardware (workstation PCs and their components), software (workstation operating systems and application programs), database management systems (DBMSs), and networking (network server PCs and their components, network operating systems, and network applications). CBE Labs has three employees in each workgroup, along with Vice President of Testing and Evaluation Georgia Burns and one administrative assistant. Hardware and software being tested are not considered part of CBE Labs equipment.

CBE Labs uses its own equipment to store the data resulting from testing and evaluations to create *The C/B/E Networker*, and to run the business applications necessary to manage the organization. Harold Evans, Vice President of Publishing, manages the Publishing workgroup, overseeing a staff of three and an administrative assistant.

CBE Labs needs to update the company's LAN. Although it could simply upgrade its existing software to newer versions, the administrators have decided they do not want to be locked into software simply because they already own a version of it. The purchasing decision will be a "zero-based" decision, in which all network operating systems will be evaluated. The company expects to use three servers in the new network: one for lab data and reports, one for publishing *The C/B/E Networker*, and one for company administration. The company needs e-mail, fax capability, and Internet access in the network. All workstations will run Windows 2000 or Windows XP and need to access large databases stored on the servers. Some applications will run from the servers, but most standardized user applications (word processing, spreadsheet, and presentation graphics software) will be loaded on the users' workstations. Finally, the company's existing network is a client-server network using a NetWare 5.1 server. Management wouldn't mind if the new network could accommodate the existing server and NetWare license, but this is not a requirement.

### Choosing the New Network

Apply the flowchart shown in Figure 1-9 to determine which network operating system CBE Labs should use. The number of users is more than 15, so you initially branch to the right at the Size decision point. The organization will store centralized data on the servers, so you branch to the right at the Central data decision point. At the File size decision point, you have to consider whether large database files will be kept on the servers. The answer is yes, so you branch to the right and choose NetWare 6 as the NOS.

However, CBE Labs might also be using client-server applications. Windows 2000 Server is considered a better application server NOS than NetWare. That doesn't mean NetWare doesn't perform well as an application server, only that Windows 2000 Server performs better in that task because its GUI interface is familiar to users. (There are also many more applications available for Windows 2000 than for NetWare.) You can still run client-server applications if needed, so NetWare 6 is your choice for the NOS.

## THE CERTIFIED NOVELL ADMINISTRATOR (CNA)

The microcomputer networking field is an exciting arena with new developments occurring almost daily. The rapid growth of this field has created the need for network professionals—trained people who can be trusted with the responsibilities of creating and maintaining LANs and WANs. By passing Novell's qualifying exam, network administrators demonstrate their competency at NetWare administration. Passing the exam earns the network administrator the designation of **Certified Novell Administrator (CNA)**. Originally called the Certified NetWare Administrator program, Novell developed the CNA program in 1992 to help define the role of network administrators in a NetWare environment A CNA is considered qualified to be the network administrator of a network system that uses Novell products, such as NetWare, GroupWise, and ZENworks. Because the Internet plays a vital role in most networks, the new CNA program also requires the administrator to have a basic understanding of Internet services and security. The program provides a standard of knowledge and performance that helps ensure the quality of network administration and support.

CNA was originally Certified *NetWare* Administrator, and CNE was Certified *NetWare* Engineer. Similarly, NDS was originally *NetWare* Directory Services. The name changes reflect a broadening of Novell's outlook and product line. You can be certified in Novell products other than NetWare, and eDirectory is being developed to work with other network operating systems, such as Unix and Windows 2000.

As a CNA, your job is to direct your organization's networking services and support to meet the processing needs of microcomputer users. To develop the CNA program, Novell researched the job duties of thousands of NetWare network administrators around the world to determine the common tasks that network administrators needed to perform on a regular basis. The sections that follow summarize Novell's research. They will help you understand the typical duties of a network administrator and give you an overview of the NetWare knowledge and skills you'll need to become a CNA.

 Current information on the CNA and other Novell certifications programs can be found on Novell Education's Web site at *www.education.novell.com*. A current list of test objectives for the CNA exam and other CNA-related information, can be found at the Novell Web site. The content of these programs and exams changes periodically, so it's a good idea to get the latest information from Novell before taking the CNA exam.

## Understanding NetWare Components and Commands

A NetWare administrator needs a solid foundation in the components of a NetWare network and how they interoperate. When a problem—such as the message "File server not found"—occurs on a workstation attached to the network, the network administrator must be able to troubleshoot the network and isolate the cause of the error by drawing on his or her knowledge of the network components.

 Novell expects that all CNAs understand basic computer hardware and operating systems as well as network systems. For that reason, information on computer hardware and network systems has been included in Chapters 2 and 3 of this book.

Just as a mechanic must learn how to use the tools necessary to maintain and repair an automobile, a CNA must learn how to use the many NetWare commands and utilities to perform network maintenance and repair tasks, such as creating users, granting access rights, listing directory information, and working with printers. Starting with this chapter and continuing throughout the book, you learn how to use the commands and utilities that are the CNA's essential tools.

## Supporting Client Workstation Environments

The majority of computers attached to NetWare networks today run some version of the Windows operating system, so as a CNA, you'll need to know how to install and configure the client software to attach these workstations to the network and establish communications. With the rapid advances in microcomputer technology that require organizations to add new computers and replace existing ones each year, one of your main tasks will be installing and updating client software regularly.

Your organization might also need to provide network support for Apple Macintosh and Unix-based computers. Although Novell does not currently require a CNA to install client software on these operating systems, you'll need to be able to identify how NetWare software components can be used to attach Unix and Macintosh computers to a NetWare network.

## Managing Novell eDirectory Services

One of the most important features in NetWare 6 is Novell eDirectory Services, previously called Novell Directory Services (NDS). On a NetWare network, a user connects to the network itself rather than to a server (or group of servers). This requires a comprehensive, logical network design and tools for administering the resources (such as disk space and printers) for the entire network. Novell eDirectory Services is the system you use to create, maintain, and administer the network design and resources. The logical network design is called the directory tree. eDirectory is actually a database of information about the network and is built on the X.500 standard for a network global database. You'll learn about X.500 and eDirectory in detail in Chapter 4.

Novell eDirectory Services is proving a useful network design and administration tool, and Novell is licensing eDirectory to other companies, such as Hewlett-Packard and Santa Cruz Operations (SCO), for use in their network operating systems and software products. Part of Novell's OneNet strategy has been to make eDirectory available for Windows 2000, Windows NT, and Linux operating systems. Using eDirectory on a variety of network operating systems makes it possible to access and manage servers as a single, uniform network.

## Managing the Network File System

A network file system uses a directory structure to define how the server's data storage is organized. You might already know how a good directory structure on your workstation's local hard disk makes it easier to run applications and access files. On a server, a good directory structure becomes even more important because many users share the same storage device. As a result, one of a CNA's most important tasks when installing a new server is planning and implementing an efficient directory structure to support users' processing needs. In this book, you'll learn the essential NetWare file system components and design techniques that will help you create and maintain a workable network directory structure.

## Establishing and Maintaining Network Users and Security

NetWare has a sophisticated security system that enables the network administrator to give users access to information while still protecting special information from unauthorized access. To implement this security system, you need to create a user account for each person who will access the network and then assign the appropriate security restrictions, such as passwords and other limitations you feel are necessary, to protect user accounts from unauthorized access. To access files on the network, users need access rights to eDirectory objects and the directories and files they will be using. As a CNA, you will assign these rights. In Chapters 9 and 10, you'll learn how to use NetWare utilities and commands to create users and how to assign rights to access eDirectory objects and the network file system. Because organizational structures continually change, your ongoing tasks will include adding and deleting users and modifying the rights assigned to users and groups.

## Setting Up and Maintaining Network Printing

Perhaps one of the most complex and demanding tasks of a network administrator is creating and maintaining the network printing environment. Network printing has become an increasingly important issue on networks with sophisticated applications, such as desktop publishing and "what you see is what you get" (WYSIWYG) word processors and spreadsheets. These applications require expensive laser and inkjet printers, which are often shared to control costs. As a CNA, you'll need to continually upgrade your network printing environment to support faster and more sophisticated printers and applications as they become available. In this book, you'll learn how to use the NetWare printing components and tools for installing and maintaining a network printing environment to meet your users' needs.

## Loading and Updating Application Software

An important ongoing job of the network administrator is installing and upgrading application software packages that run on client workstations. Whenever possible, you should install applications on the server so that they can be shared and centrally maintained. However, some applications will not run from a server or will run much more efficiently when installed on the workstation's local hard drive. As a CNA, you'll need to be familiar with installing and configuring many different application software packages and know how to support these packages on the server or local workstations. These functions are covered in Chapter 13.

A CNA must continually obtain and install software upgrades and respond to user questions and problems. As a result, CNAs often find they need strong interpersonal skills to work with frustrated or angry users. Yet another responsibility is policing copyright licenses of application software to be sure your organization always has enough licenses to cover the number of users running the applications. This task is essential because your company can be sued and fined if it's found in violation of copyright laws. To make the CNA's job easier, some companies produce software that counts the number of users currently using a software package and does not allow more users than the number you have identified according to your software licenses.

## Creating an Automated User Environment

Novell requires CNAs to know how to use NetWare login script files and ZENworks policies when setting up and maintaining a network environment. In Chapter 12, you'll learn how to use NetWare login scripts and ZENworks to create a user-friendly network environment that allows users on your network to log in to the server easily.

## Developing and Implementing a Backup and Recovery System

Information is the lifeblood of an organization, and as a CNA, you will be the guardian of the information stored on the LAN system. One of the worst nightmares a CNA can have is a server crash that loses all the network information stored on its hard drives. To prevent this catastrophe and let you sleep more easily, you need to ensure that your server environment is as reliable as possible. You also need a good backup system to restore all the programs and data on your server after a major system failure. In Chapter 2, you'll learn about fail-safe measures that can be implemented on NetWare servers and how you can develop system specifications that will provide a reliable and fault-tolerant system. No matter how reliable or fault tolerant a system is, however, you still need to be prepared for a worst-case scenario, such as your building being destroyed or the equipment being damaged by an electrical failure or lightning. In Chapter 8, you'll learn how to plan for disasters by implementing a backup and recovery system using Novell Storage Services and other utilities.

## Managing the Server and Monitoring Network Performance

A NetWare server has its own operating system and console commands that enable a network administrator to control the server environment and run special software called NetWare Loadable Modules (NLMs) to perform certain tasks or add new services. Therefore, a CNA needs to spend some time each week at the server console using console commands and utilities to monitor server activity, add new services, and modify or configure existing ones.

With the addition of users to the network, large printing loads, and the ever-increasing demands of high-speed workstations for graphics applications, network performance can sometimes falter. As a CNA, you'll regularly need to monitor your network system and the server to detect performance bottlenecks or problems and determine whether hardware or configuration changes are necessary. In Chapter 13, you'll learn about several common network problems caused by insufficient hardware and discover how to configure your server and workstations to improve performance and avoid problems.

1

## Managing Internet Services and Security

One of the benefits of implementing a LAN is that it can be used to give all users access to the Internet. Although being able to access information on the Internet is important to an organization's operations, it also means exposing the network's computers to security threats and computer virus attacks. As a result, an important task of a CNA involves being able to implement firewalls, virus-protection software, and other procedures to help eliminate the loss of data and user productivity caused by outside hackers gaining access to computers on the local network. In Chapter 14, you'll learn about implementing these security measures.

## Implementing and Maintaining E-mail Services

E-mail and other collaborative functions, such as scheduling and calendaring, are important parts of any organization's operation. Novell offers a powerful, reliable e-mail and communication software product called GroupWise, used by many NetWare-based organizations. As a CNA, you'll be required to learn the basic tasks of implementing and managing a simple GroupWise system; these tasks are covered in Chapter 15.

## CHAPTER SUMMARY

❐ A computer network is formed when two or more computers are connected so that they can communicate electronically with each other. Local area networks (LANs) are located in one site; wide area networks (WANs) connect two or more LANs.

❐ The network administrator is responsible for managing and operating the network. Networks use servers, which are specialized computers that provide network services. Examples are network servers, print servers, and application servers.

❐ Networks are widespread in many organizations because they cut costs by letting users share expensive hardware and software, save time by making it easier for users to work together, offer shared access to database and document files, provide a more secure environment to protect sensitive data from unauthorized access, provide a more reliable storage system to prevent loss of data and time, and offer a communication system that can be used for e-mail and scheduling applications and to access minicomputer and mainframe computer systems.

❐ Networks consist of three major categories of components: the computer hardware and cable system, protocols or rules to control communication, and software to provide and access network services and resources.

❐ Network operating systems (NOSs) can be classified into two types: peer-to-peer and client-server. Peer-to-peer operating systems do not require a dedicated server; instead, they share data among the client workstations. Because client-server operating systems have dedicated servers, they can be more efficient and reliable platforms for storage of centralized files.

❏ When selecting an operating system for your network, consider such factors as the number of users and workstations, the type of operating systems and applications to be used by the client workstations, and the need for high-speed centralized data storage.

❏ To succeed as a network administrator, you need a good understanding of the hardware and software components in a network system and how they interoperate. The basic hardware components of a network consist of the server, cable system, network cards, uninterruptible power supply, client workstations, and shared printers. The software components of a network consist of the card driver program, which directly controls the network interface card; the protocol stack, which formats the data transmitted between computers; the client program, which provides an interface between applications and the network; and the network operating system, which runs on the server and provides the shared network services.

❏ As a CNA, your responsibilities will include such activities as supporting client workstation applications, creating and maintaining the network directory structures, creating and maintaining the eDirectory database and directory tree, establishing network users and security, setting up and maintaining the network printing environment, managing the server console, maintaining a user-friendly environment, and implementing a fail-safe backup and recovery system.

## KEY TERMS

**application service** — A network service that runs software applications on a server for use by networked workstations.

**cable system** — The physical wire system used to connect computers in a local area network.

**centralized processing** — A processing method in which program execution takes place on a central host computer rather than at a user workstation.

**Certified Novell Administrator (CNA)** — A network administrator who has taken and passed the Novell CNA exam.

**client** — When referring to Windows 2000/XP, a client is the software providing network connectivity for the workstation, which is called a network interface card (NIC) driver in NetWare.

**client-server** — A network operating system that uses a separate computer as a dedicated server, which acts as a central storage unit for client workstations.

**client-server applications** — A type of application in which part of the application runs on the network server and part of the application runs on the client workstations.

**client workstation** — A networked computer that runs user application software and is able to request data from a file server.

**computer network** — Two or more computers connected together so they can communicate.

1

**dedicated** — A server that only performs services for other workstations.

**distributed processing** — A processing method in which application software is executed on the client workstations.

**dotted decimal notation** — A method of writing TCP/IP addresses that separates each byte (represented by a decimal number) with a period.

**duplexing** — A method of synchronizing data on storage devices attached to different controller cards.

**eDirectory security** — A security system that controls access and management of objects in the eDirectory database.

**e-mail application** — A software application that allows network users to send messages to each other.

**file server** — A server computer that provides file and print servers to client workstations. Also called a NetWare file server in earlier versions of NetWare.

**file service** — A network service that provides access to shared files on a server computer.

**file system security** — A security system that prevents unauthorized users from accessing or modifying file data.

**host** — A computer or other device that is provided with a unique IP address on a TCP/IP network.

**hub** — A central connection device in which each cable of a star topology network is connected together.

**Internet** — An information highway that is not controlled by any single organization and is used worldwide to connect business, government, education, and private users.

**intranet** — A computer network based on Internet technology (TCP/IP), but designed to meet the needs of a single organization.

**local area network (LAN)** — A high-speed, limited-distance communication system designed to support distributed processing.

**mainframe computer** — Large computers in which the processing power is in the computer and users access it via terminals.

**message service** — A network service that transfers messages and notifications between networked computers.

**metropolitan area network (MAN)** — A communication system that uses fiber optics or microwave to connect computers in the same geographic location.

**minicomputer** — A scaled down version of a mainframe computer in which processing power is within the centralized computer and accessed via terminals. Minicomputers can also run network operating system software that allow them to act as servers to PCs attached to the local area network.

**Native File Access Protocol (NFAP)** — A Session-layer protocol that enables clients to use other protocols to access files stored on a NetWare server.

**NetBEUI** — Microsoft's network protocol stack, integrated into Windows for Workgroups, Windows 95/98, and Windows NT. It consists of NetBIOS and Service Message Blocks (SMBs) at the session layer and NetBIOS frames (NBFs) at the transport layer. NBF can be replaced with NetBIOS over TCP/IP (NBT) for direct communication over TCP/IP-based networks.

**NetWare Core Protocol (NCP)** — The NetWare protocol that provides session- and presentation-layer services.

**network administrator** — The netwo rk user in charge of the network and all its resources, who is responsible for maintaining, allocating, and protecting the network.

**network-centric** — A network in which a user logs in only once to the network itself, not to each network server he or she needs access to.

**network interface card (NIC)** — An adapter card that attaches a computer system to the physical network cable system.

**network interface card driver** — The software that controls a network interface card (NIC) and access to the network.

**nondedicated** — A server that can run applications for a local user while still providing network services for attached workstations.

**OneNet** — Novell's strategy of making multiple networks, consisting of diverse clients and services, work together as one network.

**packet** — A group of consecutive bits sent from one computer to another over a network.

**peer-to-peer** — A network system in which each computer can act as both a server and client.

**print service** — The software component of the network printing environment that makes printing happen by taking jobs from user workstations and sending them to a networked printer.

**protocol** — Rules that define the formatting and transmission of data across network systems.

**protocol stack** — The software used to send and receive packets among networked computers.

**scheduling application** — A software application used to create and maintain personal and workgroup time schedules.

**security service** — The service used to authenticate user logins.

**server** — A network computer used for a special purpose such as storing files, controlling printing, or running network application software.

**server-centric** — A network in which a user logs in to each network server that he or she needs access to, instead of logging in only once to the network itself.

**Service Message Blocks (SMB)** — The Microsoft protocol that provides session- and presentation-layer services to client computers.

**system console** — The monitor and keyboard on a network server.

**system console security** — A security system that prevents unauthorized users from accessing the system console.

**terminal** — A user workstation that connects to a mainframe computer or minicomputer without a CPU of its own so that the mainframe computer or minicomputer must do all the processing.

**terminal service** — A network service that allows applications to be run on the server while the user workstation acts as a graphical window to the application running on the server.

**Transmission Control Protocol/Internet Protocol (TCP/IP)** — TCP/IP is the most common communication protocol used to connect heterogeneous computers over both local and wide area networks. In addition to being used on the Internet, the Unix operating system uses TCP/IP to communicate between host computers and file servers. Today, NetWare 6 uses TCP/IP as its native protocol, with IPX/SPX as an option.

**wide area network (WAN)** — Two or more local area networks in geographically separated locations connected by telephone lines.

## REVIEW QUESTIONS

1. Two or more computers connected so that they can communicate electronically with each other are known as which of the following?

   a. NIC

   b. NOS

   c. system

   d. network

2. Computer networks that exist in one location are called which of the following?

   a. LAN

   b. NOS

   c. system

   d. network

3. A LAN supports processing by doing which of the following? (Select all that apply.)

   a. providing access to a centralized computer

   b. allowing terminals to run programs on a mainframe computer

   c. providing access to the Internet

   d. allowing microcomputers to access centralized data and resources

4. Which of the following is a network type that connects networks existing in two or more distant locations?

   a. LAN

   b. distributed network

   c. NOS

   d. WAN

5. List two advantages of using a LAN for centralized data storage.

6. Identify two areas in which a LAN can be used to save personnel time.

7. In many networks, sharing which of the following will result in the most direct cost savings?

   a. hardware

   b. application software

   c. data

   d. fax machines

8. A network operating system that enables client workstations to share files while still accessing other client resources is called which of the following?

   a. peer-to-peer network

   b. distributed network

   c. centralized network

   d. client–server network

9. True or False: A network operating system requires a server.

10. List two advantages of peer-to-peer network operating systems.

11. List two advantages of client-server network operating systems.

12. A network in which a new user's account must be created on every server is called which of the following?

   a. client–server network

   b. distributed network

   c. network-centric

   d. server-centric

13. List the seven network hardware components.

14. Which of the following allows the server to run programs for the client?

   a. terminal server

   b. application server

   c. client–server network

   d. peer-to-peer network

15. True or False: The software component controls communications on the network cable.

16. Which of the following software components formats the information transmitted between computers?

    a. NOS

    b. client software stack

    c. protocol stack

    d. NIC driver

17. Which of the following software components provides access to shared files and other resources? (Select all that apply.)

    a. disk driver

    b. NIC driver

    c. client

    d. protocol stack

18. Which of the following software components acts as an interface between the network card and the workstation operating system?

    a. NOS

    b. client

    c. protocol stack

    d. NIC driver

19. List four types of NetWare security.

20. Which of the following are CNA responsibilities?

    a. deciding where to place the quality control database to allow shared access by several users throughout an organization

    b. making a new printer available to users in the Sales Department

    c. making it possible for the users in the Sales Department to easily select the new sales printer from their workstations

    d. determining why certain workstations cannot log in to the new server

    e. providing computers in the Sales Department with the ability to run the new PowerPoint presentation software

    f. determining how much memory the server computer is using for file caching

    g. maintaining regular lunch hours

    h. adding users to the e-mail system

    i. modifying the logical network design to accommodate the addition of a new server purchased for the sales group

    j. defining the requirements for the accounting system software

## HANDS-ON PROJECTS

### Project 1-1: Recording Network Information

Your instructor has created a user account for you on the network so that you can perform the exercises and project assignments in this book. Your instructor will supply information about your user account. Record the following information, and submit it to your instructor as a written report:

eDirectory tree name:

User name:

Last name:

Full name:

Student reference number:

Context:

Home directory location:

Volume name:

Home directory path and name:

Your instructor will take your class on a tour of your local area network. Use what you learn during this tour to gather the following information, and submit it to your instructor as a written report:

Network Server Information

   Name:

   Operating system:

   Memory (in MB):

   Disk capacity (in MB/GB):

   NIC and protocol:

   UPS:

Network Printer Information

   Printer name:

   Type:

   Location:

   Attachment method:

Your Client Workstation

Name (if any):

Operating system:

Memory (in MB):

Disk capacity (in MB/GB):

NIC and protocol:

## Project 1-2: Logging in to the Network

1. Your instructor will explain how to log in to your local workstation and the network. Record the steps on a separate sheet of paper.

2. Use the steps you recorded to log in to the network.

## Project 1-3: Setting Your Password

You can assign a password to provide more security for your user name. Be sure to assign a password you can remember, or you will have to ask your instructor or lab supervisor to reassign a new password. When you enter your password, it is displayed onscreen as asterisks. Use these steps to assign a password:

1. Start your computer, and log in to the Novell network using your assigned Admin user name and password.

2. If necessary, log on to your Windows workstation.

3. Hold down the **Ctrl**, **Alt**, and **Delete** keys to display the NetWare Security dialog box.

4. Click the **Change Password** button to open the Change Password dialog box.

5. To change your password on both the workstation and the Novell tree, hold down the **Ctrl** key and click to select only the workstation and the Novell classroom tree.

6. Enter your existing password in the Old Password text box.

7. Enter your new password in both the New Password and Confirm New Password text boxes.

8. Click **OK** to change the passwords.

9. If necessary, click **Close** to return to the NetWare Security dialog box, and then click **Cancel** to return to the Windows desktop.

## Project 1-4: Logging out of the Network

1. Your instructor will explain how to log out of your network. Record the steps on a separate sheet of paper.

2. Use the steps you recorded to log out of your network.

---

# CASE PROJECTS

## Case 1-1: Selecting a Network Operating System for the J.Q. Adams Corporation

The J.Q. Adams Corporation, a medium-sized company with more than 15 employees, manufactures office equipment and supplies and sells its products to companies that retail them. J.Q. Adams does not sell directly to the end user. The company is planning to downsize its quality-control system from a minicomputer to a LAN. Part of this system involves collecting information, such as quantities produced and inspection results from the shop floor, and saving them in a central database. Product defects from returned goods will also be coded and stored in a separate database. These database files are expected to become quite large, and it is crucial that the collection process not be interrupted during daily operations. Other computers in the office will have access to this data for use in spreadsheet and database software to produce reports and analyze production problems.

Along with this reorganization of the quality-control system, the information systems manager at J.Q. Adams has decided to expand the LAN to include administrative operations. He plans to use two servers, one for administration and one for production, connected by the LAN. Administration users will use word processing, spreadsheet, database, and accounting software.

Given the preceding information, use the flowchart shown previously in Figure 1-9 to help select the best network operating system for the J.Q. Adams Corporation. Write a memo to your instructor documenting your decision. In the memo, explain your decision by diagramming your path through the flowchart and writing a brief paragraph justifying your selection.

## Case 1-2: Selecting a Network Operating System for the Jefferson County Courthouse

Jefferson County is preparing to install a network in the Jefferson County Courthouse. The network will connect 12 users in the Social Services Department so that they can implement e-mail and group scheduling applications while sharing access to two laser printers. The 12 users include Janet Hinds, the program administrator; Tom Norihama, her assistant; Lisa Walsh, the receptionist; Terry Smith, the department secretary; and eight social workers. Terry Smith is familiar with advanced features of the word processing package and often does final editing of the documents created by the social workers. As a result, social workers need to send documents periodically to Terry's computer so that she can finalize them for printing.

1. Given the preceding information, use the flowchart shown previously in Figure 1-9 to help select the best network operating system for the Jefferson County Courthouse Social Services Department. Write a memo to your instructor documenting your decision. In the memo, explain your decision by diagramming your path through the flowchart and writing a brief paragraph justifying your selection.

   The Jefferson County Courthouse also houses the county's courtroom facilities. There are three courtrooms that support the operations of 4 judges, 4 bailiffs, 6 court reporters, and 12 administrative staff. Each judge has his or her own office. The bailiffs share an office, but each has a separate desk. A similar situation applies to the court reporters. The administrative staff is in four offices, and each has a desk. If a network were installed, each employee would have a client workstation on his or her desk. In addition, the administrative personnel would require four more workstations set up at windows where they deal with the public. A database of legal documents would be created and stored on the network, and this database is expected to grow very large over time. It is not clear whether a client-server database application would be used.

2. How would your decision change if Jefferson County also included the county court system in the network? What difference does it make if a client-server application is used for the database? Use the flowchart in Figure 1-9 to help select the best network operating system for the Jefferson County Courthouse with each database option. Write a memo to your instructor documenting your decision for each option. In the memo, explain your decision for each option by diagramming your path through the flowchart and writing a brief paragraph justifying your selection.

CHAPTER

# 2

# MICROCOMPUTER
# HARDWARE

**After reading this chapter and completing the exercises,
you will be able to:**

♦ Identify the hardware components that make up a
microcomputer system

♦ Compare and contrast microprocessors used on workstations and
NetWare servers

♦ Describe the purpose of and use of expansion buses, I/O ports,
and interrupts in a microcomputer system

♦ Compare and contrast storage systems used on NetWare servers

♦ Apply knowledge of computer hardware components when developing NetWare server specifications

In Chapter 1, you learned about networks and the basic components of a
LAN. LANs support distributed processing on a variety of computer systems, so network administrators must have a solid background in the fundamentals of microcomputer hardware and software components. Each new
generation of software applications demands more processing power, and
microcomputer systems are based on complex and evolving technologies.
Components from many manufacturers are combined to build a microcomputer. To help you make sense of the many concepts and terms used in
today's computer environments, this chapter provides a basic background in
microcomputer terminology and concepts to keep you abreast of developments in microcomputer hardware and software. This knowledge will enable
you to develop specifications for purchasing PC workstations and NetWare
servers. In addition, the information in this chapter provides a basis for configuring network interface cards (NICs) and evaluating NetWare server performance, topics discussed in more depth in future chapters.

47

# THE MICROCOMPUTER

The microcomputer is commonly called a "personal computer" (PC). People who use PCs are referred to as "end users" or just "users." PCs used by users are often referred to as "PC workstations" or just "workstations."

> The term "workstation" is sometimes used to refer to microcomputers that are more powerful than the normal PC. These workstations generally run the Unix operating system and are often used for graphics-intensive work, such as the engineering drawings produced by computer-aided design (CAD) systems. Often, only the context of the discussion indicates which type of workstation is referred to.

## The System Board

The **system board** (also called the "motherboard" or "mainboard") is the most important component of a microcomputer because it links all the individual system components. Its design directly affects the performance of a computer system. Figure 2-1 illustrates a system board and its major components. The following sections describe the system board components and discuss how they are linked by buses.

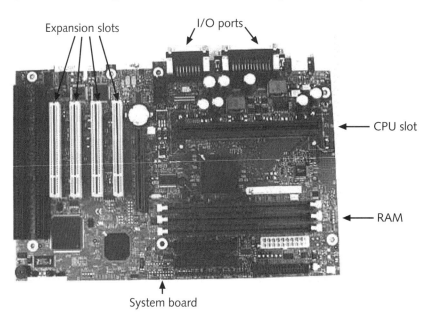

**Figure 2-1**   System board components

## The System Board Buses

The system board circuits that connect components are called **buses**, which are pathways for electronic communication between the parts of the computer. You can visualize them as a set of wires running together (in "parallel") from component to component. In actuality, circuits etched into the system board are used instead of wires, but the idea is the same. Buses vary in size (the number of "wires") and speed, and are usually referred to by names that reflect their purpose. In this section, you learn about the local bus, the data bus, the address bus, and the expansion bus. A typical bus structure is shown in Figure 2-2.

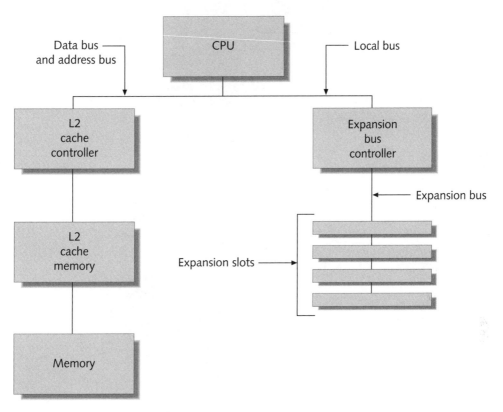

**Figure 2-2**   A system board bus structure

**The Local Bus**   The system board circuits connecting the CPU to memory and other system board components are referred to as the computer's **local bus**. The local bus is closely associated with the functions of the microprocessor chip and is designed to support the data and address bus of a specific microprocessor.

**The Data Bus**   As shown in Figure 2-3, the **data bus** is the highway that transfers data bits to and from microprocessor registers, where the microprocessor stores the data it uses. Just as the number of lanes on a highway determines the amount of traffic flow, the size of the data bus determines the number of bits that can be transferred into the micro-processor at one time.

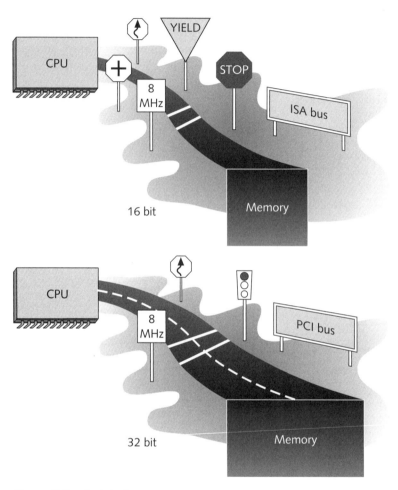

**Figure 2-3** A data bus

**The Address Bus** Just as each box in a post office is given a unique number to iden-tify it, each byte in the computer's memory is identified by a binary number called an **address**. The microprocessor uses an address to identify the memory byte it is transfer-ring data to or from. The **address bus** carries the memory byte's address from the microprocessor to the memory unit. When the memory unit receives the address and a signal to read, it responds by placing that memory byte's contents on the data bus. The number of bits in the address bus determines the maximum amount of memory the microprocessor can access directly. If an address bus consists of only two wires, for exam-ple, its maximum binary number is 11. A computer with this address bus is limited to a maximum of 4-byte addresses: 00, 01, 10, and 11. In the binary system, each additional bit on the address bus doubles the amount of memory capacity, so a 3-bit address bus has a maximum of 8-byte addresses: 000, 001, 010, 011, 100, 101, 110, and 111. The 16-bit address bus commonly found on microprocessors before 1980 could access only 64 KB of RAM; the 20-bit address bus on the 8088 can access up to 1 MB; the 24-bit address bus on the 80286 and 80386SX could access up to 16 MB; and the 32-bit address bus on the 80386DX, 80486, Pentium, and Pentium Pro could access up to 4 GB. The new 64-bit bus in Pentium II, III, and 4 processors can access 64 GB of memory.

**The Expansion Bus**   Some microcomputer components, such as video display controllers and NICs, are not usually built into the system board. Instead, these components are built on separate cards, called **expansion cards**, which are inserted into an **expansion slot** on the system board. Network connections are commonly made by inserting a NIC into one of the expansion slots. The **expansion bus** connects the expansion card slots to the system board's components. The expansion bus connection is made through a specialized chip set on the system board that controls the operation of the expansion bus and the expansion cards attached to it. There are several types of expansion buses, which are discussed in "Expansion Slots," later in this chapter.

**Direct Memory Access**   A **direct memory access (DMA) channel** is the part of the local bus used to automate data transfer between the computer's memory and external devices, such as disk drives and NICs. DMA channels are assigned to specific devices, so when you are configuring a device such as a NIC, be sure to assign an unused DMA channel number.

Because local buses are designed to support a specific microprocessor, upgrading the microprocessor chip on the system board is impossible in older microcomputers. For example, if you wanted to upgrade a system from an Intel 80386SX to an Intel 80486 processor, you needed to replace the system board. Later, system boards were designed for microprocessor upgrading. However, these system boards still had the original local bus built into them, which limited the performance of the upgraded system. For example, Intel sold a Pentium microprocessor to replace 80486 processors on properly designed system boards. But these boards were designed with a 32-bit data bus, whereas the Pentium is designed to work with a 64-bit data bus. Typically, the cost of a new processor with a system board was only slightly more than a processor alone, so replacing just the processor was cost-effective only for the latest models.

## The Central Processing Unit (CPU)

The **central processing unit (CPU)**, also referred to as a **microprocessor**, is the brain of the microcomputer system. Built into the silicon of modern microprocessors are more than three million transistors forming circuits that interpret and control program instructions and perform arithmetic and logical operations.

Experts say that etching all the circuit paths onto a microprocessor chip is comparable to mapping all the highways and streets of Los Angeles onto the head of a pin.

This section describes the different types of microprocessor chips and explains their limitations and capabilities. To compare microprocessors, you need to understand the parameters that determine their performance and functionality: clock speed, word size, instruction set, and the parameters of data bus size and address bus size, which have already been discussed.

**Clock Speed**    If the microprocessor is the brain of the computer, the clock is the heartbeat of the system unit, and its beats synchronize all the operations of the internal components. The microprocessor's **clock** is used to provide timed signal pulses called **cycles**. Each clock cycle consists of an electronic pulse transmitted to each component of the system unit to trigger and synchronize processing within the computer system. Each clock pulse causes the microprocessor's circuits to perform part or all of an instruction. Simply stated, the computer does something only when the clock ticks. Snap your fingers as you would to an old '50s tune. Each time your fingers snap, the CPU could carry out an instruction. The faster you click, the more instructions the CPU can perform.

Pentium chips can carry out two instructions per clock cycle.

Clock speed is measured in millions of cycles per second, called megahertz (MHz), or billions of cycles per second, called gigahertz (GHz). A **wait state** is a clock cycle during which the processor does not perform any operations; wait states were necessary to slow down high-speed processor chips and allow them to work with slower devices. (Contemporary hardware no longer requires wait states.) In general, higher clock rates mean faster processing speeds. The processing speed, when combined with the speed of a computer's disk storage and video card, determines its throughput performance.

**Word Size**    A microprocessor chip holds instructions and data temporarily in storage areas called **registers**. Each processor chip has several registers for various purposes. A microprocessor's **word size** is the number of bits each register can hold. A larger word size enables a microprocessor to work on more data per clock cycle. Older processor chips, such as Intel's 8088 and 80286, had 16-bit registers. The Pentium, Pentium Pro, and Pentium II had 32-bit registers. Newer processor chips, such as Pentium III and Pentium 4, have 64-bit registers.

**Instruction Set**    The **instruction set**, also called the **machine language**, is the group of commands that the microprocessor chip has been designed to process. All software must be converted to the microprocessor's machine language before it can run. This is often accomplished with the aid of a special program called a **compiler**, which converts English-like commands to the binary language of the processor chip. DOS machine-language programs use the .com or .exe filename extension. On a NetWare server, machine-language programs have the .nlm extension.

A machine-language program can run only on the processor for which it was designed. Intel and Motorola processors, for example, have very different instruction sets, making it impossible for the Motorola chip to run a machine-language program written for an Intel chip. The NetWare 3.2, 4.11, and 5.0 operating systems were written for the instruction set of an Intel 80386 microprocessor, so they cannot run on earlier Intel processors. NetWare 4.11, 5.0, 5.1, and 6 are Pentium-aware, and a Pentium II or above is *required* to run NetWare 6 server software.

The software takes advantage of the faster Pentium instruction set if it finds the system has a Pentium-class processor. Computers with Intel and most Motorola chips are classified as **complex instruction set computers (CISC)** because their instructions have a wide range of formats and because one instruction can require many clock cycles. The resulting speed of the microprocessor is often expressed in **millions of instructions per second (MIPS)**.

Companies such as Cyrix and Advanced Micro Devices (AMD) produce Intel-compatible processor chips used in some IBM-compatible systems. They include the Cyrix III (133)/700 and the AMD K7 ATHLON 650/700/750 MHz line. They perform just as well (and often better) and are much cheaper than comparable Intel chips. They are an effective alternative for CPUs on NetWare servers and on workstations for general office applications.

To maximize speed, many engineering workstations running CAD applications (such as SUN workstations) are based on processors called **reduced instruction set computers (RISC)**. RISC processors are fast and efficient because their instructions are all the same length, and each instruction performs a very specific process. There are also fewer instructions than on a CISC chip. The disadvantage of RISC processors is that software development is more complex, requires sophisticated compilers to convert programs to machine-language format, and might perform slower with general office applications.

The biggest advantage of RISC-based over CISC-based computers is the increased speed of floating-point math calculations. This speed advantage is the reason RISC-based processors are often used in workstations that run engineering, CAD, or scientific applications.

A **math coprocessor** is an extension of a chip's basic instruction set that allows the microprocessor to perform more complex arithmetic operations, such as square root and trigonometric functions. Math coprocessors are built into the 80486DX, Pentium, Pentium Pro, and Pentium II processors. Pentium III and Pentium 4 computers contain a floating point and a multimedia unit, which offer superior performance for mathematics-intensive applications.

Math coprocessors can increase the speed of spreadsheet programs and applications used for engineering and CAD applications, which typically perform many square root and trigonometric calculations.

## Intel Microprocessors

The Intel family of microprocessor chips is probably the best known because of the wide acceptance of IBM-compatible computers based on this processor design. Knowing the processors' capabilities and limitations can help you make the best use of existing systems on a network and select the correct processor chip when you need to buy a new system.

The Intel 8088 processor chip, included in the IBM PC introduced in 1981, started the IBM PC-compatible industry. The 8088 has a 4 MHz clock speed, a 20-bit address bus that can access up to 1 MB of RAM, and a 16-bit register system. It allowed designers to create everything a PC user would need in the then-foreseeable future. Running the instruction set that comes with the original Intel 8088 microprocessor is referred to as operating in **real mode**. Real-mode instructions use 16-bit data registers and can directly access only one million bytes of memory. The DOS operating system—and the thousands of DOS software applications still in use—was designed specifically for the original 8088 microprocessor. That means even if you have the latest and fastest Intel processor chip, your workstation computer is limited to 640 KB of RAM and 16-bit instructions when it runs DOS-based software in real mode.

The need for more powerful processor chips led to the development of the 80286 processor, which offered seven times the performance of the 8088 processor while providing compatibility for real-mode programs. The 80286 microprocessor introduced in 1984 in the IBM AT added three new capabilities:

- The address bus was increased to 24 bits allowing for up to 16 MB of system RAM.

- The clock speed was increased to between 8 and 20 MHz.

- It can switch between real mode and protected mode.

Real-mode operation allows the microprocessor to act like a very fast 8088; **protected mode** enables it to run multiple programs more reliably by preventing one program from affecting the operation of another. For example, if you are using real mode to run a new program on your computer and the program attempts to write data into memory cells used by DOS, the computer could crash and interrupt all other applications. When the new program is run in protected mode, however, its attempt to write the data is recognized as invalid and is terminated, although other programs continue to operate normally.

The 80386 chip represented an important advance over earlier chips yet retained compatibility with software written for the older processors. Although the design is now dated, it was popular, and you might still encounter workstation computers based on the 80386 processor chip. Although the 80386 is capable of 32-bit processing (because of its 32-bit internal registers and data paths), most PC add-on boards and software were

2

designed for older 8- or 16-bit processors, so they are unable to make optimum use of the 80386's 32-bit capability. Other features of the 80386 include:

- The use of **virtual memory**, which allows hard disk space to simulate a large amount of internal RAM. Although the use of virtual memory slows the computer's throughput, it enables you to run large programs that would not otherwise fit in existing RAM.

- The addition of **virtual real mode**, which enables multiple real-mode programs to run simultaneously.

- The ability to run at a variety of clock speeds ranging from 16 to 40 MHz.

Beginning with NetWare 3.1x, the NetWare server required an 80386 or later processor because the NOS was written for the virtual real-mode instruction set.

All new Intel-based workstations and NetWare servers you install are based on Pentium II or above microprocessors. The Pentium microprocessors provide compatibility with software written for earlier processors but have the increased computing power needed for high-speed graphics-based software (such as Windows). In fact, Pentium 4 computers can perform all the instructions our old friend the 8088 could, but 5000 times faster! They can also support the powerful NetWare servers that accommodate multiple high-speed workstations and communications services.

The 80486 chip was a supercharged version of the 80386 chip that incorporated more than one million transistor components. Many workstations you'll encounter as a network administrator still contain this processor. The 80486 included the following features:

- Clock speeds were higher, ranging from 33 to 100 MHz.

- An 8 KB high-speed memory cache (L1 cache) allowed the processor to access commonly used memory locations without going through the slower external data bus.

- A math coprocessor was built in.

There were two main versions of the 80486 chip. The 80486SX was a less expensive version of the 80486DX chip and did not include the math coprocessor.

Intel's Pentium chip represented a major leap ahead of earlier Intel chips by incorporating two 80486-type microprocessors on a single chip that could process two instructions simultaneously. The first Pentium chip operated at 60 MHz with 32-bit registers and more than three million transistors. The Pentium 4 chip operates at 2.4 GHz and has over 42 million transistors. The Pentium math coprocessor has been redesigned to achieve a 300% improvement in geometric computations over 80486 chips, allowing graphics-intensive applications to operate much faster.

Intel has usually tried to move users to each new microprocessor as quickly as possible. With the Pentium, however, Intel has continued developing the chip to extend its useful life span. The result is the Pentium MMX microprocessor, a version of the Pentium released in late 1996 that has been enhanced to speed up multimedia functions. In fact, software must be specifically written to take advantage of the MMX capability or there will be no performance enhancement. The need for multimedia processing is increasing as more software products are delivered on CD-ROM and as Internet content includes more audio, video, and 3D components.

The Intel Pentium Pro processor was designed for optimal performance with 32-bit software while maintaining compatibility with previous Intel processors. It still used a 32-bit word, but its design included 5.5 million transistors in the chip, and it operated at speeds of up to 200 MHz. The Pentium Pro chip also included a 256 KB L2 cache to accelerate data input. One of the Pentium Pro's main features is called dynamic execution. **Dynamic execution** combines three processing techniques: multiple branch prediction, dataflow analysis, and speculative execution. In multiple branch prediction, the Pentium Pro looks several programming steps ahead to predict which steps will be processed next. Dataflow analysis is then used to set up an optimized schedule for performing the program steps, which leads to speculative execution to perform the steps as scheduled by the dataflow analysis. Table 2-1 lists the basic specifications of the Intel family of microprocessors for easy comparison.

**Table 2-1**    Microprocessor Specifications

| Processor | Word Size | Data Bus | Address Bus | Maximum Clock Speed | Math Coprocessor | Millions of Instructions per Second |
|-----------|-----------|----------|-------------|---------------------|------------------|-------------------------------------|
| 8088 | 16 | 8 | 20 | 10 MHz | No | 0.33 |
| 80286 | 16 | 16 | 24 | 20 MHz | No | 3 |
| 80386SX | 32 | 16 | 24 | 33 MHz | No | 5 |
| 80386DX | 32 | 32 | 32 | 33 MHz | No | 11 |
| 80486SX | 32 | 32 | 32 | 33 MHz | No | 41 |
| 80486DX | 32 | 32 | 32 | 100 MHz (DX4) | Yes | 80 |
| Pentium | 32 | 64 | 32 | 200 MHz | Yes | >100 |
| Pentium MMX | 32 | 64 | 32 | 233 MHz | Yes | >100 |
| Pentium Pro | 32 | 64 (+8 ECC) | 36 | 200 MHz | Yes | >100 |
| Pentium II | 32 | 64 (+8 ECC) (effective 128 with DIMMS) | 36 | 450 MHz | Yes | >300 |
| Pentium III | 32 | 64 (+8 ECC) (effective 128 with DIMMS) | 36 | 1.33 GHz | Yes | >500 |
| Pentium 4 | 32 | 64 (+8 ECC) (effective 128 with DIMMS) | 36 | 2.53 GHz | Yes | >1,700 |

2

The Pentium Pro ran best with a true 32-bit operating system, such as Windows NT Workstation or OS/2. If Windows 95 was used as the operating system, performance suffered because Windows 95 (despite its advertising) had a significant amount of 16-bit code. The Pentium Pro cannot handle 16-bit code directly but must emulate this ability. A Pentium system running Windows 95, therefore, can actually outperform the Pentium Pro system when using older 16-bit user applications.

The Intel Pentium 4 processor is now the most common processor on new systems. It offers an enhanced L1 cache of 8 KB, plus 512 KB of L2 cache. Intel offers the chip in 2.53 GHz, 2.40 GHz, and 2.26 GHz versions, although it anticipates higher speeds in future releases.

As you can see from Table 2-1, CPUs' speed, power, and complexity have been increasing at a tremendous rate. Gordon Moore, co-founder with Robert Noyes of Intel, stated in 1965 that the data density of integrated circuits would double every 12 months for 10 years. This prediction was revised in 1975 to every 18 months, and has certainly held true for microprocessors and for other computer components. Dr. Moore's statement became known as "Moore's Law." What is amazing about Dr. Moore's prediction is that in 1965 he predicted that a processor's speed would be at 1 GHz by the year 2000, and he was correct!

For NetWare 6, running a Pentium 700 MHz or better is preferable. If more money is available in the budget, put it into additional RAM. NetWare performance can increase dramatically when RAM goes from 256 MB (the minimum on NetWare 6) to 512 MB or even 1 GB.

## Other Microprocessors

Some workstations you will encounter as a network administrator are not based on Intel or Intel-compatible microprocessors. Apple Macintosh computers are based on the Motorola 68000 line of microprocessors; Apple PowerMac computers are based on the PowerPC microprocessor. These processors are not covered in this book.

## Interrupts and I/O Ports

For input from and output to the computer system, you need to be able to attach such devices as keyboards, printers, monitors, network cards, and the mouse. These devices are commonly known as **peripherals** because they are added on to the system board. The microprocessor must control and monitor each peripheral device—from the hard disk to the keyboard—attached to the system board. Interrupts and input/output (I/O) ports conduct the monitoring. To configure adapter cards correctly, you need to know how interrupts and I/O ports work.

**Common Interrupts**  An **interrupt request (IRQ)** is a signal that a device or controller card sends to the processor to inform it that the device or controller needs attention. Your telephone is a good example of how an interrupt request works in a computer. When the phone rings, it means that someone is trying to contact you, and you normally try to answer it as soon as possible before you lose the opportunity to speak with the caller. On a network, when a packet arrives at a NetWare server's network card, it signals the server by "ringing" its interrupt. When the NetWare server detects the interrupt signal of a packet arrival, it temporarily stops its work and spends a few microseconds putting the data packet from the network card into memory before returning to its work.

Each device in a computer system needs its own unique interrupt so that the processor does not misinterpret the source of the interrupt signal. If your doorbell is wired so that it also causes your telephone to ring, you cannot be sure which to answer when you hear them. A wrong guess results in the loss of information. In a similar way, two devices using the same interrupt number in a computer system cannot interact correctly with the processor, and your system performance will be sporadic at best.

Because of the limited amount of system interrupt numbers, assigning unique numbers to every category of computer peripheral is impossible. There are some general usage guidelines for system interrupts, however. Figure 2-4 shows interrupt numbers used on several of the most common system devices. Each manufacturer allows you to adjust the interrupt setting of its peripheral device, so you can choose an interrupt setting that does not conflict with other system devices.

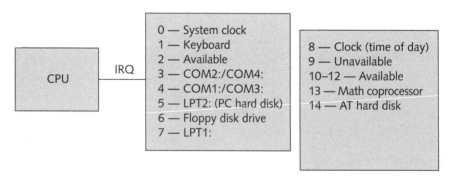

**Figure 2-4**   Common interrupt usage

**Input/Output Ports**  An **input/output (I/O) port** is a memory location that the processor uses to send control commands to a peripheral device and read back status information. To communicate with each device separately, each peripheral attached to the computer system needs a unique I/O port address range. Table 2-2 lists I/O port addresses for several common peripherals. To avoid conflicts with other devices in a computer, each peripheral controller card manufacturer offers a number of different I/O port address options. The network administrator's job includes assigning unique I/O port settings for network cards.

**Table 2-2**   Common Device Configurations

| Device | Interrupt | I/O Address |
|--------|-----------|-------------|
| COM1 | 4 | 3F8-3FFh |
| COM2 | 3 | 2F8-2FFh |
| COM3 | 4 | 3E8-3EF |
| COM4 | 3 | 2E8-2EF |
| LPT1 | 7 | 378-37Fh |
| LPT2 | 5 | 278-27Fh |
| Hard disk controller | 14 | 1F0-1F8<br>170-177 |
| Network interface card | 3 | 300-31Fh |

The **parallel port** connects the computer to a parallel cable, which transfers data from the computer to a peripheral device 8 bits at a time on parallel wires. The parallel port is commonly referred to as the "printer port" because almost all printers use a standard parallel port interface. This makes it easy to plug almost any printer into a computer's parallel port. The parallel cable attaches to a 25-pin connector on the back of the computer and a larger 36-pin card edge connector on the printer. The Centronics printer company standardized the use of the parallel port for printers. As a result of the Centronics standard's early popularity, all IBM-compatible computer and printer manufacturers now include the Centronics parallel port on their systems.

In contrast to parallel ports, which transmit an entire byte at one time, the **serial port** on IBM-compatible computers sends only 1 bit of data at a time. One advantage of the serial port is its ability to send information between devices over long distances by using only a few wires in a twisted-pair cable. With serial ports, devices such as modems can be attached to translate bits into an analog signal compatible with telephone systems, thereby allowing a worldwide range of computer communications.

The **Universal Serial Bus (USB)** port is now available on most computer systems. This bus enables multiple devices to be connected to the same port. Also, it is up to 10 times faster in throughput (up to 12 Mbps) than the earlier specification. However, the hardware devices connected to it must be manufactured to support USB or they won't gain any advantage from using the port.

The speed of the serial signal is the **baud rate**. Standard serial port baud rates on a computer range from 300 to 115,000 baud. For digital signals, the baud rate is usually equal to the number of bits per second (bps). Modems commonly use a combination of methods that vary the amplitude and phase of an analog signal to send data over telephone lines, where the bps rate is much higher than the baud rate. Baud rate no longer applies to modems as it did many years ago.

Serial communication can be synchronous or asynchronous. **Synchronous communication**, commonly used with LAN cards to send packets of 1500 or more bytes between computers, takes place at very high speeds ranging from 4 to more than 100 megabits per second (Mbps). Synchronous ports are generally quite expensive because they require special control and timing circuitry.

Asynchronous communication is much simpler, sending only one character at a time. Modems often use **asynchronous communication** to transmit information between microcomputers or between a microcomputer and the Internet or an online information service provider, such as America Online or CompuServe. In asynchronous communication, each character is transmitted separately and is encapsulated with a start and stop bit and an optional **parity bit** for error checking (see Figure 2-5). The parity bit is set to odd (off) or even (on). Even parity means that the total number of 1 bits, including the parity bit, is even. Take, for example, the ASCII character "C" in uppercase (0100 0011). Notice there are three 1s in this binary form. To meet the requirements of even parity, you add a 1 to the parity bit field so that the number of 1s equals four—therefore, an even number of them.

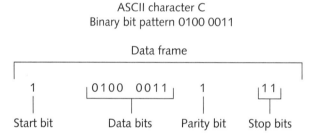

ASCII character C
Binary bit pattern 0100 0011

Data frame

1          0100  0011      1          1 1

Start bit      Data bits      Parity bit    Stop bits

**Figure 2-5**    An asynchronous data frame

If one of the bits is accidentally changed during transmission by a bad cable or noise on the line, the receiving computer detects an error because the number of 1 bits is no longer even. Parity works only if an odd number of bits are in error. However, you will never know which bit or bits are in error.

Most system board manufacturers build one or more asynchronous ports into their IBM-compatible systems. These ports are generally referred to as COM1 through COM4, have either 25-pin or 9-pin connectors, and are located on the back of the computer. The Electronic Industry Association (EIA) standardized two types of serial port connectors, known as RS232 connectors, in the early days of computing. Data terminal equipment (DTE) connectors are used on computers, and data communications equipment (DCE) connectors are used on modems. That means a simple connector-to-connector cable can connect a computer to a modem, as shown in Figure 2-6. Most of the 25-pin connections on the RS232 cable are not used by standard PC serial communications and allow a 9-pin connector to consist of only the required pin connections. A special type of RS232 cable called a **null modem cable** is used to connect two DTE computers without the use of a modem. Note that the null modem cable pictured at the bottom of Figure 2-6 has certain wires crossed so that signals from the sending computer can go to the correct connectors on the receiving computer.

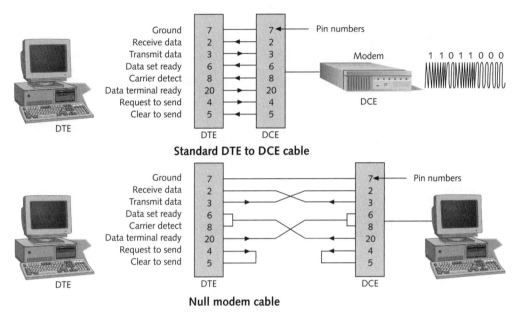

**Figure 2-6**   RS232 serial cables

## Expansion Slots

As you learned earlier in this chapter, expansion slots connect add-in cards, such as video cards and NICs, to the system board. They are connected to other components by the expansion bus. As microprocessor capabilities have improved, the demands placed on the expansion bus have grown, and its architecture has changed and improved over time. Part of the change in the expansion bus consists of changes in the expansion slot's connectors, as illustrated in the connector types shown in Figure 2-7. Notice that an expansion card designed for one expansion bus system cannot be used in another because of differences in the design of the expansion slot connectors.

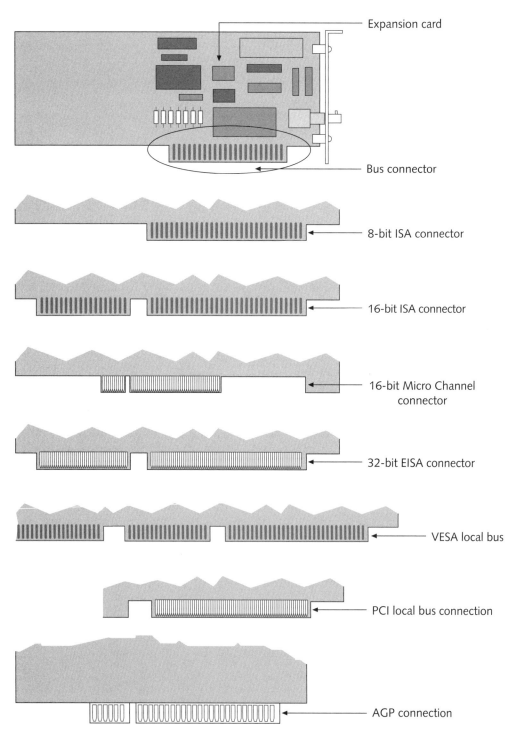

**Figure 2-7**   Common PC connector types

**ISA Bus**   The **Industry Standard Architecture (ISA) bus** was introduced in 1984 with the IBM AT computer. It supported 16-bit data and 24-bit address buses running at 8 MHz. The system board contained a local bus that supported up to 32-bit data and address paths at high clock speeds (such as 33 MHz) between the microprocessor and memory. Many lower-cost PCs used the ISA bus because it provided satisfactory performance for many applications and for low-end NetWare servers. (In fact, most system boards still include one or more ISA slots for backward-compatibility.) The main disadvantage of the ISA bus was seen in graphics applications that required high-speed video processing. Because a video card placed in an ISA expansion slot was limited to a 16-bit data bus and an 8 MHz clock speed, Windows or graphics-based applications ran slowly, even on Pentium-based computers. Check the system's manual or examine the system board to determine whether a system has an ISA bus. ISA slots on the system board have 16-bit card slots composed of two sockets placed together, one containing 31 pins and the other 18.

**Micro Channel Bus**   IBM's **Micro Channel bus** architecture can support 32-bit expansion slots running at high clock speeds (such as 33 MHz). A major advantage of the Micro Channel architecture was that it kept card configuration information in **complementary metal-oxide semiconductor (CMOS) memory** on the system board, allowing software instead of hardware to set card options and configurations. Because a small battery backs up the CMOS memory, these card settings are preserved when the computer is turned off.

Micro Channel was developed for IBM's PS/2 line, but lack of success with that line and with licensing the architecture forced IBM to discontinue using Micro Channel architecture in its PCs. (IBM now uses Intel's Peripheral Component Interface (PCI) bus in its products.) However, you might encounter a few older PCs with the Micro Channel bus still in use.

ISA and PCI cards cannot be used in Micro Channel slots. Cards designed for the ISA bus cannot be used on a Micro Channel computer because the expansion slots are different.

**EISA Bus**   When IBM introduced its Micro Channel bus, other PC manufacturers who wanted to sell systems with the increased performance of IBM's 32-bit bus slots were required to pay IBM royalties as well as redesign their systems. As a counteraction, a number of IBM-compatible computer manufacturers cooperated on the design of an enhanced version of the ISA bus that would support 32-bit expansion cards and higher clock speeds. The result was the **Extended Industry Standard Architecture (EISA) bus**, which supported 32-bit data and address expansion slots that could support adapter cards at 8 MHz clock speeds. Because the EISA bus was an extension of the ISA bus, it included 16-bit expansion slots that accepted older ISA cards. Of course, ISA cards placed in these slots still used the limited ISA address and data bus sizes.

In the end, however, consumers responded to Intel's PCI bus initiative rather than EISA, in part because vendors in the EISA consortium, although agreeing on a standard, did not develop consistently compatible cards for the EISA bus. Users were continually frustrated that EISA cards would not work in an EISA system board. Although Intel suffered many of the same problems with the PCI bus, there were fewer instances. Users began to migrate to the new PCI standard.

**Bus mastering**, a technique first used in EISA and Micro Channel bus systems and now included with the PCI bus, enables adapter cards to run independently of the CPU and to access memory and other devices without interrupting the CPU's work. Bus mastering is an important option to consider when selecting a NetWare server. Much of a NetWare server's processing involves moving information to and from memory, and bus mastering can greatly improve performance by making the system's CPU available more frequently.

**VESA Bus**   Not long after the 80486 chip was introduced, IBM-compatible system board manufacturers struggled to provide systems that would enable video and hard-drive peripherals to match the increased speed of the latest microprocessors. The Video Electronics Standards Association (VESA) cooperated with Intel to design a new system bus architecture that would allow peripheral cards, such as the video adapter, to have direct access to the system board's local bus at the same clock speed as the system board. With the advent of the Pentium chip, Intel's PCI bus became the commonly used expansion bus. You might encounter the VESA bus in PC workstations and NetWare servers that have an 80486 microprocessor. The **VESA bus** consisted of an extension to the 16-bit ISA slot, enabling the slot to be used for either a VESA-compatible device or a 16-bit adapter. With this extension, a card could be placed in a VESA slot to become part of the system board's local bus and achieve much faster data transmission. VESA slots can be included on 80486 system boards that have ISA or EISA expansion slots. On PC workstations running graphics-intensive applications, a system's VESA slot was most often used for the video card, which increased the performance of graphics-based applications. On NetWare servers, which must be able to move many large blocks of data to and from the disk and network cards, the VESA slot was often used for high-speed disk controllers and NICs.

**PCI Bus**   The latest local bus designed by Intel is called the **Peripheral Component Interface (PCI) bus**. The PCI bus improves on the older VESA bus design by avoiding the standard input/output bus and using the system bus to take full advantage of the Pentium chip's 64-bit data path. In addition, the PCI bus runs at the 60 or 66 MHz speed of the processor (compared with the 33 MHz maximum speed of the VESA bus). (It currently has a 133 MHz version called PCI-X.) Most new systems support five to six slots on the system board, and future systems are being designed that will provide eight or more PCI slots.

Intel will continue to develop the PCI bus, which will be used as a standard expansion bus in new workstations and servers. Combination buses will be the normal configuration, as the PCI bus is usually combined with an ISA bus (on PC workstations) or an EISA bus (on servers).

2

As speedy as the PCI bus is, it still isn't fast enough for onscreen video. To further enhance the display of full-motion video, Intel introduced the **Accelerated (or Advanced) Graphics Port (AGP)** specification. System boards with AGP can support adapters tailored for the delivery of high-speed, high-resolution video data. (You can see an example of an AGP slot in Figure 2-1, just to the right of the white PCI slots in the middle of the board.)

## Memory

The purpose of the computer's primary memory unit is to store software and data in a manner that allows the microprocessor unit to access each storage cell directly. Memory consists of millions of tiny switches built into silicon memory modules that can be turned on or off to represent a binary one or zero. The memory switches are arranged in groups of eight to form memory cells called bytes. Every byte is assigned a unique number or address that distinguishes it from other memory bytes. Each memory byte can then be used to store one character of data or part of an instruction. The microprocessor accesses memory by sending the address number of the desired byte on the address bus and then receiving the contents of the memory cells on the data bus. On a 32-bit data bus, four sequential memory bytes can be sent to or from the microprocessor with one memory access.

**Memory Types**   Four primary types of memory are used in microcomputer systems: RAM, ROM, CMOS, and high-speed cache. Each memory type has a specific function in processing information in a computer system:

- **Random access memory (RAM)** is considered a volatile form of memory because it depends on constant power; when the power is turned off, the contents of RAM are erased. A computer's RAM is its primary workspace, where programs and data are stored during processing. With more RAM, workstations can run larger and more complex software applications. A NetWare server uses additional RAM for file and directory caching. (File caching, the process of storing often-used disk information in memory, is discussed in detail later in this chapter.) Because memory is more than 100 times faster than disk access time, the amount of memory available for file caching directly affects the performance of a NetWare server.

- **Extended data output (EDO) RAM** is faster than older RAM and was the standard RAM used in Pentium, Pentium Pro, and Pentium II microcomputers. As of this writing, **synchronous dynamic RAM (SDRAM)** is the most common RAM in computers. It differs from earlier types of RAM in being able to support higher clock speeds (up to 133 MHz). It synchronizes with the CPU's bus, making it about twice as fast as EDO RAM.

- **Rambus dynamic (RD) RAM** uses a Rambus In-line Memory Module (RIMM) instead of a Dual In-line Memory Module (DIMM), discussed later in this chapter. A RIMM is similar to a DIMM, but it has a special memory bus installed to increase speed. Why the big concern over increasing speed? Processors are getting so fast that memory is having trouble keeping up. RDRAM chips can achieve a data rate speed of 800 MHz and are supported by Pentium 4 processors.

A special type of RAM, Video RAM (VRAM), is used in graphics cards.

When adding RAM to a microcomputer, check the specifications in the PC's user guide to be sure you add the correct type of RAM for that microcomputer. The RAM should be both the same type (EDO RAM, SDRAM, RDRAM, VRAM) and the same speed (60 ns [nanoseconds], 70 ns, and so forth).

- **Read-only memory (ROM),** as its name suggests, cannot be changed. On most microcomputer systems, ROM is used to store boot instructions and control such basic hardware functions as inputting data from the keyboard or accessing the disk drive. Because they cannot be changed, instructions stored in ROM are referred to as firmware. Because ROM is slower than RAM, most 80386 and later microprocessors allow moving the contents of ROM into RAM during booting, a process known as RAM shadowing. **RAM shadowing** can significantly increase the speed of such hardware-oriented operations as accessing the screen and keyboard.

- The original IBM PC bus contained switches for setting configuration options, such as memory capacity, disk drives, and video. Today's system boards contain a built-in setup program to store this configuration information in a special memory type called CMOS. CMOS memory uses very little power, and its contents can be maintained with a small on-board battery when the computer's power is off. The CMOS battery is recharged whenever the system is powered. If you add a new disk drive or more memory, you need to run a setup program to update your computer's CMOS configuration. Many CMOS setup programs are built into the system board's ROM and can be run by pressing a certain key sequence (such as the Esc key) while the computer system is starting. Some computers need to be started with a special disk to change the CMOS configuration settings.

2

Be aware that the CMOS battery can completely discharge when a computer is turned off for an extended time, causing loss of configuration information. It can also die because of old age. In either case, documenting CMOS settings and keeping them in a safe place is wise so that you can restore them when needed.

- **Cache memory** is very high-speed memory made of chips called **static RAM (SRAM)**. Most RAM consists of relatively inexpensive chips called **dynamic RAM (DRAM)**. Although inexpensive, DRAM bears a hidden cost: It needs a special clock cycle to maintain its memory contents. Because of this extra refresh cycle, DRAM is slower than SRAM because it requires wait states when used with processors running at speeds above 20 MHz. SRAM's speed advantage over DRAM makes it more suitable for caching the most recently used memory locations. It increases the speed of processing by allowing the processor to access data or instructions without using wait states. High-speed (33 MHz and above) computers typically need and use 128–256 KB of cache memory to improve their performance. Intel's 80486, Pentium, Pentium Pro, and Pentium II microprocessors use built-in cache. The 80486 has 8 or 16 KB of cache memory, the Pentium has 16 KB, and the Pentium Pro has 16 KB built into the microprocessor chip. This is known as the level 1 (L1) cache (primary cache). Additional cache, known as the level 2 (L2) cache (secondary cache), can often be installed on the system board to increase system performance. Typically, 128–256 KB of L2 cache is used with the 80486 and Pentium. The Pentium Pro uses a built-in L2 cache of 256–512 KB. The Pentium II, III, and 4 have a 512 KB L2 cache.

**SIMMs**    Most RAM is currently supplied on small memory cards called **single in-line memory modules (SIMMs)**, shown in Figure 2-8. SIMMs are arranged on the system board in banks. A bank can contain from one to four SIMM sockets, and a computer's system board contains several memory banks. Memory is added in banks by filling all SIMM sockets in the bank with the same type of SIMM chip because SIMMs of different capacities cannot be mixed within a bank. (For example, a 4 MB SIMM cannot be mixed with a 16 MB SIMM.) The number of SIMM banks determines the maximum amount of memory that can be placed on the system board and the ease of memory expansion. If a memory board does not contain enough SIMM banks, you can replace existing SIMMs with ones of higher capacity to expand the computer's memory.

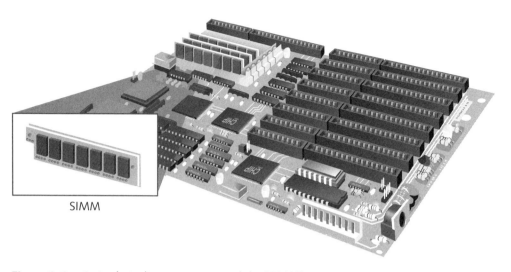

SIMM

**Figure 2-8**   A single in-line memory module (SIMM)

In addition to obtaining the correct capacity for the SIMMs, make sure the SIMMs are the same speed (60 ns is typical, but many systems have 70 ns). The speed of most SIMMs ranges between 60 ns and 80 ns. When adding SIMMs to a computer, check the system's manual to verify the correct chip speeds. Some SIMMs are marked with the speed. Finally, make sure you match the type of RAM used in the PC. If the PC was purchased with EDO RAM, use EDO RAM when you add memory.

**DIMMs**   The Pentium II also supports **dual in-line memory modules (DIMMs)**, a combination of two SIMMs that are read alternately in memory-access cycles. The result is an effective data bus of 128 bits over the Pentium Pro's normal 64-bit data bus. DIMMs come as 168-pin modules with a speed of 10 ns.

**Memory Usage**   For the most part, Windows 95 automates memory management that you previously had to specify with statements in the Config.sys and Autoexec.bat files. The same memory models and terms, however, apply because Windows 95 must still support old DOS applications. DOS was designed to run on an 8088 processor in real mode, so it's limited to managing 1 MB (1024 KB) of RAM. As shown in Figure 2-9, DOS uses the first 640 KB of this 1 MB memory area, referred to as **conventional memory**, to run software applications. The memory between 640 KB and 1 MB, called **upper memory**, is reserved for hardware use. For example, your video card uses part of its upper memory to store data displayed on the screen. The network administrator might need to use this memory area when configuring certain NICs. The memory above 1 MB, called **extended memory**, is available to microprocessors running in protected or virtual mode. DOS requires an extended memory manager, such as the Himem.sys driver, to take advantage of that memory. Operating systems that do not rely on DOS— Windows NT workstation, Unix, OS/2, and NetWare—can access extended memory directly, without the need for special drivers.

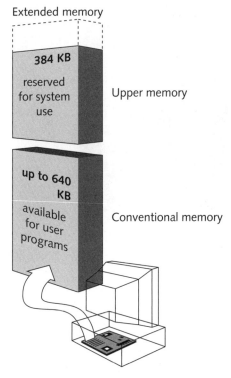

**Figure 2-9**   A memory map

# Storage Systems

Advances in disk storage systems have been as important to the development of micro-computer systems as the improvements made to processors and memory. Instructions and data need to be retrieved from disks and placed in RAM before the processor chip can act on them. Therefore, both the speed and the capacity of disk storage are critical to a computer system's performance. A NetWare server's major function involves the shared use of its hard disk drives. As a result, the NetWare operating system is specifically designed to maximize the performance and reliability of its disk storage system. In the following sections, you learn the basic terminology and concepts needed to understand and configure disk systems.

## Magnetic Disk Drives

The **magnetic disk drive** is the component of the disk storage system in which data is stored by means of magnetic fields representing ones and zeros. The disk's recording surface is coated with a metal oxide that retains magnetic fields. The polarity of each magnetic field is used to represent a one or a zero. To perform record and playback func-tions on disk surfaces, recording heads containing electronic magnets are attached to a device called an **access arm** that allows the recording heads to move back and forth across the disk surface, as shown in Figure 2-10.

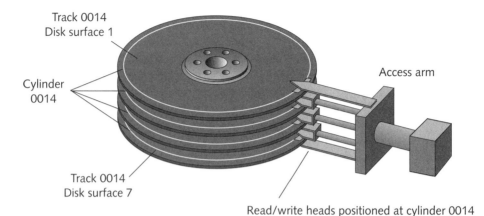

**Figure 2-10**   Disk drive components

The disk surface is divided into concentric circles called **tracks**. The set of recording tracks that the recording heads can access without repositioning the access arm is referred to as a **cylinder**. A track, which can contain a large amount of data, is divided into smaller recording areas called **sectors**, as shown in Figure 2-11. Reading or recording information in sectors, which are small, specific areas, allows efficient access to information.

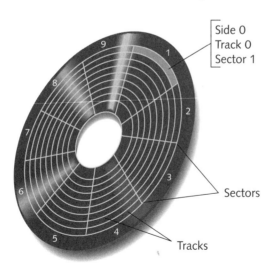

**Figure 2-11**   Disk tracks and sectors

2

## Floppy Disk Drives

Microcomputer floppy disks used to be available in two sizes: 5¼ inches or 3½ inches. Although 5¼-inch disks are obsolete, you still need to be familiar with their proper use and handling because many files have been archived on 5¼-inch disks. The 3½-inch floppy disk is today's standard because it offers higher densities, more reliability, and easier storage. Table 2-3 compares the storage capacities of 5¼-inch and 3½-inch floppy disks. However, even the venerable 3½-inch floppy is close to vanishing from newer PCs. Most software is now shipped on CD-ROM. Sharing files almost always requires more capacity than a 3½-inch disk can handle. For that reason, some vendors are offering Iomega's Zip drives with 100 MB of capacity per disk in their systems. Others offer a new, higher-density disk with 120 MB of storage, called the LS-120 (or SuperDisk), which is standard in many of the new computer systems today.

**Table 2-3**    Floppy Disk Capacity

| Size | Density | Number of Tracks | Number of Sectors | Capacity |
|------|---------|-----------------|-------------------|----------|
| 5¼" | Double | 40 | 9 | 360 KB |
| 5¼" | High | 80 | 15 | 1200 KB or 1.2 MB |
| 3½" | Double | 80 | 9 | 720 KB |
| 3½" | High | 80 | 18 | 1400 KB or 1.4 MB |

## Hard Disk Drives

A hard drive is so named because it contains one or more rigid aluminum platters coated with a metal oxide that holds magnetic fields. Each platter has a read/write head positioned above and below each disk surface. Rotating the disk surface at high speeds causes the read/write head to fly just above the disk surface. Because the recording head on hard drives does not touch the disk surface, hard drives do not wear out, as floppy disks do, and can last for several years.

 You cannot assume that your data will always be safe on a hard disk. Component failure, software bugs, and operator errors can and will eventually cause data loss, so establishing a regular backup plan for data stored on hard disks is critical.

For information to be recorded or retrieved on the hard disk, the recording head must first be positioned on the correct track. The time it takes to perform this operation is called the **seek time**. After it is positioned, the read head begins looking for the requested sector. The time it takes for the sector to come into position is called the **rotational delay**. When the requested sector comes under the read head, it is read into a computer memory buffer. This is called the **transfer time**. The seek time plus the rotational delay plus the transfer time yields the **access time**. On hard disk drives, the access time is measured in milliseconds (ms). Most current hard disk drive access times range between 9 and 12 ms. The access time for floppy disks is close to 300 ms, making hard disk drives 10 to 25 times faster.

Once installed, a new hard disk needs to be partitioned for use by the operating system. With the exception of Windows, which uses a DOS partition, each operating system requires its own hard disk partition. Partitioning establishes boundaries within which an operating system formats and stores information on a hard disk. Several different operating system partitions can exist on the same hard disk. When you install NetWare on the NetWare server, for example, you need to create one partition for DOS and another for NetWare. Generally, the DOS partition is very small—about 400 MB—because it is needed only to start the computer and load the NetWare operating system. The NetWare partition contains the storage areas used to store the data and software that will be available to the network. After the partition areas are established, each operating system needs to format its partition for its own use. In DOS, this is done with the FORMAT program. Use the NetWare Install Wizard to partition and format the disk drive for the NetWare server.

The directory area of the disk partition contains the names and locations of files and other information about each file stored in the partition. Storing an entire file can require many sectors scattered throughout the partition. DOS 6.22 and earlier operating systems used a **file allocation table (FAT)** to link all the sectors belonging to one file. Windows 95 (and the included DOS 7.0) uses a 32-bit **virtual file allocation table (VFAT)**, which is backward-compatible with the older FAT. Windows 2000, XP Professional, and Server all use a 32-bit version of FAT called FAT32, but encourage users to implement New Technology File System (NTFS) as the standard file system, if they want to take advantage of its file compression, security, encryption, and many other features. Microsoft recommends using FAT32 only if the system will be dual-booted, meaning older operating systems, such as Windows 95/98, still need to run on the Windows 2000/XP operating system computer. For example, any data stored on the NTFS partition would not be accessible if the system was started in Windows 98.

When adding information to an existing file, the new sectors can be located anywhere in the disk partition. The FAT or VFAT allows the computer to find all sectors for a file. When you load a file from the disk, the computer first reads the directory to determine the location of the first sector. Then it reads each sector of the file, as specified by the FAT or VFAT. The NetWare network operating system also uses a FAT, and the NetWare server keeps the entire FAT and the most frequently accessed directory sectors in memory.

## Disk Interfaces

Disk interfaces, or **controller cards**, enable a system's microprocessor to control the hard and floppy disk drives in a computer and provide a path for data to be transferred between the disk and the memory. The disk controller card can plug into one of the expansion bus slots in a computer's system board but is usually built into the system board's circuits. There are several types of disk controller cards. This section describes the most common ones: the IDE/EIDE/ATA controllers found in most workstations today, and the SCSI controller cards often used in NetWare servers and high-end workstations. To configure the NetWare operating system correctly, a network administrator must be able to distinguish between different controller cards.

Currently, two major types of **Integrated Drive Electronics (IDE)** hard disk controller cards are on the market: IDE and enhanced IDE. IDE controller cards are often referred to as "paddle cards" because most of the control electronics are built into the disk drive. Because few circuits are required for the IDE disk controller, most IDE controller cards come with a floppy disk controller and serial, parallel, and game ports.

Standard IDE controllers can control up to two hard disk drives and support drive capacities between 40 and 528 MB, along with transfer speeds of 3.3 MB/sec and data access speeds of less than 18 ms. Because of their low cost and high performance, IDE controllers became very popular and were used on most desktop computers. Although IDE controllers and drives are appropriate for small to medium NetWare servers with a total disk capacity of less than 528 MB, most NetWare servers use SCSI or enhanced IDE controller cards.

**Enhanced IDE (EIDE)** controllers and drives offer **Logical Block Addressing (LBA)**, which allows them to provide up to 8.4 GB (billion bytes), well above the standard IDE limit of 528 MB. Enhanced IDE also offers transfer rates of up to 13.3 MB/sec and access times of 8.5 ms. The EIDE speed improvements are achieved by increasing the disk drive rotational speed from 3000 rpm to more than 10,000 rpm, by using better read/write heads, and by using an advanced technology that allows the access arm to move from track to track in one-tenth the time. To take advantage of the increased transfer speed, the EIDE card must be installed in a PCI expansion slot. EIDE also provides for up to four devices, including nondisk peripherals such as CD-ROM or tape drives. The increased speed and capacity of the EIDE disk system, combined with the ability to connect up to four devices, make it a good choice for many NetWare server environments.

Ultra DMA or ATA-33 is a newer implementation of EIDE. It offers a 33 MB/sec transfer speed, but requires special drivers with Windows 95 to recognize the drive. There is even a proposed upgrade called ATA-66 with a 66 MB/sec speed that could be ready for delivery in the next year.

The **small computer system interface (SCSI)** is a general-purpose interface card that can control hard disks, tape backup systems, CD-ROM drives, and floppy disks, as shown in Figure 2-12. Up to seven SCSI devices can be chained together and attached to a single SCSI control card. The last device in each chain has a terminator enabled to properly end the cable segment. Multiple SCSI controllers can coexist in the same computer.

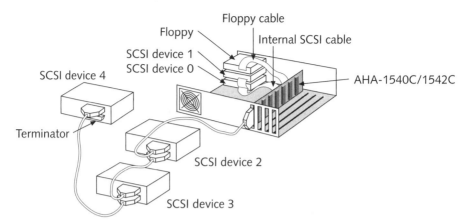

**Figure 2-12**    The SCSI drive interface

SCSI hard disk capacities normally range from 18 GB to 40 GB or more. Because they are more complex, SCSI controller cards and drives are generally more expensive than comparable ATA drives. SCSI controllers use a parallel form of communication, sending 8 or more bits to a drive at one time, resulting in higher transfer rates to and from the drive. Other controllers use serial communication, transferring only 1 bit at a time.

**SCSI-2**, an upgrade to the original SCSI specifications, provides a more standard command set and additional commands to access CD-ROM drives, tape drives, optical drives, and several other peripherals. A SCSI-2 feature called **command queuing** allows devices to accept multiple commands and carry them out in the order the device deems most efficient. This feature is particularly important for NetWare servers that could have several workstations simultaneously making requests for information from the disk system. Another feature of the SCSI-2 controller is a high-speed transfer option called Fast SCSI-2, which at 40 Mbps is nearly twice as fast as previous SCSI transfer speeds. In addition, the SCSI-2 controller can further increase transfer speeds by using a 16-bit data bus called Wide SCSI-2 between the SCSI-2 controller card and devices. This 16-bit data bus transfers twice as much data between the controller and disk drive as could be transferred using the original 8-bit data bus on standard SCSI controllers.

Because SCSI-2 controller cards accommodate more devices and provide larger storage capacities, they are often the choice for NetWare servers on medium to large networks requiring more than 10 GB of hard disk and support for CD-ROM drives and tape drives. SCSI-2 drives have the following advantages over EIDE drives for use in a NetWare server:

- SCSI-2 supports as many as seven devices chained to a single adapter; EIDE supports a maximum of four devices attached to two controller cards.

- SCSI-2 provides multitasking via command queuing, which results in better performance when multiple disk requests are pending.

- The variety of SCSI-2 storage peripherals is far greater than what EIDE offers, especially for special devices, such as magneto-optical drives sometimes used for data archiving.

SCSI evolution has not stood still with the development of SCSI-2. The work on the **SCSI-3** standard started in 1993 when SCSI-2 was already 8 years old and still not ratified. The standards for SCSI-1 and SCSI-2 were released as single documents, but SCSI-3 was divided into many documents defining different aspects of the standard. This was necessary because SCSI-3 tried to integrate many new technologies, and the already large document of the SCSI-2 specification would have grown into unmanageable dimensions, with too many people working on it at the same time. Dividing the document into several related subdocuments made it possible to develop substandards at different speeds yet retain a coherent standard.

Because many significant advances in SCSI technology have been developed since SCSI-2 was adopted, the SCSI-3 specification is still in the process of being ratified. For the first time, the SCSI specification incorporates serial interconnection schemes and SCSI's traditional parallel interconnect. Although the SCSI-3 standard has not yet been ratified, several SCSI-3 technologies are on the market and some have already seen several generations of SCSI-3 standards; for example, SCSI-3 Parallel Interface (SPI) has gone from SPI (Ultra) to SPI-4 (Ultra320) and SPI-5 (Ultra640), which is still under development. From the parallel side, Fast-20 Wide SCSI, also referred to as "Ultra" SCSI, is the technology that SCSI users implement initially because Ultra SCSI-3 is backward-compatible with SCSI-2 and SCSI-1 systems and peripherals. Ultra SCSI doubles the Fast SCSI bus clock rate from 10 MHz to 20 MHz and transfers data over a 16-bit Wide SCSI bus to produce SCSI data transfers rates up to 40 MB/sec.

From the serial interconnect side, SCSI-3 includes three new technologies: Serial Storage Architecture (SSA), Fibre Channel, and IEEE P1394. These Serial SCSI technologies offer SCSI users faster data transfer rates, more devices per bus, longer cables, and simplified connectors. Unfortunately, serial SCSI is not backward-compatible with SCSI-1 or SCSI-2 devices. Later additions to the SCSI-3 architecture are iSCSI, which uses Ethernet as the transport medium, and Inifiniband, which is expected to gradually replace PCI as the interconnect between processors and devices.

Serial SCSI's impressive data transfer rates makes it ideal for disk array applications. Therefore, the serial SCSI architects designed these serial interconnects to support true **hot swapping** without the use of special connectors. Hot-swapping support enables users to remove and insert new devices without powering down the system.

## RAID Systems

A network administrator is concerned with data integrity because network downtime can result in loss of revenue for an organization. Therefore, the NetWare server must be as reliable as possible. A popular way to increase the reliability of the NetWare server disk system is to use a **redundant array of independent disks (RAID)**. RAID protects against data loss caused by a bad disk drive. Fault tolerance (discussed later in this chapter) is the term associated with RAID since a recovery can be made if a "fault," or hard disk crash, occurs. An old adage in the high-tech industry states: Administrators should have two things in their arsenal—a good fault-tolerance disaster-recovery plan and a good resume. If the fault-tolerance disaster-recovery plan fails, they'll need the good resume!

There are three levels of RAID systems in general use: 1, 3, and 5. RAID level 1 is the most common; it uses multiple disk drives and controllers with software to provide the basic disk mirroring and duplexing (discussed later in the chapter) available with NetWare. RAID level 3 is a hardware solution that takes each byte of data off several drives; one drive is used for parity checking and error correcting. If a drive fails in a RAID level 3 system, the parity drive can be used to reconstruct each data byte on the replacement drive.

The more sophisticated RAID level 5 system takes data off the drives by sector. The parity information is embedded in the sectors, eliminating the use of a dedicated parity drive. Many RAID systems also support hot-swapping, which allows a drive to be replaced while the computer is running. With hot-swapping, the network administrator can replace a malfunctioning disk drive and have the system resynchronize the drive without interrupting network services. The hot-swapping feature can be well worth its extra cost when your NetWare server needs to support mission-critical applications that cannot be interrupted.

## CD-ROM Drives

**Compact disc read-only memory (CD-ROM)** technology differs from magnetic disk drives in that it uses light from low-intensity laser beams to read binary ones and zeros from the disk platter instead of sensing magnetic fields on hard and floppy disk surfaces. Data is permanently recorded on a CD-ROM at the factory. The main benefit of a CD-ROM is its storage capacity. A standard CD-ROM can store more than 680 MB of data, which makes CD-ROMs an excellent way to distribute and access large software applications, collections of programs, or other data-intensive files, such as sound, graphic images, and video.

CD-ROMs store data using microscopic "pits" arranged in a single spiral track that winds continuously from the outside to the inside of the disk, much like the tracks on old vinyl phonograph records. There are about 2.8 billion pits on a single CD-ROM spiral track. When a CD-ROM is accessed, the drive uses a laser beam to measure the reflections off the pits in the spiral track. These reflections vary in intensity as the light reflects off the pits. The fluctuations in the reflected light are then converted into digital ones and zeros.

Many users need access to CD-ROMs on their workstation computers. This can be accomplished by installing CD-ROM drives on each workstation, by sharing CD-ROM drives from the network NetWare server, or by a combination of both strategies. CD-ROM drives are attached to a computer through either a SCSI or an IDE/EIDE bus interface controller card.

CD-ROM technology also includes two writable versions: CD-R and CD-RW. CD-R is a write-once medium, meaning that once you record on the disc, you cannot erase that information. CD-RW is a rewritable system, meaning you can erase data you record on the device. All CD-RW devices can record CD-Rs as well as CD-RW media.

 If you try to store information on a CD-ROM, you'll see a "Write Protected" error message because the device is read-only.

The main advantage of attaching one or more shared CD-ROM drives to a NetWare server rather than running the discs at each workstation is that it reduces the cost of multiple CD-ROM titles. When a shared CD-ROM drive is attached to the NetWare server, NetWare assigns it a drive pointer so that the information can be accessed and shared across the network, just like any other data on the NetWare server's hard disks.

### DVD-ROM Drives

The **Digital Versatile Disc (DVD)**, the successor to the CD-ROM, represents the merging of three technologies: computer, audio, and video. DVDs come in two basic types: DVD-video, for home entertainment, and DVD-ROM, targeted for computer application. DVD technology uses the same size disc as CD-ROM—the diameter is 120 millimeters for both—but it stores 4.7 GB of data (8.5 GB double-sided).

 Although DVD-ROM drives can read DVD-video discs, your PC might not be capable of handling the video data stream fast enough to display it in real time on your monitor.

DVD-ROM also uses a data format called **Universal Data Format (UDF)**. Windows XP Professional reads UDF discs without added drivers. Windows 95 and earlier devices, however, require special software to read the contents of UDF discs.

 When you purchase a system with DVD-ROM drives, look for the MultiRead logo. This tells you that the drive can read all other types of 120-mm optical media, including CD-ROM, CD-R, and CD-RW. Look for the MultiRead logo on new CD-ROM systems as well because there's no guarantee that the system can read CD-RW discs.

## Video Monitors

A network administrator can be called on to make decisions about the types of monitors and adapter cards to be used in workstation computers. This section provides an overview of the video-system information you need to meet the requirements of Novell's network administrator exam.

A computer's ability to display graphics depends on the video adapter and type of monitor connected. A **pixel** (or picture element) is a point on the screen that can be turned on or off. It is composed of three very small dots—one red, one green, and one blue. The dots are adjusted and combined to create the pixel's color and intensity. The **resolution** of a video adapter is measured by the number of pixels on each line and on the number of lines. For example, a resolution of $320 \times 200$ indicates 320 pixels per line with 200 lines, for a total of 64,000 pixels.

**Dot pitch** is a measurement of how close together the dots making up each pixel are placed. A smaller dot pitch results in a clearer and crisper display screen. A dot pitch of 0.28 or less is generally desirable for a video monitor.

 Noninterlaced monitors are preferable to interlaced monitors. An interlaced monitor scans every other line on the screen, causing more eyestrain. Noninterlaced monitors have a faster scanning system that scans each line from top to bottom to create a smoother screen image. Most monitors today are noninterlaced.

## VGA

The **video graphics array (VGA)** adapter and monitor is typical in older systems. VGA supported all previous video modes and both monochrome and color monitors. A monochrome monitor was often the best choice for an inexpensive monitor for a NetWare server computer because it could be plugged directly into a standard VGA interface card and produced a good-quality text display. One big difference between VGA and previous video adapters was its use of analog signals rather than the digital RGB interface. The more expensive analog signal creates many more color variations over the same number of wires.

## Super VGA (SVGA)

The **Super VGA (SVGA)** adapter is an enhanced version of the VGA adapter that offers better resolution and more color combinations. Additional memory is usually required on VGA adapters to provide the enhanced capabilities. Super VGA adapters can display 256 colors with a resolution of $800 \times 600$, or up to $1024 \times 768$ when used with 16 colors. Most monitors sold today are SVGA monitors, and NetWare 6 requires SVGA or better.

## XGA

The **eXtended Graphics Array (XGA)** is the latest in monitor technology for laptops and notebook computers. It offers up to $1024 \times 768$ resolution, similar to the SVGA standard, but with additional colors (such as 65,536 colors versus 16 for an SVGA adapter at $640 \times 480$ resolution).

## Graphics Accelerators

Because of the increasing graphics demands in programs, video card manufacturers started building video adapters with a microprocessor called a **graphics accelerator** to speed up graphics operations. Accelerators are now found on most graphics cards and are often built into the system board. Graphics adapters based on accelerators feature resolutions of $1024 \times 768$, $1280 \times 1024$, and $1600 \times 1200$, with up to 16.7 million colors. To further enhance the display of onscreen video, system boards with the new AGP specification mentioned earlier can support adapters tailored for delivering high-speed video data.

# Power System

Because all system components depend on electricity to operate, the power system is the most important part of any computer system. Power problems can often cause intermittent computer crashes and losses of data, which cannot be tolerated on a NetWare server. A network administrator needs to be familiar with the components that make up a NetWare server's power system. In the following sections, you learn about the major power components and how you can use them to provide reliable power to a NetWare server.

## Power Supply

A power supply that does not have enough amps or that does not filter out power irregularities can cause system errors or crashes. Because a NetWare server often has multiple high-capacity hard drives and many other peripherals, such as CD-ROM drives, tape drives, and NICs, the power supply must be able to support the amperage that all these devices require. A NetWare server should have a **switching power supply** of at least 400 watts. A switching power supply stops working if there's a serious component failure or a short in the system. A built-in surge suppressor and a power filter help protect system components from damage caused by voltage spikes during electrical storms or by your computer running on the same power line as other high-power electrical equipment, such as motors and copy machines.

## Power Line

The first rule in supplying good power to a NetWare server is to have an electrician install a separate power line from the main fuse box to the server room. This power line should have no other equipment or computers attached to it. Avoid attaching laser printers or copy machines to the same power line the NetWare server uses because these devices can create power fluctuations and electrical noise that can harm the system.

## Power Filters

The second line of defense in the power system is a good power filter that removes any noise or power surges from the incoming line. It's a good idea to have your local power company or an electrician use a voltage monitor on your incoming power for several days to determine the extent of any electrical noise or power surges in the NetWare server room. You can use the voltage monitor information to buy the correct power filter to protect your server from unwanted electrical noise and surges.

## Uninterruptible Power Supply

Each NetWare server should be protected from brownouts and blackouts by an **uninterruptible power supply (UPS)**. A UPS contains a battery that automatically supplies power in the event of a commercial power failure. Depending on the battery capacity, a UPS unit can supply power to the server for up to 30 minutes after commercial power fails. The capacity of most UPS systems is measured in volt-amps (VA). Volt-amps are calculated by multiplying the number of amps needed times the voltage. To determine the correct size of the UPS needed for a server, list each piece of equipment to be protected (CPU, monitor, external drives, and so on). Include its nameplate-rated wattage or VA. Then total all wattage and VA to determine the total wattage and total volt-amps necessary—this total must be less than or equal to the UPS's recommended output.

Another important feature of a UPS is its ability to send a signal to the computer informing it that the system has switched to battery backup power. NetWare has a UPS monitoring feature that informs the NetWare server how much time the UPS battery will last and shuts itself down before all power is drained from the battery. Because a NetWare server keeps a lot of information in RAM cache buffers, if a system's power is turned off before the NetWare server is shut down, important information could easily be lost. In many cases, the NetWare server cannot mount its disk volumes after an unexpected crash, so the network administrator must perform a volume fix.

Use your UPS capacity wisely. Attach your server, monitor, and any disk subsystems to the unit, but don't attach a high-demand device, such as a laser printer, on the same unit. Remember, the UPS is intended to handle a power failure or brownout, not serve as a portable generator.

## THE WORKSTATION

Now that microcomputers have been covered, it's time to consider the user's workstation. Each user's workstation should provide network connectivity to ensure that the user can handle any job responsibilities. Although many operating systems can be used on workstations—Windows 95/98, Windows NT Workstation, Macintosh System 7.5/8—the focus in this book is on Microsoft Windows 2000 Professional/Windows XP Professional because these operating systems are the most widely used as of this writing.

## Windows 2000 Professional/XP Professional Microprocessor Requirements

Microsoft recommends a Pentium 166 MHz or higher microprocessor for Windows 2000 Professional and a Pentium 300 MHz (233 MHz minimum required) or higher clock speed for its newer Microsoft XP Professional operating system. As of this writing, most new PCs have at least a 2 GHz Pentium CPU, so this minimum is easily met for new PC purchases. Network administrators typically purchase (or recommend for purchase, if they don't have purchasing authority) an entry-level PC for most employees. The exact specifications of an entry-level PC differ from company to company, and they change over time as new hardware components push down the price of older components.

 A good general rule is to set the price you want to pay for the workstation and then buy the hardware configuration closest to that amount. As prices of existing components continually fall, you'll get nowhere waiting for the "best" system as new technology replaces the old.

## Windows 2000 Professional/XP Professional Memory Requirements

Although Microsoft claims that both operating systems support a minimum of 64 MB of RAM, the practical minimum is 128 MB or, even better, 256 MB. This amount lets you run Windows and several other applications simultaneously without undue delays.

## Workstation Storage Requirements

The size needed for a workstation's hard drive is determined by the number and size of applications, programs, and data files that will be stored on the workstation. Currently, most new PCs are being shipped with at least 20 GB hard drives, and many have hard drives with a capacity of 40 GB or more. These hard drives give you plenty of room to install Windows 2000 Professional/XP Professional and application software and still have enough disk space for most users' current storage needs.

## THE NETWARE SERVER

As explained in Chapter 1, NetWare's main function is providing network resources, such as file and print services, to client workstations. The NetWare server can be enhanced with specialized hardware and software to give better performance, security, and reliability than can be expected from a peer-to-peer NOS.

Microcomputer manufacturers often offer microcomputers labeled as LAN servers. These microcomputers offer features not found in microcomputers designed as user workstations, and should be purchased for NetWare servers whenever possible. They include more RAM, a larger hard drive, and a pre-installed NIC. Most important, they have a larger case designed to incorporate additional hard drives, interface cards, supplemental power supplies, and larger fans for cooling.

## NetWare Server Microprocessor Requirements

A NetWare 6 server requires a minimum of a Pentium II microprocessor. However, performance will be slow, so a faster CPU is preferred. Novell recommends a Pentium III 700 MHz processor. A NetWare server typically is used more for input and output operations (reading and writing files) than for computations. Therefore, server performance can often be enhanced more by adding memory or a faster NIC than by using the fastest processor. Some applications, however, run on the server. A client-server database such as Oracle runs part of the program (the server portion) on the NetWare server and other parts of the program (the client) on user workstations. In this case, a faster processor might be important for reasonable application performance.

A good general rule is that when you are purchasing a new NetWare server, you should buy one with a microprocessor at least equivalent to the microprocessor in the standard PCs you are buying for your users. For example, if the standard PCs you buy use a Pentium 4 1.3 GHz CPU, your NetWare server should have at least a Pentium 4 1.3 GHz chip. Don't skimp on the processor in the server; your network depends on it.

## NetWare Server Memory Requirements

The NetWare server uses extended memory to run the NOS, to run the utility modules called NetWare Loadable Modules (NLMs), and to keep information frequently accessed from the hard disk available in RAM. Adding more memory to a NetWare server generally increases NetWare server performance because it allows more disk information to be kept in RAM, thereby reducing read and transmission time. Adding memory to a NetWare server does not enhance the performance of applications stored and used on the individual workstations. Because each workstation's memory is managed by its own local operating system, the NetWare server provides only data and communication services. To run NetWare 6, the NetWare server should have at least 256 MB of RAM. This is the absolute minimum; normally, the NetWare server requires more RAM. Novell recommends 512 MB RAM for optimal performance.

Microcomputers designed as LAN servers are often available with a kind of RAM called **error checking and correcting (ECC) memory**. ECC memory uses algorithms that increase a server's ability to continue operating despite a single-bit memory error, by correcting minor memory errors. If a company's NetWare server controls a mission-critical application, ECC memory can be worth its expense. A **mission-critical application** is one that an organization depends on for its day-to-day operation. In a mail-order business, for example, the order-entry system is considered mission-critical because a system failure directly influences the company's profits.

 The Pentium Pro, Pentium II, Pentium III, and Pentium 4 microprocessor's data bus supports ECC by adding 8 bits of ECC circuits beyond the 64 bits used for the data to support ECC.

# NetWare Server Storage Requirements

When selecting a hard disk system for your NetWare server, first determine the storage capacity your server requires. Allow at least 2 GB for the NetWare 6 operating system files and print jobs. Next, determine which software packages you want to store on the NetWare server and record how much storage space each package needs. To determine the required data storage, identify each application and estimate its current storage requirement and future growth over the next three years. Determine how much space each user will be allowed for personal data storage needs and any shared document storage areas, and add them to obtain the estimated total data requirements. After estimating the storage requirements, add at least 25% to 50% for expansion and overhead to obtain the total hard disk capacity you'll need.

# Performance Features

A NetWare server's performance is determined by how fast it can respond to requests for data from client workstations. The major factors affecting server performance are its ability to keep frequently used information in memory, the speed of its disk system, and, if the first two are adequate, the speed of its processor unit. NetWare is the best-performing NOS in the industry because it was designed to operate on a NetWare server, so it does not contain the additional overhead associated with general-purpose operating systems, such as DOS, Unix, or Windows NT. Some of the NetWare performance features are file caching, directory caching, and elevator seeking.

## File Caching

**File caching** is the process by which NetWare increases the speed of response to requests for disk information. It does this by keeping the most frequently accessed disk blocks in memory. Because the computer's memory is about 100 times faster than the disk system, retrieving a block of data from the file cache greatly improves server performance. As a general rule, at least 50% of the computer's memory should be allocated to file caching, resulting in more than 70% of data requests being handled from the computer's memory rather than read directly from the disk.

## Directory Caching

**Directory caching** is the process of keeping the directory entry table and file allocation table (FAT) for each disk volume in the memory of the computer. Like file caching, directory caching increases server performance by allowing it to find filenames 100 times faster than when the directory information is read directly from disk. In addition to directory caching, NetWare also uses a process called **directory hashing** to create a binary index system that improves file lookup time by as much as 30%. Figure 2-13 illustrates how NetWare's caching system handles requests from two different workstations to run the WP.exe program. In Step 1, the server loads the directory cache and FATs with directory information from the disk volume and then builds the hash table. In Step 2, the first request arrives from Workstation A for the WP.exe file. The server looks up the WP.exe file in the hash table and then uses the directory table and FAT to identify the necessary disk blocks. Because the cache buffers are empty, the server reads the necessary disk blocks into the cache and then sends the WP.exe file to Workstation A. In Step 3, a second request, from Workstation B, is received for the WP.exe file. This time, after looking up the filename in the hash table, the server finds that the needed disk blocks are in the cache buffers. The server immediately sends the data directly to Workstation B from the file cache, saving the time needed to read the WP.exe file from disk.

## Elevator Seeking

At any given time, the multitasking NetWare server environment might be responding to several data requests from different client workstations. **Elevator seeking** is the process of minimizing the amount of disk drive head movement by accessing the information in the sequence of the head movement rather than in the order in which the requests were received. Elevator seeking gets its name from the way an elevator works when picking up people on different floors. Imagine that an elevator is at the top of a 10-story building when someone on the second floor pushes the down button. As the elevator passes the eighth floor, another person on the fifth floor pushes the down button. The elevator stops at the fifth floor first and then the second floor, even though the person on the second floor pushed the down button first. After picking up the person on the fifth floor, the elevator finally moves to the second floor.

## Fault Tolerance

**Fault tolerance** is a system's ability to continue operating satisfactorily despite errors or other problems. The NetWare server environment was designed with four levels of fault tolerance in its disk system to continue server operations in the event of physical errors on disk drives or controller cards.

**Step 1. Loading directory and FAT buffers**

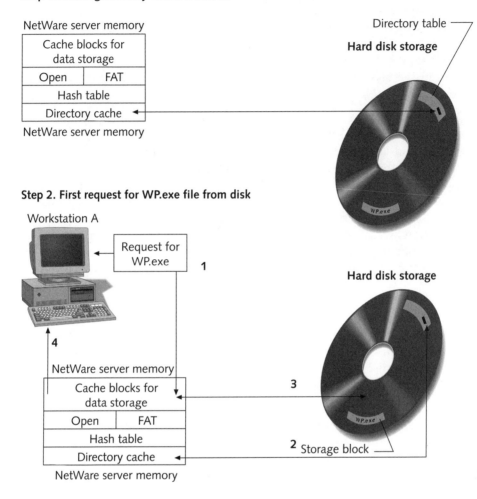

**Step 2. First request for WP.exe file from disk**

**Step 3. Second request for WP.exe from cache**

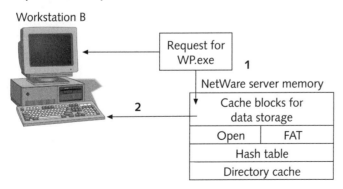

**Figure 2-13**    Cache memory

A hard disk's directory information is vital in enabling the server to locate information on the disk system. NetWare's first level of fault tolerance is set by providing second copies of the directory entry table and FAT on different locations of the disk drive. If a storage block in one of the tables is damaged, NetWare automatically switches to the duplicate table to retrieve the requested directory information. The faulty sector is then listed in the disk's bad block table, and the data in the bad sector is stored in another disk location.

Certain recording sectors of the disk's surface can become unreliable as a disk drive ages. To ensure that data written to the disk is stored in a good storage sector, NetWare implements a read–after–write verification process. If data cannot be reliably written to a disk sector after three attempts, NetWare implements the second level of fault tolerance, referred to as a "hot fix." A **hot fix** involves redirecting bad and unreliable disk storage sectors to another location on the disk surface. When NetWare first formats a new disk drive, a certain percentage of the disk capacity (2% by default) is reserved for the hot fix redirection area, allowing the disk drive to continue normal operation despite bad sectors that might develop on the disk surface. Step 1 in Figure 2-14 illustrates the NetWare server attempting to write a data buffer to disk block 201 and receiving a disk error when the data is read back during the read-after-write verification process. In Step 2, the data in the cache memory buffer is written to the redirection area and the NetWare server remaps block 201 to point to the block in the redirection area. Network administrators are responsible for monitoring NetWare servers to determine how many blocks have been redirected and when the disk drive should be replaced. In Chapter 14, you'll learn how to use the NetWare MONITOR utility to track the condition of the redirection area and determine when a disk drive should be replaced.

The third level of fault tolerance is the continued operation of the NetWare server despite a complete failure of the disk system. NetWare protects a NetWare server from major failures of the disk storage system in two ways. The first method, called **mirroring**, involves attaching two drives to the same disk controller card and then having one disk synchronize with the other disk as data is written or removed from it. After the disks have been mirrored, NetWare automatically keeps the information updated on both drives so that in a failure of one disk drive, the server can continue normal operation by using the second drive. The network administrator can then replace the defective drive at a convenient time, and NetWare will resynchronize the data on the new drive without requiring the administrator to restore any information from the backup tape. Figure 2-15 illustrates the use of disk mirroring to protect a server against failure of a disk drive. Disk mirroring works well, but requires each block to be written twice by the controller card, which can slow the performance of the NetWare server. With disk mirroring, a failure of the controller card makes data on both drives unusable.

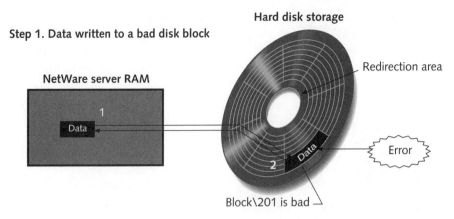

Step 1. Data written to a bad disk block

Hard disk storage

NetWare server RAM

Redirection area

Error

Block\201 is bad

Step 2. Hot fix redirection area used

Hard disk storage

Hot fix redirected

NetWare server RAM

Redirection area

Block\201 bad—Redirected

**Figure 2-14**   NetWare's hot fix feature

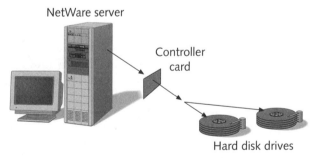

NetWare server

Controller card

Hard disk drives

**Figure 2-15**   Disk mirroring

With the second method, **disk duplexing**, NetWare provides fault tolerance for the disk drive and controller card. Disk duplexing uses two disk drives and two controller cards, as illustrated in Figure 2-16. Disk duplexing increases performance over disk mirroring in that one disk write operation can write data to both disk drives. Another advantage of disk duplexing over a single-disk drive is that it improves a NetWare server's performance. Both controllers are requested to find data, and then the information from the drive closest to the data location is read first. In a sense, implementing disk duplexing is like doubling the number of disk heads, thereby increasing disk read performance.

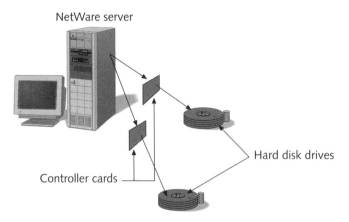

**Figure 2-16**    Disk duplexing

The fourth level of fault tolerance in NetWare is, in essence, **server duplexing**, or **clustering**. Here, two NetWare servers on the network duplicate each other exactly. If one system fails, the other instantly takes over and users never know there's been a problem. This feature is important for mission-critical applications on LANs, so it appeals to organizations that cannot afford any interruption in network services. Novell has included a clustered solution in NetWare 6 at no additional cost. Out of the box, Novell Clustered Services (NCS) includes licenses for two cluster nodes. If you want more than that, you need to purchase additional licenses.

## File Compression

NetWare server disk storage capacity is always limited, no matter how much capacity you have. NetWare 6 provides a **file compression** capability so that files can be compressed to a smaller size. As a network administrator, you can control how long a file stays inactive before it's compressed, and it will be automatically uncompressed when a user opens it again. The compression cycle can be scheduled to take place during low-use hours for the server.

NetWare offered file compression beginning with NetWare 4.1. Several third-party vendors also provide similar functionality for NetWare 3.x systems.

2

## Block Suballocation

NetWare 6 helps conserve hard disk space by using block suballocation. On a hard disk, files are stored in blocks, with each block holding a set number of bytes. In NetWare 3.2, for example, the default block size is 4 KB. Therefore, a file must be stored in 4 KB blocks, which leads to a problem with small files: A file with only one character in it (1 byte) takes up one block of 4 KB of storage—wasting a lot of disk space. The problem gets worse with larger block sizes, so NetWare 6 uses different default block sizes depending on volume size, as shown in Table 2-4.

**Table 2-4**   Default Block Sizes

| Volume Size | Default Block Size |
| --- | --- |
| 1–31 MB | 4 KB |
| 32–149 MB | 16 KB |
| 150–499 MB | 32 KB |
| 500 or more MB | 64 KB |

NetWare 6 solves this problem with **block suballocation**, which allows large block sizes to be divided into 4 KB sub-blocks when necessary. For example, if the block size is 64 KB, and a file contains 65 KB, the file is stored in one 64 KB block and one 4 KB sub-block (a total of 68 KB), instead of in two 64 KB blocks (a total of 128 KB).

Note    Although the problem of wasted disk space caused by large block sizes existed in NetWare 3.x, there were no tools to fix it. Beginning with NetWare 4.1, Novell added block suballocation to the network administrator's tools to solve the problem.

# CHAPTER SUMMARY

- Microcomputer systems are like any other computer system. They perform four basic processes: input, processing, storage, and output. Input devices take information and commands from the outside world and convert them into the binary one and zero system used in digital computers. The system unit of the computer, made up of several components, enables the computer to process input data and produce information. The computer's system board ties all the system unit components together.

- The most important component on the system board is the brain of the system unit, the microprocessor chip, also known as the central processor unit (CPU). The CPU fetches instructions and data from memory and then performs the requested function. IBM-compatible computers are based on the Intel line of microprocessors.

- The power of a microprocessor chip is based on several factors, including clock speed, word size, instruction set, and bus size. Most IBM-compatible computers today use the Pentium, Pentium Pro, or Pentium II microprocessor. The Pentium Pro and Pentium II offer a Dynamic Execution feature that improves performance.

❑ The system board components are tied together by a bus structure. The local bus supports the data and address buses, and the expansion bus supports the expansion slots, which attach peripheral controller cards. The ISA expansion bus was designed with 16-bit data and 24-bit address buses running at 8 MHz. The EISA bus was an enhanced version of the ISA bus that allowed 32-bit buses and higher clock speeds. IBM used a proprietary bus, called the Micro Channel, that provided 32-bit bus access at high clock speeds and an automatic configuration utility that made installing cards easier. PCI is called a local bus because it provides direct access to the CPU and memory at much higher speeds than either EISA or Micro Channel.

❑ The system board uses I/O ports and interrupts to communicate with peripheral devices such as keyboards, video monitors, modems, disk drives, and network cards. Parallel ports are most frequently used to connect printers, whereas serial ports provide longer-distance communication.

❑ Memory is the primary storage area for the microcomputer system. All instructions and data must be stored in memory before they can be processed by the CPU. RAM is the computer's work area, used primarily to contain instructions and data that are being processed.

❑ Hard disk storage consists of the controller card and drive. Hard drives are based on either IDE/EIDE/ATA or SCSI controller cards. IDE is a popular controller for Windows workstations and small to medium NetWare servers. The EIDE or ATA controllers provide higher speed and increased storage capacity (up to 8.5 GB) and support up to four devices. SCSI-2 controller cards can be used to attach up to seven different types of devices, including disk drives, CD-ROM drives, and tape drives. They allow for higher capacity and faster drives than IDE and are used for larger NetWare servers requiring multiple devices and more than 10 GB of disk space.

❑ CD-ROMs allow 680 MB to be stored permanently on a removable disk. CD-ROMs are used to store a variety of data including sound, text, graphics, and video. Because so much material is available on CD-ROMs, sharing them on a network has become an important function controlled by the network administrator. DVD-ROM is an improvement of the CD-ROM technology. Functionally, it is similar, but it holds up to 4.7 GB of data.

❑ The power system of the computer is critical to proper operation. Insufficient or faulty power supplies can cause computers to lock up or give parity error messages. An uninterruptible power supply (UPS) uses a battery to provide continuous power to the computer for a short time after a commercial power failure. All NetWare servers need to be protected by a UPS and power filters.

❑ User workstations using Windows 2000 Professional or Windows XP Professional need at least a Pentium 166 MHz or 233 MHz CPU, respectively, and 64 MB of RAM. Hard drive storage of at least 2 GB is preferred if applications and data will be stored on the PC.

2

❐ Novell designed the NetWare network operating system specifically as a LAN server operating system, with performance features such as high-volume file caching, directory caching and hashing, and elevator seeking. NetWare also includes such fault-tolerant features as hot fixes, disk mirroring, disk duplexing, and server duplexing. To conserve disk space, NetWare provides automatic file compression and block suballocation.

❐ NetWare 6 requires a Pentium III 700 MHz or better CPU. The NetWare server uses its RAM to run the operating system and cache information from the hard disk for faster access. Although a NetWare server with a small disk drive can run with as little as 256 MB of RAM, this is the absolute minimum; normally, you need more RAM. A large server using multiple protocols might need up to 2 GB of RAM. Although placing additional RAM on a NetWare server does not directly affect which applications can be run on the workstation, it does affect network performance. A shortage of memory in a NetWare server can cause it to crash or lock up the network.

# KEY TERMS

**Accelerated** or **Advanced Graphics Port (AGP)** — A new type of connector on system boards for attaching high-performance screen adapter cards.

**access arm** — A device used on disk drives to position the recording heads over the disk track.

**access time** — The time required for a storage device to locate and transfer a block of data into RAM.

**address** — When referring to a workstation's memory, a number used to identify the location of data in the computer system.

**address bus** — The number of bits sent from the CPU to the memory, indicating the memory byte to be accessed. The size of the address bus determines the amount of memory that can be directly accessed. The 20-bit address bus on the 8088 computer limited it to 1 MB. The 24-bit address bus on 80286 and 80386SX computers provides for up to 16 MB. The 32-bit address bus used on 80386DX and above computers can access up to 2 GB of memory.

**asynchronous communication** — A form of communication in which each byte is encapsulated with start and stop bits and then sent separately across the transmission media.

**baud rate** — A measurement of the number of signal changes per second.

**block suballocation** — A method that allows data from more than one file to be placed in a single data block.

**bus** — An electronic pathway that connects computer components.

**bus mastering** — A technique used by certain high-speed adapter cards to transfer data directly into a computer's RAM.

**cache memory** — The memory area used to temporarily hold data from lower-speed storage devices to provide better access time.

**central processing unit (CPU)** — Sometimes referred to as the "brain" of the computer. It is where most calculations and processing are done.

**clock** — A device in the system unit of a computer that sends out a fixed number of pulses or signals per second. The clock pulses are used to synchronize actions in the system unit. The clock speed is measured in billions of cycles per second, called gigahertz (GHz). The faster the clock speed, the more work a system unit can do per second.

**clustering** — A form of server duplexing, in which two or more servers can act as one. Novell's clustering supports up to 32 computers.

**command queuing** — A method of storing commands for future processing.

**compact disc read-only memory (CD-ROM)** — A data storage device that uses the compact disc format and can store about 680 MB of data. The data is recorded by the manufacturer and cannot be altered by the user.

**compiler** — A program that converts source commands to a form that the computer can run.

**complementary metal oxide semiconductor (CMOS) memory** — A type of memory capable of holding data with very little power requirements. This type of memory stores configuration data that is backed up by a battery on the system board. The battery prevents CMOS from being erased when power is turned off.

**complex instruction set computer (CISC)** — A computer with a microprocessor that uses instructions in a wide range of formats and can require more that one clock cycle to complete.

**controller card** — An adapter card used to control storage devices, such as disk drives.

**conventional memory** — The first 640 KB of memory used by DOS to run application programs.

**cycle** — The time it takes a signal to return to its starting state.

**cylinder** — The number of disk tracks that can be accessed without moving the access arm of the hard drive mechanism.

**data bus** — The "highway" that leads from a device to the CPU. Computers based on 80286 and 80386SX have 16-bit data bus architecture compared to 32 bits on the 80386DX and 80486 computer models and 64 bits on Pentium-based computers.

**Digital Versatile Disc (DVD)** — An upgraded version of CD-ROM, often called DVD-ROM, which holds up to 4.7 GB of data in the current versions.

**direct memory access (DMA) channel** — A device used to transfer data between RAM and an external device without taking time from the processor.

**directory caching** — A method of improving hard disk access time by keeping the directory entry table (DET) and file allocation table (FAT) in memory.

**directory hashing** — A method of improving access time by indexing entries in the directory entry table.

**2**

**disk duplexing** — A RAID 1 fault-tolerance methodology, in which two disks and two disk controllers are used.

**dot pitch** — A measurement of the spacing between color spots on video monitors. A smaller dot pitch provides sharper images.

**dual in-line memory module (DIMM)** — A combination of two SIMMs that are read alternately in memory-access cycles.

**dynamic execution** — A feature of the Intel Pentium Pro CPU. It consists of three processing techniques: multiple branch prediction, data flow analysis, and speculative execution.

**dynamic RAM (DRAM)** — A common form of dynamic memory chip, used in computer RAM, that requires a refresh cycle to retain data contents.

**elevator seeking** — A technique used in NetWare file servers to increase disk access performance by smoothly moving an access arm across a hard disk surface to read and write the requested data blocks in the sequence they are encountered rather than in the sequence received.

**Enhanced IDE (EIDE)** — A disk drive system that improves on the standard IDE system by supporting up to four disk drives with higher-drive capacities (above the 528 MB limitation of IDE), and faster performance.

**error-checking and correcting (ECC) memory** — A type of RAM that can automatically recognize and correct memory errors.

**expansion bus** — The system board bus that allows expansion cards plugged into expansion slots on a computer's system board to connect the adapter cards to the rest of the computer.

**expansion card** — A circuit board that plugs into an expansion slot and extends the computer's capabilities, such as a network interface card or modem.

**expansion slot** — An electrical connection on the system board into which expansion cards are plugged.

**extended data output (EDO) RAM** — A faster version of RAM now standard in Pentium, Pentium MMX, and Pentium Pro computers.

**eXtended Graphics Array (XGA)** — A video adapter that is the latest in monitor technology for laptops and notebook computers. It offers up to $1024 \times 768$ resolution, similar to the SVGA standard, but with additional colors.

**Extended Industry Standard Architecture (EISA) bus** — A system board expansion bus that supports ISA cards and high-speed 32-bit cards for increased performance.

**extended memory** — Memory above 1 MB. This memory requires special software to access it.

**fault tolerance** — A measurement of how well a system can continue to operate despite the failure of certain hardware components.

**file allocation table (FAT)** — A table stored on a disk used to link the storage blocks belonging to each file.

**file caching** — A method used by a NetWare file server to increase performance by storing the most frequently accessed file blocks in RAM.

**file compression** — A method of coding the data in a file to reduce file size.

**graphics accelerator** — A video adapter with a microprocessor programmed to speed up graphics operations.

**hot fix** — A NetWare feature for copying data on bad and unreliable disk storage sectors to a reserved redirection area, located in a different area on the hard disk.

**hot swapping** — A fault-tolerant system that allows a disk drive to be replaced without shutting down the computer system.

**Industry Standard Architecture (ISA) bus** — A system board bus structure that supports 16-bit data and 24-bit address buses at 8 MHz clock speed. This bus was developed for the IBM AT computer in 1984 and is still popular. However, used with high-speed processors, it reduces the performance of expansion cards.

**input/output (I/O) port** — An interface used to transfer data and commands to and from external devices.

**instruction set** — The set of binary command codes a CPU chip can recognize and execute.

**Integrated Drive Electronics (IDE)** — A type of hard disk controller that can control up to two hard drives with capacities up to 528 MB.

**interrupt request (IRQ)** — A signal sent from an external device to notify the CPU that it needs attention.

**local bus** — The internal address, data, and instruction buses of the system board, often used to refer to a high-speed expansion bus structure that allows adapter cards to operate close to the speed of the internal system board.

**Logical Block Addressing (LBA)** — A feature of the Enhanced Integrated Drive Electronics (EIDE) interface that allows EIDE drives to provide up to 8.4 GB of storage.

**machine language** — A program consisting of binary codes that the CPU can directly interpret and execute.

**magnetic disk drive** — The component of the disk storage system in which data is stored by means of magnetic fields representing ones and zeros.

**math coprocessor** — An extension of the CPU that enables it to perform mathematical functions and floating-point arithmetic.

**Micro Channel bus** — A system board design patented by IBM that allows for 32-bit expansion cards along with automatic card configuration.

**microprocessor** — The central processing unit (CPU) of a microcomputer system.

**millions of instructions per second (MIPS)** — A measure of speed for computer CPUs.

**mirroring** — A disk fault-tolerance system that synchronizes data on two drives attached to a single controller card.

**mission-critical application** — An application that's necessary to perform the day-to-day operations of a business or an organization.

**null modem cable** — A special type of RS232 cable used to connect two DTE computers without using a modem.

**parallel port** — A communications interface that transfers 8 or more bits of information at one time.

**parity bit** — A ninth bit added to a byte for error-checking purposes.

**peripheral** — An external device, such as a printer, a monitor, or a disk drive.

**Peripheral Component Interconnect** or **Interface (PCI) bus** — The current expansion bus design by Intel used in older 80486, Pentium, Pentium MMX, and Pentium Pro computers. It is a local bus design that moves data at 60 to 66 MHz.

**pixel** — A picture element; the smallest point on a monitor screen that can be addressed individually for color changes and so forth.

**protected mode** — The mode used by 80286 and above processor chips that allows access to up to 16 MB of memory and the ability to run multiple programs in memory without one program conflicting with another.

**RAM shadowing** — A method of increasing computer system performance by copying instructions from slower ROM to high-speed RAM.

**rambus dynamic RAM (RDRAM)** — A type of memory that has a transfer rate up to 800 MHz.

**random access memory (RAM)** — The main work memory of the computer, used to store program instructions and data currently being processed.

**read-only memory (ROM)** — Memory that is set at the factory and cannot be erased. ROM stores startup and hardware control instructions for your computer.

**real mode** — The processing mode used by 8088 computers.

**reduced instruction set computer (RISC)** — A computer with a microprocessor that uses instructions in a uniform format that require only one clock cycle to complete. A RISC workstation provides high performance for CAD workstations and scientific applications by using a simplified and highly efficient set of instructions that lends itself to parallel processing.

**redundant array of independent disks (RAID)** — A method of writing data across several disks that provides fault-tolerance.

**register** — A storage location inside the microprocessor unit.

**resolution** — A measurement of the number of bits on a display screen. Higher resolution produces better screen images.

**rotational delay** — The time required for a disk sector to make a complete circle and arrive at the disk drive's read/write head.

**SCSI-2** — An advanced version of the SCSI controller specification that allows for higher speed and more device types.

**SCSI-3** — Also referred to as Ultra Wide SCSI. Uses a 16-bit bus and supports data rates of 40 MBps.

**sector** — A physical recording area on a disk recording track. Each recording track is divided into multiple recording sectors to provide direct access to data blocks.

**seek time** — A measurement of the amount of time required to move the recording head to the specified disk track or cylinder.

**serial port** — A communication port that sends 1 bit of data per time interval.

**server duplexing** — A fault-tolerance technique that uses two identical servers so that if one goes down, the other is still available.

**single in-line memory module (SIMM)** — A memory circuit that consists of multiple chips and provides the system board with memory expansion capabilities.

**small computer system interface (SCSI)** — A general-purpose controller card bus that can be used to attach disk drives, CD-ROMs, tape drives, and other external devices to a computer system.

**static RAM (SRAM)** — Static RAM provides high-speed memory that can operate at CPU speeds without the use of wait states. SRAM chips are often used on high-speed computers in order to increase system performance by storing the most frequently used memory bytes.

**SuperVGA (SVGA)** — Video systems that provide higher resolutions (800×600 pixels and higher) and additional color combinations (up to 16.7 million colors) than the VGA systems.

**switching power supply** — A power supply used with most computers that will cut off power in the event of an electrical problem.

**synchronous communication** — A serial communication system that sends data in blocks or packets; each packet includes necessary control and error checking bits.

**synchronous dynamic RAM (SDRAM)** — High-speed random access memory (RAM) technology that can synchronize itself with the clock speed of the CPU's data bus. Used in high-end systems.

**system board** — The main circuit board of a computer system that contains the CPU, memory, and expansion bus (also called the motherboard).

**track** — A circular recording area on a disk surface.

**transfer time** — The time required to transfer a block of data to or from a disk sector.

**uninterruptible power system (UPS)** — A battery backup power system that can continue to supply power to a computer for a limited time in the event of a commercial power failure.

**Universal Data Format (UDF)** — A specification for how data is stored on storage media. Originally intended for all storage devices, it is most commonly used on CD-ROM and DVD-ROM discs.

**Universal Serial Bus (USB)** — An upgraded specification for the venerable serial port, providing for multiple devices to be attached on the same port and at higher speeds.

**upper memory** — The memory above 640 KB used by controller cards and by DOS when loading device drivers into high memory.

**VESA bus** — An older fast local bus expansion bus designed by the Video Electronics Standards Association, now largely replaced by PCI.

**video graphics array (VGA)** — A standard video circuit used in many conventional PCs that provides up to 640 × 320 resolution and up to 256 different colors.

**virtual file allocation table (VFAT)** — A 32-bit extension to the standard FAT introduced in Windows 95/98 and MS-DOS 7.0.

**2**

**virtual memory** — Allows the computer system to use its disk drive as though it were RAM, by swapping between disk and memory.

**virtual real mode** — An instruction mode available in 80386 and above microprocessors that allows access to 2 GB of memory and concurrent DOS programs running at the same time.

**wait state** — A clock cycle in which the CPU does no processing. This allows the slower DRAM memory chips to respond to requests from the CPU.

**word size** — The number of bits in the microprocessor's registers.

## REVIEW QUESTIONS

1. Which of the following is the amount of storage capacity needed to record one character of data in the computer's memory?

   a. bit

   b. word

   c. byte

   d. bus

2. Which of the following is the "brain" of a microcomputer system?

   a. clock

   b. bus

   c. CPU

   d. DIMM

3. Which of the following is the heartbeat of the system unit?

   a. clock

   b. CPU

   c. DIMM

   d. bus

4. On newer computer systems, clock speed is measured in which of the following?

   a. Kbps

   b. Mbps

   c. MHz

   d. GHz

5. Devices that are attached to a computer system are referred to as which of the following?

   a. peripherals

   b. parts

   c. expansion slots

   d. IRQs

6. Which of the following enables multiple devices to be connected to a computer?

   a. peripheral

   b. interrupt

   c. data bus

   d. expansion bus

7. _____ memory is used to store configuration information on the system board and is backed up by battery power.

   a. SCSI

   b. Rambus

   c. CDOS

   d. CMOS

8. Which of the following is the recommended amount of memory that NetWare 6 needs?

   a. 64 MB

   b. 128 MB

   c. 256 MB

   d. 512 MB

9. A NetWare server uses which of the following to keep the most frequently accessed blocks of data in memory?

   a. file caching

   b. directory caching

   c. block caching

   d. ROM caching

10. After low-level formatting, a drive needs to be _____ for use by an operating system.

    a. high-level formatted

    b. partitioned

    c. portioned

    d. Fdisked

2

11. Video resolution is measured by the number of _____.

   a. bits

   b. bytes

   c. pixels

   d. dot pitch

12. True or False: A monitor with a 0.28-dot pitch has a higher-quality image than one with a 0.35-dot pitch.

13. A NetWare server uses which of the following to make more efficient use of hard disk space?

   a. bit encryption

   b. CMOS

   c. file caching

   d. file compression

14. Disk mirroring is an example of which of the following?

   a. reflective backup

   b. RAID 1

   c. RAID 5

   d. vanity backup

15. Which of the following is used to link all disk sectors belonging to one file?

   a. CMOS

   b. data bus

   c. file allocation table (FAT)

   d. expansion bus

16. Which of the following chips can achieve a data rate speed of 800 MHz and is supported by Pentium 4 processors?

   a. DIMM

   b. SIMM

   c. RDRAM

   d. EDORAM

17. Novell recommends a Pentium _____ with a(n) _____ MHz processor speed for NetWare 6.

   a. II, 500

   b. III, 500

   c. II, 700

   d. III, 700

18. Redirecting bad and unreliable disk storage sectors to a new location is referred to as which of the following?

    a. fix it

    b. hot fix

    c. elevator seeking

    d. clustering

19. Disk duplexing uses _____ disk(s) and _____ controller card(s).

    a. 2, 2

    b. 2, 1

    c. 1, 2

    d. 4, 2

20. NetWare 6 helps conserve hard disk space by using which of the following?

    a. RAID 1

    b. RAID 2

    c. block suballocation

    d. binary inversion

21. Which of the following should you consider when purchasing a UPS for a NetWare server? (Select all that apply.)

    a. The UPS will support the volt-amps of the equipment attached.

    b. The UPS has a battery life of at least 2 hours.

    c. The UPS has a connection signal to the NetWare server.

    d. The UPS is connected to a gas-powered generator.

22. Which of the following is the measurement of distance between pixels?

    a. pixel width

    b. dot pitch

    c. pitch

    d. twips

23. The time it takes for the recording head to be positioned on the proper track of a hard disk is referred to as which of the following?

    a. rotational delay

    b. access time

    c. seek time

    d. rational delay

24. Which of the following is the process of minimizing the amount of disk drive head movement by accessing the information in the sequence of the head movement rather than in the order in which the requests were received?

    a. disk caching

    b. hot fix

    c. rotational delay

    d. elevator seeking

25. Server duplexing in NetWare 6 is implemented as which of the following?

    a. RAID 1

    b. RAID 5

    c. DSS

    d. NCS

26. Which of the following enables multiple devices to be connected to the same port?

    a. CMOS

    b. PCI

    c. USB

    d. DVD

27. Which of the following enables the user to remove and insert new devices without powering down the system?

    a. hot swapping

    b. hot fix

    c. RAID 1

    d. elevator seeking

28. NetWare 6 requires _____ or better monitors.

    a. XGA

    b. VGA

    c. PGA

    d. SVGA

29. True or False: Microsoft recommends a Pentium 166 MHz or higher for Windows 2000 Professional and XP Professional computers.

30. The size of the hard disk drive needed in a workstation is determined by which of the following? (Select all that apply.)

    a. number of stored applications

    b. size of stored applications

    c. available RAM

    d. processor speed

## HANDS-ON PROJECTS

### Project 2-1: Determining Workstation Hardware Configuration

Use the instructions in the following numbered steps, or use other hardware documenting programs (supplied by your instructor), to determine information about the hardware environment of your Windows XP Professional workstation. Copy the Computer Worksheet from Appendix B (shown in Figure 2-17) to use in this project.

1. Click **Start**, **Programs**, **Accessories**, **System Tools**, and **System Information** to open the System Information dialog box.
2. Click the **System Summary** folder, and use the information there to enter the required information on your Computer Worksheet.
3. Double-click the **Hardware Resources** folder to expand it. Note any information required on your worksheet and click the available options, such as IRQs, Memory, and so forth, and enter pertinent information on your worksheet.

---

**Computer Worksheet**

**Specification developed by:** _____

**SYSTEM INFORMATION**

**Computer make/model:** _____

**CPU:** _____ **Clock speed:** _____ **Bus:** _____

**Memory capacity:** _____

**DISK INFORMATION**

**Disk controller**

Type: _____

Manufacturer/model: _____

| Drive address | Type | Manufacturer | Cyl/Hd/Sec | Speed/Capacity | DOS Partition size |
|---|---|---|---|---|---|
| _____ | ____ | _____ | __/__/__ | _____ | _____ |

**DEVICE INFORMATION**

| Device name | IRQ | I/O port |
|---|---|---|
| _____ | _____ | _____ |
| _____ | _____ | _____ |
| _____ | _____ | _____ |

**Figure 2-17**    The Computer Worksheet

## CASE PROJECTS

### Case 2-1: Developing Workstation Specifications for J.Q. Adams

The J.Q. Adams Corporation wants to develop a specification for an entry-level PC workstation for the company. As the network administrator for this company, you have been asked to develop this specification. New workstations will run the Microsoft Windows XP Professional operating system and need to be able to run word processing applications and do basic spreadsheet calculations. The workstations will require about 2 GB of local disk storage for software and work files plus access to the network.

1. Write a memo to your instructor containing the specifications. Attach a copy of the worksheet shown in Figure 2-18 (copy this worksheet from Appendix B).

2. Some new workstations are intended for word processing and desktop publishing applications that need high-resolution graphics and a more powerful microprocessor. These workstations will require about 1.6 GB of local disk storage for software and work files. They will have access to the network so that they can share data files and access network printers. Write a memo to your instructor containing the specifications. Attach a copy of the worksheet in Figure 2-18.

3. To obtain the information for the worksheet, use the instructions from Project 2-1 and expand the Components option from the System Summary dialog box. Write a memo to your instructor containing the specifications. Attach a copy of the worksheet in Figure 2-18.

## Bid Specification Form

Specification developed by: _____

### SYSTEM INFORMATION

Computer make/model: _____

CPU: _____ Clock speed: _____ Bus: _____

Memory capacity: _____

Estimated cost: _____

### DISK INFORMATION

**Disk controller**

Type: _____

Manufacturer/model: _____

| Drive Address | Type | Manufacturer | Cyl/Hd/Sec | Speed/Capacity | DOS Partition Size |
|---|---|---|---|---|---|
| _____ | ___ | _____ | __ / __ / __ | _____ | _____ |

### NETWORK CARD INFORMATION

| Network type | Manufacturer ID | I/O port | Interrupt |
|---|---|---|---|
| _____ | _____ | _____ | _____ |

### NON-NETWORK DEVICE INFORMATION

| Device name | IRQ | I/O port |
|---|---|---|
| _____ | _____ | _____ |
| _____ | _____ | _____ |
| _____ | _____ | _____ |
| _____ | _____ | _____ |

**Figure 2-18**    The Bid Specification Form

## Case 2-2: Determining NetWare Server Disk Requirements for J.Q. Adams

**2**

The J.Q. Adams Corporation wants to store catalog information on a NetWare server to give all computers access to the information. Currently, the catalog comes on a CD-ROM, and copying it to the server's hard disk will require about 500 MB of disk storage. The company also wants to move a customer database, which currently takes up 250 MB of disk space, to the NetWare server, along with a word-processing program.

1. What type of disk controller and disk system would you recommend for this application? Write a memo to your instructor containing the specifications and describing why you made the choices you did.

2. Given the NetWare server disk requirements you just recorded, how much RAM will the J.Q. Adams NetWare server storing this data require? Write a memo to your instructor stating the requirements.

## Case 2-3: Developing NetWare Server Specifications for J.Q. Adams

The J.Q. Adams Corporation wants to purchase a new NetWare server to replace its existing NetWare server and has budgeted $10,000 for the new computer. Its current NetWare server is an 80486DX computer with 16 MB of RAM and a 500 MB hard disk drive. The company's system is running out of storage space, and the NetWare server runs slowly when it performs network printing. The company recently experienced some disk errors on the NetWare server that required an employee to restore data from backups and then re-enter a day's worth of transactions. If possible, the company wants to avoid disk errors causing this type of problem in the future. As the company's network administrator, you have been asked to select a computer system that will meet these needs within the requested budget.

The new system will need to support at least 4 GB of usable hard drive space. Write a memo to your instructor containing the specification. Attach a copy of the worksheet shown in Figure 2-19 (copy this worksheet from Appendix B).

If you think you need to spend more than $10,000 for the new server, develop two specifications: one for the system you think is necessary and one priced under $10,000. In your memo, explain why the better system is needed and why the system that stays within budget is inadequate.

**NetWare Server Worksheet**

Specification developed by: _____

**SYSTEM INFORMATION**

Computer make/model: _____

CPU: _____ Clock speed: _____ Bus: _____

Memory capacity: _____

Estimated cost: _____

**DISK INFORMATION**

**Disk controller**

Type: _____

Manufacturer/model: _____

| Drive Address | Type | Manufacturer | Cyl/Hd/Sec | Speed/Capacity | Partition Size DOS NetWare | Mirrored with Controller Drive |
|---|---|---|---|---|---|---|
| _____ | __ | _____ | __/__/__ | _____ | __ __ | _____ |

**NETWORK CARD INFORMATION**

| Network type | Manufacturer ID | I/O port | Interrupt |
|---|---|---|---|
| _____ | _____ | _____ | _____ |

**NON-NETWORK DEVICE INFORMATION**

| Device name | IRQ | I/O port |
|---|---|---|
| _____ | _____ | _____ |
| _____ | _____ | _____ |
| _____ | _____ | _____ |

**Figure 2-19**    The NetWare Server Worksheet

# 3

# DESIGNING THE NETWORK

**After reading this chapter and completing the exercises, you will be able to:**

♦ Describe the process of transmitting data on a NetWare LAN

♦ Identify and describe the hardware and software that connect computers to a NetWare LAN

♦ Apply your knowledge of LAN systems to develop a recommendation for a network system

As a network administrator, you must understand the hardware and software components that make up a local area network so that you can recommend and implement network systems and troubleshoot network problems. Chapter 1 introduced you to the hardware and software components of a LAN and the criteria for selecting a network operating system (NOS). In Chapter 2, you learned about the microcomputer hardware in PC workstations and NetWare servers. In this chapter, you learn how computers exchange data and increase your understanding of LANs by studying network cabling systems, network topologies, and protocols. As a network administrator, you'll probably be the main source of network information for your organization. You will help make important decisions about buying hardware and software when the LAN is implemented or expanded, so you need a good background in how computers use LANs to communicate and the options and standards currently available for such communication.

## LAN COMMUNICATIONS

Computers communicate over LANs by sending blocks of data called packets. Each packet contains the information to be transmitted and control information that the receiving computer uses to identify and process data in the packet. Hardware and software perform the complex task of transmitting data packets over a network, but the concepts can be broken down into easy-to-understand steps. For LAN communication to occur, standards must allow products from different manufacturers to work together. The term **interoperability** refers to the capability of different computers and applications to communicate and share resources on a network. Several organizations help set and control recognized standards that provide worldwide interoperability. Because many of the products needed to implement your network system depend on standards these organizations have developed, you should become familiar with their basic functions. The two major organizations that govern LAN standards are the **International Standards Organization (ISO)**, which works on LAN communication software models, and the **Institute of Electrical and Electronic Engineers (IEEE)**, which works on physical cable and access method standards. In this chapter, you learn about the LAN standards these institutions maintain and how the standards affect network products you'll work with as a network administrator.

## OSI Model

You'll need to understand the components of a network system and how they work together to recommend and implement a LAN. Just as dividing a complex computer program into separate modules helps you write the code, separating the LAN communication process into logical tasks or modules makes it easier to understand and work with. The ISO introduced the **Open Systems Interconnect (OSI) model** in 1980 to help standardize network system implementation. This seven-layer model acts as a blueprint to help network designers and developers build reliable network systems that can interoperate. As a network administrator, you need to know the basic levels and functions of the OSI model to understand LAN communication and to select and configure hardware and software. The OSI model helps illustrate the basic principles of network communication, which will help you troubleshoot and identify network problems.

As Table 3-1 shows, the seven layers of the OSI model range from the application software level to the physical hardware level. By following the layers, you can implement network software in structured modules, giving you more flexibility in designing and configuring network systems.

**Table 3-1**    OSI Model

| OSI Layer | Action | Result |
|-----------|--------|--------|
| Application | Interact with user and application processes. | Application program runs. |
| Presentation | Convert input to ASCII, data compression, and encryption. | Syntax of input checked and message formatted. Message packet formed. |
| Session | Make initial connection with receiving computer, maintain communication during session, and end session when complete. Control data flow by sequencing packets. Add packet sequence numbers. | Packet sequence number added to message packet. |
| Transport | Add identification and acknowledgment fields to the message and assign port addresses, such as port 80 for HTTP or port 110 for POP3. | Segment package formed. |
| Network | Determine the best route to the destination computer and add network address to the packet. | Datagram packet formed. |
| Data link | Add the physical address of the destination computer. | Ethernet frame formed. |
| Physical | Transmit packet one bit at a time. | Electronic signals representing bits appear on the cable system. |

The phrase "All People Seem To Need Data Processing" will help you remember the OSI layers from the application layer (Layer 7) to the physical layer (Layer 1). However, because many hardware vendors refer to a product using the OSI layer number, such as a Layer 3 switch, it might be easier to memorize the layers from Layer 1 to Layer 7, using the phrase "Please Do Not Throw Sausage Pizza Away."

At the application layer, a user initiates a request for network services, such as a word-processing program to access a shared document stored on the NetWare server. Starting with the application layer, each layer is responsible for performing certain network processing and control operations and then passing the data packet on to the next layer down. Each layer communicates with its peer layer on the receiving computer. For example, the transport layer on one computer includes control information in the network packet that the transport layer on the receiving computer uses to acknowledge receipt of the packet. At the bottom of the OSI model, the physical layer consists of the network cards and cables that actually carry the data packet's signals, representing ones and zeros, from one machine to another. The OSI functions can be compared to sending a letter via the postal system.

## Application Layer

The **application layer** consists of software that users interact with, enabling them to do their work without becoming involved with the full complexity of the computer or network systems. Word processors and spreadsheets are good examples of application software. Using the application layer is like using a word processor to write and print a letter. The word processor is the application you use to format and type the letter.

## Presentation Layer

The purpose of the **presentation layer** is to organize the data in machine-readable form. Your computer's desktop operating system is the software component that takes input from devices and converts it into a format the machine can process. The resulting block of information is called a **message packet**. The information in the message packet is then sent for processing to the presentation layer on the receiving computer.

Presentation layer software can also compress information to save space and transmission time. For increased security, the presentation layer can also encrypt data with a password, or key, making it difficult for an intruder to capture and access the information. Banking companies often use encrypting software to secure electronic fund transfers.

The presentation layer can be compared to the mechanics of a word processor, which makes it possible for your keystrokes to be printed. The result is a formatted, printed letter ready for delivery like a message packet.

## Session Layer

The **session layer's** purpose is initiating and maintaining a communication session with the network system. It supplies a valid user name and password so that you can log in to the NetWare server and be granted access to network resources. The session layer's job is much like a company's mail delivery schedule that has been arranged with the local post office. To use the mail service, an organization contacts the post office and sets up an address and a schedule for delivery and pickup services. This process corresponds to the session layer initiating a login session with a NetWare server.

## Transport Layer

The **transport layer's** main function is end-to-end delivery, and it uses two protocols for this function: **Transmission Control Protocol (TCP)** and **User Datagram Protocol (UDP)**. TCP requires acknowledgments from the receiver to ensure reliable delivery, and UDP is used when reliable delivery is not needed. UDP allows for faster data transmission. TCP can be slow because an acknowledgment is needed before data is transmitted. Most programs that use UDP rely on the higher layers of the OSI model to make sure data is transmitted. Many e-mail applications use UDP, but have the e-mail application resend data that gets lost along the way. The transport layer surrounds the message packet with the necessary acknowledgment and identification fields to create a **segment** packet. It then sends the segment packet to the network layer to complete the addressing requirements.

3

 The transport layer on some multitasking computers can put parts of several message packets from different applications into one segment, a process called **multiplexing**. Multiplexing can save communication costs because one cable connection can carry information from several applications simultaneously.

## Network Layer

The **network layer** supplies the information needed to route packets through the proper network paths to arrive at the destination address. To route packets to a destination computer efficiently, the network layer uses **network addresses**, which identify each group of computers on your network system. The network layer then creates a **datagram packet** by encapsulating, or wrapping, the information in the segment packet with the necessary packet routing information. The datagram packet is then sent to the data link layer for delivery.

 When designing a NetWare network system, establish a network address for each cable system used in your network.

In postal delivery, a zip code identifying the destination post office location is necessary to route a letter through the system. Similarly, the network address identifies the destination location in a network. The network layer's task is comparable to looking up the correct zip code for the destination city and then correctly marking the zip code and receiver's name and street address on the envelope. After the zip code has been added to the letter, the envelope can be taken to the post office for delivery.

## Data Link Layer

The **data link layer** is the computer network's delivery system and is responsible for using the destination address to send the packet through the requested network cable system. Using the information from the network layer, the data link layer creates a packet, called a **frame**, that encapsulates the datagram packet with control information, including the source and destination physical addresses.

The manufacturer permanently assigns a **physical address**, sometimes referred to as media access control (MAC) addresses, to each network interface card (NIC). Each physical address is a 6-byte hexadecimal number divided into two parts: The first 3 bytes identify the manufacturer, and the second 3 bytes are a unique number to differentiate the card from all the other cards the manufacturer has produced. For example, if a NIC has the hexadecimal physical address 0B00AA123456, 0B00AA is a code assigned to the manufacturer, and 123456 is the unique number that the manufacturer assigns to the card. For more information on the hexadecimal numbering system, see Appendix D.

Type the command IPCONFIG /ALL at the command prompt of your XP Professional workstation to see what your computer's MAC address is. The MAC address is identified as the physical address and displayed in hexadecimal notation, such as 00-00-0c-12-34-56.

The data link layer transmits the frame to the physical layer. Continuing with the example of the postal system, after the letter is placed in the mailbox, it is the responsibility of the postal system to deliver the letter. Based on the zip code and address information, a postal employee or machine determines which post office the letter gets sent to. The letter is then placed in a delivery truck to be taken to the correct post office.

The IEEE 802 committee, which is the IEEE group that works on network standards, divides the data link layer into two sublayers: the **logical link control (LLC) layer** and the **media access control (MAC) layer**. The LLC layer interfaces with the network layer, and the MAC layer provides compatibility with the NIC that the physical layer uses.

### Physical Layer

The **physical layer** consists of the network cable system and connectors, which are responsible for sending the data frame packet out as a series of bits. The bits appear as electrical signals on the network cable system. In the postal system example, the physical level consists of aircraft, trucks, and trains that physically deliver the letter to the designated post office.

## Sending a Message

On a NetWare network, the NetWare server receives all messages and then distributes them to users. This is similar to the way the post office receives mail and then distributes it to individual mailboxes. The steps discussed in the following paragraphs (summarized in Table 3-2) explain how the OSI model allows NetWare to send a message from one user to another.

**Table 3-2** Sending a Message

| OSI Layer | Representation | Function |
|---|---|---|
| Application | | An e-mail application is used to send the recipient a message. |
| Presentation | Translator → 1010110110 101101001 01100011 Message packet | The presentation layer converts input to binary ASCII code and creates the message packet. |
| Session | Server: "ready" Workstation: "OK" | The session layer establishes a communication session with the receiving computer. A sequence number is added to the message packet. |
| Transport | 1010110110 101101001 01100011 Message packet — Segment packet — Certified | The transport layer adds identification and acknowledgment fields to form the segment packet, which provides "certified delivery." |
| Network | Network A Router table Network address → "Datagram" | The network layer adds routing information to the network containing the destination computer. The network address is added to the segment packet to form a datagram packet. In routing devices, the network layer process is responsible for determining the most efficient path to the destination network. The network layer process in your computer assigns a valid address containing information about source and destination networks that routing devices use for path selection. After the packet has reached the correct network, the data link layer is responsible for getting the packet to the correct destination station/device by using the physical address (MAC address). |
| Data link | Physical address To address → From address → Frame | The data link layer adds the physical address of the source and destination computers to create an Ethernet frame. |
| Physical | → To network | At the physical layer, the NIC converts bits to electronic signals and transmits them on the cable system. |

An e-mail application works with the presentation layer to convert the message to the proper ASCII format for creating a message packet. The formatted message packet is then combined with the recipient's user name and passed to the session layer. On a NetWare workstation, the session layer sets up and maintains a connection between the Windows client and the NetWare operating system. A session is originally established when you start your computer and run the NetWare software that attaches it to the NetWare server. When the session is established, the session layer maintains your workstation's connection to the network by responding to requests from the NetWare server. When the session layer receives the message packet, it checks the status of the network connection, adds any control information that the NetWare software needs, and sends the message to the transport layer. A major function of the transport layer is guaranteeing delivery of the message packet to the recipient's computer. It does this by placing control information in the packet, much as you would fill out paperwork if you were sending a registered letter through the postal system. The control information uniquely identifies the packet and tells the receiving computer how to return an acknowledgment. The new packet with the transport control information is called a segment. The transport layer on the recipient's computer processes the segment heading information to acknowledge that the segment packet has been received successfully. After adding its control information, the transport layer passes the segment packet to the network layer.

In the computer, the network layer is responsible for determining the correct route for sending the packet. In a NetWare network, each cable system is assigned a unique network address similar in purpose to the postal system's zip codes. The network address allows packets to be routed quickly and efficiently to the cable system containing the destination computer. The network layer in each computer keeps a table—similar to a zip code reference book—with the correct network address of all NetWare servers. In this example, the network layer looks up the recipient NetWare server's address and then creates a datagram packet by encapsulating the segment information with control information, including the network address of the recipient's NetWare server.

The data link layer and its two sublayers—the LLC and the MAC—perform different functions. The LLC layer defines how data is packaged for the network and links the physical layer with the higher layers of the OSI model. The MAC layer defines the media access method—that is, it asks, "How do I access the cable or media?" The MAC layer also provides a unique identifier for the network card, aptly called a MAC address. The data link layer is concerned with the computer's physical address, whereas the network layer is concerned with the logical address, such as an IP address. The data link layer encapsulates the datagram packet received from the network layer with heading information, including error-checking codes and addresses for the destination and source computers. The data link layer then sends the data frame to the NIC for transmission, working closely with the NIC to make sure the data frame is transmitted successfully. If an error occurs during transmission, the data frame is sent again. After several unsuccessful attempts, the data link layer reports an error back to the network layer, stating that it could not deliver the packet.

A computer network's physical layer consists of hardware devices, such as NICs, connectors, and cable systems, which are responsible for transmitting the message bit by bit across the network system. The task of transmitting the frame can be compared to the job of a telegraph operator. Just as the telegraph operator must wait for a line to become available to translate message characters into Morse code's dots and dashes, so too the physical layer must wait for the cable to become available and use the NIC to transmit the frame by encoding the binary digits into the correct electronic signals.

 The IEEE organization sets the standards for controlling access on the physical network and determining the electronic signals used. Later in this chapter, you'll learn the standards used on different network systems.

## Receiving a Message

A data packet received from the network goes up the OSI stack, reversing the steps used in transmission, starting with the physical layer and proceeding to the application layer. The NIC transmits the frame to the physical layer, which sends the bits throughout the network. Because the NetWare server must receive and retransmit all messages, the frame is actually addressed so that the server initially receives it. When the NIC in the specified NetWare server recognizes its address, it reads the data frame and passes the bits of data to the data link layer. In the mail delivery example, this is comparable to unloading the letter at the destination post office.

The data link layer uses the error-checking codes to perform a **cyclic redundancy check (CRC)**, in which a mathematical algorithm compares bits received to the CRC code contained in the frame packet. If the calculated CRC matches the CRC in the data frame, the frame is assumed to be valid and the datagram packet is unpacked and passed to the network layer. If the CRCs do not match, the frame is considered bad, and an error is logged with the NetWare server.

The network layer on the NetWare server then checks the information in the datagram packet's heading. After confirming that the packet does not need to be sent to another server, it unpacks the segment packet and sends it to the transport layer. The transport layer checks the control information in the segment packet heading, extracts the message packet, and—depending on the control information—creates and sends an acknowledgment packet segment to your computer. This process is much like a recipient signing to confirm receipt of a registered letter. The transport layer on the sending computer is then informed that the packet has been successfully delivered. The transport layer extracts the message information and passes it to the correct NetWare session layer.

The NetWare server's presentation and application layers process the message information and retransmit the message to the recipient's computer, which receives and displays it onscreen. After reading the message, the recipient can remove the message from the screen and continue with the current application.

# NETWORK COMPONENTS

You can apply your knowledge of how information flows from one computer to another to understanding the components and product options available at each level of the OSI model. Knowledge of the common network components and product options will help you make good decisions in selecting, maintaining, and troubleshooting network systems. In the following sections, you learn about the network components in the physical, data link, and network layers of the OSI model, what product options are commonly used today, and some trends that might affect network products in the near future.

## Physical Layer Components

The physical layer components of a network system consist of the hardware that sends electrical signals from computer to computer. Occasionally, network administrators must install cables between computers, so you'll likely be involved in network hardware selection decisions and will need to be familiar with the options for connecting computers. Understanding the network cable system also enables you to isolate network problems that result from a faulty cable component.

The two aspects of the physical network system are the **media**, the transmission systems used to send electronic signals, and the **topology**, the physical geometry of the network wiring. In the following sections, you learn about some common network media and topologies and their advantages and disadvantages.

### Network Media

Network media consist of the communication systems used to transmit and receive bits of information. Most network media used today are in the form of cables or wires that run to each computer in the network. These types of media are often called **bounded media** because the signals are contained in, or "bounded by," a wire. Another medium type, which is much less common in LANs, involves beaming signals between computers with radio and light waves. These types of transmission media are called **unbounded media**. Although unbounded media are generally used in wide area network (WAN) systems and involve satellite and microwave links over hundreds or thousands of miles, many businesses and home users are now using specialized types of unbounded media, such as infrared and narrowband radio. At one time, wireless LANs were cost prohibitive for most home users, but at the time of this writing, they can be implemented for under $300!

Consider three major factors when selecting a medium for your network system: bandwidth, resistance to electromagnetic interference, and cost. A network medium's **bandwidth** is a measure of its capacity in number of bits per second that can be transmitted. A general rule is that the higher the bandwidth, the more traffic and higher speed the network medium can support.

**Electromagnetic interference (EMI)** refers to a medium's susceptibility to interference from outside electrical or magnetic fields. Networks that operate near high levels of electrical and magnetic fields, such as those given off by power plants or large pieces of electrical equipment, need to install a medium with a high EMI resistance that can carry the network signals reliably without interference.

Cost of installation is the final factor to consider when selecting a medium. If more than one medium meets an organization's bandwidth and EMI specifications, the final decision depends on the cost of installing the system. Some media types—such as fiber optics—are relatively expensive to install and maintain compared to other media types, so even though fiber has a very high bandwidth and virtually no EMI problems, it's not a common medium in most LAN connections to the desktop; however, it's used in many LANs as backbone cabling.

The following sections describe some of the most common network mediums and compare these systems in terms of bandwidth, EMI, and cost to help you select the best medium for a network system.

**Twisted-Pair Cable**   Twisted-pair cable is probably the most common form of bounded medium in use on LANs. **Twisted-pair cable** can be unshielded or shielded and consists of pairs of single-strand wire twisted together, as shown in Figure 3-1.

**Shielded twisted-pair (STP) cable**

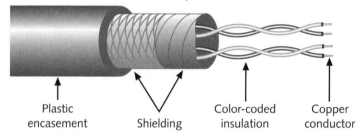

Plastic encasement        Shielding        Color-coded insulation        Copper conductor

**Unshielded twisted-pair (UTP) cable**

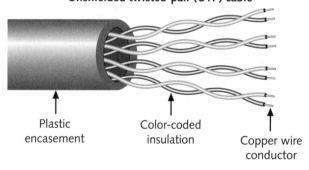

Plastic encasement        Color-coded insulation        Copper wire conductor

**Figure 3-1**   Twisted-pair cable

Twisting the wires together reduces the possibility of a signal in one wire affecting a signal in another. Normally, if two wires run side by side, the electrical signal in one wire creates a magnetic field that can induce a small current in the nearby wire. This causes "noise" and results in errors on the network. Twisting the wires eliminates this noise by canceling out the magnetic field. Fifty or more pairs of twisted wire can be put together in one large cable called a **bundled pair**.

Twisted-pair cabling comes in different categories:

- *Category 1*—Phone cable before 1983. Not used for data transfer.

- *Category 2*—A data-grade cable used in older networks with speeds up to 4 Mbps.

- *Category 3*—Another data-grade cable, which can be used with 10BaseT Ethernet but no faster.

- *Category 4*—A better grade of cable for data speeds up to 16 Mbps (the token ring network standard).

- *Category 5 ("Cat 5")*—**Category 5 cable** is four-wire, 100-ohm cable useful for networks to 100 Mbps in Fast Ethernet. Efforts are being made to upgrade this speed to 1000 Mbps (Gigabit Ethernet). However, vendors are proposing a new standard, Cat 6, for this faster speed.

- *Category 5E ("Cat 5E")*—This addendum to Category 5 cable incorporates enhanced performance requirements, and Category 5E cable is the recommended choice for network cabling. It supports applications that use full-duplex transmission schemes, such as Gigabit Ethernet.

- *Category 6 ("Cat 6")*—Category 6 cable offers a new performance range for unshielded and shielded twisted-pair cabling. It is intended to specify the best performance that UTP and STP cabling solutions can be designed to deliver, and is backward-compatible, meaning that applications running on lower categories of cable will be supported. The measured frequency range extends to 250 MHz, in contrast to Category 5's 100 MHz, and performance is far better than Category 5E at the same frequencies.

 Not all Cat 5 cabling is the same. If your cable is more than three years old, test to ensure that your Cat 5 cable will support 100 Mbps or faster.

One problem of **unshielded twisted-pair (UTP) cable** is that external electrical voltages and magnetic fields can create noise inside the wire. The noise, or EMI, is unwanted current that can result when the twisted-pair cable lies close to a fluorescent light fixture or an electrical motor. To reduce EMI, **shielded twisted-pair (STP) cables** are surrounded by a metal foil that acts as a barrier to ground out the interference. Connecting the cable ground to the building's grounding system is important in getting the STP cable to work. Unfortunately, the shield of STP cable changes the wire's electrical characteristics, reducing the distance and speed at which the network's signal can be transmitted.

Two types of connectors can be used on the ends of twisted-pair cable: RJ-45 plugs and IBM data connectors, shown in Figure 3-2. RJ-45 plugs are similar to the modular RJ-11 plugs commonly used to connect telephones to wall jacks and are generally preferred for unshielded cable because of their low cost and ease of installation. IBM engineered the data connector as a universal connector for use with STP cables. Although the data connector is rather large and difficult to install, it provides a reliable connection for high-speed signals and has the advantage of being able to connect cables without the use of special cable connectors.

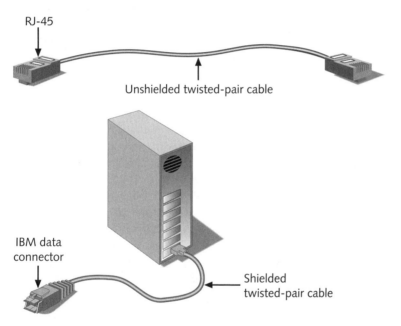

**Figure 3-2**    Connectors for twisted-pair cable

In general, UTP media are more common, less expensive, and more readily available than other bounded media. Twisted-pair cable is also available in different varieties that affect the speed at which signals can be sent over the cable. Signal speed is measured in millions of bits per second (Mbps).

Do not confuse me*gabits* with me*gabytes*. They are quite different. Although the rule is 8 bits to 1 byte, a handy rule of thumb for measuring data throughput is to make the calculation with 10 bits (to cover overhead) rather than 8 bits. That means a 10 Mbps signal actually transmits about 1 MB (one million bytes) of data.

Table 3-3 lists the common types of twisted-pair cable, their associated transmission speeds, and typical usage.

**Table 3-3**   Twisted-Pair Cable Specifications

| Wire Type | Speed Range | Typical Use |
| --- | --- | --- |
| 4 | Up to 20 Mbps | Data |
| 5 | Up to 100 Mbps | High-speed data |
| 5E | Up to 1000 Mbps | High-speed data |
| 6 | Up to 1000 Mbps | High-speed data |

Companies installing twisted-pair cable normally provide the correct type of cable for your networking needs. If you are evaluating a building's existing wiring for use in your network, however, you should have a wire expert evaluate the cable to determine whether it can support the required network speeds.

The major disadvantages of twisted-pair cable, especially UTP, are its sensitivity to EMI and increased susceptibility to wiretapping by intruders. Wiretapping involves using sniffer equipment to detect signals on the cable by sensing the electrical fields. A wiretapper can also physically splice into the cable to access network signals. If your organization is concerned about possible security violations from wiretapping or if it needs to run network cable near electrical motors or generators, consider using STP cable or some other medium that is more secure and less vulnerable to EMI.

**Coaxial Cable**   **Coaxial cable**, commonly called "coax," is made of two conductors, as shown in Figure 3-3. The name *coaxial* derives from the two conductors in the cable sharing the same axis. At the center of the cable is a fairly stiff wire encased in insulating plastic. The plastic is surrounded by the second conductor, which is a wire mesh tube that also serves as a shield. A strong insulating plastic tube forms the cable's outer covering.

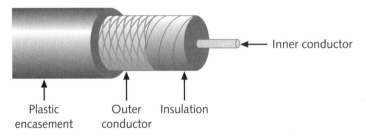

**Figure 3-3**   Coaxial cable

Coaxial cable is available in a variety of types and thicknesses for different purposes. Table 3-4 lists the varieties of coaxial cables, their electrical resistance, and their typical use. Generally, thicker cable is used to carry signals longer distances but is more expensive and less flexible. Compared to twisted-pair, coaxial cable supports higher data rates and is less susceptible to EMI and wiretapping. However, coaxial cable is generally more expensive, harder to install, and more susceptible to damage caused by linking. In the past, many networks were wired with coaxial cable. Today, twisted-pair cable's increased bandwidth, higher flexibility, and lower cost are influencing most organizations to select UTP rather than coaxial cable as the medium for new network installations. See the "Linear Bus Topology" section later in this chapter for more information on coaxial cable use.

**3**

**Table 3-4**   Coaxial Cable Types

| Cable Type | Resistance | Typical Use |
|------------|-----------|-------------|
| RG-8 | 50 ohms | Thick Ethernet networks |
| RG-58 | 50 ohms | Thin Ethernet networks |
| RG-59 | 75 ohms | Cable TV and IBM broadband networks |
| RG-62 | 93 ohms | ARCNet networks |

**Fiber-Optic Cable**   As shown in Figure 3-4, **fiber-optic cable** looks similar to coaxial cable. It consists of light-conducting glass or plastic fibers at the center of a thick tube of protective cladding (wrapping) surrounded by a tough outer sheath. One or more fibers can be bounded in the center of the fiber-optic cable. Pulses of light are transmitted through the cable by lasers or light-emitting diodes (LEDs) and received by photo detectors at the far end. Fiber-optic cables are much lighter and smaller than coaxial or twisted-pair cables and can support much higher data rates, from 100 Mbps to more than 2000 Mbps. Because light signals do not attenuate (lose strength) over distance as quickly as electrical signals, fiber-optic cables can carry high-speed signals over long distances. Fiber-optic transmission is not susceptible to EMI and is very difficult to tap. The principal disadvantages of fiber-optic cable are relatively high cost, lack of mature standards, and the difficulty of finding trained technicians to install and troubleshoot it.

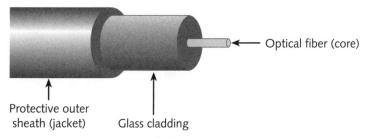

Optical fiber (core)

Protective outer
sheath (jacket)        Glass cladding

**Figure 3-4**   Fiber-optic cable

Fiber-optic cable comes in two varieties: single-mode and multimode. Single-mode (or single-index monomode) supports a single frequency of light, so it supports a much longer cable length than multimode. Multimode supports several frequencies of light, so it has a higher total carrying capacity with current technology than does single-mode. Today, most products take advantage of multimode fiber.

Fiber-optic cable is used primarily to connect servers as a kind of backbone to share data at high speeds. Occasionally, a workstation is connected using fiber-optic cable for high-speed access to large data files. It can also be used when you need maximum protection from EMI or wiretapping. Figure 3-5 shows a backbone connecting several high-volume NetWare servers or minicomputers to form a backbone network. A **backbone network** is a cable system used primarily to connect a host computer to NetWare servers, each of which can have its own local network. Fiber makes a good backbone network because it allows NetWare servers to be spread out over long distances and still provide a high-speed communication system that's safe from EMI or differences in grounding among buildings. A backbone can also be used to connect networks between buildings, such as on a campus or in an industrial park.

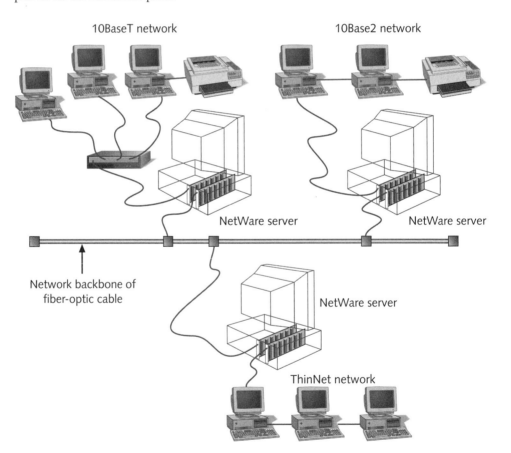

**Figure 3-5**   Backbone network

**Infrared**  **Infrared** is a wireless medium based on infrared light from LEDs. Infrared signals can be detected by direct line-of-sight receivers or by indirect receivers capturing signals reflected off walls or ceilings. Infrared signals, however, cannot penetrate walls or other opaque objects and are diluted by strong light sources. These limitations make infrared most useful for small, open, indoor environments, such as a classroom or a small office area with cubicles.

Infrared transmission systems are cost-efficient and capable of high bandwidths, similar to those in fiber-optic cable. As a result, an infrared medium can be a good way of connecting wireless LANs when all computers are located in a single room or office. Infrared eliminates the need for cables and allows computers to be easily moved, as long as they can always be pointed toward the infrared transmitter/receiver, normally located near the ceiling, as shown in Figure 3-6.

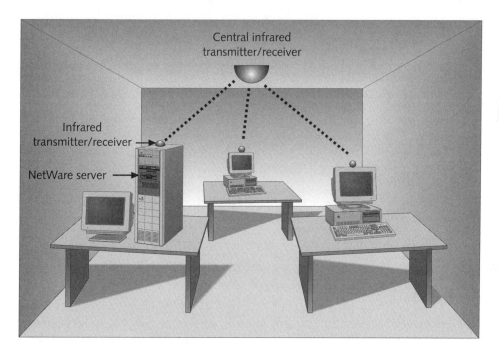

**Figure 3-6**   Infrared wireless network

Although the high frequency of infrared waves can accommodate high data transfer rates, advances in infrared technology have been slow because of limitations in connecting computers separated by walls. Growth of infrared media is expected to accelerate as other radio frequencies become increasingly congested. A large pool of potential infrared installations exists in the networking of classroom computers and limited home or small business applications.

**Narrowband Radio**   **Narrowband radio transmission** is another way wireless LANs can transmit data. Radio waves are used to transmit the data, so the line-of-sight focusing that infrared requires is not needed. The workstation must still be located within a reasonable distance from the base station or hub, or the transmission quality can be poor. In other words, you can have the same problem you have with cell phones: "Can you hear me? Can you hear me?"

**Comparing Network Media**   Table 3-5 summarizes network media in terms of cost, ease of installation, transmission capacity, and immunity to EMI and tapping. The cost comparisons are based on costs of media and other required hardware. The numbers given for maximum transmission capacity might be deceiving because they are based on the signaling technology's current use, not on the media's raw bandwidth potential. In the case study projects at the end of this chapter, you have an opportunity to apply this information to selecting cable systems.

**Table 3-5**   Network Media Summary

| Medium | Cost | Installation | Capacity/Speed | Immunity from EMI and Tapping |
|---|---|---|---|---|
| Unshielded twisted-pair cable | Low | Simple | 1–100 Mbps | Low |
| Shielded twisted-pair cable | Moderate | Simple to moderate | 1–100 Mbps | Moderate |
| Coaxial cable | Moderate | Simple | 10–1000 Mbps | Moderate |
| Fiber-optic cable | Moderate | Difficult | 100–2000 Mbps | Very high to high |
| Infrared | Moderate | Simple | 10–100 Mbps | Subject to interference from strong light sources |

## Repeaters

Network cable systems consist of one or more cable lengths, called segments, that have termination points on each end. (Do not confuse them with terminators, which are described in the "Linear Bus Topology" section later in this chapter.) **Repeaters** are hardware devices used for linking network segments. Repeaters work at the physical layer of the OSI model, receiving signals from one network segment and retransmitting them to the next segment. In the past, the common Ethernet hub was fundamentally a multiport repeater. Now, each wire extending from the hub is considered a separate segment, with the hub and the end computer (or sometimes connecting to another hub, called "cascading") as the termination points. The hub of a star network topology, for example, can act as a repeater, receiving a signal from one computer cable and broadcasting it on the other cables. Each computer in a ring topology acts as a repeater, receiving the signal from the "upstream" computer and retransmitting it to the next computer on the ring. Repeaters can also connect two linear bus segments. (You'll see an example of how repeaters are used in the "Ethernet Networks" section later in this chapter.) This use of repeaters increases a linear bus network's fault tolerance because a bad connector or cable on one segment does not prevent computers on other segments from communicating. As a network administrator, you should be aware of the role of repeaters on your network for easy maintenance and troubleshooting of network problems. Repeaters actually increase collisions, so you should be careful using them. It is for this reason that repeaters are becoming obsolete and are being replaced with switches (described in the "Switches" section later in this chapter).

## Network Topologies

Choosing the method to connect networked computers is an important aspect of a network system that uses bounded media. The physical geometry or cable layout used to connect computers in a LAN is the network topology (or just "the topology"). As a network administrator, you'll need to be familiar with your network's topology to attach new computers or isolate network problems to a faulty segment of the cable. As shown in Figure 3-7, the linear bus, ring, and star are the three major topologies for connecting computers in a LAN. In the following sections, you learn about each topology and how it affects network systems in terms of cost, reliability, and expandability.

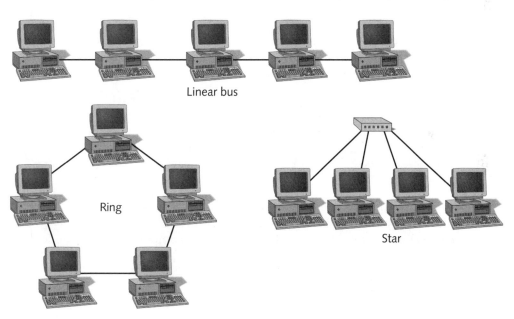

**Figure 3-7**   Topologies

**Star Topology**  The **star topology** derives its name from the fact that all cables on the network radiate from a central component, or device, usually identified as a hub. The hub device connects the network cables and passes the signals from one cable to the next. The type of hub you need depends on the access system used by the network cards (described in the "Data Link Layer Components" section later in this chapter). Most star topologies use a switch as the central component because switches are inexpensive and reduce collisions (discussed in the "Data Link Layer Components" section later in this chapter). Although star topologies cost more because of the amount of wire needed, they are generally more reliable and easier to troubleshoot than other topologies. Because each cable in a star topology is a separate component, the failure of one cable does not affect the operation of the rest of the network. Troubleshooting for star topologies is easy because a network cable problem can be quickly isolated to the cable "run" on which a network device is exhibiting errors. Another advantage of the star topology is the ease of adding or removing devices on the network without affecting the operation of other computers—using unallocated access ports on the hub, you simply plug or unplug cables.

 The star topology has become the most popular way to wire computers together because of its exceptional flexibility and reliability.

What is the disadvantage of using a star topology? Because each computer is connected to the central device, if the central device fails, the entire network fails. Although this is a remote possibility, as a network administrator you need to be aware of it and have a contingency plan in place.

Star networks are usually wired with a **patch panel**, as shown in Figure 3-8. In a patch panel system, a wire runs from each potential computer location in the building through a drop cable to a central patch panel. A **patch cable** is then used to connect a device in any given location to the hub, which is most likely a switch. A patch panel system makes it easy to move a computer to another location and to connect or disconnect computers from the network for troubleshooting.

Star topologies are generally implemented with twisted-pair cable rather than coaxial cable because of the lower cable cost, increased flexibility, and smaller size. With RJ-45 connectors on twisted-pair cable, connecting computers to wall outlets and between hubs and patch panels is easy.

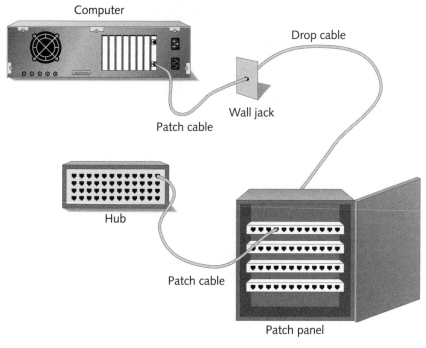

**Figure 3-8**   Patch panel system

**Linear Bus Topology**   The **linear bus topology** connects computers in series by running a cable from one computer to the next. The method of attaching the computers to the "bus" depends on the network card and cable system. When coaxial cable is used, each computer is usually attached to the bus cable by means of a T-connector, as Figure 3-9 shows. When twisted-pair cable is used, each network card usually contains two RJ-45 female connectors that allow twisted-pair cable to be run from one computer to the next. Each end of a linear bus network requires a terminator to prevent echo signals from interfering with communication signals. Coaxial cable's resistance and size are important factors and depend on the requirements of the network cards (described in the "Data Link Layer Components" section later in this chapter).

The primary advantages of a linear bus topology are the small amount of cable needed and the ease of wiring computers clustered in locations such as classrooms or computer labs. The two biggest disadvantages of a bus network are adding or removing computers and troubleshooting. Adding or removing a computer from a bus network often involves interrupting communication on the network segment. Troubleshooting the network is difficult because when a cable component failure causes a network error, it often disrupts communications on the entire network segment and requires special test equipment to locate the faulty network component. Therefore, linear bus networks are generally limited to smaller applications or are used when linking computers is particularly cost effective.

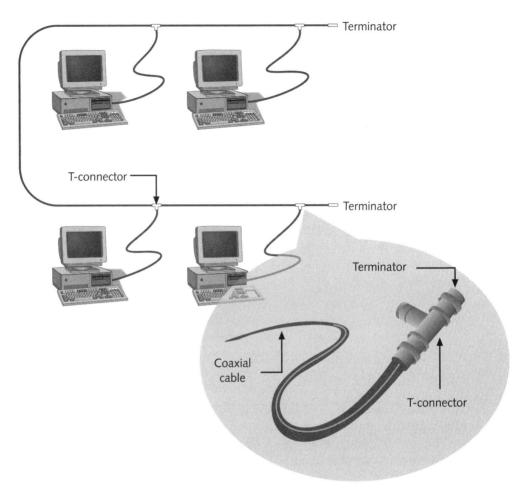

**Figure 3-9**    Coaxial cable network

 Star networks are gradually replacing linear bus networks in many organizations because star networks are easier to troubleshoot. A broken wire in a star network configuration affects only one workstation. In a linear bus network, however, all computers on the cable segment fail when the cable is disconnected or broken anywhere in the network.

**Ring Topology**    A **ring topology** is similar to a linear bus topology, except that the ends of the cable are connected instead of terminated. As a result, signals on the ring topology travel around the network in one direction until they return to the device from which they originated. In a ring topology, each computer in the ring receives signals and then retransmits them to the next computer in the ring. Because the signals are regenerated at each device along the network, they can travel longer distances, as long as another computer is located within the distance limit of each NIC's transmitter.

The disadvantage of a ring topology is the extra cable needed to complete the ring's circle when computers are spread out in a serial fashion. The ring topology also has the same disadvantage as the linear bus in terms of interrupting network transmissions to add or remove workstations. However, often it's easier to troubleshoot a ring topology than a linear bus topology because each computer on the ring receives and then retransmits a signal. The troubleshooter can use software that quickly determines which computer is not receiving the signal. The damaged cable component can then be isolated to the cable segment between the computer that does not receive the signal and its "upstream" neighbor.

**Comparing Topologies**    Table 3-6 compares the three popular network topologies in terms of wiring needs, ease of expansion, fault tolerance, and troubleshooting. The type of topology and cable system you select is closely linked to the type of network cards supported on the network.

**Table 3-6**    Topology Comparison

| Topology | Wiring | Expansion | Fault Tolerance | Troubleshooting |
|---|---|---|---|---|
| Star | Requires the most wire because a cable must be led from each computer to a central hub | Easy to expand by using a patch panel to plug new computers into the hub | Highly fault tolerant because a bad cable or connector affects only one computer | Easiest to troubleshoot by removing suspect computers from the network |
| Linear bus | Usually requires the least amount of cable because the cable is connected from one computer to the next | Difficult to expand unless a connector exists at the location of the new computer | Poor fault tolerance because a bad connector or cable disrupts the entire network segment | The most difficult to troubleshoot because all computers can be affected by one problem |
| Ring | Requires more wire than a linear bus because cable ends must be connected, but requires less than a star | Difficult to expand because the ring must be broken to insert a new computer | Poor fault tolerance because a bad connector or cable disrupts the entire network segment | Fairly easy to troubleshoot with software that can identify which computer isn't receiving the signal |

# Data Link Layer Components

The data link components control the way the network cable system transmits and receives signals. As a result, the components you select for the data link layer of your network determine which network topologies and cable types you can use. Conversely, when you want to use an already existing cable system, you should select data link products that best support it. The data link layer components consist of the NICs and card driver programs.

## Network Interface Cards

The NIC acts as an interface between the network's data link and physical layers by converting the commands and data frames from the data link layer into the correct signals for the connectors on the physical cable system. Most NICs are integrated into the motherboard on newer computer systems, especially laptops, but can still be purchased as separate interface cards.

**Driver software** is needed to control the NIC and provide an interface between the data link layer and the network layer software. Novell has developed a set of driver specifications called the **Open Data Interface (ODI)** to provide this software interface. With ODI-compatible drivers, multiple programs running on the workstation or the NetWare server can share the NIC. For example, ODI drivers enable the NetWare server to communicate with both Apple Macintosh and IBM PCs attached to the same network.

In contrast, Microsoft networks use a driver interface called **Network Driver Interface Specifications (NDIS)** between network card drivers and Microsoft's network operating system. NDIS-compatible drivers enable software developers to write programs for use on Windows operating systems without requiring them to write instructions to control the network card—the NDIS drivers perform the hardware functions for them. Microsoft's approach results in fewer programming requirements for applications developers and more standardized and reliable networking functionality in those applications.

Because there are two types of driver interfaces, ODI and NDIS, be sure the network cards for your network contain the correct driver for the type of NOS you will be supporting. NetWare 6 comes with ODI-compatible driver programs for many popular NICs, but some cards are not supported. The manufacturer of an unsupported card should supply a disk with the ODI-compatible driver program that will interface its NIC to a NetWare server or workstation. In Chapter 6, you'll learn about the standard card drivers included with NetWare and how to install them on the server or workstation computers.

 Whenever possible, try to obtain NICs that work with the standard NetWare ODI drivers to make it easier to install and maintain your network system. Despite their low cost, avoid off-brand NICs because their nonstandard drivers are difficult to maintain and troubleshoot.

For NICs and drivers from different manufacturers to communicate with each other, certain data link standards, controlled by committees within the IEEE, need to be followed. The two major committees that affect LANs are the **IEEE 802.3** and **IEEE 802.5**. In addition to controlling types of signals, data link standards control how each computer accesses the network. Because only one signal can be sent on the network cable at any one time, a **media access method** is necessary to control when computers transmit, to reduce **collisions** that can occur when two or more computers try to transmit at the same time. Collisions cause network errors by distorting data signals and making them unreadable. Media access methods used on today's LANs are token passing or contention based.

The **token passing method** enables only one computer to transmit a message on the network at any given time. This access to the network is controlled by a **token**, which is a special packet passed from one computer to the next to determine which machine can use the network. When a computer needs to transmit data, it waits until it receives the token packet and then transmits its data frame packet on the network. After the transmission is completed, the transmitting computer releases the token. The next computer on the network can then pick it up and transmit it. In actual implementation, the token passing system is complex, involving token priorities, early release of tokens, and network monitoring and error-detection functions. As a result, NICs based on the token passing method are generally more expensive.

 IBM originally developed the token passing technology, which has been standardized by the IEEE 802.5 committee.

In the **contention access method**, a node transmits a message whenever it detects that the channel is not in use. Think of the contention access method in terms of CB radio use. When no one is talking on a CB radio channel, you are free to transmit your message. When someone else is talking on the radio channel, however, you must wait for the transmission to end before you start your own. The main problem with contention-based access arises when two or more computers sense an open channel and start transmitting at the same time. A collision results, and the colliding computers must wait a few microseconds before retransmitting their messages. On a computer network, this contention system is called **Carrier Sense Multiple Access with Collision Detection (CSMA/CD)**, and the IEEE 802.3 committee has standardized it into several different product types, based on speed and cable type. The three most popular IEEE 802.3 committee standards—10BaseT, 100BaseT, and 10Base2—are described later in the "Ethernet Networks" section.

A contention system works well when network traffic is light, but its performance can drop off quickly under heavy network transmission loads. Token-based systems perform better under heavy loads because the performance does not drop off as abruptly. The following sections describe the types of NICs and data link standards currently in use and compare the network topology, performance, and access methods of these products.

## Token Ring Networks

IBM originally designed the token ring system for use in industrial environments that required reliable high-speed communications. Today, a token ring (shown in Figure 3-10) is widely considered to be the best network system in terms of overall performance and reliability.

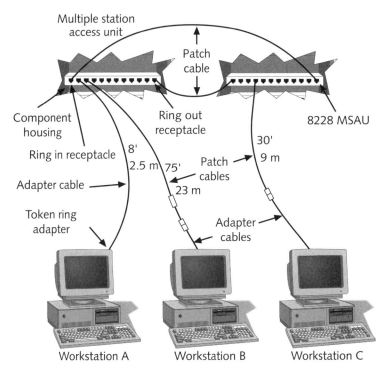

**Figure 3-10**   Token ring network

 Standard token ring cards were originally transmitted at 4 Mbps. Today, however, most token ring cards use 16 Mbps transmission speeds. You cannot mix cards running at 4 Mbps with cards running at 16 Mbps on the same token ring network.

The token ring system shown in Figure 3-10 consists of workstations connected by twisted-pair cables to a central hub, called a **multiple station access unit (MSAU)**. Although it appears to be a star arrangement, the network signals actually travel in a ring, which is why it's often called a star ring. A signal originating from Workstation A in Figure 3-10, for example, is transmitted to the MSAU first. The MSAU relays the signal to the cable for Workstation B. After receiving the signal, Workstation B retransmits the signal and returns it to the MSAU. The MSAU then relays the signal to Workstation C, and Workstation C transmits the signal back to the MSAU, where it is relayed back to its source, Workstation A. If the wire running from the MSAU to Workstation B is broken, or if Workstation B is shut down, a relay in the MSAU automatically passes the signal to Workstation C. Therefore, the token ring system is resistant to breakdowns.

 The IBM token ring network is often called a star ring because it combines the physical topology of a star with the logical topology of a ring.

The advantages of token ring systems are speed, expandability, and fault tolerance. Token ring systems are usually easy to troubleshoot because bad connections or cable runs can be quickly isolated. Disadvantages include the extra wiring the star topology requires and the higher cost of most token ring cards compared to other types of network cards. Token ring networks are quite expensive when added to the cost of an MSAU for every eight computers on your network. For this reason, the token ring is not gaining in market share over Ethernet systems.

## Ethernet Networks

The term "Ethernet" originally applied to networks using a linear bus topology and CSMA/CD on coaxial cable. This system is also known as 10Base2. However, several variations of the specification have been created, and now the term **Ethernet** is used as a general reference to the entire family of variations. The members of the Ethernet family discussed here are 10Base2, 10BaseT, 100BaseT, and 1000BaseT.

**10Base2 Networks** The **10Base2** network, shown in Figure 3-11, is based on the linear bus topology on coaxial cable and uses the CSMA/CD system standardized by the IEEE 802.3 committee. The term "10Base2" stands for 10 Mbps baseband using digital baseband signals over a maximum of two 100-meter (328-foot) coaxial cable segments. Network professionals often refer to 10Base2 as **ThinNet** because of its thin coaxial cable. The term **baseband** describes a computer network that carries **digital signals**; a **broadband** system carries **analog signals**, like the signals used for television and radio transmissions. In 10Base2, thin RG-58 coaxial cable with T-connectors can attach up to 30 machines to a single cable run, which is called a segment. According to the 10Base2 standards, a segment cannot exceed 607 feet, and no more than five segments can be joined by repeaters to form the entire network. A maximum of three of the five segments can have workstations attached, which is usually called the "5-4-3 rule." The "5" refers to the maximum amount of segments allowed, the "4" refers to the maximum amount of repeaters allowed, and the "3" refers to the maximum amount of segments that can contain workstations.

10Base2 cards use the same CSMA/CD system and 10 Mbps speed as 10BaseT cards. Some manufacturers supply cards that can be configured for the twisted-pair 10BaseT system or the RG-58 cable bus. However, 10Base2 networks are not as prevalent today because of the low cost and ease of setup with 10BaseT or 100BaseT networks.

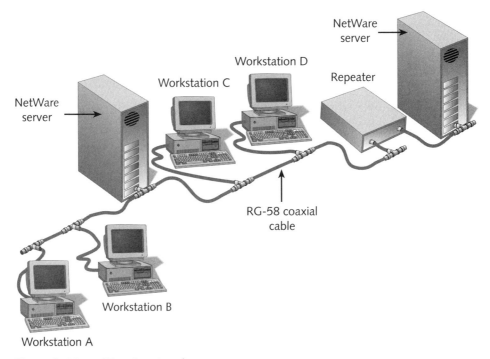

**Figure 3-11** 10Base2 network

 Thick coaxial cable is sometimes used instead of thin coaxial cables. Networks using thick coaxial cable are referred to as 10Base5, Thick Ethernet, or ThickNet. These networks are not common for the same reason that 10Base2 networks are becoming obsolete. Both ThinNet and ThickNet, however, are still good choices when longer distances need to be covered and sophisticated equipment is not available, such as fiber-enabled switches or routers. ThickNet coaxial cable can transmit data over 1600 feet. Try doing that with twisted-pair cable!

**10BaseT Networks** The 10BaseT network (shown in Figure 3-12) is currently popular in business offices because it combines the flexibility of the star topology with the lower cost of the CSMA/CD channel access method. The IEEE 802.3 designation of **10BaseT** stands for 10 Mbps baseband network using twisted-pair cable.

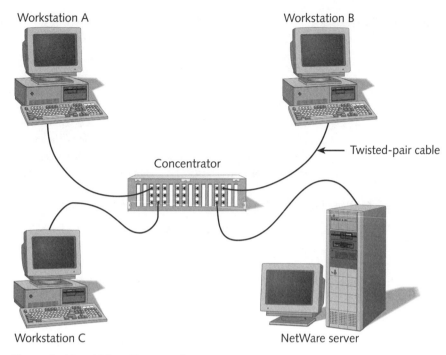

**Figure 3-12**     10BaseT network

A 10BaseT network uses a central hub in a star topology to connect all machines with twisted-pair cabling. Hub devices today can be multiport Ethernet repeaters or switches. Although the 10BaseT network uses the same star topology as a token ring network, the 10BaseT signals are not sent from one station to the next as in token ring. The CSMA/CD method, standardized by the IEEE 802.3 committee, is used to broadcast the signals to all stations simultaneously. You can easily convert a cable system designed for token ring to support 10BaseT by replacing the MSAUs with concentrators. The concentrator acts as a repeater, receiving signals on one cable port and then retransmitting those signals on all other ports. When two or more network stations attempt to transmit at the same instant, a collision occurs, and the stations must retransmit after waiting a random period of time. You look at network devices that reduce these collisions in the "Bridges" and "Switches" sections later in this chapter.

The advantages of 10BaseT include high performance under light-to-medium network loads and low costs for network cards because of the relative simplicity of the CSMA/CD system. Although 10BaseT performance can be faster than token ring under light loads, it is more easily slowed because of collisions when many stations are transmitting on the network. Another disadvantage of the 10BaseT system is additional cost for concentrators and the star topology wiring.

**100BaseT Networks**    The 100BaseT network systems, also referred to as Fast Ethernet, are extensions of the 10BaseT system and are overseen by the IEEE 802.3 committee. They use the same star topology and the CSMA/CD media access method. The designation **100BaseT** indicates a 100 Mbps baseband network using twisted-pair cable or IBM STP cable. (The **100BaseFX** designation indicates a 100 Mbps baseband network using fiber-optic cable.) 100BaseT networks appear identical to 10BaseT networks. The advantages of 100BaseT include higher performance for networks requiring fast data transmission, such as those using video. The disadvantages include shorter maximum cable run lengths in some cable systems, which is a necessary tradeoff to gain the extra speed, and higher costs for the hubs and NICs capable of handling the higher speed.

**1000BaseT Networks**    **1000BaseT** networks have the following features:

- Allow half and full duplex operation at speeds of 1000 Mbps
- Use the 802.3 Ethernet frame formats
- Use the CSMA/CD access method with support for one repeater per collision domain
- Address backward-compatibility with 10BaseT and 100BaseT technologies

Because the fundamental features of the 802.3z specification have been stable during the last stages of the standardization process, network vendors have been able to build and deliver quality, mature products to the marketplace for many months. The Gigabit Ethernet Alliance and other independent organizations have sponsored numerous interoperability demonstrations, giving customers confidence in using Gigabit Ethernet products in their production networks.

## Comparing Network Systems

Selecting a network system is a complex task that depends on such variables as type and location of computers, existing wiring, and the amount of load expected on the network. In many organizations, multiple network systems, connected with bridges and routers (described in the next section), are necessary to meet the needs of different departments. Table 3-7 summarizes the major network systems.

**Table 3-7**   Network System Comparison

| Network System | Cable Types | Topology | Maximum Number of Nodes | IEEE Standard | Speed | Access | MethodDistance |
|---|---|---|---|---|---|---|---|
| Token ring | UTP, STP, fiber | Star | 96 | 802.5 | 4–16 Mbps | Token | 150 feet (50 meters) per cable run |
| 10Base2 | Coaxial | Linear bus | 30 per segment with maximum of three populated segments | 802.3 | 10 Mbps | CSMA/CD | 607 feet (185 meters) per segment |
| 10BaseT | UTP | Star | 512 | 802.3 | 10 Mbps | CSMA/CD | 328 feet (100 meters) per cable run on UTP Cat 3 & 4; 450 feet ) (150 meters) on UTP Cat 5 |
| 100BaseT | UTP, STP | Star | 512 | 802.3 | 100 Mbps | CSMA/CD | 328 feet (100 meters) per cable run on UTP Cat 3 & 4; 328 feet (100 meters) on UTP Cat 5; 328 feet (100 meters) on STP type 1 |
| 1000BaseT | UTP, STP | Star | 512 | 802.3z | 1000 Mbps | CSMA/CD | 328 feet (100 meters) per cable run on UTP Cat 5E & 6; 328 feet (100 meters) on UTP Cat 5E; 328 feet (100 meters) on STP type 1 |

If you decide to install new cable above a ceiling or in walls, be sure to obtain cable that meets your local building codes. Some cable is not allowed in suspended ceilings, whereas others are not permitted where heating/air-conditioning ducts are nearby. (You need what is called "plenum grade" for such cables.)

## Bridges

A **bridge** operates at the data link layer of the OSI model. That means the bridge sees only the packet's frame information, which consists of the sender and receiver addresses and error-checking information. During network operation, the bridge watches packets on both networks and builds a table of workstation node addresses for each network. When it sees a packet on one network that has a destination address (MAC address) for a machine on the other network, the bridge reads the packet, builds new frame information, and sends the packet out on the other network. Because bridges work at the data link layer, they are used to connect networks of the same type. For example, a bridge can connect two different token ring networks and allow more than 100 users to access the same NetWare server. Another use for a bridge might be to break a heavily loaded Ethernet or 10BaseT network into two separate networks to reduce the number of collisions on any one network system. For example, if the destination MAC address is on the same side of the bridge as the source MAC address, the bridge does not pass the frame to the other side. The bridge keeps track of all those MAC addresses, so it knows when it has to forward the frame to the other side. In other words, if you were in Manhattan and wanted to send a message to someone else located in Manhattan, would you drive over the Brooklyn Bridge into Brooklyn to deliver the message? Well, a bridge would make the same decision as you: It wouldn't go to Brooklyn. This prevents unnecessary traffic from going over the bridge, thus reducing collisions.

## Switches

A **switch** operates at the data link layer of the OSI model, just as a bridge does, and uses MAC addresses, just like bridges, to determine where to send those frames. Think of a switch as a multiport bridge. Each port on a switch behaves like a miniature bridge, so you can have hundreds of computers connected to a switch instead of a hub. In this way, each computer has its own dedicated bandwidth. No sharing means no collision problems like those discussed in the "Repeaters" section. Most network engineers connect their NetWare servers to the 100 Mbps port on the switch and connect all their clients to dedicated 10 Mbps ports on the switch. Clients with a little more money to spend connect their servers to 1000 Mbps ports and their client computers to 100 Mbps ports. If you have a 16-port switch, you have created 16 separate collision domains instead of the one collision domain that would be created by using a repeater. The more collision domains you have, the better. If there is only one collision domain, all 16 users will contend for the wire to send data because it can accommodate only one user at a time.

# Network Layer Components

## Routers

Routers are needed to create more complex internetworks. A **router** operates at the network layer of the OSI model, so it has access to the datagram information containing the logical network address and control information. Remember, bridges and switches operate at the data link layer and have access to frame information containing the physical address (MAC address). When a router is used, each network must be given a separate network address. Remember that a network address is similar in function to a zip code. Just as each postal area has a unique zip code, each network system must have a unique network address. The router information in the datagram packet allows a router to find the correct path and, if necessary, break up a datagram for transmission on a different network system. Two disadvantages of routers are that they require a little more processing time than bridges and network packets must use a datagram format that the router can interpret. By default, routers do not forward broadcast traffic to different networks, so this device helps not only with the collision problem that bridges and switches deal with, but also with the broadcast traffic traversing your network.

Networks with different network topologies generally are connected with routers, whereas networks of the same topology are connected with bridges. Novell uses routers in its NetWare servers to allow up to eight different network cards to be installed in a single NetWare server computer. This enables you to use the NetWare server to connect networks of different types and topologies to form an internetwork.

Each network system presented in this chapter has unique limitations. In some cases, you want to take advantage of features found in two different products. For example, in a school environment, you might want the Ethernet system in the computer labs to take advantage of the economical coaxial wiring arrangement. If other computers in the building are located many feet apart in completely separate areas, however, you can create two separate networks: Ethernet for the lab and token ring for the office. You then connect the networks so that they share access to the same NetWare server. In other cases, dividing a large network into two or more smaller networks might be necessary to overcome performance problems or cabling distances or to accommodate large numbers of users. For example, if your network is having too many collisions, you can incorporate a bridge or switch into your design. If, on the other hand, broadcast traffic is bringing the network to its knees, you can bring in a router to help reduce the traffic. A good understanding of these components and why or when they should be used will make your job as a network administrator a lot easier. After all, users won't tell you there are too many collisions on the network, but they *will* tell you the network is too slow. After you determine whether the problem is caused by collisions or excessive broadcast traffic, you will know what to do about it.

Use repeaters to maintain a strong, reliable signal throughout the network system. To connect separate network systems, use routers; to connect two segments of a network, use bridges. The resulting connected networks are called an **internetwork**. Repeaters, bridges, switches, and routers are shown in Figure 3-13.

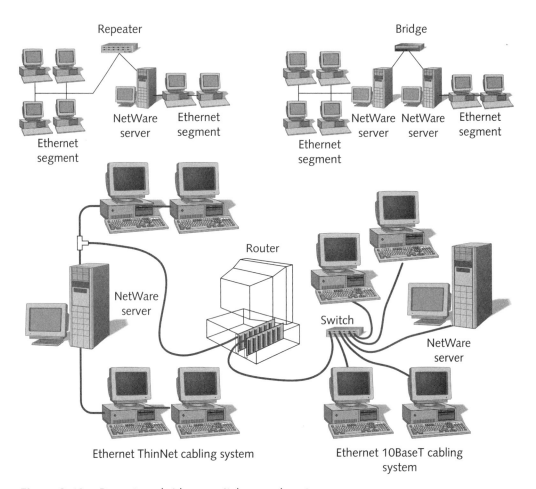

**Figure 3-13**    Repeaters, bridges, switches, and routers

## Protocol Stacks

The network's protocol stack is responsible for formatting requests to access network services and to transmit data. Delivering data packets throughout a network system is the responsibility of its data link and physical layer components; the functions of the network, transport, and session layers are built into a network operating system's protocol stack.

NetWare 6's default protocol is TCP/IP, or IP for short. Administrators need to know how to configure an IP network with NetWare. In the past, Novell's IPX/SPX protocol stack was commonly used to support clients on NetWare networks. You can install IP, IPX, or both on a NetWare LAN. Because today's networks often need to support protocol stacks of computers running other operating systems, network administrators should also be familiar with the common protocol stacks that operating systems such as Macintosh, Unix, and Windows use. In the following sections, you learn about protocol stacks and some of their advantages and disadvantages, which will help you make informed recommendations on which protocol stacks should be supported on a network.

## TCP/IP

As Table 3-8 shows, TCP/IP covers the network and transport OSI layers, as does IPX/SPX. Unlike IPX/SPX, however, TCP and IP don't overlap in the transport layer.

**Table 3-8**    The TCP/IP Protocol

OSI Model Layers

|  | Physical | Data Link | Network | Transport | Session | Presentation | Application |
|---|---|---|---|---|---|---|---|
| TCP |  |  |  | X |  |  |  |
| IP |  |  | X |  |  |  |  |
| Ethernet | X | X |  |  |  |  |  |
| Token ring | X | X |  |  |  |  |  |
| Others | X | X |  |  |  |  |  |

TCP/IP is responsible for formatting packets and routing them between networks using IP, which is more sophisticated than IPX in fragmenting packets and transmitting over WAN links. When IP is used, each workstation is assigned a logical network and node address. IP allows packets to be sent out over different routers and reassembled in the correct sequence at the receiving station. TCP operates at the transport layer and guarantees packet delivery by receiving acknowledgments. The acknowledgment system lets the sender and receiver establish a window for the number of packets to acknowledge. This results in better performance than in WANs because each packet need not be individually acknowledged before another is sent.

Today, TCP/IP is commonly used on many LANs as well as the Internet. NetWare 6 servers use IP rather than IPX as the native protocol. (NetWare 4.x can also use IP if the correct NLMs are loaded and configured.) NetWare uses TCP/IP to communicate with workstations, to provide Internet services, and to route TCP/IP packets between network cards. The need to implement TCP/IP on a NetWare network is growing rapidly because of the Internet's exploding popularity and the need for network administrators to provide a single protocol for all network services.

To communicate on a network, each computer needs to be assigned an IP address and a subnet mask. The primary drawback of TCP/IP has been the need to manually configure the address for each node on the network. This method is prone to error and could lead to problems, such as duplicate IP addresses errors or incorrect subnet masks being assigned to a workstation. Fortunately, you can use Dynamic Host Configuration Protocol (DHCP) to automate these tasks.

## Dynamic Host Configuration Protocol

DHCP is a network protocol that enables a DHCP server to automatically assign an IP address to an individual computer's TCP/IP stack software. DHCP assigns a number dynamically from a defined range of numbers (a scope) configured for a given network.

When using automatic address assignment, an IP address range can be established on a server running DHCP. Network entities then "lease" IP addresses from the DHCP server when they first start up and renew their IP addresses every several days, depending on the configuration of the DHCP service. With DHCP, an administrator can also permanently assign the same IP address to a particular user each time the user starts his or her computer. The range of IP addresses that the DHCP service is configured to distribute is referred to as the "scope." For example, CBE Labs currently uses a DHCP service running on the NetWare 6 server to automatically assign IP addresses in the range of 192.169.1.10 to 192.168.1.200. Figure 3-14 shows the range of IP addresses the administrator assigned to the DHCP service running on the Constellation server.

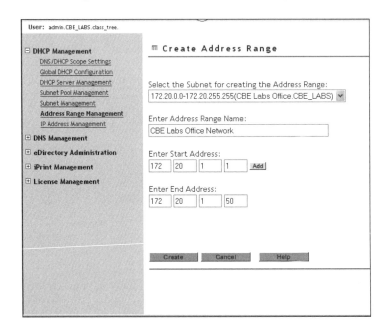

**Figure 3-14**    Configuring a DHCP scope in iManager

It is still possible to get duplicate IP addresses on a network using DHCP if multiple DHCP servers are configured and the "scopes" overlap. Use caution when defining scopes. Moreover, if there are printers or servers using static IP addresses on the network, be sure to exclude those IP addresses from the scope.

In addition to providing a client with an IP address and a mask, the DHCP address scope can be configured to assign other TCP/IP settings to client computers, such as the address of the default gateway or router (see Figure 3-15) as well as the Domain Name Service

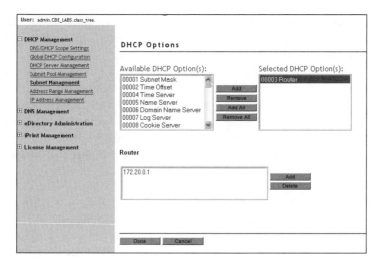

**Figure 3-15**   Configuring an IP gateway in iManager

(DNS) server, discussed later in this chapter. DHCP's sole purpose is to enable the administrator to configure users' workstations without having to sit in front of their PCs.

Take a look at the mechanics of DHCP operation. When a client is configured to obtain an IP address automatically, it starts up and sends out a request for a DHCP server, as shown in Figure 3-16.

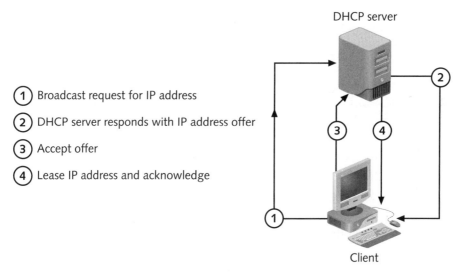

**Figure 3-16**   Using DHCP to obtain an IP address

Any DHCP servers on the same network cable respond with an available IP address that the client can lease. The client takes the first response it receives and sends a packet back to the DHCP server requesting the IP address. The DHCP server then acknowledges the request and leases the IP address information to the client. If the client receives no DHCP responses, it assigns itself an available IP address from the Microsoft-reserved, class B network, 169.254.0.0, with the subnet mask 255.255.0.0. The Microsoft automatic IP address assignment limits connectivity to the LAN of the client computer. In other words, only clients on the 169.254.0.0 network would be able to communicate with each other. Because no gateway address is configured, the client computer cannot connect to the Internet or other networks.

If a DHCP server were located on a different network cable, the client's request would not be heard because routers, by default, do not forward broadcast traffic. However, a router can be configured as a DHCP relay agent, which would forward the client's request for an IP address to the DHCP server located on a different network cable.

To view the IP address information assigned to a client configured to obtain its address automatically, enter the IPCONFIG /ALL command in the command-prompt window (see Figure 3-17). If you change the DHCP scope configuration, such as changing the IP address of the gateway or DNS server, you can force the client to obtain the new information without restarting by entering the following commands in a command-prompt window:

```
IPCONFIG /RELEASE
IPCONFIG /RENEW
```

```
(C) Copyright 1985-1999 Microsoft Corp.

C:\>ipconfig /all

Windows 2000 IP Configuration

        Host Name . . . . . . . . . . . . : TS
        Primary DNS Suffix  . . . . . . . :
        Node Type . . . . . . . . . . . . : Broadcast
        IP Routing Enabled. . . . . . . . : No
        WINS Proxy Enabled. . . . . . . . : No

Ethernet adapter Local Area Connection:

        Connection-specific DNS Suffix  . :
        Description . . . . . . . . . . . : AMD PCNET Family PCI Ethernet Adapter
        Physical Address. . . . . . . . . : 00-50-56-72-32-22
        DHCP Enabled. . . . . . . . . . . : No
        IP Address. . . . . . . . . . . . : 172.20.1.200
        Subnet Mask . . . . . . . . . . . : 255.255.0.0
        Default Gateway . . . . . . . . . : 172.20.0.60
        DNS Servers . . . . . . . . . . . : 172.20.0.60
```

**Figure 3-17**    Using the IPCONFIG command

PING *ip-address* is another useful command when testing TCP/IP communications. The PING command allows you to send packets to another computer specified by its IP address or name and wait for replies. By default, the PING command sends four 32-byte packets. If there's no reply in the default time period, a "Request timed out" error message usually means one of the following conditions exists:

- The target computer is not on.

- The target computer does not have the IP protocol configured.

- The target computer has a different IP address than the one used in the PING command.

- Either the target computer or the sending computer has an incorrect mask or gateway configuration.

> If a client configured to obtain its IP address from a DHCP server is not able to communicate on the network, use the IPCONFIG /ALL command to check its IP address. If it's assigned an IP address in the 169.254.0.1 to 169.254.255.254 range, the client was unable to communicate with the DHCP server. Check to see that the DHCP server is up and running on the network. If the IPCONFIG /ALL command shows that the client's IP address is configured, but the subnet mask indicates all zeros (0.0.0.0), the IP address is in use on the network and you have a duplicate IP address problem.

## Domain Name System (DNS)

Identifying and configuring the Domain Name System (DNS) for the network is another important part of implementing TCP/IP. No one wants to have to remember the IP addresses of other computers and Web servers they need to access; it's much easier to use names. An additional advantage of using names is that the same name can be used to access a server even if the server's IP address changes. The DNS resolves TCP/IP names into IP addresses by having the client computer send a request to its assigned DNS server. The DNS server then looks up the name and returns the IP address to the client computer. TCP/IP names are often referred to as "domain names" because they include the server's name and the name of the domain where the server is located. The Universal Resource Locator (URL) you use to access a Web site from your browser is an example of a domain name. For example, to access Novell's support site, you could enter the URL *http://support.Novell.com*; "support" is the name of the server, and "Novell.com" is the name of the domain the server resides in.

Domain names can be private or public. Private domain names are maintained on a local DNS server and are not available to computers outside the organization. To work on the Internet, public domain names need to be registered through an ISP. When a domain name is registered on the Internet, the computer's name and IP address is placed in a DNS server and made accessible to all computers attached to the Internet. As shown in Figure 3-18, the Internet Corporation for Assigned Names and Numbers (ICANN) organizes domain names on the Internet into a hierarchical structure based on the organization's type, location, and name.

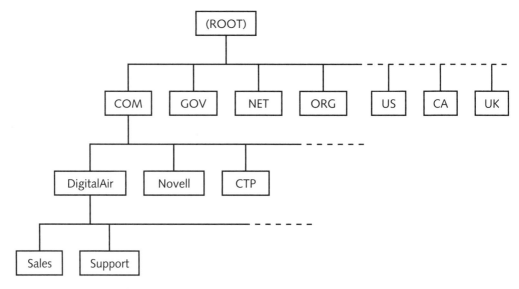

**Figure 3-18**    DNS domains

The .com domain is reserved for commercial businesses, the .org domain is generally used only by nonprofit organizations, the .gov domain is used for governmental agencies, and the .net domain contains names of Internet service providers. Top-level domains are also divided by country. There are over 200 top-level country domains, such as .vs, .jk, .ca, and .fr. The list of top-level domains keeps growing as new types are defined; some new types include .tv, .biz, .info, and .aero. To enable outside users to access the CBE Labs Web site stored on the CBE_ADMIN server by name, the administrator registered the domain name "cbe_admin.cbe.com" with the IP address 198.12.28.50.

 You can find more information on domain names and the registration process at *www.interNIC.net*.

There are thousands of computer domain names on the Internet, and keeping all the names on a single master DNS server would be impossible to manage. As a result, DNS servers typically contain only the names of computers in a single domain. The names for a domain are stored in a **zone file**, which contains all computer names for a specific domain. For example, the Novell DNS server stores the domain names of only the servers in the Novell.com domain in its Novell.com zone, and the Microsoft DNS server keeps track of the Microsoft.com server names in its Microsoft.com zone.

Top-level Internet domains are stored on 13 DNS servers referred to as the Internet (Root) servers. When a user makes a request for a server such as support.novell.com, the request is first sent to the DNS server specified in the client computer's TCP/IP configuration. The local DNS server checks its cache to see whether the name has been used recently. If the support.novell.com name is not in the cache, the local DNS server performs a lookup process (see Figure 3-19).

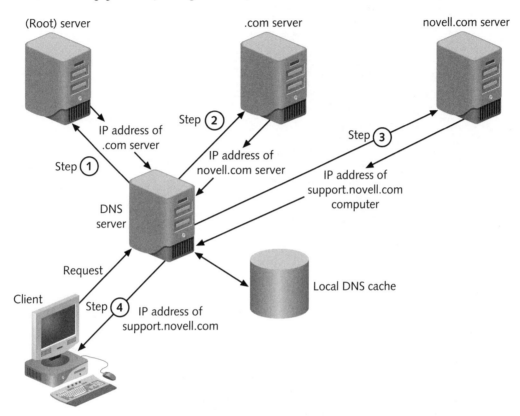

**Figure 3-19**   The DNS lookup process

In Step 1, the local DNS server sends a request to the (Root) server for the IP address of a DNS responsible for the .com domain. After receiving the IP address of the .com domain server, in Step 2, the local DNS server sends a request to the .com domain server for the IP address of the server responsible for the novell.com zone. In Step 3, the local DNS server sends a request to the novell.com server asking for the IP address of the support.novell.com computer. Step 4 involves the local DNS server returning the IP address of the support.novell.com computer to the local client, which then sends a packet directly to the support.novell.com computer using the IP address it was given.

Because they are available only to computers on your network, private domain names are much simpler to set up and manage. To implement private domain names in the CBE Labs network, you would install DNS on the NetWare 6 server and use iManager to create a zone file for the "cbe.com" domain and add a record for the CBE_ADMIN server, as shown in Figure 3-20.

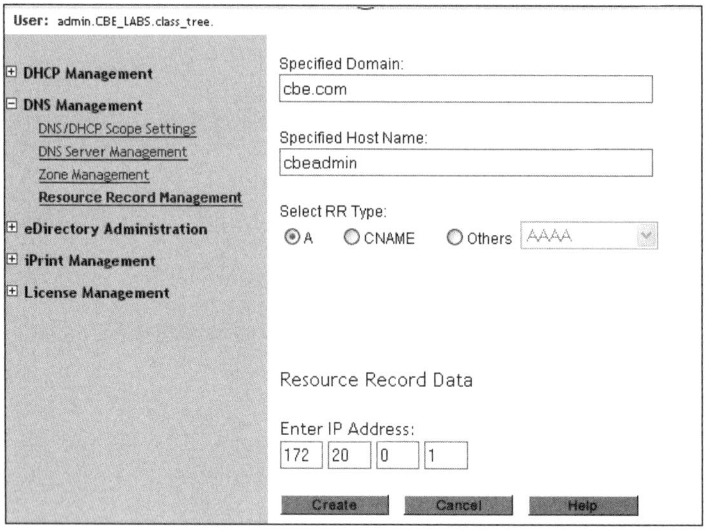

**Figure 3-20**    Using iManager to implement private domain names

After setting up the NetWare 6 DNS server, configure the computers on the CBE network to use the IP address of the CBE_ADMIN server as the primary DNS server and the address of the DNS server maintained by the ISP as the secondary name server. To configure DNS server information manually for each computer, use the Preferred DNS server text box in the Internet Protocol (TCP/IP) Properties dialog box, as shown in Figure 3-21.

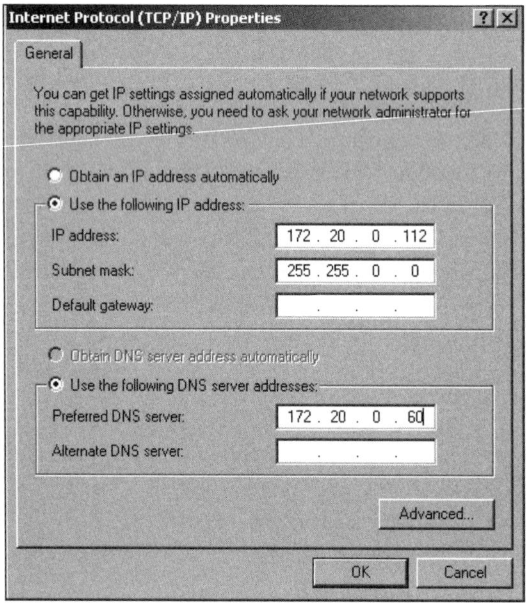

**Figure 3-21**    Configuring DNS server information manually

The information in the Alternate DNS server text box specifies the IP address of a sec-ond server that the client can use if the primary DNS server does not respond and times out. Instead of manually setting the primary and alternate DNS server IP addresses in each client computer, configure the DHCP server scope (see Figure 3-22) to automat-ically assign the DNS server addresses each time a computer starts.

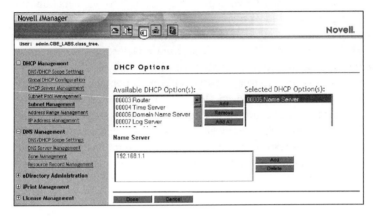

**Figure 3-22**    Configuring the DHCP server scope

When a request is made for a domain name, the client computer consults its IP con-figuration to determine the IP address of its primary and alternate DNS servers. If the primary DNS server does not respond within a set time period, the client computer sends the request to the alternate DNS server. You select the DNS server maintained by the ISP as the alternate name server. In this way, users can still access the Internet domain names if the Constellation server is down. If the alternate DNS server does not respond, an error message is displayed, letting the user know that a DNS server is not available. When a DNS server receives a request from a client, it first checks to see whether it has the requested server's name and IP address in its memory cache. DNS servers keep a temporary list, or cache, of recently accessed names in memory to respond faster. If the name is not in the cache, the DNS server checks to see whether it has a copy of the zone file that contains the name and IP address information for all com-puters in the requested domain. When the DNS server has a zone file for the requested domain, it looks up the requested name and returns the IP address. If the name is not found in the zone file, an invalid name message is returned to the user. If the DNS server does not contain a copy of the zone file, it forwards the request to the Internet Domain Name Resolver, which returns the IP address of the server that contains the zone file for the requested domain.

For example, if you enter the URL *http://support.novell.com* in your Web browser, the request is sent to the CBE_ADMIN server. Because the server does not contain a copy of the novell.com domain, it forwards the request to the (Root) DNS server and obtains the address of the DNS server that has the zone file for the Novell domain. The

CBE_ADMIN server then queries the Novell DNS server to obtain the IP address of the support.novell.com server. Finally, the CBE_ADMIN server returns the IP address for the support.novell.com server to your Web browser, which uses the IP address to access the Novell support home page.

> DNS servers usually support two types of zone files: forward lookup and reverse lookup. Forward lookup zone files contain various record types, the most popular being the "A," or host record. A host record contains the host name and associated IP address, such as www.novell.com 192.168.1.1. A Mail Exchange (MX) record is associated with the e-mail server's IP address, so you can send an e-mail to tsimpson@novell.com. A CNAME record (canonical name record), usually called an alias record, enables you to give more than one address name to an associated server. For example, users could access a server named helpdesk.novell.com as www.helpdesk.com. Reverse lookup zones provide address-to-name mapping. Some applications require the host name of a connecting computer where an IP address is given. Pointer (PTR) records provide for this type of reverse lookup.

## IPX/SPX

The IPX/SPX protocol is Novell's proprietary system that implements the session, transport, and network OSI layers, as shown in Table 3-9. Notice that IPX/SPX is not a true implementation of the OSI model because IPX and SPX functions overlap in the transport layer. This layer overlap is true of many older protocol stacks used before the OSI model was developed and standardized.

**Table 3-9**   Novell IPX/SPX and NCP Protocols

### OSI Model Layers

|           | Physical | Data Link | Network | Transport | Session | Presentation | Application |
|-----------|----------|-----------|---------|-----------|---------|--------------|-------------|
| TCP       |          |           |         |           | X       | X            |             |
| SPX       |          |           |         | X         | X       |              |             |
| IPX       |          |           | X       | X         |         |              |             |
| Ethernet  | X        | X         |         |           |         |              |             |
| Token ring| X        | X         |         |           |         |              |             |
| Others    | X        | X         |         |           |         |              |             |

**Internetwork Packet eXchange (IPX)** is the NetWare protocol that manages packet routing and formatting at the network layer. To function, IPX must be loaded on each network workstation and on the NetWare server. In addition to IPX, each workstation and NetWare server must have loaded a network card driver to transmit the frames containing the packets. IPX software and the network card driver are brought together during the network installation process, which is described in Chapter 6. In addition to IPX,

NetWare uses two protocols to provide network services: **Sequential Packet eXchange (SPX)** and NetWare Core Protocol (NCP).

The key advantage of IPX (and the reason Novell developed it, despite IP's ready availability) is that it offers automatic addressing for network nodes. Despite improved IP address automation, administrators still have to manually configure addresses for one or more nodes on an IP network. With IPX, the addresses are done for you.

SPX operates at the OSI transport layer and guarantees delivery of packets by receiving an acknowledgment for each packet sent, but this involves additional overhead. IPX/SPX is not the recommended protocol of choice, and Novell recommends using TCP/IP, which is the default. NCP works at the session and presentation layers at the workstation through the Novell client software. The client establishes and maintains network sessions, directs information and requests from the workstation, and formats them for the NetWare server. On the NetWare server, NCP provides network services, such as login, file sharing, printing, security, and administrative functions.

Novell has incorporated many improvements into its client software for DOS, Windows, and Macintosh workstations. Unless there's a reason that older client software must be used at your site, you should upgrade all workstations to the newest client software to prevent potential error conditions. The software is available free from Novell's Web site at *www.novell.com*.

## NetBEUI

The NetBEUI protocol, Microsoft's own protocol stack, is integrated into Windows for Workgroups, Windows 95/98, and Windows NT products. Of the protocols described in this section, NetBEUI is the easiest to use. It has few features, however, and cannot be used in large internetwork environments because it does not support the network layer needed for routing packets between networks. As a result, NetBEUI is limited to only the most basic of networking—communicating with other computers attached to the same network cable system.

Avoid using NetBEUI except in peer-to-peer networking on small networks of fewer than 10 to 15 workstations.

The NetBEUI protocol stack consists of **Network Basic Input/Output System (NetBIOS)** and service message blocks (SMBs) at the session layer and **NetBIOS frames (NBF)** at the transport layer, as Table 3-10 shows. SMBs and NetBIOS offer a well-defined standard method for servers and workstations to communicate with each other. Many peer-to-peer applications have been written to interface with NetBIOS so that an application can span multiple computers. Because NetBIOS-based applications are popular, Novell supplies a NetBIOS interface to work with its IPX/SPX protocol. This interface allows workstations to run peer-to-peer applications while still accessing services from NetWare servers.

**Table 3-10**     NetBEUI Protocol

**OSI Model Layers**

|  | Physical | Data Link | Network | Transport | Session | Presentation | Application |
|---|---|---|---|---|---|---|---|
| NetBIOS/SMB |  |  |  |  | X |  |  |
| NBF or NBT |  |  | X | X |  |  |  |
| Ethernet | X | X |  |  |  |  |  |
| Token ring | X | X |  |  |  |  |  |
| Others | X | X |  |  |  |  |  |

Because NetBEUI's NBF does not maintain routing tables, it is extremely small and fast, making it useful for networks ranging from 2 to 50 devices. Because the NBF does not support packet routing, however, the protocol is limited to communication among computers attached to a single network. NetBEUI allows the replacement of NBF with **NBT (NetBIOS over TCP/IP)**, which enables the protocol stack to communicate directly over large TCP/IP-based networks.

## AppleTalk

The **AppleTalk** protocol suite was originally developed so that Macintosh computers could communicate in peer-to-peer networks. It currently provides connectivity for a variety of computer systems, including IBM PCs running MS-DOS, IBM mainframes, and various Unix-based computers. The AppleTalk protocol suite was developed after the OSI model was conceived, so it can be mapped reasonably well to the OSI layers, as shown in Table 3-11.

On the data link layer, the **Apple Address Resolution Protocol (AARP)** connects the AppleTalk protocol stack to the Ethernet, 10BaseT, or token ring protocol. AppleTalk uses the **Datagram Delivery Protocol (DDP)** to support routing packets between networks. In addition, AppleTalk uses zones to organize the names of service providers logically on large internetworks. Zones limit the number of service providers present at one time, which simplifies users' choices.

Because Macintosh and the AppleTalk protocol are so popular, Novell has included AppleTalk support with NetWare 6. Loading AppleTalk on a NetWare server allows Macintosh or other computers using AppleTalk to see the NetWare server as another AppleTalk service provider.

**Table 3-11** AppleTalk Protocol

**OSI Model Layers**

| | Physical | Data Link | Network | Transport | Session | Presentation | Application |
|---|---|---|---|---|---|---|---|
| Filing Protocol (AFP) | | | | | | X | |
| Apple Session Protocol (ASP) | | | | | X | | |
| Apple Transition Protocol (ATP) | | | | X | | | |
| Datagram Delivery Protocol (DDP) | | | X | | | | |
| AARP (Apple Address Resolution Protocol) | X | X | | | | | |
| Local Talk | X | X | | | | | |
| Ethertalk (Ethernet) | X | X | | | | | |
| Token Talk (token ring) | X | X | | | | | |

**3**

**Note** On NetWare 4.x and later versions, you can use any combination of PC and Macintosh clients. The NetWare license you purchase determines the total number of users who can simultaneously log in to the network (for example, a 100-user NetWare license allows 100 simultaneous logins), but it doesn't matter whether the workstation is a PC or a Macintosh.

In the NetWare 6 environment, Macintosh workstations can also log in to eDirectory. However, Mac workstations must load and run MacIPX, which enables the Macintoshes to use the IPX protocol. For a Macintosh workstation to use eDirectory, IPX is required.

## CHAPTER SUMMARY

❐ Network communication depends on packets of information being passed from one computer to another. Understanding how information packets flow through a network system means knowing the functions of the seven layers of the Open Systems Interconnect (OSI) model. Each layer of the OSI model is responsible for a particular function, and this modular approach makes it easier to understand and work with network components.

❐ Cable types used with today's LANs include shielded and unshielded twisted-pair cable, coaxial cable, and fiber-optic cable. Infrared and narrowband radio transmission are used in wireless networks. The physical geometry of a bounded medium is called its topology. Major physical topologies include ring, linear bus, and star.

❐ Regardless of the type of topology used, only one machine can transmit on a network at any given time, and with some, a method of access control must be used to avoid data collisions. Network access control methods can be contention based or token based. Ethernet 10Base2, 10BaseT, 100BaseT, and 1000BaseT networks use a contention system, in which computers attempt to transmit whenever they sense an open period on the network. On busy networks, however, when two or more machines sense an open period and try to transmit at the same time, a collision occurs. With the CSMA/CD system, each machine waits a random time period before retrying its transmission.

❐ Token ring networks use the token passing system. A token is passed around the network when no data packet is being transmitted. A machine needing to transmit must wait for the token. When it receives the token, it can transmit its packet without any collisions. Collisions cause CSMA/CD systems to slow under heavy network transmission loads, but token passing systems offer more uniform, predictable performance. Repeaters, bridges, switches and routers are devices that enable administrators to expand networks and reduce collisions or broadcast traffic.

❐ Protocols are the languages used to implement the OSI layers. Popular protocols you'll encounter as a network administrator include Novell NetWare's IPX/SPX; TCP/IP, used by Unix and the Internet; NetBEUI, used in Windows-based networks; and AppleTalk, for Macintosh computers. NetWare 6 servers use the IP protocol by default. Earlier versions used IPX/SPX by default, but could also be configured to handle TCP/IP and AppleTalk. TCP/IP is becoming a popular protocol for use in Unix environments and international WANs, such as the Internet.

# KEY TERMS

**10Base2** — A 10 Mbps linear bus implementation of CSMA/CD Ethernet using coaxial cable with T-connectors to attach networked computers. A terminator is used at each of the coaxial cable wire segments.

**10BaseT** — A 10 Mbps star implementation of CSMA/CD Ethernet using twisted-pair wires to connect all stations to a central concentrator.

**100BaseFX** — A 100 Mbps star implementation of CSMA/CD Ethernet using fiber-optic cables to connect all stations to a central concentrator.

**100BaseT** — A 100 Mbps star implementation of CSMA/CD Ethernet using twisted-pair wires to connect all stations to a central concentrator.

**1000BaseT** — A 1000 Mbps star implementation of CSMA/CD Ethernet.

**analog signal** — A signal carried by a broadband system, such as radio or television.

**Apple Address Resolution Protocol (AARP)** — A component of the AppleTalk protocol that works at the physical and data link layers.

**AppleTalk** — Apple's network protocol developed to enable Macintosh computers to work in peer-to-peer networks.

**application layer** — The top software layer of the OSI model that interacts with the user to perform a communication process on a network.

**backbone network** — A network cable system used to connect network servers and host computer systems. Each network server or host can contain a separate network card that attaches it to client computers.

**bandwidth** — A measurement of the range of signals that can be sent across a communications system.

**baseband** — A digital signaling system that consists of only two signals, representing one and zero.

**bounded media** — A type of cable that confines the signal within eletromagnetic shielding.

**bridge** — A device used to connect two segments of a network. Operates at the data link layer.

**broadband** — A signaling system that uses analog signals to carry data across the media.

**bundled pair** — Fifty or more pairs of twisted wire put together in one large cable.

**Carrier Sense Multiple Access with Collision Detection (CSMA/CD)** — A media access control method used on Ethernet networks in which a computer waits for the media to have an open carrier signal before attempting to transmit. Collisions occur when two or more devices sense an open carrier and attempt to transmit at the same time.

**Category 5 cable** — A network cable specification most commonly used today with 10BaseT and 100BaseT.

**coaxial cable** — A thick plastic cable containing a center conductor and shield.

3

**collision** — An event that occurs when two or more nodes attempt to transmit on the network at the same time. After the collision, the nodes wait a random time interval before retrying.

**contention access method** — A media access method in which computer nodes are allowed to talk whenever they detect that the channel is not in use. This often results in collisions between packets. In Ethernet, this becomes the Carrier Sense Multiple Access with Collision Detection (CSMA/CD) method.

**cyclic redundancy check (CRC)** — An error-checking system that enables a receiving computer to determine whether a block of data was received correctly; the system applies a formula to the data and checks the results against the value supplied by the sending computer.

**Datagram Delivery Protocol (DDP)** — A component of the AppleTalk protocol that works at the network layer.

**datagram packet** — The packet created at the network layer by wrapping the information in the segment packet with packet routing information.

**data link layer** — The OSI software layer that controls access to the network card.

**digital signal** — A signal that can have a value of only zero or one.

**driver software** — When referring to a network interface card (NIC), the software needed to control the NIC and interface between the data link layer and the network layer software.

**electromagnetic interference (EMI)** — An undesirable electronic noise created on a wire cable when it runs close to a strong power source or magnetic field.

**Ethernet** — A network system that uses the CSMA/CD access method to connect networked computers. Originally, the term also meant only the 10Base2 system, but now refers to the entire Ethernet family, including 10BaseT, 100BaseT, and 100BaseFX.

**fiber-optic cable** — A cable made of light-conducting glass fibers that allows high-speed communications.

**frame** — An information packet at the data link layer.

**IEEE 802.3** — A standard issued by the Institute of Electrical and Electronic Engineers specifying an Ethernet protocol.

**IEEE 802.5** — Similar to 802.3, except that it specifies a token ring standard.

**infrared** — An unbounded media system that uses infrared light to transmit information. Commonly used on television remote control devices and small wireless LANs.

**Institute of Electrical and Electronic Engineers (IEEE)** — A U.S. professional organization that has established network standards, including those for LAN topologies.

**International Standards Organization (ISO)** — The group responsible for administering the OSI model.

**internetwork** — One or more network cable systems connected by bridges or routers.

**Internetwork Packet Exchange (IPX)** — The NetWare protocol that manages packet routing and formatting at the network layer.

**interoperability** — The ability of computers on different networks to communicate.

**linear bus topology** — A LAN topology that consists of a coaxial cable segment that connects computers by running from one machine to the next with a terminating resistor on each end of the cable segment.

**logical link control (LLC) layer** — A sublayer of the OSI model's data link layer, used in interfaces with the physical layer.

**media** — The device or material used to record and retrieve data.

**media access control (MAC) layer** — A sublayer of the OSI model's data link layer, used in interfaces with the network layer.

**media access method** — A method of controlling when a device can transmit data over a local area network. Common access methods include token ring and CSMA/CD.

**message packet** — A packet containing data being sent via the network from one user to another.

**multiple station access unit (MSAU)** — A central hub device used to connect IBM token ring network systems.

**multiplexing** — Placing multiple message packets into one segment.

**narrowband radio transmission** — An unbounded media system that uses radio waves to transmit information.

**NetBIOS frames (NBF)** — One component of Microsoft's NetBEUI protocol.

**NetBIOS over TCP/IP (NBT)** — An alternate component of Microsoft's NetBEUI protocol that enables its use with TCP/IP networks.

**network address** — An address used by the network layer to identify computers on the network.

**Network Basic Input/Output System (NetBIOS)** — The system developed by IBM, now used in Microsoft's NetBEUI protocol.

**Network Driver Interface Specifications (NDIS)** — A set of standard specifications developed by Microsoft to allow network card suppliers to interface their network cards with the Microsoft Windows operating system.

**network layer** — An OSI software layer that is responsible for routing packets between different networks.

**Open Data Interface (ODI)** — A set of standard specifications developed by Novell to allow network card suppliers to interface their network cards with multiple protocols, including the IPX protocol used with the NetWare operating system.

**Open Systems Interconnect (OSI) model** — A model for developing network systems consisting of the following seven layers: application, presentation, session, transport, network, data link, and physical.

**patch cable** — A cable segment used to connect a network card to the main cable system.

**patch panel** — A panel that consists of a connector for each cable segment, used to connect the cable segments with a central hub.

**physical address** — A unique hexadecimal network interface card (NIC) address coded into the NIC's electronics. This first part of the address identifies the manufacturer, and the second part is a unique number for that manufacturer.

**physical layer** — A layer of the OSI model, consisting of the cable system and connectors.

**presentation layer** — The OSI layer responsible for translating and encoding data to be transferred over a network system.

**repeater** — A network device for connecting multiple network cable segments.

**ring topology** — A cable system in which the cable runs to each computer and then back to the first, forming a circle.

**router** — A device used to connect complex networks consisting of different topologies. Routers operate at the network layer.

**segment** — When referring to packets on a network, the name of an information packet at the transport layer. When referring to the physical network structure, a single cable run.

**Sequential Packet eXchange (SPX)** — The NetWare protocol that operates at the transport layer.

**session layer** — The OSI software layer that establishes and maintains a communication session with the host computer.

**shielded twisted-pair (STP) cable** — A type of twisted-pair cable that has electromagnetic shielding, and is thus less susceptible to external electrical interference.

**star topology** — A cable system in which the cables radiate out from central hubs.

**switch** — A device operating at the data link layer that functions like a multiport bridge.

**ThinNet** — An Ethernet network system that uses T-connectors to attach networked computers to the RG-58 coaxial cable system.

**token** — A special packet sent from one computer to the next to control which computer can transmit when using a token passing media access method.

**token passing method** — A media access method that requires a computer to obtain the token packet before transmitting data on the network cable system.

**topology** — The geometry of a network cable system.

**Transmission Control Protocol (TCP)** — A transport layer protocol that is reliable and requires acknowledgements.

**transport layer** — The OSI layer responsible for reliable delivery of a packet to the receiving computer; requires some sort of acknowledgment to ensure delivery.

**twisted-pair cable** — Cable consisting of pairs of wires twisted together to reduce errors.

**unbounded media** — A type of twisted-pair cable that has no electromagnetic shielding, and is thus susceptible to external electrical interference.

**unshielded twisted-pair (UTP) cable** — A type of twisted-pair cable that has no electromagnetic shielding, so it is susceptible to external electrical interference.

**User Datagram Protocol (UDP)** — A transport layer protocol that is unreliable and requires no acknowledgment.

**zone file** — A file that contains all computer names for a specific domain.

**3**

## REVIEW QUESTIONS

1. Which of the following standards organizations works on physical cable standards?

   a. ISO

   b. FBO

   c. IEEE

   d. EIII

2. Which of the following layers of the OSI model provides guaranteed delivery of segment packets?

   a. physical

   b. logical

   c. data link

   d. transport

3. The data link layer is responsible for which of the following?

   a. segmentation

   b. encryption

   c. media access control

   d. ASCII conversion

4. Starting with Layer 1, write each layer of the OSI model:

   Layer 1: _____

   Layer 2: _____

   Layer 3: _____

   Layer 4: _____

   Layer 5: _____

   Layer 6: _____

   Layer 7: _____

5. Which of the following unbounded media would be well suited for use in a classroom?

   a. fiber optic

   b. coaxial

   c. twisted pair

   d. infrared

6. Which of the following is the most common form of bounded medium?

   a. fiber-optic cable

   b. unshielded twisted-pair (UTP) cable

   c. infrared

   d. satellite

7. Which of the following network cables is similar to the wire used to connect your telephone to the phone system?

   a. UTP

   b. STP

   c. fiber

   d. infrared

8. Which of the following devices operates on the physical layer of the OSI model?

   a. repeater

   b. router

   c. switch

   d. bridge

9. Which of the following devices operates on the network layer of the OSI model?

   a. repeater

   b. router

   c. bridge

   d. hub

10. All computers are attached to the same cable segment in which of the following networks?

    a. linear bus

    b. star

    c. ring

    d. WAN

11. An MSAU is used on which of the following network systems?

    a. star

    b. WAN

    c. token ring

    d. Ethernet

12. True or False: Under the CSMA/CD access method, only one node is given permission to transmit a message on the network at any given time.

13. True or False: The token passing access method performs best under heavy loads.

14. Which of the following devices reduces the amount of collisions on a network? (Select all that apply.)

    a. repeater

    b. hub

    c. bridge

    d. switch

15. Which of the following devices reduces the amount of broadcast traffic on a network?

    a. router

    b. hub

    c. bridge

    d. switch

16. What does the "T" in 10BaseT stand for?

    a. thousand

    b. twisted

    c. Telnet

    d. ten

17. Which of the following operates at the physical layer of the OSI model and relays messages from one segment to another? (Select all that apply.)

    a. hub

    b. router

    c. switch

    d. repeater

18. Which of the following operates at the network layer of the OSI model and can be used to connect networks of different topologies?

    a. router

    b. repeater

    c. bridge

    d. switch

19. How long is a MAC address?

    a. 4 bytes long

    b. 6 bits long

    c. 48 bits long

    d. very long

20. True or False: DHCP resolves host names to IP addresses.

21. Write the command you would enter at a workstation to view the full details of your IP configuration.

22. If a DHCP client is not able to access a DHCP server and it needs to issue itself an IP number, the IP address would be in the range of which of the following?

    a. 10.0.0.1 to 10.255.255.255

    b. 192.168.0.1 to 192.168.255.254

    c. 169.254.0.1 to 169.254.255.254

    d. 172.31.0.1 to 172.63.255.255

23. Which of the following is a proprietary protocol used in NetWare networks?

    a. IPX/SPX

    b. TCP/IP

    c. AppleTalk

    d. ARCNet

24. Which of the following is the default protocol that provides NetWare network services in NetWare 6?

    a. IPX/SPX

    b. TCP/IP

    c. AppleTalk

    d. ARCNet

25. TCP operates at which layer of the OSI model? (Select all that apply.)

    a. network

    b. transport

    c. fourth

    d. sixth

# HANDS-ON PROJECTS

This chapter has focused on the services provided in the OSI model and discussed the hardware and software components of a network. In these projects, you use some of the commands you learned to view and test your workstation's configuration and document the hardware components and topology used in your classroom. Each of the following projects asks you to write a memo to your instructor discussing the results of each exercise. Depending on which projects you complete, you might be able to combine these memos into one. Your instructor will tell you exactly how to report the results of your work.

## Project 3-1: Determine Classroom's Topology

Now that you are familiar with various network devices, determine what topology and devices are being used in your classroom:

◻ Is there a hub (repeater)?

◻ Is there a switch?

◻ Is there a router?

◻ How many workstations are there?

◻ What type of cabling is used?

Next, document the IP configuration of your classroom network:

1. Record the IP address assigned to your classroom server.

2. Identify which of the following TCP/IP application services are running on your network:

   ◻ DHCP

   ◻ DNS

   ◻ Web Server

   ◻ NAT

3. Record the IP address of your classroom DNS server, if available.

4. Record the IP address range assigned to the student workstations.

5. Record an IP address, a subnet mask, and a default gateway that can be manually assigned to your computer.

6. If you have an Internet connection, record the Internet IP address assigned to your network. Identify whether the Internet address is registered to your network or assigned temporarily.

7. Write a memo to your instructor discussing the topology your classroom is using. Include all hardware devices, servers, workstations, and the cabling system.

## Project 3-2: Obtaining an IP Address

Manually configuring IP addresses can be tedious and error prone. To configure your workstation to obtain an IP address from a DHCP server, perform the following steps:

1. Right-click **My Network Places**, and then click **Properties** to open the Network and Dial-up Connections dialog box.

2. Right-click the **Local Area Connection** icon, and then click **Properties** to open the Local Area Connection Properties dialog box.

3. Scroll down, if necessary, and click **Internet Protocol (TCP/IP)**, and then click **Properties** to open the Internet Protocol (TCP/IP) Properties dialog box shown in Figure 3-23.

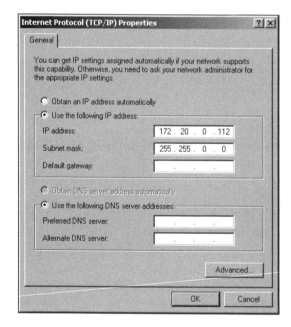

**Figure 3-23**    The Internet Protocol (TCP/IP) Properties dialog box

4. Click the **Obtain an IP address automatically** radio button, and then click **OK** to save the settings and return to the Local Area Connection Properties dialog box.

3

5. Click **OK** again to save your changes and then close the Network and Dial-up Connection dialog box. The system then obtains an IP address from the DHCP server or assigns itself an unused host address in the 169.254.0.0 network address range if no DHCP server is available.

6. Write a memo to your instructor discussing IP address configuration and the advantages of using DHCP for automatic IP address configuration. In your discussion, include information about automatic IP address assignment.

## CASE PROJECTS

### Case 3-1: The J.Q. Adams Network System

As described in Chapter 1, the J.Q. Adams Corporation would like to update its network system to collect quality-control information from the shop floor and save it on the central NetWare server for processing by other computer users. J.Q. Adams currently has 12 computer workstations in the business office, two data collection workstations in production, and two data collection workstations in shipping/receiving. Two NetWare servers (one already owned by the company and one being purchased) are located in the wire and phone equipment room. The computers in the production shop face the problem of increased electrical interference from motors and other equipment. J.Q. Adams needs your help in recommending a topology and network system that will meet its requirements. Draw the necessary cable runs on the floor plan shown in Figure 3-24.

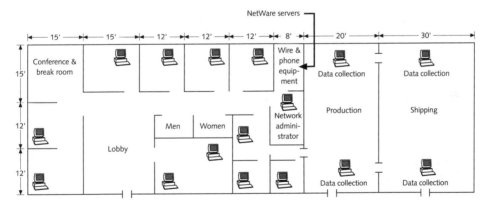

**Figure 3-24**   The J.Q. Adams Corporation network

Select the topology and network system. Draw a proposed network cable system based on the building layout shown in Figure 3-24. Write a memo to your instructor recommending a topology and network system and discussing your justification for this selection. Attach your proposed network cable system.

## Case 3-2: The Jefferson County Courthouse Network

As described in Chapter 1, the social workers in the Jefferson County Courthouse are planning a network system to let 12 users communicate and share files and printers. Plans are also being developed to add users in other departments to the network to meet the communication needs of the entire courthouse. For this reason, the NetWare 6 NOS has been chosen, and a new NetWare server has been ordered.

The floor plan for the first floor of the courthouse is shown in Figure 3-25. Given this floor plan, recommend a topology and network system that will best meet the current needs of the social workers and allow easy network expansion in the future.

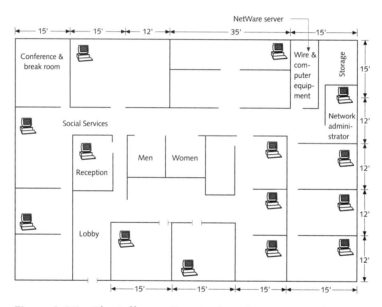

**Figure 3-25** The Jefferson County Courthouse network

Select the topology and network system. Draw a proposed network cable system based on the building layout shown in Figure 3-25. Write a memo to your instructor recommending a topology and network system and discussing your justification for this selection. Attach your proposed network cable system.

# 4

# PLANNING THE eDIRECTORY DIRECTORY TREE

## After reading this chapter and completing the exercises, you will be able to:

♦ Describe the components of the X.500 Directory Information Model and identify commonly used directory services, including eDirectory, Active Directory, and Netscape

♦ Describe the components of Novell's eDirectory system

♦ Explain the use of each object in an eDirectory tree

♦ Design an eDirectory tree

♦ Use NetWare Administrator to create objects in an eDirectory tree

♦ Plan the partitioning of an eDirectory tree

In previous chapters, you studied what a Certified Novell Administrator (CNA) needs to know about a LAN's hardware and software components. Although knowledge of general computer networking and hardware concepts is essential, as a CNA, you'll be concerned with administering NetWare network operating systems, so you need to go beyond the general concepts in previous chapters to a specific knowledge of NetWare 6. As described in Chapter 1, a fundamental component of the NetWare 6 operating system is the eDirectory service. In this chapter, you start learning about directory services in general and NetWare 6 eDirectory in detail.

## INTRODUCTION TO DIRECTORY SERVICES

In Chapter 1, you learned that a directory service provides a central means of storing, managing, and accessing information about network objects. Just as printed directories with alphabetical or categorical lists of information are important tools in library and telephone services, electronic directories supply information to network services and clients.

The purpose of electronic directories is not much different from that of printed directories—that is to provide names, locations, and other information about people and organizations. In a LAN or WAN, this directory information can be used for e-mail addressing, user authentication (such as logins and passwords), or network security (user access rights). A directory also contains information on a network's physical devices (PCs, servers, printers, routers, and communication servers, for example) and the services available on a specific device (such as operating systems, applications, shared file systems, and print queues). This information is accessible to computer applications and readable for end users.

Directory services can also play an important role in integrating different network operating systems into one system that can be centrally administered and accessed. Having resources from many different operating systems, such as Windows, NetWare, and Unix, work together as one network makes it convenient for users to access information any time, from any computer, without needing to know how to interact with a different system environment. Novell defines a directory as a combination of a database and services that provide the following network capabilities:

- Integrate diverse systems to provide centralized organization and management

- Give users access to data and resources they need to perform their jobs

- Help provide connectivity between users, both within the organization and across the Internet

- Coordinate organization and network information and resources

 Although Novell uses "Directory" (uppercase) to refer to the directory service technology and "directory" (lowercase) to refer to the folder structure when discussing file storage, in this book "directory service" refers to the technology, and "directory database" refers to the database of network objects.

The **directory database** is made up of **entries** that store information about network objects in containers organized into a hierarchical tree structure. **Directory services** provide the discovery, security, storage, and relationship-management functions that make the information in the database valuable. Several directory services are available from different vendors. A common element of these services is their roots in the X.500 directory standard originally developed in 1988 by the International Organization for Standardization (ISO) and International Telecommunication Union (ITU) committees.

As a CNA, you'll be required to know the basics of the X.500 standard and identify examples of the following common directory services:

- Novell eDirectory

- Microsoft Active Directory

- Netscape Directory Server 4

In the following sections, you learn the basics of the X.500 standard and review examples of using Active Directory and Netscape Directory Server.

# X.500 Directory Standard

Early network directories were usually developed for a particular application. In these proprietary directories, system developers had little or no incentive to work with any other system. In an effort to increase productivity, system users and administrators sought ways to share access and maintenance of directory databases with multiple applications and operating system environments. From this search came the concept of the directory as a collection of open systems that cooperate to hold a logical database of information. In this new view, users of the directory, including people and computer programs, would be able to read or modify the information or parts of it, as long as they had the authorization to do so. This idea grew into the definition of X.500.

The ITU and ISO originally developed the Open Systems Interconnect (OSI) model described in Chapter 3 to standardize the functional layers that make network communications work between different operating systems and hardware environments. In the client-server environment of the OSI model's application layer, directory functionality (administration, authentication, and access control) was initially developed to handle management of e-mail addresses and the OSI Message Handling application (X.400). However, it was recognized as having potential use with many applications, so it was defined as a separate module or standard: ITU-T Recommendation X.500 (also known as ISO/IEC 9594: *Information Technology—Open Systems Interconnection—The Directory*).

Using the OSI model as a foundation, the ITU later created specifications for a series of recommendations known as **X.500** that define directory services. The first X.500 specification—the Directory Information Model, released in 1988—was a basic model showing how directory service information should be displayed to the user. With the release of the 1993 X.500 specification, the ITU provided some additional models to describe directory services, as shown in Table 4-1.

The X.500 directory model describes a directory as a collection of systems that work in a client-server relationship to represent information about network objects in the real world. In the X.500 directory architecture, the client queries and receives responses from one or more servers in the server's directory service, with the Directory Access Protocol (DAP) controlling communication between the client and the server.

**Table 4-1**  Directory Service Models

| Model | Description |
| --- | --- |
| User Information Model | Describes how data from the directory should be displayed and accessed by the user |
| Directory Functional Model | Describes the overall operation of the directory service components |
| Operational and Administrative Information Model | Describes directory service administration functions |
| DSA Information Model | Explains how Directory System Agents (DSAs) work together to provide directory access |
| Directory Distribution Model | Describes how the DSAs distribute information between themselves |
| Directory Administrative Authority Model | Describes how the directory is administered |
| Security Model | Describes authentication and access control |

The X.500 directory model contains many components, but the following are the most vital to the operation of a basic directory:

- Directory Information Base (DIB)
- Directory Information Tree (DIT)
- Directory User Agent (DUA)
- Directory System Agent (DSA)
- Directory Access Protocol (DAP)
- Directory Service Protocol (DSP)
- Directory Information Shadowing Protocol (DISP)

Figure 4-1 illustrates the interrelationship between these directory components. In the following sections, you learn how these basic components work together to create a complete directory service.

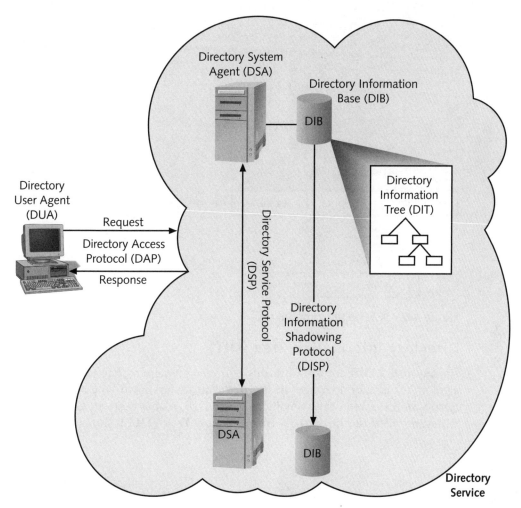

**Figure 4-1** X.500 directory service components

## Directory Information Base (DIB)

As described earlier, the directory database is made up of entries that contain information about objects in the real world, such as users, printers, computers, and data volumes. These objects are collectively known as the **Directory Information Base (DIB)**. Within the DIB, each entry is made up of a collection of information fields called attributes. As shown in Figure 4-2, an entry is made up of several attributes, each with one or more values that define information about the network object.

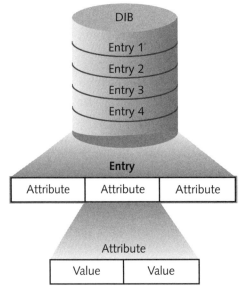

**Figure 4-2**   X.500 DIB components

## Directory Information Tree (DIT)

Entries in the DIB are stored in one or more containers that act like folders in the file system. Just as subfolders are arranged within folders in the file system, the hierarchical relationship between the containers in the DIB enable them to be arranged into a tree structure called the **Directory Information Tree (DIT)**, shown in Figure 4-3.

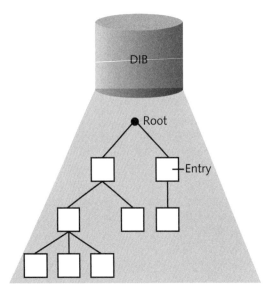

**Figure 4-3**   Structure of the X.500 DIT

To keep the directory organized, a set of rules known as the **Directory Schema** is enforced to ensure that information in the DIB is not damaged or lost as modifications are made. The Directory Schema defines a set of attributes and valid object classes. An object class defines a type of network object, such as a user or printer, and includes all attributes that make up that type of object. The Directory Schema prevents entries from having incorrect attribute types and forces all entries to be members of a defined object class.

## Directory User and Service Agents

The X.500 specification takes a client-server approach in communicating information to the directory. The directory client, called the **Directory User Agent (DUA)**, provides the standardized functionality that supports searching or browsing through directory databases and retrieving directory information. The DUA's functionality can be implemented in all types of user interfaces through dedicated DUA clients, Web server gateways, or e-mail applications. DUAs are currently available for almost all types of workstations (DOS, Windows, Macintosh, OS/2, and Unix, for example).

Processing a DUA request for information from the directory service consists of four steps, as illustrated in Figure 4-4. In the first step, the DUA, usually running on a user workstation, acts as the client to send the user's request to the **Directory System Agent (DSA)** running on a server. Next, the DSA uses a collection of services and protocols that manage specific portions of the DIB to search and find the requested information. Third, the information is retrieved from the DIB and sent back to the DSA. The last step is sending the retrieved information from the DSA back to the DUA, where it's presented to the user.

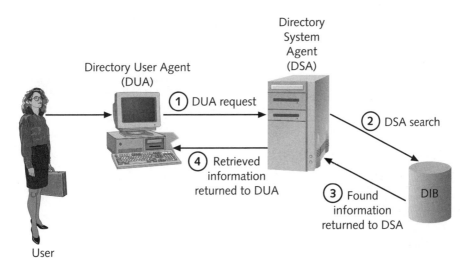

**Figure 4-4**   Directory agents

## Directory Service Protocols

Directory service protocols handle formatting and communicating requests and responses between DUAs and DSAs. The Directory Service Protocol (DSP) controls the interaction between two or more DSAs so that users can access information in the directory without knowing the exact location of a specific piece of information. The Directory Access Protocol (DAP) controls communication between a DUA and a DSA. As shown in Figure 4-5, the DAP handles formatting and transmitting data between the DUA and the DSA.

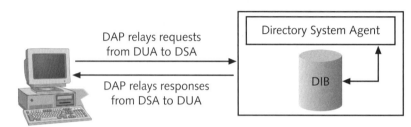

**Figure 4-5** The Directory Access Protocol

If a DSA cannot fulfill a DUA's request, it passes the request to another DSA. The DSP controls communication between DSAs, as illustrated in Figure 4-6.

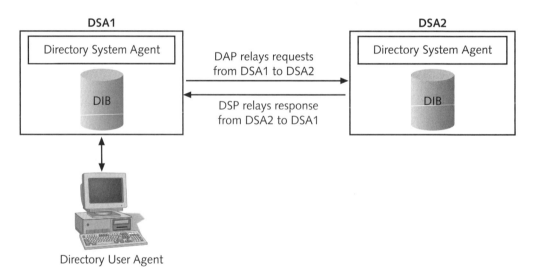

**Figure 4-6** The Directory Service Protocol

In X.500 terminology, the process of distributing and synchronizing the DIB among multiple locations is called **shadowing**. The Directory Information Shadowing Protocol (DISP) is a special DSP that's responsible for keeping multiple copies of the DIB synchronized, as shown in Figure 4-7.

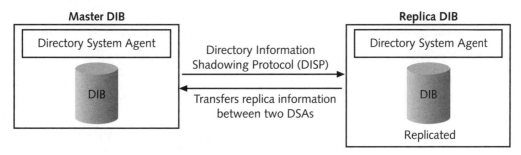

**Figure 4-7** The Directory Information Shadowing Protocol

## LDAP Directory Standard

Approved in 1988, the X.500 directory standard has matured under the ITU's aegis and was enhanced in the 1993 edition, currently in use. Although the coverage was comprehensive, users have criticized it as being too complex and, therefore, too difficult to implement. Until recently, few "pure" X.500 implementations were in operation.

The University of Michigan addressed the issue of the X.500 DAP being too complex for most directory implementations by developing a simpler TCP/IP-based version of X.500 DAP for use on the Internet: **Lightweight Directory Access Protocol (LDAP)**. LDAP specifies a common set of directory operations and commands that can be implemented on multiple vendor platforms. Novell, Microsoft, and Netscape currently support LDAP functions in their directory services. Using LDAP, a user can log in to a Novell network and access resources on NetWare *and* Windows servers. For example, a workstation can use an LDAP client running on a Netscape browser to submit a login request to an LDAP service running on a NetWare 6 server. After being logged in, the user's workstation can send additional LDAP requests to access data from the NetWare server that the user has rights to view. To print the data on a printer attached to a Windows server, the LDAP client running on the user's workstation sends a login request to the Windows LDAP service, and after being authenticated, uses the Windows-based network printer. Because of this flexibility, most major suppliers of e-mail and directory services software have expressed interest in LDAP, which is fast becoming a de facto directory protocol for the Internet.

Although LDAP started as a simplified component of the X.500 directory, it's being developed into a complete directory service. Using Internet naming services, developers are building layers of security and adding capabilities of X.500 directory components. Some analysts fear that when the missing functionality is added (such as security control, data replication between multiple sites, and characters sets more complex than plain ASCII), LDAP will be as complex as the X.500 suite is said to be.

LDAP also provides a standard naming convention that separates object types by commas. An LDAP-compatible DUA uses standardized rules and naming conventions when formatting a request independent of the NOS and then sends the request to an LDAP-compatible DSA running on a server computer. The DSA processes the LDAP request based on the standard set of services and returns the result to the DUA. In this way, any vendor's directory can be made LDAP compatible by including the ability to process LDAP requests based on that directory service's structure. Netscape Directory Server, Microsoft Active Directory, and eDirectory are all compliant to varying degrees with LDAP standards, making it possible to transfer and share information between directory services. The Lightweight Directory Interchange Format (LDIF) file is another important protocol based on the LDAP model. Both Novell and Microsoft use LDIF files for importing objects from text files into the directory database. In Chapter 9, you'll learn how to use an LDIF file to import new user accounts into eDirectory.

Installing a directory service has become an essential part of setting up a network system. Some directory services, such as Netscape Directory Server and Novell eDirectory, can run on multiple types of operating systems, making it possible to integrate varying platforms into one directory system. Other vendors' directory services, such as Microsoft Active Directory, are specialized to use features of only that vendor's operating system and cannot be installed on different platforms. However, other client environments, such as Linux and Macintosh, can access and manage Microsoft Active Directory information because it offers LDAP compatibility. In the following section, you learn how to plan for installing and implementing eDirectory on a NetWare server.

## NOVELL EDIRECTORY SERVICES

For a network administrator, the heart of NetWare 6 is **eDirectory**, previously called Novell Directory Services (NDS). eDirectory gives the network administrator the capabilities and tools to manage network resources, such as NetWare servers, users, and printers, from an organizational perspective. eDirectory is an LDAP-compatible directory service and database that maintains information about all network resources. The database is properly referred to as the "Novell eDirectory database," but it is often shortened to directory database or just eDirectory. All three terms refer to the same part of the eDirectory service.

 NDS's original name was NetWare Directory Services. Novell changed the name to Novell Directory Services in early 1996 to reflect the growing use of NDS on NOSs other than NetWare. You will still find references to NetWare Directory Services in many publications, including older Novell documentation.

### Earlier NetWare Versions

NetWare versions before NetWare 4 also had a database, called the **bindery**. Because it contained data about resources on only one server, it was described as server-centric. Each NetWare 3.x server had its own bindery, and a network administrator could work with only one bindery at a time. eDirectory is network-centric, so it provides a central location for storing data about network resources. A network-centric system makes it easier for users to use the network and for network administrators to manage the network. For example, if you have three servers in your network, you can manage all three by using eDirectory, as shown in Figure 4-8.

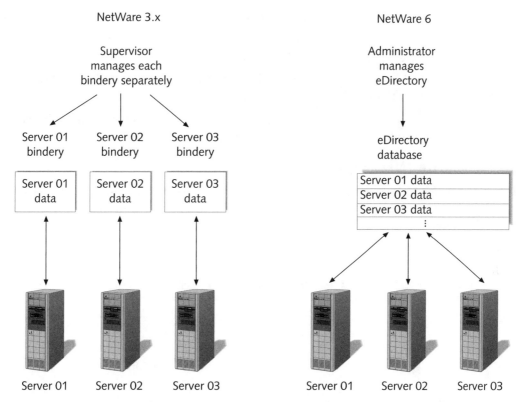

**Figure 4-8**    Managing the NetWare 3 bindery versus eDirectory

When you upgrade a NetWare 3.x server to NetWare 6, most bindery data is automatically added to the directory database. This saves you from having to re-create all the data about your users and groups and makes upgrading a NetWare server more straightforward.

## eDirectory Architecture

Novell's new eDirectory service, based on X.500 standards, offers several additional features over the previous Novell Directory Services (NDS) system, including:

- ConsoleOne management of objects, partitions, replicas, and directory schema
- Client libraries and LDAP tools for Linux, Solaris, and Tru64 Unix
- An import/conversion export (ICE) engine to import or export LDIF files and perform server-to-server migration

- A merge utility for combining eDirectory trees

- The iMonitor utility to monitor and diagnose servers in the tree from a Web browser

- The Index Manager utility to create and manage eDirectory database indexes

- The Filtered Replica Wizard for creating filtered replicas to reduce synchronization traffic between servers

- The ability to run on multiple platforms, including NetWare, Windows NT, Windows 2000/XP, Linux, Solaris, and Tru64 Unix

Understanding how eDirectory works and how it's different from earlier NDS implementations is important to effectively managing and troubleshooting the eDirectory service.

## Earlier NDS Operation

Earlier NDS versions that shipped with NetWare 4 and 5 use the RECMAN database, which consists of data and stream files located in a hidden directory on the SYS volume, as shown in Figure 4-9.

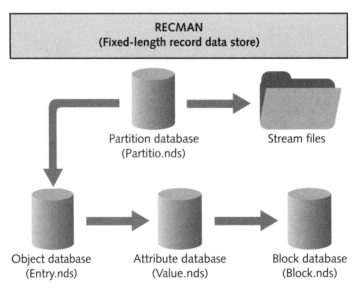

**Figure 4-9**  The RECMAN database

The RECMAN database files use fixed-length record data-storage methods and are used for the following purposes:

- The Partitio.nds file contains a list of the database partitions, which includes the schema and any external references.

- The Entry.nds file contains records for the properties of each object.

- The Value.nds file contains the property values for each object.

- The Block.nds file is used to hold overflow value data from the Value.nds file.

NDS uses Novell's Transaction Tracking System (TTS) to ensure that database transactions, such as creating new objects or changing objects' property values, are completely posted to each file in the RECMAN database. If a system problem prevents all files from being correctly updated, TTS backs out the incomplete transaction from all affected files. The transaction can be reapplied later.

**4**

The database files are the main difference between the NDS versions that shipped with NetWare 4 and 5. Table 4-2 lists the database filenames for both NDS versions.

**Table 4-2** NDS Filenames in NetWare 4 and 5

| NetWare 4 NDS Filenames | NetWare 5 NDS Filenames |
|---|---|
| Entry.nds | 0.dsd |
| Value.nds | 1.dsd |
| Block.nds | 2.dsd |
| Partitio.nds | 3.dsd |

## eDirectory Operation

Instead of the fixed-length record files used in previous versions of NDS, eDirectory uses **FLexible and Adaptive Information Manager (FLAIM)**, a highly scalable indexed database developed to store information for the GroupWise 5 e-mail system. As illustrated in Figure 4-10, the structure and purpose of files in the FLAIM database are different from the NDS database system.

- The NDS.db file acts as the control file for the database and contains the rollback log used to abort incomplete transactions.

- The 00000001.log file in the SYS\NetWare\NDS.rfl directory tracks completed transactions and the current transaction. By default, the 00000001.log file is installed in No Keep mode, which means transactions are eventually overwritten and no additional log files are created. The log file can be changed to Keep mode if additional backup is required. In Keep mode, additional log files named 0000002.log, 00000003.log, and so on are created when specified log file conditions, such as maximum size, are met.

- The NDS.xx files contain all records and indexes stored on the server. When an NDS.xx file reaches the maximum of 2 GB, additional files named NDS.02, NDS.03, and so on are created for the remaining data. Limiting NDS files to 2 GB allows scalability yet still offers high performance. The following indexes are maintained in NDS.xx files to enhance performance:

  - Attribute substring indexes for the CN and uniqueID fields

  - Attribute indexes for the Object Class field

  - Attribute indexes that include strings beginning with CN, uniqueID, Given Name, and Surname

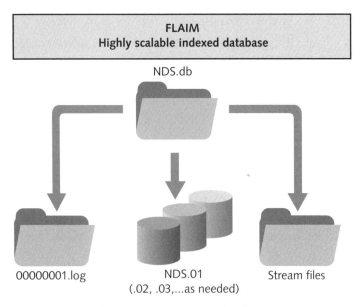

**Figure 4-10**   The eDirectory FLAIM database

- The Stream files have an .nds extension and are named with hexadecimal characters (0-9, A-F). Stream files hold information such as print job configurations and login scripts.

Instead of the TTS system used to back out incomplete transactions in the NDS system, the FLAIM database system uses log files to back out and roll forward transactions in the event of a system failure. Completed transactions, called **committed transactions**, are placed in the log file. Non-committed, or incomplete, transactions may or may not be placed in the log file. In a system failure, eDirectory can roll forward to reapply the committed transactions in the log file that might not have been fully written to the disk. Earlier versions of NetWare can be updated to use eDirectory 8.6 to take advantage of its higher performance and scalability. These enhancements, along with eDirectory's ability to run on multiple operating systems, make it the most versatile and scalable directory service available today. In Chapter 6, you'll learn how to install eDirectory on a new NetWare 6 server and upgrade NetWare servers running earlier versions of NDS to the new eDirectory system.

The directory database is divided into sections called partitions. Partitions are distributed among the servers in the network so that if you lose a single server, you don't lose the entire directory database. The partitions are replicated, which means that a copy of one partition, called a replica, is stored on one or more additional servers. This creates backup copies of the partitions so that the network data is safe, even if the server containing the original copy of the partition stops working. These concepts are discussed in more detail in "eDirectory as a Replicated, Distributed Database," later in this chapter.

Even though replicas are stored on other servers, you still need to make tape backup copies of your server's hard drives. The other files (programs and data) on the server are *not* replicated and must be backed up. (The tape backup copies, of course, also contain the eDirectory partition data.)

 Do not confuse eDirectory replicas with what Novell calls Novell Replication Services, which also uses the terms "replication" and "replicas" to refer to data replication from one storage device to another.

**4**

## Benefits of eDirectory

eDirectory offers several benefits beyond those of earlier domain services or the bindery services in NetWare 3.x:

- *Login*—Using eDirectory, the user logs in to the directory service and is then given access to whatever resources he or she has rights to. If those resources are files on three different file servers, the user will have access to the servers where those resources are located, as Figure 4-11 shows.

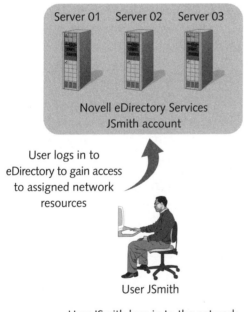

**Figure 4-11**   Logging in to the eDirectory database

- *Administration*—With eDirectory, you can work with all your network resources at the same time, using a variety of administration tools, including the iManager utility for administering eDirectory from a Web browser.

- *Security*—eDirectory uses the RSA encryption algorithm, which enables a secure, encrypted single login to the network.

- *Reliability*—Because the directory database is distributed and replicated, eDirectory provides fault tolerance for the network. For example, because information about users will be stored on at least two servers, a single server failing doesn't prevent users from logging in to the network and accessing the resources they have rights to.

- *Scalability*—**Scalability** gives you the capability to work with systems of different sizes. eDirectory works equally well in small networks with only one server or global networks with hundreds of servers. If your network expands, eDirectory can easily handle the expansion. No matter how large or small the network, eDirectory can still be administered from one location.

## eDirectory and the Network File System

As a network administrator, you must understand that eDirectory is *not* a network file system. A **network file system** is used to organize file storage on the network. When you plan a network file system, you plan the set of volumes, directories, and subdirectories to be created on the servers' hard drives for storing system, application, and data files. (In Chapter 5, you'll learn more about network file systems.) When working with eDirectory, however, you create a logical design for administering network resources.

## eDIRECTORY COMPONENTS

The visual and logical design created to organize data in the directory database is called the **eDirectory tree** (or just "directory tree"). In computer terminology, the word *tree* refers to a **hierarchical structure** for organizing data or information. A tree starts at a single point, called the **[Root]**, and branches out from there. The tree usually is drawn inverted, meaning that unlike a real tree, the [Root] is at the *top* of the diagram. A familiar example of a tree structure is a family tree, shown in Figure 4-12.

The root of the tree is usually shown in square brackets—[Root]—to match its onscreen appearance in NetWare Administrator.

In the Burns family tree, the [Root] of the tree is the marriage of Franklin Burns and Dorothy Stevenson. Branches of the tree lead to their children, Michael and Susan. Additional branches lead to the children of Michael and his wife, Mary Richards, and to the children of Susan and her husband, William Taylor. Because the [Root] of the tree is at the top of the diagram, this is an inverted tree.

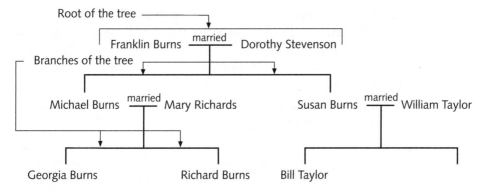

**Figure 4-12**    Burns family tree

## eDirectory Directory Trees

The same inverted tree structure is seen in the directory tree of F.D. Roosevelt Investments, Inc., as shown in Figure 4-13.

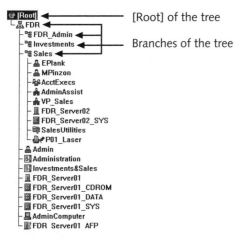

**Figure 4-13**    The directory tree of F.D. Roosevelt Investments, Inc.

The directory tree starts at the [Root] at the top of the diagram and branches down. The directory tree's hierarchical structure makes it easy for a network administrator to create a graphic representation of the organization and the location of network resources. For example, in Figure 4-13, the directory tree begins at the [Root], and then branches to an object named FDR, which represents the F.D. Roosevelt Investments organization. From FDR, the tree branches to the three organizational subdivisions of FDR: FDR_Admin (Administration), Investments, and Sales. Other branches from FDR lead to network resources: the user named Admin (the NetWare administrator), a NetWare server (FDR_Server01), and three volumes on the server (FDR_Server01_CDROM, FDR_Server01_DATA, and FDR_Server01_SYS). Branches from Sales lead to additional network resources.

The directory tree links eDirectory objects into an organized and understandable structure; the term **object** (also called an "entry") is a general term, referring to any network resource in your network. An object is *not* the network resource itself; it is an eDirectory representation of the resource used to store data about the resource in the directory database. Objects can be associated with **logical entities** or **physical entities**:

- *Physical entities*—Things that have a physical existence, such as users, NetWare servers, and printers.

- *Logical entities*—Things that exist as a logical or mental creation, such as print queues, rather than a true physical entity. An important type of logical entity is the **organizational entity**, which represents a structural part of an organization, such as a group, an Organizational Unit, or the organization itself.

The term "object" comes from object-oriented programming languages, such as Smalltalk and C++. Many of the concepts developed for object-oriented programming languages have been carried into database-management system development. The object-oriented database has evolved based on these concepts. Other software, such as Microsoft Active Directory, also uses the concept of objects, and you can expect to encounter objects in an increasing number of programs.

Objects are represented in the directory tree by icons, symbols that help you recognize what an object represents. In Figure 4-13, object icons represent the organization itself (FDR), subdivisions of the organization (FDR_Admin, Investments, and Sales), users (Admin, EPlank, and MPinzon), a group of users (AcctExecs), positions in the organization (VP_Sales and AdminAssist), a NetWare server used by FDR (FDR_Server01), and three volumes on the NetWare server (FDR_Server01_CDROM, FDR_Server01_DATA, and FDR_Server01_SYS).

The directory tree is a graphic representation of the data in the directory database. Data in the directory database *must* be associated with an object in the directory tree. In fact, you enter data into the directory database by creating directory tree objects and assigning the data to those objects. The directory tree must be given a name, called the directory tree name, when you first create the tree. When you log in to eDirectory, you do so by logging in to the directory tree by name.

## eDirectory Objects, Properties, and Property Values

An eDirectory object always represents some definable network element, either physical or logical, for which you can record data. For example, for a user, you can record the login name, last name, first name, and so on. For a printer, you can record the printer name and the printer agent that sends it print jobs. For a group, you can record the names of the group members.

The types of data collected in objects are called **properties** (also called "attributes"). The data itself is called the **property value**. For example, FDR's vice president of sales is Edgar

Plank. Because Edgar is a network user, the FDR directory tree has a User object named EPlank (which is Edgar's login name). One property of a User object is the user's Login Name, and for Edgar the property value for Login Name is EPlank. As shown in Table 4-3, the directory database stores the properties and property values for each object in the directory tree.

**Table 4-3**   Objects, Properties, and Property Values

| Object: Property | User Property Value |
|---|---|
| Login Name | EPlank |
| Last Name | Plank |
| Full Name | Edgar Plank |
| **Object: Property** | **User Property Value** |
| Login Name | MPinzon |
| Last Name | Pinzon |
| Full Name | Maria Pinzon |
| **Object: Property** | **User Property Value** |
| Server Name | FDR_Server01 |
| Network Address | 080009 3D45F8 |
| **Object: Property** | **User Property Value** |
| Printer Name | P01_Laser |
| Network Address | 080009 12CF89 |

There are two general categories of eDirectory objects: container objects and leaf objects. **Container objects**, as the name implies, contain or hold other objects. **Leaf objects** cannot contain any other objects—they are the "leaves" at the ends of the "tree branches." Figure 4-14 shows the FDR directory tree with container and leaf objects marked.

Container objects are used primarily to organize network resources (users, groups, NetWare servers, and so forth), which are represented by the leaf objects. For example, in the FDR directory tree, FDR_Admin is a container object that enables the resources of the FDR Administration group to be grouped together for easy management. In Figure 4-14, all employees in Administration (EFranklin and SSamuelson) have their associated User objects located in the FDR_Admin container. The network administrator can easily keep track of all Administration personnel this way, and the same concept applies to other container objects and the leaf objects they contain.

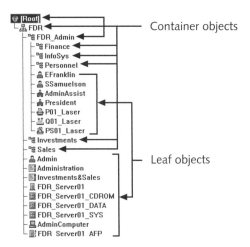

**Figure 4-14**   The FDR directory tree showing container and leaf objects

## Container Objects

As shown in Table 4-4 and Figure 4-15, several types of container objects can be used in a directory tree. Of these container objects, the most common are Tree, Country, Organization, and Organizational Unit.

**Table 4-4**   eDirectory Container Objects

| Object Name | Description | Typeful Abbreviation | Required/ Optional | Can Contain: |
|---|---|---|---|---|
| Tree or [Root] | Represents the beginning or root of the eDirectory tree. Can also be referred to as [Root] in command-line utilities. | [Root] | Required | Country, Organization, Alias (leaf object) |
| Country | This container object can optionally be used to organize an international eDirectory tree using standard country codes. | C | Optional | Organization, Alias (leaf object) |
| Organization | An eDirectory tree must contain at least one Organization container to house network entities. | O | Required | Organizational Unit, leaf objects |
| Organizational Unit | Organizational Unit containers are used to divide entities in an Organization into a departmental structure. | OU | Optional | Organizational Unit, leaf objects |

**Table 4-4**    eDirectory Container Objects (continued)

| Object Name | Description | Typeful Abbreviation | Required/ Optional | Can Contain: |
|---|---|---|---|---|
| Domain Controller | This optional container holds Domain Name System (DNS) entities, such as name servers and zones. | DC | Optional | DNS objects |
| License Container | This special container created during installation holds license objects. | LC | Required | License certificates |
| Role Based Service | This security container is used to store tasks and users and tasksauthorized to perform those tasks. | RBS | Required | Security roles |
| Security | This container holds global security policies that relate to login, authentication, and public key management. | S | Required | Authentication policies and public key objects |

> **Note**
> eDirectory also has an unused container object called Locality, used to specify geographical locations within a country. The Locality object is included in eDirectory for X.500. If implemented, the Locality object would be optional, could be contained in the Tree ([Root]) and Organization objects, and could contain Organization and Organizational Unit objects. It could not contain leaf objects.

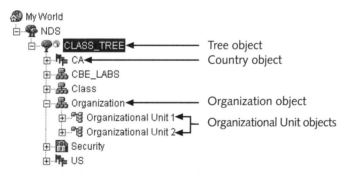

**Figure 4-15**    eDirectory container objects in a directory tree

## Tree or [Root]

The **Tree object** (also referred to as the **[Root] object**) is always the first object in the directory tree, and there is only one Tree object in each directory tree. The Tree object has no properties—its function is to be the highest access point in the directory tree.

When you first create a directory tree during NetWare 6 installation, you assign the directory tree name and create the Tree object. The Tree object is used by all other NetWare 6 servers added to the tree. There *must* be a Tree object in a directory tree, and you cannot modify or delete the Tree object after it's created. For example, the Tree object is the first object in the directory tree shown in Figure 4-15. The Tree object can contain Country objects, Organization objects, and Alias objects. (The Alias object is a leaf object described in "General-Purpose Leaf Objects," later in this chapter.)

 In network file systems, there is another root: the root directory. The root directory is the first directory on a hard disk or NetWare volume. For example, the root directory of the C: drive on a PC is C:\. Although both systems use the term *root*, they refer to two very different things.

## Country

The **Country object** organizes the directory tree for organizations operating in more than one country. The Country object uses a unique industry-standard two-letter code to designate each country. For example, in Figure 4-15, CA designates Canada. The Country object is optional, but if it's used, it must be used immediately after the [Root] object and before an Organization object. The Country object can contain Organization objects and Alias objects.

 Although Novell includes the Country object for X.500 compliance, generally it's not used. If you need to include countries in your directory tree, use the Organization object or Organizational Unit object with a country name instead. This method gives you more flexibility. For example, you could have a Sales Organizational Unit object that branches into two other Organizational Unit objects named United States and Europe.

## Organization

The **Organization object** provides the first level of organizational structure for the directory tree. You must use at least one Organization object in your directory tree. There is usually only one Organization object in the directory tree, representing the company or organization that built the network. For example, in Figure 4-13, there is only one Organization object, FDR. This, of course, represents the company F.D. Roosevelt Investments, the company that built and uses the network. You can, however, have more than one Organization object in your eDirectory tree if the organizational structure requires it. The Organization object can contain Organizational Unit objects and leaf objects.

## Organizational Unit

The **Organizational Unit object** subdivides the organizational structure of the directory tree. You are not required to use any Organizational Unit (OU) objects, as with the Organization object. However, the OU object is useful for creating organizational structure in directory trees, and you will probably use it frequently. For example, in Figure 4-13, the directory tree for F.D. Roosevelt Investments uses three OU objects to subdivide the company into administration (FDR_Admin), investments (Investments), and sales (Sales), for ease of network administration. The OU object can contain other OU objects and leaf objects. In fact, the OU object's ability to contain other OU objects makes it the main "building block" of a directory tree.

### Domain Controller

The **Domain Controller object** is used to further organize objects related to the Domain Name System (DNS), such as DNS servers, zones, and host computers.

### License Container

The **License Container object**, created in the tree during server installation, is used to store server and user connection license certificates. You'll learn more about licensing in Chapter 13.

### Role Based Service

The **Role Based Service object** holds role and task objects needed to grant users specific rights in the directory database. For example, it holds the eDirectory Administration and Printer role objects, which include tasks to create user and group accounts. Network administrators can delegate administrative tasks, such as creating users or managing network printing, to specific users by making the user a member of the appropriate role.

### Security

The **Security object**, created in the tree during server installation, is used to hold objects for providing public and private security certificates needed for public key encryption.

## Leaf Objects

Leaf objects represent network resources and are used to store data about those resources. You can use many types of leaf objects in directory trees. To understand how to use leaf objects, it helps to group them according to their purpose. As Table 4-5 shows, leaf objects can be categorized as user-related, server-related, printer-related, and general-purpose.

**Table 4-5**    Leaf Object Groups

| Leaf Object Group | Purpose |
| --- | --- |
| User-related | Manage network users |
| Server-related | Manage NetWare servers and their associated volumes |
| Printer-related | Manage printers and their associated queues and print servers |
| General-purpose | Manage other types of objects |

Leaf objects must be located in a container object, and they cannot contain any other objects. Before you create a leaf object, select the container object that will hold it by clicking on that container object in the directory tree. When a leaf object is created, it is always assigned to the active or selected container object.

 eDirectory enables software companies to create extra leaf objects that are added into eDirectory when the new software is installed. The leaf objects listed here are the standard NetWare 6 objects, but as a network administrator, you might have to become familiar with others associated with the software products you install.

## User-Related Leaf Objects

**User-related leaf objects** have properties that enable network administrators to manage users on their networks. User-related leaf objects, shown in Table 4-6 and Figure 4-16, include the User object, the Group object, the Organizational Role object, the Profile object, and the Template object.

**Table 4-6**    User-related Leaf Objects

| Object | Purpose |
| --- | --- |
| User | Represents a network user |
| Group | Represents a group of users |
| Organizational Role | Represents a position in an organization |
| Profile | Provides a common login script for a group of users |
| Template | Used to create users with a common set of property values |

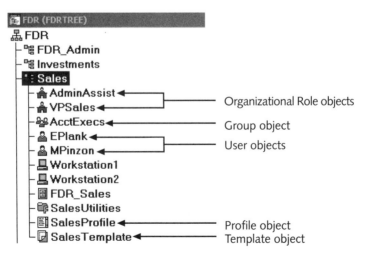

**Figure 4-16**    User-related leaf objects in a directory tree

**User**    The **User object** represents each network user. As a network administrator, you use the User object to record and manage data about each of your users. About 67 properties are associated with the User object. Two of them, Login Name and Last Name, are mandatory and must be specified when you create a user. As you create each user, a User object icon representing that user is added to the directory tree.

To create users, you must be logged in to the network as a user. This requires that at least one user account be automatically created when NetWare 6 is installed. In fact, exactly one account is created, for a user named Admin, and the Admin User object is added to the directory tree. Admin is the network administrator and is assigned the necessary rights to create and manage the directory tree and the network file structure. You will use the Admin user account in later chapters to create objects in the directory tree.

**Group**    The **Group object** is not a container, but a leaf object that represents multiple network users. It is used to record and manage data about each designated group on your network. You must specify the Group Name property when you create a group. No groups are automatically created during NetWare 6 installation.

Groups are useful when you want to assign a network resource to several users. For example, you could create a group for users who need to use a certain printer, and give the group, rather than each individual user, the right to use the printer. Each group member then gets to use the printer because of his or her membership in the group, as Figure 4-17 shows.

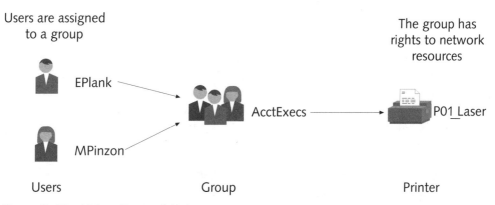

**Figure 4-17**    Using Group objects

**Organizational Role**    The **Organizational Role object** represents a position in an organizational structure, such as president, chief financial officer (CFO), or sales manager. You use the Organizational Role object to record and manage data about each organizational role in your directory tree. When you create the Organizational Role object, you must specify the Organizational Role name. Organizational roles are not created automatically during NetWare 6 installation.

Organizational roles are useful when a position in the organization has certain rights and resources available to it regardless of the person in that position. You can easily assign a user to an organizational role, and that user then automatically gets all the rights of that role. For example, Edgar Plank is the vice president of sales for FDR. Instead of assigning the rights of the vice president of sales to the User object EPlank, the FDR network administrator has created an Organizational Role object named VP_Sales and assigned the rights to that object. The network administrator then assigns the user EPlank to the role of vice president, so EPlank can do whatever the vice president can do. This is illustrated in Figure 4-18. If another user named Martha Truman becomes vice president of FDR, the network administrator can remove EPlank from the role of vice president and assign MTruman to the role. Then she will automatically have the associated rights.

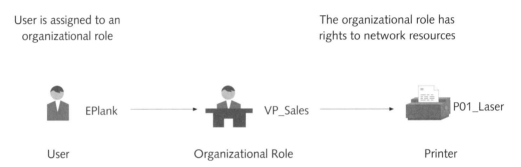

User is assigned to an organizational role

The organizational role has rights to network resources

EPlank — User

VP_Sales — Organizational Role

P01_Laser — Printer

**Figure 4-18**   Using Organizational Role objects

**Profile**   The **Profile object** is used to run login scripts and assign resources to groups of users. Login scripts (explained in more detail in Chapter 12) are a series of NetWare commands that automatically run when the user logs in to the network. Although you can create login scripts for Organization objects, Organizational Unit objects, and User objects, you cannot create a login script for a Group object. The Profile object gives the network administrator a tool for creating login scripts for groups of users. You must specify the Profile Name when you create a profile. Profiles are not automatically created during NetWare 6 installation.

NetWare clients contain a default login script that runs if no other login scripts have been created. The default login script provides access to the basic network resources that a user needs, and it is sufficient for user access during the network's initial development.

Although the Profile object is a useful tool for network administrators, you might confuse the Group object and the Profile object. They are conceptually similar because both are used with "groups" of users. To understand the differences between these two objects, remember that:

- Users are assigned to groups as members of the group, and groups are used primarily to give those members access to network resources.

4

- Profiles are assigned to users (not groups), and profiles are used primarily to give users a login script. Although many users can share a profile, there is no formal "membership" in a profile.

For example, in FDR's directory tree, the Investments & Sales Profile object is the source of the login script for users in the Investments and Sales OUs because they all can use a common login script. However, each OU has a Group object for granting access to department-specific network resources to users in that department: The InvestmentManagers Group object is Investments, and the AcctExecs Group object is Sales. As shown in Figure 4-19, GSakharov and EPlank, therefore, share a common login script through the Profile object but have their access to other network resources controlled by their departmental groups.

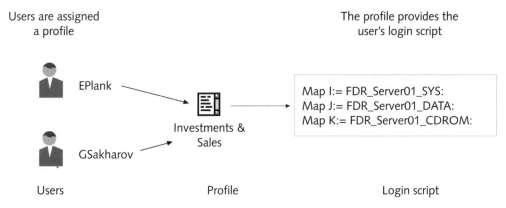

Users are assigned                                                   The profile provides the
   a profile                                                           user's login script

EPlank

Investments &
Sales

GSakharov

Map I:= FDR_Server01_SYS:
Map J:= FDR_Server01_DATA:
Map K:= FDR_Server01_CDROM:

Users                          Profile                          Login script

**Figure 4-19**   Using the Profile object

If Group objects could have login scripts, the same login requirements and resource assignments could have been provided by using just the InvestmentManagers and AcctExecs groups. This would, of course, have required two separate copies of the same login script. But groups cannot have login scripts, so Profile objects are needed.

**Template**   The **Template object** is used to define a common set of values for multiple users. When creating a new user, you can select a template to automatically supply the new user account with a set of property values. For example, users in the Accounting Department can be created with a different template than users in the Marketing Department, giving users in each department a set of values unique to their department.

## Server-Related Leaf Objects

**Server-related leaf objects** have properties that enable you to manage the NetWare servers on your network. Table 4-7 lists the server-related leaf objects (illustrated in Figure 4-20).

**Table 4-7**    Server-related Leaf Objects

| Object | Purpose |
| --- | --- |
| NetWare Server | Represents a network's NetWare server |
| Volume | Represents a hard disk volume on a server |
| License Certificate | Represents a user connection or server license |
| LDAP Group | Stores configuration data applied to a group of LDAP servers |
| LDAP Server | Stores configuration data for an LDAP server |
| AFP Server | Represents an AppleTalk File Protocol server that operates as a node in eDirectory |

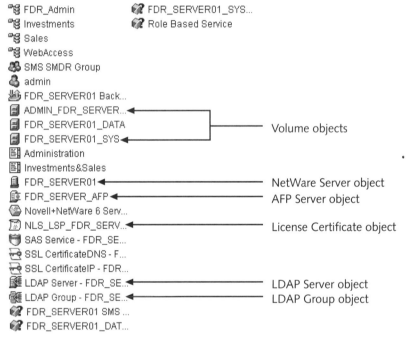

**Figure 4-20**    Server-related leaf objects in a directory tree

**NetWare Server**    The **NetWare Server object** represents each server on the network that's running a version of NetWare. This object is also referred to as an **NCP Server object** (NCP stands for NetWare Core Protocol). You must create and place the NetWare Server object in the directory tree so that the server's volumes, directories, subdirectories, and files are available to users. The NetWare Server object is created for each NetWare 6 server during NetWare installation.

Whenever you create a NetWare Server object, you must specify the NetWare server name. For example, when FDR installs NetWare 6 on the NetWare server named FDR_SERVER01, the server name FDR_SERVER01 is used to create a NetWare

Server object named FDR_SERVER01 (see Figure 4-20). During the installation process, NetWare prompts you for the server's location in the directory tree. In this case, you specify the location of FDR_SERVER01 as the FDR Organization object.

**Volume**   Volumes, which you will study in detail in Chapter 5, are the physical hard disk storage spaces in NetWare servers. The **Volume object** represents a volume in the directory tree. Volumes and their associated Volume objects are created during NetWare 6 installation. When they are created, you must specify a volume name, and this same name is used to create the Volume object name. The name of the Volume object is always the server's name, followed by an underscore, followed by the volume name:

> ServerName_VolumeName

For example, NetWare requires that a volume named SYS (short for "system") be created during installation. Therefore, when FDR installs NetWare 6 on FDR_SERVER01, a Volume object named FDR_SERVER01_SYS is created. The Volume object is placed in the same directory tree location as the server, which in this case is the Organization object FDR. You'll learn about managing file systems in Chapter 8.

**License Certificate**   License certificates are placed in the License Container object when they are initially installed. A NetWare 6 server requires one license certificate for the server, and one or more license certificates for user connections. Each user's **License Certificate object** contains five or more license connections. When users log in, they are assigned an available user connection license from a license certificate. The user account keeps the license until the license is revoked or the user has not logged in for an extended period. This method of license assignment is similar to the "per user" licensing method used with Windows NT and Windows 2000 NOSs, with the exception that the license is kept with the user's account for at least 90 days. When all user licenses have been assigned, no new users can log in to the eDirectory tree. If a user does not log in during the default 90-day period, his or her license is made available for assignment to another user account.

**LDAP Server**   The **LDAP Server object** stores configuration information for an LDAP service running on a NetWare server. During installation, an LDAP Server object named LDAP Server *server_name* (*server_name* is the name of the NetWare 6 server) is created in the same container as the NetWare Server object.

**LDAP Group**   The **LDAP Group object** is used to store configuration information that is common to multiple LDAP servers. The LDAP Group object configures the class and attribute mappings and security policies on the servers assigned to it.

**AFP Server**   The **AFP Server object** is used to represent an AppleTalk File Protocol (AFP) server, a NetWare server that runs special modules so that it can provide file and print services to Macintosh workstations. You can use this object to store data about the AFP server, such as a description and network address. An AFP Server object in a directory tree indicates that Apple Macintosh workstations are attached to the network, and the AFP server acts as a router connecting the Macintosh workstations to the rest of the network. FDR is running AFP modules on the FDR_SERVER01 NetWare server to connect the Macintosh computer named AdminComputer to the network.

## Printer-Related Leaf Objects

**Printer-related leaf objects**, listed in Table 4-8, enable you to manage network printing. NetWare 6 supports both the legacy queue-based printing system in earlier NetWare versions and the latest version of Novell Distributed Print Services (NDPS). When a user wants to print a document or a spreadsheet on a network printer using NDPS, he or she begins by using the application's printing procedure. The application generates the print data, or the material to be printed. The print data is sent to a NetWare printer agent, the software component of NDPS that transfers output from the client and controls the physical printer. Printer agent software can be loaded on a NetWare server or embedded as firmware inside a network-attached printer. The printer agent sends the print data to the printer, and the output is printed. The print job flows as indicated by the arrows in Figure 4-21.

**Table 4-8** Printer-related Leaf Objects

| Object | Purpose |
| --- | --- |
| NDPS Broker | Provides network support services used by NDPS printing |
| NDPS Manager | Provides a platform for printer agents to run on the NetWare server |
| NDPS Printer | Represents a printer object that users can install on their workstations |
| Print Queue | Represents a network print queue used to store print jobs sent from non-NDPS clients |
| Non-NDPS Printer | Represents a network printer that is attached using the queue-based printing system |
| Print Server | Provides configuration information for the print server software that controls the queue-based printing system |

NDPS is backward-compatible with software that requires older Novell print queues and/or print servers, and it will support network printers that run directly attached to the network using print server software. (You can also create Print Server and Print Queue objects if you want to run the older print services in NetWare 6.)

Chapter 11 covers NetWare printing in detail. The examples used in this chapter are intended to help you learn about directory tree objects, not about all the possible details of setting up printing on a NetWare network.

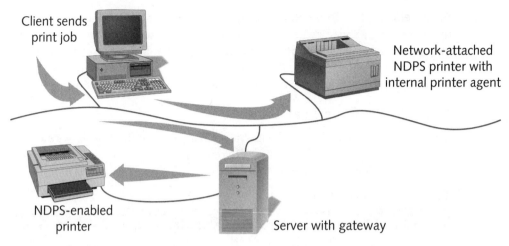

**Figure 4-21**    The NDPS printing system

**NDPS Broker**    Each eDirectory tree should have at least one **NDPS Broker object** to provide the following three network support services: the Service Registry Service, used to find printing services on the network; the Event Notification Service, used to send messages from printer agents to users and operators; and the Resource Management Service, used to download print drivers to workstations.

**NDPS Manager**    The **NDPS Manager object** is used to run printer agent software on the NetWare server. Each brand of printer requires a specific printer agent. For example, Hewlett-Packard (HP) offers a printer agent, as does Lexmark. NetWare also ships with a default printer agent for use with generic printers. You should name the NDPS Manager object after the brand and class of printer it will support, such as HP4_Agent.

**NDPS Printer**    The **NDPS Printer object** is used to represent an actual printer. This object must be created and placed in the directory tree so that you can link a printer to a printer agent. You must name the printer when you create the NDPS Printer object. For example, FDR has a laser printer used by the administration group that is referred to as P01_Laser (the "P" stands for printer, and "01" gives a number to the printer).

**Print Queue Object**    A **Print Queue object** represents a storage area to hold print jobs for client computers that use the queue-based printing system. The print queue object contains configuration information about the print queue, including its location and a list of print queue users and operators. NDPS printer agents can be configured to get print jobs from print queues and print them on the appropriate print device.

**Non-NDPS Printer**    The **Non-NDPS Printer object** is used to represent queue-based printers for backward-compatibility with the earlier queue-based printing system. The non-NDPS printer object stores configuration information about the printer, including its attachment method, port usage, and associated print queue.

**Print Server**   The **Print Server object** is used to store configuration information that the print server software needs to control queue-based printing. In queue-based printing, the print server is responsible for taking print jobs from a print queue and sending them to the printer associated with that print queue. You'll learn how to set up a queue-based printing system and create and configure the Print Server object in Chapter 11.

## General-Purpose Leaf Objects

There are many other types of leaf objects that have different purposes based on the software products you install on the network. The additional leaf objects you should be aware of are shown in Table 4-9.

**Table 4-9**   General-purpose Leaf Objects

| Object | Purpose |
| --- | --- |
| Alias | Refers to another eDirectory object in another part of the directory tree |
| Unknown | Represents a corrupted object that cannot be recognized |
| Application | Represents an application software package that can be run or installed from the server |
| Computer | Represents a user workstation on the network |
| Directory Map | Represents a reference to a directory or subdirectory on a volume |

**Alias**   The **Alias object** refers to another object in a different part of the directory tree. The Alias object is useful when NetWare tracks a user's current location or context in the directory tree. (Context is discussed in "Naming eDirectory Objects," later in this chapter.) Referring to an object not in the same location can be a complex procedure, but using an Alias object in the same location can be helpful. The Alias object contains the location reference to the original object, so the user has to refer only to the Alias object to access the original object. For example, the Investments workgroup at FDR also needs to use the laser printer. The network administrator has created an Alias object named P01_Laser in the Investments OU (see Figure 4-22) to simplify how users in the Investments workgroup specify the location of the laser printer.

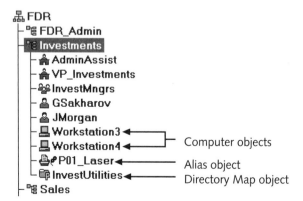

**Figure 4-22**   An Alias object in a directory tree

**Unknown** If an eDirectory object becomes corrupted so that eDirectory can't recognize it, eDirectory renames it and identifies it as an **Unknown object**. As the network administrator, you'll need to re-identify the object, delete the Unknown object, and re-create the correct object for the network resource.

> Unknown objects might occur when using utilities (such as NetWare Administrator or ConsoleOne) to view a NetWare 6 tree without installing the correct snap-ins. Snap-ins contain instructions about certain object types that are needed to process information about the object. Even if an object is valid, utilities cannot recognize it without the correct snap-in. Because Novell has stopped developing snap-ins for NetWare Administrator and ConsoleOne, you must use iManager to manage some new NetWare 6 objects.

eDirectory is extensible, which means that Novell and other vendors can add new objects to it. For example, a software vendor could create objects indicating that the software is installed on the network and provide software management capabilities. As a network administrator, you need to be aware of any new objects that can be used in directory trees.

**Application** The **Application object** represents a software application available on the network. Application objects help simplify administrative tasks, such as assigning rights, customizing login scripts, and automatically installing applications on user workstations. In Chapter 12, you'll learn how to use Novell's Z.E.N.works to work with Application objects.

**Computer** The **Computer object** represents a user workstation on the network and is used with Z.E.N.works to manage and centrally configure workstations.

**Directory Map** The **Directory Map object** is used to reference a single directory in the network file system. This object is a useful management tool for creating and managing login scripts, and you'll learn more about it when you study login scripts in Chapter 12. Figure 4-22 shows an example of a Directory Map object. The network manager for FDR has created the InvestUtilities Directory Map object to refer to the location of utility programs for investment managers in the Investments OU.

# Naming eDirectory Objects

Each eDirectory object has a name that uniquely identifies it within the directory tree. In this section, you learn about object names and the naming conventions used in eDirectory.

## Common Names

eDirectory uses a set of **name types**, which are descriptions of the type of object being named, and each name type has an abbreviation. The Country object (abbreviated as C), the Organization object (abbreviated as O), and the Organizational Unit object (abbreviated as OU) all have equivalent name types. There is no name type for the Tree or [Root] object, and all leaf objects are referred to by the **common name (CN)** name type. Each leaf object has the object name that appears in the directory tree. For example, the common name for the EFranklin User object is EFranklin.

## Context

The position or location of an object in the directory tree is called the object's **context**. Context is specified as the path from the [Root] to the object. For example, consider the context of the User object EFranklin in the FDR directory tree shown in Figure 4-23.

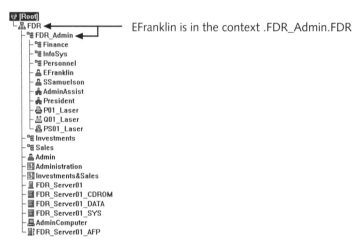

**Figure 4-23**    Context of user object EFranklin

Starting at EFranklin, you can see that she is in the FDR_Admin OU, which is in the FDR Organization, which is directly below the [Root]. Her context is

        .FDR_Admin.FDR

The context of an object reads from left to right, starting at the lowest level of the tree and working upward to the [Root]. Notice that the [Root], however, is not included in the context. The leading period in the context (the period in front of FDR_Admin) indicates that the path begins at the [Root]. Periods are also used to separate object names. A trailing period (the period after an object name) indicates a shift up one level in the directory tree. For example, the FDR_Admin OU object is one level lower in the directory tree than the FDR Organization object; the period after FDR_Admin in the context shows the shift from one level to the next.

Although each object has a fixed context in the directory tree, a user often wants to view different parts of the directory tree while working on the network. The part of the directory tree that the user is actively working with is called the user's **current context**. The context of an object never changes, but a user's current context does as he or she works with different parts of the directory tree. This is why the leading period in a context is important—a context *with* a leading period is read starting at the [Root], regardless of the user's current context. A context *without* the leading period would be read starting at the user's current context.

## Object Names

The complete name of any object is the object name plus the object's context. This is called the object's **distinguished name**, which specifies the path to the object starting at the [Root] object. As shown in Figure 4-24, this is EFranklin's distinguished name:

    .EFranklin.FDR_Admin.FDR

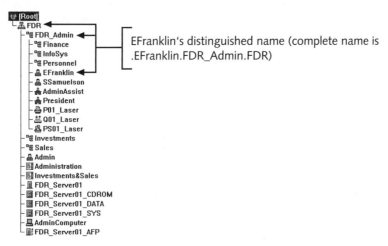

**Figure 4-24**    EFranklin's complete name

A name specification that includes the object abbreviations is referred to as a **typeful name**. For example, the user EFranklin could be identified by using the typeful distinguished name .CN=EFranklin.OU=FDR_Admin.O=FDR. The two-letter abbreviation preceding the name of an object identifies the object's type. For example, CN= identifies EFranklin as the common name for a leaf object, the OU= identifies FDR_Admin as an Organizational Unit container object, and the O= identifies FDR as an Organization container object. (To see the abbreviation for and definition of each eDirectory object type, refer back to Table 4-4.) Names without the object abbreviations are called **typeless names**. Therefore, *.CN=EFranklin.OU=FDR_Admin.O=FDR* is a typeful name, and *.EFranklin.FDR_Admin.FDR* is a typeless name.

Although the physical length of a distinguished name is almost unlimited, typing names longer than 50 characters is not practical. A distinguished name shows the path to an object from the [Root], but a **relative distinguished name** can be much shorter because it specifies only the path to an object from the workstation's current context. For example, if the current context is .FDR, the relative distinguished name for Eleanor

Franklin is *EFranklin.FDR_Admin* without a leading period (not a path from the [Root]) or a trailing period (no need to move up a directory tree level).

 Novell has developed a new function called **contextless login**. A user who wants to log in to the network has to type only a valid user name to start the process, instead of a name and a context. If more than one user on the system has that name, Novell offers the user a list to choose from. The user still must supply a valid password to complete the login.

## Object Names and Logging in to the Network

Directory tree context and distinguished names have important uses in NetWare 6. When you use Novell Client to log in to a NetWare 6 network, you log in to the directory tree. For your login to succeed, you must enter your **login name** (which is the same as the name of your User object in the tree), your password, and the correct context for your User object. Using the Advanced button in the Novell Login window to change the Context settings (see Figure 4-25) is one way to do that.

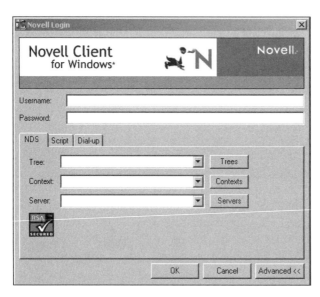

**Figure 4-25**  The Novell Login window

If Eleanor Franklin of F.D. Roosevelt Investments wants to log in to the FDR directory tree without using the Advanced button to change the Novell Client settings, she could enter her distinguished name in the Username field, as shown here:

        .EFranklin.FDR_Admin.FDR

 You can easily designate the tree and context for login by modifying Novell Client user settings, which NetWare checks during the login process. You'll study Novell Client software settings in Chapter 6.

# DESIGNING THE DIRECTORY TREE

When administering a NetWare 6 network, one of the network administrator's main responsibilities is designing the directory tree. Now that you understand the components of directory trees, you are ready to put these components together to create a directory tree. You should keep these three important design principles in mind when designing a directory tree:

- Use agreed-on network standards, such as naming conventions.
- Balance tree depth and tree width.
- Use a design approach that matches the directory tree to the organization.

## Defining Network Standards

Using network standards minimizes confusion as more servers are installed, more users are added, and new directory tree objects appear in the directory tree. **Network standards** are agreements about how to operate the network. For example, user names should be standardized. It's confusing if one network administrator creates user names based on the user's first initial and last name, such as *EFranklin*, and another administrator creates user names based on the user's last name and first initial, such *FranklinE*.

### Naming Conventions

One of the most important areas for network standards is naming conventions. A consistent and meaningful way of assigning names to users, servers, printers, print queues, print servers, and other network resources can minimize confusion for the network administrator. Before naming conventions are discussed, however, you need to be aware of the rules for naming eDirectory objects.

First, because the complete or distinguished name of an object includes the context where the object is located, object names need be unique only in their container. For example, FDR could have two users named Eleanor Franklin with the login name EFranklin as long as they worked in different parts of the organization. An Eleanor Franklin in Administration would be *.EFranklin.FDR_Admin.FDR*, and an Eleanor Franklin in Sales would be *.EFranklin.Sales.FDR*. But what happens if both end up in the same department? This would be a problem, so avoid it by using unique object names for each object. For example, an Admin User object in the FDR directory tree has the distinguished name *.Admin.FDR*. If the FDR administration OU object was named simply *Admin* instead of *FDR_Admin*, its distinguished name would also be *.Admin.FDR*, which would create two objects with the same distinguished name. Because each eDirectory distinguished name must be unique, the problem is resolved by naming the OU *FDR_Admin*, thus creating the name *.FDR_Admin.FDR*, which is unique.

Second, you can use up to 64 characters in the object name. An eDirectory name can use both uppercase and lowercase letters but is not case sensitive. For example, *EFRANKLIN*, *EFranklin*, and *efranklin* are identical as far as eDirectory is concerned.

Third, you can use some special characters, spaces, and underscores. However, underscores are displayed as spaces, so *Eleanor_Franklin* and *Eleanor Franklin* are identical as far as eDirectory is concerned.

NetWare 6 allows some network clients, such as standalone print servers, to connect to the network in bindery emulation mode, which means they behave as though they were attached to a NetWare 3.x server, which supports only 47 characters in object names. In this case, eDirectory object names longer than 47 characters are truncated to 47 characters.

NetWare does not allow the following characters in names:

/   slash

\   backslash

,   comma

;   semicolon

*   asterisk

?   question mark

For clients running in bindery emulation mode, spaces in names are converted to underscores. You should not use the other characters in the preceding list for client names that will connect to the NetWare server in bindery emulation mode.

If you use spaces in eDirectory object names, you must enclose the name in quotation marks when using command-line utilities, which could be reason enough for not using spaces in object names. Using the underscore eliminates this problem and helps ensure compatibility for bindery emulation clients.

You should develop consistent ways of naming eDirectory objects. An important consideration is length. Remember that users might have to use the names you (as the network administrator) create when entering a distinguished name for an object, so shorter names are better than longer ones. Typing *.EFranklin.FDR_Admin.FDR* is easier than typing *.Eleanor_Franklin.FDR_Administration.FDRoosevelt_Investments*, for example.

## User Name Considerations

User login names should always be created in the same way to make it easier to locate user names. For example, if all user names start with the first letter of the user's first name, you know you need to look for E to find Eleanor Franklin. Without consistency, you won't be sure which letter to look for. You have several choices for consistent naming methods:

- Use just the user's last name: Franklin
- Use the user's first initial and last name: EFranklin
- Use the user's first and last names: Eleanor_Franklin
- Use the first three characters of the user's first name and the first three characters of the user's last name: EleFra
- Use the user's first name and the first character of the user's last name: EleanorF

How you choose to create user names depends on your and your users' preferences. It also depends on how many users you are managing and how difficult it is to maintain the uniqueness of the user name. For example, a small network might have only one John Smith, but a larger organization could easily have two or more employees named John Smith. There are many ways to create user names that will work—the important consideration is consistency.

## Print System Considerations

When working with some object types, it's a good idea to include a code in the name that identifies the object type. NetWare printing is a good example. If you start printer names with the code "P," you can easily identify the object type from the object name. You can also include a number, location, or type in the name to help identify the object.

For example, FDR can name a laser printer P01_Laser, which includes a number and the type of printer. If this printer is going in Room 201 and is an HP LaserJet IV, the name could be P01_Rm201_HPLJIV. The same ideas work with servers and other eDirectory objects that have a physical existence on the network.

## Directory Tree Name Considerations

It's possible to have more than one NetWare eDirectory tree visible to network users in a WAN. For example, a company might not have implemented a companywide NetWare 6 network, and two of the company's divisions might each have a NetWare LAN. If these LANs are connected to a corporate backbone to form a WAN, NetWare users see both directory trees and can log in to one or both LANs.

Directory tree names need to be unique if there is more than one tree in a WAN. The "shorter is better" idea also applies here—a user might need to specify the tree name during login. For example, F.D. Roosevelt Investments could use FDR as the tree name of its directory tree.

Another consideration when implementing an eDirectory tree that will be used with DNS name servers is creating a directory tree name compatible with DNS naming conventions. That means special characters, such as underscores, although acceptable in eDirectory, should not be used in tree names if the eDirectory tree is to be placed on an Internet or internal DNS server.

## Balance Depth Versus Width

The term "depth" refers to the number of levels in a directory tree. The term "width" refers to the number of branches at any level, but particularly at the first level of a directory tree. When designing a directory tree, be careful not to create more levels (depth) than necessary because each level adds another term to an object's distinguished name. If there are too many levels, the names become unwieldy. What user wants a name like this?

```
JMartin.QualityControl.Prod.Ops.Plant16.Region2.DivisionIII.
EastCoast.JKHCompany
```

> Novell considers five to eight levels reasonable, but notes that eDirectory can handle as many levels as necessary to reflect an organization's structure.

In contrast, using too few levels creates a very flat directory tree (width) that probably won't clearly show the actual structure of most organizations. You're aiming for a directory tree design that reflects the organization's structure yet balances the tree's depth and width.

## APPROACHES TO DIRECTORY TREE DESIGN

You can take several different approaches to designing a directory tree. You can reflect the actual structure of the organization, you can build on the geographic locations of the organization, or you can use a combination of the two.

## Organizational Structure Approach

Because resources within an organization are allocated and accounted for according to the organizational chart, the actual structure of an organization provides one approach to designing the directory tree. Two possible organizational structures focus on functional areas and workgroups.

### Functional

Most businesses can be organized around the classic functional areas of business: operations, marketing, finance, and personnel. Although this list doesn't include every possible OU (for example, executive administration and support units, such as information systems, are not included), it does cover most of them. Other OUs can be added, and the four main units broken down into other OUs as necessary. Figure 4-26 shows a directory tree for Wilson Manufacturing, a company that manufactures home furniture. The directory tree is based on a functional structure. As you'll see in the figure, the InfoSystems OU has been added to the four typical functional areas. Other OUs have been subdivided into other OUs. For example, the Marketing OU contains OUs for Sales and Advertising, and the Operations OU has been subdivided into Production, Quality Control, Receiving, and Shipping.

### Workgroups

Some organizations prefer to focus on project workgroups composed of members from functional areas, and the directory tree structure needs to show the resources assigned to each workgroup. Figure 4-27 shows a directory tree for South Atlantic Coast Publishing, a book publisher that uses workgroups for different book topic areas: Education, Fiction, Nonfiction, and Trade.

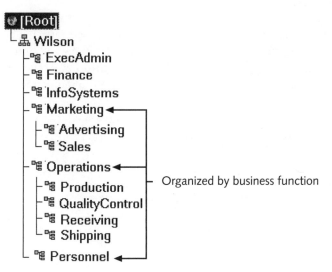

**Figure 4-26** The Wilson Manufacturing directory tree

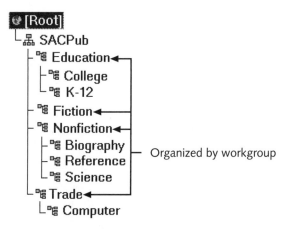

**Figure 4-27** The South Atlantic Coast Publishing directory tree

## Geographic Approach

Some organizations create their primary organizational structure based on geographic location. In each location, the directory tree can then reflect a functional or workgroup structure. You might want to use the Country object in this situation, although it's not absolutely necessary. Figures 4–28 and 4–29 show directory trees for International Metals, a company that produces a variety of metal products in several countries. The directory tree in Figure 4–28 uses Country objects for Australia, Canada, Egypt, and the United States, but the directory tree in Figure 4–29 uses the Organization object to represent the countries. When using the Country object, you are limited to the standardized two-letter code for that country.

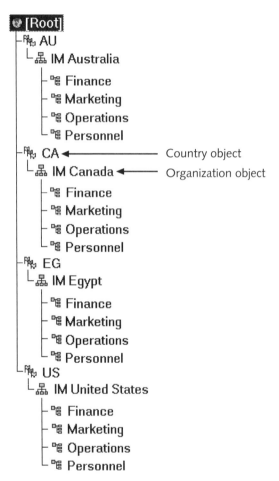

**Figure 4-28**    The International Metals directory tree with Country objects

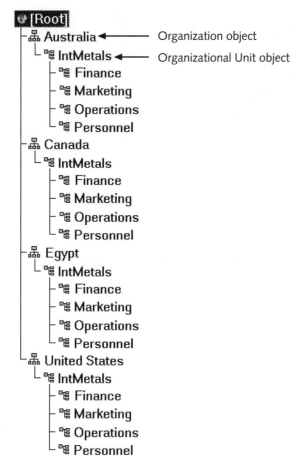

Figure 4-29    The International Metals directory tree without Country objects

## Combination Approach

You might find yourself in a situation that requires combining the functional area, workgroup, and geographical approaches. A company organized along functional lines might still have some special workgroups or units in other geographical locations that need to be represented in the directory tree. For example, Wilson Manufacturing recently bought a lumber mill in Canada to ensure a steady supply of wood to the company. Although now part of the company (*not* a separate organization), this operation is entirely different from Wilson's main business. The network administrator decided to show the network resources for the Canadian operation by using a geographical extension to Wilson's directory tree, as shown in Figure 4-30.

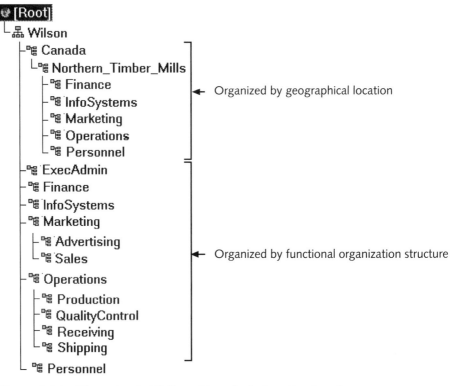

**Figure 4-30**    The extended Wilson Manufacturing directory tree

# The CBE Labs Tree Design Process

 This section describes the general process of designing a directory tree. In Chapter 7, you'll use NetWare Administrator to create this tree on your network.

To understand the use of objects in an eDirectory tree, you'll follow the process of designing a directory tree model for Cunningham, Burns, and Evans Laboratories (CBE Labs). This small, independent consulting firm tests computer hardware and software and then reports the results in its publication, The *C/B/E Networker*. You observed CBE Lab's procedure for choosing a new NOS in Chapter 1, and more details about the company are discussed in that chapter. Figure 4-31 shows the organizational chart for CBE Labs.

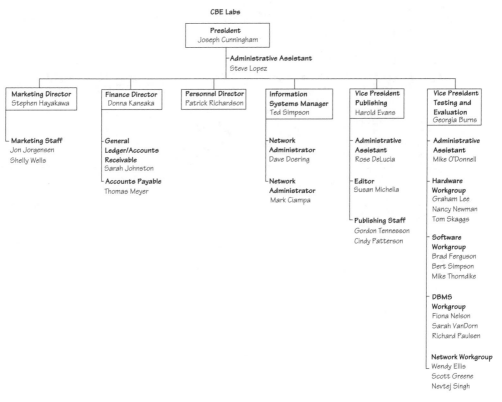

**Figure 4-31**   The CBE Labs organizational chart

## Building a Directory Tree Model

The CBE Labs information systems manager and the CBE Labs network administrators have selected a combination directory tree structure for CBE Labs. The directory tree reflects the CBE Labs workgroup-oriented organizational chart and uses traditional business functional divisions within the administration workgroup. Using this structure, the CBE Labs organizational chart shown in Figure 4-31 should provide the basis for building the directory tree model.

## Determining Container Objects

Construction of the directory tree model begins with determining what the container objects will be. Based on the organizational chart, the network administrator chose the container objects for CBE Labs (listed in Table 4-10).

In a directory tree, the container tree levels below a designated container are called the **children** of that container, and the designated container object is called the **parent**. These terms are relational—the container above a container is its parent and the container object below it are its children. Therefore, the CBE_Labs Organization object is the parent of the Organizational Unit objects listed in Table 4-10, and the Organizational

Unit objects are children of CBE_Labs. A directory tree with the container objects in Table 4-10 would look like Figure 4-32.

**Table 4-10**  CBE Labs Directory Tree Container Objects

| Object Type | Object Name | Branch Of |
|---|---|---|
| Organization | CBE_LABS | [Root] |
| Organizational Unit | CBE_Labs_Admin | CBE_LABS |
| Organizational Unit | Pubs | CBE_LABS |
| Organizational Unit | Test&Eval | CBE_LABS |
| Organizational Unit | Marketing | CBE_Labs_Admin |
| Organizational Unit | Finance | CBE_Labs_Admin |
| Organizational Unit | Personnel | CBE_Labs_Admin |
| Organizational Unit | InfoSystems | CBE_Labs_Admin |
| Organizational Unit | Hardware | Test&Eval |
| Organizational Unit | Software | Test&Eval |
| Organizational Unit | DBMS | Test&Eval |
| Organizational Unit | Network | Test&Eval |

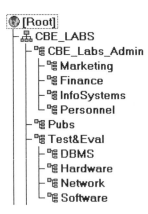

**Figure 4-32**  Container objects in the CBE Labs directory tree

## Adding Leaf Objects

After the structure of the directory tree is established by creating the container objects, the leaf objects must be added. The CBE Labs tree will use the following types of leaf objects: Users, Groups, Organizational Roles, NetWare Servers, and Volumes.

**Users**  The first user to be added to the CBE Labs directory tree will be the Admin user. NetWare 6 automatically creates this User object during the installation process. Although the Admin object can be placed anywhere in the directory tree structure, it's usually located near the [Root] of the tree. The CBE Labs Admin object will be placed in the CBE_LABS Organization container. Table 4-11 shows the CBE Labs user names to be included in the OU objects.

**Table 4-11** CBE Labs Organizational Unit Users

| Organizational Unit Objects | User Objects |
| --- | --- |
| Administration | JCunningham<br>SLopez |
| Finance | DKaneaka<br>SJohnston<br>TMeyer |
| InfoSystems | DDoering<br>MCiampa<br>TSimpson |
| Marketing | JJorgensen<br>SHayakawa<br>SWells |
| Personnel | PRichardson |
| Pubs | CPatterson<br>GTennesson<br>HEvans<br>RDeLucia<br>SMichelia |
| Test&Eval | GBurns<br>MODonnell |
| DBMS | FNelson<br>RPaulsen<br>SVanDorn |
| Hardware | GLee<br>NNewman<br>TSkaggs |
| Network | NSingh<br>SGreene<br>WEllis |
| Software | BFerguson<br>BSimpson<br>MThorndike |

**Groups**    The CBE Labs directory tree will include the Group objects shown in Table 4-12 in its OU objects.

**Table 4-12**    CBE Labs Organizational Unit Groups

| Organizational Unit Objects | Group Objects |
| --- | --- |
| Finance | Financers |
| ISMgrs | NetworkAdmins |
| Marketing | Marketers |
| Pubs | Publications |
| Test&Eval | Testing&Eval |

**Organizational Roles**    Another object type you will use is the Organizational Role object. CBE Labs will use the Organizational Role objects shown in Table 4-13.

**Table 4-13**    CBE Labs Organizational Role Objects

| Organizational Unit Objects | Organizational Role Objects |
| --- | --- |
| CBE_Labs_Admin | AdminAssist<br>President |
| Finance | Finance Director |
| InfoSystems | InfoSystems_Manager<br>Network_Admin |
| Marketing | Marketing_Director |
| Personnel | Personnel_Director |
| Pubs | AdminAssist<br>VP_Pubs |
| Test&Eval | AdminAssist<br>VP_Testing&Evaluation |

**NetWare Servers**    CBE Labs will use three NetWare servers. A year ago the original NetWare server was upgraded from NetWare 3.11 to NetWare 5.1 and is running out of capacity. To maximize performance, implement new Internet applications, and provide for future growth, management at CBE Labs recently approved the acquisition of two NetWare 6 servers. These two servers will be installed in a new eDirectory tree, and the NetWare 5.1 server will be upgraded to eDirectory 8.6 and added to the tree. Although the NetWare 5.1 server was named Ranger after a U.S. Navy aircraft carrier at the request of the president of the company, Joseph Cunningham, who served in the U.S. Navy, Ted believes server names should reflect the server's location and function. As a result, the server to be used primarily for administration and business functions will be named CBE_ADMIN, and the server to be used primarily for the Testing and Evaluation Department will be named CBE_EVAL. Additional servers in these departments could include a number after them, such as CBE_ADMIN_02, or include a three-letter abbreviation for their function. For example, if a new server is added to administration for the Accounting Department, it could be named CBE_ADMIN_ACC. Other options Ted considered were including the software version as part of the server name or using the abbreviation SRV. For example, the CBE_ADMIN server could be named CBE_ADMIN_NW6 or CBE_ADMIN_SRV. The problem with using that version is that when the server is upgraded, the version number could change, requiring a rather complex server name change. Although each network manager has his or her own preference for naming servers, Ted thought using an abbreviation such as SRV after the server name would be an unnecessary addition to the length of the server's name. Because all personnel at CBE Labs will use the CBE_ADMIN server, Ted placed it high in the directory tree, in the CBE_LABS Organization object.

Because DNS does not allow the underline character, server names to be used for both eDirectory and DNS should not contain underline characters.

**Volumes**   CBE_ADMIN and CBE_EVAL have three volumes each—SYS, DATA, and CDROM—but RANGER has only a SYS volume. All personnel will access the system volume for CBE_ADMIN, referred to as the SYS volume and with a common name of CBE_ADMIN_SYS. The Volume object for the CBE_ADMIN_SYS volume will be located with the CBE_ADMIN object in the CBE_LABS Organization container. CBE_ADMIN and CBE_EVAL also have DATA and CDROM volumes, represented by DATA and CDROM Volume objects.

## EDIRECTORY AS A REPLICATED, DISTRIBUTED DATABASE

One of the main security concerns in the NetWare 6 environment is protecting the directory database. Because the directory database contains all the information necessary for users to log in and use the network, losing this data would be catastrophic. Novell's solution assumes that there is more than one server in the network. With more than one NetWare server, the directory database is broken into parts, and those parts are stored on different NetWare servers. For even better protection, copies of each part of the directory database are stored on additional NetWare servers. The parts of the database are called *partitions*, and the copies are called *replicas*. A database that is stored in sections on different computers is called a **distributed database**. The directory database is a replicated, distributed database. To maintain current data in each of the replicas, NetWare 6 updates all replicas using a process called *replica synchronization*.

## Partitions

A **partition** is a logical division of the directory database based on the directory tree. A partition starts at an Organization or Organizational Unit branch of the directory tree and includes all leaf objects in that container plus all subsequent container and leaf objects in that branch of the tree. The data for each object is also included in the partition, but no data about the file system is included in a partition. Partitions cannot overlap, and an eDirectory object can be in only one partition. There should be at least one NetWare 6 server in each partition. Figure 4-33 shows the partitioned Wilson Manufacturing directory tree.

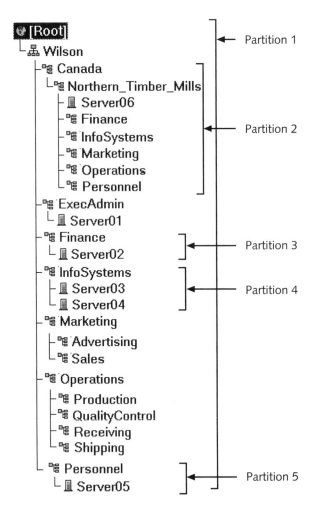

**Figure 4-33**    The partitioned Wilson Manufacturing directory tree

There are five partitions in the Wilson Manufacturing directory tree. The [Root] is included in the first partition, which is created when the first NetWare 6 server is installed. This partition is called the **[Root] partition**. Other partitions receive names based on the name of the container object in the partition closest to the [Root]. A partition is called a **child partition** if it is lower in the directory tree than another partition (**subordinate** to another partition), which is called the **parent partition**. In the Wilson Manufacturing directory tree, the [Root] partition is the parent partition, and all the other partitions are child partitions.

The term "partition" is also used to mean a *physical subdivision of a hard drive.* Be careful not to confuse the two uses of the word "partition."

## Replicas

A **replica** is a copy of a partition. Replicas are stored on NetWare 6 servers to ensure eDirectory fault tolerance and provide faster access on a WAN. Fault tolerance is achieved because a user can log in to the network even when the server containing the replica of the user's account is not available. The problem with using a replica located across a WAN is that login speed might be reduced because of the WAN's slower speed. Faster access on a WAN is achieved when the replica of a user's data is on a server physically close to the user. For example, if a WAN links offices in San Francisco and New York, a user in San Francisco can log in to the network faster by accessing the replica on the San Francisco NetWare server. There are five types of replicas: Master, Read/Write, Read-Only, Subordinate Reference, and Filtered.

**Master Replica**   The **Master replica** is the main copy of the partition. There can be only one Master replica for each partition. The Master replica can be read from and written to and is also the place where other partition operations occur, including creating, merging, moving, and repairing partitions and creating and deleting replicas.

**Read/Write Replica**   The **Read/Write replica** is a copy of the Master replica that can be read from and modified. You can create as many Read/Write replicas as you want, but the actual number you create will be determined by the size of your network and the number of NetWare servers in the network. Read/Write replicas can be used for authenticating user login, so you must have enough replicas to permit users to log in to the network if NetWare servers become inaccessible.

**Read-Only Replica**   The **Read-Only replica** is a copy of the Master replica that can only be read from; however, Read-Only replicas cannot be used for user login. You can create as many Read-Only replicas as you want, but these copies are not as useful as Read/Write replicas. Servers that are running bindery services cannot have a Read-Only replica—they must have a Master or Read/Write replica.

Because of the user login and bindery services limitations, a Read/Write replica is usually more efficient than a Read-Only replica. With the Read/Write replica, users can authenticate logins and set up bindery services later, if needed.

**Subordinate Reference Replica**   The **Subordinate Reference replica** is based on the parent partition/child partition system. If a parent partition has a Master, Read/Write, or Read-Only replica on a NetWare server and a child partition does not have a replica on that NetWare server, NetWare 6 automatically adds a nonmodifiable replica of the child partition called the Subordinate Reference replica. If you later put a Read/Write or Read-Only replica of the child partition on the server, NetWare 6 automatically removes the Subordinate Reference replica. This built-in safety measure ensures that there are enough replicas of all the partitions.

**Filtered Replica**    The **Filtered replica** is similar to a Read/Write replica except it uses a filter to specify what types of objects are included in the replica. Filtered replicas are most useful for remote sites, where the filter reduces the number of objects to be synchronized on the remote server.

### Replica Synchronization

Changes to the directory database can be made initially in either the Master replica or a Read/Write replica of a partition. When someone changes an eDirectory object, a copy of the change is sent from the partition where the change was first recorded, to all other replicas of the partition. This update is necessary to ensure that the directory database is **consistent**. However, because updating all the replicas takes some time, the directory database is said to be **loosely consistent** at any given moment. This updating procedure is called **replica synchronization.** Replica changes are classified as an **Immediate sync** or a **Slow sync**. By default, Immediate syncs occur within 10 seconds of the change and include adding or deleting new objects and making changes to object properties such as passwords, names, and group membership. Slow syncs are intended to keep replicas loosely synchronized for repetitive updates, such as user login time or change of network address properties. By default, slow syncs are scheduled to occur within 22 minutes of the change.

## Designing Partitions and Replica Distribution

The purpose of partitioning the directory database is to achieve fault tolerance and faster access on a WAN. The number of partitions that must be created depends on what it takes to achieve those goals, but you should have at least two read/write replicas for every master replica if possible.

NetWare 6 automatically creates some partitions and replicas for you. A new partition is created during NetWare 6 installation if you create a new Organization object or OU object during the installation and if the NetWare Server object corresponding to the new NetWare 6 server is a leaf object in the new branch. The new partition starts in the new container object and includes all branches of that container object. A master replica for this partition is created and stored on the NetWare server. For example, when you install your first NetWare 6 server, you must create an Organization object. When you do so, NetWare creates a partition based on that Organization object and places a master replica on the server.

When you install NetWare 6 on a server whose corresponding Server object is a leaf in an Organization or OU object that's already in a partition, NetWare 6 creates a Read/Write replica of that partition on the new server. However, to reduce synchronization traffic on the network, NetWare creates only three replicas of a partition automatically. If you install more than three servers in a partition, replicas will exist only on the first three. You can, however, add more if you want the additional security of having extra copies of the partition with additional NetWare servers. When adding more replicas, make sure you consider the network traffic necessary to keep the replicas synchronized. When users log in or out, change passwords, or make changes to the objects in a replica, this information is transmitted to each server containing a copy of the context where the user account is located. When servers are on the same network cable, this traffic is usually not a problem; however, when servers are located across routers or across WAN links, the extra packets can slow the performance of network connections. As a result, it is important to reduce the number of replicas located on remote servers.

4

 In a small LAN, partitioning gains little access time, and a single partition can be sufficient. If you have at least three servers, you can have a Master replica and two Read/Write replicas, which gives you the necessary fault tolerance.

In larger LANs and in WANs, partitioning improves user access and can reduce network synchronization traffic. To accomplish this, store the Master replica containing the user's data on a server in the partition that contains the user's User object. When an eDirectory tree spans a WAN with multiple servers located on both sides, synchronization traffic can be reduced by dividing the directory database into at least two partitions, as shown previously in Figure 4-33. Partitioning also can help create fault tolerance when you store Read/Write replicas in partitions other than the one containing the Master replica.

 The Master replica of a partition need not be stored on a server in that partition. A large organization can place *all* Master replicas on one server. A tape backup of this server then backs up all the Master replicas for the entire directory database.

## Chapter Summary

- ◻ Directory services play an important role in administering and managing networks consisting of diverse operating systems and locations. Most directory services are based on the X.500 standard, which defines protocols for the Directory Information Base, Directory Information Tree, Directory User Agent, and Directory Service Agent.

- ◻ eDirectory is network-centric; that is, it deals with the entire network. Users log in to the network, not to an individual server. The benefits of this approach include easier network administration, improved network security, increased reliability, and scalability (the ability to work with any size network).

- ◻ The logical design of eDirectory is the directory tree, a hierarchical tree structure containing objects that represent the network's organizational structure and resources. The directory tree, which is given a directory tree name during NetWare 6 installation, consists of eDirectory objects. Objects represent physical, logical, or organizational entities, including Organizations and Organizational Units. Objects have properties, which are the types of data associated with each object. Each property can store one or more property values.

❐ The directory tree consists of container objects and leaf objects. Container objects provide organizational structure for the directory tree. They can contain other container objects or leaf objects. Leaf objects represent network resources, such as users and printers. They cannot contain other objects.

❐ Container objects include [Root], Country, Domain Controller, Security, License Container, Organization, Organizational Unit, and Role Based Service. Leaf objects can be classified by function for easier understanding: user-related, server-related, printer-related, and general-purpose.

❐ The location of an object in the directory tree is the object's context, the path from the [Root] to the object. Context is combined with an object's name to create the distinguished name, which is the complete name of the object. If object type abbreviations are included in the name, it is called a *typeful name*. Names without abbreviations are called *typeless names*.

❐ When designing a directory tree, first establish naming conventions to provide a uniform method of naming network objects. Limit the depth of the directory tree so that objects' distinguished names are not too long. You can base the directory tree design on functional or geographic principles or a combination of the two.

❐ The directory database can be divided into sections called *partitions*. The partitions can and should be copied to other servers to ensure fault tolerance and faster network response times on a WAN. The copies are called *replicas*. There are five types of replicas: Master, Read/Write, Read-Only, Subordinate Reference, and Filtered. Partitions and replicas are created automatically when NetWare 6 is installed, but the network administrator should actively manage them to ensure good network performance and security.

# KEY TERMS

**AFP Server object** — An eDirectory informational leaf object that represents a network's AppleTalk File Protocol server in the directory tree.

**Alias object** — An eDirectory leaf object that represents an eDirectory leaf object located in another part of the directory tree.

**Application object** — An eDirectory used to represent an application available on the network.

**bindery** — The NetWare 3.1x files that contain security information, such as user names, passwords, and account restrictions. The bindery files, stored on NetWare 3.1x servers in the SYS:System directory, consist of NET$OBJ.SYS, NET$PROP.SYS, and NET$VAL.SYS.

**child partition** — In eDirectory, a partition that is below (farther away from the [Root]) a parent partition in the directory tree structure. The child partition is subordinate to the parent partition.

**children** — In eDirectory, container levels that are subordinate (farther away from the [Root]) to another container. The superior (closer to the [Root]) container level is called the parent.

**committed transaction** — A completed directory service transaction that is placed in the log file.

**common name (CN)** — The name type associated with an eDirectory leaf object.

**Computer object** — An eDirectory object used to represent workstations in a network.

**consistent** — The same throughout. When referring to eDirectory, all the replicas of a partition must be updated so that they are consistent. Because the updating process takes time, the directory database is said to be loosely consistent at any moment in time.

**container object** — An eDirectory object that contains other eDirectory objects. The main eDirectory container objects are [Root], Country, Organization, and Organizational Unit.

**context** — The location of an eDirectory object in the directory tree.

**contextless login** — A NetWare login during which the user does not have to specify a context. Instead, NetWare is configured to understand the User object's context or the user selects it from a list of valid users.

**Country object** — An eDirectory container object that represents a country in the directory tree.

**current context** — The user's current location in the eDirectory tree.

**directory database** — A database used to store information about network objects.

**Directory Information Base (DIB)** — The name of the X.500 directory database.

**Directory Information Tree (DIT)** — A tree structure for the DIB containers that represents the hierarchical relationship between entries.

**Directory Map object** — An eDirectory server-related leaf object that is used in the directory tree to reference a drive mapping

**Directory Schema** — A set of rules for ensuring that the information in the DIB is not damaged or lost.

**directory service** — Software that provides discovery, security, relational management, storage, and retrieval of directory database information.

**Directory System Agent (DSA)** — Software running on a server that consists of a collection of services and protocols for managing specific portions of the DIB.

**Directory User Agent (DUA)** — Runs on the user workstation and acts as a client to send requests from the user to the directory service.

**distinguished name** — The complete name when referring to an eDirectory object, consisting of the object's common name plus the object's context. A distinguished name always shows the path to the object from the [Root]. An example of a distinguished name is .EFranklin.FDR_Admin.FDR.

**distributed database** — A database split into parts, with each part residing on a different server.

**Domain Controller object** — An eDirectory container object used to hold DNS entities, such as name servers and zones.

**eDirectory** — The Novell LDAP-compatible directory service system implemented in NetWare 6.

**4**

**eDirectory tree** — The visual and logical design used to organize data into a hierarchical structure.

**entry** — A record in the directory database that stores information on a network object.

**Filtered replica** — Similar to the Read/Write replica in eDirectory, except it filters the types of objects included in the replica.

**FLexible and Adaptive Information Manager (FLAIM)** — The database system used to store eDirectory tree objects.

**Group object** — An eDirectory user-related leaf object that is used in the Directory tree to manage groups of users.

**hierarchical structure** — A logical organizational structure that starts at one point, called the [Root], and branches out from the starting point. Points in the structure are logically above or below other points on the same branch.

**Immediate Sync** — A type of replica synchronization that occurs by default within 10 seconds of adding or deleting new objects and making changes to object properties.

**LDAP Group object** — An eDirectory object that contains configuration information and security policies for LDAP services running on one or more NetWare servers.

**LDAP Server object** — An eDirectory object that contains configuration information for the LDAP service running on a NetWare server.

**leaf object** — An eDirectory tree object that cannot contain other objects. Leaf objects are used to store data about network resources, such as NetWare servers, volumes, users, groups, and printers.

**License Certificate object** — An eDirectory object that represents user or server connections.

**License Container object** — An eDirectory object that houses server and user license certificates.

**Lightweight Directory Access Protocol (LDAP)** — A simplified version of the X.500 protocol that specifies a common set of directory operations and commands that can be implemented on multiple vendor platforms.

**logical entity** — In eDirectory, a network resource that exists as a logical or mental creation, such as an organizational entity that models the structure of an organization.

**login name** — The name a user enters at the login prompt or in the Novell Client Login window when logging in to the network. The login name is also the name displayed for the user's User object in the eDirectory tree.

**loosely consistent** — The same throughout, more or less. When referring to eDirectory, all partition replicas need to be updated so that they are consistent. Because the updating process takes time, the directory database is said to be loosely consistent at any moment in time.

**Master replica** — In eDirectory, the main copy of a partition. There is only one Master replica for each partition. A Master replica can be read from and written to, and can be used for login purposes.

**name type** — An eDirectory descriptor of object types. There are four name types: Country (abbreviated as C), Organization (abbreviated as O), Organizational Unit (abbreviated as OU), and common name (which refers to all leaf objects and is abbreviated as CN). There is no name type for the [Root] object.

**NCP Server object** — Another name for the NetWare Server object. NCP is an abbreviation for NetWare Core Protocol.

**NDPS Broker object** — An eDirectory object that contains configuration information for the Service Registry Service, Event Notification Service, and Resource Management Service.

4

**NDPS Manager object** — An eDirectory object that represents the NDPS Manager software used to provide a platform for running printer agents on a NetWare server.

**NDPS Printer object** — An eDirectory object that represents the printer agent for a physical printer.

**NetWare Server object** — An eDirectory object used to represent a network's NetWare server in the directory tree.

**network file system** — The logical organizational structure of file storage on network volumes.

**network standard** — An agreement about how to operate a network.

**Non-NDPS Printer object** — An eDirectory object that represents a network printer using queue-based printing.

**object** — In eDirectory, the representation of a network resource in the directory database; it appears as an icon in the directory tree. eDirectory objects can be associated with physical entities and logical entities.

**Organization object** — An eDirectory container object used to organize the structure of the directory tree; it can contain Organizational Unit objects and leaf objects.

**organizational entity** — In eDirectory, a logical entity that models the structure of an organization.

**Organizational Role object** — An eDirectory user-related leaf object used in the directory tree to manage users' privileges by associating them with specific positions, such as president, vice president, and so on, in an organizational structure. The privileges are assigned to the Organizational Role object, and the users assigned to that role inherit those privileges.

**Organizational Unit object** — An eDirectory container object used to organize the structure of the directory tree; it can contain other Organizational Unit objects and leaf objects.

**parent** — In eDirectory, a designated container level that has other subordinate container levels (farther away from the [Root]). The subordinate container levels are called children. In the network file system, a parent is a data set such as a directory or subdirectory.

**parent partition** — In eDirectory, a partition that is above (closest to the [Root]) a child partition in the directory tree structure.

**partition** — A logical division of the directory database based on the directory tree structure.

**physical entity** — In eDirectory, a network resource that has a physical existence, such as a NetWare server.

**printer-related leaf object** — In eDirectory, a group of leaf objects used to manage printers in a network.

**Print Queue object** — An eDirectory object that represents a holding area in which print jobs are kept until the printer is available to print them. In NetWare, a print queue is a subdirectory on an assigned volume.

**Print Server object** — An eDirectory object that stores configuration information for queue-based printing software.

**Profile object** — An eDirectory user-related leaf object used in the directory tree to manage users' login scripts. The login script is stored in the Profile object, and the users assigned to that profile use the login script.

**property** — An aspect of an eDirectory object, such as the user's last name for the User object. The actual last name—for example, Burns—is the property value.

**property value** — In eDirectory, an actual value of an eDirectory object property. For example, the user's last name is a property of the User object, and an actual user's last name—for example, Burns—is the property value.

**Read-Only replica** — In eDirectory, a copy of the Master replica that can only be read from, not written to, and cannot be used for login purposes.

**Read/Write replica** — In eDirectory, a copy of the Master replica that can only be read from and written to, and can be used for login purposes.

**relative distinguished name** — In eDirectory, this name specifies the path to the object from an object other than the [Root]. An example of a relative distinguished name is EFranklin.FDR_Admin. Note that there is no leading period because the path is not from the root of the tree.

**replica** — In eDirectory, a copy of a partition. There are five types of replicas: Master, Read/Write, Read-Only, Subordinate Reference, and Filtered.

**replica synchronization** — In eDirectory, the process of updating all replicas of a partition so that they are consistent.

**Role Based Service object** — Allows the network administrator to provide specific types of administrative tasks to selected users.

**[Root]** — The starting point of a hierarchical structure, such as a tree, that starts at one point (the [Root]) and branches out from there. When referring to eDirectory, [Root] is the [Root] object.

**[Root] object** — The starting point of the eDirectory tree.

**[Root] partition** — The partition of the eDirectory tree that contains the [Root] object.

**scalability** — The capability to work with systems of different sizes.

**Security object** — An eDirectory container object that holds global policies for login security and authentication using public key encryption.

**server-related leaf object** — In eDirectory, a group of leaf objects used to manage servers in a network.

**shadowing** — The X.500 process of distributing and synchronizing the DIB among multiple locations.

**Slow sync** — An eDirectory replica synchronization process that by default occurs within 22 minutes of including information, such as login time, change of network address, or updated properties.

**subordinate** — Below or under. In eDirectory, a child partition is a partition that is below (farther away from the [Root]) a parent partition in the eDirectory tree structure. The child partition is subordinate to the parent partition.

**Subordinate Reference replica** — In eDirectory, a copy of the Master replica that NetWare 6 automatically generates to make sure a child partition has a replica on the NetWare server containing a replica of the parent partition. The Subordinate Reference replica cannot be modified. Subordinate reference replicas are used to ensure that there are enough replicas of all partitions.

**Template object** — An eDirectory object used to define a common set of attributes that can be applied to new user accounts.

**Tree object** — An eDirectory object that represents the beginning of the eDirectory database structure. This object is also referred to as a [Root] object.

**typeful name** — When an eDirectory object's distinguished name is written with name type abbreviations, it's referred to as a typeful name. An example of a typeful name is .CN=EFranklin.OU=FDR_Admin.O=FDR.

**typeless name** — When an eDirectory object's distinguished name is written without name type abbreviations, it's referred to as a typeless name. An example of a typeless name is .EFranklin.FDR_Admin.FDR.

**Unknown object** — An eDirectory miscellaneous object used in the directory tree to identify corrupted objects that eDirectory cannot recognize.

**User object** — An eDirectory user-related leaf object used in the directory tree to manage network users.

**user-related leaf object** — In eDirectory, a group of leaf objects used to manage users in a network.

**Volume object** — An eDirectory server-related leaf object used in the directory tree to manage volumes on NetWare servers.

**X.500** — Specifications developed by International Telecommunication Union (ITU) that define directory service functions and format.

# REVIEW QUESTIONS

1. In the X.500 model, which of the following components is responsible for initiating a request for directory services information?

   a. DIB

   b. DSP

   c. DUA

   d. DUP

2. The X.500 protocol used to communicate between different directory servers is known as which of the following?

    a. DIB

    b. DSP

    c. DUA

    d. DUP

3. Which of the following is made up of objects called entries?

    a. DIB

    b. DSP

    c. DUA

    d. DUP

4. Which of the following is a set of rules that makes sure the directory remains well formed as modifications are made?

    a. protocol

    b. DUP

    c. Directory Schema

    d. DSP

5. Which of the following is the process of distributing the X.500 directory information base between servers?

    a. synchronizing

    b. replicating

    c. shadowing

    d. stabilizing

6. _____ is a database that contains network resources and tools for using the data in the database.

7. Which of the following is *not* a benefit of using eDirectory?

    a. administration

    b. security

    c. scalability

    d. simplicity

8. The directory database uses which of the following to represent network resources?

    a. objects

    b. properties

    c. values

    d. records

9. The types of data stored for each resource are called which of the following?

   a. objects

   b. properties

   c. values

   d. records

10. Which of the following is used primarily to organize network objects?

    a. containers

    b. logical entities

    c. partitions

    d. leaf objects

11. Which of the following is used to represent network objects and resources?

    a. containers

    b. replicas

    c. Organizational Units

    d. leaf objects

12. Which of the following objects is created first when a NetWare 6 server is installed in a new tree? This object is assigned the name of the directory tree.

    a. Country

    b. Root

    c. Organization

    d. Server

13. From the list below, identify four container objects.

    a. Security

    b. Root

    c. Group

    d. Role Based Service

    e. Volume

    f. Profile

    g. Domain

14. Which of the following is *not* a user-related leaf object?

    a. Template

    b. NDPS Broker

    c. Profile

    d. Organizational Role

15. Which of the following is *not* a server-related leaf object?

    a. LDAP Group

    b. Volume

    c. NDPS Broker

    d. License Container

16. For each object in the Objects column, give the number from the Object Groups column that matches which object group the object belongs to.

    | **Objects** | **Object Groups** |
    |---|---|
    | a. Print Server object | 1. Printer-related leaf object |
    | b. Unknown object | 2. Server-related leaf object |
    | c. Computer object | 3. General-purpose leaf object |
    | d. NDPS Manager object | |
    | e. License Certificate object | |
    | f. LDAP Group object | |

17. Which of the following is the term for the location of an object in a directory tree?

    a. container

    b. domain

    c. path

    d. context

18. For each object type, list its associated abbreviation:

    a. Country _____

    b. Organization _____

    c. Organizational Unit _____

    d. All leaf objects _____

19. An object's complete name is also called which of the following?

    a. relative name

    b. common name

    c. distinguished name

    d. leaf name

20. The name *CN=GWashington.OU=WhiteHouse.O=USGovernment.C=US* is a(n) _____ name, and *GWashington.WhiteHouse.USGovernment.US* is a(n) _____ name.

    a. distinguished, relative

    b. typeful, typeless

    c. typeless, typeful

    d. relative, distinguished

**4**

21. For each of the following names, indicate whether it is an acceptable name in NetWare 6:

    a. Joan*Jones (Yes or no?)

    b. Joan_Jones (Yes or no?)

    c. Joan_Smith_who_lives_at_100_Armstrong_avenue_CocoBeach_Florida (Yes or no?)

    d. Joan/Jones (Yes or no?)

22. The directory database can be divided into sections called which of the following?

    a. containers

    b. replica

    c. pools

    d. partitions

23. Copies of partition sections are called which of the following?

    a. containers

    b. replica

    c. pools

    d. partitions

24. True or False: A License Container is an example of a leaf object.

25. Which of the following objects would be used to hold login scripts of special groups of users?

    a. Profile

    b. Application

    c. Group

    d. Organizational Role

## HANDS-ON PROJECTS

### Project 4-1: X.500 Components

In this project, use Figure 4-1 to create and label a diagram that includes the following X.500 directory service components:

Directory System Agent (DSA)

Directory User Agent (DUA)

Directory Access Protocol (DAP)

Directory Service Protocol (DSP)

Directory Information Base (DIB)

Directory Information Tree (DIT)

After you have created your diagram of the X.500 components, identify and label the following eDirectory components in your diagram:

NetWare server

NetWare client

Master replica

Read/Write replica

An Organization object

An Organizational Unit object

### Project 4-2: Documenting the CBE Labs eDirectory Tree Structure

In this project, you use what you have learned about the CBE Labs tree structure to document the tree design for your version of the CBE Labs organization. Your design should include the following OUs: CBE_Labs_Admin, Pubs, Test&Eval, Finance, InfoSystems, Marketing, Personnel, DBMS, Hardware, Network, and Software. Refer to Table 4-10 and Figure 4-32 when designing your tree, and submit your design to your instructor when you're finished. You will create these OUs in Chapter 7's projects.

# CASE PROJECTS

## Case 4-1: The Jefferson County Courthouse Network

The Jefferson County Courthouse network is proceeding according to plan. The network proposal includes 12 users in the Social Services Department, including Janet Hinds, the program administrator; Tom Norihama, her assistant; Lisa Walsh, the receptionist; Terry Smith, the department secretary; and eight social workers. The group will use one NetWare server. Because the network might be expanded later to include other courthouse functions, NetWare 6 was selected as the NOS for its scalability. After discussions with Janet, the following decisions have been made:

1. The name of the directory tree will be JCCH.

2. No Country or Locality objects will be used, and there will be only one Organization object: JCCH.

Create a proposed eDirectory directory tree for the project, referring to Figure 4-34. When designing your model, remember that a directory tree is used for managing network resources and does not necessarily mirror a company's organizational chart. In your proposal, discuss the following issue: With only one server, there can be only one partition with a Master replica. Because you don't have fault tolerance with Read/Write replicas on other servers, how will you protect the data in the directory database?

Turn the proposal in to your instructor in memo form.

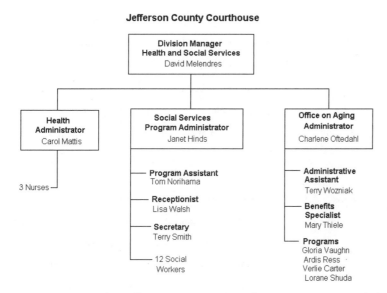

**Figure 4-34**   The Jefferson County Courthouse organizational chart

## Case 4-2: The J.Q. Adams Corporation Directory Tree

The J.Q. Adams Corporation is expanding its networking plans. Donna Hulbert, president of Adams, has decided to use two NetWare 6 servers in the network. One will be dedicated to administration tasks and the other to supporting production. After conferring with the appropriate people at J.Q. Adams, the following decisions have been made:

1. The name of the directory tree will be ADAMS.
2. No Country or Locality objects will be used, and there will be only one Organization object: ADAMS.
3. Partitions of the directory tree will be created for administration and production.

Figure 4-35 shows an organizational chart for J.Q. Adams. Prepare your proposal for the eDirectory tree. When designing your model, remember that a directory tree is used for managing network resources and does not necessarily mirror a company's organizational chart. Include proposed partitions and replicas.

Turn the proposal in to your instructor in memo form.

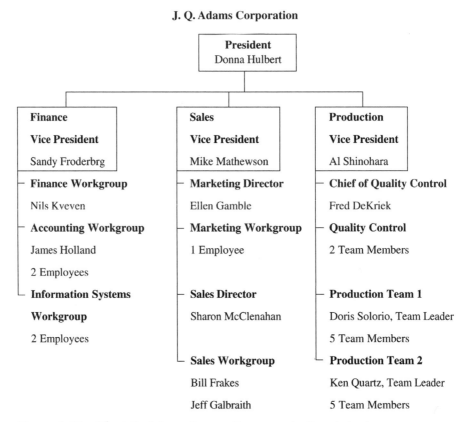

**Figure 4-35**   The J.Q. Adams Corporation organizational chart

# PLANNING THE NETWORK FILE SYSTEM

**After reading this chapter and completing the exercises, you will be able to:**

♦ Describe the components of the NetWare file system

♦ Explain the purpose of each NetWare-created directory and Novell-suggested directory

♦ Apply directory design concepts to developing and documenting a directory structure for an organization

♦ Identify NetWare and Windows utilities used to view volume and directory information

One of a network administrator's most important tasks is designing a network file system that meets an organization's needs. The design must be completed before installing NetWare and setting up the network system. The file system should be designed to allow a smooth workflow for users. Also, it must not disrupt the information flow that existed before the network was implemented. Network administrators use the network file system to manage and control system, application, and data files on the network. Therefore, a good network file system design is necessary to facilitate a network's setup, use, and growth.

## NETWORK FILE SYSTEM COMPONENTS

In Chapter 4, you learned about Novell eDirectory Services and the eDirectory tree, a logical organizational view of the entire network that enables a network administrator to manage and control network resources. A network file system, in contrast, is a design for storing files on one or more hard disks in your NetWare servers. The term "network file system" refers to how file storage is structured across all NetWare servers in the network. "File system" refers to the file storage structure on an *individual* NetWare server. The network file system is the sum of *all* the NetWare server file systems. The NetWare file system offers the following advantages that help facilitate network file system design and implementation:

- Centralized management of data and backups ensures that duplicate copies of data are always automatically available for restoring lost or damaged files.

- Improved security prevents users from modifying or accessing data they are not responsible for maintaining.

- Improved reliability and fault tolerance enable data to be backed up at regular intervals and allow recovery if data is lost or a NetWare server goes down.

- Shared and private storage areas facilitate the creation of workgroups, so users can easily share and transfer files without having to carry disks between machines. Users can take advantage of private storage areas to save their work in a secure area of the NetWare server.

- Using common clients and operating systems enables users to access the data and documents they need from computers attached to any interconnected network.

Novell has improved the network file system in NetWare 6 by implementing **Novell Storage Services (NSS)** version 3. As you will learn in this section, NSS version 3 (NSS3) offers several improvements over earlier file systems, making it the ideal choice for most NetWare 6 storage needs.

 The NetWare 5 version of NSS was more complex to implement and did not support the SYS volume, so it was typically used only with very large data volumes. Because of the improvements made to version 3 of the NSS file system, NetWare 6 now uses NSS by default for the SYS volume.

As illustrated in Figure 5-1, the main components of the NSS3 file system are disk partitions, storage pools, and volumes. The disk drive is first divided into one or more partitions. The partition space from one or more drives is then combined to form storage pools. A single storage pool can contain space from one or more disk partitions. After a storage pool is created, volumes can be defined within that storage pool. In Chapter 8, you will learn how to create disk partitions, storage pools, and volumes.

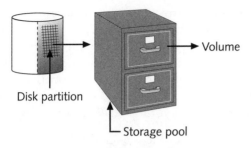

**Figure 5-1**    NSS3 file system components

5

# Disk Partitions

Formatting and managing storage on a physical disk drive requires dividing the disk drive into one or more **partitions**. Originally, a disk drive could have a maximum of four disk partitions defined, but with NSS3, you can have an almost unlimited number of NSS partitions. When installing NetWare 6 on a new server, the installation program requires a DOS partition of at least 200 MB, with a recommended size of 1 GB (described in Chapter 6). In addition, the installation program creates a 4 GB SYS volume for operating system files. Leaving some unpartitioned space for future expansion is a good idea when planning how to allocate the remaining drive space. The unpartitioned space can be used later to create new storage pools or extend the space of existing storage pools. For example, Figure 5-2 shows how the storage space for a 60 GB disk drive could be configured into one DOS partition, two NSS volumes, and 14 GB of unpartitioned free space. By leaving approximately 14 GB unpartitioned, the administrator has the option of extending the SYS or DATA partition in the future.

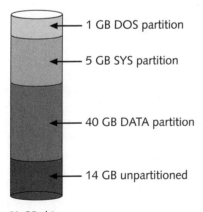

60 GB drive

**Figure 5-2**    Sample disk partitions

You can use ConsoleOne or NetWare Remote Manager to create and manage partitions. Because NSS partitions are considered part of the NetWare server's disk storage, they do not appear as separate objects in the eDirectory tree; instead, you access them by clicking on the NetWare Server object, as shown in Figure 5-3. Notice in Figure 5-3 that the existing disk partitions are displayed in the left-hand pane, with information about the selected partition displayed in the center of the window. Use the option buttons on the right to create new partitions, delete partitions, show device information, or establish mirroring between partitions of equal size. In Chapter 8, you'll learn how to use ConsoleOne to view partition information through the NetWare Server object.

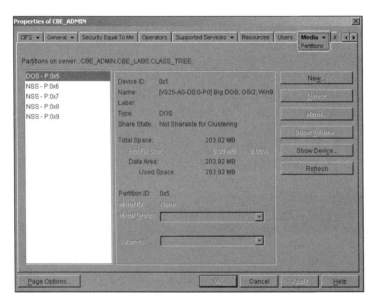

**Figure 5-3**   Viewing partition information

*In NetWare 6.5, storage management services are performed using either iManager or NSSMU as described in Appendix D.*

## Partition Fault Tolerance

Having all operating system files and data on one drive creates a potential single point of file service failure if the drive or its controller card fails. As described in Chapter 1, fault tolerance is the system's ability to continue functioning despite the failure of a major component. With NetWare, you can enable the Hot Fix or Mirror features, as shown in Figure 5-4, to provide increased reliability when you create an NSS partition. The Hot Fix option increases partition reliability by detecting bad disk blocks and then automatically redirecting the data being written to those blocks to another area of the disk called the reserved area. The size of the reserved area is specified when you enable the Hot Fix option on a new partition. The only two disadvantages of Hot Fix are the relatively small amount of space reserved for bad blocks and the small amount of server processing time required to redirect data requests to the hot fix area. Unless disk space is a real problem, you should always enable the Hot Fix option when creating partitions.

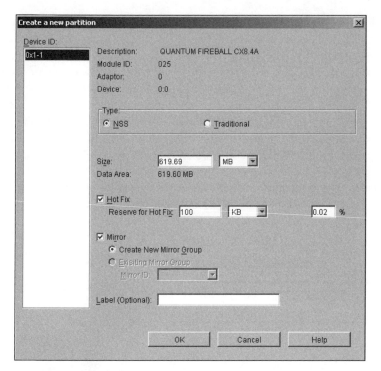

5

**Figure 5-4**     The Create a new partition dialog box
*In NetWare 6.5, storage management services are performed using either
iManager or NSSMU as described in Appendix D.*

As described in Chapter 2, RAID 5 disk systems provide hardware-based fault tolerance
in the event that one of the disk drives in the RAID system fails. On RAID 5 systems,
data from the failed drive is automatically reconstructed by the disk system using a mathematical algorithm and control information stored on the other drives. Although many
new servers use RAID 5 disk systems, they can be expensive for use on small servers. As
a less expensive alternative, the NSS file system can be configured to provide fault tolerance through implementing the Mirror feature. The NSS Mirror feature uses RAID
level 2 to automatically keep the data on two partitions (located on different drives) synchronized by writing data to both partitions. If one of the drives fails, the data is still
available from the mirrored drive. You can use the Mirror option shown in Figure 5-4
to create a new mirror group or add the new partition to an existing mirror group. When
adding a partition to an existing mirror group, observe the following rules:

- Only NSS partitions can be mirrored.

- The new partition's data area must be the same size as the existing partition in
  the group. If the partitions are different sizes, NetWare automatically increases
  the Hot Fix area of the larger partition to make the data areas the same size.

- The partitions you add to a group cannot be part of an existing partition
  group; they must be individual mirrored objects.

The term "duplexing" describes the process of mirroring disk partitions that exist on separate physical disks on separate controller cards, whereas "mirroring" means that the separate drives are attached to the same controller card. By using two controller cards, duplexing provides faster speeds and continuous operation in the event of a controller card failure. For example, to ensure maximum speed and reliability, an administrator could attach two 60 GB drives to separate controller cards on the server to duplex the SYS and DATA partitions (see Figure 5-5). If one of the drives or controllers fails, the system continues reading and writing to the other drive. When the problem is fixed, NetWare automatically rebuilds the new drive so that the two drives are the same.

The process of enabling duplexing is the same as mirroring; the only difference is that the two partitions are located on disks attached to different controller cards.

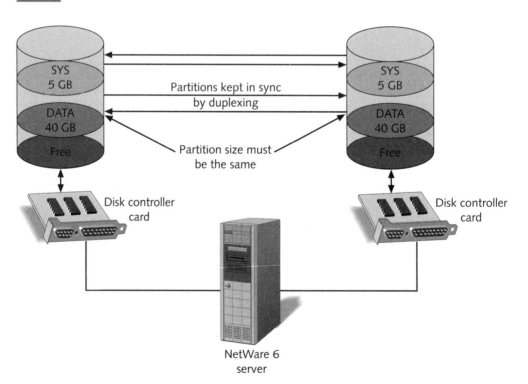

**Figure 5-5** Duplexing partitions

## Storage Pools

After a disk has been partitioned, the next job in setting up an NSS file system is creating one or more storage pools. As shown in Figure 5-6, **storage pools** are created from disk partitions and can be extended by adding disk partitions. After space from a disk partition is added to a storage pool, it cannot be removed without deleting the storage pool. When a disk partition is added to a storage pool, the amount of free space in the pool is increased by the size of the disk partition. If you're adding a new disk partition from a second drive to an existing storage pool, consider mirroring or duplexing the new partition on another disk to prevent a drive failure from bringing down the entire storage pool. Leaving some unpartitioned space on a new drive gives you the option of extending a storage pool without adding another drive. The space in the storage pool is then divided into one or more NSS logical volumes. During installation, a storage pool named SYS is created for the SYS volume to hold operating system files and programs. To separate the operating system files from the organization's data, the network administrator must create one or more additional storage pools.

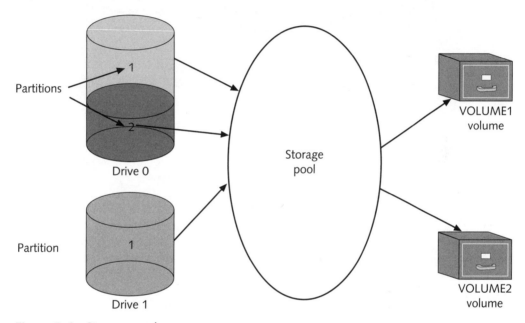

**Figure 5-6**    Storage pools

  You can have only one storage pool on a partition that you set up, but you can place unlimited logical volumes in the storage pool array. Storage pools can be increased in size by adding space from disk partitions, but they cannot be reduced.

## Volumes

**Volumes** are the basic storage unit that the network file system uses to give users access to network directories and files. NetWare 6 supports traditional volumes and the new NSS volumes. **NSS volumes** are usually preferred over traditional volumes because they offer additional capacity and high-speed mounting. Table 5-1 compares NSS and traditional volumes.

**Table 5-1** NSS Versus Traditional Volumes

| Feature | Traditional Volume | NSS Volume |
| --- | --- | --- |
| Maximum number of volumes | 64 | 255 |
| Maximum number of files | 16 million | Unlimited |
| Memory required to mount 20 GB volume | 320 MB of RAM | 32 MB of RAM |
| Mounting speed | Several minutes for large volumes | Less than one minute, even for very large volumes |
| Support for file compression | Yes | Yes |
| Support for block suballocation | Yes | No |
| Support for large block sizes (more than 4 KB) | Yes | No |
| Support for clustering | No | Yes |
| Support for data shredding | No | Yes |
| Support for user space restrictions | Yes | Yes |
| Support for directory space restrictions | Yes | Yes |
| Support for hot fixes | Yes | Yes |
| Support for automatic error correction and data recovery | No | Yes |
| Support for Modified File List feature | No | Yes |
| Software RAID support | No | Yes |

As listed in Table 5-1, before NSS, the traditional file system supported up to 64 volumes per server and 16 million files per volume. In contrast, NSS3 supports up to 255 mounted volumes per server and a virtually unlimited number of files per volume.

The increased speed of mounting NSS volumes on the server is a benefit that network administrators will appreciate. In the past, mounting a volume involved loading the file allocation table (FAT) into the server's memory. On large volumes, this process could take several minutes and require megabytes of RAM; for example, a 10 GB volume could take 160 MB of RAM to mount. Instead of a large FAT, NSS uses a more memory-efficient file allocation system called **balanced trees (B-trees)**. Using B-trees, large volumes of over 400 million files can be mounted in just seconds and require a maximum of only 32 MB of RAM. In addition, with the B-tree system, NetWare can retrieve any file blocks that are not memory in just four processor cycles, making NSS much faster than previous file system versions.

## NSS Volumes

NSS volumes are logical divisions of an NSS storage pool and are contained in one or more disk partitions. You can give NSS volumes a specific size, up to the storage pool's maximum size, or you can allot an initial size and then allow them to grow until they reach the size of the storage pool. Configuring a volume to allow this type of growth enables you to extend the volume size in the future by simply adding another partition to the storage pool. For example, assume that your SYS volume is the only volume in a storage pool consisting of one 10 GB disk partition. If the SYS volume is allowed to grow to the size of the storage pool, its maximum size will be 10 GB. If you add another 5 GB partition to the storage pool later, the SYS volume size can grow to a maximum of 15 GB.

In addition to faster mounting and lower server memory requirements, NSS volumes incorporate several new features and attributes that make them beneficial for network storage. Most of these features and attributes can be specified when you create the NSS volume (as shown in Figure 5-7) or later through the volume's Properties dialog box.

**5**

The new features in NSS3 volumes are not compatible with earlier NSS NetWare utilities, such as NWCONFIG and NSS Menu.

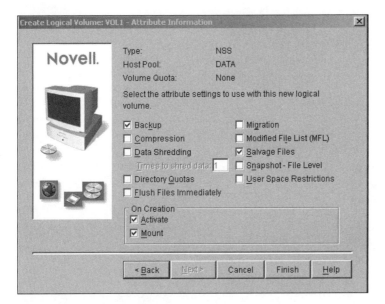

**Figure 5-7**    Setting options when creating a volume

As a Certified Novell Administrator (CNA), you should understand how the following NSS volume features benefit the network file system. In Chapter 8, you'll learn how to use ConsoleOne to view and configure NSS volume features and attributes.

**Clustering**    Although mirroring and duplexing can provide fault tolerance if a drive or controller fails, the server's hardware could still cause loss of network services. To provide fault tolerance in the event of a server failure, NSS supports Novell's NetWare 6 Clustering Services. **Server clustering** allows volumes to be shared among two or more servers, as shown in Figure 5-8. Shared volumes are usually placed on a networked storage device that's attached to a high-speed **storage area network (SAN)**. As illustrated in Figure 5-8, a SAN is a specialized network that often uses very high-speed fiber cable to connect two or more servers to a storage system. If one of the clustered servers has a hardware failure, another server automatically takes over the role of making the data on the shared volume available to network users. The process of switching from the failed server to an operational server is called **failover** and occurs in a matter of seconds.

Another possible source of downtime is the failure of a disk drive in the network storage device. Networked storage devices usually use hardware-based RAID 5 technology to provide fault tolerance in case there's a hardware failure on one of the network storage device's disk drives.

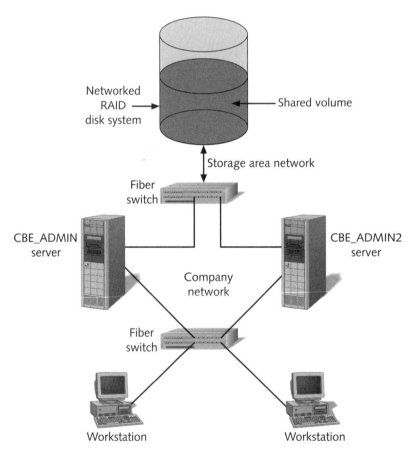

**Figure 5-8**    Server clustering

**Overbooking**    Assume that you have a 40 GB storage pool to be divided into two volumes: one for accounting data and another for sales data. After analyzing the storage needs for each department, you conclude that the Sales Department will eventually need 35 GB, but the Accounting Department could get by with 15 GB. Although no one volume can exceed the storage pool size, **overbooking** allows the sum of all volumes in the storage pool to be larger than the pool size; therefore, with this feature, you could create a SALES volume of 35 GB and an ACCOUNTING volume of 15 GB. If both volumes grow to their capacity, you could expand the storage pool size by adding more disk partitions. For example, assume you want to create a 1.5 GB volume named VOL3 within a storage pool named DATA, which has 1.6 GB available. When you create the new volume, you can specify its size in the selected storage pool, as shown in Figure 5-9. Notice that the Total Quotas column for the DATA pool has 2.2 GB already allocated to other volumes. With overbooking, you can specify a size for the new volume up to the capacity shown in the Available column, despite the total quotas exceeding the pool size. Of course, the storage pool will be filled before all volumes can reach their allocated sizes. If this happens, you can increase the pool size by adding more partitions.

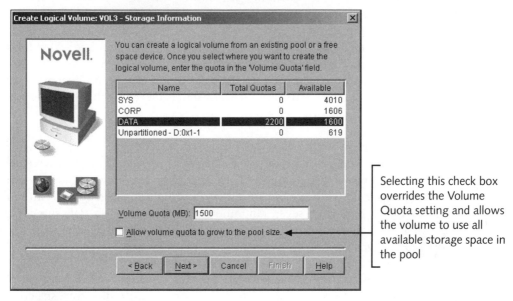

**Figure 5-9**    Overbooking volumes when specifiying the storage pool size

**Flush Files Immediately**    You can select the Flush Files Immediately attribute during or after volume creation. It causes a file to be saved to disk immediately after it is closed, instead of waiting for the next server disk write cycle. Writing closed files to disk immediately decreases the chance of data loss if the server has a hardware or power failure.

**File Snapshot**    In the past, backing up file servers that are accessed 24-7 created problems with getting good backups of open files. For example, if a backup program is running while a file is being changed, the backup will contain an incomplete copy of the new data. NSS offers a solution to this problem through the use of its file snapshot capability. To enable this feature, select the Snapshot – File Level attribute during or after volume creation. This option keeps the most recent copy of a closed file for backup purposes and ensures that if your data is lost between backup copies, you can restore a valid copy of the previously closed file.

**Modified File List**   Previous versions of the NetWare file system determined which files needed to be backed up by setting the Archive attribute flag (described in Chapter 10) whenever a file's data changed. This system required the backup utility to scan all filenames for attribute flags to determine which files to back up. When you create NSS3 volumes, you can optionally select the Modified File List attribute to have the volume track the names of any files that have changed since the last backup. Using this feature can speed up making a differential file system backup (where only the files that changed are backed up) of large volumes, as described in Chapter 8.

**File Compression**   A feature common to both traditional and NSS volumes is file compression. Like other volume attributes, although you can enable the File Compression attribute during or after volume creation with the ConsoleOne utility, once it's enabled, it cannot be turned off. When file compression is enabled on a volume, the server automatically compresses all files that have not been used for a specified period. By default, the server compresses files that have not been used for seven days if the compression produces at least a 5% savings in disk space. In Chapter 10, you'll learn how to change attribute settings to selectively enable or disable compression on individual files and directories.

**Data Shredding**   With the NetWare file system, you can easily recover deleted data files by using the NetWare salvage capability. If you need to destroy sensitive data for security purposes, however, enabling the Data Shredding attribute can add an extra level of security to your network file system by overwriting any purged files with random data patterns. By writing up to seven random patterns over the data, data shredding makes it impossible to access information from deleted files with disk editor software, such as Norton Disk Doctor.

**Disk Space Restriction**   By default, administrators could restrict space that traditional volumes used on the basis of individual users or an entire directory structure. Because managing user restrictions and directory quotas on very large volumes requires extra processing time, however, disk space restrictions are optional on NSS volumes. When creating NSS volumes, administrators can decide whether they want to be able to restrict volume space by selecting the User Space Restrictions or Directory Quota options when the volume is created or modified.

**Salvage Files**   As with disk space restrictions, administrators have the option of salvaging deleted files on NSS volumes. When a file is deleted from a volume that supports salvaging files, the filename and data are kept until the space is needed for new files. When new space is needed, the space from the oldest deleted files is used first. On a large volume, it could be months before the operating system reuses the space from a deleted file. Deleted files can be salvaged, or undeleted, until the operating system reuses the space or the file is purged. With NSS volumes, network administrators have the option of salvaging files on a volume-by-volume basis when a volume is created or modified. Although being able to salvage deleted files can be important on volumes that contain shared user data, the additional processing time required to maintain deleted files might not be worthwhile for volumes that contain application software or highly secure documents. For example, the SYS volume contains NetWare applications and system files that sometimes need to be updated. Updating the NetWare operating system with a new service pack deletes and replaces older program files with newer ones. It is highly unlikely you would want to salvage old system programs after installing a newer version because mixing the old software with the new software can cause system errors. In addition, many applications create and delete temporary files that you would not want to salvage. As a result, to save processing time on volumes such as SYS, you might want to turn off the Salvage Files attribute to improve system performance. Security can also be a reason to turn off this attribute. Some volumes may contain sensitive information, and salvaging the deleted files might mean that the information in them could be accessed. Turning off the Salvage Files attribute on these volumes can help increase security on deleted files.

## Traditional Volumes

Although NSS volumes offer many advantages over traditional volumes, when you upgrade a NetWare server to NetWare 6, any existing volumes remain traditional. Traditional volumes can be converted to NSS volumes by creating an NSS volume and transferring data from the traditional volume to the new NSS volume. Because traditional volumes are created directly from disk partitions, they do not offer the flexibility and scalability of NSS volumes that are created from storage pools. When creating traditional volumes, certain options, such as block size and suballocation, are not available on NSS volumes. Data is written to the disk in units called blocks. A **block** is the amount of data written to or read from the disk at one time. Block size is set when a storage pool or traditional volume is created and ranges from 4 KB to 64 KB. Although the block size on storage pools is automatically set to 4 KB when the storage pool is created, you can set the block size on traditional volumes when you create the volume. Larger block sizes can speed up disk access because it takes fewer disk requests to read or write large files. As a result, network administrators often prefer to use large block sizes for traditional volumes containing large files, such as those used in desktop publishing or other graphical presentation applications.

In addition to customizing the block size, traditional volumes offer a suballocation feature not currently available with NSS volumes. Without suballocation, each block in a volume can be assigned to only one file, meaning that small files on volumes with large block sizes waste disk space; for example, if you stored a 1 KB file on a volume with 16 KB blocks, 15 KB of disk space would be wasted. This problem is solved in traditional volumes by **suballocation**, which divides a block into 512-byte units as a way to store data from multiple files in the same block. When using suballocation, a file must always start at the beginning of a block; other files can then use the space remaining in the block as necessary. Figure 5-10 illustrates using suballocation to store three files on a traditional volume named VOL1. File1 requires 2.5 KB and occupies the first five suballocation units in Block 1.

File2 requires 1.5 KB and occupies the first three suballocation units in Block 2. File3 requires 7 KB and uses all of Block 3, along with three suballocation units in Block 1 and three suballocation units in Block 2.

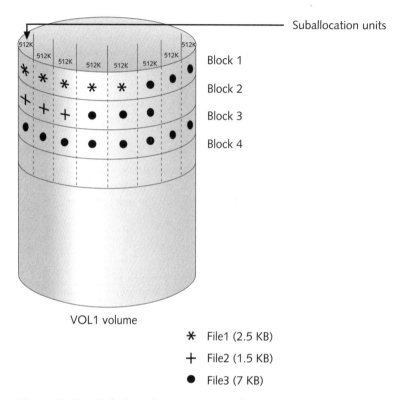

VOL1 volume

✻  File1 (2.5 KB)

╋  File2 (1.5 KB)

●  File3 (7 KB)

**Figure 5-10**  Suballocation in traditional volumes

## Viewing NSS Information

As a network administrator, you need to know how much space has been used on a volume so that you can make decisions about the location of new network directories and plan for system expansion. Before NetWare 6, viewing and managing file system information often required the administrator to use the NWCONFIG utility from the server console. With NetWare 6, administrators can create, manage, and view disk partitions, storage pools, and volumes from a workstation with the Windows-based ConsoleOne utility or through a Web browser running the NetWare Remote Manager utility. In Chapter 13, you'll learn how to use Remote Manager to monitor and maintain the server environment and access server and file system information. In Chapter 8, you'll learn how to use ConsoleOne to view information on partitions, storage pools, and Volume objects.

A Volume object represents each NetWare volume in the eDirectory system. These objects play an important role in eDirectory by linking eDirectory tree objects and the network file system. Before you can use ConsoleOne to access the network file system, you need to have an eDirectory object for each physical network volume. These eDirectory Volume objects are created during the NetWare installation and, by default, are placed in the same container as their NetWare server. For example, the default Volume object name for the SYS volume on the CBE_ADMIN server is CBE_ADMIN_SYS. You might want to create additional Volume objects in other contexts to improve access to data and applications. After an eDirectory Volume object has been created, you can view configuration information about the volume or access its directories and files by selecting the Volume object from the eDirectory database.

# Directories and Subdirectories

The storage space in each NetWare volume can be organized into directories and subdirectories. A **directory** is a logical storage area on a volume. A **subdirectory** is a further division of a directory. In Windows, directories are called **folders**. Creating directories within a NetWare volume is like hanging folders in the drawer of a file cabinet. Directories and subdirectories help you keep files organized in a volume, just as folders help you organize files in a file cabinet's drawer. An important network administrator responsibility is designing a directory structure for each volume that separates software and data according to functionality and use. NetWare's SYS volume contains several system-created directories that play important roles in the operation of the NetWare server. Novell also recommends an additional set of directories to help build a suitable directory structure for organizing software and data files. These directories are discussed in the following sections.

## System Directories

When you install NetWare 6, a number of system directories (see Figure 5-11) are created to store system files and utilities. To become a CNA, you need to understand how NetWare uses these required directories and where certain types of NetWare system files are stored. This section explains these directories and provides examples of their use in NetWare.

The actual system-created directories on your server can vary based on installation options, so the structure of your SYS volume might be different from the one shown in Figure 5-11.

The SYS:Login directory contains files and programs that can be accessed before logging in. Think of this directory as NetWare's reception area. Just as you enter a reception area when you first go into a business office, when a user first connects to the network, he or she is attached to the Login directory of a NetWare server. Workstations gain access to the Login directory only and have limited access to files and programs stored in that directory.

Many network administrators like to use the SYS:Login directory to store common files and programs used by many workstations during the startup process. With this method, you can update new releases of programs simply by copying the new software into the Login directory rather than copying it to each workstation's hard disk drive.

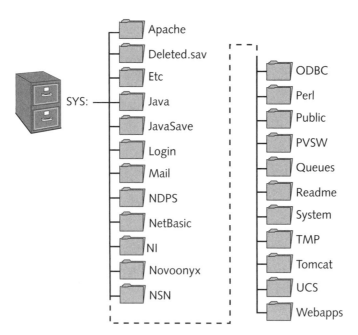

**Figure 5-11**    NetWare system-created directories

The SYS:Public directory contains utility programs and files that are available to all network users after they have logged in. Many of these programs and files are necessary for users to access and use network services. The NDIR.exe, NLIST.exe, WHOAMI.exe, NCOPY.exe, and LOGOUT.exe programs are examples of NetWare utilities that can be run from the Public directory. For a network administrator, the Public directory is like a toolbox, containing many utilities you need to perform such network tasks as creating new users, managing files, assigning access rights, and working with printers.

The SYS:System directory contains NetWare operating system files and utilities that are accessible only to users such as Admin users who have been given supervisory privileges on the network. Novell uses the dollar symbol ($) in all filenames that contain system information. For example, the Sys$Log.err file is the system error log.

The SYS:Etc directory contains TCP/IP configuration files. Examples of files stored in the Etc directory are Hosts and Hostname. The Hosts file stores the names and IP addresses of computers on the network, and the Hostname file contains the DNS name of the NetWare server. Log files used to record entries from IP services, such as DNS, and the NetWare console are also found in this directory.

In NetWare 6, the SYS:Mail directory is used for backward-compatibility with the NetWare 3 bindery, which used the Mail directory to hold a subdirectory for each user.

As Figure 5-11 shows, in addition to the required directories, many other system directories are created on the SYS volume. Table 5-2 describes the most common directories created during a typical system installation. As a CNA, you should be aware of these directories and their purposes.

**Table 5-2**   NetWare System Files

| Directory | Description |
|---|---|
| Apache | Contains system files for the Apache Web server, which is used to host many OneNet services, including Novell NetStorage and Novell Portal Services. |
| Deleted.sav | Contains deleted files from directories that no longer exist. |
| Etc | Contains sample configuration files for TCP/IP-based protocols. |
| Java | Stores support files for Java language applications used on the server. |
| JavaSave | Stores support files for Java language applications used on the server. |
| Login | Contains files and programs used to log in. |
| Mail | Used for backward-compatibility with earlier NetWare versions. |
| NDPS | Contains support files and software for Novell Distributed Print Services (NDPS). |
| NetBasic | Contains system files needed to support the NetBasic language applications. |
| NI | Contains NetWare server installation files. |
| Novoonyx | Contains installation and support files for Novell's Enterprise Web Server. |
| NSN | Contains Novell Script for NetWare files. |
| ODBC | Contains driver files for ODBC.ini based software. |
| Perl | Stores Web Server scripts written in the PERL language. |
| Public | Contains system utilities, such as NetWare Administrator, and support files. |
| PVSW | Contains client license files. |
| Queues | Contains print queue storage areas. |
| Readme | Used to store system Readme files. |
| System | Contains operating system files. |
| Tomcat | Contains files related to configuring and running the Tomcat Servlet Engine. |
| UCS | Contains a variety of NetWare Loadable Modules (NLMS) used by the NetWare server. |
| Webapps | Contains HTML and other files needed for remote management of Novell applications, such as Novell NetStorage. |

**5**

To help users recover lost files, a network administrator should be aware of the purpose of the Deleted.sav directory. The SYS:Deleted.sav directory is automatically created on each NetWare volume and is the part of the NetWare file recovery system that allows a file to be recovered even after the directory that contained the file has been deleted. When files are deleted from a NetWare volume, the blocks on the hard disk that contained the file's information are not immediately reused (as would happen on your local DOS drive). Instead, as NetWare requires more disk space, it reuses disk blocks from the files that have been deleted the longest, so you can recover files even after they have been deleted for some time. Normally, a file must be recovered in the directory from which it was deleted, but if that directory has been removed, you might still find the file in the Deleted.sav directory. In Chapter 8, you'll have an opportunity to practice salvaging deleted files.

## Suggested Directories

The required directories are automatically created during installation and give the NetWare operating system the storage areas it needs to perform its functions. In addition to the required directories, an organization will probably need storage areas in the NetWare server disk volumes. The network administrator is responsible for planning, creating, and maintaining the directory structure for organizing the network's data and software on the NetWare server. Novell suggests that in addition to the required directories, three basic types of directories should be part of an organization's file system: application directories, user home directories, and shared directories. The following sections explain how these directories, shown in Figure 5-12, can be used to meet an organization's storage needs.

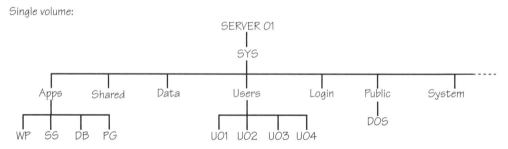

**Figure 5-12**   Novell-suggested directories

**Application Directories**   Network administrators must create directories and subdirectories for the applications and data that network users need. The first rule in organizing directories is to keep data and software separate whenever possible. This means you need to define a directory for each software application stored in the NetWare server. Software applications fall into two basic categories: general-purpose packages, such as Microsoft Word, Microsoft Excel, and Lotus 1-2-3, and special-purpose or vertical applications, such as payroll or order-entry software. Often many users in an organization need general-purpose software, so these applications are usually stored in directories on the server's SYS volume. Special-purpose applications are often restricted to small groups of users or departments; such applications contain their own data directories and files and sometimes require large amounts of data storage. To restrict access or keep the SYS volume from filling up, some network administrators store special-purpose applications, such as payroll or inventory, in a separate data volume.

**Home Directories**   Each user needs a private **home directory** in which to store files and documents. When planning disk storage needs, anticipate the space users need to store personal projects and files for their work. Generally, only the owner of a home directory has access rights to it; store files needed by multiple users in shared directory areas. The location of user home directories depends on the design of the directory structure. If the server has only one volume (SYS), the home directories can be placed in a general-purpose directory named Home or Users, as shown in Figure 5-12. Alternatively, you can place Home or Users (and all other data subdirectories) in a Data directory, as Figure 5-13 shows. User home directories can also be separated by workgroup, as described later in the "Organizing the DATA Volume" section.

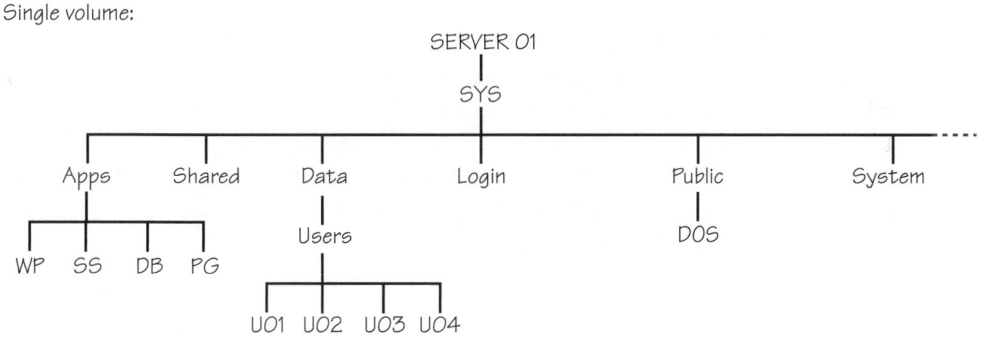

Single volume:

**Figure 5-13**    Using a Data directory

If the server has more than one volume, use the additional volumes for data storage, and locate the home directories there, as shown in Figure 5-14.

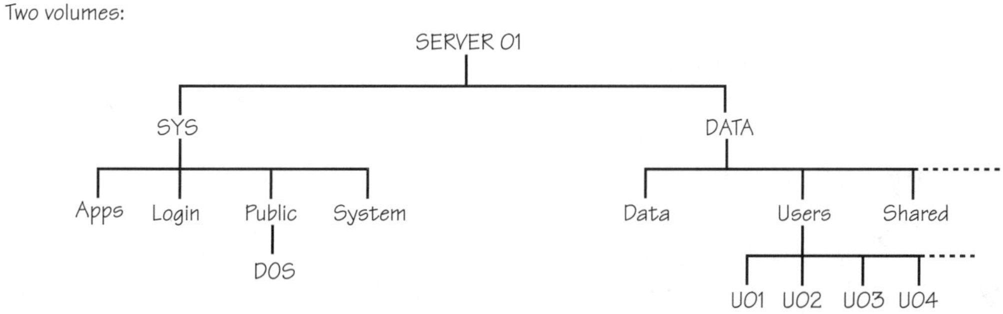

Two volumes:

**Figure 5-14**    Using a DATA volume

User home directories should be named with the user's login name so that the network administrator can assign a drive letter to the user's home directory when the user logs in. In Chapter 12, you'll learn how to use NetWare login scripts to automate the process of mapping drives to user home directories.

**Shared Directories**    An important benefit of using a network is being able to share files. As a network administrator, you need to establish shared work directories that allow multiple users to work with common files and documents. Shared work directories enable one user to save a file and another user working on the same project to access it. Word-processing documents and spreadsheet program worksheets stored in a shared directory are available to only one user at a time. Special software is needed to let multiple users access a file at the same time, to prevent one user's changes from overwriting someone else's changes. Figure 5-12 shows a general-purpose shared directory named Shared that's available for all users. Later in the "Design the Directory Structure" section, you'll learn how to design a departmental directory structure that includes shared directories for each workgroup.

**Web Service Directories** NetWare 6 offers a number of Web-based services for accessing information from the Internet. Some of these services, such as Enterprise Web Server, FTP Server, and iFolder, require special directories to be created during installation. Enterprise Web Server and FTP Server can be used to host a company Web site, and the iFolder service allows users to synchronize files stored on local computers with the server. If you are planning to implement any of these services, you need to allocate a storage space for the service on a NetWare volume.

## Files

Files contain the actual blocks of data and software that can be loaded from the disk storage system into the computer's RAM. Every NetWare volume contains a **directory entry table (DET)** and a file allocation table (FAT) to keep track of each file's name and location on the disk volume. The DET also stores file attributes and access rights. Access rights control what operations a user can perform on a file or directory. Attributes are special flags that identify how the file is to be viewed or processed. Examples of common file attributes used in DOS and Windows are Read-Only, Hidden, and System. NetWare has additional attributes, such as Sharable and Delete-Inhibit. In Chapter 10, you'll learn more about NetWare file access rights and attributes.

## Directory Paths

To access files, you need to specify the location of the directory or file in the NetWare file system. The **default drive** and **default directory** are the drive and directory you are currently using. A **directory path** is a list of file system components that identifies the location of the directory or file you want to access. A **complete directory path**, also called an **absolute directory path**, contains the NetWare server's name, volume name, directory, and all subdirectories leading to the target object. For example, the complete path to the U01 home directory shown in Figure 5-12 is SERVER01/SYS:Users\U01. A partial directory path, also called a **relative directory path**, lists only the locations leading from the default directory to the target object. Assume, for example, that your default directory is the SYS volume. In this case, the partial directory path is specified as \Users\U01. Network administrators often need to use both complete and partial paths when working with the NetWare file system, whether they're using Windows utilities or DOS. To drill down into folders to locate a file, you need to know which folders to look into.

### Complete Path

When specifying the complete directory path to an object, start with the NetWare server's name followed by a slash and then the name of the volume followed by a colon. Next, specify directories and subdirectories by using a forward slash (/) or a backslash (\) to separate the directory and subdirectory names. Although you can add a slash between the volume and directory names, some programs misinterpret the volume name as a directory name. Therefore, it is best *not* to include a slash after the colon in a volume's name.

To avoid confusion when you enter DOS paths (or enter paths into the Windows Run dialog box), consistently use backslashes between directory and subdirectory names in NetWare paths because DOS does not accept forward slashes as part of directory paths on local disk drives.

Windows command prompts normally do not accept NetWare complete directory paths because they contain unfamiliar objects, such as the NetWare server name and volume name. For example, the following command output shows that the DIR command will display the directories in a NetWare path (here it is G:), but an attempt to use the COPY command to copy files from drive A: to Eleanor Franklin's home directory (EFRANKLN) fails because the COPY command does not recognize the SYS volume as part of the target directory path.

```
G:\> DIR USERS

Volume in drive G is SYS
Directory of G:\USERS

EFRANKLN       <DIR>          12-15-98      9:10a
SSAMLSN        <DIR>          12-15-98      9:10a
EPLANK         <DIR>          12-15-98      9:10a
MPINZON        <DIR>          12-15-98      9:10a
GSAKHARV       <DIR>          12-15-98      9:10a
JMORGAN        <DIR>          12-15-98      9:10a

G:\> COPY A:\*.* SYS:USERS\EFRANKLIN
The filename, directory name, or volume label syntax is incorrect.
```

The actual error message might vary based on your version of Windows.

The result of this COPY command is an error message that reads "The filename, directory name, or volume label syntax is incorrect." The Windows command prompt cannot correctly interpret SYS as a valid part of the directory path. The same is true when typing in a directory path, as in the Windows Run dialog box. Type G: in the preceding example, and Windows knows how to retrieve the information. Type CBE_ADMIN\SYS, however, and an error message appears stating that you have an incorrect path.

## Universal Naming Convention (UNC) Paths

NetWare directory paths can also be specified by using **Universal Naming Convention (UNC)** paths originally developed for Microsoft networks. A UNC path includes the server name preceded by two backslashes (sometimes called "wacks") and followed by the volume name and directory path preceded by backslashes. For example, the URL for the U01 home directory would be \\SERVER01\SYS\Users\U01. UNC paths can be used with both Windows and NetWare commands. For example, to copy all files from the A: drive to EFranklin's home directory, you could enter the command:

```
G:\> COPY A:\*.*   \\CBE_ADMIN\SYS\Users\EFranklin
```

## SYS File System eDirectory Objects

Three of the eDirectory objects you studied in Chapter 4 represent parts of the file system—the NetWare Server object, the Volume object, and the Directory Map object. Each NetWare server in the network is represented by a NetWare Server object. For NetWare 6 servers, the NetWare Server object is automatically created and added to the eDirectory tree when NetWare 6 is installed on the server. The server must be named at the time NetWare 6 is installed, and this name is used as the name of the NetWare Server object. In Chapter 6, you'll learn more about installing NetWare 6.

When a volume is created and named, NetWare also creates a Volume object and places it in the same context in the eDirectory tree as the NetWare Server object where the volume is physically located. The Volume object is named by combining the name of the NetWare server and the name of the volume. For example, when the SYS volume is created on Server01, a Volume object named Server01_SYS is placed in the same container holding the NetWare Server object Server01.

You can use eDirectory Volume objects in file system directory paths by typing the Volume object's relative or distinguished name followed by a colon and the directory path. For example, the path to EFranklin's home directory could be entered as this:

```
.CBE_ADMIN_SYS.CBE_LABS:Users\EFranklin
```

## DIRECTORY STRUCTURE

Once you understand the components of a file system, you can design a directory structure to meet an organization's processing needs. Designing a directory structure is like creating a blueprint for a building. Just as a blueprint helps a builder determine the construction details and necessary materials, a directory structure design helps a network administrator allocate storage space and implement the network file system. Designing the directory structure involves two steps:

1. Defining the directories and subdirectories needed

2. Placing those directories in the file system structure

Before you design an organization's directory structure, you need to analyze the processing needs of users in the organization to determine which directories will be needed. When creating the directory structure, be aware that there is no single best approach that all network administrators use. Instead, each network administrator develops his or her own unique style for defining and arranging directories. The following sections explain the concepts and techniques that will help you develop your own style for creating good directory structures.

## Define Workgroups

The first step in designing a directory structure is determining the storage needed for the services the NetWare server will provide to network users. To do this, you'll work with the information systems personnel at Cunningham, Burns, and Evans Laboratories (CBE Labs), the same company you worked with in Chapters 1 and 4.

To determine storage needs, start by examining an organizational chart to determine the computer users and any workgroups. On the CBE Labs organizational chart, you can immediately see three main workgroups: administration, publications, and testing and evaluation. In addition, administration can be divided into marketing, finance, personnel, and information systems. Testing and evaluation can be divided into hardware, software, database, and network.

## Define NetWare Server Use

Although small networks might have only one NetWare server, a typical network has two or more. When more than one NetWare server is on the network, each server's use must be defined. For example, Ted Simpson, the information systems manager at CBE Labs, has recommended installing two new NetWare 6 servers and upgrading the existing NetWare 5.1 server to NetWare 6. Management has approved buying the two new servers that will run the NetWare 6 operating system and upgrading the existing NetWare 5.1 server. Ted needs to decide how to use the three servers.

The purpose of CBE Labs is to test computer components and then report the results, so the main server needs are for the testing and evaluation workgroup and for the publishing workgroup. Ted decides to allocate one NetWare 6 server to testing and evaluation and one NetWare 6 server to publishing. This leaves administrative tasks and companywide requirements, such as e-mail, to be taken care of. Ted realizes that the testing and evaluation workgroup will need all the capacity of its NetWare server, but the publishing workgroup will use only part of its server capacity. By allocating one NetWare 6 server as a combined administration/publishing server, many administration needs can be filled. However, the Finance Department needs resources for the accounting system. This system is already running on the NetWare 5.1 server. Ted decides to leave the accounting application on the NetWare 5.1 server and then upgrade that server to NetWare 6 in the future.

Many network administrators create naming schemes for the NetWare servers in their networks. As you learned in Chapter 4, because CBE Labs President Joseph Cunningham served as an officer in the U.S. Navy, CBE Labs named its original server after the U.S. Navy aircraft carrier *Ranger*. However, in an attempt to make server names more meaningful, Ted instructed David Doering, the network administrator, to name the new servers based on their function and location. For example, the administration/publishing NetWare 6 server will be named CBE_ADMIN, and the testing and evaluation NetWare 6 server will be named CBE_EVAL. The NetWare Server Planning Form in Figure 5-15 shows the three servers, their proposed functions, and the volumes they will contain.

 Underline characters cannot be used in a server name if that name will be used for a DNS server.

| NetWare Server Planning Form | | | |
|---|---|---|---|
| **Created By:** | *Ted Simpson* | *Date:* | *9/15/03* |
| **Organization:** | *CBE Labs* | | |
| **NetWare Servers:** | | | |
| **NetWare Server Name:** | *CBE_ADMIN* | | |
| **NetWare Operating System:** | *6.0* | | |
| **Volumes:** | *SYS* | | |
| | *DATA* | | |
| | *CDROM* | | |
| | | | |
| **Purpose:** | *CBE_ADMIN is the main administration and publishing NetWare server.* | | |
| **NetWare Server Name:** | *CBE_EVAL* | | |
| **NetWare Operating System:** | *6.0* | | |
| **Volumes:** | *SYS* | | |
| | *DATA* | | |
| | *CDROM* | | |
| | | | |
| **Purpose:** | *CBE_EVAL is the main testing and evaluation labs NetWare server.* | | |
| **NetWare Server Name:** | *RANGER* | | |
| **NetWare Operating System:** | *5.1* | | |
| **Volumes:** | *SYS* | | |
| | | | |
| | | | |
| | | | |
| **Purpose:** | *RANGER is the secondary administration NetWare server and is used for accounting applications and data.* | | |

**Figure 5-15**    CBE Labs NetWare Server Planning Form

Both of the new servers, CBE_ADMIN and CBE_EVAL, have two hard drives, which will become a SYS volume and a DATA volume. Each also has a CD-ROM drive, and NetWare 6 will treat a CD-ROM in this drive as a volume. Each CD-ROM will have a separate volume name, but for planning purposes these volumes will be referred to as CDROM. The existing NetWare 5.1 server, RANGER, already has a large SYS volume that will be updated to NetWare 6.

## Define Directories

After you identify the network users and workgroups, you need to determine—through discussions with the users and department managers—what applications and data storage areas they will need. Getting users involved early in the directory design process helps ensure that the result will serve their needs.

Directories can be divided into four general categories: general-purpose applications, vertical applications, shared data, and home directories. A **general-purpose application** is a software program—such as a word processor, spreadsheet, or CAD product—that many different users access to create and maintain their own files and documents. A **vertical application** is a software program that performs a specialized process, such as payroll, order entry, or manufacturing requirements planning. Vertical applications are normally restricted to a department or a limited number of users and give multiple users access to shared database files in the application's directory structure.

Shared data areas enable users to exchange files by saving the files where multiple users can access them. In designing directory structures, a network administrator can include a **local shared directory**, which restricts access to shared files to the users of the workgroup concerned with them. The network administrator can also provide a **global shared directory** so that workgroups can share files.

As described in Chapter 1, NetWare 6 includes new OneNet services that help make data more accessible to users, independent of the network or operating system they are using. One of these utilities, called iFolder, allows users to keep data on their local workstation or laptop synchronized with data stored centrally on the server. Keeping data synchronized with the server makes centralized backups and access to information from multiple locations possible. To implement iFolder, you must identify a volume for storing the centralized data for all users. When planning the network file system, the network administrator needs to identify the volume to be used for iFolder data and the amount of space to be allocated.

You will follow this process for CBE Labs. Ted Simpson has discussed network use with the CBE Labs staff and has gathered the following information:

- The Finance Department uses a payroll application for weekly payroll processing. In addition, all finance users use a spreadsheet package to work on budgets, and only the finance users share these budget spreadsheet files.

- Each user in testing and evaluation has his or her own computer and uses it to access test results stored in a specialized Structured Query Language (SQL) database. The testing and evaluation users periodically share word-processing document files when working together on a report.

- Testing and evaluation users have a specialized hardware analysis program that they use to evaluate hardware.

- The publishing personnel use word-processing and desktop publishing software to work on shared documents such as the company's main publication, *The C/B/E Networker*. Publishing personnel also work with the testing and evaluation personnel to help format and print special test reports for customers.

- All staff members at CBE Labs need access to a word-processing program to produce correspondence and memos. To make work easier, everyone would like to share common word-processing templates, forms, and customer lists.

- All staff members at CBE Labs need access to the company's e-mail program, a shared fax program, and Internet tools.

- CBE Labs has purchased a Windows XP software suite, Office XP, which includes a word processor, an electronic spreadsheet, a presentation graphics program, and a database program. Enough licenses were purchased so that everyone at CBE Labs can use the suite.

- Because several users need to be able to access network files from their laptop computers while away from the office, Ted has decided to implement the iFolder service on the CBE_ADMIN server and store the user files on its DATA volume. Placing the iFolder files on the DATA volume will help ensure that the SYS volume has adequate space for the operating system.

- CBE Labs plans to make certain information available to the Internet through its own Web server. Ted has provided a Web directory on the DATA volume to hold the Internet data.

Using information from his discussions, Ted has filled out the Directory Planning Form shown in Figure 5-16. Next, he needs to allocate volume space for the applications and data storage needs. The general-purpose software directories for CBE Labs include the software suite application that all employees need, the company's e-mail program, and the company's shared fax software. Vertical applications at CBE Labs include the payroll system that administration uses, the SQL database and the hardware analysis software that testing and evaluation uses, and the desktop publishing application that publishing uses. Ted decides to put application directories for the general-purpose software on the CBE_ADMIN_SYS volume, along with the desktop publishing program. He also decides to put the testing and evaluation applications on the CBE_EVAL_SYS volume and the accounting software on the RANGER_SYS volume. This arrangement puts each application on the NetWare server assigned to the workgroup using the software.

# Directory Planning Form

| Created By: | Ted Simpson | Date: | 9/15/03 |
|---|---|---|---|
| Organization: | CBE Labs | | |

## Workgroups:

| Workgroup Name: | Workgroup Members |
|---|---|
| Everyone | All CBE Labs users |
| Administration | 13 Administration users |
| Publications | 5 Publications users |
| Testing and Evaluation | 14 Testing and Evaluation users |
| Marketing | 3 Marketing users |
| Finance | 3 Finance users |
| Personnel | 1 Personnel user |
| Information Systems | 3 Information Systems users |
| Hardware | 3 Hardware users |
| Software | 3 Software users |
| Database | 3 Database users |
| Network | 3 Network users |

## Directories:

| Description | Type | Users | Estimated Size |
|---|---|---|---|
| WINOFFICE | general-purpose application | everyone | 3 GB |
| E-mail | general-purpose application | everyone | 3 GB |
| Fax | general-purpose application | everyone | 25 MB |
| Internet | general-purpose application | everyone | 50 MB |
| Payroll | vertical application | finance | 25 MB |
| SQL database | vertical application | testing & eval. | 100 MB |
| Hardware analysis | vertical application | testing & eval. | 50 MB |
| Desktop publishing | vertical application | publishing | 50 MB |
| CBE shared | shared data | everyone | 100 MB |
| Workgroup shared | shared data | 11 workgroups | 50 MB each |
| Test data | shared data | 4 testing & eval. workgroups | 100 MB |
| Reports | shared data | testing & eval. | 100 MB |
| Payroll data | shared data | finance | 250 MB |
| Desktop publishing documents | shared data | publishing | 100 MB |
| Budgets | shared data | 2 admin. workgroups | 25 MB each |
| Reports | shared data | 3 admin. workgroups | 25 MB |
| Home directories for each user | private data | 32 staff users | 40 MB per user |

**Figure 5-16**    CBE Labs Directory Planning Form

Ted plans to put data directories on the DATA volumes of the CBE_ADMIN and CBE_EVAL servers and on a Data directory of the RANGER server. Figure 5-16 shows these data needs. Shared directories include a Shared directory for all users that contains common word-processing forms, templates, and customer lists needed by all users; Budgets directories for general administration and finance; Reports directories for three administration workgroups, TestData directories for each testing and evaluation workgroup to hold the results of the groups tests; and a Reports directory for testing and evaluation. Ted will use separate workgroup-shared work directories to hold each workgroup's working papers. Although Ted could set up just one shared directory for the entire company, multiple directories will keep the files separate, making it easier for staff to locate and use only the files they need.

## Design the Directory Structure

After you have figured out which directories are needed, you are ready to design the layout and determine the location of the directories within the NetWare server's volumes. To design the directory structure for your NetWare server, you must first define the data and software directories your users need to perform their processing functions.

Then you organize these directories into a logical and easy-to-use structure that will provide a foundation for your network's file system. In the following sections, you learn how to analyze directory needs for an organization and see two major ways to organize a directory structure: department oriented and application oriented. You'll also find forms and techniques that will help you design and document your directory structures.

### The NSS Volume Design Form and Directory Design Form

As the example in Figure 5-17 shows, the NSS Volume Design Form is used to document each volume's directory structure and all directories branching from the root of the volume. This form can also show subdirectory structures, as shown in Figure 5-17's Market directory. In addition to laying out the directory structure, the NSS Volume Design Form contains fields for specifying total volume capacity and volume attributes, such as file compression and user space restrictions.

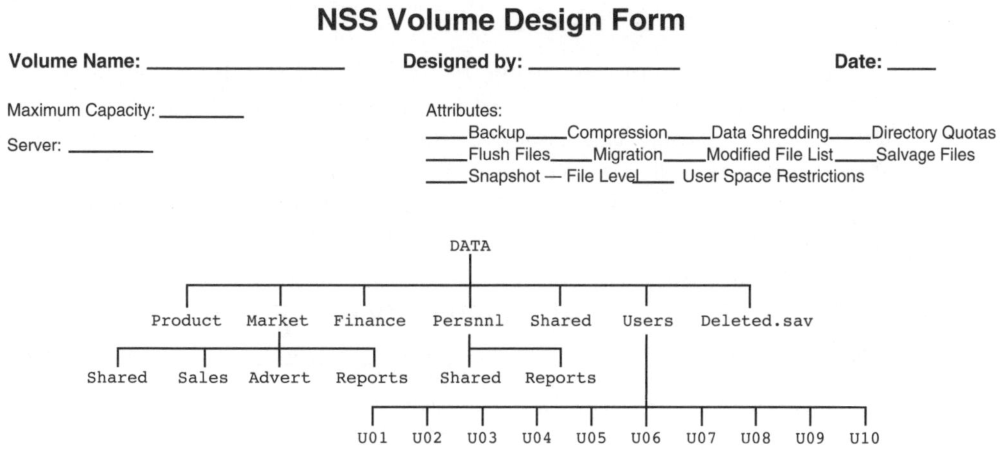

## NSS Volume Design Form

Volume Name: _____     Designed by: _____     Date: _____

Maximum Capacity: _____

Server: _____

Attributes:
____Backup____Compression____Data Shredding____Directory Quotas
____Flush Files____Migration____Modified File List____Salvage Files
____Snapshot — File Level____ User Space Restrictions

```
                              DATA
        ┌───────┬───────┬───────┬───────┬───────┬─────────┐
     Product  Market  Finance Persnnl  Shared  Users   Deleted.sav
    ┌────┬────┐      ┌────┐        ┌─────┬────┐
 Shared Sales Advert Reports    Shared Reports
                  ┌────┬────┬────┬────┬────┬────┬────┬────┬────┐
                 U01  U02  U03  U04  U05  U06  U07  U08  U09  U10
```

**Figure 5-17**   Sample NSS Volume Design Form

When diagramming a directory structure, often you'll find it's difficult to draw all directories and subdirectories for a volume on one sheet of paper. The NSS Volume Design Form does not have enough space for you to diagram more complex directories. However, you can use separate forms for subdirectories so that you can make alterations to a subdirectory without having to redraw an entire diagram. The example in Figure 5-18 shows how you could use the Directory Design Form for the Product directory structure (shown previously in Figure 5-17).

| Directory Design Form | | | |
|---|---|---|---|
| **Created By:** | *Ted Simpson* | **Date:** | *9–15–03* |
| **Volume:** | *SERVER01_DATA:* | **Capacity:** | *6 GB* |
| **Directory:** | *Product* | **Capacity:** | *350 MB* |
| **Subdirectory Structure Diagram** | | | |

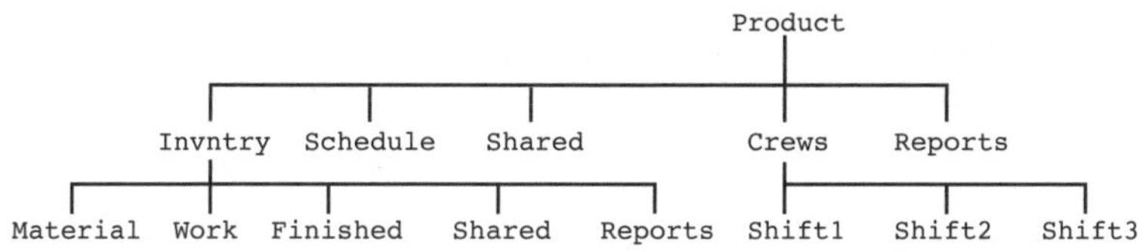

```
                              Product
            ┌───────┬───────┬───────┬───────┐
        Invntry Schedule Shared   Crews   Reports
      ┌────┬────┐     ┌────┐   ┌────┬────┬────┐
  Material Work Finished Shared Reports Shift1 Shift2 Shift3
```

**Figure 5-18**   Sample Directory Design Form

## Organizing the SYS Volume

The simplest method for organizing the SYS volume is to branch all directories from the root of the SYS volume, as illustrated in Figure 5-19's sample structure. The lack of hierarchy in this directory design, however, makes it difficult to group directories by function or to manage and assign special trustee rights. In addition, storing all files in the SYS volume can cause the NetWare server to crash if not enough disk space is available for the operating system.

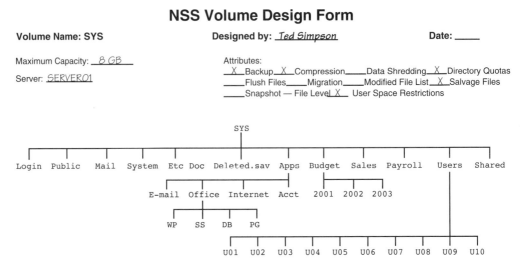

**Figure 5-19**    Simple SYS volume directory design

To avoid these pitfalls, many network administrators separate the SYS volume from data storage by using a DATA volume. This method not only frees up adequate space in the SYS volume for system functions, but also simplifies backup procedures and lets you perform maintenance activities on the DATA volume without taking the SYS volume offline.

In a multiple-volume design, many network administrators place directories for operating system and general-purpose applications in the SYS volume. Figure 5-20 illustrates this multiple-volume approach applied to the CBE Labs SYS volume structure on the NetWare server CBE_ADMIN. Notice that all the general-purpose application packages and special-purpose applications have been placed in separate subdirectories under the Apps directory, which will make it easy for the network administrator to assign access rights. The directories for the CBE Labs data will be located in a separate DATA volume. Because the data directories will grow in size, placing them in a separate volume will enable the network administrator to monitor and maintain adequate storage space in the DATA volume.

## NSS Volume Design Form

**Volume Name: SYS**                     **Designed by:** _Ted Simpson_                     **Date:** _____

Maximum Capacity: _8 GB_

Server: _CBE_ADMIN_

Attributes:
_X_Backup_X_Compression_____Data Shredding_X_Directory Quotas
_____Flush Files_____Migration_____Modified File List_X_Salvage Files
_____Snapshot – File Level_X_User Space Restrictions

```
                              SYS
   ┌──────┬──────┬──────┬──────┬──────────┬──────┬──────┬──────┐
 Login  Public System  Mail        Deleted.sav    Etc    Doc   Apps
                                 ┌──────┬──────┬──────┬──────┐
                                Fax  E-mail Internet WinOffice PagePub
                                              ┌────┬────┬────┐
                                             WP   SS   PG   DB
```

**Figure 5-20**    CBE Labs CBE_ADMIN_SYS volume

## Organizing the DATA Volume

Network administrators generally use two methods to organize directories in a DATA volume: by application or by department/workgroup. The method you select depends on your personal preference and on the size and type of processing the organization performs. Generally, smaller network file systems can be organized by using an application-oriented structure that branches all directories from the root of the volume. This keeps the design simple and easy to manage. In larger file systems with multiple workgroups and many data directories, often a departmental structure makes it easier to maintain security and locate data. A departmental structure places data directories as subdirectories under workgroup directories. In some cases, a combination of both methods work best for an organization.

 Whatever design method you use for data directories, a good rule of thumb is to have no more than six subdirectory layers and no more than 16 subdirectories in any one directory. This rule also helps reduce typing long names and allows you to see all directories on a computer monitor at the same time.

**Application-Oriented Structure** An **application-oriented structure** groups the directories by application rather than by department or workgroup. All user home directories, for example, can be placed in a common directory called Users. The shared directories can then be grouped according to use, and applications not placed on the SYS volume can be placed in separate directories at the root of the DATA volume. Figure 5-21 shows the application-oriented method applied to the DATA volume.

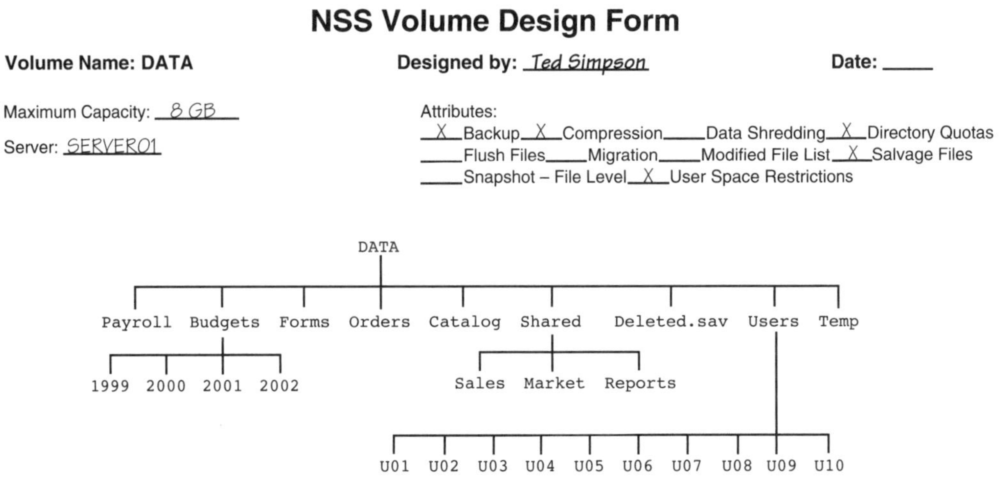
NSS Volume Design Form
Volume Name: DATA
Designed by: Ted Simpson
Date: ____
Maximum Capacity: 8 GB
Server: SERVER01
Attributes:
X Backup X Compression ____ Data Shredding X Directory Quotas
____ Flush Files ____ Migration ____ Modified File List X Salvage Files
____ Snapshot – File Level X User Space Restrictions
DATA
Payroll
Budgets
Forms
Orders
Catalog
Shared
Deleted.sav
Users
Temp
1999
2000
2001
2002
Sales
Market
Reports
U01
U02
U03
U04
U05
U06
U07
U08
U09
U10

**Figure 5-21** DATA volume with an application-oriented structure

The advantage of an application-oriented structure is that it's fairly shallow, which makes it easier to locate files without going through multiple layers of directories. In large directory structures, however, the shallow nature of the application-oriented structure can actually be a disadvantage because it's difficult to know which departments use which directories. In an application-oriented structure, the network administrator needs to make more trustee assignments because rights will not automatically be granted for users to access directories with the software applications they need.

**Departmental Structure** In a **departmental structure**, user home directories, shared work directories, and applications are located within the workgroups and departments that control them. Directories containing files available to all users are located at the root of the volume. Figure 5-22 shows the organization of directories for a DATA volume using a departmental structure. A Shared directory is located at the root of the DATA volume to contain files that the entire organization uses. The Shared work directories located in each workgroup's directory structure provide separate shared file access for each department. A major difference between the departmental- and application-oriented structures is the location of the user home directories. Notice in Figure 5-22 that the user home directories are located under each department directory instead of being placed together under a general Users directory.

**Combined Structure** It is also possible to combine the two approaches. A common way of doing this is to use the departmental structure for most of the volume organization but consolidate all user home directories in a common Users directory. This method has the advantage of maintaining a logical structure for creating directories associated with departmental functions while making user directories easier to manage by locating them in one place. CBE Labs will use this approach for the CBE_ADMIN_DATA: volume, as Figure 5-23 shows.

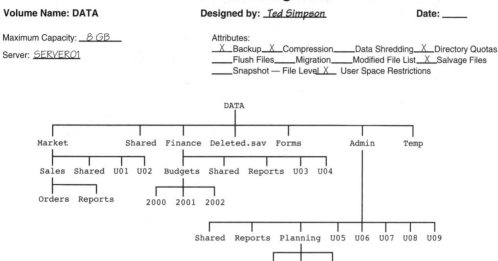

**Figure 5-22**    DATA volume with a departmental structure

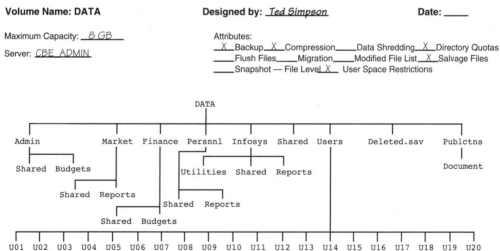

**Figure 5-23**    CBE_ADMIN_DATA volume with a combined structure

The other CBE Labs volumes will be organized the same way, as shown in the directory structures of the CBE_EVAL_SYS: and CBE_EVAL_DATA: volumes in Figures 5-24 and 5-25. The RANGER_SYS: volume follows the same guidelines but includes a Data directory because RANGER has no DATA volume. Figure 5-26 shows the RANGER_SYS: volume.

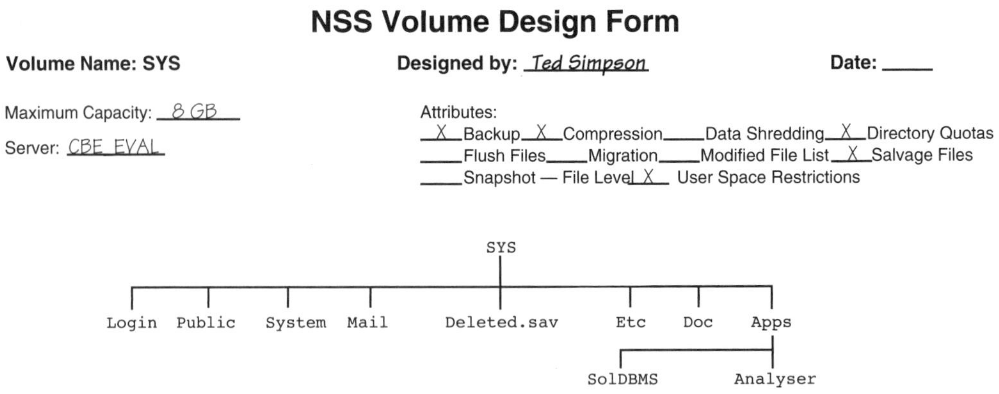
NSS Volume Design Form
Volume Name: SYS
Designed by: Ted Simpson
Date:
Maximum Capacity: 8 GB
Server: CBE_EVAL
Attributes:
X Backup X Compression Data Shredding X Directory Quotas
Flush Files Migration Modified File List X Salvage Files
Snapshot — File Level X User Space Restrictions
SYS
Login
Public
System
Mail
Deleted.sav
Etc
Doc
Apps
SolDBMS
Analyser

**Figure 5-24** CBE_EVAL_SYS volume

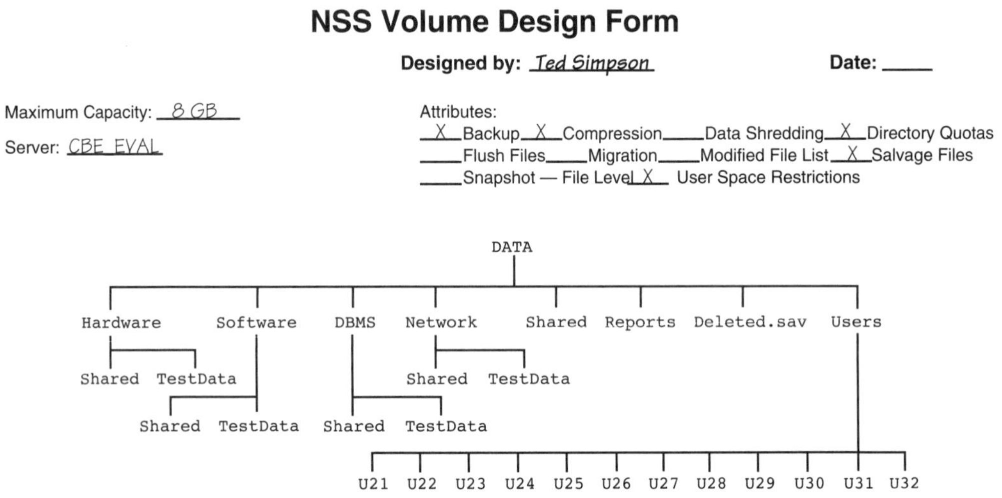
NSS Volume Design Form
Designed by: Ted Simpson
Date:
Maximum Capacity: 8 GB
Server: CBE_EVAL
Attributes:
X Backup X Compression Data Shredding X Directory Quotas
Flush Files Migration Modified File List X Salvage Files
Snapshot — File Level X User Space Restrictions
DATA
Hardware
Software
DBMS
Network
Shared
Reports
Deleted.sav
Users
Shared
TestData
Shared
TestData
Shared
TestData
Shared
TestData
Shared
TestData
U21 U22 U23 U24 U25 U26 U27 U28 U29 U30 U31 U32

**Figure 5-25** CBE_EVAL_DATA volume

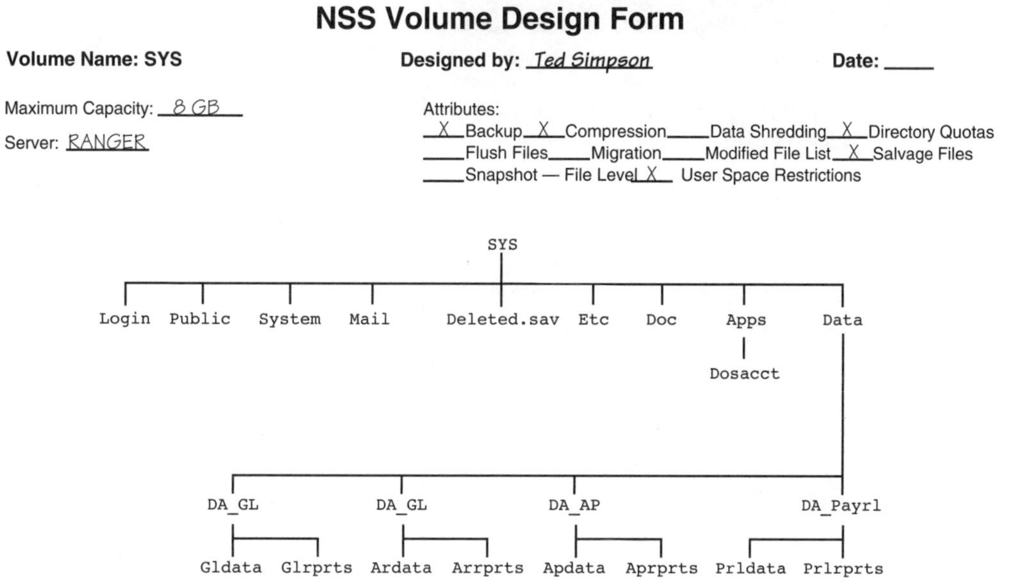

## NSS Volume Design Form

**Volume Name: SYS**                    Designed by: _Ted Simpson_                    Date: _____

Maximum Capacity: _8 GB_

Server: RANGER

Attributes:
_X_Backup_X_Compression____Data Shredding_X_Directory Quotas
____Flush Files____Migration____Modified File List_X_Salvage Files
____Snapshot — File Level_X_ User Space Restrictions

```
                              SYS
   ┌──────┬───────┬──────┬──────────┬─────┬─────┬──────┬──────┐
 Login  Public  System  Mail  Deleted.sav  Etc  Doc  Apps   Data
                                                      │       
                                                   Dosacct    

        ┌──────────────┬──────────────┬───────────────────────┐
      DA_GL          DA_GL          DA_AP                    DA_Payrl
    ┌────┴────┐    ┌────┴────┐    ┌────┴────┐          ┌────┴────┐
 Gldata  Glrprts Ardata  Arrprts Apdata Aprprts   Prldata  Prlrprts
```

**Figure 5-26**    RANGER_SYS volume

# NETWARE FILE AND DIRECTORY UTILITIES

NetWare provides several ways to create and manipulate files and directories and to view information on them, including Windows Explorer and the NetWare Services utility available through the Windows taskbar or by right-clicking Network Neighborhood on the Windows desktop. NetWare also maintains support for **command-line utilities**, programs you run by typing a command at the DOS prompt or in the Windows Run dialog box. One command-line utility that remains useful is NDIR. The following sections describe how to use Windows Explorer and NDIR to find information about the volumes and directory structures on a NetWare server.

## Windows Explorer

You can view NetWare volumes and their contents by opening Windows Explorer, selecting My Network Places, and then double-clicking the Novell Connections icon. You will then see your eDirectory tree object and the servers available to you (depending on your rights). Double-click any server, and the volumes within it appear in the pane on the right.

For volume information, such as space used, purgeable space (space taken up by deleted files, which could be reused), or the number of directory entries, right-click the volume name and choose Properties. If you click the NetWare Volume Statistics tab, volume and directory information are represented as pie charts, as shown in Figure 5-27.

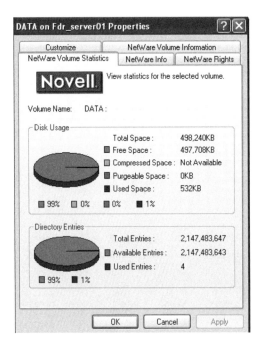

**Figure 5-27**    Checking volume information in Windows Explorer

You can use Windows Explorer to reorder files by access date, size, or extension. This can simplify a copy or delete operation for multiple files or directories. As a network administrator, you can also modify user rights to directories by right-clicking the directory, choosing Properties, and selecting the NetWare Rights tab.

For file information, right-click any file stored in the NetWare volume and choose Properties. As a network administrator, you can view and set rights for access to this file and change its attributes. You can view the file's attributes on the NetWare Info tab, as shown in Figure 5-28, or click the NetWare Rights tab to view or set file system rights.

## Command-Line Utilities

Although the majority of file system functions are most easily performed in Windows Explorer, there are times when command-line utilities are more efficient or can be used in script files to automate a process. Table 5-3 lists several commonly used command-line utilities.

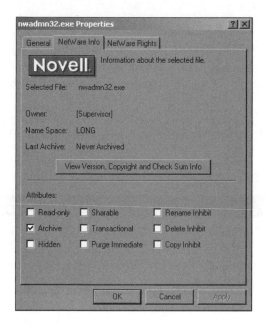

**5**

**Figure 5-28**   Checking rights and attributes in Windows Explorer

**Table 5-3**   Common Command-line Utilities

| Command | Description | Sample |
|---------|-------------|--------|
| CAPTURE | Used to redirect a physical printer port, such as LPT1, to a network print queue | To redirect the output from LPT1 to the print queue named LASER_Q with a timeout of 5 seconds and no banner:<br>CAPTURE Q=LASER_Q TI=5 NB |
| CX | Used to change or display the current context | To change the current context of your workstation to the CBE_Labs_Admin.CBE_LABS container:<br>CX  .CBE_Labs_Admin.CBE_LABS |
| FILER | A menu-based utility used to manage NetWare 3 file systems | |
| LOGIN | A command-line utility used to log in a new user | To log in as DDoering:<br>LOGIN .DDoering.InfoSystems.CBE_Labs_<br>Admin.CBE_LABS |
| LOGOUT | Logs the current user out of the network | |
| MAP | Maps a drive letter to a network path | MAP  L:=CBE_ADMIN_DATA:InfoSys |
| NDIR | Lists network directory information | See "The NDIR Command" section in this chapter |
| NCOPY | Copies files between NetWare volumes | NCOPY SYS:\APPS\*.*  DATA:APPS |
| NLIST | Lists information on eDirectory objects | NLIST PRINTER<br>NLIST VOLUME |

## The NDIR Command

NetWare's NDIR command in NetWare 6 is similar to, but much more powerful than, the DOS DIR command. For example, the DIR command does not list NetWare file attributes, such as last accessed or owner. This is the syntax of the NDIR command:

```
NDIR [path] [/options] [/?] [/VER]
```

As shown in the syntax, the NDIR command has several parameters that you can use, listed in Table 5-4.

**Table 5-4**    NDIR Command Parameters

| Parameter | Use This Parameter To: |
| --- | --- |
| path | See the directory path to the volume, directory, subdirectory, or file |
| /? | Access help about NDIR. If this parameter is used, all others are ignored. |
| /VER | See the version number of the NDIR command. If this parameter is used, all others are ignored. |

The NDIR command has many options for sorting and displaying files, such as by size and by date of last access. You can also display files created after or before a certain date. One of the most important NDIR options lets you display a list of files in directories and subdirectories by owner (that is, who created them), a capability not currently available with Windows Explorer. As an administrator, you will need this capability to identify which users are using space on the network in which files. To display a list of files by owner, enter the following command at the DOS command line:

```
NDIR /SORT OW
```

NetWare then lists the files in the current directory by owner in alphabetical order. If you want to include all subdirectories as well, enter this command:

```
NDIR /SUB /SORT OW
```

If the directory listing is long (which is likely), you can redirect the output to a file with this command:

```
NDIR /SUB /SORT OW >dirlist.txt
```

In this command, *dirlist.txt* can be any name you want, as long as it's a valid filename for your server. (NetWare places the file in the directory from which you ran the command. You can then read the file with Notepad or another text editor.)

After you have this list, you can examine it to determine who owns what files. You can then inform users of the files they have on the system and get feedback on which ones can be deleted. Often people forget they have created and stored files in various locations, and other users are reluctant to delete them, so the files take up space unnecessarily. A quick review using NDIR can find these files.

Table 5-5 lists some of the most useful options available with the NDIR command-line utility.

The /SORT option has a reverse function, /REV SORT *option*, in which *option* is one of the SORT options (AC, AR, CR, OW, SI, and so forth). For example, NDIR /REV SORT SI displays a list of files sorted from largest to smallest (the reverse of the /SORT SI command).

**Table 5-5** NDIR Options

| Option | Use This Option To: |
| --- | --- |
| /VOL | See volume information. |
| /SPA | See space information. |
| /DO | See a list of directories only. |
| /FO | See a list of files only. |
| /FI | See a list of every copy of the specified files in the current directory and the directories listed in the current path. |
| /SUB | Include all subdirectories below the specified directory. |
| /DA | See date information. |
| /D | See file detail information. |
| /R | See file attributes and user rights information. |
| /COMP | See file compression information. |
| /L | See long filenames in namespaces that support long filenames. |
| /MAC | See Apple Macintosh files. |
| /SORT | Sort the list of files in ascending order (A to Z, earliest to latest, smallest to largest). |
| /REV SORT *option* | Sort in descending order (Z to A, latest to earliest, largest to smallest). |
| /SORT AC | Sort by access date. |
| /SORT AR | Sort by archive date. |
| /SORT CR | Sort by creation or copy date. |
| /SORT OW | Sort by owner. |
| /SORT SI | Sort by size. |
| /SORT UP | Sort by last update date. |
| /SORT UN | Display without sorting (stop sorting). |

5

## The NetWare File Copy Utility

When you view your directories and files in Windows Explorer, you can copy them in a variety of ways:

- Drag and drop the file or directory to a new location.
- Right-click the file and select Copy, and then paste it to a new location.
- Right-click the file, and then select NetWare Copy.

The first two perform a standard Windows copy operation. The NetWare Copy option is quite different and should not be confused with Windows copy operations. NetWare Copy preserves the rights specified for the file, whereas Windows ignores them and does not place them on the new copy of the file. Also, with NetWare Copy, all file attributes are preserved, but with standard Windows copy procedures, NetWare file attributes are not carried over. A file attribute is a flag, stored in the directory along with the file's name and location, that gives the file certain characteristics, such as making it Read-Only, Hidden, or Sharable.

Many CNAs have found the DOS command line very efficient over the years. Many still use versions of DOS for brevity or because some industrial devices still support DOS. One utility to avoid is the DOS XCOPY function. You should always use NCOPY. One interesting behavior that contrasts these two utilities is that XCOPY must cache files in the client workstation's local memory during the read function and then write the data to the target after memory is full. If you are working with NCOPY, your client memory is not used for caching purposes.

## Renaming Directories

A network administrator sometimes needs to change the name of an existing directory or subdirectory to make it more meaningful or to avoid conflicts with other directory or filenames. You can right-click the directory name in Windows Explorer, choose Rename, and type in the new name of the directory.

## CHAPTER SUMMARY

- The basic components of the Novell Storage System (NSS) include partitions, storage pools, volumes, directories, and files.

- Storage pools are made up of one or more physical disk partitions. The volume is the logical division of the storage pool and is comparable to a file cabinet drawer in that it holds folders and files. Each server is required to have a minimum of one NSS volume named SYS consisting of at least 2 GB, with 4 GB recommended.

- When NetWare is installed on your server, the required SYS volume and system directories are created automatically. Some of the NetWare required directories include Login, Public, System, Mail, Etc, and Deleted.sav. Each serves a specific purpose.

- In addition to the directories created by NetWare, the network administrator should create directories for application software, shared data, and personal user home directories.

- There are two major methods of arranging directories: by application and by department. Application-oriented structures are grouped around applications; departmental structures are grouped around workgroups.

❏ A path is used to specify the location of a file or directory in the NetWare file system. A complete path contains all components of the directory structure leading to the specified file or directory.

❏ You can use command-line utilities or Windows Explorer to work with the NetWare file system. Novell Client for Windows adds some features to Windows to enhance working with the NetWare file system and allow you to access volume, directory, and file information on NetWare servers and to rename and delete files and directories from NetWare volumes.

# KEY TERMS

**absolute directory path** — Another name for a complete directory path, which identifies the location of a file or directory by specifying the path: NetWare Server/Volume:Directory\Subdirectory[\Subdirectory].

**application-oriented structure** — A directory structure that groups directories and subdirectories according to application or use rather than by department or owner.

**balanced trees (B-trees)** — The NSS file system storage access method used to provide fast access to files stored on NSS volumes.

**block** — When referring to a database, a collection of data records that can be read or written from the computer RAM to a storage device at one time. When referring to a hard disk, a storage location on the physical disk volume consisting of 4 KB, 8 KB, 16 KB, 32 KB, or 64 KB.

**command-line utility** — A NetWare utility that performs a specific function from the DOS prompt given specific command-line parameters. Examples are NDIR, NCOPY, and MAP.

**complete directory path** — Identifies the location of a file or directory by specifying the path: NetWare Server/Volume:Directory\Subdirectory[\Subdirectory].

**default directory** — The directory from which data will be accessed when no path is supplied.

**default drive** — The drive from which data will be accessed when no path is supplied.

**departmental structure** — A directory structure that groups directories and subdirectories according to the workgroup or department that uses or controls them.

**directory** — When referring to the network file system, a logical storage unit on a volume; called a "folder" in Windows.

**directory entry table (DET)** — A table on a storage device that contains the names and locations of all files.

**directory path** — A list of network file system components, such as the names of directories and subdirectories, identifying the location of data on a storage device.

**failover** — The process used in server clustering to automatically switch an NSS volume from a failed server to an operational server.

**folder** — When referring to the network file system or a user's workstation, the Windows term for a directory or subdirectory.

**general-purpose application** — An application package, such as a word processor or a spreadsheet, used to perform many different functions.

**global shared directory** — A directory in which all users in an organization can store and retrieve files.

**home directory** — A private directory in which a user typically stores personal files and works on projects that are not shared with other users.

**local shared directory** — A directory in which all users of a department or workgroup can store and retrieve files.

**Novell Storage Services (NSS)** — The file system used primarily by NetWare 6. In NSS, logical volumes are created from storage pools that consist of one or more disk partitions.

**NSS volume** — A logical division of a storage pool used to organize information in the NSS file system.

**overbooking** — The process in which the total space assigned to two or more NSS volumes exceeds the space available in the storage pool.

**partition** — A physical storage area on a disk drive that is formatted for a particular file system.

**relative directory path** — Identifies the location of a file or directory by specifying all directories and subdirectories starting from the user's current default directory location.

**server clustering** — A setup in which two or more servers can share a common disk system, making the data available in case one of the servers has a hardware failure.

**storage area network (SAN)** — A specialized network that often uses very high-speed fiber cable to connect storage devices to two or more servers.

**storage pool** — An NSS file system component used to group one or more partitions into a storage area that can be divided into one or more volumes.

**suballocation** — A method used on traditional volumes to save disk space by dividing blocks into 512-byte units as a way to store information from multiple files in the same block.

**subdirectory** — A division of a directory, when referring to the network file system.

**Universal Naming Convention (UNC)** — A naming system that specifies the path to a shared directory with two backslashes, the server name, a single backslash, and the name of the shared folder.

**vertical application** — A software application designed for a specific type of processing. Vertical applications are often unique to a certain type of business, such as a dental billing system or an auto parts inventory system.

**volume** — The major division of the NetWare file system consisting of the physical storage space on one or more hard drives or CD-ROMs of a file server.

# REVIEW QUESTIONS

1. Which of the following are logical divisions of NSS storage pools?

   a. pools

   b. partitions

   c. volumes

   d. containers

2. List the three major components of the NSS file system:

   _____

   _____

   _____

3. Which of the following volumes is required on all NetWare 6 servers?

   a. DATA

   b. SYSTEM

   c. SYS

   d. PUBLIC

4. Which of the following is *not* a directory created when NetWare is installed on a server?

   a. Etc

   b. Email

   c. NDPS

   d. Apache

   e. Webapps

5. Which of the following directories contains files and programs that can be accessed and run before logging in to the network?

   a. Public

   b. System

   c. Login

   d. Etc

6. Which of the following directories contains NetWare utility programs that are available to all users after they log in?

   a. Public

   b. System

   c. Login

   d. Etc

5

7. Which of the following directories contains operating system files that are not available to users?

   a. Public

   b. System

   c. Login

   d. Etc

8. List three types of directories that Novell suggests you create in the file system:

   _____

   _____

   _____

9. True or False: Larger file systems are easier to manage when using a departmental directory structure design.

10. What is the advantage of leaving some unallocated disk space when creating partitions for a NetWare 6 server?

11. Which of the following eDirectory objects is used to access the file system from eDirectory?

   a. root

   b. storage pool

   c. volume

   d. partition

12. Which of the following is a physical amount of storage on one or more hard disk drives or other storage media?

   a. root

   b. storage pool

   c. volume

   d. partition

13. Which of the following fault-tolerance capabilities should you consider before spanning a partition over multiple disk drives?

   a. hot fix

   b. duplexing

   c. clustering

   d. backup attribute

14. How many characters is the maximum length for a volume name?

   a. 12

   b. 15

   c. 50

   d. 255

15. Which of the following are *not* valid characters in a volume name? (Select all that apply.)

    a. $

    b. #

    c. ,

    d. (

    e. +

16. Which of the following directories contains files and utilities available only to the administrator?

    a. Public

    b. System

    c. Login

    d. Etc

17. Which of the following is not an option when creating NSS volumes?

    a. compression

    b. block suballocation

    c. salvaging files

    d. data shredding

18. Which of the following directories is created in each volume to contain deleted files?

    a. Salvage.sav

    b. System

    c. Deleted.sav

    d. Queue.sav

19. Under what conditions are files placed in the directory containing deleted files?

20. Which of the following system-created directories is used for backward-compatibility with NetWare 3 servers?

    a. Login

    b. Queues

    c. Mail

    d. Etc

21. Given the directory structure shown in Figure 5-29, write a complete path to the Jan02.wk1 file.

22. Use the directory structure in Figure 5-29 to write a UNC path to the directory containing the Catalog directory.

**5**

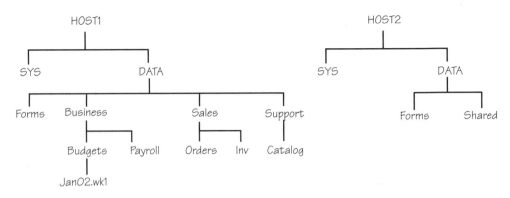

**Figure 5-29**   Sample directory structure

23. In a(n) _____ directory structure, the user home directories are located in a common directory called Users.

    a. departmental

    b. user oriented

    c. system oriented

    d. application oriented

24. Use the directory structure shown in Figure 5-29 to write the steps to change your current directory from the Forms directory on the NetWare server HOST1 to the Payroll directory on HOST1.

25. Which of the following is a disadvantage of storing data files in the SYS volume?

    a. Space on the SYS volume is needed for print queues.

    b. The SYS volume could fill up and halt server operations.

    c. The SYS volume has a maximum size of 4 GB.

    d. It's difficult for users to access data files on SYS without giving them Supervisor rights to the server.

## HANDS-ON PROJECTS

### Project 5-1: Documenting Your CBE Labs DATA Volume Structure

In this project, you use the Volume and Directory Design Forms (copied from Appendix B) to document the directory structure for your CBE Labs DATA volume, using the directory names and structure supplied in this chapter. You'll use the forms in Chapter 8 to create your CBE Labs directory structure. To keep your directory structure separate from other students, your Volume Design Form should show your structure on the STUDENTS volume within a subdirectory named CBEDATA in your ##DATA directory, as shown here:

```
CBE_ADMIN\STUDENTS volume

        ##DATA
          |
        CBEDATA
          |
```

## Project 5-2: Checking Volume Information

As a network administrator, you need to know how to find information to make such decisions as determining the location for installing a new application on the NetWare server. In this project, you use Windows Explorer and/or NDIR to obtain volume information about a NetWare server on your network. Include this information and the commands and steps you used in a memo to your instructor.

1. Use Windows Explorer and create a memo to your instructor that documents the following information for each volume on your classroom server:

   |  | Bytes | Percent Used |
   |---|---|---|

   Total volume space:

   Space used by entries:

   Deleted space not yet purgeable:

   Space remaining on volume:

2. Use NDIR to determine the following information about the SYS volume. Record the NDIR commands you use in your memo to your instructor.

   Amount of space in use by compressed files:

   Amount of space saved by compressed files:

   Amount of space available in the volume:

3. Calculate the available amount of unused disk space without any deleted files being purged, and include that amount in your memo.

4. Use the information from Step 3 to answer the following question: Will saving a 100 KB file on the SYS volume require reclaiming space from deleted files? Briefly explain your reasoning.

## Project 5-3: Checking Directory Space

Use Windows Explorer and/or NDIR to determine the amount of disk space available at the root of your NetWare server's SYS volume. Include this information and the commands and steps you used in a memo to your instructor.

## Project 5-4: Checking Directory Information

Use Windows Explorer or NDIR to determine the amount of disk space used by each directory on the root of your NetWare server's SYS volume. Include this information and the commands and steps you used in a memo to your instructor.

## Project 5-5: Checking Directory Structure

Use My Network Places to list the directory structure of the CBE_ADMIN\DATA: directory. Use a copy of the NSS Volume Design Form (see Figure 5-17) to document all subdirectories in the directory structure. Include this information and the commands and steps you used in a memo to your instructor.

## Project 5-6: Obtaining NetWare File and Directory Information

Create a memo to your instructor that contains the following information and the commands and steps you used:

1. Which volume contains the PG subdirectory?

2. All files with the filename extension .frm located in the CBE_ADMIN:DATA directory structure, including file attributes and owner information.

3. The total size of all files with the extension .exe that are located in the CBE_ADMIN:SYS\Public directory.

4. The number of files in the SYS:Etc directory.

5. The NDIR command you use to display all files with the file extension .frm located in the CBE_ADMIN\DATA:Publctns directory structure, displaying files only.

6. The NDIR command you use to display all files with the file extension .frm located in the CBE_ADMIN\DATA:Publctns directory structure, sorted by size.

## Project 5-7: Working with Explorer and NetWare Copy

In this project, you practice using Windows Explorer and the NetWare Copy option to find and copy files into the directories you have created. Use Windows Explorer to verify that the files have been copied successfully into the specified directory locations.

1. Change to your ##ADMIN directory and create a subdirectory named Letters.

2. Suppose you need to copy all form files from the DATA volume into the Letters subdirectory you just created. Because form files use the .frm extension, you can use the Windows Explorer Arrange option to find and display all the form filenames. Record the steps you use and the path to the .frm files in your memo to your instructor.

3. Use the NetWare Copy option to copy the .frm files you recorded in Step 2 into the Letters directory you created. Record the steps you used in your memo to your instructor.

4. Use Windows Explorer to rename the Letters directory as Docs. Record the steps you used in your memo to your instructor.

## CASE PROJECTS

### Case 5-1: Creating a Network File Structure for the Jefferson County Courthouse

The Jefferson County Courthouse network is proceeding according to plan. The network proposal is still for just the 12 users in the Social Services section. The 12 users include the program administrator, Janet Hinds; her assistant, Tom Norihama; the receptionist, Lisa Walsh; the department secretary, Terry Smith; and eight social workers. The group will use one NetWare 6 server. From discussions with Janet, the following decisions have been made:

❐ The NetWare server will have only one volume, a 6 GB SCSI drive.

❐ The county is providing a license for a Windows-based suite of software that includes a word processor, an electronic spreadsheet, and a presentation graphics program. No personal database program is included in this package. This program is named Office99, and the three programs are abbreviated as WP, SS, and PG.

❐ The county has purchased a database management system named DBSys and has contracted for an application to be developed in DBSys that can be used to track the social services workers' cases. DBSys requires a directory named DBSys, and the application requires a subdirectory named Tracker under that directory. In addition, a data directory named Trkrdata is required, and this directory must have three subdirectories named TForms, TTables, and TReports.

❐ The staff needs a Shared directory and a Reports directory that all members of the staff can access.

❐ Each member of the staff requires a Home directory that only he or she can access.

Create a proposed network file system for the Jefferson County Courthouse. Document your proposal with a NetWare Server Planning Form, a Directory Planning Form, NSS Volume Design Forms, and Directory Design Forms as needed (see Appendix B). Turn in the proposal to your instructor in memo form, with copies of your work forms attached.

## Case 5-2: Creating a Network File Structure for the J.Q. Adams Corporation

The J.Q. Adams Corporation network development is proceeding according to plan. The network will use two NetWare 6 servers, one dedicated to administration and one to production. The J.Q. Adams Corporation organizational chart is shown in Chapter 4, Figure 4-35. From discussions with Donna Hulbert, the following decisions have been made:

◻ Each NetWare server has two volumes: SYS and DATA. Each is a 4 GB SCSI drive.

◻ The company has purchased a license for a Windows-based suite of software that includes a word processor, an electronic spreadsheet, and a presentation graphics program. There is no personal database program included in this package. This program is named Office99, and the three programs are abbreviated as WP, SS, and PG. This application will reside on the administration NetWare server.

◻ The company has purchased an accounting system named AcctSys. This application and all its data will reside on the administration NetWare server. This application requires a program directory named AcctSys. It also requires a data directory named ASdata, and this directory must have subdirectories named AS_GL, AS_AP, AS_AR, and AS_PR.

◻ The company has purchased an inventory tracking system that will reside on the production NetWare server. Named InvTrack, this application requires a program directory named InvTrack. In addition, it requires a data directory named ITdata, and this directory must have subdirectories named ITForms, ITTables, and ITRprts.

◻ The staff needs a Shared directory and a Reports directory that all members of the staff can access on the administration server.

◻ Each staff member requires a Home directory on the administration server that only he or she can access.

Create a proposed network file system for the J.Q. Adams Corporation. Document your proposal with a NetWare Server Planning Form, a Directory Planning Form, NSS Volume Design Forms, and Directory Design Forms as needed (see Appendix B). Turn in the proposal to your instructor in memo form, with copies of your work forms attached.

# 6

# INSTALLING NETWARE 6

**After reading this chapter and completing the exercises, you will be able to:**

♦ Describe the steps to install NetWare on the server

♦ Document the NetWare server environment

♦ Identify and load common disk and local area network (LAN) drivers

♦ Use the NetWare Install Wizard to create NetWare disk partitions and volumes

♦ Load and unload NetWare Loadable Modules (NLMs)

♦ Use NetWare console commands to check your server installation and configuration

♦ Install Novell Client software, which allows a Windows workstation to access a NetWare server

♦ Identify other methods available for users to access a NetWare server by using Native File Access Protocol (NFAP)

Now that you have designed your eDirectory tree and network file system, you are ready to get down to the business of working with NetWare and setting up your network. A network administrator must know the software components that make the network operate and be able to configure the NetWare operating system. In this chapter, you learn about loading and running NetWare 6 on a server and Novell Client on the attached workstations.

NetWare installation can be divided into two major parts: server and workstation. Server installation involves loading the NetWare operating system on the server's hard drive, setting up the NetWare partitions on each drive, creating volumes, loading the necessary drivers to access the network interface cards (NICs), and doing the initial work with the eDirectory tree. Workstation installation involves loading software and drivers on users' workstations so that they can access the NetWare server and use the network.

Although a Certified Novell Engineer (CNE) is expected to be able to install the NetWare NOS on a server, a Certified Novell Administrator (CNA) is expected only to administer the installation after it is done. Therefore, this chapter explains what NetWare installation accomplishes so that you can understand the results of the installation and how it affects the network. The installation steps, however, are not covered in detail. On the other hand, a CNA is expected to be able to install client software on the workstations. The current Novell Client is available in Windows 2000 and Windows XP Professional versions. It makes full use of the 32-bit computing power of current microprocessors and uses memory more effectively. In this chapter, you learn how to install and configure Novell Client for Windows XP Professional.

# NetWare Network Operating System Installation

There are eight main steps in installing NetWare 6 on a server:

1. Define and document the network layout and hardware configuration of your server.

2. Install NetWare server hardware and configure the hardware.

3. Partition and install DOS on the bootable hard drive.

4. Launch the NetWare Install Wizard and perform the steps under DOS.

5. Complete the NetWare installation under the NetWare NOS, including:

   ■ Load disk and CD-ROM drivers.

   ■ Load LAN drivers and protocols.

   ■ Create NetWare hard drive partitions and volumes.

6. Install eDirectory.

7. Create and modify the startup configuration files, Startup.ncf and Autoexec.ncf.

8. Choose optional installation options.

In the following sections, you review the installation steps and learn about their effects on the NetWare server.

## Defining and Documenting the NetWare Server Environment

Before you start the NetWare server installation, you must document the network system and your server's hardware configuration. Chapters 4 and 5 covered the initial parts of the NetWare server installation plan: planning the eDirectory tree and preparing the network file system's volume and directory design. Now you need to complete the plan by documenting the network layout and NetWare server hardware configuration.

## Defining the Network Layout

Defining the network layout requires understanding and documenting the network system in which the NetWare server will be installed. A **network layout** consists of the following components:

- The NetWare server's name and internal network number

- The network topology and network cards used

- The IP address of each device on the network where the NetWare server is to be connected

- The frame type to be used on each network cable system

You can obtain most of this information by walking around the existing network or from decisions you make during installation. A good way to do this on existing networks is to make a simple pencil sketch of the network system that includes the network layout information. Figure 6-1 illustrates a network layout consisting of a NetWare server attached to a single Ethernet 10BaseT hub.

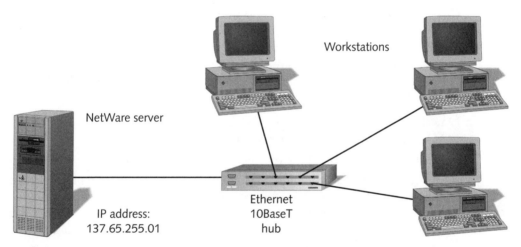

**Figure 6-1**    A network with a single NetWare server

A **NetWare server name** is a unique identification of the server, distinguishing it from other machines on the network. Each NetWare server must have a name that is meaningful *and* unique. When assigning a NetWare server name, consider including the server's location and function as part of its name. For example, the primary NetWare server at F.D. Roosevelt Investments could be named FDR_SERVER01. NetWare server names can be from 2 to 47 characters long and can include alphanumeric characters, hyphens, and underscores. You cannot use spaces or any of the following characters in the server name:

```
= < > [ ] " * + , ? | : ; / \
```

Valid NetWare server names include, for example, FDR_SERVER01, CBE_ADMIN, and FDR_NW-50_Server. However, FDR SERVER01 (using a space instead of an underscore), FDR+SERVER01 (using the + symbol), and FDR[SERVER01] (using square brackets) are not valid names.

A NetWare server must also be assigned a unique **internal network number**. The IPX internal network number for each file server must be unique and is a hexadecimal number of one to eight digits (1 to FFFFFFFE). The NetWare operating system uses this number for communication among its device drivers. Although you can assign your own internal network number, most installations use the random server number suggested by the NetWare installation program. Some network administrators use the server program's serial number as the internal network number. This method keeps the serial number handy when you need to contact Novell for NetWare OS software upgrades.

Both the NetWare server name and the internal network number are unique, so either is enough to identify the NetWare server. However, they are used for different purposes: Users refer to the NetWare server by name (while accessing resources in the tree, for example), but the network software uses the internal network number.

Chapter 3 defined a network address as a number assigned to each LAN system and used to route packets between networks. The IPX external network number uniquely identifies a network cable segment. It is a hexadecimal number of one to eight digits (1 to FFFFFFFE) and is assigned when the IPX protocol is bound to a network board in the server. The terms "network number" and "network address" are often used to refer to the IPX external network number.

Novell stations must be assigned a single unique 48-bit address. This address is normally the MAC address from one of the LAN interfaces. An individual station can be connected to several physical networks but always has only one station address.

Each network must have a unique 32-bit number. There is no organization responsible for maintaining and assigning Novell network numbers. It is up to the network administrator to ensure that each network in the internetwork has a unique network number. A number of schemes are used for assigning network numbers, including the following:

- *Using telephone numbers*—Use the telephone number of the office or building where the network is physically located, or the telephone number of a local support person responsible for the network. If the number is less than 8 digits long, add zeros to the left of the number. For example, the network in a laboratory with the telephone extension 8631 could be assigned the network number 00008631. The advantage of this method is that contact information is readily available if there's a network problem.

- *Using IP subnet addresses*—If the internetwork also runs IP, each network should have an administrator-assigned IP subnet address, which is guaranteed to be unique. Converting each of the four numbers in the IP subnet address to hexadecimal numbers and concatenating them can generate a unique Novell network number. For example, the IP subnet address 192.168.35.32

(mask is 255.255.255.224) when converted to hexadecimal is c0.a8.23.20, so the Novell network number is c0a82320. To determine the internal network number for a NetWare 386 server, add "1" to the network number of the LAN the server is connected to. For example, a server connected to network c0e723c0 would be assigned an internal network number of c0e723c1. This number is guaranteed to be unique because no valid IP subnet address generates an odd hexadecimal number.

It is also normal to give file servers a textual name, so a full host designation will look like this:

    [00000012:008048804d32] ENGINEERING

In this example, the host name is ENGINEERING, its station (MAC) address is 008048804d32, and its network number is 12.

Network addresses must also be set for all devices capable of transmitting router information packets (RIPs) or Service Advertising Protocol (SAP) packets, including routers and file servers. Each workstation does not need to have an assigned network number. It already has a unique host number by virtue of its MAC address. For details on how to change the network address on a file server, consult the Novell documentation supplied with Netware. LAN addresses are necessary because several LANs can be connected to a common backbone to form an internetwork or can be joined via telephone lines to form a WAN. However, because TCP/IP has become standardized as the network protocol, NetWare now distinguishes resources by using their unique IP addresses.

In addition to using IP addresses, a network must have one or more packet frame types assigned to it. As Chapter 3 explained, a frame type defines the formatting of the physical packet transmitted over the network. It does not matter if the network is IP-only, IPX-only, or a mixture of both. Each protocol typically uses one or two packet frame types. To communicate on the network, all machines must use the same frame type. NetWare 6 defaults to using the Ethernet_II frame type, which supports IP. The two most common Ethernet frame types used with NetWare in the past are IEEE 802.3 and IEEE 802.2. IEEE 802.2 is a more up-to-date frame type than 802.3 and is the default for NetWare 6 when using IPX. If you are installing a NetWare server on an existing network with machines that use IEEE 802.3, you can convert all workstations and servers to IEEE 802.2, or you can load both frame types on your new server.

Loading two frame types is a good temporary solution until you can get all machines converted to IEEE 802.2. This approach slows down performance, however, because each frame type must be treated as a separate logical network. Many administrators continue to use IPX to maintain backward-compatibility with IPX-dependent applications or because they are unwilling to take the "plunge" into the world of IP. NetWare provides many tools, including compatibility mode and Service Locator Protocol, to overcome the limitations of earlier NetWare versions in dealing with IP. If possible, take the plunge and use the Ethernet_II frame type in a pure IP environment for performance and ease of management.

Adding a second NetWare server to an existing network creates a **multiple NetWare server network**, as Figure 6-2 shows. Although each NetWare server is given a unique name and IP address (or internal network number with IPX), they both use the same network address and frame type for the LAN cable system on which they communicate.

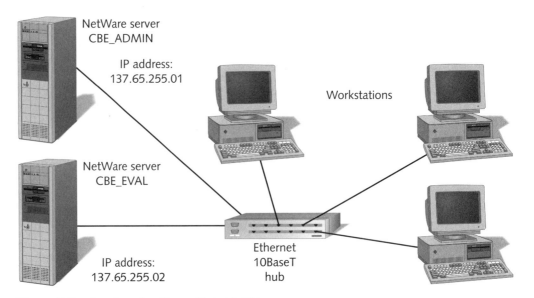

NetWare server
CBE_ADMIN

IP address:
137.65.255.01

Workstations

NetWare server
CBE_EVAL

IP address:
137.65.255.02

Ethernet
10BaseT
hub

**Figure 6-2**   A network with multiple NetWare servers

Multiple networks can be connected to form an internetwork. As discussed in Chapter 3, an internetwork consists of networks connected by bridges, switches, and routers. Figure 6-3 illustrates an internetwork created by adding a different network topology to the system. Notice that each network cable system in the internetwork is assigned a different network address. The NetWare server SUPERIOR is referred to as an "internal router" because it transfers packets between networks in addition to performing its usual NetWare server activities. This requires that the server contain two or more network cards, one for each type of media access protocol, and is sometimes a cheaper solution than purchasing a router.

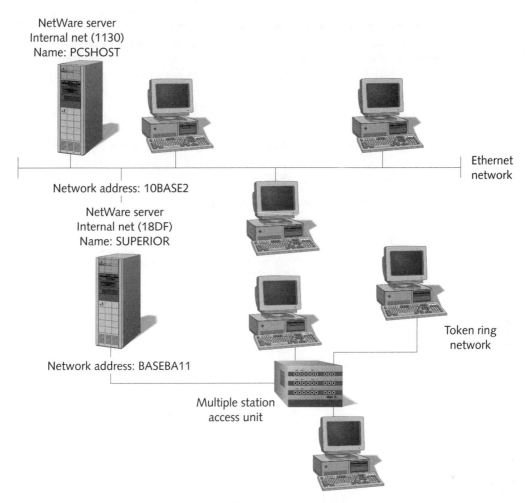

NetWare server
Internal net (1130)
Name: PCSHOST

Network address: 10BASE2

NetWare server
Internal net (18DF)
Name: SUPERIOR

Network address: BASEBA11

Ethernet
network

6

Token ring
network

Multiple station
access unit

**Figure 6-3**   A sample internetwork with token ring and Ethernet

## Completing the NetWare Server Planning Form

After you have identified the network system, you should record the NetWare server's name and internal network number, the network address, and the frame type for each network card to be placed in the NetWare server. During installation, you also need the following NetWare server hardware information:

- Name of the disk driver program for each disk controller card
- Each disk controller card's settings, including interrupt and I/O port
- Capacity and configuration of each hard drive attached to a disk controller
- Name of the network card driver program to be used with each network card
- Each network card's settings, including interrupt, I/O port, and memory address range
- IP information, including IP address, subnet address, and gateway

You can find this information in the documentation supplied with the NetWare server and network cards. If you cannot find it there, your hardware vendor can provide the necessary hardware settings. This information is best documented by filling out a NetWare Server Planning Form like the one shown in Figure 6-4. (A blank copy of this form is in Appendix B.)

## NetWare Server Planning Form

Page 1 of 2

### Server Identification

**File server name:** *CBE-ADMIN*          **Server ID #:** _____

**Domain name:** *cbeadmin.com*                Random _X_ or Assigned _____

### System Information

Computer make/model: _____

CPU: *Intel Pentium III*    **Clock Speed:** *1.5 GHz*  **Bus:** *PCI*

Memory capacity: *512 MB*

### Disk Driver Information

**Disk Controller 1**

   Type: *SCSI*                      Manufacturer/model : *Adaptec 2940*

   Interrupt: *5*    I/O address: *340-343*      DMA channel: *3*

   Memory address: _____ - _____

   Disk driver name: *AHA2940*

| Drive Address | Type | Manufacturer | Speed Capacity |
|---|---|---|---|
| 0 | SCSI | Western Digital | 12 ms/60GB |

**Disk Controller 2**

   Type: *SCSI*                      Manufacturer/model : *Adaptec 2940*

   Interrupt: *11*    I/O address: *350-353*      DMA channel: *3*

   Memory address: _____ - _____

   Disk driver name: *AHA2940*

| Drive Address | Type | Manufacturer | Speed Capacity |
|---|---|---|---|
| 0 | SCSI | Western Digital | 12 ms/20GB |

### Partition Information for Initial Installation

| Partition | Type | Pool/Volume/Capacity |
|---|---|---|
| 1 | NSS | SYS_Pool/SYS/4GB |

### Network Card Information

| Card Number | Network Type | Manuf. ID | LAN Driver | Bus | I/O Port | Memory Address | IRQ/DMA |
|---|---|---|---|---|---|---|---|
| 1 | 100BaseT | Microdyne | NE2000 | PCI | 300 | 0D000 | 10/None |

**Figure 6-4**   The NetWare Server Planning Form

**NetWare Server Planning Form**

Page 2 of 2

<u>Protocol Information</u>

**Network card:** Microdyne, card number 1
**TCP/IP frame type:** Ethernet II
**IP address:** 192.168.1.51
**Subnet mask:** 255.255.255.0
**Gateway:** 192.168.1.1

\_\_\_\_\_ **IPX protocol**

    **Frame type(s):** _802.2_     _____   _____

       **Network address:** _1EEE8022_   _____   _____

<u>Server Context</u>

Tree name: _CLASS_TREE_      Organization: _CBE_LABS_     Organizational Unit: _____

<u>Installation Component Options:</u> ("D" are installed by default)

    _D_   **Novell Certificate Server (Only one per tree)**

    _D_   **NDS iMonitor Services**

    _D_   **NetWare Remote Manager**

    _D_   **Storage Management Services**

    _D_   **ConsoleOne 1.3.2**

    _X_   **iPrint/NDPS**

    \_\_\_   **NetWare Enterprise Web Server**

    \_\_\_   **NetWare Web Manager**

    \_\_\_   **NetWare FTP Server**

    \_\_\_   **NetWare Web Search**

    \_\_\_   **Novell DNS/DHCP Services**

    \_\_\_   **WAN Traffic Manager Services**

    _X_   **Novell Native File Access Protocol**

    _X_   **Novell Advanced Audit Service**

    \_\_   **NetWare WebAccess**

    \_\_\_   **Novell iFolder Storage Services**

    \_\_\_   **eDirectory iManager Service**

    \_\_\_   **Novell NetStorage**

<u>Port Usage</u>

| Service | IP Address | Ports | |
|---------|-----------|-------|---|
| iFolder | _____ | \_\_\_\_ | \_\_\_\_ |
| NetStorage | _____ | \_\_\_\_ | \_\_\_\_ |
| iPrint | _____ | \_\_\_\_ | \_\_\_\_ |

**Figure 6-4** The NetWare Server Planning Form (continued)

6

The NetWare Server Planning Form has nine main sections: Server Identification, System Information, Disk Driver Information, Partition Information for Initial Installation, Network Card Information, Protocol Information, Server Context, Installation Component Options, and Port Usage.

**Server Identification**   Record the installer's name, the name of the NetWare server, and the internal network number in this section.

**System Information**   Enter the computer's make and model, the microprocessor type, clock speed, memory capacity, and types of expansion slots in this section. Although you won't need this information during NetWare installation, you do need to know that your NetWare server meets or exceeds the minimum requirements for the NetWare version you are installing. (You learned the minimum requirements for a NetWare 6 server in Chapter 2.) This information is also useful after initial installation if you add server options or upgrade the NetWare server software.

**Disk Driver and Partition Information**   The Disk Driver Information section of the NetWare Server Planning Form contains documentation for up to two disk controller cards in your NetWare server, which you need during server installation. In addition, the capacity and partition size information for each disk drive is helpful in planning disk mirroring and duplexing. (Disk mirroring or duplexing requires that each mirrored NetWare partition be the same size.) The settings for the cylinder, head, and sector of IDE disk drives are stored in the Complementary Metal-Oxide Semiconductor (CMOS). You might need this information to reconfigure the CMOS after a battery or system failure.

Recording this information isn't just for your own knowledge. System failures frequently occur during vacations or weekends when the administrator is not accessible. Having hardware configuration information available on site can speed the recovery process and reduce user downtime while the network is offline. Many common IDE/ATA drive specifications are now available on the Web at the drive vendor's Web site as a further resource.

You need the controller card information to load the correct disk driver software during installation and to provide NetWare with the necessary configuration parameters. In addition, knowing the hardware configuration information, such as interrupt, I/O port, and DMA channel, can help you avoid hardware conflicts when you install other hardware, such as LAN cards.

One of the first steps in installing NetWare on a server is loading the correct disk driver program to give the NetWare operating system access to the server's hard drives. The Install Wizard auto-detects most common controllers and disk drives during the configuration process. You need to verify that the wizard has correctly identified your hardware, but you won't have to go hunting for drivers as in the past. You must also determine the amount of disk storage to be allocated to DOS and the NetWare partition later in the installation. You can enter that information in the form, too.

**Network Card Information**   Often, it is the network administrator's job to install network cards in the NetWare server and workstations. The network card information section of the NetWare Server Planning Form contains important information identifying the network cards and their configurations. Your first concern is obtaining cards that are appropriate for the network system you are installing and ensuring that the network cards are Novell certified to work with your version of NetWare. One way of saving the trouble of maintaining a CD/floppy disk library and carrying it around in your tool bag is to make a subdirectory structure on your server's boot partition where all the updated drivers and the card's original electronic documentation could reside.

Do not trust a vendor or reseller's promise that its "plug-and-play" PCI card will work with NetWare. Even when the card is listed as approved for NetWare, it might have been tested with only one brand of PCI system board. You could end up spending hours trying to get NetWare to recognize a "plug-and-play" card without success. Your best bet is to use known brands and ask for configurations the reseller or hardware vendor has already tested.

Next, you need to identify the correct network card driver to load during NetWare installation to enable sending and receiving packets. To help you load the correct driver, Novell has included NIC drivers for many of the common network cards. You will have a chance to locate and download the correct driver for your NIC in Case Project 6-1.

To avoid hardware conflicts with other devices in the computer, each NIC installed in the NetWare server must be set to use a unique interrupt, I/O port, and memory address. Because you might need to enter these hardware settings when first installing the card driver, documenting the interrupt, I/O port, and memory address of each NIC on the NetWare Server Planning Form is useful.

**Protocol Information**   Because IP is NetWare's native protocol, you need to record information about your computer's IP address for future reference. Each device using IP must have its own unique addressing information. If two devices have the same IP address, they cannot connect with the network.

It's important to record your IP information. If your network administrator is not available or months have passed since you configured your machine, reconstructing the information is not easy. Unlike drive specifications or drivers, you cannot get this information from a vendor's Web site or documentation because each site has a unique IP address.

Determining and selecting IP addresses is beyond the scope of this book; however, Appendix D provides more background on IP addressing concepts. Typically, your IT Department or network administrator assigns these addresses to coordinate with the rest of your network's IP addresses and facilitate connecting to the Internet. If your network is an isolated system that won't be connected to another IP network, such as the

Internet, several private address ranges are available: 10.0.0.1 to 10.255.255.254, 172.16.0.1 to 172.31.255.254 and 192.168.0.1 to 192.168.255.254. These addresses are sometimes referred to as "non-routable" IP addresses and are often used by businesses to shield their systems from the outside world. Also, companies can save a lot of money by using a private network internally and implementing **Network Address Translation (NAT)** on their NetWare servers. NAT translates the internal private network IP address to a public IP address (owned by the company) that is routable. So NAT enables you to hide your private intranet from the Internet, while still giving you the capability to access the Internet. In fact, NAT can allow up to 15,000 users to access the Internet using a single registered IP address. For more information on NAT, see Novell's online documentation.

## NetWare Server Installation

After you have identified the network system and hardware specifications and filled out the NetWare Server Planning Form, you are ready to roll up your sleeves and start the NetWare installation. The time spent planning and documenting the network and NetWare server environment will pay off by helping you avoid the problems caused by loading wrong drivers or entering incorrect card configurations.

### NetWare Server Preparation

Before installing the NetWare NOS, you must install all the necessary hardware. If your NetWare server is not shipped with all the hardware installed (such as disk drives, CD-ROMs, disk controller cards, and NICs), you need to install and configure them. The hardware manufacturer should provide the necessary instructions and materials. (Typically, you do this to add another hard drive or NIC to the existing hardware.)

Before you start the Install Wizard, you should know that NetWare 6's Server CD is bootable. Most drives include firmware that enables the CD-ROM drive to act as a boot drive, just as a floppy disk drive can. This specification, called El Torito, is standard with most PCs. If your hardware supports the El Torito specification on the CD-ROM drive, you can have the soon-to-be NetWare server system start from the CD. This is the installation method covered in this chapter, and it eliminates having to create a DOS partition because the Install Wizard automatically creates one for you. The NetWare 6 Install Wizard runs only from DOS, not from Windows or the MS-DOS prompt in Windows. You will let the NetWare installation program create this DOS partition for you, after starting your system from the CD. Novell suggests a minimum DOS partition of 200 MB. However, you should create a larger DOS partition to store a core dump for diagnostic purposes. Novell recommends a minimum of 1 GB for the DOS partition.

 Although DOS is initially used to start the NetWare server, after NetWare has started, it functions as a completely separate operating system that directly controls the computer hardware.

The final step in preparing the NetWare server is making sure that the date and time have been set accurately in the CMOS. NetWare 6 uses this information when the NOS takes control of the server.

## NetWare Installation Methods

You can install NetWare 6 from a CD in the server's CD-ROM drive or from a copy of NetWare 6 located on another server on the network (either from a CD in a CD-ROM drive or from files copied onto a server volume). If another NetWare server is available on the network, installing from files copied to a volume on that NetWare server is the fastest installation method. The explanations in this chapter assume that only one new NetWare server is available.

NetWare 6 can be installed as an upgrade, a new server, or a pre-migration server. You should select the pre-migration option when a destination server will receive information from an existing server through the migration process. For example, you can upgrade a NetWare 5.1 server by moving all its data and eDirectory information to a new server running NetWare 6. (See Novell's online documentation for more information on the migration process.) This chapter covers a new server installation. Don't forget that if you reformat the hard drive to create a new DOS partition and blank space for NetWare, you will also erase your CD-ROM drivers. Copy them to a separate disk before reformatting.

## Customizing the Installation

Novell provides two options for installing NetWare 6 on a new NetWare server: an express installation and a custom installation. The express installation means you accept the defaults that the Install Wizard provides for your network. Normally, the defaults, which include LAN, mouse, and disk drivers auto-discovered, a 4 GB SYS volume, a United States keyboard, and so forth, are perfectly acceptable on a small network. Customizing the installation gives network administrators more control by enabling them to specifically name or set configuration options that NetWare handles automatically during an express installation. The following sections give an overview of the NetWare 6 installation process.

## The First NetWare 6 Server in the eDirectory Tree

Now that the NetWare server is ready, you can install the NetWare 6 NOS. If this is the first copy of NetWare 6 installed in your network, this installation creates eDirectory for the network, which includes creating and naming the eDirectory tree and the eDirectory administrator. When additional NetWare 6 servers are installed in the network, they are added into the existing eDirectory tree and administered by the previously created network administrator. In the following sections, you look at the steps David Doering, the network administrator for CBE Labs, took to install NetWare 6 on his server.

## The Character-Based Portion of the Installation

The character-based portion of the Install Wizard is responsible for the following:

- Initiating a NetWare server installation

- Letting the user select a New Server install, an upgrade of an existing NetWare NOS to NetWare 6, or a pre-migration install

- Copying NetWare DOS files to the DOS partition of the NetWare server's startup hard drive

- Letting the user specify a language, mouse, and video type for the NetWare server

- Creating the Startup.ncf file to load the correct hardware drivers

 The extension .ncf stands for **NetWare Command File (NCF)**.

- Creating the Autoexec.ncf file to load additional drivers

- Adding the ability to automatically start the NetWare server to the Autoexec.bat file

First, David configured the BIOS to start from the CD-ROM and then performed the following steps to create the DOS partition:

1. First, he inserted the CD into the server and then began the server software installation by starting from the CD-ROM.

2. When the language selection window displayed (see Figure 6-5), he pressed Enter to accept the default English language.

3. He selected the Accept License Agreement option, and then pressed Enter.

4. To create a DOS partition, he selected the Create a new boot partition option, and then pressed Enter.

5. He pressed Enter to accept the default partition size of 200 MB, selected Continue, and then pressed Enter to create the DOS partition.

 You must use the keyboard to select the Continue option because in this part of the installation, the mouse driver is not yet available.

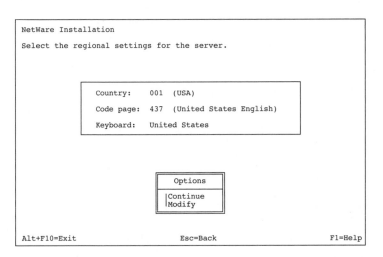

```
NetWare Installation

Select the regional settings for the server.




                    Country:    001  (USA)

                    Code page:  437  (United States English)

                    Keyboard:   United States




                          Options
                          Continue
                          Modify


 Alt+F10=Exit                  Esc=Back              F1=Help
```

**Figure 6-5**   Choosing the language, code page, and keyboard

    6. After the DOS partition was created, he pressed the spacebar to restart the server.

    7. After the system restarted, the DOS partition was automatically formatted and the initial file copying began.

The installation program copies files to the C:\Nwserver directory on the DOS partition and then starts the NetWare server kernel and proceeds with the text-based installation. During this phase, you need to select your installation method, identify the disk and network card drivers, and create the SYS volume. David performed the following steps during the initial installation of the CBE_ADMIN server:

    1. After reading the JReport runtime License Agreement, he pressed F10 to continue and display the NetWare Installation window.

    2. After pressing Enter to select the Custom installation option, he pressed the down arrow key to highlight Continue and pressed Enter to open the Server Settings window containing the server ID number, reboot, and SET options.

    3. He recorded the server ID number on the NetWare Server Planning Form, and then pressed Enter to continue with the default server settings.

    4. He pressed Enter to continue with the default regional settings, including country, code page, and keyboard.

    5. He again pressed Enter to continue with the default mouse type and video mode settings (see Figure 6-6) and start the initial file copying.

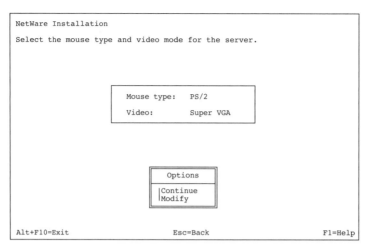

**Figure 6-6**    Choosing the mouse and video type

6. Initial files were then copied to the server's C:\Nwserver directory. Next, NetWare displayed the window listing device types and driver names, similar to the one in Figure 6-7.

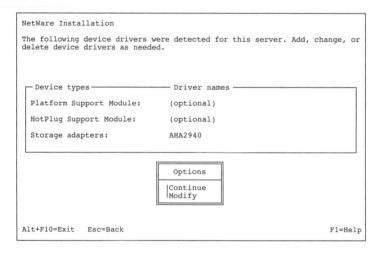

**Figure 6-7**    Selecting device types and drivers

7. Because NetWare 6 detected the Adaptec AHA2940 adapter, David simply highlighted the Continue option and pressed Enter to load the detected storage drivers. If the storage drivers had not been automatically detected, he could have used the Modify option to select the correct ones from the list.

8. After the storage device drivers were loaded, a window displayed showing the detected network boards (see Figure 6-8).

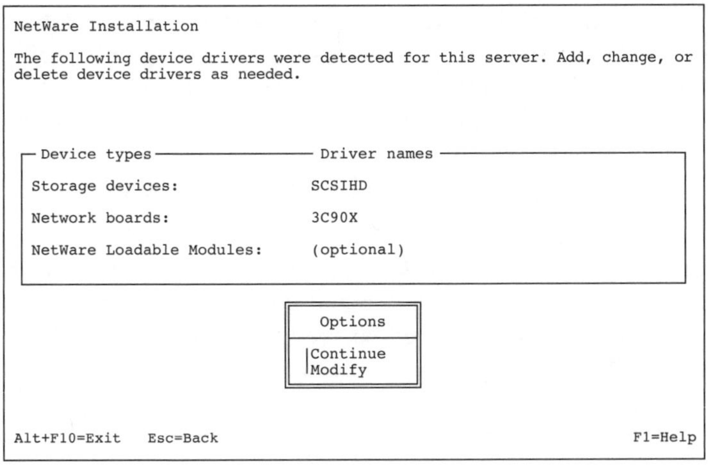

```
┌─────────────────────────────────────────────────────────────────────────┐
│ NetWare Installation                                                      │
│                                                                           │
│ The following device drivers were detected for this server. Add, change, or│
│ delete device drivers as needed.                                          │
│                                                                           │
│                                                                           │
│   ┌ Device types ──────────────── Driver names ─────────────────┐         │
│   │ Storage devices:             SCSIHD                          │         │
│   │                                                              │         │
│   │ Network boards:              3C90X                           │         │
│   │                                                              │         │
│   │ NetWare Loadable Modules:    (optional)                      │         │
│   │                                                              │         │
│   └──────────────────────────────────────────────────────────────┘       │
│                                                                           │
│                        ┌────────────────────┐                            │
│                        │      Options        │                            │
│                        ├────────────────────┤                            │
│                        │ Continue            │                            │
│                        │ Modify              │                            │
│                        └────────────────────┘                            │
│                                                                           │
│ Alt+F10=Exit   Esc=Back                                  F1=Help          │
└─────────────────────────────────────────────────────────────────────────┘
```

**Figure 6-8**    The network card information window

9. Because he purchased a Novell-certified NIC, David simply verified that the correct driver was detected, highlighted the Continue option, and pressed Enter to continue the installation. If your NIC is not automatically detected, you can use the Modify option and follow these steps to install a NIC driver from a floppy disk:

- Highlight the Modify option, and press Enter.

- Press the down arrow key to highlight the Network Boards field, and press Enter to display the Drivers window.

- Press Insert to display a list of known network board drivers.

- Press the down arrow key to find and highlight your network board, and then press Enter. If your network board is not included in the list, press Insert to display the Path to be Scanned window. Insert a floppy disk containing the drivers, and press Enter again to scan for the driver files. Press Enter to select your driver file.

- Press Enter to return to the Drivers window.

- Press the down arrow key to select the Return to driver summary option, and then press Enter. Your new driver should now appear in the Drivers window.

- Press the down arrow key to return to the Options menu.

- Highlight the Continue option, and press Enter to load the selected network and disk drivers.

NetWare 6 is quite good at detecting common network cards and includes a wide range of drivers, so you should not encounter many problems. Unfortunately, if there are difficulties, they crop up here as NetWare attempts to communicate with the board. If it cannot detect the card, NetWare states that no card was found. This might indicate a problem with the PCI card or, most likely, a problem with an incorrect slot selected. You can toggle to the console screen, check the slot that Novell selected, and make any necessary changes. The worst-case scenario is that you might have to purchase another brand of NIC, such as SMC or 3COM, but usually this isn't the case because NetWare supports about 50 LAN drivers. Remember, this is your server. Get the fastest PCI network board you can afford, and be sure to purchase a Novell-certified NIC and use the proper driver. You should check your vendors periodically for any upgraded drivers to help improve your server's performance.

Each LAN driver results in a LOAD *LANdriver* statement being created in the Autoexec.ncf file. The LOAD *LANdriver* command includes any module parameter values needed for the LAN driver to be loaded correctly. LAN drivers use the set of module parameters listed in Table 6-1 to specify information about NICs. You can modify the LOAD *LANdriver* commands after the installation process by editing the Autoexec.ncf file. Figure 6-9 shows an example of an Autoexec.ncf file with LOAD *LANdriver* commands.

**Table 6-1**    LAN Module Parameters

| Module Parameter | Use This Parameter To |
| --- | --- |
| DMA = *number* | Set the direct memory access (DMA) channel. |
| FRAME = *frametype* | Set the frame type used with the board. |
| INT = *number* | Set the interrupt number (IRQ) used by the board. |
| MEM = *number* | Set the memory address used by the board. |
| NAME = *name* | Assign a name to this configuration of the board. |
| PORT = *number* | Set the I/O (input/output) port used by the board. |
| NODE = *address* | Set a node address for the board. Usually not needed because each board is encoded with a unique address. |
| RETRIES = *number* | Set the number of retransmissions the board will make for frames that fail to reach their destination. |
| SLOT = *number* | Specify the EISA, MCA, or PCI slot in which the board is installed on the system board. |

The LOAD *DISKdriver* commands are located in Startup.ncf; the LOAD *LANdriver* commands are located in Autoexec.ncf.

```
NetWare Configuration


                          File: AUTOEXEC.NCF

# If you change the name of this server, you must update
# all the licenses that are assigned to this server. Using
# NWAdmin, double-click on a license object and click on
# the Assignments button. If the old name of
# this server appears, you must delete it and then add the
# new server name. Do this for all license objects.
SERVERID 774CD4E
LOAD IPXRTR
LOAD 3C90XC.LAN SLOT=2 FRAME=ETHERNET_802.2  NAME=3C90XC_1_E82
BIND IPX 3C90XC_1_E82 NET=6C364633
LOAD 3C90XC.LAN SLOT=10008 FRAME=ETHERNET_802.2  NAME=3C90XC_2_E82
BIND IPX 3C90XC_2_E82 NET=83FA0432
LOAD IPXRTRNM
```

**Figure 6-9** LOAD *LANdriver* commands in the Autoexec.ncf file

The initial installation continued with these steps:

1. After the installation software detected the drive's free space, David could have chosen to modify the default settings, but he decided to accept them.

2. To accept the default size of 4 GB, he highlighted Continue and pressed Enter to begin the file-copying process. During file copying, the installation program creates the system directories on the SYS volume, and then copies files from the CD to the correct directories. After file copying is finished, the installation software starts the GUI console to complete the installation.

Even though your system might support a bootable CD, the CD-ROM drive must still be able to read ISO9666-formatted CDs. Otherwise, even though the installation might have been successful to this point, it would abort abruptly with the error "Could not mount CD" displayed. You are then taken to a Temporary: prompt at the system console. To avoid this, be sure your hardware is compliant with NetWare 6 before installing it.

## The GUI-Based Portion of the Installation

At this point, the Install Wizard is ready to move out of the character-based screens and into GUI mode. You can use your mouse to highlight and select items, if you like. If you use the keyboard, note that accepting the contents of a field and window is a two-step process. For example, if you type the name of your server and press Enter, you might expect to move to the next window. However, with the Install Wizard, pressing Enter just moves the active component to the Next button at the bottom of the window. To continue to the next window, you need to press Enter again or click Next.

You use the GUI installation mode to supply most of the server setup and configuration information. The GUI installation can be subdivided into three general phases:

- Server Setup
- eDirectory (NDS) Installation
- License and Component Installation

**Server Setup Phase**    In the server setup phase, you supply the server name, create additional volumes, select protocols, supply IP address information, enter the server's DNS name and domain, and identify your time zone. This phase begins with asking for the server name and then obtaining the initial encryption license information. Before performing this phase, you should have access to a license that contains the Novell Cryptographic License file (extension .nkf) for your server. David used the following steps in the server setup phase:

1. When asked for the server name, he entered CBE_ADMIN, and then clicked Next to display the Encryption license window.

2. In the Encryption license window, he clicked the Browse button and navigated to the directory on the floppy disk containing his license files. He then clicked the NFK license file and clicked OK to place the filename and path in the Location text box.

3. He clicked Next to accept the encryption license and display the Configure File System window, similar to the one in Figure 6-10.

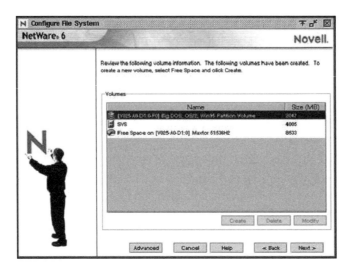

**Figure 6-10**    The Configure File System window

4. Because David was planning to create additional storage pools and volumes later, he clicked Next to accept the existing information and display the Protocols window, similar to the one in Figure 6-11.

If you were creating additional volumes in Step 4, you would select the Free Space item in the Volumes list and click the Create button.

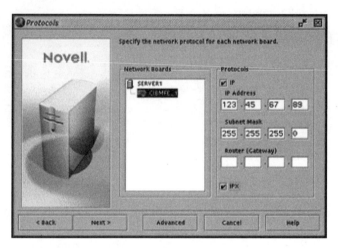

**Figure 6-11**   The Protocols window

5. He clicked the IP check box and entered the server's IP address and subnet mask, as defined on the NetWare Server Planning Form.

6. To install support for the IPX protocol, he clicked the IPX check box and then clicked the Advanced button to document the network address assigned to each network frame type on the NetWare Server Planning Form. He wanted to be sure that the network address detected for each frame type was the same for all servers using IPX.

The network board is the one David configured during the earlier part of the installation. The protocol choices are IP and IPX. You can install either or both. For most networks, you install IP only, and your network administrator supplies the correct IP addresses. (If you choose to install IPX, it defaults to use the 802.2 frame type and a random internal network number.)

The default frame type for NetWare 6 is Ethernet_II (which supports TCP/IP). If you decide to include IPX support, NetWare also installs the Ethernet 802.2 frame type.

Each selected protocol is bound to a LAN driver with a BIND protocol statement in the Autoexec.ncf file. This is the syntax of the BIND command:

```
BIND protocol[TO] LAN driver | board name [driver
parameters . . . ] [protocol parameters . . . ]
```

The BIND *protocol* command includes any parameter values needed. Table 6-2 lists the parameters that can be used with BIND.

**Table 6-2**    BIND Command Parameters

| Parameter | Use This Parameter To: |
| --- | --- |
| *protocol* | Specify the network protocol—for example, IPX. |
| *LAN driver | board name* | Specify the LAN driver name or the name assigned to the NIC in a LOAD *LANdriver* statement. |
| *driver parameters* | Specify the LAN module parameters used to identify an NIC. The simplest to use is the NAME = *name* parameter. |
| *protocol parameters* | Specify the parameters necessary for the protocol. For the IPX protocol, the NET=IPX external network number parameter is required. |

After the installation process is finished, you can modify the LOAD driver commands by editing the Autoexec.ncf file. (Refer back to Figure 6-9 to see an example of an Autoexec.ncf file with LOAD *LANdriver* commands.) Each frame type driver that is bound results in a BIND *frametype* statement being created in Autoexec.ncf. The Install Wizard then asks you to specify your time zone. Note that the supplied list of time zones is based on Greenwich Mean Time, not listed alphabetically, so you might have to search a little to find your exact time zone. Choosing the right one is essential to keeping eDirectory correctly synchronized.

Continuing with the server setup phase, David performed the following steps:

1. After documenting the IPX address information, he clicked OK to return to the Protocols window and then clicked Next to display the Domain Name Service window.

2. He entered cbehost in the Host name text box and cbeadmin.com in the Domain text box. Because he had no DNS server on the network, he left the Verify the DNS information check box and Name Server text boxes blank, clicked Next, and responded to the DNS warning by clicking OK.

3. After completing the DNS information, he selected his time zone in the Time Zone window, and then clicked Next to begin the eDirectory installation.

**eDirectory (NDS) Installation Phase**    This installation phase involves installing eDirectory and identifying the tree and context information for the server. In either case, you are asked to enter the context for the new server. When creating a new tree, the installation program asks for the context and password of the Admin user. By default, the

Admin user account is created in the same context as the server it's installed into. Be sure to write down the following information, which is displayed in a summary window:

- eDirectory tree name
- Server context
- Administrator name

David installed eDirectory on the CBE_ADMIN server by performing the following steps:

1. To create a new eDirectory tree, he clicked the New NDS tree option, and then clicked Next to display the tree information window.

2. In the tree window, he entered the following data:
   - Tree name: CLASS_TREE
   - Context for server: CBE_LABS
   - Admin name: admin
   - Admin context: O=CBE_LABS
   - Password: He started with a password of "novell" and then changed the password later to something more secure.

3. David then clicked Next to install eDirectory and display a summary window. He recorded the following information for later reference:
   - eDirectory tree name
   - Server context
   - Administrator name

4. After documenting the preceding information, he clicked Next to close the summary window and display the Licenses window.

**License and Component Installation Phase**   The final phase of the installation process is locating and selecting the NetWare server and connection licenses and then selecting any additional components to install. Your NetWare 6 license is on the LICENSE floppy disk in a file with the extension .nlf. NetWare prompts you for the disk and then copies the license to the server. (Remember, you can use this license only once in a given tree. If you try to reuse this license for another server, NetWare will detect the attempt.)

The word "final" can be misleading when discussing NetWare installation. In fact, installation is an ongoing process. Network administrators must be aware not only of how NetWare 6 installation affects the network, but also the importance of **support packs (SPs)**, which usually become available soon after a new version is released. Netware 5.1 had at least four such SPs. Some are critical to the operation of your system, and others are patches to repair security vulnerabilities (discussed in Chapter 14) that have been discovered along the way.

As of this writing, there is already an SP2 for NetWare 6 and probably more on the way. As improvements to the NetWare operating system are made, SPs become available. Administrators should periodically check the *www.novell.com* or *support.novell.com* sites for any new releases or patches to the current system. Newsgroups, such as *novell.community.chat* and *novell.support.newsflash*, are also excellent ways to keep abreast of changes and improvements to the NOS and are just a mouse click away. To see which version of NetWare and SP is running on your server, simply type "Version" at your system console prompt.

David performed the following steps to complete the installation of the CBE_ADMIN server by installing the Novell license and selecting the initial server components:

1. Only a single server license can be installed during NetWare 6 installation; user licenses are installed later with iManager. When the Licenses window was displayed, he noticed that multiple licenses were listed in the Licenses to be installed section.

2. At this time, only server licenses can be installed. Because more than one license was listed in the Licenses to be installed section, he clicked each license to see its description. He then clicked the Remove button to remove all user licenses, leaving only the NetWare 6 Server License in the window.

3. He clicked Next after verifying the license information to display the Components Selection window.

As a general rule, it's best to select a minimum number of additional components at first and install additional features by using the GUI console. If you plan to have Microsoft, Unix, and/or Macintosh clients accessing your NetWare server, this is where you have the opportunity to install the Native File Access Protocol (NFAP), discussed later in the chapter in the "Novell Client Software Installation" section.

## Using NetWare Console Commands at the Server

To become a CNA and effectively operate a server console, you need to know how to use the basic **console commands** built into the NetWare operating system, so you should know the purpose of the console commands in Table 6-3. The following sections describe these console commands in more depth and provide examples of using the commands to perform server operations.

**Table 6-3**    Essential Console Commands

| Command Syntax | Description |
|---|---|
| BIND *protocol* TO *drive\|board_name* [*drive_parameters*] | Attaches a protocol to a LAN card. Replace *protocol* with the protocol name (IPX or IP, for example). Replace *drive\|board_name* with the name of the NIC or an optional name assigned to the network board. You can optionally replace *drive_parameters* with the hardware settings that identify the NIC (such as I/O port and interrupt). |

**Table 6-3**    Essential Console Commands (continued)

| Command Syntax | Description |
|---|---|
| LOAD [*path*]*module_name* [*parameters*] | Loads an NLM in the file server's RAM. Optionally replace *path* with the DOS or NetWare path leading to the directory containing the module to be loaded. Replace *module_name* with the name of the NLM you want to load. Optional parameters can be entered depending on the module being loaded. |
| CONFIG | Displays configuration information about each network card, including hardware settings, network address, protocol, and frame type. |
| DISPLAY SERVERS | Displays all servers in the file server's IPX router table, including the number of routers (hops) to get to each server. This command is not available unless IPX is selected during server installation. |
| MEMORY | Displays the total amount of memory available to the file server. |
| SET TIME | Allows you to change the file server's current system date and time. |
| CLS or OFF | Clears the file server console screen. |
| DISABLE/ENABLE LOGIN | Prevents or enables new user logins. |
| BROADCAST | Sends the specified message to all currently logged in users. |
| DOWN | Closes all files and volumes, disconnects all users, and takes the file server offline. |
| MOUNT *volume_name* [ALL] DISMOUNT *volume_name* | Places a volume online or offline. Replace *volume_name* with the name of the volume you want mounted, or use ALL to mount all NetWare volumes. |
| MODULES | Lists all currently loaded modules starting with the last module loaded. |
| SECURE CONSOLE | Provides additional security to help protect the server from unauthorized access. |
| SEND "*message*" [TO] *user_name\|connection_number* | Sends a message to a specified user. Replace *message* with the message line you want to send, and replace *user_name\|connection_number* with the name of the currently logged in user or the connection number assigned to the user. The connection number can be obtained from the Connection option of the MONITOR NLM. |

6

**Table 6-3**    Essential Console Commands (continued)

| Command Syntax | Description |
|---|---|
| UNBIND protocol [FROM] LAN_driver\|board_name | Removes a protocol from a LAN card. Replace protocol with the name of the protocol stack (such as IPX) you want to remove from the card. Replace LAN_driver\|board_name with the name of the driver program that has been loaded for the network card or the name assigned to the network card by the LOAD command. |
| UNLOAD module_name | Removes an NLM from memory and returns the memory space to the operating system. Replace module_name with the name of the currently loaded module, given in the MODULES command. |
| VOLUMES | Displays a list of all mounted volumes along with the volume type (NSS or traditional) and supported name spaces. |
| PROTOCOLS | Displays a list of all currently loaded protocols. |
| HELP command | Displays information on the specified command. For example, to get information on the syntax and use of the BIND command, enter HELP BIND, and press Enter. |

### The BIND [*protocol*] TO [*driver*] Command

The BIND command attaches a protocol stack to a network card and is necessary so that workstations using that protocol can communicate with the file server. Replace the *protocol* parameter with the name of the protocol stack you want to attach to the network card. Replace *driver* with the name of the network card. For example, TCP/IP can be bound to the NE2000 card driver by entering the command BIND IP TO NE2000 and then supplying the network address, as shown in Figure 6-12.

```
CBE_ADMIN
CBE_ADMIN
CBE_ADMIN:BIND IP TO NGRPCI_1_EII ADDR=172.20.0.60 MASK=255.255.0.0

TCPIP-6.3-112: Wed Mar 20 08:07:37 2002
Bound to board 2 with IP address 172.20.0.60 and mask FF.FF.00.00.
IP LAN protocol bound to NETGEAR FA310TX Fast Ethernet PCI Adapter driver

 3-20-2002   8:07:39 am:    SLP-2.2-0
    SLPTCP bound to 172.20.0.60

CBE_ADMIN
```

**Figure 6-12**    Sample BIND command

### The CONFIG Command

The CONFIG command displays information about the server and network card configuration, as shown in Figure 6-13.

```
File server name: CBE_ADMIN
IPX internal network number: 0774CD4E
Server Up Time: 2 Hours 11 Minutes 19 Seconds

3COM Etherlink PCI
    Version 5.30a   June 28, 2000
    Hardware setting: Slot 2, I/O ports DC00h to DC3Fh, Memory FF020400h to FF0
2047Fh, Interrupt Ah
    Node address: 0050DA63EBBE
    Frame type: ETHERNET_802.2
    Board name: 3C90XC_1_E82
    LAN protocol: IPX network 6C364633
Press ESC to terminate or any other key to continue
```

**Figure 6-13**  Sample CONFIG command

Notice that in addition to displaying the file server's name and internal network address, the CONFIG command displays the following information about each network adapter in the file server:

- Name of the LAN driver

- Board name assigned when the LAN driver was loaded

- Current hardware settings, including interrupt, I/O port, memory address, and DMA channel

- Node (station) address assigned to the network adapter

- Protocol stack that was bound to the network adapter

- Network address of the cabling scheme for the network adapter

- Frame type assigned to the network adapter

You should use the CONFIG command before installing network adapters in the server so that you have a current list of all hardware settings on the existing network boards. This will help you to select unique interrupt and I/O address settings for the new cards. In addition, the CONFIG command can be used to determine the network address of a cable system before adding another server to the network. If you accidentally start another server using a different network address for the same cable system, router configuration errors between the servers will interfere with network communications.

## The DISPLAY SERVERS Command

The DISPLAY SERVERS command, shown in Figure 6-14, can be useful when using IPX to determine whether the server is correctly attached to a multiserver network. This command, included with IPX, is not available if only TCP/IP is loaded.

```
CBE_ADMIN:display servers
  BSER4.00-7.0  0   CBE_ADMIN    0   CBE_ADMIN    0   CBE_ADMIN    0
  CBE_ADMIN     0   CLASS_TREE__ 0   CLASS_TREE__ 0
There are 7 known services.
CBE_ADMIN:
```

**Figure 6-14**  Sample DISPLAY SERVERS command

When a server using IPX is first started, it sends out broadcasts advertising its services to all machines on the network. From these broadcasts, the servers and workstations on the network build lists that include the names of all servers and eDirectory trees on the network. The DISPLAY SERVERS command also lists other services, such as print servers and NDPS Brokers. If a new server does not appear in other server lists, and the new server does not "see" the other servers on the network, your server is not communicating properly with the network. The most common problems are that IPX has not been bound to the network card or the NIC driver is using a different frame type than other servers. Another common problem when using TCP/IP is that the server has been configured with the wrong network address or subnet mask.

If the new server shows up on other servers, but no servers are showing up on the new server, it could mean that the network card in the new server has a conflicting interrupt or memory address and cannot receive network packets from other servers. You should use the CONFIG command to check for an overlapping interrupt or memory address.

## The DISABLE/ENABLE LOGIN Commands

The DISABLE LOGIN command prevents new users from accessing services on the NetWare server. Before shutting down the server, you should issue the DISABLE LOGIN message to prevent any additional users from accessing the server, and then use the BROADCAST command to send a message to all logged-in users telling them that the server will be shutting down in the specified time period and they should close all files and log out of the server. If the DISABLE LOGIN command is not issued, new users might log in to the server after the message was broadcast and not be aware the server was shutting down shortly. Another use of the DISABLE LOGIN command is to temporarily prevent users from logging in while you perform maintenance work, such as loading new drivers or backing up the system. After the work is finished and the server is ready for use, you can issue the ENABLE LOGIN command to allow users to log in again and use the server.

## The DOWN Command

The DOWN command deactivates the NetWare server operating system, removes all workstation connections, and returns the server to the DOS prompt. Before issuing the DOWN command, you should disable new logins and broadcast a message to all users, as shown in Figure 6-15. If active sessions exist at the time you try to shut down the server, the NetWare operating system issues a warning message asking if you want to terminate active sessions.

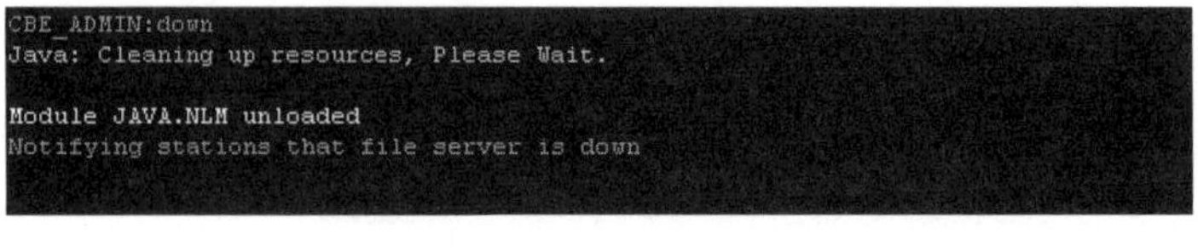

```
CBE_ADMIN:down
Java: Cleaning up resources, Please Wait.

Module JAVA.NLM unloaded
Notifying stations that file server is down
```

**Figure 6-15**    Shutting down a server

If you see this message, you should cancel the DOWN command, use the MONITOR utility (described in "Using the MONITOR Module," later in this chapter) to determine which connections have open files, and then send a message to users to log out. If no one is at any workstations and data files have been left open, you might need to go to individual workstations to close files and log the users out. Therefore, be sure to remind users that their workstations should not be left unattended while data files are open.

## The LOAD Command

The LOAD command loads an NLM into memory and runs it. By default, the LOAD command searches for the requested module in the SYS:System directory unless a different path is specified. Valid paths can include NetWare volume names and DOS local drive letters. When a module is loaded into memory, it remains there until the console operator ends the program or uses the UNLOAD command to remove the software from memory. Optional parameters can be placed after the LOAD command, depending on the needs of the module being loaded.

Beginning with NetWare 5 and continuing with NetWare 6, using the LOAD command to run an NLM is no longer necessary. If you simply type the name of the NLM, the system automatically performs the loading process.

## The MODULES Command

The MODULES command lists all currently loaded modules and their names, version numbers, and dates. The modules are listed in sequence, starting with the last module loaded and ending with the first module loaded. The MODULES command is also useful for quickly checking a module's version number and date to determine NetWare compatibility or to look for network problems known to be caused by defective versions of certain modules.

## The MOUNT and DISMOUNT Commands

Mounting a volume is the process of loading information from the volume's directory entry table (DET) into the file server's RAM, thereby making the volume available for access by users and the file server's operating system. The MOUNT command is needed to mount a volume that has been taken offline with the DISMOUNT command or that did not mount correctly when the file server was started. Normally, the MOUNT ALL command is inserted into the file server's Autoexec.ncf startup file during installation and attempts to mount all volumes when the file server is started. However, in some cases, such as after a file server crash, some volumes might not mount because of errors in their file allocation tables (FATs) or DETs. When this happens to traditional volumes, you must use the VREPAIR module (see "NetWare Loadable Modules (NLMs)" later in this chapter for more information) to correct the FAT problem and then use the MOUNT command to bring the repaired volume online. When working with NSS volumes, you must dismount the volume and then use the NSS /poolrebuild command (described in the next section) rather than VREPAIR to identify and correct NSS pool and volume problems.

## The NSS /poolrebuild Command

The NSS command has a number of options for viewing and repairing the state of NSS components, such as pools and volumes. For example, the NSS /poolrebuild=*poolname* command can be used to rebuild the SYS volume pool when server errors occur. You need to deactivate the pool and all volumes in the pool before the rebuild. The rebuild copies any errors into an error file named volume_name.rlf at the root of the server's SYS volume. Every time you rebuild an NSS volume, the previous error file is overwritten. Novell recommends using the NSS /poolrebuild command only as a last resort to recover the file system because it could result in lost data. Therefore, you should verify that you have a good backup of the volume before using this command.

## The SECURE CONSOLE Command

The SECURE CONSOLE command adds the following security features to help protect the server from unauthorized access:

- Prevents loading NLMs from other sources, such as floppy disks, the DOS partition, or CDs.

- Allows only the console operator to modify the date and time.

- Prevents keyboard entry into the internal debugger software. This is important because programmers could use the debugger to change operating system parameters.

## The SEND Command

The SEND command on the server console is used to send a message to a specific client. The most common use of the SEND command is to request a user to log out before shutting down the file server. Messages can be sent to a user's login name or connection number. For example, to send a message to a user at connection number 9, enter the following command:

```
SEND "Server going down in 5 minutes" TO 9
```

## The SET TIME Command

The SET TIME command is used to change the current server time or date. In a multiple server network tree consisting of 30 or fewer servers, a single server is designated as a Reference server. All other servers on the network synchronize their time to the Reference server, so in a multiple-server network, you should change time only at the Reference server. Novell recommends checking the time from DOS or CMOS and then making any corrections before starting the Server.exe program. The following commands show several ways of using SET TIME to change the file server's current date and time to 3:00 P.M., October 30, 2003:

```
SET TIME 10/30/2003 3:00pm

SET TIME October 30, 2003 3:00pm

SET TIME October 30, 2003

SET TIME 3:00
```

## The UNBIND Command

The UNBIND command is used to unload a protocol stack from a LAN driver, causing the server to stop communicating with other machines using that protocol. The most common use of the UNBIND command is to take a defective server off the network. If, for example, you have bound the IPX protocol to a LAN driver and used the wrong network number for the cable system, almost immediately, the servers on the network will complain that another router is calling the network a different name. To stop this problem, you can use the UNBIND command to remove the protocol from the network card and then reissue the BIND command using the correct network address.

# NetWare Loadable Modules (NLMs)

One of NetWare's strengths is its use of **NetWare Loadable Modules (NLMs)** to add functionality to the core operating system. Because NLMs play such an important role in tailoring the NetWare network, CNAs must be familiar with the standard NLMs included with the NetWare operating system. As shown in Table 6-4, NLMs can be classified into four general categories based on their function, with each category having its own extension.

**Table 6-4**    NLM Categories

| Category | Extension | Description |
| --- | --- | --- |
| Disk drivers | .ham and .cdm | Controls access to the NetWare disk partitions. Commands to load these modules are usually placed in the Startup.ncf file. |
| LAN drivers | .lan | Each network card must be controlled by a compatible LAN driver. Commands to load these modules are placed in the Autoexec.ncf file. |
| Namespace | .nam | Contains logic to support other workstation-naming conventions, such as those used with Macintosh, OS/2, or Unix-based computers. Commands to load namespace modules are usually placed in the Startup.ncf file. |
| General-purpose | .nlm | Adds services and functions to the file server's operating system. |

In addition to the special modules for controlling disk and network cards, NetWare comes with a number of general-purpose NLMs in the SYS:System directory with the extension .nlm. These NLMs can be used for a wide range of capabilities, as shown in Table 6-5. In the following sections, you learn about several of these modules that CNAs must be able to use to manage their network file servers.

**Table 6-5**    General-purpose NLMs

| NLM | Purpose |
| --- | --- |
| CDROM.NLM | Used to mount a CD when it's first inserted in the server's CD-ROM drive. After this module is loaded, it automatically detects the removal and insertion of CDs. |
| NWCONFIG.NLM | Used to work with NetWare partitions, volumes, and system files. |
| MONITOR.NLM | Used to monitor file server performance, hardware status, and memory usage. |
| REMOTE.NLM | Used to view and operate the NetWare server console from a remote workstation. Requires a password. |
| RSPX.NLM | Allows the REMOTE module to send and receive console screen commands over the local network cable. |
| RCONAG6.NLM | Provides an IP-based remote Java console for use with ConsoleOne (described in Chapter 7). |
| SCRSAVER.NLM | Provides a way to lock the server console with a password. To access the server console, the operator must enter the specified password or the Admin user's password. |
| VREPAIR.NLM | Checks the specified traditional volume for errors and allows the operator to write corrections to the disk volume. This command works only with traditional volumes. To correct problems with NSS volumes, use the NSS /rebuild command. |
| DSREPAIR | Checks the eDirectory tree replicas for any problems and synchronizes all replicas with the master. See the "Migrating an Existing Server to Netware 6" in Appendix C for an example of using DSREPAIR. |

## Using the MONITOR Module

The **MONITOR utility** module is useful for monitoring and configuring system performance. In this section, you learn how to use it to lock the server console and to view server performance, connection information, and disk and network statistics. After loading the MONITOR utility, the main monitor screen, shown in Figure 6-16, is displayed.

The screen displays the version and date of the NetWare operating system and several important system parameters about your server's available memory and performance. The lower half of the screen displays a menu of monitor options. You can view a menu of Available Options (shown in Figure 6-17) by pressing the Tab key.

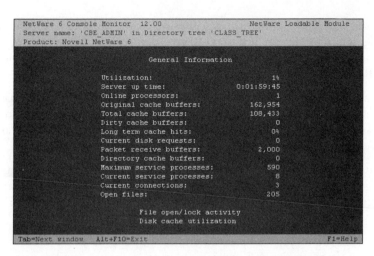

```
NetWare 6 Console Monitor  12.00              NetWare Loadable Module
Server name: 'CBE_ADMIN' in Directory tree 'CLASS_TREE'
Product: Novell NetWare 6

                        General Information

            Utilization:                        1%
            Server up time:              0:01:59:45
            Online processors:                    1
            Original cache buffers:         162,954
            Total cache buffers:            108,433
            Dirty cache buffers:                  0
            Long term cache hits:                0%
            Current disk requests:                0
            Packet receive buffers:           2,000
            Directory cache buffers:              0
            Maximum service processes:          590
            Current service processes:            8
            Current connections:                  3
            Open files:                         205

                     File open/lock activity
                     Disk cache utilization

 Tab=Next window   Alt+F10=Exit                          F1=Help
```

**Figure 6-16**    The console screen for the MONITOR utility

```
NetWare 6 Console Monitor  12.00              NetWare Loadable Module
Server name: 'CBE_ADMIN' in Directory tree 'CLASS_TREE'
Product: Novell NetWare 6

                        General Information

            Utilization:                        1%
            Server up time:              0:01:56:13
            Online processors:                    1
            Original cache buffers:         162,954
            Total cache buffers:            108,434
            Dirty cache buffers:                  0


                        Available Options

              ┌─────────────────────────────┐
              │ Connections                 │
              └─────────────────────────────┘
                Storage devices
                Volumes
                LAN/WAN drivers
                Loaded modules
                File open/lock activity
                Disk cache utilization

 Tab=Next window   Enter=Select option   Alt+F10=Exit    F1=Help
```

**Figure 6-17**    The Available Options menu

Some of the system parameters and items in the General Information menu are described in the following list:

- *Utilization*—Shows the percentage of time the processor is busy. In most cases, utilization should be less than 70%.

- *Server up time*—Measures the length of time the server has been running since it was last started.

- *Original cache buffers*—Contains the number of buffers (in 4 KB blocks) available when the server was first started.

- *Total cache buffers*—Contains the number of buffers currently available for file caching. If the number is less than 40% of the original cache buffers, your server is running low on memory and you should unload modules or add more RAM as soon as possible.

- *Dirty cache buffers*—Contains a count of the number of buffers that have had modifications but are waiting to be written to disk. A high number of dirty cache buffers indicates that the disk system is bogging down, and a faster disk or an additional disk controller card might be necessary.

- *Current disk requests*—Shows how many requests for disk access are currently waiting to be processed. Like the dirty cache buffers, this number can be used to determine whether disk performance is slowing down the network.

- *Packet receive buffers*—Indicates the number of buffers established to receive packets that the server has received and are waiting to be serviced. If this number approaches the default maximum of 10,000, your file server is falling behind in servicing incoming packets and, therefore, slowing down the network. You might need to get a faster server, increase the disk speed, or add more memory, depending on the other statistics.

- *Directory cache buffers*—Indicates the number of buffers that have been reserved for disk directory blocks. Increasing the number of available directory cache buffers when the server first starts can sometimes improve its performance.

- *Service processes*—Indicates the number of "task handlers" that have been allocated for station requests. If the number of station requests in the packet receive buffers exceeds a certain limit, the server adds extra task handlers to process the requests. Of course, this in turn reduces the amount of memory and processing time for other activities. If the number of service processes approaches the default maximum of 570, and you have a high processor utilization rate, you might need to unload NLMs or add another file server to decrease the load on the current server.

- *Connections*—Quickly shows how many stations are turned on and connected to the server. A station does not have to be logged in to appear in this statistic because any computer accessing the server from the local network or Internet uses up a connection on the file server.

- *File open/lock activity*—Helps determine whether any files are currently open before shutting down the server.

The server's Utilization, Total cache buffers, Packet receive buffers, and Dirty cache buffers can give you a quick picture of your server's health; simply verify that utilization is under 70%, total cache buffers are at least 50% of the original cache buffers, and dirty cache buffers are less than 30% of the total cache buffers. Table 6-6 summarizes the MONITOR statistics, including certain key values.

**Table 6-6** MONITOR Statistics

| Statistic | Description | Values |
|---|---|---|
| Utilization | Percentage of time the processor is being used. | Generally should not be higher than 80%. |
| Server up time | Length of time the NetWare server has been running since it was last started. | Used to determine when the server was last started. |
| Online processors | Number of enabled processors | Used to verify whether all CPUs are running when using a multi-processor system. |
| Original cache buffers | Number of cache buffers available when the server is first started; represents the amount of memory in your server after the NetWare kernel is loaded. | Used along with total cache buffers to determine the amount of memory the server is using. |
| Total cache buffers | Number of buffers available for file caching. | Decreases as modules are loaded into memory. (Novell recommends that total cache buffers be at least 40% of the original cache buffers.) |
| Dirty cache buffers | Number of buffers containing information that needs to be written to disk. | If consistently 30% or more of total cache buffers, check the disk system's speed to see if installing additional disk controllers or faster drives would improve speed. |
| Long term cache hits | Number of times the server found requested data in memory instead of having to read it from disk. | For best performance, should be 80% or higher; adding more memory can increase long term cache hits. |
| Current disk requests | Number of disk requests in a queue waiting to be serviced. | A consistently high value along with a high number of dirty cache buffers could indicate a slow disk system. |
| Packet receive buffers | Number of buffers available to receive requests from workstations. | Default value of 2,000 should be more than enough; on smaller networks with fewer than 50 workstations, can be decreased to 1,000 to provide more memory for cache buffers. |
| Directory cache buffers | Number of buffers allocated for directory caching. | Normally does not need to be adjusted. |
| Service processes | Number of task handlers allocated for user workstation requests. | Normally does not need to be adjusted. |

6

**Table 6-6**   MONITOR Statistics (continued)

| Statistic | Description | Values |
|---|---|---|
| Current connections | Number of licensed and unlicensed connections currently in use by the server. | Should consistently be less than the number of connections in the license; if the value approaches the maximum available licensed connections, additional connections might need to be purchased. |
| Open files | Number of files being accessed via the network server in user workstations. | Tracking this value can help determine server usage. |

In addition to the General Information window, the MONITOR utility contains several menu options for viewing information about your server's performance and operation. Selecting the Connections option displays a window showing all active connections and the name of the user currently logged in. If no user is logged in to a given connection number, the message "NOTLOGGED-IN" appears next to the connection number. You can use this option to check for user activity before shutting down the server. You can also disconnect a user by highlighting the user name and pressing the Delete key. To view information about any connection, select the connection number and press Enter.

The Volumes option lists all mounted volumes and the percentage of volume space used. The LAN/WAN drivers options displays information on all LAN drivers loaded, including driver name, frame type, port, and interrupt. The System resources option is a convenient way to view the percentage of cache buffers used. The Disk cache utilization option, used to open the Cache Utilization Statistics window, shown in Figure 6-18, is a good way to determine whether your server has enough memory.

Novell recommends that the long term cache hits should be more than 90%. If this figure is less than 90%, adding more memory or unloading NLM will improve server performance.

Select the Server parameters option to modify server configuration parameters, such as the maximum number of packet receive buffers or server time type.

The preceding commands all run at the server console. CNAs should memorize these commands; however, most of what you do as a network administrator is not performed at the server console screen, but from a workstation or client.

To see a list of all commands available at the system console, type "Help."

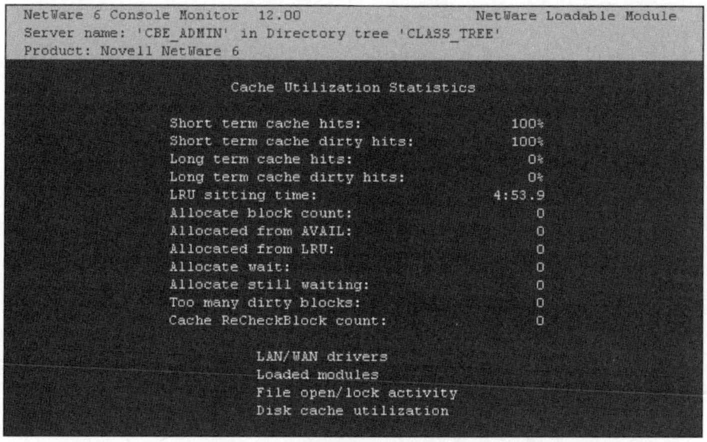

```
NetWare 6 Console Monitor  12.00                 NetWare Loadable Module
Server name: 'CBE_ADMIN' in Directory tree 'CLASS_TREE'
Product: Novell NetWare 6

                      Cache Utilization Statistics

              Short term cache hits:            100%
              Short term cache dirty hits:      100%
              Long term cache hits:               0%
              Long term cache dirty hits:         0%
              LRU sitting time:                4:53.9
              Allocate block count:                 0
              Allocated from AVAIL:                 0
              Allocated from LRU:                   0
              Allocate wait:                        0
              Allocate still waiting:               0
              Too many dirty blocks:                0
              Cache ReCheckBlock count:             0

                   LAN/WAN drivers
                   Loaded modules
                   File open/lock activity
                   Disk cache utilization
```

**Figure 6-18**   The Cache Utilization Statistics window

The next section discusses the installation of the software that enables administrators to manage the network from workstations.

## NOVELL CLIENT SOFTWARE INSTALLATION

As a CNA, one of your responsibilities is to install and configure user workstations on your network. To communicate and access network services, a user's computer requires a NIC along with the client and protocol software components, as shown in Figure 6-19. Before setting up the client computers for your network, you need to understand the role that each of these software components plays in the network communication process.

The NIC driver controls the NIC so that it can send and receive packets over the network cable system. Information on the correct driver program for use with your NIC should be included in the operating manual. Most common NIC drivers are included with Windows 2000 or Windows XP. You can refer to the Microsoft Hardware Compatibility List for a list of NIC manufacturers compatible with your version of Windows. Often Windows automatically detects the NIC and loads the drivers for you. If drivers for your NIC are not included in Windows, you can click the Have Disk button from the driver installation window to load the drivers from the manufacturer's disk or CD.

Communication protocols are responsible for formatting the data in a network packet and routing packets between different networks. In the past, communication protocols were closely linked to the client software. For example, early versions of the Novell client required Novell's IPX/SPX protocol to communicate with NetWare servers, but Microsoft clients and servers required NetBEUI/NetBIOS protocols. Because TCP/IP is needed to access Internet services, many networks required the administrator to install and manage multiple protocols on the same network cable system. Supporting multiple

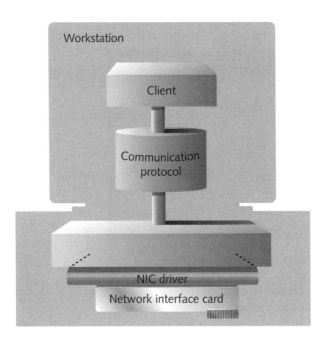

**Figure 6-19** Client components

protocols on a single network requires more time and can cause extra traffic, thus reducing network performance. Because modern clients can use any of the major protocols to access network services, most networks today use TCP/IP to access both local services and the Internet.

Network services need both client and server software components to operate. The client software component must work closely with the local operating system and the server to provide access to network services. The client software formats a request and then uses a network protocol to send that request to a server. A service running on the server processes the request and then sends the results back to the client. As shown in Figure 6-20, each type of network operating system requires its own client to be loaded on the workstation to communicate with services running on the server. To access services on Windows servers, Microsoft clients use the Common Interface File System (CIFS) to format service requests. Before NetWare 6, accessing file services on NetWare servers required the workstation to have the Novell client to format requests with the NetWare Core Protocol (NCP). Unix clients use the Network File System (NFS) protocol to access files on other Unix systems, and Apple clients use AppleTalk Filing Protocol (AFP) to access file services on other Apple computers. Web browsers such as Internet Explorer are clients that use the HTTP and Web Distributed Authority and Versioning (WebDAV) protocols to access resources and services running on Web servers.

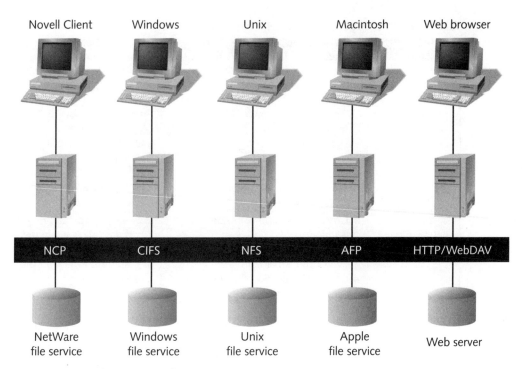

**Figure 6-20**   Client protocols

An important part of Novell's OneNet strategy is providing network services that are compatible with the variety of clients shown in Figure 6-20. Although previous NetWare versions depended on the Novell client being installed on user workstations, NetWare 6 adds direct support for Web browser clients and for native file access from Windows, Apple, and Unix workstations. Another client accessing NetWare servers is the Microsoft Client Services for NetWare client, included with all versions of the Windows operating system. With multiple client alternatives for accessing NetWare servers, network administrators can select a client that best suits the needs of users' workstation environments and applications. Table 6-7 lists the clients that can be used with Windows to access NetWare 6 servers.

**Table 6-7**   NetWare Client Options

| Client | Advantages | Disadvantages |
|---|---|---|
| Web client | ■ Allows access to NetWare services and administrative tasks from any computer attached to the Internet.<br>■ Does not require a Novell client on the workstation. | ■ Does not yet provide access to all NetWare services and resources. |

**Table 6-7**    NetWare Client Options (continued)

| Client | Advantages | Disadvantages |
|--------|-----------|---------------|
| Microsoft client | ■ No additional clients required on the Windows computer.<br>■ Users view the NetWare server in the same way as other Windows servers. | ■ Requires NFAP to be installed on the NetWare server.<br>■ Uses different passwords that are not as secure as Novell Client passwords.<br>■ Users might have to maintain multiple passwords.<br>■ Does not allow access to certain NetWare services and administrative utilities. |
| Microsoft NetWare client | ■ Easy to install and configure on Windows.<br>■ Requires less administrative overhead to maintain.<br>■ Uses the same Novell eDirectory user names and passwords as Novell Client. | ■ Does not allow access to certain NetWare services and administrative utilities.<br>■ Requires IPX/SPX on the NetWare server. |
| Novell Client | ■ Provides access to all NetWare services and administrative utilities. | ■ Requires more administrative time to install and maintain.<br>■ Might conflict with some Windows features. |

To make accessing NetWare file services simpler in a multi-client environment, NetWare 6 includes Novell's new NFAP, which enables NetWare 6 servers to process file service requests formatted by non-Novell clients, such as Microsoft, Apple, and Unix. This allows Macintosh computers using AFP, Unix computers using NFS, and Windows computers using CIFS to access files on a NetWare server just as they would on a server or host running their own operating system. So a Macintosh user sees an Apple server, a Unix user sees a Unix host, and the Windows user sees a Windows server. However, this access is still controlled by NetWare's own security and directory service. Using Novell's NFAP helps simplify network administration by eliminating the need to install Novell Client on computers that simply need to access files on NetWare servers. To provide access directly from Windows, Unix, and Apple clients, the NetWare 6 server needs to have NFAP installed by selecting the NFAP option during server installation, as described earlier in this chapter, or by adding it later using the install feature of the server console. Although supporting Apple and Unix clients is important in many networks, in this chapter, you learn how to use NFAP to work with Microsoft clients.

As shown in Table 6-7, accessing certain eDirectory or application services on a NetWare server still requires Novell Client to be installed on the workstation. Because eDirectory services are necessary to provide the best security and administer certain eDirectory objects and services, Novell Client still plays an important role in a Novell network. In

"The Novell Client" section later in this chapter, you also learn how the Novell client is installed and configured on user workstations.

## Web Browser Clients

Web browsers, such as Internet Explorer and Netscape, are clients that use HTTP and WebDAV to make requests to Web servers. Today, many Internet applications are being written to provide access to data and services from Web browsers. An important part of Novell's OneNet strategy is to allow administrators and users to use their Web browsers as clients to manage the network and access file and print services. In this book, you will learn about a number of Web-enabled applications that are part of NetWare 6, including iManager, Remote Manager, iFolder, and iPrint. In Chapter 13, you will learn how to use Remote Manager and how to configure iFolder so that users can access their files from any location using browser software. In Chapter 7, you will use the iManager utility, and in Chapter 11, you will learn how the Internet Printing Protocol is used to set up and maintain the network printing environment.

6

## Using the Microsoft Client

The Microsoft client is needed to access shared resources and services from other Windows-based computers. It is optional on Windows 9x, but is automatically installed with the Windows 2000 and XP operating systems. Because the Microsoft client is so common on desktop computers, it is a natural choice for accessing NetWare file services on workstations that do not need additional Novell services.

As you learned in Chapter 1, in peer-to-peer networks, Windows servers are organized into workgroups. For Microsoft clients to access the NetWare server, NFAP makes the NetWare 6 server appear to the Windows client as another Windows server in a workgroup. During NFAP installation, a Microsoft server name and workgroup is assigned to the NetWare 6 server along with the volumes to be shared with the Microsoft clients. The default method is to share all volumes and place the NetWare server in the WORKGROUP workgroup, using a Microsoft server name that includes the NetWare server name followed by an underscore character and a "W." For example, the Microsoft server name for CBE_ADMIN would be CBE_ADMIN_W. A user can access data volumes on the NetWare server by browsing the network with My Network Places or entering the Universal Naming Convention (UNC) path for the data volume. A UNC path has two backslashes preceding the server name and a backslash separating the server and shared volume name. For example, the name for the DATA volume on the CBE_ADMIN_W server would be \\CBE_ADMIN_W\DATA.

When a computer running a Microsoft client attempts to access a NetWare 6 server running NFAP, the Windows client submits its local user name and password to the NetWare server in the same way it would attempt to log on to a Microsoft server. Access is granted if the user account and password exist on the NetWare server. If the user account and password on the NetWare server do not match the user account and password used to log on to the Microsoft client, an Enter Network Password dialog box opens, requesting the user to enter his or her user name and password for the CBE_ADMIN_W server.

In addition to a user's eDirectory password that the Novell client needs, NetWare keeps a separate password for each user account to use when logging on from Microsoft clients. Keeping separate passwords for use with NFAP is necessary because the Microsoft client uses a different password encryption system than Novell's eDirectory-based clients do. Novell refers to NFAP passwords as simple passwords because they do not have the same security encryption used with the Novell eDirectory passwords. If users log in from two different computers, one using only the Microsoft client and another using the Novell client, they need to maintain separate passwords, one password for the Novell client and a simple password for use with the computer that has only the Microsoft client.

## The Novell Client

Although the Microsoft NetWare client can be used to log in and access basic NetWare file and print services, it does not have all the capabilities of the Novell client that ships with NetWare 6. For example, Novell Client offers the following advantages over using the Microsoft NetWare client when logging in to a NetWare 6 server:

- Easy access to network services through the addition of the Novell menu in the taskbar and extra NetWare options in My Computer, Network Neighborhood, and Explorer menus
- More secure passwords
- The ability to use NetWare utilities, such as ConsoleOne (see Chapter 7 for more on this utility) and NetWare Administrator
- Support for ZENworks application services

As shown in Table 6-8, over time there have been several versions of the Novell client for different operating system environments. Earlier versions of the Novell client required the use of IPX/SPX to communicate with NetWare servers. As a result, there are still applications that need IPX/SPX to operate. The Novell client that ships with NetWare 6 offers backward-compatibility with earlier clients and applications by supporting the IPX/SPX application interface over TCP/IP.

**Table 6-8**    Novell Clients

| Novell Client Version | Description |
| --- | --- |
| NetX | The NetX client, used with DOS and Windows 3.1, provided network access using only IPX/SPX; the NetX client acted as a shell to the DOS environment, enabling it to use network services. It was loaded with the Autoexec.bat file to run the NIC driver, load the protocol, and run the client. |

**Table 6-8**    Novell Clients (continued)

| Novell Client Version | Description |
| --- | --- |
| Client 32 | Client 32, an early version of Novell Client, was used with Windows 95. Like the NetX client, Client 32 depended on IPX/SPX to access NetWare servers. Client 32 used the capabilities of a 32-bit operating system to enhance the client's features and performance. Because operating systems such as Windows 95 are more network-aware than DOS, Client 32 worked with the operating system to provide access to NetWare services instead of acting as a DOS shell. |
| Novell Client | Novell Client is an improved version of Client 32 that provides access to NetWare services by using IPX/SPX or TCP/IP. Versions of Novell Client are available for Windows 9x/2000/NT/XP computers. The latest Novell Client version is required if you need to use NetWare 6 management tools, such as ConsoleOne, and access application services, such as ZENworks. |

6

Installing Novell Client from a CD on every workstation in a network would be a time-consuming task for most organizations. Fortunately, Novell offers multiple installation or upgrade methods to make the job of implementing Novell Client easier. As a network administrator, you can select any of the following methods to install Novell Client, depending on the workstation's configuration and your personal preferences:

- *Install from CD*—This method is best used on new workstations that are not currently connected to the network. If the workstation has a CD-ROM drive, Novell Client can be installed quickly from the client CD.

- *Install from the network*—Another good use of Novell NFAP is installing Novell Client on a new Windows computer. With NFAP, a new computer can log in to the network using only the default Microsoft client. Novell Client can then be installed from a shared copy of the client installation software on the NetWare server. Installing from the network is faster and more convenient than installing from a CD.

- *Automatic Client Upgrade (ACU)*—You can use the ACU method to automate upgrading older Novell Client versions to the latest Novell Client when a user logs in from the workstation.

- *Install from the Novell Web site*—You can download the latest client from Novell's Web site. This method is preferred because the client software is updated frequently, thus ensuring that you have the newest and most enhanced version. You will perform this type of installation later in Project 6-3, but take a look at the steps David used to install Novell client:

  1. From his XP Professional workstation, he clicked the Internet Explorer icon and connected to *www.novell.com*. When he searched for product downloads, he saw the top 10 downloads available from Novell, as shown in Figure 6-21.

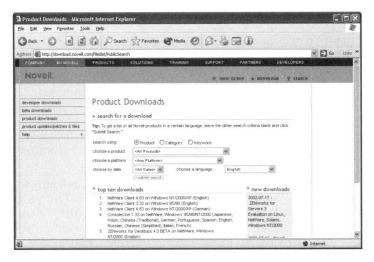

**Figure 6-21**    Available downloads

2. He selected a location on his PC to download the file.

 **Tip** Create a folder on your desktop with a descriptive name, such as NW Client, and download the file to that location. There's nothing worse than down-loading a large file and forgetting where you sent it.

3. After the file was downloaded and expanded, he located the Setupnw file and double-clicked it, as shown in Figure 6-22.

**Figure 6-22**    The Setupnw file

4. After he selected the Typical option, all the necessary files were installed on his PC (a process that could take several minutes). When prompted to restart his PC, he clicked the Reboot button.

5. When XP Professional started, he saw the Novell Login window (see Figure 6-23). He had to click the Advanced button before he could enter all the information shown in the figure.

**Figure 6-23**    The Novell Login window

Now that Novell Client has been installed, you can use this client to log in to your network.

## Logging In

Before accessing resources or services on a network, users must authenticate themselves by providing a valid user name and password to the client software. The client software then uses this information to authenticate users to the network. Novell uses the term **logging in** for the process of entering an authorized user name and password before gaining access to the network. To access a local Windows 2000/XP workstation, Microsoft also requires a valid user name and password, and refers to this authentication process as **logging on** to the workstation. As a result, when you access the Novell network from a Windows 2000/XP workstation, you need to perform two authentication processes. First, you log in to the network using Novell Client. Novell Client then attempts to log on to the local Windows 2000/XP workstation with the user name and password you supplied to Novell Client. If the local workstation has a user account with this user name and password, the user is automatically logged on. However, if the local workstation doesn't have a user account that matches the Novell Client user name and password, the user sees a Windows logon window and must enter a valid user name and password to authenticate to the local workstation before proceeding.

To allow users to access the Novell network, the network administrator needs to create a user account in Novell's eDirectory for each user. To make accessing the local workstation easier, the network administrator can also create a user account on the Windows 2000/XP workstation with the same user name and password as the Novell user name. Because Novell's eDirectory service stores user accounts in containers stored in a tree structure, users must supply their user names and passwords when logging in, along with the container and tree where their user names are located. The location of the container in eDirectory is referred to as its "context." Figure 6-23 showed the Novell Login window after David clicked the Advanced button. Notice that the window contains text boxes called Username, Password, Tree, Context, and Server. It also contains the Windows tab, used to specify the local user name for logging on to the Windows 2000/XP workstation (see Figure 6-24). The user name entered in this tab must exist on the local computer and is initially set to Administrator. The local user name determines the rights and desktop environment users will have on the local workstation. If multiple users share a workstation, you should create a local user account for each user.

**Figure 6-24**    The Windows tab of the Novell Login window

By default, the Username text box contains the name and context of the last user who logged in from your workstation. If no one has logged in since the client was installed, the Username text box is blank. The Password text box is where you enter the password associated with your user account. This field is kept blank to prevent someone else from logging in as the previous user. Your password is used like a signature, allowing eDirectory to verify that you are the actual user of the account. Clicking the Advanced button enables you to select the tree and context information identifying the location of your user account. Use the Context text box to specify the path leading to the container where your user name is stored. You can use the buttons to the right of each text box to browse for a tree, container, or server instead of typing in the object's exact name. The list arrows next to each text box enable you to select from previously used trees and contexts. You will have the opportunity to use Novell Client as well as other methods to gain access to your network throughout this book's projects.

## Viewing NetWare Resources

Now that David has installed the client software, he can view a list of the NetWare connections by using NetWare's extensions to My Network Places and Windows Explorer. When he right-clicks the My Network Places icon on the desktop or in Windows Explorer, a shortcut menu appears, as shown in Figure 6-25. Note the additions, or extensions, to the menu.

**Figure 6-25**    NetWare extensions

David wants to view the current network connections, so he clicks Explore on the shortcut menu, and then clicks the Novell Connections entry shown in Figure 6-26.

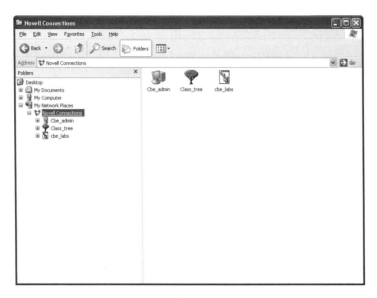

**Figure 6-26**    Current network connections

He can also view additional information, while in Explorer, by expanding the Entire Network icon, as shown in Figure 6-27.

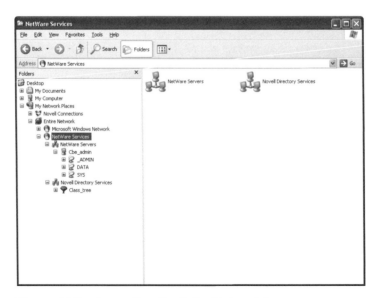

**Figure 6-27**    Expanding the Entire Network icon

## Verifying the Installation

After completing the server and workstation installation, you should restart your workstation to load the new parameters. If you see a "NetWare server not found" message, the most common causes are a defective cable, a faulty Ethernet connector, an incorrect frame type, an interrupt being used by both the network card and some other device in the server or workstation, a faulty hub, or the IP protocol not being properly bound to the network card on the NetWare server.

 Sometimes the reason for a problem can be so obvious that it escapes you. Take, for example, the case of a network administrator who spent some time looking for the cause of a "NetWare server not found" message only to discover that someone had broken into the NetWare server room and actually stolen the server. In this case, the workstation was literally correct: The NetWare server could not be found!

After verifying that the NetWare server and workstations are communicating correctly, you can continue setting up the network by establishing the NetWare server's directory structure, user accounts, and security, as described in the following chapters. Installation is an ongoing process that enhances the NetWare server and expands the network to incorporate additional workstations.

Is it necessary to install the Novell client on all computers? Then answer is no. In fact, Novell has done an excellent job of making it possible for many different clients to connect to a NetWare server without client software. The following section explains how a Microsoft client can access resources on a NetWare server without NFAP.

## The Microsoft Client Service for NetWare

As you learned previously, NFAP enables computers with only Microsoft, Macintosh, or Unix client software to access files on a NetWare server by using NFAP's simple password system. The simple passwords used by the Microsoft client are not as secure as the Novell eDirectory passwords used by the Novell client and require users who have both Novell Client and the Microsoft client installed to maintain two passwords. Another alternative to installing the Novell client on Windows computers is to use Microsoft's NetWare client. Windows 9x, Windows 2000, and Windows XP all come with an optional NetWare client that enables users to access services on NetWare 6 servers. If you install the Microsoft NetWare client, users can access NetWare files and printers with their eDirectory user names and passwords. Using the Microsoft NetWare client rather than the full Novell Client helps keep the computer configuration simpler because the Microsoft NetWare client requires less maintenance to configure. In addition, using the Microsoft NetWare client can reduce the chance of system failures caused by system conflicts with the Novell client. The disadvantage of the Microsoft NetWare client is that it does not support ZENworks applications or administrative utilities, such as NetWare Administrator or ConsoleOne. In addition, the Microsoft NetWare client requires the

NetWare 6 server to use IPX/SPX. If you are planning to use only TCP/IP on your network, the Microsoft NetWare client will not be able to access NetWare servers.

## CHAPTER SUMMARY

❒ The NetWare installation process is divided into two major operations: installing the NetWare server software and installing the workstation software. Installing NetWare on a server can be divided into eight main steps. Step 1 involves planning the network layout and documenting the network environment and NetWare server hardware configuration. Step 2 is installing and configuring the NetWare server hardware. Step 3 includes partitioning the boot drive and installing DOS. In Step 4, you complete the portion that runs under DOS, which includes loading the correct disk drivers, local area network (LAN) drivers, and protocols and creating drive partitions and volumes. In Step 5, you work with the main steps of the Install Wizard that runs under NetWare 6. Step 6 is installing Novell eDirectory Services and creating the eDirectory tree. Step 7 is editing the Startup.ncf and Autoexec.ncf startup files, and Step 8 is choosing additional installation options.

❒ For the NetWare server to connect to the network, disk drivers and network interface card (NIC) LAN drivers must be correctly loaded into the NetWare NOS. Similarly, network protocols must be bound to the NICs. The commands to bind network protocols to NIC are stored in the Startup.ncf and the Autoexec.ncf files so that they will run automatically when the NetWare server is started. MONITOR.NLM is a useful tool for monitoring the NetWare server's performance.

❒ To access the NetWare server, the workstation requires three software components: the network card driver, which provides the data link process of transmitting and receiving packets over the network cable system; the protocol stack, which is responsible for formatting packets through the OSI network, transport, and session layers (in NetWare 6, TCP/IP is the default protocol); and the client software that supplies an interface from Windows to the NetWare server. Novell Client acts as a front end for Windows and directs all application and user requests for NetWare services to the network server. All three components are included with the installation process for Novell Client. Novell Client software can also improve network performance and security by using packet burst mode and packet signatures.

❒ Novell Client software is available in versions for Windows 95/98/2000, NT, and XP. The client files are on the Novell Client/ZENworks CD included with NetWare 6. They can also be downloaded free from Novell's Web site. Installing Novell Client for Windows XP Professional is an auto-run function from the CD, or you can run the Setupnw program located in the client folder if you have downloaded the files from Novell. After installation, you can configure Novell Client by setting parameters in the Novell Client for Windows Properties dialog box.

❐ Novell frequently issues updates and patch files to the NetWare NOS and Novell Client files. After installation, periodically you need to download and install any necessary updates.

❐ You use the Novell Login window provided with Novell Client to log in to eDirectory trees and NetWare servers. You can log in to more than one eDirectory tree when using Novell Client.

❐ After installing the workstation software, you should restart the computer and attempt to log in to the NetWare server. When first loaded, Novell Client attempts to attach to an eDirectory tree and a default NetWare server. If the workstation does not receive a response from a NetWare server in a few moments, it returns a "NetWare server not found" error message. The most common causes of this error message are a bad cable, incorrect frame type, overlapping interrupt assignments, or the IP protocol not being properly bound to the network card on the NetWare server.

6

# KEY TERMS

**console command** — A command function built into the NetWare kernel Server.exe program and, therefore, is always in memory.

**internal network number** — A network address used internally by NetWare to communicate with its software components.

**logging in** — The process of authenticating yourself to a Novell network by supplying a user name and password.

**logging on** — The process of authenticating yourself to a Windows network by supplying a user name and password.

**MONITOR utility** — A NetWare console utility that displays essential information about NetWare server performance.

**multiple NetWare server network** — A network with more than one NetWare server attached.

**NetWare Command File (NCF)** — A file similar to a DOS batch file in that it contains console commands and program startup commands that the operating system will run. Startup.ncf and Autoexec.ncf are two examples.

**NetWare Loadable Module (NLM)** — A program that can be loaded and run on the NetWare server. There are four types of NLMs, identified by their three-letter extension. The filename extension .NLM is used for general-purpose programs; .DSK is for disk drivers; .LAN, for network card drivers; and .NAM for name space support modules.

**NetWare server name** — The name that a NetWare server broadcasts over the network; when referring to eDirectory, the name of the NetWare Server object.

**Network Address Translation (NAT)** — An Internet standard that maps internal private IP addresses to Public IP addresses.

**network layout** — An installation-planning document that consists of the following information: the NetWare server's name and internal network number, the network topology and NICs, IP addresses of all devices connected to the network, and the frame type used on the cable system.

**support pack (SP)** — An update to software that fixes or improves on current software.

## REVIEW QUESTIONS

1. Which of the following commands assigns a protocol to a LAN driver?

   a. BIND

   b. CONFIG

   c. LOAD

   d. NETBIND

2. A(n) _____ is used internally by the NetWare operating system to communicate with its device drivers.

3. A NetWare server's name can be from _____ to _____ characters.

   a. 1, 255

   b. 2, 255

   c. 1, 47

   d. 2, 47

4. All devices that communicate with each other over a network cable system must use the same _____.

   a. packet frame type

   b. IP number

   c. IPX number

   d. hostname

5. A network containing two different NetWare servers is referred to as which of the following?

   a. external network

   b. internal network

   c. bridged network

   d. multiple NetWare server network

6. Multiple networks connected by routers are called which of the following?

   a. Internet

   b. intranet

c. internetwork

d. multinetwork

7. A NetWare server that connects two different networks is referred to as using which of the following?

a. internal router

b. multihomed switch

c. external router

d. multihomed bridge

8. Which of the following is an invalid IPX network address?

a. A

b. 10BaseT

c. 1AB216A15

d. 1EEE8025

9. Which of the following console commands would show the total file memory available on the file server?

a. DISPLAY SYSTEM

b. MEMORY

c. SYSTEM

d. RESTART

10. Which of the following key combinations is used to switch the server console from one active module to another?

a. Alt+Esc

b. Ctrl+Alt+Delete

c. Alt+Tab

d. Esc+Shift+6

11. Where are updated Novell files and patches available?

12. Which of the following commands is used at the DOS prompt to start the NetWare NOS on a NetWare server?

a. START

b. Autoexec.ncf

c. SERVER

d. REBOOT

13. Which of the following server commands closes all files and volumes, disconnects all users, and takes the file server offline?

   a. DOWN

   b. CLOSE

   c. EXIT

   d. BYE

14. The _____ command attaches a protocol stack to a network and is necessary so that workstations using that protocol can communicate with the file server.

15. Novell's OneNet strategy allows administrators to use their _____ as clients to manage the network and access file and print services.

16. The _____ controls the NIC so that it can send and receive packets over the network cable system.

17. Microsoft clients use which of the following to access services on Windows?

   a. NCP

   b. NFS

   c. CIFS

   d. AFP

18. Which of the following eliminates the need to install Novell Client software on workstations that will simply access files from NetWare servers?

   a. NFAP

   b. CIFS

   c. AFP

   d. FAA

19. Which of the following clients requires NFAP to be installed on the NetWare 6 server?

   a. Microsoft client

   b. Web browser client

   c. Microsoft NetWare client

   d. Novell Client

20. Another alternative to installing the Novell client on Windows computers is to install which of the following?

   a. ZENworks on the client

   b. ATP on the client

   c. Microsoft NetWare client

   d. NFAP on the client

# HANDS-ON PROJECTS

## Project 6-1: Using Console Commands

To perform this project, you need to have access to your server's system console. An important task for every network administrator is developing and maintaining documentation on the network and server configurations. Use the following steps to record the requested server and network information, and summarize your findings in a written report to your instructor.

1. Use the **CONFIG** command to record the following server data:

   ❏ Server name

   ❏ Internal IPX number (if your server is using IPX protocol)

   ❏ Network card driver

   ❏ Interrupt

   ❏ Port

   ❏ Network address

   ❏ Node address

   ❏ Frame type

   ❏ Bindery context

   ❏ Currently mounted volumes

   If IPX is not installed on your server, skip the following step.

2. If using the IPX protocol, enter the **DISPLAY SERVERS** command, and record up to two servers.

3. Use the **MEMORY** command, and record your server's amount of RAM.

4. Use the **VOLUMES** command, and record the name of each volume.

## Project 6-2: Testing a NetWare 6 Installation

For this project, you need access to a NetWare server console you have recently installed or one provided by your instructor. Table 6-9 presents a set of console commands that were not discussed in the chapter. Try the commands on the console, and record the results. Write a short memo to your instructor, including the following information for each console command:

1. Briefly describe its purpose and why you might use it after performing an installation.

6

2. Report and interpret the results of the console command.

**Table 6-9**    Selected NetWare Console Commands

| Command | Purpose |
|---------|---------|
| SPEED | Use this command to display the speed of the NetWare server's processor. |
| MEMORY | Use this command to display the amount of installed memory. |
| MODULES | Use this command to display a list of the modules that are currently running on the NetWare server. The output includes the name, description, and version number (for .DSK, .LAN, and .NLM modules). |
| VOLUMES | Use this command to display a list of the mounted volumes on the NetWare server. The output uses the following flags:<br>Cp–File compression is enabled.<br>Sa–Block suballocation is enabled.<br>Mg–Data migration is enabled. |
| DISPLAY SERVERS | Use this command to display a list of all NetWare servers and services that are broadcasting SAP packets. Services will include NetWare servers, eDirectory, print servers, Storage Management Services (SMS) devices, and Structured Query Language (SQL) servers. The output includes the network address of the server and the number of hops to the server, where a hop is defined as the number of routers the packer must pass through to get to the destination. |
| DISPLAY IPX NETWORKS | Use this command to display a list of networks recognized by the NetWare server. The output includes the IPX external network number followed by the number of hops to the network and the time in tics (1/18th of a second) it takes for a packet to get to that address. |

## Project 6-3: Installing Novell Client for Windows XP Professional on a Workstation

In this project, you install Novell Client for Windows XP Professional by downloading the most recent version available from Novell. First, check the Novell Support Connection Web site for the most recent Novell Client version. Next, you'll download this file and install it on your PC. To complete this project, you need the following components, which you instructor will supply:

❏ A workstation with a LAN card, a CD-ROM drive, a hard drive, and Windows XP Professional installed

❏ Internet access at the workstation and a Web browser with FTP capabilities

1. Use your Web browser to connect to the Novell Support Connection Web site at *http://support.novell.com*.

2. Browse the Web site to see what information is available.

3. Download the most recent file for Novell Client for Windows XP Professional. Your instructor will provide additional information about where to store this file.

4. Your instructor will give you instructions on how to expand the contents of the file you downloaded.

## Project 6-4: Customizing the Novell Client

In this project, you have been asked to customize the Novell clients in each department to default to the department's container, which will make it easier for users to log in. You'll also explore some of the options available when customizing Novell Client. Record the information requested during these steps, and submit it to your instructor as a written report.

1. If necessary, start your computer to open the Novell Login window.

2. Click the **Workstation only** check box, and log on to your local Windows computer with your Windows local administrator user name and password.

3. Right-click **My Network Places**, and then click **Properties** to open the Network Connections dialog box.

4. Right-click **Local Area Connection**, and then click **Properties** to open the Local Area Connections dialog box.

5. Record the items listed under this heading: This connection uses the following items.

6. Click the **Novell Client for Windows** item to highlight it, and then click the **Properties** button to open the Novell Client for Windows Properties dialog box.

7. If necessary, click the **Client** tab to select it, as shown in Figure 6-28. Notice the text boxes for First network drive, Preferred server, and Preferred tree. You can use these text boxes to change the initial settings when a user first logs in. The Client tab also contains the version number of the client and the latest service pack. This information is important to ensure that the client is current. The bottom section of the Client tab contains the default context where eDirectory will look to find the user name.

6

**Figure 6-28**    The Novell Client for Windows Properties dialog box

8. Verify that the First network drive is set to F and that the Preferred tree text box contains CLASS_TREE.

9. Change the default context to point to your ##ADMINOU container in the CLASS Organization:

   a. Click in the **Tree** text box, and then enter **CLASS_TREE**.

   b. Click in the **Name context** text box, and then enter **.##ADMINOU.CLASS**.

   c. Click the **Add** button to insert the context into the Name context pane (see Figure 6-29). If tree and context information is already listed, select the entry and click **Remove**.

10. Click the **Advanced Login** tab, where you set which options are displayed when you click the Advanced button during login. Record the current settings.

11. Click the **Advanced Menu Settings** tab, where you can set the options available on various menus. Click the **Change Password** option (if it's not highlighted by default) and then record the description.

12. Click the **Advanced Settings** tab, where you control parameters used to communicate on the network. Click the **File Caching** option and then record its description.

**Figure 6-29**    Changing the default context

13. Click the **Contextless Login** tab, which is used to specify a global catalog of objects. The global catalog makes it possible to log in or access a resource without specifying which container the user account or resource is located in.

14. Click **OK** to close the Novell Client for Windows Properties dialog box.

15. Click **Close** to close the Local Area Connection Properties dialog box.

16. Close all open windows, and log off.

## CASE PROJECTS

### Case 6-1: Documenting the NIC and Driver

You have been tasked to document your server's NIC card and to download the most updated driver. After determining the NIC's manufacturer, locate the company's site and download the correct driver. Write a memo to your instructor detailing the steps you took to complete the task. Include any problems you encountered and how you solved them.

## Case 6-2: Building a Server Baseline

Although the CBE network is performing fine, increased demands and equipment failures could cause future performance problems. To help identify performance problems that might occur, determine the server's nominal performance by using the MONITOR utility to build a baseline showing server performance during typical work periods. In this project, use the MONITOR utility over a period of a few days to determine server baseline statistics. To do this project, you need access to the MONITOR utility from the server console or through the remote console facility. Your instructor will provide instructions on accessing the MONITOR utility. Summarize your findings in a written report to your instructor.

# 7

# CREATING THE eDIRECTORY TREE STRUCTURE

**After reading this chapter and completing the exercises, you will be able to:**

♦ Use NetWare utilities to work with the eDirectory tree structure

♦ Create, move, rename, and delete container objects

♦ Install and use NetWare Administrator, ConsoleOne, and iManager to browse the eDirectory tree, view object properties, and create new objects

♦ Use ConsoleOne to view and work with partitions and replicas

♦ Rename eDirectory trees

**A**fter the server installation is finished, it's time to set up the eDirectory tree structure. You planned the eDirectory tree in Chapter 4 and created the first portions of it during the NetWare 6 installation in Chapter 6. Now you need to create the tree's organizational structure and add network resources in their proper organizational context. To do this, you need to understand the NetWare commands and utilities used to create, navigate, and display the eDirectory tree. In Chapter 9, you'll add users, groups, and organizational roles to the tree.

## NETWARE UTILITIES

You need to be familiar with Novell's management utilities to work with the eDirectory tree. In previous releases of NetWare, implementing and managing the eDirectory tree required running the NetWare Administrator utility on a computer with the Novell client installed. In NetWare 5, Novell introduced the ConsoleOne utility, which was written using the Java language so that it could run on multiple platforms, including the NetWare server's console. With NetWare 6, Novell has introduced a new network management tool called iManager that can be used in addition to NetWare Administrator and ConsoleOne. With this utility, network administrators can manage their eDirectory trees from a Web browser, such as Internet Explorer, instead of having to use a workstation with the Novell client. Because the iManager utility does not require the Novell client running on a Windows-based computer, it is an integral part of Novell's OneNet vision, allowing network management from any client on a connected network.

The version of iManager that ships with NetWare 6 is referred to as a "pre-release" utility because it offers only limited eDirectory object management. Until Novell is able to incorporate all management tasks into iManager, network administrators need to be able to use the legacy Novell Client utilities—ConsoleOne and NetWare Administrator—to perform certain management tasks. Each utility has its advantages and disadvantages. For example, ConsoleOne has the most capability to manage NetWare 6 features, NetWare Administrator provides high performance on older computers, and iManager can be used from any network through a standard Web browser. Because of the utilities' different capabilities, a Certified Novell Administrator (CNA) needs to be familiar with all three utilities. Although ConsoleOne is the primary utility used in this book, you'll also learn how to use NetWare Administrator and iManager to perform network tasks, and the activities in this book introduce you to using all three utilities. In the following sections, you learn how to install NetWare Administrator and ConsoleOne and then use these utilities to view the CBE Labs tree structure that David Doering, the network administrator, designed.

### NetWare Administrator

To run **NetWare Administrator (NWAdmin)**, you need a Windows 9x, 2000, or XP workstation with at least 64 MB of RAM and the Novell Client software. Although the Microsoft client enables users to access NetWare file and print services, it does not have the necessary components to run ConsoleOne or NetWare Administrator. During server installation, the NetWare Administrator software is loaded into the Public directory of the server's SYS volume. David used the following steps to create a NetWare Administrator shortcut on his desktop:

1. He started his client computer and logged in with Administrator rights.

2. Next, he opened the Z:\Public\Win32 folder by following these steps:

   a. He double-clicked the My Computer icon.

b. He double-clicked the Z: drive.

c. He double-clicked the win32 folder.

3. He right-clicked the nwadmin32 program, and then clicked Send to, Desktop (create shortcut) to create a shortcut on his desktop.

Now that NetWare Administrator is available on your desktop, you can use this tool to browse the eDirectory tree, view object properties, and create new objects. After logging in and double-clicking the Nwadmin32 shortcut, you'll see a window similar to Figure 7-1. You can open a new browse window by clicking the Close button and selecting Tools, NDS Browser from the menu bar. This opens the Set Context dialog box, where you can see your workstation's current context in the tree. If you want to change to one level higher, click the browse button next to the Context text box, and double-click the up arrow in the Browse context section of the Select Object dialog box (see Figure 7-2).

7

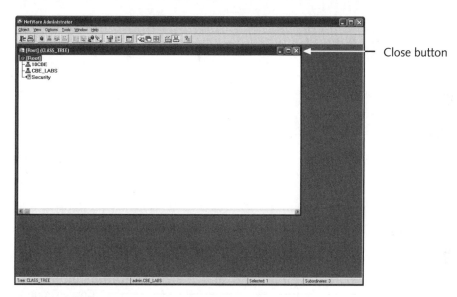

Close button

**Figure 7-1**   The NetWare Administrator browse window

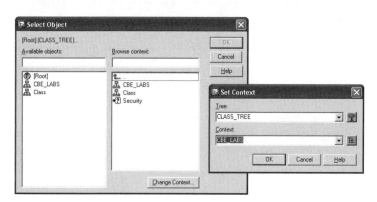

**Figure 7-2**   The NetWare Administrator Select Object dialog box

The NetWare Administrator utility contains a number of buttons on its toolbar for performing various activities, as illustrated in Figure 7-3. As with any new tool, you should spend some time working with it and getting familiar with what each button does. You see how David uses this utility to perform some eDirectory management tasks in the "Working with Container and Leaf Objects" section, but for now, take a look at another utility called ConsoleOne.

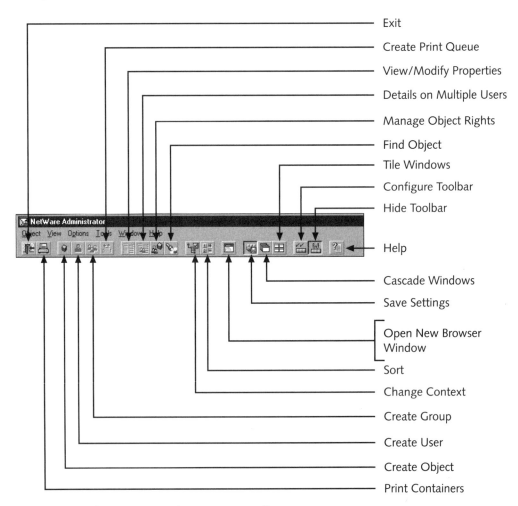

**Figure 7-3**    The NetWare Administrator toolbar

# ConsoleOne

**ConsoleOne** remains the primary utility for managing most aspects of the NetWare 6 eDirectory tree. ConsoleOne requires a workstation to have Novell Client installed and at least 128 MB of RAM and a 300 MHz processor to run effectively. Although the

ConsoleOne software can be run directly from the NetWare 6 server's SYS volume; loading the ConsoleOne files across the network is slower and uses up network bandwidth. It's much faster to start ConsoleOne if you install it on your local computer. As mentioned in Chapter 6, to get the latest version of NetWare products, go to the *www.novell.com/download* Web site. Look for the most recent ConsoleOne version, and follow the same instructions you would use to download the Novell Client software. After downloading, you should create a shortcut icon on your desktop for easy access. David decided to copy the ConsoleOne installation files to the Client directory of the SYS volume to make it easier to install on additional workstations. He used these steps to install ConsoleOne on his workstation:

1. He logged in to the workstation as Administrator.

2. He started the ConsoleOne installation program in the Public\Client\ConsoleOne directory of the server's SYS volume with these steps:

    a. He double-clicked My Computer, and then double-clicked the Public on 'Cbe_admin\Sys' (Z:) drive to open the Public folder.

    b. He double-clicked the Client folder to open it.

    c. He double-clicked the c1.exe icon (for the Win Setup program) to start this program.

    d. He clicked the Novell ConsoleOne option to display the installation options for ConsoleOne, and then clicked the Novell ConsoleOne 1.3 option to open the WinZip Self-Extractor – Welcome to ConsoleOne window.

3. He clicked the Setup button to start unzipping the ConsoleOne files and to display the Welcome window of the ConsoleOne Installation Wizard.

4. He read the information in the Welcome window, and then clicked the Next button to continue.

5. He viewed the License Agreement window, and then clicked the Accept button to continue.

6. He clicked Next to accept the default installation directory. Then he clicked Next to accept the default components to install, clicked Next to install in English, selected I DO in the License window, and clicked Next.

7. He clicked the Finish button to complete the installation and waited for the files to be copied to his local hard drive.

The file-copying process normally takes several minutes, so it's a good time to take a short break. The Installation Complete window is displayed after all files are copied to your local computer and a shortcut to start ConsoleOne is added to your desktop.

8. He clicked the Close button and waited for the WinZip window to close and return him to the Client Installation ConsoleOne options.

9. ConsoleOne uses snap-ins to extend its ability to manage network objects. To enable the full features of ConsoleOne, David needed to install the snap-in files by following these steps:

   a. He clicked the NetWare 6 ConsoleOne Snapins option to open the WinZip Self-Extractor dialog box.

   b. He verified that the path shown in the WinZip Self-Extractor dialog box pointed to the location where he placed the ConsoleOne software.

   c. He clicked the Unzip button to extract the files to his ConsoleOne folder, and waited while the files were extracted.

   d. When David saw the message indicating that the files were successfully unzipped, he clicked OK to exit the snap-in installation, and then clicked the Close button to close the WinZip Self-Extractor dialog box.

   e. He then clicked the Exit button to close the Novell Client Installation window.

When David double-clicks the ConsoleOne icon on his desktop, he will see a window similar to Figure 7-4.

**Figure 7-4**    The ConsoleOne window

On the left is the Navigation frame, which displays structure objects, such as containers, servers, and volumes. On the right is the Object frame, which displays leaf objects, such as users, groups, and printers. If necessary, you can click the + symbol to the left of an icon to expand it. Before seeing ConsoleOne in action, however, take a look at one more utility you can use to manage eDirectory.

## iManager

You've worked with ConsoleOne and have become comfortable with its graphical user interface (GUI). You decide you need a vacation and are sitting in your Maui hotel room when the telephone rings. "I know you're on vacation, but could you please add a new Organizational Unit container called TV_Sales under the Marketing Organizational Unit?" the desperate voice asks. Is this possible from your laptop computer that doesn't have ConsoleOne installed? Yes, it is. There are several tools for such a task, but **iManager** gives you the ability to do your job without having to use ConsoleOne or any other client software. In fact, all you need is a Web browser. When NetWare 6 is installed, an IP address is configured for several components: iFolder, iManager, Apache Web Server, and so forth. It is beyond the scope of this book to discuss all these installation components, but you should understand the process of how to manage your NetWare server from any remote location. iManager is based on the **eDirectory Management Framework (eMFrame)**, which is a Web application you can use to easily build modular eDirectory management services called plug-ins. eMFrame plug-ins define management roles and implement tasks associated with those roles. eMFrame is implemented as a Java servlet and uses WebAccess technology developed for GroupWise. Its features are also accessible from a command prompt and through scripts.

First, take a look at a fast way to get a little information from Novell about iManager. To connect to your server, simply enter https://*ip_address*:2200/eMFrame/iManager.html as a URL (replacing *ip_address* with the IP address of your NetWare server).

Remember to stay current on updates. If you have not installed SP1 on your server, you might see iManager referred to as iManage.

7

To connect to your server, enter https://*ip_address*:2200/eMFrame/iManager.html as the URL, and click Yes to accept the security certificate for this site. You'll be prompted to log in to your server, as Figure 7-5 illustrates.

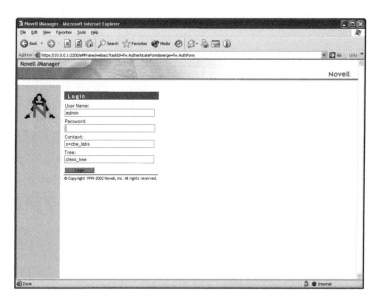

**Figure 7-5**    The iManager Login window

After logging in, you see a welcome window like the one in Figure 7-6. You get a chance to create an object using iManager in the section "Creating eDirectory Container Objects."

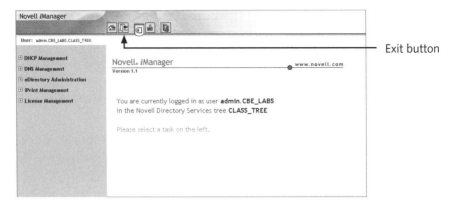

**Figure 7-6** The iManager window listing your task options

## WORKING WITH CONTAINER AND LEAF OBJECTS

Now that you have been introduced to the management utilities, you'll see how David uses NetWare Administrator to create an Alias object in the CBE_LABS Organization, and how he uses the iManager and ConsoleOne utilities to establish his CBE tree structure by creating an Organizational Unit (OU) and a user account.

### Creating eDirectory Container Objects

You use the same basic procedure to create any eDirectory object. All the objects covered in this section have been discussed in detail in Chapter 4. Here, you are concerned with how the different NetWare utilities can be used to manage these objects. You can use any of these methods in ConsoleOne:

- Click the container for the object, click the New Object icon on the toolbar, and then select the type of object you want to create.

- Right-click the container object for the object, point to New, and then click Object on the shortcut menu to open the New Object dialog box. In the Class list, click the type of object you want, and click OK. In the New *ObjectType* dialog box, enter the necessary property values, and then click the OK button.

- Click the container object and press the Insert key.

 The type or class of objects listed in the New Object dialog box's Class list will vary—only the types of objects you can create in the selected container are displayed for you to choose from. When you choose an object type, the corresponding New *ObjectType* dialog box for the object type opens. *ObjectType* is the name of the object you choose in the Class list. For example, if you are creating an OU object, the New Organizational Unit dialog box opens.

## The [Root] Object

The [Root] object is the only exception to the steps just described for creating a new eDirectory tree object. You create the [Root] object *only* during installation of the first NetWare 6 server in the eDirectory tree. The [Root] object stores the name of the eDirectory tree. At this point, you cannot modify the [Root] object itself.

You can rename the eDirectory tree by using the DSMERGE utility, discussed later in this chapter in the "Modifying and Managing the eDirectory Tree" section.

## The Country Object

As Chapter 4 discusses, Country objects are optional, and network administrators often prefer to use Organization objects with geographic names instead of Country objects. The names of Country objects are limited to a standard two-letter code, some of which Table 7-1 shows. The codes are CCITT X.500 standard country codes. The Online Documentation shipped with NetWare 6 lists additional country codes.

**7**

**Table 7-1**    Examples of Country Codes

| Country | Code | Country | Code |
|---------|------|---------|------|
| Australia | AU | Mexico | MX |
| Brazil | BR | New Zealand | NZ |
| Canada | CA | Philippines | PH |
| China | CN | Puerto Rico | PT |
| Denmark | DK | Russian Federation | RU |
| Egypt | EG | Saudi Arabia | SA |
| France | FR | Spain | ES |
| Germany | DE | Switzerland | CH |
| India | IN | United Kingdom | GB |
| Japan | JP | United States | US |

Although many administrators prefer to use Organization objects with geographic names, you might want to add Country objects to the eDirectory tree to represent overseas branches of a company. For example, CBE Labs has just created a European branch with an office in England, so David used these steps to create a United Kingdom Country object in the tree:

1. He logged in with administrative privileges and started ConsoleOne.

2. He clicked the [Root] object, and then clicked the New Object button on the toolbar to open the New Object dialog box, shown in Figure 7-7. (He could also have right-clicked the [Root] object, pointed to New, and then clicked Object on the shortcut menu, shown in Figure 7-8.)

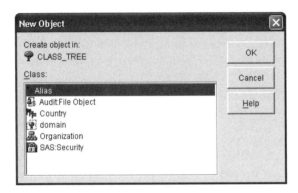

**Figure 7-7** The New Object dialog box

Notice that the list of object types displayed in the Class list varies, depending on which type of new objects you are creating. In this case, you can create only an Alias, an Audit: File Object, a Country, a domain, an Organization, or an SAS: Security object.

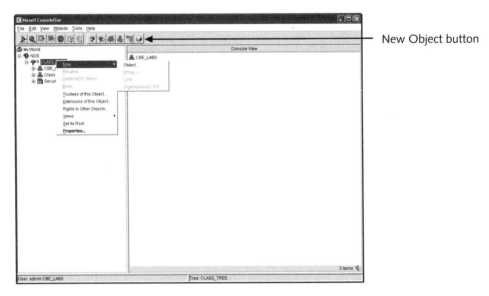

New Object button

**Figure 7-8** Creating a new object in ConsoleOne

3. He clicked Country, and then clicked OK to open the New Country dialog box, shown in Figure 7-9.

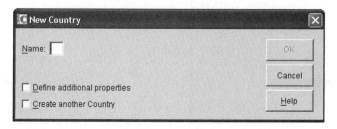

**Figure 7-9**    The New Country dialog box

4. In the Name text box, he typed the country code (gb) for the United Kingdom.

5. He clicked OK, and the gb Country object was added to the directory tree, as shown in Figure 7-10.

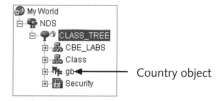 ———— Country object

**Figure 7-10**    The Country object added to the directory tree

## The Organization Object

You can add Organization objects directly below the [Root] or below a Country object in the directory tree. To add an Organization object to a directory tree, select Organization in the Class list, and specify a name for the organization.

David wants to create the CBE_LABS_Europe Organization object below the gb Country object, to indicate the new European operation. To create this Organization object, he used these steps in Console One:

1. He clicked the gb Country object, and then clicked the New Object button on the toolbar to open the New Object dialog box with the Class list of available objects displayed, as shown in Figure 7-11.

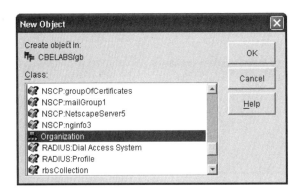

**Figure 7-11**    Creating a new Organization object

2. He clicked Organization, and then clicked OK to open the New Organization dialog box.

3. In the Name text box, he typed CBE_LABS_Europe.

4. He clicked OK, and then double-clicked the gb Country object to display the CBE_LABS_Europe object (see Figure 7-12).

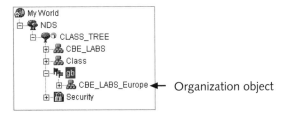

**Figure 7-12**    The CBE_LABS_Europe Organization object added to the directory tree

## The Organizational Unit Object

You can add OU objects directly below an Organization object or another OU object in the directory tree. Take a look at how David used iManager to add OU objects to his directory tree:

1. He started Internet Explorer and opened the iManager utility by following these steps:

   a. He entered the URL https://*ip_address*:2200/eMFrame/iManager.html, replacing *ip_address* with the IP address or DNS name assigned to his server, and then clicked Yes to accept the security certificate for the site.

   b. He logged in with his user name and password.

   c. He clicked the + symbol to the left of eDirectory Administration to display the list of tasks he is authorized to perform.

2. David created the InfoSystems OU by following these steps:

   a. He clicked the Create Object link to open the Available Classes window.

   b. He clicked the Organizational Unit item, and then clicked the Next button to open the Create Organizational Unit window, similar to the one in Figure 7-13.

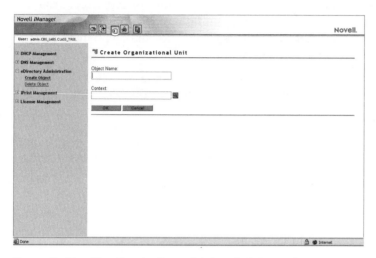

**Figure 7-13**   The Create Organizational Unit window

   c. He entered InfoSystems in the Object Name text box.

   d. He clicked the browse button next to the Context text box, and then clicked his Organization in the browse window that opened to insert it into the Context text box.

   e. He clicked OK to create the object and display the Create Object request succeeded message box.

   f. He clicked OK to acknowledge the message and return to the iManager task list.

3. He repeated Step 2 to create the Test&Eval OU and the Finance OU.

4. He clicked the Exit button on the iManager toolbar to return to the Novell Login window.

5. He closed his Web browser by clicking File, Close on the menu bar.

6. Finally, he logged off Windows.

## Working with eDirectory Leaf Objects

### The Alias Object

An Alias object is a pointer to the real object located in another container. These objects are useful when you need to access physical resources, such as files and printers, from different contexts (several departments in a company, for instance). Using Alias objects enables you to create a single object containing information about a resource and then access that object from other containers. The following steps show how David used NetWare Administrator to create an Alias object for the server:

1. He started NetWare Administrator by double-clicking Shortcut to nwadmin32, and then clicked Close to exit the Welcome to NetWare Administrator window.

If the option to see the Welcome to NetWare Administrator window has been disabled, NetWare Administrator bypasses this window on subsequent startups.

2. He opened a browse window in NetWare Administrator to show the contents of his CBE_LABS container.

3. He clicked the container, and then pressed the Insert key to open the New Object dialog box, similar to the one in Figure 7-14.

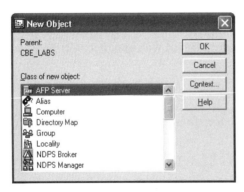

**Figure 7-14**    Selecting an object type in the New Object dialog box

4. He double-clicked Alias in the Class list to open the Create Alias dialog box (see Figure 7-15).

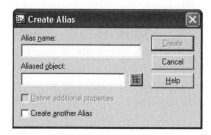

**Figure 7-15**   The Create Alias dialog box

5. He typed CBEHOST in the Alias name text box.

6. He clicked the browse button next to the Aliased object text box to open the Select Object dialog box, and used the Browse context section to navigate to the CBE_LABS container.

7. He double-clicked the CBE_ADMIN NetWare Server object in the Available objects section to insert it into the Aliased object text box.

8. In the Create Alias dialog box, he clicked the Create button to create the alias server object.

9. He double-clicked his new Alias object to open the NetWare Server: CBE_ADMIN dialog box.

10. He clicked the Cancel button to return to NetWare Administrator. His NetWare Administrator window looked like the one shown on Figure 7-16.

**Figure 7-16**   The NetWare Administrator window with the CBEHOST Alias object

## The Volume Object

Volumes are the basic logical components of the network file system. A server's disk space is divided into one or more volumes, much as a file cabinet is divided into one or more drawers. Every NetWare server is required to have one volume named SYS that contains operating system files and utilities. The network administrator then creates additional volumes to store user data and applications. Volume objects point to the physical data volumes on the server and are used to access data and store volume configuration and status information. When a new volume is created on the server, a corresponding Volume object is created in the server's eDirectory container. Additional Volume objects can then be created in other containers to make it easier to access volume data and statistics without browsing the tree or changing your current context. David wanted to create a Volume object on the CBE Labs server named CBEHOST_SYS that points to the SYS volume on his server, just as an Alias object points to an actual physical object on a server. To do this, David used Netware Administrator to perform these steps:

1. He clicked his CBE_LABS container to highlight it.

2. He pressed the Insert key to open the New Object dialog box.

3. He scrolled down the Class list and double-clicked Volume to open the New Volume dialog box.

4. He entered CBEHOST_SYS in the Volume name text box.

5. He clicked the browse button next to the Host server text box to open the Select Objects dialog box.

6. He double-clicked the CBEHOST alias in the Available objects section.

7. He clicked the Physical Volume list arrow to display a list of all volumes on the CBEHOST server.

8. He clicked the SYS volume, and then clicked the Create button. A CBEHOST_SYS Volume object was then displayed in his CBE_LABS container.

## The User Object

Even though you are a network administrator, you are also considered a network user when you perform such tasks as word processing or sending e-mail messages. When you log in with the Admin user name, you risk accidentally changing the system configuration or erasing or corrupting server files. In addition, if the workstation from which you're logging in has a computer virus in memory, the virus could infect program files on the server, causing the virus to quickly spread throughout the network. To reduce the chance of these problems occurring, you should create a separate user name for everyday tasks, such as e-mailing or word processing, and log in as Admin only when you need to maintain or configure the network. After creating the InfoSystems OU, David realized that he did not have a separate user name account, so he used ConsoleOne to create a standard user account:

1. He clicked the InfoSystems OU he created earlier.

2. He clicked File on the ConsoleOne menu bar, pointed to New, and then clicked User to open the New User dialog box (see Figure 7-17).

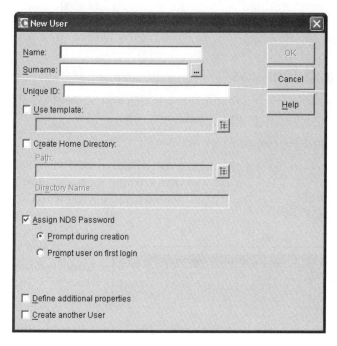

**Figure 7-17** The New User dialog box

3. In the Name text box, he entered a user name consisting of the first letter of his first name followed by his last name, and then entered his last name in the Surname text box.

4. He clicked the Create Home Directory check box.

5. He clicked the browse button to the right of the Path text box.

6. He clicked the up arrow to view all Organizations, and then clicked the CBE_ADMIN_SYS volume.

7. He clicked OK to enter the path to his home directory.

8. He clicked OK to create his user account and home directory.

9. In the Set Password dialog box, he entered and confirmed a password for his user account, and then clicked the Set Password button.

10. He closed ConsoleOne by clicking the Exit ConsoleOne button.

11. He logged out to display a new Novell Login window.

## MODIFYING AND MANAGING THE EDIRECTORY TREE

As a network administrator, you often need to modify an existing eDirectory tree. Common modification tasks include creating new containers and leaf objects, deleting objects, moving objects, renaming container and leaf objects, and moving sections of the directory tree. In some instances, you might have to rename a tree or merge trees, but these tasks should only be performed after careful planning and evaluation. You might also need to add servers to your network to improve performance, and you may need to view partitions and replicas.

### Viewing Partitions and Replicas

David wants to identify partitions and find the servers that contain replicas of partitions. To do so, he used the following steps in ConsoleOne:

1. He double-clicked his ConsoleOne desktop shortcut.

2. He changed the ConsoleOne window to the Partition and Replica view by clicking the CLASS_TREE object, and then clicking View, Partition and Replica View on the menu bar. Each Organization's partition has a special icon (see Figure 7-18).

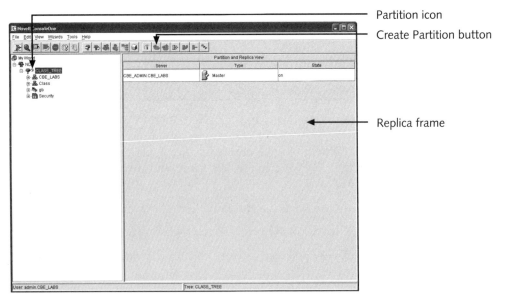

**Figure 7-18**   The Partition and Replica view in ConsoleOne

3. He clicked his CBE_LABS Organization to view all replicas of his partition in the Replica frame.

To create a partition using ConsoleOne, David followed these steps:

1. In the ConsoleOne Partition and Replica view, he selected the CBE_Labs_Admin OU.

2. He clicked the Create Partition button on the ConsoleOne toolbar to open the Create Partition dialog box. (He could also have clicked Edit, Create Partition on the ConsoleOne menu bar.)

3. He clicked OK to create a partition from the CBE_Labs_Admin container (see Figure 7-19).

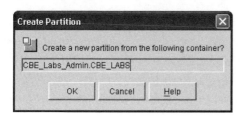

**Figure 7-19**    The Create Partition dialog box

4. After the system performed its checks, the Creating Partition message box displayed with Close and Cancel buttons (see Figure 7-20). David did not click either button, but waited for the partition creation to finish. After a short time, the partition was created, and a partition icon appeared to the left of the container.

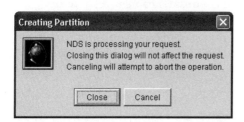

**Figure 7-20**    The Creating Partition message box

## Renaming Objects

Network administrators often need to rename an eDirectory object. For example, David wanted to rename the Test_Eval OU to Test&Eval, so he used these steps in ConsoleOne:

1. He right-clicked the Test_Eval OU, and then clicked Rename on the shortcut menu to open the Rename dialog box.

2. He typed Test&Eval in the New name text box, as shown in Figure 7-21.

3. He clicked OK.

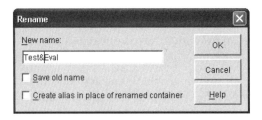

**Figure 7-21**    The Rename dialog box

## Moving Leaf Objects

Often you need to move a leaf object, such as a User object or a Printer object, from one container to another. Doing this changes the object's context, but eDirectory automatically makes the necessary changes in the property values. To move an object using ConsoleOne, you can use either method:

- Click the object, click File, Move on the menu bar, enter the new destination, and then click OK.

- Right-click the object, click Move on the shortcut menu, browse to the new destination, and then click OK.

## Deleting Objects

Managing and modifying the directory tree often requires that you delete an object. Deleting most leaf objects, such as Users and Printers, presents no problem. Deleting a NetWare Server object, however, demands consideration of eDirectory partitions and replicas because NetWare 6 automatically copies the eDirectory database to a new server installed on your network. To delete a container object, you must first delete or move all objects in the container. To delete an object using ConsoleOne, you can use any of these methods:

- Click the object, press Delete, and then click Yes when asked to confirm.

- Click the object, click File, Delete NDS Object on the menu bar, and then click Yes when asked to confirm.

- Right-click the container for the object, click Delete NDS Object on the shortcut menu, and then click Yes when asked to confirm.

## Renaming an eDirectory Tree

As a network administrator, occasionally you need to work with the eDirectory tree as a whole, instead of with its component parts. This happens when you need to rename the eDirectory tree if, for example, the company name changes. You might also need to combine two eDirectory trees into one tree if, for instance, management decides to consolidate the multiple directory trees in your internetwork for easier administration. It is important to understand that only the Tree objects are merged. In other words, leaf and container objects maintain their own identities in the newly created merged tree, and object names do not change in the containers. The target tree is the name of the tree that merges into the source tree. Confused? Don't worry. For CNAs, merging trees is not a daily occurrence. However, if you do need to merge two trees, remember that Novell's online resources are only a mouse click away at *http://support.novell.com*. The online documentation gives you a step-by-step approach to merging and renaming trees, and the ramifications of doing both.

## DSMERGE.NLM

The utility used to manage eDirectory trees is **DSMERGE.NLM**. To run this NetWare Loadable Module (NLM), load it at the console prompt by typing the following console command and then pressing Enter:

    LOAD DSMERGE

When the module is loaded, it appears as shown in Figure 7-22.

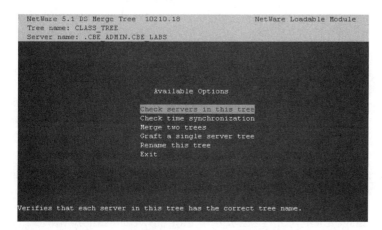

```
NetWare 5.1 DS Merge Tree  10210.18          NetWare Loadable Module
Tree name: CLASS_TREE
Server name: .CBE_ADMIN.CBE_LABS




                    Available Options

                 Check servers in this tree
                 Check time synchronization
                 Merge two trees
                 Graft a single server tree
                 Rename this tree
                 Exit




Verifies that each server in this tree has the correct tree name.
```

**Figure 7-22**   The main menu in DSMERGE

You can rename a directory tree by selecting the Rename this tree menu item. You must load DSMERGE on the NetWare server where the Master replica of the [Root] partition is stored for this tree. When you choose the Rename this tree menu item, you must log in to the tree from the server as the Admin user and use the complete name of the Admin account (that is, Admin.CBE_LABS, not just Admin). DSMERGE then asks for the tree's new name. After you enter it, press F10, press Enter, and then click Yes to finish renaming the tree. You'll need to change the Tree statement on each NetWare client workstation after this, or your help desk telephone will be ringing off the hook.

## CHAPTER SUMMARY

◻ To set up and manage a network, NetWare network administrators must master the NetWare commands and utilities. This chapter described the different types of NetWare tools available to the network administrator: command-line utilities, graphical utilities, supervisor utilities, menu utilities, console commands, and NetWare Loadable Modules (NLMs). Console commands and NLMs are used from the server's console; command-line utilities, menu utilities, and graphical utilities run at workstations.

◻ Graphical utilities use the Windows graphical user interface (GUI). The term *supervisor utilities* refers to any utility stored in the SYS:System directory that the network administrator uses for system administration.

◻ The ConsoleOne graphical utility is the preferred tool for working with eDirectory. It enables you to do just about everything you need to do with eDirectory, using an easy Windows interface.

◻ You can also use NetWare Administrator (NWAdmin) to display portions or all of an eDirectory tree. You can also open additional browser windows to display different sections of the eDirectory tree in separate browser windows. A maximum of 10 browser windows can be open at one time.

◻ eDirectory is initially created during the installation of NetWare 6 servers. After all NetWare 6 servers in a network have been installed, the eDirectory tree contains the [Root] object, one or more Country objects (optional), at least one Organization object, one or more Organizational Unit (OU) objects (optional), the Admin User object, a NetWare Server object for each NetWare 6 server installed, a SYS volume object for each NetWare 6 server installed, and a Volume object for each additional volume created during server installation (optional).

◻ To complete the organizational structure, you typically add container objects to the eDirectory tree. Container objects include the [Root], Country, Organization, and OU objects. Using ConsoleOne, you can create, rename, and delete container objects and manage their properties. You cannot, however, simply move a container object to another part of the tree.

◻ iManager is a Web-based tool, which gives you the ability to manage your NetWare server using a Web browser.

◻ The server console utility DSMERGE.NLM is used to rename eDirectory trees. NetWare utilities, including ConsoleOne, NWAdmin, and iManager, support multiple eDirectory trees for administration and sharing resources.

## KEY TERMS

**ConsoleOne** — Both a server and workstation Java-based NetWare utility that can be used to perform administrative tasks.

**DSMERGE.NLM** — The utility used to manage eDirectory trees.

**eDirectory Management Framework (eMFrame)** — A Web application for building modular eDirectory management services called plug-ins. eMFrame plug-ins define management roles and implement tasks associated with those roles.

**iManager** — A browser-based utility for managing eDirectory and configuring iPrint, NetWare Licensing, and DNS/DHCP.

**NetWare Administrator (NWAdmin)** — A graphical utility that runs in Windows, used to perform administrative tasks. Novell is attempting to phase out this utility with its newer product, ConsoleOne.

## REVIEW QUESTIONS

1. eDirectory can be maintained by using which of the following utilities?
   a. NWAdmin
   b. iManager
   c. ConsoleOne
   d. all of the above

2. Which of the following do you use to access iManager?
   a. ConsoleOne
   b. server console
   c. command line
   d. Web browser

3. Which of the following is a pointer to the real object located in another container?
   a. alias
   b. leaf
   c. branch
   d. root

4. To rename the tree after an installation, you must use which of the following?
   a. ConsoleOne
   b. iManager
   c. NWAdmin
   d. DSMERGE

5. Which of the following protocols is used to access network servers from a Web browser?
   a. NCP
   b. IPX
   c. HTTP
   d. NSF

6. The location of an object in the eDirectory tree is referred to as its
   _____.

7. Which of the following is a field that can contain information about an object?
   a. leaf
   b. property
   c. value
   d. container

8. To finish creating an object, you must supply which of the following values in the New *ObjectType* dialog box?
   a. container
   b. leaf
   c. property
   d. class

9. The telephone number of the user Bob Jones is 555-1473. This telephone number is defined in eDirectory as which of the following?
   a. property
   b. class
   c. value
   d. object

10. You can rename a directory tree by using which of the following tools?
    a. iManager
    b. DSMERGE
    c. ConsoleOne
    d. A directory tree cannot be renamed.

11. You create country codes by using which of the following tools?
    a. DSMERGE
    b. NDIR
    c. NWAdmin
    d. The administrators does not create country codes.

12. Organization objects can be created directly below which objects in eDirectory? (Select all that apply.)
    a. [Root]
    b. leaf
    c. Country
    d. Organizational Unit

13. An Organizational Unit object is created directly below which objects in eDirectory? (Select all that apply.)

    a. Organization

    b. Organizational Unit

    c. [Root]

    d. leaf

14. Which of the following is an example of a leaf object? (Select all that apply.)

    a. Organizational Unit

    b. Organization

    c. User

    d. Printer

15. Which utility enables an administrator to delete objects from eDirectory?

    a. NWAdmin

    b. iManager

    c. ConsoleOne

    d. all of the above

16. True or False: To function properly, iManager software requires additional memory and Novell Client software to be installed on a workstation.

17. Explain how to rename eDirectory objects using ConsoleOne.

18. Explain how to delete objects from eDirectory using ConsoleOne.

19. While attending a Novell seminar in Utah, you are asked to create the User object TSmith in an OU to be named Temp-Employees. Write down the steps to create both the User object and OU object.

20. To install NWAdmin on your PC, you must do which of the following?

    a. Purchase client software from Novell.

    b. Install NetWare 6 on your PC and select the NWAdmin Only option.

    c. Browse to the Z:\Win32 folder using your PC and locate the Nwadmin32.exe file.

    d. Visit *www.novell.com/download* and install the latest version.

## HANDS-ON PROJECTS

### Project 7-1: Using ConsoleOne to View and Create New Objects

In this project, you use ConsoleOne to create new OUs and several User objects. Use the directory tree design you created in Chapter 4's projects for your version of the CBE Labs organization.

1. Log in to the network with your assigned ##Admin user name.

2. Double-click your desktop shortcut to start ConsoleOne.

3. In the Navigation frame, expand the **CLASS_TREE** tree and the **CLASS** Organization.

4. Right-click your **##ADMINOU**, point to **New**, and write down the available options.

5. Click **Organizational Unit** on the shortcut menu to open the New Organizational Unit dialog box.

6. Enter **CBE_LABS** in the Name text box, and then click **OK**. The CBE_LABS OU should appear under the ##ADMINOU container in the ConsoleOne window.

7. Right-click the **CBE_LABS** OU, point to **New**, and click **Organizational Unit** on the shortcut menu. Referring to the directory tree you designed in Chapter 4, continue creating the OUs needed to populate your CBE Labs tree. Also create an additional OU named Temp.

You might need to expand the CBE_LABS OU by clicking the + icon.

8. In the Temp OU you just created, create three User objects:

   a. Right-click the **Temp** OU, point to **New**, and click **User** to open the New User dialog box.

   b. In the Name text box, enter your user name, consisting of the first letter of your first name followed by your last name, and then enter your last name in the Surname text box.

   c. Click OK to create your user account.

   d. When you see the Set Password dialog box, type **password** in the New Password text box and then type **password** again in the Retype Password text box. Click the **Set Password** button.

   e. Repeat these steps to create two temporary users named Charlie Parker and Howard Roberts.

If you want to test one of the accounts you created, be sure to log in as that user and select the correct context for that user.

9. Close ConsoleOne by clicking the **Exit ConsoleOne** button on the toolbar.

10. Log out.

11. Write a memo to your instructor listing the steps you used to create the objects in eDirectory with ConsoleOne. Include the options you have on the New shortcut menu when creating a new eDirectory object.

## Project 7-2: Using iManager to Delete Objects from eDirectory

In this project, you use iManager to remove the objects created in Project 7-1. You have been asked to remove these objects while you are out of the office on a business trip.

1. Bypass the Novell Client login to simulate operating from your hotel room. If you're using Windows XP Professional, click the **Workstation only** check box in the Novell Login window, enter your local Windows user name and password, and click **OK**.

2. Start your Internet Explorer or Netscape program, and open the iManager utility by following these steps:

   a. After starting your browser program, enter the URL **https://ip_address:2200**, replacing *ip_address* with the IP address or DNS name assigned to your classroom server.

   b. If you see any Security Alert message boxes, write down the message, and then click **Yes** or **OK** to continue. Click the **CBE_ADMIN** link under the eDirectory iManager heading.

   c. Enter your **##Admin** user name (replacing ## with your assigned student number) in the User Name text box, enter your password, enter the correct context and tree name, and click the **Login** button.

3. Click the small **+** icon to expand the eDirectory Administration item, and click the **Delete Object** link.

4. In the Delete Object window, click the small magnifying glass icon to browse for the objects to delete. You might need to click the small arrow to the left of each container object to expand it.

5. Locate the Temp OU you created earlier.

6. In the Delete Object window, note the name in the Object name text box, and click **OK**. Write down the error message you see, and click **OK**.

7. In the Delete Object window, browse to the Temp OU, and select one of the User objects. Click **OK** to delete the object. Repeat these steps to remove each user, and then delete the **Temp** OU.

**7**

Notice that you are not prompted with a warning or verification screen when attempting to delete an object.

8. Write a memo to your instructor describing the steps you took to remove objects from eDirectory with iManager and include the other information you were asked to write down during the steps.

Be sure to mention that a container object cannot be deleted from eDirectory until it becomes a leaf object.

## CASE PROJECTS

### Case 7-1: Creating the Jefferson County Courthouse Directory Tree Organizational Structure

In Chapter 4, you designed an eDirectory tree for the Jefferson County Courthouse. The network administrator has installed the NetWare 6 server and is ready to finish creating eDirectory. Your job is to put your directory tree plan into practice, using the design you created in Chapter 4.

1. Start ConsoleOne.

2. Using the steps you've learned in this chapter, create a JCCH OU under your ##ADMINOU.

3. Create the rest of the Jefferson County Courthouse directory tree structure you designed in Chapter 4. Because you cannot add the server objects directly, describe the steps you would take to create them in the tree.

4. Print a copy of your completed directory tree.

5. Write a memo to your instructor describing the steps you used, and attach a copy of your printed directory tree.

### Case 7-2: Creating the J.Q. Adams Corporation Directory Tree Organizational Structure

In Chapter 4, you designed an eDirectory tree for the J.Q. Adams Corporation. The network administrator has installed its two NetWare 6 servers and is ready to finish creating the directory tree. Your job is to put your directory tree plan into practice, using the design you created in Chapter 4.

1. Start ConsoleOne.

2. Using the steps you've learned in this chapter, create an ADAMS OU under your ##ADMINOU.

3. Create the rest of the J.Q. Adams directory tree structure you designed in Chapter 4. Because you cannot add the server objects directly, describe the steps you would take to create them in the tree.

4. Print a copy of your completed directory tree.

5. Write a memo to your instructor describing the steps you took, and attach a copy of your printed directory tree.

7

# 8

# CREATING THE NETWORK FILE SYSTEM

**After reading this chapter and completing the exercises, you will be able to:**

- ♦ Create and manage file system objects, including Novell Storage Services (NSS) storage pools and volumes
- ♦ Use Windows and NetWare utilities to implement a directory structure
- ♦ Describe the use of network and search drive pointers and establish a drive pointer usage plan for your network system
- ♦ Use NetWare utilities to manage files and directories
- ♦ Identify NetWare backup software options and define a backup strategy for network data

**A**fter the server installation is complete, it's time to set up the network file system. To do this, you need to understand the NetWare commands and utilities used to create and maintain the NetWare file system. Chapter 5 introduced you to using Window Explorer and a few NetWare commands to view file system information; in this chapter, you learn how to work with the NetWare and Windows commands and utilities needed to manage the network file system.

The information in this chapter is divided into five major categories: working with NSS objects, directory management, drive pointers, file management, and backing up network data. The NSS objects section describes the process used to create the storage pools and volumes needed for the files system. In the directory management section, you apply Windows commands you're already familiar with to the NetWare file system to create the network directory structure and use ConsoleOne to view and create directories. In the drive pointers section, you use Windows Explorer to access network drives, use the DOS MAP command to manage drive pointers, and learn ways to plan drive pointer use in your network system. In the file management section, you learn about Windows and NetWare utilities that help you manage files on your NetWare servers.

This book assumes that you are already comfortable using Windows file and directory management tools. Windows file management is not covered in depth in this chapter.

## CREATING NSS STORAGE POOLS AND VOLUMES

In Chapter 5, you learned how to design the server's file system using volumes, directories, and subdirectories. In this section, you learn how to use ConsoleOne to create and manage NSS storage pools and volumes. You'll continue to watch David Doering, a network administrator for CBE Labs, as he creates the NSS storage pools and volumes to contain the directory structures. Recall that CBE Labs has two NetWare 6 servers, CBE_ADMIN and CBE_EVAL, and one existing NetWare 5 server, RANGER. Both CBE_ADMIN and CBE_EVAL have SYS and DATA volumes, but RANGER has only a SYS volume. Because CD-ROMs provide their own directory structures, the network administrator doesn't need to worry about those directory structures—just the structure for volumes on hard disks.

At CBE Labs, the Administration and Publishing workgroups use the CBE_ADMIN server, so the CBE_ADMIN_SYS volume stores a major set of application software, including the company's e-mail, fax, and Internet software. In addition, CBE_ADMIN_SYS stores a shared copy of the company's Windows-compatible desktop publishing software, PageMaker. CBE Labs also keeps a copy of the Office XP package on the volume so that the software can be installed on users' workstations from the network instead of from disks.

The CBE_ADMIN_DATA volume stores administration and publishing data. A Shared directory is maintained at the root level so that users can easily transfer files to each other, and Shared subdirectories are maintained for each administration section so that administration groups can share files (The Publishing workgroup has no access to these directories.) Finally, private directories are maintained for each user in the Administration and Publishing workgroups under the Users directory.

The lab workgroups use CBE_EVAL. Therefore, the CBE_EVAL_SYS volume stores the applications the lab workgroups share, including a SQL database management system (DBMS) program and the Analyzer program, which evaluates hardware and software. The CBE_EVAL_DATA volume stores test and evaluation data and reports. As on CBE_ADMIN_DATA, a Shared directory is kept at the root level so that users can easily transfer files to each other, and Shared subdirectories are kept for each lab workgroup for file sharing among groups. In addition, a Reports subdirectory holds the final lab reports; everyone at CBE Labs can access this directory. For example, the publishing group picks up copies of reports from this directory to publish in *The C/B/E NetWorker*. Private directories are kept for each user in the lab workgroups under a Users directory.

The Finance Department uses RANGER, the NetWare 5 server, to run the accounting system. The RANGER_SYS volume contains the program files in the Apps\Dosacct subdirectory, and the Data directory holds the subdirectories for the program's data files. There is no need for a Shared directory or User directories on RANGER_SYS.

Chapter 5 showed the volume design forms for each volume in the CBE Labs network. For reference, Figures 8-1 and 8-2 show the volume design forms for the CBE_ADMIN_SYS and CBE_ADMIN_DATA volumes. (Blank copies of these forms are available in Appendix B.)



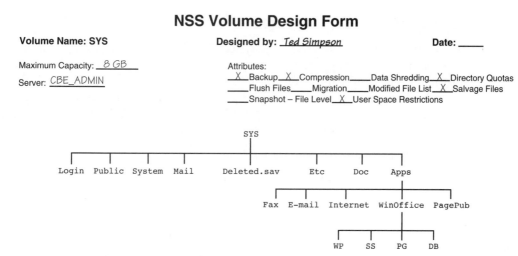

NSS Volume Design Form
Volume Name: SYS
Designed by: Ted Simpson
Date:
Maximum Capacity: 8 GB
Server: CBE_ADMIN
Attributes:
X Backup X Compression ___ Data Shredding X Directory Quotas
___ Flush Files ___ Migration ___ Modified File List X Salvage Files
___ Snapshot – File Level X User Space Restrictions
SYS
Login
Public
System
Mail
Deleted.sav
Etc
Doc
Apps
Fax
E-mail
Internet
WinOffice
PagePub
WP
SS
PG
DB

**Figure 8-1** CBE_ADMIN_SYS volume

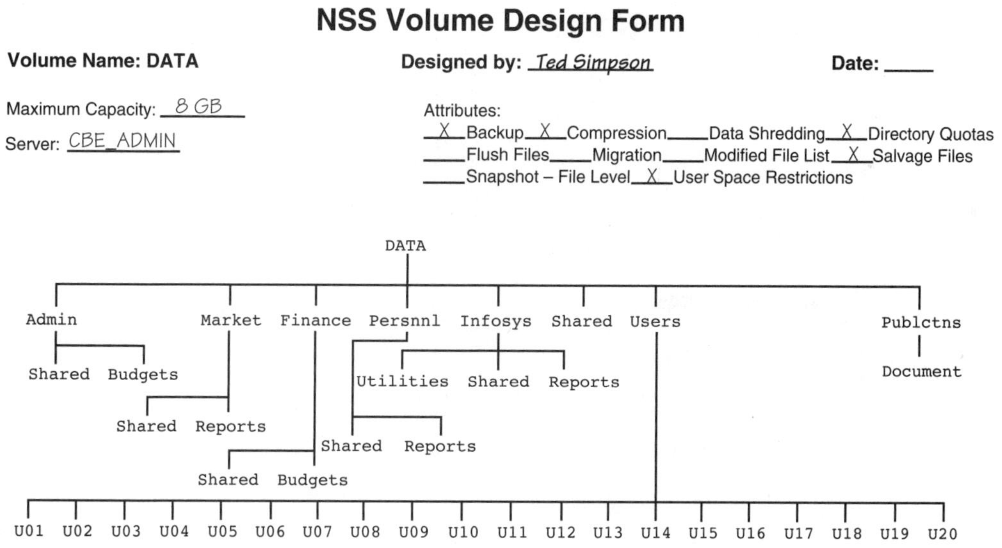

NSS Volume Design Form
Volume Name: DATA
Designed by: Ted Simpson
Date:
Maximum Capacity: 8 GB
Server: CBE_ADMIN
Attributes:
X Backup X Compression ___ Data Shredding X Directory Quotas
___ Flush Files ___ Migration ___ Modified File List X Salvage Files
___ Snapshot – File Level X User Space Restrictions
DATA
Admin
Market
Finance
Persnnl
Infosys
Shared
Users
Publctns
Shared
Budgets
Utilities
Shared
Reports
Document
Shared
Reports
Shared
Reports
Shared
Budgets
U01 U02 U03 U04 U05 U06 U07 U08 U09 U10 U11 U12 U13 U14 U15 U16 U17 U18 U19 U20

**Figure 8-2** CBE_ADMIN_DATA volume

After defining the storage needs for the network file system, David established the network file system by first creating the NSS volume named DATA. Because NSS volumes exist within storage pools, creating the DATA volume involved three steps: creating a new disk partition, assigning the partition to a new storage pool, and creating the NSS volume. In the following sections, you learn how to use ConsoleOne to view and create NSS objects.

## Preparing to Use ConsoleOne

To manage the server's physical disk system from a workstation using ConsoleOne, you need to turn off the File Caching option on the client so that you can update the server information in "real" time without caching previous information. Although file caching can increase operating speed when multiple users are accessing the same file, it can cause problems when viewing or updating server information in real time. David used the following steps to turn off file caching on his workstation:

1. He right-clicked My Network Places, and then clicked Properties.

2. He right-clicked the Local Area Connection icon, and then clicked Properties.

3. He clicked Novell Client for Windows, and then clicked Properties to open the Novell Client for Windows Properties dialog box.

4. He clicked the Advanced Settings tab to display the Parameter groups list shown in Figure 8-3.

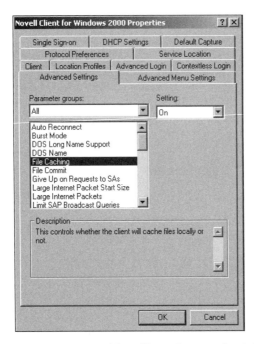

**Figure 8-3**    Disabling file caching in the Advanced Settings tab

5. He clicked the File Caching parameter, clicked the Setting list arrow, and then clicked Off in the list of options.

6. He clicked OK and then clicked Close to save the configuration settings and close the Local Area Connection Properties dialog box.

7. He clicked Yes to restart his computer.

## Viewing Partition Information

After turning off File Caching, you can use ConsoleOne to view and modify file system information. David used the following steps to view information on partitions, storage pools, and NSS volumes:

1. First, he first logged in to the Novell network with the Admin user name and password.

You must be logged in as a user with administrative rights to access server file system information.

2. He started ConsoleOne and expanded the tree icon by clicking the "+" symbol.

3. He expanded the CBE_LABS Organization, right-clicked the NetWare Server object, and then clicked Properties to open the server's Properties dialog box. He then used the scroll button to display the Media tab, as shown in Figure 8-4.

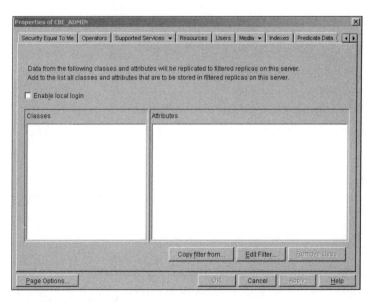

**Figure 8-4**    The server's Properties dialog box

4. He clicked the Media tab's down arrow to display the media options shown in Figure 8-5.

**Figure 8-5**   Options on the Media tab

5. He clicked the Partitions option to display the Partitions tab (see Figure 8-6).

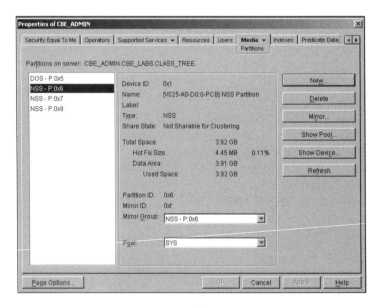

**Figure 8-6**   Viewing partition information

6. He clicked the first NSS partition to view the partition values. To display information on partitions that are part of the mirror group, he clicked the Mirror button to open the Partition Mirror Group dialog box shown in Figure 8-7.

If two partitions are mirrored or duplexed, their partition IDs are listed in this dialog box. In addition to viewing the information in the Group Status section, you can click one of the mirrored partitions to view its status information to determine whether it is in sync with the mirror group.

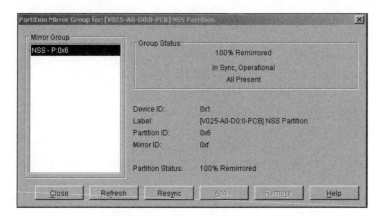

**Figure 8-7**   The Partition Mirror Group dialog box

7. He clicked the Close button to return to the Partitions tab.

8. To view device information, David selected a partition and then clicked the Show Device button to display a tab similar to the one in Figure 8-8. (Note that the name on the Media tab has changed to Devices.)

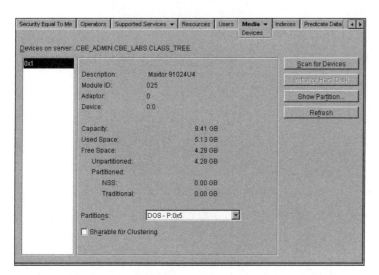

**Figure 8-8**   Viewing device information

9. He clicked Cancel to return to the ConsoleOne window.

## Viewing Storage Pool Information

As described in Chapter 5, storage pools are used to combine the space from one or more partitions. This space is then allocated to create logical volumes. Monitoring the size and status of storage pools is an important part of maintaining the network file system. To view information on existing NSS storage pools, David used the following steps:

1. He started ConsoleOne and expanded the necessary containers to display the NetWare Server object.

2. He right-clicked the NetWare Server object, and then clicked Properties to open the server's Properties dialog box.

3. He clicked the Media tab's down arrow to display the media options.

4. He clicked the NSS Pools option to display a tab showing all storage pools on the selected server.

5. He clicked the SYS storage pool to view its information, similar to the CBE_ADMIN SYS storage pool shown in Figure 8-9.

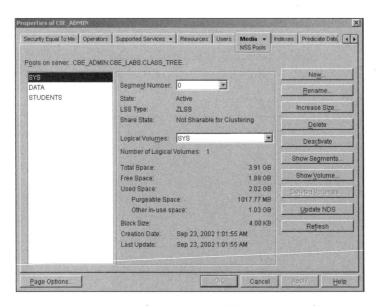

**Figure 8-9**    Viewing information on NSS storage pools

6. He clicked the Show Segments button to open the Segment Information for SYS dialog box, which displayed information on the partition segments that make up the SYS storage pool, as shown in Figure 8-10. When he had finished checking the information, he clicked Close to return to the NSS Pools dialog box shown previously in Figure 8-9.

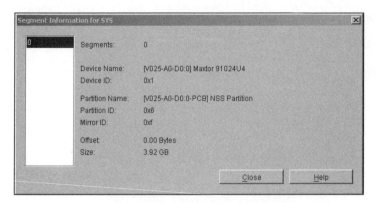

**Figure 8-10**    Viewing information on partition segments in a storage pool

7. He clicked the Increase Size button to add partitions to the storage pool, as shown in Figure 8-11, and then clicked the Finish button to return to the NSS Pools dialog box.

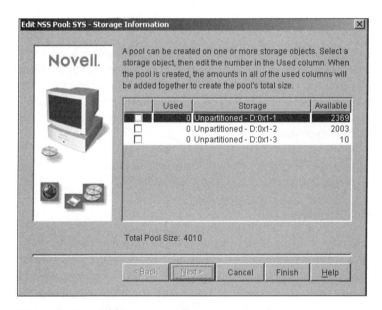

**Figure 8-11**    Adding space to a storage pool

8. He clicked the Show Volume button to see information on all volumes contained in the storage pool (see Figure 8-12).

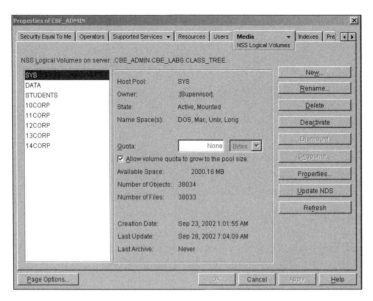

**Figure 8-12**    Viewing information on volumes in the storage pool

Note that using the Show Volume button changes the Media tab to the NSS Logical Volumes option. To return to the NSS Pools window, click the Media tab's down arrow and then click the NSS Pools option. The Deactivate button can be used to take the storage pool offline. Deactivating the storage pool is necessary before performing certain maintenance options, such as running the NSS REBUILD utility.

9. After viewing the NSS pool information, David clicked the OK button to save any changes and return to the ConsoleOne window.

## Viewing Volume Information

The eDirectory database and file system are two separate environments, and the Volume object acts as a link between the two. As a result, you can use the Volume object in ConsoleOne or NetWare Administrator to manage the network file system. Remember that to keep the server functioning, you need to make sure the SYS volume does not run out of space. Network administrators should periodically use ConsoleOne, Windows Explorer, or Remote Manager (described in Chapter 13) to check the status of the SYS volume.

### Using ConsoleOne to View Volume Information

ConsoleOne supplies the most information about NSS volumes. David used the following steps to view this information:

1. First, he logged in to the Novell network with the Admin user name and password.

2. Next, he started ConsoleOne, expanded the Tree object, and then expanded the CBE_LABS Organization to locate the SYS volume.

3. He right-clicked the Volume object and then clicked Properties to open the volume's Properties dialog box. He clicked the Statistics tab to view volume statistics (see Figure 8-13).

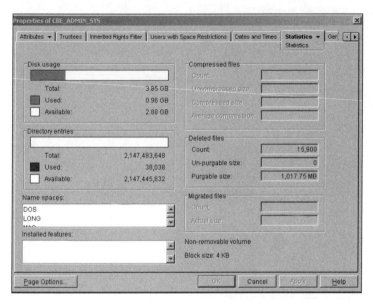

**Figure 8-13**    The CBE_ADMIN_SYS volume Statistics window

4. He clicked the Dates and Times tab to view volume creation and modified dates.

5. He clicked the Statistics tab to display the space usage and the volume's block size and compression or suballocation status, as shown in Figure 8-13.

6. He clicked the Users with Space Restrictions tab to view or enter user space restrictions for that volume. To add a space restriction for a user, David clicked the Add button and then selected the user's account and entered the maximum space that users will be allowed on the volume.

7. Finally, he clicked OK to save changes and return to the ConsoleOne window.

## Using Windows Explorer to View Volume Information

Windows Explorer also enables you to see information about a selected volume. These are the general steps:

1. Open Windows Explorer.

2. Right-click the volume name you want.

3. Choose Properties on the shortcut menu.

4. Click NetWare Volume Information to open the Properties dialog box to the NetWare Volume Information tab, as shown in Figure 8-14.

**Figure 8-14**   The NetWare Volume Information tab

Again, you'll see a variety of information about the current volume. One important statistic displayed in the ConsoleOne Statistics tab but not shown in Windows Explorer is the amount of space taken up by deleted files (called "Purgable size" in Figure 8-13). NetWare recovers this space automatically when it runs out of free space on the volume. Comparing the amount of purgeable space a volume has to its available space gives you an idea when this volume will be full.

## Creating the DATA Partition

In previous NetWare versions, the NWCONFIG utility was used to create and maintain partitions from the server console. Because NWCONFIG is not compatible with the NSS3 file system, ConsoleOne or Remote Manager is used to manage file system components in NetWare 6. Remote Manager is one of Novell's new Web browser utilities that complies with Novell's OneNet vision of making network management possible from any networked computer. The following steps illustrate the process David used to create the DATA partition with ConsoleOne. Your instructor will demonstrate this process for you. If you like, you can follow along on your computer, but keep in mind that certain screens or options are not available if you are not logged in as the eDirectory tree administrator.

1. First, David logged in to the network with the Admin user name and password and started ConsoleOne.

2. In the ConsoleOne Navigation frame, he expanded the Tree object and the CBE_Labs Organization to display the CBE_ADMIN server object.

3. Because partitions are part of the NetWare server, not separate objects in the eDirectory tree, he right-clicked the CBE_ADMIN server object, and then clicked Properties to open the Properties of CBE_ADMIN dialog box.

4. He clicked the down arrow on the Media tab and clicked the Partitions option to display the Partitions on server CBE_ADMIN dialog box.

5. To create a new partition, he clicked the New button to open the Create a new partition dialog box, similar to the one in Figure 8-15.

8

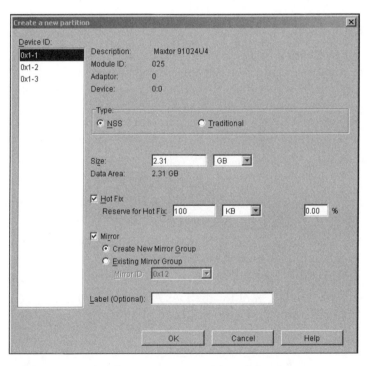

**Figure 8-15**   The Create a new partition dialog box

6. He then entered the size of the partition and accepted the default options of Hot Fix and Create New Mirror Group. When creating a mirrored partition on the second drive, he will change the default option by clicking the Existing Mirror Group radio button and then identifying the partition created in this dialog box.

 Entering a name in the Label text box is optional but can be helpful in locating a particular partition. You need to remember the name assigned to the partition to select it when creating or adding to a storage pool.

7. After entering the necessary data, he clicked OK to create the new partition and return to the Media Partitions tab.

8. After clicking the new partition and verifying that it was successfully entered in the Partitions text box, he clicked Cancel to return to the ConsoleOne window.

## Creating a Storage Pool

Like partitions, in NetWare 6 you can create and manage storage pools by using ConsoleOne from a local computer or Remote Manager from a browser. David used the following steps in ConsoleOne to create the DATA storage pool on the CBE_ADMIN server. Your instructor will demonstrate this process for you. If you like, you can follow along on your computer, but keep in mind that certain screens or options are not available if you are not logged in as the eDirectory tree administrator.

1. To create a storage pool for the DATA volume, David logged in to the CLASS_TREE tree as the Admin user, and then started the ConsoleOne utility.

2. He used the Navigation frame to expand the CBE_Labs Organization container, right-clicked the CBE_ADMIN server object, and clicked Properties.

3. In the Properties of CBE_ADMIN dialog box, he clicked the down arrow on the Media tab and then clicked the NSS Pools option to display the Pools on server CBE_ADMIN dialog box.

4. To create a new storage pool for the DATA volume, he clicked the New button to start the Create a New Pool Wizard, shown in Figure 8-16.

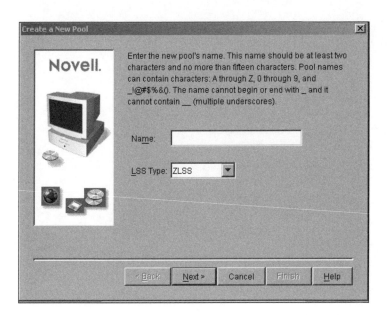

**Figure 8-16**     The Create a new NSS Storage Pool dialog box

5. He entered the name DATA and then clicked the Next button to display the Storage Information window (see Figure 8-17), which shows the existing disk partitions and their available space and identification.

If a DATA pool already exists on your server from the classroom setup process, your instructor might want to demonstrate creating an NSS pool named DATA2.

6. He clicked in the check box next to the NSS – M:0x14-1 partition, and then clicked Next to display a summary window.

7. He clicked Finish to create the DATA storage pool, using the default Activate on Creation option.

8. After he verified that the new DATA storage pool appeared with the SYS pool in the Media NSS Pools tab, he clicked Cancel to return to the ConsoleOne window.

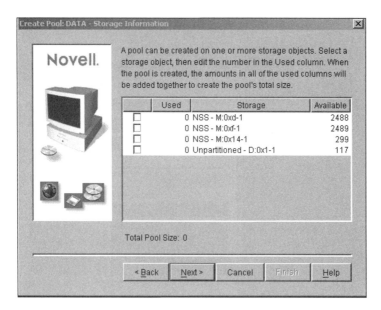

**Figure 8-17**   NSS Storage Pool Information dialog box

## Creating an NSS Volume

Before establishing the directory structure, David needed to create a volume in the DATA storage pool. By default, when you create a volume, a corresponding volume object is created in the same container as the server. To make accessing and managing volumes more convenient, David also created volume objects in other Organizational Units (OUs). The following list shows the steps David took in ConsoleOne to create a logical NSS volume (the DATA volume) on the CBE_ADMIN server. Your instructor will demonstrate this process on your classroom server. If you like, you can follow along on your computer, but keep in mind that certain screens or options are not available if you are not logged in as the eDirectory tree administrator.

1. After logging in to the CLASS_TREE tree as the Admin user and starting ConsoleOne, David expanded the CBE_LABS Organization in the Navigation frame, right-clicked the CBE_ADMIN server, and clicked Properties.

2. He clicked the down arrow on the Media tab and then clicked the NSS Logical Volumes option to display the NSS Logical Volumes on server CBE_ADMIN dialog box.

3. To create a new volume, he clicked the New button to start the Create a New Logical Volume Wizard.

4. He entered DATA in the Name text box and clicked Next to open the Storage Information window (see Figure 8-18) that lists the existing storage pools.

A DATA volume should already exist on your server from the classroom setup process, so your instructor might demonstrate creating a NSS logical volume with another name, such as DATA2.

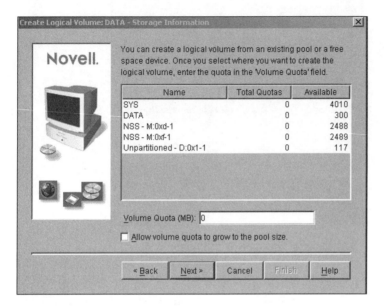

**Figure 8-18**   The Storage Information window

5. After selecting the DATA storage pool, he clicked the Allow volume quota to grow to the pool size check box. To create multiple volumes in the pool, he could use the Volume Quota (MB) text box to set a limit for the volume.

 As described in Chapter 5, although a single volume's quota cannot exceed the size of the storage pool, when you're creating multiple volumes in a pool, overbooking allows the sum of all volume quotas to be larger than the pool size.

6. After entering the volume storage information, he clicked Next to display the Attribute Information window, similar to the one shown in Figure 8-19.

7. In addition to the default Backup and Salvage Files options, he clicked the Directory Quotas and User Space Restrictions check boxes to restrict directory sizes to the capacities he allotted in Chapter 5.

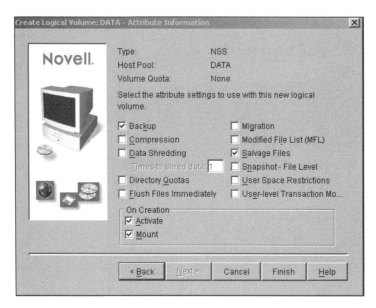

**Figure 8-19**   The Attribute Information window

8. After selecting the options he needed, he clicked Finish to create the volume.

9. After verifying that the volume was created, he clicked Cancel to return to the ConsoleOne window.

## DIRECTORY MANAGEMENT

### Windows Directory Management Commands

In Windows, directories and subdirectories are called folders. To create them, you use the File, New, Folder command on the Windows Explorer menu. David needs to create a Pagepub subdirectory under an Apps directory. To create these directories in Windows Explorer, David used the following steps:

Only your instructor will be able to perform the following steps exactly as shown. You can follow along using your own user directory as the Root of SYS.

1. He logged in to the Novell network with his Admin user name and password.

2. He clicked Start, Programs, Accessories, Windows Explorer and maximized the Windows Explorer window to full screen (see Figure 8-20).

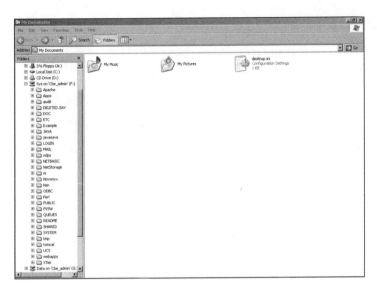

**Figure 8-20**   Windows Explorer

**Note**

Some organizations use another letter, such as G:, as the initial network drive. If necessary, substitute your network drive letter for F: in these steps.

3. David did the following to change the mapping of his F: drive to point to the root of the SYS volume:

a. He right-clicked the F: drive and clicked the Novell Map Network Drive option to open the Map Drive dialog box.

b. He clicked the Choose the drive letter to map list arrow and clicked the F: drive.

c. He modified the Enter the network path to the resource text box to read "\\CBE_ADMIN\SYS."

d. He clicked the Map button and then clicked Yes when asked to connect to the "\\CBE_ADMIN\SYS" path. The contents of the SYS volume were then displayed.

4. He clicked File, New, Folder to create a new folder (subdirectory) called Apps. The new folder then appeared in the Contents of the F:\ window. (The title New Folder is highlighted in edit mode so that you can change the folder name.)

5. He typed Apps as the new folder name, and then pressed Enter.

6. He double-clicked the Apps folder, and then clicked File, New, Folder. He typed "Pagepub" as the new folder name, and pressed Enter.

7. He closed Windows Explorer.

8

## ConsoleOne Directory Management

You can also create directories and subdirectories with the ConsoleOne utility. Although directories are not eDirectory objects, directories can be created for Volume objects and other directories, and displayed in the ConsoleOne tree view. To view the directory structure for a Volume object in ConsoleOne, follow these general steps:

1. Double-click the Volume object icon when the directories are not displayed.

2. Double-click each directory icon to display the subdirectories (and files) in that directory.

3. Repeat Step 2 on each subdirectory until the entire directory tree is displayed.

To create a directory using ConsoleOne, follow these general steps:

1. Click the volume or directory that will contain the directory, and then press Insert.

   *or*

   Click the volume or directory that will contain the directory, and then click File, New, Object on the menu bar.

   *or*

   Right-click the volume or directory that will contain the directory, and then click New, Object on the shortcut menu.

   *or*

   Click the volume or directory that will contain the directory, and then click the New Object button on the ConsoleOne toolbar.

2. Select Directory, and then click OK. In the New Directory dialog box, type the name of the directory, and then click the OK button.

## Creating the Directory Structure

Except for the user home directories, which are created automatically with user accounts, David used ConsoleOne to create the directory structures shown previously in Figures 8-1 and 8-2 for the SYS and DATA volumes. David used the following steps to create the Admin directory and its subdirectories on the DATA volume. (The directory structure shown in Figures 8-1 and 8-2 was created during your classroom server setup. Your instructor might demonstrate the process of creating these directories using different volumes.)

1. First, David logged in with the Admin user name and password and started ConsoleOne.

2. Next, he expanded the Tree object and the CBE_LABS Organization to display the Volume objects.

3. He clicked the CBE_ADMIN_DATA Volume object and then clicked the New Folder button on the ConsoleOne toolbar to open the New Directory dialog box, as shown in Figure 8-21.

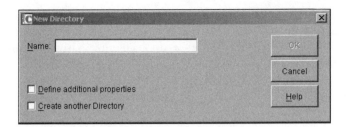

**Figure 8-21**    The New Directory dialog box

4. He then entered Admin in the Name text box and clicked OK to create the Admin directory and return to the ConsoleOne main window.

5. David followed these steps to create the subdirectories of Admin:

    a. He double-clicked the Admin directory and then clicked the New Folder button to open the New Directory dialog box.

    b. He entered Budgets in the Name text box and then clicked the Create another Directory check box.

    c. He clicked OK to create the Budgets directory and return to the New Directory dialog box.

    d. He entered Shared in the Name text box and clicked OK to create the Shared directory and return to the New Directory dialog box.

    e. After both subdirectories were created, he clicked the Cancel button to close the New Directory dialog box and return to the ConsoleOne main window.

6. He repeated Steps 3–5 to create the rest of the directory structure on the SYS and DATA volumes.

Using this process, David created the rest of the directories and subdirectories needed in the directory structures on each volume. Note that even though Figure 8-2 shows subdirectories for each user, he did not create them at this time. The user home directories are created when the User object is created for each user, which you'll learn how to do in Chapter 9. (Your instructor might have completed the structure on the server during the classroom setup procedure. In the end-of-chapter projects, you'll re-create a similar structure in your own home directory.)

## DRIVE POINTERS

In both NetWare and Windows environments, drive pointers play an important role in accessing files located on different devices and directories. A **drive pointer** is a letter of the alphabet used to reference storage areas in the file system. By default, Windows reserves the first five drive pointers (A–E) for storage devices on the local workstation, so these letters are often called **local drive pointers**. Letters A and B are reserved for floppy disk drives, C and D are normally used for hard disks, and E is often a CD-ROM drive (although D and E are often reserved for CD-ROM drives or other external storage devices).

As shown in Figure 8-22, Novell Client adds a number of options to My Network Places and Windows Explorer that enable you to work with network drive pointers and perform other tasks, such as logging in as a different user, viewing network connections, and redirecting output to network printers.

**Figure 8-22**    The Novell client options for My Network Places

In addition to these options, Novell Client includes a NetWare N icon in the taskbar that contains options for working with drive pointers, changing passwords, and sending messages (see Figure 8-23). Both My Network Places and the Novell taskbar icon are important tools for network administrators and users to establish and maintain drive pointers.

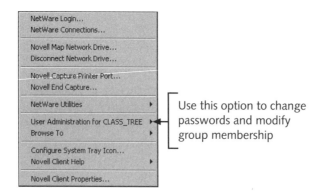

**Figure 8-23**    Novell taskbar icon options

Planning and implementing a proper set of network and search drive pointers are essential steps in setting up a successful network environment. Later in this section, you learn some tips and suggestions for organizing drive pointer use for your file system.

Think of NetWare **drive mappings** as similar to Windows shortcuts. Just as a shortcut must point to a specific directory to find a given application, a NetWare drive pointer points to a directory for a NetWare application.

In the past, planning drive mappings was a crucial administrator task. Because there can be a maximum of only 26 drives (one for each letter), the administrator didn't have much room to play around. Worse, each time an administrator or a user installed a new application, it often grabbed a mapping for itself. It isn't too hard to imagine a user with more than 16 applications plus another set of five or six data directories. Add all the local drive letters, and mappings became a scarce commodity.

Fortunately, drive mappings are in much less critical demand in Windows. Some organizations require them, especially to support older programs. In some network systems, you might not need any drive mappings. However, most networks require at least some search drive or regular drive mappings to access network data and software utilities.

A **network drive pointer** can be one of three types: regular, root, or search. Regular and root drive pointers are usually assigned to directories containing data files; search drive pointers are assigned to network software directories. Network drive pointers make it easier to access data files without needing to specify a complete path. A **complete path** includes the volume name followed by all necessary directories and subdirectories. Network drive pointers enable applications and DOS commands that do not recognize volume names to access data and programs on multiple volumes and servers.

■ A **regular drive pointer** is assigned to a directory path and shows all directories and subdirectories leading to the storage area. A regular drive pointer should be assigned to each volume and to commonly used directories so that applications that cannot use NetWare complete paths are able to access the data in any volume.

■ A **root drive pointer** looks to the user or application as though the directory path were at the root of the drive or volume. Figure 8-24 shows an example of two drive pointers, using Windows Explorer. Notice how the search drive pointer displays the volume name, whereas the root drive pointer shows the exact name of the directory (and its path). Making a drive letter a root drive prevents a user from accidentally changing the drive pointer to a different directory location.

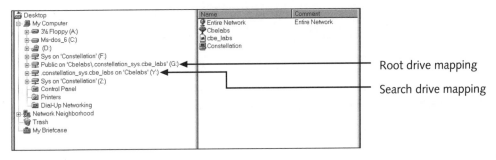

**Figure 8-24**    Root and search drive pointers

- DOS programs use **search drive pointers** to locate files. As a network administrator, you'll also find that search drive pointers are useful for providing quick access to third-party command-line tools. Typically, the primary search drive points to the NetWare 6 server's SYS:Public directory. For most applications, Windows shortcuts or menu options in the application provide the primary link to start an application.

 Windows applications do not need search drives because the application icon's parameters provide the path to the Windows application. Therefore, as more workstations use Windows, there will be less need for NetWare search drives.

If your program requires a search drive, you can select that option when mapping the drive. In the Map Drive dialog box shown in Figure 8-25, select the Map Search Drive check box. Notice the option to reconnect the mapped drive at login (the check box called Check to always map this drive letter when you start Windows), thus making the drive mapping permanent. Otherwise, the mapping lasts only until the user logs in again.

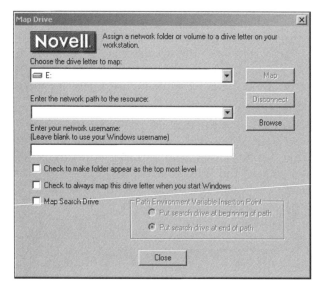

**Figure 8-25**   The Map Drive dialog box

 Any changes a user makes to his or her drive mappings apply only to that user, not to other users on the network.

NetWare supports up to 16 search drives, as shown in Figure 8-26. This user limitation was a key reason that operating systems moved away from the drive pointer model and to the Universal Naming Convention (UNC) used in Windows.

**Network and Search Drive Pointers**

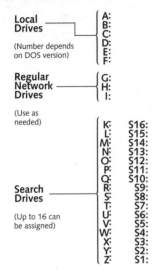

**Figure 8-26**    Drive pointer usage chart

Search pointers can be changed accidentally by using the DOS [CD] command or by traversing folders in Windows. This could cause the search pointer to "point" somewhere else, thus preventing access to some command-line utilities. To help prevent this problem, use the ROOT option when mapping search drives.

In general, most network administrators use regular and root drive pointers to map drive letters to data directories and use search drive pointers only to map drives to directories containing software or utilities that run from the command prompt. In the next section, you learn how CBE Labs planned the use of regular and search drive pointers for the organization's network.

## Planning Your Drive Mappings

Now that you have learned about the kinds of drive mappings NetWare uses, it's time to consider when and why you would use them. You need to plan a minimum set of drive pointers that are assigned a standard set of drive letters in your network blueprint. Then you implement these mappings using group or personal login scripts. After users log in, they will find that their workstation automatically includes those mappings.

First, determine what regular and root drive pointers you need for easy access to any shared and private files. Keep these drive pointers to a minimum because most users cannot keep track of more than five different drive pointers. Typical drive pointers for each user should include the following:

- *A drive pointer to the root of each volume*—These drive pointers let users change to another volume quickly without drilling up and down through layers in Windows Explorer. When using a two-volume structure, many network administrators map one drive letter to the SYS volume and another drive letter to access the DATA volume.

- *A drive pointer to the shared work directories that are available to all users*—For example, if you create a shared directory named Work on the root of the DATA volume, any user can access files in this directory by clicking on the mapping to the DATA volume. Similarly, if you create a shared word-processing forms directory named Forms on the root of the DATA volume, then mapping a drive to the DATA volume enables any user to access a common word-processing form.

- *A root drive pointer mapped to the user's home directory*—This drive letter, usually H: for "home" or U: for "user," is the starting point for users' personal data storage. Each user will have a different path mapped to his or her home drive letter. Using a root drive pointer is important because it enables users to create subdirectories within their home directories, and then move around within those subdirectories in Windows Explorer without interfering with other users.

- *A root drive pointer mapped to the user's workgroup directory*—This drive pointer lets users access shared files within their workgroups. Users in the Business Department, for example, can have their L: drive mapped to DATA:Business. The Sales Department users can have their L: drive mapped to the DATA:Sales directory. If you create a Work directory for each department, every user in the system can get to his or her workgroup's shared work directory by using the path L:\Work.

- *Application drive pointers*—Although some older DOS-based applications require their own search drive pointers, Windows-based software that runs from a network drive uses regular or root drive pointers. When you plan for drive pointers that will be used to run applications from the server, keep in mind that all users who run the application will want to have the same drive pointer letter because the software might be installed to use a specific drive letter for accessing its data and work files.

Network administrators also need to plan search drive pointers to let users access frequently used utilities and software packages. When planning search drive use, keep the total number of search drives to fewer than eight to provide better performance and reduce the chance of conflicts with regular drive pointers.

As mentioned, users running Windows do not need search drives mapped to Windows applications because the paths to these directories are already stored in the properties of the Windows folders or icons. As a minimum, most network administrators will want to create the following search drive mappings:

- Search drive to the SYS:Public directory

- Search drive to the network's Windows directory if Windows is being run from the network

A properly planned set of drive pointers includes the search drives needed to run any older DOS-based software packages and utilities and a standard set of regular drive pointers that give users easy access to data storage directories containing files they need for work. The Drive Mapping Planning Form in Figure 8-27 includes the following drive pointers for each user:

- The H: drive pointer to the user's home directory lets each user access his or her own private data easily.

- The J: drive pointer mapped to each user's local department or workgroup lets users access their department's shared work files by using the path J:\Work.

- The G: drive pointer to the SYS volume gives each user access to software or utilities stored in the SYS volume.

- The I: drive pointer mapped to the root of the DATA volume gives each user access to the organization's global data structure. For example, a user can access the organization's global work directory with the path I:\Work or access the organization's shared forms directory with the path I:\Forms. If a department wants its own Forms directory, that directory can be accessed with the path J:\Forms.

- The K: drive pointer is mapped to each user's shared workgroup data.

**8**

| Drive Mapping Planning Form | | |
|---|---|---|
| **Organization:** | CBE Laboratories | |
| **Planned By:** | Ted Simpson | |
| **Date:** | 9/15/2003 | |
| | | |
| **GROUP:** | **Everyone** | |
| **Letter:** | **Description of Use:** | **Path:** |
| S1: | NetWare Utilities | CBE_ADMIN/SYS:PUBLIC |
| S2: | | CBE_ADMIN/SYS: |
| G: | Global SYS volume | CBE_ADMIN/SYS: |
| I: | Global Data volume | CBE_ADMIN/DATA:SHARED |
| | | |
| **GROUP:** | **Marketing** | |
| **Letter:** | **Description of Use:** | **Path:** |
| H: | User data | CBE_ADMIN/DATA: |
| | | USERS/%Username |
| J: | Workgroup data | CBE_ADMIN/DATA:MARKET |
| K: | Workgroup shared data | CBE_ADMIN/DATA: |
| | | MARKET/SHARED |
| | | |
| **GROUP:** | **Finance** | |
| **Letter:** | **Description of Use:** | **Path:** |
| H: | User data | CBE_ADMIN/DATA: |
| | | USERS/%Username |
| J: | Workgroup data | CBE_ADMIN/DATA:FINANCE |
| K: | Workgroup shared data | CBE_ADMIN/DATA: |
| | | FINANCE/SHARED |
| | | |
| **GROUP:** | | |
| **Letter:** | **Description of Use:** | **Path:** |
| | | |
| | | |
| | | |
| | | |
| | | |

**Figure 8-27**    A sample Drive Mapping Planning Form

# Mapping Drive Pointers with Windows Explorer

You can create drive pointers in Windows by using Windows Explorer. To create a drive pointer, right-click on the directory you want to map and choose Novell Map Network Drive from the shortcut menu.

Creating routine drive mappings in the user's login script saves the trouble of re-creating them each session. To do this, you use NetWare Administrator to include a MAP command in the User object's Login Script property.

For example, David could map the root of the SYS volume on the CBE_ADMIN server to the K: drive by following these steps:

1. Click Start, Programs, Accessories, Windows Explorer to start Windows Explorer.

2. To display all the available network connections, expand My Network Places. Double-click Novell Connections, and click the + symbol next to CBE_ADMIN.

3. Right-click the folder icon for SYS to display the shortcut menu.

4. Click Novell Map Network Drive to open the Map Drive dialog box shown previously in Figure 8-25.

5. Click the Choose the drive letter to map list arrow, and then click K: to select the K: drive.

6. Click the Map button to create the drive mapping. The mapping appears in the list of drives under My Computer.

You can also map a drive by clicking Tools, Map Network Drive on the Windows Explorer menu bar. However, this action starts a Windows wizard, not NetWare. So mapping a drive here would apply only to that particular workstation. Otherwise, the process is similar to mapping with NetWare: Select the drive you want to map from the Drive drop-down list. Select the mapping you want by clicking the browse button next to the Folder text box (or, if you know the mapping path, type it directly in the Folder text box). When entering the mapping, you use UNC pathnames. As described in Chapter 5, UNC pathnames include the server and volume name as part of the path by using double backward slashes in front of the NetWare server name, a single backward slash between the server and volume names, and a single backward slash between the volume name and the directory name (instead of a colon). The syntax looks like this:

`\\ServerName\Volume\Directory\Subdirectory`

You can also specify the server name and volume name by using Novell syntax:

`ServerName\Volume:Directory\Subdirectory`

Notice that when using Novell syntax, the server name is not preceded by two backward slashes and the volume name ends in a colon. The advantage of the Novell syntax is that it also works with earlier NetWare server and client versions.

## Mapping and Removing Drives in Windows Using NetWare

Now that you're familiar with the theory of drive mapping, you can learn how to create and manage those mappings in Windows. Keep in mind that many, if not most, of your applications will now be delivered or installed as icons on the Windows desktop, so you won't need to map drives nearly as often as in previous NetWare versions.

You've looked at drive mapping using Windows tools. When you install the Novell client, you also install some important enhancements to this basic function. In particular, you can map root drives and search drives from the Windows desktop. To map either drive type, right-click the My Network Places icon on your Windows desktop. NetWare displays the menu shown previously in Figure 8-22.

Note that this menu includes a Map Network Drive option for Windows as well as options marked with the Novell *N*. If you choose the Novell version for mapping a drive, NetWare opens a dialog box similar to the one shown previously in Figure 8-25. Note the three check boxes at the bottom of this dialog box: Check to make folder appear as the top most level, Check to always map this drive letter when you start Windows, and Map Search Drive. The Check to make folder appear as the top most level check box is also referred to as a root drive mapping because the mapping makes the folder appear as though it's the beginning of the volume. By default, NetWare performs a regular mapping unless you select this check box. If you want the drive mapping to be performed each time a user logs in, click the Check to always map this drive letter when you start Windows check box, or add the drive mapping to the login script (described in Chapter 12). To complete the drive mapping, type the pathname or browse to your drive path, and then click Map.

Removing a drive mapping in Windows is simple. Right-click the icon of the mapped drive in My Computer or Windows Explorer, and then choose Disconnect. NetWare automatically removes the mapping.

## Using the MAP Command

Network administrators use MAP, a versatile DOS command-line utility, to create, modify, and delete regular and search drive pointers. Although you'll use Windows desktop tools more often to handle pointers, you need to be familiar with the basic MAP command used in login scripts to control a user's drive mappings at login. A login script is a set of NetWare commands stored in eDirectory that run when the user logs in to the Novell network. In this section, you learn the required network administrator tasks and see the syntax of the MAP command associated with each task and an example of the command's use.

This is the basic syntax of the MAP command:

```
MAP [option] /VER [drive:=] [path] [?]
```

You can use several parameters, listed in Table 8-1, with the MAP command.

**Table 8-1** MAP Command Parameters

| Parameter | Use This Parameter To: |
| --- | --- |
| drive: | Specify the drive letter. |
| path | Specify the path to the directory being mapped. Include: NetWare server name Volume name Directory path on volume |
| /? | Access help about MAP. If this parameter is used, all others are ignored. |
| /VER | See the version number of the MAP command. If this parameter is used, all others are ignored. |

You can use several options with MAP, as listed in Table 8-2.

**Table 8-2**   *MAP Command Options*

| Option | Use This Option To: |
|--------|---------------------|
| INS | Insert an additional search drive mapping. You can also type the word INSERT. |
| DEL | Delete the drive mapping. |
| N | Use the next available drive letter for mapping. You can also use the word NEXT. |
| R | Create a root drive mapping. You can also use the word ROOT. |
| C | Change the type of drive mapping from regular to search or search to regular. |

Table 8-3 gives examples of using the MAP command to perform tasks at the DOS command line or in a user's login script. (Remember, you must press Enter after typing each command.)

**Table 8-3**   *Examples Using the MAP Command*

| Task | Example |
|------|---------|
| View current mappings | MAP |
| Create regular drive mappings | MAP G:=CBE_ADMIN_SYS: |
| Create a root drive mapping | MAP ROOT J:=CBE_ADMIN_SYS:Apps\Office |
| Change a drive mapping | MAP J:=J: (This has the effect of changing the root mapping shown in the preceding example into a regular drive mapping.) |
| Create a search drive mapping | MAP S16:=CBE_ADMIN_SYS:PUBLIC |
| Remove a drive mapping | MAP DEL J: (This deletes the drive mapping on J:.) |

## Creating Regular Drive Pointers

To use the MAP command to create a new drive letter, enter this command:

```
MAP drive:=[path]
```

In this command, *drive* can be any letter of the alphabet (A–Z). You can replace *path* with a complete or partial NetWare path leading to the target directory. If you omit the path, the MAP command assigns the specified drive pointer to the current path. For example, if David wants to assign drive L: to the DATA:Market directory on CBE_ADMIN using the physical volume name, he would enter the following MAP command to specify a complete path:

```
MAP L:=CBE_ADMIN/DATA:Market
```

The slash between the server name and the volume name specifies that the path points directly to the DATA volume on the CBE_ADMIN server. To map drive L: to the

DATA:Market directory using the distinguished name of an eDirectory Volume object name in the path, he could enter the following MAP command:

```
MAP L:=.CBE_ADMIN_DATA.CBE_LABS:Market
```

The name .CBE_ADMIN_DATA.CBE_LABS tells the MAP command to look in the eDirectory database for the Volume object named CBE_ADMIN_DATA, and then use that object to locate the physical server and volume.

You can also use an existing drive map as part of the path, as shown in the following command, which assigns the drive letter N to the DATA:Market\Reports directory by using the L: drive pointer, which is mapped to the DATA:Market directory as a starting point:

```
K:\>MAP N:=L:Reports
```

Notice that there is no slash between the drive letter (L:) and the path (Reports). Placing a slash in the command would cause the system to search the root of the DATA volume for the Reports directory. Because no Reports directory exists in the root of the DATA volume, an error message indicating an invalid path would be displayed.

 If you use a local drive pointer (A–F), the MAP command asks if you want to override the local pointer with a network path. If you answer yes, the local drive pointer accesses the network path rather than the local drive.

The N option can be used with the MAP command to instruct Novell Client to map the next available drive letter to the specified path. For example, you can use the following MAP command to assign the specified path to the next available drive letter:

```
MAP N [path]
```

Notice that no colon is used after the N option. Placing a colon after the N would cause the client to attempt to map drive letter N: to the specified path instead of automatically selecting the next available drive letter. You can also use the word NEXT instead of just N. This command is useful when you want to map an unused drive letter to a directory path and you do not care what letter is used. Suppose, for example, you want to map a drive to the Shared subdirectory of the Market directory. The MAP NEXT command, as shown in Figure 8-28, maps the next available drive letter—in this case, H:—to the User subdirectory.

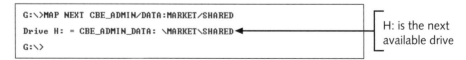

```
G:\>MAP NEXT CBE_ADMIN/DATA:MARKET/SHARED
Drive H: = CBE_ADMIN_DATA: \MARKET\SHARED          H: is the next
G:\>                                               available drive
```

**Figure 8-28**    Creating a regular drive mapping using the N option of the MAP command

## Why Create Root Drive Pointers?

A root drive pointer looks to the user or application as though the drive pointer were at the beginning of a drive or volume. Root drive pointers are useful for two reasons:

- Some applications access files only from the root of a directory path. This can be a problem for network administrators because users are not usually given rights to the root of a volume and also because you might want to keep the application contained in a certain directory in the structure. NetWare solves this problem by letting network administrators or users map a drive to a "fake" root containing the application.

- Root drive pointers make it more difficult for a user or application to change the drive pointer to another location inadvertently. For example, if a user's home directory is mapped to a regular drive pointer and the user issues a CD\ command, the mapping of the drive pointer is changed to the root of the current volume. Root drive mappings, in contrast, appear to DOS as the beginning of a drive, causing the CD\ command to return to the directory the root drive is mapped to instead of going to the root of the volume.

**8**

## Creating Search Drive Pointers

Search drives are pointers to directories where programs are stored on the network. A workstation already has one or more search drives mapped to local directories. You can assign a maximum of 16 search drives, starting with S1 and ending with S16. You can add new search drives to the list by using the MAP command to assign the next available search drive number or to insert the new search drive between two existing search drives. The syntax of the MAP command that adds new search drives is as follows:

```
MAP INS S#: = [path]
```

When you add a search drive to the end of the list, you do not include the INS option and you replace # with the next available search drive number from 1 through 16. If you skip search drive numbers, the MAP command automatically assigns the next available number. When you add a new search drive, NetWare automatically assigns the next available drive letter, starting with Z: for S1 and ending with K: for S16. For example, suppose you have the following search drives mapped:

```
S1:=Z:. [CBE_ADMIN\SYS:\Public]
S2:=Y:. [CBE_ADMIN\SYS:\Public\Win32]
S3:=C:\DOS
```

The next available search drive is Search4 (S4). To map search drive S4 to the SYS:Apps\WinOffice directory, you can use the following MAP command:

```
MAP S4:=SYS:Apps\WinOffice
```

When adding new search drives, you cannot skip search drive numbers. For example, if you attempt to map the preceding search drive to S5 before S4 is mapped, NetWare automatically uses the next sequential search drive number (in this case, S4). Figure 8-29 shows an example of trying to add a search drive mapping that skips numbers.

 Because NetWare does not skip search drive numbers, you can use the command MAP S16:=[*path*] if you want to add a search drive to the end of the search list and cannot remember the number of the last search drive.

```
F:\>MAP S10:=CBE_ADMIN/SYS:APPS
S6: = X:. [CBE_ADMIN_SYS: \APPS]

F:\>MAP

Drives A,B,C,D,E map to a local disk.
Drive F: = CBE_ADMIN_SYS: \
Drive G: = CBE_ADMIN_DATA: \
Drive H: = CBE_ADMIN_DATA:MARKET\SHARED \
Drive L: = CBE_ADMIN_DATA:MARKET \
Drive Y: = CBE_ADMIN_SYS: \
-----        Search Drives     -----
S1: = Z:. [CBE_ADMIN_SYS: \PUBLIC]
S2: = C:\NOVELL\CLIENT32
S3: = C:\WINDOWS
S4: = C:\WINDOWS\COMMAND
S5: = C:\QTW
S6: = X:. [CBE_ADMIN_SYS: \APPS]

F:\>
```

New search drive is designated S10

Because S6 does not exist, new search drive is designated S6 instead of S10

New search drive in list of drive mappings

**Figure 8-29**    Adding a new search drive mapping

When inserting a search drive between two existing drives, include the INS option and replace # with the number of the search drive before the one where you want the new drive placed. When you set up search drives, assign the lower search drive numbers to the most commonly used paths. This makes the system more efficient by reducing the number of directories NetWare has to search through when it looks for a program file.

For example, assume you have the following search drives mapped:

```
S1:=Z:.[CBE_ADMIN\SYS:Public]
S2:=Y:.[CBE_ADMIN\SYS:Apps\PagePub]
S3:=X:.[CBE_ADMIN\SYS:Apps\WinOffice]
```

Suppose you want to use the word-processing program in the Apps\WinOffice\WP directory and still maintain the other search drive mappings. To make the word-processing directory first in the search order, you could use the MAP INS command shown in Figure 8-30 to create a new search mapping. This resequences the other search drives, as displayed by the MAP command.

Notice that the drive letter W: is assigned to the new search drive and that, although the other search drives are renumbered, they retain their drive letter assignments. The DOS MAP commands shown in Figure 8-30 illustrate the way the search commands affect the DOS path. NetWare keeps track of search drive numbers by their sequence in the DOS path. Because drive W: is now the first drive in the path, it becomes S1.

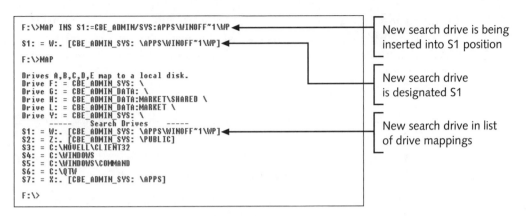

```
F:\>MAP INS S1:=CBE_ADMIN/SYS:APPS\WINOFF~1\WP
S1: = W:. [CBE_ADMIN_SYS: \APPS\WINOFF~1\WP]
F:\>MAP
Drives A,B,C,D,E map to a local disk.
Drive F: = CBE_ADMIN_SYS: \
Drive G: = CBE_ADMIN_DATA: \
Drive H: = CBE_ADMIN_DATA:MARKET\SHARED \
Drive L: = CBE_ADMIN_DATA:MARKET \
Drive Y: = CBE_ADMIN_SYS: \
          -----    Search Drives    -----
S1: = W:. [CBE_ADMIN_SYS: \APPS\WINOFF~1\WP]
S2: = Z:. [CBE_ADMIN_SYS: \PUBLIC]
S3: = C:\NOVELL\CLIENT32
S4: = C:\WINDOWS
S5: = C:\WINDOWS\COMMAND
S6: = C:\QTW
S7: = X:. [CBE_ADMIN_SYS: \APPS]
F:\>
```

New search drive is being inserted into S1 position

New search drive is designated S1

New search drive in list of drive mappings

**Figure 8-30**    Inserting a search drive mapping

## Using Directory Map Objects

A Directory Map object is a server-related leaf object that the network administrator can use in a MAP command to simplify administration of drive mappings. This object contains the path you would normally use in a drive mapping. By using the Directory Map object in a MAP command, you are providing the drive-mapping path as the path contained in the Directory Map object.

For example, David wants to map a drive to the files shared among all CBE Labs personnel. These reports are stored in the CBE_ADMIN_DATA:Admin\Shared directory. To map a regular drive, he would use the following command:

```
MAP ROOT P:=CBE_ADMIN_DATA:Admin\Shared
```

To map a drive using a Directory Map object, David first creates the Directory Map object and enters the volume and path data needed for the drive map. For example, he could create a Directory Map object named SharedFiles in the CBE_Labs_Admin OU of the CBE_LABS Organization. He would use the following MAP command:

```
MAP P:=.SharedFiles.CBE_Labs_Admin.CBE_LABS
```

If David wants to move these files to another location later, he can change the drive mapping by simply changing the Volume and Path property values stored in the Directory Map object. This is easier than finding every use of the regular mapping in all the login scripts that use the drive mapping. For this reason, you will usually want to create Directory Map objects to use in drive mappings. You can create these objects with ConsoleOne or NetWare Administrator. After creating them, you can use them in any MAP command.

8

David wants to create a Directory Map object named SharedFiles in the CBE_Labs_Admin OU. The Directory Map object will contain the path CBE_ADMIN_ DATA:Admin\Shared. To create the SharedFiles Directory Map object, David used these steps:

1. He started ConsoleOne.

2. He expanded the eDirectory tree to show the CBE_Labs_Admin OU and its contents.

3. He clicked the CBE_Labs_Admin OU, and then clicked the New Object button on the toolbar to open the New Object dialog box.

4. He clicked Directory Map, and then clicked OK to open the New Directory Map dialog box (see Figure 8-31).

**Figure 8-31**    The New Directory Map dialog box

5. He entered SharedFiles in the Name text box.

6. He clicked the Volume text box to activate it, and then clicked the browse button to the right of the Volume text box to open the Select Objects dialog box.

7. He browsed the eDirectory tree to locate and select the CBE_ADMIN_DATA Volume object. The name of the object appeared in the Selected Object text box.

8. He clicked OK. The volume name CBE_ADMIN_DATA.CBE_LABS appeared in the Volume text box of the New Directory Map dialog box.

9. He clicked the Path text box to activate it, and then clicked the browse button to the right of the Path text box to open the Select Objects dialog box again.

10. He navigated to the Admin directory and clicked the Shared directory to select it. He clicked OK to fill in the Path text box of the New Directory Map dialog box, as shown in Figure 8-32.

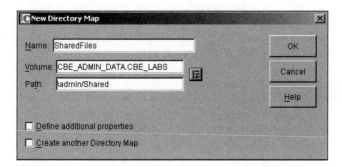

**Figure 8-32**    Entering a Directory Map path

11. He clicked OK to create the Directory Map object SharedFiles and add it to the eDirectory tree.

Before testing the Directory Map object, David used ConsoleOne to add the following MAP command to the login script:

```
MAP P:=.SharedFiles.CBE_Labs_Admin.CBE_LABS
```

You will learn how to work with MAP commands in login scripts in Chapter 12.

# FILE MANAGEMENT

After you have your network file system in place and have created drive mappings, you can install applications and users can put their data on the network. The directories and subdirectories of the network file system are used for storing application and data files. As a network administrator, you must manage these files and their directories. In this section, you study some tools that will help you accomplish this.

## Viewing NetWare Directory and File Attributes

To see information about directory and file attributes, run Windows Explorer. Select a network directory, and display its contents. Right-click on a file or directory, and you see a menu with the Properties option at the bottom. Click on it, and NetWare will display information about the current directory or file. The NetWare Info tab of the Properties dialog box also provides a way to set file or directory attributes. For example, Figure 8-33 shows NetWare information about the CBE_ADMIN/SYS:Public directory.

Notice that the following information about a file or directory appears in the NetWare Info tab:

■ The Owner field displays the name of the user who created the directory. Administrator authority is required to change the information in this field.

- The Creation Date field tells you the date and time the directory was created and can be changed only if you are logged in with Administrator authority.

- The Attributes section displays the attributes available for this directory or file. With a check mark, it indicates which ones are active. As an administrator, you can click the boxes to enable or disable any of these attributes. They include Read-only, Hidden, Compression variables, and Purge Immediate (used when you need the space).

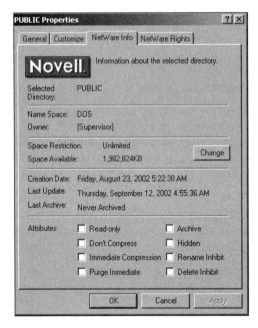

**Figure 8-33**    The NetWare Info tab for a directory

The NetWare Rights tab (see Figure 8-34) provides fields that an administrator can use to determine who has access rights in the selected file or directory. To change this information, you must be logged in with a user name that has administrative rights to modify the directory trustee assignments. (Chapter 10 explains the access rights shown in this tab in more detail.)

- The Trustees list displays all users and groups who have been assigned rights to this directory.

- Clicking the Inherited Rights and Filters button displays a list of access rights that the directory will allow to flow into it from its parent directories.

- The Effective Rights section is for information purposes only and shows the rights that the currently logged in user has to the selected directory.

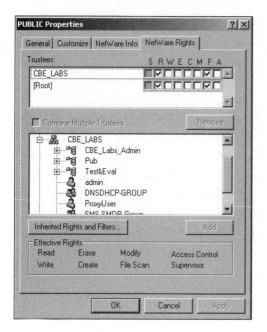

**Figure 8-34**    The NetWare Rights tab for a directory

You can also display file property information about a specific file by right-clicking the file and choosing Properties, as Figure 8-35 shows.

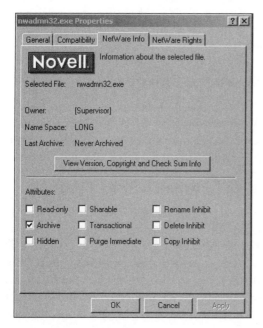

**Figure 8-35**    The NetWare Info tab for a file

The NetWare Info tab for a file offers the following functions, similar to the options for a directory:

- In the Attributes section, you can add or remove attribute flags for this file by clicking the check boxes associated with the attributes.

- The Owner field identifies the user who originally created the file. Only an administrator user can change the contents of the Owner field. This is normally done if the name of the user who originally created the file is deleted from the system.

- The Name Space field shows whether the file uses a DOS (eight-character) or LONG filename space. (Windows uses the LONG option.)

- In the NetWare Rights tab, the Inherited Rights and Filters and Trustees areas function the same way they do in the directory's Properties dialog box (shown previously in Figure 8-34).

- As in the directory's Properties dialog box, the Effective Rights section in the NetWare Rights tab is for information purposes only and cannot be changed, even by the administrator.

- In the General tab, the Size field shows the file size in bytes.

- The Created date field (as well as the Modified and Accessed date fields in the case of files) is for informational purposes and cannot be changed.

 If you want to work with several files, Ctrl-click each filename and then right-click and choose Properties. NetWare displays a tabbed Properties dialog box, similar to the one for a single file, but shows only the combination of rights/trustees for the selected files.

## Windows-Based NetWare File Management

You can use Windows Explorer to copy, move, and delete local and network files. You should already know how to use Windows Explorer to do these functions. Used with Novell Client, Windows Explorer can also be used to assign and control trustee rights. In this section, you see how to use Windows-based tools for file management.

### Using Windows to Salvage and Purge Deleted Files

You can use Windows to salvage or purge files from network directories. (Naturally, you'll need appropriate rights in the directory you're trying to purge or salvage.) Salvaging a file is quite similar to the Windows Recycle bin; you retrieve a file or files that have been deleted but you now want to restore. Salvaging has similar limitations to the Recycle bin, in that if you wait too long, you might not be able to salvage a file. A purge is like emptying the Recycle Bin—it irrevocably removes the deleted files from the network volume. After you run Purge on a directory or file, you cannot use Salvage to recover it.

To perform a Salvage or Purge operation, select the directory you want by opening My Computer or My Network Places, and then double-clicking the corresponding network volume. Right-click the directory you want (the one containing the file or files you want to recover), and NetWare displays a menu similar to the one in Figure 8-36.

**Figure 8-36**    The shortcut menu options for a directory

NetWare offers you a choice of Salvage Files or Purge Files. If you choose Salvage Files, the Salvage Network Files dialog box opens (see Figure 8-37). If there are no files that can be salvaged from this directory, this dialog box will be blank.

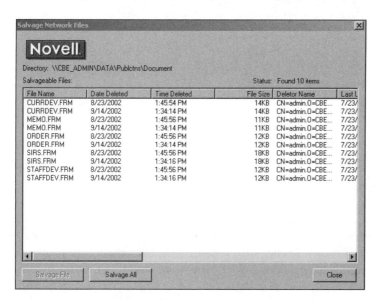

**Figure 8-37**    The Salvage Network Files dialog box

The importance of the Salvage feature is its ability to recover files that have been deleted even when the directory structure in which the file was stored no longer exists.

If you choose Purge Files, the Purge Network Files dialog box opens, listing all deleted files (see Figure 8-38). You can choose one or more files to purge, or you can click the Purge All button. You can also click the Purge Subdirectories button to purge deleted files from all subdirectories of the selected directory.

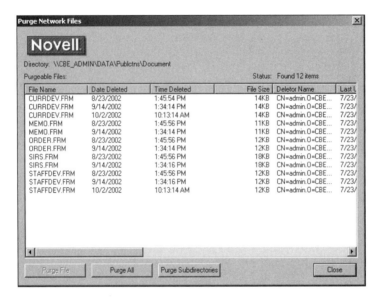

**Figure 8-38**     The Purge Network Files dialog box

After you purge a file, it is removed from the file system and can only be retrieved from a backup. So choose carefully when performing a Purge All or Purge Subdirectories operation.

## BACKING UP NETWORK DATA

An organization's data plays a critical role in today's highly competitive and rapidly changing world of business and industry. A company robbed of its information would certainly suffer major losses and could even be forced out of business. Therefore, as a network administrator in an organization that relies on the network for data storage and retrieval, you become the "keeper of the flame," in that you're responsible for much, if not all, of your organization's critical data files. As a network administrator, management counts on your knowledge to provide a reliable storage system, secure from unauthorized access and protected from accidental loss caused by equipment failure, operator error, or natural disaster. After planning and implementing the network storage system, you need to establish a regular backup system and policy to protect the system from loss of valuable data.

## The Storage Management System

NetWare includes the **Storage Management System (SMS)** for backing up even complex networks consisting of data residing on multiple file servers and on DOS and OS/2 workstations. The NetWare server that runs the backup program and has the attached tape or other backup media is referred to as the **host server**. Other servers and client workstations being backed up are referred to as **target servers**. When using the SMS system, the term "parent" refers to a data set, such as a directory or subdirectory, and the term "child" refers to a specific subset of a data set, such as a file or program. SMS uses NetWare Loadable Modules on the host server to communicate with modules on target devices, read the information from the target devices, and send it to the backup media, as shown in Figure 8-39.

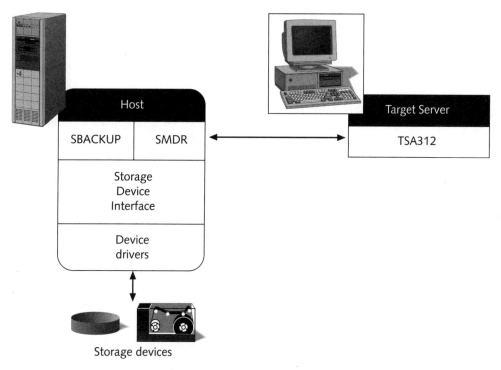

**Figure 8-39**     The NetWare 6 SMS backup process

The NetWare SMS consists of the following software components that can be run on NetWare servers as well as DOS or Windows workstations:

- Storage device drivers are loaded on the host server and control the mechanical operation of various storage devices and media, such as tape drives.

- The Target Server Agents (TSAs) are loaded on the target servers and communicate with the SBACKUP program running on the host server. The purpose of the TSA is to get information from the target server's volumes and send it to the SBACKUP program running on the host server. A server can act as host *and* target by running both the SBACKUP and TSA software.

- Workstation TSAs are run on DOS or OS/2 workstations to back up data on the local drives across the network.

- The enhanced SBACKUP utility is the main NetWare-provided software, which runs on the host server or Windows workstation. It works with the SMS architecture to control the backup process and transfer data to and from the host server.

- In addition to the SBACKUP software that runs from the server console, NetWare includes the NWBACK32 program, which runs on a Windows workstation. It is used to create backup jobs processed by the Backup/Restore NetWare Loadable Modules (NLMs) running on the NetWare server.

## Other Backup Software Packages

A number of other companies offer specialized backup software packages with several features and benefits. The most common third-party backup systems are ARCserve and Backup Exec. As a CNA, you should be aware of their basic features, described in the following sections.

**ARCserve for NetWare** ARCserve for NetWare (currently marketed as Brightstor ARCserve Backup for NetWare) fully supports eDirectory and the NSS storage system to provide enterprise-wide backups. ARCserve has the following features:

- *Cross-platform capability*—Enables ARCserve to back up data from and restore data to computers connected to the NetWare network.

- *Backup storage selection*—Lets you protect your data by storing it in more than one location.

- *File interleaving*—Enables you to back up several servers at one time.

- *Media pooling*—Allows you to separate media into groups, which are used to create certain backup jobs.

- *Server-to-server copying*—Gives you the advantage of a duplicate server to help reduce downtime; also called "server mirroring."

- *User-defined scripts*—Enables you to configure backups once and reuse them when needed.

- *Databases*—Gives you quick access to data on the backup media and information about jobs performed by ARCserve.

- *Reports and logs*—Provides a complete history of operations.

ARCserve consists of both server and client components. The client component, ARCserve Manager, runs on the Windows workstation and handles all backup and restore sessions. ARCserve Manager also performs such tasks as copying files from one server to another, accessing the ARCserve utilities, and viewing information about past and current jobs.

The server component of ARCserve, called ARCserve Server, runs on the NetWare server console and processes all unattended jobs scheduled by ARCserve Manager and all jobs submitted from the ARCserve server. ARCserve Server has the following subcomponents:

- The Schedule component manages jobs you schedule through ARCserve Manager.

- Job Processing Modules scan the queue and, when a job is ready to print, dynamically load the NLMs required for the print job.

- Tape Server Modules communicate with your tape drives and enable you to view the tape server log and current activities.

- Databases keep track of workstations and servers on the network, the jobs you have run, and all the files backed up, copied, or restored.

ARCserve client agents run on Windows workstations and allow you to back up and restore Windows, DOS, and Windows workstations. Optional client agents are available for Macintosh and Unix workstations.

**VERITAS Backup Exec for NetWare**   Like ARCserve, Backup Exec supports NSS and eDirectory and lets you back up and restore NetWare server volumes, workstation drives, and non-volume objects, such as binderies and registries. Backup Exec offers the following features and benefits:

- The ability to act as a data management system for Novell networks.

- An administrative console for NetWare servers.

- A Java-based administrative console so that you can access your NetWare server from any Windows workstation. This console provides the following functions:

  - Configuring default options for your media server

  - Managing your devices and media

  - Viewing scheduled and active jobs

  - Obtaining histories of completed jobs

  - Running general reports

8

- Back up and restore Windows 2000/XP systems.

- Policy-based backup allows you to store all settings for a job in a policy that can be viewed and reused. With this feature, you can save all backup job settings, except files and target devices, as a policy that you then apply to specific resources, making it easier to create new backup jobs.

- Enhanced device management simplifies how you organize and allocate storage devices attached to your media server.

- Multiple catalog views give you the choice of a catalog-based (tape) view or a volume-based view of the backed-up data. Volume-based views make it easier to locate and identify damaged or deleted files for restoring.

- Backup jobs can be submitted from the Administrative Console program running on a Windows workstation or Administrative Console for NetWare running on a server.

As with ARCserve, Backup Exec uses both server and workstation components. The Bestart.ncf file in the SYS:System directory is used to load the Backup Exec job engine software on the media server (the server that hosts a backup device, such as a tape drive). The job engine then processes jobs submitted from the Administrative Console running on a workstation.

 Backup Exec is designed to work with earlier NetWare versions as well as NetWare 6. When Backup Exec is installed, it determines the NetWare version running on the media server and then adds the necessary lines to the Bestart.ncf file.

The Bestop.ncf file removes the Backup Exec job engine from the media server's memory. You should run this file before shutting down your server. If you are running Administrative Console for NetWare on the server, you need to manually exit this program before shutting down the server.

## Establishing a Backup System

Having a reliable and tested backup system is one of the best medicines a network administrator can have to ensure a good night's sleep, so spending some extra time planning and testing the backup system is well worth it. Establishing a successful backup system involves six steps:

1. Determine your network's storage needs.

2. Determine a backup strategy.

3. Assign a backup user.

4. Run the backup software on a scheduled basis.

5. Test the backup.

6. Develop a disaster recovery procedure.

In the following sections, you learn how David applied these steps to setting up the backup system for the CBE Labs network.

## Determining Storage Needs

The first step in establishing a backup system for your network is calculating how much data needs to be copied to the backup tape on a daily basis by determining which volumes and directories you plan to back up. If possible, you should try to obtain an SMS-compatible tape backup system with enough capacity to store your daily backup on one tape cartridge. In a single-file server environment, the file server acts as both the host and target devices, requiring you to load the SBACKUP and TSA modules on the same server. An advantage of having a file server as both host and target devices is that a file server backing up its own data runs almost four times faster than a host file server backing up data across the network from another target file server. As a result, when implementing SMS in a multiple-file server environment, you should plan on making the server that stores the most data the host system.

## Determining a Backup Strategy

Depending on backup storage needs, one of the three backup strategies shown in Table 8-4 is normally used.

**Table 8-4**    Backup Strategies

| Type of Backup | Data to Back Up | Status of Archive Attribute |
|---|---|---|
| Full | All data, regardless of when or if it has been previously backed up | Cleared |
| Incremental | Files created or modified since the last full or incremental backup | Cleared |
| Differential | All data modified since the last full backup | Not cleared |

With the **full backup** strategy, all data is copied to the backup tape each night. This backup strategy will work well for CBE Labs because the current size of files to be included on the backup does not exceed one tape cartridge. The advantage of the full backup strategy is that if a crash occurs, only the previous day's backup needs to be restored. The disadvantage is the need for a large tape capacity and the time required to perform backups.

The **incremental backup** strategy takes the least amount of time for each backup because only the data files that have changed that day are copied to the backup tape. When using the incremental backup strategy, a full backup is made at the beginning of the week and an incremental backup is made each day. The disadvantage of this strategy is that all incremental backup tapes must be restored if data is lost. For example, if a crash occurs on Thursday, you need to restore the Monday full backup first, followed by the Tuesday and Wednesday incremental backups.

A compromise between the full backup and the incremental backup is the **differential backup** strategy, in which all files that have changed since the last full backup are copied to the backup tape. That means the size of the tape backup increases as the week progresses. The advantage of the differential strategy is that if a crash occurs later in the week, only the full backup and the last day's differential backup need to be restored.

Currently, David is using the full backup strategy for CBE Labs to make a complete backup of all data and the eDirectory database each day. In the future, as CBE's data storage requirements grow beyond the space of one tape cartridge, David recommends implementing a differential backup strategy to reduce the backup time and eliminate the need for someone to change tapes in the middle of the night.

## Assigning a Backup User

Although you can log in as Admin to perform the backup, most network administrators prefer creating a separate user name for backups. Creating a separate user name has the advantage of allowing you to assign other people to perform the backup and limits the number of times you need to log in to the network as Admin. The user name you create to perform the backup must have the following access rights and privileges:

- To back up the file system, the user name needs to have Read, File Scan, and Modify rights to the volumes and directories included in the backup. The Modify right is necessary for the backup program to reset the Archive attribute after backing up data files. When assigning these rights to the directory, you need to be aware of any Inherited Rights Filters (IRFs) that might block these rights from a subdirectory you want to back up. (See Chapter 10 for more information on these attributes and IRFs.)

- To back up the eDirectory database, the backup user name needs to have the Browse Entry and Read attribute rights to the containers included in the backup.

- The person performing the backup needs to know the password used on the host server and the passwords assigned to any target servers or clients.

## Running the Backup Software

After you have decided on a backup strategy and created any necessary user names, your next step is testing the SMS installation by backing up your server data and then testing the backup by restoring selected files from the backup tape. In the following steps, David leads you through the backup process using SMS from the server console. If you have access to the server console, you can follow along to back up your network data:

1. To load the enhanced SBACKUP utility, David loads the Storage Manager Device Redirector software by entering the command LOAD SMDR.

2. After the SMDR software is loaded, he loads the target agents for backing up NetWare server data and the eDirectory database with these commands:

```
LOAD TSA600
LOAD TSANDS
```

3. After loading the target service agents, he finishes the initialization by loading the Storage Management System Device Interface software with this command:

```
LOAD SMSDI
```

4. The SMS uses job queues to store backup and restore jobs until they are to be run. Just as a print queue enables a print job to wait for a printer to be available, the job queue enables you to enter a job and have it run later that night or when the backup device is available. To load the job queue software, David enters this command:

```
LOAD QMAN
```

5. To load the enhanced SBACKUP software on the server, he enters the following two commands to display the main menu backup options:

```
LOAD SBSC
LOAD SBCON
```

6. Next, he selects Job Administration and then Backup to display the Backup Options menu shown in Figure 8-40.

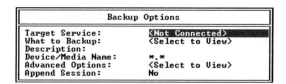

**Figure 8-40**    SBACKUP options

7. Next, he selects the Target Service option to choose the NetWare server running the Target Service Agent. When prompted for the target server's user name, he enters the Admin user name and password for the CBE_ADMIN server. The enhanced SBACKUP utility takes a few moments to attach to that target. Next, the Backup Options form appears. To perform a full backup, David selects the default values. Other options include incremental and differential backups.

8. Next, he selects what he wants to back up from the List of Resources and enters a descriptive name for the backup session.

9. Finally, he selects the backup media to start the backup process.

## Testing the Backup

After a successful backup, the next step in testing your backup system is to try restoring selected files from the backup media. A complete restore is often not feasible because of time constraints and the possible loss of data if the restore process fails. Before doing a major restore, you should restore test files that are not needed or files that have been copied to another disk storage device. To restore selected files, select Job Administration from the main SBCON menu, select the Restore option from the main SBCON menu and then enter the path to the working directory you used when the backup tape was created. Next, select the option Restore from session files, and select the session you named previously when the backup was created.

After the restore screen has been completed, start the restore process. The selected files should be copied back to their appropriate directories. When the restore is finished, log in from a user workstation and verify that the files have been correctly restored.

## Developing a Disaster Recovery Procedure

After the backup system has been tested, the next step in implementing a reliable disaster recovery plan is to develop a tape rotation procedure and backup schedule. Having a multiple-tape rotation procedure that enables you to save certain backups for a long time is an important part of a disaster recovery plan because it gives you a way to go back to an earlier backup to recover files and to be able to store backup tapes outside the building. Sometimes you must be able to recover a file from an earlier backup if a software virus, an operator error, or a software bug corrupts it, and the damage to the file is not discovered for several days or weeks. If you were rotating your backups between just a few tapes, by the time the error was discovered, a backup copy of the corrupted file would have overwritten the original backup with the valid file. To help prevent this problem, IS Manager Ted Simpson has recommended a tape rotation system consisting of 20 tapes, as shown in Figure 8-41.

Four tapes are labeled Monday through Thursday and are rotated each week. Four tapes are labeled Friday1 through Friday4, with Friday1 used on the first Friday of the month, Friday2 on the second, Friday3 on the third, and Friday4 on the fourth. In addition, 12 tapes are labeled January through December. These tapes are rotated each year and can be used on the last Friday of each month by replacing the Friday# tape with the correct monthly backup. Another alternative, if someone is available to change the tape, is to make the monthly backup on the last Saturday of each month. Storage for backup tapes is also important in case of a fire or damage to the building; many administrators store weekly backups in a fireproof vault and keep monthly backup tapes off-site in a secure location, such as a safety-deposit box.

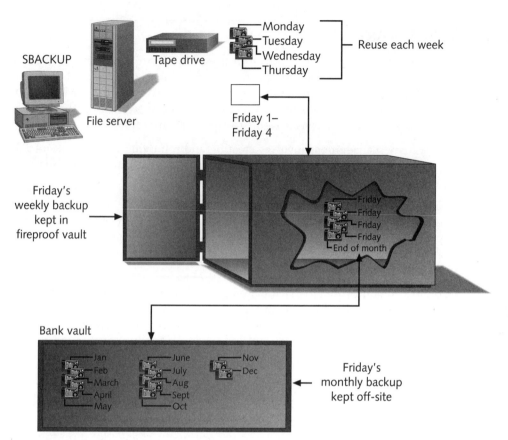

**Figure 8-41** Tape rotation procedure

The final step in implementing the backup system is setting up a time for the backup to be performed and ensuring that no users are logged in during the backup process. To prevent interference with user work schedules, many network administrators like the backup to start each night at about 12:00 A.M. To keep night owls from working late and to prevent users from leaving their workstations logged in during the backup, all user accounts, except the user name used to back up the system, should have a time restriction to prevent accessing the network between 12:00 A.M. and 5:00 A.M. This five-hour interval should be enough time to create your backup. If you need extra time, you can set the backup to begin at 11:00 P.M. or perhaps to end at 6:00 A.M., as long as the user time restrictions are also set for the longer backup period.

Congratulations! You have learned how to set up a basic network file system to organize and backup an organization's data. In subsequent chapters, you'll learn how to create and secure user accounts and give users access to data and applications.

## CHAPTER SUMMARY

❑ File system management involves creating Novell Storage Services (NSS) objects, such as partitions, storage pools, and volumes. These objects can be created, viewed, and managed with ConsoleOne or the new NetWare Remote Manager utility. To access file system objects in ConsoleOne, you need to turn off the File Caching option and have Supervisor rights to the NetWare server.

❑ Directory management involves creating and removing directories and subdirectories on volumes in the network. This is known as creating and maintaining the directory structure for each volume.

❑ Drive pointers are letters assigned to local drives and network directories for working with the file system and accessing software stored in other directories. The drive pointers A–E are normally reserved for local drives. Regular and root drive pointers are assigned to directories that contain data files; search drive pointers are assigned to software directories.

❑ Users can add or delete drive mappings with the Windows NetWare utilities or by using Windows Explorer. In addition to Windows Explorer and My Network Places, the N icon in the taskbar displays a menu with the option for Novell Map Network Drive. When a user logs in, drive pointers are set through the login script.

❑ The MAP command is the utility network administrators use to create and maintain drive pointers in login scripts. As a network administrator, you should be able to use the MAP command to create regular and search drive mappings.

❑ A Directory Map object is used in the eDirectory tree to simplify the mapping of drive pointers when the mapped directory might change location in the file directory structure. By mapping a drive to the Directory Map object, the network administrator can change the drive pointer in just one place, the Directory Map object properties, when the directory location changes.

❑ Network administrators should establish standards for drive pointer use to prevent conflicts and software configuration problems. As a general rule, you should establish for each user a set of drive pointers that includes a regular drive pointer to the root of each volume, a root drive pointer to the user's home directory, and another root drive pointer to the shared work area for the user's workgroup. In addition to the required search drive to the SYS:Public directory, search drives need to be allocated for any older DOS-based software packages.

❑ File management involves copying, moving, deleting, salvaging, and purging files in directories. Several NetWare utilities are useful in file management. The importance of the Salvage feature is its ability to recover deleted files even when the directory structure in which the file was stored no longer exists. Purging files permanently erases deleted files and frees up disk space. When you are low on disk space, purging deleted files can often improve the NetWare server's performance. You can use Windows Explorer and NetWare Administrator to salvage and purge deleted files.

❑ Backing up data is a critical function that should be performed daily on any network system. NetWare 6 includes the Storage Management System (SMS) for backing up data and eDirectory objects with a full, differential, or incremental backup strategy. You load and run backup software at the host server, with Target Service Agents (TSAs) running on the server and workstations to be backed up. The TSA600 agent is used to back up network data to the host, and the TSANDS agent backs up eDirectory objects.

## COMMAND SUMMARY

| Command | Syntax | Definition |
|---------|--------|------------|
| **MAP** | MAP d:= [*path*] | Creates regular drive mappings |
| | MAP N [*path*] | Creates a regular drive mapping using the next available drive letter |
| | MAP d:=[*path*] | Creates root drive mappings |
| | MAP S#:=[*path*] | Adds a search drive to the end of the search list |
| | MAP INS S#:=[*path*] | Inserts a search drive before an existing drive number |
| | MAP DEL *d*: | Removes regular, root, or search drive pointers |
| | MAP C *drive* | Changes a search drive mapping to a regular drive mapping and vice versa |

This summary of the MAP command contains only basic parameters, not all possible options.

## KEY TERMS

**complete path** — A directory path that includes the server, volume, and all necessary directories and subdirectories leading to the file or folder.

**differential backup** — A backup strategy in which only files that have changed since the last full backup are copied to the backup tape. When performing a differential backup, the SBACKUP utility backs up all files that have the Archive attribute enabled but does not reset the Archive attribute, thus making it easier to restore all data after a disaster.

**drive mapping** — The assignment of a drive pointer to a storage area on a hard disk.

**drive pointer** — A letter of the alphabet that is used to reference storage areas in the file system.

**full backup** — A backup strategy in which all data is copied to the backup tape daily, regardless of when it changed.

**host server** — The NetWare server that runs the backup program and has the attached tape or other backup media.

**incremental backup** — A backup strategy that backs up only the files that have changed (the Archive attribute is on) that day, and then resets the Archive attribute on all files that are backed up.

**local drive pointer** — A drive pointer (normally A: through F:) that is used to reference a local device on the workstation such as a floppy or hard disk drive.

**network drive pointer** — A network drive pointer is a letter that is assigned to a location on a NetWare server and controlled by NetWare, normally G: through Z:.

**regular drive pointer** — A network drive pointer that is normally assigned to a file storage directory on the NetWare server.

**root drive pointer** — A regular drive pointer that appears to DOS and applications as though it were the beginning or "root" of a drive or volume.

**search drive pointer** — A network drive pointer that has been added to the DOS path. Search drives are usually assigned to directories containing software to make the software available to run from any other location.

**Storage Management System (SMS)** — The NetWare backup service that includes several NetWare Loadable Modules and workstation software that enables the host server to back up data from one or more target devices by using SBACKUP NLM.

**target server** — A server whose data is backed up by a host server.

---

# REVIEW QUESTIONS

1. Which of the following utilities is used to create a Volume object? (Select all that apply.)

   a. Windows Explorer

   b. NetWare Remote Manager

   c. ConsoleOne

   d. NetWare Administrator

2. Volumes are created within which of the following?

   a. partitions

   b. storage pools

   c. directories

   d. containers

3. Which of the following drive pointers are used to reference data storage locations on the server?

   a. search

   b. root

c. regular

d. system

4. Which of the following drive pointers are used to reference software storage directories on a server?

a. search

b. root

c. regular

d. system

5. Write the steps to view all drive mappings.

6. Write the MAP command to create a new root drive pointer H that will point to the SERVER01/DATA:Users\John directory.

7. Write the MAP command to add a search drive pointer to the SERVER01/SYS:Software\WP directory.

8. True or False: The path of a search drive pointer can be changed from the SYS:Software\WP directory to the SYS:Software\Utility directory without deleting the existing search drive.

9. Given the directory structure shown in Figure 8-42, write the MAP commands needed to map drives to the marked areas.

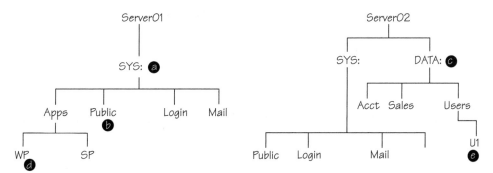

**Figure 8-42**   Sample directory structure

a.

b.

c.

d.

e.

10. What is (are) the advantage(s) of using a Directory Map object instead of a direct drive pointer mapping?

11. Describe how you would use a Directory Map object to create a drive pointer to directory (c) in Figure 8-42.

12. Describe how you would use a Directory Map object to create a drive pointer to directory (d) in Figure 8-42.

13. A user or network administrator can map drive pointers on a user's PC using the _____ or the _____.

14. True or False: Users can create their own drive pointers using Windows Explorer.

15. Deleted files can be recovered using which of the following functions from Windows Explorer?

    a. System

    b. Salvage

    c. Undelete

    d. Purge

16. To permanently remove deleted files from a volume, you would use which of the following functions?

    a. System

    b. Salvage

    c. Undelete

    d. Purge

17. Which of the following backup strategies backs up only files that have been created or modified since the last full backup?

    a. full

    b. incremental

    c. differential

    d. system

18. Other servers or client workstations that are being backed up are referred to as which of the following?

    a. child servers

    b. host servers

    c. target servers

    d. parent servers

19. Which of the following Target Service Agents must be loaded on a server to back up the data files?

    a. TSANDS

    b. TSA600

    c. SBCON

    d. SMS

20. To back up the file system, the user name for logging in to the network must have which of the following rights?

  a. Full Control

  b. Read and File Scan

  c. Read, File Scan, and Modify

  d. all rights except Supervisor and Access Control

# HANDS-ON PROJECTS

## Project 8-1: Using ConsoleOne to Create Your Directory Structure

In this project, you use ConsoleOne to create the directory structure shown in Figure 8-2 in a directory named CBEDATA located in your ##DATA home directory. The directories in this structure will be used in subsequent Hands-on Projects and Case Projects.

1. Log in to the network with your student user name.

2. Start ConsoleOne and expand the **CLASS_TREE** tree and **CBE_LABS** Organization.

3. Expand the **CBE_ADMIN_STUDENTS** volume to display your ##DATA directory.

4. Create a directory within your ##DATA directory named **CBEDATA**.

5. Map drive letter G: to your CBEDATA directory.

6. Use the procedure described in this chapter to create your version of the CBE Labs directory structure within your CBEDATA directory.

Use Windows to display the contents of your home directory and all subdirectories. Compare these directory listings with the one you produced in Step 4. Make sure all subdirectories are included.

## Project 8-2: Using Windows Explorer to Copy Files

In this project, you practice using Windows Explorer to copy files from one directory on the server to another directory location.

1. Start Windows Explorer and map drive letter I: to the CBE_ADMIN_DATA volume. If necessary, use Windows Explorer to map drive letter G: to your ##DATA directory located on the CBE_ADMIN_STUDENTS volume.

2. Copy all files from the Publctns\Document directory located on the DATA volume to your CBEDATA\Publctns\Document directory located on drive G:.

3. Copy all files from the Admin\Budgets directory located on the DATA volume to your CBEDATA\Admin\Budgets directory located on drive G:.

4. Exit Windows Explorer.

## Project 8-3: Using Windows Explorer to Rename Files and Directories

In this project, you practice using Windows Explorer to change the names of files and directories.

1. If you have not already done so, start Windows Explorer and change to your ##DATA\CBEDATA directory.

2. In the Admin\Budgets subdirectory, change the name of the worksheet file Earn01.xls by replacing the "01" in the filename with the current year (for example, Earn2003). Change the name of the Tax02.xls file by replacing the "02" in the filename with the current year (for example, Tax2003).

3. Create a subdirectory under Budgets called Forms. Rename this subdirectory **Ctiforms**.

4. After completing the name changes, use Windows Explorer to display a directory listing of the Budgets subdirectory.

5. Use Windows Explorer to display the entire structure of your ##DATA\ CBEDATA directory.

## Project 8-4: Salvaging Files

In this project, you practice using the Salvage option in NetWare Administrator to recover deleted files. You use Windows Explorer to delete the files from the Sample\ Budgets subdirectory, and then salvage them with NetWare Administrator.

1. Start Windows Explorer.

2. Navigate to your ##DATA\CBEDATA\Admin\Budgets subdirectory.

3. Select two files, and delete them.

4. Exit Windows Explorer.

5. Start Windows Explorer.

6. Navigate to your ##DATA\CBEDATA\Admin directory and right-click the **Budgets** subdirectory.

7. Click **Salvage Files** on the shortcut menu to display files sorted by deletion time.

8. Highlight the files you deleted in Step 3 and then click the **Salvage File** button.

9. Close the Salvage Network Files dialog box, and exit Windows Explorer.

10. Summarize your results in a memo to your instructor.

## Project 8-5: Using the MAP Command

In this project, you use the login script MAP command to create regular and search drive mappings, and then test the search drive. Create a memo to your instructor that includes the information requested in the following steps.

1. In your memo, record the MAP command you plan to use to create each of the drive mappings for the following sample directory areas:

   a. A regular drive pointer to the STUDENTS volume

   b. A root drive pointer to the Budgets subdirectory of your student ##DATA\ CBEDATA directory

   c. A root drive pointer to your user name's home directory

   d. A search drive pointer after the last existing search drive that points to the SYS:Apps\WinOffice\DB directory

"WinOffice" is over eight characters long, so you might need to enter "WinOff~1" for the directory name.

2. Open a command-prompt window by clicking **Start**, **Run**, entering **Command** in the Open text box, and clicking **OK**. Use the PATH command to record any existing search drive paths in the memo to your instructor. Use MAP commands to create the drive mappings you defined in Step 1.

3. In your memo, record the drive letter used by the new search drive mapping. Use the PATH command to verify that the new search drive is added to the search paths. Record your findings.

4. Use Windows Explorer to test your search drive mapping by opening a command-prompt window and typing the command **DB.BAT**. Record the results of testing your search drive.

5. Delete the search drive you tested in Step 4. Record the steps you use to delete your search drive mapping.

6. Use My Network Places functions to display the revised drive list. Verify that the search drive has been deleted. Record the remaining drive mappings in the memo to your instructor.

## Project 8-6: Creating a Directory Map Object with ConsoleOne

In this project, you create a Directory Map object using ConsoleOne.

1. Start ConsoleOne.

2. Expand your **##ADMINOU** container and your **CBE_LABS** OU. Click your **CBE_Labs_Admin** OU to display all its objects in the Object frame.

8

3. Create a Directory Map object named **##Budgets** that maps a drive pointer to your CBE_ADMIN\STUDENTS:##DATA\CBEDATA\Admin\Budgets subdirectory.

4. Exit ConsoleOne.

5. Write a MAP command to use the ##Budgets Directory Map object in a root drive mapping.

6. Use MAP commands to create the drive mapping you defined.

7. Create a memo to your instructor containing the steps you used to create the ##Budgets Directory Map object and the MAP command for testing this Directory Map object.

## CASE PROJECTS

### Case 8-1: Implementing the J.Q. Adams Directory Structure

In this case project, you create the directory structure you designed in Case 5-2 for the J.Q. Adams company within your ##DATA home directory.

1. Log in with your ##Admin user name and password.

2. If necessary, map a drive to your ##DATA directory.

3. Create a subdirectory named ADAMDATA within your ##DATA home directory.

4. Create your J.Q. Adams directory structure within your ##DATA\ ADAMDATA folder.

5. Document your directory structure in a memo to your instructor.

### Case 8-2: Setting Up a Drive Pointer Environment for the J.Q. Adams Corporation

The J.Q. Adams Corporation would like you to set up a drive pointer environment for the administrative users of its network. To be able to access his or her home directory directly without accidentally changing to another location, each user needs a drive pointer. In addition, all users in each department need to be able to easily access the Shared directory and the organization's Report directory. All users in the company need to be able to run either the word-processing or spreadsheet software stored in the Software directory.

1. Fill out a copy of the Drive Mapping Planning Form shown in Figure 8-27. (You can copy a blank form from Appendix B.)

2. In a memo to your instructor, describe the MAP commands you would use to implement the drive pointers you planned in Step 1.

## Case 8-3: Implementing the Jefferson County Courthouse Directory Structure

In this case project, you create the directory structure you designed in Case 5-1 for the Jefferson County Courthouse within your ##DATA home directory.

1. If necessary, log in with your ##Admin user name and password.

2. If necessary, map a drive to your ##DATA directory.

3. Create a subdirectory named JCCHDATA within your ##DATA home directory.

4. Create your Jefferson County Courthouse directory structure within your ##DATA\JCCHDATA folder.

5. Document your directory structure in a memo to your instructor.

8

# MANAGING USERS, GROUPS, AND LOGIN SECURITY

**After reading this chapter and completing the exercises, you will be able to:**

♦ Use ConsoleOne to establish login security by setting restrictions on user accounts

♦ Use ConsoleOne, NetWare Administrator, and iManager to create and manage User, Group, and Organizational Role objects

♦ Use NetWare 6 utilities to manage objects

**A**s you learned in previous chapters, Novell's eDirectory uses a global database to store information on network objects, such as users, groups, printers, and volumes, so that they are accessible to all NetWare servers. In this chapter, you learn how to set up login restrictions and create user accounts for an organization. You also learn how to secure user accounts against intruders, how to use templates and the NDS Import/Export wizard to create user accounts more efficiently, and how to move User objects to other locations in your eDirectory tree. Delegating tasks to other users is another important task for network administrators, and you learn how to use Organizational Role objects to delegate privileges to user accounts.

## ESTABLISHING LOGIN SECURITY

In addition to establishing a network file system and eDirectory structure, a network administrator must secure the network so that users are limited to accessing only the network resources and services they have been authorized to use. Login security is sometimes called "initial access security" because it provides the basis for all security systems by ensuring that only authorized users have access to network resources. In the following sections, you learn how to protect user accounts from unauthorized access by implementing the following login security measures:

- User names
- Passwords and password restrictions
- Time and station restrictions
- Login restrictions

### User Names

When NetWare 6 is first installed and started, one user name and account, Admin, is automatically created, and the Admin User object is added to the eDirectory tree. The Admin user has access to all network services, including the entire eDirectory tree and file system. Initially, the network administrator logs in as Admin and then creates the eDirectory tree, the directory structure, other users, groups, and access restrictions. In this section, you learn to assign user names and access privileges and to properly construct the user environment.

After creating the eDirectory tree and network file system, the network administrator needs to create a User object in the eDirectory tree for each user. The administrator can then assign access to network resources by granting access privileges to the User objects.

User names can be up to 64 characters. NetWare 6 defaults to having long filename support, so there is no problem with longer user names. However, you might want to limit their length to make it easier for users to type them at login time. One of the first considerations in creating user names is developing a consistent way to construct them from users' actual names. Two common methods are used. One is to use the first letter of the user's first name followed by the first seven letters of his or her last name, for a total of eight letters. For example, the user name for Mary Read is MREAD. The advantage of this method is that the user name is very similar to the user's actual name. The disadvantages are that most last names must be truncated and that two or more users often have the same first initial and last name. For example, the user name for Michael Read would also be MREAD.

The second method for creating user names is to use the first three letters of the user's first name, followed by the first three letters of the user's last name. In this method, Mary Read's user name becomes MARREA. This way, user names are uniformly a consistent length, and there's a smaller chance of duplicates. A disadvantage of this method is that the user names are less recognizable. Other naming systems are described in the "Creating User Objects from Templates" section later in this chapter. Whichever system you choose, be as consistent as possible.

## Passwords

Although user names and assigned privileges provide initial access to the server and delegate network management duties, they do little to prevent unauthorized access to restricted information or server functions. Networks need additional security to restrict who can use the server, to protect information and the integrity of the server environment. After user names, the next barrier in a security system is passwords on user accounts. You create the password for the Admin account during installation.

In NetWare 6, passwords can be up to 39 characters; if you let users change their own passwords, you can increase password security by requiring some or all of the password restrictions described in the following section.

 NetWare provides additional security against hackers guessing user names and passwords. Instead of displaying a message that an attempted login user name is invalid or does not exist, NetWare simply denies the login attempt. This feature makes it more difficult for people to guess user names because they can never be sure if they have entered a correct user name and wrong password, or if they have just entered an incorrect user name.

### Password Restrictions

Passwords that are known only to the user are a necessary part of login security to authenticate the person logging in as a valid user. Although NetWare passwords can be up to 39 characters, passwords have a way of becoming common knowledge among other users and thus lose their effectiveness at authenticating users. To help keep passwords secret, they need to be at least six to eight characters long and be changed periodically. Because users often neglect this task, administrators can use NetWare **password restrictions** (see Figure 9-1) to require users to change passwords within a given time period. Password restrictions include options to set minimum password length, force password changes, require users to come up with a different password each time they change, and limit the number of grace logins users have after their password expires. These password restrictions are described in the following sections.

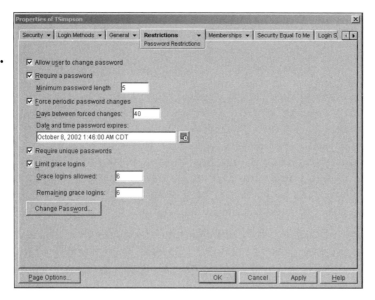

**Figure 9-1**    The Password Restrictions dialog box

**Set Minimum Password Length**    To prevent the use of passwords that are short and easy to guess, most network administrators follow Novell's recommendation of at least a five-character minimum for password length. Because of the more sophisticated password-breaking programs currently available, many network administrators are increasing the default minimum to six to eight characters to make passwords more difficult to decrypt. In this section, you will learn how to use ConsoleOne to change the minimum length of passwords assigned to existing or newly created users.

**Force Periodic Password Changes**    If a user's password becomes known to co-workers, it no longer provides protection against unauthorized access to that user's account. Having users periodically change passwords reduces this problem. You can force selected user accounts to change passwords by limiting the time period a password remains valid. As shown in Figure 9-1, NetWare's default is 40 days between password changes. However, because this time period is often too short for most users, they resort to writing down their current passwords near their work areas, where others could easily find and use them. (Under the keyboard and in a desk drawer are common hiding places.) This defeats the purpose of forcing periodic password changes to increase server security, so as the network administrator, you might decide to increase the time between password changes. In addition, encourage good password and login habits by periodically reminding users not to record password information near workstations and to log out whenever they leave workstations unattended.

**Require Unique Passwords**   Another way to increase password security is to require users to enter a different password each time they change their password. When you require unique passwords, the server keeps track of the user's last 10 passwords and rejects a new password that repeats one of the previous 10. NetWare's unique passwords option prevents users from rotating between a few favorite passwords, making it more difficult for intruders to log in with a known password. Network administrators often combine this option with forced periodic password changes to increase the safety of security-sensitive user accounts, such as the Admin account or an account assigned to a payroll clerk.

**Limit Login Grace Periods**   When a password has been set to expire, the user has six grace logins to continue using the expired password. This default grace period prevents users from being accidentally locked out from the network after their passwords expire, and it also keeps users from using an expired password indefinitely. Each time a user logs in after password expiration, NetWare displays a reminder that the current password has expired and states the remaining number of grace logins. Six grace logins are adequate for most server installations, but the network administrator can change this number on an individual basis or change the default value assigned to all new user names when they are created.

## Time and Address Restrictions

Despite all your efforts, you cannot prevent users from revealing their passwords to other people or keep them from writing down their passwords and leaving them on desks or in wastebaskets. To increase security in case someone detects a user's password, NetWare offers account restriction options that include time and station restrictions for user accounts. With these restrictions, you can keep users who work with highly secure data, such as payroll information and customer lists, from logging in except during specified time periods or from certain workstations. With time and station restrictions in effect on a user's account, a potential intruder who knows a user's password would have to enter the building during normal business hours to log in as that user.

### Time Restrictions

**Time restrictions** enable the network administrator to increase a user's account security by limiting the times during which the account can be used (see Figure 9-2). This prevents someone who knows a user's password from logging in and accessing the network after business hours. Time restrictions can be set in half-hour increments. For example, you can restrict a payroll clerk to using the server only between 8 A.M. and 4:30 P.M. on weekdays. Time restrictions are important on high-security accounts, such as a payroll clerk's, because they keep intruders from accessing sensitive payroll information during non-business hours. Later in this section, you learn how to use ConsoleOne to set time restrictions on a user account.

9

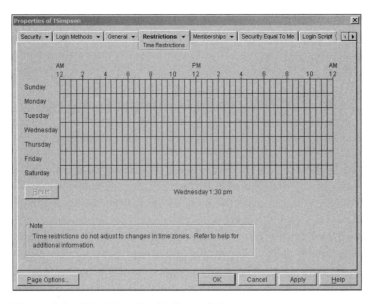

**Figure 9-2**   The Time Restrictions dialog box

## Address Restrictions

**Address restrictions** can be used to limit on which workstations a user can log in to the network (see Figure 9-3). The NetWare default is that a user can log in from any workstation and be logged in to the network at several workstations simultaneously. The Admin user or other users with appropriate Administrator privileges can change these defaults.

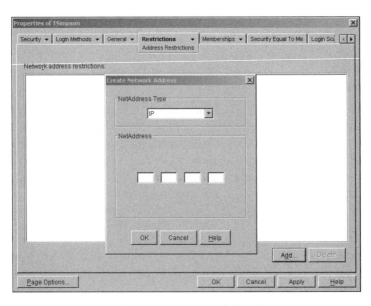

**Figure 9-3**   The Address Restrictions dialog box

Restricting a user account to a specific network and workstation node address increases security for highly sensitive information. A payroll clerk, for example, can be required to log in only on the workstation located in his or her office and only during normal office hours. For intruders to access the payroll data, they would need to know the payroll clerk's user name and password to enter the office during normal business hours and log in to the server from the clerk's workstation. These limitations prevent all but a very bold intruder or a very well-trusted employee from making such an attempt, and other employees would likely notice his or her actions.

Of course, if your Admin password is generally known to network users, all security efforts are in vain—anyone with the Admin password can log in from any workstation and have access to the entire network. So you might want to enhance Admin account security by requiring any Administrator-equivalent user names to access the network from only two workstations that you can constantly monitor. Having your Admin account operate from two different workstations, or having an Administrator-equivalent user name that operates on a separate workstation address, enables you to access the server with Administrator privileges if one workstation is out of order.

## Login Restrictions

As shown in Figure 9-4, login restrictions are conditions defined by the administrator to restrict user accounts from logging in through disabling the account, setting an account expiration date, or limiting the number of concurrent workstations a user can be logged in from.

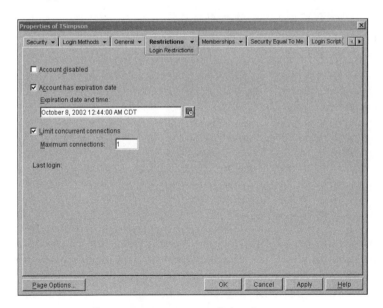

**Figure 9-4**    The Login Restrictions dialog box

## Account Disabled

When an account is disabled, no one can log in to the server with that user name until the account is reactivated. A network administrator needs to know how account restrictions can be used to disable an account, set an account expiration date, or limit the number of workstations an account can be logged in from concurrently.

## Account Expiration Date

NetWare's account expiration date is used to set a date after which the user account becomes disabled. This is a good way to establish temporary user accounts that you do not want accessed after a certain date. Student user accounts, for example, can be set to expire at the end of a semester or school year. After the expiration date, if a user attempts to log in with an expired user name, NetWare requires a password and then displays a message that the account has been disabled. Figure 9-5 shows a login attempt with an expired user name. Note that before issuing the error message, NetWare requires you to enter a password.

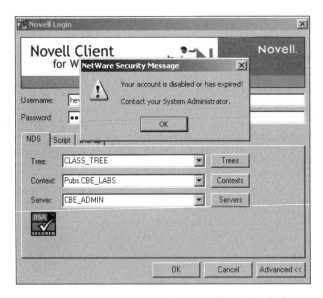

**Figure 9-5**    Attempting to log in with a disabled user account

## Limit Concurrent Connections

By setting a user name to be valid for logging in simultaneously from several workstations, the network administrator can create a general-purpose user name for multiple users. In most situations, however, limiting user accounts to one workstation at a time is important for the following reasons:

- Logging in from multiple workstations can cause software errors with some programs because certain control files cannot be shared, so a user can't access them simultaneously from more than one location.

- Restricting the user name to one workstation at a time helps users who move between multiple workstations remember not to leave a workstation unattended—and thus open to access by unauthorized users.

- Limiting a user account to access from a single workstation prevents an intruder who knows a user's name and password from logging in at an unattended workstation and gaining unauthorized access to the server.

## Implementing User Account Restrictions

By establishing password, time, and station restrictions, network administrators can use user account restrictions to help ensure that the user logging in is actually an authorized user. In this section, you learn about these account restrictions and how they can be used to increase network security.

As a network administrator, you can use ConsoleOne to set password, time, and station restrictions on existing users, or you can use templates (described later in the "Creating User Templates" section) to apply standard restrictions to new users. Because you cannot set time and station restrictions on an Organizational Unit (OU), using account restrictions with templates saves time because you can automatically apply these template-configured restrictions to all users created with that template. In the following examples, you learn how David Doering, the network administrator for CBE Labs, established account restrictions for the Admin user account. In the "Creating User Objects from Templates" section of this chapter, you learn how to use templates with a set of standard login restrictions to create new user accounts.

Because the Admin user account has all rights to manage the network, one of the most important security needs on your network is login security for this user account. To help secure the Admin user account, David used ConsoleOne to set the following restrictions:

- Require a minimum length of eight characters for the password.

- Require passwords to be changed every 60 days.

- Limit the Admin user account to being logged in from only one workstation at a time.

- Restrict the Admin user account to using only specific workstations.

David used the following steps to set these restrictions:

1. After logging in with the Admin user name and password, he started ConsoleOne and expanded the tree and CBE_LABS Organization by clicking the + symbol to the left of each object.

2. He then clicked the CBE_LABS Organization to display the objects in the Object frame.

3. Next, he right-clicked the Admin user name and click Properties to open the Properties of admin dialog box, similar to the one in Figure 9-6.

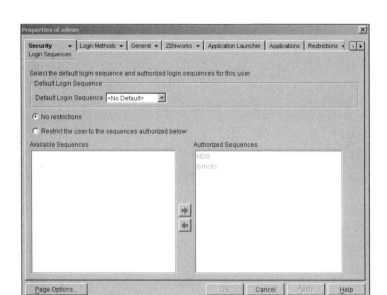

**Figure 9-6** The Properties of admin dialog box

4. To create an address restriction that limits the Admin user to logging in only from selected workstations, he did the following:

a. He clicked the down arrow on the Restrictions tab to display the restrictions options shown in Figure 9-7.

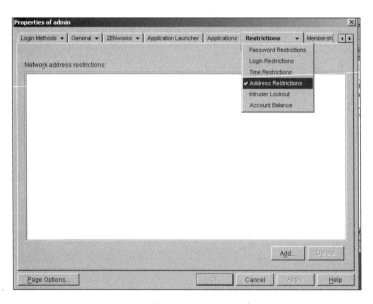

**Figure 9-7** Options on the Restrictions tab

b. He clicked the Address Restrictions option to open the Network address restrictions dialog box.

c. He clicked the Add button to open the Create Network Address dialog box.

d. He selected IP in the NetAddress Type list box.

e. He entered the IP address of the administrative workstation in the NetAddress fields, as shown in Figure 9-8.

f. He clicked OK to save the entry and return to the Network address restrictions dialog box.

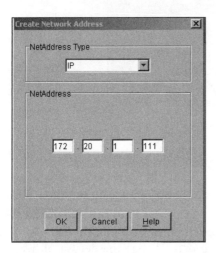

**Figure 9-8**    The Create Network Address dialog box

5. To limit the Admin user to logging in from only one station at a time, David did the following:

a. He clicked the down arrow on the Restrictions tab, and then clicked the Login Restrictions option to open the Login Restrictions dialog box shown in Figure 9-9.

b. He clicked the Limit concurrent connections check box.

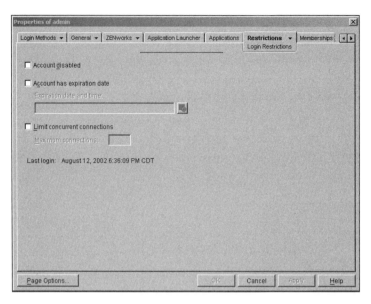

**Figure 9-9** The Login Restrictions dialog box

6. David did the following to require the Admin user to enter a new unique password of at least eight characters every 60 days:

a. He clicked the down arrow on the Restrictions tab, and then clicked the Password Restrictions option to open the Password Restrictions dialog box.

b. He clicked the Require a password check box, and then entered 8 in the Minimum password length text box to change the default of five characters.

c. He clicked the Force periodic password changes check box, and then entered 60 in the Days between forced changes text box.

d. He clicked the Require unique passwords check box to require a different password each time.

e. He clicked the Limit grace logins check box, and accepted the default of allowing the user six additional logins with the password after the password expires, as shown in Figure 9-10.

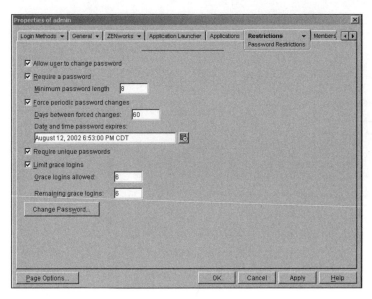

**Figure 9-10**    The Password Restrictions dialog box

9

7. David then used the following steps to set time restrictions on the Admin user account:

a. He clicked the down arrow on the Restrictions tab, and then clicked the Time Restrictions option to open the Time Restrictions dialog box shown previously in Figure 9-2.

b. He moved his mouse to the upper-left position in the time chart and then dragged to the right until he reached the 5:00 column to restrict the Admin user account from accessing the network weekdays between 5:00 A.M. and 11:59 A.M. He continued to drag down to the Saturday row. After highlighting the designated area, he released the mouse button to select the highlighted area.

 Each column represents a time period of 30 minutes, starting with the time displayed when the column is highlighted. For example, highlighting the 11:30 A.M. column would restrict the user from logging in during the 11:30 A.M. to 11:59 A.M. time period.

c. He repeated this process to highlight the 11:30 P.M. column for all days of the week, as shown in Figure 9-11.

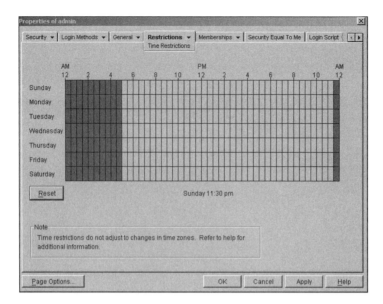

**Figure 9-11** Setting time restrictions for the Admin user account

8. After securing the Admin account, David clicked OK to save the account restrictions and return to the ConsoleOne main window.

In the end-of-chapter projects, you perform a similar process to set account restrictions on one of your user accounts.

## Implementing Intruder Detection Limits

Another potential login security problem is an intruder who is able to successfully guess user passwords. Forcing user passwords to be longer than four characters and training users to create non-obvious passwords that contain numbers as well as characters can go a long way toward preventing password guessing. Having non-obvious passwords is critical because intruders could get lucky with guesses, or, even more frightening, they might have a password-guessing program that can send hundreds of password combinations into a computer in just a few seconds. An effective way to deter password guessing from intruders or software is to implement the NetWare Intruder Detection feature in each OU container.

**Intruder detection** works at the container level by setting a limit on the number of incorrect login attempts that can be made on a user account in that container during a specified time period. To work with Intruder Detection, right-click on the container in ConsoleOne, select Properties, click the down arrow on the General tab, and then click the Intruder Detection option to open the Intruder Detection dialog box shown in Figure 9-12.

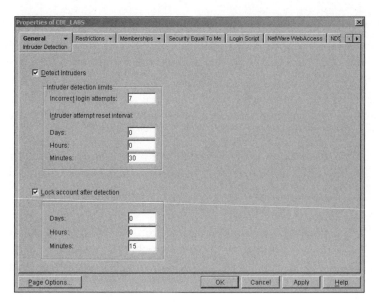

**Figure 9-12**   The Intruder Detection dialog box

The Incorrect login attempts text box is used to set the number of invalid login attempts the user can make before the account is locked.

The Intruder attempt reset interval text box is used to specify the amount of time from the first invalid login attempt until the counter is reset. For example, the default of 30 minutes means that if the user makes fewer than seven invalid login attempts in 30 minutes, the counter will be reset and the user can make seven more attempts in the next 30 minutes. Within an hour, the user could potentially make 14 incorrect login attempts.

After selecting the Lock account after detection check box, you can fill in the text boxes below to configure how long the account stays locked. After the time specified has elapsed, the account is again available for the user. If you leave the time field blank, the user account will be locked out until the administrator uses ConsoleOne to unlock it. For example, given the default settings, when a potential intruder reaches seven incorrect login attempts within a 30-minute time period, the user's account will be locked for 15 minutes, and the time and station address of the login attempt is recorded on the user's account. The user account will become available again at the end of the 15-minute lockout time period, or the Admin user can free the account at any time.

David used the following steps to set intruder detection for CBE Labs users:

1. After starting ConsoleOne, he expanded the Tree object and the CBE_LABS Organization.

2. To set intruder detection on the InfoSystems container, he did the following:

a. He expanded the CBE_Labs_Admin OU, right-clicked the InfoSystems OU, and then clicked Properties to open the Properties of InfoSystems dialog box.

b. He clicked the down arrow on the General tab and clicked the Intruder Detection option to open the Intruder Detection dialog box shown in previously in Figure 9-12.

c. He clicked the Detect Intruders check box.

d. He entered 5 in the Incorrect login attempts text box to change the default from seven attempts.

e. He entered 10 in the Minutes text box.

f. He clicked the Lock account after detection check box, and then entered 2 in the Minutes text box to change the default time.

g. He clicked the OK button to save the intruder detection settings for the InfoSystems OU.

Setting intruder detection on the container that holds the Admin user name could result in the Admin user name being locked out for the specified time period, causing you to temporarily lose administrative access to the network. To help prevent this problem, David created a backup administrative account that can be used to manage the network and then renamed the Admin user to make it more difficult for users to make invalid login attempts on the administrative user account. You learn how to create a backup administrative account and rename the Admin user in the "Increasing Admin User Security" section.

## CREATING USER, GROUP, AND ORGANIZATIONAL ROLE OBJECTS

After establishing password restrictions and setting an intruder detection policy for the OUs, David's next task was creating the user and group accounts needed for each department. Group objects play an important role in network administration because they make it possible for network administrators to give similar privileges to several users at once, instead of assigning rights separately to each user. In NetWare 6, you can use ConsoleOne, NetWare Administrator, or the new iManager Internet utility to create and manage User and Group objects. Which utility you use depends on your personal preference and needs. If you're working from the LAN using a computer with the Novell Client software, you'll find that ConsoleOne and NetWare Administrator have more options and are easier to use. As an essential part of Novell's OneNet strategy, the iManager utility enables network management functions to be performed on any computer, regardless of how it's attached to the network or its installed client. For example, if you're logging in to your company's network via the Internet or are working from a local computer that does not have Novell Client installed, you need to use iManager to manage the eDirectory system and create new user accounts.

In previous chapters, you learned how to use Novell's ConsoleOne utility to create and manage objects in the eDirectory database. In the following sections, you learn how to use ConsoleOne to create User and Group objects and manage multiple user accounts. In the "Managing eDirectorym with iManager" section, you learn how iManager can be used to create and manage user and group accounts from any computer with Internet access.

## Increasing Admin User Security

Securing access to the network is an important responsibility of the network administrator, and Novell has provided NetWare with many features you can use to meet this responsibility. As a CNA, you'll need to know how to set up NetWare security options that meet the security needs of your users. As you learned in the previous section, attempting to log in as the network administrator without the correct authentication credentials can lock out the Admin user account, making it unavailable for the lockout duration you established. Some network administrators rename their Admin user accounts to make it harder to hack and to help prevent locking out the Admin user, but this method makes it harder to use certain utilities that default to using the Admin user name. However, if your server will be attached to the Internet, the additional security of renaming the Admin user can be worth the inconvenience. For this reason, Novell recommends renaming the Admin user as part of securing the network.

Another security responsibility is having a backup Administrator account that you can use to administer the network if your primary Admin user account becomes disabled or deleted. You can also use this backup account if the network administrator leaves the company, taking the Admin user name and password with him or her, or if he or she is incapacitated for any reason. When creating a backup administrator account, the CEO or office manager should keep the name and password secure. David used the following steps to create a backup Administrator account:

1. He logged in with the Admin user name and password, started ConsoleOne, and expanded the CBE_LABS Organization.

2. To create a backup administrator named CKent in the InfoSystems OU, David did the following:

   a. He expanded the CBE_Labs_Admin OU and then clicked the InfoSystems OU to display the objects in the Object frame.

   b. He clicked the New User button on the ConsoleOne toolbar to open the New User dialog box.

   c. He entered CKent in the Name text box.

   d. He entered Kent in the Surname text box.

   e. He left all other fields and options blank, as shown in Figure 9-13, and clicked OK to open the Set Password dialog box.

9

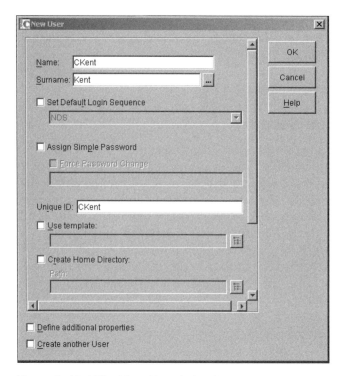

**Figure 9-13**    The New User dialog box

      f. He typed a password for the CKent user in both the New Password and Retype Password text boxes.

      g. He clicked the Set Password button to create the CKent user.

   3. To make CKent security-equivalent to the Admin user, David did the following:

      a. He clicked the CBE_LABS Organization to display all objects in the Object frame.

      b. He right-clicked the Admin user name and clicked Properties to open the Properties of admin dialog box.

      c. He scrolled to the right and clicked the Security Equal to Me tab.

      d. He clicked the Add button to open the Select Objects dialog box and navigated to the InfoSystems OU.

      e. He clicked on the newly created CKent user and then clicked the OK button to add CKent to the Security Equal to Me dialog box.

      f. He clicked the OK button to save the changes and return to the ConsoleOne main window.

In Chapter 10, you'll learn how David uses trustee assignments to assign administrative rights to the CKent user.

Because Admin is the default name of the NetWare 6 administrative user, intruders often attempt to log in using the Admin user name and a variety of password combinations. At best, this can lock the Admin user account, or, if the intruder gets lucky, provide complete access to the network. To help prevent this type of hacking, Novell recommends renaming the Admin user account. The following steps describe how David renamed the Admin user account:

1. He clicked the CBE_LABS Organization to display all objects in the Object frame.

2. He right-clicked the Admin user name, and then clicked the Rename option.

3. He entered CBEAdmin in the New name text box and then clicked OK to return to the ConsoleOne window, where the Admin user name then appeared as CBEAdmin in the Object frame.

4. He exited ConsoleOne and logged out.

**9**

Because renaming a user account that you are currently logged in as removes your administrative rights, after renaming the Admin user, you need to log out and then log back in as the CBEAdmin user to regain administrative rights.

From now on, David will need to log in with the CBEAdmin user name instead of Admin to perform administrative functions.

## Defining and Creating Groups

Groups are leaf objects that represent one or more user accounts listed in the Membership property. Groups are useful when you want to assign the use of some network resource to several users. For example, at CBE Labs, all users who work in the administrative office need access to certain programs and data files. These users also share access to a laser printer. Rather than assigning the access rights for these resources to individuals, the network administrator can create a group named Admin_Staff and assign the access rights to the group. All members of this group automatically get access to the resources.

You can create groups as needed in container objects and assign users to a group regardless of the Group object's context and the User object's context. Group membership can also be a property value in a user template, providing all users created with the template have membership in the specified Group objects. Access to network resources can be granted to multiple users by assigning rights to a group or container object (see Chapter 10 for more in-depth information); this method is more streamlined than assigning the same rights to multiple users individually.

Groups are also a convenient way to change user job responsibilities. For example, Gordon Tennesson and Susan Michelia currently have responsibility for the CBE company Web site. To give them rights to maintain the Web site, David created a group called WebMgrs and made both Gordon and Susan members. In the future, if Susan gets too busy with other editing jobs, another user could be assigned the responsibility by simply removing Susan and adding the new user to the WebMgrs group. In the "Hands-on Projects" section, you'll find a Group Planning Form, listing the groups and their members that David implemented in the CBE Labs network, and you'll create those groups for your version of the CBE network.

Because user accounts can be assigned group membership when they are initially created, when setting up the CBE Labs network, David simplified the task of assigning users to groups by creating the Group objects first, and then assigning each user to his or her corresponding group when the user account was created. If you create Group objects after the user accounts have been created, you need to perform the additional step of assigning users to their groups. The following example shows you how David used ConsoleOne to create the ISMgrs group and then add existing users:

1. After logging in with the CBEAdmin user name and password, David started ConsoleOne and expanded the CBE_LABS Organization.

2. To create the ISMgrs group in the InfoSystems OU and make CKent a member, he did the following:

   a. He expanded the CBE_Labs_Admin OU, clicked the InfoSystems OU in the Navigation frame, and then clicked the New Group button on the ConsoleOne toolbar to open the New Group dialog box (see Figure 9-14).

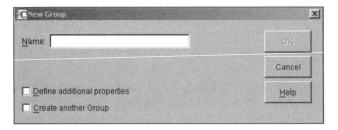

**Figure 9-14** The New Group dialog box

   b. He entered the group name ISMgrs in the Name text box, and then clicked the Define additional properties check box.

   c. He clicked OK to create the group and open the Properties of ISMgrs dialog box shown in Figure 9-15.

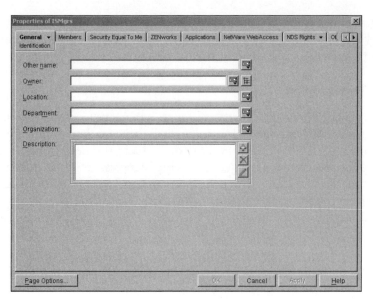

**Figure 9-15**    The Properties of ISMgrs dialog box

d. He clicked the Members tab, and then clicked the Add button to open the Select Objects dialog box shown in Figure 9-16.

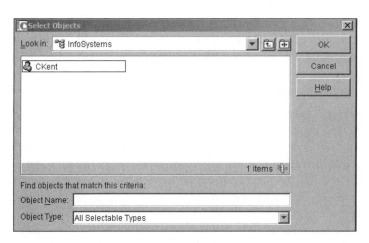

**Figure 9-16**    The Select Objects dialog box

e. He clicked the CKent user name, and then clicked OK to add this user to the ISMgrs group.

f. He clicked OK to save the changes and return to the ConsoleOne window.

David repeated this procedure to create the remaining groups in their respective OUs. He did not add users to these groups because the user accounts will be automatically added by using templates, as described in the next section.

## Creating User Templates

Now that the necessary groups have been created, David needs to create accounts for all users. Although he could create each user individually, this method is time consuming, and it's easy to miss a setup task, such as forgetting to add the new user to a group or omitting certain account restrictions. Missing setup steps can result in the user being unable to access certain data files or having nonstandard login restrictions. Therefore, establishing user templates to simplify and standardize creating user accounts is an efficient method for network administrators to use. A **user template** defines certain standard settings you want to establish for each user created with that template. In most organizations, users have account restrictions and a home directory where they can create and manage their own files; with user templates, network administrators can easily define these restrictions and home directory locations for all users created in that container.

Another practical use of templates is changing the default file system and eDirectory rights NetWare provides to new users. In Chapter 10, you'll learn about file system and eDirectory security and how users are granted rights to work with or manage files and eDirectory information. For example, when you create new users, NetWare grants them all rights to their home directories as well as rights to change their personal login scripts. As you'll learn in Chapter 12, login scripts contain commands that run each time a user logs in. Because Mark Ciampa, another CBE network administrator, will be responsible for maintaining all login scripts, Ted Simpson, the information systems manager, does not want users to be able to change the login scripts Mark sets up for them.

By default, new users can give other users authority in their home directories. To maintain better security, Ted does not want users to be able to change the security assignments to their home directories. By using templates, David can change the default file system and eDirectory security settings for new users to ensure the file system and eDirectory security Ted has deemed necessary. Figure 9-17 shows the worksheet with the template requirements David created for users in the CBE Labs Information Systems Department. By removing Supervisor and Access Control rights from the user home directories, users will not be able to grant rights to others. In addition, providing only Read rights to the Login Script property will prevent users from changing their login script commands. Using the "T_" prefix before each template name helps identify the object as a template and makes the name different from corresponding group names. In the end-of-chapter projects, you'll create similar template forms for the other user templates David identified for the CBE_Labs_Admin OU.

User Template Planning Form

Department: Information Systems

| | |
|---|---|
| Template name | T_IS |
| Context | .OU=InfoSystems.OU=CBE_Labs_Admin.O=CBE_LABS |
| Home directory path | CBE_ADMIN_DATA:Users |
| Minimum password length | 8 |
| Require unique passwords | Yes |
| Days between password changes | 90 |
| Grace logins | 6 |
| Valid login times | 5:00 a.m. until 11:59 p.m. |
| Concurrent connections | 1 |
| Groups | ISMgrs |
| Users | TSimpson, DDoering, MCiampa |
| Rights to Login Script | Read |
| Rights to home directory | All rights except Supervisor and Access Control |

9

**Figure 9-17**   The User Template Planning Form for the Information Systems Department

David performed the following steps to create the T_IS template in the InfoSystems OU:

1. After logging in, he started ConsoleOne, and then expanded the tree, the CBE_LABS Organization, and the CBE_Labs_Admin OU.

2. Next, he clicked the InfoSystems OU, and created the T_IS template by following these steps:

   a. He clicked File, New, Object on the menu bar to open the New Object dialog box.

   b. He scrolled down and double-clicked the Template object to open the New Template dialog box.

   c. He entered T_IS in the Name text box, and then clicked the Define additional properties check box.

   d. He clicked OK to create the template and open the Properties of T_IS dialog box, as shown in Figure 9-18.

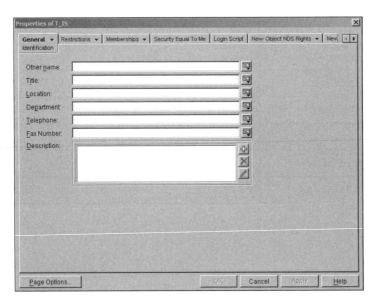

**Figure 9-18**    The Properties of T_IS dialog box

3. David then set the home directory path for the InfoSystems users by doing the following:

   a. He clicked the down arrow on the General tab, and then clicked the Environment option.

   b. To set the home directory path, he clicked in the Volume text box, and then clicked the browse button to the right to open the Select Object dialog box.

c. He clicked the up arrow to navigate to the CBE_LABS Organization and then double-clicked the CBE_ADMIN_DATA volume object to display all the directories on the DATA volume.

d. To create home directories in the Users directory, he clicked the Users folder object and then clicked OK. The Environment dialog box then looked similar to the one in Figure 9-19.

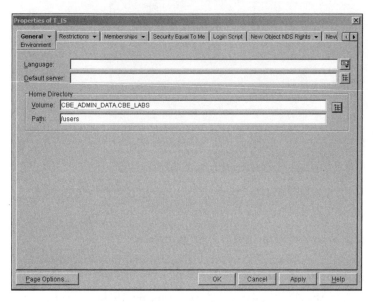

**Figure 9-19**   The home directory information in the Environment dialog box

4. David set the password restrictions for the InfoSystems template as defined in the User Template Planning Form.

5. He did the following to set the login restrictions specified on the User Template Planning Form:

a. He clicked the down arrow on the Restrictions tab, and clicked the Login Restrictions option to open the Login Restrictions dialog box.

b. He clicked the Limit concurrent connections check box to limit new user accounts to being logged in from only one computer at a time (see Figure 9-20).

6. To set the time restrictions shown in the User Template Planning Form, he used the Restrictions tab to block out 11:59 A.M. until 5:00 A.M., as described previously in the "Implementing User Account Restrictions" section.

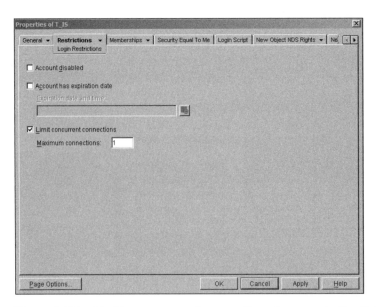

**Figure 9-20**    Limiting concurrent connections for users in the T_IS template

7. He did the following to add the group memberships specified in the User Template Planning Form to the T_IS template:

a. He clicked the down arrow on the Memberships tab and clicked the Group Membership option.

b. He clicked the Add button, and then double-clicked the ISMgrs group.

c. He clicked the Apply button to save the changes without returning to the main ConsoleOne window.

8. He changed the Login Script property rights to Read with these steps:

a. He clicked the down arrow on the New Object NDS Rights tab and then clicked the Rights To Other Objects option to open the NDS Objects dialog box.

b. He clicked <New Object>, and then clicked the Assigned Rights button to open the Rights assigned to <New Object> dialog box.

c. He clicked the Add Property button, selected the Login Script property, and clicked OK to place the Login Script property in the Property list box with default Read and Compare rights (see the Rights column in Figure 9-21). He then clicked OK in the Rights assigned to <New Object> dialog box.

d. He clicked the Apply button to save the new trustee assignment without returning to the main ConsoleOne window.

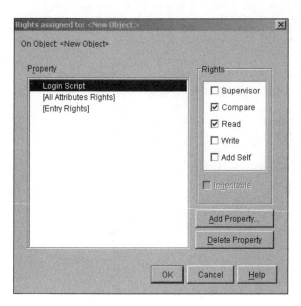

**Figure 9-21** The Rights assigned to <New Object> dialog box

9

9. To remove the Supervisor and Access Control rights from the user home directories, David did the following:

a. He scrolled to the right and clicked the New Object FS Rights tab to display existing trustee assignments.

b. He clicked to clear the Supervisor and Access Control check boxes, as shown in Figure 9-22.

10. After completing the template configuration, he clicked OK to save the changes and return to the main ConsoleOne window.

David repeated this process to create and configure templates for the other departments of the CBE_Labs_Admin OU. In the end-of-chapter projects, you'll create and configure these templates for your version of the CBE Labs network.

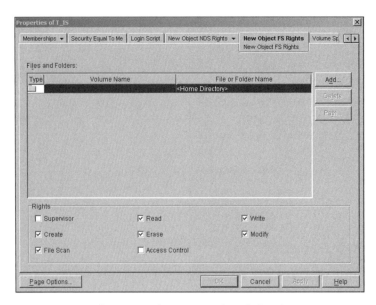

**Figure 9-22**  The New Object FS Rights dialog box

## Creating User Objects from Templates

In NetWare, users are given login names by creating a user object in an eDirectory container for every network user. In addition to login names, you can use eDirectory to keep track of many other fields of information, called properties, about each user. As you learned in previous activities, at a minimum, User objects must be assigned a login name and a last name; other properties, such as title, address, home directories, passwords, and time restrictions, are optional. Because certain properties, such as the location of the user's home directory or password requirements, are often common for many users, using templates can make creating User objects easier and more standardized. Before creating users, you should develop a user naming convention and identify which information properties you want to enter on each user account. Popular naming conventions include the following:

- *User's last name followed by the first initial of the first name*—For example, Ted Simpson would have the user login name SimpsonT.

- *First letter of the user's first name followed by the last name*—For example, Mark Ciampa would have the user login name MCiampa.

- *User's first name followed by the first letter of the last name*—For example, David Doering would have the user login name DavidD.

- *First three characters of the first name, middle initial, and first three letters of the last name*—For example, Ted L. Simpson would be TedLSim.

For the CBE Labs network, IS Manager Ted Simpson decided to have user login names consist of the first letter of the first name followed by the user's last name. Another important consideration is what to do when your naming system has two users with the same login name. NetWare can support multiple user accounts with the same login name as long as the users' accounts exist in different OUs. For example, if you have the user Mark Ciampa in the Information Systems Department and the user Mike K. Ciampa in the Test&Eval Hardware Department, you could create a user account named MCiampa in the InfoSystems OU for Mark and another MCiampa account in the Hardware OU for Mike. Novell's eDirectory can keep each user separate because they exist in different contexts. Although NetWare can work with two or more users having the same login name, this setup can create conflicts when accessing the network from other environments, so you should select a naming convention that creates user login names that are unique throughout the tree. For example, Ted and David plan to add a number to the end of any duplicate user names to keep them unique. In the preceding example, Mike's login name would become MCiampa2.

To define the user accounts, Ted developed the User Planning Form shown in Figure 9-23, which lists users in the InfoSystems OU, their context, and their template requirements. Ted used the Initial eDirectory and Simple Password column to define the password initially given to user accounts. The eDirectory password is used to log in from the Novell client, and the simple password is used to access the server from a Windows computer that doesn't have the Novell client installed (see the discussion of Native File Access Protocol in Chapter 6).

**9**

David performed the following steps to create the users in the InfoSystems OU using the T_IS template:

1. After logging in, he started ConsoleOne and expanded the Tree object and the CBE_LABS Organization.

2. To create a user account for Ted Simpson in the InfoSystems OU, he did the following:

The TSimpson user is created by this book's setup instructions, so for demonstration purposes, your instructor should use a different name, such as MSimpson, for the user account.

a. He expanded the CBE_Labs_Admin OU, and then clicked the InfoSystems OU.

b. He clicked the New User button on the ConsoleOne toolbar to open the New User dialog box.

c. He entered TSimpson in the Name text box.

d. He pressed the Tab key to advance to the Surname text box, and entered Simpson.

**User Planning Form**

Company: <u>CBE Labs</u>

Created by: <u>Ted Simpson</u>

Department: <u>Information Systems</u>

| User Name | Login Name | Initial eDirectory and Simple Password | Context | Template Name | Home Directory | Groups | Additional Properties |
|---|---|---|---|---|---|---|---|
| Ted Simpson | TSimpson | Novell | InfoSystems.CBE_Labs_Admin.CBE_LABS | T_IS | CBE_ADMIN_DATA:Users | ISMgrs | |
| David Doering | DDoering | Novell | InfoSystems.CBE_Labs_Admin.CBE_LABS | T_IS | CBE_ADMIN_DATA:Users | ISMgrs | |
| Mark Ciampa | MCiampa | Novell | InfoSystems.CBE_Labs_Admin.CBE_LABS | T_IS | CBE_ADMIN_DATA:Users | ISMgrs | |

**Figure 9-23**   The User Planning Form

e. He clicked the Assign Simple Password check box so that users could use NFAP to access the server without Novell Client.

f. He clicked the Force Password Change check box and entered the initial password (shown on the User Planning Form) in the text box directly under the check box.

g. He clicked the Use template check box, clicked the browse button to the right, and then double-clicked the T_IS template.

h. He clicked the Create another User check box, as shown in Figure 9-24.

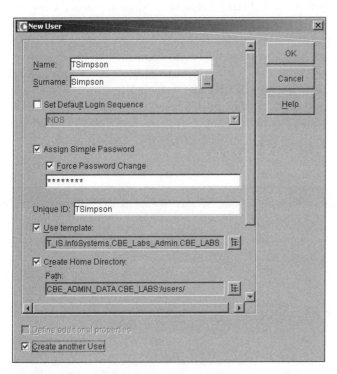

**Figure 9-24** The New User dialog box

i. He clicked OK to create Ted's user account and open the Set Password dialog box.

Simple passwords are set with the Remote Manger utility, as described in Chapter 13.

j. He entered the initial password shown on the User Planning Form in both the New password and Retype password text boxes, and clicked the Set Password button to create the new user and return to the New User dialog box.

David repeated this procedure to create user accounts for the remainder of the users on the User Planning Form, and then clicked Cancel to return to the ConsoleOne main window. In the end-of-chapter projects, you'll use the same steps to create these users in your version of the CBE Labs network.

## Using LDAP to Import Objects

eDirectory uses the industry-standard X.500 naming system to store information on network objects, so information can be exported or imported from other directory systems, such as Windows 2000 Active Directory, that are also X.500 based. The Lightweight Directory Access Protocol (LDAP) is a simplified version of X.500 that makes it easier for compatible systems to exchange directory information. NetWare 6 includes an LDAP import and export wizard with ConsoleOne that network administrators can use to transfer information to and from eDirectory by using **Lightweight Directory Interchange Format (LDIF)** files, which are simple ASCII text files that use a standardized syntax to add, change, or delete objects. The basic syntax of an LDIF file consists of a distinguished name, a change type, an object class, and attribute values, as shown in Table 9-1.

**Table 9-1**   LDIF Command Syntax

| Command Line | Purpose |
|---|---|
| dn: *distinguished name* | Distinguished name of object to be created, modified, or deleted |
| changetype: *Add* | Specifies the type of change: add, modify, or delete |
| ObjectClass: *object class* | Specifies an object class to be used with this entry; an object can have multiple object classes defined for it |
| uid: *username* | The user's login name |
| cn: *common name* | The user's last name |
| ACL: *access control list* (rights to eDirectory) | Assign a new user's entry rights to certain properties with multiple ACL entries (described in Chapter 10) |
| groupMembership: *groups* | Distinguished name of Group objects the user will be added to |

LDAP distinguished names are specified differently than eDirectory distinguished names. They use a typeful format with commas to separate the components instead of the periods used with eDirectory distinguished names. Unlike eDirectory distinguished names, LDAP distinguished names do not start with a period. For example, Ted Simpson's LDAP distinguished name would be specified as follows:

```
cn=TSimpson,ou=InfoSystems,ou=CBE_Labs_Admin,o=CBE_LABS
```

The changetype field specifies the action, such as Add, Modify, or Delete. The object class specifies the type of object being created or modified, such as user, container, or printer. The attribute fields specify information properties that are unique to the specified object class. Examples of attributes for a user object include givenName, fullName, and title. CBE labs has several computers in the Testing and Evaluation Department that are used mostly for entering data. Instead of creating user accounts for each user who can enter data on these stations, Ted has recommended having a generic account for each station based on its function. Although David could use ConsoleOne to create the accounts for the computer stations in the Testing and Evaluation Department, because these accounts will be very similar, he decided to use an LDIF file to create the accounts. Using an LDIF file makes it easy to add stations in the future by simply editing the file to add the new station name and location. Figure 9-25 shows an example of an LDIF file David used to create two accounts, named TestEval1 and TestEval2, in the Test&Eval OU.

**Figure 9-25** A sample LDIF file for creating user accounts in the Test&Eval OU

 A copy of the stations.ldif shown in Figure 9-25 is included in the CBE_ADMIN_DATA:InfoSys\Utility directory of the classroom server.

The following steps describe how David used the LDIF Import capability of ConsoleOne to import the new accounts shown in Figure 9-25:

1. After logging in with the CBEAdmin user name and password, he started ConsoleOne and expanded the Tree object and the CBE_LABS Organization.

2. He clicked the Test&Eval OU to highlight it.

3. He then clicked Wizards, NDS Import/Export on the ConsoleOne menu bar to open the NDS Import/Export Wizard.

4. In the Select Task dialog box, he verified that the Import LDIF File radio button was selected, and then clicked the Next button to open the Select Source LDIF File dialog box.

5. He inserted the floppy disk with the LDIF file, clicked the browse button, and selected the A: drive letter to display all files on the root of the floppy disk.

6. He double-clicked the Stations.ldif file to include it in the Select Source LDIF File text box.

7. He clicked the Advanced button, clicked the Exit on Error check box to remove the check mark, and clicked OK.

8. He clicked the Next button to open the Select Destination LDAP Server dialog box shown in Figure 9-26.

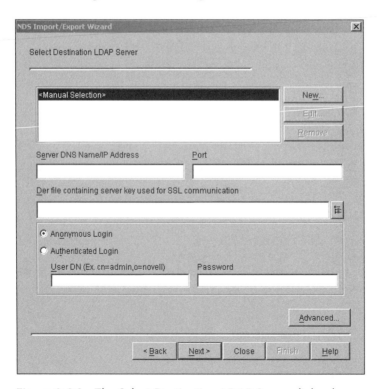

**Figure 9-26**    The Select Destination LDAP Server dialog box

9. In the Server DNS Name/IP Address text box, he entered the IP address of the CBE_ADMIN server, entered 389 in the Port text box, clicked the Authenticated Login radio button, and entered cn=CBEAdmin,o=CBE_LABS in the User DN text box, making sure he separated the entries with commas.

10. He entered the Administrator password in the Password text box and clicked the Advanced button to open the Advanced Options dialog box shown in Figure 9-27.

**Figure 9-27**    The Advanced Options dialog box

11. He clicked the Allow forward references check box so that the LDAP server could create objects in the sequence it needs them, and then clicked OK to return to the NDS Import/Export Wizard (see Figure 9-28).

12. He then clicked the Next button to display summary information, verified his entries, and clicked the Finish button to import the users.

13. After the users were created, he verified the results shown in the completion window and then clicked Close to return to ConsoleOne.

David was happy that he got a clean report from the Import/Export wizard with no errors; he has learned through experience that it pays to be meticulous when creating batch files. If the report had shown any errors, he would have made the necessary correction to his Stations.ldif file, deleted any users the import process had created, and then repeated the preceding steps.

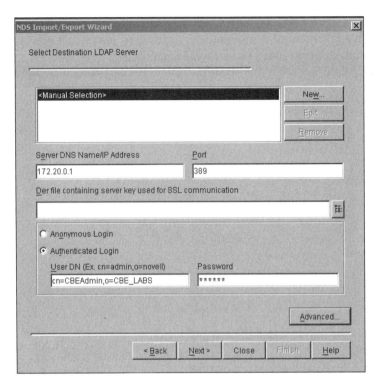

**Figure 9-28**    The completed Select Destination LDAP Server dialog box

## Establishing Organizational Role Objects

As described previously, Group objects are a convenient way to give users the rights they need for certain job responsibilities. However, because Group objects generally represent several users who share common privileges, they can be misleading if they're used to represent positions in the company. For example, a group called CEO could indicate that several people shared the task of being the corporate executive. To improve flexibility in assigning rights and privileges to company positions, NetWare 6 offers another type of leaf object: the Organizational Role object. Ted asked David to create separate Organizational Role objects to perform administrative functions in each department, as shown in Table 9-2.

**Table 9-2**   Organizational Roles for CBE Labs

| Organizational Role | Context | Occupant |
|---|---|---|
| President | CBE_Labs_Admin.CBE_LABS | JCunningham |
| AdminAssist | CBE_Labs_Admin.CBE_LABS | SLopez |
| VP_Pubs | Pubs.CBE_LABS | HEvans |
| Editor | Pubs.CBE_LABS | SMichelia |
| AdminAssist | Pubs.CBE_LABS | RDeLucia |
| VP_Test&Eval | Test&Eval.CBE_LABS | GBurns |
| AdminAssist | Test&Eval.CBE_LABS | MODonnell |
| Marketing_Director | Marketing.CBE_Labs_Admin.CBE_LABS | SHayakawa |
| Finance_Director | Finance.CBE_Labs_Admin.CBE_LABS | DKaneaka |
| Personnel_Director | Personnel.CBE_Labs_Admin.CBE_LABS | PRichardson |
| InfoSystems_Manager | InfoSystems.CBE_Labs_Admin.CBE_LABS | TSimpson |
| SysOp | InfoSystems.CBE_Labs_Admin.CBE_LABS | CKent |
| Network_Admin | InfoSystems.CBE_Labs_Admin.CBE_LABS | DDoering, MCiampa |

**9**

Because the user accounts assigned to these positions will change and could include multiple users, Ted does not want to assign the rights to individual users. With the Organizational Role object, however, you can assign rights to an object rather than a specific user. The Occupant property of the Organizational Role object performs a similar function to a Group object's Membership property: You can add any user, or multiple users, to the Organizational Role object's Occupant property to gain the associated rights and privileges given to the Organization Role object. If the job duties are given to another employee, you simply need to make the new employee an occupant of the Organizational Role object. Another good use for an Organizational Role object is to assign rights to a backup Administrator account that can be used in case your Admin user name is disabled. In Chapter 10, you'll learn how to assign the rights needed to enable the Organizational Role objects to perform their required functions. David used the following steps to create the SysOp Organizational Role object and make the CKent user an occupant:

1. After logging in as the CBEAdmin user, he started ConsoleOne and expanded the Tree object and the CBE_LABS Organization.

2. He did the following to create an Organizational Role object named SysOp:

   a. He expanded the CBE_Labs_Admin OU, and then clicked the InfoSystems container.

   b. He clicked the New Object button on the toolbar to open the New Object dialog box, scrolled down, and double-clicked the Organizational Role object to open the New Organizational Role dialog box.

c. He entered SysOp in the Name text box, and then clicked the Define additional properties check box.

d. He clicked the OK button to create the SysOp object and open the Properties of SysOp dialog box shown in Figure 9-29.

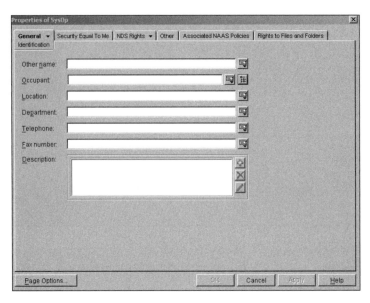

**Figure 9-29**    The Properties of SysOp dialog box

e. He clicked the browse button to the right of the Occupant text box to open the Select Object dialog box displaying the InfoSystems users.

f. He double-clicked CKent to make him the occupant of the SysOp Organizational Role object.

g. He clicked OK to save the changes and return to the main ConsoleOne.

David continued using this process to create the remaining Organizational Role objects shown in Table 9-2. You'll use this process in the end-of-chapter projects to create the remaining Organizational Role objects for the CBE_Labs_Admin OU.

## MANAGING OBJECTS

The work of a network administrator is never done. After creating the initial User, Group, and Organizational Role objects, you'll have the ongoing tasks of changing object configurations, adding new objects, and deleting, renaming, or moving existing objects. In the following sections, you learn how to use iManager to work with the eDirectory tree from a Web browser and how to save time by using ConsoleOne to make changes to multiple user accounts at once.

## Deleting and Renaming User Objects

Deleting a leaf object with ConsoleOne is as easy as clicking on the object and pressing the Delete key. However, after the object is deleted from the tree, its internal object ID is removed and cannot be restored. To restore the object, you have to create another object with the same name and then grant that object all the rights and memberships the original object had. For example, when an employee leaves the company and is replaced by another person with the same job function, renaming the original employee's user account and home directory is usually easier than deleting the old user account and creating a new one. Deleting container objects is more work because you must first delete or move all leaf objects from the container before the system allows the container to be deleted. Instead of deleting an existing container and then creating a new one, you may find it easier to move the container and then rename it as described in the following section.

## Managing eDirectory with iManager

One of Novell's objectives with the OneNet strategy is to make it easier to manage and maintain the organization's network from any computer, regardless of the type of computer you're working on or the network system it is attached to. The iManager utility is one of the new utilities that make managing and maintaining eDirectory possible from an Internet browser. To run iManager, start your Web browser and then enter the https URL for your server, followed by port number 2200. For example, if your server is assigned the IP address 172.20.0.60, enter "https://172.20.0.60:2200" in the Address field. The "https" tells the browser to use the Secure Socket Layer (SSL) for a secure connection, and the port number 2200 tells the NetWare Web server to open the Web Manager page shown in Figure 9-30.

9

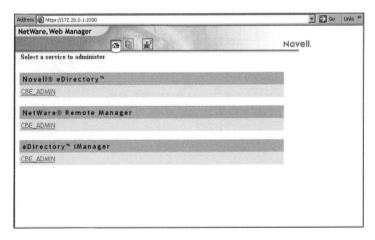

**Figure 9-30**    The NetWare Web Manager window

The SSL protocol provides a secure connection between the browser and the Web server by using public and private keys, as described in Chapter 14.

Before displaying the NetWare Web Manager window, you might see a security alert message stating that you are about to view pages over a secure connection. You can click the In the future, do not show this warning check box, and then click OK to continue. You might see another security alert message informing you that the security certificate was issued by a company you have not chosen to trust. Security certificates (discussed in more depth in Chapter 14) accompany the key sent from the server to the client to encrypt data before sending it over the Internet. The certificate authorizes the key as being issued from a server in a valid organization. Many Internet companies obtain certificates from recognized Internet authorities that are included with Internet Explorer. This message is displayed because your browser software does not have your NetWare server in its trusted certification authority file. You can click the View Certificate option to view the certificate information and then install the certificate. Click Yes to accept the security certificate and continue.

To use iManager, you need to click the server name, CBE_ADMIN, displayed under the eDirectory iManager heading to open the iManager Login window shown in Figure 9-31.

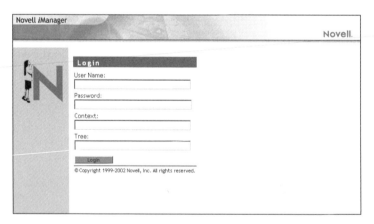

**Figure 9-31**   The iManager Login window

To maintain eDirectory objects in iManager, you need to log in with the administrator's user name and password or be logged in as a user who has been delegated the authority to perform administrative tasks through Novell's Role Based security. (In Chapter 13, you'll learn how to use Role Based security to assign administrative roles to other objects.) Figure 9-32 shows the iManager window after logging in as the network Admin user.

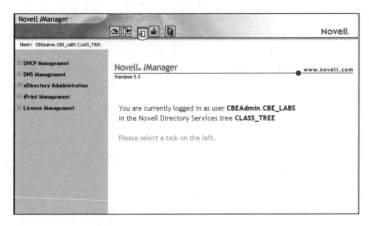

**Figure 9-32**    The iManager main window

## Using iManager Role Based Security

The roles a user can perform are displayed in the column on the left in Figure 9-32. Role Based security consists of groups of administrative tasks, called **administrative roles**, that can be assigned to certain users, enabling them to perform tasks within a particular context in the eDirectory tree. The administrative roles in NetWare 6 include the following:

- *DHCP Management*—Perform tasks necessary to set up and manage Dynamic Host Configuration Protocol services on NetWare 6 servers.

- *DNS Management*—Perform tasks necessary to set up and manage Domain Name System services on NetWare 6 servers.

- *eDirectory Administration*—Perform basic eDirectory administration tasks, such as creating users and groups.

- *iPrint Management*—Perform tasks such as creating printer objects and enabling iPrinter access (see Chapter 11 for more information).

- *License Management*—Performs tasks that include maintaining and managing NetWare server licensing (see Chapter 13 for more information).

 To perform the projects in this book, Role Based security was used to give your ##Admin student user name the administrative roles necessary to manage users and printers in your organization.

Roles can also be used to reduce the need to log in as the network administrator. Logging in as the network administrator over the Internet can increase the likelihood of security leaks or making mistakes such as accidentally changing or deleting network objects. Delegating roles is a good way to decrease the need to log in with the network administrator user name; you can substitute a user name that has been assigned only the necessary permissions. For example, if you're working on network printers, log in to the network with the user name that has only that role. Using the iPrint role will prevent you from accidentally deleting or changing the configuration of another object.

For example, last month David took a vacation to Virginia to explore the Blue Ridge Parkway. Unfortunately, he had to leave for his trip before he had finished setting up user accounts for the network. Ted approved his vacation request, however, because David would still be able to finish his work while traveling by taking advantage of Novell's OneNet strategy and using Role Based security. To avoid logging in over the Internet with the Admin user name and password, David used Role Based security in iManager to grant his user name the rights to manage the eDirectory tree.

While in Virginia, he learned that Ted wanted him to create two user accounts for the temporary employees the company is hiring in the IS Department to help with updating system documentation. He also needed to create a group called TempEmpl for those users. To do this, David used a computer in his hotel lobby to log in to the CBE Labs network via the Internet and create user accounts named Temp1 and Temp2 and the TempEmpl group account, as described in the following steps:

1. He started Internet Explorer and in the Address text box, entered the URL https://*IP_address*:2200, and then pressed Enter (replacing *IP_address* with the IP address assigned to the CBE Labs network).

2. He clicked OK and Yes to respond to the security alert messages and display the NetWare Web Manager window.

3. He clicked the CBE_ADMIN server link under the eDirectory iManager heading to open a Login window similar to the one shown previously in Figure 9-31.

4. He entered the CBEAdmin user name and password and the Context and Tree information, and then clicked the Login button to log in and display the iManager window.

5. He expanded the eDirectory Administration role by clicking the + symbol to the left of that role to display the eDirectory options shown in Figure 9-33.

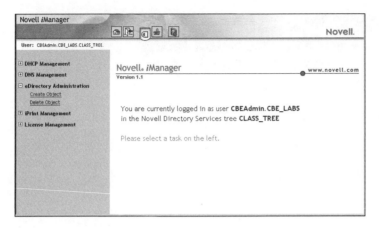

**Figure 9-33**    The options for the eDirectory Administration role

6. He did the following to create a group for the temporary users:

    a. He clicked the Create Object link to open the Available Classes window.

    b. He clicked the Group object class, and then clicked the Next button to open the Create Group window shown in Figure 9-34.

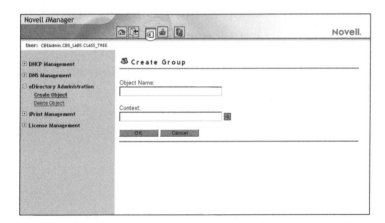

**Figure 9-34**    The Create Group window

    c. He entered TempEmpl in the Object Name text box.

    d. He clicked the browse button next to the Context text box, and clicked the down arrow to the left of the CBE_LABS Organization to view all the OUs.

    e. He clicked the down arrow to the left of the CBE_Labs_Admin container to expand it, as shown in Figure 9-35.

    f. He clicked the InfoSystems OU to place it in the Context text box.

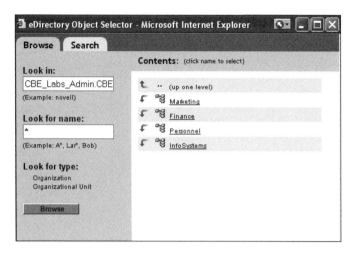

**Figure 9-35**    Selecting a context for the TempEmpl group

      g. He clicked OK to create the group.

      h. He clicked OK again to close the Create Object request succeeded message box and return to the iManager main window.

   7. To create user accounts named Temp1 and Temp2, David did the following:

      a. He clicked the Create Object link under the eDirectory Administration role to open the Available Classes window.

      b. He clicked the User object class, and then clicked the Next button to open the Create User window shown in Figure 9-36.

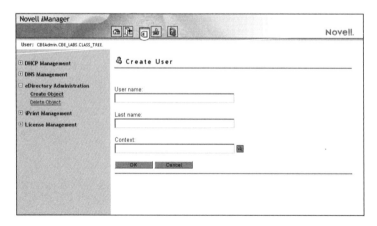

**Figure 9-36**    The Create User window

   c. He entered Temp1 in the User name text box.

   d. He entered Temporary Employee 1 in the Last name text box.

   e. He clicked the browse button and then clicked InfoSystems to select the InfoSystems.CBE_Labs_Admin context.

   f. He clicked OK to create the user.

   g. He clicked OK to close the Create User request succeeded message box, and return to the iManager main window.

8. David repeated Step 7 to create an account named Temp2.

9. He ended the iManager session by clicking the Exit button to return to the Login window, and closed Internet Explorer.

## Updating Multiple User Accounts

As a network administrator, you'll often find that after creating user accounts, you need to make changes that affect several different users, such as preventing users from being logged in to the network between 11:59 P.M. and 5:00 A.M. so that you can perform a network backup. To make this job easier, you can use NetWare Administrator or ConsoleOne to simultaneously modify multiple user accounts. In ConsoleOne, to change properties common to several users, such as an address or login restriction, you can select multiple users by pressing the Ctrl key and clicking user names, highlighting a group or template object, or highlighting a container, and then selecting File, Properties of Multiple Objects on the menu bar. If you highlight a group or container object, all users in that group or container will be modified. If you highlight a template object and select Properties of Multiple Users, all user accounts created with that template will be modified. After returning from his vacation, David used the following steps to create home directories and apply password and time restrictions for the temporary accounts he created in iManager:

1. After logging in as the administrator, he started ConsoleOne and expanded the tree and CBE_LABS Organization. He expanded the CBE_Labs_Admin OU and clicked the InfoSystems OU to display all User objects in the Object frame.

2. Next, he selected the Temp1 and Temp2 accounts by clicking on the Temp1 user account, holding down the Ctrl key, and clicking on the Temp2 object to highlight both users.

3. He clicked File, Properties of Multiple Objects on the menu bar to open the Properties of Multiple Objects dialog box, shown in Figure 9-37.

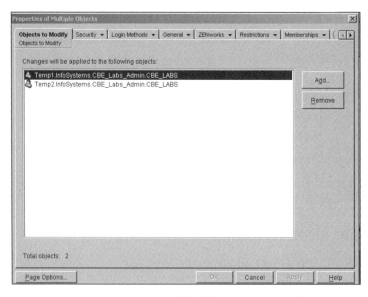

**Figure 9-37**    The Properties of Multiple Objects dialog box

    4. To create home directories for the user accounts, he did the following:

        a. He clicked the down arrow on the General tab, and then clicked the Environment option.

        b. He clicked the browse button to the right of the Volume and Path text boxes to open the Select Object dialog box, and used the up arrow to navigate to the CBE_LABS Organization, as shown in Figure 9-38.

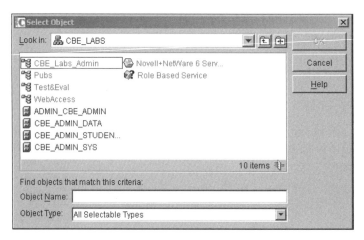

**Figure 9-38**    Selecting a path for home directories in the Select Object dialog box

c. He double-clicked the CBE_ADMIN_DATA volume to expand it, clicked the Users folder, and then clicked OK to display the Home Directory path.

d. He clicked the Apply button to create the user home directories without returning to the main ConsoleOne window.

5. He did the following to add users to the TempEmpl group:

a. He clicked the Memberships tab to open the Memberships dialog box.

b. He clicked the Add button to open the Select Objects dialog box.

c. He clicked the TempEmpl group, and then clicked OK to add the group to the Memberships dialog box.

6. To set password restrictions for the selected users, he did the following:

a. He clicked the Restrictions tab to open the Password Restrictions dialog box.

b. He clicked to remove the check mark from the Allow user to change password check box.

7. Last, he clicked OK to save the changes and return to the main ConsoleOne window.

## Moving Objects

As you'll learn in Chapter 10, when users become a member of an OU, they often gain rights to access files and use eDirectory objects. In addition, login scripts are usually associated with OUs to provide drive mappings and workstation setups for all users in an OU. When moving objects, keep in mind that moving an object to a different location can change the drive mappings and workstation setups users have when they log in and can affect users' rights to access files and other network objects, such as printers.

To move a leaf object, such as a User, Group, or Volume, you simply need to select the object in ConsoleOne and choose File, Move on the menu bar. Moving container objects is more difficult because NetWare moves only partitions. To move an OU from one location to another, you must make the container a separate partition first, as described in the next section. You can then move the container's partition to another location and merge it back into the tree. In the following sections, you learn how to use ConsoleOne to move user and container objects.

### Moving a Container Object

When managing the structure of the eDirectory database, sometimes you need to move a container object from one location to another within the eDirectory hierarchy to make access to resources easier, for example. As you'll learn in Chapter 10 on eDirectory security, when a container becomes a subcontainer of another container, the subcontainer has access rights to objects in the parent container. For example, the InfoSystems container is currently a subcontainer of the CBE_Labs_Admin container, but Ted has suggested that the InfoSystems container be made a separate container to prevent accidental access to the CBE_Labs_Admin OU's resources. Before moving the InfoSystems OU, David must identify any rights that the InfoSystems users gain from assignments made to the CBE_Labs_Admin OU so that these rights can be assigned directly to the InfoSystems OU, as described in Chapter 10.

Moving a container object is more complex than moving a leaf object because it changes the hierarchy of the eDirectory tree, thereby reorganizing the eDirectory database. In Chapter 4, you learned that the eDirectory database is divided into one or more partitions, starting with the [Root] partition. Each partition is a separate physical file called a replica, which is located on one or more NetWare servers. The main reason for creating additional partitions is to divide a large eDirectory database into smaller files or replicas for more efficient access. However, partitioning eDirectory also makes it easier to move containers. By making a container a separate partition, it becomes a separate file that can be moved and synchronized to another location in the hierarchical structure of the eDirectory database. To move the InfoSystems container object to another location in the eDirectory tree, David needed to perform only these three steps:

1. He used the following steps in ConsoleOne to create a partition that starts with the container to be moved (the InfoSystems OU, shown in Figure 9-39):

   a. He clicked the container to be moved (InfoSystems).

   b. He clicked the Partition and Replica View option from the ConsoleOne View menu.

   c. He clicked the Create Partition button and clicked OK to create a separate InfoSystems partition. After the partition was created, the InfoSystems OU was displayed with the partition icon shown in Figure 9-39.

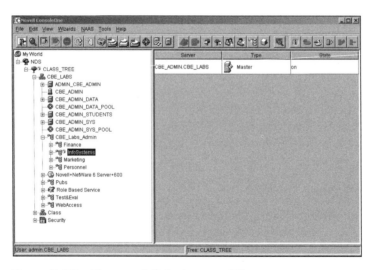

**Figure 9-39** The new InfoSystems partition

2. After a partition was created for the container, he used the following steps in ConsoleOne to move the container's partition to the new location:

a. He right-clicked the InfoSystems OU, and then clicked Move to open the Move dialog box shown in Figure 9-40.

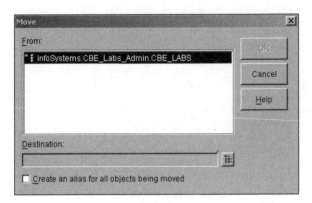

**Figure 9-40**   The Move dialog box

b. Next, he clicked the browse button next to the Destination text box to navigate up the tree and select the CBE_LABS Organization.

c. He clicked OK twice to move the InfoSystems partition. After closing the CBE_LABS Organization and expanding it again, CBE_LABS appeared with the relocated InfoSystems OU, as shown in Figure 9-41.

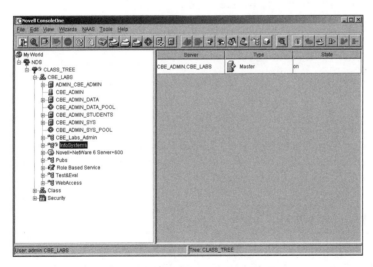

**Figure 9-41**   The InfoSystems partition moved to a new location

3. He clicked the InfoSystems container's partition, clicked the Merge Partition button (looks like the Create Partition button with an up arrow added), and clicked OK to merge the InfoSystems partition back into the main tree, as shown in Figure 9-42.

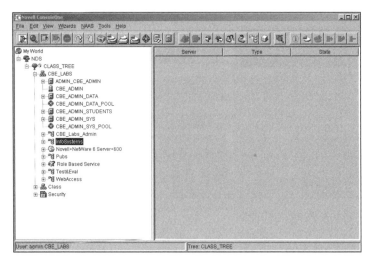

**Figure 9-42**    The InfoSystems partition after merging back into the main tree

When moving container objects, remember that creating and merging partitions requires changes to the [Root] of the eDirectory tree. Therefore, NetWare requires that your user name have Supervisor rights to the root of the eDirectory tree, as described in Chapter 10.

## CHAPTER SUMMARY

❏ The eDirectory tree is the skeleton of the NetWare 6 network system, providing the structure that contains all network objects. As a result, network administrators must know how to implement the eDirectory system by creating the necessary objects and establishing a login security system. ConsoleOne is a powerful and easy-to-use Windows-based utility for setting up and securing the network. The iManager utility can also be used to create and maintain User and Group objects from a Web browser.

❏ Login security consists of account restrictions, intruder detection, and authentication. Account restrictions include password, time, and station restrictions and can be set for User and Template objects. Intruder detection, enabled on a container-by-container basis, helps protect against intruders guessing user passwords by locking user accounts after a specified number of incorrect login attempts have been made in a given time period.

❏ User templates make creating User objects more efficient. You can use them to define the path to users' home directories and set common account and password restrictions.

❏ LDAP provides a way of exchanging directory information between X.500-compatible systems, such as eDirectory and Microsoft Active Directory, by using LDIF files. You can use LDIF files as a quick way to create User objects.

❏ Novell supplies an Organizational Role object that's useful when assigning rights to certain user accounts. Organizational Role objects are similar to groups, except that they usually represent positions in the organization. If another user is assigned the responsibilities, you simply need to change the occupant of the organizational role to give him or her the required rights.

❏ When managing an eDirectory system, you often need to move objects from one container to another. Although moving leaf objects is fast and easy, moving a container from one location to another requires the administrator to create a partition starting at the container to be moved, move the partition to the new location, and then merge the new partition with the parent partition of the container it has been moved into.

9

# KEY TERMS

**address restrictions** — Used to limit a user to logging in from only certain workstation addresses.

**administrative role** — A group of administrative tasks that can be assigned to Admin users so that they can perform administrative functions, such as managing eDirectory, printing, licensing, and DHCP/DNS services.

**intruder detection** — A part of login security that works at the container level by setting a limit on the number of incorrect login attempts that can be made on a user account in that container during a specified time period.

**Lightweight Directory Interchange Format (LDIF)** — An ASCII text file that use a standardized syntax to add, change, or delete objects in LDAP-compatible directory systems.

**password restrictions** — Can be used to force users to periodically change passwords, set minimum password lengths, and use a different password each time they change.

**time restrictions** — Used to limit the times that a user can be logged in to the network.

**user template** — A property that defines standard settings and configures restrictions for each user in a particular container.

## REVIEW QUESTIONS

1. A template can be used to automate all of the following except _____ when creating a user's account.

    a. creating a user home directory

    b. setting address restrictions

    c. setting the number of invalid login attempts

    d. setting the user rights to their home directory

2. Which of the following allows the network administrator to define standard settings, such as the location of home directories and password restrictions for new users?

    a. groups

    b. templates

    c. organizational roles

    d. LDIF files

3. List the three steps for moving the InfoSystems container from the CBE_Labs_Admin container to the CBE_LABS container.

    _____

    _____

    _____

4. Which of the following is *not* a component of login security?

    a. time restrictions

    b. station restrictions

    c. access rights

    d. intruder detection

5. List three types of login restrictions.

    _____

    _____

    _____

6. Which of the following security measures allows you to set the maximum number of times a user can enter an incorrect password?

    a. password restriction

    b. account restriction

    c. intruder detection

    d. authorization

7. Which of the following is *not* a password restriction?

   a. unique passwords

   b. maximum password length

   c. require password changes

   d. minimum password length

8. A NetWare user name can be up to —————————— characters.

9. Which of the following NetWare 6 utilities can be used to move a container to another location in the eDirectory tree?

   a. ConsoleOne

   b. NDSMgr

   c. NetWare Administrator

   d. iManager

10. Which of the following objects should be used to provide a backup Administrator account?

    a. Group

    b. Organizational Role

    c. Organizational Unit

    d. administrative role

11. Following the naming conventions identified in this chapter, write four possible user names for Mark A. Ciampa.

    _____

    _____

    _____

    _____

12. Which of the following defines certain standard settings you want to establish for multiple users?

    a. Organizational Role object

    b. user template

    c. administrative role

    d. import

13. Which of the following is *not* an administrative role?

    a. eDirectory Administration

    b. iPrint Management

    c. DNS Management

    d. Disk Storage Management

9

14. Which of the following protocols can be used to transfer objects between X.500–compatible directories?

    a. LDIF

    b. LDAP

    c. TCP

    d. IP

15. Which of the following utilities can be used to import an LDIF file?

    a. LDAP

    b. ConsoleOne

    c. iManager

    d. Both b and c

16. Intruder detection is implemented at which of the following levels?

    a. user

    b. [Root]

    c. container

    d. server

17. A user is granted rights to use iManager to create eDirectory objects through which of the following?

    a. eDirectory security

    b. Role Based security

    c. membership in the Admin group

    d. login security

18. Which of the following is the best technique for giving a user the rights needed for a particular position in the company?

    a. Give the Organizational Unit the necessary rights.

    b. Create a Group object that has the rights and make the user a member.

    c. Create an Organizational Role that has the rights and make the user an occupant.

    d. Make the user security-equivalent to another user who has been given the necessary rights.

19. In an LDIF file, which of the following fields specifies information properties that are unique to a certain object class?

    a. attribute

    b. property

    c. name

    d. entry

20. Which of the following tasks can you perform from iManager? (Select all that apply.)

   a. create a new user or group

   b. make users members of a group

   c. delete users and groups

   d. create Organizational Role objects

## HANDS-ON PROJECTS

### Project 9-1: Renaming User Accounts

An important part of securing your internal network is renaming your Administrator user account. Follow the steps described in this chapter to rename your ##ADMIN user account to ##iiiADMIN (iii represents your initials).

1. Start your computer and log in with your assigned ##ADMIN user name and password.

2. Start ConsoleOne and expand the **CLASS_TREE** tree and your **##ADMINOU** OU.

3. Follow the steps in this chapter to rename your ##ADMIN user name so that it includes your initials after your student number.

4. Exit ConsoleOne and log out.

5. Test your account by logging in with your new administrative user name.

6. After testing your account, repeat Steps 2 through 4 to change your user name back to ##ADMIN.

7. Log out.

### Project 9-2: Creating an Alternate Admin User

It is important to have a backup administrative user account that you can use to manage the system if your main administrative user account becomes locked or disabled. In this project, use the following steps to create another user in your ##CBE OU and then make that user security-equivalent to your administrative user.

1. If necessary, log in with your newly renamed administrative user name and password.

2. Start ConsoleOne, expand the **CLASS_TREE** tree, expand the **CLASS** Organization, expand your **##ADMINOU** OU, and expand your **CBE_LABS** OU.

3. Use the steps in this chapter to create a new user named ##CKent within your CBE_LABS OU.

9

4. Follow these steps to make your ##CKent user security-equivalent to your administrative user:

   a. Click your **##ADMINOU** OU to display all users in the Object frame.

   b. Right-click your **##ADMIN** user account and click **Properties**.

   c. Click the **Security Equal To Me** tab to open the Security Equal To Me dialog box.

   d. Click the **Add** button to open the Select Objects dialog box.

   e. Navigate to the **CBE_LABS** OU within ##ADMINOU, and double-click your **##CKent** user to add it to the dialog box.

   f. Click **OK** to save your changes.

   g. Exit ConsoleOne and log out.

5. Test your account by logging in as your ##CKent user and then use ConsoleOne to create another user named ##LLane in your CBE_LABS.##ADMINOU container.

6. Log out after completing your tests.

## Project 9-3: Setting User Account Restrictions

To provide good internal security, it's important that users select passwords of at least eight characters and change their passwords regularly. Certain key accounts should be further secured by restricting them to logging in only during certain time periods and from certain workstations. Use the steps described in this chapter to add the following password, time, and station restrictions to your ##CKent user account:

   ❏ Require a minimum length of eight characters for the password.

   ❏ Require passwords to be changed every 60 days.

   ❏ Limit the backup administrator to being logged in from only your workstation from 6:00 A.M. until 10:00 P.M.

## Project 9-4: Creating Groups

Use the steps described in this chapter to create a group named ISMgrs in your InfoSystems.CBE_LABS OU and then make your ##CKent user a member of the ISMgrs group. Create the group accounts for both the CBE_Labs_Admin and InfoSystems OUs shown in Table 9-3. Do not add any group members at this time. Based on your instructor's direction, optionally create the other groups in Table 9-3. Note that all contexts are relative to your ##ADMINOU OU.

**Table 9-3**    Groups and Group Membership for CBE Labs

| Group | Context | Members |
|---|---|---|
| WebMgrs | InfoSystems | GTennesson, SMichelia |
| Executives | CBE_Labs_Admin.CBE_LABS | JCunningham, HEvans, GBurns |
| Admin_Assists | CBE_Labs_Admin.CBE_LABS | SLopez, RDeLucia, MODonnell |
| Admin_Staff | CBE_Labs_Admin.CBE_LABS | JCunningham, SLopez, SHayakawa, JJorgensen, SWells, DKaneaka, SJohnston, TMeyer, PRichardson, TSimpson, DDoering, MCiampa |
| Pub_Staff | Pubs.CBE_LABS | HEvans, RDeLucia, SMichelia, GTennesson, CPatterson |
| Lab_Staff | Test&Eval.CBE_LABS | GBurns, MODonnell, GLee, NNewman, TSkaggs, BFerguson, BSimpson, MThorndike, FNelson, SVanDorn, RPaulsen, WEllis, SGreene, NSingh |
| Hardware_Staff | Hardware.Test&Eval.CBE_LABS | GLee, NNewman, TSkaggs |
| Software_Staff | Software.Test&Eval.CBE_LABS | BFerguson, BSimpson, MThorndike |
| DBMS_Staff | DBMS.Test&Eval.CBE_LABS | FNelson, SVanDorn, RPaulsen, GBurns |
| Network_Staff | Network.Test&Eval.CBE_LABS | WEllis, SGreene, NSingh |

## Project 9-5: Creating User Templates

Copy the User Template Planning Form from Appendix B, and define user templates for the following OUs in your CBE_LABS.##ADMINOU.CLASS OU:

- ◘ T_Executive within your CBE_Labs_Admin OU

- ◘ T_AdminAsst within your CBE_Labs_Admin OU

- ◘ T_IS within your InfoSystems.CBE_Labs_Admin OU

- ◘ T_Finance within your Finance.CBE_Labs_Admin OU

- ◘ T_Marketing within your Marketing.CBE_Labs_Admin OU

- ◘ T_Personnel within your Personnel.CBE_Labs_Admin OU

Each user template should identify at least one group created in Project 9-4 and provide the restrictions shown in Table 9-4.

**Table 9-4**  Restrictions to Apply to User Templates

| Minimum password length | 8 |
|---|---|
| Require unique passwords | Yes |
| Days between password changes | 90 |
| Grace logins | 6 |
| Valid login times | 5:00 A.M. until 11:59 P.M. |
| Concurrent connections | 1 |
| Rights to Login Script | Read |
| Rights to home directory | All rights except Supervisor and Access Control |

Use the steps described in this chapter to create user templates for each department in the preceding list.

# Project 9-6: Creating User Accounts

In this project, use the templates you defined in Project 9-5 to identify and create the user accounts in each OU listed in Table 9-5. Note that all entries in the Organizational Unit Context column are relative to your ##ADMINOU.CLASS OU.

**Table 9-5**  User Accounts for the CBE_Labs_Admin OU

| Organizational Unit Context | User/Title |
|---|---|
| CBE_Labs_Admin.CBE_LABS | Joseph Cunningham/President<br>Steve Lopez/Admin Assistant |
| InfoSystems.CBE_Labs_Admin.CBE_LABS | Ted Simpson/IS Manager<br>Dave Doering/Network Administrator<br>Mark Ciampa/Network Administrator |
| Finance.CBE_Labs_Admin.CBE_LABS | Donna Kaneaka/Director<br>Sarah Johnston/Accounts Receivable<br>Thomas Meyer/Accounts Payable |
| Personnel.CBE_Labs_Admin.CBE_LABS | Patrick Richardson/Director |
| Marketing.CBE_Labs_Admin.CBE_LABS | Stephen Hayakawa/Director<br>Jon Jorgensen/Sales Representative<br>Shelly Wells/Sales Representative |

1. Copy the User Planning Form from Appendix B.
2. Fill in the User Planning Form, identifying an account for each user listed in Table 9-5.
3. Log in with your administrative user name and start ConsoleOne.

4. Expand your **CBE_LABS.##ADMINOU** OU and follow the steps described in this chapter to create the accounts on your User Planning Form, using Project 9-5's templates.

5. Exit ConsoleOne and log out.

6. Test your user accounts by verifying that you can log in as each of the users you created in this project.

## Project 9-7: Creating Organizational Role Objects

In this project, follow the steps described in this chapter to create the Organizational Role objects listed in Table 9-6. Note that all contexts in the Context1 column are relative to the CBE_LABS.##ADMINOU.CLASS OU.

**Table 9-6**    Organizational Role Objects for the CBE_Labs_Admin OU

| Organizational Role | Context1 | Occupant(s) |
|---|---|---|
| President | CBE_Labs_Admin | JCunningham |
| AdminAssist | CBE_Labs_Admin | SLopez |
| Finance_Director | Finance.CBE_Labs_Admin | DKaneaka |
| InfoSystems_Manager | InfoSystems.CBE_Labs_Admin | TSimpson |
| Network_Admin | InfoSystems.CBE_Labs_Admin | DDoering |
| Marketing_Director | Marketing.CBE_Labs_Admin | SHayakawa |
| Personnel_Director | Personnel.CBE_Labs_Admin | PRichardson |

1. If necessary, log in with your administrative user name and password.

2. Start ConsoleOne and expand the **CLASS_TREE** tree, your **CLASS** Organization, and your **##ADMINOU** and **CBE_LABS** OUs.

3. Follow the steps described in this chapter to create the Organizational Role objects in Table 9-6 and add the designated user as the occupant.

4. Exit ConsoleOne and log out.

## Project 9-8: Working with iManager

In this project, follow the steps described in this chapter to use iManager to create users and groups.

1. If necessary, log out to display the Novell Login window.

2. To simulate working from a remote computer, click the **Workstation only** check box and log in using the user name and password for your local Windows XP workstation.

3. Start Internet Explorer.

4. Enter **https://ip_address:2200** (replacing *ip_address* with the IP address of your classroom CBE_ADMIN server). If necessary, respond to the Security Alert message boxes by clicking **OK** or **Yes** and pressing **Enter**.

5. Click your **CBE_ADMIN** server under the eDirectory iManager heading.

6. Log in by entering your administrator's user name, password, context, and tree.

7. Follow the steps in this chapter to create a group named ##TempEmpl in your InfoSystems OU.

8. Follow the steps in this chapter to create the following user accounts in your InfoSystems OU:

   ❐ ##Temp01

   ❐ ##Temp02

9. Exit iManager and log out from your workstation.

10. Attempt to log in as the two users you created in this project.

## Project 9-9: Updating Information for Multiple User Accounts

Knowing how to use the multiple update feature can save you a lot of time and reduce the number of possible errors when entering the same information for several users. In this project, use ConsoleOne's multiple update feature to enter the following information for the users you created with iManager in Project 9-8:

   ❐ Make users members of the ##TempEmpl group.

   ❐ Set time restrictions so that the accounts can be used only during normal hours (8:00 A.M. to 4:00 P.M.).

   ❐ Prevent temporary employees from changing their passwords.

1. Log in with your administrative user name and password.

2. Start ConsoleOne and expand the **CLASS_TREE** object, the **CLASS** Organization, and your **##ADMINOU** and **CBE_LABS** OUs.

3. Expand your **CBE_Labs_Admin** OU, click your **InfoSystems** OU, and then follow the steps in this chapter to set the restrictions in the preceding list.

4. Exit ConsoleOne and log out.

5. Log in as ##Temp01.

6. Attempt to change your password and record the results.

7. Log out.

## Project 9-10: (Optional) Importing Users from LDIF Files

In this project, use the steps described in this chapter to import computer accounts for the Testing and Evaluation Department computers:

1. If necessary, log in with your administrative user name and password.

2. Start ConsoleOne and expand the **CLASS_TREE** object, your **CLASS** Organization, and your **##ADMINOU** and **CBE_LABS** OUs.

3. If necessary, create an OU named **Test&Eval** within your CBE_LABS OU.

4. Click your **Test&Eval** OU to display all objects in the Object frame.

5. If necessary, create a group named **LabStaff** within your Test&Eval OU.

6. Use Notepad to create the LDIF file shown in Figure 9-25. (Your instructor might supply a copy of this file.)

7. Be sure to modify the contexts in the file to replace all instances of o=CBE_LABS with **ou=CBE_LABS.ou=##ADMINOU.o=CLASS**.

8. Follow the steps in this chapter to import the TestEval1 and TestEval2 user accounts.

9. Use the Properties of Multiple Users page to give both accounts a password of **novell**.

10. Exit ConsoleOne and log out.

11. Test the accounts by logging in as the TestEval1 and TestEval2 users.

12. Log out.

## Project 9-11: (Optional) Enabling Intruder Detection

In this project, you use ConsoleOne to enable intruder detection for your ##CBE OU. Because Administrator privileges are necessary to enable intruder detection, you need to log in to the server with a user name that has Administrator equivalency. Your ##ADMIN account should already have these privileges. If not, your instructor will tell you which user name to use.

1. Log in with your Administrator-equivalent user name.

2. Start ConsoleOne.

3. In your InfoSystems container, create a user named **##JOHN** without a home directory. Set a password of **PASSWORD** on the ##JOHN account.

4. Open your InfoSystems OU Properties dialog box, and select Intruder Detection on the General tab to enable these settings:

    Incorrect login attempts: **3**

    Intruder attempt reset interval: Days: **0**; Hours: **0**; Minutes: **15**

    Under the Lock account after detection check box: Days: **0**; Hours: **0**; Minutes: **5**

9

5. Close the dialog box and log out.

6. Attempt to log in as ##JOHN with an incorrect password. Repeat this until you get a message that you are locked out of the system. Report the message you received to your instructor.

## CASE PROJECTS

### Case 9-1: Creating Users for the Jefferson County Courthouse Network

In this case project, you apply what you have learned about login security and creating user and group accounts to creating the following users and groups in the Social Services OU you created in Chapter 4 for your Jefferson County Courthouse project.

1. Copy the Group Planning Form from Appendix B and use it to identify the groups needed in the Social Services Department.

2. Copy the User Template Planning Form from Appendix B and use it to configure at least one user template for the Social Services users.

3. Use a copy of the User Planning Form from Appendix B to identify the Social Service users defined in Case Project 4-1.

4. Use ConsoleOne to create the groups, templates, and users you have identified within your JCCH.##ADMINOU.CLASS structure.

### Case 9-2: Creating Users for the J.Q. Adams Corporation Directory Tree

In this case project, you apply what you have learned about login security and creating user and group accounts to creating the users identified in the J.Q. Adams organizational chart (shown previously in Figure 4-35).

1. Copy the Group Planning Form from Appendix B and use it to identify any groups needed in the J.Q. Adams organizational chart.

2. Copy the User Template Planning Form from Appendix B and use it to configure at least one user template for each of the following divisions shown in the J.Q. Adams organizational chart:

   ◻ Finance

   ◻ Sales

   ◻ Production

3. Use a copy of the User Planning Form from Appendix B to identify the J.Q. Adams users.

4. Use ConsoleOne to create the groups, templates, and users you have identified within the appropriate containers of your ADAMS.##ADMINOU.CLASS structure.

## CHAPTER 10

# MANAGING TRUSTEE ASSIGNMENTS AND FILE ATTRIBUTES

**After reading this chapter and completing the exercises, you will be able to:**

♦ Identify the components of NetWare trustee rights (eDirectory and file system) security

♦ Calculate the effective rights obtained from a combination of trustee assignments, group rights, and inherited rights and how the Inherited Rights Filter is used to selectively block inherited rights

♦ Identify and assign entry and attribute rights for the eDirectory system

♦ Identify directory attributes and use ConsoleOne and the FLAG command to implement directory attributes

After user accounts have been created and secured, NetWare's next level of security involves giving users access to eDirectory and the NetWare file system. This is the trustee assignments and file attributes security level. Initially, new users have rights only to work in their home directories and run programs from the SYS:Public directory. An important responsibility of a network administrator is providing users with rights to access the network eDirectory objects, directories, and files they need while still protecting sensitive network information. If you have worked with previous versions of NetWare, not much has changed in the area of rights and trustee assignments. This chapter serves as a good review of those concepts. However, if this is your first look at NetWare's method of securing files, directories, and eDirectory objects, this chapter offers a thorough explanation.

Trustee assignments control who has rights to access network resources after the user has logged in to the network. Access rights are like a set of keys given to a new employee. Just as keys provide access to rooms, access rights give users access to directories that contain files they need to use. You can also protect directories and files in NetWare security. In addition to controlling access to them through trustee assignments, the network administrator can assign directory and file attributes to a directory, file, or group of files. These attributes can be attached as another means of limiting user access. In this chapter, you learn how to use access rights and attributes to give users the effective access to network resources they need.

Most software applications allow file sharing for workgroup computing. Therefore, the network administrator needs to balance file system security and integrity with providing shared access to directories containing files used simultaneously by more than one workstation.

## TRUSTEE ASSIGNMENTS

In this section, you learn about trustees, rights, and assignments and how to use them in planning eDirectory and file system security. You'll also become familiar with NetWare and Windows tools for managing trustee assignments.

## Trustees, Rights, and Assignments

A **trustee** is a user who has been given access to eDirectory objects, directories, or files. The user is called a trustee because the user is responsible for the security of the objects, directories, or files to which he or she has access.

The term **rights** describes the type of access the user has been given. For example, the file system's File Scan right lets users see directory and file listings, and the Read right lets users see (but not change) the contents of a file. NetWare 6 has entry rights, attribute rights, directory rights, and file rights. Table 10-1 summarizes these rights, which are discussed in more detail later in this chapter.

**Table 10-1** Types of NetWare 6 Trustee Rights

| Type of Rights | Trustee Access |
| --- | --- |
| Entry rights | Trustee can work with an eDirectory tree object as a whole but can't work with the properties of that object |
| Attribute rights | Trustee can work with the properties of an eDirectory tree object but must first be granted necessary entry rights to the object |
| Directory rights | Trustee can work with a file system directory and, generally, the files in that directory, although this can be blocked by assigned file rights and the file's Inherited Rights Filter (discussed later in this chapter) |
| File rights | Trustee can work with a file |

Although NetWare Administrator uses the terms "object rights" and "property rights," ConsoleOne uses the term "entry rights" to describe a trustee's object rights and the term "attribute rights" to describe a trustee's rights to an object's properties. In this chapter, the term "entry rights" is used to describe rights given to an object, and the term "attribute rights" is used to describe rights given to an object's properties.

The terms **grant** and **assign** are used interchangeably to describe giving rights to a trustee. Therefore, you make the user JCunningham a *trustee* of the CBE Labs eDirectory tree by *granting* or *assigning* him specific eDirectory entry rights. The term **trustee assignment** refers to the rights given to the user; for example, the trustee assignments given to JCunningham determine what access he has to eDirectory tree objects and the network file system's directories and files. A **trustee list** is the set of trustee assignments for an eDirectory object, directory, or file; it is used to determine who can access the object, directory, or file. The trustee list of an eDirectory object is stored in a property of the object, the **access control list (ACL)**.

As a network administrator, you use trustee assignments to control which users have access to the network resources, thus maintaining network security by giving access *only* to users who need it. Trustee assignments are the network administrator's main tool for controlling network resources and maintaining system security after a user has logged in to the network.

**10**

Typically, the notation for Novell rights is to use only the first letter of the right enclosed in brackets, as shown in Table 10-2. This notation is used in this chapter.

## Entry Rights

**Entry rights** give the user access to eDirectory objects. They do not, however, give access to the object's properties. Table 10-2 summarizes the NetWare 6 entry rights.

**Table 10-2**   NetWare 6 Entry Rights

| Right | Effect on Object |
| --- | --- |
| Supervisor [S] | Grants the user all rights and all attribute rights to the object. |
| Browse [B] | Lets the user see the object in the eDirectory tree and have the object's name show up in search results. |
| Create [C] | Applies only to container objects. Lets the user create new objects in the container but does not let the user create attribute rights for the objects. |
| Delete [D] | Lets the user delete the object from the eDirectory tree. If the object is a container object, it must be empty before it can be deleted. |
| Rename [R] | Lets the user rename the object. |
| Inheritable [I] | Lets all rights be inheritable within the container (the NetWare 6 default). Applies only to container objects. If this right is deselected, then rights are not inherited by child containers. |

The **Browse [B] right** enables users to see objects in the eDirectory tree. By not granting this right, the network administrator can control which parts of the eDirectory tree users can see. For example, consider the CBE Labs eDirectory tree in Figure 10-1.

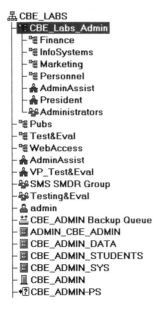

**Figure 10-1**    The CBE Labs eDirectory tree

Users in the Test&Eval and Pubs OUs might not need to see other sections of the eDirectory tree, such as the Finance, Marketing, and Personnel OUs. By controlling the Browse right for users in Test&Eval and Pubs, the network administrator can make these three OUs invisible to those users.

The **Create [C] right**, which applies only to container objects, lets users create objects within a container object. However, it does not allow the user to set property values in the objects. The **Delete [D] right** lets users delete an eDirectory tree object. However, before you can delete a container object, you must delete all objects in it—you cannot delete a container object with objects in it. The **Rename [R] right** lets users change the name of an object, which changes the object's complete name.

The **Inheritable [I] right** changes the way rights flow down the eDirectory tree. By default in NetWare 6, all rights flow down (are inheritable) from a parent container to its child containers or leaf objects. The Inheritable right applies only to container objects because leaf objects do not contain subordinate objects to inherit rights. If the Inheritable right is removed, the container's child containers will not inherit rights granted to the parent container. By using the Inheritable right, an administrator can effectively create a "dead-end" container for special purposes. For example, you might want to grant certain rights to a container, but you don't want those rights to trickle down to subordinate containers. In other words, you made the container a dead-end, in which rights apply only to it and nowhere else. Typically, however, the Inheritable right is left at the default active setting.

The **Supervisor [S] right** gives the user all other entry rights and Supervisor rights to all properties of the object. Therefore, a user with Supervisor rights to an object can change any property settings for that object.

## Attribute Rights

**Attribute rights** let users access the property settings of eDirectory objects. Before you can grant attribute rights to a user, the user must have entry rights to the object. Table 10-3 summarizes the NetWare 6 attribute rights.

**Table 10-3**    NetWare 6 Attribute Rights

| Right | Effect on Property |
|---|---|
| Supervisor [S] | Grants the user all rights to the property. |
| Compare [C] | A special case of the Read right that allows the user to compare the value of a property field to a fixed value returning true or false, without being able to view a property's contents. |
| Read [R] | Lets the user see the value of the property. Includes Compare. |
| Write [W] | Lets the user change, add, or delete the value of the property. Includes Add/Remove Self. |
| Add/Remove Self [A] | Lets users add or delete themselves to or from the user list in objects that have user lists. The user can't change other property values. Included in Write. |

**10**

The **Compare [C] right** lets users test the values of a property against a reference value—for example, whether a printer in the eDirectory tree is a color printer. When a user with Compare rights tests a property value (such as color), a true (equals test value) or false (doesn't equal test value) response can be returned, although the value stored in the property setting is never displayed. For example, you could ask a woman wearing sunglasses if her eye color (property) was brown (comparison) and get a true or false answer, but you wouldn't be able to see her eye color (property). The **Read [R] right** lets users actually see the value of the property setting. The Compare right is included in the Read and Write rights, so when you grant the Read and Write rights to users, you also grant the ability to make comparisons.

Although the Read right lets users see the value of the property setting, it doesn't allow them to change the value. To change values, users must have the **Write [W] right**, which includes the Add/Remove Self right that enables trustees to change information in attribute fields. The **Add/Remove Self [A] right** enables trustees to make themselves members of a group or remove their user names from a group. For example, if you give all users the Add/Remove Self right to a mail group, they can make their user names members of a group that receives copies of e-mails, or remove their names from the group when they no longer want to receive those e-mails.

As with entry rights, the **Supervisor [S] right** gives a user all rights to the property. Note that attribute rights can be assigned individually for each object property, so different users can have different access to an object's property values or to all properties. Granting the Supervisor entry right to an object normally grants the Supervisor attribute right to all the object's properties. (This assignment can, however, be changed with the Inherited Rights Filter [IRF], discussed later in the "The Inherited Rights Filter" section.)

## Directory and File Rights

**Directory rights** control access to the directories and subdirectories in the network file system, and **file rights** control access to the files in these directories and subdirectories. The same eight rights are used for both directory and file rights. Note that the rights can be assigned to individual files and directories. Normally, users have the same access to files in a directory as they do to the directory, but you can modify this access by using file rights on specific files or by using an IRF on a file. Table 10-4 summarizes the NetWare 6 directory and file rights.

**Table 10-4**  NetWare 6 Directory and File Rights

| Right | Effect on Directory | Effect on File |
|---|---|---|
| Supervisor [S] | Grants all rights to the specified directory and all subdirectories. Cannot be changed or blocked by a trustee assignment or an IRF. | Grants all rights to the specified file. |
| Read [R] | Lets the user read files or run programs in the directory. | Lets the user read or run the specified file or program without having Read rights at the directory level. |
| Write [W] | Lets the user change or add data to files in the specified directory. | Lets the user change or add data to the specified file without having Write rights at the directory level. |
| Create [C] | Lets the user create files and subdirectories. | Lets the user salvage the specified file if it is deleted. |
| Erase [E] | Lets the user delete files and remove subdirectories. | Lets the user delete the specified file without having Erase rights at the directory level. |
| Modify [M] | Lets the user change file and subdirectory names and use Windows Explorer, ConsoleOne, or NetWare Administrator to change attribute settings on files or subdirectories. | Lets the user change the name or attribute settings of the specified file without having Modify rights at the directory level. |

**Table 10-4**    NetWare 6 Directory and File Rights (continued)

| Right | Effect on Directory | Effect on File |
|---|---|---|
| File Scan [F] | Lets the user obtain a directory of file and subdirectory names. | Lets the user view the specified filename on a directory listing without having File Scan rights at the directory level. |
| Access Control [A] | Lets the user grant access rights to other users for the specified directory. | Lets the user grant access rights to the specified file without having Access Control rights at the directory level. |

Being able to assign access rights to a specific file means the network administrator can let users update a file or database in a directory while blocking rights to other files in that storage area.

The **Read [R] right** and **File Scan [F] right** are often used together to enable users to access files or run programs in a specified directory. All users are given Read and File Scan rights to the SYS:Public directory. With the **Create [C] right** to a directory, a user can create subdirectories as well as new files in the specified directory. The Create right lets a user copy files into the directory as long as no other file in the directory has the same name. Granting the Create right to an existing file might seem meaningless, but it does enable the user to salvage the file if it's deleted. Be aware that assigning the **Erase [E] right** to a directory lets a user not only delete files but also remove the entire directory and its subdirectories.

There's an important difference between the Write right and the Modify right. The Write [W] right allows users to change or add data to an existing file; the **Modify [M] right** lets users change a file's name or attributes only—it has nothing to do with changing the file's contents. The **Access Control [A] right** lets a user determine which users can access the directory or file by granting access rights to other users. With the Access Control right, users can assign all rights except Supervisor [S]. You should not give the Access Control right to other users because allowing users to grant rights to other users can make it difficult for you to keep track of file system security.

Having the **Supervisor [S] right** is not quite the same as having all rights because it applies to all subdirectories and cannot be changed at a lower directory. If you need to grant the equivalent of [S] to a trustee, but you want a filter to block those rights at a subordinate directory or file, grant the [R W C E M F A] set of rights. This assignment gives the trustee the equivalent of [S] without the ability to pass through an IRF. The Supervisor right differs from other rights in that only the Admin user or another user who has Supervisor rights to the directory can assign it.

10

Users who have the Access Control right in a directory but not the Supervisor right can accidentally restrict themselves from working in the directory by assigning themselves fewer rights to the directory or a subdirectory than they need. To avoid this, grant the Access Control right to a user only when it's absolutely necessary for him or her to assign rights to other users.

By looking at specific situations, you can better understand which access rights are necessary to perform tasks in the network file system. Table 10-5 lists typical operations for files and directories and the access rights required to perform them.

**Table 10-5    Rights Required for Common Operations**

| Operation | Typical Command/Program for Performing Operation | Rights Required |
|---|---|---|
| Read a file | WordPad | Read |
| Obtain a directory listing | Windows Explorer | File Scan |
| Change the contents of data in a file | WordPad | Write |
| Write to a closed file using a text editor that creates a backup file | EDIT (DOS command) | Write, Create, Erase, Modify (Modify not required if creating a new file) |
| Run a program file | WordPad | Read |
| Create and write to a new file | WordPad | Create |
| Copy a file from a directory | Windows Explorer | Read, File Scan |
| Copy a file into a directory | Windows Explorer | Create |
| Copy multiple files to a directory with existing files | Windows Explorer | Create, File Scan |
| Create a subdirectory | Windows Explorer | Create |
| Delete a file | Windows Explorer | Erase |
| Salvage deleted files | Windows Explorer, ConsoleOne, or NetWare Administrator | Read and File Scan on the file and Create in the directory or on filename |
| Change attributes | NetWare Administrator or ConsoleOne | Modify |
| Rename a file or subdirectory | Windows Explorer | Modify |
| Change the IRF | NetWare Administrator or ConsoleOne | Access Control |
| Make or change a trustee assignment | NetWare Administrator or ConsoleOne | Access Control |

Directory trustee assignments are kept track of in the directory entry table (DET) of each volume. A DET for a file or directory can hold up to six trustee assignments. If you assign more than six trustees to a directory, an additional entry is made in the DET for that directory name. However, keeping trustee assignments to six or fewer for each directory is a good idea.

You can usually do this by assigning a group as a trustee and making users who need access to the directory members of the group. File trustee assignments are also tracked in the DET. If you assign more than six trustees to a file, you need an additional entry in the DET for that filename.

## Assigning eDirectory Rights

**Assigned rights** are granted directly to a user or another eDirectory object. It is always the user who actually exercises trustee rights. The rights that a user has to an object, an object's properties, a directory, or a file are called **effective rights**. Effective rights are the functions a user can perform on an object, on a property, or in a specific directory or file. A user's effective rights are often the same as his or her trustee assignments and are the result of one or more of the following factors:

- A trustee assignment is made to the *user*.

- The user is a member of a *group,* and the group has trustee assignments.

- The user occupies an *organizational role,* and the organizational role has trustee assignments.

- The user's User object is located in a *container object* that has trustee assignments.

- The user has been given *security equivalence* to another user who has trustee assignments.

- Subordinate container objects and directories inherit the user's trustee assignments granted in a parent container object or directory. This inheritance applies, however, only if no rights are specifically assigned for that object or directory. A subsequent assignment of rights is discussed in more detail in the following sections.

The following sections discuss ways of gaining effective rights. Although all techniques for managing trustee assignments are similar, it's easier to understand trustee assignment management by discussing entry and attribute rights separately from directory and file rights.

# Managing Entry Rights and Attribute Rights

When you are assigning entry and attribute rights, you make the assignment by using the object (Object A) to which access is being granted or the object (Object B) that's getting access to Object A. For example, if you want a user to have rights in a container object, the trustee assignment can be granted to the user in the container object's dialog box or in the user's dialog box.

## Granting Trustee Assignments to a User

The simplest and most straightforward way for a user to gain effective rights is to be granted a trustee assignment. To see a simple example of granting user trustee assignments, take a look at F.D. Roosevelt Investments, Inc. (FDR Investments), a small investment brokerage

10

house that manages a variety of mutual funds. FDR Investments has three business units: Administration, Sales, and Investments. Figure 10-2 shows its organizational chart, and Figure 10-3 shows the eDirectory tree.

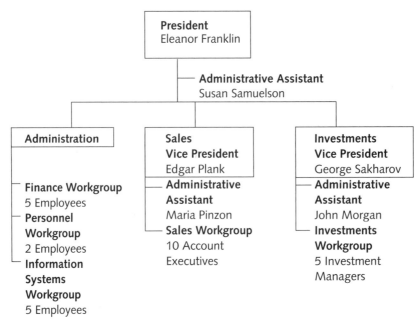

**F.D. Roosevelt Investments**

**Figure 10-2**    The organizational chart for F.D. Roosevelt Investments, Inc.

**Figure 10-3**    The FDR eDirectory tree

Paul Drake, the lead account executive, needs to manage eDirectory objects in the Sales OU, so he will be granted the Supervisor entry right to the Sales OU. The Supervisor entry right gives the trustee the Supervisor right to all properties of that object, as Figure 10-4 shows.

|  | Trustee Assignments |  | Object:  Sales |
|---|---|---|---|
| P Drake: | User | Entry Rights | [S          ] |
|  | Effective Rights |  | [S B C D R] |
|  | User | Attribute Rights:<br>All Properties | [          ] |
|  | Effective Rights |  | [S C R W A] |

**Figure 10-4**   Paul's entry and attribute rights

Now consider another example: implementing entry and attribute rights at CBE Labs. Georgia Burns, vice president of Testing and Evaluation, is very knowledgeable about network administration. To expedite administering the Test&Eval branch of the CBE Labs eDirectory tree, she will be given rights to administer the Test&Eval OU. Therefore, she must be given the Supervisor right to the Test&Eval OU. Figure 10-5 shows the Test&Eval branch of the CBE Labs eDirectory tree.

**10**

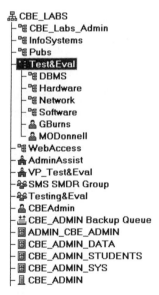

**Figure 10-5**   The Test&Eval branch of the CBE Labs eDirectory tree

To assign Georgia trustee rights from the Test&Eval object's dialog box, David Doering, the network administrator for CBE Labs, performed the following steps:

1. He started NetWare Administrator and logged in with Administrator privileges.

2. He clicked the Test&Eval OU, and then clicked Object, Trustees of this Object on the menu bar to open the Trustees of Test&Eval dialog box (see Figure 10-6).

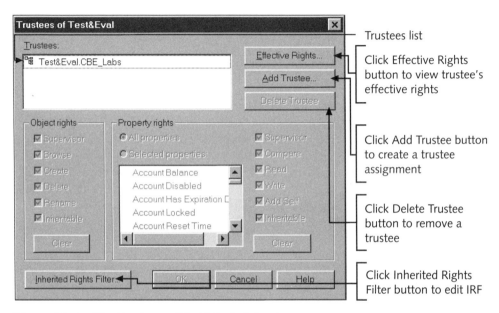

**Figure 10-6**   The Trustees of Test&Eval dialog box

 Note that the object is a trustee of itself. Check marks indicate that the right is granted; empty check boxes indicate that it is not. Grayed-out check boxes indicate that the right is not applicable to the selected object—this usually occurs when no objects have been selected.

3. He clicked the Add Trustee button to open the Select Object dialog box.

4. He browsed the tree to locate the GBurns User object, clicked to select it, and clicked OK to make GBurns a trustee of the Test&Eval OU (see Figure 10-7). He then clicked OK to close the Trustee of Test&Eval dialog box.

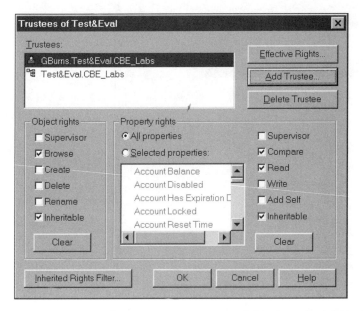

**Figure 10-7**    Making GBurns a trustee of the Test&Eval OU object

10

Now take a look at David performing the same task in ConsoleOne. Remember, as an administrator, you should know more than one way to perform a task. Although NetWare Administrator is a great tool for administrators, ConsoleOne is also an efficient tool for managing your eDirectory tree. To grant Georgia trustee rights to the Test&Eval OU object from the Test&Eval OU object, David used the following steps in ConsoleOne:

1. He logged in with Administrator privileges and started ConsoleOne.

2. He clicked the Test&Eval OU, and then clicked File, Trustees of this Object on the menu bar to open the Properties of Test&Eval dialog box to the Trustees of this Object tab (see Figure 10-8).

3. To see the object's assigned rights, he clicked the Assigned Rights button to open the Rights assigned to: Test&Eval.CBE_LABS dialog box (see Figure 10-9). He then clicked Cancel to return to the Properties of Test&Eval dialog box.

Check marks indicate the right is granted; empty check boxes indicate that the right is not applicable to the selected object, which usually occurs when no objects have been selected.

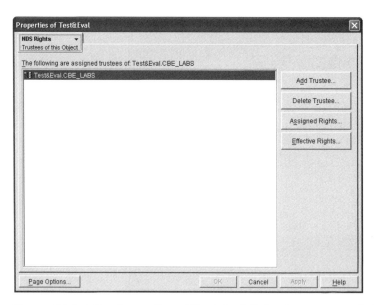

**Figure 10-8** The Properties of Test&Eval dialog box in ConsoleOne

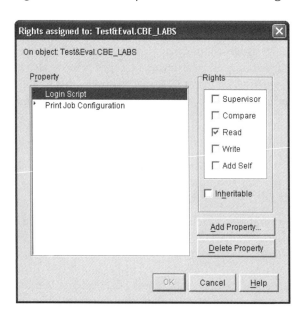

**Figure 10-9** The Rights assigned to: Test&Eval.CBE_LABS dialog box

4. He clicked the Add Trustee button to open the Select Objects dialog box.

5. He selected the GBurns User object, and then clicked OK in the Select Objects and Rights assigned to dialog boxes to make GBurns a trustee of the Test&Eval OU object, as Figure 10-10 shows.

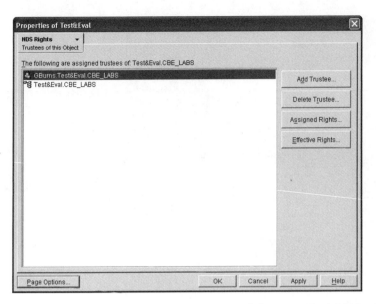

**Figure 10-10** Making GBurns a trustee of the Test&Eval OU in ConsoleOne

Now that Georgia Burns is a trustee of the Test&Eval OU, her specific rights can be assigned. Remember that the Compare right is included in the Read right, so nothing is gained by assigning the Compare right if the Read right has already been assigned. Georgia Burns needs the Supervisor entry right. This assignment includes the Supervisor attribute right to all properties, but explicitly granting the Supervisor attribute right to all properties in the dialog box, too, serves as a visual reminder of the rights granted to the trustee. To grant Georgia Burns entry and attribute rights to the Test&Eval OU object, David followed these steps in NetWare Administrator after logging in:

1. He opened the Trustees of Test&Eval dialog box, as described previously, and clicked GBurns.Test&Eval.CBE_LABS in the Trustees list.

2. In the Object rights section, he clicked to select the Supervisor check box, and clicked to deselect the Browse check box. (Although it isn't necessary to deselect the Browse right, it gives a clearer picture of the trustee's rights.)

3. In the Property rights section, he clicked the All properties radio button.

4. In the Property rights section, he clicked the Supervisor check box to select it, and clicked to deselect the Compare and Read check boxes. (Again, it isn't necessary to deselect the Compare and Read rights, but it offers a clearer picture of the trustee's rights.) The Trustees of Test&Eval dialog box then looked like the one shown in Figure 10-11.

5. He clicked OK to close the Trustees of Test&Eval dialog box.

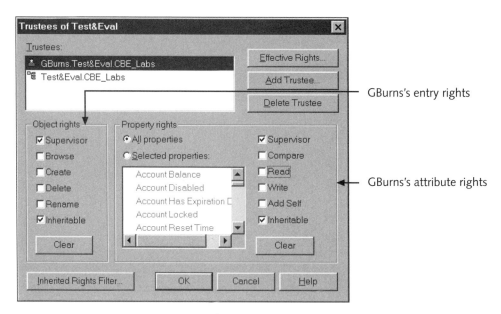

**Figure 10-11** GBurns's entry and attribute rights to Test&Eval

The Trustees of *ObjectName* dialog box gives the network administrator a quick way of checking a trustee's effective rights to an object. David used these steps in NetWare Administrator to view Georgia's effective entry and attribute rights to the Test&Eval OU:

1. He clicked Object, Trustees of this Object on the menu bar.

2. He clicked GBurns.Test&Eval.CBE_LABS in the Trustees list.

3. He clicked the Effective Rights button to open the Effective Rights dialog box (see Figure 10-12).

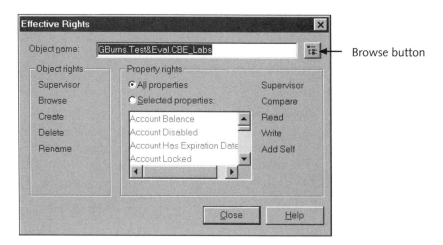

**Figure 10-12** The Effective Rights dialog box

Notice that Georgia Burns has all entry and attribute rights to the Test&Eval OU. Rights not assigned would be grayed out. You can use the Browse button to check the effective rights of other objects in the eDirectory tree to the current object.

4. He clicked the Close button to close the Effective Rights dialog box and return to the Trustees of Test&Eval dialog box.

5. He clicked Cancel to close the Trustees of Test&Eval dialog box.

Now take a look at David doing the same thing, but using ConsoleOne again. Remember that NetWare Administrator uses the terms "object rights" and "property rights." Therefore, when you're assigning entry rights, you use the column labeled "Object rights"; when you're assigning attribute rights, you use the column labeled "Property rights" (refer back to Figure 10-11). To grant Georgia entry and attribute rights to the Test&Eval OU, David did the following:

1. He started ConsoleOne, right-clicked the Test&Eval OU, and clicked Trustees of this Object on the shortcut menu.

2. He clicked GBurns.Test&Eval.CBE_LABS in the Trustees list, and clicked the Assigned Rights button.

**10**

3. To grant Georgia entry rights, he verified that [Entry Rights] was selected in the Property section and clicked the check boxes in the Rights column (see Figure 10-13).

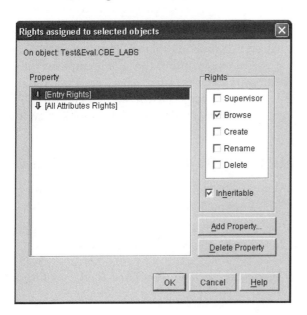

**Figure 10-13** Selecting an entry right to assign

4. He clicked the [All Attributes Rights] item, clicked the Supervisor check box to grant Supervisor attribute rights (see Figure 10-14), and then clicked OK.

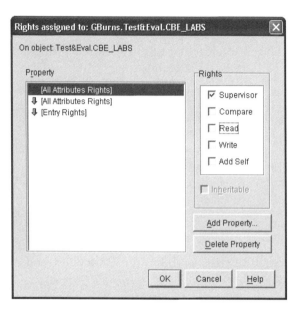

**Figure 10-14** Selecting an attribute right to assign

5. In the Properties of Test&Eval dialog box, he clicked OK to save the assignment.

You should now have a sense of how these two tools can perform the same tasks and how each tool shows the same information in a different format. The goal of this chapter is to show you how to manage trustee assignments without too much emphasis on which tool to use. The rest of this chapter demonstrates tasks using either NetWare Administrator or ConsoleOne, not both. The end-of-chapter projects will strengthen your ability to use both of NetWare's eDirectory management tools. For now, take a look at another way of assigning trustee rights.

## Assigning Trustee Rights to an Object from the Trustee Object

You can also assign attribute and entry trustee rights from the object being granted the trustee assignment. To do so, follow these general steps in NetWare Administrator:

1. Click the object name or icon to select it. Then click Object, Rights to Other Objects on the menu bar to open the Search Context dialog box.
*or*
Right-click the object name or icon, and then click Rights to Other Objects to open the Search Context dialog box.

2. Use the Search Context dialog box to configure the search for the trustee's rights to other objects in the eDirectory tree and to search for the trustee rights.

3. Use the settings in the Rights to Other Objects dialog box to manage trustees and trustee rights assignments.

When the trustee assignment is made from the User object (or other trustee object), NetWare first searches the eDirectory tree to find and list the objects for which the user has rights assigned. The context for this search—the whole tree or a branch of it—is specified as part of the search. Searching the eDirectory tree takes time, so it's faster to limit the search to a specific area of the tree, when possible. Normally, you should limit the search context to only the part of the eDirectory tree that includes the objects for which you are granting trustee rights to the user. To use this method to give Georgia her trustee assignment to the Test&Eval OU, David did the following:

1. He started NetWare Administrator.

2. First, he removed the trustee assignment he made earlier to GBurns. He clicked the Test&Eval OU, and then clicked Object, Trustees of this Object on the menu bar.

3. In the Trustees of Test&Eval dialog box, he clicked GBurns in the Trustees list.

4. He clicked the Delete Trustee button.

5. He then clicked Yes to accept the deletion. This removed the trustee assignment he made earlier.

6. He clicked OK to close the Trustees of Test&Eval dialog box.

7. He expanded the tree to locate the GBurns User object. He clicked to select it, and then clicked Object, Rights to Other Objects on the menu bar to open the Search Context dialog box, shown in Figure 10-15.

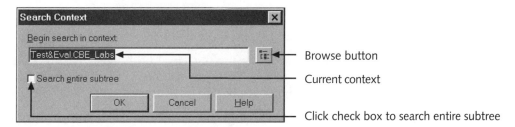

**Figure 10-15**     The Search Context dialog box

8. He clicked the browse button to open the Select Object dialog box, selected the CBE_LABS Organization, and then clicked OK.

9. In the Search Context dialog box, CBE_LABS was displayed in the Begin search in context text box. He clicked the Search entire subtree check box, and then clicked OK. NetWare searched for object trustee assignments for GBurns, and then the Rights to Other Objects - User: GBurns dialog box opened, as Figure 10-16 shows.

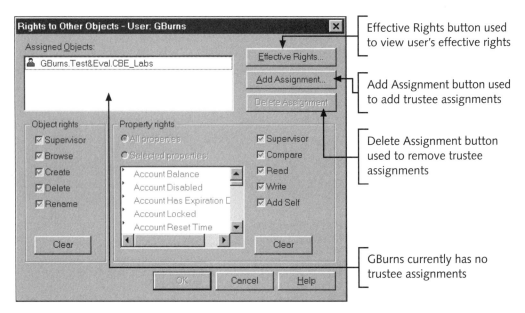

Effective Rights button used to view user's effective rights

Add Assignment button used to add trustee assignments

Delete Assignment button used to remove trustee assignments

GBurns currently has no trustee assignments

**Figure 10-16**    The Rights to Other Objects - User: GBurns dialog box

 Note that there are no assigned objects at this time because these steps are simply illustrating the initial assignment of trustee rights to the Test&Eval OU object to Georgia Burns.

10. He clicked the Add Assignment button to open the Select Object dialog box.

11. He browsed the tree to locate the Test&Eval OU object, clicked to select it, and then clicked OK to assign GBurns trustee rights to the Test&Eval OU object, as shown in Figure 10-17. He saved the assignment by clicking OK.

You could also assign Georgia Burns's specific entry and attribute rights in the Rights to Other Objects dialog box, which works much the same way as granting trustee rights in the Trustees of *ObjectName* dialog box. Note that in Figure 10-17 the Rights to Other Objects dialog box shows that the same default rights have been granted: the Browse entry right and the Compare and Read attribute rights to all properties.

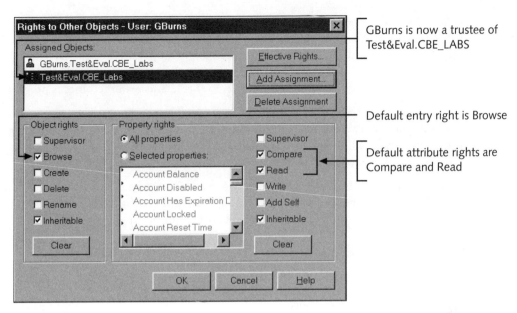

GBurns is now a trustee of Test&Eval.CBE_LABS

Default entry right is Browse

Default attribute rights are Compare and Read

**Figure 10-17** GBurns assigned as a trustee of the Test&Eval.CBE_LABS OU

## Granting Trustee Assignments to a Group

Groups consist of users who have common network requirements, and grouping users can simplify trustee assignments. When a group is made a trustee of an object, all members of that group are also considered trustees of the object and, therefore, have the same rights as the group. A user's effective rights in a directory then combine his or her own trustee assignment with any rights he or she has as a group member.

A special case of a group is the **[Public]** trustee object. When [Public] is made a trustee of an object, *every* object in the eDirectory tree—users, groups, OUs, and so on—inherits the same [Public] rights to the object. In addition, [Public] rights are available to users who have loaded Novell Client but haven't logged in to the network yet. When you install NetWare 6, [Public] becomes a trustee of the [Root] object and gets the Browse entry right, so by default, anyone with access to your network can see your whole eDirectory tree *before* logging in to the network!

If you don't want all users, logged in or not, to see your eDirectory tree, you must delete [Public] as a trustee to the [Root] of the eDirectory tree.

Novell recommends making a container object an object's trustee rather than giving the [Public] object trustee rights to an object. This narrows the granting of rights to only the users, groups, and other objects in that container. Granting rights to only a specific container also means that users have to be logged in before receiving rights, which would not be the case with granting rights to [Public].

Take a look at some simple examples from FDR Investments of using groups to assign trustee rights. FDR has removed the [Public] trustee assignment from the [Root] of the eDirectory tree and has granted the AcctExecs group the Browse [B] entry right and Compare and Read [C R] attribute rights for the Sales OU. This lets the AcctExecs group see all objects in their branch of the eDirectory tree and read the object's property values.

In addition, the AcctExecs group is being given the right to let group members add themselves to ACLs for objects in the Sales OU. This will be especially useful for printing problems because all members of the group will have more control of the printing process with the workgroup's laser printer.

What effective rights does Maria Pinzon, the administrative assistant for Sales, have to the Sales OU? As Figure 10-18 shows, because Maria doesn't have any trustee assignments as a user, her effective rights are determined by her group membership.

|  | Trustee Assignments |  | Object: Sales |
|---|---|---|---|
| MPinzon: | User | Entry Rights | [ ] |
|  | Group: AcctExecs | Entry Rights | [ B ] |
|  | Effective Rights |  | [ B ] |
|  | User | Attribute Rights: All Properties | [ ] |
|  | Group: AcctExecs | Attribute Rights: All Properties | [ C R A ] |
|  | Effective Rights | All Properties | [ C R A ] |

**Figure 10-18**   Maria's entry and attribute rights to the Sales object

What effective rights does Paul Drake have to the Sales OU? As shown in Figure 10-19, Paul's Supervisor entry right and Supervisor attribute right still give him rights to the object and its properties.

|  | Trustee Assignments |  | Object: Sales |
|---|---|---|---|
| PDrake: | User | Entry Rights | [S ] |
|  | Group: AcctExecs | Entry Rights | [ B ] |
|  |  |  | [S B C D R] |
|  | User | Attribute Rights: All Properties | [S ] |
|  | Group: AcctExecs | Attribute Rights: All Properties | [ C R A] |
|  | Effective Rights | All Properties | [S C R W A] |

**Figure 10-19**   Paul's entry rights to the Sales object

Returning to CBE Labs, the Testing and Evaluation Lab_Staff workgroup has been granted permission to link some of the servers it tests to the CBE Labs network. To facilitate managing the servers and their associated volumes in the CBE Labs eDirectory tree, the NetWare servers and their associated volumes will be placed in the Network OU. The Lab_Staff group members will have Supervisor rights to the Network OU so that they can create and manage objects as needed in this section of the eDirectory tree.

The Network OU is used as an example in this section, but is not configured on your system. However, if you would like to follow the steps David used to grant trustee assignments to the Network OU, you can create this container.

Assigning rights to groups uses the same process as assigning rights to individual users. Entry and attribute rights are granted using the object to which access is being granted or the object that's receiving the trustee assignment. The same steps for granting Georgia trustee rights to the Test&Eval OU are used to grant the Lab_Staff group a trustee assignment to the Network OU. To grant the Lab_Staff group trustee rights to the Network OU from the Network OU object, David did the following:

1. He logged in and started NetWare Administrator.

2. He right-clicked the Network OU, and clicked Trustees of this Object to open the Trustees of Network dialog box.

Notice that the shortcut menu includes the commands Rights to Other Objects and Trustees of this Object. You can use this shortcut menu to open the Rights to Other Objects dialog box or the Trustees of *ObjectName* dialog box.

3. He clicked the Add Trustee button to open the Select Object dialog box.

4. He clicked the Lab_Staff Group object, and then clicked OK to make this group a trustee of the Network OU, as shown in Figure 10-20.

To grant the Lab_Staff group entry and attribute rights to the Test&Eval OU, David did the following:

1. He made sure that Lab_Staff.Test&Eval.CBE_LABS was selected in the Trustees list.

2. In the Object rights section, he clicked the Supervisor check box to select it, and clicked the Browse check box to clear it.

3. In the Property rights section, he made sure the All properties radio button was selected.

**10**

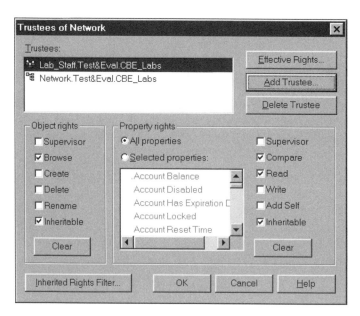

**Figure 10-20** The Trustees of Network dialog box

4. In the Property rights section, he clicked the Supervisor check box to select it, clicked the Compare and Read check boxes to clear them (see Figure 10-21), and then clicked OK to close the Trustees of Network dialog box.

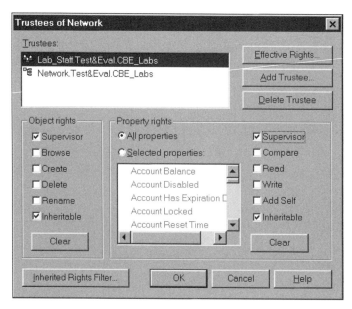

**Figure 10-21** The Network group's entry and attribute rights

## Granting Trustee Assignments to an Organizational Role

You can also create assigned rights by granting trustee assignments to an Organizational Role object. These rights are then available to any user who occupies the organizational role. The advantage of this method is that when a new person takes over a job, you don't have to remove trustee assignments from one user and create them for another—you simply change the occupant of the position. Because trustee assignments belong to the position, they are available only to the person(s) occupying the position. The user's effective rights are the combination of his or her user trustee assignments, group memberships, and organizational roles occupied.

Take a look at using trustee assignments with Organizational Role objects at FDR Investments. Edgar Plank, vice president of Sales, is the occupant of the VP_Sales organizational role in the FDR eDirectory tree. He is also a member of the AcctExecs group, which has the Browse [B] entry right and Compare and Read [C R] attribute rights for the Sales OU. Edgar has no trustee assignments granted directly to him. The VP_Sales Organizational Role object is granted the Create, Delete, and Rename [C D R] entry rights and the Supervisor attribute right to all properties [S C R W A].

What effective rights does Edgar Plank have to the Sales OU? As Figure 10-22 shows, because he doesn't have any trustee assignments as a user, his effective rights are determined by his group membership and the organizational role he occupies.

**10**

|  | Trustee Assignments |  | Object: | 🖳 Sales |
|---|---|---|---|---|
| EPlank: | User | Entry Rights | [         ] | |
| | Group: AcctExecs | Entry Rights | [B       ] | |
| | OrgRole: VP_Sales | Entry Rights | [C D R ] | |
| | Effective Rights | | [B C D R] | |
| | User | Attribute Rights: All Properties | [          ] | |
| | Group: AcctExecs | Attribute Rights: All Properties | [C R   A] | |
| | OrgRole: VP_Sales | Attribute Rights: All Properties | [S         ] | |
| | Effective Rights | All Properties | [S C R W A] | |

**Figure 10-22**    Edgar's entry rights to the FDR object

Paul Drake does not occupy any organizational role in the eDirectory tree. What effective rights does he have to the Sales OU? As Figure 10-23 shows, Paul's Supervisor entry and attribute rights still give him rights to the object and its properties.

| | Trustee Assignments | | Object: | Sales |
|---|---|---|---|---|
| PDrake: | User | Entry Rights | [S | ] |
| | Group: AcctExecs | Entry Rights | [ B | ] |
| | OrgRole: None | Entry Rights | [ | ] |
| | Effective Rights | | [S B C D R] | |
| | User | Attribute Rights: | | |
| | | All Properties | [S | ] |
| | Group: AcctExecs | Attribute Rights: | | |
| | | All Properties | [ C R   A] | |
| | OrgRole: None | Attribute Rights: | | |
| | | All Properties | [ | ] |
| | Effective Rights | All Properties | [S C R W A] | |

**Figure 10-23**  Paul's entry rights

At CBE Labs, Georgia should be granted Supervisor entry and attribute rights to the Test&Eval branch of the eDirectory tree because of her acknowledged skill as a network administrator. However, network administration skills are a requirement for this position so that whoever occupies the position of vice president for Testing and Evaluation can administer the Test&Eval branch of the eDirectory tree. Therefore, it makes sense to assign the Supervisor entry and attribute rights for that branch to the VP_Test&Eval Organizational Role object. Whoever occupies that organizational role will automatically have the necessary rights. Furthermore, the network administrator won't have to delete the trustee assignment for one User object and assign it to another.

David has not removed the [Public] trustee assignment to the [Root] object. Taking this into account, Figure 10-24 shows Georgia's effective rights to the Test&Eval OU after the trustee assignment has been shifted. David needs to delete the trustee assignment for the GBurns User object to the Test&Eval OU and add the VP_Test&Eval object as a trustee. Because the GBurns User object occupies the VP_Test&Eval organizational role, Georgia will have the same access to network resources she had before.

You make trustee assignments for organizational roles in exactly the same way you would for users and groups—using the Trustees of *ObjectName* dialog box or the Rights to Other Objects dialog box. You can also delete trustee assignments with the Delete Trustee button in the Trustees of *ObjectName* dialog box or the Delete Assignment button in the Rights to Other Objects dialog box.

| GBurns: | User | Entry Rights | [ | ] |
|---|---|---|---|---|
| | [Public] trustee | Entry Rights | [ B | ] |
| | Group: Lab_Staff | Entry Rights | [ | ] |
| | OrgRole: VP_Test&Eval | Entry Rights | [S | ] |
| | Effective Rights | | [S B C D R] | |
| | | | | |
| | User | Attribute Rights: | | |
| | | All Properties | [ | ] |
| | [Public] Trustee | Attribute Rights | | |
| | | All Properties | [ | ] |
| | Group: Lab_Staff | Attribute Rights: | | |
| | | All Properties | [ | ] |
| | OrgRole: VP_Test&Eval | Attribute Rights: | | |
| | | All Properties | [S | ] |
| | Effective Rights | All Properties: | [S C R W A] | |

**Figure 10-24**    Georgia's entry rights

To delete Georgia's trustee assignment and grant the VP_Test&Eval organizational role trustee rights to the Test&Eval OU from the Test&Eval OU object, David did the following:

1. He started NetWare Administrator.

2. He clicked the Test&Eval OU, and then clicked Object, Trustees of this Object on the menu bar to open the Trustees of Test&Eval dialog box.

3. He clicked GBurns.Test&Eval.CBE_LABS in the Trustees list (see Figure 10-25).

**10**

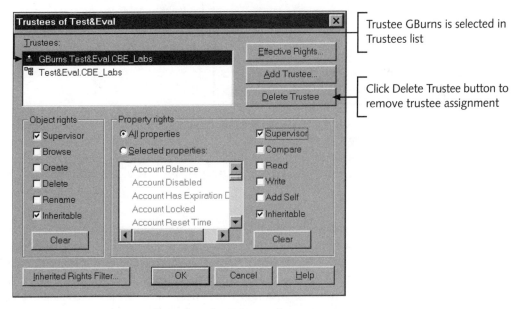

**Figure 10-25**    GBurns selected in the Trustees list

4. He clicked the Delete Trustee button and then clicked Yes to confirm deleting the trustee assignment.

5. He clicked the Add Trustee button to open the Select Object dialog box.

6. He clicked the VP_Test&Eval Organizational Role object, and then clicked OK to make this object a trustee of the Test&Eval OU.

7. In the Object rights section, he clicked the Supervisor check box to select it, and then clicked to clear the Browse check box.

8. In the Property rights section, he made sure the All properties radio button was selected.

9. In the Property rights section, he clicked the Supervisor check box to select it, and then clicked to clear the Compare and Read check boxes (see Figure 10-26).

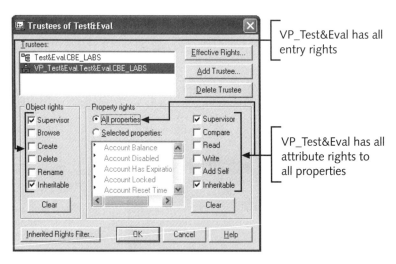

**Figure 10-26**    The VP_Test&Eval Organizational Role object's entry and attribute rights to Test&Eval

10. He clicked OK to close the Trustees of Test&Eval dialog box.

## Inherited Rights

To decrease the number of trustee assignments you need to make, NetWare allows trustee entry and attribute rights granted in a container to flow down to any subcontainers or leaf objects. The process of rights flowing down the tree structure is referred to as **inherited rights**. In an eDirectory tree, inherited rights in a container are rights that were granted to a container higher in the eDirectory tree. These rights are then available to any object in the subordinate container, as shown in Figure 10-27. Without inheritance, you would need to make multiple trustee assignments to containers and subcontainers.

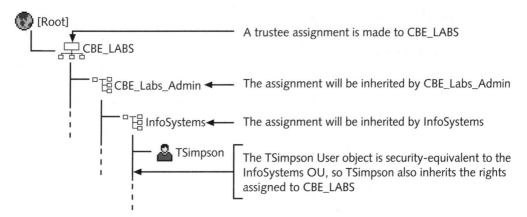

**Figure 10-27**     Inherited rights and container objects

Inherited entry and attribute rights can be blocked by using an **Inherited Rights Filter (IRF)**. In addition, each property has its own IRF that can be used to block rights to just that property. The main difference between eDirectory security and file system security (discussed in the "Managing Directory Rights and File Rights" section) is that with eDirectory security, you can block a container or leaf object from inheriting Supervisor rights.

Any object in a container object is automatically security-equivalent to the container object because of its context in that container. However, you can also create **security equivalence** by directly assigning it; to do this, you open the object's dialog box in NetWare Administrator and go to the Security Equal To page. Granting access rights in the Security Equal To page is similar to granting access rights by making a user a member of a group. Note that making Object A security-equivalent to Object B grants Object A only the rights *specifically granted* to Object B, not to any rights that Object B has because of security equivalence. That is, if Object B is security-equivalent to Object C, Object A does not have the rights that Object B is granted by being security-equivalent to Object C. A common use of security equivalence is to grant certain users Supervisor rights on the network by making them security-equivalent to the Admin user.

 Although an object is security-equivalent to all container objects in the object's complete name, the container objects are not displayed in the list box called "Security Equal to" on the Security Equal To page.

Eleanor Franklin, the president of FDR, has asked the network administrator to grant her Supervisor rights on the network so that she has free reign to check information as needed. To do this, the network administrator has made her security-equivalent to the Admin object. Regardless of any other rights Eleanor has assigned to her, her security equivalence to Admin grants her full Supervisor rights throughout the network.

Edgar Plank has also been made security-equivalent to the Admin user. Although he occupies the VP_Sales organizational role in the eDirectory tree and is a member of the AcctExecs group, he has no trustee assignments granted directly to him. What effective rights does Edgar have to the Investments OU? He doesn't have any trustee assignments as a user, and the rights he has because of his group membership and organizational role occupancy are only for the Sales OU. As Figure 10-28 shows, however, his security equivalence to Admin grants him full access to the Investments OU.

|  | Trustee Assignments | | Object: ⬛ Investments |
|---|---|---|---|
| EPlank: | User | Entry Rights | [          ] |
|  | Group: AcctExecs | Entry Rights | [          ] |
|  | OrgRole: VP_Sales | Entry Rights | [          ] |
|  | Container: FDR | Entry Rights | [          ] |
|  | Security Equivalence: Admin | Entry Rights | [S B C D R] |
|  | Effective Rights | | [S B C D R] |
|  | User | Attribute Rights: | |
|  |  | All Properties | [          ] |
|  | Group: AcctExecs | Attribute Rights | |
|  |  | All Properties | [          ] |
|  | OrgRole: VP_Sales | Attribute Rights: | |
|  |  | All Properties | [          ] |
|  | Container: FDR | Attribute Rights: | |
|  |  | All Properties | [          ] |
|  | Security Equivalence: Admin | Attribute Rights: | |
|  |  | All Properties | [S C R W A] |
|  | Effective Rights | All Properties: | [S C R W A] |

**Figure 10-28**    Edgar's entry rights to the Investments object

Now take a look at an example at CBE Labs. Ted Simpson, the information systems manager for CBE Labs, needs to have the security equivalence of the Admin user. To make Ted security-equivalent to the Admin user, David did the following:

1. He started NetWare Administrator.

2. He double-clicked the TSimpson User object in the InfoSystems OU to open the User: TSimpson dialog box.

3. He scrolled through the page buttons, and clicked the Security Equal To button to display the Security Equal To page, as Figure 10-29 shows.

Although Ted Simpson has security equivalence to the InfoSystems, CBE_Labs_Admin, and CBE_LABS container objects, none of them is listed in the Security Equal to list box. Group memberships, however, give a member security equivalence to the group, so that security equivalence does appear in the Security Equal to list box.

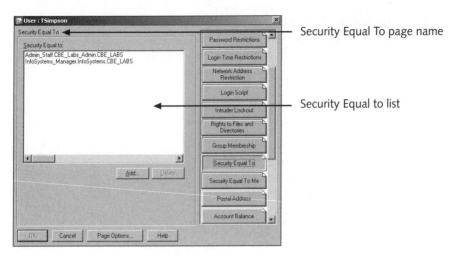

Figure 10-29    The Security Equal To page

4. He clicked the Add button to open the Select Object dialog box, browsed the tree to locate his Admin User object, and clicked to select it (see Figure 10-30).

**10**

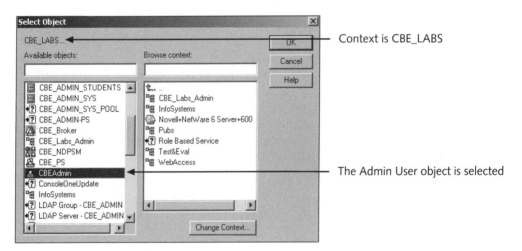

Figure 10-30    Selecting the Admin object

5. He clicked OK to add the Admin.CBE_LABS object to the Security Equal to list box (see Figure 10-31), and clicked OK to close the User:TSimpson Object dialog box.

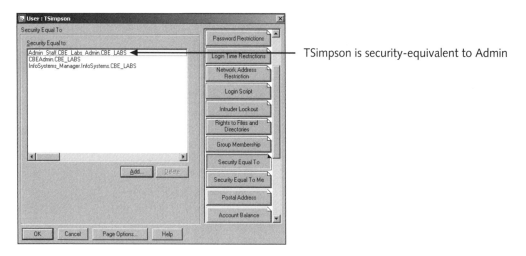

TSimpson is security-equivalent to Admin

**Figure 10-31**   The completed Security Equal To page

Users should not be able to add themselves to their own Security Equal to list box. Otherwise, they could assign themselves security equivalence to the Admin user or another network administrator.

You can grant trustee rights to container objects: the [Root] object, Country objects, Organization objects, and OU objects. These rights will be directly available to any user, group, or organizational role that's in the container object because each object in a container object has security equivalence to the container object. When Object A is security-equivalent to Object B, Object A is granted all the rights that Object B has been granted. Therefore, because the User object GBurns is located in the Test&Eval OU container, GBurns is security-equivalent to Test&Eval.CBE_LABS and automatically has all rights granted to that container object.

Actually, it's a little more complex. An object in a container is security-equivalent to all container objects in the object's complete name. So GBurns is also security-equivalent to CBE_LABS, as Figure 10-32 shows.

Assigning rights to container objects is a powerful way to control trustee assignments. Every object in the container object, or in child container objects in the eDirectory tree, has the access rights of the trustee assignments granted to the container. Therefore, all users, groups, and organizational roles in a container have the same access to network resources created by trustee assignments to the container.

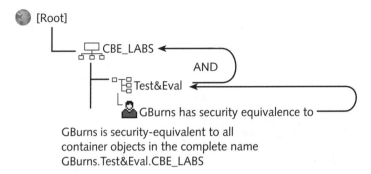

GBurns is security-equivalent to all
container objects in the complete name
GBurns.Test&Eval.CBE_LABS

**Figure 10-32**   Security equivalence and container objects

For example, although the network administrator for FDR Investments has removed the [Public] trustee from the [Root] of the eDirectory tree, he still wants to let users browse the tree. To do this, he has assigned the Browse [B] entry right to the FDR Organization. He has also assigned the FDR Organization Compare and Read [C R] attribute rights to all properties so that users can see property values of objects in the eDirectory tree.

In the FDR eDirectory tree, Edgar Plank occupies the VP_Sales organizational role and is a member of the AcctExecs group. He has no trustee assignments granted directly to him. What effective rights does he have to the FDR Organization? He doesn't have any trustee assignments as a user, and the rights he has because of his group membership and organizational role occupancy are only for the Sales OU. As Figure 10-33 shows, his effective rights are determined by the rights granted to the FDR Organization and by his security equivalence to this object because it's part of his complete name— EPlank.Sales.FDR.

| | Trustee Assignments | Object: ⌾ FDR | |
|---|---|---|---|
| EPlank: | User | Entry Rights | [      ] |
| | Group: AcctExecs | Entry Rights | [      ] |
| | OrgRole: VP_Sales | Entry Rights | [      ] |
| | Container: FDR | | [ B    ] |
| | Effective Rights | | [ B    ] |
| | | | |
| | User | Attribute Rights: | |
| | | All Properties | [      ] |
| | Group: AcctExecs | Attribute Rights: | |
| | | All Properties | [      ] |
| | OrgRole: VP_Sales | Attribute Rights: | |
| | | All Properties | [      ] |
| | Container: FDR | Attribute Rights: | |
| | | All Properties | [ C R  ] |
| | Effective Rights | All Properties: | [ C R  ] |

**Figure 10-33**   Edgar's entry rights

You can see another example of effective rights with the Test&Eval OU in the CBE Labs eDirectory tree. To let all CBE Labs employees in Test&Eval see objects in the Test&Eval OU, you need to make the trustee assignment only to the Test&Eval OU itself. However, it turns out that NetWare automatically makes a container object a trustee of itself, but leaves entry and attribute rights undefined. Undefined rights are indicated by grayed boxes next to the entry and attribute rights, as Figure 10-34 shows.

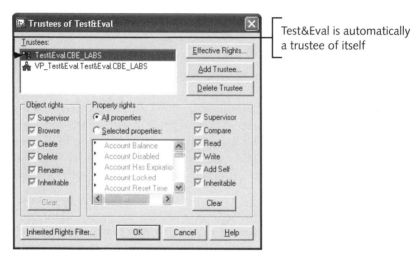

Figure with annotation: "Test&Eval is automatically a trustee of itself"

**Figure 10-34**    The Test&Eval OU as a trustee of itself

Therefore, the network administrator is the one who must assign rights to objects in a container, typically the Browse [B] entry right and the Compare and Read [C R] attribute rights. To change trustee rights for a container object, you would use the process for assigning rights already discussed.

You've learned about trustee assignments made directly to the user or to a group or organizational role associated with the user. You've also seen how making trustee assignments to the [Public] trustee and setting security equivalence to container and leaf objects are ways to gain access to network resources. Generally, the user's effective rights are the sum of all these rights. However, calculating a user's effective rights is a little more complex because of inherited rights. Inherited rights are available in the eDirectory tree because an object is security-equivalent to each container in its complete name. However, inherited rights differ from security equivalence because inheritance works only if no direct trustee assignments are made to an object.

Take a look at how inherited rights are used at FDR Investments. Maria Pinzon is a member of the AcctExecs group but has no trustee assignments granted directly to her. AcctExecs has the Browse [B] entry right and the Compare, Read, and Add/Remove Self [C R A] attribute rights for all properties to the Sales OU. No rights are granted to the [Public] trustee. The FDR network administrator has just granted the Browse [B] entry right and the Compare and Read [C R] attribute rights for all properties to the FDR Organization. What effective rights does Maria have to the Sales OU object? Because she has specific trustee assignments for the AcctExecs group, the rights granted to the FDR Organization have no effect on her rights in the Sales OU, as Figure 10-35 shows.

| | Trustee Assignments | Object: Sales | |
|---|---|---|---|
| MPinzon: | User | Entry Rights | [          ] |
| | Group: AcctExecs | Entry Rights | [ B        ] |
| | [Public] trustee | Entry Rights | [          ] |
| | Container: Sales | Entry Rights | [          ] |
| | Container: FDR | Entry Rights | NO EFFECT |
| | Effective Rights | | [ B        ] |
| | User | Attribute Rights: All Properties | [          ] |
| | Group: AcctExecs | Attribute Rights: All Properties | [ C R  A ] |
| | [Public] trustee | Attribute Rights: All Properties | [          ] |
| | Container: Sales | Attribute Rights: All Properties | [          ] |
| | Container: FDR | Attribute Rights: All Properties | NO EFFECT |
| | Effective Rights | All Properties: | [ C R  A ] |

**Figure 10-35**   Maria's effective rights in Sales

What effective rights does Maria have to the Investments OU? Her group membership has no specific rights granted here. Therefore, her rights are those inherited from the trustee assignments granted to the FDR Organization, as shown in Figure 10-36.

Maria inherited attribute rights from the FDR container object. However, attribute rights are inherited only if they are granted to all properties of the object. For example, if the FDR Organization had been granted only the Compare and Read [C R] attribute rights to object names instead of to all properties, containers lower in the eDirectory tree would not inherit these rights. Therefore, if no trustee assignment is made for a user or group in a container, the user or group inherits rights from the parent container. Making a new trustee assignment to the user or group to which the user belongs can modify a user's effective rights in a container. The rights in the new trustee assignment will override the inherited rights for that group or user name in the specified container, as in Maria's rights to the Sales OU.

|  | Trustee Assignments |  | Object: 🖿 Investments |  |  |
|---|---|---|---|---|---|
| MPinzon: | User | Entry Rights | [ |  | ] |
|  | Group: AcctExecs | Entry Rights | [ |  | ] |
|  | [Public] trustee | Entry Rights | [ |  | ] |
|  | Container: Sales | Entry Rights | [ |  | ] |
|  | Container: FDR | Entry Rights | [ B | | ] |
|  | Effective Rights |  | [ B |  | ] |
|  | User | Attribute Rights: |  |  |  |
|  |  | All Properties | [ |  | ] |
|  | Group: AcctExecs | Attribute Rights: |  |  |  |
|  |  | All Properties | [ |  | ] |
|  | [Public] trustee | Attribute Rights: |  |  |  |
|  |  | All Properties | [ |  | ] |
|  | Container: Sales | Attribute Rights: |  |  |  |
|  |  | All Properties | [ |  | ] |
|  | Container: FDR | Attribute Rights: |  |  |  |
|  |  | All Properties | [ C R | | ] |
|  | Effective Rights | All Properties: | [ C R |  | ] |

**Figure 10-36**    Maria's effective rights in Investments

## The Inherited Rights Filter

When you make a specific trustee assignment in a container, the assignment overrides any rights inherited from a parent container. You can also block rights from being inherited even if no specific trustee assignment is made. When you do not want a child container to inherit trustee assignments, NetWare enables you to block rights from being inherited by providing an IRF for each container object and directory. The IRF blocks selected rights from passing into the lower container object's structure. When you first create a container, the IRF allows all rights to be inherited. Thereafter, removing rights from the IRF prevents the container or directory from inheriting rights no longer specified in the IRF.

The IRF filters rights inherited from a higher container object, but does not affect a trustee assignment made in the current container object.

An IRF is created for every object and is used to determine which rights a trustee inherits. You can picture the IRF as a series of gates—one for each right (see Figure 10-37).

Entry Rights IRF:

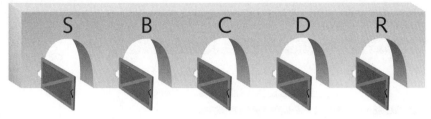

Attribute Rights IRF:

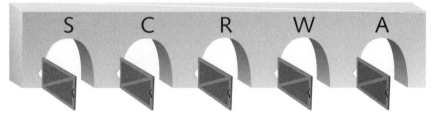

**Figure 10-37** The Inherited Rights Filter for entry and attribute rights

Initially, as Figure 10-37 shows, the IRF allows all rights to be inherited—all the gates are open. You can also see this in NetWare Administrator's Inherited Rights Filter dialog box (see Figure 10-38). Figure 10-39 shows an IRF for entry rights in ConsoleOne.

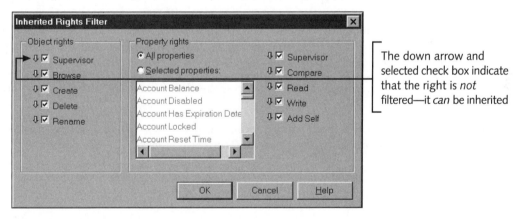

**Figure 10-38** The Inherited Rights Filter dialog box in NetWare Administrator

In Figure 10-38, all the check boxes are selected and a down arrow appears next to each check box, indicating that the right is not being filtered. That is, the gate is open and the right can be inherited. To filter a right—to prevent it from being inherited—clear the corresponding check box in the Inherited Rights Filter dialog box for the object. This "closes the gate" and stops inherited rights from getting through.

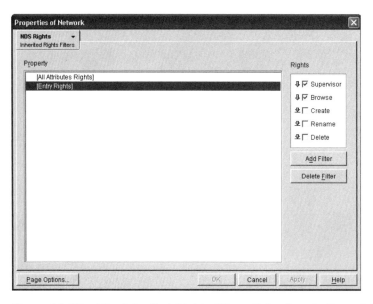

**Figure 10-39**    The Inherited Rights Filters dialog box in ConsoleOne

For example, the Lab_Staff group at CBE Labs now has Supervisor rights to the Network OU. The group does not want other users to be able to modify this object or its properties. Therefore, the group will use the IRF for the Network object to block the Create, Delete, and Rename [C D R] entry rights and the Supervisor, Write, and Add/Remove Self [S W A] attribute rights from being inherited. Then the "gates" to Network will look like Figure 10-40.

In NetWare Administrator, you can access the IRF for an object through the Trustees of *ObjectName* dialog box by following these general steps:

1. Click the object name or icon, and then click Object, Trustees of this Object on the menu bar to open the Trustees of *ObjectName* dialog box.
   *or*
   Right-click the object name or icon, and then click Trustees of this Object to open the Trustees of *ObjectName* dialog box.

Network Entry Rights IRF:

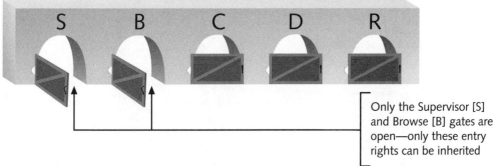

Only the Supervisor [S] and Browse [B] gates are open—only these entry rights can be inherited

Network Attribute Rights IRF:

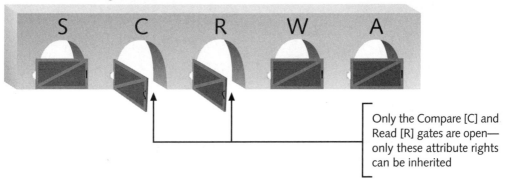

Only the Compare [C] and Read [R] gates are open—only these attribute rights can be inherited

**Figure 10-40**     Network's IRF for entry and attribute rights

    2. Click the Inherited Rights Filter button.

    3. Use the settings in the Inherited Rights Filter dialog box to manage inherited entry and attribute rights.

To set the IRF for the Network OU, David did the following:

    1. He started NetWare Administrator.

    2. He browsed the tree to locate the Network OU and clicked to select it.

    3. He clicked Object, Trustees of this Object on the menu bar to open the Trustees of Network dialog box, as Figure 10-41 shows.

    4. He clicked the Inherited Rights Filter button to open the Inherited Rights Filter dialog box.

    5. In the Object rights section, he clicked the Create, Delete, and Rename check boxes to clear them. In the Property rights section, he clicked the Supervisor, Write, and Add Self check boxes to clear them (see Figure 10-42), and then clicked OK to return to the Trustees of Network dialog box.

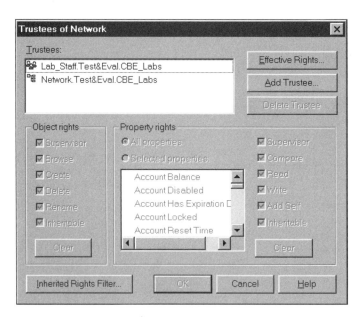

**Figure 10-41** The Trustees of Network dialog box

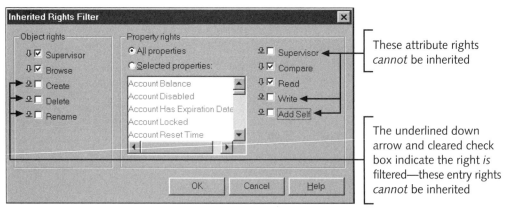

**Figure 10-42** The completed Inherited Rights Filter dialog box for the Network OU

Notice in Figure 10-42 that each down arrow has been replaced by an arrow with a line under it for all rights that are being filtered out. This symbol and the cleared check box indicate a filtered out or blocked ability to inherit a trustee right. Remember that the IRF only reduces rights; it doesn't add to them.

When you are calculating a trustee's effective rights for an object, you must subtract any inherited rights filtered out by the object's IRF. Remember, however, that the IRF blocks only inherited rights, not the rights that can be directly granted to an object. Remember that if trustee rights are directly granted to an object, the grant stops all inherited rights so that the IRF has no effect. The IRF blocks only inherited rights when such rights can, in fact, be inherited.

For example, Maria Pinzon, a member of the AcctExecs group at FDR Investments, has no trustee assignments granted directly to her. AcctExecs has the Browse [B] entry right and the Compare, Read, and Add/Remove Self [C R A] attribute rights for all properties to the Sales OU only, not other branches of the eDirectory tree. There are no rights granted to the [Public] trustee.

The FDR network administrator has granted the Browse [B] entry right and the Compare and Read [C R] attribute rights for all properties to the FDR Organization. However, because the Investments group has decided that it doesn't want users reading property values for objects in the Investments OU, the network administrator has also implemented an IRF for the Investment OU that blocks all attribute rights except Supervisor [C R W A]. What effective rights does Maria have to the Investments OU? Her group membership has no specific rights granted. Therefore, her rights are those she inherits from trustee assignments granted to the FDR Organization, minus those blocked by the IRF, as Figure 10-43 shows. Maria inherited the Compare and Read [C R] attribute rights to Investments from the FDR container object. However, the IRF blocks these attribute rights, so Maria has no attribute rights to Investments.

**10**

Handle the Supervisor right carefully in IRFs. Novell's Technical Support groups claim that many of the calls they receive are related to incorrect use of IRFs. Although the Supervisor right cannot be removed from an IRF for a directory or file (as you'll learn in the "Managing Directory Rights and File Rights" section), it can be removed from an IRF for an object. This lets you split administrative duties throughout the eDirectory tree. For example, CBE Labs could have two network administrators for its offices in Great Britain and the United States. Blocking the Supervisor right appropriately by using IRFs would ensure that each network administrator had control of only his or her portion of the CBE Labs eDirectory tree.

There is a potential problem, however. If no trustee was assigned Supervisor rights to an object and the object's IRF blocked inherited Supervisor rights, the object would be cut off from anyone's control. To help prevent this problem, Novell has designed the NetWare 6 utilities so that you cannot block the Supervisor entry right unless some object has been granted specific Supervisor rights to the object.

|  | Trustee Assignments |  | Object: Investments |
|---|---|---|---|
| MPinzon: | User | Entry Rights | [        ] |
|  | Group: AcctExecs | Entry Rights | [        ] |
|  | [Public] trustee | Entry Rights | [        ] |
|  | Container: Investments | Entry Rights | [        ] |
|  | Container: FDR | Entry Rights | [ B     ] |
| LESS | IRF: Investments | Entry Rights | [        ] |
|  | Effective Rights |  | [ B     ] |
|  | User | Attribute Rights: All Properties | [        ] |
|  | Group: AcctExecs | Attribute Rights: All Properties | [        ] |
|  | [Public] trustee | Attribute Rights: All Properties | [        ] |
|  | Container: Investments | Attribute Rights: All Properties | [        ] |
|  | Container: FDR | Attribute Rights: All Properties | [ C R     ] |
| LESS | IRF: Investments | Attribute Rights: All Properties | [ C R W A] |
|  | Effective Rights | All Properties: | [        ] |

**Figure 10-43**    Maria's effective rights in Investments

Unfortunately, the Supervisor right can be assigned to any object, including the object that will have the IRF set. For example, you could assign the Supervisor entry right to the Test&Eval OU in the CBE Labs eDirectory tree and then block the Supervisor right in the Test&Eval OU's IRF. Because the Supervisor entry right had been assigned, this would be permitted. Doing so, however, would cut off the Test&Eval branch of the tree because a user cannot access the granted Supervisor right—you can't log in as an OU, only as a User object. So be careful to assign an object's Supervisor entry right to a User object before using the object IRF. In general, IRFs should be used only when absolutely necessary. A network administrator can usually control access to network resources by directly assigning trustee rights without using IRFs.

## eDirectory Default Rights

The eDirectory security system is powerful and flexible, allowing network administrators to tailor their systems to meet special needs. Knowing what rights are available by default and where they come from is important in planning for eDirectory security needs and troubleshooting the eDirectory security system. When eDirectory is installed on the first server, the [Public], [Root], and Admin objects are created. The Admin object is assigned the Supervisor entry right to the root of the new eDirectory tree, thereby making Admin a supervisor of the entire network, including all servers. Giving the Supervisor entry right to a NetWare Server object automatically gives that user Supervisor file system rights to the server's volumes and file system. In addition to the Admin user assignment, during installation the [Public] trustee is given the Browse entry right all the way to the root of the tree, so users can view all objects in the tree by using the CX /T /A /R command before logging in. If this creates a security problem in your organization, remove [Public] as a trustee of the root of the tree, and assign the Browse entry right to individual users, groups, or containers. You can give all users who have logged in to the network rights to browse the entire tree by making the [Root] object a trustee of the tree with Browse entry rights.

## Managing Directory Rights and File Rights

Directory and file rights control access to the network file system resources. The same concepts and techniques you learned for trustee assignments of entry and attribute rights can be applied to directory and file rights. Trustee assignments for directories and files can be made to the same objects that can have trustee assignments for objects and properties. When you are assigning directory and file rights, the assignment is made by using the user's User object or the directory or file object's dialog box. Granting trustee rights to a directory automatically grants the same rights to all files in that directory. To change the trustee rights for a file in that directory, you must change the rights assigned for that specific file.

10

Although granting the Supervisor directory or file right automatically grants all directory and file rights, many network administrators specifically grant all other rights, too, when granting the Supervisor right.

### Rights Assigned to the User

As with entry and attribute rights, the simplest and most straightforward way for a user to gain effective rights is to be granted a trustee assignment as a user. A simple example follows; then you'll see how trustee assignments are made at CBE Labs. Figure 10-44 shows the Volume Design Form for the FDR_SERVER01_DATA volume.

Paul Drake needs to be able to manage the Sales directory and its subdirectories on the FDR_SERVER01_DATA volume. He will be granted all rights—including the Supervisor right—to the Sales directory. When the Supervisor right is granted in the directory, it gives Paul the Supervisor right to all files in that directory, as Figure 10-45 shows.

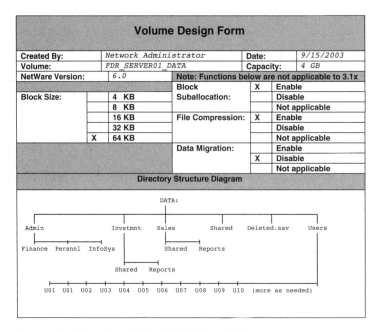

**Figure 10-44** The FDR_SERVER01_DATA volume

| | | Trustee Assignments | | Object: 🖳 Sales | |
|---|---|---|---|---|---|
| PDrake: | | User | Directory Rights | [S ] | |
| | | Effective Rights | | [S R W C E M F A] | |
| | | User | File Rights: | [S ] | |
| | | | | may be modified for each file as needed | |
| | | Effective Rights | | [S R W C E M F A] | |

**Figure 10-45** Paul's effective rights in Sales

Now consider another example: assigning directory and file rights at CBE Labs. Georgia Burns will be given all rights (Supervisor and all others) so that she can administer the CBE_EVAL_SYS and CBE_EVAL_DATA volumes. Figure 10-46 shows the recommended directory structure for CBE_EVAL_SYS; Figure 10-47, the recommended directory structure for CBE_EVAL_DATA.

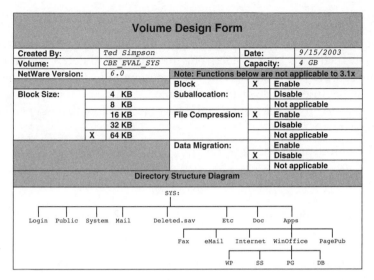

**Figure 10-46**    The Volume Design Form for the CBE_EVAL_SYS volume

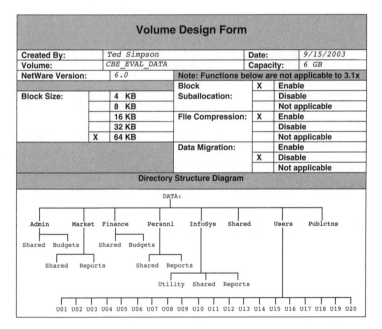

**Figure 10-47**    The Volume Design Form for the CBE_EVAL_DATA volume

10

## Assigning Trustee Rights to a Directory or File from the Trustee Object

As with entry rights, you're assigning trustee rights from the object being granted the trustee assignment, such as a User object. This procedure is different from assigning trustee rights through the object that access is being granted to (such as a directory or a container object) because you do it from the object's dialog box. To grant directory and file trustee rights to an object from the trustee object, follow these general steps in NetWare Administrator:

1. Click the object, and then press Enter.

   *or*

   Click the object, and then click Object, Details on the menu bar.

   *or*

   Right-click the object, and then click Details on the shortcut menu.

2. Switch to the Rights to Files and Directories page.

3. Click the Find button to open the Search Context dialog box and search the eDirectory tree for existing trustee assignments in the desired context.

4. Click the Add button and use the Select Object dialog box to select the directory or file for which trustee rights are being granted.

5. Click the corresponding check boxes in the Rights section to select or deselect the rights to be granted.

6. Click OK.

When the trustee assignment is made from the User object (or other trustee object), NetWare can first search the eDirectory tree to find and list the directories and files for which the user has rights assigned. The context for this search—all of the tree or a branch of it—is specified as part of the search. Searching the eDirectory tree takes time, so it's faster to limit the area of the tree that needs to be evaluated. Normally, you should limit the search context to only the part of the eDirectory tree that includes the objects for which you are granting trustee rights to the user. This step is not required for adding a new trustee assignment, but it's helpful to see what assignments have already been made so that you aren't inadvertently duplicating a previous assignment.

To see how this method works, take a look at how David gave Georgia Burns her trustee assignment to the root of the CBE_EVAL_DATA volume:

1. He started NetWare Administrator.

2. He right-clicked the GBurns User object, and then clicked Details to open the User: GBurns dialog box.

3. He scrolled through the page buttons, and clicked the Rights to Files and Directories button to open the Rights to Files and Directories page, as Figure 10-48 shows.

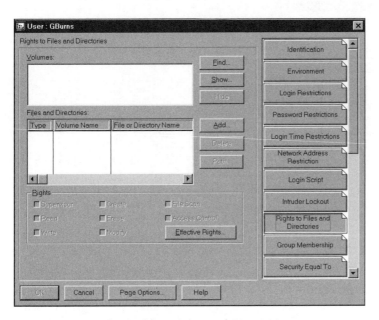

**Figure 10-48** The Rights to Files and Directories page

4. He clicked the Find button to open the Search Context dialog box, and then clicked the browse button to open the Select Object dialog box. He clicked the Test&Eval OU, and then clicked OK.

5. In the Search Context dialog box, Test&Eval.CBE_LABS was displayed in the Begin search in context text box. He clicked the Search entire subtree check box, and then clicked OK. NetWare searched for directory and file trustee assignments for Georgia Burns, and then displayed them in the Volumes list and the Files and Directories list. As Figure 10-49 shows, the only existing trustee assignment for GBurns is to her home directory on the CBE_EVAL_DATA volume.

Notice that if you were using an alias for CBE_EVAL_DATA, the NetWare Administrator window would show the actual server and volume name: CBE_ADMIN_DATA.

10

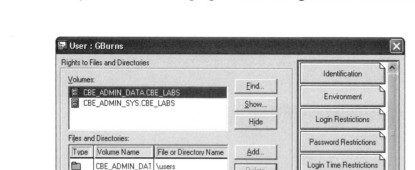

**Figure 10-49**    The User: GBurns dialog box showing current directory and file trustee rights

 The eDirectory configuration in your test network might vary from the one shown in the figures. For example, if there's no actual second server in your test network, you will have only an Alias object to represent CBE_EVAL. In this case, the actual assignment will be to the CBE_ADMIN_DATA volume, even though NetWare Administrator and other Novell utilities might show the Alias object's name.

6. He clicked the Add button to open the Select Object dialog box.

7. He selected the CBE_EVAL_DATA Volume object, and then clicked OK to assign GBurns default trustee rights of Read [R] and File Scan [F] to the root of the CBE_EVAL_DATA:\ directory.

 If you are using an Alias object for CBE_EVAL_DATA, NetWare Administrator does not show this assignment at first, but this is only temporary. When you save this configuration and then reopen this page, the assignment will show the "true" server and volume name, not the CBE_EVAL_DATA alias.

8. He clicked all the cleared check boxes in the Rights section to assign GBurns all trustee rights to this directory (see Figure 10-50), and clicked OK.

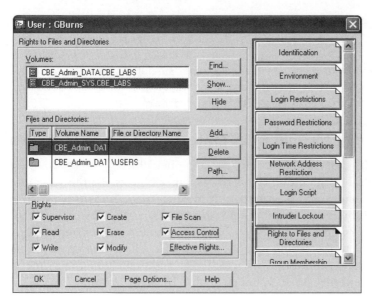

**Figure 10-50**    GBurns assigned all trustee rights to the CBE_EVAL_DATA:\ directory

## Rights Assigned to Groups, Profiles, and Organizational Roles

**10**

Directory and file rights can also be assigned to groups and organizational roles, just as entry and attribute rights were assigned. In addition, you can grant trustee rights to Profile objects. You have already learned that the Profile object is similar to the Group object, with the advantage of being able to have its own login script. Assigning directory and file rights to a Profile object is a convenient method of assigning directory and file rights to those who use the Profile object's login script.

The methods discussed earlier for assigning directory and file rights to users are also used for granting rights to groups and organizational roles. When you decide whether to assign rights to an organizational role, a group, or individual users, the same advantages still apply: It is easier to administer rights to organizational roles and groups. By granting rights to organizational roles and groups, users automatically get appropriate rights if they need them, and removing a user from a group or organizational role effectively removes the user's rights.

For example, Georgia Burns has decided to give the Lab_Staff group Read and File Scan rights [R F] to the CBE_EVAL_DATA volume. The Lab_Staff group keeps its data in this volume, and these rights will let everyone see what files exist and be able to open and read them. However, [R F] rights will not let users change, delete, or rename the files, so Georgia must grant these additional rights to the Lab_Staff group, which also needs these rights to the Network directory (and its subdirectories). Therefore, Georgia will grant the Lab_Staff group Write, Create, Erase, and Modify rights [W C E M] to the Network directory. Because trustee assignments made in one directory are inherited by (flow down to) subdirectories, the Network group will inherit the same rights in the Network\Shared, Network\Testdata, and Network\Reports subdirectories.

 The Network directory and its subdirectories are not configured on your system. However, you can create them if you want to follow the steps David uses later in this chapter to set an IRF for this directory.

## Rights Assigned to Container Objects and Security Equivalence

You can assign directory and file rights to container objects just as you assigned entry and attribute rights. For granting rights to container objects, use the same methods you used to assign directory and file rights to individual users. Security equivalencies work the same way. If Object A is security-equivalent to Object B, Object A is granted all the directory and file rights that Object B has been granted. For example, because Ted is security-equivalent to the Admin user at CBE Labs, he effectively has the same directory and file rights as the Admin user. This gives Ted all rights, including the Supervisor right, to all directories and files on all volumes of all CBE Labs servers.

## Reduce Use of IRFs

The need for an IRF as part of your security plan might indicate that you have placed a directory requiring more security within a general-purpose directory and that you need to rethink your directory structure design. It's usually easier to troubleshoot explicit trustee assignments than trace the use of IRFs. However, inherited rights work almost the same for directory and file rights as they do for entry and attribute rights, with one important exception: The IRF cannot block the Supervisor [S] right for directory and file rights. Figure 10-51 illustrates a way to visualize IRFs for directory and file rights.

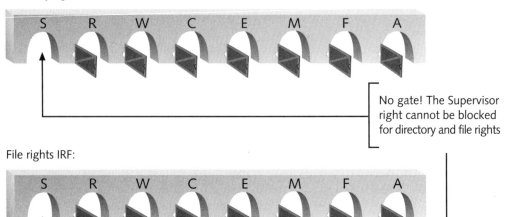

**Figure 10-51**    The Inherited Rights Filter for directory and file rights

The IRF for a directory or file is accessed through the *ObjectName* dialog box. To use NetWare Administrator to modify the IRF for directory or file trustee rights of a directory or file, follow these general steps:

1. Click the directory, filename, or icon, and then click Object, Details on the menu bar to open the *ObjectName* dialog box.
   *or*
   Double-click the directory, filename, or icon to open the *ObjectName* dialog box.
   *or*
   Right-click the object name or icon, and then click Details to open the *ObjectName* dialog box.
   *or*
   Click to select the directory or file, and then press Enter.

2. Click the Trustees of this Directory or Trustees of this File button.

3. On the Trustees of this Directory or Trustees of this File page, use check boxes in the Inheritance filter section to set the IRF. A selected check box enables the right to be inherited; a cleared check box blocks inheritance.

4. Click OK.

The method of setting an IRF for directories and files is the same as setting an IRF for objects and properties. The IRF default is all check boxes selected, which lets all rights be inherited, and you must clear a check box to block the right's inheritance. The only difference is the directory and file Supervisor right, which cannot be blocked.

For example, the Lab_Staff group at CBE Labs wants only those users who have specifically been granted rights to the CBE_EVAL_DATA:Network directory to be able to use that directory. To set the IRF for this directory, David did the following:

1. He started NetWare Administrator.

2. He expanded the eDirectory tree to view the directories on the CBE_EVAL_ DATA volume. He clicked the Network directory object to select it, and then clicked Object, Details on the menu bar.

3. He clicked the Trustees of this Directory button to display the Trustees of this Directory page, as Figure 10-52 shows.

4. Looking at the Inheritance filter section, he noticed that all the check boxes were selected. The Supervisor check box was selected *and* grayed out, indicating that he could not change the setting for this right. He clicked all the check boxes except Supervisor to block those rights from being inherited, as Figure 10-53 shows, and then clicked OK.

**10**

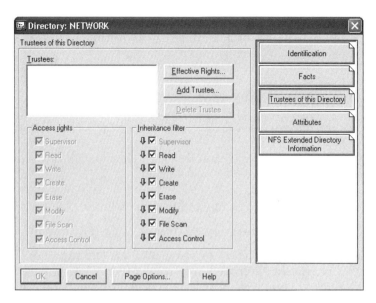

**Figure 10-52**    The Trustees of this Directory page

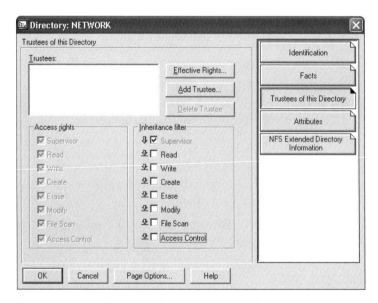

**Figure 10-53**    The completed Trustees of this Directory page

  Notice that in Figure 10-53, each down arrow next to a check box has been replaced by an arrow with a line under it for all rights being filtered out. This symbol and the cleared check box indicate a filtered out or blocked ability to inherit a trustee right.

As with entry and attribute rights, users' effective rights are a combination of their assigned and inherited rights, and it's always a *user* who actually uses trustee rights. You can calculate a user's effective directory or file rights to a directory or file as follows:

1. Combine the assigned rights from trustee assignments made to:

   - The *user*
   - The user as a member of a *group*
   - The user as a member of a *profile*
   - The user as an occupant of an *organizational role*
   - The user as an occupant of a *container object*
   - The user as security-equivalent to other objects

   If the user has assigned rights granted to the directory or file, the assigned rights take precedence over inherited rights, inherited rights do not apply, and the IRF has no effect. This combination of rights is the user's effective rights.

2. If the user has no assigned rights granted, the user's trustee assignments granted in a parent container object or directory are inherited. The inherited rights must be checked against the IRF for the directory or file. The inherited rights not blocked by the IRF are the user's effective rights.

Take a look at how inherited rights work in the FDR Investments file system. Maria Pinzon is a member of the AcctExecs group, but has no trustee assignments granted directly to her. AcctExecs has the Read, Write, Create, Erase, Modify, and File Scan directory rights [R W C E M F] to the FDR_SERVER01/DATA:Sales directory. There is an Everyone group at FDR, and Maria, along with everyone else, is a group member. The Everyone group has Read and File Scan rights [R F] to FDR_SERVER01/DATA: (the [Root] directory on the DATA volume). No directory or file rights are granted to the [Public] trustee. No other trustee assignments affect Maria directly, but IRFs could limit her inherited rights. What effective rights does she have to the FDR_SERVER01/DATA:Sales directory? Because she has specific trustee assignments to Sales from the AcctExecs group, the rights granted to the Everyone group to the [Root] directory have no effect on her rights in the Sales directory, as Figure 10-54 shows.

|          | Trustee Assignments | Object: 📁 Sales | |
| --- | --- | --- | --- |
| MPinzon: | User | Directory | [           ] |
|  | Group: AcctExecs | Directory | [ R W C E M F ] |
|  | [Public] trustee | Directory | [           ] |
|  | Group: Everyone | [Root] of DATA | [ R       F ] |
|  | IRF: | Directory | [           ] |
|  | Effective Rights |  | [ R W C E M F ] |

**Figure 10-54**   Maria's effective rights in the Sales directory

What effective rights does Maria have to the FDR_SERVER01/DATA:Admin directory? Because she has no specific trustee assignments to Admin from the AcctExecs group, the rights granted to the Everyone group to the [Root] directory will be inherited, subject to an IRF. There is no IRF for Admin, however. Figure 10-55 shows Maria's rights in the Admin directory.

| | Trustee Assignments | Object: 📁 Admin | | |
|---|---|---|---|---|
| MPinzon: | User | Directory | [ | ] |
| | Group: AcctExecs | Directory | [ | ] |
| | [Public] trustee | Directory | [ | ] |
| | Group: Everyone | [Root] of DATA | [ R | F ] |
| | IRF: | Admin | [ | ] |
| | Effective Rights | | [ R | F ] |

**Figure 10-55**     Maria's effective rights in the Admin directory

What effective rights does Maria have to the FDR_SERVER01/DATA:Invstmnt directory? Because she has no specific trustee assignments to Invstmnt from the AcctExecs group, the rights granted to the Everyone group to the [Root] directory will again be inherited, subject to an IRF. Invstmnt does have an IRF, which blocks the Read, Write, Create, Erase, Modify, File Scan, and Access Control [R W C E M F A] directory rights. Figure 10-56 shows Maria's rights in the Invstmnt directory. In this case, the IRF completely blocks any rights Maria would have had in the Invstmnt directory. She cannot see or use this directory, any of its subdirectories, or any of the files in any of those directories.

| | Trustee Assignments | Object: 📁 Invstmnt | | |
|---|---|---|---|---|
| MPinzon: | User | Directory | [ | ] |
| | Group: AcctExecs | Directory | [ | ] |
| | [Public] trustee | Directory | [ | ] |
| | Group: Everyone | [Root] of DATA | [ R | F ] |
| | IRF: | Directory | [ R W C E M F A ] | |
| | Effective Rights | | [ | ] |

**Figure 10-56**     Maria's effective rights in the Invstmnt directory

# Planning Directory Tree and File System Security

Computing effective rights can be a complex task when multiple container, profile group, and user trustee assignments are involved. Good strategies in planning eDirectory tree and file system security include using as few trustee assignments as possible and keeping IRFs to a minimum. If you need to use an IRF, you might need to rethink your assignment of rights, the organization of your eDirectory tree, or the directories in your file system. Imagine, for example, that you are a network administrator for a company and your predecessor created a directory structure in which word-processing files were stored in subdirectories of the Software\WP directory, as Figure 10-57 shows.

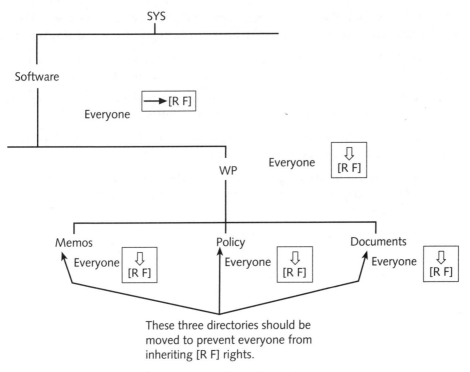

**Figure 10-57**   The directory structure for Software\WP

Your predecessor created a Group object named Everyone (all users are added to the group) and made this group a trustee of Software with [R F] rights, so all users inherit [R F] rights to the document subdirectories. This creates a security problem because all users have the ability to read any document. To eliminate this problem, set the IRFs of the document subdirectories to block the inherited rights and then grant appropriate users the necessary trustee assignments to these subdirectories. Although this solution will work, it doesn't address the real problem: Data directories and software directories should be in separate locations. The best solution in this example is to move the document subdirectories to another location in the file system.

To help keep trustee assignment security as simple and effective as possible, a network administrator should follow two simple strategies:

- Plan rights from the top down.
- Plan trustee assignments in this order: groups, profiles, organizational roles, and container objects.

Remember that rights are inherited from parent containers into subordinate containers and from parent directories into subordinate subdirectories and files. Planning the eDirectory tree and the network directory structure from the top down takes advantage of this principle. The following guidelines can help you use a top-down strategy:

- At the top of your directory structure, place directories that are least often accessed. Place the most frequently accessed directories at the bottom.

- Start planning rights at the department or highest-level directory, and work down to the subdirectories and files within it.

- Grant only the rights the user or group needs at any given level of the eDirectory tree or the file system.

- Use the inheritance principle. Use IRFs to protect objects and directories against trustees inheriting unwanted rights, but keep IRFs to an absolute minimum.

- Create and use an Everyone group.

When planning trustee assignments, start by assigning rights to the groups and profiles with the most users. Often, it's helpful to create an Everyone group and assign common trustee rights for all users to this group. Next, assign rights to other groups and profiles. It helps to think of profiles as simply another type of group—a group created specifically to enable assigning resources on login via the login script. Therefore, profiles often group together users who can benefit from common directory and file trustee assignments. Organizational roles can also be thought of as a type of group (although often a group with only one member). Use organizational roles to allocate specialized resources that occupants of that role need. Container objects provide the basis for yet another type of group: people who share a common location in the organizational schema. Their common resource needs can be the basis for trustee assignments.

Finally, make individual user trustee assignments to keep user trustee assignments to a minimum. Usually, some group or organizational role is more appropriate for assigning trustee rights. Some network administrators go to the extreme of never making trustee assignments to users; they make the trustee assignment to a group name instead, and then make the user who needs the access rights a member of that group. When assigning trustee rights to groups and users, follow the same pattern as when you planned rights assignments:

1. Assign rights to groups, starting with the Everyone group.

2. Assign rights to profiles.

3. Assign rights to organizational roles.

4. Assign rights to container objects.

5. Assign rights to individual users.

# DIRECTORY AND FILE ATTRIBUTES

**Attributes** are flags or codes that can be associated with files and directories. They indicate to the NetWare operating system what type of processing can be performed on the associated file or directory.

> Attributes apply only to file system components (directories and files). They do not apply to eDirectory objects.

For additional protection against accidental change or deletion, the network administrator often places attributes on directories and files. Attributes can also specify certain processing, such as making a file shareable or purging all files that have been deleted from a directory. Attributes override users' effective rights in a directory or file. If a file is flagged with the Read Only attribute, the only operations you can perform on the file—no matter what your effective rights are—are Read and File Scan. If, for example, a user has the Supervisor right to the Sales directory, he or she would inherit all access rights to the files and subdirectories in the Sales structure. If a file named Zipcode.dat is stored in the Sales directory and flagged with the Read Only attribute, this user has only Read access to the Zipcode.dat file. Because this user has a Supervisor trustee assignment to the Sales directory, however, he or she can use the Modify right to remove the Read Only attribute and then change or even delete the Zipcode.dat file.

**10**

## Attribute Security

Table 10-6 lists in alphabetical order all the attributes NetWare 6 uses, along with their corresponding abbreviations and whether they can be applied to directories, files, or both.

**Table 10-6**    NetWare 6 Directory and File Attributes

| Attribute | Applies To | Abbreviation |
| --- | --- | --- |
| Archive Needed | File | A |
| Can't Compress | File | Cc |
| Compressed | File | Co |
| Copy Inhibit | File | Ci |
| Delete Inhibit | File, Directory | Di |
| Don't Compress | File, Directory | Dc |
| Don't Migrate | File, Directory | Dm |
| Don't Suballocate | File | Ds |
| Execute Only | File | X |
| Hidden | File, Directory | H |
| Immediate Compress | File, Directory | Ic |
| Index | File | I |

**Table 10-6**    NetWare 6 Directory and File Attributes (continued)

| Attribute | Applies To | Abbreviation |
| --- | --- | --- |
| Migrated | File | M |
| Normal | File, Directory | N |
| Purge | File, Directory | P |
| Read Only | File | Ro |
| Read Write | File | Rw |
| Rename Inhibit | File, Directory | Ri |
| Shareable | File | Sh |
| System | File, Directory | Sy |
| Transactional | File | T |

Of these 21 attributes, 4 are from DOS: Archive Needed (A), Hidden (H), Read Only (Ro in NetWare, just R in DOS), and System (Sy in NetWare, just S in DOS). NetWare supports the 4 DOS attributes and adds 17 more.

 NetWare 6 also enables the Read Audit and Write Audit attributes, but Novell does not use them yet. Although these attributes can be assigned to files, Novell has not yet defined their use, so network administrators do not use them.

## Archive Needed

The **Archive Needed (A)** attribute is automatically assigned to files when their contents are modified and is one of the four DOS attributes NetWare supports. Copy or backup utilities can remove this attribute after the file is copied to another storage location. This attribute is important in controlling what files are copied to a backup disk. You can back up only files that have been changed since the last backup.

## Can't Compress

The **Can't Compress (Cc)** attribute is a status flag showing that the file can't be compressed with NetWare file compression because the compression wouldn't save a significant amount of disk space. Although displayed on attribute lists, the Cc attribute can't be set by a user—NetWare automatically sets it.

## Compressed

Like Can't Compress, the **Compressed (Co)** attribute is a status flag displayed in attribute lists, but it can't be set by the user. The Co attribute shows that the file is compressed with NetWare's file compression.

## Copy Inhibit

The **Copy Inhibit (Ci)** attribute protects specified files from being copied by Macintosh users. Setting this attribute prevents Macintosh computers running the Apple Filing Protocol v2.0 and above from copying the file.

## Delete Inhibit

The **Delete Inhibit (Di)** attribute prevents a file or directory from being deleted. If assigned to a file, the file's contents can be changed or the file renamed, but the file cannot be deleted unless a user who has been granted the Modify [M] right first removes the Delete Inhibit attribute. This attribute is useful for protecting an important data file from accidentally being deleted while still enabling its contents to be changed. Consider setting the Delete Inhibit attribute on your organization's permanent files, such as customer, payroll, inventory, and accounting files. Setting the Delete Inhibit attribute on a directory prevents the directory's name from being removed but does not prevent its contents or files and subdirectories from being deleted. You might want to protect the fixed parts of your organization's directory structure from being modified by flagging all main directories with the Delete Inhibit attribute.

## Don't Compress

The **Don't Compress (Dc)** attribute is used to keep files or directories from being compressed by NetWare's file compression. The Dc attribute can be set by the user.

## Don't Migrate

Migration is used to move files that haven't been used for a long time to secondary storage media, such as DAT tape or optical disks. NetWare 6 has two attributes that work with migration systems: Migrated (discussed later in the chapter) and Don't Migrate. The **Don't Migrate (Dm)** attribute is set by the user to keep a file from being migrated, regardless of how long it has been on a volume without being used. For example, you don't want NetWare system files migrated even if you haven't used them. When the Dm attribute is set for a directory, none of the files in that directory can be migrated. For example, by setting the Dm attribute for the *ServerName*/SYS:System directory, you don't have to set the Dm attribute for every file in the System directory.

## Don't Suballocate

NetWare's block suballocation scheme is used to save disk space, and normally you should use this feature. If certain files shouldn't be stored with block suballocation, however, use the **Don't Suballocate (Ds)** attribute to prevent its use.

## Execute Only

Whereas the Copy Inhibit attribute keeps Macintosh files from being copied, the **Execute Only (X)** attribute protects software files from being illegally copied. This attribute can be set only on .exe and .com files by an administrator-equivalent user. Once set, Execute Only cannot be removed, even by the administrator, so don't assign this attribute to files unless there are backup copies. Some program files do not run when they are flagged (X) because they need to copy information into the workstation's memory, and the Execute Only attribute prevents this. Because this attribute cannot be removed, you need to delete the file and reinstall it from another disk to get rid of the attribute flag.

## Hidden

The **Hidden (H)** attribute is a DOS attribute used to hide files and directories from DOS utilities and certain software applications. However, the NDIR and NCOPY commands display hidden files and directories and show the H attribute, when it is enabled. One way to help protect software from illegal copying is to use the Hidden attribute to hide software directories and files from normal DOS utilities. If you move the NCOPY and NDIR commands from the SYS:Public directory to the SYS:System directory or some other location, standard users will not have access to them.

 Another way to protect the NCOPY and NDIR commands from unauthorized use is to place an IRF on the files in question to prevent users from inheriting the [R F] rights to these files and then make a specific trustee assignment to a special group. Only members of the special group can then use the NCOPY and NDIR commands.

The Hidden attribute can be especially useful when you have Windows workstations because it's easy for users to explore the directory structure with Windows Explorer. By hiding directories and files, you can make the file structure much less accessible.

## Immediate Compress

The **Immediate Compress (Ic)** attribute is set for files and directories that you want compressed as soon as possible. Before compressing the file, NetWare 6 normally waits until the file hasn't been used for a specific period. Immediate Compress causes a file, or files in a directory and its subdirectories, to be compressed as soon as the operating system can, without waiting for a specific event (such as a time delay). For a directory, files flagged with Don't Compress are unaffected by the (Ic) attribute.

## Index

NetWare automatically sets the **Index (I)** attribute when a file reaches a certain size in relation to the block size on the volume. (As a minimum, this would be any file that exceeds 64 file allocation table [FAT] entries.) Because NetWare handles indexing, users cannot modify the Index attribute.

## Migrated

The **Migrated (M)** attribute is a status flag set by NetWare after a file has been migrated. A file that appears in a listing with the (M) attribute has actually been moved to another storage medium and is no longer physically on the volume. When you try to work with this file, it must be retrieved from the other storage medium and recopied to the volume. If the other storage medium is easily accessible, such as a DAT tape already in the DAT tape drive, the retrieval can be fairly quick. However, if the file is stored on a medium that's more difficult to access, such as a DAT tape stored in a different building, you must retrieve the storage medium first and place it in the correct drive before it can be recopied to the volume.

## Normal

If none of the attributes are set, the file or directory is considered to be **Normal (N)**.

## Purge

The **Purge (P)** attribute can be assigned to a directory so that the NetWare file server immediately reuses the space from any files deleted in that directory. When this attribute is assigned to a directory, any file deleted from the directory is automatically purged and its space reused. The (P) attribute is often assigned to directories containing temporary files so that the temporary file space can be reused as soon as the file is deleted.

**10**

## Read Only

The **Read Only (Ro)** attribute applies only to files and protects file contents from being modified. The (Ro) attribute performs a function similar to opening the write protect tab on a disk. Files containing data that's not normally changed—such as a zip code file or a program file—are usually flagged Read Only. When you first set the Read Only attribute, the Rename Inhibit and Delete Inhibit attributes are also set by default. If you want to let the file be renamed or deleted but don't want its contents changed, you can remove the Rename Inhibit and Delete Inhibit attributes.

## Read Write

The **Read Write (Rw)** attribute applies only to files. It is the opposite of Read Only, and indicates that file contents can be added to or changed. When files are created, the Read Write attribute is automatically set, letting the contents of the file be added to or changed. When file attributes are listed, either Rw or Ro is listed.

## Rename Inhibit

You can assign the **Rename Inhibit (Ri)** attribute to files or directories. When assigned to a file, it protects the filename from being changed. During installation, many software packages create data and configuration files that might need to be changed, but those filenames must remain constant for the software to operate properly. After installing a software package that requests certain file or directory names, it's a good idea to use the (Ri) attribute on these files and directories to keep someone from changing the file or directory name and causing an error or a crash in the application. Using the (Ri) attribute on a directory keeps the directory name from being changed, while still allowing files and subdirectories in that directory to be renamed.

## Shareable

When files are created, they are available to only one user at a time. Suppose you create a spreadsheet file called Budget2002.wk1 on the server and a coworker opens it with a spreadsheet program. If you try to access this file, you'll see an error message that the file is in use or not accessible. With spreadsheet files and word-processing documents, if more than one user can access the file at one time, any changes one user makes can be overwritten by another user. Program files and certain database files, however, should be made available to multiple users at the same time. For example, you would want as many users as have licenses to be able to run the word-processing software you installed or perhaps have access to a common database of customers. To let a file be opened by more than one user at a time, the **Shareable (Sh)** attribute for that file must be enabled. Normally, you need to flag all program files as (Sh) after an installation. Most program files are also flagged as Read Only (Ro) to prevent users from deleting or making changes to the software. To prevent multiple users from making changes to the file at the same time, most document and data files are not flagged as Shareable.

## System

The **System (Sy)** attribute is often assigned to files that are part of the NetWare operating system. Like the Hidden attribute, the (Sy) attribute hides files from DOS utilities and software packages, but also marks the file as being for operating system use only.

## Transactional

The **Transactional (T)** attribute can be assigned only to files; it indicates that the file will be protected by the **Transaction Tracking System (TTS)**. The TTS ensures that when changes or transactions are applied to a file, either all transactions are completed or the file is left in its original state. The TTS is particularly important for database files—when a workstation is updating a record and crashes before the update is finished, the file's integrity is protected. Assume, for example, that a NetWare server is used to maintain an online order entry system containing customer and inventory files. When an order is entered, at least two transactions are necessary: one to update the customer's account balance and the other to record the inventory item to be shipped. While you are entering the order, the workstation you're using crashes after it updates the customer balance, so it fails to record the item on the shipping list. TTS cancels the transaction and restores the customer's balance to its original amount, enabling you to reenter the complete order.

Because TTS is used by application software, using the Transactional attribute does not implement TTS protection—you also need to have the proper system design and application software.

## Setting Directory Attributes

To set directory and file attributes using NetWare Administrator or ConsoleOne, select the directory or file object in the eDirectory tree and then open the *ObjectName* dialog box. The *ObjectName* dialog box for a directory or file contains an Attributes page, with a set of check boxes to set attributes. For files, NetWare also displays another set of check boxes (which cannot be changed by the user) that show whether a file can or can't be compressed (Cc attribute), is or isn't compressed (Co attribute), and is or isn't migrated (M attribute). To set directory and file attributes from the directory or file object itself, follow these general steps in NetWare Administrator:

1. Click the directory or file object, and then press Enter.
   *or*
   Click the directory or file object, and then click Object, Details on the menu bar.
   *or*
   Right-click the directory or file object, and then click Details on the shortcut menu.

2. Switch to the Attributes page.

3. Click the check boxes in the Directory attributes or File attributes section corresponding to the attributes to be set.

4. Click OK.

For example, David has decided to protect the files in the CBE_ADMIN/SYS:Public directory from accidental erasure and renaming by using Delete Inhibit (Di) and Rename Inhibit (Ri). Setting these attributes means that users cannot delete or rename the files in the Public directory. To set directory attributes for the CBE_ADMIN_SYS:Public directory from the CBE_ADMIN_SYS:Public directory object, David did the following:

1. He started NetWare Administrator and expanded the tree until the directories on the CBE_ADMIN_SYS volume were visible.

2. He right-clicked the CBE_ADMIN_SYS:Public directory and clicked Details to open the Directory: public dialog box.

3. He clicked the Attributes button to display the Attributes page (see Figure 10-58).

**10**

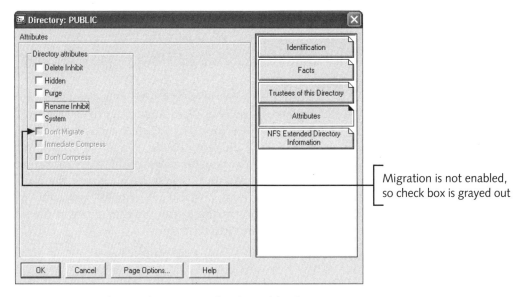

Migration is not enabled, so check box is grayed out

**Figure 10-58**    The Attributes page for the Public directory

4. He clicked the Delete Inhibit and Rename Inhibit check boxes in the Attributes section to set those attributes (see Figure 10-59), and clicked OK.

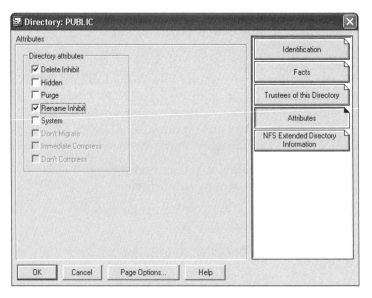

**Figure 10-59**    Setting attributes for the CBE_ADMIN_SYS:Public directory

# Using the FLAG Command

Just as the RIGHTS command is useful for documenting or setting access rights from the DOS prompt, the NetWare FLAG command-line utility is useful for documenting and setting directory and file attributes. The FLAG command has two different options to work with file or directory attributes. As a network administrator, you should know how to use the FLAG command's directory and file options to work with attributes.

## Setting and Documenting Directory Attributes

The FLAG command uses the /DO parameter to set and view directory attributes:

```
FLAG [path] [+/-] [attribute_list] /DO
```

You can replace [attribute_list] with one or more of the directory attributes shown previously in Table 10-6. Use the + operator if you want to add the attribute to the directory, or the - operator to remove the attribute from the directory. The [path] parameter is optional, and if you enter only the FLAG /DO command, you'll see a list of the attribute settings for all subdirectories of the current directory. To see how this command works, take a look at the command David entered to view the attribute settings applied to the Utility directory (see Figure 10-60).

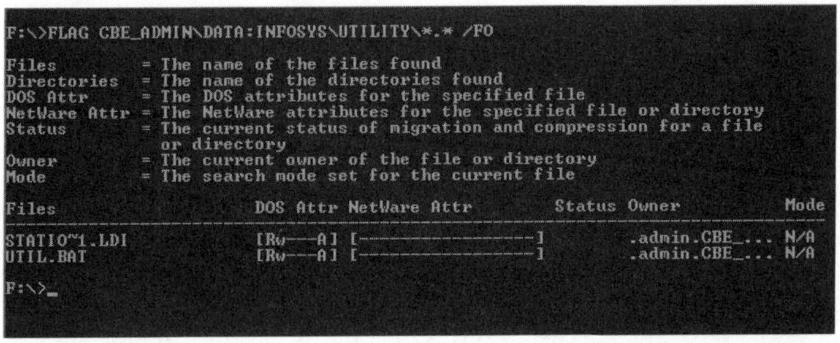

**10**

```
F:\>FLAG CBE_ADMIN\DATA:INFOSYS\UTILITY\*.* /FO
Files         = The name of the files found
Directories   = The name of the directories found
DOS Attr      = The DOS attributes for the specified file
NetWare Attr  = The NetWare attributes for the specified file or directory
Status        = The current status of migration and compression for a file
                or directory
Owner         = The current owner of the file or directory
Mode          = The search mode set for the current file

Files                    DOS Attr NetWare Attr        Status Owner        Mode

STATIO~1.LD1             [Rw---A] [--------------]     .admin.CBE_... N/A
UTIL.BAT                 [Rw---A] [--------------]     .admin.CBE_... N/A

F:\>_
```

**Figure 10-60**    Viewing attribute settings with the FLAG command

David decided that these two files should be set to Read Only to prevent users from editing them. Figure 10-61 shows the command he entered. Notice that the Delete Inhibit and Rename Inhibit attributes are enabled by default when you use the Read Only attribute.

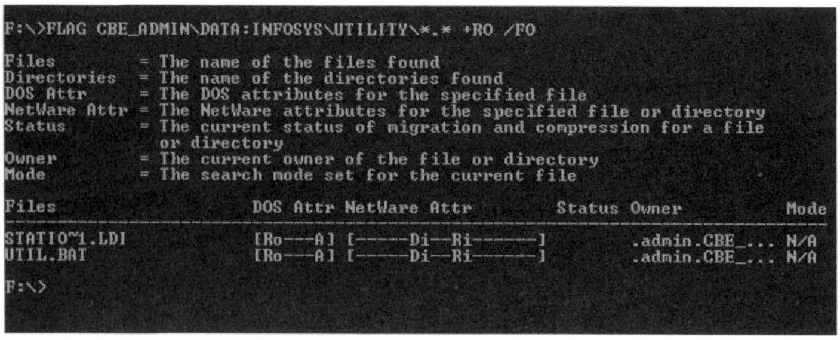

```
F:\>FLAG CBE_ADMIN\DATA:INFOSYS\UTILITY\*.* +RO /FO
Files          = The name of the files found
Directories    = The name of the directories found
DOS Attr       = The DOS attributes for the specified file
NetWare Attr   = The NetWare attributes for the specified file or directory
Status         = The current status of migration and compression for a file
                 or directory
Owner          = The current owner of the file or directory
Mode           = The search mode set for the current file

Files                     DOS Attr NetWare Attr        Status Owner          Mode
------------------------------------------------------------------------------------
STATIO~1.LDI              [Ro---A] [-----Di--Ri------]        .admin.CBE_...  N/A
UTIL.BAT                  [Ro---A] [-----Di--Ri------]        .admin.CBE_...  N/A

F:\>
```

**Figure 10-61**    Setting files to Read Only with the FLAG command

You use the FLAG command to view or change the attributes of files in the specified directory. You can replace the path with a complete or partial path leading to the file or files. If you specify no path, you access files in the current directory. You can replace the filename in the path with the name of the file you want to access, or you can use global (*) and wildcard (?) characters to access several files. If no filename is specified, the FLAG command affects all files in the specified path. To see a list of the attributes on all files in the current directory, simply type FLAG and press Enter. Replace the flag list field with the letters, separated by spaces, of the attributes you want to set.

## CHAPTER SUMMARY

❏ Just as a warehouse needs to be secured with locks and keys, the NetWare eDirectory and file systems must also be secured. Trustee assignments provide access rights that, like keys, give users entry to the eDirectory tree and server storage areas they need to access.

❏ Entry rights allow users to view and manage objects in the eDirectory tree, and consist of Supervisor, Browse, Create, Delete, Rename, and Inheritable.

❏ Attribute rights allow users to access and maintain information stored in an object, and consist of Supervisor, Read, Compare, Write, Add/Remove Self, and Inheritable.

❏ Directory and file rights provide access to the file system directories and files, respectively. Trustee assignments can be made to User objects, Group objects, Profile objects, Organizational Role objects, and container objects.

❏ Effective rights for a user are a combination of rights given to the User object combined with rights given to any other object the user is associated with. Granted trustee rights are then inherited by all container objects in the eDirectory tree subordinate to the container where the trustee assignment was made, or the subdirectories and files in the directory for which the trustee assignment was made. As a result, a user's effective rights often consist of inherited rights that have flowed down to a container object, directory, or file from a trustee assignment made in a higher-level container object or directory.

❑ Each object, directory, and file has an Inherited Rights Filter (IRF) to control what rights it inherits from higher-level objects and directories. When an object, directory, or file is first created, the IRF enables all rights to be inherited. Later, you can remove rights from the IRF to block them from being inherited.

❑ NetWare Administrator and ConsoleOne are used to set and view trustee assignments and IRFs.

❑ Attributes play an important role in file system security because they enable you to protect directories and files from operations such as deletion, renaming, and copying. Attributes can also be used to control file sharing, suballocation, compressing, purging, and migrating.

❑ The same graphical utilities—NetWare Administrator and ConsoleOne—for setting and viewing trustee assignments are used to set and view attributes. The FLAG command-line utility provides a comprehensive tool for managing directory and file attributes from the DOS prompt.

## COMMAND SUMMARY

**10**

| Command | Definition |
| --- | --- |
| FLAG | When used without any options, the FLAG command displays the attribute settings of all files in the current directory. To set attributes on files, replace the path with the path and name of a file, or use global file identifiers (such as *) and replace attributes with one or more of the following attribute flags separated by spaces (attributes marked (Dir) work with both directories and files): |

| | |
| --- | --- |
| ALL | Set all attributes (Dir) |
| A | Archive Needed |
| Ci | Copy Inhibit |
| Di | Delete Inhibit (Dir) |
| Dc | Don't Compress (Dir) |
| Dm | Don't Migrate (Dir) |
| Ds | Don't Suballocate |
| H | Hidden (Dir) |
| Ic | Immediate Compress (Dir) |
| N | Normal (Dir) |
| P | Purge (Dir) |
| Ri | Rename Inhibit (Dir) |

Ro     Read Only

Rw     Read Write

Sh     Shareable

Sy     System (Dir)

T      Transactional

X      Execute Only

Options that can be used include:

/C     Continuous output

/D     View details

/DO    Directories only

/FO    Files only

/M = mode

/NAME = name (change the owner)

/S     Include subdirectories

## KEY TERMS

**Access Control [A] right** — A NetWare file and directory right that allows a user to assign rights to other users.

**access control list (ACL)** — A property of an eDirectory object that stores the trustee list for that object.

**Add/Remove Self [A] right** — An eDirectory attribute right that lets users add themselves to or remove themselves from the object's access control list.

**Archive Needed (A)** — A NetWare file attribute set by the computer whenever the contents of a file have changed.

**assign** — The act of giving rights to a trustee. *See also* grant.

**assigned rights** — The set of rights granted or assigned to a trustee.

**attribute** — A flag that NetWare uses to determine the type of processing that can be performed on files and directories.

**attribute rights** — The set of rights to the properties of an eDirectory object that can be granted to a trustee. Attribute rights include Supervisor [S], Compare [C], Read [R], Write [W], and Add/Remove Self [A].

**Browse [B] right** — An eDirectory entry right that enables a trustee to see the object in the eDirectory tree and have the object's name appear in search results.

**Can't Compress (Cc)** — A NetWare file attribute used to flag files that can't be compressed.

**Compare [C] right** — An eDirectory attribute right that enables a trustee to compare a value to the value of the property, but not see the value itself. (The Read [R] right is needed to see the value.)

**Compressed (Co)** — A NetWare file attribute used to flag files that are compressed.

**Copy Inhibit (Ci)** — A NetWare file attribute that prevents Macintosh computers from accessing certain PC file types.

**Create [C] right** — An eDirectory entry right that lets a user create new objects in a container (applies to container objects only). Also a NetWare directory and file right that allows users to create new files and subdirectories.

**Delete [D] right** — An eDirectory entry right that enables users to delete the object from the eDirectory tree.

**Delete Inhibit (Di)** — A NetWare attribute that prevents a file or directory from being removed.

**directory rights** — The set of rights to directories in the network file system that can be granted to a trustee. Directory rights include Supervisor [S], Read [R], Write [W], Create [C], Erase [E], Modify [M], File Scan [F], and Access Control [A].

**Don't Compress (Dc)** — A NetWare file attribute used to flag files that you do not want compressed.

**Don't Migrate (Dm)** — A NetWare file attribute used to flag files that you do not want migrated.

**Don't Suballocate (Ds)** — A NetWare file attribute used to flag files that you do not want suballocated.

**effective rights** — A subset of access rights that controls which disk processing a user can perform on a directory or file. Effective rights consist of a combination of rights the user has as a user and as a member of groups, container objects, and so on.

**entry rights** — The set of rights to eDirectory objects that can be granted to a trustee. Entry rights include Supervisor [S], Browse [B], Create [C], Delete [D], Rename [R], and Inheritable [I].

**Erase [E] right** — A NetWare directory and file right that allows users to delete files and remove subdirectories when assigned to a directory.

**Execute Only (X)** — A NetWare file attribute that can be used with executable (.com and .exe) program files to prevent the files from being copied yet still allow users to run them.

**file rights** — The set of rights to files in the network file system that can be granted to a trustee. File rights include Supervisor [S], Read [R], Write [W], Create [C], Erase [E], Modify [M], File Scan [F], and Access Control [A].

**File Scan [F] right** — A NetWare directory and file right that allows users to view file and directory names.

**grant** — To give trustee rights to a user, a group, or another eDirectory object. *See also* assign.

**Hidden (H)** — A NetWare attribute used to prevent a file or directory from appearing on directory listings.

**10**

**Immediate Compress (Ic)** — A NetWare file attribute used to flag files that should be compressed immediately instead of waiting for the standard waiting period to elapse.

**Index (I)** — NetWare automatically sets this attribute when a file reaches a certain size in relation to the block size on the volume.

**Inheritable [I] right** — An eDirectory entry right that changes the way rights flow down the eDirectory tree.

**inherited rights** — Rights that flow down into a container object, directory, or file from a higher level.

**Inherited Rights Filter (IRF)** — Each container object, directory, and file contains an IRF that controls what access rights can flow down to the container object, directory, or file from a higher level.

**Migrated (M)** — A NetWare file attribute used to flag files that have been migrated.

**Modify [M] right** — A NetWare directory and file right that allows users to change file and directory attributes and rename files and subdirectories.

**Normal (N)** — A NetWare file attribute used to identify files that have no attributes set.

**[Public]** — A special trustee, [Public] is similar to a group. When [Public] is made a trustee of an object, every object in the eDirectory tree inherits the [Public] rights. In addition, [Public] rights are available to users who are not even logged in to the eDirectory tree, as long as they have Novell Client running on their computers.

**Purge (P)** — A NetWare file or directory attribute that specifies the storage space of a file that is to be made available for immediate reuse by the server.

**Read Only (Ro)** — A NetWare file attribute that prevents data in a file from being erased or changed.

**Read [R] right** — An eDirectory attribute right that enables a trustee to see the property values of an object. Also a directory and file right that allows users to open and read data from a file or run programs.

**Read Write (Rw)** — A NetWare file attribute that allows data in a file to be modified or appended to.

**Rename Inhibit (Ri)** — A NetWare file or directory attribute that prevents changing the name of a file or directory.

**Rename [R] right** — An eDirectory entry right that enables users to change an object's name.

**rights** — When referring to eDirectory or the network file system, the type of access that has been granted or assigned to a user, who is called a *trustee*. In eDirectory, there are entry rights and attribute rights; the network file system has directory rights and file rights.

**security equivalence** — An eDirectory object assignment that grants one object the same set of rights as another object.

**Shareable (Sh)** — A NetWare file attribute that allows multiple users to access or update data in a file at the same time.

**Supervisor [S] right** — A NetWare access right that provides a user with all rights to an eDirectory object and its properties and the entire directory structure. Once assigned, the Supervisor right cannot be restricted on the network file system (directory and file rights), but it can be restricted for eDirectory rights (entry and attribute rights).

**System (Sy)** — A NetWare file attribute used to flag system files.

**Transaction Tracking System (TTS)** — A NetWare fault-tolerance system that returns database records to their original value if a client computer system fails while processing a transaction.

**Transactional (T)** — A NetWare file attribute that enables transaction tracking on a database file.

**trustee** — A user given access to eDirectory objects or network file system directories and files. Access is given when rights are assigned or granted to the user or another eDirectory object the user is associated with.

**trustee assignment** — The set of eDirectory or file system rights granted to a user.

**trustee list** — The set of trustee assignments for an eDirectory object or a network file system directory or file.

**Write [W] right** — An eDirectory attribute right that enables users to change, add, or delete the value of the property. Also a directory or file right that allows users to change or add data to a file.

**10**

# REVIEW QUESTIONS

1. Which of the following tools can be used to manage eDirectory?

    a. ConsoleOne

    b. NetWare Administrator

    c. iManager

    d. DOS

2. True or False: Trustee assignments define a user's access to eDirectory and the NetWare file system.

3. To simplify trustee assignments, an administrator can do which of the following?

    a. create groups

    b. create subordinate rights

    c. delete the [Public] object

    d. delete eDirectory

4. The purpose of entry rights is to do which of the following?

    a. control user access to eDirectory objects

    b. control access to eDirectory properties

    c. organize the tree structure

    d. create a hierarchical file structure

5. Which of the following rights enables a user to create eDirectory objects in a container object?

   a. Delete Inhibit (Di)

   b. Create [C]

   c. Archive [A]

   d. Browse [Br]

6. What is the purpose of directory rights?

   a. give eDirectory rights to all users

   b. control user access to directories and subdirectories in the network file system

   c. control access to eDirectory

   d. restrict access to eDirectory

7. Which of the following directory rights enables a user to see file and subdirectory names?

   a. Compare [C]

   b. Comparable (C)

   c. File Scan [F]

   d. Archive (A)

8. Which of the following directory rights enables a user to assign rights to other users?

   a. Rights [R]

   b. Assign [A]

   c. Access Control [A]

   d. Assign Rights [AS]

9. What is the purpose of file rights?

   a. restrict all access to system files

   b. restrict all access to [Public] files

   c. control user access to files in the network file system

   d. File rights were eliminated in NetWare 6.

10. Which of the following rights enables users to read a file if they do not have the necessary directory rights?

    a. Read [R]

    b. Read File [R]

    c. Read Directory [R]

    d. Users cannot read a file if they do not have directory rights.

11. Which of the following file rights enables a user to change data within an existing file?

    a. Change [C]

    b. Archive [A]

    c. Read [R]

    d. Write [W]

12. Which of the following directory rights cannot be revoked or blocked within the directory structure in which it is defined?

    a. Administrator [A]

    b. Admin [A]

    c. Supervisor [S]

    d. Self [S]

13. What is the purpose of attribute rights?

    a. control user access to the property value settings of eDirectory objects

    b. control user access to all objects

    c. control user access to [Public] objects

    d. control all rights to properties

14. Which of the following consists of a subset of the access rights and controls which functions a user can perform in a directory or file?

    a. directory rights

    b. attribute rights

    c. access rights

    d. effective rights

Figure 10-62 shows the eDirectory tree for FDR Investments. Use this eDirectory tree as the basis for answering Questions 15–20. [Public] has no rights in the tree.

15. You work in administration and have been given the [B C D] rights to the FDR Organization and the [S B C D R] rights to the FDR_Admin OU. What are your effective rights in the Finance.FDR_Admin.FDR OU? Why do you have these rights?

16. You work in administration and have been given the [B C D] rights to the FDR Organization and the [S B C D R] rights to the FDR_Admin OU. What are your effective rights in the Sales.FDR OU? Why do you have these rights?

17. You work in sales and are a member of AcctExecs. You have been given the [B] right to the FDR Organization and [B C D R] rights to the Sales.FDR OU. In addition, AcctExecs has the [S] right to Sales.FDR. What are your effective rights in the Sales.FDR OU? Why do you have these rights?

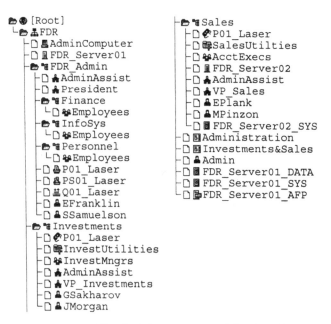

**Figure 10-62**   The FDR Investments eDirectory tree

18. You are the new VP for investments and are a member of InvestMngrs. You have been given the [B] right to the FDR Organization and the [B] right to the Investments.FDR OU. In addition, InvestMngrs has [C D] rights to Investments.FDR. As VP for investments, you have the [R] right for Investments.FDR. What are your effective rights in the Investments.FDR OU? Why do you have these rights?

19. You are a member of the AcctExecs group that has been granted [R W F] rights to the Business directory and have a trustee assignment of [R C F] to this directory. What are your effective rights in the Business directory?

20. You have been given a trustee assignment of [R C F] to the Business directory and a trustee assignment of [W E] to the Business\Spdata\Budgets subdirectory. What are your effective rights in the Business\Spdata subdirectory?

# HANDS-ON PROJECTS

These projects assume that each student has been given a home directory for class work in the STUDENTS:##DATA directory.

## Project 10-1: Working with Access Rights

In this project, you practice assigning access rights to a directory and then attempt to perform several disk operations in that directory to see how access rights affect use of the file system. In the following steps, make sure you substitute your assigned student number for the ## symbol. Write down your results (and answer any questions) as you're working through the steps, and turn them in as a report to your instructor.

1. Log in with your assigned student user name, open Windows Explorer, and find your ##DATA directory.

2. Create subdirectories called Chap10 and SP in your ##DATA directory.

3. Use Windows Explorer to copy all files with the .txt extension from your local Windows directory to the Chap10 and SP subdirectories.

4. Use NetWare Administrator to create a user named ##User10 anywhere in your tree.

5. Use NetWare Administrator to assign ##User10 the Access Control right to Chap10 and Read and File Scan rights to ##DATA\SP.

6. Log out.

7. Log in as ##User10 and change to the ##DATA\Chap10 directory.

8. Log out and log in as administrator. Use Windows Explorer to view the files. Record your results.

9. Use NetWare Administrator to grant ##User10 only File Scan rights to Chap10.

10. Log in as ##User10 and repeat Step 8. Record your observations.

11. Try to read the contents of a file by using the TYPE *filename* command at the command prompt. Record your results.

12. Log in as administrator and use NetWare Administrator to give ##Group10 the Read right to the Chap10 directory.

13. Log in as ##User10 and repeat Step 11. Record your observations.

14. Try creating a subdirectory called Practice. Record your observations.

15. Log in as administrator and use NetWare Administrator to give ##User10 only the Create and Access Control rights to the Chap10 directory.

16. Log in as ##User10 and repeat Step 14. Record your results.

17. What two methods could you use to make the directories visible?

18. Try using Windows Explorer to copy any file from SYS:Public to the Chap10 directory. Record your results.

19. Log in as administrator and add the File Scan right to ##Group10 so that ##User10 has effective rights of [R C F A] in the Chap10 directory. Log in as ##User10 and then repeat Step 18. Record your observations.

20. Log in with your assigned ##Admin user name and delete any users and groups you created in this project.

## Project 10-2: Using the Inherited Rights Filter

In this project, you create a directory structure and two users and then use NetWare utilities to grant trustee assignments and set up an IRF to observe how effective rights are inherited. Write down your results (and answer any questions) as you're working through the steps, and turn them in as a report to your instructor.

### Part 1: Create a Directory Structure and Users

1. Log in with your assigned student user name, open Windows Explorer, and find your ##DATA directory.

2. If you have not already done so, create a Chap10 subdirectory in your ##DATA directory.

3. Create two directories in the Chap10 directory named Orders and Users.

4. Create two users called ##Clerk1 and ##Clerk2 anywhere in your tree. Create home directories for these users in the Chap10\Users directory.

5. Create a group named ##Clerks. Make ##Clerk1 and ##Clerk2 members of this group.

6. Give the ##Clerks group Read and File Scan rights to the Chap10 directory.

7. Make ##Clerk1 a manager of the Chap10 directory structure by granting the user name the Supervisor right.

8. Make ##Clerk2 a trustee of the Chap10 directory with [W C E M] rights.

9. Log out.

### Part 2: Check Effective Rights

1. Log in as ##Clerk2.

2. Use ConsoleOne or NetWare Administrator to record your effective rights in these directories:

| Directory Path | Effective Rights |
|---|---|
| Chap10 | |
| Chap10\Orders | |
| Chap10\Users | |

3. Log out.

### Part 3: Modify Trustee Assignments

In this part of the project, you observe how making a new trustee assignment to the group of which a user is a member changes the effective rights to a subdirectory that user inherits.

1. Log in with your assigned student user name, and change to your ##DATA directory.

2. Use ConsoleOne or NetWare Administrator to assign the ##Clerks group no rights to the Chap10\Orders subdirectory.

3. Log out.

4. Log in as ##Clerk2

5. Record your effective rights in the Chap10 directory.

6. Record your effective rights in the Chap10\Orders subdirectory.

7. Why didn't your effective rights in the Chap10 directory flow down to the Chap10\Orders directory?

8. Log out.

## Part 4: Use IRFs to Change Effective Rights

1. Log in with your assigned ##Admin user name.

2. Use NetWare Administrator to remove all rights except File Scan and Supervisor from the IRF of the Chap10\Users directory.

3. Use NetWare Administrator to enable the Chap10\Orders directory to inherit only Read and File Scan rights.

4. Log out.

5. Log in as ##Clerk2.

6. Use ConsoleOne or NetWare Administrator to record your effective rights in the following subdirectories:

| Directory Path | Effective Rights |
| --- | --- |
| Chap10 | |
| Chap10\Orders | |
| Chap10\Users | |

7. Log out.

8. Log in as ##Clerk1.

9. Use ConsoleOne or NetWare Administrator to record your effective rights in the following subdirectories:

| Directory Path | Effective Rights |
| --- | --- |
| Chap10 | |
| Chap10\Orders | |
| Chap10\Users | |

10

## CASE PROJECTS

## Case 10-1: J.Q. Adams Corporation Security

You are the network administrator for J.Q. Adams, and Lois, John, and Ann are employees who work in the Business Department. Figure 10-63 shows the Business Department's directory structure. Write down your results (and answer any questions) as you're working through the steps, and turn them in as a report to your instructor.

Students must have all rights to their home directories, including Supervisor and Access Control, to complete these projects. Your instructor or network administrator might need to set these rights for you.

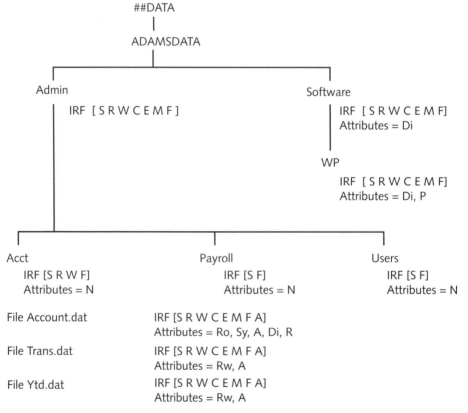

**Figure 10-63**    The J.Q. Adams Business Department directory structure with IRF assignments

## Step 1: Creating a Structure

To perform this project and answer the questions, use the directory structure you created for J.Q. Adams in Chapter 8. If you have not created it yet, create one in your STUDENTS:##DATA student work area.

1. Log in with your assigned student user name.

2. Using NetWare Administrator, create the directory structure shown in Figure 10-63, if you didn't create it in Chapter 8.

3. Set the IRFs for each directory, as indicated in Figure 10-63.

4. Set the Delete Inhibit attribute on each directory in the ADAMSDATA structure.

5. Print a copy of your directory structure, including the IRFs for each directory.

6. Use NetWare Administrator to display the attributes for each directory and subdirectories.

7. Press the Print Screen key to print the window showing your directory attributes.

## Step 2: Working with Files

In this project, you need to create the general ledger files for the Acct directory and use FLAG commands to set attributes to meet the requirements specified in the problem.

1. Use Notepad to create the Account.dat file in the Acct directory with the following contents:

   This is the Accounts database.

   General ledger accounts and their descriptions are stored here.

2. Use Notepad to create the Trans.dat and Ytd.dat files shown in Table 10-7.

   Trans.dat:

   This is the Accounts transaction file.

   Debit and credit entries are stored here.

   Ydt.dat:

   This is the year-to-date summary file.

   End-of-year totals are stored here.

**Table 10-7**   File and Directory Attribute Requirements

| Directory/File | Attribute Requirements |
| --- | --- |
| Account.dat | Protect the file from being changed and enable shared access |
| Trans.dat | Protect the file from being erased or renamed, but allow changes to the contents |
| Ytd.dat | Protect the file from being erased or renamed, but allow changes to the contents |
| Software: | Hide this directory |
| Software\WP: | Immediately purge any deleted files |

10

3. Use the appropriate utility to set the file and directory attributes described in Table 10-7. Record each command or utility you used.

   Account.dat file:

   Trans.dat file:

   Ytd.dat file:

   Software:

   Software\WP:

4. Use the NDIR command to obtain a hard copy of all files in the Acct directory.

5. Use NetWare Administrator to display the directory attributes. Use the Print Screen key to print the screen.

## Step 3: Creating Users and Groups

In this project, you create the users and groups needed for the J.Q. Adams Business Department. Be sure to replace the ## symbols in each user name with your assigned student number.

1. Create the ##Admin group in an appropriate part of the ADAMS tree. Assign the group [R F] rights to the ADAMSDATA directory. (This will be the default setting.)

2. Create the user accounts shown in Table 10-8 having home directories in the ADAMSDATA\Admin\Users subdirectory. Make all users members of the ##Admin group.

**Table 10-8**    J.Q. Adams User Accounts

| User | User and Home Directory Name |
| --- | --- |
| John Combs | ##JCombs |
| Lois Kent | ##LKent |
| Ann Bonny | ##ABonny |

## Step 4: Assigning Trustee Rights

In this project, you use NetWare Administrator to grant trustee assignments for the ADAMSDATA directory structure to the Business Department users you created.

1. Start NetWare Administrator.

2. Because John is the administrator of the Business Department, grant him the Supervisor right in the ADAMSDATA\Admin\Users subdirectory.

3. Make Ann a trustee of the Payroll directory by giving her all rights to the Payroll directory.

4. Make Lois a trustee with [R W C E F] rights to the Acct directory.

5. If you haven't already done so, grant the ##Admin group [R F] rights to the ADAMSDATA directory.

6. Print a hard copy of the trustee assignments for each ADAMSDATA directory.

## Step 5: Determining Effective Rights

In this project, you use NetWare commands to answer questions on the user's effective rights to the directory structure. Write down which command you used to determine the rights and who you were logged in as when you used the command. In addition, explain why the user or group has these rights and how the rights were obtained. When you're finished, turn in the report to your instructor.

1. What are John's rights in Payroll?

   Command used:

   Logged in as:

   Explain how John got these rights.

2. Explain what you would do if you no longer wanted John to have all rights to the Payroll subdirectory but still have Supervisor rights in the other subdirectories of the ADAMSDATA structure.

3. What are Ann's rights in the Acct directory?

   Command used:

   Logged in as:

   Explain how Ann got these rights.

4. What are Ann's rights in the Payroll directory?

   Command used:

   Logged in as:

   Explain how Ann got these rights.

5. What are Lois's rights in the Acct directory?

   Command used:

   Logged in as:

   Explain how Lois got these rights.

6. Are Lois's rights in the Acct subdirectory sufficient for her to keep the files updated? If not, explain why, and grant her the necessary rights. Record how you did it.

7. Log in as John and determine what his effective rights are to the Account.dat file:

   Command used:

   Logged in as:

8. Try to use Notepad to change the contents of the Account.dat file. Record your results.

9. Explain briefly what John must do if he needs to add information accounts to the Account.dat file.

10. Use the appropriate utility to implement the solution you defined in Step 9. Record the option you used.

11. Ann needs to post payroll transactions to the Trans.dat file. Briefly explain what steps you should follow to enable Ann to post to the Trans.dat file but not give her access to the other files in the Acct directory.

# 11

# IMPLEMENTING AND MANAGING NETWORK PRINTING

**After reading this chapter and completing the exercises, you will be able to:**

♦ Explain how printers are accessed on a network and set up a queue-based printing system, including print queues, printers, and print servers

♦ Use NetWare Administrator and iManager to create and configure Novell Distributed Print Services components, describe how to install printers on user workstations, and explain how to troubleshoot print services

♦ Use iPrint to create and install printers that users can access and manage across networks

♦ Use NetWare Administrator and iManager to manage network printers

As described in Chapter 1, sharing printers is an important benefit of implementing a network system. Network printing offers cost savings, increased workspace for users, and multiple printer-selection options. To become a CNA, Novell requires you to know how to use the original queue-based printing system, the Novell Distributed Print Services (NDPS) system, and the new iPrint printing system to set up, customize, and maintain the printing environment on your network. As part of Novell's OneNet strategy, iPrint makes it possible to install, access, and configure network printers through a Web browser. This chapter covers the printing concepts and skills needed to understand and implement network-printing environments using these three printing systems.

## QUEUE-BASED PRINTING

As shown in Figure 11-1, the basic function of network printing is to take output formatted by an application running on the user's workstation and send it to a shared printer attached to the network.

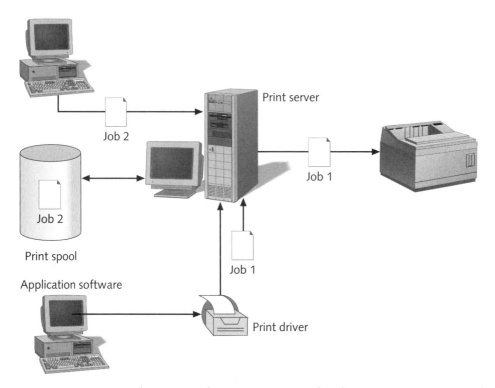

**Figure 11-1** Network printing: The print server spools Job 2 to a storage area until Job 1 finishes printing

Because a physical printer can print output from only one application at a time, network printing must provide a way to control the flow of output from multiple user applications to a single network printer. Usually, this is done by sending output from a user's workstation to a print job on a server, where it's held until the network printer is available. The process of sending output from a user's workstation to a print job is referred to as **spooling**. As illustrated in Figure 11-1, the **print server** software actually makes network printing happen by retrieving print jobs and sending them to the assigned network printer. When a network printer finishes printing output for one application, the print service retrieves the next application's print job for that printer and sends it to the printer. With print spooling, applications can quickly send their output to a network printer and continue processing information without waiting for the output to be physically printed.

## Queue-Based Printing System Components

Available since NetWare 3, **queue-based printing** was designed to support simple print-ers and DOS-based applications. Because many NetWare networks still use queue-based printing systems, as a CNA you'll be required to know their basic components and oper-ation. Before implementing a queue-based printing environment for your network, you need to understand how the basic printing components work together. In the following sections, you learn how these four queue-based printing objects are implemented in a NetWare printing environment:

- Print queue
- Printer
- Print server
- Client

### Print Queues

A **print queue** is a network object that represents a holding area for storing output from workstations in a form ready to send directly to a printer. As shown in Figure 11-2, a print queue allows multiple workstations on a network to use the same printer by stor-ing the printer output from each client as a separate print job. After being stored in the print queue, print jobs are printed one at a time as the printer becomes available.

**11**

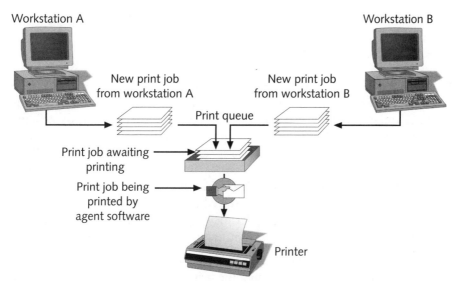

**Figure 11-2**    Queue-based printing

In queue-based printing, print jobs are files containing output formatted for a specific printer. In many ways, having a client send output to a print queue is similar to storing files on a volume. For example, when saving a file on the server, the data is transferred from the client to the server and then stored in a file located in the specified directory. Because an application's printer output is actually data being transmitted to the printer, placing a job in a print queue is a similar process, in which the printer data from the application is stored in a file called a print job. Just as data files are stored in directories, print job files are located in special print queue directories, as illustrated in Figure 11-3.

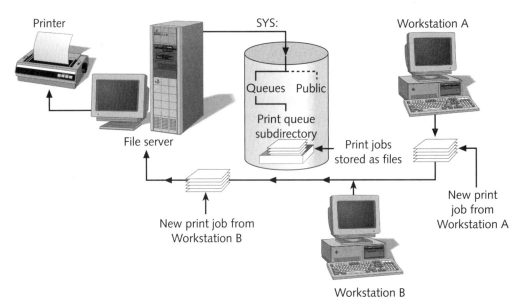

**Figure 11-3**    A NetWare print queue

In a NetWare queue-based printing system, network print queues are subdirectories of the Queues directory and can be placed on any volume. As described later in this section, print queues are created in NetWare Administrator. When setting up a queue-based printing environment, at least one print queue is created for each networked printer. For user workstations that need to print to a specific printer, you use the Add Printer Wizard to specify that users send their output to a print queue. DOS-based applications can be directed to send their output to a print queue with the NetWare CAPTURE command-line utility. After print jobs have been stored in the print queue, the printer assigned to the print queue prints jobs in the order they were received. After a job has been printed, it's automatically deleted from the print queue.

One of the tasks involved in network printing is managing jobs in print queues. By default, the network administrator who created the print queue is made the print queue operator, authorized to rearrange the sequence of print jobs, remove a print job, or place a print job on hold. NetWare also allows other users besides network administrators to be print queue operators. You might want to give other users in your organization the title of print queue operator to delegate the work of managing jobs on several print queues.

## Printers

To successfully format and print information on a printer, the application running on the user workstation must be configured with the correct printer driver for the printer's make and model. Because of the variety of makes and models available, you should have this information for your network's printers so that you can correctly configure network printing, thus ensuring that formatted output goes to the correct printer. For example, a user's workstation might be configured to support both a Lexmark Optra Plus laser printer and an HP Deskjet ink-jet printer. When a user selects the Lexmark Optra Plus laser printer and prints a document, the network printing configuration must be set up to ensure that the output is sent to the laser printer for which it was formatted.

Printers can be attached to the network in one of the following three ways, as illustrated in Figure 11-4:

- Remote attachment through a workstation

- Local attachment to the print server

- Direct attachment to the network cable

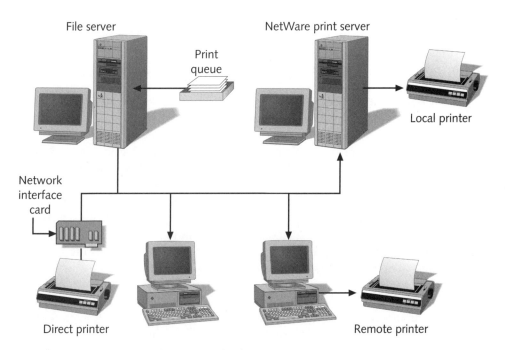

**Figure 11-4**    Printer attachment methods

When configuring the network printing environment, carefully consider each attachment method to weigh its advantages and determine how it will affect the way printers are distributed on the network. Many network administrators use a combination of printer attachments, based on the type of printer and its use. The following sections describe the three printer attachment options and how they affect network printing.

**Remote Attachment**   Remote printers, which are attached to other clients on the network, are called **manual load printers** because you must manually load software on the client workstation to connect the printer to the print server. After the software has been loaded on the client, print jobs can be sent to its remote printer, using the network cable to transmit packets of printed data from the print server to the client with the remote printer attached. NetWare includes the NPTWIN95 utility, which can be loaded only on Windows 95/98 client workstations that have an attached network printer. NPTWIN95 receives packets of printer output directed to it from the print server and prints the output on the attached network printer; the printing doesn't interfere with anyone using that Windows 95/98 client workstation for other processing. The advantage of using manual load printers attached to client workstations is that you can select a convenient location for the printer, making it easier for users to retrieve their printed output. The disadvantages of manual load printers include the lack of support for printers attached to Windows 2000 or XP workstations, the additional setup time to load NPTWIN95 on Windows 95/98 workstations, the need to leave the client workstation on to access network printers, and the possible decrease in printing performance for large graphics print jobs. This decrease is caused by applications running on the client workstation and the extra load created on the network cable when sending output from the print queue on the server to the network printer attached to the workstation.

**Local Attachment**   Locally attached printers are attached directly to a printer port on the server running the print server software (PSERVER.NLM). In NetWare, these printers are called **automatic load printers** because output is sent directly from the print server to the local printers through ports on the server. Automatic load printers can be attached to the parallel port (LPTn) or serial port (COMn) of the server running the print server software. Compared to manual load printers, the advantages of automatic load printers include better printing performance and less network traffic. The improved performance is a result of less software overhead because the print server does not have to communicate with a client workstation running NPTWIN95. Network traffic is reduced because print jobs do not need to be sent from the print server to a printer attached to a client workstation somewhere on the network.

**Direct Attachment**   A popular alternative to using remote printers attached to a client workstation is to attach the printer directly to the network cable with a special network card for the printer or to use a dedicated print server device, such as HP's JetDirect products. Dedicated print server devices have a network port, one or more printer ports, and built-in software that enable them to receive print jobs from the network and print them on attached printers. Many high-speed laser printers have an option that includes a network card for attaching printers directly to the network cable. With the direct attachment option, the printer can become its own print server and print jobs directly from a NetWare print queue. The direct printer attachment is often used in networks that need high-speed laser printers, which don't operate efficiently when attached as remote printers.

The main disadvantage of attaching printers directly to the network is the cost and availability of the network attachment option for each printer. Another possible disadvantage of making each directly attached printer its own print server is the need to use an additional network connection for each print server device. Because your NetWare license supports a limited number of network connections, having several direct-attachment printers acting as independent print servers could potentially cause your server to reach the maximum licensing limit. If this happens, additional users will not be allowed to log in. You can usually get around the use of extra license connections by configuring the directly attached printers as remote printers controlled through a common NetWare print server, as described in the following section.

Before setting up any network printing system, identify the printers in terms of printer type, location, name, and attachment method. For example, assume that CBE Labs has an existing HP LaserJet 5si PostScript printer that Ted Simpson wants all users in the InfoSystems Organizational Unit (OU) to be able to share. Because the NetWare server is located near the Information Systems Department, David decided to attach the printer locally to the NetWare server. He plans to develop a more sophisticated printing system using NDPS, but for simplicity's sake, he decided that for now, he could implement queue-based printing to share the new printer. Table 11-1 contains the information he used to identify the new printer, including its name, make and model, and attachment method.

**Table 11-1**    Queue-Based Printer Information

| Printer Name | Make/Model 1 | Port and Interrupt | Location | Users | Print Queue Name/Volume | eDirectory Context | Operator |
|---|---|---|---|---|---|---|---|
| IS_P | HP LaserJet 5si PostScript | LTP1 Polled | Server AutoLoad | ISMgrs group | IS_Q CORP volume | .InfoSystems. CBE_Admin. CBE_LABS | ISMgrs group |

## Print Servers

A print server makes queue-based network printing happen by taking print jobs from print queues on NetWare servers and sending them to the assigned printer, as shown in Figure 11-5.

Printers can be attached directly to the print server as with local printers, attached remotely through a client running the NPTWIN95 software, or directly attached to the network through a device such as the HP JetDirect. Print servers are also responsible for sending control commands to the printers and reporting printer status to the print server operator. In NetWare queue-based printing, each print server is defined by an eDirectory Print Server object containing the print server name and the names of up to 255 printer objects. After the Print Server object has been created and configured, the NetWare print server software can be loaded and run as a nondedicated print server from the file server by loading PSERVER.NLM.

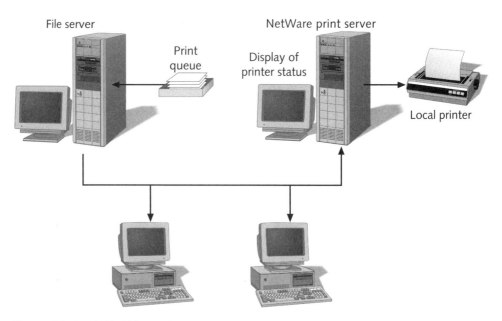

**Figure 11-5**    A NetWare print server

## Setting Up Queue-Based Printing

Setting up a simple queue-based network printing system involves these basic steps:

1. Create a print queue for each printer.

2. Create an eDirectory Non-NDPS Printer object to represent each printer.

3. Define a Print Server object to send output from the print queues to the corresponding printer.

4. Load the print server and any remote printer software.

Because Novell is moving toward performing network administration tasks through iManager, printer management tasks were not added to ConsoleOne. Until iManager is fully implemented, you need to use NetWare Administrator to perform many of the tasks for creating and managing the NetWare printing environment. In the following examples, you see how David used NetWare Administrator to implement queue-based printing for the existing InfoSystems printer shown in Table 11-1.

### Creating a Print Queue

After defining the names and eDirectory contexts for the printer, print queue, and print server, David used NetWare Administrator to create the queue-based printing objects:

1. After logging in with the CBEAdmin user name and password, he started NetWare Administrator and opened a browse window to the CBE_LABS Organization.

2. To create a Print Queue object named IS_Q in the InfoSystems container, he did the following:

   a. He clicked the InfoSystems OU, and pressed Insert to open the New Object dialog box.

   b. He scrolled down and double-clicked the Print Queue object to open the Create Print Queue dialog box shown in Figure 11-6.

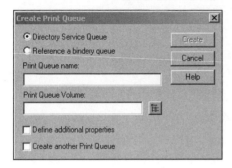

**Figure 11-6**   The Create Print Queue dialog box

   c. He entered the print queue name, IS_Q, in the Print Queue name text box.

   d. To select a volume for the print queue job storage, he clicked the browse button next to the Print Queue Volume text box.

   e. He double-clicked the up arrow in the Browse context section to navigate to the CBE_LABS Organization.

   f. To help prevent the SYS volume from filling up, he double-clicked the CBE_ADMIN_DATA Volume object in the Available objects section.

   g. He clicked the Define additional properties check box and then clicked the Create button to create the print queue and open the Print Queue: IS_Q dialog box shown in Figure 11-7.

   h. To make the ISMgrs group the manager of the print queue, he clicked the Operator button, clicked the Add button to open the Select Object dialog box, and double-clicked the ISMgrs group to add it as a print queue operator.

3. To display the print queue users, he clicked the Users button, and noted that the CBEAdmin user and the InfoSystems OU were listed in the Users list box, as shown in Figure 11-8.

By default, the container where the print queue is located is made a user of the print queue. Because the InfoSystems OU is a user, all users in that OU can send output to this print queue.

4. He completed the process by clicking OK to save the changes and return to the NetWare Administrator browse window.

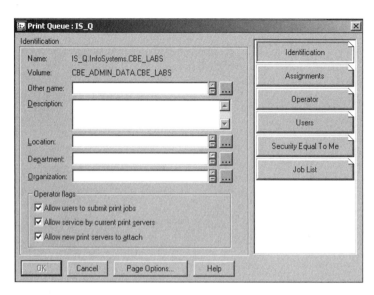

**Figure 11-7**    The Print Queue dialog box

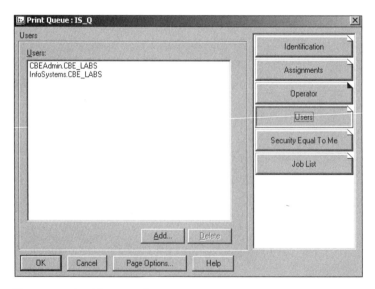

**Figure 11-8**    Viewing the print queue users

## Creating a Printer Object

After David created the print queue and defined the users and operators, his next step was to create and define the Non-NDPS Printer object and then identify the printer attachment method, the port and interrupt to be used, and the print queue the printer will get its output from. He used the following steps in NetWare Administrator to create and define the IS_P printer object listed in Table 11-1:

1. To create a printer object named IS_P in the InfoSystems container, he did the following:

    a. He clicked the InfoSystems OU, and then pressed the Insert key to open the New Object dialog box.

    b. He scrolled down and double-clicked the Printer (Non NDPS) object to open the Create Printer dialog box.

    c. He entered IS_P in the Printer name text box and clicked the Define additional properties check box.

    d. He clicked the Create button to create the printer object and open the Printer (Non NDPS): IS_P dialog box shown in Figure 11-9.

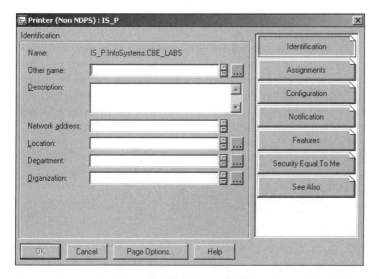

**Figure 11-9**    Configuring the Non-NDPS Printer object in the Printer (Non NDPS): IS_P dialog box

2. To configure the printer object to receive output, he identified the print queue and attachment method by performing the following steps:

    a. He clicked the Assignments button, and clicked the Add button to open the Select Object dialog box.

    b. He double-clicked the IS_Q print queue in the Available objects section to add it to the Print queues assignment list box, as shown in Figure 11-10.

    c. He clicked the Configuration button to display the configuration information (see Figure 11-11).

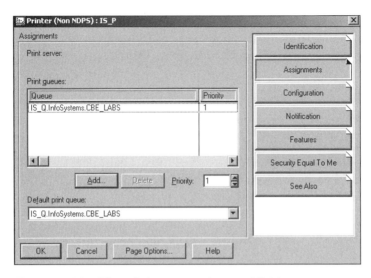

**Figure 11-10** The print queue assignment list box

Note

Notice that by default the printer is defined as a parallel printer with a text banner type. The service interval of 5 specifies that the print server will check the print queue every five seconds to see if there are any jobs to be printed. By default, the printer starts with forms type 0 mounted. The "Minimize form changes within print queues" setting tells the printer to print all jobs with forms number 0 before checking for jobs with forms number 1, and so on.

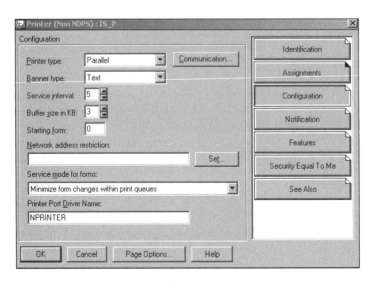

**Figure 11-11** Viewing configuration information for the printer

d. To set the attachment method and port information, he clicked the Communication button to open the Parallel Communication dialog box shown in Figure 11-12.

 Notice that the default port is LPT1 with the polled interrupt setting. With the polled method, the computer checks the printer frequently to see if it's ready. This method prevents the printer from interrupting the computer processor every time it's ready to print and can provide better server performance. Notice that the connection type is also defined by default.

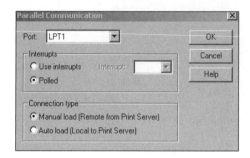

**Figure 11-12**    The Parallel Communication dialog box

e. Because the printer will be attached directly to the server, he clicked the Auto load (Local to Print Server) radio button.

f. He clicked OK to save his changes and return to the Printer (Non NDPS): IS_P dialog box.

3. He clicked OK to return to the NetWare Administrator browse window.

## Creating and Configuring a Print Server

For queue-based printing to work, the print server software needs to know what printers it controls and who the print server operators and users are. To supply this information to the print server software, you create and configure an eDirectory Print Server object. David used the following steps in NetWare Administrator to create a print server for the CBE_LABS Organization and then configured it to manage the existing IS_P printer:

1. To create a Print Server object named CBE_PS in the CBE_LABS Organization, he did the following:

a. He clicked the CBE_LABS Organization, and pressed Insert to open the New Object dialog box.

b. He scrolled down and double-clicked the Print Server (Non NDPS): object to open the Create Print Server dialog box.

c. He entered CBE_PS in the Print Server name text box, and clicked the Define additional properties check box.

11

d. He clicked the Create button to create the Print Server object and open the Print Server dialog box shown in Figure 11-13.

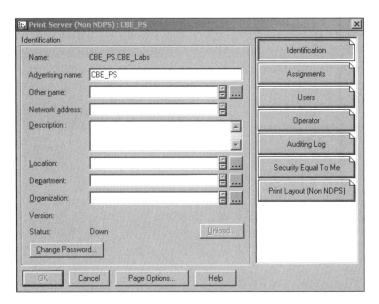

**Figure 11-13**   The Print Server (Non NDPS): CBE_PS dialog box

2. To assign the IS_P printer to the new print server, he did the following:

a. He clicked the Assignments button, and then clicked the Add button to open the Select Object dialog box.

b. He navigated to the InfoSystems OU in the Browse context section.

c. He double-clicked the IS_P printer in the Available objects section to add it to the Printers list box, as shown in Figure 11-14.

A non-NDPS print server can service up to 255 printers.

3. He clicked the Users button and verified that the CBE_LABS Organization was listed as the user of the print server (see Figure 11-15).

By default, the container where the print server is created becomes a user of the print server. Because David created the print server in the CBE_LABS Organization, all users in the Organization and all its OUs will be users of the print server.

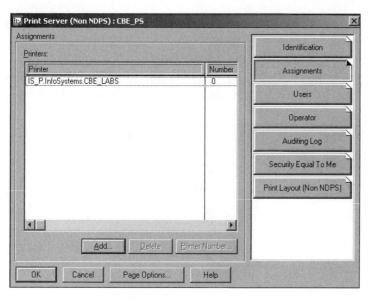

**Figure 11-14**   Viewing the printers for CBE_PS

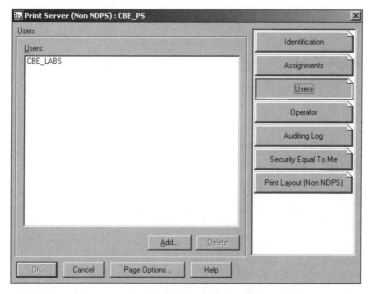

**Figure 11-15**   Viewing the users for CBE_PS

4. By default, the administrative user who creates the print server automatically becomes the print server operator and can perform functions such as stopping and starting print server functions. David performed the following steps to add the ISMgrs group as another operator of the new print server:

a. He clicked the Operator button to open the Operators dialog box and then clicked the Add button to open the Select Object dialog box.

b. He used the Browse context section to navigate to the InfoSystems OU and then double-clicked the ISMgrs group in the Available objects section to add the group to the Operators list box, as shown in Figure 11-16.

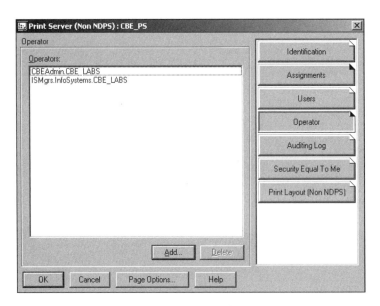

**Figure 11-16**   Viewing the operators for CBE_PS

5. He clicked OK to save the print server configuration and return to NetWare Administrator.

## Loading the Print Server

Before network printing can start, you need to run the print server software on the NetWare server. The print server software runs as a module on a NetWare server and uses the configuration and security information from a Print Server object in the eDirectory database to control its operations. Only one print server module can be loaded on a NetWare server at a time. The print server module can be set up to load automatically from the Autoexec.ncf file (described in Chapter 6) when the server starts, or can be loaded manually from the server console. In the following example, David loaded the CBE_PS print server from the server console:

 In Chapter 13, you'll learn how to use Remote Manager to add the commands in the Autoexec.ncf file needed to load a print server.

1. On the server console, he pressed Ctrl+Esc to display the Current Screens menu.

2. He selected option 1 to display the System Console screen and entered the following command (see Figure 11-17):

   ```
   LOAD PSERVER.  CN=CBE_PS.O=CBE_LABS
   ```

```
CBE_ADMIN:LOAD PSERVER
Loading Module PSERVER.NLM                              [    OK    ]
CBE_ADMIN:
CBE_ADMIN:
CBE_ADMIN:LOAD PSERVER  .CN=CBE_PS.O=CBE_LABS
```

**Figure 11-17**  Loading PSERVER on the NetWare 6 server console

The print server software displayed a menu showing options to view printer status and print server information, as shown in Figure 11-18.

Available Options

Printer Status
Print Server Information

**11**

**Figure 11-18**  The Available Options menu

3. He selected the Printer Status option and pressed Enter twice to open a status window for the IS_P printer (see Figure 11-19).

4. He noticed that the "Out of paper" message was displayed because the printer was not connected to the server's LPT port. After he correctly connected the printer, the "Out of paper" message was cleared.

Printer messages might vary based on the server's configuration.

5. He pressed the down arrow key to select the Printer control option, and then pressed Enter to see the tasks listed in Figure 11-20.

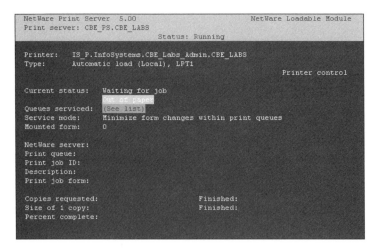

**Figure 11-19**    Viewing the printer status

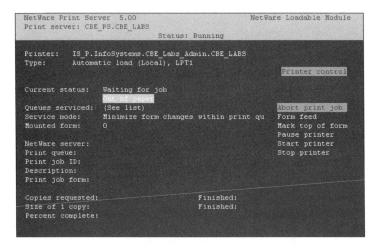

**Figure 11-20**    Tasks available for the Printer control options

6. After using the Form feed option to verify that the print server and printer were properly communicating, he pressed the Esc key twice to return to the Available Options menu.

7. The following steps describe how to unload the print server if you need to make changes to the configuration:

a. Highlight Print Server Information in the Available Options menu, and press Enter to open the Print Server Information and Status window shown in Figure 11-21.

b. Press Enter to display the Print Server Status Options menu.

c. Select the Unload after active print jobs option, and press Enter to unload your print server and return to the server console screen.

You can also unload the print server by entering the UNLOAD PSERVER command from the NetWare 6 server console. The disadvantage of using this command is that any print jobs currently bring printed might be lost.

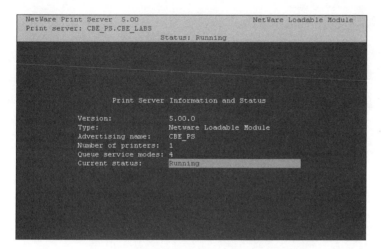

**Figure 11-21**    The Print Server Information and Status window

## Adding a Non-NDPS Printer to the Workstation

Before users can send output to the networked printer, the printer and associated drivers need to be added to the workstations. There are two methods you can use to add a non-NDPS network printer to the Windows workstation. First, create a network printer by using the Add Printer function. Second, redirect a local printer port to the NetWare print queue. Redirecting a local printer port to a print queue enables older applications written for a local printer to send output to a network printer. The disadvantage of redirecting output is that you have to be sure the network printer uses the same print driver as the local printer. If you send output to a network printer that's formatted for another type of printer, you might generate a lot of garbage output. It's usually better to create a network printer that uses the correct print driver for the printer you have selected. To set up the IS_P printer on his workstation, David did the following:

1. He clicked Start, Settings, Printers and Faxes to open the Printers dialog box.

2. He clicked the Add Printer icon under Printer Tasks to start the Add Printer Wizard, and then clicked the Next button to continue.

3. He clicked the Network printer radio button, and then clicked Next.

4. He clicked the Next button to open the Browse for Printer dialog box.

5. In the Shared printers list box, he double-clicked the NetWare Network item, and then double-clicked the Novell Directory Services item to display the CBE_LABS Organization.

6. He double-clicked the CBE_LABS Organization to display the OUs, and then navigated to the InfoSystems OU and double-clicked it to display the printer and print queue objects shown in Figure 11-22.

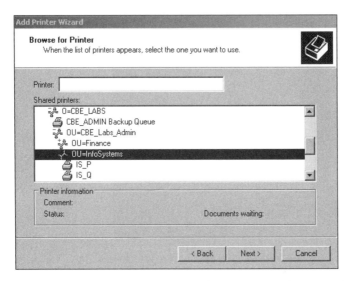

**Figure 11-22** Viewing printer and print queue objects in the Add Printer Wizard

7. He clicked the IS_Q print queue object, and then clicked Next to display a message informing him that the server did not have the correct printer drivers installed. He clicked OK to close the window and open the Printer Selection dialog box.

8. He selected the manufacturer and printer identified for the InfoSystems printer, and clicked OK to continue.

If you receive a message that the driver is already installed, click the Keep existing driver (recommended) radio button, and then click the Next button to enter the printer name.

9. He responded with Yes to use the InfoSystems printer as the default, and then clicked the Next button to display the summary window.

10. He clicked the Finish button to return to the Printers dialog box, with the new printer displayed.

# Troubleshooting Queue-Based Printing

Despite your best efforts, with so many components working together, things can go wrong and cause network-printing problems. As with any form of problem solving, a systematic, logical approach usually produces the best results. Typically, when you begin troubleshooting a network-printing problem, you should gather information about the problem and how it occurs. Part of this process is determining whether printing worked in the past. If printing has been working, look for anything that has changed, such as printer drivers, changes to printer or print queue configurations, or physical moving of equipment. If the printing process has not been used previously, look for problems in the initial setup and configuration. For example, one of the most common problems in setting up queue-based printing is forgetting to assign the printer to a print queue. If this happens, print jobs are sent to the print queue but are not printed. The most obvious sign of this problem is a lot of print jobs in the print queue. If printing has been working in the past, before spending a lot of time digging into the details, try these Novell-recommended quick-fix techniques:

1. If the printer status is offline or out of paper:

   a. Turn the printer off and on and retry the output.

   b. Check the printer self-test to make sure the printer functions properly.

   c. Check the printer cover and paper feed.

   d. Check the cable type and connections.

   e. Test the cable with a working printer.

2. If printer output is garbled:

   a. Check the printer software setting and language.

   b. Check for the correct printer driver installed at the workstation.

   c. Turn the printer off and on, and then retry the output.

3. If print jobs are not going to the print queue:

   a. Check the print queue setting for the printer on the user workstation.

   b. Check the language setting on the printer.

If the queue-based printing problems cannot be corrected with these quick fixes, determine whether the problem occurs before or after the print queue. You can use the following steps to determine whether the printing problem occurs before or after the print job reaches the print queue:

1. Stop print jobs from leaving the print queue by performing the following steps:

   a. If necessary, log in as the network administrator or print queue operator, start NetWare Administrator, and expand the container where the print queue is located.

11

    b. Right-click the print queue, and click Details to open the Print Queue dialog box.

    c. Click the Allow service by current print servers check box to disable this option.

    d. Click OK to save the setting and minimize NetWare Administrator.

    e. Use an application such as Notepad to send a job to the printer.

    f. Maximize NetWare Administrator, right-click the printer, and click Details.

    g. Click the Job List button to display the print jobs.

2. If the print job never arrives at the print queue or if the print job status indicates "Adding" and does not change to "Ready," the problem is probably in the workstation. Check the printer redirection for the workstation by performing these steps:

    a. Click Start, Settings, Printers and Faxes to open the Printers dialog box.

    b. Right-click the printer you're checking, and then click Properties.

    c. Click the Ports tab, and verify that the print queue is correctly identified in the Port and Printer columns.

3. If the print job is placed in the print queue and is in the Ready status, perform the following steps to enable service by the print server and monitor the printer status:

    a. Use NetWare Administrator to clear the Allow service by current print servers check box, as described in Step 1c.

    b. In the Print Queue dialog box, click the Assignments button, and verify that the print queue is assigned to a printer and print server.

    c. Verify that the print server is loaded on the NetWare server by going to the server console and pressing Ctrl+Esc to display all modules. If necessary, load the print server as described in the previous section.

4. If the print job is printed, but there's no output from the printer, do the following:

    a. Turn the printer off and on.

    b. Check the printer cable.

    c. Check the printer language settings.

    d. Check the print server configuration, and then unload and reload the print server. Reloading the print server can sometimes correct printing problems.

Printing problems can be tricky to find and could require a lot of checking and experimenting. The more experience you have, the more quickly you'll recognize common problems and be able to figure out solutions. If the problem persists, try re-creating the printer objects and then adding the new printer to the workstation. For a number of reasons, printer objects have been known to become corrupted, and the only solution is to re-create them. As with all troubleshooting, change only one item at a time, and then test the system. Making multiple changes can further complicate the problem, making it harder to solve.

# IMPLEMENTING NOVELL DISTRIBUTED PRINT SERVICES

Although queue-based printing works fine for small networks in which the printer can be attached to the server, setting up and maintaining queue-based printing on larger, more complex networks, with printers attached directly to the network cable, is a lot of work. **Novell Distributed Print Services (NDPS)** system is the result of a joint effort between Novell, Hewlett-Packard, and Xerox to develop a truly distributed network printing system based on the International Standards Organization 10175 Document Printing Application standard. Because most printer manufacturers support this standard, NDPS will support existing and future printer products. NDPS is an improvement over earlier NetWare printing solutions because it makes network printing easier to configure, use, and manage. As part of Novell's OneNet strategy, the NetWare 6 NDPS system also supports iPrint, which is based on the new Internet Printing Protocol (IPP) standard. Because iPrint uses IPP standards, NDPS printers can be accessed and managed across the Internet and within the corporate intranet.

NDPS is designed to simplify setting up and maintaining network printing by taking advantage of new client software and more sophisticated printers. In NDPS printing, each printer is represented by an agent that can advertise itself on the network. Printer agents can run on the NetWare server or be embedded within the network printer. An NDPS printer with embedded printer agent software enables you to simply connect the printer to the network to make it available to all users. The NDPS printer agent running on the NetWare server or the printer communicates directly with NDPS-compatible clients on user workstations so that users can spool output directly to a print job stored on a NetWare server. NDPS makes installing printers on user workstations easier by automatically downloading the necessary printer driver to the user's workstation during printer installation. NDPS has some additional key advantages over the queue-based system, including:

- *Automatic detection of NDPS-aware printers*—NDPS printers can be plugged into the network cable or hub and automatically announce their presence. This makes them immediately available for printing. (See the "Creating a Public Access Printer Agent" section later in this chapter.)

- *Automatic download of drivers to clients*—NDPS distributes the correct printer drivers to the workstation automatically when a user logs in. This eliminates the common complaint that a user can access a printer but doesn't have the correct driver for it.

**11**

■ *Bidirectional communications with printers*—**Bidirectional communication** lets clients, printers, and administrators exchange information about printers and print jobs. With bidirectional communication, you can manage NDPS printers from NetWare Administrator rather than through a proprietary management tool (such as software supplied by a printer vendor that works only with that vendor's printers) or from the printer's own keypad. Users can view the status of print jobs in real time, determine error conditions, or see when the printer is simply out of paper, for example. In the past, this information could be determined only by actually going to the printer or using a vendor-supplied tool. Bidirectional communication enables more options—via e-mail, pop-up messages, or records in an event log—for notifying users and administrators about the status of printing tasks. Third-party software supports fax notices and pager notifications, too.

In the following sections, you learn about the NDPS components and how to plan and implement an NDPS printing system.

## NDPS Components

Before implementing the NDPS network-printing environment for the CBE network, you need to understand the basic NDPS components and how they work together. As shown in Figure 11-23, the NDPS components consist of:

■ Physical printers

■ Brokers

■ NDPS Manager

■ NDPS printer agents

■ Gateways

In the following sections, you learn how these NDPS components are implemented in an NDPS printing environment and how to apply these techniques to setting up two printers: one for the CBE Labs Information Systems Department and another for all users. In the end-of-chapter projects, you use the concepts and techniques you have learned to plan and implement NDPS printing for your version of the CBE network.

### Physical Printers

Printers come in a wide variety of makes, models, and capabilities. To correctly format data and take advantage of a printer's capabilities, user workstations need to have the correct software driver loaded for the printer model they are using. To configure network printing correctly, network administrators need to define the make and model of each printer used on the network. Because NDPS directly supports a limited number of printer makes and models, Ted recommended purchasing printers included in the NDPS printer list to make configuring printers easier. CBE was already using Lexmark printers, so Ted recommended purchasing the Lexmark Optra R printers for network printing.

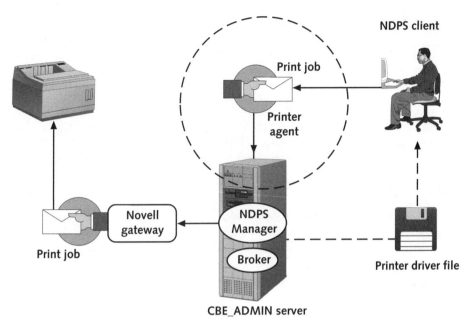

**NDPS client**

**Print job**

**Printer agent**

**Novell gateway**

**NDPS Manager**

**Broker**

**Print job**

**Printer driver file**

**CBE_ADMIN server**

**Figure 11-23**    NDPS components

You also need to identify how each printer will be attached to the network. As in queue-based printing, NDPS printers can be physically attached to the network in one of three ways:

- Local attachment to the server

- Remote attachment through a workstation

- Directly to the network cable

## Brokers

Printer agents need to register their printing services on the network and be able to send messages to users and operators. The NDPS **Broker** component provides these services to the printer agents running on the network and includes the following services for all printer agents:

- *Resource Management Service (RMS)*—This service stores network resources, such as software drivers, fonts, and forms, in a central location and then provides these resources to clients that request them. NDPS uses RMS to download printer drivers and other setup information, such as banners, to NDPS clients.

- *Event Notification Service (ENS)*—Printer agents use this service to send printer status messages to users via pop-up messages, e-mail, or log files.

**11**

- *Service Registry Service (SRS)*—This service allows NDPS printers to advertise their presence so that NDPS clients can access them. SRS also maintains printer information, such as the device type, device name, and network address. SRS reduces network traffic because it eliminates the need for each printer to broadcast its presence on the network by sending out Service Advertising Packets (SAPs) at frequent intervals.

Before creating and running printer agents, a Broker must be running on the local network. A Broker consists of both the NDPS Broker eDirectory object and software loaded on the server. Later in this section, you learn how to create and load a Broker object.

## NDPS Manager

Because most printers currently on the market do not have embedded printer agents, NetWare includes NDPS Manager, which you can run on your NetWare server to manage printer agents for printers without embedded printer agents. With NDPS Manager, any printer can be attached to the network with the local, remote, or direct attachment methods described in the queue-based printing section. Printer agent software running on NDPS Manager transfers data from the user's workstation to the printer through a printer gateway. NetWare includes NDPS printer gateways for a variety of printer models and attachment methods.

Each physical printer in NDPS must be represented on the network by a printer agent. NDPS-enabled printers have printer agent software embedded in the physical printer. Printers that aren't NDPS-enabled don't have their own embedded printer agents, so their printer agent software must run on a NetWare server. **NDPS Manager** consists of software and an eDirectory object used to create, manage, and run printer agents for printers without embedded printer agents. NDPS Manager's eDirectory object contains configuration information that tells the NDPS Manager software where to store print jobs and which users have rights to perform management tasks. After the NDPS Manager object is created, the NDPSM software must be loaded on the server to create and run printer agents. NDPS Manager also enables administrators to manage and configure printer agents from the NetWare server console. Figure 11-24 shows the relationship between NDPS Manager, printer agents, and physical printers.

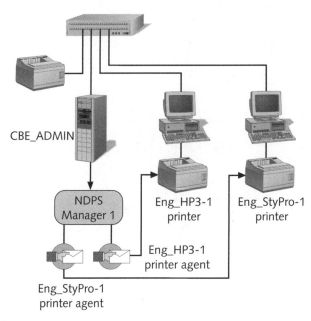

**Figure 11-24**   NDPS Manager

   Only one NDPS Manager at a time can be loaded on a NetWare server.

There's no limit on the number of printer agents that can be controlled from one NDPS Manager, but a large network can have multiple NDPS Managers running on separate NetWare servers to delegate administrative tasks or reduce network traffic across routers and WANs, as shown in Figure 11-25.

Because the CBE Labs printers do not have embedded printer agent software, before creating printer agents, David created an NDPS Manager object named CBE_NDPSM in the CLASS_TREE container. The CBE_NDPSM object contains the configuration and security information needed to load the NDPS Manager software. When configuring the CBE_NDPSM object, David selected the DATA volume rather than the SYS volume as the location for the print job database. Using a volume other than SYS for storing print jobs protects the SYS volume from filling up with print jobs waiting to be printed. If the SYS volume becomes full, the NetWare server will go down, with the possible loss of data and productivity.

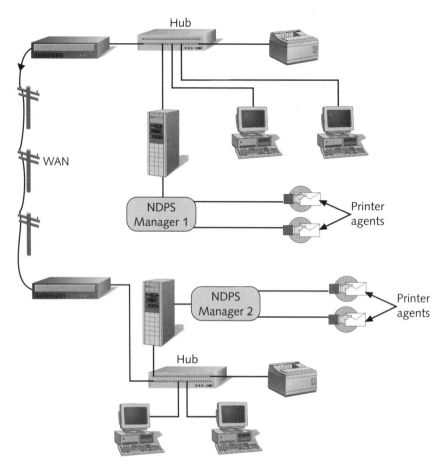

**Figure 11-25** Multiple NDPS Managers

## Printer Agents

**Printer agents** are software that represent network printers, forming the core of the NDPS architecture; each physical printer on the network must be represented by a printer agent. To configure and manage NDPS, you need to understand and work with printer agents, which perform the following three basic functions for a networked printer:

- Receive spooled output from applications running on client workstations and store the output as a print job in a database on the NetWare server

- Act as a print server by taking print jobs from the server database and printing them on the printer

- Provide printer status and control information to network clients through the Broker

With NDPS-embedded printers, the printer agent is contained in the printer itself. For non–NDPS-embedded printers, such as the CBE network printers, the printer agent is contained in the NDPS Manager software running on the NetWare 6 server. This software acts as a liaison between the physical network printer it represents and the client workstation, as shown in Figure 11-26. When a user prints to a network printer, the output first goes to the printer agent representing that printer, which spools the output to a database on the NetWare server until the printer is ready. When the printer is available, the printer agent takes a print job from the database and then transmits (through its assigned gateway) the print job and any configuration commands to the network printer.

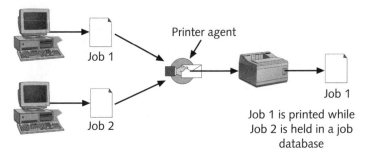

**Figure 11-26**   The NDPS printer agent

To spool printer output and work with other network services, a printer agent must be configured with basic printer information, including a name that references the physical printer, the printer's make and model, and the gateway for the printer attachment method. To access printers using iPrint's Internet Printing Protocol (IPP), printer agents must also be IPP enabled. When the first printer agent on an NDPS Manager is IPP enabled, NetWare automatically loads the IPPSRVR.NLM module to handle IPP-based printing functions. Printer agents that are not IPP enabled are accessible only to users who have Novell Client loaded.

**Types of Printer Agents**   Printer agents can be classified as public access or controlled access. As the name implies, **public access printers** are available to anyone with an attachment to the network. These printers are the easiest to set up because they do not require a corresponding eDirectory object. Using public access printers is advisable in the following circumstances:

- When you have a high-trust/low-risk network, such as in a workgroup or small office

- When you don't need NDPS's improved print job notification feature

- When you don't need to distribute printer drivers to many desktops

- When you have an NDPS-enabled printer

11

For example, CBE Labs would like to have a printer available for all employees to use when their department printer is busy or down. To accommodate this need, David is planning to install one of the Lexmark Optra R printers in a central location and then create a public access printer agent named PUB_OptR_1 for it.

Because public access printers are less secure, Novell does not encourage their use in NetWare 6 and they are not included in the CNA test objectives.

**Controlled access printers** provide more security and manageability, but for each controlled access printer, you need to create and configure an eDirectory object and then grant access to that object for the appropriate users or groups. Controlled access printers are accessible only to certain users and/or groups that the administrator defines, so they have the following advantages:

- Tighter security on who uses the printer

- Easier management of print jobs and the printer

- The option to automatically distribute printer drivers to users

A controlled access printer does, however, require creating and configuring an eDirectory object. Because most printers are not NDPS enabled, and because printer use needs to be managed in most networks, usually you'll create and administer controlled access printers. To restrict use of the InfoSystems printer to only IS users, David decided to create a controlled access printer agent named IS_OptR_1 for the InfoSystems printer. The context of a controlled access printer agent object is important in making it available to users. By default, the container in which a printer agent is created becomes a user of the printer, thereby making the printer available to all users in that container and its subcontainers. To make the IS_OptR_1 printer accessible only to users in the Information Systems Department, for example, David is planning to create the printer agent in the InfoSystems OU.

## Gateways

Before creating the printer agent, David needed to define a gateway for connecting the printer agent to the physical printer. As described earlier, for printer agent software running on NDPS Manager to access a physical printer, the printer agent needs to use one of the gateways shown in Figure 11-27.

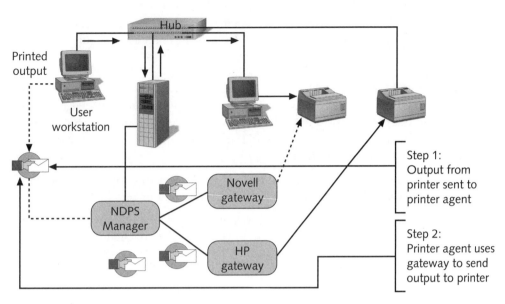

**Figure 11-27**   The NDPS gateway

As you can see in the diagram, **gateways** connect physical printers to their associated printer agents running on NDPS Manager. Gateways ensure that printer agents can communicate with physical printers regardless of the attachment method or port connecting the printer to the network. When you create a printer agent, in addition to selecting the NDPS Manager to host the agent, you need to identify the gateway and the physical printer's make, model, and connection information (port and address). To send output from the printer agent to the correct printer, you configure a gateway with the connection information that identifies the correct physical printer. The method for identifying the physical printer depends on the gateway type. For example, printers attached to the network through dedicated print server interfaces, such as the HP JetDirect print servers at CBE, use specialized gateways supplied by the printer manufacturers. These gateways typically require you to identify the printer by the IP address assigned to the dedicated print server interface.

NetWare 6 ships with several gateways, including the HP gateway, Xerox gateway, EpsonNet gateway, Lexmark IP gateway, IPP gateway, and Novell gateway. Other companies are developing gateways for their printers using Novell's System Development Kit.

**The HP and Xerox Gateways**   The HP gateway software connects printer agents to network-attached printers via an HP JetDirect print server or an HP JetDirect card. This gateway can be configured to locate all printers attached to the network via the HP JetDirect print server or JetDirect card and automatically create printer agents for them. On a large network with many directly attached printers, using this method instead of manually creating printer agents for each printer can save a lot of time. The Xerox gateway is similar in function to the HP gateway, except that it's designed to find and configure Xerox printer products.

**The Novell Gateway**    The Novell gateway consists of two major components: the Print Device Subsystem (PDS) and the Port Handler (PH). The PDS translates control information, such as commands for landscape or duplex printing, to the appropriate escape code sequence for the printer. The PH directs output to the correct physical printer with one of the following methods:

- *Local ports*—The PH enables printer agents to communicate with printers attached to the gateway computer's parallel or serial port.

- *Remote printers*—The PH provides communication between a printer agent and a remote printer. The remote printer can be attached to a client running remote printer software or directly attached via a dedicated print server device, such as HP's JetDirect or Intel's NetPort.

- *Print queue*—For devices that support printing only from a queue-based system, the PH can send printer output from a printer agent to a specified print queue serviced by a dedicated print server device, such as earlier versions of Intel's NetPort or HP's JetDirect products.

# Defining an NDPS Printing Environment

Now that you have had a chance to become more familiar with network printing and NDPS components, the first step in setting up a network-printing environment is to define the network printers to be implemented on the network. Before getting into the specifics of setting up NDPS, you should develop an overall plan for network printing. First, define printing needs for your network through this process:

1. Define the printing requirements of each user's applications.

2. Determine printer types, locations, and attachment methods.

3. Define names for all printers and identify any required print queues.

4. Plan the eDirectory context for each printer object.

In the following sections, you learn how David applied these steps to designing an NDPS network printer environment for CBE Labs.

## Step 1: Defining Printer Requirements

The first step in defining a printing environment is to identify the number and types of network printers that the organization will need. To do this, you need to analyze the requirements of each user's software and printing needs. Table 11-2 summarizes the printing needs for departments in the CBE_Labs_Admin OU.

**Table 11-2** CBE_Labs_Admin OU Printing Requirements

| All Users | All users should have access to a companywide Lexmark Optra R printer. This printer can be used if their department's printer is down or busy and will be connected directly to the network via an HP JetDirect printer interface. |
|---|---|
| InfoSystems | The department's Lexmark Optra R laser printer will be connected to the NetWare 6 server first and then later connected directly to the network via a JetDirect printer interface. This printer should be available only to InfoSystems users. |
| Finance | The department's Lexmark Optra R laser printer will be connected directly to the network and available to all Finance users and members of the Admin_Staff group to print correspondence and finance reports. |
| Administrative Staff | The department's Lexmark Optra R laser printer will be connected directly to the network and be available to all administrative staff to print correspondence and finance reports. |

After identifying printing needs, the next step is identifying each network printer agent and the gateway for attaching it to the NDPS Manager. In a multiserver environment, you should also consider how many NDPS Managers will be needed to reduce network traffic across routers. David used the NDPS Printer Definition Form, shown in Figure 11-28, to identify the printer agents, gateways, and NDPS Managers in the CBE network.

**NDPS Printer Definition Form**

NDPS Manager: *CBE_NDPSM*
Server: *CBE_ADMIN*
Managers: *CBEADMIN*

eDirectory Context: *CBE_LABS*
Database Volume: *DATA*

| Printer Name | Make/Model | NDPS Printer Classification | eDirectory Context | Attachment Method | Gateway Type | Port and Interrupt | Associated Print Queue | Users | Operators |
|---|---|---|---|---|---|---|---|---|---|
| IS_OptR_1 | Lexmark Optra R | Controlled access | .InfoSystem.CBE_Labs _Admin.CBE_LABS | File server | Novell | LPT1 Polled | IS_Q | InfoSystems container | ISMgrs group |
| PUB_OptR_1r | Lexmark Optra R | Public access | | Direct using JetDirect interface | HP gateway | | Pub_Q | All users | ISMgrs group |
| FIN_OptR_1 | Lexmark Optra R | Controlled access | .Finance.CBE_Labs_A dmin.CBE_LABS | Direct using JetDirect interface | HP gateway | | Fin_Q | Finance container | ISMgrs group Admin_Assists group |
| ADM_OptR_1 | Lexmark Optra R | Controlled access | .CBE_Labs_Admin.CB E_LABS | Direct using JetDirect interface | HP gateway | | Adm_Q | Admin_Staff group Executives group | ISMgrs group Admin_Assists group |

**Figure 11-28** The NDPS Printer Definition Form

The top part of the NDPS Printer Definition Form identifies the NDPS Manager object and the NetWare server that will run the NDPSM software. Because an NDPS Manager can support an unlimited number of printer agents, one server running the NDPS Manager software is usually enough for most organizations, except when the network is connected over a WAN. For example, if CBE Labs had a department connected across a T1 line, David would need to use a separate NDPS Printer Definition Form for that department. The form includes columns for identifying the printer model and the users and applications for each network printer attached to a print server. To keep the printing system as simple as possible, David standardized the network printers' make and model when purchasing new equipment.

After analyzing the CBE users' needs, David installed one laser printer for generating word-processing documents and reports in each department. In addition, he installed a public access laser printer available to all users for printing graphs and presentation material. By creating NDPS printer agents for these printers, they will be available on the network.

## Step 2: Determining Printer Location and Attachment Method

After identifying the printers that will meet users' projected printing requirements, the next consideration is their physical location and how they will be attached to the network. There are several rules David considered when planning locations and attachment methods for printers:

- Place the printer close to the user who is most responsible for it.

- Determine whether the printer will be a local printer attached to the server, a remote printer attached to a client, or a printer directly attached to the network.

- Identify the printer port and interrupt each printer is going to use.

- Avoid attaching remote printers to clients that are not running 32-bit operating systems, such as Windows 95, 98, or 2000/NT.

- Use a direct attachment option for printers commonly accessed by multiple users.

The NDPS Printer Definition Form shows how David has identified the attachment method and location information for each printer in the CBE network. Notice that the form shows the gateway to be used and the printer port/interrupt used with Novell gateways to connect the printer to the network. All printers except the InfoSystems printer will be attached directly to the network using the printer's own network card or an HP JetDirect print server. The Lexmark Optra R printer Ted purchased for the IS Department did not have a built-in network card, so David decided to attach it to the NetWare server using the Novell gateway. Because the server is located within the Information Systems area, users in that department can easily retrieve their printed output. Later, when he receives the JetDirect print servers, he will move the printer from the server and create a new printer agent using the HP gateway to reduce the server load.

## Step 3: Defining Printer Names

To keep your printing system as simple as possible, select printer and print queue names that will enable you to quickly identify the printer when working with the printing environment. One method is defining one- to six-character codes that identify the printer's location, model, and number and separating the codes with hyphens or underscores. For example, David used FIN_OptR_1 to identify the first Lexmark Optra R laser printer installed in the Finance Department. If additional Optra laser printers are installed in the Finance Department, their names would be FIN_OptR_2 and FIN_OptR_3.

When naming your printers in the end-of-chapter projects, you need to precede the printer name with your assigned ## student number for all students to share the same NDPS Manager program.

Notice that the NDPS Printer Definition Form also contains a column for print queue names. If a printer agent is required to support non-NDPS clients, a print queue must be created. In this case, the print queue name should be the same as the printer agent name, followed by an underscore and the letter Q. Each print queue consists of a subdirectory in the Queues directory. Because any NetWare volume can be used to store print queues, you need to assign each one to the NetWare volume where its Queues directory is located when you're defining print queues.

To prevent print queues containing many large print jobs from filling up the SYS volume, Novell recommends that you place large print queues on a volume other than SYS.

It's a good idea to physically label each printer in the office with its assigned name. This makes it easier for the network administrator and users to identify printers when working with the printing system.

## Step 4: Planning the eDirectory Context

As with all network objects, you need to define printers, print queues, and print servers in the eDirectory tree. Before you can implement network printing, you need to plan where you'll place printing objects in the tree structure. When users in multiple containers use an object, such as a printer or the print server manager, it should be placed in a container that's a parent of the user containers. For example, as shown in the NDPS Printer Definition Form, David has placed the NDPS Manager object in the CBE_LABS Organization so that it can service printers and users in any subcontainer.

Placing printers and print queues in the same container as users makes access more convenient because users can select the printer by name instead of specifying its context. For example, if the FIN_OptR_1 laser printer object is placed in the Finance container, all users in the Finance Department could send output to the printer simply by specifying the printer's name. Users whose current eDirectory contexts are located in another department's container would have to browse to the printer or use a distinguished name for the printer. Another reason for placing printer agents in the container where they are most frequently accessed is that the container storing the printer agent becomes a user of that printer agent by default. If necessary, you can make other users, groups, or containers users of a printer agent object through NetWare Administrator, as described in the following section. Notice in the NDPS Printer Definition Form that

David has located printers in the Finance or Information Systems Departments and given the Admin_Staff group rights to the Finance laser printer so that management users can access this printer if their printer is down. In the end-of-chapter projects, you'll use the information shown previously in Figure 11-28 to create NDPS printers for your version of the CBE Labs network.

# Implementing NDPS Printing

Because of Novell's OneNet strategy, NDPS printer management tasks have been included in iManager rather than ConsoleOne; NetWare Administrator still retains the NDPS management functions from earlier NetWare versions. Although either NetWare Administrator or iManager can be used to create NDPS objects, David elected to use iManager to get more experience with Novell's OneNet strategy.

## Creating NDPS Broker and NDPS Manager Objects

After planning the NDPS printing system, David started creating the network NDPS Broker object and then loading the Broker software on the CBE_ADMIN server. He performed the following steps in iManager to create an NDPS Broker object for the CBE_ADMIN server:

1. He started Internet Explorer and entered the URL https://*ip_address*:2200 (replacing *ip_address* with the IP address of the CBE_ADMIN server).

2. He clicked the CBE_ADMIN server object under the iManager heading to open the Login window.

3. He logged in with the CBEAdmin user name and password,

4. He expanded the iPrint Management heading to display the options shown in Figure 11-29.

**Figure 11-29**    The iPrint options in iManager

5. He clicked the Create Broker option to open the Create Broker window shown in Figure 11-30.

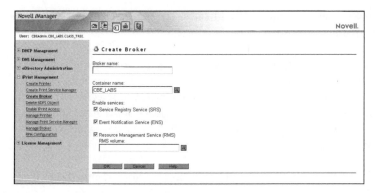

**Figure 11-30**    The Create Broker window

6. He entered the name CBE_Broker in the Broker name text box.

7. He verified that the CBE_LABS Organization was displayed in the Container name text box.

8. He clicked the browse button next to the RMS volume text box to open the eDirectory Object Selector window.

9. He clicked the CBE_ADMIN_SYS volume to place it in the RMS volume text box.

10. He clicked OK to create the Broker object, and then clicked OK to close the "Create Broker succeeded" message and return to the iManager window.

11. Next, he clicked the Create Print Service Manager option to open the Create Manager window shown in Figure 11-31.

**Figure 11-31**    The Create Manager window

12. He entered CBE_NDPSM in the Manager name text box.

13. He verified that the CBE_LABS Organization was displayed in the Container name text box.

14. To select the volume for the print job database, he clicked the browse button next to the Database volume text box to open the eDirectory Object

Selector window, and then clicked the CBE_ADMIN_DATA volume to place it in the Database volume text box.

The Database volume text box is used to specify the volume where the print jobs will be stored. Depending on the number of networked printers, print jobs can consume a lot of disk space, making it important to select a volume that has enough free space. Placing the print job database on a data volume rather than the SYS volume helps prevent filling up the SYS volume, which could halt server operations.

15. He clicked OK to create the NDPS Manager object, and then clicked OK to close the "Create Manager request succeeded" message box and return to the iManager window.

16. He clicked the Exit button on the toolbar to return to the iManager Login window. He then closed Internet Explorer and logged out.

**Loading Broker and NDPS Manager Software** Before creating the other NDPS objects, the Broker and NDPS Manager software need to be loaded on the NetWare server. David used the following steps in Remote Manager to load this software on the CBE_ADMIN server:

1. First, he started his Web browser and entered the URL https://*ip_address*:2200 (replacing *ip_address* with the IP address assigned to the CBE_ADMIN server) to open the NetWare Web Manager window.

2. Next, he clicked the CBE_ADMIN server object under the NetWare Remote Manager heading to open the Login window.

3. He entered the CBEAdmin user name and password, and then clicked OK to open the NetWare Remote Manager window, similar to the one in Figure 11-32.

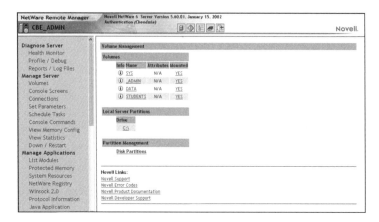

**Figure 11-32** The NetWare Remote Manager window

4. He clicked the Console Screens link under the Manage Server heading on the left to open the Current Screens window.

5. He clicked the System Console link, clicked in the command text box, and entered the command LOAD BROKER .CBE_BROKER.CBE_LABS.

6. He then clicked the Execute Command Line button to load the Broker software.

7. After the Broker window displayed, he entered LOAD NDPSM .CBE_NDPSM.CBE_LABS in the command text box (see Figure 11-33), and clicked the Execute Command Line button again to load the NDSPM Manager software.

```
CBE_ADMIN:
CBE_ADMIN:LOAD BROKER .CBE_BROKER.CBE_LABS
Loading Module BROKER.NLM                        [    OK    ]
CBE_ADMIN:
CBE_ADMIN:LOAD NDPSM .CBE_NDPSM.CBE_LABS
Loading Module NDPSM.NLM                          [    OK    ]
CBE_ADMIN:
```

**Figure 11-33**  Loading the Broker and NDSP Manager software

8. After loading the Broker and NDPSM Manager software, he closed the CBE_ADMIN - System Console window and returned to Remote Manager.

9. He clicked the Exit button on the Remote Manager toolbar, and clicked Yes to end the remote management session and close Internet Explorer.

## Adding Printer Drivers to the Broker

The Broker's Resource Management Service can be used to add printer drivers to the network. For example, after creating and loading the CBE_Broker, David used the following steps to add a printer driver for the HP DeskJet 880C printer to the Broker's RMS:

1. He logged in to the Novell network with his CBE Admin user name and password, started NetWare Administrator, and expanded the CBE_LABS Organization.

2. He double-clicked the CBE_Broker object and clicked the Resource Management (RMS) button to open the Resource Path dialog box.

3. He clicked the Add Resources button to open the Manage Resources dialog box.

4. He clicked the Windows 2000 Printer drivers button to display the list of current resources.

5. He clicked the Extract From File button to display all Windows 2000 printer drivers on his workstation.

6. He scrolled down and clicked the HP DeskJet 880C printer type, and clicked OK.

7. He inserted his Windows CD into the workstation to copy the drivers to the RMS database.

8. He clicked the Continue Anyway button when the Hardware Installation message box displayed.

9. After the files were copied, he clicked OK to return to the Resource Path dialog box, and clicked Cancel to return to NetWare Administrator.

## Creating Printer Agents

After the NDPS Manager is running, you can continue to set up NDPS printers by creating the printer agents and gateways. In the following examples, you see how David used NetWare Administrator to create both controlled access and public access printer agents for the CBE Labs network.

**Creating a Controlled Access Printer Agent**    To prevent users from printing to network printers in other departments, David created a controlled access printer agent for each department's printer in the department OU, as shown on the NDSP Printer Definition Form. Although printer agents can be created with iManager, he used NetWare Administrator because it has more options for selecting gateways and configuring the printer attachment. In the following example, you see how he used NetWare Administrator to create a controlled access printer agent for the InfoSystems OU using the Novell gateway:

1. After logging in as the CBEAdmin user, he started NetWare Administrator and opened a browse window to the CBE_LABS container.

2. Next, he clicked the InfoSystems OU, and then pressed Insert to open the New Object dialog box.

3. He scrolled down and double-clicked the NDPS Printer object to open the Create NDPS Printer dialog box (see Figure 11-34).

4. He entered IS_OptR_1 in the NDPS Printer Name text box and verified that the Create a New Printer Agent radio button was selected.

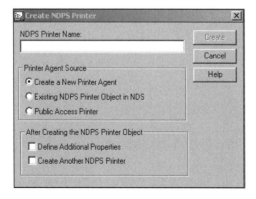

**Figure 11-34**    The Create NDPS Printer dialog box

5. He clicked the Define Additional Properties check box, and then clicked the Create button to open the Create Printer Agent dialog box, shown in Figure 11-35.

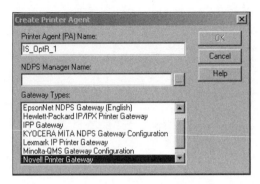

**Figure 11-35**    The Create Printer Agent dialog box

6. He clicked the browse button next to NDPS Manager Name to open the Select Object dialog box. In the Browse context section, he navigated to the CBE_LABS Organization. He double-clicked the CBE_NDPSM object in the Available objects section to place it in the NDPS Manager Name text box.

7. He verified that Novell Printer Gateway was selected in the Gateway Types list, and then clicked OK to open the Configure Novell PDS for Printer Agent dialog box, shown in Figure 11-36.

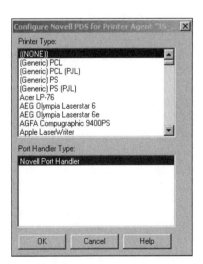

**Figure 11-36**    The Configure Novell PDS for Printer Agent dialog box

8. He scrolled down and clicked Lexmark Optra R in the Printer Type list box, and then clicked OK to open the Configure Port Handler for Printer Agent dialog box shown in Figure 11-37.

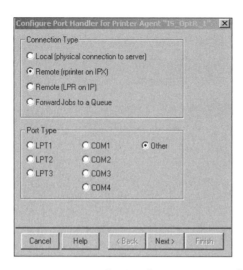

**Figure 11-37**    The Configure Port Handler for Printer Agent dialog box

9. In the Connection Type section, he clicked the Local (physical connection to server) radio button, and in the Port Type section, clicked the LPT1 radio button used to connect the printer to the NetWare server's printer port.

10. He clicked the Next button to set controller type and interrupts, as shown in Figure 11-38. In this dialog box, he clicked the interrupt used by the NetWare server for the LPT1 printer port he selected.

Unless you're sure of the interrupt number used by your client workstation's LPT port, click the None (polled mode) option.

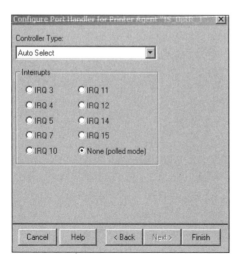

**Figure 11-38**    Configuring the controller type and interrupt

11. He clicked the Finish button to create the printer agent for the IS_OptR_1 printer.

12. While the system creates and loads the printer agent, usually a Loading Printer Agent wait message is displayed. Because a printer was not currently connected to the new printer agent, however, David saw a message indicating that the printer needed attention. Because this problem will be corrected later by loading the remote printer software, he clicked OK to continue.

13. The Select Printer Drivers dialog box opened, which is used to identify the printer driver for the client to use when formatting output for this printer. David clicked the Windows 2000 Driver tab and verified that Lexmark Optra R was selected in the Printer Drivers list box (see Figure 11-39).

 At this time, he could also select the Windows 95/98 and Windows NT 4 Driver tabs to select printer drivers for users accessing the printer from those operating systems.

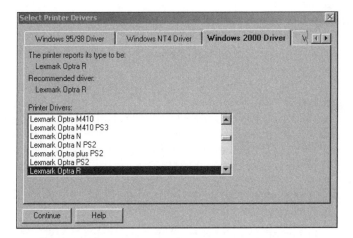

**Figure 11-39**   The Select Printer Drivers dialog box

14. He clicked the Continue button to open the Information - NDPS summary window. After verifying the entries, he clicked OK to continue.

15. Because no printer was currently connected to his workstation, he saw an error message informing him that printer details could not be viewed. He clicked OK to continue and open the NetWare Printer Control dialog box for the IS_OptR_1 printer (see Figure 11-40).

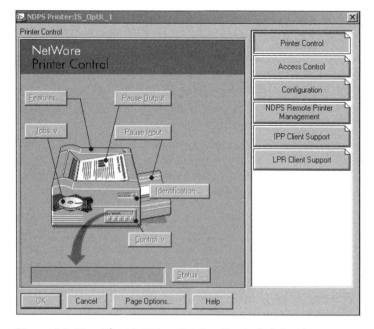

**Figure 11-40**    The NetWare Printer Control dialog box

16. By default, the container that the printer agent is created in becomes a member of the Users list, and the Admin user is made the Manager. Making the container where the printer is created a User allows all users in that container and its subcontainers to access the printer. To change the default Users or Managers, David clicked the Access Control button to open the Access Control dialog box shown in Figure 11-41.

17. To make his user name an Operator of the printer, David did the following:

   a. He clicked the Operators icon to display the current operators, and then clicked the Add button to open the Select Object dialog box.

   b. He double-clicked his user name in the Available objects section to add it to the Current Operators list box.

18. After completing the printer agent setup, he clicked the Printer Control button to return to the NetWare Printer Control dialog box. He clicked OK to save his changes and return to the NetWare Administrator browse window.

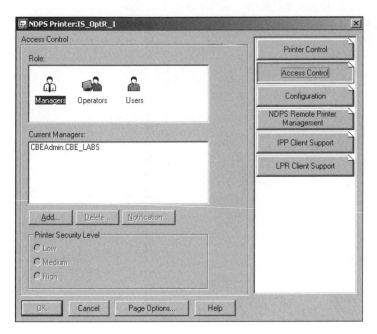

**Figure 11-41**     The Access Control dialog box

**Creating a Public Access Printer Agent**     To make a Lexmark printer accessible to all users in case their department printer is down or busy, Ted purchased another Lexmark Optr R printer and a HP JetDirect printer interface. Because the new printer will be available to all users, David decided to create a public access printer agent for it. Public access printer agents are created in much the same way as controlled access printer agents, except you select the NDPS Manager object instead of the OU. He used the following steps in NetWare Administrator to create a public access printer agent that uses the HP gateway to send output to the new printer:

1. To create the public access printer within the NDPS Manager, he expanded the CBE_LABS Organization and then double-clicked the CBE_NDPSM object to open the NDPS Manager dialog box.

2. He clicked the Printer Agent List button to display the Printer Agent List page, similar to the one shown in Figure 11-42.

**11**

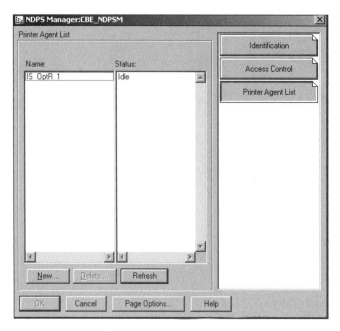

**Figure 11-42**    The Printer Agent List page

3. He clicked the New button to open the Create Printer Agent dialog box shown previously in Figure 11-35.

4. He entered PUB_OptR_1 in the Printer Agent (PA) Name text box and verified that the CBE_NDPSM print service manager was selected in the NDPS Manager Name text box.

5. He clicked Hewlett-Packard IP/IPX Printer Gateway in the Gateway Types list, and then clicked OK to open the Configure HP Printer Gateway for PA "PUB_OptR_1" dialog box shown in Figure 11-43.

6. He scrolled down and clicked the Lexmark Optra R printer type in the Printer Type list box, and then clicked the IP Printer radio button to display all the Jet Direct interfaces currently connected to the network.

To identify a printer by IP address, click the Specify Address or name radio button, and then enter the IP address assigned to the JetDirect interface. If you do not know the IP address, you can click the Printer/JetDirect radio button to display a list of JetDirect interfaces that have been automatically detected on the network. Some JetDirect interfaces can have multiple printer ports. On these types of interfaces, you must enter the port number of the JetDirect interface used to connect the printer.

7. He selected the JetDirect interface attached to the PUB_OptR_1 printer, and then clicked OK.

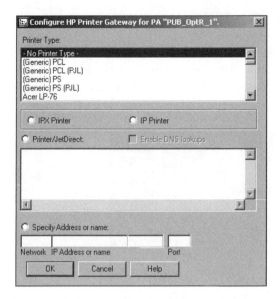

**Figure 11-43**    Configuring the HP gateway

If a JetDirect interface is not found or the printer is not connected or turned on, you'll see a message indicating that the printer needs attention. This problem will be corrected later by connecting the JetDirect printer.

11

8. After the printer agent was created, the Select Printer Drivers dialog box opened, and he identified the printer driver by clicking the Windows 2000 Driver tab and verifying that the Lexmark Optra R was selected.

9. He clicked the Continue button to open the Information - NDPS summary window. When he was satisfied with the selections, he clicked OK to create the printer and return to the Printer Agent List page shown previously in Figure 11-42.

10. After verifying that the printer was listed, he clicked Cancel to return to NetWare Administrator.

## Installing NDPS Printers from User Workstations

After setting up the NDPS printing components for all the CBE Labs printers, David's next task was installing network printers on user workstations. As with queue-based printing, to use an NDPS printer, a workstation must have a printer driver and client. Applications use the driver to format data correctly for the printer's type and model, and the printer client is responsible for sending output to the network printer agent. As with queue-based printers, you can manually install a network printer on a user's workstation with the Add Printer function in the Windows Printers dialog box. Manually adding printers to user workstations can be time-consuming for network administrators and might require extra training to instruct users on how to add their own printers. A preferred alternative is having Novell Client automatically install the NDPS printers when users log in. To automatically install printers on user workstations, use NetWare Administrator to add printers to the NDPS Remote Printer Management page, shown in Figure 11-44.

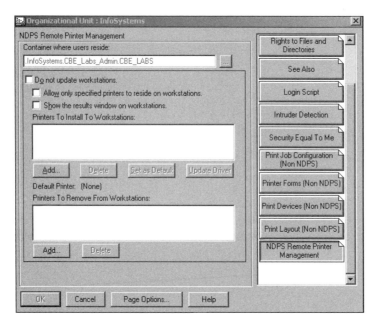

**Figure 11-44**    The NDPS Remote Printer Management page

When you add a printer to the Printers To Install To Workstations section, it's installed upon login on the workstation of any user in that container. For example, if you add the IS_OptR_1 printer to the Printers To Install To Workstations section, when users in the InfoSystems OU, such as Mark Ciampa, log in, Novell Client checks to see whether the IS_OptR_1 printer has been installed; if not, Novell Client automatically installs the printer. In the following example, David added the IS_OptrR_1 printer to the Printers To Install To Workstations section for the InfoSystems OU:

1. He started NetWare Administrator and opened a browse window to the CBE_LABS Organization.

2. He right-clicked the InfoSystems OU, and then clicked Details to open the Organizational Unit: InfoSystems dialog box.

3. He scrolled down and clicked the NDPS Remote Printer Management button to display the Printers To Install To Workstations section.

4. He clicked the Add button to display the Available Printers options, clicked the IS_OptR_1 printer, and clicked OK to add it to the Printers To Install To Workstations section.

5. He clicked OK to save the changes and return to NetWare Administrator.

When users from the InfoSystems OU log in, Novell Client will automatically install the IS_OptR_1 printer and download the printer driver software.

## Troubleshooting NDPS Printing

Many of the basics you learned about troubleshooting queue-based network printing problems apply to NDPS printing. Novell recommends the following "quick fixes" for solving problems that occur when setting up NDPS printing:

1. Attempt to resolve any error messages received at the server, printer agent, or client by using the following suggestions:

   ■ If the error message says the client could not connect to the printer agent, verify that the NDPS Manager and Broker are both loaded and running. If they are both loaded, unload and then load the NDPS Manager.

   ■ Verify that the Autoexec.ncf file contains a LOAD NDPSM command and that the correct distinguished name of the NDPS Manager is specified.

   ■ If the client receives a message that a print job was rejected, check to see that the spooling volume for the printer agent has enough free space. If possible, use a volume other than SYS and set a limit on the spooling space.

2. If a network-printing problem is limited to a single workstation, check the following:

   ■ Check the printer's job list to ensure that the job is getting to the spooling volume.

   ■ Review any changes made since the printer agent was properly working.

   ■ Check the printer configuration.

3. If a network-printing problem affects several workstations, check the following:

   ■ In Novell Printer Manager, check the Printer Information dialog box for any NDPS error messages.

   ■ Check for printer error conditions (printer beeps or LCD panel lights) and error messages.

   ■ Turn the printer off and on. If the job is still in the printer agent job list, delete it.

In addition to the preceding checks, the following tables contain tips for troubleshooting NDPS printing based on the scope of the printing problem. Table 11-3 contains suggestions on isolating specific NDPS printing problems for a single workstation that's unable to print to an NDPS printer that other workstations are using successfully.

**11**

**Table 11-3** Isolating Single-Workstation Printer Problems

| Condition | Possible Problem | Action |
|---|---|---|
| The user workstation is printing to a print queue, but the printer receives no output. This could happen for non-NDPS clients, such as DOS or Macintosh computers. | The print queue is not being serviced by a printer agent or queue-based print server. | Use NetWare Administrator to verify that the print job is in the print queue. Verify that the print queue is being serviced by a print server or printer agent. If necessary, associate the print queue with the appropriate NDPS printer agent and verify that the printer agent is printing jobs for other workstations. |
| | The print job is being sent to the wrong print queue. | Check the printer configuration on the workstation to be sure it's associated with the correct print queue. |
| | The printer is using an incorrect print driver, causing the print device to disregard the print job. | Check the printer configuration on the workstation to make sure the printer is using the correct driver for the printer agent that services the corresponding print queue. |
| Print jobs do not appear in the printer agent's job list. | The Windows printer configuration is not correct. | Click Start, Settings, Printers and Faxes and check the printer status to see if any problems are evident. |
| | | Check the driver and printer port configuration. The port should be configured to print to the correct printer agent or print queue. |

Table 11-4 contains suggestions for troubleshooting problems that could prevent an NDPS printer from printing jobs for all workstations.

**Table 11-4** Isolating NDPS Printer Problems

| Condition | Possible Problem | Action |
|---|---|---|
| Printer agent problem | Printer agent is unable to connect to the print device. | Check the printer status on the server console or through NetWare Administrator. |

**Table 11-4**     Isolating NDPS Printer Problems (continued)

| Condition | Possible Problem | Action |
|---|---|---|
| Printer not connected | The printer agent is configured as a local printer on the Novell gateway, and the printer is not attached to the server or is turned off. | Attach or turn on the printer and retry printing. |
| | The printer agent is configured as a remote printer on the Novell gateway, and the NPTWIN95 remote printer software is not loaded or the computer hosting the printer has been shut down. | Load the NPTWIN95 software on the workstation hosting the print device and connect it to the correct printer agent. Start the computer hosting the print device and retry. |
| I/O error | The printer agent is configured as a local printer on the Novell gateway, using the same port as a printer agent that's already loaded. | Determine which printer agent should be using that printer port on the server and then delete the incorrectly configured printer agent and re-create it, using a different gateway or printer port. |
| | The printer agent is configured as a direct attached printer using a printer interface, and the printer interface is not connected to the network or is powered down. | Reconnect or power on the printer interface and try again. If necessary, wait until there's no printer activity, and then unload and load the NDPS Manager on the server. |
| | The printer agent is configured as a printer attached directly to the network, using a gateway such as the HP JetDirect, and the printer interface is disconnected from the network or powered off. | Reconnect the printer interface and then power it off and on. If the status does not change after a few minutes, wait until there's no printing activity and then unload and reload the NDPS Manager on the server. |
| Printer not found | The printer gateway is not available, or the print device is disconnected from the gateway. | Reconnect the printer to the printer interface and retry. |
| Printer offline | The printer is out of paper or turned off. | Make sure the print device is on, and check for any error messages on the print device panel. |
| | The printer cable is defective or disconnected. | Check the printer cable to make sure it's securely attached to the print device and interface. If the printer still shows offline status, test and replace the printer cable. |

11

**Table 11-4**    Isolating NDPS Printer Problems (continued)

| Condition | Possible Problem | Action |
|---|---|---|
| Printer status is grayed out | NDPS Manager is not loaded. | Load the NDPS Manager on the server console. |
| | The wrong NDPS Manager is loaded. | If you have multiple NDPS Managers in your tree, verify that the correct NDPS Manager for the printer is loaded. If necessary, unload the incorrect NDPS Manager and load the correct one. |
| | The new printer agent encountered an error when first loading. | If a print device or interface is not attached to the network, the printer is turned off, or the remote printer software has not yet been loaded on a Windows 95/98 computer, you'll see an error message when creating the printer agent and the status will be grayed out in the Printer Control dialog box. Close the Printer Control dialog box, and then reopen it to view the printer status. |
| Jobs print but remain in the job list | User or operator hold is on. | Click the Configuration button in the Printer Control dialog box, and then modify the Job Hold settings of any job configurations listed in the Printer Configurations dialog box. |
| Jobs removed from the job list but not printed | Incorrect driver language. | Verify that the correct printer driver is configured for the printer agent. Incorrect drivers can cause the printer to disregard print jobs. |
| | Cable problem. | Faulty printer cables or broken wires can prevent data from reaching the print device. Test and replace the printer cable. |
| Jobs not displayed in the job list | Workstation printer configuration problem. | Check the printer configuration on the workstation to make sure it's using the correct driver and is printing to the correct printer agent or print queue. |

**Table 11-4**    Isolating NDPS Printer Problems (continued)

| Condition | Possible Problem | Action |
|---|---|---|
|  | Users do not have rights to print to the printer. | Verify that the printer agent is in the same container as the users who are printing. Verify that users who are not in the same container as the printer agent have been added to the access control list. |

An important part of any printer troubleshooting is tracking print jobs from the workstation to the printer agent. In the end-of-chapter projects, you practice the steps for tracking print jobs by walking through two sample problems.

## IPRINT AND INTERNET PRINTING PROTOCOL

To use NDPS printers, the user's workstation must have a printer driver installed and configured to send output to a printer agent. In earlier versions of NetWare, the Novell client software had to be installed on the user's workstation before NDPS printer agents could be installed and accessed. In NetWare 6, Novell has removed the requirement for the Novell client and replaced it with the iPrint system. As part of Novell's OneNet strategy, **iPrint** makes network printing independent of the client software and type of network connection. By using the industry-standard **Internet Printing Protocol (IPP)**, iPrint enables users to print from anywhere to anywhere. With iPrint, users can use a Web browser to locate printers and then automatically download and install the latest printer drivers on their workstations. The iPrint system consists of three major components (see Figure 11-45):

- A print provider consisting of a set of browser plug-ins installed on the Web browser of a user's workstation to communicate with the IPP server software.

- The IPP server software installed on the NetWare 6 server during server installation. The IPP server software, which consists of the IPPSRVR.NLM module, is automatically loaded on the server when the first iPrint printer is configured.

- A set of HTML pages on the NetWare server that enable users to install the iPrint client and to set up and access network printers.

**11**

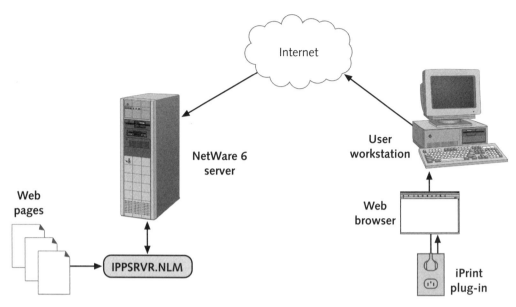

**Figure 11-45** iPrint components

In the following sections, you learn the benefits of iPrint, how to use iManager to enable your public access printer agent for IPP printing, and how to use iPrint to install and access printers from your workstation.

## Benefits of iPrint

In addition to using the recognized industry-standard IPP printing protocol, iPrint provides the following benefits that promise to make it the primary future printing protocol.

- *Global access to printers*—Mobile employees, customers, and business partners can use iPrint from their Web browsers to access IPP-enabled printers from any location, whether using the LAN in the office building, an Internet connection from home, or a remote connection from a conference thousands of miles away.

- *Lower costs*—Without iPrint, users needed to fax or e-mail documents to the office. Faxing a document often results in expensive phone charges and produces a lower quality image. E-mailing requires the recipient to open and print the document using a compatible application, which takes up valuable employee time and resources.

- *Secure printing*—By integrating IPP with eDirectory, iPrint ensures that only authorized users can send output to IPP-enabled printers. In addition, high-security encryption prevents outside intruders from accessing document contents.

- *Centralized management*—Using iManager with the iPrint management tools, network administrators can control all printers from a single location, even if printers are made by different manufacturers and are located at multiple sites.

■ *Convenient printer selection*—Users can use the iPrint plug-in from their Web browsers to view available printers and printer status or find a printer that meets certain printing requirements, such as a color ink-jet or high-speed laser printer. Network administrators can use iPrint Map Designer to create facility maps that show the location and types of printers around the network. Users can then access this map to send output to the printer that best meets their needs.

# Enabling Printers for iPrint

For an existing NDPS printer agent to be accessed from iPrint using IPP, the printer must first be IPP enabled. Enabling a printer agent identifies and connects it to the IPPSRVR software running on the NetWare 6 server. If this software is not running, it's automatically loaded when the first printer agent is IPP enabled. You can use NetWare Administrator or iManager to enable an existing NDPS printer. David used the following steps in iManager to enable the PUB_OptR_1 printer for iPrint access:

1. He started Internet Explorer and entered the URL https://*ip_address*:2200 (replacing *ip_address* with the IP address of the CBE_ADMIN NetWare 6 server). He clicked OK and Yes to display the NetWare Web Manager menu.

2. He clicked the CBE_ADMIN server under the iManager heading to open the Login window.

3. He entered the CBEAdmin user name, password, and context in the corresponding text boxes, and then clicked the Login button.

4. He expanded the iPrint Management heading, and then clicked the Enable iPrint Access link to display the NDPS Manager text box.

5. He clicked the browse button next to the NDPS Manager text box to open the eDirectory Object Selector window, and then double-clicked the CBE_NDPSM object to place it in the NDPS Manager text box.

6. He clicked OK to open the Printer Agents window, similar to the one in Figure 11-46.

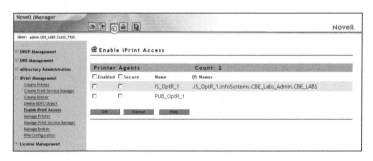

**Figure 11-46**    The Printer Agents window

7. He clicked the check boxes in the Enabled column next to the PUB_OptR_1 and IS_OptR_1 printers.

8. He clicked the check box in the Secure column for the IS_OptR_1 printer to increase security for that printer.

9. He clicked OK to open the Results window, and then clicked OK to return to the iManager menu.

10. To end the session, he clicked the Exit button on the iManager toolbar, and then closed Internet Explorer.

## Creating Printers from iManager

Creating NDPS printers from iManager is a two-step process. First, use iManager to create and enable the printer agent. Currently, iManager allows the selection of only the Novell IPP printer gateway, which is designed to act as an interface between the printer agent and the IPP-enabled client; you cannot assign a gateway to a printer agent running on the NDPS print service manager. Therefore, the second step in setting up a printer from iManager is to assign the printer agent a gateway from the NDPS print service manager.

### Part 1: Creating the Printer Agent

David used the following steps in iManager to create a printer agent for the FIN_OptR_1 printer:

1. He started Internet Explorer and entered the URL https://*ip_address*:2200 (replacing *ip_address* with the IP address of the CBE_ADMIN server). He clicked OK and then Yes to display the NetWare Web Manager menu.

2. He clicked the CBE_ADMIN server under the iManager heading to open the Login window.

3. He entered the CBEAdmin user name, password, and context in the corresponding text boxes, and then clicked the Login button.

4. He expanded the iPrinter Management heading and then clicked the Create Printer link under the iPrint Management heading to open the Create Printer dialog box shown in Figure 11-47.

5. He entered FIN_OptR_1 in the Printer name text box and clicked the browse button to change the container name to Finance.CBE_Labs_Admin.CBE_LABS.

6. He selected the CBE_NDPSM printer service manager in the Manager name text box.

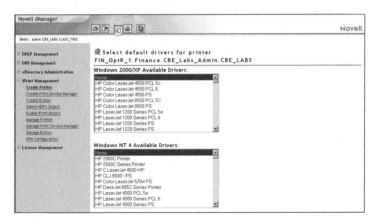

**Figure 11-47**    The Create Printer dialog box

The only gateway types shown in the Gateway type window are the Novell IPP gateway (IPP on IP) and the Novell LPR gateway (LPR on IP). If a printer has embedded IPP gateway software, selecting the Novell IPP gateway type is all that's needed to send output to the printer. If the printer does not directly support the IPP gateway, it is necessary to use the Print Service Manager to select a gateway type, as described in "Part 2: Selecting an NDPS Driver."

7. Because the printer will be using an NDPS gateway to emulate the IPP gateway functions, he selected the Novell IPP gateway (IPP on IP) option and then clicked Next to display the Printer URL text box.

8. He entered FIN_OptR_1.Finance.CBE_Labs_Admin.CBE_LABS, the distinguished name for the printer, in the Printer URL text box, and clicked Next to load the printer and open the Select default drivers for printer dialog box shown in Figure 11-48.

**Figure 11-48**    Selecting a printer driver

9. He clicked the Lexmark Optra R driver in the Windows 2000/XP Available Drivers window and then scrolled down and clicked Next to display the "Create Printer request succeeded" message.

10. He clicked OK to return to the iManager window. To close his session, he clicked the Exit button to return to the Login window, and then closed Internet Explorer.

## Part 2: Selecting an NDPS Printer Agent

David used the following steps in Remote Manager from his workstation to access the NDPS print service manager and create a printer agent for the FIN_OptR_1 printer agent:

1. He started Internet Explorer and entered the https://*ip_address*:2200 URL (replacing *ip_address* with the IP address of the CBE_ADMIN server) to access the NetWare Web Manager home page.

2. He clicked the CBE_ADMIN server under the NetWare Remote Manager heading and logged in with the CBEAdmin user name and password to display the NetWare Remote Manager main window.

3. He clicked the Console Screens link to display a list of modules currently running on the server.

4. He clicked NDPS Manager to display the NDPS Manager Printer Agent list showing the newly created FIN_OptR_1 printer.

5. At the bottom of the window, he clicked the UP button to highlight the FIN_OptR_1 printer, and then clicked the ENTER button to open the printer agent information window shown in Figure 11-49.

6. He clicked the DOWN button to highlight the Configuration: (See Form) option and then clicked the ENTER button to open a configuration window.

7. He clicked the DOWN button again to highlight the Configuration Utilities: (See List) option and clicked the ENTER button to display a list of gateway types.

8. David wanted the output to be displayed on the server's console screen to test the printer. To select the server console as the output device, he did the following:

   a. He clicked the DOWN button and then clicked ENTER to select the Novell Printer Gateway.

   b. He clicked the DOWN button and then clicked ENTER to select Generic PCL as the printer type.

   c. He clicked the ENTER button and then clicked ENTER to select the default Novell Port Handler.

   d. He clicked the DOWN button and then clicked ENTER to select Local Printer as the connection type.

   e. He clicked the DOWN button and then clicked ENTER to select SCREEN as the port type.

```
NDPS Manager  v3.00c                        NetWare Loadable Module
NDPS Manager: .CBE NDPSM.CBE LABS

Printer Agent:          FIN OptR 1
  Status and Control:   Error Printing
  Status Details:       Printer Not Connected
  Information:          (See Form)
  Configuration:       (See Form)
  Current Medium:       Any Medium


Job Name:
  ID:
  Requested Medium:


  Kbytes Sent:                    of
  Copies Sent:                    of

  Percentage Sent:


Displays printer control options such as Pause, Resume, and Shutdown.

Enter=Select option    Esc=Previous menu    Alt+F10=Exit              F1=Help
```

F1 F2 F3 F4 F5 F6 F7 F8 F9 F10 | ALT-F10

Send Command Line

UP | DOWN | INSERT | HOME | PGUP | TAB | BACKSPACE

LEFT | RIGHT | DELETE | END | PGDN | ENTER | ESC

**Figure 11-49**   The NDPS Manager printer agent information window

9. After setting the gateway, he received a message informing him that the printer agent needed to be shut down and restarted for the change to take effect. He clicked the ENTER button to clear the message and return to the printer agent configuration window.

10. He clicked the ESC button to return to the printer agent information window.

11. David did the following to restart the printer:

   a. He clicked the UP button to highlight the Status and Control field and then clicked the ENTER button to display the Printer Control menu.

   b. He clicked the DOWN button to highlight the Shutdown Printer option and then clicked the ENTER button.

   c. With the Status and Control field now showing "Shut Down," he again clicked the ENTER button to display the Printer Control menu listing only the Start Up Printer option.

   d. He clicked the ENTER button to restart the printer with the new gateway.

12. He clicked the ESC button to return to the main NDPS printer agent list and then closed Internet Explorer to return to the NetWare Remote Manager window. He clicked the Exit button and clicked Yes to close his session and exit Remote Manager.

## Installing the iPrint Client and IPP Printers

With Novell's iPrint system, you can install the printer driver and client on a user workstation from your Web browser. Using iPrint simplifies setting up a network printer and enables computers to print to NDPS printers without using Novell Client. On the NetWare server, iPrint works through the IPPSRVR.NLM software and a set of HTML pages available from the NetWare Web server. Installing a printer on the user workstation involves three steps:

1. Access the iPrint Web site from the workstation browser by entering the URL for the NetWare Web server and a port number. Port number 631 is used to access public access printers that do not require a user name, and port number 443 is used for controlled access printer agents that require a valid user name.

2. Download the IPP client software from the NetWare Web server to the user workstation. This process is performed automatically the first time an IPP printer is installed on the workstation.

3. Install a printer for the IPP-enabled printer agent. The printer consists of an IPP connection to the printer agent and the correct driver software for formatting the printer output at the workstation.

David installed the PUB_OptR_1 printer on his workstation, and then used iManager to verify that print jobs were sent to the printer:

1. He started Internet Explorer, entered the URL http://*ip_address*:631/ipp (replacing *ip_address* with the IP address of the CBE_ADMIN server), and pressed Enter.

2. When he saw the iPrint client installation message box, he clicked OK, and then followed these steps to install the iPrint client on his workstation:

   a. In the File Download dialog box, he clicked the Open button to run the program and extract the files.

   b. He clicked OK to select the English language and start the iPrint Installation Wizard.

   c. When he saw the Welcome window, he clicked Next to open the license agreement window.

   d. After reading the agreement, he clicked Yes to accept it and open the Select Program Folder dialog box.

   e. He clicked Next to accept the default Novell iPrint folder location and begin the file copying.

   f. He clicked Yes in the ReadOnly File Detected message boxes to overwrite the indicated files.

   g. After the installation was finished, he verified that the Yes, I want to restart my computer now radio button was selected, and then clicked the Finish button to restart his computer.

3. After the computer restarted, he logged in with the CBEAdmin user name and password.

4. He started Internet Explorer and entered the iPrint URL shown in Step 1 to display a list of IPP-enabled printers (see Figure 11-50).

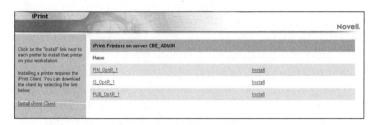

**Figure 11-50**    The list of IPP-enabled printers on the CBE_ADMIN server

5. He clicked the Install link next to the PUB_OptR_1 printer and then clicked OK to begin the installation.

6. After the printer was installed, he clicked OK to close the "Printer has been installed successfully" message and return to the iPrint Printers list.

7. To test the printer, he minimized Internet Explorer and then did the following:

  a. He clicked Start, Settings, Printers and Faxes to verify that the printer was installed.

  b. He made the PUB_OptR_1 printer the default printer.

  c. He closed the Printers and Faxes window and started Notepad.

  d. He created and printed a short document.

  e. He closed Notepad and then maximized Internet Explorer.

8. To display the existing print jobs, he clicked the PUB_OptR_1 printer to display the Job list, shown in Figure 11-51. He exited Internet Explorer to return to the Windows desktop, and logged out.

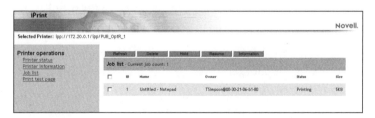

**Figure 11-51**    Displaying the existing print jobs

## Using the iPrint Map Utility

For users to access NDPS printers, they need to have iPrint or Novell Client, along with the printer drivers they will access, installed on their workstations. However, users occasionally need to send output to printers in other locations not included in the automatic printer setup. Although David plans to train users on how to use iPrint to select and install printers, this process can be confusing when users don't know the name of the printer they want to use. To make printer selection easier, Novell offers the iPrint Map Designer utility for placing printer icons on a facility map. The map can be displayed in a browser window, and users can select and install a printer by simply clicking the location of the printer they want to send output to. In this section, you learn how to use the iPrint Map Designer utility to construct a map of your CBE Labs printers and to install printers on user workstations. Using this utility involves the following steps:

1. *Scan in a map of the facility and save it as a GIF or JPG file.* David scanned in a copy of the CBE facility plan and saved it as a GIF file in the SYS:Login\ Ippdocs\Images\Maps folder. Storing the image in this folder is important so that the default iPrint Web server configuration can access it.

2. *Use iPrint Map Designer to add existing printers to the facility map.* After saving the scanned image, David used the latest version of Internet Explorer (IE version 5.5 is required to use this utility) to run the Maptool.htm file on the NetWare 6 server. This file is used to place icons representing printers on a scanned image. Each icon has the IPP address of the associated printers, a description, and a title. He used the CBE floor plan and the iPrint Maptool interface to place each printer on the floor plan.

3. *Save the facility map in a folder accessible to users.* After adding all the printers, David saved the floor plan map in the Login\Ippdocs directory as an HTML file. By placing the printer map in the Login directory, all users can access it to select and install printers on their computers, even if they are using a computer in another part of the country.

In the following example, David used the facility map to create a printer map for the CBE network:

1. He did the following to create a facility printer map with iPrint Map Designer:

   a. He started Internet Explorer.

   b. He opened iPrint Map Designer by clicking File, Open on the menu bar, entering F:\Login\ippdocs\maptool.htm, and pressing Enter.

   c. He clicked the Background list arrow to display existing maps and selected the Office.gif file to display the facility map (see the sample map shown in Figure 11-52).

   d. In the Printer icon list box, he clicked laser_5.gif to display a small laser printer icon (see Figure 11-52).

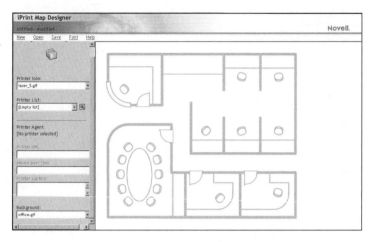

**Figure 11-52**    The iPrint Map Designer utility

2. He clicked the browse button next to the Printer List text box to open the Change printer list dialog box.

3. He entered the IP address of the CBE_ADMIN server, and clicked OK to open the Login window.

4. He logged in with the CBEAdmin user name and password and then clicked the Printer List list arrow to display the IPP-enabled printers.

5. He did the following to place the FIN_OptR_1 printer in the Finance Department:

   a. He dragged the printer icon to a location in the Finance Department, as shown in Figure 11-53.

   b. He entered https://*ip_address*/ipps/FIN_OptR_1 in the Printer URL text box and Finance Laser in the text box called Mouse over text.

6. He repeated Step 5 to place the other printers in their corresponding locations.

7. He saved the facility printer map by clicking Save, selecting the F: drive, and navigating to the Login\Ippdocs directory.

8. He entered the filename CBEPrinters.htm and clicked the Save button.

9. To test the printer, he started Internet Explorer and entered the URL http://*ip_address*:631/Login/Ippdocs/CBEPrinters.htm.

10. The CBE floor plan displayed, showing the printers in the locations he had placed them. He checked each printer by placing his cursor over the printer icon on the map and verifying its description.

11

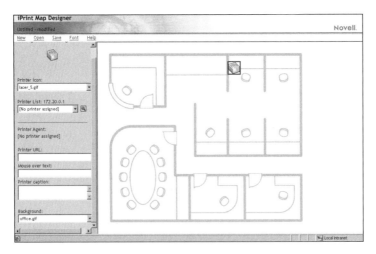

**Figure 11-53** Placing a printer icon on the facility map

11. He clicked the FIN_OptR_1 laser printer and installed it on his workstation.

12. After completing the installation, David closed Internet Explorer. He clicked Start, Settings, Printers and Faxes to open the Printers dialog box, and verified that the FIN_OptR_1 printer was installed on the workstation.

13. He closed the Printers dialog box and logged out.

# Troubleshooting iPrint Printing Problems

Because iPrint is based on NDPS, certain iPrint printing problems, such as being unable to download and install the IPP plug-ins for the browser, might be caused by NDPS setup problems. When you have problems using iPrint, be sure to refer to the NDPS troubleshooting tips earlier in this chapter to help determine whether the problems are NDPS related. There are four general types of problems you might encounter when implementing and working with Novell's iPrint system. In the following sections, you learn how to identify each of these problem types and some ways to correct them.

## Browser-Related Problems

The most common iPrint browser-related problem is client workstations running an older browser version. To operate the iPrint client, you need to have Internet Explorer version 5.5 or later or Netscape 4.7 or later. With older browser clients, you cannot select printers from floor maps or perform administrative tasks, such as modifying floor map layouts.

## Security Issues

A common problem when accessing iPrint printers is supplying the correct port number. If the printer is accessed through a secure port, be sure to use the default port 443.

For public access printers, use port 631. Also, verify that "http," not "https," is used in the URL for connecting to the iPrint printer.

### Printer Map Problems

If you are unable to find the printer floor map, make sure the required .gif or .jpg map files have been copied into the SYS:Login\Ippdocs\Maps directory.

### Printer Drivers

When installing an iPrint printer, you might get an error message stating that the necessary printer driver is not available. If this occurs, you can use the following steps in iManager to specify the drivers to install on the workstation:

1. Start iManager.

2. Click the Print Management link, and then click the Manage Printer option.

3. Enter the NDPS printer name or browse the tree and select the printer object to manage.

4. Select the Drivers tab.

5. Select the appropriate client operating system(s) where the printer will be used.

6. Select the correct driver for the printer make and model.

7. Click Apply and then click OK to complete the change.

8. Exit iManager.

## MANAGING PRINTERS AND PRINT JOBS

Network administrators can manage NDPS printing with iManager or NetWare Administrator. As a CNA, you'll be expected to manage NDPS printing by performing such tasks as securing printers, configuring printer notification, changing the order of print jobs, and adding new printer drivers to the RMS database. Users can also run iManager from their Web browsers and view the status of their print jobs, delete them, or put them on hold. Although users can perform many of the same tasks from Windows Control Panel, using iManager makes it easier to find and select network printers and gives them access to printers across the Internet.

## Setting Printer Security

In "Defining an NDPS Printing Environment," earlier in this chapter, you learned that by default, all users in the same container as the NDPS printer agent have rights to use that printer. Users in other containers must be assigned rights by using the Access Control button to add users, groups, or containers (shown previously in Figure 11-41).

This security measure prevents unauthorized users from sending output to a printer, but it does not prevent intruders from intercepting and reading data, which is a concern when printing across the Internet. To prevent data from being intercepted, it must be encrypted. NetWare 6 provides the three printer security levels shown in Table 11-5 that affect the security of data transmitted across the network.

**Table 11-5**    NetWare 6 NDPS Printer Security Levels

| Level | Description |
|---|---|
| Low | Security is enforced only by the client applications. |
| Medium | Security is enforced by the NDPS Manager only when print data integrity is involved. Otherwise, security is enforced by the client application. |
| High | Security is always enforced by the NDPS Manager for all operations. |

By default, the printer security level is set to Medium. When printing sensitive data across a WAN or the Internet, you should change the security setting to the High level, even though it slows performance and increases server overhead. Use iManager to change the security level by following these steps:

1. Start your Web browser and load iManager as described in previous sections.

2. In iManager, expand the iPrint Management heading and click the Manage Printer link.

3. Browse to and select the printer to be secured.

4. Click Access Control and then click Security.

5. Select the security level.

6. Save your changes by clicking OK.

David set the security level to High on the IS_P printer by performing the following steps:

1. He logged in to the Novell network with his DDoering user name and password.

2. He started his Web browser and entered the URL https://*ip_address*:2200 to display the NetWare Web Manager home page.

3. He clicked the CBE_ADMIN server under the eDirectory iManager heading and logged in to iManager with his CBEAdmin user name and password.

4. He expanded the iPrint Management heading and clicked the Manage Printer link to display the NDPS Printer text box used to select the printer to be managed.

5. He selected the IS_OptR_1 printer with these steps:

    a. He clicked the browse button next to the NDPS Printer text box to display the eDirectory Object Selector window, and then navigated to the InfoSystems OU.

    b. He double-clicked the IS_OptR_1 printer.

6. After selecting the printer, he clicked OK and then clicked Yes to display the Manage Printer window shown in Figure 11-54.

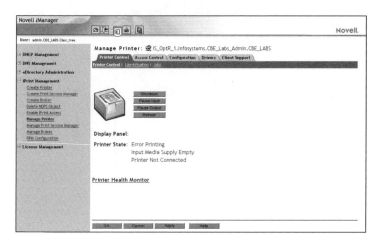

**Figure 11-54**    The Manage Printer window

7. He clicked the Access Control tab to display the roles shown in Figure 11-55.

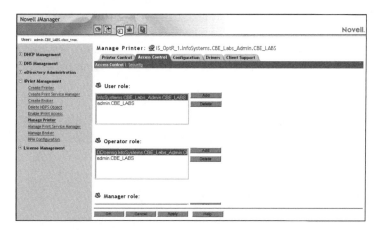

**Figure 11-55**    The Access Control tab

8. He clicked the Security link to display the security level settings shown in Figure 11-56.

9. He clicked the High security level, and then clicked the Apply button to display the "Success - Your changes have been saved" message box. He clicked OK to return to the iManager window.

10. To end his session, he clicked the Exit button and then closed the Web browser when the Login window displayed.

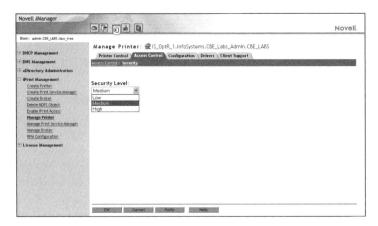

**Figure 11-56**   The security level settings

## Setting Print Job Notifications

With event notification, messages can be sent to users who need to be notified of a printer event that occurs during the processing and printing of a job. For example, print operators should be notified when a printer they are responsible for runs out of paper, has a paper jam, or runs low on toner. Notifications can be classified as job-owner notifications or interested-party notifications and sent with a variety of delivery methods, including pop-up messages, e-mail, and log files. Job-owner notifications inform users when their job has printed; interested-party notifications are usually sent to print operators to inform them of printer problems, such as paper jams or empty paper trays.

### Configuring Notifications

You can configure job-owner notifications with NetWare Administrator. To receive pop-up messages, user accounts must be configured with the default server to be used in the Advanced section of the Novell Login window (see Figure 11-57).

David set the default server for all users in the InfoSystems OU and then configured notifications for the IS_OptR_1 printer by performing these steps:

1. He logged in with the CBEAdmin user name and password.

2. He started NetWare Administrator and expanded the CBE_Labs_Admin and InfoSystems OUs.

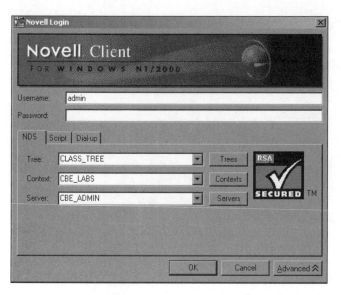

**Figure 11-57**     The Advanced section of the Novell Login window, showing the default server

3. He set the default server for all users in the InfoSystems OU to CBE_ADMIN by using these steps:

   a. He selected all user names in the InfoSystems OU by pressing the Ctrl key and clicking each user name.

   b. He then clicked Object, Details on Multiple Users on the menu bar to open the Details on Multiple Users dialog box.

   c. He clicked the Environment button to display the Environment page shown in Figure 11-58.

   d. He clicked the browse button next to the Default server text box and double-clicked the CBE_ADMIN server.

   e. He clicked OK to save the changes, and clicked Yes to apply changes to all selected users and return to the main NetWare Administrator window.

4. He right-clicked the IS_OptR_1 printer and clicked Details to display the Printer Control dialog box.

5. He clicked the Access Control button to display the Access Control page shown in Figure 11-59.

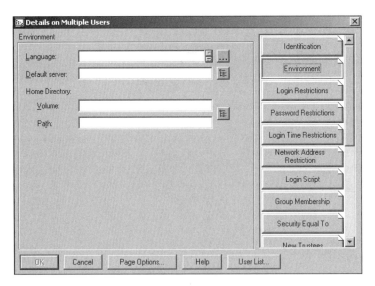

**Figure 11-58**    The Environment page in NetWare Administrator

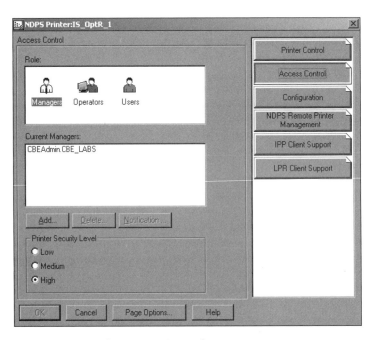

**Figure 11-59**    The Access Control page

6. To send pop-up notifications on printer problems to his DDoering user account, David did the following:

   a. He clicked the Operators icon to display the operators of the IS_OptR_1 printer.

   b. He clicked his DDoering user name and then clicked the Notification button to open the Notification dialog box showing job and printer notification options.

   c. He clicked the Pop-Up Notification tab to display a tree listing the current pop-up notifications.

   d. He clicked the + symbol to expand the Printer item and then clicked the Errors, Warnings, and Printer State Changed check boxes, as shown in Figure 11-60.

   e. He clicked OK to save the changes and return to the Access Control page.

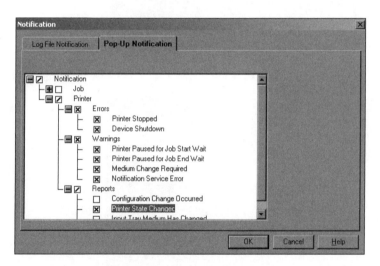

**Figure 11-60**    Selecting pop-up notifications

7. To send pop-up job notifications on print job status to users, he did the following:

   a. He clicked the Users icon to display the users of the IS_OptR_1 printer.

   b. He clicked the InfoSystems OU and then clicked the Notification button to open the Notification dialog box.

   c. He clicked the Pop-Up Notification tab, expanded the Job item, and then expanded Errors and Warnings, as shown in Figure 11-61.

   d. He expanded the Reports item and clicked the check boxes shown in Figure 11-62.

   e. He clicked OK to save the changes and return to the Access Control page.

8. After all notifications were configured, he clicked Cancel to return to the main NetWare Administrator window. He then exited NetWare Administrator and logged out.

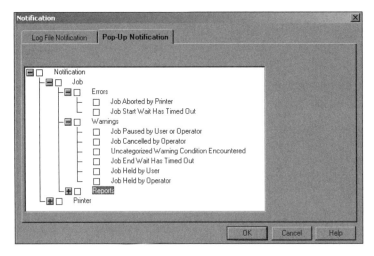

**Figure 11-61**    Options under Errors and Warnings on the Pop-Up Notification tab

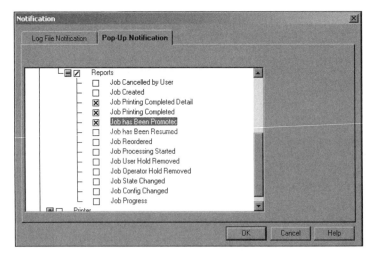

**Figure 11-62**    Selecting pop-up notifications to send to users

## Managing Print Jobs

You can manage print jobs with NetWare Administrator or iManager. In NetWare Administrator, you can open a dialog box showing all print jobs for the selected printer. You can view the status of the job, including job owner, submission date, and size by double-clicking it. You delete the job by clicking the Jobs menu and selecting Cancel Printing.

If you need to reorder print jobs, such as when a senior manager wants a report generated immediately, you can highlight the rush job, and then move it to the top of the queue. To do this, David used the following steps:

1. He started NetWare Administrator and expanded the InfoSystems OU.

2. He right-clicked the IS_OptR_1 printer and clicked Details to open the NetWare Printer Control dialog box shown in Figure 11-63.

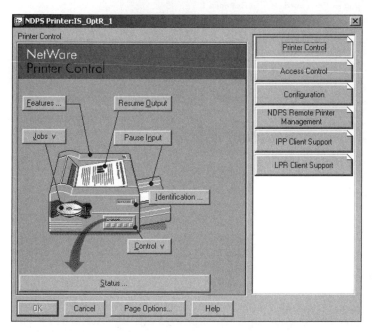

**Figure 11-63**    The NetWare Printer Control dialog box

3. He clicked the Pause Output button to pause printing.

4. He clicked the Jobs v button and clicked the Job List option to open the JOB LIST dialog box shown in Figure 11-64.

5. To change which job would print next, he clicked the Workload job and then clicked the Job Options v button to display a list of options (see Figure 11-65), including deleting the job, changing the job sequence, or moving the job to another printer.

6. To change the job sequence, he clicked Reorder. In the Reorder dialog box, he entered 1 in the Job Position text box (see Figure 11-66), and clicked OK.

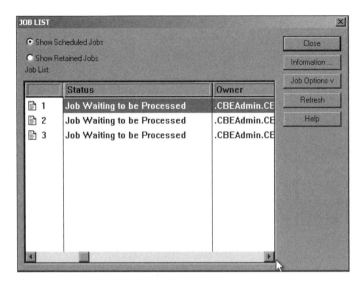

**Figure 11-64**    The JOB LIST dialog box

**Figure 11-65**    The Job Options v list

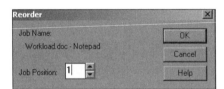

**Figure 11-66**    Reordering a print job

7. He clicked Close to return to the NetWare Printer Control window.

8. He clicked the Resume Output button to restart the printer, and then clicked Cancel to return to the main NetWare Administrator window. He exited NetWare Administrator and logged out.

You can also use iManager to view, delete, and rearrange print jobs. For example, David used the following steps in iManager to pause the IS_OptR_1 printer, rearrange the print jobs, and then resume printing:

1. He started his computer and logged in to the Novell network with his DDoering user name and password.

2. He started his Web browser and loaded iManager.

3. After logging in with the CBEAdmin user name and password, he expanded the iPrint Management heading and clicked the Manage Printer link.

4. He entered the distinguished name IS_OptR_1.InfoSystems.CBE_Labs_Admin.CBE_LABS in the NDPS Printer text box and clicked OK to display the Manage Printer window shown previously in Figure 11-54.

5. To pause the printer, he clicked the Pause Output button.

6. He clicked the Jobs link to display the Job List window shown in Figure 11-67.

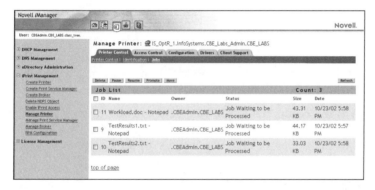

**Figure 11-67**    The Job List window in iManager

7. To make TestResults2.txt print before the existing print jobs, he clicked the check box next to that job and then clicked the Promote button. TestResults2.txt was moved to the top of the job list, followed by Workload.doc and TestResults1.

8. He clicked the Printer Control link and then clicked the Resume Output button to restart printing.

9. He clicked the Exit button and closed his Web browser window.

## CHAPTER SUMMARY

❏ The queue-based printing system is included with NetWare 6 to provide backward-compatibility with earlier NetWare versions. Queue-based printing involves creating print queue objects and at least one print server. Each printer is defined in the print server and must be associated with at least one print queue. Output is sent from user workstations to a print queue. The print server software, running on the NetWare server, takes jobs from a print queue and sends them to the associated printer.

❏ In cooperation with Hewlett-Packard and Xerox, Novell has developed a new network printing environment called Novell Distributed Printing Services (NDPS). As a CNA, you'll need to know the printing components and utilities that make up NDPS and be able to set up and maintain a NetWare printing environment consisting of an NDPS Manager, printer agents, gateways, Brokers, print queues, and client workstations.

❏ Printer agents are software that make up the core of NDPS. Client workstations send formatted printer output to printer agents, which then control the physical printer. When setting up NDPS, you need to create and configure one printer agent for each physical printer.

❏ As part of Novell's OneNet strategy, iPrint uses Internet Printing Protocol (IPP) to enable printers to be installed, accessed, and managed anywhere from a Web browser. iPrint consists of three components: the IPPSRVR module on the NetWare server, a Web browser client, and NDPS printers enabled for IPP access.

❏ NDPS Manager is the component used to create and run printer agents. By using specialized gateways, NDPS printers can be remotely attached to client computers, locally attached to the server, or attached directly to the network.

❏ Because not all clients are immediately compatible with NDPS, Novell offers backward-compatibility with older clients via print queues, which consist of a directory on the file system for holding print jobs until the printer is ready.

❏ The first task in establishing the printer environment is to define the printing requirements for your network; to do this, assess printing needs for each user's applications and determine the types and number of printers required, their location on the network, and their attachment method.

❏ After defining the printing environment, the next step is installing the printing system. NetWare Administrator is used for most of the work of setting up and maintaining the NetWare printing system. To install the printing system, you need to create the NDPS Manager and printer agents. The printer configuration can also include a notification list of user names to receive printer messages.

❏ Managing printers involves using NetWare Administrator or iManager to perform such tasks as arranging and deleting print jobs, configuring printer notifications, and setting printer security.

# KEY TERMS

**automatic load printer** — A printer that's attached directly to the server's printer port or a port on the workstation.

**bidirectional communication** — Communication between a printer agent and the client that enables clients to locate printers based on printer type and availability.

**Broker** — An NDPS component responsible for sending printer messages and notifications by using the Event Notification System (ENS), Resource Management Service (RMS), and Service Registry Services (SRS).

**controlled access printer** — An NDPS printer that exists as an object in the eDirectory tree. By default, only users in the same container as the controlled access printer can send output to it.

**gateway** — The NDPS component that works with the printer agent to send output from the printer agent to the network print device.

**Internet Printing Protocol (IPP)** — An industry-standard protocol that enables printers to be installed, managed, and accessed from a Web browser.

**iPrint** — Novell's implementation of the IPP protocol that makes it possible to access and manage NDPS printers through a Web browser.

**manual load printer** — A remote printer attached to a port on a networked workstation and controlled by the print server.

**NDPS Manager** — The NDPS component that manages the printer agent for printers that do not have one embedded.

**Novell Distributed Print Services (NDPS)** — A new printing system developed by Hewlett-Packard and Novell that makes it more convenient to configure and access network printers.

**print queue** — A network object representing a holding area where print jobs are kept until the printer is available. In NetWare, a print queue is a subdirectory of the Queues directory, located in the volume specified during print queue creation.

**print server** — A component of queue-based printing that manages network printers by taking jobs from print queues and sending them to the correct network printer.

**printer agent** — The software component of NDPS that transfers output from the client workstation and controls the physical printer.

**public access printer** — An NDPS printer that's attached to the network but does not have an eDirectory object. Any user attached to the network can send output to a public access printer without having to log in to the network.

**queue-based printing** — A printing system implemented in NetWare 3 that's designed to support simple printers and DOS-based applications.

**spooling** — Sending output from a user's workstation to a print job.

11

## REVIEW QUESTIONS

1. Which of the following network printing components provides backward-compatibility by holding printed output until the printer is ready to print?

   a. print server

   b. print queue

   c. gateway

   d. printer agent

2. Which of the following queue-based printing components controls print jobs on the physical printer?

   a. print server

   b. print queue

   c. gateway

   d. printer agent

3. Which of the following utilities can be used to create print queues?

   a. NetWare Administrator

   b. ConsoleOne

   c. iManager

   d. Remote Manager

4. In the queue-based printing system, user workstations send their output to which of the following?

   a. print server

   b. print queue

   c. gateway

   d. printer agent

5. Which of the following NDPS printing components manages each physical printer?

   a. print server

   b. print queue

   c. gateway

   d. printer agent

6. Which of the following must be running before you can create printer agents? (Select all that apply.)

   a. NDPS Manager

   b. IPPSRVR

   c. Broker

   d. print server

7. A network printer attached to a client is called a(n) _____ attached printer.

   a. locally

   b. directly

   c. system

   d. remote

8. Which of the following is the first step in setting up a network printing environment?

   a. create printer agents

   b. create and load the NDPS Broker

   c. create and load the NDPS Manager

   d. install the IPP client on your administrative workstation

9. Which of the following utilities can be used to create printer agents? (Select all that apply.)

   a. iManager

   b. Remote Manager

   c. ConsoleOne

   d. NetWare Administrator

10. A printer attached to a server is referred to as which of the following?

    a. manual load printer

    b. local printer

    c. directly attached printer

    d. system printer

11. "Automatic load printers" is the term Novell uses for _____ attached printers.

    a. locally

    b. remote

    c. directly

    d. IPP

12. Printer agents that can be accessed without logging in are referred to as which of the following?

    a. automatic load printers

    b. controlled access printers

    c. public access printers

    d. global printers

13. The _____ URL is used to access the iManager utility.

**11**

14. Which of the following NDPS components helps clients find network printer agents?

    a. NDPS Manager

    b. printer agent

    c. Broker

    d. print queue

15. Novell's iPrint is based on which of the following industry standards?

    a. IPP

    b. 802.3

    c. IEEE

    d. X.500

16. True or False: Most printers today have embedded printer agents.

17. List two steps for using iManager to create an IPP-enabled printer agent.

    _____

    _____

18. The _____ URL is used to access the iPrint installation utility.

19. Remote printers are also called which of the following?

    a. automatic load printers

    b. controlled access printers

    c. manual load printers

    d. global printers

20. List the two steps for implementing an NDPS Manager on a NetWare server.

    _____

    _____

21. Which of the following is *not* a step in implementing network printing?

    a. define printer names

    b. define the context for NDPS objects

    c. create a Printers container

    d. create and load NDPS Manager

22. The _____ directory contains the URL for the iPrint Map Designer utility.

23. NetWare provides _____ security levels.

    a. 3

    b. 5

    c. 2

    d. unlimited

24. Before setting up print job notifications for a user account, you need to do which of the following?

   a. make the user a print operator

   b. set the user account's default server

   c. add the user to the printer's notification list

   d. load the pop-up message handler on the NetWare server

25. Which of the following can be done using the version of iManager that ships with NetWare 6? (Select all that apply.)

   a. create new printers

   b. pause a printer

   c. resequence print jobs

   d. set up print job notification

   e. add print operators and managers

---

## HANDS-ON PROJECTS

### Project 11-1: Defining NDPS Printers

Copy the NDPS Printer Definition Form from Appendix B and use it to define each printer and print queue, along with operators and users, to meet the printing needs for the CBE_Labs_Admin OU, as defined in Tables 11-2 and 11-6. Include the network printers on the NDPS Printer Definition Form shown previously in Figure 11-28. If your lab has a laser printer attached to the network, use it instead of the Lexmark Optra R mentioned in the table. When naming the printers, be sure to include your assigned student number before each printer name.

**Table 11-6**  Personnel/Marketing Network Printing Needs

| Department | Network Printing Needs |
| --- | --- |
| Personnel | The department's Lexmark Optra R laser printer will be connected directly to the network and available to Personnel Department users. Users in the Executives group should also be able to send output to the Personnel Department printer. |
| Marketing | Until they are attached directly to the network by using a JetDirect print server, the Lexmark Optra R laser printer in the Marketing Department will be attached to Jon Jorgensen's computer. |

After completing your NDPS Printer Definition Form, have your instructor verify it against the answer key. Make any necessary changes to include all the printer information in the master NDPS Printer Definition Form so that you'll be able to do the projects in later chapters.

## Project 11-2: Setting Up Network Printing

In this project, you apply what you learned in this chapter about using NetWare Administrator to create eDirectory objects in your containers for the printer agents and print queues on your NDPS Printer Definition Form. You'll create your CBE printer objects within your .CBE_LABS.##ADMINOU.CLASS container structure. If you do not have access to a user account that has Supervisor rights to the classroom CBE_NDPSM Manager, create the PUB_OptR_1 printer as a controlled access printer in your CBE_LABS OU.

## Project 11-3: Enabling IPP Access to Printers

Use the steps described in this chapter to enable IPP for each of your printers.

## Project 11-4: Testing Your Printing Setup

In this project, use NetWare Administrator and iPrint to install the printers in Table 11-7 as described in this chapter.

**Table 11-7**   CBE_Labs_Admin OU Printers

| Printer | Installation Method |
|---|---|
| ##IS_OptR_1 | Use NetWare Administrator to include this printer in the NDPS Remote Printer Management page of the InfoSystems container. |
| ##FIN_OptR_1 | Use NetWare Administrator to include this printer in the NDPS Remote Printer Management page of the Finance container. |
| ##PER_OptR_1 | Use Internet Explorer to install this printer with iPrint. |
| ##ADM_OptR_1 | Use Internet Explorer to install this printer with iPrint. |

Test each of your printers by sending output to the printer and then use iManager to verify that the results have been sent to the correct printer.

## CASE PROJECTS

## Case Project 11-1: Performing a Print Queue Services Quick Setup

Follow these steps to do a quick setup for the CBE print services:

1. If necessary, start your workstation, and log in with your administrative user name and password.
2. Start NetWare Administrator, and open a browse window to the CLASS Organization.
3. Click your **##ADMINOU** container.
4. Click **Tools**, **Print Services Quick Setup (Non-NDPS)** on the menu bar.

5. Record the following information:

- ◻ Print server name

- ◻ Printer name

- ◻ Type:

- ◻ Print queue name

6. Change the printer name to **##PR** (## represents your assigned student number).

7. Click the **Create** button to create the queue-based printing system.

8. Document your results in a memo to your instructor.

9. Add the ##PR printer to your desktop.

## Case Project 11-2: Troubleshooting Network Printing

In this project, your instructor will create one of the "bugs" described in the "Troubleshooting NDPS Printers" section in the printing system you set up. Your job is to use the techniques and fixes explained in this chapter to find, document, and correct the problem. Record your findings in a memo to your instructor.

## Case Project 11-3: Creating a Printer Map

Use the procedure described in this chapter to create a printer map document for your CBE network printers. Use the Office.gif file and then save your printer plan with the name ##CBEPrinters (replacing the ## with your assigned student number). Be able to demonstrate to your instructor how to install your PUB_OptR_1 printer using your printer map.

**11**

## Case Project 11-4: Jefferson County Courthouse Printing Setup

In this project, you fill out an NDPS Printer Definition Form for your Jefferson County Courthouse project. The printer form should define two printers (one ink-jet and one laser printer) that will be available for all users in the Social Services Department. Terry Smith and your ##Admin user name should be included in the list of printer managers and operators.

1. Use iManager to create the following NDPS printer objects in the JCCH.##ADMINOU.CLASS container:

- ◻ A Broker named ##JCCH_Broker

- ◻ An NDPS Manager named ##JCCH_NDPSM

2. Create your JCCH printers in the contexts you specified on your NDPS Printer Definition Form. Unless your NDPS Manager is loaded on the server, you'll need to use the classroom NDPS Manager when creating your printer agents instead of the NDPS Manager you created in Step 1.

3. Enable IPP on the department's laser printer.

4. Use NetWare Administrator to set the laser printer's security level to High.

5. Create a printer map that shows the locations of the Social Services printers.

6. Add your JCCH printers to your workstation.

7. Create a memo to your instructor that describes the names and locations of your JCCH printers and the method you used to add the printers.

# 12

# MANAGING THE USER DESKTOP ENVIRONMENT

**After reading this chapter and completing the exercises, you will be able to:**

♦ Identify the four types of login scripts and how they are used to map network drive letters, provide informational messages, and run special programs

♦ Identify and use login script variables and commands to write, enter, and document login scripts

♦ Identify user and network requirements for login scripts and write, test, and debug login scripts

♦ Install and use Zero Effort Networking for Desktops to help manage the user environment, and maintain a consistent desktop environment with Policy Package objects

**A**fter the network directory structure has been established and secured, the user accounts created, and the applications installed, the next challenge for the network administrator is making this complex system easy to access and use. Administrators can configure Windows workstations with user profiles, which allow several users to share the same hardware but have different workstation configurations. Novell's Zero Effort Networking for Desktops provides another means of configuring workstations remotely and simplifies managing a user's profile. Another way is to use login scripts, which run at the time the user logs in to the network. Login scripts make it possible for users to log in to a server and access network services by establishing drive mappings, providing informational messages, and running special programs. Establishing the user environment is an important aspect of a network administrator's job. In this chapter, you learn how to establish login scripts for your network system and how to manage user profiles and configure workstations remotely with ZENworks.

## NetWare Login Scripts

As you learned in Chapter 8, unless you select the option to reconnect drive mappings when you log in, any drive mappings you establish during a network session are effective only until you log out of the network. The next time you log in, you must reconnect each drive pointer you want to use. Requiring users to establish their drive pointers not only means they need more technical knowledge about the system, but also takes time away from productive work and can cause problems when they don't select the correct drive letters for accessing software or files. To solve these problems, Novell has provided **login scripts** for establishing users' network environments each time they log in. As shown in Figure 12-1, a NetWare login script consists of a set of NetWare login command statements that Novell Client processes when a user logs in.

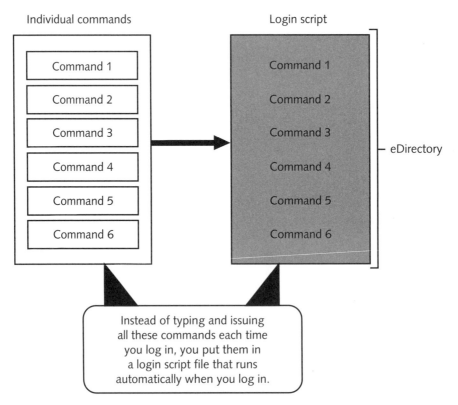

**Figure 12-1** NetWare login script processing

The command statements in a login script file form a program that the client software processes after a user successfully logs in with a valid user name and password. As illustrated in Figure 12-1, the login script commands are stored in eDirectory and sent to the user's workstation from the server. The workstation processes each command statement, one at a time, starting with the first command. As shown in Figure 12-2, the Novell Login window contains a Script tab with options for controlling how login script commands are processed.

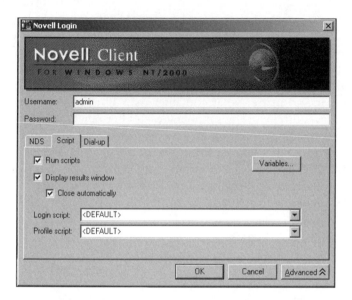

**Figure 12-2**    The Script tab of the Novell Login window

You use the Run scripts check box to control whether the user's workstation processes login script commands. If you enable the Display results window option, a message is displayed for each login script command that's processed. If you want users to view messages from login scripts, you need to select this option. Selecting the Close automatically option closes the Results window after all login script commands have been processed.

When testing login scripts, you should select the Display results window option and disable the Close automatically option so that you can verify the results of your login script commands and check for any error messages. The most common problem when testing login scripts is drive mapping commands that don't work because of insufficient rights to the directory in the MAP command. So when implementing login script commands, you might need to review the user's file system rights, described in Chapter 10.

If users aren't getting any network drive mappings, check to make sure the Run scripts option is enabled on their workstations. If they are getting some network drive mappings but not others, check to make sure they have at least Read and File Scan rights in the directories being mapped in the login script.

12

## Types of Login Scripts

To understand how NetWare stores and processes login scripts, you need to be aware of the types of login scripts and their purpose. For maximum flexibility, NetWare has four types of login scripts: container, profile, user, and default. Having multiple login scripts enables the network administrator to give all users a standard environment, yet allows some flexibility to meet individual user needs. A **container login script** is a property of a container; the network administrator uses it to provide standard setups for all users in that container. **Profile login scripts** are eDirectory objects containing login commands common to multiple users, no matter what container their User object is in. NetWare allows for individual user requirements by supplying each User object with its own **user login script** property containing additional statements that run after the container and profile login script commands. The **default login script** is a set of commands in Novell Client used to establish a default working environment for users who don't have a user login script defined. To become a CNA, you'll need to know how these login scripts work together and the sequence in which they run to set up a reliable, efficient login script system for your network. The flowchart in Figure 12-3 illustrates the relationship between the NetWare login script types.

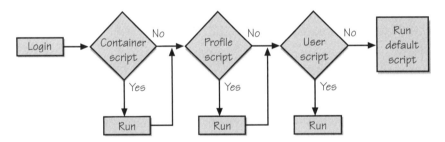

**Figure 12-3**   NetWare login script types

When a login script is created for a container, its commands are carried out when users in that container log in to the network. After all commands in the container login script run, NetWare determines whether the user is assigned to a Profile object. If so, NetWare performs any login script commands included in the Profile object's Login Script property. After checking for a profile assignment, the last step is to run the commands in the user login script or default login script. If a user does not have a user login script, Novell Client performs the commands in the default login script.

A good way to remember the sequence of login script processing is the acronym CPU, for *c*ontainer, *p*rofile, *u*ser login scripts.

It's important to remember that the login script commands processed last take precedence, which means drive mappings made in the user or default login script file can overwrite drive mappings made by the container login script. As a result, many network administrators disable the processing of the default script and remove the rights of users to change their personal login scripts. In the following sections, you learn more about container, profile, user, and default login scripts and how to disable the processing of default login script commands.

## Container Login Scripts

The container login script is a property of the container object, used to enter login script commands that run for each User object housed in that container. The purpose of container login scripts is to map a search drive to the Public directory and set up drive pointers that all users in a container access. When a user logs in to the network, Novell Client looks for login script commands in that user's container. Only the login script commands in the user's home container are carried out; login script commands in parent containers are not. For example, login script commands in the CBE_LABS container aren't run by users in the .Finance.CBE_Labs_Admin or InfoSystems containers. That means each container's login script should include all the commands needed to set up a standard working environment for users in that container. Because the CBE tree structure has users in several different OUs—for example, Finance contains Donna Kaneaka, Thomas Meyer, and Sarah Johnson, and InfoSystems contains David Doering, Mark Ciampa, and Ted Simpson—you need to create container login scripts for each container that has user accounts.

## User Login Scripts

The user login script is located in the User object's Login Script property. Unless the EXIT command is issued in the container or profile login script, Novell Client runs any login script commands in the user's Login Script property. If there are no login script commands in the user's Login Script property and the NO_DEFAULT command hasn't been issued, Novell Client runs the default login script commands.

By default, either the network administrator or the user can access and maintain the user login script by using ConsoleOne or NetWare Administrator to select the Login Script property in the user's Properties dialog box. If you don't want users to be able to modify their own login script commands, you can use the Selected properties option in ConsoleOne to remove the Write attribute right (discussed in Chapter 10) from the user's Login Script property.

Placing commands in user login scripts makes maintaining the login script environment more difficult because changes could require accessing many separate user login script files. Many network administrators prefer to place most commands in container or profile login scripts to reduce the need for user login scripts whenever possible.

12

## Default Login Scripts

The default login script consists of several login script commands built into Novell Client. If there's no user login script file for the user currently logging in, Novell Client runs the default login script commands. The purpose of the default login script is to provide basic drive mappings for users until container and profile scripts have been established. The statements that make up the Novell Client default login script include the following:

- MAP *1:=SYS: (maps the first network drive to the SYS volume)
- MAP INS S1:=SYS:Public (maps the first search drive to the Public directory)

After the network administrator has established a container login script that includes the basic drive mappings for the network, he or she must prevent the default login script from running so that drive mappings in the container login script aren't overwritten or duplicated. NetWare has three basic ways to stop the default login script from running:

- Place the NO_DEFAULT statement in the container or profile login script.
- Provide a user login script for each user on the network, even if the user login script contains only the EXIT command.
- Include an EXIT command in the container or profile login script. The EXIT command ends the login script process and, therefore, prevents all subsequent login scripts from running. Placing the EXIT command in the container login script usually isn't a good option, however, because it also prevents profile login scripts from running.

Although some network administrators avoid large or complex login scripts, most prefer having one large container login script program to manage a user's network environment, instead of having lots of user and profile login scripts that require looking in many different places when problems occur. Decide on the method that's best for you and your network based on your network environment and personal preference.

## Profile Login Scripts

The purpose of a profile login script is to enable you to create a standard set of login commands performed only by selected users. Profile login scripts are set up by creating a Profile object in a container and then entering the login script command in the Profile object's Login Script property. Profile login scripts are independent from the container object, so they have the advantage of being available to users in any container because those users are granted Read attribute rights to the Profile object's Login Script property. In Figure 12-4, suppose that users DDoering, TSimpson, and MCiampa need the same login script as SLopez. Because you want these four users to have the same login script but don't want to make the script part of the CBE_Labs_Admin container script, you can create a Profile object, give these four users Read rights to that object, and have the profile login script assigned to them. Whenever they log in, the profile login script would run. (Only one profile login script per user runs.)

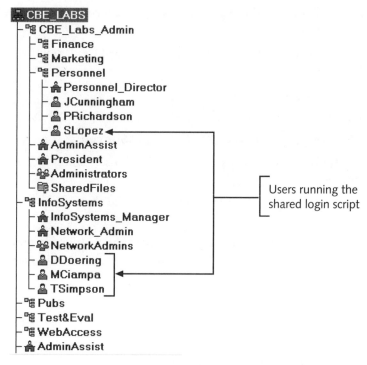

**Figure 12-4**   The CBE Labs eDirectory structure

Currently, the WebMgrs group has users from several departments who need to work together on the CBE Web site. To give the group members a drive mapping to the InfoSys\Shared directory, David Doering, the network administrator, could place a MAP command in each department's container login script. David thought a better solution would be implementing a WebProfile login script containing the necessary login commands for the WebMgrs group and attaching the WebProfile object to each group member. He used the following steps to assign the WebProfile login script to GTennesson, a member of the WebMgrs group:

1. He logged in with his CBEAdmin user name and password.

2. He started ConsoleOne and expanded CLASS_TREE, CBE_LABS, and the CBE_Labs_Admin OU.

3. He clicked CBE_Labs_Admin to display all existing objects.

4. He clicked the New Object button on the ConsoleOne toolbar to open the New Object dialog box.

5. He scrolled down and clicked the Profile object type, and then clicked OK to open the New Profile dialog box.

6. He entered WebProfile in the Name text box, and clicked the Define additional properties check box.

7. He clicked OK to create the Profile object and open the Properties of WebProfile dialog box.

8. He clicked the Login Script tab.

9. He entered the following command in the Login Script text box:

```
MAP ROOT W:=CBE_ADMIN/DATA:InfoSys\Shared
```

10. He clicked Apply and then Close to save the login script and return to the main ConsoleOne window.

11. David used these steps to grant the WebMgrs group the rights to read the profile login script:

    a. In the ConsoleOne window, he right-clicked the WebProfile object, and then clicked Properties to open the Properties of WebProfile dialog box.

    b. He clicked the NDS Rights tab to display the trustees of the WebProfile object.

    c. He clicked the Add Trustee button to open the Select Objects dialog box.

    d. He clicked the WebMgrs group, and then clicked OK to open the Rights assigned to selected objects dialog box.

    e. He clicked the [All Attributes Rights] item, and verified that the Read and Compare rights were selected.

    f. He clicked OK to place the new trustee assignment into the Trustees list box.

    g. He clicked OK to save his changes and return to the main ConsoleOne window.

12. David used these steps to attach the WebProfile object to the GTennesson user account:

    a. He clicked the Pubs OU to display all User objects.

    b. He right-clicked GTennesson in ConsoleOne's Object frame, and then clicked Properties to open the Properties of GTennesson dialog box.

    c. He scrolled to the right and clicked the Login Script tab to display the Login Script text box.

    d. He clicked the browse button next to the Profile text box to open the Select Object dialog box.

    e. He clicked the up arrow to move up one level and then double-clicked the CBE_Labs_Admin OU.

f. He clicked the WebProfile object, and then clicked OK to place it in the Profile text box.

g. He clicked OK to save the changes to the user login script and return to the main ConsoleOne window.

13. He exited ConsoleOne, and logged out to display a new Login window.

14. He logged in as GTennesson in the Pubs.CBE_LABS context.

15. He double-clicked the My Computer icon, and verified that the drive was mapped to the InfoSys\Shared directory.

 If your drive mapping fails, make sure you have made GTennesson a member of the WebMgrs group and the WebMgrs group has rights to the InfoSys\Shared directory.

In the future, other users can easily be added to help manage the Web site by adding their user names to the WebMgrs group and then associating their user names with the WebProfile object.

## LOGIN SCRIPT PROGRAMMING

12

Creating login scripts is much like writing programs with any programming language. You need to learn the valid commands and the syntax, or rules, for formatting the commands. In addition, like any other programming language, login script commands can use variables, so one command can have multiple values. In the following sections, you learn how to use login script commands and variables to create sophisticated login scripts that can set up user drive mappings and display announcements and other messages to users.

David is a member of the InfoSystems OU along with Mark Ciampa and Ted Simpson. Instead of creating separate login scripts for the three of them, he decides to create a container login script (shown in Figure 12-5) for the InfoSystems OU so that each user receives the same drive mappings and messages when logging in.

Notice that the script contains statements to display a greeting message and establish a network environment by mapping the drive pointers you identified in Chapter 4. Take a look at the steps David used to create this container login script:

1. He logged in with his CBEAdmin user name and password.

2. He started ConsoleOne and expanded CLASS_TREE and the CBE_LABS Organization.

3. He right-clicked the InfoSystems OU, and then clicked Properties to open the Properties of InfoSystems dialog box.

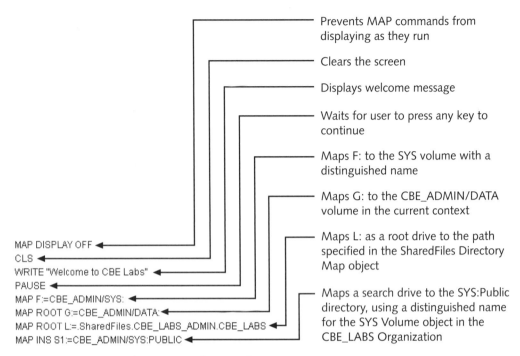

Prevents MAP commands from displaying as they run

Clears the screen

Displays welcome message

Waits for user to press any key to continue

Maps F: to the SYS volume with a distinguished name

Maps G: to the CBE_ADMIN/DATA volume in the current context

Maps L: as a root drive to the path specified in the SharedFiles Directory Map object

Maps a search drive to the SYS:Public directory, using a distinguished name for the SYS Volume object in the CBE_LABS Organization

```
MAP DISPLAY OFF
CLS
WRITE "Welcome to CBE Labs"
PAUSE
MAP F:=CBE_ADMIN/SYS:
MAP ROOT G:=CBE_ADMIN/DATA:
MAP ROOT L:=.SharedFiles.CBE_LABS_ADMIN.CBE_LABS
MAP INS S1:=CBE_ADMIN/SYS:PUBLIC
```

**Figure 12-5**   A sample container login script

4. He used the following steps to enter the login script:

   a. He clicked the Login Script tab to display the Login Script text box.

   b. He entered the login script commands shown in Figure 12-5.

   c. He clicked OK to save the login script and return to the main ConsoleOne window.

5. He exited ConsoleOne and logged out.

6. In the Novell Login window, David changed the context to InfoSystems.CBE_LABS, and entered his user name and password in the Username and Password text boxes.

7. David used the following options to set up Novell Client so that he could check his login script results:

   a. He clicked the Advanced button, and then clicked the Script tab to display the options shown previously in Figure 12-2.

   b. He clicked to clear the Close automatically check box so that the Login window wouldn't automatically close.

8. He clicked OK to log in. The Results window, similar to the one in Figure 12-6, displayed the welcome message.

**Figure 12-6**    The Results window

9. He pressed the spacebar to continue and noted that the drive mappings were added to his Results window.

10. He identified any drive letters that were repeated.

Repeated drive letters could mean that the default login script is running or that the user has a personal user script that is changing drive mappings. David will disable the default login script later.

11. He clicked the Close button to close the Results window and logged out.

## Login Script Variables

Login script programs consist of a limited number of command statements in the NetWare login script language. As a CNA, you'll need to know how to use this language to design and write login scripts for your organization. As in other programming languages, you can use variables with many of the command statements in the NetWare login script language. A **login script variable** is a reserved word in the login script language whose value can change for each user logging in. By using login script variables, you can write a login script program that works for many different users and workstations.

Check Novell's Web site at *http://novell.com* for more information on login script commands and variables.

Because login script variables play an important role in writing login script programs to meet the needs of many different users, you should gain an understanding of how they are used in login script command statements so that you can successfully learn the NetWare login script language. Login script variables can be divided into types based on their use: date, time, user, workstation, and user-defined variables. The following sections discuss how each type is used and describe the variables associated with each type.

When using login script variables in commands, you must capitalize the variable and precede it with a percent sign (%). (See the section "Using Login Script Variables" later in this chapter for more information.)

## Date Variables

**Date variables** contain information about the current day of the week, month, and year in a variety of formats, as shown in Table 12-1. These variables can be useful when displaying current date information or checking for a specific day to perform tasks. For example, the InfoSystems users need to meet at 10:00 A.M. each Monday to review weekly work projects. Using the %DAY_OF_WEEK variable, you could write login script commands to display a reminder message on Monday morning. When using date variables, note that their values are stored as fixed-length ASCII strings. For example, the %DAY variable contains the day number of the current month and ranges from 01 to 31, but the %NDAY_OF_WEEK variable contains values ranging from 1 to 7.

**Table 12-1**    Date Variables

| Variable | Description |
|---|---|
| DAY | Day number of the current month, with possible values from "01" to "31" |
| DAY_OF_WEEK | Name of the current day of the week, with possible values of "Monday," "Tuesday," "Wednesday," and so on |
| MONTH | The number of the current month, with possible values from "01" for January to "12" for December |
| MONTH_NAME | The name of the current month, with possible values from "January" to "December" |
| NDAY_OF_WEEK | The current weekday number, ranging from "1" for Sunday to "7" for Saturday |
| SHORT_YEAR | The last two digits of the current year, such as "02" or "03" |
| YEAR | The full four-digit year, such as "2003" or "2004" |

## Time Variables

The **time variables**, shown in Table 12-2, offer a variety of ways to view or check the login time.

**Table 12-2**   Time Variables

| Variable | Description |
|---|---|
| AM_PM | Day or night (A.M. or P.M.) |
| GREETING_TIME | Used for displaying welcome messages, with possible values of "Morning," "Afternoon," or "Evening" |
| HOUR | The current hour of the day or night in the range of "01" through "12" |
| HOUR24 | The current hour in 24-hour mode, ranging from "01" for 1 A.M. to "24" for 12 A.M. |
| MINUTE | The current minute, ranging from "00" to "59" |
| SECOND | The current second, ranging from "00" to "59" |

The %GREETING_TIME variable is most often used in WRITE statements to display welcome messages. The difference between the %HOUR24 variable and the %HOUR variable is that %HOUR requires using the %AM_PM variable to determine whether the specified time is before or after noon. %HOUR24 uses a 24-hour clock, so hour 12 is noon, hour 13 is 1 P.M., and so forth. When checking for a specific time, %HOUR24 is often easier to use. For example, if you want all users who log in before 3:00 P.M. to be notified of a special meeting, you could write login script commands using %HOUR24 to compare the current login hour to 15. If %HOUR24 is less than 15, the login script commands would display a message about the meeting.

## User Variables

The **user variables**, shown in Table 12-3, enable you to view or check the user's login name, full name, or hexadecimal user ID that's given to the user in eDirectory.

**Table 12-3**   User Variables

| Variable | Description |
|---|---|
| FULL_NAME | The user's full name, as defined by SYSCON or USERDEF |
| LOGIN_NAME | The user's unique login name |
| USER_ID | The hexadecimal number NetWare assigns for the user login name |
| HOME_DIRECTORY | The path to the user's home directory |

The %LOGIN_NAME and %FULL_NAME variables can be used to personalize greeting messages by including the user's name. The %HOME_DIRECTORY variable is useful for mapping a drive letter that points to the user's home directory. David uses this variable to automate the process of mapping drive letter H: to his home directory.

12

## Workstation Variables

The **workstation variables** are shown in Table 12-4. The %MACHINE, %OS, and %OS_VERSION variables are most commonly used in the system login script when mapping a search drive to the correct DOS version used on the workstation. The %STATION variable contains the connection number assigned to the user's workstation; sometimes software packages use this variable to separate the user's temporary files by including the station number as part of the temporary filename. The %P_STATION variable contains the actual node address of the workstation logging in and can be used in login script files to carry out certain processing tasks on specific workstations. For example, suppose only workstation address 000DC03D7D27 is used to run the new CAD software. In the login script, you could write commands to use the %P_STATION variable to check for the station address 000DC03D7D27, and then set up the necessary drive mappings and start the CAD software. The %NETWORK_ADDRESS variable can be used to display or check the IPX address of the cable attached to the workstation the user is logging in from.

**Table 12-4**   Workstation Variables

| Variable | Description |
| --- | --- |
| OS | The workstation's operating system; default value is "MSDOS" |
| OS_VERSION | The version of DOS used on the workstation processing the login script, such as "V6.20" |
| MACHINE | The long machine name that can be assigned in the Shell.cfg or Net.cfg file; default value is "IBM_PC" |
| P_STATION | The node address of the network card in the workstation, expressed as a 12-digit hexadecimal value |
| SMACHINE | The short machine name that can be assigned in the Shell.cfg or Net.cfg file; default value is "IBM" |
| STATION | The connection number of the current station |
| SHELL_TYPE | The workstation's shell version number |
| NETWORK_ADDRESS | The network address of the cabling system the user's workstation is attached to, expressed as an eight-digit hexadecimal number |
| FILE_SERVER | The name of the current file server |

Workstation variables are most often used to establish drive mappings for software utility directories based on the client workstation's hardware or operating system.

## User-Defined Variables

Based on the workstation or applications they need to run, more advanced network users might want to modify certain login script parameters when they log in. Novell Client offers **user-defined variables**, represented with a number preceded by a percent sign, as a way for users to enter parameters for their login scripts. To enter these variables, click the Variables button in the Script tab of the Novell Login window, and you'll see a dialog box like the one shown in Figure 12-7. Because the first variable parameter, %1, is reserved for system use, user-defined variables start with %2.

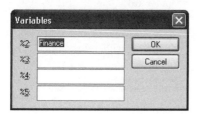

**Figure 12-7**   User-defined variables

When testing software for different departments, David needs to be able to modify the drive mapping for drive letter L: to point to the departments' shared work directories. To be able to select a department's directory path when he logs in, he decided to use the %2 user-defined variable to represent the department name. David entered the following command in his personal login script to map drive letter L: to the department name that's stored in the %2 variable:

```
MAP ROOT L:=CBE_ADMIN/DATA:\%2
```

When he logs in, the client workstation will perform all commands in the InfoSystems OU container login script and then carry out the preceding command, substituting the department name he specified for the %2 variable. For example, if he enters "Finance" for %2 in the Variables dialog box, the MAP command would become the following:

```
MAP ROOT L:=CBE_ADMIN/DATA:\Finance
```

# Using Login Script Variables

As described previously, a login script variable is a reserved word that's replaced with an actual value when the login script is processed. To assign a drive pointer to each user's home directory without login script variables, you would have to create a separate user login script for each user that contains a MAP command to his or her home directory, as shown in Figure 12-8.

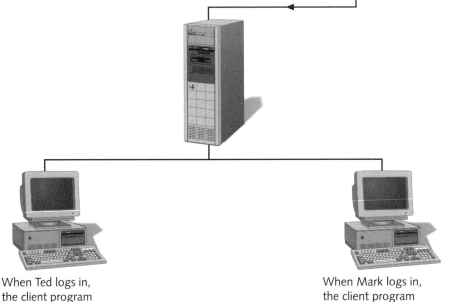

**Script for Mark**

MAP DISPLAY OFF
WRITE "Welcome to CBE Labs"
MAP INS S1:=CBE_ADMIN/SYS
MAP F:=/CBE_ADMIN/SYS:
MAP G:=CBE_ADMIN/DATA:InfoSys
#CAPTURE Q=IS_Q NB NT TI=5
MAP H:=CBE_ADMIN/DATA:Users\MCiampa
DRIVE H:

**Script for David**

MAP DISPLAY OFF
WRITE "Welcome to CBE Labs"
MAP INS S1:=CBE_ADMIN/SYS
MAP F:=CBE_ADMIN/SYS:
MAP G:=CBE_ADMIN/DATA:InfoSys
#CAPTURE Q=IS_Q NB NT TI=5
MAP H:=CBE_ADMIN/DATA:Users\DDoering
DRIVE H:

**Script for Ted**

MAP DISPLAY OFF
WRITE "Welcome to CBE Labs"
MAP INS S1:=CBE_ADMIN/SYS
MAP F:=CBE_ADMIN/SYS:
MAP G:=CBE_ADMIN/DATA:InfoSys
#CAPTURE Q=IS_Q NB NT TI=5
MAP H:=CBE_ADMIN/DATA:Users\TSimpson
DRIVE H:

When Ted logs in, the client program runs his script.

When Mark logs in, the client program runs his script.

**Figure 12-8** Using individual user login scripts

As you can see, creating a separate login script for each user involves a lot of extra work and redundancy. An alternative is creating a single login script that works for all users in the OU. Notice in Figure 12-8 that each user's directory name is the same as his or her login name. As you learned in Chapter 4, when creating new users with ConsoleOne, each user's home directory is given the same name as the user's login name by default. The path to the user's home directory is then stored as a property of the user account in the eDirectory database. When users' home directory paths are included with their user account information, you can substantially reduce the number of statements in the login script by using the %HOME_DIRECTORY variable in the MAP command statement, as shown in the following example:

```
MAP H:=%HOME_DIRECTORY
```

A container login script is processed by any user in the container when he or she logs in to the network. The percent sign (%) in front of the variable name is necessary to tell Novell Client to substitute the path to the user's home directory for the %HOME_DIRECTORY variable during the login process. Notice, too, that the login script variable name is entered in all uppercase letters.

Because many login script command statements require variable names to be capitalized, it's a good practice to capitalize all login script variable names.

Therefore, when David logs in, the Novell Client software running on his workstation replaces the %HOME_DIRECTORY variable with the path to his home directory, and the H: drive letter is mapped to the InfoSys\DDoering home directory. When Ted Simpson logs in, the Novell Client software on his workstation replaces the %HOME_DIRECTORY variable with the user name TSimpson, causing his H: drive letter to be mapped to the InfoSys\TSimpson directory.

Take a look at how David uses login script variables to display the current date in the greeting message and assign a drive pointer to the home directory for each user in InfoSystems:

**12**

1. David logged in with his CBEAdmin user name and password.

2. He started ConsoleOne and expanded CLASS_TREE and CBE_LABS.

3. He right-clicked the InfoSystems OU, and then clicked Properties to open the Properties of InfoSystems dialog box.

4. He used these steps to modify the InfoSystems container script:

   a. He clicked the Login Script tab.

   b. He modified the login script to add the following greeting message before the PAUSE statement:

   ```
   WRITE "Good %GREETING_TIME, %LOGIN_NAME"
   ```

   c. He modified the login script to add the following command to the end of the login script, so that drive letter H: would be mapped to the user's home directory:

   ```
   MAP H:=%HOME_DIRECTORY
   ```

d. He verified that the login script looked like the one in Figure 12-9 and then clicked OK to save the login script changes and return to the ConsoleOne main window.

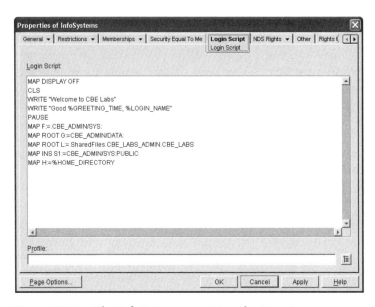

**Figure 12-9**    The InfoSystems container login script

5. He exited ConsoleOne and logged out to display a new Login window.

6. He used these steps to verify that the login script window would not close automatically:

a. He clicked the Advanced button, and then clicked the Script tab to display the login script options.

b. He made sure the Close automatically check box was cleared to disable this option.

c. He clicked the NDS tab and changed the context to his .InfoSystems.CBE_LABS container.

7. He logged in as the TSimpson user.

8. He verified that there were no error messages, and then clicked Close to close the Results window.

9. He double-clicked the My Computer icon to verify that the correct drive mappings had been set.

10. He closed the My Computer window and logged out.

# Writing Login Scripts

In many ways, creating login scripts is similar to writing a computer program. As in any programming language, there are specific valid commands that cause the computer to perform certain processing, and there are rules that must be followed for the commands to be processed. These rules are commonly referred to as the **syntax** of the programming language. In the following sections, you learn the valid syntax for the NetWare login script commands and examine examples of how to use the commands to perform common login functions. Before studying the login script commands, you should be aware of these general rules for their use:

- Only valid login script command statements and comments can be placed in a login script file.

- Login script command lines can be a maximum of 150 characters.

- Long commands can be allowed to "wrap" to the next line if there's not enough room on one line.

- Novell Client reads the login script commands one line at a time, and only one command is allowed on any command line.

- Commands can be entered in either uppercase or lowercase letters, except for variable values that are enclosed in quotation marks, which must be preceded by a percent sign (%) and typed in uppercase letters.

- Comments are entered by preceding the text with the command REM, an asterisk (*), or a semicolon (;).

## The CLS Command

The CLS command is used to clear the screen. Normally, it's a good idea to precede messages to users by clearing the screen and firing multiple phaser blasts (see "The FIRE PHASERS Command," later in this chapter), which gets users' attention and makes the message more likely to be read. You might want to follow the message with another CLS command to remove the message from the screen. If you do, be sure to follow the message with a PAUSE command, or users will not have time to read it.

## The MAP Command

The MAP command is perhaps the most important login script command because it automatically sets up both regular and search drive mappings that a user needs to access files and software in the NetWare environment. The syntax and use of the MAP login script command is very similar to the MAP command-line utility described in Chapter 8, except that you can use identifier variables and relative drive letters as part of the MAP login script command, as follows:

```
MAP [option] [drive:=path;drive:=path] [variable]
```

The semicolon in the MAP command is optional, used only to separate drive mappings when multiple drive letters are being mapped.

You can replace [*option*] with one of the parameters in Table 12-5.

**Table 12-5**    MAP Command Options

| Optional Parameter | Description |
|---|---|
| ROOT | Used to make a drive appear as the root of a volume to DOS and application programs, and must be used for Windows Explorer to point to the subdirectory; including the ROOT parameter on all drive mappings is usually a good practice |
| INS | Used to insert a new search drive at the sequence number you specify and renumber any existing search drives |
| DEL | Used to remove the specified regular or search drive mapping |

The [*drive:*] parameter must be replaced with a valid network, local, or search drive. In addition to using a specific drive letter, you can use a relative drive specification, such as *1: to indicate the first network drive, *2: for the second network drive, and so on. If the workstation's first network drive letter is F:, *1 will be replaced with F:, and *2: will be replaced with G:. On the other hand, if a workstation's first network drive is L:, *1: will be replaced with L:, and *2: will be replaced with J:. Replace [*path*] with a full directory path, beginning with a DOS drive letter or NetWare volume name.

With the login script version of the MAP command, you can place additional drive mappings on the same line by separating them with semicolons. For example, if you wanted to map the F: drive to the SYS volume and the G: drive to the DATA volume, you could do so with this MAP command:

```
MAP F:=SYS:;G:=DATA:
```

Other special MAP command statements include MAP DISPLAY OFF and MAP ERRORS OFF. The MAP DISPLAY OFF command prevents MAP commands from being displayed on user workstations and is often included at the beginning of a login script command to reduce the amount of information displayed on users' workstations. The MAP ERRORS OFF command prevents the display of error messages generated by MAP commands that specify invalid paths. This command is useful if you include drive mapping commands in a login script that you know won't be valid for all users. Rather than have users confused by receiving error messages that don't affect them, you can include the MAP ERRORS OFF command before the MAP commands containing the invalid drive paths. When first testing login scripts, however, you need to see the results of MAP commands and any error messages. Therefore, you should wait until after login scripts have been tested and debugged to add the MAP DISPLAY OFF and MAP ERRORS OFF commands.

## The NO_DEFAULT Command

The NO_DEFAULT login script command prevents the default login script commands from running when users do not have their own login scripts. However, after you implement a login script system, running the default login script can overwrite your drive mappings and cause multiple drive mappings and error messages. As a result, it's important to include the NO_DEFAULT command at the beginning of each container's login script to prevent the default script from running. David used the following steps to prevent the default login script from running:

1. He logged in with his CBEAdmin user name and password.

2. He started ConsoleOne and expanded CLASS_TREE and CBE_LABS.

3. He right-clicked the InfoSystems OU, and then clicked Properties to open the Properties of IS dialog box.

4. He clicked the Login Script tab to display the existing login script.

5. He added the following command to the beginning of the InfoSystems container login script:

   NO_DEFAULT

6. He clicked OK to save the changes and return to the main ConsoleOne window.

7. He logged out to display a new Novell Login window.

8. He used these steps to log in as TSimpson:

   a. He entered TSimpson in the Username text box.

   b. He entered the password for TSimpson in the Password text box, and then clicked the Advanced button.

   c. He clicked the NDS tab and changed the context to the InfoSystems.CBE_LABS container. (Note that changing the context isn't always necessary.)

   d. He clicked OK to log in.

   e. He read the welcome message, and then pressed the Enter key to continue. (You can press any key to continue.)

9. He noted that no additional login script commands were displayed in the Results window when the default login script was disabled, so he clicked Close to close the Results window.

10. He double-clicked the My Computer icon and noted that no duplicate paths existed.

11. He closed the My Computer window and logged out.

12

## The CONTEXT Command

Accessing network resources is much easier when your current context is set to the container holding the objects you need to use, which is usually accomplished with the Advanced button in the Novell Login window. However, if a user logs in using his or her distinguished user name, the client workstation's current context isn't changed. By using the CONTEXT login script command, however, you can change the client workstation's current context to another container when a user logs in. The syntax of the CONTEXT command includes the typeful distinguished name of the container that will become the default context. For example, to set the default container to the InfoSystems OU, you would enter this command:

```
CONTEXT .OU=InfoSystems.O=CBE_LABS
```

Being able to automatically change the context is important when using Directory Map objects and volume names in the login script MAP commands. If the context is not changed to the correct container, the Directory Map object might not be found or the wrong volume could be used in the MAP command. For example, David often needs to log in from other users' workstations to test software. To use his distinguished name instead of selecting the context in the Novell Login window each time he logs in, David inserts the preceding CONTEXT command in the InfoSystems container login script immediately after the PAUSE command. He then logs in and receives a new login window, similar to Figure 12-10, after pressing the spacebar.

**Figure 12-10**    The Results window with a welcome message and context information

## The WRITE Command

The WRITE command is used to display simple messages enclosed in quotation marks on users' workstations. Messages can also contain identifier variables and special control strings, as shown in the WRITE command syntax:

```
WRITE "text [control string] [%variable]"
```

Common login script variables often used with the WRITE command include %GREETING_TIME and %LOGIN_NAME. The %GREETING_TIME variable contains the current time expressed as "Morning," "Afternoon," or "Evening." Many network administrators include a WRITE statement such as the following, with a greeting message at the beginning of the login script to display the login time and user's full name:

```
WRITE "Good %GREETING_TIME, %LOGIN_NAME"
```

Important messages that you want to be sure all users see and acknowledge should be followed with the PAUSE statement, as shown here:

```
WRITE "File server will be coming down today, March 1, at
5:00 p.m. for a maintenance call."
PAUSE
```

David decided to modify the InfoSystems OU login script to include this WRITE statement:

```
WRITE "It's %HOUR:%MINUTE %AM_PM on %DAY_OF_WEEK,
%MONTH/%DAY/%YEAR"
```

**12**

Always test login scripts you create before releasing them to your customers because it is easy to make a mistake while typing in the commands. To test his login script, David logged in and saw the Results window shown in Figure 12-11.

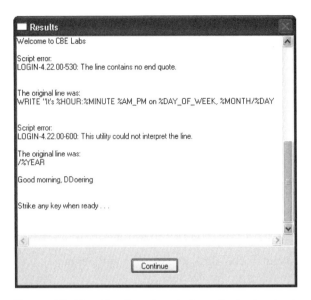

**Figure 12-11**    The Results window displaying login script errors

The reason he received an error is because he forgot that commands must appear on one line and accidentally pressed Enter before entering the %YEAR variable, so he needed to modify the WRITE statement, as shown in Figure 12-12.

```
NO_DEFAULT
MAP DISPLAY OFF
CLS
WRITE "Welcome to CBE Labs"
WRITE "It's %HOUR:%MINUTE %AM_PM on %DAY_OF_WEEK, %MONTH/%DAY/%YEAR"
WRITE "Good %GREETING_TIME, %LOGIN_NAME"
PAUSE
CONTEXT .OU=InfoSystems.O=CBE_LABS
MAP F:=.CBE_ADMIN/SYS:
MAP ROOT G:=CBE_ADMIN/DATA:
MAP ROOT L:=.SharedFiles.CBE_LABS_ADMIN.CBE_LABS
MAP INS S1:=CBE_ADMIN/SYS:PUBLIC
MAP H:=%HOME_DIRECTORY
```

**Figure 12-12**    The InfoSystems login script with the correct syntax

David tested the script again by logging in as TSimpson and was happy to see the window shown in Figure 12-13. Although at first you will probably spend more time debugging your login scripts than creating them, don't worry; the more scripts you write and debug, the faster you will get and the fewer errors you will see. There are two schools of thought in this area. Some people think the system should debug any errors in their scripts, so they enter them quickly, test them by running them, and correct any errors after looking at the Results window. They might do this several times before getting the script to function as it should. Others check their syntax carefully before saving and running the script; they look for missing % signs, spelling errors, and so forth, before running the script. There is no right or wrong way, as long as you get the script to work in a timely fashion. Decide what works best for you.

**Figure 12-13** The Results window with time variables

## The DISPLAY and FDISPLAY Commands

The DISPLAY and FDISPLAY (for "filtered display") commands are used to show the contents of an ASCII text file onscreen when the login script runs. This is the proper syntax for both commands:

DISPLAY (or FDISPLAY) [*directory path*] *filename*

If the [*filename*] specified is in the current directory, or if a search drive has been established to the directory containing the [*filename*], the directory path is not needed. However, in the following example, even though a search drive has been created for SYS:Public, the Welcome.msg file is in the Message subdirectory. Therefore, you need to include the FDISPLAY command as shown to make sure the message file is found:

```
MAP INS S1:=SYS:Public
FDISPLAY SYS:Public\Message\Welcome.msg
PAUSE
```

An error message is displayed if the file specified in the DISPLAY command does not exist or if the user does not have the necessary permissions to the file.

You should follow the DISPLAY or FDISPLAY command with a PAUSE statement to give the user time to read the message file. The difference between DISPLAY and FDISPLAY is that the FDISPLAY command "filters" and formats the contents of the specified filename so that only the ASCII text is displayed. FDISPLAY does not display tab characters, but converts them into spaces to make the output more readable. The DISPLAY command, on the other hand, displays the exact characters contained in the file, including "garbage" characters, such as printer or word-processing edit codes. Using FDISPLAY with files created with word-processing packages is usually preferable; however, if you use a word-processing package, be sure to save the file in ASCII text format, or not even FDISPLAY will be able to read it. This allows you to create text files with messages you want to be displayed on various days of the week. For example, David can create text files with Notepad (or any word processor); name them Monday.txt, Tuesday.txt, Wednesday.txt, Thursday.txt, and Friday.txt; and store them in the Shared folder he created earlier. Each text file can contain a message for that day, such as "Monday morning staff meeting in conference room at 8:00 A.M." He could then add the following statement in the InfoSystems OU login script before the PAUSE command:

```
DISPLAY CBE_ADMIN/DATA:Shared\%DAY_OF_WEEK.txt
```

When TSimpson logs in, he receives a welcome window similar to Figure 12-14. He logged in on a Monday, so the Monday.txt file was displayed because Monday replaced the %DAY_OF_WEEK variable.

**Figure 12-14**   The Results window after using the DISPLAY command to display a text file message

## The # and @ Commands (Execute a DOS Program)

The external program execution (# and @) commands are used to load and run an .exe or .com program without exiting Novell Client. The # command stops the login script from processing until the specified program has finished running, but the @ command starts the executable program and then continues processing login script commands while the executable program runs in the background. The @ command is useful if you want to load continuously running programs, such as virus detection software, into the computer's memory. Using the # command in this case would cause the login script to "hang" because the virus detection software runs continuously in memory and does not exit back to the login script processor.

The # command cannot be used to run a batch or script file; only executable programs, such as .exe or .com files, can be run from the login script.

When using the # command, after the program finishes, the next login script command line runs. This is the syntax for the # and @ commands:

```
@ [path] filename [parameters]
# [path] filename [parameters]
```

You can optionally replace [*path*] with a full directory path, using a DOS drive letter or NetWare volume name to specify the location of the DOS program. If a network drive letter is used, make sure a previous login script MAP command is used to map the drive letter to a valid NetWare path. You must replace *filename* with the name of the .com or .exe program you want to run. The extension is not necessary. Depending on the program you're running, you can replace [*parameters*] with any parameters that should be passed to the specified program.

The external program execution character (#) is important because it lets you run other command-line utilities or DOS commands from inside the login script. For example, the # command could be used to run the CAPTURE program to establish a default network printer for DOS and Windows 3.11 clients, as described in Chapter 11. Because CAPTURE is not a login script command, the # command can be used to run the CAPTURE program with the appropriate parameters.

## IF ... THEN ... ELSE Statements

Network administrators often use the IF login statement to customize a login script for specific users or groups and to perform special processing when a certain condition, such as a specific day, time, or station, exists. The syntax of a simple IF statement is as follows:

```
IF condition THEN command
```

The *condition* parameter is replaced with a conditional statement that has a value of true or false. Conditional statements usually consist of an **identifier variable** and a value

**12**

enclosed in quotation marks. Examples of several common conditional statements are shown in Table 12-6.

**Table 12-6**   Common Conditional Statements

| Condition | Description |
|---|---|
| MEMBER OF "group" | This statement is true if the user is a member of the specified group. |
| DAY_OF_WEEK= | This statement is true if the name of the day is Monday. Possible values range from "Sunday" through Saturday. Uppercase or lowercase letters can be used. |
| DAY="05" | This statement is true on the fifth day of the month; valid day values range from "01" to "31." You must include the leading zero for day numbers lower than 10. |
| MONTH="June" | This statement is true for the month of June. You can replace "June" with any valid month name from January to December. Either uppercase or lowercase letters are accepted. |
| NDAY_OF_WEEK="1" | This statement is true on Sunday, which is the first day of the week. Valid weekday numbers range from "1" to "7." |

The *command* parameter can be replaced with any valid login script command statement. For example, a simple IF statement with a single condition can be written as follows:

```
IF DAY_OF_WEEK="FRIDAY" THEN WRITE "Hurrah, it's Friday!"
```

More complex IF statements can consist of multiple commands followed by the END statement. When using complex IF statements containing multiple commands, you should use the BEGIN command after THEN, and then place the commands after the IF statement, as shown in the following example:

```
IF condition THEN BEGIN
    command 1
    command 2
    command n
END
```

When using a multiple-command IF statement, all commands between the IF statement and the END statement are performed when the condition is true. For example, to prevent the error message produced by your CBE_Labs_Admin OU login script attempting to map a home directory when the Admin user logs in, you can use an IF statement similar to the following:

```
IF MEMBER OF "ISMgrs" THEN BEGIN
MAP ROOT P:=CBE_ADMIN/DATA:
END
```

Sometimes it's best to combine multiple conditions by using AND or OR. When using OR to connect two conditions, the login commands are performed if *either* condition is true. For example, if you wanted all members of *either* the WebMgrs group or the ISMgrs group to be informed of a weekly meeting, you could use this statement:

```
IF MEMBER OF "ISMgrs" OR MEMBER OF "WebMgrs" THEN BEGIN
    WRITE "Weekly Web development meeting will be in conference
room 100 starting at 10:00 a.m."
    PAUSE
END
```

The word AND is used when you want both statements to be true before processing the commands. For example, suppose you wanted to remind all ISMgrs users of a meeting on Friday morning. Before displaying the reminder, you would want to make sure the user was a member of the Marketing department, the day was Friday, and the login time was before noon. To do this, you could use AND to connect these three conditions with the following statement:

```
IF MEMBER OF "ISMgrs" AND DAY_OF_WEEK="Friday" AND
HOUR24 < "12" THEN
```

The optional word ELSE is a helpful feature of the IF statement because it allows you to choose between sets of commands based on a certain condition. For example, the following IF...THEN...ELSE command could be used if all members of the WebMgrs group need to have their I: drive pointer mapped to the InfoSys\Web directory, but all other users in the InfoSystems OU should have their I: drive pointer mapped to the InfoSys\Shared directory:

```
IF MEMBER OF "WebMgrs" THEN
    MAP I:=CBE_ADMIN/DATA:InfoSys\Web
ELSE
    MAP I:= CBE_ADMIN/DATA:InfoSys\Shared
END
```

**12**

## The EXIT Command

The EXIT command stops the login script from running and returns control to the client workstation, so no additional login script commands are processed after the EXIT command is issued. Be careful about using this command in a container because it is possible to inadvertently prevent all other login scripts from running.

## The FIRE PHASERS Command

The purpose of the FIRE PHASERS command is to make a noise with the PC speaker to alert the user of a message coming in or a condition encountered in the login process. You should limit the use of the FIRE PHASERS command to important messages, however; otherwise, users get used to the sound and will probably miss the message. You can control the length of the phaser blast with the following command:

```
FIRE [PHASERS] n [TIMES]
```

You can replace *n* with a number from 1 to 9 to represent how many successive times the phaser sound is made. The words PHASERS and TIMES are optional and can be omitted from the FIRE login script command. FIRE PHASERS is often used with the IF statement to notify the user of a certain condition. For example, you could use the FIRE PHASERS command in an IF statement to remind users of a special meeting time, as follows:

```
IF DAY_OF_WEEK="Tuesday" AND HOUR24 < "11" THEN
    WRITE "Department meeting at 11:30 a.m."
    FIRE PHASERS 2 TIMES
    PAUSE
END
```

Some people find the sound generated from the FIRE PHASERS command to be annoying, so use it only when you think it's necessary to get users' attention. After all, the sound of 20 to 30 workstations beeping simultaneously can be unpleasant.

## The REM Command

The REM command can be used with the asterisk (*) or the semicolon (;) to place a comment line in the login script. The login process skips any line that begins with REM, REMARK, *, or ;. Using comments in your login script can make the script much easier for you or another administrator to read and understand, but placing a comment on the same line as other login script commands causes errors when the script runs. To make your work easier to identify and maintain, you should use REM statements to include your name, last modified date, and a brief description of the commands in each section in the script. For example, you should precede each section of your login script with a comment identifying the function of that section, as in the following example:

```
REM Login Script for InfoSystems OU
REM Written by David Doering
REM Last modified 2/19/03
;
* Preliminary Commands
MAP DISPLAY OFF
;
```

The name helps other programmers identify the author in case there are questions about how the login script works. There is nothing worse than trying to figure out what others were thinking when they wrote a login script and neglected to document their work. A sentence or two, explaining what the script does, can be a lifesaver for someone who has to maintain your work.

The last modified date identifies the latest version of login script command listings, and command descriptions help other programmers understand the function of command sequences in the login script. As your login scripts grow, they can become overwhelming to read, so adding some blank comment lines helps improve their readability.

## Documenting Login Scripts

The best way to document your login scripts for troubleshooting and planning is to print hard copies of each container and profile login script. Unfortunately, ConsoleOne and NetWare Administrator don't have options for directly printing login scripts. However, you can use the NLIST command-line utility to print login scripts to a printer attached to your computer, or highlight the login script commands and use the Ctrl+C and Ctrl+V key combinations to copy and paste the commands to Notepad or WordPad. The format of the NLIST command is as follows:

```
NLIST "object type" = context SHOW "Login Script" > PRN
```

Replace *object type* with "Organization" or "Organizational Unit" and replace *context* with the path to the container. For example, to print the contents of the InfoSystems OU login script on your locally attached printer, you would use the following command:

```
NLIST "Organizational Unit" = .InfoSystems.CBE_LABS SHOW "Login
Script" > PRN
```

Using the copy-and-paste method is the fastest and easiest way to print your login scripts. For example, David used the following steps to print a copy of the InfoSystems OU login script:

1. He logged in with his CBEAdmin user name and password.

2. He clicked Start, Settings, Printers and Faxes, and set the CBE_LABS printer as his default printer.

3. He started ConsoleOne and expanded the CLASS_TREE and CBE_LABS containers.

4. He right-clicked the InfoSystems OU, and then clicked Properties to open the Properties of InfoSystems dialog box.

5. He clicked the Login Script tab to display the login script commands.

6. He highlighted all the login script commands in the Login Script text box, held down the Ctrl key, and then pressed C to copy the selected commands to the Clipboard.

7. He started Notepad by clicking Start, Programs, Accessories, Notepad.

8. He clicked in the Notepad window, and then pressed Ctrl+V to paste the commands into the Notepad window.

9. He clicked File, Print on the Notepad menu bar and then clicked Print in the Print dialog box to print the login script to the default printer.

You might want to consider punching some holes in the copy you print, placing it in a loose-leaf binder, and labeling it "CBE Login Scripts."

**12**

## IMPLEMENTING LOGIN SCRIPTS

Now that you have learned the syntax and function of the login script commands and seen how login scripts are stored and carried out, you need to learn how to apply login scripts to setting up a network environment for each user's workstation when he or she logs in. Implementing a login script system for your network requires four basic steps:

1. Identify the login script requirements for each container and user.

2. Write the script commands.

3. Enter the script commands.

4. Test the login script.

### Identifying Login Script Requirements

To design a login script system, you start by identifying a standard set of regular and search drive mappings that all users will need to run software and access data in the network file system. Next, identify any special setup needs for each workgroup in the organization, such as mapping all members of the WebMgrs group to the I: drive. Finally, identify any special setups that are unique for certain users. For example, a user might need to be reminded of a meeting with the company president that takes place only twice a year.

If most of the user workstation setup needs are the same for groups of users (and they generally are), you can meet those needs through the container and profile login script commands. If your network has many special or individualized setup requirements, decide if you want to create a container or profile login script containing only the essential commands, such as mapping a search drive to SYS:Public. Then implement user login scripts to handle the workstation setup for each user.

Just as network administrators differ in the ways they design a directory structure, they also implement login script systems differently, depending on their preferences and experience. The important thing is to develop a workable strategy that meets the needs of your organization and your personal preferences.

### Writing Login Scripts

After you identify your login script needs and strategy, the next step is to write the login script commands. You might find it helpful to use a login script worksheet, similar to the one in Figure 12-15. (You can find a blank form of this worksheet in Appendix B.)

---

**Container Login Script Worksheet**

Organization: ____CBE Labs_____          Page __1__ of __1__

Developed by:__David Doering_____   Date:__2/19/03_____

Container Context: InfoSystems.CBE_LABS_____

---

**REM General Commands**

REM Created by: David Doering
REM Last modified: 2/19/03
NO_DEFAULT
MAP DISPLAY OFF
CONTEXT .InfoSystems.CBE_LABS
MAP ROOT G:=CBE_ADMIN/DATA:
MAP H:=%HOME DIRECTORY
MAP L:=.SharedFiles.CBE_Admin_Labs.CBE_LABS
MAP INS S1:=CBE_ADMIN/SYS:Public
CLS
WRITE "Good %GREETING_TIME, %LOGIN_NAME"
WRITE "Welcome to CBE Labs"
DISPLAY CBE__ADMIN/DATA:Shared\%DAY_OF_WEEK.TXT
IF DAY OF WEEK="Monday" and HOUR24 < "09" THEN BEGIN
    WRITE "Weekly systems meeting at 9:00 a.m. in conference room"
    FIRE PHASERS 2
END
PAUSE

---

**REM Commands for ISMgrs and NetworkAdmins Groups**

IF MEMBER OF "ISMgrs" OR MEMBER OF "NetworkAdmins" THEN BEGIN
  WRITE "Weekly systems meeting will be in conference room 100 starting at 10:00 a.m."
END
IF MEMBER OF "ISMgrs" THEN
    MAP ROOT P:=CBE_ADMIN/DATA:
END

---

**REM Commands for WebMgrs Group**

IF MEMBER OF "WebMgrs" THEN BEGIN
  MAP I:=CBE_ADMIN/DATA:Publctns
ELSE
  MAP I:=CBE_ADMIN/DATA:Shared
END

---

**REM End of Login Script Commands**

---

**Figure 12-15**   The Container Login Script Worksheet for CBE Labs

The worksheet is divided into sections, using REM statements to define the start of each section. The General Commands section contains any initializing commands, such as NO_DEFAULT, MAP DISPLAY OFF, and MAP INS S1:=CBE_ADMIN\SYS:Public. In addition, this section can be used to clear the screen and display a greeting message to the user. Notice how the CLS command is used to clear the screen before displaying messages. This section also contains drive mappings and messages for all users in the container. Notice the use of the SharedFiles Directory Map object created in Chapter 8 to map drive L: to the CBE_ADMIN/DATA:Shared folder. Using the Directory Map object enables the InfoSys directory to be changed to another volume without modifying the login script.

The REM Commands for *<workgroup name>* Group sections contain login script commands that are performed only for users who are members of the specified group. In the InfoSystems container script worksheet, if a user is a member of the ISMgrs workgroup, he or she receives a P: drive mapping to the CBE_ADMIN/DATA: volume. The End of Login Script Commands section can be used to contain any commands that all users perform before exiting the login script.

## Testing and Debugging Login Scripts

After the login scripts have been entered, you should test the login script system for at least one user in each workgroup by logging in with that user's name and checking to be sure all commands are carried out correctly. When establishing login scripts, do not be discouraged if everything does not work correctly the first time. Although proper planning and design can eliminate many possible problems, small errors caused by missing or invalid login script commands, incorrect paths, or lack of user access rights can still be irritating. Consider using the MAP DISPLAY ON and MAP ERRORS ON commands during this debugging stage. After verifying that the script is working correctly, you can turn both features off.

When all login scripts have been debugged, document drive mappings and other special setup commands that are performed for each workgroup or user.

 Because users need to know certain drive mappings to effectively access data and applications through the network file system, you should give users the documentation or training they need to use the workstation environment the login script creates. The time spent in documenting and training users in how to use the system will pay off later in fewer problems and support calls.

## MANAGING USER ENVIRONMENTS WITH ZENWORKS FOR DESKTOPS

You have learned how to use login scripts to help create consistent, standardized drive pointers for users each time they log in to the network. However, login scripts are only part of the solution for making the network easy to use and maintain; users also need a consistent desktop environment and access to required applications from any workstation they work on. In the past, network administrators had to install applications and modify workstation configurations on many different machines to accommodate users' varying needs of users. Manually installing applications and setting up or restoring user desktops can be a labor-intensive task that takes time away from other network administration priorities. Novell's **Zero Effort Networking (ZENworks) for Desktops (ZfD)** package enables network administrators to centrally monitor and manage software and workstation configurations so that users have easy mobility among workstations. In the following sections, you learn what a CNA needs to know about using the Novell ZENworks package to set up and manage user desktop environments.

## ZENworks for Desktops 3 Overview

The cost of hardware and software is only a small part of the total cost of owning a computer. In addition to the physical and software components, the cost of ownership, which is becoming a major concern for many organizations, includes the ongoing costs of maintaining and upgrading the computer hardware, software installation and configuration, troubleshooting, and user support and training. Although the Windows environment makes it easy for users to interact with and personalize their desktop computers, because of its complexity, it can actually increase the total cost of ownership (TCO); network administrators, therefore, must spend more time configuring, managing, and supporting Windows environments. Configuration time can also increase when users move to different workstations, yet want to access their same desktop environments. In a large network, another concern is providing help desk support for users when they have problems or questions.

Novell's ZfD makes the network easier for users to work with and reduces the time administrators have to spend at each user workstation. In addition, ZfD offers a remote-control capability that gives you a secure way to take control of a client workstation's display, keyboard, and mouse; in this way, you can help a user fix a problem or change a configuration without having to physically go to that workstation. The ZfD product consists of client and server components that enable network administrators to use eDirectory Services to centralize configuration information for applications, users, and workstations; this method reduces the time and repetitiveness of workstation configuration and management.

**12**

### Benefits and Features

ZfD has benefits in the following areas of network management:

- *Application management*—ZfD includes an Application Launcher, which enables you to centrally distribute, upgrade, and manage applications on any Windows-based workstation attached to your network.

- *Workstation management*—The Workstation Manager component allows you to store user and desktop configurations for Windows workstations in eDirectory. Because ZfD uses eDirectory to extend Windows features, such as policies, printers, and user profiles, these features are manageable from a centralized location by using ConsoleOne.

- *Remote control*—With ZfD, you can securely manage and interact with workstations from a remote location. This makes troubleshooting user problems and changing configurations much more convenient on large networks.

## Hardware and Software Requirements

To use ZfD, your server must be running NetWare 4.11 or higher with the latest support packs installed. Windows 95/98 workstations need to have Novell Client 3.3 or later installed, and Windows NT/2000 workstations need to have at least Novell Client 4.8 or later installed. Following are the minimum hardware requirements for workstations; keep in mind that these are *minimum* hardware requirements that might not provide adequate performance:

- Processor: Pentium 75 MHz or higher

- Memory: 16 MB for Windows 95/98 or 128 MB for Windows NT/2000

- Hard disk space: 4 MB (workstation) or 24 MB (full installation)

In addition, to configure and manage ZfD, you need to use ConsoleOne because NetWare Administrator and iManager do not currently have ZfD management capabilities.

# Installing ZENworks

Before taking advantage of the ZENworks features, you need to install ZfD on your server and, if necessary, update the client on workstations. David installed ZfD on the CBE_ADMIN server with the following procedure:

1. Because the ZfD installation needs to replace certain Java utilities on the server, before starting the installation, David went to the server console and entered the command UNLOAD JAVA to stop Java applications on the server. If this is not done, the ZfD installation program issues an error message.

2. Next, he logged in to the network from his workstation with the CBEAdmin user name and password so that he would have Supervisor rights to the network.

3. After successfully logging in, he inserted the ZENworks for Desktops CD into the workstation's CD drive. The installation wizard automatically started and displayed the language selection window.

4. He clicked the English language option to display the installation options and then clicked the Install ZENworks option.

5. He clicked Next in the Novell Product Installation window to display the License Agreement window.

6. After reading the agreement, he clicked Accept to display the Install Prerequisites window. After reading the prerequisites, he clicked Accept to continue.

7. To be able to select specific options, he clicked the Custom radio button, and then clicked Next to continue.

8. He clicked the Clear All button and selected only the following components:

   ■ Application Management

   ■ Automatic Workstation Import

   ■ Workstation Management

9. After selecting these components, he clicked Next to display the installation window.

10. He clicked Next to install Files, Schema Extensions, and NDS Objects.

11. He clicked Next to select the default CLASS_TREE, and then clicked Next again to accept the CBE_ADMIN server.

12. He then verified that the English language was selected, and clicked Next to continue.

13. He verified that None was selected for the Import/Removal role of the CBE_ADMIN server, and then clicked Next to display the installation summary window.

14. He clicked Finish to begin installing the displayed components.

15. When he saw the message asking whether to replace newer files, he clicked the Never overwrite newer file radio button, and then clicked OK.

16. After all files were copied, he read and closed the log file to complete the installation.

17. He then closed all open windows and logged out.

18. To finish the installation, he restarted the server by entering the command RESTART SERVER at the server console.

19. To be able to manage the ZENworks system, he needed to update ConsoleOne on his workstation. To do this, he used the following steps:

    a. He logged in to the CBE_ADMIN server from his workstation, using his administrative user name and password.

    b. He used My Computer to navigate to the Z:\public\ZENWORKS folder and double-clicked the C1Update application.

    c. He clicked the browse button to set the source path to Z:\mgmt\ConsoleOne\1.2.

    d. He clicked the Autosearch button to find the destination path for the ConsoleOne files on his workstation.

Sometimes it's necessary to edit the destination path to remove the bin\ConsoleOne.exe path. The final destination path should be similar to C:\Novell\ConsoleOne\1.2.

12

  e. He clicked Next to display his selections, verified the selected paths, and clicked Start to update his ConsoleOne snap-ins for use with ZENworks.

  f. After the snap-ins were copied, he closed the ZENworks folder window, and logged out.

## MANAGING WORKSTATIONS

In addition to installing and configuring applications on each workstation, network administrators need to be able to maintain a consistent desktop environment and keep track of each client's hardware and software configurations. The key to managing Windows desktop environments is using policies, which are powerful Windows desktop management tools that allow user workstations to be customized for individual user needs. However, when implementing a network with many Windows computers, managing workstation and user policies with the local policy-editing program in Windows 2000 Professional/ Windows XP Professional can be a time-consuming chore. ZENworks makes Windows policies easier to manage and more powerful by adding Policy Package objects to eDirectory.

**Policy Package objects** enable you to manage the way users access their workstations and connect to the network. There are two types of policy packages: Workstation policies and User policies. With Workstation policies, you can configure settings such as the path to Windows setup files, file and printer sharing, workstation passwords, and run options. Run options can be used to configure which applications automatically run on a workstation regardless of which user logs in. For example, you could use a Workstation policy package to specify that workstations automatically start Novell Application Launcher (NAL.exe) instead of placing the command in a container login script. User policy packages affect users' access to workstations and their desktop restrictions, regardless of where they log in to the network. You can use User policy packages to define restrictions, such as hiding the Entire Network option in Network Neighborhood or hiding the Run or Find commands, for example. You can also define a desktop environment, including wallpaper, screensavers, sounds, and colors.

When a policy package is applied to a Windows 95/98 workstation, the restrictions made to the workstation's Registry are applied to the next user, unless he or she has a policy that changes the Registry settings. As a result, if the Admin user logs in to a 95/98 workstation that a restricted user had previously used, the restriction is applied to the Windows environment for the Admin user, too. For example, if the previous user was restricted from using the Windows Start, Run option, the Admin user would also be unable to run programs from the Start, Run option. As a result, when setting up restricted User policy packages, you should create an open policy package that enables all Windows functions and then associate the open policy with your Admin user. In this way, when you log in as the Admin user from a restricted workstation, you will have access to all Windows features. Before setting up the User policy packages, David created an open access policy package and associated it with his Admin user account. He used the following steps to create an open access workstation environment for network administrators:

1. He logged in with his CBEAdmin user name and password.

2. He started ConsoleOne and expanded CLASS_TREE and the CBE_LABS Organization.

3. He used these steps to create an open policy package for his CBEAdmin user account:

   a. He clicked CBE_LABS Organization, and then clicked the New Object button on the ConsoleOne toolbar to open the New Object dialog box.

   b. He scrolled down and double-clicked Policy Package to start the Policy Package Wizard.

   c. He clicked the User Package object in the Policy Package pane on the left, and then clicked the Windows 2000 Group Policy item in the Policies pane on the right.

   d. He clicked the Next button to display the Policy Package Name and Container text boxes.

   e. He entered Admin Policy in the Policy Package Name text box, and verified that CBE_LABS container was displayed in the Container text box.

   f. He clicked the Next button to display the Summary dialog box.

   g. He clicked the Define Additional Properties check box, and then clicked the Finish button to open the Properties of Admin Policy dialog box.

   h. He clicked the down arrow on the Policies tab, and then clicked the Win95-98 option to open the Win95-98 User Policies dialog box, similar to the one in Figure 12-16.

4. He used these steps to configure the user policy package to reset all restrictions:

   a. He clicked the User Extensible Policies check box, and then clicked the Properties button to open the User Extensible Policies dialog box.

   b. In the ADM Files section, he clicked the \zen\admfiles\admin.adm file to display the associated policies.

   c. In the Policies section, he double-clicked the Control Panel policy (and expanded each item under that policy) to show all the options, as shown in Figure 12-17.

12

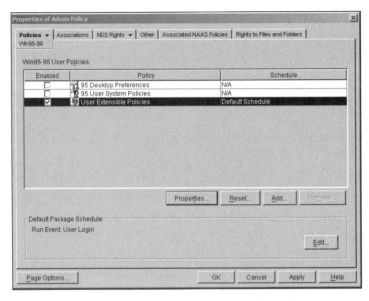

**Figure 12-16** The Win95-98 User Policies dialog box

A gray check box indicates that the policy setting will not be changed on the user workstation. A check mark in the check box indicates that the policy will be applied. A clear (white) check box indicates that the policy will be reset.

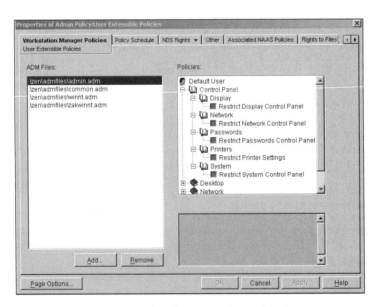

**Figure 12-17** Options for the Control Panel policy

    d. He double-clicked each check box until it was white (clear with no check mark) to reset all Control Panel restrictions for the Admin user.

    e. He scrolled down the list in the Policies section, and double-clicked the Shell policy to view all the options.

    f. He double-clicked each policy under the Restrictions policy until it was white (clear with no check mark) to reset all restrictions.

    g. He double-clicked the System policy, double-clicked Restrictions to view all the options, and double-clicked each policy check box until it was white (clear with no check mark) to reset all restrictions.

    h. He clicked OK to save his changes and return to the Policies tab of the Properties of Admin Policy dialog box.

5. He used these steps to reset all restrictions on the Windows NT/2000 policies:

    a. He clicked the down arrow on the Policies tab, and then clicked the WinNT-2000 option.

    b. He clicked the User Extensible Policies check box, and then clicked the Properties button to open the User Extensible Policies dialog box.

    c. He clicked the \zen\admfiles\admin.adm file to display the associated policies.

    d. He expanded each policy and removed any restrictions by double-clicking the check box until it was white (clear with no check mark).

    e. He clicked OK to save the new policy settings and return to the Policies tab of the Properties of Admin Policy dialog box.

6. He used these steps to associate the Admin Policy package with his CBEAdmin user account:

    a. He clicked the Associations tab to open the Associations dialog box.

    b. He clicked the Add button to open the Select Objects dialog box.

    c. He double-clicked the CBEAdmin user to associate the policy with his administrative user name.

7. He clicked OK to save his changes to the Admin policy and return to the main ConsoleOne window.

8. He exited ConsoleOne and logged out.

You can also configure a standard user desktop for users in your organization that might restrict them from using the Run command, the Start menu, and even Control Panel. You might want to give all users in one department a standard company wallpaper, instead of allowing them to have pictures of their families or pets displayed on their monitors. These types of policy packages can sometimes annoy your users, but they have proved to reduce the number of help calls in an organization. After implementing login scripts and policy

**12**

packages for your company, your network users can log in with a consistent desktop and use a standard set of drive pointers to access the network file system.

## CHAPTER SUMMARY

- ❑ Establishing a workstation environment and providing access to network files are important responsibilities for a network administrator. NetWare offers a powerful way to automate workstation setups through the use of login scripts.

- ❑ NetWare login scripts contain commands to provide drive mappings and other workstation setup functions needed during login. Novell supplies a set of commands that can be included in login script files to map drive letters, set a workstation's DOS environment, display messages and files, run other programs, and issue certain commands based on specified conditions.

- ❑ By using login script variables with commands, you can create general-purpose login scripts that work for multiple users. Login script variables are divided into date variables, such as %DAY_OF_WEEK; time variables, such as %HOUR24; user variables, such as %HOME_DIRECTORY; workstation variables, such as %OS and %OS_VERSION; and user-defined variables, such as %2, which enable users to enter a parameter. The percent sign preceding a variable name tells NetWare to substitute the value of the variable when the login script command runs.

- ❑ Novell Client can run four types of NetWare login scripts: container, profile, user, and default. The container login script is a property of the container object, and its commands run first when users in that container log in. After the container login script has ended, if the login script processor identifies a Profile object for a user, the login script commands in the Profile object run. Last, the system checks for commands in the user's Login Script property. If no user login script exists, the login script processor runs the default login script commands stored in the client software.

- ❑ When possible, most login script commands should be stored in the container login script. By including the NO_DEFAULT command in the container login script, you can prevent NetWare from running the default login script. If you place the EXIT command at the end of the container login script, the login script processing will end and no profile, user, or default login scripts will run. Creating a login script for each user prevents the default login script from running and provides extra security.

- ❑ You maintain container, profile, and user login scripts in NetWare Administrator or ConsoleOne. To create or modify a container login script, select a container's Login Script property. Implementing a profile login script requires creating a Profile object and then granting users the Read attribute right to the Login Script property. To create or modify a user login script, select the User object and click the Login Script tab in the Properties dialog box.

- ❑ When testing login scripts, make sure the user has access rights to the directory paths in the MAP statements.

❏ With ZENworks for Desktops (ZfD), network administrators can centrally manage user desktop configuration and applications through the use of User and Workstation policies.

❏ Policy Package objects are created in the eDirectory tree and associated with the appropriate users. You should create an open policy package for the Admin user that enables all workstation functions so that user workstation restrictions aren't applied.

# KEY TERMS

**container login script** — A login script stored in a container object and used by all users in the container unless the user is assigned a profile login script or has a user login script.

**date variable** — A login script variable that contains date information, such as month, day of the week, and year.

**default login script** — The login script that's used if no other login script exists for a user.

**identifier variable** — A login script variable used in login script commands to represent such information as the user login name, date, time, and DOS version.

**login script** — A set of NetWare commands performed each time a user logs in to the file server.

**login script variable** — A reserved word that can be used to substitute values into login script statements to modify processing.

**Policy Package object** — An eDirectory object used to manage the way users access their workstations and connect to the network. Policy Package objects can consist of Workstation policies or User policies.

**profile login script** — A login script stored in a Profile object and used by all users assigned to that script.

**syntax** — The rules of a programming language and of NetWare login scripts.

**time variable** — A login script variable that contains system time information, such as hour, minute, and A.M./P.M.

**user-defined variable** — A login script variable that enables users to enter parameters for their personal user login scripts.

**user login script** — A login script stored in a User object; this script runs for only a single user.

**user variable** — A login script variable containing information about the currently logged in user, such as the user's login name, full name, or hexadecimal ID.

**workstation variable** — A login script variable containing information about the workstation's environment, such as machine type, operating system, operating system version, and station node address.

**Zero Effort Networking (ZENworks) for Desktops (ZfD)** — A Novell product that enables network administrators to centrally manage users' desktop environments.

12

## REVIEW QUESTIONS

1. Which of the following is the main purpose of login scripts?

   a. setting the user's desktop environment

   b. mapping drive letters

   c. providing informational messages

   d. running applications

2. Which of the following login script files would most likely contain the NO_DEFAULT command?

   a. default

   b. user

   c. container

   d. profile

3. Which of the following commands is used to display the contents of an ASCII text file onscreen? (Select all that apply.)

   a. DISPLAY

   b. WRITE

   c. MESSAGE

   d. FDISPLAY

4. Which of the following commands is used to display a brief message onscreen?

   a. DISPLAY

   b. WRITE

   c. MESSAGE

   d. FILE

5. Which of the following login scripts runs first to standardize the environment for all users in a department directory?

   a. default

   b. user

   c. container

   d. profile

6. Which of the following login scripts provides drive mappings and other setup commands that are common to users in multiple containers?

   a. default

   b. user

   c. container

   d. profile

7. The default login script runs if there is no _____ login script.
   a. default
   b. user
   c. container
   d. profile

8. Which of the following commands can be used in a container login script to stop the default login script from running but allow profile or user scripts to run?
   a. NO_DEFAULT
   b. EXIT
   c. SKIP_DEFAULT
   d. EXIT /NO_DEFAULT

9. In addition to the command used in Question 8, describe three other ways you can prevent the default login script commands from running.

10. Suppose the first network drive on your workstation is L:. Which drive letter would the MAP *3:=DATA login script command use to access the DATA volume?

11. Write a login script command that displays a "Welcome to CBE" message containing today's date, including the day, month, and year.

12. Write a condition that could be used to determine whether a user is logging in on the third day of the week.

13. Write a MAP command that uses variables to map H: as a root drive pointer to the user's home directory.

14. Which of the following login script variables can be used to change the default drive to the user's home directory on drive H:?
   a. %LOGIN_NAME
   b. %CONTEXT
   c. %HOME_DIRECTORY
   d. %PATH

15. Which of the following commands prevents the output of MAP commands from being displayed?
   a. MAP OFF
   b. DISPLAY OFF
   c. MAP DISPLAY OFF
   d. NO_OUTPUT

16. Write a command to output the login script commands from the CBE Organization to a file named CBE.txt.

**12**

17. Write a login script command to display a greeting message that includes the user's login name and general time of day in the format "Good afternoon (morning, evening), DDoering."

18. Write a command to display the contents of the DailyMst.txt file located in the SYS:Public directory.

19. List the login scripts in the sequence they run.

20. True or False: You use Workstation policies to hide the Entire Network option in My Network Places.

21. Write a login script command that sets the context of the workstation to the Sales OU of the ACME Organization.

22. When configuring the User policy package, which of the following is true?

    a. A gray check box indicates that the policy setting will change on the user's workstation.

    b. A clear (white) check box indicates that the policy will be reset.

    c. A gray check box indicates that the policy setting will be reset.

    d. A check mark in the check box indicates that the policy setting will change on the user's workstation.

23. A user logs in and sees no network drive mappings. What is most likely the problem?

    a. The Run scripts option isn't selected in Novell Client.

    b. There are insufficient file system rights for this user.

    c. There are insufficient eDirectory rights for this user.

    d. The MAP command contains the wrong path.

24. Which of the following is not a feature of ZENworks for Desktops?

    a. application management

    b. server management

    c. policy management

    d. remote-control capabilities

---

# HANDS-ON PROJECTS

## Project 12-1: Documenting the Container Login Script on Your Server

In this project, you demonstrate your knowledge of login script commands by examining the login scripts on your server and explaining the purpose of each of its commands.

1. Log in to the server with your assigned student user name.

2. View container, profile, and user login scripts with NetWare Administrator or ConsoleOne, and record the scripts. If the login script is empty, describe typical commands that would go into such a script.

3. Next to each login script command, briefly describe the command's function in the login script.

## Project 12-2: Practicing with Login Script Commands

In this project, you practice writing and testing several login script commands by creating a practice user and then providing that user with a user login script.

1. Log in with your assigned student user name.

2. Open Windows Explorer, and use it to view and document the directory structure of your assigned server.

3. Create a new user named **##USER** (replacing ## with your assigned student number).

4. Expand the **CBE_ADMIN_STUDENTS** volume to display your ##DATA directory, and create a subdirectory called Work. Grant the new user Read, File Scan, Write, Create, and Delete rights to your ##DATA\Work directory.

5. Enter all the required drive mappings in the user's login script that will let this user run NetWare utilities and issue DOS external commands.

6. Log out and test the login script you have created by logging in as ##USER.

7. Log in with your assigned student user name. Start ConsoleOne and open your own User object. Select your ##DATA Login Script page.

8. Write the necessary command to display the daily message file based on the day of the week. For example, on Monday the login script should display a message called MONDAY.MSG; on Tuesday, display TUESDAY.MSG; and so on. Record the command you use.

9. Assume that the user's birthday is today and include an IF statement that will display a short "Happy Birthday" message along with phaser fire (sound blasts) on today's date. Record the IF command you use.

10. Write a command to map a root drive to your \##DATA\Work directory. Record the command you use.

11. At the end of the user login script, write an EXIT command to run the SESSION program on a Windows 95/98 workstation. Record the EXIT command you use.

12. Test the login script by logging in as ##ADMIN again.

13. Use My Computer or another option to check the drive mappings.

14. Print a hard copy of the login script and a memo containing the commands you recorded for your instructor to check.

## CASE PROJECT

### Case 12-1: Designing a Container Login Script for the J.Q. Adams Corporation

In this project, you write a container login script for J.Q. Adams that performs the following functions:

- ❐ Creates a drive mapping to each volume on the JQA_Server01 NetWare server.

- ❐ Includes a search drive mapping to the WP and SS subdirectories of WinOffice for all users.

- ❐ For Production Department users, provides a drive mapped to the InvTrack/Itdata subdirectory and root drive mapping to the InvTrack subdirectory.

- ❐ Before noon on Mondays, displays a message for all Production Department users reminding them of the weekly meeting in conference room 210A.

1. Write a memo to your instructor describing the commands used to create the container login script and what steps you would take to prevent any other login scripts from overriding your mappings.

2. For extra credit, what step or steps would you have to take to actually run this login script using the existing CBE_ADMIN server and volumes?

# CHAPTER
# 13

# ACCESSING AND MANAGING THE NETWORK WITH NOVELL'S ONENET UTILITIES

> **After reading this chapter and completing the exercises, you will be able to:**
>
> ♦ Implement and use iFolder to access files and directories
>
> ♦ Set up and use NetStorage to access network files
>
> ♦ Use NetWare 6 remote management tools, including Remote Manager, RConsoleJ, and iMonitor, to access and manage the NetWare 6 server from your workstation
>
> ♦ Explain NetWare 6 licensing and be able to view and install NetWare license information using iManager

**A**fter David Doering finished setting up the network printing system for the CBE Labs network, he installed the necessary application software on user workstations and then began training users on the new network system. An important consideration for the marketing and administrative users is being able to use NetWare 6 to access their documents and data files when they are away from the office. For example, Joseph Cunningham, the president of CBE Labs, spends time away from the office visiting other facilities and customer sites. In addition, the Marketing staff needs to be able to access the customer database and other documents from notebook computers that aren't always attached to the network. Novell has solved many of these access problems by including new utilities with NetWare 6 as part of its OneNet strategy. These utilities—iFolder and NetStorage—enable users to access network data from any remote computer. In this chapter, you learn how to use iFolder and NetStorage to give users access to their documents and data files from any location. In addition, you learn how to use Novell's OneNet utilities to remotely monitor and manage the NetWare 6 server and maintain server licenses from your Web browser.

# WORKING WITH IFOLDER

Login scripts provide drive mappings for users to access network data, but they are not effective unless the user's computer is attached to the network. Users with laptop computers often need to access data and files when they're away from the office or not attached to the network, and traveling users might want to access files from other computers located outside the organization. One of the goals of Novell's OneNet strategy is to ensure that users have access to their network data and resources independent of the network connection. As illustrated in Figure 13-1, **iFolder** is an important part of the OneNet strategy because it enables files to be kept on a local computer or laptop and synchronized with the network—across the Internet or when the user's computer is reattached to the local network.

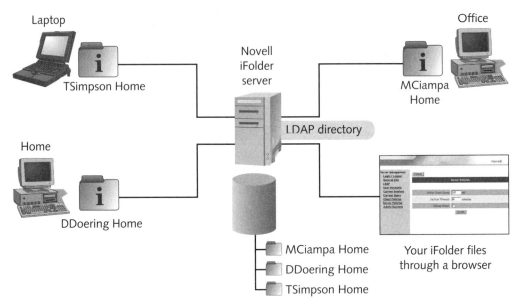

**Figure 13-1**    The iFolder service

With iFolder, users can have automatic, secure, and transparent synchronization of files between their hard drives and the iFolder server. Before David installed iFolder, CBE Labs users either copied the files they needed to their laptops or attached the files to e-mail messages so that they could access files from remote locations. After iFolder is installed and configured, users can access the latest version of their data from the computers they regularly use or through a Java-enabled browser on a computer attached to the Internet. Being able to access their files from any computer, from any location, has helped eliminate the file-overwriting errors and time-consuming tasks often involved with manually copying files between local computers and the network. Novell lists the following benefits of implementing iFolder:

- A simple and secure way to access, organize, and manage files from any computer without having to be logged in to the network

- Secure access to files using a Web browser, allowing users to access their files from computers at other locations

- Encryption of sensitive files stored on the server, protecting them from unauthorized access

- The ability to work on files offline and have them automatically synchronized to the server the next time the computer is logged in to the network

- The ability to run on Windows NT 4.0/2000 servers running Microsoft Internet Information Server (IIS) as well as NetWare 6 and 5.1 servers (Novell plans to support Linux and Solaris servers in future iFolder releases)

- Automatic synchronization of locally stored data across multiple workstations (users can directly access their files from any workstation with the iFolder client, or use a Web browser to download their files from the iFolder server)

In the following sections, you learn about the iFolder components and how to set up and configure iFolder so that you can access and synchronize files between computers.

## iFolder Components and Installation

The iFolder software consists of a server component, a Novell Client component, and a Java applet component. These three components work together to give users access to their iFolder files from anywhere in the world, even if their computer is temporarily offline from the network. iFolder is also helpful when users need access to their files but the server is unavailable because of network connection problems or other hardware failures. Because changes are made to the local files and then synchronized to the server, users can continue to work on their documents until the server is back online. In the following sections, you learn how to implement the iFolder components on a Novell network.

### The iFolder Server Component

The iFolder server component, the central piece of the iFolder system, is required to synchronize files between workstations and allow access to files over the Internet. The server component also supplies a Server Management console and an iFolder Web site. Network administrators can use the Server Management console to perform administrative tasks for all iFolder user accounts. The iFolder Web site, where the iFolder client software can be downloaded, makes it possible for users to view and download iFolder files through the Java applet running on their Web browsers. Novell has designed the iFolder server component so that in the future it can be installed and run from other server platforms, such as Windows NT or Windows 2000. The iFolder server component can be installed on the NetWare 6 server during or after server installation, and the server must meet the following minimum requirements:

- The iFolder server must have 10 MB of free space on the SYS volume.

- The iFolder server needs to have the Root Certificate to issue the public keys required to securely encrypt data transmissions with public key cryptography, as described in Chapter 14. If necessary, copy the Root Certificate from the Certificate Authority to the server that will host iFolder.

- If using DNS names for your iFolder server, verify that the DNS name and corresponding IP address of the iFolder server are in the SYS:Etc\Hosts file of the server hosting the iFolder service.

To keep the initial installation of the NetWare 6 server (described in Chapter 6) as simple and straightforward as possible, David chose to install the iFolder server component after installing NetWare 6 by performing the following steps:

1. First, he inserted the NetWare 6 CD into the CBE_ADMIN server.

2. He pressed Ctrl+Esc and entered 1 to select the System Console screen (described in Chapter 6).

3. He entered the command CDROM, and then pressed Enter to mount the CD as a volume on the server.

4. After mounting the NetWare 6 Installation volume, he again pressed Ctrl+Esc and entered the appropriate number to select the X Server - Graphical Console.

5. At the graphical console, he clicked Novell and then clicked Install to display the Installed Products window.

6. He clicked Add to display the Source Path window. After using the browse button to select the NETWARE6 volume, he clicked OK. The installation files were then copied to the server.

7. After the file copying was finished, the Components window displayed check marks to indicate the default installed components. David clicked Clear All to prevent reinstalling existing components. Next, he clicked the Novell iFolder Storage Services check box, and then clicked Next to display a login window.

8. He entered the CBEAdmin user name, password, and context in the appropriate text boxes and clicked OK to log in.

9. After he successfully logged in, the Configure IP-based Services window displayed, showing the IP address assigned to the iFolder service. To access the iFolder service without specifying a port number, David chose to give the iFolder service its own IP address. For example, because the CBE_ADMIN server and iPrint services were using the IP address 172.20.0.1, and the Apache-based services were using 172.20.0.2, he entered 172.20.0.3 for the iFolder service.

Using a separate IP address for the iFolder service makes it easier for users to access and provides more flexibility if the service needs to move to another server in the future. For more information on Apache services, see Chapter 14.

10. After entering the IP address for the iFolder service, he clicked Next to display the LDAP Configuration window.

11. The iFolder service uses the LDAP service to process user login requests. By default, the LDAP service uses port number 389 for clear text packets and port number 636 for SSL-encrypted packets. Port 636 is a good choice if the iFolder and the LDAP server are running on different servers to encrypt communications and data transferred across the wire between the LDAP server and the iFolder server. Because iFolder and LDAP are running on the CBE_ADMIN server, David left the default port number of 389. (Selecting port 636 would require more post-installation steps to complete the setup and would not significantly enhance security.)

12. In addition to the port number selection, the LDAP Configuration window contains an option to allow clear text passwords. David checked the iFolder installation documentation and learned that if he were using port 389, the LDAP Group object must be marked to allow clear text passwords. He clicked the Allow Clear Text Passwords check box, and then clicked Next to save the LDAP configuration options and display the iFolder Server Options window.

13. The iFolder Server Options window contains fields for the location of user data, the network domain, and the administrator's name and e-mail address. By default, the installation program places users' iFolder data in the iFolder directory on the SYS volume. To prevent the SYS volume from filling up with user files, David entered DATA:\iFolder in the User Data text box to place users' iFolder files on the DATA volume.

14. He verified that CBEAdmin was entered in the Admin Name text box. He then entered the IP address of the CBE_ADMIN server for the network domain, entered cbeadmin@cbelabs.com for the e-mail address, and clicked Next.

15. When the Summary window displayed, he clicked the Customize button and did the following to customize the LDAP service so that it could find users in all OUs of the CBE_LABS Organization:

    a. In the Product Customization window, he expanded the NetWare 6 Services option and then clicked the Novell iFolder Storage Services item.

    b. He clicked the Configure button to display the Advanced settings window.

    c. He clicked the iFolder Primary LDAP Settings tab and verified the following:

        ■ That the IP address of the server (CBE_ADMIN) was entered in the LDAP Host field (if DNS is installed, this entry should be the DNS name of the iFolder server).

        ■ That O=CBE_LABS was entered in the LDAP Login Dn Context text box.

    d. He clicked the 389 (clear text) radio button for the LDAP port setting.

    e. To have the iFolder server search for user accounts in the OUs, he clicked the Subcontainer Search check box. Although this option enables the iFolder server to find user accounts in department OUs, some additional post-installation steps (described in the following example) are needed for iFolder to perform subcontainer searches.

**13**

   f. He clicked OK to save the changes and display the iFolder Primary LDAP Settings message box. After reading the information message, he clicked OK again to close the message box and return to the Product Customization window.

   g. He clicked OK to return to the summary window.

16. David verified the contents of the summary window and clicked Finish to complete the iFolder installation. During the file-copying process, he received a Product Conflict message telling him that he had a newer or identical copy of LDAP Services on the server. He clicked No to prevent replacing the existing LDAP Services.

17. After all files were copied to the server, he read the Installation Complete message and then clicked Close to return to the Novell X Server graphical console. After completing the iFolder installation, he needed to reinstall the latest support pack to apply any changes to the newly installed iFolder service.

The iFolder installation program automatically adds commands to the server's Autoexec.ncf file to start the iFolder service when the server boots.

Next, David needed to assign the iFolder service the rights required to search subcontainers for user names. He could assign the [Public] object Browse and Read rights to the tree's Common Name (CN) property, or create an LDAP proxy user account with Browse and Read rights to the tree CN object and then add the proxy user to the LDAP group. An **LDAP proxy user** is a special user account that has been given rights to read information from the eDirectory tree. When this account is added to the LDAP server group, the LDAP server uses the account to log in to the eDirectory tree to search for user name information. For servers connected to the Internet, an LDAP proxy user is more secure than giving the [Public] object rights to read user names. Because the CBE Labs server will host Internet services (see Chapter 14), David decided to use a LDAP proxy user instead of giving the [Public] object rights to read user names. He used the following steps to create an LDAP proxy user and configure the iFolder service:

   1. He started his administrative workstation, logged in with the CBEAdmin user name and password, and then started ConsoleOne.

   2. After expanding the tree and CBE_LABS Organization, he used ConsoleOne to create a user named ProxyUser (with no password or home directory) within the CBE_LABS Organization.

   3. After creating the ProxyUser account, he did the following to add it as a trustee of the tree with Read and Browse rights:

   a. He right-clicked the tree object and then clicked Properties.

   b. He clicked the Add Trustee button to open the Select Objects dialog box.

c. He double-clicked the CBE_LABS Organization and then double-clicked the ProxyUser user account to open the Rights assigned to selected objects dialog box. He then clicked the [All Attributes Rights] entry in the Property list box.

d. Because the default rights would allow the ProxyUser account to read all attribute information, thus creating a possible security problem, he cleared the Read check box and did the following to give the user account rights to read only the CN property:

- He clicked the Add Property button and then clicked the Show all properties check box.

- He scrolled down and clicked the CN property and then clicked OK to add the CN property to the Property list box in the Rights assigned to selected objects dialog box (see Figure 13-2).

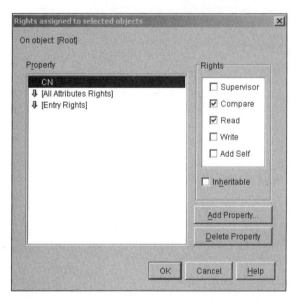

**Figure 13-2**    Assigning rights to the Proxy User account

- He clicked the Inheritable check box to allow all subcontainers in the tree to inherit this assignment.

e. He clicked OK to return to the Trustees dialog box.

f. He clicked OK to save the new trustee assignment changes and return to the main ConsoleOne window.

4. To complete the setup, David added the ProxyUser account to the LDAP Group object by performing these steps:

a. He clicked the CBE_LABS Organization to display all objects.

      b. He right-clicked the LDAP Group - CBE_ADMIN object in the Object frame and then clicked Properties to open the Properties of LDAP Group - CBE_ADMIN dialog box (see Figure 13-3).

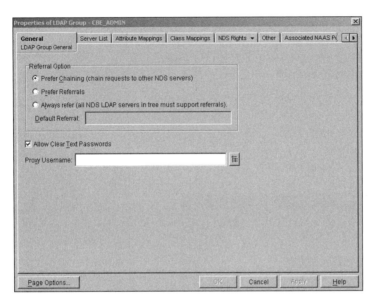

**Figure 13-3**    The Properties of LDAP Group - CBE_ADMIN dialog box

      c. He used the browse button next to the Proxy Username text box to locate the ProxyUser account he created previously.

      d. He clicked the ProxyUser account and then clicked OK to place it in the Proxy Username text box.

      e. He clicked Apply and Close to save the changes and return to the ConsoleOne main window.

    5. He exited ConsoleOne and logged out.

## The Novell iFolder Client Components

After iFolder has been installed on the NetWare server, users can begin using it to access their files from any computer. Except for installing the iFolder server and optionally changing the default configuration parameters, administrators don't need to perform any setup for users. Two iFolder client components are available: the iFolder client and the iFolder Java applet. Users can install and use the Novell iFolder client or access iFolder from their Web browser with the iFolder Java applet. In this section, you learn how to access iFolder using both the Novell iFolder client and the Java applet. The iFolder client must be installed on a computer running Novell Client, but the Java applet can be installed on any computer that has a Java-enabled Web browser, such as Netscape or Internet Explorer. Either the iFolder client or Java applet must be installed on any workstation used to access iFolder files. The iFolder clients are installed from the Web site located on the NetWare 6 server. In the following sections, you learn about the capabilities of each iFolder client component and how to install them on your workstations.

The iFolder client component can be installed on Windows 9x/Me, Windows NT, or Windows 2000/XP to perform the following tasks:

- Allow access to synchronized files through the workstation's My Documents\iFolder directory

- Use a restore bin to contain files that have been deleted from other computers

- Allow access to files from a computer that's not connected to the network

- Update data across multiple workstations

- Minimize bandwidth usage by using delta block synchronization to update only the data blocks that change in a file

- Allow encryption of files stored on the server

- Encrypt files on the client so that confidential files can be securely transmitted to a server and stored in an encrypted state

**The Windows iFolder Client**  Before using iFolder from the Windows desktop, the iFolder client software must be installed. Installing the iFolder client places an iFolder option on the taskbar for configuring and managing iFolder client settings. With minimum training, users can easily install the Novell iFolder client on their workstations. The iFolder service automatically creates a user account on both the iFolder server and the client workstation the first time the user logs in to iFolder. Creating a user account can optionally place an icon on the user's computer desktop that points to the user's iFolder home directory, located in My Documents\iFolder\userid\Home. The iFolder directory acts like any other directory on the user's hard drive, allowing users to place data in the iFolder directory by simply dragging and dropping files or folders or by saving files directly to the My Documents\iFolder\userid\Home directory. Users can open and edit files in the iFolder directory the same way as any other file on the computer. Applications associated with the file in the iFolder directory must be installed at the local workstation. For example, if you have a Word document in your iFolder directory, you need to have Microsoft Word installed on your local workstation to access the document files. When a user places a new file or folder in his or her iFolder directory, it's automatically synchronized to the user account storage area on the iFolder server, so the user can view and access it from any workstation using iFolder's Windows or Web browser client. Any changes made to files in the iFolder directory, from any workstation, are automatically synchronized to the iFolder server, ensuring that users are always working with the latest copy of the file or folder. The user or network administrator can determine the frequency of synchronizing iFolder directories by right-clicking the iFolder icon and selecting iFolder Preferences.

**13**

**Note**

If you are installing the iFolder client on a Windows 95 workstation, you must have the Winsock 2 update from Microsoft installed.

To install the iFolder client on his Windows workstation, David did the following:

1. After logging in to the Novell network, he started his Web browser software, entered the URL https://*ip_address* (replacing *ip_address* with the IP address of his iFolder server), and clicked Yes to display the iFolder Welcome window, shown in Figure 13-4.

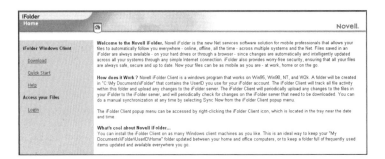

**Figure 13-4**    The iFolder Welcome window

2. He clicked the Download link to display the File Download dialog box.

3. He clicked the Open button to extract the files and display the Novell iFolder Setup welcome window.

4. He clicked Next to display the Language selection dialog box.

5. He clicked Next to accept the default English language and display the license agreement window.

6. He read the license agreement, and then clicked File, Close on the menu bar to close the license agreement window.

7. He clicked Yes to accept the license agreement and display the Destination Location dialog box.

8. He clicked the Next button to copy files into the default C:\Program Files\Novell\iFolder location and display the completion window.

9. He clicked the Finish button to end the installation and display the Readme text file.

10. He closed the Readme file window, and then clicked Finish again to restart his computer.

When a user logs in for the first time after the iFolder client is installed, the Novell iFolder Setup Complete dialog box opens (see Figure 13-5).

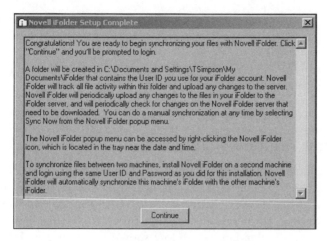

**Figure 13-5**    The Novell iFolder Setup Complete dialog box

After reading the information and clicking the Continue button, the Novell iFolder Login window shown in Figure 13-6 is displayed.

**Figure 13-6**    The Novell iFolder Login window

**The iFolder Java Applet Component**    The iFolder Java applet enables users to perform file operations, such as copy, delete, rename, download, and upload, between any Java-enabled browser and their iFolder server account. To use iFolder from a Web browser, users need to agree to download a Java applet script named the JVMD.tmp to the browser the first time the iFolder server is accessed. An advantage of the iFolder Java applet is that by using a Web browser, users can access their iFolder files from a computer that does not have iFolder or Novell Client installed. With the iFolder Java applet, users no longer have to bring along laptops while on the road because they can use any computer with Internet access to download and work on their files. The iFolder Java applet works well in organizations where users often travel between different facilities. For example, when the Marketing users travel from the CBE home office to a customer facility, they can simply use the computers and software at the customer location to access their iFolder files.

You can use Netscape 4.7 or later or Internet Explorer 5 or 5.5 to download the iFolder Java client. Netscape 6 is not supported with this release.

## Using iFolder from the Windows Desktop

After iFolder has been installed on the NetWare server, users can begin accessing their files from any computer. Before using iFolder, a user account needs to be created on both the iFolder server and the iFolder client workstation. To simplify this process, an iFolder user account is created automatically the first time a new user logs in to the iFolder server. Notice in the iFolder Login window shown previously in Figure 13-6 that the "Place a shortcut to the iFolder on the desktop" check box is selected by default. If you do not want this shortcut, clear this check box.

Another important option when creating an iFolder account is encrypting the iFolder data with a pass phase. When users create iFolder accounts, they are given the option to encrypt files (see Figure 13-7) with a pass phrase. As a network administrator, you should communicate to your users the importance of iFolder encryption. When iFolder data is synchronized and stored on the iFolder server with no encryption, the contents of iFolder are not secure because none of the data is encrypted. However, if you enable users to create encrypted iFolders, the contents of their personal folders will be secure. Contents in encrypted iFolders are transmitted and stored in encrypted format on the iFolder server.

**Figure 13-7**    The Novell iFolder New Internet Folder Setup dialog box

iFolder uses the Blowfish encryption scheme that Bruce Schneier created in 1993. It is a fast symmetric block cipher designed as an alternative to the Data Encryption Standard (DES). In encryption, fast is good. Blowfish can use keys from 32 bits to 448 bits to encrypt data. Novell uses 128-bit keys for iFolder encryption. When you create a folder that uses encryption, you must supply a pass phrase. iFolder uses it to generate the 128-bit key, which is then used to encrypt and decrypt your iFolder data. Novell also provides a 56-bit version of iFolder for use in France.

The pass phrase is like a password, but in iFolder you use a password to log in to your iFolder account and a pass phrase to encrypt your iFolder contents.

iFolder security is so tight that only those with explicit rights to a folder can see its files or even its directory structure because it, too, is encrypted. Additionally, because the iFolder data is encrypted on both the network wire and the hard disk, users can securely access encrypted iFolder accounts across the Internet.

David logged in and created an iFolder user account for himself with the following steps.

1. First, he entered his user ID (DDoering) in the User ID text box and his password in the Password text box.

2. Next, he clicked the Login button. Because no account existed for DDoering, the Novell iFolder New Internet Folder Setup dialog box shown previously in Figure 13-7 displayed.

3. To automatically display the iFolder Login window, he clicked the Enable automatic login at startup check box and then clicked OK to open the Novell iFolder Get Pass Phrase dialog box (see Figure 13-8).

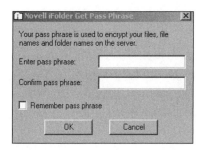

**Figure 13-8**    The Novell iFolder Get Pass Phrase dialog box

4. He entered a pass phrase (used to encrypt data on the iFolder server) of at least eight characters, and then clicked the Remember pass phrase check box to avoid having to enter a pass phrase each time he logs in. After he clicked OK, the iFolder server searched the CBE Labs tree for David's user account.

Because the ProxyUser account has Read rights to the CN property of all objects in the tree, the iFolder server was able to find the DDoering user account in the InfoSystems.CBE_LABS container. If there were multiple DDoering user accounts in the tree, the iFolder server would attempt to log in using the first DDoering user it finds. To make sure users can be found, all users must have unique names, even if their user accounts are located in different contexts.

5. After David successfully logged in, an iFolder icon named DDoering Home was created on his workstation.

To test iFolder, David used the following steps to copy the StaffDev.frm file from the Publctns\Document directory on the DATA volume to his iFolder drive:

1. He double-clicked My Network Places and then double-clicked the Novell Connections icon to display the CBE_ADMIN server object.

2. He double-clicked the CBE_ADMIN server object and then double-clicked the DATA volume object to display all directories on the DATA volume.

3. He double-clicked the Publctns directory and the Document directory to display all files in the Document window.

4. He right-clicked the StaffDev.frm file, and then clicked Copy.

5. He right-clicked the DDoering Home icon on his desktop, and then clicked Paste.

6. He double-clicked his DDoering Home icon to verify that the StaffDev.frm file had been added, as shown in Figure 13-9.

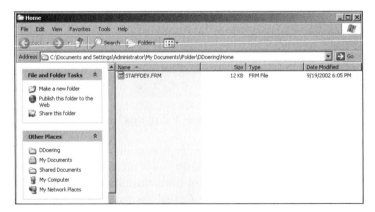

**Figure 13-9**    A sample iFolder Internet home directory

7. He closed the iFolder home directory window.

## Using iFolder from a Web Browser

As you learned in the previous example, the iFolder client can be useful when users need to maintain access to their files on multiple computers or access their files from a laptop that's offline. However, often it's not practical to install the iFolder client and place the iFolder directory on remote computers that users don't access frequently. For example, Stephen Hayakawa, the marketing director, needs to access certain documents when visiting customer locations and does not want to install the iFolder client and iFolder home directory icon on these computers because he might not use the same computer the next time he visits the location. To test the iFolder browser client, David used the following steps to access his iFolder files from Internet Explorer:

1. He started his Internet Explorer software, entered the URL http://*iFolder_ip_ address* (replacing *iFolder_ ip_address* with the IP address assigned to his iFolder server), and then pressed Enter.

2. He clicked the Login link under the Access your Files heading, and then clicked Yes to proceed with the security certificate.

3. Because this was the first time he had accessed iFolder from a Web browser, he saw a security warning asking him to install and run the JVMD.tmp script. He clicked Yes to install the script and display the Login window.

4. He entered his user name, password, and pass phrase to encrypt the data.

5. He clicked the Connect button to log in and display the iFolder Home directory.

6. He double-clicked his Home directory to expand it and verified that the StaffDev.frm file was listed, as shown in Figure 13-10.

**13**

**Figure 13-10**    The contents of iFolder displayed in a browser window

7. To copy the StaffDev.frm file to the My Documents folder of his local computer, David did the following:

   a. He clicked the StaffDev.frm filename and then clicked the Download link to open the Save As dialog box.

  b. He clicked the My Documents folder and clicked the Save button to save the file on his local computer.

8. He uploaded a file to iFolder by following these steps:

  a. He clicked the Home directory in the iFolder client, and then clicked the Upload link to display the Novell iFolder Upload dialog box.

  b. He navigated to the folder containing the file to be uploaded.

  c. He clicked the filename in the list, and then clicked the Open button. The new file was uploaded to his iFolder window.

9. He clicked the Logout button to end his iFolder session and closed Internet Explorer.

## Managing iFolder

In addition to installing the iFolder software on the NetWare 6 server and clients, it's also important to customize the iFolder server and clients by performing the following tasks:

- Customize the iFolder Web site
- Use the Server Management console to manage iFolder user accounts and perform common iFolder administrative tasks
- Optimize the iFolder server
- Secure user accounts by using security options to specify which types of personal iFolders you will allow users to create on your iFolder server (unencrypted or encrypted with pass phrase)

### Customizing the iFolder Web Site

The iFolder Web site contains the iFolder Client Quick Start Guide and other important information about using the Novell iFolder system. In addition, the iFolder Web site is where users download the iFolder client and access their iFolder files through a Java-enabled browser. Because users in your organization will be accessing the iFolder Web site, you might want to customize the iFolder Web page to fit your organization's internal needs. To access the default iFolder Web site, users simply need to enter the iFolder server's IP address or DNS name in their browsers.

### Using the Server Management Console

The **Server Management console** enables network administrators to perform administrative tasks, such as managing iFolder user accounts and customizing activity between the server and iFolder clients. To access the Server Management console from his Web browser, David entered https://*iFolder_ip_address*/iFolderServer/Admin (replacing *iFolder_ip_address* with the IP address assigned to the iFolder service during installation) and then logged in with his administrative user name and password (see Figure 13-11).

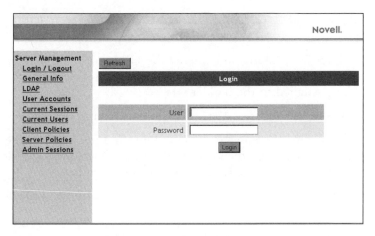

**Figure 13-11** The Login window of the Server Management console

After logging in, administrators can view and modify iFolder user accounts and perform the following administrative tasks:

- View general server information.

- View and change LDAP settings.

- View and manage user account information. The Server Management console enables administrators to remove user accounts, change disk storage quotas for users on the iFolder server, and set polices for individual users.

- View client connections to see which users are currently accessing the iFolder service.

- Set specific policies for your iFolder clients and servers.

- Configure client policies that will be applied by default to iFolder clients, such as remembering passwords and password phrases so that iFolder users cannot change them, or hiding certain iFolder client options. For example, you could increase security by hiding the option that requests users to select encryption of the iFolder data so that the data will always be encrypted without users being aware of it. Client policies include settings such as Automatic sync, Synchronize to server delay (in seconds), Synchronize from server interval (in seconds), Remember password, and Remember pass phrase. You can configure these and all other settings so that users do not have the option to change your initial settings. You can also use the default settings and allow users to configure their own settings via their iFolder client.

- Remove an iFolder user account.

- Restore a user's iFolder data to another iFolder server.

13

Before having users access iFolder, David checked the iFolder server settings by performing these steps:

1. He started Internet Explorer and entered the URL https://*iFolder_ip_address*/ *iFolderServer/Admin* in the Address text box (replacing *iFolder_ip_address* with the IP address assigned to the iFolder service).

2. He responded to the Security Alert messages by clicking OK and Yes.

3. In the Login window, he entered the user name and password for the iFolder Administrator account, and then clicked the Login button to log in to the iFolder server and display the General Information window.

4. He clicked the LDAP link to display the LDAP window shown in Figure 13-12.

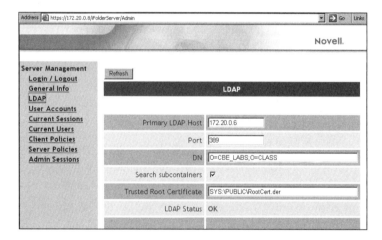

**Figure 13-12**   Viewing configuration information in the LDAP window

5. He clicked the User Accounts link to display the User Account window shown in Figure 13-13.

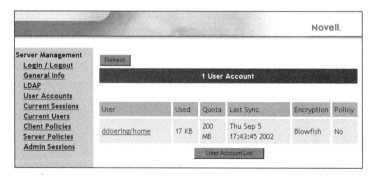

**Figure 13-13**   Viewing information in the User Account window

6. He clicked the Client Policies link to display the Client Policies window shown in Figure 13-14.

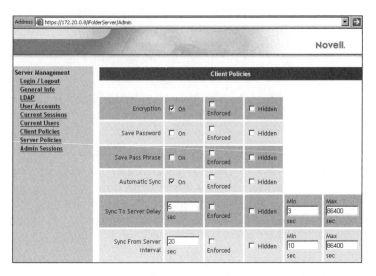

**Figure 13-14**    Viewing client policy information in the Server Management console

7. He clicked the Server Policies link to display the Server Policies window shown in Figure 13-15.

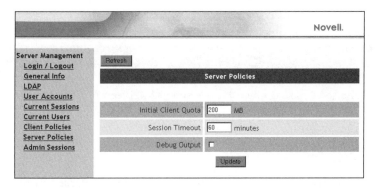

**Figure 13-15**    Viewing server policy information in the Server Management console

8. After verifying all the iFolder server settings, he clicked the Login/Logout link, and then clicked the Logout button to end his iFolder management session. He exited Internet Explorer and logged off the local workstation.

## Optimizing the iFolder Server

David did not encounter any problems with the default performance of the iFolder server because the CBE Labs network has a limited number of iFolder users. However, as the number of users increases, and the amount of storage space managed by iFolder grows, network administrators need to consider improving the performance of the iFolder server in the following ways:

- Add more RAM to the server to provide more memory for caching iFolder data. Because memory cache is many times faster than disk access, increasing RAM can significantly improve speed when synchronizing data to the iFolder clients.

- Add another server to split the processing load. Although the iFolder service could be moved to another server, moving other files and applications from the iFolder server to a new server might be easier.

- Increase the number of threads available to the NetWare 6 Apache Web server. **Threads** are processes that the CPU is working on, and a multi-CPU server can work on multiple threads at the same time. Increasing the number of threads makes more CPU processing available for iFolder requests instead of other Web server work. Although Novell recommends that one thread be allocated for each iFolder client, iFolder has been tested with up to 25 clients per thread.

- Set quotas limiting the amount of disk space allocated to each user. Allocating large amounts of disk space to users can decrease the iFolder server's performance.

- Change the default synchronization delay parameters when you have many users and need to improve iFolder performance (see Table 13-1).

**Table 13-1** iFolder Synchronization Delay Parameters

| Default Delay Parameters | Suggested Delays for Large Numbers of Users |
| --- | --- |
| 5-second delay after file activity | 30-second delay after file activity |
| 20-second delay after server-polling interval | 1-minute delay after server-polling interval |

## INSTALLING AND USING NETSTORAGE

Although iFolder can give users access to their data from any networked or remote computer, it requires installing the iFolder client or Java applet on users' computers and placing files in the iFolder directory. Because some users need to access files in shared directories on the server, placing these files in the iFolder client is not practical. In addition, when visiting other sites, installing the iFolder client or even the Java applet on those computers isn't always feasible.

**Novell NetStorage** solves some of these problems by giving users secure access to files on the NetWare server from any Internet location; it does this by using an existing Web browser or Microsoft Web Folders, with no additional client or applet to download or install on the user's workstation. Web Folders, available as of Internet Explorer 5, enable users to navigate to network files and folders much as they would use Windows Explorer on their local drive. NetStorage offers the following features:

- Allows users to securely copy, move, rename, delete, read, and write files between any Internet-enabled computer and the Novell network.

- Supports Internet standards such as HTTP, HTTPS, HTML, XML, and WebDAV, making it compatible with most client computer systems, including Windows, Macintosh, and Linux.

- Includes the ability to process a user's container, profile, or user login script for drive mapping; the drive mappings appear on a Web page in the form of folders. For example, a user's home drive mapping of MAP H:=%HOME_ DIRECTORY in the login script appears on the Web page as a folder named HOME@H.

- Supports contextless and context-based logins to eDirectory, so users can log in with their short names (such as DDoering) or fully distinguished names (such as .DDoering.InfoSystems.CBE_Labs_Admin.CBE_LABS).

- Includes a plug-in (called a "gadget" in Novell) for NetWare WebAccess so that users can access network files and folders through the NetWare WebAccess page.

In the following sections, you learn how to set up and use Novell NetStorage so that users in your organization can access and manage network files.

## Installing Novell NetStorage

Like iFolder, Novell NetStorage can be installed during or after NetWare 6 installation. As with iFolder, David preferred to install NetStorage after the NetWare 6 installation to keep the initial installation as simple as possible. To install and use Novell NetStorage, there must be at least one NetWare 6 server in the eDirectory tree where NetStorage will be installed, and workstations must have a minimum of Netscape 4.7 or Internet Explorer 5 installed. Because NetStorage is configured during installation, any changes you need to make to the initial configuration can be made only by removing and reinstalling NetStorage. To avoid reinstalling, make sure the following information is available before starting the NetStorage installation:

- Identify the IP address or DNS name of the primary NetWare 6 server. The primary server must have a Master or Read/Write replica of the eDirectory tree. NetStorage does not need to be installed on the primary server, but you need to identify this server in the NetStorage Install window. The primary server comes into play when a user attempts to log in to NetStorage. During the login process, NetStorage searches the eDirectory database on the primary server to locate the user name and password. When NetStorage finds the user in the eDirectory database, it authenticates the user to eDirectory.

**13**

- Identify the eDirectory context of users who will use NetStorage. NetStorage searches for user accounts in the context(s) you specify in the NetStorage Install window. The context is indicated by inserting a colon after the primary server's IP address or DNS name and then entering the container's distinguished name. For example, to search for users in the CBE_ADMIN server, David specified 172.20.0.1:CBE_LABS.

- In addition to the primary context, the NetStorage Install window contains two more fields for specifying the primary servers and eDirectory contexts from additional eDirectory trees that the NetStorage service will support.

- The final field in the NetStorage Install window is where you specify the IP address or DNS name of your iFolder server. For users to access their iFolder files through NetStorage, you must specify the iFolder server.

After identifying the CBE_ADMIN server as the primary NetStorage server and obtaining its IP address and DNS name, David installed NetStorage by performing these steps:

1. He picked a time over the weekend when the server was not needed because installing NetStorage requires shutting down the server and restarting. To start the installation, he inserted the NetWare 6 CD into the CBE_ADMIN server, pressed Ctrl+Esc, and entered 1 to select the System Console screen.

2. He entered the command CDROM, and then pressed Enter to mount the CD as a volume on the server.

3. Next, he pressed Ctrl+Esc and entered the appropriate number to select the X Server - Graphical Console.

4. At the graphical console, he clicked Novell and then Install to display the Installed Products window.

5. He clicked Add to display the Source Path window, clicked the Browse button to select the NETWARE6 CD volume, and then clicked OK. The installation files were then copied to the server.

6. Next, the Components window was displayed with check marks indicating the default installed components. He clicked Clear All to prevent reinstalling existing components, clicked the Novell NetStorage check box, and then clicked Next to display a login window.

7. After David logged in to the network with his CBEAdmin user name and password, the LDAP Configuration window displayed.

8. He verified that 389 was entered in the Clear Text Port text box and 636 was entered in the SSL Port text box.

9. He clicked the Allow Clear Text Passwords check box to enable this option, and then clicked Next to display the NetStorage Install window.

10. He verified that the IP address and context of the CBE_ADMIN server (172.20.0.1:CBE_LABS) was entered in the Primary Server text box, that the

IP address of the iFolder service (172.20.0.1) was entered in the iFolder Server text box, and that port 80 was entered in the iFolder Port text box. He clicked Next to display the installation summary window.

11. After verifying that Novell NetStorage and NetWare Port Resolver were listed in the summary window, he clicked Finish to copy the NetStorage files and complete the installation. When he received a Product Conflict message, he clicked No to continue the installation.

12. When the Installation complete message box displayed, he clicked Close to return to the graphical console. After finishing the installation, he restarted the server by entering RESTART SERVER at the console command prompt. When the server restarted, the NetStorage module (NCPL.NLM) automatically loaded from the Autoexec.ncf file.

## Using Novell NetStorage

Starting NetStorage on the server side happens automatically when the server restarts. To use NetStorage from the client side, the date and time on the server *must* match very closely with the date and time on user workstations. If the time on the workstation differs too much from that on the server, file updates might not be properly synchronized with the changes made from the local network. If workstations are logging in using Novell Client, the client software automatically sets the workstation date and time to match the server. If users are logging in to local workstations that don't have Novell Client installed, the workstation time must be set close to the server's time for NetStorage to properly synchronize changes made to network data.

After the date and time conditions are met, users can use Microsoft Web Folder or a Web browser to access NetStorage services. To access NetStorage services from a Web browser, enter the URL http://*ip_address*/oneNet/NetStorage (replacing *ip_address* with the IP address or DNS name of the NetWare server running Novell NetStorage). The NetStorage service then prompts users to enter their eDirectory user names and passwords. After logging in, NetStorage reads user login scripts, drive mappings, and User object properties to determine the location of home directories. The NetStorage Web page then displays the network files and folders currently accessible to the user. After users have logged in to NetStorage, they will see folders and files that can be manipulated in much the same way as in Windows Explorer. The same procedures are used to expand and collapse directories and to open, move, delete, copy, and rename files. Unlike Windows Explorer, local files and folders are not accessible from the NetStorage window. In addition, users cannot map drives or change login scripts from the NetStorage Web page.

After installing NetStorage on the CBE_ADMIN server, David tested the system by logging in to the NetStorage server with his DDoering user name and then verifying access to his files and folders:

1. He logged on to his local Windows workstation by clicking the Workstation only check box and entering his local user name and password.

**13**

2. He started Internet Explorer, entered the URL http://*ip_address*/oneNet/ NetStorage, and pressed Enter.

The *ip_address* represents the IP address assigned to the Apache server running on the NetWare 6 server. Be careful when you enter the URL because it is case sensitive.

3. When the Enter Network Password window displayed, David entered his Novell distinguished user name (.DDoering.InfoSystems.CBE_LABS) and password to log in and display the NetStorage opening page for his user name, as shown in Figure 13-16.

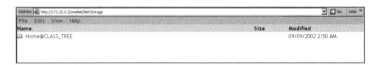

**Figure 13-16**    The NetStorage opening page

4. He double-clicked his Home directory and then clicked the Folder View option to display the directory's contents, as shown in Figure 13-17.

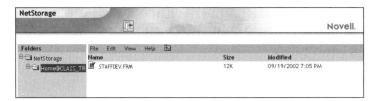

**Figure 13-17**    Viewing the contents of a user's NetStorage Home directory

5. To edit the StaffDev.frm file using the word-processing application, he double-clicked the filename.

6. After saving the changes, he closed NetStorage by clicking File, Logout on the menu bar.

# USING NETWARE 6 REMOTE MANAGEMENT UTILITIES

An important part of Novell's OneNet strategy is enabling network administrators to manage the network and server from any networked computer, so Novell has included the iManager, Remote Manager, iMonitor, and RConsoleJ remote management utilities with the NetWare 6 operating system. In Chapters 9 and 11, you learned how to use iManager to create users, groups, and printers from a Web browser. You have also been introduced to using Remote Manager for administrative tasks, such as creating volumes and accessing the server console. As its name implies, iMonitor provides network monitoring and diagnostic capabilities to help you identify and isolate network and server performance problems. In the following sections, you learn more about using Remote Manager, RCONSOLEJ, and iMonitor to manage and monitor your server and network performance.

## The Remote Manager Utility

**Remote Manager**, perhaps the most powerful of NetWare 6's remote management utilities, enables you to monitor your server's health, change configuration parameters, and perform diagnostic and debugging tasks. To use Remote Manager, the server and workstation must meet the software requirements shown in Table 13-2.

**Table 13-2**   Remote Manager Software Requirements

| Software | Requirement |
| --- | --- |
| NetWare operating system | NetWare 5.1 or later |
| Browser | One of the following:<br>Netscape 4.5 or later<br>Internet Explorer 5 or later<br>NetWare server browser |
| NLMs loaded on the server | PORTAL.NLM and HTTPSTK.NLM |

To access Remote Manager, start your Web browser and enter the URL https://*server_ip_address*:8009 or http://*server_ip_address*:8008 to go directly to the Remote Manager login page. You can also enter https://*server_ip_address*:2200 to display the NetWare Web Manager window shown in Figure 13-18, and then select your server under the NetWare Remote Manager heading.

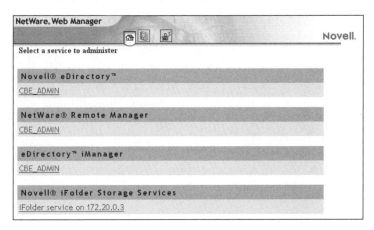

**Figure 13-18**   Selecting a service in NetWare Web Manager
*When using NetWare 6.5, you will see the NetWare 6.5 Welcome as shown in Figure D-17.*

After you log in with the administrative user name and password, Remote Manager's opening page is displayed (see Figure 13-19).

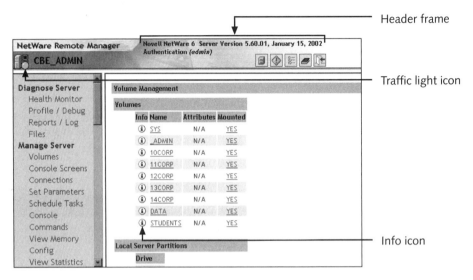

Figure 13-19    The Remote Manager opening page

If the Java Virtual Machine (JVM) is not installed on your Web browser, you will see an Install on Demand window with a Download button that you can use to download the JVM needed to display certain information, such as the traffic light icon to indicate server health (described in this section).

Notice that the Remote Manager window is divided into several sections. The overall health indicator in the upper-left corner of the page (the traffic light icon in Figure 13-19) gives you a quick look at your overall server health. The header frame at the top of the page contains general server information and icons used to exit Remote Manager and to view volumes, the health monitor, and configuration information. The navigation frame at the left side lists general tasks you can perform in Remote Manager and supplies links to specific pages for performing these tasks. The main content frame in the middle of the window changes depending on which link you click in the header or navigation frame. The online help frame displays help information for the content being viewed in the main content frame. In the following sections, you learn how to use these frames to diagnose your server's health, manage NetWare servers and volumes, check server application usage, view server hardware configurations, access Novell eDirectory information, and monitor license usage.

## Monitoring Server Health and Performance

The overall health indicator in the upper-left corner of the Remote Manager opening page displays one of the following colors to give a quick indication of the overall server status:

- *Green*—Represents a server in good health.

- *Yellow*—Provides a warning of possible problems with the server's health or performance.

- *Red*—Represents a server in bad health, which requires the administrator's response.

- *Black*—Indicates that communication with the server has been lost (the server might be down).

If the overall health indicator is not green, you can click the Health Monitor link under the Diagnose Server heading to view the status of individual indicators (see Figure 13-20).

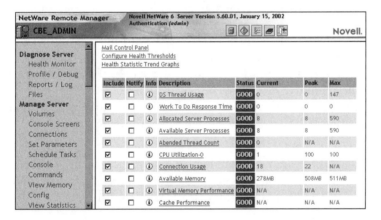

**Figure 13-20**    Viewing the status of health monitor indicators

If an indicator is yellow or red, it needs attention. For example, if the available memory indicator is yellow or red, it indicates that the system is running short of memory. You can view more detailed information about the indicator by clicking on it to see a graph of memory usage, as shown in Figure 13-21.

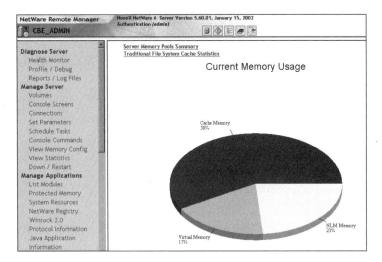

**Figure 13-21**    The Current Memory Usage graph

In this example, the memory usage is in good shape, with more than half the memory reserved for caching files. If the cache memory drops below 30% of the total memory, it might indicate that RAM should be added to the server. If NLM memory usage is more than the cache memory, you might be able to correct the problem by unloading some unneeded modules. For example, exiting the X Server graphical console can free up quite a bit of memory. Click the Back button in your browser to return to the Health Monitor window.

To determine which NLMs are currently loaded, you can click the Reports/Log Files link and then click the View Config Report button to view server configuration settings and a list of currently loaded modules (see Figure 13-22).

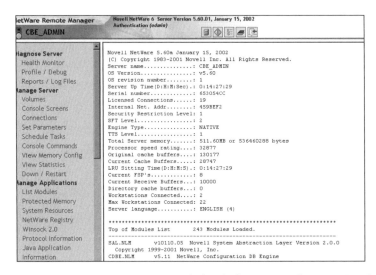

**Figure 13-22**    Viewing currently loaded NLMs in the Run Config Report

When viewing the Health Monitor window (shown previously in Figure 13-20), you can click the Configure Health Thresholds link to view or set suspect and critical values for a variety of indicators, as shown in Figure 13-23.

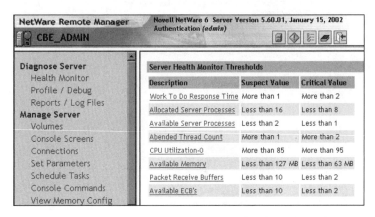

| NetWare Remote Manager | Novell NetWare 6 Server Version 5.60.01, January 15, 2002 |
| --- | --- |
| CBE_ADMIN | Authentication *(admin)* |

| Server Health Monitor Thresholds | | |
| --- | --- | --- |
| **Description** | **Suspect Value** | **Critical Value** |
| Work To Do Response Time | More than 1 | More than 2 |
| Allocated Server Processes | Less than 16 | Less than 8 |
| Available Server Processes | Less than 2 | Less than 1 |
| Abended Thread Count | More than 1 | More than 2 |
| CPU Utilization-0 | More than 85 | More than 95 |
| Available Memory | Less than 127 MB | Less than 63 MB |
| Packet Receive Buffers | Less than 10 | Less than 2 |
| Available ECB's | Less than 10 | Less than 2 |

Diagnose Server
  Health Monitor
  Profile / Debug
  Reports / Log Files
Manage Server
  Volumes
  Console Screens
  Connections
  Set Parameters
  Schedule Tasks
  Console Commands
  View Memory Config

**Figure 13-23**    Setting suspect and critical values for indicators

The Suspect Value column identifies the criteria for displaying a yellow indicator, and the Critical Value column identifies the criteria for displaying a red indicator. To change the criteria, click the indicator, enter the new suspect or critical value, and then click OK.

## Server File System Management

Server management includes managing volumes and user connections, viewing and setting parameters, viewing system statistics, managing memory, and accessing current console screens. Being able to access the server console screens remotely is a powerful management feature when troubleshooting or repairing NetWare server problems. In addition to being able to view and change system configurations in Remote Manager, you can view volume information, mount or dismount volumes, and perform many file management tasks, such as uploading, downloading, renaming, and deleting files. Being able to manage the server from remote locations has been convenient for David when he's away from the office. For example, while at Comdex in Las Vegas, he needed to replace a .dll file for an application. He used the following steps to access volume information and upload and rename the .dll file.

1. He started the Web browser software on the computer in his hotel room and entered the URL https://*ip_address*:8009 (replacing *ip_address* with the IP address of the CBE_ADMIN server).

2. He logged in with the CBEAdmin user name and password to display the NetWare Remote Manager window.

3. Under the Manage Server heading in the main window, he clicked the Volumes link to display the Volume Management window.

**13**

4. To get information on the SYS volume, he clicked the Info icon next to the SYS volume to view the Volume Information window (see Figure 13-24).

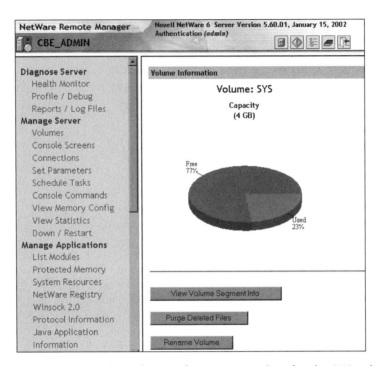

**Figure 13-24**    The Volume Information window for the SYS volume

5. To return to the volume list, he clicked the Back button.

6. He clicked the SYS volume to view the directory information shown in Figure 13-25.

**Figure 13-25**    Viewing directories on the SYS volume

7. He clicked the Public directory to view its contents (see Figure 13-26) and clicked the Upload link to display the upload window shown in Figure 13-27.

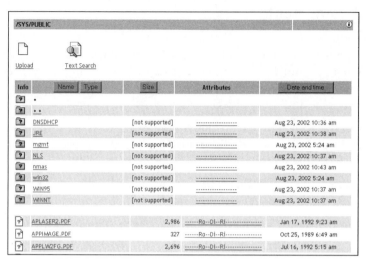

| Info | Name | Type | Size | Attributes | Date and time |
|------|------|------|------|------------|---------------|
| ? | . | | | | |
| ? | .. | | | | |
| ? | DNSDHCP | | [not supported] | ------------------ | Aug 23, 2002 10:36 am |
| ? | JRE | | [not supported] | ------------------ | Aug 23, 2002 10:38 am |
| ? | mgmt | | [not supported] | ------------------ | Aug 23, 2002 5:24 am |
| ? | NLS | | [not supported] | ------------------ | Aug 23, 2002 10:37 am |
| ? | nmas | | [not supported] | ------------------ | Aug 23, 2002 10:43 am |
| ? | win32 | | [not supported] | ------------------ | Aug 23, 2002 5:24 am |
| ? | WIN95 | | [not supported] | ------------------ | Aug 23, 2002 10:37 am |
| ? | WINNT | | [not supported] | ------------------ | Aug 23, 2002 10:37 am |
| ? | APLASER2.PDF | | 2,986 | ------Ro--Di--Ri------------- | Jan 17, 1992 9:23 am |
| ? | APPIMAGE.PDF | | 327 | ------Ro--Di--Ri------------- | Oct 25, 1989 6:49 am |
| ? | APPLW2FG.PDF | | 2,696 | ------Ro--Di--Ri------------- | Jul 16, 1992 5:15 am |

**Figure 13-26**    The contents of the Public directory

The contents of the Public directory will vary based on your server's configuration.

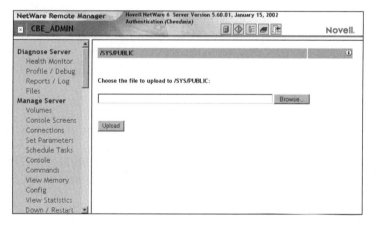

**Figure 13-27**    The upload window in Remote Manager

8. He clicked the Browse button and navigated to the folder containing the .dll file to upload.

9. He double-clicked the .dll file to place it in the Choose the file to upload to /SYS/PUBLIC text box, and clicked the Upload button to copy the file.

10. After the file was copied, he clicked the Exit button to end his session and then clicked Yes to confirm.

## eDirectory Management

When working with a remote server, sometimes you need to find and view objects. Although iManager is used for most eDirectory maintenance and management functions, Remote Manager does enable administrators to browse the eDirectory tree and view or delete objects. David used the following steps in Remote Manager to browse the CBE eDirectory tree and view objects:

1. He started the Web browser on the computer in his hotel room and entered the URL https://*ip_address*:8009 (replacing *ip_address* with the IP address of the CBE_ADMIN server).

2. He logged in with the CBEAdmin user name and password to display the NetWare Remote Manager window.

3. He clicked the Access Tree Walker link under the Manage eDirectory heading and then expanded the tree and CBE_LABS Organization (see Figure 13-28).

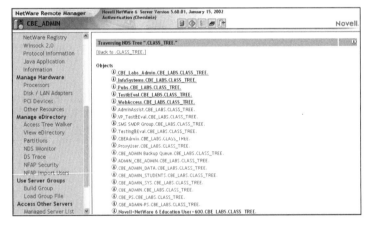

**Figure 13-28** Using the Tree Walker feature to view details on the eDirectory tree

4. To view information on Ted's user account, David clicked the InfoSystems OU to display all user accounts in the Information Systems Department. He clicked the Info icon to the left of the TSimpson user to display the user information window shown in Figure 13-29.

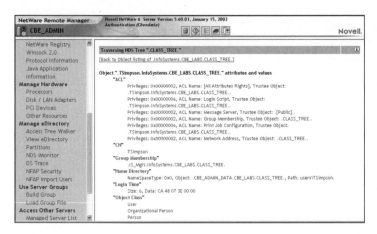

**Figure 13-29**    Viewing user account details

5. After viewing the user information, he clicked the Exit button to end the Remote Manager session.

## Server Hardware Management

Using Remote Manager, you can view your server's current hardware configuration settings, which is useful when diagnosing problems or planning for new equipment. For example, David found a 1 GB network card at Comdex that he wanted to install in the CBE_ADMIN server. He used the following steps in Remote Manager to view the server's hardware configuration so that he could check the slots and interrupts to determine the feasibility of installing the new network card:

1. He started the Web browser on the computer in his hotel room and entered the URL https://*ip_address*:8009 (replacing *ip_address* with the IP address of the CBE_ADMIN server).

2. He scrolled down the navigation frame to the Manage Hardware heading and clicked the Processors link to display the Processor Information window (see Figure 13-30).

3. Under the Manage Hardware heading, he clicked the Disk/LAN Adapters link and then clicked the Info icon next to Network Adapter to display a window similar to the one in Figure 13-31.

4. Under the Manage Hardware heading, he clicked the Other Resources link to display the Hardware Resources window.

5. He clicked the Interrupts link to display the Interrupts window (see Figure 13-32).

**13**

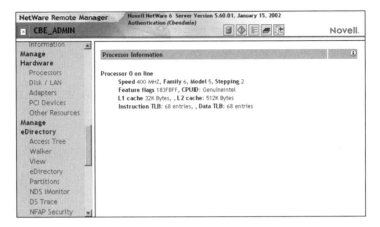

**Figure 13-30**    The Processor Information window

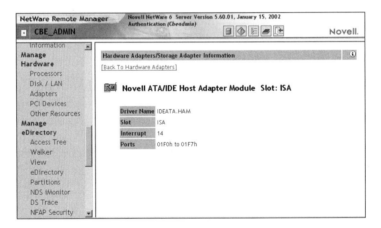

**Figure 13-31**    Viewing information on network adapters

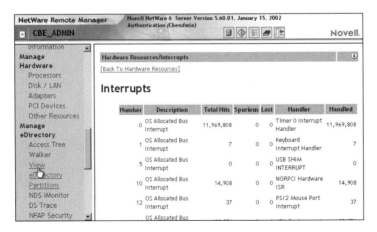

**Figure 13-32**    Viewing settings for interrupts

6. After checking all the hardware settings, he clicked the Exit button to end the Remote Manager session.

## The iMonitor Utility

Like Remote Manager, the **iMonitor** utility provides monitoring and diagnostic capabilities for all servers in the eDirectory tree. As you learned in the previous section, Remote Manager provides only minimum information on the eDirectory tree, but iMonitor is designed to be a major troubleshooting tool for monitoring and repairing eDirectory tree problems. Monitoring and diagnosing the eDirectory tree requires the administrator to be able to look at partitions and replicas on a server basis. iMonitor can be run on any platform that supports eDirectory 8.6, including NetWare, Windows NT/2000, Linux, and Solaris. On NetWare 6 servers, iMonitor is started from a link in Remote Manager. Like Remote Manager, iMonitor listens on the default HTTP port 8008. Upon login, the user's port is redirected to 8009. To run iMonitor, your server and workstation must meet the requirements shown in Table 13-3.

**Table 13-3**      iMonitor Software Requirements

| Software | Requirement |
| --- | --- |
| Browser | Internet Explorer 4 or later<br>Netscape 4.06 or later<br>NetWare server console browser |
| Platform | NetWare 5 support pack 5 or later<br>Windows NT/2000<br>Linux<br>Solaris<br>Tru64 Unix |
| eDirectory | Version 8.6 or higher |

**13**

Although the eDirectory tree is an extremely stable and reliable platform, occasionally problems can occur as a result of replication errors caused by communication media failure or server hardware problems. David used the following steps in iMonitor to perform some common eDirectory monitoring and management tasks:

1. He started iMonitor from Internet Explorer by entering the URL https://
   *ip_address:2200* (replacing *ip_address* with the IP address of the CBE_
   ADMIN server).

2. In the Security Alert message box, he clicked Yes to display the NetWare Web Manager window.

3. He clicked the CBE_ADMIN server name under the Remote Manager heading and entered the CBEAdmin user name and password to display the NetWare Remote Manager window.

4. He scrolled down to the Manage eDirectory heading and clicked the NDS iMonitor link to display the Agent Summary window (see Figure 13-33).

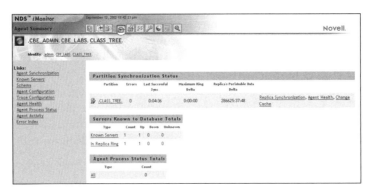

**Figure 13-33**    The Agent Summary window in iMonitor

5. A useful eDirectory troubleshooting technique is performing a DSTRACE on the eDirectory tree transactions to look for error conditions or messages that can be used to identify and correct a problem. David used DSTRACE to check the integrity of the CBE Labs tree by performing the following steps:

a. He clicked the Trace Configuration link, and then clicked Yes in the Security Alert message box to display the Trace Configuration window, shown in Figure 13-34.

b. In the DS TRACE Options section, he left the default options shown in Figure 13-35 selected and clicked the Submit button to start the trace.

c. In the Trace History section, he clicked the View icon (see the magnifying glass in Figure 13-36) to display the output shown in Figure 13-37.

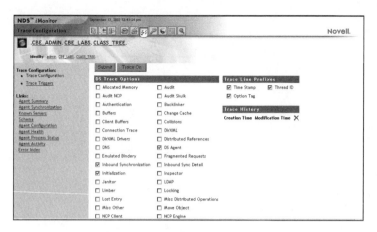

**Figure 13-34**    The Trace Configuration window

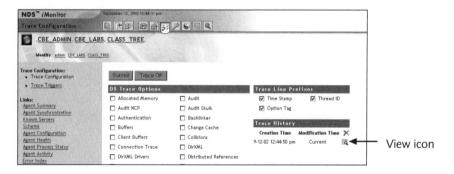

**Figure 13-35**    DS Trace default options

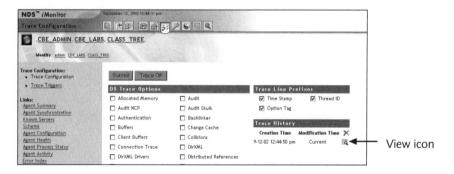

**Figure 13-36**    Selecting the View icon to see the trace report output

13

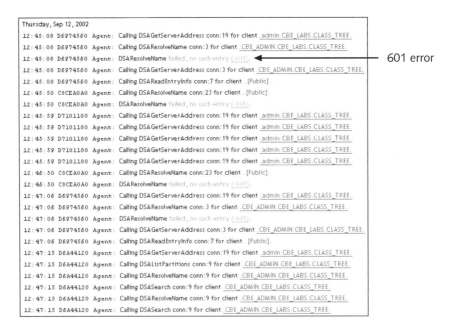

**Figure 13-37** A sample DS Trace report

d. He noted that a DSAResolveName had failed (see the 601 error in Figure 13-37). He clicked on the message to see a help window (see Figure 13-38), explaining that the possible cause of the problem was an eDirectory object name that no longer existed in the specified context. He determined that the problem was caused by a user attempting to log in from the wrong context or by access attempts to deleted objects.

**Figure 13-38** The help window explaining possible causes for errors

e. To end the trace, he clicked the Trace Configuration link (shown previously in Figure 13-38) to display the Trace Configuration window. He then clicked the Trace Off button.

6. Another eDirectory troubleshooting aid is checking to make sure eDirectory replicas are synchronized on the servers. David used the following steps in iMonitor to view the replica synchronization status on the network:

a. He clicked the Agent Synchronization link under the Links heading to display the Agent Synchronization summary window (similar to the one in Figure 13-39).

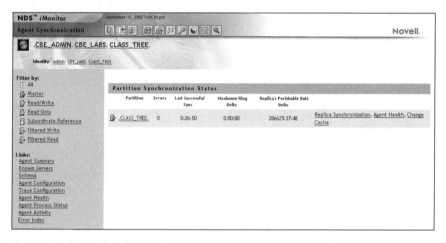

**Figure 13-39**   The Agent Synchronization summary window

b. The Partition Synchronization Status section contains information on each partition. For example, to view information on the CLASS_TREE partition, he clicked that partition and scrolled down to the Replica section, as shown in Figure 13-40.

c. He clicked the Home NetWare Manager button (a server icon with a bull's-eye) on the iMonitor toolbar to return to Remote Manager.

7. The DSREPAIR utility plays a major role in identifying and fixing inconsistencies in the eDirectory partition replicas. David used the following steps to run DSREPAIR and view the DSREPAIR log for any possible problems. Because this process can interrupt normal server operations, he picked a time when no users were accessing the network.

a. He scrolled down and clicked the NDS iMonitor link under the Manage eDirectory heading to return to the iMonitor window.

b. He clicked the Repair button (a wrench icon) to display the NDS Repair Switches window shown in Figure 13-41.

13

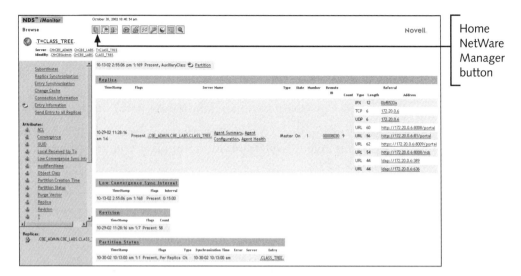

Home
NetWare
Manager
button

**Figure 13-40**    Viewing information in the Replica section

Repair button

**Figure 13-41**    The NDS Repair Switches window

    c. With the default Repair Local DIB check box selected, he clicked the Start Repair button to perform the repair process on the local Directory Information Database (DIB). During the repair process, any status messages were displayed in the iMonitor window.

8. He closed iMonitor by clicking the Logout button.

## The RConsoleJ Utility

You can use the **RConsoleJ** utility to access the server console from ConsoleOne. Although you can use Remote Manager to perform the same server operations, if you are currently using ConsoleOne and are logged in as the Admin user, with RConsoleJ you don't need to start a Web browser and log in to the server again to access the server console from ConsoleOne. RConsoleJ includes the following components:

- *RConsoleJ Client*—This component is a Java-based utility running on a Java-enabled workstation or NetWare server. From the RConsoleJ Client, you can remotely control and monitor all NetWare console operations.

- *RConsoleJ Agent*—This component (RCONAG6.NLM) is a utility running on the target NetWare server, which can be connected over IP, IPX, or IP/IPX running the RConsoleJ Agent. The RConsoleJ Agent services all RConsoleJ Client requests and advertises its services using Service Location Protocol (SLP) packets sent to all client workstations on the network.

- *RConsoleJ Proxy Agent*—This component (RCONPRXY.NLM) is a utility running on a NetWare server. It routes all IP packets to IPX and vice versa.

To use RConsoleJ, the RCONAG6.NLM module must be loaded at the server you want to access. RCONAG6.NLM sets the password, TCP port, and IPX/SPX port that will be used to gain access to the target server. To run RConsoleJ at the workstation, you need to be logged in as the Admin user and running ConsoleOne at the workstation. David used the following steps in RConsoleJ to access the CBE_ADMIN server console:

1. First, he loaded the RConsoleJ software on the CBE_ADMIN server and assigned a password by using these steps:

   a. He went into the server room and pressed Ctrl+Esc on the CBE_ADMIN server to display the Current Screens list.

   b. He entered the number 1 and pressed Enter to display the System Console screen.

   c. He entered the LOAD RCONAG6 command, and then pressed Enter to load the software module and display the Enter a password prompt.

   d. He entered a password, and then pressed Enter.

   e. He pressed Enter again to accept the default TCP port number 2034.

   f. He pressed Enter again to use the SPX port number 16800.

   g. Finally, he pressed Enter again to use the default port number 2036 for a secured connection. The RConsoleJ module loaded, and he returned to the system console. He left the server room and returned to his office.

2. He started his workstation and logged in with the CBEAdmin user name and password, started ConsoleOne, expanded the CBE_LABS Organization, and clicked the CBE_ADMIN Server object.

3. He started RConsoleJ by clicking Tools, Remote Console on the menu bar to open the Novell RConsoleJ dialog box shown in Figure 13-42.

**13**

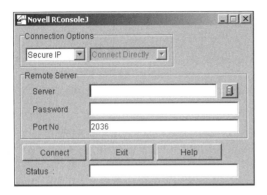

**Figure 13-42**    The Novell RConsoleJ dialog box

4. He clicked the browse button next to the Server text box to display a list of remote servers running the RCONAG6 module.

5. He clicked his CBE_ADMIN server, and then clicked OK to return to the Novell RConsoleJ dialog box.

6. He entered the password assigned to the RConsoleJ module, and clicked the Connect button to log in.

7. He clicked OK to accept the certificate and display the console screen.

8. To display a list of screens to access, he clicked the down arrow next to the Server Screens text box, as shown in Figure 13-43.

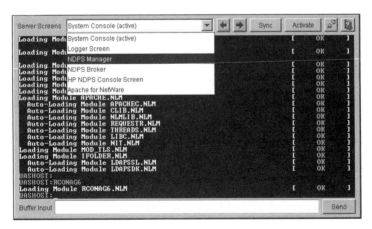

**Figure 13-43**    Viewing a list of available console screens

9. After viewing the status of the NDPS Manager, David clicked the Disconnect button to the right of the Activate button to exit the RConsoleJ session.

10. He closed the RConsoleJ dialog box, exited ConsoleOne, and logged out.

# MANAGING NETWARE LICENSING SERVICES

In previous versions of NetWare, clients have access to NetWare servers through a licensed connection system known as **Server Connection Licensing (SCL)**. In SCL, each pre–NetWare 6 server is assigned a number of connections based on the installed license certificates. When a user connects to a pre–NetWare 6 server, one of the license connections is allocated to that client for the duration of the user's session. When the user logs out and turns off the workstation, the licensed connection is made available for another client to attach to that server. In the SCL system, organizations need to purchase licenses for the total number of concurrent users on each NetWare server. For example, if CBE Labs had 50 employees who connected to two servers, the organization would need to purchase 100 connection licenses (50 for each server).

The Novell Licensing Services (NLS) that ship with NetWare 6 support a new type of licensing system: **User Access Licensing (UAL)**. With the UAL system, users gain access to network services by connecting to the network rather than an individual server. When they first log in to the server, User objects receive a permanent license unit, so they can access network services on any network server in the tree at any time from any computer. That means a user needs only one license, regardless of the number of servers he or she needs to log in to. In the new UAL model, an organization purchases licenses for the total number of User objects in the tree, instead of purchasing licenses for each server. When users log in to the network, they obtain a license unit reserved for a minimum of 90 days. If a user does not log in within the 90-day time period, the license is released and made available to the next user who needs it. The 90-day limit begins each time a user logs in to the network. Unlike the SLC model, in which print servers and other network resources required licensed connections, in the UAL model, non-user objects, such as printers and ZENworks, do not use user licenses. The major disadvantage to the UAL model is in networks that have public access, such as schools, libraries, or other facilities, requiring many user accounts that often don't log in at the same time. For example, a school with accounts for several hundred students might have only 50 who log in at one time because of a limited number of workstations. In this type of environment, purchasing licenses for each possible user would be prohibitively expensive. As a result, because NetWare 6 does not support the SCL model, the best alternative in environments that support many unlicensed users is creating a few generic user accounts for all non-licensed users.

**13**

## Planning License Installation

If License Certificate objects are not well placed in the eDirectory tree, some NLS clients might not have access to licensing services. Place license certificates as close as practical to actual users but high enough in the eDirectory tree so that everyone who needs to access them can. For example, CBE Labs has purchased another license certificate for the Testing and Evaluation Department. To make this license available to department users, David installed the certificate in the Test&Eval OU. When users from any subcontainer of Test&Eval log in, NLS will search up the tree and find the license certificate to the Test&Eval OU and then use that license certificate to assign a license connection to the user.

Consider the following guidelines when installing license components.

- Place server license certificates so that NLS servers do not have to traverse slow WAN links to access license units. Place user certificates so that NLS does not have to traverse WAN links when users are authenticating to the tree.

- Place at least one License Service Provider object in a container near the root of the tree. Also, consider loading license service provider software on servers where many or most users log in to in the eDirectory tree. These two actions distribute requests for license units.

- Identify license certificates that many users throughout the eDirectory tree will use. Place these license certificates in a context near the root of the eDirectory tree.

- Identify license certificates that a small group will use. Place these license certificates in the same eDirectory context as those users' objects.

- Identify license certificates that larger groups will use. Place these certificates in the eDirectory context closest to the root for the group.

Because managing network use in the UAL model is a priority, network administrators can use the new NetWare Usage tool in Remote Manager to view the total number of licenses and to generate reports showing user access information. In addition, you can use iManager to view license certificates and install additional licenses. Because the server installation software installs Novell Licensing Services but not the license certificates, network administrators need to know how to use iManager to install UAL license certificates separately. In the following sections, you learn how David used iManager to install his license certificates and see how to use Remote Manager's NetWare Usage tool to monitor license usage data.

## Using iManager to Install and View License Certificates

When NetWare 6 is first installed, NLS adds a License Container object to the tree in the same context as the new NetWare server. License Certificate objects are then added to the License Container. There are two types of NetWare license certificates: NetWare 6 Server certificates and NetWare 6 User certificates. The **NetWare 6 Server certificate** is installed during the NetWare 6 server installation and is necessary for the server to run. The **NetWare 6 User certificate** is a UAL license certificate that supports user connections to the network. NetWare 6 User certificates are not installed during server installation, but need to be added with iManager after the server is up and running. You install license certificates by accessing envelope files (.nlf files). If you purchase and install additional license certificates, they are also added to the eDirectory tree as objects in the License Container object. With envelopes, you can install more than one license certificate at a time into License Container objects. For example, if you have purchased three products in a suite, you can use an envelope to simultaneously install license certificates for all three products. David used the following steps to install his NetWare 6 User certificates:

1. First, he started his administrative workstation and logged in to the network with the CBEAdmin user name and password.

2. Next, he started his Web browser, entered the URL https://*ip_address*:2200 (replacing *ip_address* with the IP address of the CBE_ADMIN server), and clicked Yes to open the NetWare Web Manager portal.

3. He clicked the CBE_ADMIN server under the iManager heading to display the Login window.

4. He entered CBEAdmin in the User Name text box and his password in the Password text box.

5. After verifying that the context was set to CBE_LABS and the Tree text box contained the correct tree name, he clicked the Login button to log in and display the Novell iManager window.

6. He expanded the License Management option and then clicked the Install a License link to display the Install a License window, similar to the one in Figure 13-44.

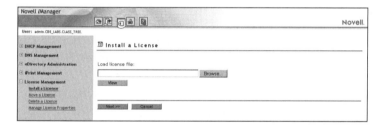

**Figure 13-44**    The Install a License window

7. He inserted the license certificate disk into the floppy disk drive and clicked the Browse button next to the Load license file text box to display the Choose file window.

8. He navigated to the floppy disk and double-clicked the license file named 65234114.nlf to insert the license file into the Load license file text box.

 Each license file is uniquely named with a serial number and the extension .nlf, which stands for "Novell license file."

9. He clicked the View button to verify the license file in the NetWare 6 User certificate, as shown in Figure 13-45.

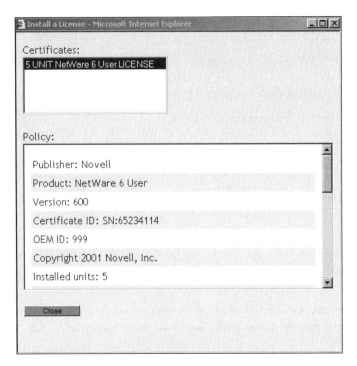

**Figure 13-45**    Verifying license file information

10. He clicked the Close button to return to the Install a License window, and then clicked the Next button to display the certificates listed in the license file.

11. He clicked the check box next to the NetWare 6 User License (see Figure 13-46), and then clicked the Next button to display the window for specifying where to install the certificate.

**Figure 13-46**    Selecting a certificate to install

12. To place the certificate in the same context as the CBE_ADMIN server, he clicked the browse button next to the Location text box, navigated to the root of the tree, and clicked the CBE_LABS Organization to place it in the

Location text box (see Figure 13-47). Placing the license in the Organization object that contains the servers allows the servers to allocate units from the license certificates.

**Figure 13-47**     Selecting the license location

13. Next, he clicked the Install button to install the NetWare 6 license certificate. After the installation completed, the system displayed a "Successfully installed the following licenses" message box.

14. He noted that the license was correctly installed and then clicked the Done button to return to the Novell iManager window.

15. After installing the NetWare 6 User license certificate, he used iManager to document information on his existing licenses by following these steps:

    a. He clicked the Manage License Properties link to display the Manage License Properties window.

    b. He clicked the eyeglass icon next to the Object name text box, and navigated to the CBE_LABS Organization, as shown in Figure 13-48.

**13**

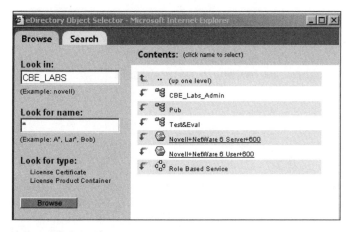

**Figure 13-48**     The eDirectory Object Selector dialog box

c. He expanded the Novell+NetWare 6 User+600 License Container object and clicked on a License Certificate object to insert it into the Object name text box. He then clicked OK to display information about that license and clicked Yes to view through the browser (see Figure 13-49).

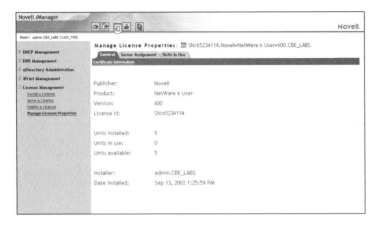

**Figure 13-49** The Manage License Properties window

d. He clicked the Server Assignment tab to display the Server text box shown in Figure 13-50. He noticed that the license was not assigned to any server. A license can be assigned to a specific server or available to all servers in the organization. Licenses not assigned to a specific server are available for use by any server in the CBE_LABS Organization. By leaving the Server text box blank, he made the license units available for the CBE_ADMIN or CBE_EVAL server to use.

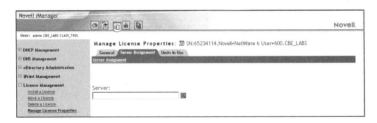

**Figure 13-50** The Server Assignment tab

e. To view the users who are currently assigned license units, David clicked the Units In Use tab, as shown in Figure 13-51. A license is assigned to a user when he or she first logs in. The license assignment then stays with that user until the user is inactive for 90 days, or the administrator releases the assignment by selecting a license assignment and clicking the Remove button.

f. After verifying the license information, he clicked OK to return to the Novell iManager window.

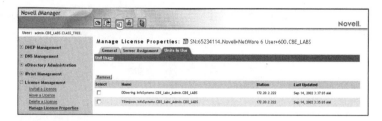

**Figure 13-51**    The Units In Use tab

16. He clicked the Exit button to end the Novell iManager session and return to the Login window.

17. He clicked File, Close to exit Internet Explorer and return to the Windows desktop.

# Using Remote Manager to View License Information

Network administrators should monitor license usage so that they can prevent problems caused by a lack of licenses. With the license usage information option in Remote Manager, administrators can view or print license usage reports. David used the following steps to check license usage on the CBE network:

1. He started his Web browser software and entered the URL https://*ip_ address*:8009 (replacing *ip_address* with the IP address assigned to the CBE_ADMIN server) to display the Login window.

2. He logged in to NetWare Remote Manager with the CBEAdmin user name and password.

3. In the NetWare Remote Manager window, he scrolled down to the NetWare Usage heading and clicked the Usage Information link to display the NetWare Usage Information window (see Figure 13-52).

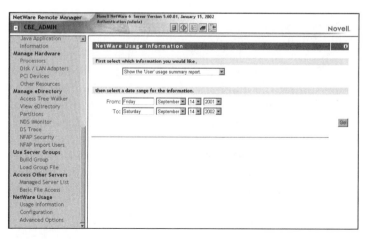

**Figure 13-52**    The NetWare Usage Information window

4. He clicked the Go! button to display a usage report similar to the one in Figure 13-53.

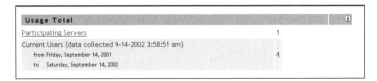

**Figure 13-53**    A sample license usage report in Remote Manager

5. After viewing the usage report, he clicked the Exit button to exit NetWare Remote Manager and then clicked Yes to close the Web browser window.

## Troubleshooting Novell Licensing

As network systems have become larger with more servers and services that need to be accessed from multiple networks, licensing has become more complex and can be a source of network problems. As a CNA, you should be aware of the following common network license problems and what actions you can take to correct them.

**Problem:** The server console displays "Unable to get a Server Base license."

**Possible cause:** The server license certificate is not attached to the server or is located in a subcontainer of the server's context.

**Action:** Delete and reinstall the server license certificate. If you use iManager, you must manually make a server assignment while installing the license certificate.

**Problem:** Users do not have access to license units, so they have no drive mappings when they log in.

**Possible cause:** There are no more user licenses certificates available in the license container, or NLS cannot find the license container holding the user license certificates.

**Action:** In the UAL model, when a user logs in, NLS searches up the tree from the user's context looking for user license certificates. When a user license certificate is located, the user is assigned an available license. The license is assigned to the user's account for a period of at least 90 days. As a result, having a user license certificate for each user account (not just for the number of users who will be logged in at one time) is important. If necessary, add more user license certificates to the license container. Another possible problem is that the user license certificates are located in a license container that's not located in the users' context or in a parent container. NLS searches up the tree starting from the user account's current context. If a license container is located in another branch of the tree, NLS will not find it. In this case, it's necessary to move one or more license certificates from the license container to the users' context.

**Problem:** The system reports that duplicate licenses are installed in the eDirectory tree.

**Possible cause:** In earlier NLS versions, you installed a license certificate, deleted it, and then reinstalled it elsewhere in the eDirectory tree. When the earlier NLS process walks the eDirectory tree and looks for certificates, NLS encounters the deleted certificate and considers it a duplicate.

**Action:** Use Deployment Manager (described in Appendix C) to upgrade the server to the latest NLS version.

Congratulations! You're now part of the Novell OneNet world. Knowing how to access and manage data and network configurations from anywhere, anytime, will give you some valuable skills for your network management career. Look for Novell to be advancing this technology rapidly in future releases.

## CHAPTER SUMMARY

- By storing files on the local computer and synchronizing them with the network, the iFolder service enables users to access their files from multiple workstations without having to be logged in to the network.

- To use iFolder, you must first install the iFolder service on a server and then install the iFolder client or a Java applet on the user workstation.

- The iFolder Java applet enables users to access their files from a Web browser without having to install the iFolder client on the workstation.

- The NetStorage service provides access to user files and folders from a Web browser without the need to install any component on the user workstation.

- Remote Manager enables the administrator to perform a number of administrative tasks on the server from anywhere by using a Web browser.

- Remote Manager makes it possible to access server volumes, configuration parameters, the eDirectory tree, and hardware information from any computer.

- iMonitor offers many of the capabilities of Remote Manger, along with the flexibility to be used from multiple platforms, including Windows NT/2000, Linux, and Sun Solaris.

- The RConsoleJ utility provides remote access to server consoles from ConsoleOne and can be used to access and manage your servers without using the server console or starting a Web browser.

- NetWare 6 uses a new license system called User Access License (UAL). UAL differs from previous license systems in that it assigns a license to a user account that can be used to access all NetWare servers in the tree. Previous versions of NetWare used the Service Connection License (SCL) model, which required each server to have licenses for as many users as could be attached to it. Although the UAL system is an advantage for organizations with multiple servers, it can create problems for organizations that have many users that infrequently log in.

▢ Licenses can be added and managed with iManager. License usage information can be viewed in Remote Manager with the Usage Information option.

---

# KEY TERMS

**iFolder** — A NetWare service that enables files to be kept on a local computer (or one that's not attached to the network) and synchronized with the network.

**iMonitor** — A Novell OneNet utility that enables a network administrator to work with the eDirectory system from a Web browser and perform such tasks as checking for eDirectory replica synchronization, tracing eDirectory activity, viewing error reports, and performing repair operations.

**LDAP proxy user** — A user account that's a member of the LDAP server group and provides the LDAP server with rights to read certain information from the eDirectory tree.

**NetWare 6 Server certificate** — A license certificate installed during the NetWare 6 server installation that is necessary for the server to run.

**NetWare 6 User certificate** — A UAL license certificate that supports user connections to the network. This certificate is not installed during the NetWare 6 server installation; it's installed later by using iManager.

**Novell NetStorage** — A NetWare service that gives users secure access to files on the NetWare server from any Internet location.

**RConsoleJ** — A NetWare Java-based remote console tool that enables an administrator to access a server's console screen from ConsoleOne.

**Remote Manager** — A Novell OneNet utility that enables a network administrator to manage a NetWare server console from a Web browser.

**Server Connection Licensing (SCL)** — The license model used by pre–NetWare 6 servers that requires each server to have a license for each connection, including connections made by printers and other non-user resources.

**Server Management console** — The iFolder component that enables network administrators to perform administrative tasks, such as managing iFolder user accounts.

**thread** — A process that's currently being worked on by the CPU.

**User Access Licensing (UAL)** — The NetWare 6 licensing system, in which each user account is provided with a fixed license to access any server in the tree the first time the user logs in.

# REVIEW QUESTIONS

1. Which of the following OneNet utilities allows access to network data from a Web browser without adding a client to the user workstation?

   a. iFolder

   b. NetStorage

   c. RConsoleJ

   d. iManager

2. Which of the following OneNet utilities allows access to server console screens from a Web browser?

   a. Remote Manager

   b. RConsoleJ

   c. iManager

   d. iMonitor

3. Which of the following OneNet utilities provides secure and transparent synchronization of files between the local hard disk and the server?

   a. iFolder

   b. NetStorage

   c. WebDAV

   d. Remote Manager

4. Which of the following utilities can be used to access the server console from ConsoleOne?

   a. iMonitor

   b. RConsoleJ

   c. RConsole

   d. Remote Manager

5. Which of the following is *not* a benefit of iFolder?

   a. secure access to network files from any computer using only a Web browser or Microsoft Web Folder

   b. automatic synchronizing of data across multiple workstations

   c. encryption of sensitive files to protect them from unauthorized access

   d. the ability to work on files offline

6. True or False: The iFolder server component cannot be installed during NetWare 6 installation.

13

7. The iFolder client can be installed on which of the following platforms? (Select all that apply.)

   a. Linux

   b. Windows NT

   c. Windows 2000

   d. Windows 9x

   e. Windows 3.1

   f. Windows Me

8. Accessing iFolder files from a Web browser requires which of the following?

   a. the iFolder client on the workstation

   b. a Java applet installed in the Web browser

   c. no additional software

   d. Internet Explorer 5.5 or later installed on the workstation

9. Client iFolder policies can be used to do which of the following? (Select all that apply.)

   a. enforce encryption

   b. set user quota limits

   c. save passwords and phrases

   d. force password changes after the specified number of days

   e. set session timeout values

10. Server iFolder policies can be used to do which of the following? (Select all that apply.)

    a. set initial disk quotas

    b. set session timeout values

    c. enforce encryption

    d. save passwords and phrases

    e. force password changes after the specified number of days

11. If you have multiple CPUs on your server and many iFolder user accounts, you could help increase iFolder Apache server performance by doing which of the following?

    a. increasing the disk quota limits

    b. adding additional iFolder servers

    c. increasing the number of threads

    d. reducing the default synchronization interval

12. Which of the following options can be performed by right-clicking the iFolder icon in the taskbar? (Select all that apply.)

    a. logging in or out

    b. changing passwords

    c. viewing disk quotas

    d. setting synchronization intervals

13. True or False: To access iFolder files using a Web browser, you first need to download the file to your local disk.

14. True or False: To access NetStorage files using a Web browser, you first need to download the file to your local disk.

15. Which of the following requirements must be met to use NetStorage on a client? (Select all that apply.)

    a. The NetStorage client software must be downloaded and installed on the client.

    b. The date and time settings must be close to the server's date and time.

    c. NetStorage must be installed on the server.

    d. The context(s) for the user accounts must be specified during NetStorage installation.

16. True or False: To change the configuration of NetStorage, you need to reinstall it.

17. When using Remote Manager, a black light in the overall health indicator indicates which of the following conditions?

    a. The server is in good health.

    b. The server is in suspect health.

    c. The server requires administrator response.

    d. The server is not responding.

18. Which of the following utilities can be used to view printer agent error messages?

    a. iMonitor

    b. iManager

    c. Remote Manager

    d. RConsoleJ

19. You can use the Configure Health Thresholds link in the Health Monitor window to do which of the following?

    a. view the criteria for green, yellow, and red indicator lights

    b. set the suspect and critical values

    c. view interrupt usage

    d. view memory usage

13

20. Which of the following utilities is used to help troubleshoot eDirectory problems?

    a. iManager

    b. RConsoleJ

    c. iMonitor

    d. NDS Manager

## HANDS-ON PROJECTS

David's test of the iFolder and NetStorage services paved the way to their use in the CBE organization. In the following projects, you continue to work with iFolder, NetStorage, and Remote Manager to simulate scenarios in your CBE Lab network operations.

### Project 13-1: Installing iFolder Client

After hearing about the capabilities of iFolder, Joseph Cunningham, the president of CBE Labs, and Steve Lopez, the administrative assistant, were anxious to begin using iFolder so that they could access their files when traveling to customer facilities. In this project, you simulate installing the iFolder client on Steve's notebook computer. Record the steps you perform for use in Case Project 13-1, where you will write a memo to the CBE staff telling them how to install iFolder to access their files.

1. Obtain the IP address of your iFolder service, and record it on your memo. (You can get the IP address from your instructor or by pressing Ctrl+Esc while at the server console and then selecting the Apache for NetWare option.)

2. If necessary, start your computer, and log in with your administrative user name and password.

3. Start your Web browser software, and enter the URL **https://ip_address** (replacing *ip_address* with the IP address of your iFolder server) to display the iFolder Welcome window.

4. Follow the steps described in this chapter to install iFolder on your Windows computer. Document these steps for use in Case Project 13-1.

### Project 13-2: Creating iFolder User Accounts

After installing the iFolder client, David tested the system by creating an iFolder user account for his user name. In this project, you follow the process described in this chapter to create an iFolder user account for the TSimpson user you created in Chapter 9. Record the steps you perform on a separate paper for use in Case Project 13-1, where you create a memo to the CBE personnel staff telling them how to use iFolder.

## Project 13-3: Using iFolder

The CBE organization's first real test of the iFolder service came when Marketing Director Stephen Hayakawa wanted to work on his year-end spreadsheet while traveling. To do this, he must install the iFolder client on his notebook and then copy the files to his iFolder directory. In this project, you simulate this task by performing the following steps:

1. Log in as your Stephen Hayakawa user.

2. Create an iFolder user account and pass phrase for Stephen.

3. Copy the BegYear and EndYear worksheet files to your iFolder directory:

   a. Use My Network Places to navigate to the CBE_ADMIN server.

   b. Double-click the DATA volume, and navigate to the Admin\Budgets folder.

   c. Copy all the files with the extension .xls into Stephen's iFolder directory.

4. Log out.

5. Simulate being offline by clicking the **Workstation only** check box to log on to your local Windows 2000 computer.

6. Use iFolder to open the EndYear file and make some changes. (You should use Notepad to add some text to the end of the file.)

7. Save the file and close iFolder.

8. Log out.

9. Simulate being back in the office by logging in to Novell Client with Stephen's user name and password.

10. Right-click the **iFolder** icon on the taskbar and click the **Sync Now** option to update your changes.

11. Verify your changes have been synchronized with the server and write a memo to Stephen explaining how to use iFolder to access files while away from the office and then synchronize them with the server when he returns.

12. Log out.

**13**

## Project 13-4: Using iFolder from Internet Explorer

When accessing iFolder files from a computer outside the organization's network, often it's not feasible to load the iFolder client. You might not have sufficient rights to install the iFolder client on the computer you want to use, or perhaps you don't want to leave iFolder files on computers outside your company. The solution to this problem is to access your iFolder through a Web browser as described in this chapter. For example, Stephen Hayakawa needs to know how to access the EndYear file in his iFolder client when working from a hotel-based computer. In this project, you work with another student to access your iFolder files from his or her computer without creating an iFolder client on the other Windows workstation.

1. Change Windows workstations with your lab partner.

2. If necessary, create a folder named Temporary on the local computer's C: drive.

3. Start Internet Explorer from your lab partner's computer and then access the iFolder account you created for your Stephen Hayakawa user in Project 13-3.

4. Download the EndYear file to the Temporary directory you created in Step 2.

5. Make some changes to the file.

6. Use the iFolder Java applet to upload the modified file to Stephen's iFolder directory.

7. Close Internet Explorer.

8. Delete the EndYear file from the Temporary folder.

9. Create a memo to your Stephen Hayakawa user that lists the steps for using iFolder from a computer outside the company network. Turn the memo in to your instructor.

## Project 13-5: Using NetStorage

A real test of the NetStorage service came when Stephen went on a trip to a customer site and wanted to download some files for the salespeople to analyze. To make the files available to Stephen, Steve Lopez wants to copy files into Stephen's home directory so that he can download them with NetStorage. In this project, test and document a procedure for Steve and Stephen to use:

1. Log in with your ##Admin user name and password.

2. Copy the Order.frm file from the DATA:Publctns\Document directory to Stephen's home directory, and then log out.

3. Simulate Stephen working from a remote computer by clicking the **Workstation only** check box to log on to your Windows 2000/XP computer.

4. Follow the steps in this chapter to use your Web browser to access NetStorage and log in with Stephen's user name and password.

5. Download the Order.frm file to your local computer.

6. Change the file.

7. Upload the revised Order.frm file back to your home directory.

8. Record the steps you performed for use in Case Project 13-2.

## Project 13-6: Using Remote Manager

While attending a computer conference in Orlando, Florida, you want to upload some software you've purchased to a new folder in the Apps directory of the CBE_ADMIN server. In this project, you perform the following steps to create a subfolder in the Apps directory and then copy files from your local workstation to the folder.

1. Simulate being at a remote computer by clicking the **Workstation only** check box to log on to your Windows 2000/XP computer.

2. Start your Web browser software, and log in to Remote Manager by entering your ##Admin user name and password in the appropriate text boxes.

3. Click the **STUDENTS** volume, and then navigate to your ##DATA directory.

4. Find the "." entry located at the top of the Name column. This entry is used to work with the current folder. To create a subfolder within the currently selected Apps folder, click the Info icon to the left of the "." to display information about your folder.

5. Scroll down and enter **LanMan** in the New name text box to the right of the Create Subdirectory button.

6. Click the **Create Subdirectory** button to display the newly created LanMan folder in the directory listing.

7. Click the **LanMan** folder, and then click the **Upload** button to upload the Freecell.exe program in the Windows\System32 folder of your Windows workstation to your LanMan folder.

8. Exit Remote Manager, and log out.

## Project 13-7: Viewing License Information

**13**

For this project, you need access to a user account with Supervisor rights to the CBE_LABS Organization.

In this project, use the steps described in this chapter to create a memo to your instructor that shows the license units in use. The memo should identify number of units in use, the number of units available, user accounts assigned to the first five license units, and the steps you used to obtain the information.

## CASE PROJECTS

### Case 13-1: Novell OneNet Utilities

In this project, create a memo to the CBE staff that describes the new Novell iFolder and NetStorage utilities and how they can use them to access their data when away from the office.

### Case 13-2: Using iFolder Memo

In this project, use the steps you recorded in Projects 13-2 through 13-4 to create a memo to the CBE staff describing how to install iFolder, create a new user account, and then how to copy files to their iFolder clients and synchronize them with the server.

### Case 13-3: Using NetStorage Memo

In this project, use the steps you recorded in Project 13-4 to create a memo to Steve Lopez and Stephen Hayakawa describing how they can use NetStorage to allow Stephen to download and work with files that Steve copies to his home directory (see Project 13-5).

# IMPLEMENTING AND SECURING NETWORK SERVICES

**After reading this chapter and completing the exercises, you will be able to:**

♦ Describe NetWare 6 Internet/intranet services, including Net Services and Web Services components

♦ Install and configure Novell Web Services components

♦ Describe public key cryptography and use the Novell Certificate Authority service to export public and private keys

♦ Describe internal and external security policies and strategies, including firewalls, virus protection, and defense against denial-of-service attacks

**A**s you have learned in previous chapters, Novell's OneNet strategy uses the Internet to make network services and information available from anywhere at any time. To support the OneNet features of NetWare 6, network administrators need to understand the components that make Internet services available on a NetWare 6 server. They also need to know how to implement these services and secure them from unauthorized access and attacks. In addition to Internet services, NetWare 6 includes Web and FTP services that you can install and configure to deliver information to the Internet. In this chapter, you learn about the Internet service components available with NetWare 6, how to implement Enterprise Web Server and FTP Server, which are part of Novell's Web services, and how to implement internal and external security strategies.

## NetWare 6 Internet Service Components

Novell is a leader in Internet/intranet services that help simplify the implementation of business networks by providing a common set of services for accessing data and resources with a variety of workstation and server operating systems. The NetWare 6 Internet service components can be divided into Net Services and Web Services components, as shown in Figure 14-1.

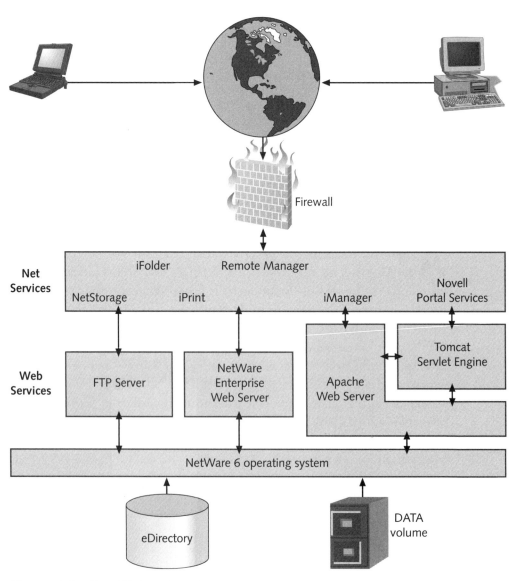

**Figure 14-1**    Novell Internet services

**Web Services** are TCP/IP-based applications that give users access to network data and services through Web sites and FTP servers. To access a Web service, users need to have the correct client software running on their computers. For example, to access a Web site, you need to run a Web browser, such as Internet Explorer or Netscape.

**Net Services** components extend the capabilities of standard Web services and include many of the services you have worked with already, such as iFolder, NetStorage, iPrint, iManager, and Remote Manager. As illustrated in Figure 14-1, a network can be configured so that requests for Net Services originating at user workstations or laptops are sent via the Internet to a firewall running on a server or router. After being checked through the firewall, the request is routed to the appropriate services based on its IP address and port number. IP addresses are used to direct a packet to the correct computer, but port numbers are used to transfer information in the packet to the correct application. When an application starts, it registers a port number with TCP/IP. The TCP/IP protocol stack uses this port number when a workstation receives a packet to determine which application running on the workstation should get the packet's information. Table 14-1 lists commonly used applications and their default well-known port numbers. Each type of application has a designated, or "well-known," port number. The Internet Corporation for Assigned Names and Numbers (ICANN) assigns these well-known port numbers to application endpoints that communicate with the Internet's Transmission Control Protocol (TCP) or User Datagram Protocol (UDP). For example, a remote job entry application has port number 5, HTTP has port number 80, and Post Office Protocol Version 3 (POP3), commonly used for e-mail delivery, has port number 110. When one application communicates with another application at a host computer on the Internet, it specifies the other application in each data transmission by using its port number.

Well-known ports cover the range of possible port numbers from 0 through 1023. Registered ports are numbered from 1024 through 49151. The remaining ports, referred to as dynamic ports or private ports, are numbered from 49152 through 65535.

**14**

**Table 14-1**    Commonly Used Port Numbers

| Port Number | Application |
| --- | --- |
| 21 | File Transfer Protocol (FTP) |
| 23 | Telnet |
| 25 | Simple Mail Transfer Protocol (SMTP) |
| 80 | Web server |
| 110 | Post Office Protocol version 3 (POP3) |

To gain access to NetWare files and resources, Novell Net Services run as applications on Web Services components, such as Apache Web Server. Novell chose Apache Web Server to host the Net Services components because it's public-domain software, meaning it's freely available and can be modified to run on other operating system platforms.

By running through Apache Web Server, Novell Net Services can be implemented on any network operating system platform that supports Apache Web Server, including Unix, Linux, and Windows 2000/XP. For example, because the iFolder service uses Apache Web Server to synchronize files with the server, it can be installed on NetWare 6, Linux, or Windows 2000 servers. In addition to processing requests for Net Services, NetWare Web Services components can make data available through a new feature called Novell Portal Services. In the following sections, you learn about Novell's Web Services components and how Novell Portal Services can be used to customize Web access.

## Apache Web Server for NetWare

Apache Web Server is open-source Web server software originally developed by the Apache Group, a nonprofit organization. Apache Web Server is free to any organization or person who wants to use it to implement Web-based services. Currently, over 60% of all Web-hosting organizations use Apache Web Server. Because it is such a common platform for implementing Web-based services, Novell made Apache Web Server an integral part of NetWare 6's Internet services, and it's installed by default during the NetWare 6 installation. Its primary purpose, however, is to provide support for Novell Portal Services and Net Services, such as iFolder and NetStorage. Because of Apache Web Server's tight integration with Novell's Net Services, it requires no special configuration by the network administrator.

The following NetWare 6 Web-based services use Apache Web Server:

- NetWare Web Manager
- NetWare Web Search Server
- NetWare WebAccess
- iFolder
- iManager

## Tomcat Servlet Engine for NetWare

NetWare 6 ships with the Tomcat Servlet Engine (also developed by the Apache Group), which is used to run Java-based Web applications. Tomcat is Java 2.2 compliant and runs on Apache Web Server. Several NetWare 6 components use Tomcat, including Novell Portal Services and NetWare Web Search Server. Although network administrators rarely need to configure or manage the Tomcat Servlet Engine, programmers developing Web-based applications often work with Tomcat because it runs on a wide variety of operating systems.

# Novell Portal Services

**Novell Portal Services (NPS)** is the leading portal strategy for delivering the right information to the people authorized to use it. A portal strategy is a shift from the standard intranet methodology of obtaining information, in which a user must search for documents (usually static Web pages) to perform an analysis. A portal provides "one view" into a company's information and displays this information as Web pages. For example, with a portal strategy, David Doering, the network administrator at CBE Labs, could use a wireless PDA to log in to the portal and get information on the Information Systems Department's five-year plan as it relates to human resource data. Using NPS, personalized Web pages can be delivered to users regardless of operating system platform or network structure. With NPS, network administrators can protect and control access to network resources, delivering personalized data to people based on their company roles, locations, and group associations. NPS enables users to easily gain access to the Web sites and applications they are authorized to use by building customized Web pages based on users' needs and access rights.

NPS consists of a number of Java applications, called **Java servlets**, that run on Apache Web Server, as shown in Figure 14-2. Java servlets are small, platform-independent, server-side programs that programmatically extend a Web server's functionality, not to be confused with **Java applets**, which are compiled applications that run within a client's Web browser. The Java servlet application programming interface (API) provides a simple framework for building applications on Web servers. Java servlets are not applications that users run; they interact with a servlet engine (an implementation of the Sun Microsystems Java 2.2 Servlet specification) through requests and responses. The servlet engine in turn interacts with the Web server by delegating requests to servlets and transmitting responses to the Web server.

The Tomcat Servlet Engine shown in Figure 14-2 is a Web server application that runs Java servlets. To run NPS, the servlet engine must support the Sun Microsystems Java 2.2 Servlet specification, which enables NPS to be installed and run on a variety of Web server platforms, as long as they support a Java 2.2-compliant Web application server.

When users access the portal service URL on a NetWare 6 server, Apache Web Server, which is hosting the portal service, sends users an authentication page consisting of an HTML form for logging in. Users then submit their user names and passwords to the Apache Web server, which passes the information to the NPS Java servlet running on the Tomcat Servlet Engine. The NPS Java servlet accesses the directory to authenticate users and build a Web page of data that's customized in its content and the way it's displayed. The data's display is based on the user's access rights and the layout format, which can be defined with Extensible Stylesheet Language (XSL). During installation, NetWare 6 automatically creates directory objects to support NPS's additional capabilities and features. NPS configuration is managed through the Portal Admin browser-based utility, so you can use Netscape Navigator 6.0 or later or Internet Explorer 5.0 or later to access this utility.

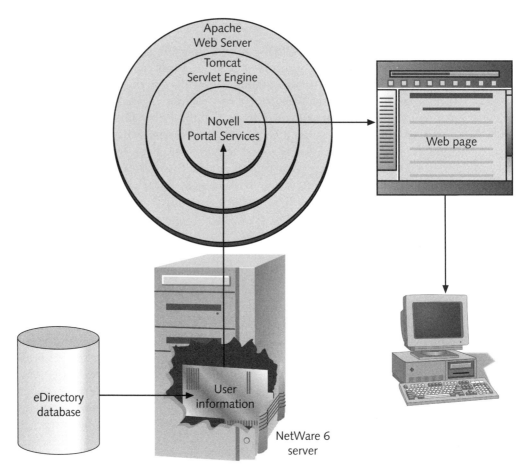

**Figure 14-2**    NPS components

Novell Web Manager is an example of an NPS application that customizes the content of browser-based management utilities, such as iManager and Remote Manager, based on users' access rights. When you access Novell Web Manager from a browser with the URL https://*ip_address*:2200 (replacing *ip_address* with the IP address of your NetWare 6 server), you get a customized Web page containing the management utilities available on your server. After you select a utility, NPS displays a login page for authenticating your user name and password and customizes the available options on the management utility's main page based on your access rights.

For example, if you log in as the network Admin user when accessing Remote Manager, you see all the program options, as shown in Figure 14-3. However, you would not see all these options if you logged on as a user without Supervisor rights to the NetWare 6 server.

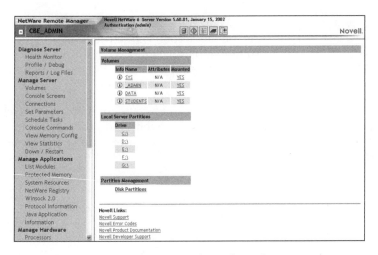

**Figure 14-3**    Remote Manager from the Admin portal

## NetWare Web Search Server

NetWare Web Search Server can make data on your network or the Internet searchable in minutes. It bridges all types of networks—from file servers to intranets and the Internet—delivering requested information in a minimum amount of time. Installed by default during the NetWare 6 installation, NetWare Web Search Server is ready to run simply by pointing it at the Web or file servers you want included in the search index. It then generates keyword indexes from the information found in the selected locations and returns timesaving keyword searches for users to find data quickly. Using a powerful yet simple template-based architecture, network administrators can customize search forms and search results pages to get the information users need.

## NetWare Enterprise Web Server

To host a company's Web or FTP site, you need to install and configure NetWare Enterprise Web Server, an HTTP-based service for sending Web pages to browsers on the Internet or within the company intranet. Enterprise Web Server is optimized to run in the NetWare environment and is a critical component in building a company's Internet or intranet information system. The following list explains the traditional categories of webs; each plays a unique role in sharing information:

- The most popular of all webs is the World Wide Web (WWW) available through the Internet. Hosting a Web server with Internet access requires a persistent Internet connection accessible to anyone running a Web browser. When using the Internet to provide access to Net Services, a firewall is required to provide security for Web servers. As described in the "Firewall External Security" section later in this chapter, firewalls prevent Internet users from accessing the company's network-based resources.

14

- Another important use of NetWare Enterprise Web Server is hosting a private intranet Web site to enhance communication and distribution of information within your company. Although employees inside your company can access both Web sites, the firewall prevents people outside the company from accessing the intranet Web site.

- NetWare Enterprise Web Server is also a necessary component in developing an extranet. An **extranet** is a combination of public and private Web sites, usually created to expedite communication and cooperation among companies that work closely together.

## FTP Server

Before the advent of HTTP and World Wide Web servers, FTP servers provided a means of transferring files from one Internet host to another. FTP servers are designed as a highly efficient and secure method of transferring files to and from Internet sites. Web servers can transfer files using HTTP, but FTP servers generally offer more efficient and reliable delivery through their specialized transfer protocol. They are also commonly used to upload content to Web sites. NetWare 6 includes FTP Server for transferring files to and from NetWare volumes, posting new content to Web sites, and downloading large documents and software.

## NetWare Web Manager

NetWare Web Manager is the portal service for configuring and managing NetWare Web Services and accessing other Web-based management tools. Because NetWare Web Manager is a Java-based browser utility, you can use it to manage Web Services from any location on the Internet. In the following section, you learn how to use NetWare Web Manager to access and configure NetWare Enterprise Web Server and FTP Server.

## INSTALLING AND CONFIGURING WEB SERVICES

As described previously, Web Services are TCP/IP applications that deliver information to clients running on user workstations. Web servers operate in a client-server relationship, in which the Web service running on the NetWare server processes requests from clients running on user workstations. A Web browser, such as Netscape Navigator or Internet Explorer, acts as a client requesting information from the Web server. A Web server uses a specified directory in the file system, referred to as the "content directory," to store all files it makes available to clients. All files in the content directory and its subdirectories are available to the browser clients. NetWare Enterprise Web Server, based on Netscape Web Server, is included on the NetWare 6 operating system CD. Other commonly used Web servers, described in the following list, are also available for hosting Web sites:

- Apache Web Server offers a solid, secure platform for hosting Web sites. Because it has open-source code, third-party companies can offer tools and enhancements to make it even more powerful and flexible.

- The iPlanet Web server is an LDAP-only server designed for user authentication and management, electronic commerce (e-commerce), extranet, and Internet applications and is the foundation for a suite of e-commerce-delivered products from the Sun-Netscape alliance. Because the same team that built the Standalone LDAP (SLDAP) server also created the iPlanet Web server, it has a fully LDAP-compliant directory capability, making it compatible with several other LDAP-compliant directory services, such as eDirectory and Microsoft Active Directory. The iPlanet Web server is designed for use on servers operating outside a corporate firewall, so it is a good choice for an Internet-based Web server that can securely deliver data to Internet users, without risking unauthorized access to data stored on servers that operate behind the corporate firewall.

- Microsoft offers two levels of its Web server product: Microsoft Personal Web Server (PWS) and Internet Information Server (IIS). To deliver Web site content for personal intranet applications, Microsoft designed PWS for use on Windows 95/98 and NT workstations and includes a limited version of IIS for Windows 2000 Professional computers. Although it offers all basic Web server functions, PWS and the Windows 2000 Professional version of IIS do not have all the security options and capabilities needed to deliver and secure company Web sites on the Internet. IIS version 5, installed automatically with Windows 2000 Server, is an integral part of Windows 2000 Internet capabilities, much as Novell uses Apache Web Server to host its Net Services. In addition to hosting Microsoft Internet services, IIS can be configured to host corporate Web sites in much the same way as NetWare Enterprise Web Server. The main disadvantage of the IIS 5 Web server is that it's a proprietary Web server that runs only on Windows 2000 servers. This tight integration can be an advantage when you're using all Microsoft-based services, but it is not open for other developers, thereby limiting your Internet service options.

**14**

## Working with NetWare Enterprise Web Server

You can install NetWare Enterprise Web Server during or after the NetWare 6 server installation. Before using Enterprise Web Server, you must use Web Manager to start the Web server and make any necessary configuration changes. First, take a look at the steps David used to install NetWare Enterprise Web Server:

1. First, he inserted the NetWare 6 CD into the CBE_ADMIN server, pressed Ctrl+Esc, and entered the appropriate number to select the System Console screen.

2. He entered the command CDROM and pressed Enter to mount the CD as a volume on the server.

3. After mounting the NETWARE6 Installation volume, he pressed Ctrl+Esc and entered the appropriate number to select the X Server - Graphical Console.

4. At the graphical console, he clicked Novell and then Install to display the Installed Products window.

5. He clicked Add to display the Source Path window, clicked the browse button to select the NETWARE6 volume, and then clicked OK. He clicked OK again in the Source Path window to copy installation files to the server. After the files were copied, the Components window was displayed with check marks indicating the default installed components.

6. He clicked Clear All to prevent reinstalling existing components, clicked the NetWare Enterprise Web Server check box, and clicked Next to display the login window.

7. He entered his CBEAdmin user name, password, and context in the corresponding text boxes, and then clicked OK to log in. Next, the Configure IP-based Services window was displayed, showing the IP address assigned to the existing Net Services.

8. He assigned a unique IP address (10.0.0.3) to the Enterprise Web Server, using the same network address range as the NetWare 6 server, and clicked Next to display the LDAP Configuration window.

9. In the LDAP Configuration window, he clicked the Allow Clear Text Passwords check box, and then clicked Next to display the Summary window.

10. After verifying that the NetWare Enterprise Web Server and NetWare Port Resolver components were listed, he clicked Finish.

11. After the installation was finished, he clicked Close to close the Installation complete message box and returned to the X Server - Graphical Console. Enterprise Web Server was then ready to configure and use.

After Enterprise Web Server is installed, NPS displays the NetWare Enterprise Web Servers option in the Web Manager window (see Figure 14-4). You'll see a window similar to Figure 14-5 after entering your user name and password.

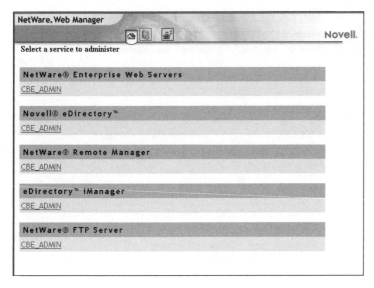

**Figure 14-4**    Selecting a service to administer in Web Manager
*When using NetWare 6.5, you will see the NetWare 6.5 Welcome as shown in Figure D-17.*

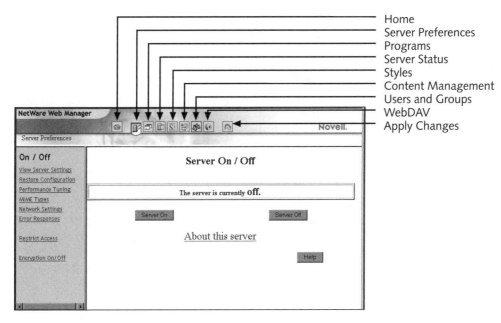

**Figure 14-5**    The Server Preferences window
*NetWare 6.5 uses Apache Manager as described in Appendix F.*

The buttons described in Table 14-2 are displayed across the top of the menu bar and represent different configuration windows.

**Table 14-2**   Enterprise Web Server Configuration Buttons

| Button Name | Description |
|---|---|
| Server Preferences | Use this option to start and stop the Web server and set the following configuration options (refer to Figure 14-5):<br>• View Server Settings<br>• Restore Configuration<br>• Performance Tuning (such as enabling DNS and caching)<br>• MIME (Multipurpose Internet Mail Extensions) Types<br>• Network Settings (such as server name, port number, and IP address)<br>• Error Responses<br>• Restrict Access<br>• Encryption On/Off |
| Programs | Use this option to set the common gateway interface (CGI) directory and file types and activate server-side Java script processing. |
| Server Status | Use this option to monitor current Web server activity and view error, archive, and access logs. |
| Styles | Use this option to set and change style sheets for Web Services. |
| Content Management | Use this option to set the current content directory path and user document directories and to create and manage virtual Web sites. |
| Users and Groups | Use this option to configure the directory service the Web server will use when authenticating users. Options include using a local database, the LDAP server, or eDirectory. |
| WebDAV | Use this option to check the status of the Web Distributed Authoring and Versioning (WebDAV) service and turn WebDAV services on or off. WebDAV allows users to edit and manage files located on a remote Web server. |
| Apply Changes | Use this option to apply the changes you have made to the currently running Web service. If this button is not clicked, the changes are not made until after the system is restarted. |

There are many configuration options and settings, but the most common tasks for network administrators are starting and stopping Web Services, changing the default path to the content directory, creating virtual Web sites, configuring document preferences, and setting up public and restricted access sites. The following sections explain how to perform these tasks. When changing the Web server's configuration parameters, remember to always save and apply the changes. To submit changes made to a form, click the Save button and then click the Save and Apply button. To reject your changes, click the Cancel button.

## Starting and Stopping Web Services

After selecting the NetWare Enterprise Web Servers option and logging in, the Server Preferences window is displayed, with options on the left side of the window to open different configuration windows. For example, in Figure 14-5 the Server Preferences window displays the Server On/Off window. Notice that the Enterprise Web server initially is set to "on." To start Enterprise Web Server, you simply click the Server On button and then click OK when the browser displays the Success message box. Sometimes you need to stop the Web server before making configuration changes; to do this, click the Server Off button or enter NSWEBDN at the NetWare 6 Server Console screen. To restart the server, click the Server On button in the Web Manager window or enter the NSWEB command at the NetWare 6 Server Console screen.

## Changing the Path of the Default Web Content

After verifying that your server is operating properly, you might need to move the Web site's contents from the default location, which is the SYS:Novonyx\SuiteSpot\Docs directory, to a directory located on a different volume. By default, the Web content directory is located on the SYS volume, which can be a problem if the Web site grows to the point that the SYS volume fills and crashes your system. To move the content directory for the CBE site, David used these steps in Web Manager:

1. He clicked the Content Management button on the NetWare Web Manager toolbar to display the Primary Document Directory window, shown in Figure 14-6.

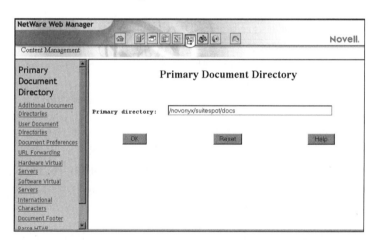

**Figure 14-6**    The Primary Document Directory window
*NetWare 6.5 uses Apache Manager as described in Appendix F.*

2. He entered the new path in the Primary directory text box and clicked OK to display the change window.

3. He clicked the Save and Apply button to save the new content directory path and apply the path to the Web server.

## Creating a Virtual Document Directory

If your company plans to run its own Web site, you might want to create a virtual document site so that departments can keep their own specialized content in a separate subdirectory of the main IS\Web content directory. For example, the CBE Labs DNS server

**14**

could have a host record called *www.cbeadmin.com* and Personnel employees could access the virtual document site called Personnel by entering *www.cbeadmin.com/personnel* as the URL. To configure NetWare Enterprise Web Server to use a virtual directory named Personnel, David used these steps in NetWare Web Manager:

1. He clicked the Content Management button on the toolbar, and then clicked the Additional Document Directories link to display the Additional Document Directories window (see Figure 14-7).

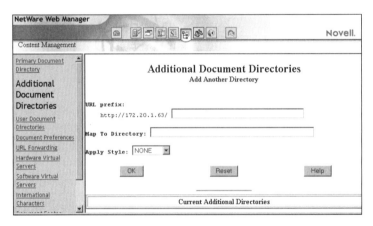

**Figure 14-7**    The Additional Document Directories window
*NetWare 6.5 uses Apache Manager as described in Appendix F.*

2. He entered Personnel in the URL prefix text box and entered the path to the Personnel directory in the Map To Directory text box.

3. After verifying that the entries were correct, he clicked OK and then clicked the Save and Apply button to apply the changes to the currently running Web server and return to the Web Manager window.

## Configuring Document Preferences

When NetWare Enterprise Web Server receives a request from a browser that does not specify the name of a page file, it uses a default index filename specified in the Document Preferences window (see Figure 14-8).

Given the configuration shown in Figure 14-8, if users enter the URL *http://cbeadmin.com* in their Web browsers, Enterprise Web Server sends back the contents of the Index.html file. You can specify multiple index filenames by separating the filenames with commas. With multiple filenames, Enterprise Web Server searches for the filenames in the order specified and then uses the first filename it finds as the home page.

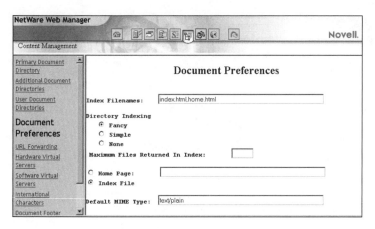

**Figure 14-8**    The Document Preferences window
*NetWare 6.5 uses Apache Manager as described in Appendix F.*

If no default index file is specified or none of the specified index filenames is found in the content directory, Enterprise Web Server can be configured to generate a page that lists all files found in the root of the document content directory and then send that listing to the Web browser. This option can be useful if you're preparing a Web site that allows users to select from multiple files. The following three directory-indexing options are available:

- *Fancy*—Generates a graphical icon that represents the type of file and includes the file size and date it was last modified. The disadvantage of using the Fancy directory indexing option is that it takes longer to prepare.

- *Simple*—Generates a simple list of filenames and returns it to the browser.

- *None*—No directory indexing will be performed. If the index filename is not found, Enterprise Web Server returns an error message.

## Setting Up Public and Restricted Access

After Enterprise Web Server is installed, anyone who accesses the server from a Web browser can open document files in the SYS:Novonyx\SuiteSpot\Docs directory or any of its subdirectories. This can be quite dangerous, and you should be aware of the possibility of unwanted intruders gaining entrance into your network through your Web site. For more details, see the "Firewall External Security" section later in this chapter. If you change the primary document directory, create additional document directories, or want to restrict access to documents, you need to click the Restrict Access link in the Server Preferences window and then scroll down to the Public Directory Designations list box (see Figure 14-9).

14

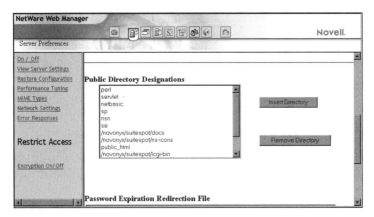

**Figure 14-9** Viewing the Public Directory Designations list box
*NetWare 6.5 uses Apache Manager as described in Appendix F.*

All users are given access to any directory in the Public Directory Designations list box. If the directory or filename being accessed exists but is not included in this list box, Enterprise Web Server displays a dialog box that asks the user to enter a user name and password for logging in. If the user account has at least Read and File Scan rights to the specified file, the Web server sends the file to the user's Web browser.

## Working with NetWare FTP Server

NetWare FTP Server is a Web Services application that enables users to transfer files to and from the NetWare volumes that have been configured as part of the FTP content. Why not use Web tools for this task, you ask? FTP, although a little rough around the edges, is still a great utility for quick file downloads and uploads and automated transfers of data that Web utilities cannot deliver. For example, you can write a script file that would download specific files from an FTP server at a specific time each day, extract and modify the data, and then upload the file to a different FTP server. Try doing that with one of the Web-based utilities, such as Web Manager or iManager.

After logging in to NetWare FTP Server, users can also navigate to other NetWare servers and volumes where they have access rights, even though the other servers are not running the FTP Server software. As with other Web-based services, FTP services require server and client components. FTP clients send requests for services to an FTP server, which then processes the request and returns results to the client. Clients connect to an FTP server by using an anonymous user name or by logging in with an authorized user name and password. Authorized users can be given access to resources that are not available to anonymous users. Typically, anonymous users are limited to downloading files and software from specific directories, whereas authorized users can upload files and access other restricted directories not available to anonymous users.

To access files on an FTP site, computers must have FTP client software. Most Web browsers have a built-in FTP client for accessing FTP servers with the URL *ftp://ip_address/dns_name*. In addition to the built-in FTP clients, a number of dedicated FTP clients are designed to work directly with FTP servers from various operating system and application environments. Many dedicated FTP clients enable the operator to enter commands directly from the FTP command prompt; other clients use a graphical environment to access the FTP server's files and directories. For example, FTP Explorer and CuteFTP are free for home and educational use. Table 14-3 compares the features and limitations of some commonly used FTP clients.

**Table 14-3**   FTP Clients

| FTP Client | Features | Limitations |
|---|---|---|
| CuteFTP (www.globalscape.com) | Easy to use and very reliable Graphical user interface Available in shareware and full versions | Limited options Does not use command prompts |
| Windows FTP command | Available by clicking Start, Run in Windows Uses command prompts | Does not have a graphical user interface More difficult to use |
| Internet Explorer | Easy access to FTP sites from the Internet Explorer Web browser | Limited commands |

Setting up NetWare FTP Server requires installing the FTP software on the NetWare 6 server and then configuring the software to provide access to the content directories. David used the following steps to install FTP on his server:

1. First, he inserted the NetWare 6 CD into the CBE_ADMIN server, pressed Ctrl+Esc, and entered the appropriate number to select the System Console screen.

2. He entered the command CDROM and pressed Enter to mount the CD as a volume on the server.

3. After mounting the NETWARE6 Installation volume, he pressed Ctrl+Esc and entered the appropriate number to select the X Server - Graphical Console.

4. At the graphical console, he clicked Novell and then Install to display the Installed Products window.

5. He clicked Add to display the Source Path window, clicked the browse button to select the NETWARE6 volume, and then clicked OK. He clicked OK again in the Source Path window to copy installation files to the server, and the Components window was displayed with check marks indicating the default installed components.

**14**

6. He clicked Clear All to prevent reinstalling existing components, clicked the NetWare FTP Server check box, and clicked Next to display the login window.

7. He entered his CBEAdmin user name, password, and .CBE_LABS context in the corresponding text boxes, and then clicked OK to display the LDAP Configuration window.

8. In the LDAP Configuration window, he clicked the Allow Clear Text Passwords check box, and then clicked Next to display the Summary window.

9. After verifying that the NetWare FTP Server and NetWare Port Resolver components were listed, he clicked Finish.

10. David received a Product Conflict message box informing him that LDAP Services version 3.20.0 was already installed and asking whether he wanted to replace the current version with the version being installed. Because the version numbers of the LDAP service being installed were the same as or older than the version currently on his system, he clicked No when asked if he wanted to replace the existing version.

11. After file copying was finished, the Installation complete window displayed the option to view the Readme file. He clicked Close to exit the FTP Server installation program and return to the X Server - Graphical Console.

The FTP service enables administrators to set access restrictions for containers and users in the SYS:\Etc\Ftprest.txt file. Restriction lines in the Ftprest.txt file contain the name of the entity and one of the following access restrictions:

- *DENY*—Denies access to the FTP server for the specified user or container.

- *READONLY*—Gives read access rights to the specified client.

- *NOREMOTE*—Restricts access to allow only local access to the client.

- *GUEST*—Allows the specified client to have only the permissions given to the Guest user account.

- *ALLOW*—Gives the specified client read and write access to the FTP server directory.

If you do modify the FTP server restrictions file, be aware of the following:

- Each line can have only one entity and its corresponding access rights. For example, the following line would give all users in the .CBE container Read Only rights to the FTP server:

  `*.CBEADMIN READONLY`

- The entities are assigned rights in the order they appear in the restriction file. If different rights apply to the same entity, those that appear last in the restriction file apply.

- If the restriction file is empty or does not exist, access is given to all users.

If David wanted to allow users in the InfoSystems OU to use FTP Server to upload files but restrict other users to Read Only access, he would edit the Ftprest.txt file in the SYS:\Etc directory using Notepad, as shown in Figure 14-10.

**Figure 14-10**    Editing the FTP restrictions file

## Accessing FTP Folders and Files

After FTP Server is up and running, you can use any FTP client to log in to the FTP server and transfer files. Use any Web browser and simply enter the URL ftp://*ip_address* (replacing *ip_address* with the IP address of your server), click the Login Anonymously check box, enter your e-mail address, and then click Login to see a window displaying all files available on the site. To enable FTP Server logging, open a Web browser and enter https://*ip_address*:2200 (replacing *ip_address* with the address of your server), click your server name under the NetWare Enterprise Web Server heading, enter your administrative user name and password, and click the Log Settings link in the column on the left (see Figure 14-11). Enabling FTP Server logging is highly recommended because you can use logging to monitor your system and look for any inconsistencies or possible break-in attempts. You can configure FTP security by clicking the Security link in the Server Preferences window (see Figure 14-12).

14

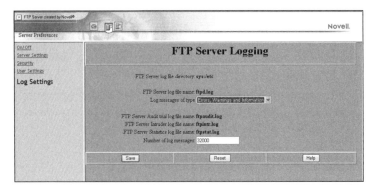

**Figure 14-11** The FTP Server Log Settings window

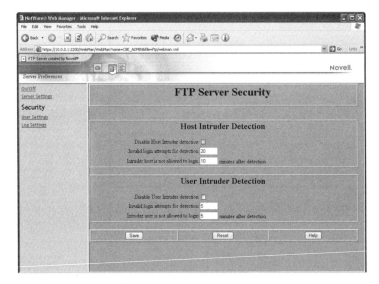

**Figure 14-12** The FTP Server Security window

Some additional features of NetWare FTP Server include the following:

- *Multiple instances of the FTP Server software*—Multiple instances of FTP Server can be loaded on the same NetWare server, providing different FTP services to different sets of users.

- *FTP access restrictions*—FTP access can be restricted at different levels through various types of access rights.

- *Intruder detection*—An intruder host or user who tries to log in with an invalid password can be detected and restricted.

- *Remote server access*—FTP users can navigate and access files from other NetWare servers in the same eDirectory tree and from remote servers, whether or not the remote servers are running FTP Server.

- *Special Quote Site commands*—These NetWare-specific commands can be used to change or view some of the NetWare server-specific parameters.

- *Firewall support*—When the FTP client is behind a firewall and the FTP server cannot connect to the FTP client, FTP Server supports passive mode data transfer and the configuration of a range of passive data ports. (Firewalls are discussed in the "Firewall External Security" section later in this chapter.)

- *Active sessions display*—You can view details of all active FTP instances at a particular time, such as a list of all instances, details of each instance, all sessions in an instance, and all details of each session.

- *Namespace support*—FTP Server can operate in both DOS and long namespaces. FTP users can dynamically change the default namespace by using one of the Quote Site commands.

- *Simple Network Management Protocol (SNMP) error-reporting service*—SNMP traps are issued when an FTP login request comes from an intruder host or from a node address restricted through eDirectory. The traps can be viewed on the management console.

- *Welcome banner and message file support*—FTP Server displays a welcome banner when an FTP client establishes a connection and displays a message file when a user changes the directory in which the file exists.

- *NetWare Web Manager management*—NetWare Web Manager can be used to administer (start and stop) the FTP server and to configure server, security, user, and log settings. These settings can then be modified from a client workstation by using a Web browser. You can also get information, such as the current server status, by viewing different logs through the Web Manager interface.

- *Cluster Services Support*—Running FTP Server on Novell Cluster Services provides benefits such as automatic restart without user intervention in case of a node failure in the cluster.

**14**

## WORKING WITH CERTIFICATE SERVICES

Providing security is a critical part of implementing services across a public network such as the Internet. In previous chapters, you have learned how file system and eDirectory security use trustee assignments to grant users the rights they need to access data and manage network objects, but still prevent unauthorized access. **Public key cryptography** is a security system that authenticates users and organizations to ensure that they are who they claim to be, and encrypts data transmissions to prevent information from being intercepted by unauthorized people. Table 14-4 shows how public key cryptography relates to file system and eDirectory security.

**Table 14-4** Network Security Systems

| Security System | Description |
|---|---|
| eDirectory security | Uses a system of granting and withholding rights to containers and objects in the eDirectory tree |
| File system security | Uses a system of granting and withholding rights to directories and files in the file system to control access to data |
| Role Based security | Assigns users to roles with a predefined set of operations the users can perform within a specified context |
| Public key cryptography | Uses authentication and encryption to secure communication and transmissions between senders and receivers |

Public key cryptography provides both authentication and encryption security through the use of mathematically related sets of digital codes called key pairs. A key pair consists of a public and private key that is unique to a person, an application, or an organization. The **private key** is kept solely by the owner of the key pair and used to create digital signatures and to encrypt and decrypt data. The **public key** is made available to all network users and used by outside entities to encrypt data sent to the key pair owner. The received data can be decrypted and read only by using the owner's corresponding private key. The owner of a key pair also uses the private key to create digital signatures. Just as a personal signature on a paper document authenticates it, a digital signature is used to authenticate an electronic document as being from a specific user or an organization. To create a digital signature, the cryptography software mathematically links the data being signed with the sender's private key. The receiver of the data can then use the sender's public key to verify the digital signature, as illustrated in Figure 14-13.

Workstation

Bank server

Transfer request
and signature

1. You authorize the transfer using your banking application.

2. Your application creates a digital signature for the transfer request using your *private* key (which only your application can access).

3. The application then sends the request and your digital signature to your bank.

4. Your bank's computer receives the request and your digital signature.

5. A system operator then validates your signature against the request using your *public* key.

If the results compute correctly, the signature is authenticated.

If not, the signature, the message, or both are assumed to be fraudulent, and the transaction is denied.

**Figure 14-13**   Digital signature authentication

An important part of public key cryptography is verifying that the public key used to encrypt data and check digital signatures is actually from the person or organization it claims to represent. One method of providing reliable public keys is to actually meet with the person or organizational representative and then exchange public keys using a physical medium, such as a floppy disk. However, this method is not feasible for e-mailing a large number of people or conducting e-commerce with other organizations, so a more efficient, practical method—the Certificate Authority (CA) service—was developed to mediate the exchange of public keys. In this service, the public key cryptography software running on an entity creates a public and private key pair. To get the public key authorized, an entity needs to send its public key and other identification information to a CA. The CA validates an owner's key pair by creating a certificate containing the owner's public key along with the CA's digital signature. As illustrated in Figure 14-14, the CA is responsible for verifying that the requesting entity's identity is established before validating the requester's public key certificate.

14

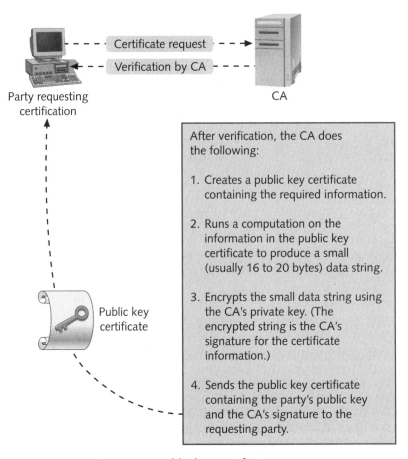

**Figure 14-14**   Creating a public key certificate

At a minimum, public key certificates contain the entity's public key, a subject name, and a CA-generated digital signature. Public key certificates generated by most commercial CAs use the X.509v3 format and contain the following information:

- The name of the user or organization (subject name)
- The public key of the user or organization
- The length of time the public key certificate is valid
- The name of the CA that signed the public key certificate (issuer)
- The digital signature created by the CA

Before using an entity's public key to encrypt data or verify a digital signature, the cryptography service running on the user's workstation checks the digital signature on the public key certificate against a list of known CAs. If the digital signature is not recognized as coming from a known CA, the cryptography service either discards the data or asks the user if he or she wants to trust the entity issuing the public key.

When planning cryptography services, determine the type of CA service your applications and users will require. The two basic types of CA services are external and internal. When using an external CA service, you need to submit requests for public key certificates to recognized organizations, which verify your identity and provide a public key certificate that can be imported into applications and clients. Using recognized external CAs is important for Web servers and other Internet services that deliver information and services to the public sector. By using public key certificates signed by recognized external CAs, your public keys will be trusted by any Web browser, thus making e-commerce transactions easier and less risky for users. On the other hand, obtaining signed public key certificates from external CAs can be expensive and time consuming when implementing internal applications and services.

Internal CA services run on a local server and can be used to automatically issue and sign public key certificates for applications and services available to authorized users of the network. For example, transactions between Novell OneNet utilities and Web Services running on a NetWare 6 server take place using public key certificates issued and signed by the internal Novell Certificate Server on the NetWare 6 server. In the next section, you learn about Novell Certificate Server and its functions.

## Novell Certificate Server

Novell Certificate Server, included with NetWare 6, integrates public key cryptography services into eDirectory and enables administrators to create, issue, and manage user and server certificates. It helps network administrators meet the challenges of public key cryptography with the following functions:

- Creating an Organizational CA in the eDirectory tree that allows your CA server to internally issue user and server certificates without going to an external CA, thereby reducing costs and the time needed to implement Net Services for your organization

- Storing key pairs in the eDirectory tree to provide security against unauthorized access and tampering, yet make public keys available to all network entities

- Allowing centralized management of public key certificates through ConsoleOne snap-ins

- Supporting commonly used e-mail clients and Web browsers

Novell Certificate Server consists of PKI.NLM (a NetWare Loadable Module) and a snap-in module for ConsoleOne that administrators use to request, manage, and store public key certificates and their associated key pairs in the eDirectory tree. In other words, PKI.NLM provides a set of services that integrate with eDirectory and interface with Novell International Cryptographic Infrastructure (NICI) so that companies will have a PKI (Public Key Infrastructure) in place on their networks. PKI refers to the technology, cryptographic framework, and services required to generate and store those public-private key pairs.

**14**

Using Novell Certificate Server, administrators can establish an Organizational CA that is specific to their organization's eDirectory tree. Because NICI is used to support all cryptography and signature functions, a single version of Novell Certificate Server can be used throughout an organization's entire intranet. NICI must be installed on both the Novell server and client to provide secure, two-way communication between applications using public key cryptography.

Novell Certificate Server is installed by default on the first NetWare 6 server installed in a tree. If an eDirectory tree already contains an older version of the Novell CA, you need to upgrade the existing certificate server to the latest NetWare 6 CA version before installing the new NetWare 6 server. You can use ConsoleOne to perform the following CA management tasks:

- Create a Server Certificate object for the server

- Request a public key certificate from an external CA

- Create a user certificate

- Create trusted root containers and objects

## SECURING NET SERVICES

Making Net Services and information available on the Internet exposes the NetWare server and user workstations to potential attacks on an organization's information system. Undoubtedly, security has become an issue for everyone. Whether it be a cyber-terrorist or a 15-year-old with lots of time on his hands, hackers, crackers, and other intruders are making network administration more complex.

Is it possible to protect your networks from outsiders? Can a security system with firewalls, proxy servers, and encryption software guarantee a secure network? Unfortunately, the answer to both questions is no. (Unless, of course, you unplug your network cable from the wall jack.) However, you can make the potential attacker work harder to get into your system than someone else's. Just as a car thief would walk to the next car if yours had a better alarm system, most hackers would jump to an easier system if yours proved to be a more formidable adversary.

Although public key cryptography secures data through encryption and identifies entities with digital signatures, it does not prevent outside hackers from attacking your system and gaining unauthorized access to network services and data. As network and data communications have become more complex, so has the level of attacks against their operations. The most common types of hacker attacks on information systems can be divided into the following general categories:

- *Intrusion*—The most common type of attack, **intrusion** involves an unauthorized person gaining access to the system through the illegal use of another user's account. Often, intruders get access to user names and passwords from knowledge gained from insiders, through guesswork, or with software that can break down passwords using mathematical or random processes. Unless users see the importance of protecting their passwords against intruders, your job becomes extremely difficult. Users who leave their passwords written on Post-Its and pasted to their keyboards or monitors make the job of protecting a network almost impossible. As an administrator, you must convince users that this behavior could jeopardize the company's data and that a hacker could log on with one of their passwords and use the system to attack government or business sites. Law enforcement authorities could then believe that your user was the culprit. Also, if potential intruders can gain access to the server console, they might be able to change the administrator's password or download a file containing user names and encrypted passwords. They can later enter this file into a program that attempts to decrypt passwords with a variety of techniques. You can best prevent intrusion by physically securing the servers and ensuring that users have passwords of at least eight characters. These measures are discussed in the "Internal Security" section later in this chapter.

- *Social engineering*—After convincing your users not to give their password information to anyone, your next step is teaching them how to resist the temptation of giving information to people outside the organization. Experts in **social engineering** are able to gather information from employees by simply behaving in a friendly manner and giving the false impression of having authority over your computers and networks. For example, an attacker could say he was with the ISO troubleshooting branch (a bogus organization) and that he has been hearing of complaints that the network response time is slow. "Are there multiple operating systems in use currently?" he asks. Your user answers, "I'm not sure, I just use NetWare 6. I think there may be others, too." This information is useful to the would-be hacker. He now knows the operating system your company uses and would then ask for the names of other employees who might be of assistance. After the intruder gets additional names, the next phone call would be more like the following: "Hello, Ted. Mike from Systems said you're the guy I need to speak with about network security." An even bolder attacker might say "Hello, Ted. I need the Telnet password of your router to add a restriction list. It should take only a few minutes." Many people have successfully used these tricks, including a world-renowned computer crime investigator. Educate your users not to give information to anyone except authorized IT personnel from your company, and tell them to refer all phone calls about system questions to you.

- *Spoofing*—Using underhanded or illegal means to gain access to a computer or network by masquerading as an authorized user or entity is called **spoofing**. This process often involves sending packets to a server that have been modified to make it seem as though they originated from an authorized entity. Spoofing was once the province of more sophisticated hackers, but hundreds of hacking sites now supply step-by-step instructions on how to manipulate the IP packets

**14**

you learned about in Chapter 3. Public key encryption helps prevent spoofed packets by requiring a digital signature that can be authenticated only by using the public key supplied by the actual entity. Because the intruder does not have the actual entity's private key, digital signatures cannot be spoofed.

- *Virus attacks*—**Viruses** are programs or macros embedded in other software or e-mail attachments. When the program or e-mail is opened, the virus code runs. Like viruses in the real world, computer viruses can spread to other computers on the network by embedding themselves in network software or sending e-mail messages to users in the infected computer's address list. Viruses can simply be nuisances that slow down a computer, or they can be more serious, attacking the local computer's software and causing data loss and system crashes. In the "Protection Against Virus Attacks" section later in this chapter, you learn more about the types of computer viruses and the measures you can take to prevent or reduce the spread of viruses on your network.

- *Denial-of-service attacks*—Although less common than intrusion or virus attacks, **denial-of-service attacks** can prevent users from accessing network services. These attacks are usually caused by a bombardment of packets sent to a server from someone without authorized access. The packet bombardment overloads memory or CPU time, causing legitimate users' connection requests to be denied. It can also be as simple as flooding a company's mail server with more e-mails than it can handle, causing the mail server to shut down. An Army base's e-mail system was shut down when a user accidentally sent an e-mail message with a graphic attachment to 4000 recipients. Most denial-of-service attacks, however, are intentional. In the "Defense Against Denial-of-Service Attacks" section, you learn about some of the common denial-of-service attacks and how you can reduce the likelihood of these attacks.

- *Information theft*—This type of attack involves illegally intercepting and reading information transmitted between computers through the use of wiretaps and sniffer software. **Information theft** is also referred to as a man-in-the-middle attack because the two computers transferring data to each other are not aware that someone is monitoring, and possibly modifying, the data as it traverses the network. The best defenses against information theft are implementing public key cryptography and keeping sensitive data on isolated or private networks.

Now look at a security plan that you can implement to protect your company from both internal and external attacks. Figure 14-15 illustrates a multiple-level security system that Ted designed for the CBE Labs network.

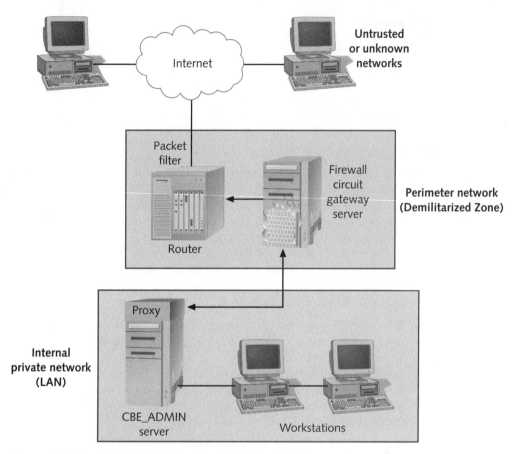

**Figure 14-15**    CBE Labs Internet security

The security plan consists of two major layers. The outer perimeter, also referred to as the Demilitarized Zone (DMZ), is where packets from the outside world first enter the CBE network. The inner layer consists of the local area network, which is secured with file system and eDirectory security, as described in previous chapters. The DMZ, the area most vulnerable to attacks, is where the Internet router and firewall software are located. If the firewall server finds no anomalies in a packet, the packet is passed to the internal router and then relayed to the appropriate service. Rather than expose the CBE_ADMIN server to attacks in the DMZ, David can install another NetWare server that would run firewall software, such as Novell's BorderManager, that includes firewall, packet filter, and proxy server components.

## Internal Security

Internal security involves placing the NetWare servers in secure locations and making sure all users have adequate passwords of at least eight characters that are changed periodically. (See Chapter 9 for more information on login security.) Depending on the nature of your business, this period could range from every two weeks to every six months. Internal security also involves making proper file system and eDirectory trustee assignments, as described in Chapter 10. The following list describes some precautions you should consider to protect your network:

- Ensure that server rooms are kept locked at all times. If unauthorized people have physical access to the server, they could load software from a disk, switch the server into debug mode to modify system settings, change the server time, or shut down the server. No matter what kind of complex password or encryption you might have on a server, any security specialist will tell you this: If they can sit in front of it, they can hack it. In some organizations, the server can be further secured by removing input devices, such as the keyboard and mouse, and even removing the monitor. The server is then remotely managed with Netware Remote Manager.

- Workstation monitors throughout your organization should not be visible from behind the user. In other words, try to position all workstations so that users are facing visitors to their cubicle or office. Many people can observe keystrokes and figure out passwords as they are entered. If some of your users have information that must be protected from others in the organization, suggest removable hard disks, which can easily be removed at the end of the day and locked in a safe or secure area.

- Keep all wiring closets locked and restrict their access to very few people in your organization. Category 5 cable is extremely susceptible to "tapping." In fact, many organizations were hacked into during the late 1980s by an inexpensive device called Mr. Microphone. The wireless microphone would output a user's voice to an AM/FM radio. An intruder could place this device over network cabling and then retrieve logins and passwords from a car radio. Technology has improved on such gadgetry, making it even easier to tap cables.

- Provide extra security by using the console screen saver and SECURE CONSOLE commands. You can activate the console screen saver by entering the command SCRSAVER on the system console and then supplying a password. To access the server console and enter commands, you provide the screen saver password or the Admin user password. The SECURE CONSOLE command provides the following security:
  - Requires that all NLMs be loaded from the SYS:System directory to prevent someone from loading software on the server with a floppy disk

- Prevents keyboard entry into the operating system debugger, which enables knowledgeable operators to change operating system configurations, thus potentially gaining access to data or shutting down the server

- Prevents the server date and time from being changed

- Change user password restrictions to require a password of at least eight characters that's changed every 60 days. Many password-cracking software programs are available to anyone who can connect to the Internet. One such brute-force program can go through approximately one million dictionary words in a couple of minutes. The program, called Imp 2.0, can be run against the Partitio.nds file (a NetWare 4.x file) and is very easy to use. Even more troubling, it's free and can be downloaded from *www.wastelands.gen.nz/*. You should be aware of such things because the only way to protect your network is to know what bored 15-year-olds know. After all, nothing is more embarrassing than having a teenager tell you the latest and greatest ways to hack a NetWare 6 server. The best protection is longer passwords that consist of alphabetic, special, and numeric characters. With each extra password character, the number of possible combinations goes up exponentially. Users should also be trained on how to create complex passwords with little or no effort because many users panic when they have to change their passwords. Here are some suggestions:

  - If the user is a musician, chords make good passwords, such as C#Dominant7 or CMajor7#5.

  - A baker or cook can use recipes, such as 1cupFlour! or 2CupsMilk! (The exclamation point is a special character that makes the password much more difficult to crack.)

- Many administrators get lazy and leave it up to the user to create passwords. Some resort to random password generator programs. If this is your approach, don't be surprised when most users continue to use simple passwords because they think it will be too difficult to remember complex ones. Show your users that this is not the case. Also, the chances are high that passwords given to a user from a password generator program will be written on Post-It notes and stuck to the monitor or keyboard.

- Review file system and eDirectory security to ensure that users have only the rights they need to perform their assigned tasks.

## Common Internal Security Violations

Despite a good security plan and documentation, it's possible for users to gain excessive rights to your system and compromise network security, through an error in trustee assignments or by unauthorized access. Users could gain unauthorized access rights to your network system in the following ways:

- Password security is your front-line defense against internal security violations. If intruders learn the password for the Admin or another user account,

**14**

they could gain unauthorized access to the network. You can implement NetWare's intruder detection option to prevent guessing at passwords and place time and station restrictions on security-sensitive user accounts to prevent intruders from logging in during off-hours or from remote workstations. (These options are described in Chapter 9.)

■ Despite your best planning and documentation, user accounts might be assigned unauthorized rights to the eDirectory tree or file system. Although administrators could inadvertently make errors in trustee assignments, intruders can make incorrect rights assignments if they have access to the server or an administrative workstation that has been left logged in. The best protection against this type of attack is to physically secure the server and always log out or lock your administrative workstation when away from your desk. In addition, you should periodically check trustee assignments and use one of the following tools to track internal security compromises:

- Novell Advanced Audit Service, included with NetWare 6, can help you track unauthorized or unusual actions by configuring policies in eDirectory containers that record certain user actions. For example, you can configure auditing to record such events as logging in with certain user accounts (such as Admin), creating objects, changing passwords or other user properties, and opening, deleting, and modifying files.

- BindView Solutions for Novell from the BindView Corporation (*www.bindview.com*) can help automate the search for user objects with too many rights and rogue Admin user accounts. The bv-Control product features the BindView RMS Console, which reports on and administers almost all aspects of network servers. Using bv-Control for eDirectory, you can perform security checks across the eDirectory tree for possible security or configuration vulnerabilities, and use the bv-Control ActiveAdmin technology to resolve any security problems. With BindView tools, you can get effective rights information and reports in minutes, generate policy compliance reports for your management staff, and check server configuration settings for potential problems.

■ Another possible security compromise involves creating a rogue Admin account that has the Supervisor right to the eDirectory tree. Typically, these accounts are created by an intruder running a program on the server console or from an administrative workstation left logged in and unlocked. One method used to create rogue Admin accounts is through the old NetWare bindery database used to store user accounts and access rights. To maintain compatibility with earlier NetWare servers, NetWare 6 still maintains a bindery database. If a Supervisor user is created in the bindery database, that account can gain the same rights to the tree as the Admin user. For example, an NLM called BURGLER.NLM can create a hidden Supervisor account in the bindery with the same rights as the eDirectory tree Admin user. This NLM can be downloaded from the Internet at no cost and is defined as a tool that administrators can use if they forget their Admin passwords. Because BURGLER.NLM must be run from the server console, the best prevention is to physically secure the server and use the SECURE CONSOLE and SCRSAVER commands to limit access to the Server Console prompt.

When an internal security problem is identified, you must know how to identify and correct it. When tracing internal security violations involving excessive rights, follow these steps to track the problem to the source:

1. Identify the user account with excessive rights and the directory or container where the rights are being used.

2. Identify the effective rights of the user in the directory or container.

3. Identify any groups the user is associated with.

4. Use ConsoleOne to display the trustee assignments in the directory or container where the user has excessive rights. Check whether the user is a trustee of the directory or container. If necessary, remove or change the user's trustee assignment.

5. Verify that the user is not security-equivalent to any other users in the trustee list for the directory or container you check in ConsoleOne.

6. Identify any groups that are trustees of the directory or container being checked. If the user is a member of a group that's granting excessive rights, remove the user from that group and then make sure he or she has only the rights needed to perform the task.

7. Check for any trustee assignments being granted to Organizational Role objects. If an Organizational Role object is a trustee, determine whether the user in question is an occupant of that organizational role. If necessary, remove the user from any roles granting excessive rights.

8. Move up one directory or container level and repeat Steps 4 through 7.

9. Continue working up the directory structure or eDirectory tree until you reach the root of the volume or tree.

10. If working with the file system, and the user has the Supervisor right at the root of the volume, check the user's effective rights to the Server object in the eDirectory tree. If the user has the Write attribute right to the Server object's ACL property, he or she will inherit the Supervisor right to all volumes on that server.

**14**

## Firewall External Security

Outside the network environment, firewalls often separate people and equipment from possible dangers. For example, an automobile's firewall separates the potentially explosive engine from the driver. In computing environments, firewalls are used in a similar way to protect your computer and data from the potential hazards of the Internet. Computer firewalls control access between the company's private network and an untrusted external entity on the Internet. **Firewalls** consist of software that run on a server or specialized hardware, such as a network router. You can configure the firewall to provide protection from external threats in the following ways:

- Enforce corporate security and access control policies by controlling the type of traffic permitted between the internal private network and the Internet.

- Keep log files of information about external traffic to better monitor the source and frequency of unauthorized access attempts.

- Provide a central point that all network traffic must pass through before reaching the internal private network. Having a single point of access eliminates the possibility of your network being open to external Internet users and allows you to redefine access policies in the event of any security breaches.

- Act as a traffic cop by permitting only selected services, such as FTP or WWW, to access the network.

- Create firewall partitions that limit security breaches or prevent intruder attacks from spreading across the company intranet.

A firewall's primary objective is to prevent entities on untrusted or unknown networks from accessing services and computers on the trusted or internal network. When configuring Internet security, the IS Department needs to identify the network address of each trusted and untrusted network. A **trusted network** consists of your organization's private network along with the firewall server and networks it covers; it can exist within the company intranet and include the network addresses of other computers and networks on the Internet that you regularly communicate and do business with. To avoid explicitly identifying trusted network addresses for users who need to get through the firewall to access services and resources on your internal network, you can implement a **virtual private network (VPN)**, which is a trusted network that sends packets over an untrusted network. An **untrusted network**, such as the Internet, is an external network whose administration and security policies are either unknown or out of your control. When you configure a firewall server, you can identify any untrusted networks that will interface with the firewall. An **unknown network** is neither trusted nor untrusted and, by default, is treated the same as an untrusted network. You can use firewall software to enable the following security measures on all untrusted and unknown networks:

- *Packet filtering*—A screening router often performs this process before allowing packets into the firewall server. **Packet filtering** looks at the destination and source IP addresses to determine whether the packet is from a trusted, untrusted, or unknown network. Packets from trusted networks are allowed into the internal network, but packets from other network addresses are routed through the firewall server. Packet filtering routers also record the interface from which the packet arrives or leaves. The Department of Defense is issued a list of IP addresses that are restricted from accessing government networks. The list is applied to routers, which check the source address of all packets attempting to enter the trusted network. This list, called an access list, looks like the following example. Although packet filtering can permit or deny a service, it cannot protect unsecured services from unauthorized access.

```
access-list 10 deny host 172.16.5.5
access-list 10 deny host 172.27.14.23
access-list 10 permit any
```

- The preceding code would restrict IP address 172.16.5.5 and 172.27.14.23 from entering the trusted network if the access list were applied to the router interface. (For more information about creating access lists, see the *CCNA Guide to Cisco Networking*, Course Technology: 2003, ISBN 0619034777.)

- *Virtual private networks (VPNs)*—VPNs enable two or more hosts to communicate over a public network using a secure channel. To maintain a secure channel, VPNs encrypt the data packets sent between hosts and provide for access controls. There are two basic types of VPNs: client and site. Client VPNs connect to the firewall using dial-in connections or through an ISP over the Internet. Site VPNs, which are usually for departments or external organizations, typically use dedicated network connections. Departments might use a VPN to create a secure connection across the company's private network or the Internet. For example, a college might want a VPN connection between departments across the campus network to prevent students who share the network from accessing confidential information, such as grades. Both intranet and Internet site VPNs can be implemented with the VPN server in the DMZ zone between the Internet and your private network or with the VPN server located on your private network behind the DMZ. VPN servers operating in the DMZ are easier to configure and require less overhead than setting up a VPN server behind the firewall. However, VPN servers in the DMZ are more difficult to secure and are at more risk from attacks than VPN servers on the private network.

- *Network Address Translation (NAT)*—This firewall technique, discussed in Chapter 6, translates private IP addresses used on the internal network to one or more registered IP addresses. NAT enables clients on the private internal network to access the Internet without having a "live" (registered) IP address. Not having an assigned IP address hides the client from outside entities, essentially hiding ports and services on the client from packets that originate

**14**

on the Internet. NAT does not require any special software on users' computers. The computers are simply configured to use the NAT server as their default gateway, causing all packets sent to Internet sites to be routed through the NAT server.

- *IPX/IP gateways*—These gateways perform the same basic function as NAT, with the addition of converting IPX protocol packets to IP. Using an IPX/IP gateway requires software on the client to place TCP/IP service requests inside IPX packets. The IPX packet is then sent to the gateway software, where the IP request is removed from the IPX packet and sent to the Internet. When a response is received, the IPX/IP gateway places the TCP/IP information in an IPX packet and returns it to the client. IPX/IP gateways allow the private internal network to use only the IPX protocol, thus totally isolating the internal network from the Internet.

- *Circuit-level gateways*—**Circuit-level gateways** usually run on a firewall server and inspect additional packet heading information, including type of service, port number, user name, and DNS name. Using service packet types enables these gateways to permit or deny connections to services based on the destination port number. Many hacker attacks are based on sending packets to open ports running on servers and workstations. Using a circuit-level gateway provides a means of stopping these packets from entering the private network. Because they operate at the session layer of the OSI model, circuit-level gateways have access to user information, so they can accept or reject packets based on the user name or group membership. Circuit-level gateways offer increased firewall security, but they might need special client software and are often slower than other firewall systems, such as NAT.

- *Proxy services*—By receiving and monitoring all network traffic, **proxy services** help prevent denial-of-service attacks and information theft and enable administrators to control most of the network traffic flowing through the firewall. If the security policy permits the client to contact the outside server, the proxy contacts the outside host on behalf of the client. Because proxy services are applications that operate by inspecting network packets at the application level, they are also referred to as "application-level gateways." A proxy service requires two components: the proxy server and the proxy client. The proxy server acts as the end server for service requests from the private network. The proxy clients run on user workstations and communicate with the proxy service rather than with untrusted or unknown networks. Clients from unknown or untrusted networks communicate through the proxy server to request access to FTP or Web Services. The proxy server checks the incoming packets and allows or disallows the packets based on the organization's security policy and procedures. Outgoing traffic is also routed through the proxy server. The proxy service determines the validity of the client's request based on the established security rules. If the policy prohibits contacting the outside server, the proxy rejects the request and informs the client of the policy violation.

As of this writing, Novell's software firewall, called BorderManager 3.7, is available for your NetWare 6 server. It is easy to use and makes protecting your internal and external network a breeze. You can set up alerts to notify you when possible attacks are being made and use BorderManager's Access Rule Definition tool, which enables you to define access rules to your network based on protocols, port numbers, source and destination IP addresses, and so forth. BorderManager has passed ICSA Labs (a company that sets standards for security products) firewall certification.

## Protection Against Virus Attacks

Viruses are often embedded in other programs or e-mail attachments. After a virus is activated by running the program or opening the e-mail attachment, it can copy itself to other programs or disk storage areas. Each virus has a different signature, which is a bit pattern made by the virus when it's embedded in a program or an e-mail attachment. Although viruses do not directly attack the NetWare operating system and services, they can use the server and network services, such as e-mail, to rapidly spread to other computers on the network. Firewalls offer security measures to help protect a network from information theft and attacks, but they are not designed to detect and prevent viruses from entering the network. When it comes to virus attacks, the best possible defense is knowing the types of virus software and how viruses enter a computer network. Viruses are classified based on how they infect computer systems:

- Boot sector viruses attack the boot record, master boot record, or file allocation table (FAT) of a hard or floppy disk. When the computer is booted from the infected disk, the virus is loaded into memory and from there copies itself to other programs, including those stored in shared directories on the server. The virus can also damage information on the local computer. Joshi and Michelangelo are examples of boot sector viruses.

- File viruses, also called Trojan horses, attack executable program files—files ending with .exe, .com, .sys, .drv, .dll, and .bin—by attaching themselves to the code in the program. The virus code waits in memory for the user to run another application and uses that event as a trigger to perform an action such as replicating itself or attacking the local computer. A Trojan horse is a destructive program often concealed as part of other software, such as a game or graphics application. Trojan horses can also contain software used for embezzlement, for example, and self-destruct after they have finished their operation.

- Macro viruses attack programs that run macros, such as spreadsheet and word-processing applications. These malicious macros start when the infected document or template is opened. The macro can erase or damage data and copy itself to other documents. A well-known example is the Melissa macro virus.

- Stealth viruses (the Tequila virus, for example) are able to disguise themselves to make it difficult for antivirus software to detect them. Passive stealth

**14**

viruses can increase the size of files while still evading detection by presenting the file's original size. Certain types of stealth viruses called encrypted viruses—Cascade, for instance—mask their code or virus signatures to make it difficult for antivirus software to detect them.

■ Polymorphic viruses are a rapidly growing type of stealth virus with built-in code to create random changes or mutations to their virus signatures, making reliable detection very difficult. SMEG is an example of a polymorphic virus.

■ Worms are independent programs that do not replicate; instead, they copy themselves to other computers over a network. Worms can infiltrate legitimate programs to alter or destroy data and degrade system performance. For example, a worm program could infect a bank's computer and initiate fund transfers to another account. Worm attacks are usually easier to identify and recover from than other types of viruses because there's only one copy of the program to search for and remove.

## Virus Prevention Techniques

Virus prevention on a network involves installing a virus protection system, making regular backups, and training users on how to reduce the risk of virus attacks. Virus protection systems scan programs on the server and user workstations and monitor program files as they are loaded to detect known virus signatures. In addition to scanning, most antivirus software warns the user of any activity that could be caused by a computer virus, such as modifying the disk boot sector or system settings.

Installing antivirus software is just half the battle, however; you must also make sure users know how their workstations might be affected by virus infections. Recognizing virus symptoms can help identify and remove new viruses before they propagate to other computers or cause more data loss. Your users should be trained to be aware of the following common symptoms of virus infection:

■ A computer that fails to start normally

■ Programs that do not start, or fail when using common commands

■ Changes in filenames or files that become inaccessible

■ Unusual words or graphics appearing on the monitor

■ Hard or floppy disks being unexpectedly formatted

■ Slow computer performance when loading or running software

To help protect against virus attacks, you should do the following:

■ Install NetWare-compatible antivirus software from one of the following vendors:

- NetShield from Network Associates (*www.mcafeeb2b.com*)

- Server Protect from Trend Micro (*www.antivirus.com*)

- Norton Antivirus Corporate Edition from Symantec (*www.symantec.com/nav*)
- Command Antivirus from Command Software Systems (*www.commandsoftware.com/products/netware.html*)

- Use the antivirus software vendor's Web site to keep the virus signature files up to date on servers and workstations.

- Configure the antivirus software to immediately send virus notifications to you and the workstation user.

- Enable the virus expiration warning to alert you when the signature files are out of date.

- Configure the server's virus-scanning software to scan both incoming and outgoing files of all types, including .exe, .dll, and .zip files.

- Install an antivirus software package that quarantines files to protect users from accessing a potentially infected file and spreading the virus.

- Train users on the importance of virus scans and, if possible, disable the option of canceling a virus check.

- Train users on common types of viruses and explain how they usually spread by running infected programs, opening e-mail attachments, booting from infected floppy disks, or downloading infected files from bulletin boards.

- Use Novell's ZENworks for Desktops to distribute the latest virus signature updates to all workstations.

- Create write-protected emergency boot floppy disks to be used if a workstation becomes infected or damaged by a virus. Keep the emergency boot floppy disks updated with the latest virus signature updates.

- Scan all incoming and outgoing e-mail messages and attachments.

- Develop a company policy to avoid downloading e-mail attachments and software that aren't work related.

- Configure the GroupWise server to filter and eliminate unsolicited "junk" e-mail that could contain a virus or malicious program.

- Train users on antivirus software operation and encourage them to install an antivirus software package on their home computers.

## Virus Removal Planning

Despite security measures and antivirus software, new viruses pop up almost daily. There's always the possibility that one could slip by your antivirus software and infect your network's computers. You can use the following procedure to isolate and remove the virus from all networked computers:

1. First, isolate all systems and floppy disks that were known to be, or suspected of being, infected with the virus.

**14**

2. Check the support site for the antivirus software to help determine the type of virus and find any suggested clean-up procedures.

3. Locate the clean floppy disk formatted with a boot system that was created earlier with the antivirus software. The clean boot disk also contains a copy of the virus-scanning software.

4. Use the clean boot disk to start all infected or suspect computers. This method ensures that no virus code is loaded into the computer memory.

5. Use the virus-scanning software on the clean boot disk to scan all physical and logical hard disks on each infected or suspect computer. Also, scan any floppy disks used with the suspect computers. During the scanning process, remove any viruses from the files and programs of infected computers.

6. After scanning and removing any virus code, restart the system and create a system backup that excludes any infected files on the workstations or server.

7. Viruses that infect program files can create problems because the virus might have replaced instructions in the program; often the program doesn't run correctly, or it might "hang" when loaded. To handle this problem, you should delete all infected programs and reload the software from the original CD. In the worst-case scenario, you might need to reformat the hard disk, reinstall the entire workstation, and restore the backups.

8. Finally, you should scan all the network drives and reload copies of the executable programs from backup tapes.

The server's boot sector and operating system files cannot be infected unless the server is started from an infected floppy disk. So you should scan all floppy disks before inserting them in the server and modify the server's CMOS to prevent it from starting from a floppy disk that might have been inadvertently left in the drive.

## Defense Against Denial-of-Service Attacks

Although denial-of-service attacks usually don't directly damage or steal a company's data, they can cost a company a lot of money by bogging down the organization's Web services, causing lost customer sales and reducing user productivity. Denial-of-service attacks are usually caused by flooding the server with packets or sending oversized packets to a service, making it crash. A properly configured firewall and software designed for Net Services security are the best defenses against denial-of-service attacks. Table 14-5 lists several known denial-of-service attacks that could affect your organization.

**Table 14-5**   Common Denial-of-Service Attacks

| Type of Attack | Description |
|---|---|
| Ping of death | The PING command is modified to send Internet Control Message Protocol (ICMP) ECHO packets that are longer than the 64 KB maximum defined in the TCP/IP RFC 791 standard. The extra bytes in the packet can cause unprotected TCP/IP software to overflow the buffer space, resulting in computer hang-ups or crashes. |
| Teardrop attack | The teardrop attack intentionally overlaps packet fragments, causing errors in fragment reassembly that can result in packets being resent repeatedly and flooding the server. |
| Land attack | The land attack sends packets with the same source and destination IP addresses, thereby flooding the service with an endless loop of packets being sent to the server. |
| SYN packet flooding | TCP connections require the following three-way handshake between the server and the client:<br>1. The client sends a packet in which the SYN flag is set in the TCP header.<br>2. The server sends a SYN/ACK (acknowledgment) packet back to the client.<br>3. The client sends an ACK packet so that data transmission can begin.<br>A TCP SYN denial-of-service condition is caused when the client fails to send the last ACK packet and intentionally sends successive TCP connection requests to the server, filling up the server's buffer. After the server's buffer is full, other client requests are rejected, resulting in a denial-of-service condition. |
| Oversized UDP packets | Like the ping of death, sending oversized UDP packets can result in buffer overflows that cause the server to hang or crash. |
| Smurf | Smurf attacks use the ICMP ECHO in response to PING broadcasts to flood the server. |

**14**

The ping of death is perhaps one of the best-known denial-of-service attacks. Normally, the Packet Internet Groper (PING) application is used as a diagnostic utility on TCP/IP networks to send ECHO packets to selected hosts and receive responses if the network and host are operational. By default, ECHO packets contain only 64 bytes of data, but the RFC standard allows up to 64 KB in a PING ECHO packet. The ping of death occurs when a PING command is sent to an IP host with more than 64 KB of data. Some older software cannot handle these large ECHO packets, which can cause the TCP/IP stack to overflow, thereby slowing down or crashing the server. It is the vendor's responsibility to ensure that its TCP/IP implementation can handle oversized ECHO packets. By going to Novell's Technical Information Web site at *http://support.novell.com*, you can verify that all of Novell's current TCP/IP products since NetWare 3.11 are designed to discard oversized packets without hanging or crashing. In addition, earlier 16-bit versions of the Novell client might pause for up to 15 seconds when receiving oversized PING packets.

Although the Novell TCP/IP stack is not affected by the teardrop attack, it might be affected by the land attack when the transport protocol is using UDP. The land attack could cause the server to hit 100% utilization. Novell currently has a TCP/IP stack fix that corrects this problem by dropping packets if the software determines that the source and destination IP addresses are the same and the IP address is not the loopback address (127.0.0.1). You can download the fix to the Ftcpsv01.exe file from the Novell site. Although this fix isn't necessary for a new NetWare 6 server, you will need to implement it on any older servers at your organization.

After ensuring that the system software in your organization has been updated to fix any known problems, your next step is to configure your firewall. If you have purchased BorderManager, you should configure its firewall to send security alerts for the following conditions and denial-of-service attacks:

- Security-sensitive NLMs being loaded or unloaded

- Oversized PING packets

- SYN packet flooding

- Oversized UDP packets

BorderManager alerts can detect many other types of denial-of-service attacks (smurf, teardrop, or land) because they all share common techniques, such as using ICMP ECHO packets, overlapping fragments, and packets with the same source and destination IP addresses to create server overloads.

## Chapter Summary

- An essential part of Novell's strategy for the future is to provide Internet services that enable clients and servers using diverse operating systems to be managed and accessed as one network. To do this, Novell has developed Net Services, which includes iFolder, NetStorage, iManager, Remote Manager, iPrint, and iMonitor. Because Net Services is written to run on top of the open-source Apache Web Server, the services can be implemented on other network operating systems, such as Windows 2000/XP, Windows NT, and Linux.

- NetWare Web Services includes Enterprise Web Server and FTP Server, which can be installed and customized to supply information and Web pages to the Internet and local intranet. The NetWare Web Manager portal is used to configure and manage both Enterprise Web Server and FTP Server. Typical Web server management tasks include specifying the primary document directory, creating virtual Web sites, setting document preferences, and specifying public and restricted access to Web content. FTP configuration tasks include setting the default FTP directory, providing anonymous access, and restricting user access to the FTP server.

❐ Using public key cryptography to encrypt data transmission and provide authentication with digital signatures is a vital component of securing information transmission on the Internet. Public key cryptography uses public and private keys to create digital signatures and encrypt and decrypt data transmissions. Clients use the public key to encrypt data, which can be decrypted only by the public key owner's private key.

❐ Certificate Authorities (CAs) issue public key certificates for verifying that the public key belongs to the entity distributing it. Clients receiving the public key certificate can then verify the owner's identity by trusting the CA's digital signature.

❐ Internet security involves protecting Web and Net Services from threats such as data theft, hacking, and computer viruses. An Internet security plan should include a firewall to isolate the internal network from the outside Internet and implement a virus protection and data recovery plan. Firewalls should be configured to detect denial-of-service attacks, such as the ping of death, SYN packet flooding, oversized UDP packets, teardrop attacks, and land attacks.

# KEY TERMS

**circuit-level gateway** — A firewall gateway that inspects packet heading information, including type of service, port number, user name, and DNS name.

**denial-of-service attack** — A form of network attack that loads the server with packets to shut down network services.

**extranet** — A network system that uses the Internet to connect different organizations for business transactions.

**firewall** — A point of access between an organization's internal private network and the Internet, used to filter packets and reduce the risk of unauthorized access to or malicious attacks on the organization's private network system and services.

**information theft** — A form of network attack that uses wire taps and sniffer software to illegally intercept data.

**intrusion** — A form of network attack that involves gaining unauthorized and illegal access to an organization's information, usually through obtaining a user's account and password.

**Java applet** — An application written in the Java programming language to run on a client workstation's Web browser.

**Java servlet** — An application written in the Java programming language to run on a Web server.

**Net Services** — A set of hardware and software components that work together to provide access to information services across the Internet or company intranet.

**Novell Portal Services (NPS)** — A Net Services component running on a NetWare server that provides customized pages or portals for users based on users' rights and personal style specifications.

14

**packet filtering** — A process performed by a screening router to determine whether a packet is from a trusted, untrusted, or unknown network.

**private key** — The digital key code used in public key cryptography that is kept solely by the owner and used to decode data and create digital signatures.

**proxy service** — A high-level firewall service that works at the application level to give clients on an organization's network both incoming and outgoing access to Internet services.

**public key** — The digital key code used in public key cryptography for clients to encrypt data being sent to a host and to verify a host's digital signature.

**public key cryptography** — An Internet security system that uses public and private keys to encrypt and decrypt data and create digital signatures for authenticating users.

**social engineering** — Social engineering can be regarded as "people hacking." Hackers use this technique to persuade targets to volunteer information or assistance instead of breaking into systems independently.

**spoofing** — A method of illegally accessing network resources or attacking a network service by creating falsified packets that appear to come from an authorized entity.

**trusted network** — A network with an IP address range that's known to be safe or can be controlled and monitored by your organization.

**unknown network** — A network that is not specified as a trusted or untrusted network in a firewall. Firewalls treat unknown networks as untrusted networks.

**untrusted network** — An IP address range that might contain hackers or other malicious entities. Packets from networks listed as untrusted are inspected by the network firewall.

**virtual private network (VPN)** — A trusted network that sends packets over an untrusted network, such as the Internet.

**virus** — A self-replicating program that can be embedded in software to propagate between computers and eventually can be triggered to affect computer performance or destroy data.

**Web Services** — A set of hardware and software components that provide WWW and FTP information services to clients located on the Internet or company intranet.

---

# REVIEW QUESTIONS

1. Which of the following OneNet utilities allows access to network data from a Web browser without adding a client to the user workstation?

   a. iPrint

   b. iManager

   c. NetStorage

   d. iFolder

2. Which of the following is an example of a Web Services component?

   a. FTP server

   b. portal services

   c. iFolder

   d. NetStorage

3. Tomcat is an example of which of the following?

   a. Web server

   b. Java servlet

   c. servlet engine

   d. FTP server

4. Which of the following Web servers does NetWare 6 use to provide Net Services? (Select all that apply.)

   a. Enterprise Web Server

   b. Apache Web Server

   c. Tomcat

   d. Web Manager

5. Which of the following provides customized Web pages to users based on their access rights and privileges?

   a. Web servers

   b. Novell Portal Services

   c. iManager

   d. Remote Manager

6. Java servlets require which of the following to run?

   a. Enterprise Web Server

   b. NetWare FTP Server

   c. NetWare Web Manager

   d. Tomcat

7. Which of the following is an example of a Java servlet?

   a. Tomcat

   b. Enterprise Web Server

   c. Novell Portal Services

   d. iFolder

8. The _____ button in the NetWare Enterprise Web Server management window is used to set access restrictions.

**14**

9. The _____ button in the NetWare Enterprise Web Server management window is used to identify a virtual Web document.

10. The _____ button in the FTP Server management window is used to configure anonymous user access.

11. In public key cryptography, which of the following keys is used to create digital signatures?

    a. public

    b. private

    c. digital

    d. certificate

12. In public key cryptography, which of the following keys is used to decrypt data packets?

    a. public

    b. private

    c. digital

    d. certificate

13. In public key cryptography, the CA is responsible for which of the following? (Select all that apply.)

    a. creating public and private keys

    b. encrypting data

    c. validating that users are who they claim to be

    d. signing and issuing public key certificates

14. Which of the following attacks involves sending very large ECHO packets?

    a. ping of death

    b. SYN packet flooding

    c. teardrop

    d. land

15. Which of the following attacks involves failure to send ACK packets?

    a. ping of death

    b. SYN packet flooding

    c. teardrop

    d. land

16. Which of the following is a form of firewall packet filtering that uses port number and service types?

    a. proxy filtering

    b. circuit-level gateway

    c. packet filtering

    d. ECHO filtering

17. Which of the following is a form of firewall security that checks only packet source IP addresses?

    a. proxy filtering

    b. circuit-level gateway

    c. packet filtering

    d. ECHO filtering

18. Which of the following is software that embeds into existing programs and e-mail messages?

    a. trojans

    b. viruses

    c. ICMP

    d. hacker

19. Firewalls can be used to screen all of the following except _____.

    a. land attacks

    b. oversized packets

    c. computer viruses

    d. SYN packet flooding

20. Which of the following is a firewall application that enables administrators to control most of the network traffic flowing in and out of the network?

    a. packet filtering

    b. circuit-level gateway

    c. proxy service

    d. VPN

21. Which of the following firewall technologies would be the best choice for your organization to control the type of information sent between the network and clients?

    a. proxy service

    b. circuit-level gateway

    c. NAT

    d. VPN

**14**

22. You are concerned about maintaining a secure channel when using the Internet to connect to servers in your facility. Which of the following firewall technologies should you implement?

a. NAT

b. circuit-level gateway

c. packet filtering

d. VPN

23. Which of the following firewall technologies can hide client IP addresses on a private network from the Internet?

a. packet filtering

b. circuit-level gateway

c. NAT

d. VPN

24. Which of the following are the three basic components of public key cryptography? (Select all that apply.)

a. VPN

b. CA

c. public and private keys

d. certificate signing request

25. Which of the following is *not* a firewall technology?

a. packet filtering

b. NAT

c. VPN

d. virus scanning

## HANDS-ON PROJECTS

In the following projects, you apply concepts and techniques from this chapter to implement Net and Web Services.

### Project 14-1: Identifying Net and Web Services

Identify each of the following types of servers as either a Web Services or a Net Services component. Briefly explain what makes each component a Net Service or a Web Service.

◘ iFolder

◘ Enterprise Web Server

- ☐ NetWare FTP Server
- ☐ Web Manager
- ☐ Novell Portal Services

## Project 14-2: Developing a Security Plan for CBE

The CBE facility is planning to implement FTP Server so that users can download software files. In this project, you develop a plan to secure the CBE facility from outside attacks. Your plan should include a diagram of the following network components and a brief description of what type of attacks you plan to prevent:

- ☐ Router
- ☐ Firewall
- ☐ CBE internal private network

# CASE PROJECTS

## Case Project 14-1: Developing a Virus Protection Plan

You have been assigned to research the antivirus software listed in this chapter, using the supplied URLs, and then make a recommendation that includes the vendor, product, and price for a 30-station network. Your recommendation should include two antivirus software packages and the reasons this antivirus software would make a good choice for the CBE network.

## Case Project 14-2: Researching Hacking Sites

You need to become informed on the latest hacking tools available over the Internet that might create vulnerability problems for your Novell-based network. Write a memo to your instructor that includes any sites you found, explains whether Novell has issued any statements on this vulnerability, and reports whether a service pack is available. Be sure to give details about the types of attacks the hacking sites are recommending, such as denial-of-service, social engineering, or Trojan horse.

14

# 15

# IMPLEMENTING MESSAGING SERVICES

**After reading this chapter and completing the exercises, you will be able to:**

♦ Identify e-mail components, protocols, clients, and servers, and install and set up the GroupWise client to send and receive e-mail

♦ Configure and manage the GroupWise system so that you can create post office users and establish mailbox security

♦ Monitor the GroupWise system and troubleshoot common GroupWise problems

Electronic messaging and workgroup applications, such as scheduling and calendaring, are essential components of today's networked offices. Novell's GroupWise software is a highly reliable and efficient electronic messaging and workgroup application system that is integrated with eDirectory to enhance network security and provide centralized management. In this chapter, you learn about GroupWise features and components by seeing how they are used to implement and manage an electronic messaging system for the CBE Labs network.

## Implementing an E-mail System

After the basic network services and security measures are in place, another important step in setting up a network is implementing an office e-mail system that can improve employee productivity and communications. Office e-mail systems can also include the following collaborative applications:

- *Scheduling*—For setting meeting dates, inviting people to events, and reserving resources, such as conference rooms and audiovisual equipment

- *Task lists*—For creating prioritized to-do lists for themselves and others

- *Reminders*—For creating notes to be displayed on specific dates

## E-mail Components

Like other network software, such as iFolder, FTP Server, and Enterprise Web Server, e-mail systems require both server and client components. As shown in Figure 15-1, the client component (referred to as the **front-end process**) runs on the user's workstation and provides an interface for communicating with the server component (referred to as the **back-end process**) to send or receive messages and attachments. The server and client software work together to provide collaborative office applications, too, such as scheduling meetings and resources, creating reminder notes, and managing to-do lists.

The post office application running on the server handles the actual delivery of e-mail messages. As illustrated in Figure 15-1, when a client sends a message, the data is first sent to the e-mail server, where the post office application interprets the recipient's address and then sends the message to the destination post office. Based on the route determined by the originating post office, the message data is sent directly to the destination server or to an intermediate server, which forwards the message to the final destination. The destination post office looks up the name of the recipient in the user list and then forwards the e-mail address to that user's mailbox. If a user name is not in the list of users on the destination server, the e-mail message is returned to the sender.

E-mail servers use software components, called agents, to assist in transferring e-mail messages. The **Message Transfer Agent (MTA)** assists the core post office software in transferring e-mail between user mailboxes and maintaining message integrity. To transfer messages, the MTA uses an algorithm for interpreting the e-mail address and finding the best route to the destination post office. You can configure the MTA to transfer mail at predetermined intervals and set criteria for selecting the best route to destination servers. The **Post Office Agent (POA)** is responsible for delivering messages from the client to the correct mailbox on the server. If the destination mailbox is located on a different server, the MTA finds the best route to the destination post office and transfers the message. The POA at the receiving server's post office then delivers the message to the correct mailbox.

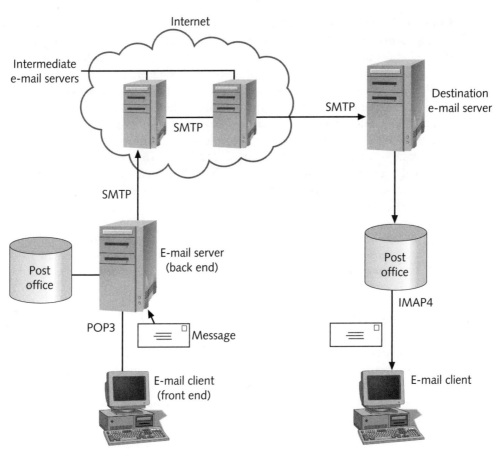

**Figure 15-1**    E-mail components

# E-mail Protocols

As you learned in Chapter 3, protocols are the rules used to transfer data and information between computer systems. In addition to using TCP/IP to transfer packets between computers, e-mail systems use specialized protocols to transmit messages from the client to the post office server and between post office servers. **Simple Mail Transfer Protocol (SMTP)** is a TCP/IP-based mail transfer protocol for transferring messages between servers. As part of the TCP/IP suite (see Appendix D for more information on TCP/IP), SMTP provides reliable delivery of e-mail messages by using TCP/IP to transfer data between servers. As illustrated in Figure 15-1, mail transfers between post offices often involve sending messages to intermediate servers. In this case, SMTP dynamically determines the route from the source server to the destination server. Because it's a mail transfer protocol, SMTP has limited capacity to store messages at the receiving end. As a result, it is always used with other protocols, such as Post Office Protocol and Internet Message Access Protocol, that provide the capability of receiving and storing messages.

15

**Internet Message Access Protocol (IMAP)** is a standard protocol for accessing and storing e-mail messages from the post office server. To help users organize messages, IMAP has features for creating mail folders on the server for cataloging sent and received messages. The latest version of IMAP (IMAP4) has advanced features that support downloading only the e-mail address and subject, so users can decide whether they want to download the entire message or just the subject header to save download time. In addition, IMAP4 offers a powerful search feature for finding messages that contain specific text embedded in the message. For example, before reporting to management about the current status of the GroupWise system, David Doering, the network administrator for CBE Labs, used the search feature to find all e-mail messages containing the word "GroupWise" and moved these messages into a separate folder so that he could reference them in the report.

The advanced IMAP features can be implemented only when using the actual client for e-mail access. When users access their e-mail accounts via the Web, they won't be able to download sender information and subject headers, for example.

**Post Office Protocol (POP)** is a standard client-server protocol for transferring e-mail messages between the client and e-mail server. POP3, the latest version of POP, contains enhancements for downloading messages to the client. Although POP and IMAP have many of the same functions, POP is referred to as a store-and-forward messaging protocol that transfers complete messages from the server to the client without giving the user the option to search and read e-mail heading information before downloading messages from the server. IMAP4, on the other hand, enables you to select transmission options and read e-mail heading information so that you can select which messages to download.

## Common E-mail Clients

To work with e-mail systems, user workstations need to have e-mail client software installed and configured. Because most e-mail systems, such as GroupWise, use the standard POP, IMAP, and SMTP messaging protocols, they are compatible with many e-mail and workgroup clients. When researching e-mail systems, David wanted to find one that was compatible with the most commonly used e-mail clients. From his investigations, he determined that the most common e-mail clients include Eudora, GroupWise, Outlook Express, Outlook 2002, Netscape Messenger, and Lotus Notes. In the following sections, you learn what David discovered about some of these common e-mail clients and their features.

### Eudora Client (Version 5.1 and Later)

Eudora is a standalone e-mail client created by Qualcomm to support all common e-mail protocols and servers. As a standalone e-mail client, Eudora has the advantage of being used on many different e-mail systems and being more resistant to e-mail viruses designed to attack more integrated systems, such as Outlook or GroupWise. After being installed on the user workstation, Eudora asks for the following e-mail server information the first time a user logs in:

- The user name and password for authenticating to the post office server
- The IP address or DNS name of the post office server
- The protocols the client application will use to connect to the post office server
- The ports used to communicate to the MTA and POA

In addition to the basic functions of sending and receiving e-mail, the Eudora client offers the following features that make it unique:

- *Eudora Shell Extensions*—This feature can be used to warn users about the potential for virus infection when running an e-mail attachment stored in the Attach directory.
- *Moodwatch*—This feature identifies potentially offensive phrases (based on user settings) and flags them with one to three chili pepper icons to denote one of the following levels:
  - One chili pepper: Message might be offensive.
  - Two chili peppers: Message is probably offensive.
  - Three chili peppers: Message is "on fire."
- *Strikeout style*—This feature, used to cross out selected text with a horizontal line, can be helpful when reviewing e-mail messages or checking off tasks in a to-do list.
- *Drag and drop*—This feature enables users to simply drag and drop attachments to e-mail messages.
- *Qualcomm PureVoice*—This add-on enables users to send messages with attached voice recordings.

## Outlook Express and Outlook 2002 Clients

Outlook Express and Outlook 2002 are the two Microsoft e-mail clients. Outlook Express, which comes bundled with Internet Explorer and is designed for personal users, is an Internet-enabled e-mail client with support for standard e-mail protocols as well as Network News Transfer Protocol (NNTP) for newsgroup access. Because it's bundled with Internet Explorer and offers many support features, many home and small-business users choose Outlook Express as their e-mail client. The full Outlook 2002 client is sold as part of the Microsoft Office Suite and is intended for use in office environments that include Microsoft Exchange Server. The Microsoft Outlook client offers all the features of Outlook Express and can also work with Microsoft Exchange Server (described in

**15**

the "Common E-mail Back-end Servers" section) to perform scheduling, calendaring, and other collaborative functions. It includes the following features:

- Automatic completion of address information

- E-mail account selection to allow users with multiple e-mail accounts to select which one to use when they start Outlook 2002

- Support for using external text editors so that users can switch between different formats, such as text, HTML, or rich text, when creating e-mail messages

- The Find feature, which offers rapid searches of folders and e-mail messages

- A mailbox cleanup feature that enables users to archive e-mail and search for messages by date, size, and other attributes to make it easier to remove items and better manage mailbox space

## Lotus Notes Client

Lotus Notes is a powerful workgroup client that includes e-mail, calendaring, scheduling, and other collaborative functions for both Windows and Macintosh computers. Lotus Notes also has a complete Web browser capability, so users can access their e-mail and other features across the Internet or intranet. Some important features of the Notes client include the following:

- Support of multiple protocols, including NNTP for newsgroup access

- Automatic name-to-address resolution

- Customized views of calendars and to-do lists

- A Notes editor for creating and printing e-mail preview documents

- Animated GIFs as a visually appealing way to access other Web sites

## GroupWise 6 Client

GroupWise 6 is a complete and integrated messaging system from Novell that includes both client and server components. In addition to the basic client features, the GroupWise 6 client offers the following advanced features to help increase user productivity:

- Supports multiple protocols, including NNTP for sending and receiving newsgroup postings.

- Facilitates migration from other clients by making it possible for users to import addresses and user account information from other e-mail clients, including Outlook and Netscape.

- Offers secure access to e-mail and user accounts through servers to support Secure Socket Layer (SSL) transmissions for encrypting data with public key cryptography, as described in Chapter 14.

- Includes the ability to have multiple account signatures, making it possible to configure GroupWise clients to send data and messages to other applications, such as banking systems, that require public key encryption for authentication (see Chapter 14 for more information on using public key cryptography).

- Provides a new **caching mode** feature that automatically stores all messages and attachments on the local hard disk, thus allowing access to e-mail without being continuously connected to the network.

- Offers **mailbox mode switching** so that users can change their mailbox modes between online, caching, and remote. In online mode, messages are stored on the e-mail server. In caching mode, e-mail is automatically downloaded to the client's local hard disk. In remote mode, users can dial into a network, access e-mail messages, and selectively download messages for offline access. Also in remote mode, the client automatically dials in and initiates a connection with the server when required to send and receive e-mail.

- Includes the **AutoComplete addressing** feature, which automatically searches the address book for matching names when a user starts typing in an e-mail address and then completes the address entry for the user.

- Offers the **document management** feature for sharing documents with a group of users and maintaining multiple versions of documents.

- Uses security certificates for securing e-mail through mail authentication.

# Common E-mail Back-end Servers

For e-mail clients to provide messaging and other collaborative services, such as calendaring and scheduling, they need to be connected to an e-mail server. E-mail servers provide post office and other services requested by clients. Simple clients, such as Eudora, are designed primarily to send and receive e-mail messages, so they can work with a variety of e-mail servers using standard protocols (POP3 and IMAP4). Performing more complex functions, such as calendaring and scheduling, requires tight integration between the e-mail client and the server. Although many back-end servers can provide basic post office functions to clients for basic e-mail, three major back-end server products offer complete collaborative office messaging solutions for scheduling, calendaring, and task-list management: Microsoft Exchange 2000 Server, Lotus Domino Mail Server, and GroupWise 6 Mail Server. Before selecting the GroupWise system, David researched several back-end e-mail systems to decide which one would best meet the needs of the CBE network. The following sections describe the basic features of the major back-end messaging servers.

## Microsoft Exchange 2000 Server

Microsoft Exchange 2000 Server is a sophisticated system that provides e-mail and many collaborative services, such as calendaring, scheduling, and document management, to integrated Outlook clients. To reduce the administrative costs of maintaining the messaging and collaborative services, Exchange 2000 Server is designed to be a highly reliable and

**15**

scalable platform with easy-to-use administrative features. Exchange also includes built-in statistical analysis tools for proactively managing the messaging environment, monitoring server performance, and troubleshooting connectivity problems. Like the GroupWise system, Exchange is designed to support collaborative services across the Internet to give users "anytime, anywhere" access. Versions of Exchange are available for Windows NT and Windows 2000 servers. Although Exchange would provide the e-mail and collaborative services that CBE needs, it would require installing and managing a separate Windows NT or Windows 2000 server.

## Lotus Domino Mail Server

Lotus Domino Mail Server is a powerful collaborative and messaging server for corporate intranets and the Internet. In addition to native support for all major Internet standards, Domino Server supports the latest in Internet messaging. Because of its easy installation and configuration, you can use the default settings to get a basic Domino mail server up and running in just a few minutes. Domino Server enables administrators to track messages across multiple domains to help determine path selection and troubleshoot delivery problems. In addition, it allows users to check the status of sent messages to determine delivery time and other tracking information. Like Exchange 2000 Server, Domino Server includes built-in statistical analysis tools for proactively managing the messaging environment, monitoring server performance, and troubleshooting connectivity problems. With Domino Server, users can integrate calendar and group scheduling features, share online work areas, and access the Web, newsgroups, and bulletin boards from any standards-based e-mail client, such as Eudora or Netscape Messenger.

## GroupWise 6 Mail Server

Because the GroupWise system has been around since the early days of microcomputer networking (it was originally part of the WordPerfect office suite in the 1980s), David found it to be the most mature workgroup collaborative office system. Realizing the vital role that e-mail, calendaring, and document management play in an organization's operations, Novell has continued to upgrade and improve the GroupWise product through its various releases (GroupWise 4.1, 5.0, 5.2, 5.5, and now 6). With its most recent release, Novell has emphasized taking advantage of the Internet to deliver integrated collaborative services to users at any location, whether at the office, at home, or on the road.

Although GroupWise 6 offers many up-to-date features and management tools, it continues to provide backward-compatibility with earlier WordPerfect versions by retaining some WordPerfect naming conventions, such as "wp" (WordPerfect) and "of" (Office) in the file prefix or extension. GroupWise functions include e-mail messaging, calendaring, scheduling, document management, task-list management, workflow organization, and support for wireless communications.

To enable users to check e-mail and use other applications while traveling, David is planning to supply personal digital assistants (PDAs) for employees in the future. David liked GroupWise's support for Wireless Access Protocol (WAP)-enabled devices because users with PDAs could easily check e-mail and use other applications while on the road. After investigating the major back-end server alternatives, David found that GroupWise 6 equaled or exceeded the alternatives in offering all the collaborative services CBE needs. In addition, one of the biggest advantages of implementing GroupWise 6 is its tight integration with eDirectory and other Novell services, which makes configuring and managing the GroupWise 6 server easier.

## Installing GroupWise 6 on the NetWare Server

To implement a GroupWise system, you need to install both server and client components first. Unlike installing iFolder or other NetWare Internet services installed from the server console (see Chapters 13 and 14), the GroupWise 6 server installation process is performed from a client workstation. Before performing the installation, it is important to identify the server that will host the GroupWise services, the storage locations, IP addresses, and ports. The GroupWise Documentation Worksheet shown in Figure 15-2 lists the information David gathered before the installation.

 It's best to keep names for the directories holding the domain directory and post office directory at eight or fewer characters. Although NetWare supports long directory names and filenames, GroupWise has problems finding directory names longer than eight characters.

The GroupWise volume drive letter identifies the drive letter that will be mapped to the volume containing the GroupWise system. For example, David used drive letter G:, the drive letter mapped to the CBE_ADMIN_DATA volume in the login script.

**15**

**GroupWise Documentation Worksheet**

GroupWise volume drive letter: ___*G:*_____

GroupWise directory structure: ____*EMail*_____

GroupWise software distributor path: ___*G:\EMail\GrpWise\Software*_____

ConsoleOne path: _____*C:\novell\consoleone*_____

GroupWise system name: _____*CBE Labs*_____

GroupWise domain name: _____*CBEWorld*_____

GroupWise domain directory path: ___*G:\EMail\GrpWise\Mail\CBEWorld*_____

GroupWise post office name: _____*CBEPO*_____

GroupWise post office directory path: _____*G:\EMail\PostOff\CBEPO*_____

Post office context: _____*O=CBE_LABS*_____

POA network address and port      IP address: ___*IP address of CBE_ADMIN*_____
                                         Client-server port: _____
                                         Message transfer port: _____
                                         HTTP port: _____

MTA network address and port      IP address: ___*IP address of CBE_ADMIN*_____
                                         Message transfer port: _____
                                         HTTP port: _____

Web Console information           User name: ___*WebAgent*_____
                                         Password: _____

**Figure 15-2**    The GroupWise Documentation Worksheet for CBE Labs

The GroupWise directory structure identifies the directory that will contain the GroupWise software and mailbox files. As a general rule, you should place this directory structure on a NetWare volume. Placing the structure on the SYS volume could fill up the system volume, causing the server to crash. GroupWise 6 needs the directory structure shown in Figure 15-3 to be created within the location you select. Ted decided to have David place the GroupWise directory structure in the EMail directory on the DATA volume of the CBE_ADMIN server to prevent filling up the SYS volume.

**Designed by**: <u>Ted Simpson</u>                    **Date**: <u>10/30/02</u>

Volume name: <u>DATA</u>     Directory Name: <u>EMail</u>     Estimated Size: <u>2 GB</u>

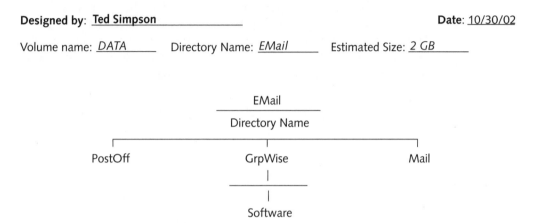

**Figure 15-3**   GroupWise directory structure

The GroupWise software distribution path identifies the path to the software directory shown in Figure 15-3. David entered the path "G:\EMail\GrpWise\Software" for the path to be used on the CBE_ADMIN server.

The ConsoleOne path identifies the location of the ConsoleOne files on the GroupWise administrative workstation. This path is important because the GroupWise installation program copies the ConsoleOne snap-ins needed to install and manage GroupWise.

The GroupWise system name information is necessary to identify the GroupWise service on the computer and should typically identify the organization. For example, David used "CBE Labs" for the GroupWise system name.

A GroupWise system can have one or more domains based on geographic or administrative needs. Each domain has its own database directory path. For example, CBE Labs could set up separate domains for the CBE_ADMIN and CBE_EVAL servers. This would be important if the servers were in different locations separated by a WAN, or if there were separate network administrators for each location. Because both servers are in the same geographic area, David decided to have one domain named CBEWorld.

The GroupWise domain directory path specifies where the domain will store its user database information. David used EMail\GrpWise\Mail\CBEWorld as the path for the CBE domain database.

15

The GroupWise post office name identifies the post office for storing the domain's messages and attachments. David chose CBEPO for the CBE domain post office.

The GroupWise post office directory path identifies where the post office data will be stored. David specified EMail\GrpWise\PostOff\CBEPO as the path to the CBE post office.

The post office context identifies the container for storing GroupWise 6 post office objects. David selected the CBE_LABS Organization as the container for storing these objects.

The POA network address and port information specify the IP address of the NetWare server that will host the post office service. David recorded the IP address of the CBE_ADMIN server. Because he plans to use the default ports, David left the client-server port, message transfer port, and HTTP port fields blank so that he could enter the default port numbers provided during the installation.

The MTA network address and port specify the IP address of the NetWare server that will host the message transfer agent service. David recorded the IP address of the CBE_ADMIN server. Because he plans to use the default ports, he left the message transfer port and HTTP port fields blank so that he could enter the default port numbers provided during the installation.

The Web Console information specifies the name and password of a user who will be able to access the Web console from a Web browser. Because this user name could be accessed over the Internet, for the best security you shouldn't specify an existing eDirectory user name and password in this field. David used "WebAgent" as the Web Console user and gave the WebAgent user an eight-character password.

## Installation Phases and Steps

The GroupWise server installation process can be divided into these five major phases:

1. *Server preparation.* In this phase, you prepare the server by creating the necessary GroupWise directory structure and drive mappings. To install and manage GroupWise, you must reserve a drive letter for the volume containing GroupWise files and directories. For example, David has reserved drive letter G: for the GroupWise DATA volume.

2. *Software installation.* In this phase, you accept the GroupWise license agreement, select the type of installation (update or new), and identify the path to the GroupWise software folders on the server and the ConsoleOne folder on the administrative workstation. After entering the required information, the GroupWise installation program examines the system and then copies the necessary files and databases to the paths you have identified. After the GroupWise files are copied to the system, ConsoleOne is started and you perform the remaining installation steps with this utility.

3. *Collect system information.* In this phase, you identify the following information:
   - Software distribution path
   - The eDirectory tree to contain the GroupWise system objects

- The GroupWise system name
- The domain name and domain database path
- The domain's post office name and path
- Language and time zone information for the domain
- POA network address and port information
- MTA network address and port information
- Optionally create post office user accounts and mailboxes at this time, or add them later (as described in the "Creating GroupWise Post Office Users" section)

4. *Create the system.* In this phase, you create the domain and post office eDirectory tree objects, copy files to the assigned directories, and create post office users and mailboxes.

5. *Install agent software.* In this phase, you copy GroupWise agent software to the SYS:System directory, set up the Web Console user, and copy files to the selected directory paths.

David used the steps in these five phases to install GroupWise on the CBE_ADMIN server:

1. Network and Server Preparation

   a. He started his workstation and logged in with the CBEAdmin user name and password.

   b. He used My Computer to verify that drive letter G: was mapped to the DATA volume.

   c. He created a directory named EMail off the root of his DATA volume.

   d. Next, he created the following required GroupWise directories as subdirectories within the existing DATA:\EMail directory structure:

      - Mail
      - PostOff
      - GrpWise
      - GrpWise\Software

   e. After creating the directory structure, he needed to grant all users rights to read the GroupWise software. He did this by using Windows Explorer to assign the [Root] container object Read and File Scan rights to the DATA:EMail\GrpWise\Software directory structure.

2. Install Software

   a. David inserted the GroupWise 6 CD into the CD drive of his administrative workstation. The GroupWise installation program automatically started and displayed the GroupWise installation options shown in Figure 15-4.

   b. He clicked the Create or update a GroupWise system option to display the Software License Agreement window showing the language selection options and license agreement.

**15**

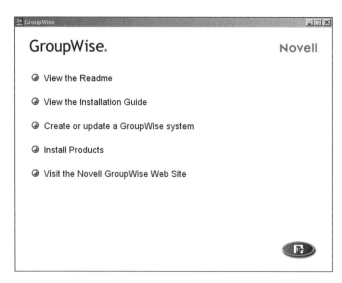

**Figure 15-4**    GroupWise installation options

    c. He clicked Yes to accept the license agreement and the default English language and display the Welcome to GroupWise Install window.

    d. After reading the installation overview in the Welcome to GroupWise Install window (see Figure 15-5), he clicked Next to display the Plan Your System window. He clicked the Installation Guide button to open an Adobe Acrobat document containing installation and update instructions. After reviewing the document, he exited Acrobat Reader and returned to the Plan Your System window.

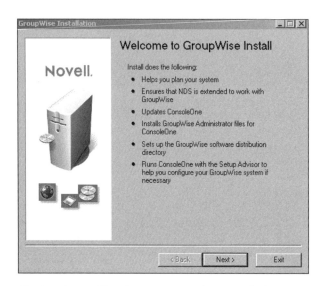

**Figure 15-5**    The GroupWise welcome window

e. He then clicked Next to continue the installation and display the Administration Options window shown in Figure 15-6.

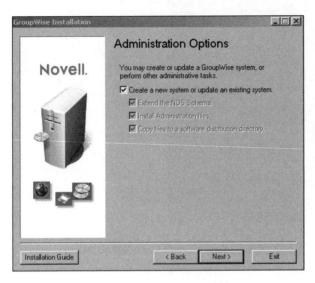

**Figure 15-6**   The GroupWise Administration Options window

f. He verified that the Create a new system or update an existing system option was selected, and then clicked Next to display the Select Tree window.

g. He selected CLASS_TREE, the CBE network tree, and clicked Next to display the NDS Will Be Extended window.

Because GroupWise was designed to work on earlier versions of NetWare using Novell Directory Services (NDS), the GroupWise documentation refers generally to NDS rather than eDirectory. In this chapter, references to NDS services in steps include the NetWare 6 eDirectory services.

15

h. He clicked Next to extend the NDS schema and display the NDS Has Been Extended completion window. He then clicked Next again to display the Select Languages dialog box.

i. He verified that English-UAS was selected, and then clicked Next to enter the path to the ConsoleOne directory, as shown in Figure 15-7.

j. He set the path to C:\Novell\ConsoleOne\1.2, and then clicked Next to display the Software Distribution Directory dialog box. He used the browse button to navigate to the G:\EMail\GrpWise\Software directory (see Figure 15-8), and then clicked Next to display the Select Software window.

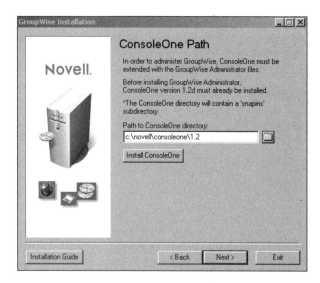

**Figure 15-7** The ConsoleOne Path dialog box

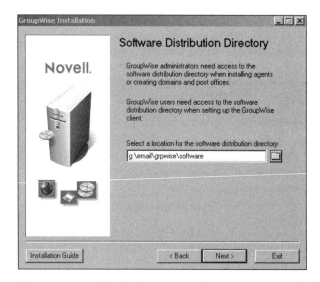

**Figure 15-8** The Software Distribution Directory dialog box

k. In the Select Software dialog box (see Figure 15-9), he clicked the Select All button and then clicked Next. The Checking Files window displayed while the installation software examined the files in the existing system.

l. After the files were checked, the Ready to Install window displayed. David clicked the Install button to begin the installation. After several minutes, all files were copied to the server and the Novell GroupWise Partner Page window (see Figure 15-10) displayed.

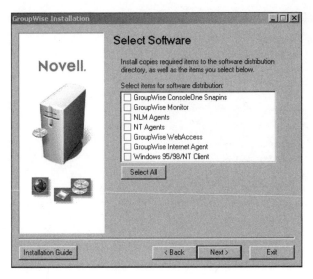

**Figure 15-9**    The Select Software dialog box

In this window, you can click the Go to GroupWise Partner Page button to view GroupWise information on the Internet.

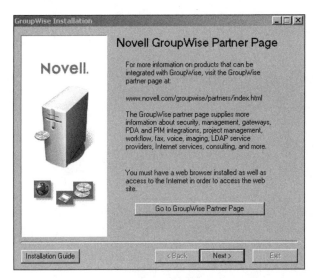

**Figure 15-10**    The Novell GroupWise Partner Page window

m. He clicked the Next button in the Novell GroupWise Partner Page window to display the Determine Next Step dialog box (see Figure 15-11). He clicked the Creating a new GroupWise system? radio button, and then clicked Next to display the Run ConsoleOne window.

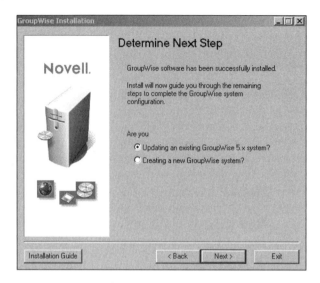

**Figure 15-11**    The Determine Next Step dialog box

       n. In the Run ConsoleOne window, David clicked the Run button to start ConsoleOne and open the GroupWise System Setup Wizard (shown in Figure 15-12) after ConsoleOne loaded. David performed each task listed in the GroupWise Setup Progress window, as described in the following steps.

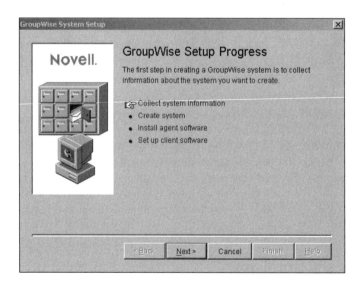

**Figure 15-12**    The GroupWise System Setup Wizard

    3. Collect System Information

       a. David verified that the Collect system information option was selected in the GroupWise Setup Progress window, and then clicked Next to display the Software Distribution Directory window.

b. He verified that g:\email\grpwise\software was entered as the path to the GroupWise software distribution directory, and clicked Next again to display the NDS Tree window.

c. He verified that tree for the CBE Labs network was listed in the Current tree text box, and then clicked Next to open the System Name dialog box asking for the name of the GroupWise system. He entered the name CBE Labs (the name he filled out earlier on his GroupWise Documentation Worksheet), and then clicked Next to open the Primary Domain dialog box.

d. He entered CBEWorld as the domain name, and then clicked Next to display the Domain Directory dialog box.

e. Filling in the GroupWise Domain Directory text box is important because it specifies the path to the GroupWise mail database, which is needed when configuring ConsoleOne. David entered the path G:\EMail\ Mail\CBEWorld (see Figure 15-13), and then clicked Next to create the directory and display the Domain Context window.

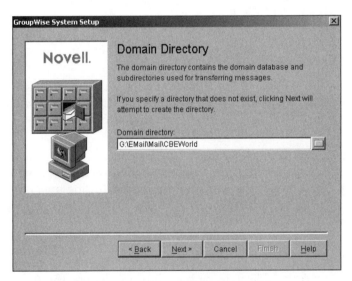

**Figure 15-13**     The Domain Directory dialog box

f. He clicked the browse button, clicked CBE_LABS Organization, and clicked OK to insert CBE_LABS into the Domain context text box, as shown in Figure 15-14. He then clicked Next to display the Domain Language dialog box.

g. He clicked Next to select the default English language and display the Domain Time Zone dialog box. He used the scroll button to select his time zone, and then clicked Next to display the Post Office Name dialog box.

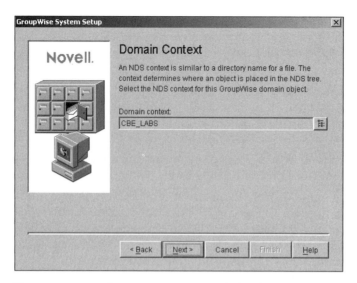

**Figure 15-14**    The Domain Context dialog box

    h. He entered CBEPO in the Post office name text box, and then clicked Next to display the Post Office Directory dialog box.

    i. He entered the path he recorded on the GroupWise Documentation Worksheet (G:\EMail\PostOff\CBEPO) to the GroupWise post office directory, and then clicked Next to create the CBEPO directory and display the Post Office Context dialog box.

    j. When prompted to provide the Post Office context, David verified that CBE_LABS was entered in the Post office context text box, and then clicked Next to display the Post Office Language dialog box.

    k. He again selected his language and time zone information, clicking Next after each entry. Next, the Post Office Link dialog box (see Figure 15-15) displayed, containing the options Direct link or TCP/IP link.

    l. He selected the TCP/IP link radio button, and then clicked Next to display the POA Network Address dialog box, shown in Figure 15-16.

    m. To be able to use port numbers to access GroupWise from a Web browser, he recorded the default port numbers for the client-server port (1677), message transfer port (7101), and HTTP port (7181) on his GroupWise Documentation Worksheet.

    n. He verified that the IP Address radio button was selected and entered the IP address of the CBE_ADMIN server in the IP Address text box (the same address he recorded on the GroupWise Documentation Worksheet).

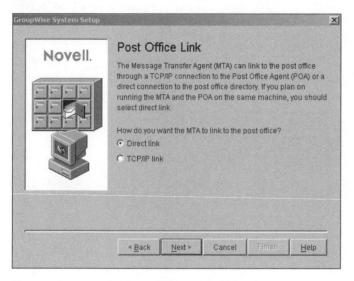

**Figure 15-15**    The Post Office Link dialog box

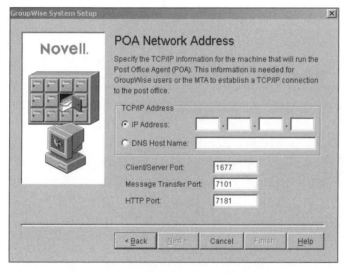

**Figure 15-16**    The POA Network Address dialog box

    o. He clicked Next to display the MTA Network Address dialog box, shown in Figure 15-17.

    p. Again, he verified that the IP Address radio button was selected. He then entered the IP address of the CBE_ADMIN server and recorded the IP address and port information on his GroupWise Documentation Worksheet.

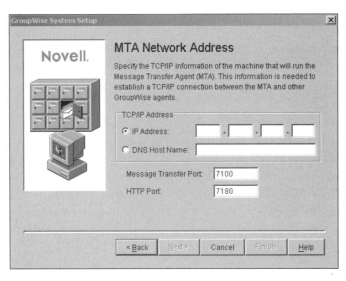

**Figure 15-17**    The MTA Network Address dialog box

q. He then clicked Next to display the Post Office Users dialog box shown in Figure 15-18. To test the system, David initially added all users in the Information Systems Department by clicking the Add button to open the Select Object dialog box, navigating to the InfoSystems OU, and highlighting all users in that container.

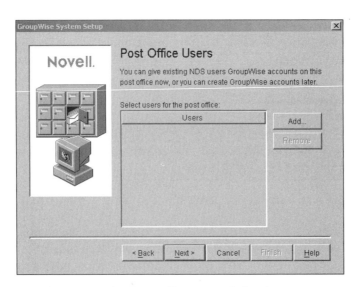

**Figure 15-18**    The Post Office Users dialog box

r. After highlighting all users in the InfoSystems OU, he clicked OK to add the users to the Post Office Users dialog box. After testing the system,

David will use ConsoleOne, as described in the "Configuring and Managing the GroupWise System" section later in this chapter, to add mail accounts for users in other departments.

Note that all users in the same post office must have unique names. Users with the same name cannot be added to the post office, even though their names are located in different contexts.

    s. After all user accounts were added to the Post Office Users window, David clicked Next to return to the GroupWise Setup Progress window.

4. Create the System

    a. David verified that the Create system option was selected, and then clicked Next to display the Summary window for the GroupWise installation, similar to the one shown in Figure 15-19.

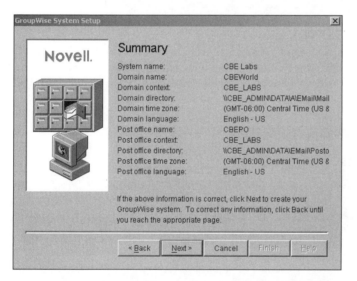

**Figure 15-19**    The Summary window for the GroupWise installation

    b. He reviewed the information in the GroupWise installation Summary window and then clicked Next to continue the setup.

    c. After creating the system, David received a message stating that the GroupWise system was successfully installed. He clicked Next to close the window and return to the GroupWise Setup Progress window.

5. Install Agent Software

    a. He verified that the Install agent software was selected, and then clicked Next to display the Select Platform dialog box (see Figure 15-20). He verified that the NetWare platform was selected, and then clicked Next to display the Installation Path dialog box.

15

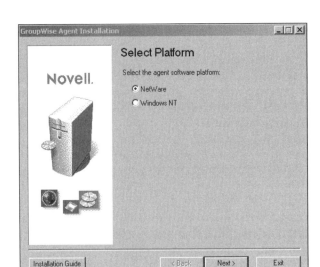

**Figure 15-20**    The Select Platform dialog box

b. He entered f:\SYSTEM in the Installation path text box, and then clicked
Next to display the Web Console Information dialog box shown in
Figure 15-21.

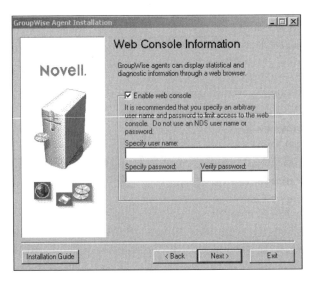

**Figure 15-21**    The Web Console Information dialog box

c. He entered WebAgent (the name recorded on his GroupWise Documentation
Worksheet) in the Specify user name text box and a password in the Specify
password and Verify password text boxes, and then clicked Next to display the
Language selection window.

d. He verified that English was selected and clicked Next to display the Summary window. After verifying that the entries were correct, David clicked the Install button to begin the file copying.

The GroupWise installation process might attempt to overwrite existing files with files from the GroupWise CD. This can be a problem if more recent files needed for NetWare 6 services are overwritten. For example, a problem David encountered was GroupWise replacing NetWare 6 LDAP files, which caused problems with other NetWare 6 services. To avoid this, prevent the replacement of existing Read Only files or reinstall the support pack after GroupWise installation.

e. During the file copying, David received the Read-Only File message box for the ldapskk.nlm file. David clicked No when asked if he wanted to replace this file. When additional Read-Only File message boxes displayed, he continued to click No to prevent overwriting the existing LDAP files.

f. When the Installation Complete dialog box displayed (see Figure 15-22), he verified that the Update AUTOEXEC file and Launch GroupWise agents now options were selected, and then clicked Finish to complete the agent software installation and return to the GroupWise Setup Progress window, where the Set up client software option was selected.

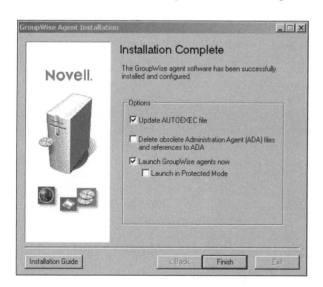

**Figure 15-22**   The Installation Complete dialog box

g. Because David is planning to install the client software separately, he clicked Cancel and then clicked Yes to exit the GroupWise installation program and return to the main ConsoleOne window.

To give students the rights to access and manage the user post office database, the instructor should use ConsoleOne to assign the Students group all rights except Supervisor and Access Control to the EMail directory.

h. After completing the login script entries, David clicked the Close button in the GroupWise window, and then exited ConsoleOne and logged out. Next, he needed to view the MTA and POA information. He moved to the CBE_ADMIN server console and pressed Ctrl+Esc to display the Current Screens window.

i. He entered the number to the left of the GroupWise MTA - CBEWorld option, and then pressed Enter to display the GroupWise MTA information window, shown in Figure 15-23.

```
CBEWorld                                       Up Time: 0 Days 0 Hrs 6 Mins
GroupWise Message Transfer Agent
  Status                        Statistics
              Total  Closed                        Total      10 Minutes
  Domains       1      0       Routed               11            11
  Post Offices  1      1       Undeliverable         0             0
  Gateways      0      0       Errors                0             0




09-25 19:36:37 DIS: MTA configuration loaded
09-25 19:36:39 CBEPO: Post office now closed
09-25 19:36:41 DIS: MTA restart in progress
09-25 19:36:41 DIS: No configuration changes detected
09-25 19:36:41 DIS: MTA restart request ignored
```

**Figure 15-23** The GroupWise MTA information window

j. After verifying that the MTA was running, David pressed Ctrl+Esc to display the Current Screens window. He entered the number to the left of the GroupWise POA - CBEPO.CBEWorld option, and then pressed Enter to display the GroupWise POA information window, similar to the one in Figure 15-24.

```
CBEPO.CBEWORLD                                 Up Time: 0 Days 0 Hrs 8 Mins
GroupWise Post Office Agent
  Status                        Statistics
  Processing    Busy  0: 0     C/S Requests:      0  Message Files:     0
  User Connections:       0    Requests Pending   0  Undeliverable:     0
  File Queues:            0    Users Timed Out:   0  Problem Messages   0

19:36:39 259
19:36:39 2A6 Initializing dispatcher
19:36:39 2A8 Initializing dispatcher
19:36:39 2AC Initializing worker
19:36:39 2AE Initializing worker
19:36:39 2B2 Initializing worker
19:36:39 2B4 Initializing worker
19:36:39 2B6 Initializing worker
19:36:39 2B8 Initializing worker
```

**Figure 15-24** The GroupWise POA information window

k. After verifying that the MTA and POA were running successfully, David used the Ctrl+Esc key sequence to select the X Server – Graphical Console and returned to his administrative workstation. The GroupWise system was then ready for David to begin the client installation and configuration.

## Setting Up GroupWise Client Computers

After installing GroupWise on the CBE_ADMIN server, David's next task was to prepare and configure user workstations by installing the GroupWise client. Having a common drive mapping, such as G:, to the GroupWise software directory is necessary to access and manage the GroupWise system. The GroupWise client installation requires a three-phase setup. In the first phase, you run the setup program and identify the installation language and directory. The setup program then copies files to your local hard drive and restarts your computer. After the computer is restarted, in the second phase, you identify your installation options and program folder. When this phase is finished, you can view the Readme file and start GroupWise. The last phase of the client installation requires entering a user name and the post office server's IP address and port number. The user name you enter becomes the default GroupWise user for the workstation.

### Phase 1: Install Messaging System

David used the following steps to install the GroupWise client on workstations in the Information Systems Department:

1. He started a user workstation and logged in with his DDoering user name and password.

2. He inserted the GroupWise CD in the CD-ROM drive and then used My Computer to navigate to the G:\EMail\Grpwise\Software\Client\Win32 folder.

3. He scrolled down and double-clicked the Setup.exe program to start the first phase of the installation process, which displays the Choose Setup Language dialog box.

4. He clicked OK to select the default English language and start the setup wizard.

5. When he received a message informing him that the messaging system was not found on his computer, he clicked Next to begin copying files. After all messaging software files were copied, the Restart Windows dialog box opened. David verified that the Yes, I want to restart my computer now radio button was selected, and then clicked OK to close the window and restart the computer.

### Phase 2: Install GroupWise Client

After the computer restarted, David logged in again with his DDoering user name and password and performed the following steps:

1. The GroupWise client installation continued with the second phase by asking him to again select the installation language.

**15**

2. David clicked OK after selecting the language to display the GroupWise Welcome window.

3. He then clicked Next to display the Setup Options dialog box shown in Figure 15-25.

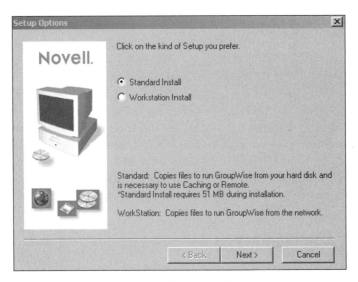

**Figure 15-25**   GroupWise client installation options

4. He verified that the Standard Install radio button was selected, and then clicked Next to display the Destination Directory dialog box.

 If you are unable to perform a standard install because of insufficient disk space (for example, the installation "freezes" or fails to proceed), select the Workstation Install option to run the software from the server.

5. He clicked Next to accept the default Destination Folder path (C:\Novell\ GroupWise) and display the Select Optional Components dialog box shown in Figure 15-26.

6. He clicked Next to select the default components and display the Select Program Folder dialog box.

7. He clicked Next to place the programs in the default GroupWise folder and display the Select StartUp Folder Software dialog box.

8. He clicked the Clear All button, and then clicked Next to display the Language Selection dialog box.

9. After verifying that the English language was selected, he clicked Next. Because Microsoft Word was installed on this client, the Software Integration dialog box opened, asking David to select applications for integration with GroupWise Document Management. He left Microsoft Word selected, and clicked Next to display the Start Copying Files summary window.

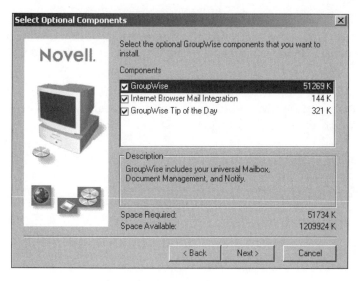

**Figure 15-26**    The Select Optional Components dialog box

10. He verified that the correct options were selected, and then clicked Next to start the file-copying process. After all files were copied, the Setup Complete dialog box opened. He clicked to clear the Yes, I want to launch GroupWise check box, and then clicked Finish to open Notepad and display the Readme file. After closing the Readme file, he verified that a GroupWise icon was displayed on his Windows desktop.

## Phase 3: Configure GroupWise Client

The final phase of the client installation involves configuring the IP address and port for the post office server. David used the following steps:

1. He started GroupWise by double-clicking the GroupWise icon on his desktop to open the Novell GroupWise Startup dialog box (see Figure 15-27).

**15**

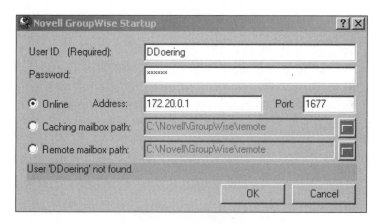

**Figure 15-27**    The Novell GroupWise Startup dialog box

2. He entered DDoering in the User ID text box and his password in the Password text box. He verified that the Online radio button was selected, and then entered the IP address for the GroupWise server in the Address text box and 1677 in the Port text box.

3. He clicked OK to display an informational tip-of-the-day message, and then clicked Close to close the tip box and view the Novell GroupWise - Mailbox window, similar to the one in Figure 15-28.

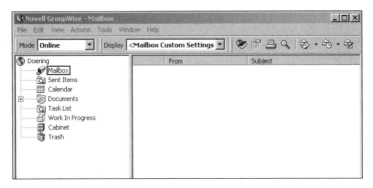

**Figure 15-28**   The Novell GroupWise - Mailbox window

4. He closed the Novell GroupWise - Mailbox window and logged out.

## CONFIGURING AND MANAGING THE GROUPWISE SYSTEM

After the basic e-mail system was operational, David took on some of the ongoing tasks of creating user accounts and distribution lists, automating e-mail functions with rules, making resources available for checkout, and monitoring GroupWise activity.

### Creating GroupWise Post Office Users

After installing and configuring the GroupWise software, an ongoing task is assigning new users to mailboxes and creating additional GroupWise post office objects, such as rules, nicknames, and distribution lists. As in the U.S. postal system, users need to be assigned to post offices to send and receive e-mail. During the GroupWise configuration, David was able to assign all users in the InfoSystems OU to the GroupWise 6 post office. To allow new users as well as users in other OUs to send and receive messages, David needed to assign them to the post office. In GroupWise, you can assign users to post offices in the following ways:

- Assign multiple eDirectory users to a post office

- Assign a single user to the post office

- Assign a new user to a post office when creating the user account

- Create a GroupWise external entity

In the following sections, you learn how David used ConsoleOne to perform these methods for assigning users to post offices.

## Assigning Multiple eDirectory Users to a Post Office

The best way to assign several users to a post office is to use ConsoleOne to select the GroupWise post office object and then use the Membership tab to add the user accounts. In the following example, you see how David used ConsoleOne to assign users to the CBEPO post office:

1. He started ConsoleOne and expanded the CLASS_TREE object.

2. He expanded the GroupWise System object, and then expanded the CBEWorld and CBEPO objects, as shown in Figure 15-29.

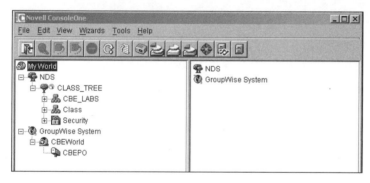

**Figure 15-29**   Expanding GroupWise objects in ConsoleOne

3. He right-clicked the CBEPO office, and then clicked Properties to open the Properties of CBEPO dialog box.

4. To view existing members, David clicked the down arrow on the GroupWise tab to display the options shown in Figure 15-30.

15

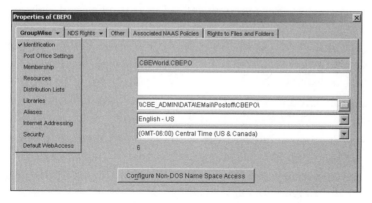

**Figure 15-30**   Options available on the GroupWise tab

5. He clicked the Membership option to display the Users window, similar to the one shown in Figure 15-31.

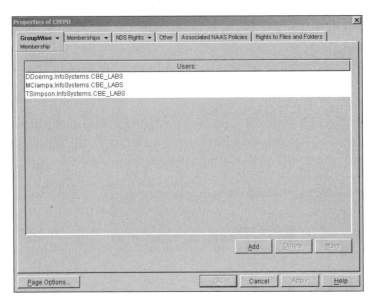

**Figure 15-31**    Viewing existing members in CBEPO

6. To create additional user post office accounts, he clicked the Add button to open the Select Objects dialog box. He navigated to the Personnel.CBE_Labs_ Admin OU and selected users by holding down the Ctrl key as he clicked on each user name. He clicked OK to add the users to the Users window.

7. After adding all users, he clicked OK to update the mailbox assignments and return to the ConsoleOne window.

## Assigning a Single eDirectory User to a Post Office

When adding only one user to the GroupWise post office, sometimes it's quicker to use the Properties dialog box for that user's account instead of expanding and right-clicking the post office object. David used the following steps to add JJorgensen to the CBE post office:

1. He navigated to the Marketing.CBE_Labs_Admin OU, right-clicked the JJorgensen User object, and then clicked Properties to open the Properties of JJorgensen dialog box.

2. He clicked the GroupWise tab to display the GroupWise account information window, similar to the one shown in Figure 15-32.

3. He clicked the browse button next to the Post Office text box to open the Select Object dialog box.

4. He double-clicked the CBEWorld object to display the CBEPO post office object shown in Figure 15-33.

5. He clicked the CBEPO post office object, and then clicked OK to insert it into the Post Office text box.

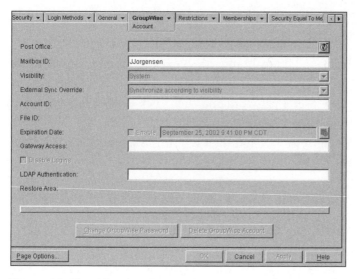

**Figure 15-32**    Viewing GroupWise account information for JJorgensen

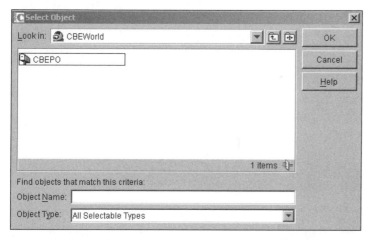

**Figure 15-33**    Assigning JJorgensen to the CBEPO post office object

> 6. He clicked the OK button to assign JJorgensen to the CBEPO post office and return to the main ConsoleOne window.

## Assigning New eDirectory Users to a Post Office

When creating new user accounts, administrators can save time by creating a GroupWise mailbox for new users at the same time. To assign a new user to a post office at the time you create the User object, follow these steps:

> 1. After starting ConsoleOne, click to highlight the container where you'll create the new user. Click the New User button to open the New User dialog box.

15

2. Enter the user's Name and Surname information.

3. If needed, select a template in the Use template text box.

4. Click the Define additional properties check box, and then click OK to create the new user account and open the Set Password dialog box.

5. Assign the new user a password and then click the Set Password button to open the Properties dialog box.

6. Click the GroupWise tab, and then repeat the steps described in "Assigning a Single eDirectory User to a Post Office" to create a GroupWise account for the new user.

7. Click OK to save your changes and return to the main ConsoleOne window.

## Creating a GroupWise External Entity

**External entities** are typically used to allow non-eDirectory users to have an account in a GroupWise post office. An external entity appears in the GroupWise address book for e-mail address purposes and in the eDirectory tree for administrative purposes. For example, there are user e-mail accounts for each of CBE's major customers, such as NASA administrators. To make it easier to send e-mail to these customers, David created external entities for the commonly used e-mail addresses. The following example shows how he created an external entity for one of these users, Jerry Tayler:

1. He started ConsoleOne and expanded the GroupWise System and CBEWorld objects.

2. He right-clicked the CBEPO object, and then pointed to New to display the list of GroupWise object types that can be created (see Figure 15-34).

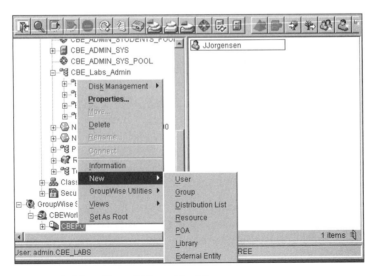

**Figure 15-34**    GroupWise object types

3. He clicked the External Entity object type to open the Create GroupWise External Entity dialog box, shown in Figure 15-35.

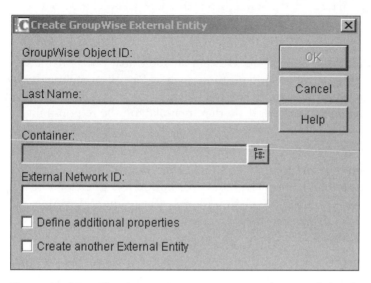

**Figure 15-35**    The Create GroupWise External Entity dialog box

4. He entered Jerry in the GroupWise Object ID text box.

5. He entered Tayler in the Last Name text box.

6. Because Jerry's user name is normally accessed by users in the Testing and Evaluation Department, David wanted to create the external entity in the Test&Eval OU. To select an OU for the external entity, he clicked the browse button next to the Container text box to navigate to the Test&Eval container and then clicked OK to add the Test&Eval OU's context to the Container text box.

7. In the External Network ID text box, he entered Jerry's e-mail address.

8. He clicked the Define additional properties check box, and then clicked OK to create the external entity and open the Properties of Jerry dialog box.

9. He entered a description for Jerry in the Title text box, and then clicked OK to save the changes and return to the main ConsoleOne window.

## Creating Additional GroupWise Post Office Objects

ConsoleOne can be used to create a variety of other post office objects, including GroupWise rules, nicknames, distribution lists, and resources. GroupWise **rules** contain actions that are applied to any incoming message that meets the specified conditions. For example, David created an out-of-the-office rule to use when he's away from the office; the rule sets up a response to e-mails with a message telling the sender when he will return. David's out-of-the-office rule returns the message "I will not be back in the office until Monday, April 15. In case of any urgent communication, please contact Ted Simpson at CBELABS.com." Rules can also be used to move incoming messages to predetermined folders based on the sender's e-mail address, subject, or character string in the message text. David uses this rule to help screen "junk" messages into a special folder so that he can quickly review and delete them.

A GroupWise **nickname** allows you to assign an additional e-mail name to a user and can be used to identify a role or job position, such as Payroll or Billing. By using nicknames, people can send messages to the role name if they don't know the name of the user currently assigned to that role. If another user takes on the responsibility of the role, the nickname can simply be removed from one user and applied to the new user. David set up nicknames for Accounting, Testing, and Marketing.

A GroupWise **distribution list** is a set of users and resources that can be addressed as a group by using a unique name. David uses distribution lists to create e-mail groups for each department and for the entire organization. If management personnel want to send an announcement to all users in the organization, for example, they can simply select the name of the company distribution list in the To field.

GroupWise **resources** are physical assets that can be checked out or scheduled. For example, David created resource objects for the conference room, company vehicle, and audiovisual equipment. Because resource objects are assigned to an owner who makes decisions on scheduling and allocating the assigned resources, they must be created in the same post office as the user account assigned to them.

After the user mailbox accounts were set up, David made the GroupWise system more efficient by creating nicknames, distribution lists, and resources. In addition, he held a brief training session to show users basic GroupWise operations, including how to create rules to help manage their incoming messages. In the following example, you see how David created a distribution list for the Information Systems Department, assigned resources for the conference room and the company vehicle, and set up a computer support nickname.

1. He started ConsoleOne, and then expanded the Tree object and the GroupWise System object.

2. To create a distribution list for the Information Systems Department, David performed the following steps:

   a. He right-clicked the CBEPO object, pointed to New, and clicked Distribution List to open the Create GroupWise Distribution List dialog box shown in Figure 15-36.

   b. He entered InfoSystems Department in the Distribution List Name text box.

   c. He clicked the browse button next to the Container text box to open the Select Objects dialog box. He navigated to the CBE_Labs_Admin.CBE_LABS OU, clicked the InfoSystems OU, and clicked OK to insert InfoSystems.CBE_Labs_Admin.CBE_LABS in the Container text box.

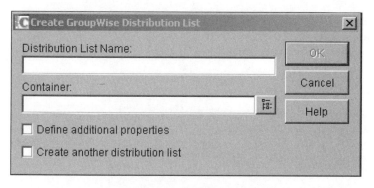

**Figure 15-36**    The Create GroupWise Distribution List dialog box

     d. He clicked OK to create the distribution list.

3. To view existing distribution lists for the CBEPO, David performed the following steps:

     a. He right-clicked the CBEPO and clicked Properties.

     b. He clicked the down arrow on the GroupWise tab and clicked the Distribution Lists option to display existing distribution lists, as shown in Figure 15-37.

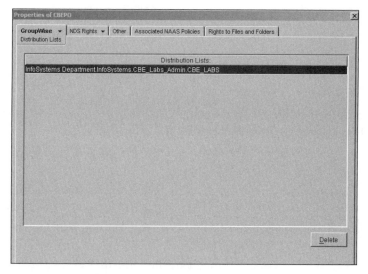

**Figure 15-37**    Viewing existing distribution lists

4. To create a new resource object in the CBE_Labs_Admin container for the conference room, David performed the following steps:

     a. He right-clicked the CBEPO object, pointed to New, and clicked Resource to open the Create GroupWise Resource dialog box shown in Figure 15-38.

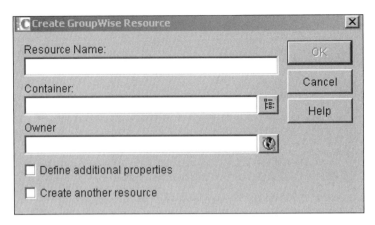

**Figure 15-38**   The Create GroupWise Resource dialog box

    b. He entered Conference Room 101 in the Resource Name text box.

    c. He clicked the browse button next to the Container text box and used the Select Objects dialog box to navigate to and select the CBE_Labs_ Admin OU.

    d. He clicked the browse button next to the Owner text box to open the Select Objects dialog box.

    e. He clicked the SLopez user, and clicked OK.

    f. He clicked OK to create the resource object and return to the main ConsoleOne window.

5. To assign a nickname of Support to his DDoering user account, he performed the following steps:

    a. He expanded the GroupWise System object.

    b. He clicked the CBEPO object to display all e-mail users.

    c. He right-clicked his DDoering user name, and clicked Properties to open the Properties of DDoering dialog box.

    d. He clicked the down arrow on the GroupWise tab, and then clicked the Nicknames option to display the Nicknames window shown in Figure 15-39.

    e. He clicked Add to open the Create Nickname dialog box shown in Figure 15-40.

    f. He clicked the browse button next to the Domain.PO text box, selected the CBEPO object, and clicked OK to return to the Create Nickname dialog box.

    g. He entered Support in the Object ID text box.

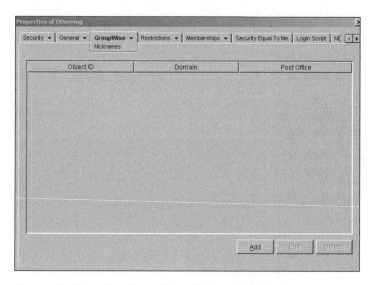

**Figure 15-39**    The GroupWise Nicknames window

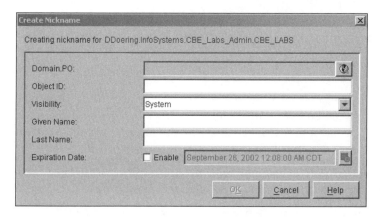

**Figure 15-40**    The Create Nickname dialog box

15

h. He entered A+ Computer Support Technician in the Given Name text box.

i. He clicked OK to add the nickname to the GroupWise Nicknames window.

j. He clicked OK to save his changes and return to the main ConsoleOne window.

## Deleting and Renaming Post Office Objects

When users leave the organization or change their names, or when you need to make modifications such as changing nicknames, removing resources that are no longer available, or deleting obsolete distribution lists, you must be able to remove and rename post office objects. User objects can be deleted from the entire eDirectory system or from just the GroupWise post office. When you use ConsoleOne to delete a User object from an eDirectory container, you are prompted to specify which attributes to delete, as shown in Figure 15-41.

**Figure 15-41** The Delete User Options dialog box

You might need to change GroupWise mailbox names if a user's name changes, if you need to implement a new naming convention for your organization, or if there are duplicate names. When you change a user mailbox name with ConsoleOne, the following changes take place throughout the entire GroupWise system:

- The user's mailbox is renamed and the address book is updated. The contents of the old mailbox are maintained with the new name.

- Distribution lists are updated with the new mailbox name.

- Any resources owned by the user are reassigned to the new user mailbox name.

- Any personal groups that contain the user name are updated as part of the nightly maintenance the POA performs.

When you rename a user mailbox, the post office database information for the user's mailbox is changed and the user database is updated. The information in the user mailbox is updated through the following process:

1. The administrator uses ConsoleOne to rename the user mailbox.

2. ConsoleOne writes the information to eDirectory, updates the domain database (Wpdomain.db), and creates an administrative message in the MTA input queue to replicate the update to other GroupWise servers.

3. The MTA transfers the administrative message to the MTA "in progress" queue and communicates the administrative message to the POA.

4. The POA creates a copy of the administrative message in the post office priority queue.

5. The POA updates the Wphost.db file for the post office to reflect the modification and deletes the administrative message from its administrative queue.

6. The POA updates the user's database with the user's new name.

## Establishing Mailbox Security

Mailbox security can be set by the administrator or by users. Users can assign passwords to their mailboxes to prevent unauthorized access and must assign a separate password as a security measure when running the client in remote or cached mode (the user's messages are stored on the local hard drive). In addition to changing and setting passwords, administrators can set post office security levels that apply to users who do not have passwords set on their mailboxes; they can be set to Low security or High security. If Low security is selected, user mailboxes without passwords are left unprotected. With the High security setting, users need to have a password for their GroupWise mailbox or log in to the Novell network before accessing their mailbox. David used the following steps in ConsoleOne to set a security level for the CBE GroupWise system:

1. In the ConsoleOne window, he expanded the GroupWise System object and then the CBEWorld object.

2. He right-clicked the CBEPO post office object and clicked Properties to open the Properties of CBEPO dialog box.

3. He then clicked the down arrow on the GroupWise tab and clicked the Security option to display the Security dialog box (see Figure 15-42).

4. In the Security Level section, he clicked the High radio button, and then clicked the NDS Authentication check box, as shown in Figure 15-42.

To allow GroupWise to be installed on other network operating systems, such as Windows NT and Windows 2000, GroupWise has its own built-in user database for authenticating user access to mailbox data. The GroupWise authentication system is not as secure as Novell's NDS or eDirectory. The NDS Authentication option in Step 4 increases security by requiring GroupWise users to log in with their eDirectory user name and password before accessing their GroupWise post offices.

5. He clicked OK to save his changes and return to the main ConsoleOne window.

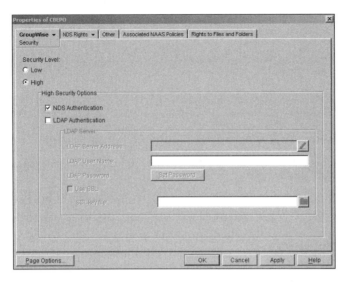

**Figure 15-42**    Selecting a security level for the GroupWise system

## MONITORING AND TROUBLESHOOTING A GROUPWISE SYSTEM

As with other computerized systems, monitoring performance and troubleshooting problems are ongoing tasks of system administration. In the following sections, you learn how to use the Web Console utility from your Web browser to view information on the performance of your GroupWise system. In addition, you learn how to identify and troubleshoot some common GroupWise implementation problems.

### Monitoring GroupWise Agents

The two major agents for monitoring and managing the GroupWise system are the Message Transfer Agent (MTA) and Post Office Agent (POA). As described previously, the MTA is responsible for transferring messages between user mailboxes located on the same or different post office servers. The POA is responsible for communication between the client and the post office server. The POA transfers messages from the client to the server and enables the client to read any new messages in the user mailbox. Both the MTA and POA are objects in the eDirectory tree that are initially created and configured during GroupWise installation. Like other eDirectory objects, you can view and modify the MTA and POA objects by using ConsoleOne. The MTA and POA also have startup files in the SYS:System directory that contain agent startup and configuration information. For example, the user name, password, and port number for the agent are stored in both the agent startup file and the eDirectory object. The MTA user name and password for the CBE GroupWise system are stored in the startup file, as shown in Figure 15-43. GroupWise shortened the name of the startup file from CBEWorld to CBEWorl.MTA to meet internal GroupWise requirements.

```
; -----------------------------------------------------------------
;   Http Enabled
;   The port number for browsers to use for http queries.
; -----------------------------------------------------------------
/httpport-7180
/httpuser-webagent
/httppassword-novell
;/httprefresh-[seconds]

; -----------------------------------------------------------------
;   Enable SSL for Https
;   Valid server certificate in PEM format obtained from a Certificate
;   Authority ( CA ), Private key must not be password protected.
; -----------------------------------------------------------------
;/httpcertfile-[file name]

; -----------------------------------------------------------------
;   Live Remote Enabled
;   The port number for live remote to use
; -----------------------------------------------------------------
;/liveremote-[port number]

; -----------------------------------------------------------------
;       Maximum Live Remote connections
; -----------------------------------------------------------------
;/lrconn-[connections]
```

**Figure 15-43**    The MTA startup file

The CBE POA user name and password are stored in the CBEPO.POA file (see Figure 15-44).

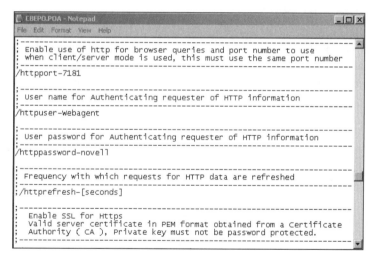

**Figure 15-44**    The POA startup file

To make the system more secure, David used ConsoleOne to place the user name and password in the eDirectory tree and then modified the startup files to remove the user name and password entries. In the end-of-chapter case project, you will have the opportunity to use ConsoleOne to view information about the MTA and POA objects in your GroupWise system.

## Identifying and Troubleshooting E-mail Problems

Problems in GroupWise e-mail systems can occur for both internal and external reasons. Internal problems are usually caused by configuration or operational problems with the client or server. Common internal problems are incorrect IP addresses, insufficient disk space for mail storage and forwarding, and incorrect routes specified for transfers between e-mail servers. External problems are often the result of problems in the connectivity channel used to transfer information between e-mail components. Common problems associated with the GroupWise system include the following:

- A corrupt mailbox database
- Shortage of mailbox space
- Queue overloads
- Connectivity problems
- E-mail virus problems

In the following sections, you learn the steps David took to prevent these possible problems.

### Corrupt Mailbox Database

E-mail databases require periodic maintenance to clean up old user names, remove incorrect addresses, and check the relationship between addresses and their related mailboxes. In his GroupWise training, David learned that periodically performing the following mailbox maintenance tasks is the best way to protect the GroupWise system from mailbox corruption:

- Validating post office databases
- Recovering databases
- Rebuilding databases and their indexes

A detailed description of performing mailbox maintenance tasks is a Certified Novell Engineer (CNE) topic that is beyond the scope of this book.

David learned that the frequency of performing these maintenance tasks depends on the network's reliability and the administrator's experience and knowledge of how often problems are likely to occur.

### Mailbox Space Problems

Not maintaining the space used by mailboxes can result in a database that consumes more space than is allocated, causing the e-mail system to run out of disk space and possibly crash. One solution is to limit the size of the mailbox database and have users download and archive e-mail to their local computers. Although this approach saves space on the server, it requires users to be at their local computers to access downloaded or archived e-mail messages and attachments. The following tasks can help manage disk space use in the post office:

- Obtaining mailbox statistics from the Web Console utility
- Reducing the size of user and message databases
- Reclaiming disk space from post office databases
- Reducing the size of library and document storage areas

## Queue Overloads

Excessive e-mail on a server, known as queue overload, can shut down the GroupWise e-mail server. The **queue** is a space in the e-mail database where the server temporarily stores outgoing messages while waiting to contact the destination server at a predefined interval. Using predefined intervals helps ensure maximum use of network bandwidth. The most common cause of queue overload is a heavy message load on an old e-mail server with slow performance. The slower hardware cannot clear the data in the queue as fast as new e-mail comes in, causing the backlog of e-mail in the queue to grow until the queue is overloaded, thus shutting down the server. Queue overloads can also be caused by slow bandwidths that prevent moving messages from the queue as fast as they are being generated or e-mail viruses that propagate by sending e-mail to all users in an address list. The attachment containing the virus code can infect other clients as it's distributed via e-mail; this type of virus attack can rapidly escalate, causing a queue overload problem.

## Connectivity Problems

Connectivity problems are often caused by faulty hardware or incorrect driver software. If a router or switch on the network is faulty, it can cause delays in transferring data from the server, causing e-mail server problems such as queue overloads. Connectivity problems can also be caused by faulty network configurations and cable layouts that cause data collisions, thus slowing data flow. Network board problems on the server are fairly easy to identify because they prevent clients from connecting to the server. To help identify possible connectivity problems, David obtained network monitor software to view network activity, including collisions, bad network connections, and defective cards. Network monitoring software, such as LANalyzer, ManageWise, and ZENworks for Servers, is available from Novell. Other organizations, such as Computer Associates and Hewlett-Packard, also provide good network monitoring tools.

**15**

## Virus Problems

E-mail systems automate many tasks to assist users when forwarding messages or opening attachments. Many e-mail virus programs, called worms, are executable programs that replicate themselves by using the resources in e-mail programs or by taking advantage of known security weaknesses in the e-mail client software. (For more information on virus prevention, see Chapter 14.) To help protect the GroupWise system against viruses, David took the following precautions:

- He installed antivirus software on the e-mail server and clients.

- He established a system of regular updates to the antivirus software.

- He trained users to use discretion when opening e-mail messages that have executable attachments. David informed users that they should not open e-mail with attachments from unknown users. E-mail messages with "suspicious" attachments, such as .exe, .scr, or .com files, should also be avoided. David also informed users that they should not ignore any warning messages from the antivirus software or system administrator.

## CHAPTER SUMMARY

- ❏ E-mail systems combined with other collaborative applications, such as calendaring, scheduling, and document management, play an important role in a network office environment.

- ❏ E-mail systems consist of client and server components that work together through special programs called agents. The Message Transfer Agent (MTA) is responsible for transferring messages between e-mail servers, while the Post Office Agent (POA) transfers messages between the client and the post office server.

- ❏ Standardized protocols for communicating between e-mail components include POP, IMAP, and SMTP. SMTP is used to transfer messages between the source and destination servers, and POP and IMAP are used to communicate between server and client.

- ❏ Common clients, also referred to as front ends, include Eudora v5.1, GroupWise, Outlook 2002, Outlook Express, and Lotus Notes. All clients support the standard Post Office Protocol version 3 (POP3) and Internet Message Access Protocol (IMAP) and have specialized capabilities for e-mail and collaborative functions.

- ❏ Common e-mail back-end server products with both e-mail and collaborative applications include Microsoft Exchange 2000 Server, Lotus Domino Mail Server, and GroupWise.

- ❏ GroupWise is installed from an administrative workstation and involves creating directories for GroupWise software and database files, copying files to the GroupWise directories, and configuring agents using an upgraded version of ConsoleOne.

- ❏ Using the GroupWise system for e-mail and collaborative applications involves installing the GroupWise client on the workstation and then logging in and starting the GroupWise client from the workstation desktop.

- ❏ GroupWise maintenance tasks include assigning users to post offices and creating additional objects, such as distribution lists, rules, and nicknames, to enhance user access and management of messaging.

❏ With the Web Console utility, you can monitor agent statistics from a Web browser for the MTA and POA to assess system performance. Using Web Console requires logging in with a user name and password supplied in the agent startup files or through eDirectory.

❏ Common GroupWise problems, such as corrupted mailboxes, queue overloads, and shortage of disk space, can often by prevented through periodic maintenance tasks, such as validating the post office database information, rebuilding post office database and index files, and installing virus prevention software.

## KEY TERMS

**AutoComplete addressing** — An e-mail client feature used to search the address book for matching names when a user enters an e-mail address.

**back-end process** — Software such as an e-mail server that processes the data or messages received from the front-end process running on a client.

**caching mode** — An e-mail client feature that automatically stores all messages and attachments on the local hard disk of the user workstation.

**distribution list** — A GroupWise object consisting of a set of users who can be addressed as a group by using a unique name.

**document management** — An e-mail client feature that enables you to share documents with a group of users.

**external entity** — An object type created to give users outside the organization an account in a GroupWise post office.

**front-end process** — Software such as an e-mail client that runs on a user's workstation and provides an interface that allows users to communicate with services running on a server.

**Internet Message Access Protocol (IMAP)** — A standardized protocol used to access and store messages from the post office server.

**mailbox mode switching** — A GroupWise client feature that enables users to change mailbox modes between online, caching, and remote.

**Message Transfer Agent (MTA)** — A software component that assists the core post office software in transferring messages between mailboxes.

**nickname** — A GroupWise object that assigns an account name to a role or position in the company.

**Post Office Agent (POA)** — An e-mail software component that is responsible for transferring messages from the client to the correct mailbox on the e-mail server.

**Post Office Protocol (POP)** — A standardized client-server protocol used for sending and receiving e-mail messages between the client and the e-mail server.

**queue** — A space in the e-mail database where the server temporarily stores outgoing messages while waiting to contact the destination server at a predefined interval.

**resource** — A GroupWise object representing a physical asset that can be checked out or scheduled, such as a conference room or a company vehicle.

15

> **rule** — A GroupWise object containing actions that are applied to incoming messages that meet certain conditions.
>
> **Simple Mail Transfer Protocol (SMTP)** — A TCP/IP-based e-mail protocol used to transfer messages between e-mail servers.

## REVIEW QUESTIONS

1. Which of the following is *not* an example of a collaborative application?
   a. scheduling
   b. calendaring
   c. FTP
   d. task management
   e. reminders

2. Which of the following is an example of a front-end process?
   a. Domino Server
   b. Web Server
   c. Eudora
   d. Exchange 2002

3. Which of the following assists the core post office software in transferring e-mail between user mailboxes and maintaining message integrity?
   a. SNMP
   b. POA
   c. SMTP
   d. MTA

4. Which of the following protocols is used to transfer messages between e-mail servers?
   a. MTA
   b. POA
   c. SMTP
   d. SNMP

5. Which of the following protocols has features for transferring only address and subject information to the e-mail client?
   a. SNMP
   b. SMTP
   c. IMAP
   d. POP
   e. IMAP4
   f. POP3

6. Moodwatch is a feature of which of the following e-mail clients?

   a. Eudora v5.1

   b. GroupWise

   c. Outlook 2002

   d. Lotus Notes

7. Mailbox mode switching is a feature of which of the following e-mail clients?

   a. Eudora v5.1

   b. GroupWise

   c. Outlook 2002

   d. Lotus Notes

8. Which of the following GroupWise objects can be used to send e-mail to a role or job position?

   a. distribution list

   b. nickname

   c. resource

   d. rule

9. Which of the following is responsible for delivering messages from the client to the correct mailbox on the server?

   a. POP

   b. SNMP

   c. MTA

   d. POA

10. Which of the following is *not* an e-mail protocol?

    a. POP3

    b. SNMP

    c. SMTP

    d. IMAP4

11. Which of the following is *not* a method used to assign a user to a post office?

    a. using ConsoleOne to access the properties of the user object

    b. using ConsoleOne to access the Membership tab from the properties of the post office object

    c. using Web Console to add users to the post office

    d. selecting the post office from the User Properties dialog box while creating the User object

15

12. Which of the following allows non-eDirectory users to have an account in a GroupWise post office?

    a. nicknames

    b. external entities

    c. alias entities

    d. resources

    e. rules

13. Which of the following is used to represent physical assets?

    a. nickname

    b. external entity

    c. alias entity

    d. rule

    e. resource

14. During installation, user names and passwords for agents are _____.

    a. stored in eDirectory

    b. stored in the Autoexec.ncf startup file

    c. stored in the agent startup file

    d. not assigned

15. The MTA object is stored in which of the following containers?

    a. GroupWise System object

    b. Post Office object

    c. CBEWorld domain object

    d. CBE Organization

16. You need to use which of the following to change the configuration of an agent object?

    a. ConsoleOne

    b. Web Console

    c. Remote Manager

    d. NetWare Administrator

17. Which of the following can be used to view statistical information about the performance of the MTA?

    a. ConsoleOne

    b. Web Console

    c. Remote Manager

    d. a text editor, such as Notepad

18. Which of the following are examples of common GroupWise e-mail problems? (Select all that apply.)

   a. incorrect IP port number assignment

   b. connectivity problems

   c. corrupt mailboxes

   d. mailbox database running out of disk space

19. Which of the following are tasks you can perform to help prevent mailbox corruption? (Select all that apply.)

   a. limiting the size of user mailboxes

   b. periodically validating mailboxes

   c. periodically rebuilding mailbox indexes

   d. installing antivirus software

20. True or False: Not providing enough memory during GroupWise installation is a common cause of queue overload problems.

## HANDS-ON PROJECTS

In the following projects, you apply concepts and techniques from this chapter to implementing e-mail services for your CBE office users. Before getting started, copy the GroupWise Documentation Worksheet from Appendix B, and fill it in (consulting your instructor, if necessary) to make sure you have all the information you need.

### Project 15-1: Installing the GroupWise Client

In this project, you follow the procedure described in this chapter to install the GroupWise client on your Windows workstation. Configure the GroupWise client to use the IP address of your classroom server, default ports, and the user name you established for yourself in your version of the CBE InfoSystems OU. Document the steps you perform and use them to create a memo to your instructor describing how to install the GroupWise client on user workstations. Turn in the GroupWise Documentation Worksheet you filled in previously.

### Project 15-2: Sending and Receiving E-mail

In this project, you work as a team with another student to send and receive e-mail. Log in with the user name you used to create your e-mail account in Project 15-1. Obtain the e-mail address of your partner's user name, send a message to your lab partner, and then retrieve your mail and respond to the message. When you're finished, create a memo to your instructor describing the use of basic e-mail functions, such as sending, receiving, deleting, and archiving e-mail. In your memo, include your responses to the information requested in the following steps:

1. When your computer restarts, log in with the user name you used in Project 15-1.

15

2. Start GroupWise by double-clicking the **GroupWise** icon on your desktop. When prompted, log in to GroupWise with the user name you used in Project 15-1.

3. Read the GroupWise 6 tip of the day, and click **Close**.

4. Place your cursor over each GroupWise button icon and record the button descriptions.

5. Click the **Create New Mail** button to open the Mail To dialog box.

6. Click the **Address** icon, and then click the **Novell GroupWise Address Book** tab, which lists users in the CBEPO post office.

7. Double-click the name of your team member, and then click **OK** to insert the user name into the To text box.

8. Enter **GroupWise Test** in the Subject text box.

9. Enter **This is a test of the GroupWise e-mail system. Please respond when you receive this message.** in the Message text box.

10. Click the **Send** button to send the message.

11. Wait for a message to appear in the Novell GroupWise – Mailbox window. Double-click the message to read it.

12. Click the **Reply** button, and then click **OK** to accept the default Reply to sender option.

13. Enter a short reply in the Message text box, and then click the **Send** button.

14. Wait for a reply to come back from your original message, and then read and delete the reply.

15. Close the GroupWise client, and log out.

## Project 15-3: Installing the GroupWise ConsoleOne Snap-ins

Before using ConsoleOne to configure and work with GroupWise objects, you must install the GroupWise snap-ins. When David installed the GroupWise server, the ConsoleOne snap-ins were automatically installed on his computer to complete the initial GroupWise installation. Other workstations used to access and configure the GroupWise objects also need to have the ConsoleOne snap-ins installed. In this project, you learn how to update ConsoleOne to include the new snap-ins and how to use ConsoleOne to perform basic GroupWise management and configuration tasks. Create a memo to your instructor that includes your responses to the information requested in the following steps:

1. If necessary, start your computer, and log in with your user name and password.

2. In this step, start ConsoleOne and describe the GroupWise objects before adding the snap-ins:

a. Start ConsoleOne, and expand your classroom tree.

b. If necessary, scroll down and expand the **GroupWise System** object.

c. Expand the **CBEWorld** object.

    d. Record the icons next to the CBEPO and CBEWorld GroupWise objects.

    e. Right-click the **CBEPO** post office object, and click **Properties** to open the Properties of CBEPO dialog box. Record the tabs you see.

    f. Click **Cancel** to close the Properties of CBEPO dialog box and return to the main ConsoleOne window.

    g. Exit ConsoleOne.

3. Use My Network Places to navigate to the \\CBE_ADMIN\DATA\EMail\ GrpWise\Software\Admin\C1Admin directory:

    a. Double-click **My Network Places,** and then double-click **Novell Connections** to display your CBE_ADMIN server.

    b. Double-click the **CBE_ADMIN** server icon to display all volumes.

    c. Double-click the **CBE_ADMIN_DATA** Volume object to display all directories.

    d. Double-click the **EMail, GrpWise, Software, Admin,** and **C1Admin** directories to display the Groupwise ConsoleOne directories.

4. Click **Edit, Select All** on the My Network Places menu bar to select all GroupWise ConsoleOne subdirectories.

5. Click **Edit, Copy** on the menu bar, and then close the C1Admin directory window.

6. Use My Computer to navigate to your C:\Novell\ConsoleOne\1.2 directory:

    a. Double-click the **My Computer icon,** and then double-click your **Local Disk (C:)** icon to display all directories on your C: drive.

    b. Double-click the **Novell, ConsoleOne,** and **1.2** directories to display the existing ConsoleOne subdirectories.

7. Click **Edit, Paste** on the My Computer menu bar, and then click **Yes to All** to copy the new ConsoleOne GroupWise software into your ConsoleOne\1.2 subdirectory.

8. Close the 1.2 directory window.

9. Start ConsoleOne. If this is the first time ConsoleOne has been started with the GroupWise snap-ins, the GroupWise Administrator dialog box opens, asking for the domain path to the GroupWise domain database. Use the following steps if you are asked to enter the path to the GroupWise domain database; otherwise, skip to Step 10.

    a. Click the **browse** button to select your M: drive, navigate to the Mail\ CBEWorld directory, and then click the **wpdomain.db** database filename.

    b. Click the **Open** button to insert the path to the wpdomain.db database into the Domain Path text box, and then click **OK** to start ConsoleOne.

10. In this step, you start ConsoleOne and observe the GroupWise objects after adding the snap-ins:

    a. If necessary, expand the **GroupWise System** and **CBEWorld** objects.

    b. Right-click the **CBEPO** post office object, and click **Properties** to open the Properties of CBEPO dialog box. Record the available tabs.

**15**

c. Click **Cancel** to close the Properties of CBEPO dialog box and return to the main ConsoleOne window.

11. Exit ConsoleOne, and log out. In your memo to your instructor, describe the differences you noticed after installing the ConsoleOne snap-ins.

## Project 15-4: Setting Up E-mail Accounts

In this project, you apply what you have learned about assigning users to the GroupWise post office to assigning all users in your CBE_Labs_Admin container and subcontainers to the CBEPO post office. Create a memo to your instructor describing the method(s) you used to create your user accounts.

## Project 15-5: Creating Additional GroupWise Objects

In this project, you create a rule that will place all incoming mail containing the word "Results" in the Subject field into a special folder:

1. Log in as one of the users in your InfoSystems OU (for example, DDoering).

2. Start GroupWise, log in with your user name and password, and then click **Close** in the Tip window.

3. Create a new mailbox folder named **Testing**.

4. Use GroupWise to create a new rule that places all incoming messages with the word "Results" in the Testing folder:

   a. Click **Tools, Rules** on the GroupWise menu bar to open the Rules dialog box.

   b. Click **New** to open the New Rule dialog box, and enter a name, such as Test Results Rule, for the new rule.

   c. In the When event is section, verify that New Item is shown in the button description and that the Received check box is selected.

   d. Click the **Define Conditions** button to open the Define Conditions dialog box.

   e. Click the **Include entries where** list arrow and then click **Subject** in the list of options.

   f. In the Subject contains text box, enter **Test**, and then click **OK** to close the Define Conditions dialog box.

   g. Click the **Mail** check box, click the **Add Action** button, and then click the **Move to Folder** option to open the Move Item to Folder Action dialog box.

   h. Click the check box next to your Testing folder, and then click the **Move** button to place "Move to Folder: Testing" in the Action window.

   i. Click **Save** to save your new rule, and then click **Close** to return to your GroupWise mailbox. Click **File, Exit** on the menu bar to close the GroupWise - Mailbox window.

5. Log out.

6. Log in as a different user and send a message containing the word "Test Results" in the Subject field to the user name you used in Step 1.

7. Log out.

8. Log in with the same user name and password used in Step 1 and start the GroupWise client.

9. Verify that the message has been placed in the new Testing folder.

10. Log out.

11. Create a memo to your instructor describing the use of rules in this project.

## Project 15-6: Creating Distribution Lists

In this project, you follow the procedure described in this chapter to create distribution lists for the Marketing and Finance departments of your CBE_LABS OU. Test your distribution list by performing the following steps:

1. Log in with your user name and password.

2. Start the GroupWise client.

3. Send an e-mail to your Marketing distribution list.

4. Log out.

5. Log in as one of the users in your Marketing OU and start the GroupWise client.

6. Read the message and log out.

Create a memo for your instructor that describes the steps your office staff should use to create and use distribution lists.

---

# CASE PROJECTS

## Case Project 15-1: Using the Novell Web Console Utility

The Novell Web Console utility enables administrators to view statistics and other configuration information about the MTA and POA running on the GroupWise server. To use Web Console to access agent information, you need to provide your Web browser with the IP address and port number of the agent you want to access. After entering this information, you enter the user name and password identified during agent installation and configuration.

In this project, you use Web Console to log in to the MTA and POA agents so that you can gather information and create a memo to your instructor describing agent configuration.

1. Start your Web browser and enter the URL **http://ip_address:7100** (replacing *ip_address* with the IP address of your GroupWise server).

15

2. If necessary, log in with the user name **WebAgent** and the password given to WebAgent by your instructor to display the Web Console window.

3. Use Web Console to document the MTA settings in Table 15-1 in a memo to your instructor.

4. Exit your Web browser.

5. Start your Web browser and enter the URL **http://*ip_address*:1677** (replacing *ip_address* with the IP address of your GroupWise server).

6. If necessary, log in with the user name **WebAgent** and the password given to WebAgent by your instructor to display the Web Console window.

7. Use Web Console to document the POA settings shown in Table 15-1 in a memo to your instructor.

8. Exit your Web browser, and log out.

**Table 15-1**   MTA and POA Statistics

| MTA Statistics | POA Statistics |
|---|---|
| Number of domains | C/S requests |
| Number of post offices | Intruder Detection setting |
| Total messages undelivered | Maximum log disk space |
| Maximum inbound TCP/IP connections | Maximum application connections |
| TCP port for inbound connection | HTTP refresh rate |
| Server name and OS date | Processor utilization |
| Messages queued | HTTP port |
| Maximum log file age | Message transfer status last opened |
| Build date for GWENN3.NLM | |

# A

# CNA Objectives

Table A-1 maps the CNA objectives to the corresponding chapter and section title where the objectives are covered in this book. Because the CNA exam undergoes frequent updating and revising, check the Novell Education Web site for the latest developments at *www.novell.com/education*.

Titles of subsections are enclosed in parentheses. Bold formatting for section titles indicates where to find the primary objective coverage.

**Table A-1** NetWare 6 Objectives Mapping

| Objective | Chapter: Section |
|---|---|
| **Section 1: Identify NetWare 6 Features and Services** | |
| 1.1: Identify the Features of NetWare 6 | Chapter 1: Network Components **(Types of Network Operating Systems)** |
| 1.2: Identify the Operating System Components of NetWare 6 | Chapter 6: NetWare Network Operating System Installation **(Defining and Documenting the NetWare Server Environment)** |
| 1.3: Describe How NetWare Relates to Other Operating Systems | Chapter 1: Network Components **(Types of Network Operating Systems)** |
| **Section 2: Install NetWare 6** | |
| 2.1: Identify Prerequisite Requirements | Chapter 6: NetWare Network Operating System Installation **(Defining and Documenting the NetWare Server Environment)** |
| 2.2: Prepare the Existing Network | Appendix C: Planning the Upgrade, **Upgrading NDS to eDirectory 8.6** |
| 2.3: Prepare the Designated Computer | Chapter 6: NetWare Network Operating System Installation **(NetWare Server Installation)** |
| 2.4: Install NetWare 6 | Chapter 6: NetWare Network Operating System Installation **(NetWare Server Installation)** |
| **Section 3: Manage NetWare 6** | |
| 3.1: Server Console Commands to Manage NetWare 6 | Chapter 6: NetWare Network Operating System Installation **(Using NetWare Console Commands at the Server)** |
| 3.2: Use Configuration Files | Chapter 6: NetWare Network Operating System Installation **(Using NetWare Console Commands at the Server)** |
| 3.3: Identify the Utilities to Remotely Manage NetWare 6 | Chapter 7: NetWare Utilities **(iManager)**; Chapter 9: Managing Objects **(Managing eDirectory with iManager)**; Chapter 13: **Working with iFolder** (all subsections), **Installing and Using NetStorage** (all subsections), **Using NetWare 6 Remote Management Utilities** (all subsections) |
| **Section 4: Install and Manage the Novell Client** | |
| 4.1: Describe the Novell Client | Chapter 6: Novell Client Software Installation **(The Novell Client)** |
| 4.2: Install the Novell Client | Chapter 6: Novell Client Software Installation **(The Novell Client)** |
| 4.3: Log in to eDirectory and the Workstation | Chapter 6: Novell Client Software Installation **(Logging In)**; Chapter 7: **Working with Container and Leaf Objects** (all subsections) |
| 4.4: Set Client Properties | Chapter 6: Novell Client Software Installation **(Logging In)** |

**Table A-1**    NetWare 6 Objectives Mapping (continued)

A

| Objective | Chapter: Section |
|---|---|
| **Section 5: Identify Directory Service Basics** | |
| 5.1: Identify Basic Directory Service Tasks | Chapter 1: Network Components **(Network Software Components)**; Chapter 4: **Introduction to Directory Services** |
| 5.2: Identify Common Directory Service Uses | Chapter 4: **Introduction to Directory Services** |
| 5.3: Describe How a Directory is Structured | Chapter 4: **Introduction to Directory Services** (all subsections) |
| **Section 6: Describe Novell eDirectory** | |
| 6.1: Identify the Role and Benefits of eDirectory | Chapter 4: **Novell eDirectory Services** |
| 6.2: Identify How eDirectory 8.6 Works | Chapter 4: Novell eDirectory Services **(eDirectory Architecture)** |
| 6.3: Identify and Describe the Composition of eDirectory | Chapter 4: **eDirectory Components** (all subsections) |
| 6.4: Identify and Describe eDirectory Object Classes | Chapter 4: **eDirectory Components** |
| 6.5: Identify the Flow and Design of the eDirectory Tree | Chapter 4: **Designing the eDirectory Tree**, Approaches to Directory Tree Design |
| 6.6: Identify eDirectory Tools and When to Use Them | Chapter 7: **NetWare Utilities** (all subsections) |
| **Section 7: Manage User Objects** | |
| 7.1: Describe the Admin Object | Chapter 4: eDirectory Components **(Leaf Objects)**; Chapter 9: Establishing Login Security **(Increasing Admin User Security)** |
| 7.2: Create User Objects | Chapter 9: **Creating User, Group, and Organizational Role Objects** |
| 7.3: Modify User Objects | Chapter 9: **Managing Objects** (all subsections) |
| 7.4: Move Objects | Chapter 9: Managing Objects **(Moving Objects)** |
| 7.5: Delete User Objects | Chapter 9: Managing Objects **(Deleting and Renaming Objects)** |
| **Section 8: Manage eDirectory Rights** | |
| 8.1: Describe eDirectory Security | Chapter 10: Trustee Assignments **(Planning Directory Tree and File System Security)** |
| 8.2: Determine How Rights Flow | Chapter 10: Trustee Assignments **(Managing Entry Rights and Attribute Rights)** |
| 8.3: Block Inherited Rights | Chapter 10: Trustee Assignments **(Managing Entry Rights and Attribute Rights)** |

Table A-1    NetWare 6 Objectives Mapping (continued)

| Objective | Chapter: Section |
|---|---|
| 8.4: Determine eDirectory Effective Rights | Chapter 10: Trustee Assignments (**Managing Entry Rights and Attribute Rights**) |
| 8.5: Troubleshoot eDirectory Security | Chapter 10: Trustee Assignments (**Planning Directory Tree and File System Security**) |
| **Section 9: Configure the User Environment** | |
| 9.1: Use Login Scripts to Configure the User Environment | Chapter 12: NetWare Login Scripts (**Types of Login Scripts**) |
| 9.2: Plan the Login Scripts for Container, Groups, and Users | Chapter 12: **Implementing Login Scripts** (all subsections) |
| 9.3: Use ZENworks for Desktops 3 to Configure the Environment | Chapter 12: Managing User Environments with ZENworks for Desktops, **Managing Workstations** |
| 9.4: Identify Common Configurations Created Through User Policies | Chapter 12: **Managing Workstations** |
| **Section 10: Implement Queue-Based Printing** | |
| 10.1: Set Up a Queue-Based Printing System | Chapter 11: Queue-Based Printing (**Setting Up Queue-Based Printing**) |
| 10.2: Set Up Queue-Based Printing in an IP-Only Environment | Chapter 11: Queue-Based Printing (**Setting Up Queue-Based Printing**) |
| 10.3: Configure Queue-Based Printing on the Workstation | Chapter 11: Queue-Based Printing (**Setting Up Queue-Based Printing**) |
| 10.4: Manage Queue-Based Printing | Chapter 11: **Queue-Based Printing** (all subsections) |
| 10.5: Troubleshoot Queue-Based Printing Problems | Chapter 11: Queue-Based Printing (**Troubleshooting Queue-Based Printing**) |
| **Section 11: Implement NDPS Printing** | |
| 11.1: Identify the Features of NDPS | Chapter 11: Implementing Novell Distributed Print Services (**Defining an NDPS Printing Environment**) |
| 11.2: Describe NDPS Components | Chapter 11: Implementing Novell Distributed Print Services (**NDPS Components**) |
| 11.3: Set Up NDPS | Chapter 11: Implementing Novell Distributed Print Services (**Implementing NDPS Printing**) |
| 11.4: Manage NDPS | Chapter 11: **Managing Printers and Print Jobs** (all subsections) |
| **Section 12: Implement Novell iPrint Printing** | |
| 12.1: Identify the Benefits and Features of Novell iPrint | Chapter 11: iPrint and Internet Printing Protocol (**Benefits of iPrint**) |
| 12.2: Describe Novell iPrint Components | Chapter 11: **iPrint and Internet Printing Protocol** |
| 12.3: Install and Configure Novell iPrint | Chapter 11: iPrint and Internet Printing Protocol (**Enabling Printers for iPrint**), Installing the iPrint Client and IPP Printers |

**Table A-1**     NetWare 6 Objectives Mapping (continued)

| Objective | Chapter: Section |
|-----------|------------------|
| **Section 13: Resolve Network Printing Problems** | |
| 13.1: Apply Quick-Fix Techniques | Chapter 11: Implementing Novell Distributed Print Services **(Troubleshooting NDPS Printing)** |
| 13.2: Troubleshoot the Most Common Problems with Printing | Chapter 11: Implementing Novell Distributed Print Services **(Troubleshooting NDPS Printing)** |
| 13.3: Troubleshoot Problems Arising from Incompatible Printer Drivers | Chapter 11: Implementing Novell Distributed Print Services **(Troubleshooting NDPS Printing)** |
| 13.4: Troubleshoot Printing Problems Arising from Incompatible Document Formats | Chapter 11: Implementing Novell Distributed Print Services **(Troubleshooting NDPS Printing)** |
| 13.5: Identify the Printing Environment | Chapter 11: Implementing Novell Distributed Print Services **(Defining an NDPS Printing Environment)** |
| 13.6: Troubleshoot NDPS-Based Printing | Chapter 11: Implementing Novell Distributed Print Services **(Troubleshooting NDPS Printing)** |
| 13.7: Troubleshoot Printing Problems in a Mixed Environment | Chapter 11: Implementing Novell Distributed Print Services **(Troubleshooting NDPS Printing)** |
| 13.8: Troubleshoot Problems with iPrint | Chapter 11: **Troubleshooting iPrint Printing Problems** (all subsections) |
| **Section 14: Evaluate NetWare File Services** | |
| 14.1: Identify Network File Service Components | Chapter 5: **Network File System Components** (all subsections) |
| 14.2: Identify Types of NetWare Volume Storage | Chapter 5: Network File System Components **(Volumes)** |
| **Section 15: Create and Access NetWare Volumes** | |
| 15.1: Create Traditional and NSS Volumes | Chapter 8: **Creating NSS Storage Pools and Volumes** (all subsections) |
| 15.2: Access Volumes through Mapped Network Drives | Chapter 8: **Drive Pointers** (all subsections) |
| **Section 16: Implement Directory and File Rights to Provide NetWare File System Security** | |
| 16.1: Identify the Types of Network Security Provided by NetWare | Chapter 1: Network Software Components **(Network Services)**; Chapter 9: **Establishing Login Security**; Chapter 10: **Trustee Assignments** |
| 16.2: Identify How NetWare File System Security Works | Chapter 10: Trustee Assignments **(Planning Directory Tree and File System Security)** |
| 16.3: Plan File System Rights | Chapter 10: Trustee Assignments **(Planning Directory Tree and File System Security)** |
| 16.4: Identify Directory and File Attributes | Chapter 10: **Directory and File Attributes** |

A

**Table A-1**    NetWare 6 Objectives Mapping (continued)

| Objective | Chapter: Section |
|---|---|
| **Section 17: Design a Network File System** | |
| 17.1: Identify Guidelines for Planning Network Volumes | Chapter 5: Network File System Components **(Volumes)**; **Directory Structure** |
| 17.2: Identify the Content and Purpose of NetWare SYS Directories | Chapter 5: Network File System Components **(Directories and Subdirectories)** |
| 17.3: Identify the Types of Directories Used for Organizing a File System | Chapter 5: **Directory Structure** |
| 17.4: Evaluate Directory Structure Types | Chapter 5: **Directory Structure** |
| **Section 18: Identify How to Back Up and Restore NetWare Systems** | |
| 18.1: Identify the SMS Backup Process | Chapter 8: Backing Up Network Data **(The Storage Management System)** |
| 18.2: Develop a Network Backup Strategy | Chapter 8: Backing Up Network Data **(Establishing a Backup System)** |
| 18.3: Evaluate Common Backup and Restore Software Used with NetWare | Chapter 8: Backing Up Network Data **(Establishing a Backup System)** |
| 18.4: Identify Protection Guidelines for Backup Data | Chapter 8: Backing Up Network Data **(Establishing a Backup System)** |
| **Section 19: Implement Novell iFolder** | |
| 19.1: Identify the Purpose and Benefits of iFolder | Chapter 13: **Working with iFolder** (all subsections) |
| 19.2: Identify How the iFolder Components Help You Access and Manage Your Files | Chapter 13: **Working with iFolder** (all subsections) |
| 19.3: Install and Configure iFolder | Chapter 13: Working with iFolder **(iFolder Components and Installation)** |
| 19.4: Manage and Optimize iFolder | Chapter 13: Working with iFolder **(Managing iFolder)** |
| **Section 20: Identify Features and Functions of Email** | |
| 20.1: Describe the Structure of Common Client/Server Email Programs | Chapter 15: Implementing an E-mail System **(E-mail Components)** |
| 20.2: Identify the Protocols Used for Sending and Receiving Email | Chapter 15: Implementing an E-mail System **(E-mail Protocols)** |
| 20.3: Identify Common Email Front-End (Client) Programs | Chapter 15: Implementing an E-mail System **(Common E-mail Clients)** |
| 20.4: Identify Common Email Back-End (Server) Programs | Chapter 15: Implementing an E-mail System **(Common E-mail Back-end Servers)** |

**Table A-1**   NetWare 6 Objectives Mapping (continued)

| Objective | Chapter: Section |
|---|---|
| **Section 21: Identify the Components of a GroupWise 6 System** | |
| 21.1: Understand How Messages are Routed in a GroupWise System | Chapter 15: Implementing an E-mail System **(E-mail Components)** |
| 21.2: Identify the GroupWise Domain Directory Structure | Chapter 15: Implementing an E-mail System **(Installing GroupWise 6 on the NetWare Server)** |
| 21.3: Identify the GroupWise Post Office Directory Structure and Files | Chapter 15: Implementing an E-mail System **(Installing GroupWise 6 on the NetWare Server)** |
| 21.4: View the GroupWise System in ConsoleOne | Chapter 15: **Configuring and Managing the GroupWise System**, Monitoring and Troubleshooting a GroupWise System |
| **Section 22: Maintain a Basic GroupWise System** | |
| 22.1: Create GroupWise Post Office Users | Chapter 15: Configuring and Managing the GroupWise System **(Creating GroupWise Post Office Users)** |
| 22.2: Create Additional GroupWise Post Office Objects | Chapter 15: Configuring and Managing the GroupWise System **(Creating Additional GroupWise Post Office Objects)** |
| 22.3: Delete Post Office Objects | Chapter 15: Configuring and Managing the GroupWise System **(Deleting and Renaming Post Office Objects)** |
| 22.4: Rename a GroupWise User | Chapter 15: Configuring and Managing the GroupWise System **(Deleting and Renaming Post Office Objects)** |
| 22.5: Establish Mailbox Security | Chapter 15: Configuring and Managing the GroupWise System **(Establishing Mailbox Security)** |
| **Section 23: Secure Your Network** | |
| 23.1: List the Steps for Developing an Effective Security Policy | Chapter 14: **Securing Net Services** (all subsections) |
| 23.2: Identify the Basic Methods for Internally Securing a Network | Chapter 14: Securing Net Services **(Internal Security)** |
| 23.3: Restrict Administrative Access to the Network | Chapter 10: Trustee Assignments **(Trustees, Rights, and Assignments**, all subsections**)** |
| 23.4: Identify How to Troubleshoot Common Internal Security Problems | Chapter 14: Securing Net Services **(Internal Security)** |
| 23.5: Identify How a Firewall Provides External Network Security | Chapter 14: Securing Net Services **(Firewall External Security)** |
| **Section 24: Protect Your Network Against Viruses** | |
| 24.1: Identify Types of Viruses | Chapter 14: Securing Net Services **(Protection Against Virus Attacks)** |
| 24.2: List the Symptoms of an Infected Computer | Chapter 14: Securing Net Services **(Protection Against Virus Attacks)** |

**Table A-1**   NetWare 6 Objectives Mapping (continued)

| Objective | Chapter: Section |
|---|---|
| 24.3: Describe What you Can Do to Prevent a Virus Attack | Chapter 14: Securing Net Services **(Protection Against Virus Attacks)** |
| 24.4: List the Steps in the Virus Removal Process | Chapter 14: Securing Net Services **(Protection Against Virus Attacks)** |
| **Section 25: Identify How Novell Products Deliver Internet Services** | |
| 25.1: Identify How Data and Services Are Delivered Over the Internet | Chapter 14: **NetWare 6 Internet Service Components** (all subsections) |
| 25.2: Evaluate the Internet Delivery Components | Chapter 14: **NetWare 6 Internet Service Components** (all subsections) |
| 25.3: Identify the Novell Products that Deliver Internet Services | Chapter 14: **NetWare 6 Internet Service Components** (all subsections) |
| **Section 26: Identify How to Implement a Web Server** | |
| 26.1: Identify How a Web Server Works | Chapter 14: NetWare 6 Internet Service Components **(NetWare Enterprise Web Server)** |
| 26.2: Evaluate Commonly Used Web Servers | Chapter 14: Installing and Configuring Web Services **(Working with NetWare Enterprise Web Server)** |
| 26.3: Identify the Process of Installing and Configuring NetWare Enterprise Web Server | Chapter 14: Installing and Configuring Web Services **(Working with NetWare Enterprise Web Server)** |
| **Section 27: Describe How to Install and Configure an FTP Server** | |
| 27.1: Describe the Role of an FTP Server | Chapter 14: Installing and Configuring Web Services **(Working with NetWare FTP Server)** |
| 27.2: Evaluate FTP Servers | Chapter 14: NetWare 6 Internet Service Components **(FTP Server)** |
| 27.3: Evaluate FTP Clients | Chapter 14: NetWare 6 Internet Service Components **(FTP Server)** |
| 27.4: Install and Configure NetWare FTP Server | Chapter 14: Installing and Configuring Web Services **(Working with FTP Server)** |
| **Section 28: Identify How Viruses Affect Web Services** | |
| 28.1: List the Factors that Encourage Attacks on Web Servers | Chapter 14: **Securing Net Services** (all subsections) |
| 28.2: Identify What a Virus Is | Chapter 14: Securing Net Services **(Protection Against Virus Attacks)** |
| 28.3: Identify Common Methods Used to Attack Web Services | Chapter 14: Securing Net Services **(Defense Against Denial-of-Service Attacks)** |
| 28.4: List the Measure You Can Take to Prevent Virus Attacks | Chapter 14: Securing Net Services **(Protection Against Virus Attacks)** |

**Table A-1**    NetWare 6 Objectives Mapping (continued)

| Objective | Chapter: Section |
|---|---|
| **Section 29: Identify the Purpose and Function of a Web Portal** | |
| 29.1: Describe How Portals are Used in the Industry | Chapter 14: NetWare 6 Internet Service Components **(Novell Portal Services)** |
| 29.2: Describe the Purpose of Novell Portal Services | Chapter 14: NetWare 6 Internet Service Components **(Novell Portal Services)** |
| 29.3: Identify Novell Portal Services Features and Benefits | Chapter 14: NetWare 6 Internet Service Components **(Novell Portal Services)** |

A

## Computer Worksheet

Specification developed by: _____

### SYSTEM INFORMATION

Computer make/model: _____

CPU: _____ Clock speed: _____ Bus: _____

Memory capacity: _____

### DISK INFORMATION

**Disk controller**

Type: _____

Manufacturer/model: _____

| Drive address | Type | Manufacturer | Cyl/Hd/Sec | Speed/Capacity | DOS Partition size |
|---|---|---|---|---|---|
| _____ | ____ | _____ | __/__/__ | _____ | _____ |

### DEVICE INFORMATION

| Device name | IRQ | I/O port |
|---|---|---|
| _____ | _____ | _____ |
| _____ | _____ | _____ |
| _____ | _____ | _____ |

## Bid Specification Form

Specification developed by: _____

**SYSTEM INFORMATION**

Computer make/model: _____

CPU: _____ Clock speed: _____ Bus: _____

Memory capacity: _____

Estimated cost: _____

**DISK INFORMATION**

**Disk controller**

Type: _____

Manufacturer/model: _____

| Drive Address | Type | Manufacturer | Cyl/Hd/Sec | Speed/Capacity | DOS Partition Size |
|---|---|---|---|---|---|
| _____ | __ | _____ | __/__/__ | _____ | _____ |

**NETWORK CARD INFORMATION**

| Network type | Manufacturer ID | I/O port | Interrupt |
|---|---|---|---|
| _____ | _____ | _____ | _____ |

**NON-NETWORK DEVICE INFORMATION**

| Device name | IRQ | I/O port |
|---|---|---|
| _____ | _____ | _____ |
| _____ | _____ | _____ |
| _____ | _____ | _____ |
| _____ | _____ | _____ |

B

## NetWare Server Worksheet

Specification developed by: _____

### SYSTEM INFORMATION

Computer make/model: _____

CPU: _____ Clock speed: _____ Bus: _____

Memory capacity: _____

Estimated cost: _____

### DISK INFORMATION

**Disk controller**

Type: _____

Manufacturer/model: _____

| Drive Address | Type | Manufacturer | Cyl/Hd/Sec | Speed/Capacity | Partition Size DOS  NetWare | Mirrored with Controller  Drive |
|---|---|---|---|---|---|---|
| _____ | __ | _____ | __/__/__ | _____ | __  __ | _____ |

### NETWORK CARD INFORMATION

| Network type | Manufacturer ID | I/O port | Interrupt |
|---|---|---|---|
| _____ | _____ | _____ | _____ |

### NON-NETWORK DEVICE INFORMATION

| Device name | IRQ | I/O port |
|---|---|---|
| _____ | _____ | _____ |
| _____ | _____ | _____ |
| _____ | _____ | _____ |

# NetWare Server Planning Form

| Created By: | | Date: | |
|---|---|---|---|
| Organization: | | | |

## NetWare Servers:

| NetWare Server Name: | |
|---|---|
| NetWare Operating System: | |
| Volumes: | |
| | |
| | |
| | |
| | |
| | |
| Purpose: | |

| NetWare Server Name: | |
|---|---|
| NetWare Operating System: | |
| Volumes: | |
| | |
| | |
| | |
| | |
| | |
| Purpose: | |

| NetWare Server Name: | |
|---|---|
| NetWare Operating System: | |
| Volumes: | |
| | |
| | |
| | |
| | |
| | |
| Purpose: | |

# Directory Planning Form

| Created By: | | Date: | |
|---|---|---|---|
| Organization: | | | |

## Workgroups:

| Workgroup Name: | Workgroup Members |
|---|---|
| | |
| | |
| | |
| | |
| | |
| | |
| | |
| | |
| | |
| | |
| | |
| | |
| | |
| | |
| | |

## Directories:

| Description | Type | Users | Estimated Size |
|---|---|---|---|
| | | | |
| | | | |
| | | | |
| | | | |
| | | | |
| | | | |
| | | | |
| | | | |
| | | | |
| | | | |
| | | | |
| | | | |
| | | | |
| | | | |
| | | | |
| | | | |

# NSS Volume Design Form

**Volume Name:** _____          **Designed by:** _____          **Date:** _____

Maximum Capacity: _____

Server: _____

Attributes:
_____Backup_____Compression_____Data Shredding_____Directory Quotas
_____Flush Files_____Migration_____Modified File List_____Salvage Files
_____Snapshot — File Level_____ User Space Restrictions

| **Directory Design Form** | | | |
|---|---|---|---|
| **Created By:** | | **Date:** | |
| **Volume:** | | **Capacity:** | |
| **Directory:** | | **Capacity:** | |
| **Subdirectory Structure Diagram** | | | |
| | | | |

# NetWare Server Planning Form

## Server Identification

**File server name:** _____     **Server ID #:** _____

**Domain name:** _____     Random ____ or Assigned ____

## System Information

Computer make/model: _____

CPU: _____     Clock Speed: _____     Bus: ___

Memory capacity: _____

## Disk Driver Information

**Disk Controller 1**

Type:____     Manufacturer/model : _____

Interrupt: ___     I/O address: _____     DMA channel: _

Memory address: _____ - _____

Disk driver name: _____

| Drive Address | Type | Manufacturer | Speed Capacity |
|---|---|---|---|

**Disk Controller 2**

Type: ____     Manufacturer/model : _____

Interrupt: ___     I/O address: _____     DMA channel: _

Memory address: _____ - _____

Disk driver name: _____

| Drive Address | Type | Manufacturer | Speed Capacity |
|---|---|---|---|

## Partition Information for Initial Installation

| Partition | Type | Pool/Volume/Capacity |
|---|---|---|

## Network Card Information

| Card Number | Network Type | Manuf. ID | LAN Driver | Bus | I/O Port | Memory Address | IRQ/DMA |
|---|---|---|---|---|---|---|---|

## NetWare Server Planning Form

Page 2 of 2

### Protocol Information

Network card:

TCP/IP frame type:

IP address:

Subnet mask:

Gateway:

\_\_\_\_ IPX protocol

    Frame type(s): _____    _____    _____

    Network address: _____    _____    _____

### Server Context

Tree name: _____    Organization: _____    Organizational Unit: _____

### Installation Component Options: _____

\_\_\_\_ Novell Certificate Server (Only one per tree)

\_\_\_\_ NDS iMonitor Services

\_\_\_\_ NetWare Remote Manager

\_\_\_\_ Storage Management Services

\_\_\_\_ ConsoleOne 1.3.2

\_\_\_\_ iPrint/NDPS

\_\_\_\_ NetWare Enterprise Web Server

\_\_\_\_ NetWare Web Manager

\_\_\_\_ NetWare FTP Server

\_\_\_\_ NetWare Web Search

\_\_\_\_ Novell DNS/DHCP Services

\_\_\_\_ WAN Traffic Manager Services

\_\_\_\_ Novell Native File Access Protocol

\_\_\_\_ Novell Advanced Audit Service

\_\_\_\_ NetWare WebAccess

\_\_\_\_ Novell iFolder Storage Services

\_\_\_\_ eDirectory iManager Service

\_\_\_\_ Novell NetStorage

### Port Usage

| Service | IP Address | Ports | |
|---|---|---|---|
| iFolder | _____ | \_\_\_\_ | \_\_\_\_ |
| NetStorage | _____ | \_\_\_\_ | \_\_\_\_ |
| iPrint | _____ | \_\_\_\_ | \_\_\_\_ |

## User Template Planning Form

Department: _____

| | |
|---|---|
| Template name | |
| Context | |
| Home directory path | |
| Minimum password length | |
| Require unique passwords | |
| Days between password changes | |
| Grace logins | |
| Valid login times | |
| Concurrent connections | |
| Groups | |
| Users | |
| Rights to Login Script | |
| Rights to home directory | |

**User Planning Form**

Company: _____

Created by: _____

Department: _____

| User Name | Login Name | Initial eDirectory and Simple Password | Context | Template Name | Home Directory | Groups | Additional Properties |
|-----------|------------|----------------------------------------|---------|---------------|----------------|--------|-----------------------|
|           |            |                                        |         |               |                |        |                       |
|           |            |                                        |         |               |                |        |                       |
|           |            |                                        |         |               |                |        |                       |
|           |            |                                        |         |               |                |        |                       |
|           |            |                                        |         |               |                |        |                       |
|           |            |                                        |         |               |                |        |                       |
|           |            |                                        |         |               |                |        |                       |
|           |            |                                        |         |               |                |        |                       |
|           |            |                                        |         |               |                |        |                       |

## Group Planning Form

| Organization: | | Page | of | |
|---|---|---|---|---|
| Developed by: | | Date: | | |

| Group Name | Members | Context | Description |
|---|---|---|---|
| | | | |
| | | | |
| | | | |
| | | | |
| | | | |
| | | | |
| | | | |
| | | | |
| | | | |
| | | | |
| | | | |
| | | | |
| | | | |
| | | | |
| | | | |

**NDPS Printer Definition Form**

NDPS Manager: _____          eDirectory Context: _____
Server: _____                 Database Volume: _____
Managers: _____  _____   _____

| Printer Name | Make/Model | NDPS Printer Classification | eDirectory Context | Attachment Method | Gateway Type | Port and Interrupt | Associated Print Queue | Users | Operators |
|---|---|---|---|---|---|---|---|---|---|
|  |  |  |  |  |  |  |  |  |  |
|  |  |  |  |  |  |  |  |  |  |
|  |  |  |  |  |  |  |  |  |  |
|  |  |  |  |  |  |  |  |  |  |
|  |  |  |  |  |  |  |  |  |  |
|  |  |  |  |  |  |  |  |  |  |
|  |  |  |  |  |  |  |  |  |  |
|  |  |  |  |  |  |  |  |  |  |
|  |  |  |  |  |  |  |  |  |  |
|  |  |  |  |  |  |  |  |  |  |
|  |  |  |  |  |  |  |  |  |  |
|  |  |  |  |  |  |  |  |  |  |
|  |  |  |  |  |  |  |  |  |  |
|  |  |  |  |  |  |  |  |  |  |

## Container Login Script Worksheet

Organization: _____          Page ____ of ____

Developed by: _____           Date: _____

Container Context: _____

**REM General Commands**



**REM Commands for _____ Groups**



**REM Commands for _____ Group**



**REM End of Login Script Commands**

## GroupWise Documentation Worksheet

GroupWise volume drive letter: _____

GroupWise directory structure: _____

GroupWise software distributor path: _____

ConsoleOne path: _____

GroupWise system name: _____

GroupWise domain name: _____

GroupWise domain directory path: _____

GroupWise post office name: _____

GroupWise post office directory path: _____

Post office context: _____

POA network address and port        IP address: _____
                                    Client-server port: _____
                                    Message transfer port: _____
                                    HTTP port: _____

MTA network address and port        IP address: _____
                                    Message transfer port: _____
                                    HTTP port: _____

Web Console information             User name: _____
                                    Password: _____

# C

# IP ADDRESSING BASICS

**A**s you learned in Chapter 3, Transmission Control Protocol/Internet Protocol (TCP/IP) is a pair of communications protocols that an application uses to send data across a network. TCP/IP also refers to an entire collection of protocols called a protocol suite, which contains applications such as e-mail, Telnet, FTP, and SNMP. One of the most important areas of TCP/IP is IP addressing. In this appendix, you learn about the classes of IP addresses, binary and hexadecimal numbering systems, and subnetting.

# IP ADDRESSING

Planning an IP address system is a critical part of implementing TCP/IP. An IP address consists of four bytes that are divided into two components: a network address and a host address. Based on the starting decimal number of the first byte, you can classify IP addresses as Class A, Class B, or Class C, as shown in Table C-1.

**Table C-1**   TCP/IP Address Classes

| Address Class | Range | Address Bytes | Number of Networks | Host Bytes | Number of Hosts |
|---|---|---|---|---|---|
| Class A | 1–127 | 1 | 127 | 3 | 16,777,215 |
| Class B | 128–191 | 2 | 16,128 | 2 | 65,535 |
| Class C | 192–223 | 3 | 2,097,152 | 1 | 254 |

Class D and Class E addresses are reserved for multicast and experimental addressing, respectively, and are not covered in this appendix.

From the preceding table, for example, you can determine that a user with an IP address of 193.1.2.3 has a Class C address, and a user with an IP address of 9.1.2.3 has a Class A address. An IP address is composed of four bytes, or octets. An octet is equal to eight bits, which equals one byte, so you sometimes see an IP address defined as four octets, instead of four bytes. The following list describes each address class in more detail:

- The first byte of a Class A address is reserved for the network address, making the last three bytes available to assign to host computers. Because a Class A address has a three-octet host address, Class A networks can support over 16 million host computers. (For more information on determining how many hosts a network can support, see the next section, "Understanding the Binary Numbering System.") The number of Class A Internet addresses is limited, so they are reserved for large corporations and governments. Class A addresses have a format of *network.node.node.node*.

- Class B addresses are evenly divided between a two-octet network and two-octet host address, allowing more than 65,000 host computers per Class B network address. Large organizations and Internet service providers are often assigned Class B Internet addresses. Class B addresses have a format of *network.network.node.node*.

- Class C addresses have a three-octet network address and a one-octet host address, resulting in more than 2 million Class C Internet addresses. Each of these addresses supports up to 254 host computers. These addresses are usually available for small-business and home use. They have a format of *network.network.network.node*.

In addition to a unique network address, each network must also be assigned a subnet mask, which helps identify the network address bits from the host address bits. Subnetting is covered in more depth in "Subnetting Your Network" later in this appendix. First, however, you need to learn binary numbers so you can understand network addresses.

## Understanding the Binary Numbering System

C

You learned base-10 math as a student, although you might not have realized it at the time. When you see the number 3742, for example, you quickly recognize it as three thousand seven hundred and forty-two. By placing each number in a column, as shown in the following lines, you can see that each number has a different value and magnitude. This numbering system uses 10 as its base and goes from right to left, multiplying the base number in each column by an exponent starting from zero. Valid numbers in base 10 are 0 through 9. That is, each column can contain any number from 0 to 9.

```
1000      100      10        1
10^3      10^2     10^1      10^0
3         7        4         2
```

As you can see, 3742 is obtained by multiplying 3 by 1000, 7 by 100, 4 by 10, and 2 by 1, and then adding the values.

The binary system, on the other hand, uses the number 2 as its base. Each *binary digit*, or *bit*, is represented by a 1 or a 0. Bits are usually grouped by eight because a byte contains eight bits. Computer engineers chose this numbering system because computers or logic chips make binary decisions based on TRUE or FALSE, ON or OFF, and so forth. With eight bits, a computer programmer can represent 256 different colors for a video card. (Two to the power of eight, or $2^8$, equals 256.) Therefore, black can be represented by 00000000, white by 11111111, and so on.

To simplify the concept of binary numbers, think of a room with two light switches, and consider how many different combinations of positions the switches could be in. For example, both switches could be "off." Also, Switch 1 could be "off" and Switch 2 could be "on." Switch 2 could be "off" and Switch 1 could be "on." Finally, both switches could be "on." A binary representation of these switch positions follows:

```
0 0 (off, off)
0 1 (off, on)
1 0 (on, off)
1 1 (on, on)
```

The two switches have four possible occurrences, or $2^x$ power; x represents the number of switches (bits) available.

## Examples of Determining Binary Values

Now that you've been introduced to the basic concepts, you can see examples of how bits are used to notate binary numbers. First, however, you must learn and memorize the columns for binary numbers, just as you did for base 10 years ago:

| 128 | 64 | 32 | 16 | 8 | 4 | 2 | 1 |

These numbers represent increasing powers of two, from right to left. Using the preceding columns, try to determine the value of an example binary number:

| 128 | 64 | 32 | 16 | 8 | 4 | 2 | 1 |
|-----|-----|-----|-----|-----|-----|-----|-----|
| $2^7$ | $2^6$ | $2^5$ | $2^4$ | $2^3$ | $2^2$ | $2^1$ | $2^0$ |
| 0 | 1 | 0 | 0 | 0 | 0 | 0 | 1 |

The byte in the preceding example represents the binary number 65. You calculate this value by adding each of the columns that contain a 1 (64+1). When you type the uppercase letter *A* on your keyboard, this sequence of ones and zeros goes to the CPU you learned about in Chapter 2.

Now try another example:

| 128 | 64 | 32 | 16 | 8 | 4 | 2 | 1 |
|-----|-----|-----|-----|-----|-----|-----|-----|
| $2^7$ | $2^6$ | $2^5$ | $2^4$ | $2^3$ | $2^2$ | $2^1$ | $2^0$ |
| 1 | 1 | 0 | 0 | 0 | 0 | 0 | 1 |

To convert the binary number to decimal (base 10), add the columns that contain 1s:

$$128 + 64 + 1 = 193$$

Adding the values in these columns can be tedious, but in the following section, you learn some tricks of the trade to help you translate binary to decimal quickly. However, make sure to memorize each binary column before working through the remaining examples in this appendix.

## Understanding Nibbles

Psychologists have found that people have difficulty memorizing numbers of seven digits or more. This is why telephone numbers have only seven digits and why a dash follows the first three numbers—the dash gives your brain a chance to pause before moving on to the next four numbers.

Likewise, binary numbers are easier to read when there is separation between them. For example, 1111 1010 is easier to read than 11111010. If you need to convert a binary number written as 11111010, you should visualize it as 1111 1010. In other words, you break the byte into two nibbles (sometimes spelled "nybbles"). A nibble is half a byte, or four bits. The four bits on the left side are called the high-order nibble, and the four bits on the right are the low-order nibble.

The following examples show you how to convert a low-order nibble to a decimal number. Note the pattern at work among the binary numbers as you proceed through the examples:

```
0000 = 0
0001 = 1
0010 = 2
0011 = 3
0100 = 4
0101 = 5
0110 = 6
0111 = 7
1000 = 8
1001 = 9
1010 = 10
1011 = 11
1100 = 12
1101 = 13
1110 = 14
1111 = 15
```

The largest decimal number you can represent with four low-order bits is 15. You should memorize these numbers if you can, especially the ones that come with convenient memory aids. For example, 1010 is equal to the decimal number 10. Just remember the phrase: "It's 10, it's 10!" 1011 is just as easy: "Not 10, but 11." You can make up your own tricks, but you can always just add the columns quickly if you forget.

You can also practice converting decimal numbers into binary numbers by using license plate numbers as you drive to work. For example, if a license plate number ends with "742," you should visualize 0111, 0100, and 0010. (You can eliminate the leading zeros after a few days of practice.) When you get comfortable with the low-order nibble and can quickly identify a sequence of four bits, you can move to the high-order side.

For example, what would the binary number 1010 1010 equal in decimal? On the low-order side, you can quickly convert 1010 to the decimal number 10. The high-order side is also 10, but it's 10 times 16, or 160. You can always add the columns if you are confused:

```
128 + 32 = 160
```

Any value in the high-order nibble is multiplied by the number 16. For example, the binary number 0010 0000 is equal to 32. You can multiply the nibble value of 2 by 16, but in this case it's easier to immediately recognize the 1 in the 32 column, which makes the answer 32.

You should memorize the following high-order nibble values, which will help you with subnetting. (For more details, see "Subnetting Your Network" later in this appendix.)

```
1000 = 128
1100 = 192
1110 = 224
1111 = 240
```

If you recognize 1111 0000 as 240, the binary number 1111 1000 should be easy to calculate as 248. By the same token, the binary number 1111 1111 is equal to the decimal 255, or 240 + 15, the largest number you can represent with eight bits.

To help you convert numbers correctly, note that all odd numbers have the low-order bit turned on. For example, 1001 cannot be an even number, such as 10 or 8, because the low-order bit is turned on. You can also guess that the number is larger than 8 because the 8 column bit is turned on. Similarly, you can identify 0101 as converting to a decimal number less than 8 because the 8 column is not turned on and as an odd number because the low-order bit is on.

There are other easy ways to memorize and break down binary numbers. For example, note that 1010 is 10, and 0101 converts to half of 10, or 5. The two numbers are mirror images of each other in binary, and one number is half of the other in decimal. In the same way, 1110 equals 14 and 0111 is 7. In the high-order nibble, 1110 equals 224, and 0111 in the high-order nibble equals 112 (half of 224). This trick helps you convert binary numbers quickly. For example, the binary number 0101 1010 equals 90. In this number, the high-order nibble converts to 80 because 1010 would equal 160. The low-order nibble converts to 10, and quick addition gives you the final answer of 90.

## Understanding Hexadecimal Numbers

Use Table C-2 at the end of this appendix to see how easily you can convert a decimal number to binary. For example, find decimal number 145 in the table, and note that the binary number in the next column is 1001 0001. If you remember your nibbles, you should see a "9" for the high-order nibble and a "1" for the low-order nibble.

Now look at the corresponding value in the Hex column, 91. "Hex" is short for hexadecimal, which is another numbering system you need to know to work with computers. Your media access control (MAC) address is written in hex, as are memory dumps. Even the Microsoft Event Viewer uses hex in some of its output, as shown in the Event Properties dialog box in Figure C-1. Note that the Bytes radio button is selected.

A hex number is written with two characters, each representing a nibble. Hexadecimal is a base-16 numbering system, so its valid numbers range from 0 to 15. Like base 2 (binary), hex uses exponents that begin with 0 and increase from right to left:

| 4096 | 256 | 16 | 1 |
|------|-----|-----|-----|
| $16^3$ | $16^2$ | $16^1$ | $16^0$ |
| A | 0 | C | 1 |

Fortunately, in hex you have to memorize only the final two columns: 1 and 16. As you can see from the preceding example, the value contains alphabetic characters—valid hex numbers range from 0 to 15, and hex solves the problem of expressing two-digit numbers in a single slot by using letters. For example, *A* represents the number 10, *B* stands for 11, *C* is 12, *D* is 13, *E* is 14, and *F* is 15.

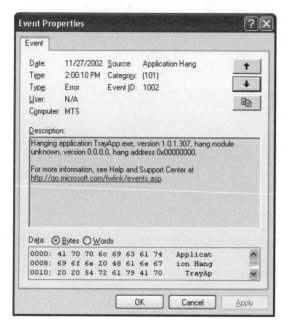

**Figure C-1**   The Event Properties dialog box, using hexidecimal output

Hex numbers are sometimes expressed with an "0x" in front of them. For example, 0x10 equals decimal number 16. As with decimal and binary numbers, you multiply the value in each column by the value of the column to determine hex numbers. In the previous example, you would simply multiply 1 by 16 to get 16. To convert a hex number to binary, you write out each nibble from left to right. For example, 0x10 would be 0001 0000 in binary, and 0x24 would be 0010 0100.

## Exercises for Determining Binary and Hexadecimal Values

To end your lesson in binary and hexadecimal numbering systems, try a few exercises. With a little practice, you can instantly convert binary numbers to hex and vice versa. For example, if you memorized the high-order nibbles for 128, 192, 224, and 240, which convert to 1000, 1100, 1110, and 1111, respectively, you can see how easy it is to quickly convert the following binary numbers into decimal:

```
1100 1000 = 192 + 8 = 200
1110 1010 = 224 + 10 = 234
```

You should have instantly recognized 1010 as the decimal number 10. Now try another example:

```
1111 0101 = 240 + 5 = 245
```

The faster you recognize the nibble, the faster you can convert it. To convert the same number to hex, you need to know that 1111 equals F and that 0101 is 5.

Don't forget the obvious as you practice these tricks of the trade. For example, if you see the binary number 0100 1010, you should quickly recognize that the high-order nibble contains the decimal value 64 because the binary 1 is in the 64 column. Once you recognize this, you can quickly add 64 and 10 to get 74.

Here's another little trick. What happens when you add a 1 to a binary number, such as 7, as shown in the following example?

```
0111 + 1 = 1000
```

Notice how the added 1 seemingly pushes all the other 1s down to 0 as it moves from right to left. When the added 1 finally reaches a 0, it replaces the 0 with itself, a 1. Confused? Try another example:

```
0011 1111 + 1 = 0100 0000
```

As you move from low order to high order, see how the added 1 serves to replace each consecutive column that contained a 1 with a 0. It then takes over the 0 in the 64 column and replaces it with the 1 that you added. By the way, this works only when you move from right to left—in other words, from low order to high order. Watch how this trick can help you translate the following binary number into decimal:

```
0111 1111 = ?
```

This number looks difficult, but if you visualize adding a 1 to it, you should see the binary number 1000 0000. You should not need more than a few seconds to determine that the number is 128. If you're still having trouble, review the binary column values until you know them without thinking. If 1000 0000 equals 128 after you added a 1 to 0111 1111, you should know that 0111 1111 equals 127.

Now try translating another binary number into decimal:

```
0011 1111 = ?
```

If you add a 1 to this binary number, you should see a 0100 0000, which means that the equivalent decimal number is 63. Now try a more difficult translation:

```
1101 1111 = ?
```

By now, you should see that if you add a 1, the binary number becomes 1110 0000, which you should have memorized as being equal to 224. Therefore, 1101 1111 must be 223.

Now put your knowledge to work with network addresses. A network address component is identified by placing a 1 in each bit that is part of the address. For example, a Class A address has a default subnet mask of 11111111 00000000 00000000 00000000 in binary, or 255.0.0.0 in decimal. The number 255 in the subnet mask identifies the entire first byte as part of the network address. (For more details on subnetting, see "Subnetting Your Network" later in this appendix.)

You can demonstrate the previous example using Boolean algebra. Don't worry; it isn't like high-school algebra. You just need to examine how the computer figures out the network portion of an address. For example, if your address is 10.4.5.7 and your subnet mask is

255.0.0.0, your network operating system will perform the following calculations. First it converts both addresses to binary:

```
    00001010.00000100.00000101.00010001
AND
    11111111.00000000.00000000.00000000
    00001010.00000000.00000000.00000000
```

C

In Boolean algebra, a 1 AND a 1 equals 1. All other combinations are equal to 0. Note that the system would identify 10.0.0.0 as the network address after performing this "AND" calculation. "All bits 0" stands for "this": "this" host (IP address with *<host number>* = 0) or "this" network (IP address with *<network number>* = 0). For example, 0.0.0.25 identifies host number 25 on "this" network, whatever the network number happens to be. On the other hand, 10.0.0.0 identifies network number 10. The host, or node, address would be 4.5.7. You can think of the 1, in a subnet mask, as a funnel that allows only 1 to pass through, and a 0 as a plug. The zeros in the last three bytes identify the last three octets as the host portion of the IP address. A Class B address has a default subnet mask of 255.255.0.0, indicating that the first two bytes (octets) represent the network portion of the address and the last two octets represent the host or node address.

A Class C address has a default subnet mask of 255.255.255.0, indicating that the first three bytes are the network address, and only the last byte can be used to represent the node. Because 0 and 255 are not valid node values, a Class C address enables up to 254 devices to access the network at the same time. Why isn't 255 a valid node address? Because there's another address of special importance: the "all bits 1" class. "All bits 1" stands for "all": "all" networks or "all" hosts. For example, 128.2.255.255 (a Class B address with a host number of 255.255) means all hosts on network 128.2. These hosts are used in broadcast messages. The IP address 205.12.13.255 would be used to send a message to all host computers on network 205.12.13.0, so the 205.12.13.255 address cannot be given to a host or node on a network. The network number 127 is reserved for the loopback address. Anything sent to an address with 127 as the value of the high-order byte (for example, 127.0.0.1) must not be routed via a network; it must be routed directly from the IP implementation's output driver to its input driver.

Now try one more example. If the network address is 172.30.5.7 and the subnet mask is 255.255.0.0, what network are you on? Without converting to binary, you know that the 172 and 30 would flow down, but that the 5 and 7 would be blocked. This information indicates that you are on the 172.30.0.0 network and that your host address is 5.7. For network administrators, this is important information; it helps them assign IP address numbers correctly so that users can connect to one another.

## Planning IP Address Assignments

When assigning IP addresses, you need to assign a unique network address to each network segment that is separated by a router. For example, suppose you have been issued two IP addresses for your business: 192.168.8.0 and 192.168.9.0. Looking at the first byte of each address, you determine both to be Class C. With a default subnet mask of 255.255.255.0, you can assign 254 host addresses to each segment. You make this calculation using the following formula:

```
2^x - 2, or 2^8 - 2, which = 254
```

Memorize this formula. You must subtract 2 in the formula because the network portion and host portion of an IP address cannot contain all 1s or all 0s. Remember, you cannot assign a network user the IP address 192.168.8.0.

When you are ready to issue an address to a user, fill out the Internet Protocol (TCP/IP) Properties dialog box shown in Figure C-2.

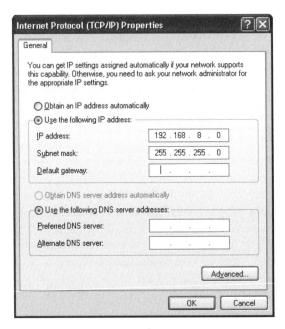

**Figure C-2**    The Internet Protocol (TCP/IP) Properties dialog box

If you issue an invalid address, you receive the error message shown in Figure C-3. Remember, you cannot give a user an address of 192.168.8.255 because it would produce all 1s in the host portion of an IP address; this address is reserved as a broadcast address to all nodes on the segment 192.168.8.0. You use "8" as the exponent in this example because there are eight bits in the fourth octet.

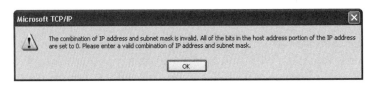

**Figure C-3**    The error message for an invalid IP address

To access entities and services on other networks, each computer must also have the IP address of its gateway. Before sending a packet to another computer, TCP/IP's Internet layer uses your computer's subnet mask to determine the destination computer's network address. If this address is different from the sending computer's network address, the sending computer relays the packet to the IP address specified in the gateway parameter. The gateway computer then forwards the packet to its next destination. In this way, the packet eventually reaches the destination computer.

For example, if your NetWare 6 server had an IP address of 192.168.8.2 and a subnet mask of 255.255.255.0, and one of your users had a workstation with an IP address of 192.168.9.200 and a subnet mask of 255.255.255.0, you would have to configure a default gateway address. The default gateway would send the user to a router, which routes the user to the different network segment, as you learned in Chapter 3. If you forgot to configure the default gateway on the user's workstation, and a user attempted to use the PING command to contact the server, he or she would get the error shown in Figure C-4.

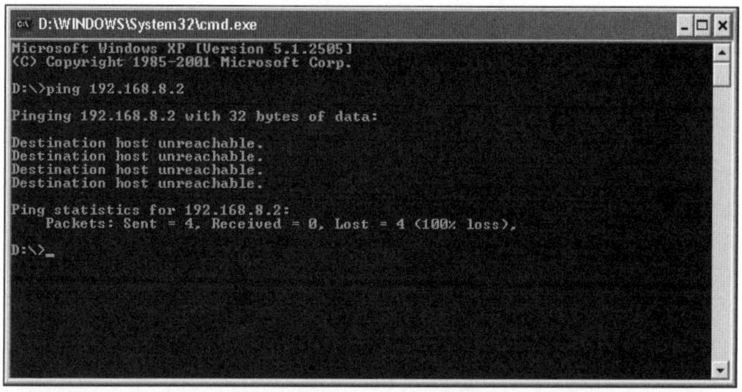

```
D:\WINDOWS\System32\cmd.exe                                    _ □ ×
Microsoft Windows XP [Version 5.1.2505]
(C) Copyright 1985-2001 Microsoft Corp.

D:\>ping 192.168.8.2

Pinging 192.168.8.2 with 32 bytes of data:

Destination host unreachable.
Destination host unreachable.
Destination host unreachable.
Destination host unreachable.

Ping statistics for 192.168.8.2:
    Packets: Sent = 4, Received = 0, Lost = 4 (100% loss),

D:\>
```

**Figure C-4**   The "Destination host unreachable" error

The error defines the problem as "Destination host unreachable." The user's workstation cannot connect to the other host, a NetWare 6 server located on a different network segment, because there is no router to help it. The router's job is to take those packets, which are not on the same network segment, and send them on their way. One reason that networks are broken into multiple segments is to reduce broadcast traffic. Too much broadcast traffic slows your network. In the preceding example, there are already two networks: 192.168.8.0 and 192.168.9.0. However, what if your business had only one IP address number assigned, and you had problems with too much broadcast traffic? In other words, sometimes you need to assign IP addresses to users that break one network segment into two or more segments, but you have only one network address to work with. This is called subnetting.

## Subnetting Your Network

If you are assigned a Class C IP address of 192.168.8.0, you have one network of 254 hosts that you can use. Remember that a Class C address uses the first three octets for the network portion of the address and leaves the last octet for the hosts. If you needed to split your network into two networks, you could "steal" or "borrow" from those host bits. This practice is called subnetting.

When subnetting, you need to know how many bits you can borrow. The number depends on how many networks you need to create. If you need to create two networks, for example, you can borrow two bits because $2^{\wedge}2 - 2 = 2$. You saw this formula in the previous section, and you can begin to see how important it is.

As another way to illustrate subnetting, remember that the original subnet mask for a Class C address is 255.255.255.0. Borrowing two bits from the last octet would change the mask to 255.255.255.192. It's a little easier to see this in binary:

```
11111111.11111111.11111111.1100 0000
```

The borrowed bits are bolded in the fourth octet for readability. These are the high-order bits, and they include the 128 and 64 columns. Now you understand why the subnet mask is 255.255.255.192. By borrowing these two bits, you can create the following networks: 00, 01, 10, and 11.

Remember, however, that you cannot have all 0s or all 1s in a network address. When you subtract 00 and 11, you are left with only two networks—01 and 10. Both networks can have 62 hosts because there are only six bits left over for host addressing. To confirm this number, use the formula again to see how many hosts you can create with 6 bits:

```
2^6 - 2 = 64 - 2 = 62
```

The 01 network becomes the 192.169.8.64 network and the 10 network becomes the 192.168.8.128 network. Remember, you have to see these network numbers as high-order bits. The 01 is 64 decimal and 10 is 128 decimal. Now you can assign IP addresses to users on either segment. For example, you can assign IP addresses 192.168.8.65 through 192.168.8.126 to one segment, and 192.168.8.129 through 192.168.8.190 to users on the other segment.

You've now found a valid range of addresses, but you might want to experiment with other ranges for practice. For example, see if you can assign an address range of 192.168.8.1 through 192.168.8.63. Because you are a binary expert now, it will make more sense if you convert the number to binary:

```
11000000.10101000.00001000.00000001 -
11000000.10101000.0000.1000.00111111
```

Note that the bits have to be set to all 0s to include the range of IP addresses in question. Unfortunately, all 0s are not allowed. Next, you can try issuing the IP address 192.168.8.64 to a user. Convert the number to binary and see if it works:

```
11000000.10101000.00001000.01000000
```

The network portion of the address looks fine, but notice that 192.168.8.64 would translate to all 0s in the host portion of the IP address. Again, this is invalid. If you then tried giving an IP address of 192.168.8.127 to a user, you would notice a similar problem after converting to binary:

```
11000000.10101000.00001000.01111111
```

The network portion looks fine, but this time the host portion contains all 1s. Again, this is not allowed, and by now you're probably becoming frustrated. Fortunately, there's a faster way of doing this without having to write out everything in binary. The following final example uses some good shortcuts, although they still require an understanding of the binary numbering system. If you skipped the section on binary numbering earlier in this appendix, you might need to review it before continuing.

## Creating Network Segments

Assume that you have been issued the Class C address of 192.168.1.0 and you need to create five network segments. You must ask yourself the following questions:

- How many bits do I need to borrow?

- How many networks will be created?

- What will the range of addresses be for each of the networks (called blocks)?

- How many hosts will be on each segment?

Using your formula, you know that borrowing three bits will give you six networks. You can also determine that the binary number is 111. Remember, these are high-order bits. If you memorized these bits, you should know that 111 equals 224 decimal. Examine the three bits and pick the lowest order bit, which is the 32 column. This becomes the block size of each segment. Write down 32, skip a line and add 32 to get 64, and continue adding 32 to each value until you get to the number of your subnet mask, which is 224 in this example.

```
32
64
96
128
160
192
224
```

Next, modify the list as shown in the following example to obtain the ranges of IP addresses in each block:

```
32  -  63
64  -  95
96  -  127
128 -  159
160 -  191
192 -  223
```

Note that 224 is missing from the previous example because it is invalid, but it was used to obtain the range of 192 to 223. Next, modify the list to show valid host addresses for each range:

```
32  -  63        33  -  62
64  -  95        65  -  94
96  - 127        97  - 126
128 - 159        129 - 158
160 - 191        161 - 190
192 - 223        193 - 222
```

Remember, the first number from each block cannot be given to a user as a host address because it is the network address. The second address in each range is the broadcast address (all 1s) and is also invalid to give as a host address. To calculate how many hosts are available in each block or range, use the formula you learned earlier. Because you borrowed three bits from the host portion, you have five bits left for host addresses ($2^5 - 2 = 30$ hosts).

As a CNA, you'll sometimes have to troubleshoot network connectivity problems. Incorrect subnet masks or mistyped IP addresses cause many of these problems, so any additional time you spend studying IP addressing and subnetting is time well spent. Use Table C-2 if you need assistance converting numbers between the decimal, binary, and hexadecimal systems.

**Table C-2**  Conversion Table

| Decimal | Binary | Hex | Decimal | Binary | Hex |
|---|---|---|---|---|---|
| 0 | 0000 0000 | 0 0 | 32 | 0010 0000 | 2 0 |
| 1 | 0000 0001 | 0 1 | 33 | 0010 0001 | 2 1 |
| 2 | 0000 0010 | 0 2 | 34 | 0010 0010 | 2 2 |
| 3 | 0000 0011 | 0 3 | 35 | 0010 0011 | 2 3 |
| 4 | 0000 0100 | 0 4 | 36 | 0010 0100 | 2 4 |
| 5 | 0000 0101 | 0 5 | 37 | 0010 0101 | 2 5 |
| 6 | 0000 0110 | 0 6 | 38 | 0010 0110 | 2 6 |
| 7 | 0000 0111 | 0 7 | 39 | 0010 0111 | 2 7 |
| 8 | 0000 1000 | 0 8 | 40 | 0010 1000 | 2 8 |
| 9 | 0000 1001 | 0 9 | 41 | 0010 1001 | 2 9 |
| 10 | 0000 1010 | 0 A | 42 | 0010 1010 | 2 A |
| 11 | 0000 1011 | 0 B | 43 | 0010 1011 | 2 B |
| 12 | 0000 1100 | 0 C | 44 | 0010 1100 | 2 C |
| 13 | 0000 1101 | 0 D | 45 | 0010 1101 | 2 D |
| 14 | 0000 1110 | 0 E | 46 | 0010 1110 | 2 E |
| 15 | 0000 1111 | 0 F | 47 | 0010 1111 | 2 F |
| 16 | 0001 0000 | 1 0 | 48 | 0011 0000 | 3 0 |
| 17 | 0001 0001 | 1 1 | 49 | 0011 0001 | 3 1 |

**Table C-2**   Conversion Table (continued)

| Decimal | Binary | Hex | Decimal | Binary | Hex |
|---|---|---|---|---|---|
| 18 | 0001 0010 | 1 2 | 50 | 0011 0010 | 3 2 |
| 19 | 0001 0011 | 1 3 | 51 | 0011 0011 | 3 3 |
| 20 | 0001 0100 | 1 4 | 52 | 0011 0100 | 3 4 |
| 21 | 0001 0101 | 1 5 | 53 | 0011 0101 | 3 5 |
| 22 | 0001 0110 | 1 6 | 54 | 0011 0110 | 3 6 |
| 23 | 0001 0111 | 1 7 | 55 | 0011 0111 | 3 7 |
| 24 | 0001 1000 | 1 8 | 56 | 0011 1000 | 3 8 |
| 25 | 0001 1001 | 1 9 | 57 | 0011 1001 | 3 9 |
| 26 | 0001 1010 | 1 A | 58 | 0011 1010 | 3 A |
| 27 | 0001 1011 | 1 B | 59 | 0011 1011 | 3 B |
| 28 | 0001 1100 | 1 C | 60 | 0011 1100 | 3 C |
| 29 | 0001 1101 | 1 D | 61 | 0011 1101 | 3 D |
| 30 | 0001 1110 | 1 E | 62 | 0011 1110 | 3 E |
| 31 | 0001 1111 | 1 F | 63 | 0011 1111 | 3 F |
| 64 | 0100 0000 | 4 0 | 96 | 0110 0000 | 6 0 |
| 65 | 0100 0001 | 4 1 | 97 | 0110 0001 | 6 1 |
| 66 | 0100 0010 | 4 2 | 98 | 0110 0010 | 6 2 |
| 67 | 0100 0011 | 4 3 | 99 | 0110 0011 | 6 3 |
| 68 | 0100 0100 | 4 4 | 100 | 0110 0100 | 6 4 |
| 69 | 0100 0101 | 4 5 | 101 | 0110 0101 | 6 5 |
| 70 | 0100 0110 | 4 6 | 102 | 0110 0110 | 6 6 |
| 71 | 0100 0111 | 4 7 | 103 | 0110 0111 | 6 7 |
| 72 | 0100 1000 | 4 8 | 104 | 0110 1000 | 6 8 |
| 73 | 0100 1001 | 4 9 | 105 | 0110 1001 | 6 9 |
| 74 | 0100 1010 | 4 A | 106 | 0110 1010 | 6 A |
| 75 | 0100 1011 | 4 B | 107 | 0110 1011 | 6 B |
| 76 | 0100 1100 | 4 C | 108 | 0110 1100 | 6 C |
| 77 | 0100 1101 | 4 D | 109 | 0110 1101 | 6 D |
| 78 | 0100 1110 | 4 E | 110 | 0110 1110 | 6 E |
| 79 | 0100 1111 | 4 F | 111 | 0110 1111 | 6 F |
| 80 | 0101 0000 | 5 0 | 112 | 0111 0000 | 7 0 |
| 81 | 0101 0001 | 5 1 | 113 | 0111 0001 | 7 1 |
| 82 | 0101 0010 | 5 2 | 114 | 0111 0010 | 7 2 |
| 83 | 0101 0011 | 5 3 | 115 | 0111 0011 | 7 3 |
| 84 | 0101 0100 | 5 4 | 116 | 0111 0100 | 7 4 |
| 85 | 0101 0101 | 5 5 | 117 | 0111 0101 | 7 5 |

**Table C-2**   Conversion Table (continued)

| Decimal | Binary | Hex | Decimal | Binary | Hex |
|---------|--------|-----|---------|--------|-----|
| 86 | 0101 0110 | 5 6 | 118 | 0111 0110 | 7 6 |
| 87 | 0101 0111 | 5 7 | 119 | 0111 0111 | 7 7 |
| 88 | 0101 1000 | 5 8 | 120 | 0111 1000 | 7 8 |
| 89 | 0101 1001 | 5 9 | 121 | 0111 1001 | 7 9 |
| 90 | 0101 1010 | 5 A | 122 | 0111 1010 | 7 A |
| 91 | 0101 1011 | 5 B | 123 | 0111 1011 | 7 B |
| 92 | 0101 1100 | 5 C | 124 | 0111 1100 | 7 C |
| 93 | 0101 1101 | 5 D | 125 | 0111 1101 | 7 D |
| 94 | 0101 1110 | 5 E | 126 | 0111 1110 | 7 E |
| 95 | 0101 1111 | 5 F | 127 | 0111 1111 | 7 F |
| 128 | 1000 0000 | 8 0 | 160 | 1010 0000 | A 0 |
| 129 | 1000 0001 | 8 1 | 161 | 1010 0001 | A 1 |
| 130 | 1000 0010 | 8 2 | 162 | 1010 0010 | A 2 |
| 131 | 1000 0011 | 8 3 | 163 | 1010 0011 | A 3 |
| 132 | 1000 0100 | 8 4 | 164 | 1010 0100 | A 4 |
| 133 | 1000 0101 | 8 5 | 165 | 1010 0101 | A 5 |
| 134 | 1000 0110 | 8 6 | 166 | 1010 0110 | A 6 |
| 135 | 1000 0111 | 8 7 | 167 | 1010 0111 | A 7 |
| 136 | 1000 1000 | 8 8 | 168 | 1010 1000 | A 8 |
| 137 | 1000 1001 | 8 9 | 169 | 1010 1001 | A 9 |
| 138 | 1000 1010 | 8 A | 170 | 1010 1010 | A A |
| 139 | 1000 1011 | 8 B | 171 | 1010 1011 | A B |
| 140 | 1000 1100 | 8 C | 172 | 1010 1100 | A C |
| 141 | 1000 1101 | 8 D | 173 | 1010 1101 | A D |
| 142 | 1000 1110 | 8 E | 174 | 1010 1110 | A E |
| 143 | 1000 1111 | 8 F | 175 | 1010 1111 | A F |
| 144 | 1001 0000 | 9 0 | 176 | 1011 0000 | B 0 |
| 145 | 1001 0001 | 9 1 | 177 | 1011 0001 | B 1 |
| 146 | 1001 0010 | 9 2 | 178 | 1011 0010 | B 2 |
| 147 | 1001 0011 | 9 3 | 179 | 1011 0011 | B 3 |
| 148 | 1001 0100 | 9 4 | 180 | 1011 0100 | B 4 |
| 149 | 1001 0101 | 9 5 | 181 | 1011 0101 | B 5 |
| 150 | 1001 0110 | 9 6 | 182 | 1011 0110 | B 6 |
| 151 | 1001 0111 | 9 7 | 183 | 1011 0111 | B 7 |
| 152 | 1001 1000 | 9 8 | 184 | 1011 1000 | B 8 |
| 153 | 1001 1001 | 9 9 | 185 | 1011 1001 | B 9 |

**Table C-2**   Conversion Table (continued)

| Decimal | Binary | Hex | Decimal | Binary | Hex |
|---|---|---|---|---|---|
| 154 | 1001 1010 | 9 A | 186 | 1011 1010 | B A |
| 155 | 1001 1011 | 9 B | 187 | 1011 1011 | B B |
| 156 | 1001 1100 | 9 C | 188 | 1011 1100 | B C |
| 157 | 1001 1101 | 9 D | 189 | 1011 1101 | B D |
| 158 | 1001 1110 | 9 E | 190 | 1011 1110 | B E |
| 159 | 1001 1111 | 9 F | 191 | 1011 1111 | B F |
| 192 | 1100 0000 | C 0 | 224 | 1110 0000 | E 0 |
| 193 | 1100 0001 | C 1 | 225 | 1110 0001 | E 1 |
| 194 | 1100 0010 | C 2 | 226 | 1110 0010 | E 2 |
| 195 | 1100 0011 | C 3 | 227 | 1110 0011 | E 3 |
| 196 | 1100 0100 | C 4 | 228 | 1110 0100 | E 4 |
| 197 | 1100 0101 | C 5 | 229 | 1110 0101 | E 5 |
| 198 | 1100 0110 | C 6 | 230 | 1110 0110 | E 6 |
| 199 | 1100 0111 | C 7 | 231 | 1110 0111 | E 7 |
| 200 | 1100 1000 | C 8 | 232 | 1110 1000 | E 8 |
| 201 | 1100 1001 | C 9 | 233 | 1110 1001 | E 9 |
| 202 | 1100 1010 | C A | 234 | 1110 1010 | E A |
| 203 | 1100 1011 | C B | 235 | 1110 1011 | E B |
| 204 | 1100 1100 | C C | 236 | 1110 1100 | E C |
| 205 | 1100 1101 | C D | 237 | 1110 1101 | E D |
| 206 | 1100 1110 | C E | 238 | 1110 1110 | E E |
| 207 | 1100 1111 | C F | 239 | 1110 1111 | E F |
| 208 | 1101 0000 | D 0 | 240 | 1111 0000 | F 0 |
| 209 | 1101 0001 | D 1 | 241 | 1111 0001 | F 1 |
| 210 | 1101 0010 | D 2 | 242 | 1111 0010 | F 2 |
| 211 | 1101 0011 | D 3 | 243 | 1111 0011 | F 3 |
| 212 | 1101 0100 | D 4 | 244 | 1111 0100 | F 4 |
| 213 | 1101 0101 | D 5 | 245 | 1111 0101 | F 5 |
| 214 | 1101 0110 | D 6 | 246 | 1111 0110 | F 6 |
| 215 | 1101 0111 | D 7 | 247 | 1111 0111 | F 7 |
| 216 | 1101 1000 | D 8 | 248 | 1111 1000 | F 8 |
| 217 | 1101 1001 | D 9 | 249 | 1111 1001 | F 9 |
| 218 | 1101 1010 | D A | 250 | 1111 1010 | F A |
| 219 | 1101 1011 | D B | 251 | 1111 1011 | F B |
| 220 | 1101 1100 | D C | 252 | 1111 1100 | F C |

**Table C-2** Conversion Table (continued)

| Decimal | Binary | Hex | Decimal | Binary | Hex |
|---------|-----------|-----|---------|-----------|-----|
| 221 | 1101 1101 | D D | 253 | 1111 1101 | F D |
| 222 | 1101 1110 | D E | 254 | 1111 1110 | F E |
| 223 | 1101 1111 | D F | 255 | 1111 1111 | F F |

# D

# UPGRADING TO NETWARE 6.5

In the high-tech world, change is usually depicted as a new version number, a code name, or a buzzword blasted over the Internet, such as one Net, .NET, Sun One, and so forth. With each change, CNAs and CNEs alike wonder whether the skills they have mastered will become outdated or obsolete. Although many changes and enhancements have been made to Novell's reliable network operating system, the skills you have learned in NetWare 6 will help with what's available in NetWare 6.5. As illustrated in Figure D-1, NetWare 6.5 includes enhancements for IT administrators, end users, and software developers. In addition to the familiar ConsoleOne and NetWare Administrator utilities you learned to use in this textbook, IT administrators will benefit from version 2.0 of iManager, which now has all the capabilities of both ConsoleOne and NetWare Administrator in one Web-based administration utility. Network administrators will also appreciate the new installation and configuration capabilities of NetWare 6.5, which simplify the task of installing specialized servers and consolidating data from multiple servers into a single data center. End users will benefit from NetWare 6.5 Virtual Office, which provides a collaborative computing environment that enables users to organize and manage teams to communicate and share resources. NetWare 6.5 also furthers Novell's commitment to the open source concept by replacing the Enterprise Web Server in NetWare 6 with a second copy of the Apache Web Server as well as including open source software and Web development tools, such as PHP, MySQL, and Perl, at no additional cost. In this appendix, you update your NetWare skills by learning about many of the new administrative, end user, and software development features of NetWare 6.5.

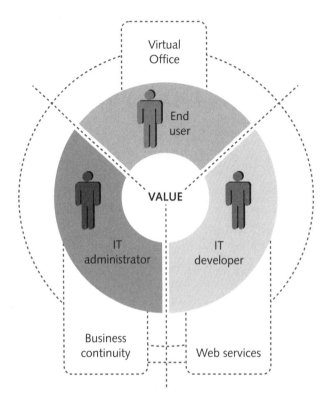

**Figure D-1**  Strategic areas of focus in NetWare 6.5

## NetWare 6.5 Installation and Upgrading Enhancements

As networks grow, installing new servers and upgrading existing servers are ongoing processes in most multiserver organizations. One way in which NetWare 6.5 provides scalability for network growth is by adding specialized servers to the eDirectory tree. These servers, which are specialized for tasks such as running an Apache Web server or iFolder and iPrint services, can often improve network performance and management in a multiserver network.

As you learned in this book, a complete customized server installation of NetWare 6 can be rather complex and time consuming if all you want to do is set up a dedicated iFolder or Domain Name System/Dynamic Host Configuration Protocol (DNS/DHCP) server. Although the basics steps in a customized NetWare 6.5 server installation are similar to those in NetWare 6, Novell offers new server installation options called "Choose a pattern" to help simplify and speed up the installation of specialized servers, as shown in Figure D-2.

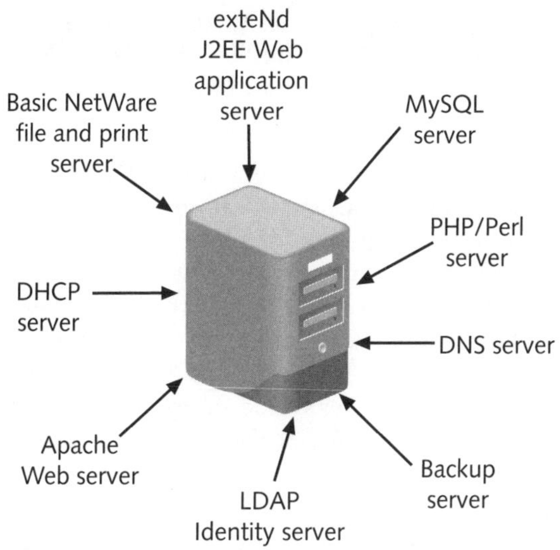

exteNd
J2EE Web
application
server

Basic NetWare
file and print
server

MySQL
server

PHP/Perl
server

DHCP
server

DNS server

Apache
Web server

LDAP
Identity server

Backup
server

**Figure D-2**    NetWare 6.5 patterned server installation options

These pattern options, shown in Figure D-3, enable administrators to select what type of server they want to install.

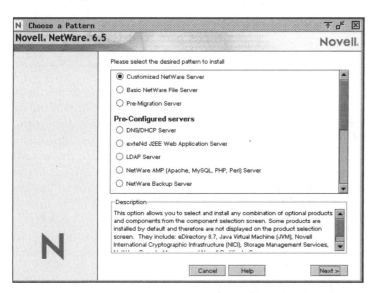

**Figure D-3**    Selecting a patterned server option in the Choose a Pattern dialog box

- The Customized NetWare Server pattern takes you through all the server installation and configuration options, allowing you to select and configure each option manually.

- The Basic NetWare File Server pattern simplifies the process of installing a server that will be used specifically as a NetWare file server by automatically selecting and configuring the options necessary to provide file services.

- Although some organizations are installing a NetWare 6.5 server as their first NetWare server, often it's more common to install a NetWare 6.5 server in an existing eDirectory tree or to upgrade a server running an older NetWare version. Because the hardware requirements for NetWare 6.5 are more demanding than earlier NetWare versions (see Table D-1), many administrators find it more feasible to install NetWare 6.5 on a new computer and then use the Novell Migration Wizard to migrate users and data from the earlier NetWare server to the new NetWare 6.5 server. Novell includes the Pre-Migration Server pattern to make it easier for administrators to install a server that's configured to be the target server for the migration process.

**Table D-1**   NetWare 6.5 Hardware Requirements

| Component | Minimum Requirement |
| --- | --- |
| Processor | Pentium II or AMD K7 (Pentium IV recommended) |
| Memory | 512 MB (1 GB recommended) |
| Disk | 200 MB DOS partition (1.2 GB recommended if you have 1 GB RAM—200 MB for DOS plus 1 GB to hold memory dumps equals a 1.2 GB partition)<br>2 GB free for SYS volume (4 GB recommended for SYS volume) |
| Monitor | Super VGA |

- The patterns under the Pre-Configured servers section are used to automate the installation of special-purpose servers. For example, if you indicate a DNS/DHCP installation, the pattern installation process asks for the information needed to install DNS/DHCP. After you supply the information, the pattern installation process quickly and automatically installs the necessary software and customizes the server to maximize DNS/DHCP performance. An important Novell strategy is to fully support open-source application development in NetWare 6.5. Because NetWare 6.5 offers so many open-source development tools, Novell has included the NetWare AMP (which stands for Apache, MySQL, PHP/Perl) server pattern to simplify installing and configuring a server specialized for open-source application development.

## Performing a NetWare 6.5 Server Installation

A new NetWare 6.5 server installation uses many of the same steps described in the textbook for a NetWare 6 installation, but the NetWare 6.5 process follows a slightly different sequence and includes some new options, such as pattern deployment, a main menu, and several enhanced login security options (described in Appendix E).

The best way to learn about the new installation process and options is to go through an installation of a NetWare 6.5 server. Assume that you work for a network consulting company, and one of your co-workers, Kathleen Stanton, has just completed a NetWare 6.5 training class. A small startup company, Rocky Ridge Enterprises, is planning to install a NetWare 6.5 server to handle its business needs. Rocky Ridge selected NetWare 6.5 because it offers a secure and open-source environment for in-house development of Web applications. The Rocky Ridge manager has purchased new server hardware that exceeds the NetWare 6.5 minimum requirements and would like your consulting company to install the NetWare 6.5 operating system and configure the server. The following sections describe the steps Kathleen uses to install a customized NetWare 6.5 server for the Rocky Ridge organization.

 If you have a computer with a blank hard disk or have VMWare installed on your workstation, you can follow these steps to practice a NetWare 6.5 installation. You can use your server to perform the activities in this appendix.

## Initial Installation Phase

As in the NetWare 6 installation process, the initial installation phase uses text-based menus and screens to select language and keyboard settings, to choose disk and LAN drivers, and to create the SYS volume. The NetWare 6.5 installation process includes a new screen, the NSS Main Menu, for creating additional partitions, pools, and volumes during this installation phase. The Main Menu can be accessed after installation by entering the command NSSMU at the server console. The following steps illustrate Kathleen's progress through the initial installation phase:

1. Kathleen inserted the NetWare 6.5 (Operating System) CD 1 into the CD-ROM drive of the server and restarted it. She chose the default options: "I" to install a new server and "A" to search for a CD-ROM driver. Next, she selected "A" for Auto terminate and then "A" for Auto Execution.

2. When the installation program started, she pressed Enter to select the option to install in English.

3. She pressed Enter again to accept the default regional settings for Country, Code page, and Keyboard.

4. Next, she read the NetWare 6.5 license agreement and then pressed the F10 key to accept and continue.

5. She pressed the F10 key again to accept the JReport runtime license agreement and display the Welcome to the NetWare 6.5 server installation window shown in Figure D-4.

**Figure D-4**    The Welcome to the NetWare 6.5 server installation window

6. To customize the installation, Kathleen pressed Enter to change the default installation type to Manual. Next, she pressed the Tab key to select the Continue option and pressed Enter to display the Prepare boot partition window.

7. The Prepare boot partition window allows the installer to create a DOS boot partition within the first 8 GB of the server's hard drive. The minimum DOS partition boot size is 200 MB, but Novell recommends adding space to hold a memory dump in case the server undergoes a hardware fault. Because this server has 1 GB of RAM, Kathleen selected the Modify option, pressed Enter, highlighted Free Space, and then pressed Enter; she typed in a size of 1200 MB for the DOS partition. She pressed Enter again, and the installation program formatted the DOS boot partition and returned to the Prepare boot partition window. Kathleen pressed Tab, selected the Continue option, and then pressed Enter to display the Server Settings window.

8. Kathleen recorded the server ID number on her installation worksheet and then pressed Enter to start the file copy process. During this process, files are copied from the Operating System CD to the DOS partition. These files include the server startup software, configuration files, and drivers.

9. After the files are copied, the installation program displays the detected platform support driver. Kathleen pressed Enter to accept and load the detected driver and display the detected HotPlug and Storage adapters.

10. Kathleen verified the detected driver and adapters and pressed Enter to display the detected storage devices. Again, Kathleen verified these devices and then pressed Enter to continue and load them.

11. Next, the installation program displays the drivers that support the detected LAN adapter. Kathleen selected the driver identified by her computer hardware configuration and pressed Enter to display the Device types and Driver names window. She pressed Enter again to accept the devices and continue loading the drivers.

12. After the drivers loaded, the installation program displayed the Create SYS Volume window shown in Figure D-5.

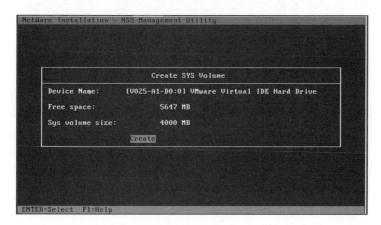

**Figure D-5**   The Create SYS Volume window

13. Kathleen pressed Enter to accept the default 4 GB SYS volume size and display the NSS Main Menu window shown in Figure D-6. This installation menu is a new addition to NetWare 6.5 and allows the installer to customize or change the configuration of devices, storage pools, and volumes without restarting the installation program.

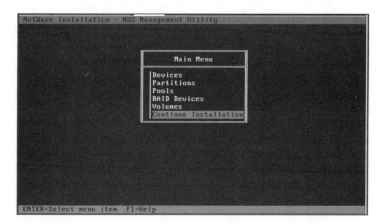

**Figure D-6**   The NetWare 6.5 main menu for installation

14. Kathleen performed the following steps to create an NSS pool named CORP for user data:

a. From the NSS Main Menu, she selected the Partitions option and pressed Enter to display the Partitions window.

b. She pressed the Insert key, selected the Free Space option, and pressed Enter to display the Select Partition Type window.

c. Next, she verified that NSS was selected and pressed Enter to display the Create Partition window.

d. She then used the arrow keys to select the Create option and pressed Enter to create a new partition and return to the Partitions window.

e. She pressed Esc to return to the NSS Main Menu.

f. Next, she selected the Pools option and pressed Enter to display the Pools window.

g. To create a new pool, she pressed the Insert key and then typed the name CORP in the Enter new pool name text box. She pressed Enter to display the Available Partitions window.

h. She pressed Enter to select the previously created partition and display the Pool Information window.

i. After creating the CORP pool, Kathleen pressed Esc to return to the NSS Main Menu.

15. Kathleen used the following steps to create a new volume named USERDATA for user data:

a. From the NSS Main Menu, she selected the Volumes option and pressed Enter to display the Logical Volumes window.

b. She typed USERDATA in the Enter new volume name text box and pressed Enter to display the Pools window.

c. She selected the USERDATA pool and pressed Enter to display the Change Volume Properties window.

d. Next, she set the Directory Quotas attribute to yes, as shown in Figure D-7.

e. She highlighted the Create option and pressed Enter to create the new volume and return to the Logical Volumes window.

f. After creating the USERDATA volume, she used the Esc key to return to the NSS Main Menu.

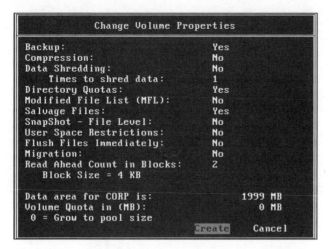

```
                  Change Volume Properties
   Backup:                            Yes
   Compression:                       No
   Data Shredding:                    No
       Times to shred data:           1
   Directory Quotas:                  Yes
   Modified File List (MFL):          No
   Salvage Files:                     Yes
   SnapShot - File Level:             No
   User Space Restrictions:           No
   Flush Files Immediately:           No
   Migration:                         No
   Read Ahead Count in Blocks:        2
       Block Size = 4 KB

   Data area for CORP is:                    1999 MB
   Volume Quota in (MB):                        0 MB
      0 = Grow to pool size
                                  Create    Cancel
```

**Figure D-7**   The Change Volume Properties window

16. After creating the USERDATA volume, Kathleen used the Esc key to return to the main menu. She selected the Continue Installation option and pressed Enter to start another file copy process. This process copies all the system files to the SYS volume and then loads the server program. She took a short break while waiting a few minutes for the files to be copied.

## Pattern Selection Phase

The pattern selection phase allows installers to select the type of server installation they want to perform and then enter the configuration information required for that type of installation. At the end of this phase, the installation process copies the necessary files into the SYS volume. The following steps show how Kathleen performed this part of the installation:

1. After the server program loaded, the Choose a Pattern dialog box shown previously in Figure D-3 was displayed. Because this server will be a general-purpose one, Kathleen left the default Customized NetWare Server radio button selected and clicked Next to display the Components dialog box shown in Figure D-8.

2. Kathleen selected the following installation options (she plans to install additional features, such as the FTP server, later):

   - Apache2 Web Server and Tomcat 4 Servlet Container (required for iPrint)
   - iPrint
   - MySQL
   - OpenSSH
   - eGuide
   - Novell iManager 2.0
   - Novell Virtual Office Framework

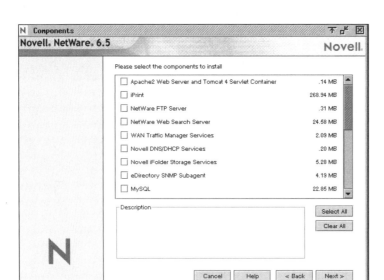

**Figure D-8**   The Components dialog box

3. After selecting these options, Kathleen clicked Next to display the installation summary window.

4. Kathleen verified that all the products she wanted to install at this time were included. Next, she clicked the Copy Files button and inserted the NetWare 6.5 (Products) CD 2 and clicked OK when prompted. Because this file copy takes almost 30 minutes, Kathleen decided to take a well-deserved break.

During the file copy process, windows with information about the selected products are displayed.

## Server Configuration Phase

During this final phase of the server installation, installers need to enter the server name, supply the license information, select and configure any network protocols to be used, identify the time zone, install eDirectory, and select any additional login methods to be used by network clients. Kathleen used the following steps to complete this final phase of the installation:

1. After finishing the file copy, the installation process displays the Enter the server name dialog box. Kathleen entered Rocky65 in the Server Name text box and then clicked Next to display the Encryption dialog box. NetWare services encrypt data by using cryptographic files (with the extension .nfk) located on the server license diskette.

You can use the Browse button to locate cryptographic files on other media. The NetWare 6.5 Products CD contains a License folder with cryptographic and license files that can be used to install an evaluation or demonstration server.

2. Kathleen inserted her license diskette and clicked Next to configure cryptography and then display the Protocols dialog box.

3. She clicked the IP check box and entered the IP address and mask for the NetWare 6.5 server. She then clicked Next to display the Domain Name Service dialog box shown in Figure D-9.

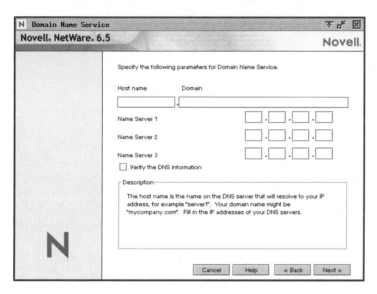

**Figure D-9**   The Domain Name Service dialog box

4. Because there's no DNS server on the local network, Kathleen left all fields blank and clicked Next. When she received a warning message informing her that some services will have limited functionality without the DNS service, she clicked OK to continue.

5. Next, she selected her time zone and clicked Next to initialize the eDirectory service and display the eDirectory Installation dialog box.

6. She clicked the Create a new eDirectory tree radio button, and then clicked Next to display the eDirectory Installation dialog box shown in Figure D-10.

7. Kathleen entered RR_TREE in the Tree Name text box and RockyRidge in the Context for Server Object text box. She then entered the password for the Admin user in the Password and Retype Password text boxes, and clicked Next to install eDirectory and display the eDirectory Summary window. She recorded the information from this window on her server installation worksheet and clicked Next to display the Licenses dialog box.

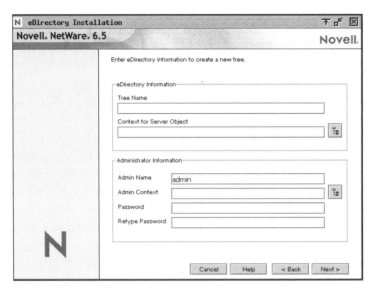

**Figure D-10**   The eDirectory Installation dialog box

8. The Licenses dialog box can be used to install licenses for the NetWare 6.5 server and users during server installation. License files have an .nlf extension and can also be installed after server installation by using iManager as described in the textbook. Because the Rocky Ridge company has an MLA server license, no user licenses are required. Kathleen used the Browse button to locate the MLA license certificate on her floppy diskette and then added it to the License(s) to be installed list box (see Figure D-11).

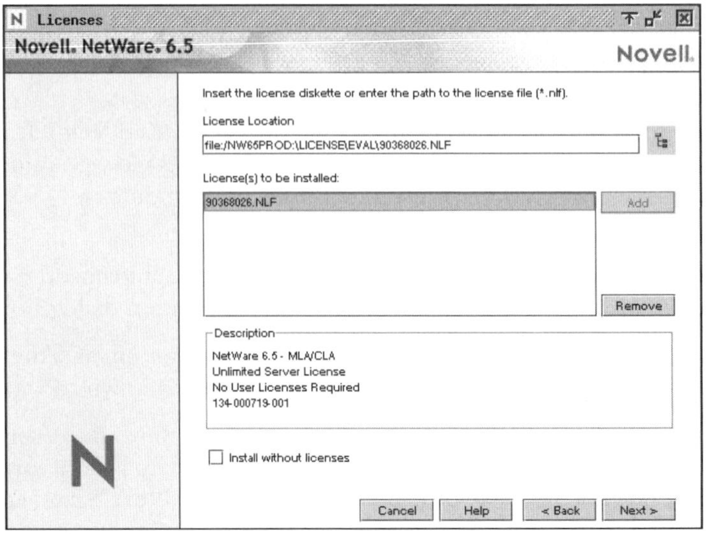

**Figure D-11**   The Licenses dialog box

A sample MLA license certificate for evaluation purposes is included on the NetWare 6.5 Products CD in the License\eval folder.

9. Kathleen clicked Next to display the MLA License Certificate Context dialog box. The Select the NDS context text box allows the installer to specify the context where licenses are installed. The licenses are then valid for all users in the selected context and below. Kathleen verified that the context was set to the RockyRidge Organization, and then clicked Next to install the licenses and display the LDAP Configuration dialog box.

10. She recorded the default clear text and SSL/TLS port numbers on her server worksheet, and then clicked Next to accept the default port settings and display the Novell Modular Authentication Service dialog box shown in Figure D-12.

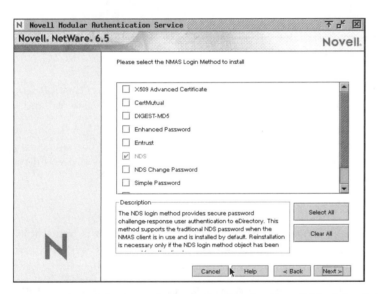

**Figure D-12**   Selecting a login method in the Novell Modular Authentication Service dialog box

11. The Novell Modular Authentication Service dialog box allows the installer to select from a variety of standard security options, described in Appendix E. In addition to the default NDS login method, Kathleen selected the Simple Password login method so that Windows client computers in the Marketing Department could log in without using the Novell client software. She then clicked Next to display the MySQL Options dialog box shown in Figure D-13.

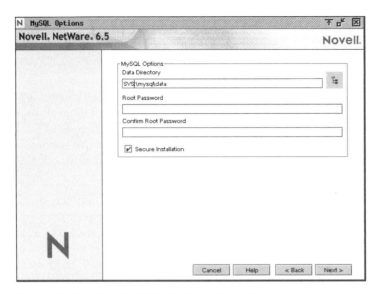

**Figure D-13**   The MySQL Options dialog box

12. She recorded the default path to the MySQL data directory on her server worksheet and then entered a password in the Root Password and Confirm Root Password text boxes.

13. After she clicked Next, the installation program finished configuring each selected service. Kathleen removed all CDs and floppy disks, and then restarted the server.

## Installing NetWare 6.5 on Blade Computers

Another enhancement in the NetWare 6.5 installation process is being able to quickly and easily install multiple NetWare servers on blade computers, which consist of one to several computers housed in a single cabinet (see Figure D-14).

In a blade system, each computer consists of a single board containing CPU, memory, disk storage, and network controller. Each server blade slides into a socket that connects it to a backplane, which supplies it with common infrastructure components, such as power supply, shared video and keyboard, CD-ROM, network switches, and system ports. Blade servers save space, improve access convenience, and reduce equipment costs and are a convenient way of clustering NetWare servers to share a common network storage device (as described earlier in the textbook).

Novell has optimized the NetWare 6.5 installation process to support simple, automated installation on multiple blade servers through the use of ZENworks images. In this textbook, you learned how to use ZENworks for Desktops to create user policies that help manage the desktop environment. With NetWare 6.5, you can also use ZENworks policies to create a server image that supplies the information for automatically installing NetWare 6.5 on a blade server.

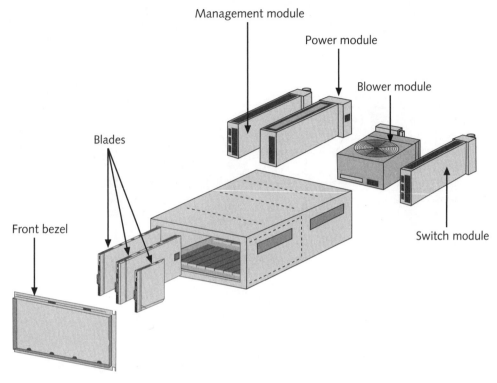

**Figure D-14**   Blade server components

## Managing Branch Offices

For large organizations, providing network services and business continuity to branch offices distributed across a wide geographical area has traditionally been an expensive undertaking. In addition, branch offices might not have the equipment or technical support staff to perform regular backups and recover from problems, resulting in possible data loss and increased support time. For example, Novell has more than 100 branch offices located around the world. In this environment, managing and maintaining servers at remote locations can involve considerable travel and administrative expense. Although consolidating servers into a corporate data center can reduce travel and administration time, it often results in unacceptable response times for users at branch offices. Novell has helped solve these problems through the Novell Nterprise Branch Office Appliance included with NetWare 6.5. As shown in Figure D-15, Nterprise Branch Office is a multifunction software appliance that enables network administrators to centralize control and reduce costs by caching eDirectory and file system information kept at the data center on one or more servers at each branch office.

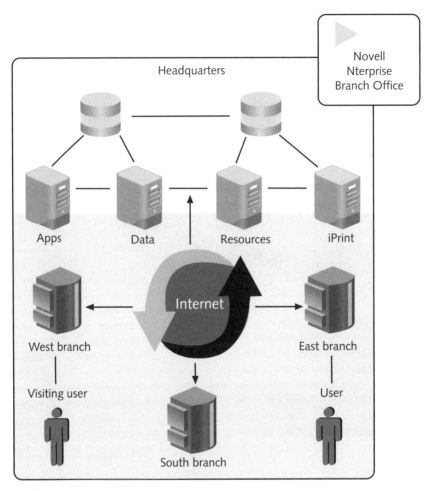

**Figure D-15** The Nterprise Branch Office Appliance

Novell refers to the Nterprise Branch Office system as an "appliance" because it requires no complex installation process; you simply insert the preconfigured Nterprise CD into the computer you want to be the branch office cached server and start it up. The Nterprise Branch Office Appliance is then copied to the hard disk, and the system is up and running. The branch office will have a local cached copy of eDirectory and frequently accessed data, thus providing high performance yet still allowing centralized system management from the data center.

As shown in Figure D-15, Nterprise Branch Office servers use standardized Internet connections to communicate with the corporate office. Using the multiple network paths available on the Internet eliminates the extra expense of dedicated WAN links and helps reduce network downtime. When a user logs in at a branch office, the Nterprise Branch Office Appliance first checks its eDirectory cache for the user name and password; if the user does not exist on the local eDirectory cache, the Nterprise appliance uses LDAP to check the corporate server's eDirectory. When the user is found, a copy of the user's eDirectory data is cached on the local Nterprise appliance, a user home directory is created, and access to shared printers and folders is granted.

## Server Consolidation

As organizations and their networks grow, network administrators often need to consolidate data from branch office servers into the corporate data center and merge older servers into new directory trees. NetWare 6.5's new Consolidation utility has options for automating the process of moving a server into another tree and consolidating data from multiple servers into a corporate data center. The NetWare 6.5 Consolidation utility can save network administrators many nerve-wracking hours of attempting these processes manually. For example, implementing Nterprise Branch Office Appliances at distributed offices requires moving the data currently at the branch office server to the corporate data center and then using Nterprise Branch Manager to set up a cache appliance at the branch office. Before implementing the Nterprise Branch Office Appliance, network administrators can use the Consolidation utility to move data from existing servers to servers in the corporate data center. After the data has been successfully consolidated in the data center, the Nterprise Branch Manager Appliance replaces the existing local servers.

Network administrators can also use the Consolidation utility to move data to a new location when implementing cluster volumes. To implement a cluster volume using NetWare 6.5, the network administrator would first create a clustered volume on a network storage device shared by two NetWare 6.5 servers and then copy the files and trustee assignments from the original data volumes. In NetWare 6, an administrator would need to manually copy all the files from the existing volume to the new clustered volume, reassign network rights to users and groups, and eventually delete the old data.

 As described in the textbook, a clustered volume is located on a network storage device that's shared among multiple servers. The advantages of having a clustered volume are improved performance (because two or more servers share the access load) and increased fault tolerance (because access to the volume is still possible if hardware failure or planned maintenance activities have caused a server to be down).

However, with the NetWare 6.5 Consolidation utility, this process is more automated and reliable; the administrator can now simply drag and drop the existing volume onto the new clustered volume. The Consolidation utility then moves the data, along with file attributes and trustee assignments, to the new location. The process is nondestructive, in that if the operation fails, the original data is still intact and the process can be restarted easily. The Consolidation utility can save network administrators much time and frustration and reduce expenses caused by administrative overhead and server downtime.

## Remote Upgrades

In today's rapidly growing network environments, upgrading servers to newer versions and installing support packs are frequent tasks for network administrators to keep organizations' information systems current. NetWare 6.5 offers the powerful Remote Upgrade utility that enables a network administrator at one location to upgrade a server at a different site simply by identifying the server to be upgraded (the target server) and the server containing the new software (called the source server). It's even possible for the source server and target servers to be in two separate sites with the network administrator at a third location. For example, a network administrator in Utah could use the Remote Upgrade utility to instruct a source server in Sydney, Australia containing a new support pack to automatically upgrade another server in Perth. This upgrade capability promises to save large organizations the time and money currently required to keep their servers upgraded with the latest software versions.

## NETWORK ADMINISTRATION AND BUSINESS CONTINUITY

In addition to installing and upgrading servers, a network administrator must perform a wide variety of tasks, including implementing and maintaining eDirectory trees, setting up and managing network users and printing, backing up data, and securing network resources. Novell refers to the network administration tasks that ensure an organization's continuous operation as the network's "business continuity needs." As networks have become more integrated and wide ranging, business continuity has become more complex to manage. The resulting increase in administrative time has resulted in extra costs for many organizations attempting to implement and maintain large networks of servers in multiple locations. After considerable research into the business continuity needs of today's integrated networks, Novell has enhanced NetWare 6.5 with several important features to reduce network administration time and costs and provide additional services, as described in the following sections.

## iManager 2.0 Enhancements

Introduced in NetWare 6, iManager 2.0 is expanded and enhanced in NetWare 6.5 to include the capabilities of both ConsoleOne and NetWare Administrator, providing enhanced administrative tasks and remote server management features, such as:

- Creating and managing eDirectory objects
- Working with eDirectory partitions
- Managing storage resources
- Running server diagnostics
- Performing intrusion detection
- Creating branch office connections
- Handling outages

In the following sections, you learn how to use iManager 2.0 to perform a variety of administrative procedures, including creating objects, working with universal passwords, viewing eDirectory partition information, and creating tasks.

## Starting iManager

iManager 2.0 has many new options and features not available with iManager 1.0. One of the first differences you'll notice is the startup process. As in iManager 1.0, to start iManager 2.0, you open your Web browser and enter the URL (*https://ip_address* or *Server_name*:2200) for your NetWare 6.5 server to display the login window shown in Figure D-16. Notice that by default the secure port 636 is used along with a Secure Sockets Layer (SSL) connection. More information about using SSL to create a secure connection is provided in Appendix E.

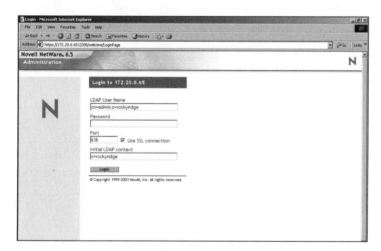

**Figure D-16**    The Administration login dialog box in NetWare 6.5

To start iManager 2.0, perform the following step after starting your browser and entering the URL stated previously:

1. If necessary, enter the user name and context of your Admin user.

2. Next, enter the password for the Admin user and then click the Login button to display the Welcome to NetWare 6.5 window, similar to the one in Figure D-17.

3. Click the + sign to expand the Network Management option and then click the iManager 2.0 option to display the Novell iManager 2.0 startup window shown in Figure D-18.

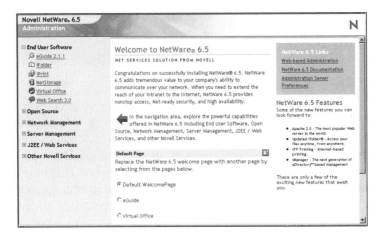

**Figure D-17**    The Welcome to NetWare 6.5 window

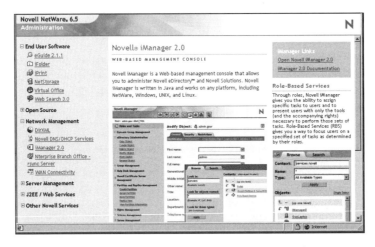

**Figure D-18**    The Novell iManager 2.0 startup window

4. Click the Open Novell iManager 2.0 link under the iManager Links heading at the upper-right to start the iManager 2.0 utility and display the Novell iManager window (similar to the window shown in Figure D-19).

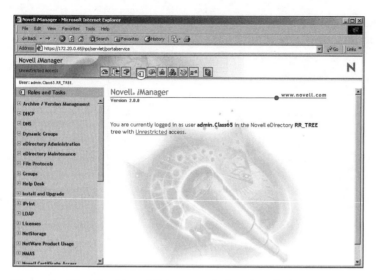

**D**

**Figure D-19**   The Novell iManager 2.0 main window

Notice all the options available in the Roles and Tasks frame on the left. These options are based on the tasks assigned to your login user name. Novell has enhanced iManager 2.0 so that administrators can now be assigned roles to perform all the administrative functions that previously required ConsoleOne or NetWare Administrator. For example, Kathleen performed the following steps in iManager to create a new DATA volume on the Rocky Ridge server. If you have supervisor rights to your NetWare 6.5 server, you can follow these steps to create a DATA volume on your server.

1. After opening her Web browser and logging in, Kathleen started iManager by following the steps described previously.

2. Next, she expanded the Storage option in the Roles and Tasks frame and clicked the Volumes option to open the Volume Management window.

3. She clicked the magnifying glass icon next to the Server text box and selected the Rocky65 server object to display the existing volumes (see Figure D-20).

4. To create a new volume named USERDATA, Kathleen clicked the New button to display the New Volume text box.

5. She entered the name USERDATA and clicked Next to open the New Volume window (similar to the one shown in Figure D-21).

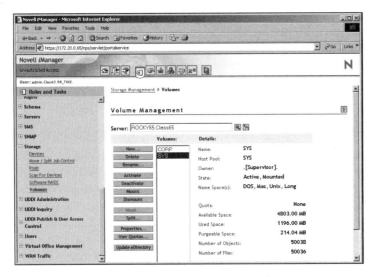

**Figure D-20**    The Volume Management window

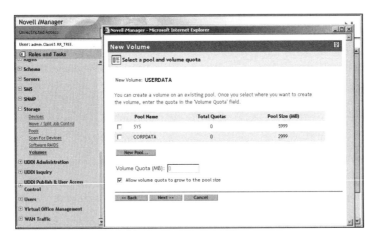

**Figure D-21**    The New Volume window

6. To assign the new USERDATA volume to the CORP storage pool and allow the volume to grow to CORP's maximum size, Kathleen clicked the check box next to CORP.

To restrict the amount of space available to the USERDATA volume, you can click to clear the Allow volume quota to grow to the pool size check box and then enter a limit in the Volume Quota (MB) text box.

7. Kathleen then clicked Next to display the Attribute information window shown in Figure D-22.

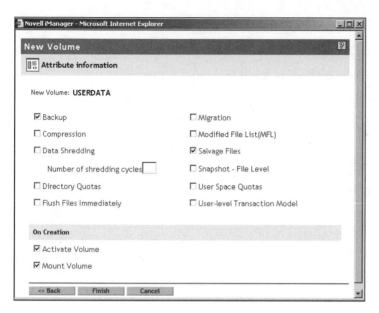

**Figure D-22**   The Attribute information window

    8. She clicked the Directory Quotas and User Space Quotas check boxes and then clicked Finish to create the new USERDATA volume and return to the Volume Management window.

    9. Kathleen clicked the Update eDirectory button to create the associated eDirectory object for the new volume, and then clicked the Home button to return to the main iManager window.

After creating the USERDATA volume, Kathleen used iManager to create user accounts with home directories on the new volume. To keep user accounts separate from other operating system objects, Kathleen decided to create an RRUSERS Organizational Unit (OU) within the RockyRidge Organization and a HOMEDIR folder on the USERDATA volume. She then created a template object to add the user accounts shown in Table D-2. To see how this is done, follow the steps in Activity D-1.

**Table D-2**   Marketing Users

| Login Name | Full Name | Comments |
|---|---|---|
| ##RWiggerts | Rosemarie Wiggerts | General Manager |
| ##CDunn | Clara Dunn | Administrative Assistant |
| ##WLocke | William Locke | Production Manager |
| ##MHeise | Mary Heise | Marketing Manager |

## Activity D-1: Creating eDirectory Objects

**Time Required:** 20 minutes

**Objective:** Use iManager to create eDirectory objects

**Description:** As the network administrator for Rocky Ridge, you have already created a USERDATA volume and now need to create the user accounts shown in Table D-2 in the RRUSERS OU. In this activity, you use iManager 2.0 to create an RRUSERS OU within your assigned container and then create the users in Table D-2 by using a template.

1. Open your Web browser and enter the URL *https://ip_address:2200* (*ip_address* represents the IP address of your NetWare 6.5 server).

2. Follow the procedure described previously to open the iManager main window.

3. Create a HOMEDIR folder in your assigned storage area by following these steps:

   a. Click the **+** symbol next to the Servers option to expand it.

   b. Click the **Launch NetWare Remote Manager** option to open the Launch NetWare Remote Manager window.

   c. Click the **Browse** button to the right of the NCP Server name text box, and use the ObjectSelector window to select your NetWare 6.5 server.

   d. Click **OK** to open the Volume Management window.

   e. Click the volume assigned to your student account to display the NetWare File Listing window, similar to the one in Figure D-23. In this figure, 10Sample represents a storage folder assigned to a student.

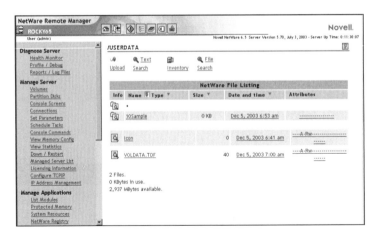

**Figure D-23**   The NetWare File Listing window in Remote Manager

f. If necessary, navigate to your assigned folder by clicking on the folder name. (For example, to open the 10Sample folder, click on the name 10Sample.)

g. Click the **Info** icon to the left of the single "." to display the Create Subdirectory button shown in Figure D-24.

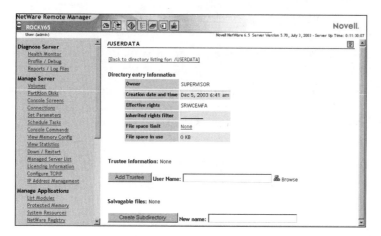

**Figure D-24**   Viewing file information

h. Enter **RRHOME** in the New name text box, and click the **Create Subdirectory** button to create the new directory and return to the Volume Management window.

i. Click the **Exit** button on the toolbar to return to the iManager window.

4. Create the RRUSERS OU in your assigned container:

a. In the Roles and Tasks frame, click the + sign to expand the eDirectory Administration option.

b. Click the **Create Object** link to open the Create Object window.

c. Click **Organizational Unit** in the Available object classes list box, and then click **OK** to open the Create Organizational Unit window.

d. Enter **RRUSERS** in the Organizational Unit name text box.

e. Click the **Browse** button (magnifying glass icon) next to the Context text box to open the ObjectSelector window.

f. If necessary, navigate down the tree until your assigned container is displayed in the Contents frame.

g. Click your assigned container to place its name in the Context text box.

h. Click **OK** to create the RRUSERS OU, and then click **OK** when the "Create Organizational Unit request succeeded" message is displayed.

5. Create the T_RRUSER user template in your RRUSERS OU:

a. Click the **Create Object** link to open the Create Object window.

b. Scroll down the Available object classes list box, click the **Template** object class, and then click **OK** to open the Create Template window.

c. Enter **T_RRUSER** in the Template name text box.

d. Click the **Browse** button next to the Context text box to open the ObjectSelector window.

e. If necessary, navigate down the tree until your RRUSERS OU is displayed in the Contents frame.

f. Click your **RRUSERS** container to place its context in the Context text box, and then click **OK** to create the object and display the "Create Template request succeeded" message. Click **OK** to return to the Novell iManager main window.

6. Configure the T_RRUSER template by performing the following steps:

a. Click the **Modify Object** link under the eDirectory Administration heading to open the Modify Object window.

b. Click the **Browse** button next to the Object name text box to open the ObjectSelector window.

c. Click the **down arrow** next to the RRUSERS OU to display the T_RRUSER template object.

d. Click the **T_RRUSER** template object to place its context in the Context text box, and then click **OK** to open the Modify Object window shown in Figure D-25.

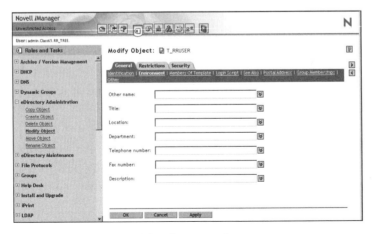

**Figure D-25**   The Modify Object window

e. Explore the tabs in the Modify Object window and notice that you can set the same parameters described in the textbook when using ConsoleOne to work with templates.

f. In the Environment tab, select the **RRHOME** folder in your assigned volume for the user home directory path.

g. Click **OK** to save your changes, and then click **OK** again to return to the iManager main window.

7. Follow these steps to create a user account for Rosemarie Wiggerts:

a. Click the **+** symbol to expand the Users options.

b. Click the **Create User** link to open the Create window.

c. Enter the user's login name, **##RWiggerts** (## represents your assigned student number), in the Username text box and **Wiggerts** in the Last name text box.

d. Click the **Browse** button next to the Context text box, and in the Object Selector window, click your **RRUSERS** OU to place it in the Context text box.

e. Click the **Copy from template or user object** check box, use the **Browse** button to navigate to your RRUSERS OU, and click your **T_RRUSER** template object.

f. If necessary, click the **Create home directory** check box to enable it. Click the **Browse** button next to the Volume text box, and then navigate to your assigned volume.

g. Click in the **Path** text box and enter the path (preceded by a backslash) to the RRHOME folder you created in Step 3.

h. Enter a password in the Password and Retype Password text boxes, and then click the **Set simple password** check box.

i. Scroll down and click the **OK** button to create the new user account and display the "Create User request succeeded" message box. Continue to the next step.

8. Create the remaining users shown in Table D-2:

a. Click the **Repeat Task** button to return to the Create User window.

b. Repeat Step 7 to create the remaining users in Table D-2. (Remember to include your assigned student number at the beginning of each user's login name.)

c. After creating the last user, click **OK** in the "Create User request succeeded" message box to return to the main iManager window.

9. Click the **Exit** button on the toolbar to exit iManager, and then close your Web browser.

## Working with Universal Passwords

In the textbook, you learned that NetWare 6 and 6.5 include the Native File Access Protocol (NFAP) feature, which makes it possible for Windows, Macintosh, and Unix workstations to access the NetWare server without installing the Novell client software. NFAP is an important feature, because many organizations want to minimize software complexity on user workstations. The downside of using the workstation's native client protocol is that certain NetWare features aren't available, such as the additional security built into Novell Client's eDirectory password encryption. When accessing the NetWare 6 or NetWare 6.5 server from a workstation that doesn't have Novell Client installed, the client computer uses its own password encryption algorithm to secure the password. This requires eDirectory to maintain two passwords, one for Novell Client encryption and another, called a "simple password," to differentiate it from the more secure eDirectory password, for native client protocols. If users need to log in from multiple workstations (some with Novell Client and some without) when using NetWare 6, they have to maintain two passwords, one for Novell Client workstations and the other for native client workstations. With NetWare 6.5, Novell simplifies the management of simple passwords by implementing a universal password option. After the universal password option is enabled in an OU, the "simple password" is automatically synchronized with the eDirectory password whenever a user in that OU logs in from a Novell client. From then on, the NetWare operating system synchronizes the two passwords, allowing the user to maintain only one password for both Novell and native client workstations. In the following activity, you enable universal passwords for your RRUSERS OU and then verify that the eDirectory password works when logging in from a Novell or Microsoft client.

## Activity D-2: Enabling Universal Passwords

**Time Required:** 10 minutes

**Objective:** Use iManager to create eDirectory objects

**Description:** To simplify installation and maintenance, most computers in the organization access the NetWare 6.5 server using only the Microsoft client. As a result, Novell Client has been installed on only two computers. To allow users to log in to the network from these computers with only one password, Kathleen decided to implement the NetWare 6.5 Universal Password feature. In this activity, you implement universal passwords in your RRUSERS OU so that users can use the same password for the Microsoft or Novell client.

1. Open your Web browser and enter the URL *https://ip_address:2200* (*ip_address* represents the IP address of your NetWare 6.5 server).

2. Follow the procedure described previously to open the iManager main window.

3. Click the **+** sign to expand the NMAS options.

4. Click the **Universal Password Configuration** link to open the Universal Password Configuration window.

5. View the current status of your RRUSERS container by following these steps:

a. Click the **Browse** button next to the Container text box to open the ObjectSelector window.

b. Click the **down arrow** to navigate through the tree until the RRUSERS OU appears in the Contents frame.

c. Click your **RRUSERS** OU to insert its context into the Container text box.

d. Click the **View** button to display the universal password's current setting, similar to the context shown in Figure D-26.

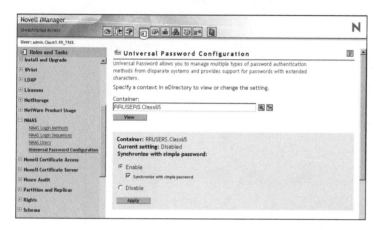

**Figure D-26** The Universal Password Configuration dialog box

6. Enable the Synchronize with simple password option:

a. Verify that the Enable radio button and the Synchronize with simple password check box are selected.

b. Click the **Apply** button to enable the Universal Password option for your RRUSERS container.

c. Click the **OK** button when the "Universal Password has been enabled" message is diplayed.

7. Click the **Exit** button to end your iManager session. Users should now be able to log in from the Microsoft or Novell client with the same password.

# File System Enhancements

Because information is the life blood of most organizations, network data must be secure, reliable, and protected against disaster. NetWare 6.5 has several enhanced features that increase an organization's ability to protect network data yet still provide high-speed, continuous access. The following sections describe how NetWare 6.5 file system enhancements can help protect an organization's most valuable asset.

## Cluster SAN Architecture

In the textbook, you learned that storage area networks (SANs) consist of one or more storage devices directly attached to a high-speed network so that multiple servers can access and share the storage devices. NetWare 6 introduced the capability of creating a volume on a SAN that was shared by a cluster of two or more servers. As shown in Figure D-27, Novell has continued to improve server cluster technology in NetWare 6.5 with enhancements.

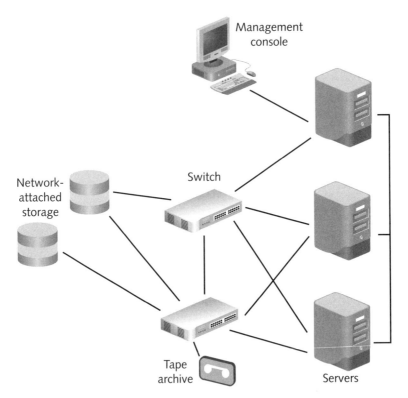

**Figure D-27**   Cluster SAN architecture

- Read-only shared volumes allow multiple servers to share the same content, which improves response time for user requests. This feature is especially useful in Web sites where downloading graphical data can bog down a single server. Changes can be made on only the master volume and automatically synchronized to the read-only volumes.

- The XML-based management console provides a way to monitor and manage the cluster environment from any computer. The XML-based interface also allows Novell to quickly adapt the management console to meet emerging industry standards for storage management.

- The quarantine of failing service function allows the cluster to remove a volume or service experiencing repeated failures.

- Maintenance Mode operation keeps a cluster together when one server is taken offline for normal maintenance. In NetWare 6 clusters, when a computer is shut down, the other computers in the cluster assume that the computer has failed and remove it from the cluster. When you bring the machine back online, it must be reinserted into the cluster. In NetWare 6.5, you can put a server into Maintenance Mode to inform the other cluster members that the machine has not failed. After maintenance is completed, you simply bring the machine back online to continue its role in the cluster. Using Maintenance Mode saves administrative time when performing normal maintenance.

## iSCSI Support

Small Computer System Interface (SCSI) technology is a major way in which network file systems are attached to servers. A new standard called Internet SCSI (iSCSI) enables SCSI protocols to be run across a high-speed TCP/IP network. Novell has implemented the iSCSI standard in NetWare 6.5 so that servers can use LAN networks to share access to SCSI disk systems. This technology allows smaller organizations to implement a SAN at reduced costs by using a NetWare 6.5 server attached to an array of SCSI disks as a network storage device. With iSCSI, NetWare 6.5 can deliver full-featured SANs for many small and medium-sized businesses by providing server clustering at reduced costs.

## Snap Shot Backups

As network storage needs have grown, tape-based backup systems (discussed in Chapter 8) have not kept up with the need for regular backups. For example, before NetWare 6.5, a server backup might have required several hours; during that time, the files being backed up must be offline to ensure that the data is correct. In a traditional backup system, open files are skipped or incorrectly copied to the backup device.

In NetWare 6.5, Novell has taken advantage of today's low-cost storage devices to make a copy of each data file to be backed up. The copy, called a "snap shot," is a picture of the actual data file at a specific time. Snap shot files can be updated frequently with little or no impact on user access to the primary data file. The snap shot file is then available to be backed up with conventional backup technology without bringing the primary file offline. Novell's snap shot technology allows data to be available around the clock, which is an important feature for NetWare 6.5 administrators.

A critical part of backing up database files is ensuring that the database is consistent before performing the backup or snap shot. To be consistent, the database must have finished its last update before the backup. To ensure database file consistency, NetWare 6.5 snap shot technology implements a set of function calls known as "freeze and thaw." By calling the freeze function, the snap shot process instructs the database application to complete its current transaction and get the database consistent for the snap shot. After the snap shot is complete, the thaw function is called to inform the database software that it can resume operation.

Another important application of the NetWare 6.5 snap shot technology is providing geographic mirroring (see Figure D-28), which combines snap shot technology and an iSCSI SAN to provide a fault-tolerant solution to data access.

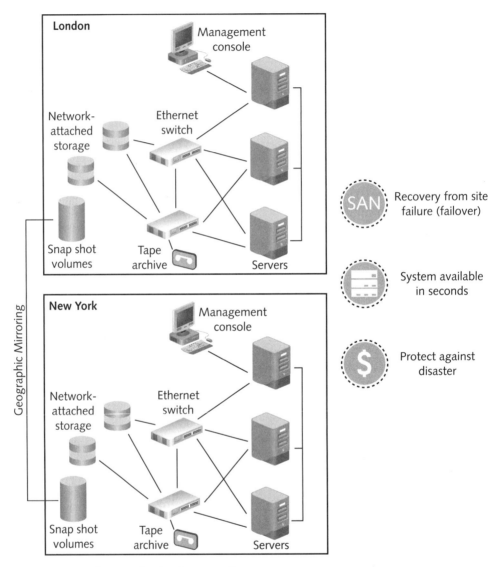

**Figure D-28** Geographic business continuance

Figure D-28 shows a cluster setup that includes London as the primary Logical Unit Number (LUN), with a mirrored copy of the London Snap Shot volume located in New York as the secondary LUN. If the London server or site fails, the New York cluster would promote the New York secondary volume as the primary volume. This system

D

would keep data available despite the loss of service at any location. This type of disaster recovery or business continuance is especially important as a result of 9/11. The federal government is planning a policy that would require financial organizations seeking FDIC insurance to demonstrate that a geographic mirror is in place. In addition, business insurance rates could substantially increase (by more than 10%) for organizations that do not have a geographic disaster recovery plan or system in place.

## END USER ENHANCEMENTS

NetWare 6.5 continues to build on Novell's one Net strategy of making network services available at anytime from anywhere. Throughout this book, you have learned about some key one Net utilities, including iManager, iPrint, iFolder, and NetStorage. In NetWare 6.5, Novell has continued to enhance these utilities and added some new capabilities called Virtual Office and Virtual Teams, described in the following sections.

## Virtual Office

Users are making more use of the Internet for real-time collaborative tasks, such as sharing data in development and design teams, analytical research, product design, and mergers or acquisitions. Needs for these collaborative tasks include messaging, data sharing, printing, and access to common task-specific applications, such as word processing and data management software. Users can become more productive when these tasks are independent of location and time, thus allowing the work experience to follow the user. As illustrated in Figure D-29, Virtual Office is an environment providing access to Novell's one Net applications, including iFolder, iPrint, and the new Novell Virtual Teams and Novell eGuide.

**Figure D-29**   The Novell Virtual Office environment

From the Virtual Office window, users can easily access their iFolder data, install and send output to their printers, interact with other users in their teams, organize and manage their contacts, and look up and access eDirectory information by using eGuide.

## Virtual Teams

As shown in Figure D-29, NetWare 6.5 Virtual Teams is a place where users can exchange and share information. You can think of Virtual Teams as a group of workers who have shared purposes, accountabilities, and work activities.

As globalization and network connectivity continue to increase, so does the need for organizations to be able to conduct work across time, space, and cultural boundaries. Virtual Teams using technology such as mediated communication systems and applications to collaborate can increase productivity for organizations that can harness these technologies. In Activities D-3 and D-4, you see how to create Virtual Teams and use them to share information.

## Activity D-3: Creating Virtual Office Teams

**Time Required:** 20 minutes

**Objective:** Use Novell Virtual Office to create teams

**Description:** The Rocky Ridge organization is working on a Web-based marketing project that involves three employees. To help communicate and share data, Rosemarie Wiggerts wants to implement a Virtual Team. In this activity, you use Virtual Office to create a Web marketing team and add the three employees.

1. On your workstation, open your Web browser and enter the URL for your NetWare 6.5 server (*https://ip_address*) to display the Welcome to NetWare 6.5 window.

2. Click the **Virtual Office** option in the left pane.

3. To log in, click the **User Login** option at the upper-right to open the Login window.

4. Enter the user name and password for your Rosemarie Wiggerts user and click the **Login** button.

5. Create a Virtual Team named RRWEBDEV:

   a. Under the Virtual Team Tasks heading on the left, click **Create Virtual Team**.

   b. In the Name text box, enter **RRWEBDEV** and click **Create**. Click **OK** to respond to the success message.

6. Members can be added to your new Virtual Team by selection or by invitation. Follow these steps to send an invitation to your William Locke and Rosemarie Wiggerts users:

   a. Under My Virtual Teams on the left, click **RRWEBDEV** to display the Virtual Team window, similar to the one in Figure D-30.

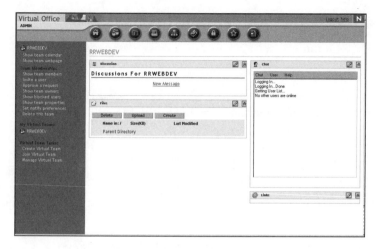

**Figure D-30**  The Virtual Team window

b. Under the Team Membership heading on the left, click the **Invite a user** option.

c. Click the **Add** button to display a search window.

d. Enter **Locke** in the Last name text box and click **Search**.

e. Click your **William Locke** user, and click **Add** to place William in the Virtual Team Invitations window.

7. Click the **Logout** link at the upper-right of the Virtual Office window.

8. Follow these steps to log in as William Locke and join the RRWEBDEV team:

a. Log in with your William Locke user name and password.

b. Click RRWEBDEV from the Virtual Team Inbox, and then click the Join button to add the RRWEBDEV team to William's My Virtual Teams list. Notice that the RRWEBDEV team is now listed under the My Virtual Teams heading located in the left column.

c. In the left options column, click the RRWEBDEV team located under the My Virtual Teams heading and explore available team information.

d. Click the **Logout** link to log out.

9. Log out.

## Activity D-4: Working with Virtual Teams

**Time Required:** 20 minutes

**Objective:** Use Virtual Teams to share information

**Description:** In this activity, you upload a file to the RRWEBDEV virtual team and then log in as another team member and download the file.

1. Log in to Virtual Office as Rosemarie Wiggerts.

2. Create a team calendar by following these steps:

   a. Click the **RRWEBDEV** team.

   b. Click the **Show team calendar** option to display a calendar window, similar to the one in Figure D-31.

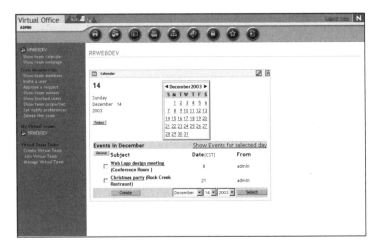

**Figure D-31** The Virtual Team Calendar window

   c. Click the **Create** button to add an event for today's date.

   d. Click **Save** to save the entry, and then click **Close** to return to the RRWEBDEV Calendar window.

3. Publish a favorite URL for all team members by following these steps:

   a. Click the **Show team webpage** option to display a Team Page window, similar to the one in Figure D-32, and then click the **Edit** button.

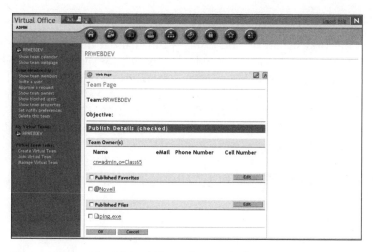

**Figure D-32**    The Virtual Team Page window

    b. Click the **Published Favorites** check box, and then click the **Edit** button to open the Current Bookmarks window.

    c. Click **Add** to open the Add Bookmark dialog box.

    d. Enter **Novell** in the Name text box, and enter **www.novell.com** in the URL text box.

    e. Click **OK** to place the bookmark in the Current Bookmarks window.

    f. Click **Save** to save the new bookmark and open a Links window. Close the Links window to return to the Virtual Team Page window.

4. To upload a file, follow these steps:

    a. Click the **Published Files** check box and then click **Edit** to open the Files window.

    b. Click the **Upload** button, and use the **Browse** button to navigate to your C:\WINNT\System32 (or C:\WINDOWS\System32) folder.

    c. Select the **Ping.exe** program and click **Open** to insert it in the File name text box.

    d. Click the **Upload** button to upload the file and notify all subscribers.

    e. After the file is uploaded, click **Close** and then close the Files window.

5. Log out.

6. Log in to Virtual Office as William Locke and verify that the calendar, URL, and Ping.exe file are available.

7. Log out and close your Web browser.

## NetWare 6.5 eGuide

Rapid changes in business structures and policies can make it difficult for users to find and access corporate information or know who to contact for support and problems. To improve access to an organization's internal information, NetWare 6.5 ships with Novell's new eGuide Web application. As shown in Figure D-33, the eGuide application enables users to search for names, addresses, fax numbers, and e-mail addresses stored in Novell eDirectory or on other LDAP-compatible directory services, such as Microsoft Active Directory, across the Internet.

**Figure D-33**    The eGuide welcome window

In addition, Novell eGuide makes use of eDirectory's self-help capabilities by enabling users to manage their personal directory information and get answers to common problems, thereby reducing administrative time and costs.

## iPrint Enhancements

As you learned in Chapter 11, using iPrint to easily find and access network printers through a Web browser is a powerful part of the one Net strategy. In NetWare 6.5, Novell has expanded iPrint's capabilities by adding the following features:

- Support for Citrix and terminal server environments enables users to print to printers both inside and outside the terminal server environment.

- The iPrint client allows users to add printers to their workstations without needing to log in with administrator rights to the local workstation.

- Although Novell Distributed Print Services (NDPS) still plays an important role in supporting iPrint printers, new gateways are making it easier to set up printing through iManager without using NetWare Administrator.

- Print auditing allows organizations to track access to printers.

- With the new printer pooling feature, multiple print devices can be accessed as one logical iPrint printer.

- Because many organizations still need support for applications that print to the LPT port, the NetWare 6.5 iPrint services allow DOS-based printers to print directly through iPrint instead of sending output to a print queue.

D

# WEB SERVICES

As you learned in the textbook, Novell has included Apache Web Server, Tomcat Servlet Engine, and NetWare Enterprise Web Server with NetWare 6.5. Novell has implemented many of its management tools as Web interfaces rather than the traditional GUI or text-mode interfaces. NetWare Remote Manager, iManager, and the like are Web-based applications or Net services that administrators use to manage their networks. The Internet has created a new breed of user, one who is sophisticated and knowledgeable. Novell understands that the learning curve to use a browser-type interface is much lower, because most administrators have experience using Internet tools, such as search engines and browsers. Web-based tools also make it possible for administrators and end users to work from anywhere in the world, with any operating system. As long as a Web browser is available, NetWare servers are available.

## Developer Tools

Previous versions of NetWare had few tools for Web or application developers. Apache Web Server is included with NetWare 6, but having a Web server without the necessary Web development tools can increase costs for businesses. NetWare 6.5 comes to the rescue with some new tools and products, described in the following sections.

### MySQL Database

MySQL is an open-source database application that thousands of Web developers currently use as the back-end database for e-commerce solutions. With NetWare 6.5, you get a commercial license for MySQL, enabling you to create a back-end database to your company's Web pages.

Not sure what a database is? To find some great books on the subject, visit *www.course.com* and search on the keyword "database."

Rhode Island became one of the first states to implement open-source technology for state government use, and many businesses are using open-source applications instead of proprietary vendor software as a cost-saving alternative. Other examples of open-source applications are Apache (Novell's default Web server), FreeBSD, Linux, and Perl.

In a MySQL database, information is stored electronically. When a customer places an order over the Web, for example, code written by a developer updates the database with information the customer enters or displays information from the MySQL database in a Web page for the customer to view. If you want to create a table to store contact information for employees working in an OU called InfoSystems, you could use the following code to create a table called tblinfosys with four columns—emp_id, emp_name, emp_email, and emp_phone—for the employee data:

```
CREATE TABLE tblinfosys (
    emp_id    int(4) NOT NULL,
    emp_name    varchar(50),
    emp_email    varchar(50),
    emp_phone    varchar (10),
    PRIMARY KEY (emp_id)
);
```

Even without any database experience, you can see that creating a table is not that complicated. In fact, your experience in writing login scripts will help you in this area.

## PHP

NetWare 6.5 includes PHP version 4.0, an open-source scripting language for creating dynamic Web pages, which can change depending on information the user enters or on code written in the script. For example, you can display a clock with the current time of day on your Web page and have it updated every second. There are literally thousands of sites you can visit with sample code, free tutorials, support groups, and newsgroups, making it a great choice for a new Web developer wondering what scripting language to learn.

PHP is a server-side scripting language, similar to Microsoft Active Server Pages (ASP), that can be used on Web servers. One of its advantages is that you can use it to connect directly to MySQL, Oracle, and DB2 databases. PHP code is usually inserted into HTML Web pages. The following example mixes HTML code with PHP code. PHP code begins with the characters <? and ends with the characters ?>, so it's easy to determine where the two codes are being used. Note the /* and */ characters in the PHP segment. These characters separate comments from the actual PHP code. As you learned when creating login scripts, comments are essential in any scripts you write.

```
<HTML>
<HEAD>
```

D

```
<TITLE>CBE Labs</TITLE>
</HEAD>

<BODY BGCOLOR="white">

<H1>InfoSystems Employees</H1>
<?
/*
PHP InfoSystems Personnel
Written by William Locke
The following code counts how many records are in the
tblinfosys table. (For simplicity, the code for connecting
to the database is omitted.) */

  $query = "SELECT COUNT(*) FROM tblinfosys";
?>
```

## Novell exteNd

Formerly called SilverStream extend, an application developed by IBM, Novell exteNd includes four software packages: exteNd Application Server, exteNd Composer, exteNd Workbench, and exteNd Director. As a Web developer, one of your tasks is formatting data for your online customers to view from their browsers. Before you can format this data, however, you need to access it. In other words, you must find out where the data is located. Is it on the company's legacy system, located in the computer room of an old dilapidated building? Or is the data on a NetWare 6.5 server running MySQL? In either case, Novell exteNd Composer can be used to access that database. You would use exteNd Director to deliver that data to your online customers. Both tools work together as a wizard and are displayed to the developer as an exteNd Workbench GUI.

 As a CNA, you probably won't be required to use many of these Web development tools. However, having a better understanding of what your NetWare server is capable of makes you a better administrator and a more valuable employee to your company.

Novell's exteNd Application Server was one of the first application servers to be Java 2 Enterprise Edition (J2EE) 1.3 certified, which requires passing more than 15,000 tests. For developers who want to deploy Java applications, this server includes all the tools needed to create anything from robust applications to interactive applets for your company's Web pages. (If needed, you can refer to Chapter 14 for an explanation of applets.) The big advantage of Java is its platform independence. As long as the computer system on which the application is running has a Java Virtual Machine (JVM), the developer has to create only one version of the program for it to run on multiple platforms. This platform independence makes Java the language of choice for the World Wide Web and the recommended programming language to study if you want to expand your computer skills. As of this writing, NetWare 6.5 includes JVM version 1.4.1.

With NetWare 6.5, administrators can create both simple Web-based applications and Web interfaces similar to iManager or Remote Manager. This gives administrators the flexibility to create their own management tools, if necessary, and to customize NetWare's management consoles by creating their own gadgets. The only limitations are the administrator's programming skills. Gone are the days of NLMs being the only method of creating applications for Novell.

NetWare 6.5 has also integrated eDirectory with Web Services, enabling you to take advantage of the security features already implemented in your network. Certificates and Secure Sockets Layer (SSL) security can be implemented with minimum coding, so your e-commerce applications can be released to your customers with reduced security risks.

NetWare 6.5 includes many new features and security enhancements that promise to make NetWare and Novell services, such as eDirectory, more prevalent in IT environments. In Appendix E, you'll learn more about the NetWare 6.5 security enhancements and how they can be used to securely access Novell services across the Internet, using a wide variety of security standards. As NetWare and Novell services continue to grow, the skills you have gained in studying to become a CNA will become even more valuable. In addition, Appendix F outlines how Novell's Nterprise for Linux can make your skills with eDirectory and iManager even more valuable in the rapidly growing Linux community.

# E

# NetWare 6.5 Security Enhancements

S ecurity can be defined as a measure of how data and resources are protected from unauthorized access. The higher the security for a resource, the more difficult it is for an intruder to gain access to that resource. Most security systems consist of a three part model: authentication, authorization, and auditing (AAA). The AAA model begins with authentication, which is the process used to positively identify an entity as being the person or system they claim to be. Authorization is the process of giving authenticated users a set of predetermined rights to the resource they are attempting to access and ensuring that the service request actually originated from the authenticated user. Authorization security in NetWare 6/6.5 is implemented through trustee assignments and Role Based Services (RBS). As described in the textbook, trustee assignments are used to grant authenticated users rights to the NetWare file system and eDirectory objects; RBS is used to give users rights to perform administrative tasks in iManager. Appendix F explains how to set up RBS in NetWare and Linux environments. Finally, auditing is the process of logging the use of each resource. Since NetWare version 2, Novell has included auditing features in NetWare for keeping track of all changes and access attempts made to network resources. For example, you can track which users access a file or printer and record the user name, date and time of access, operation performed, and success or failure of the operation. This information can be important when tracking changes or looking for an intruder. NetWare 6.5 still uses the same basic authorization and auditing security features from previous NetWare versions, but in this appendix, you learn about new features that have been incorporated into NetWare 6.5 authentication security services.

In the past, a large part of security relied on physically isolating resources and networks. Although security has always been important to implementing computerized business applications, even on isolated or internal networks, the Internet has placed new demands on security systems by removing the physical security of isolation and placing resources and applications where they are potentially accessible to nearly anyone with a computer.

Novell has a history of implementing strong security systems in the NetWare operating system products. NetWare 6.5 continues to build on the security systems Novell has included since NetWare version 2 in the mid-1980s. As described in the textbook, NetWare security systems can be divided into login security, file system security, eDirectory security, printer security, and server console security. Using the AAA model, login security provides authentication, and the other security systems provide authorization security. In addition, since NetWare version 2, Novell has always included an auditing security system for tracking access to network resources and data. An important aspect of any type of security is preventing data from being captured and read while it's being transmitted between network entities. Secure data transmission is accomplished by scrambling or encrypting the message in a way that only the receiver can decipher. In this appendix, you learn how Novell has continued to enhance network security by implementing industry open-source standards into the NetWare 6.5 operating system.

## INTRODUCTION TO ENCRYPTION SECURITY

In addition to the security options described in the textbook, security systems need to protect information from being captured and read as it's transmitted across the network. Keeping passwords and data secret is especially important when using the Internet, because intruders might have access to login and data packets as they travel across network routers and cables. Keeping passwords and data unintelligible to anyone except the intended receiver is accomplished through some type of encryption. Basically, encryption is the process of converting plain text into a secret message, which can only be read after it is decrypted by reversing the encryption process. The process used to encrypt and decrypt the message is called a cipher. The science of encrypting data, called cryptography, involves using algorithms with a special value called a key (often the user's password) to hide information from all but intended recipients by "scrambling" data packets as shown in Figure E-1. The only way to read the scrambled data packet is to decrypt the data packet by reversing the process and using the corresponding key value.

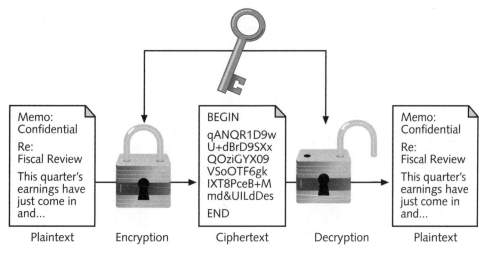

**Figure E-1**   Cryptography algorithm process

## Cryptography Techniques

The two major types of cryptography techniques, or ciphers, are symmetric ciphers and asymmetric ciphers (also called public key cryptography). When using a symmetric key cryptography technique, the same key, usually the user's password, is used to encrypt and decrypt the message or request. The advantage of symmetric cryptography is that it's simple and efficient. The problem with symmetric cryptography is that both the sender and receiver must have the same key. Securely exchanging the same key between the server and client can be a problem when communicating over public networks such as the Internet. Asymmetric ciphers or public cryptography gets around the problem of exchanging the same key by using a set of two keys: a public key and a private key. An entity's public key is exchanged with other systems and used to encrypt data being sent to that entity. The entity's private key is then used to decrypt the data that was encrypted with its public key, as illustrated in Figure E-2.

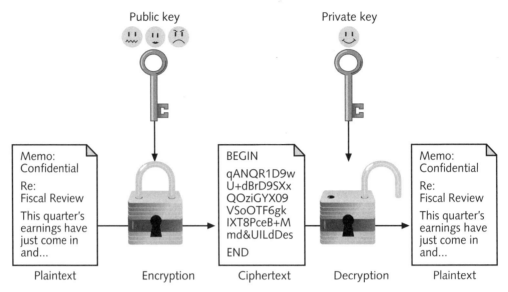

**Figure E-2**    Asymmetric cryptography process

In addition to encrypting data packets, public and private keys can be used to create and verify digital signatures. A digital signature is important because it shows that a message or request is from the actual entity, since only that entity could create a signature readable by its public key.

Private and public keys are provided to network entities or users through a certificate issued by a Certificate Authority (CA). Public Key Cryptography Standards (PKCS) provides a set of standards maintained by the RSA Data Security organization for the purpose of implementing public key cryptography on the Internet. PKCS-compatible CAs use the X.509 standard to format certificates that can be used to encrypt and decrypt data by any PKCS-compatible system. There are PKCS standards for different encryption needs. For example, PKCS#7 is an extensible message format that represents the results of cryptographic operations on data. The PKCS#12 standard is often used for encrypting login requests and is included as a NetWare 6.5 login option.

CAs can be defined as private or public. Most network operating systems, including NetWare, Windows 2000/2003, and Linux, include private CA software that allows the server to issue X.509 certificates to clients. Although a private X.509 certificate issued by the local network operating system works fine for users who have accounts on that organization's network, to operate on the Internet an organization needs an X.509 certificate that's digitally signed by a recognized CA, such as VeriSign. This digital signature is analogous to having a passport, a driver's license, or other certified picture ID rather than a company or student ID card. Although a student ID card can get you into campus activities, it isn't recognized as a valid form of ID at the airport. A digitally signed certificate is considered more valid than a locally issued certificate because a CA verifies the identity of the user or organization requesting the certificate. Just as a passport is recognized as a valid form of ID at the airport, a digitally signed certificate is accepted as valid identification by most Web browsers and servers, including Netscape, Windows Internet Explorer, and Novell NetWare 6.5.

## Encryption Protocols

A number of encryption protocols can be used to secure data and passwords transmitted across networks. Most protocols can be configured to use symmetric or asymmetric cryptographic techniques, depending on security and performance needs. When exchanging keys isn't necessary, symmetric protocols require less processing overhead, so they are often used to encrypt data transmitted on private networks, and keys for each user can be stored in a directory service on the server. Public systems that allow access by users who are unknown to the server often use asymmetric cryptography in the encryption protocol to exchange keys securely. Some protocols use a combination of symmetric and asymmetric cryptography, thus taking advantage of the security of asymmetric cryptography to exchange a key that a symmetric protocol then uses to encrypt and decrypt data packets. The following sections introduce some common protocols for securing network transmissions and securing access to your NetWare 6.5 console.

### IP Security Protocol (IPSec)

Data transmitted across the network can also be secured by performing the data encryption process at Layer 3 (the Network layer) of the Open Systems Interconnect (OSI) model, which eliminates the need to encrypt passwords. The IP Security (IPSec) protocol, developed by the Internet Engineering Task Force (IETF), secures the Network layer by using Encapsulating Security Payload (ESP) to perform encryption and decryption at the IP packet level. Either symmetrical or asymmetrical encryption can be used. Because IPSec packets have a standard TCP/IP header, they can be routed through the network using standard devices that might not be IPSec aware. The main disadvantage of IPSec is the additional processing time needed to encrypt and decrypt all IP packets. Security systems that work at a higher level can selectively encrypt sensitive data packets, thereby improving network performance.

### SSL and TLS Protocols

Secure Sockets Layer (SSL) and Transport Layer Security (TLS) are some of the most widely used protocols for securing message transmission across the Internet. Originally developed by Netscape, SSL and TLS are also supported by Microsoft and Novell as well as many other Internet application developers. Although TLS is essentially the latest version of SSL, it's not as widely available in Web browsers. Both SSL and TLS use a hybrid of the symmetric and asymmetric encryption ciphers to encrypt data packets. First, the sending computer uses the receiver's X.509 certificate to verify the receiver's identity. Next, the sender's computer randomly picks a symmetric key and then encrypts it using the public key from the receiving computer's digital certificate. The sending computer then sends the encrypted key to the receiving computer, which decrypts the data packet using its private key. After the sender and receiver identify the secret symmetric key, the computers can use this shared key to perform standard symmetric encryption of data packets more efficiently than using the asymmetric technique to encrypt and decrypt each data packet. The length of the symmetric key also plays a role in secure transactions. Web browsers that use 40- and 56-bit keys are considered to have weak encryption because these key sizes can be cracked in a short time (approximately one week on average) by using commonly available processing power along with specialized software. The 40- and 56-bit browsers are common because of U.S. government regulations on exporting strong (128-bit) cipher keys.

Key lengths are not the sole characteristic that makes the security of a key weak or strong; the security of a key also depends on the encryption algorithm. Keys based on certain encryption algorithms can be 10 to 20 times stronger for a given length than keys based on a weaker algorithm.

## The HTTPS Protocol

Secure Hypertext Transfer Protocol (HTTPS) is a secure communications protocol designed to transfer encrypted information between computers over the Web. HTTPS is essentially an implementation of the widely used HTTP protocol that uses SSL/TLS for secure data transmission. The major difference between HTTPS and SSL/TLS is that SSL/TLS is used to encrypt a persistent connection whereas HTTPS uses SSL to encrypt a single page. After a digital certificate is installed on a Web server, an SSL-enabled Web browser, such as Netscape or Internet Explorer, can connect to the Web server using HTTPS and securely exchange information. HTTP combines with SSL/TLS to enable secure communications by following these steps:

1. By accessing a URL with HTTPS, the client requests a secure transaction and negotiates an encryption algorithm.

2. The server sends the client the server's digital certificate containing the public key and a list of supported ciphers and key sizes in priority sequence.

3. The client compares the CA that issued the certificate to a list of trusted CAs and verifies that the certificate has not expired.

4. The client generates a secret symmetric key based on the list of ciphers and then encrypts the key using the server's public key and sends it to the server.

5. The server then decrypts the new symmetric session key using its own asymmetric private key.

6. After the symmetric key has been identified, both the server and client use that key along with the negotiated algorithm to secure all further communication between the two entities.

## Message Digest Security

Another important aspect of securing data transmitted across the Internet is ensuring that data has not been tampered with or changed since it left the sender. Data transmissions can be secured against tampering by using a hashing algorithm to create a fixed-length message called a message digest, as shown in Figure E-3.

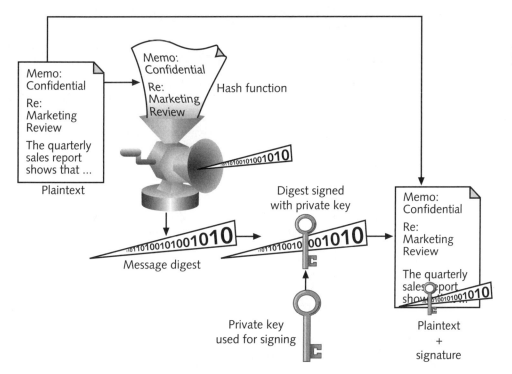

**Figure E-3**    Creating a message digest

The message digest is signed with the user's private key and appended to the message transmission. The receiver then opens the transmission and uses the sender's public key along with the hash algorithm to compute a message digest from the original message. If the message digests match, the receiver knows that no bits in the message have changed since it was signed by the sender. In some ways, a message digest is similar to the Cyclic Redundancy Check (CRC) code attached to each data packet by TCP/IP. The CRC is also calculated by applying a mathematical algorithm to the data packet's contents to create a relatively simple code consisting of 8 to 16 bits. When the packet is received, the receiver applies the same algorithm to the data packet's contents and then checks its results against the sender's CRC. If the results are different, the receiver assumes the bits in the packet were changed or damaged by the transmission process.

The difference between using a message digest and the normal CRC that TCP/IP attaches to data packets is that the CRC notifies the receiver of transmission errors, but doesn't allow the receiver to detect falsified data packets in which the hacker has modified the CRC to match the new data content. Two major hashing algorithms are in use today. Secure Hash Algorithm 1 (SHA-1), developed by the National Security Agency (NSA), produces 160-bit message digests and is considered the most secure. Message Digest 5 (MD5), developed by RSA Data Security, produces 128-bit digests and has been placed in the public domain. Because it requires no licensing, as of this writing MD5 is the most commonly used hashing algorithm, but cryptography experts fear it has flaws that could cause it to be broken in the future.

## The Secure Shell Protocol: OpenSSH

The Secure Shell (SSH) protocol is used with remote login and file transfer programs, such as Telnet and File Transfer Protocol (FTP), to provide an encrypted link between the client and server. SSH uses asymmetric public key cryptography techniques to establish an encrypted, secure connection between the user and the remote machine. After the secure connection is established, user names, passwords, and all other data can be securely transmitted over the secure connection. Because of its popularity, many network applications and operating systems, including NetWare 6.5, now support SSH ports, and free clients are available for logging on to an SSH-compatible server. Novell supports the open-source version of SSH called OpenSSH and includes it as an installation option (see the NetWare 6.5 installation section in Appendix D).

Originally, the FTP file transfer program did not ensure secure encrypted data transmission between client and server. As a result, several attempts have been made to fix FTP's security shortcomings, but they have not been widely adapted. The most commonly used file transfer program that provides encrypted security is called Secure File Transfer Protocol (S/FTP). S/FTP is not a rework of the traditional FTP, but is a new component of SSH that has the same command syntax as FTP but performs all operations over an encrypted transport. S/FTP can also use SSH features, such as public key authentication and compression. Novell has included S/FTP with OpenSSH in NetWare 6.5 to provide the following advantages over the traditional FTP service:

- Because S/FTP uses the underlying OpenSSH protocol, it offers strong authentication using a variety of methods, including X.509 digital certificates.

- By using OpenSSH, all authentication information, commands, and data transferred between the S/FTP client and the Novell server are encrypted and secured.

- S/FTP uses a single TCP connection port, making it relatively easy to configure on a firewall. On the other hand, the older FTP service uses two connection ports: the initial connection that uses port number 21 and a second reverse connection that opens a random high port number. Assigning a random port number for the second connection makes firewall configuration more difficult.

- As described in the textbook, many networks use Network Address Translation (NAT) to route packets between a secured private network and the Internet. S/FTP makes NAT configuration easier because it doesn't need to negotiate a separate IP address for the data connection, as with traditional FTP clients and servers.

Because Novell includes OpenSSH with NetWare 6.5, you can use one of several client programs to securely access the NetWare 6.5 server console. One popular choice is PuTTy. You can download the PuTTy utility from several sources, including *www.chiark.greenend.org.uk/~sgtatham/putty/download.html*. In the following activity, you use PuTTy to securly access your NetWare 6.5 server's console.

**E**

## Activity E-1: Using the OpenSSH Protocol

**Time Required:** 15 minutes

**Objective:** Use OpenSSH and PuTTy to securely access the NetWare 6.5 console

**Description:** As a consultant for the Rocky Ridge organization, you need to access the server console periodically to perform server maintenance. To do this, you have down-loaded the OpenSSH PuTTy utility and plan to use it to securely access the Rocky Ridge server console. Follow these steps to access your NetWare 6.5 server console with PuTTy:

1. At the server console, type **SSHD** and press **Enter** to start the OpenSSH ser-vice, which replaces the less secure rlogin and Telnet services.

2. At the server console, type the command **SCP** and press **Enter** to start the SCP (remote console) service. Then type **SFTP** and press **Enter** to start the S/FTP service.

3. If necessary, download the PuTTy client from *www.chiark.greenend.org.uk/~sgtatham/putty/download.html*.

4. From your workstation desktop, open the SSH-compliant client by running the PuTTy application.

5. In the Host Name text box, enter the IP address of your NetWare 6.5 server, and then click the **SSH** radio button to change the port to 22.

6. To begin the session, click **Open**.

7. If necessary, click **Yes** twice to trust the host and continue with the connection.

8. Enter your assigned Admin user name and password at the "login as:" prompt. The server console screen should then be displayed on your desktop.

9. Explore the functionality of the SSH session by using the following keyboard commands:

   - **Ctrl+Z** to open the screen list (GUI not supported)
   - **Ctrl+Z** to toggle between server screens
   - **Ctrl+Q** to display the SSH keyboard commands help screen

10. Press **Ctrl+X** and enter **y** to exit the SSH session and close the PuTTy application.

# NETWARE 6.5 AUTHENTICATION SECURITY ENHANCEMENTS

As described earlier, authentication security provides a way to ensure that the entity attempting to access the system is a valid user and is actually the user it claims to be. For example, you might know that Rosemarie Wiggerts is an employee of the Rocky Ridge company, but how do you determine that the entity attempting to gain access is actually Rosemarie? In the real world, we often identify people by checking authorized picture IDs, by verifying signatures, or by knowing the person personally. Most network authentication security relies heavily on user names and passwords to identify a valid user. For example, if an entity supplies the user name RWiggerts along with the proper password, that entity is assumed to be Rosemarie Wiggerts and is granted Rosemarie's access to the system resources. As you learned in this textbook, NetWare includes the following optional features to help strengthen authentication security:

- Minimum password lengths
- Password expiration
- Unique password
- Intruder detection
- Time restrictions
- Station restrictions

Although Novell's eDirectory uses a highly secure system of password encryption and storage, it's a proprietary system that requires the Novell client to provide the encryption services needed to access eDirectory passwords. Because NetWare 6.5 is designed to allow access from other clients, including Web browsers, Novell offers additional authentication options in the installation process (as described in Appendix D) to secure the transmission of passwords and ensure that the login attempt is from an authorized entity. In the following sections, you learn more about these login methods and how they enhance the NetWare security environment.

## NDS Passwords

The NDS password option is the default authentication method the NetWare 6.5 server uses. NDS passwords are stored in eDirectory using Novell's proprietary encryption method. An NDS password requires the Novell client to be installed on user workstations to provide the necessary encryption algorithm. As described in the textbook, when you create a user account in ConsoleOne or iManager, you have the option of entering an NDS password for the user. In NetWare 6.5, an NDS password is required for the user to log in from the Novell client. If you don't enter an initial NDS password, a message (see Figure E-4) is displayed warning you that a password is required for the user to log in.

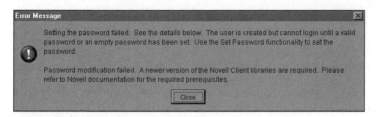

**Figure E-4**   The NDS password warning message

## Simple Passwords

In the textbook, you learned that NetWare 6 and 6.5 include Native File Access Protocol (NFAP), which allows Windows, Macintosh, and Unix workstations to access the NetWare server without having Novell Client installed. NFAP is an important feature because many organizations want to minimize software complexity on user workstations. The downside to using a workstation's native client protocol is that certain NetWare features aren't available, such as the additional security built into the Novell client's NDS password encryption. When a client workstation without Novell Client accesses the NetWare 6.0 or 6.5 server, it uses its own password encryption algorithm to secure the password. This requires eDirectory to maintain two passwords: one for Novell Client encryption and another for native client protocols, called a "simple password," to differentiate it from the more secure NDS password. NetWare stores the simple password separately from the NDS password, using a different encryption system that's compatible with the workstation's native client.

## Universal Passwords

One of the inconveniences of simple passwords is that users might need two different passwords, one for Novell Client workstations and the other for native Windows workstations. With NetWare 6.5, Novell has simplified this process by adding universal passwords. Administrators enable this option in a container of the eDirectory tree, and then eDirectory stores one password that all workstations use. When the Universal Password option is enabled in an Organizational Unit (OU), the simple password is automatically synchronized with the eDirectory password whenever a user in that OU logs in from a Novell client. The NetWare operating system keeps the two passwords synchronized so that users need to use and maintain only one password for Novell and native client workstations. Universal passwords decrease the security of NDS passwords, but because they can be enabled on a container-by-container basis, administrators can pick and choose which users need this flexibility. Because of the reduced security of native client passwords, however, the Universal Password option should not be enabled on highly sensitive user accounts that require stronger security, such as the Admin user. In the following activity, you enable universal passwords for your RRUSERS OU so that the same password will work when logging in from the Novell or Microsoft client.

## Activity E-2: Enabling Universal Passwords

**Time Required:** 10 minutes

**Objective:** Enable universal passwords

**Description:** To simplify installation and maintenance, most computers in the Rocky Ridge organization access the NetWare 6.5 server using only the Microsoft client, so the Novell client has been installed on only two computers. Kathleen has decided to implement universal passwords so that users can log in to the network using only one password. In this activity, you implement universal passwords in your RRUSERS OU:

1. Open your Web browser and enter the URL *https://ip_address:2200* (*ip_address* represents the IP address of your NetWare 6.5 server).

2. Follow the procedure described in Appendix D to open the iManager main window.

3. Click the **+** sign to expand the NMAS options.

4. Click the **Universal Password Configuration** option to open the Universal Password Configuration window.

5. View the current status of your RRUSERS container by following these steps:

    a. Click the **Browse** button next to the Container text box to open the ObjectSelector window.

    b. Click the **down arrow** to navigate down the tree until the RRUSERS OU appears in the Contents frame.

    c. Click your **RRUSERS** OU to insert its context into the Container text box.

    d. Click the **View** button to display the current setting for universal passwords, similar to the window shown in Figure E-5.

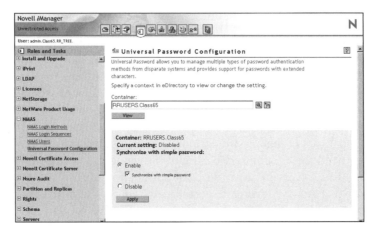

**Figure E-5**   The current setting for universal passwords

6. Enable the Synchronize with simple password option:

   a. Verify that the Enable radio button and the Synchronize with simple password check box are selected.

   b. Click the **Apply** button to enable universal passwords for your RRUSERS container.

   c. Click **OK** to complete the update.

7. Click the **Exit** button to end your iManager session. Users should now be able to log in from the Microsoft or Novell client with the same password.

## Message Digest 5 (MD5)

Message Digest 5 performs a hashing encryption method that uses a one-way function to mix the contents of a password and make it an unintelligible entry in a password table. Microsoft uses MD5 encryption in Microsoft Challenge Handshake Authentication Protocol (MS-CHAP) when logging on to Active Directory. By incorporating an MD5 login method in NetWare 6.5, Novell makes it easier for NetWare servers to co-exist in a Windows 2000 or 2003 network.

## CertMutual

As described in the textbook, Lightweight Directory Access Protocol (LDAP) is an industry-standard protocol designed to govern access to directory services over a TCP/IP network. In addition to defining a hierarchical naming system and directory information tree, LDAP provides authentication security by using a standards-based interface called Simple Authentication and Security Layer (SASL). LDAP provides three levels of authentication:

- *No authentication*—Use this option if the directory is published publicly and there is no need to restrict access to certain individuals.

- *Simple authentication*—This LDAP security option passes login information across the network in clear text, which creates a security risk because intruders could use packet-capturing software to capture and read passwords. The clear text security risk can be lessened if lower-level protocols, such as IPSec, are used for password encryption.

- *SASL*—This option uses one of several security methods, such as TLS and IPSec, to encrypt data over a connection-oriented protocol. When LDAP authentication is used, TLS/SSL is the most common method used with the LDAP version 3 included in NetWare 6.5.

## Universal Smart Card

Security tokens are authentication devices that are assigned to users to eliminate the need to type a password. They help increase security by preventing passwords from being captured at the keyboard and by providing a way to authenticate from non-keyboard devices, such as entry locks. A universal smart card is an active security token that creates an encrypted base key each time the owner tries to authenticate. A smart card is a plastic card, about the size of a credit card, that has an embedded chip with an integrated circuit containing memory and a programmable microprocessor. Universal smart cards can be plugged directly into a computer or other device and act as an employee badge, credit card, electronic building key, or access-granting certificate. In addition to storing user name and password information, smart cards can securely store personal information, such as biometric information that confirms the owner's identity, health records, digital certificates, and private/public keys. Because of the growing use of universal smart cards in IT environments, Novell has included a smart card authentication option in the NetWare 6.5 installation process.

## X.509 Certificate

As described earlier, public key cryptography uses X.509 certificates to exchange keys and verify the identity of the sender and receiver. Since NetWare version 5, Novell has included a private CA that allows network administrators to issue and use private X.509 certificates for use within an organization. In the following activity, you use iManager to create an X.509 certificate from the NetWare 6.5 CA software.

## Activity E-3: Creating an X.509 Certificate

**Time Required:** 10 minutes

**Objective:** Use iManager to create an X.509 certificate from the NetWare 6.5 CA

**Description:** Rocky Ridge wants to install an X.509 certificate on its e-mail server to enable secure message transmissions. Follow these steps to create an X.509 certificate for your NetWare 6.5 server:

1. Open your Web browser and enter the URL *https://ip_address:2200* (*ip_address* represents the IP address of your NetWare 6.5 server).

2. Follow the procedure described in Appendix D to open the iManager main window.

3. Log in with your assigned Admin user name and password.

4. Expand the **Novell Certificate Server** option and view the available certificate options.

5. Click the **Create Server Certificate** option to display the Create Server Certificate Wizard shown in Figure E-6.

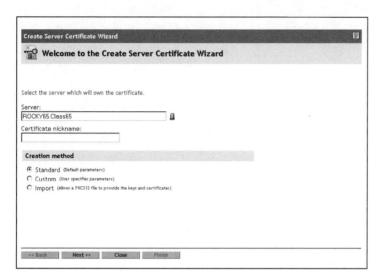

**Figure E-6**   The Create Server Certificate Wizard

6. In the Server text box, enter **ROCKY65.Class65**. (Note that the context might vary, depending on your classroom setup.)

7. In the Certificate nickname text box, enter **RRCert**.

8. Leave the Standard radio button selected as the creation method, and then click **Next**.

9. Review the summary information, and then click **Finish**.

10. When you see the message informing you that the certificate was successfully created, click **Close**.

11. Click the **Exit** button to end your iManager session, and then close your Web browser.

# F

# NOVELL SERVICES FOR LINUX

L inux is proving to be a viable enterprise-wide network operating system that can help organizations reduce costs yet still provide robust and secure network services. As a result of this track record, there's a growing demand for Linux in almost every area of the IT industry, including Web servers, e-mail servers, application servers, and user desktops. To meet the growing demand for Linux services and support, Novell and other leading vendors are bringing many new services and support to the Linux environment. In this appendix, you learn about the growing demand for Linux and how Novell is helping meet this demand through services, support, and certification.

# GROWTH OF LINUX

Most IT professionals agree that Linux and the open-source movement have changed the landscape of the IT industry. According to the market research firm IDC (*www.idc.com*), between 2002 and 2007 Linux is projected to grow at a compounded annual rate of 14%. Forrester Research (*www.forrester.com*) surveyed companies earning more than $1 billion dollars and also confirmed the growth of Linux. Of the 50 companies responding to the survey, 72% plan to increase their Linux use over the next two years, and more than half plan to use Linux in place of their existing operating systems.

An important part of the growth of Linux is open-source licensing, which enables developers to build systems with open-source software without paying royalties or other fees, as long as they release the source code with their product. According to CIO research (*www.cio.com*), 64% of 375 companies surveyed use open-source products and cite the lower total cost of ownership (TCO) as a key advantage. An article in the December 2002 issue of *CIO* magazine states that company CIOs (chief information officers) mentioned the following benefits of using open-source products: lower TCO (total cost of ownership), reduced capital investment, and increased reliability and uptime compared to existing systems. In this same article, IT executives said that open-source products offer more flexibility and faster, cheaper application development.

## Linux Benefits

Although the open-source concept has been part of academic and scientific computing for many years, only recently have many business organizations started to take it seriously. Part of the reason for this increased interest in open source has been the cutback in IT budgets and the increased costs and headaches of maintaining proprietary software licenses. In addition, many organizations are examining new open-source business applications and services in an effort to stay competitive. Some benefits organizations can reap from open-source solutions include the following:

- Support for a wide variety of hardware environments
- Reduction in software costs
- Availability, reliability, and scalability
- Reduced operating costs
- Experienced development resources
- Rapidly growing number of applications and tools

The following sections explain these benefits and how they can affect organizations.

## Hardware Choices

One of Linux's greatest strengths is its capability to run on many types of computer hardware, ranging from mainframe computers to laptops and PDAs. Many hardware vendors, such as IBM, Dell, Hewlett-Packard, and Sun Microsystems, have options to include and support Linux with their computer systems. In addition, because of Linux's efficient use of hardware resources, such as processors and memory, many organizations find they can support more users and applications with less hardware investment. Although some versions of UNIX require an expensive reduced instruction set computer (RISC) processor, Linux runs fine on Intel processors, so organizations can realize significant cost savings.

## Reduced Software Costs

Open-source Linux is free, but bundled distributions from companies such as Red Hat and SuSE can range from $50 to $1500, depending on additional features and support. However, because most commercial Linux distributions don't require user licensing, a company can save substantially by buying a single copy and installing it on several machines in the network.

## Availability, Scalability, and Reliability

Many organizations have selected Linux to run their Web applications because of its reputation for stability. Linux system uptime is often measured in years rather than days or weeks. Windows-based systems often need to be entirely shut down and restarted to install a patch or upgrade, but Linux systems generally require stopping and restarting only a single service or process. Performance and reliability are improved with Linux systems because multiprocessors are supported and because Linux servers can be linked to form computing clusters. As with NetWare 6 clusters, when any Linux computer in the cluster fails or needs to be shut down for maintenance, users of the cluster don't experience interruptions because another computer in the cluster continues to provide the downed computer's resources and services. With estimates of revenue losses running as high as $1 million per hour for some enterprises, clustering is becoming an important part of the IT environment.

## Reduced Operating Costs

In a cost-of-ownership study, the Robert Frances Group found that salaries for operators of Linux Web servers are lower than salaries for operators of proprietary operating systems (Sun Solaris, Microsoft Windows, and Novell NetWare) and that operators of Linux servers can support more machines per operator. One reason for this finding is that the same software image can run on a variety of hardware platforms, reducing the cost of training system operators and support staff when different operating systems are needed for each distinct hardware platform. For example, in an environment where servers such as the IBM AS400 are used with Sun and Intel-based workstations, multiple proprietary operating systems can require a lot of system operator time and training. In this case, running Linux on all hardware platforms can reduce administrative costs.

## Software Development Resources

Organizations using Linux benefit from the combined efforts of thousands of experienced open-source developers who collaborate on many different projects. Compared to proprietary operating systems, the open-source community of developers and experts continually improves on Linux at little or no cost to end user organizations. Because of open-source agreements, companies can modify the Linux operating system and other open-source software to enhance their capabilities, as long as the source code modifications are made available to the open-source community. This process creates constant growth in the product based on needs rather than marketing strategies.

## Applications and Tools

Linux seems to have reached a threshold at which developers are starting to see a viable market for applications and software tools. As a result, many applications from independent developers and the open-source community are readily available. Open-source applications, such as StarOffice and OpenOffice, have been designed and written to be compatible with and comparable with major proprietary products, such as Microsoft Office. Graphical desktop environments, such as Ximian Desktop, create a Windows-like look and feel and support several applications and tools, including Novell services. Other leading companies, such as Computer Associates, IBM, Oracle, PeopleSoft, Sybase, and SAP, have converted or are planning to convert their applications, tools, and databases to the Linux environment. As the number of Linux users increases, you can look for the number of software choices to continue growing rapidly.

## LINUX CONCERNS

As shown in Figure F-1, a study conducted by Forrester Research (*www.forrester.com*) showed that some of the biggest concerns organizations express when considering open-source solutions such as Linux are support, number of applications, product maturity, security, and lack of in-house skills. The following sections briefly examine these concerns.

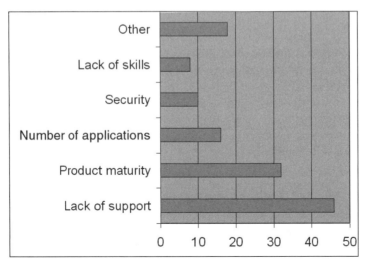

**Figure F-1**   Factors affecting adoption of open-source solutions

## Support

Concern about 24-hour support is probably one of the key factors preventing many organizations from adopting Linux and other open-source solutions. Corporate-level support must go beyond a hotline that customers can call when a problem comes up. When implementing a large-scale system, IT departments need to consider many issues, such as network infrastructure, training (technical and end user), availability, support, and data integration. Organizations tend to feel more confident having support from a large vendor with extensive experience in operating systems, networks, and IT infrastructure, such as Microsoft, Novell, or IBM.

## Number of Applications and Product Maturity

Although versions of Linux have been available for more than 10 years, only in the past few years has Linux been recognized as a viable operating system for business applications in corporate environments. The list of Linux-based business applications is growing rapidly, but the software is relatively new compared to proprietary operating systems, such as UNIX, Macintosh, or Windows. Today, most application development is based on Microsoft .NET and Java. Because it's unlikely that Microsoft .NET development software will ever be available on Linux, most Linux software developers currently use a Java or Java 2 Enterprise Edition (J2EE) environment. This could change in the future if an open-source implementation of .NET called the Mono Project becomes an alternative to Java-based development tools.

Another concern is network, system, and application management software. Linux has many excellent utilities for software distribution, metering, account management, and backup, but there's concern in the IT industry that these utilities haven't been adequately stress-tested or integrated into enterprise-wide IT environments. In addition, most existing Linux utilities operate only on Linux, making it difficult to integrate them into an enterprise-wide system consisting of Windows, NetWare, and UNIX systems. The good news is that large vendors, including Novell, are developing and converting proven software management tools to the Linux platform. Several of these solutions are discussed in the "Novell Services for Linux" section later in this appendix.

## Security

In this textbook and in Appendix E, you learned about several ways to secure a network from internal and external intruders. Organizations that deploy Linux must be assured that it can effectively meet their enterprise-wide security requirements for single login, firewalls, encryption, and virus protection. As an operating system, Linux plays a critical but limited role in authenticating user identity and ensuring that users have access only to the system resources they are authorized for. Novell eDirectory can solve many of these Linux security issues by providing a secure directory service that can be shared among many servers of different operating system types.

### Lack of Skilled Staff

Many NetWare and Windows-based IT organizations are concerned about not having the specialized skills required to effectively set up, use, and maintain the Linux operating system. Organizations currently running UNIX-based systems find that they can leverage their UNIX expertise to manage Linux systems. By implementing Novell Linux services, most NetWare-based IT organizations can make use of the skills they have developed with eDirectory and Novell utilities, such as iManager, in the Linux environment. In addition, Novell has developed the Certified Linux Engineer (CLE) program to help bring IT staff up to speed on maintaining a system that integrates Linux and NetWare servers. This certification program is discussed in more depth in the "Training and Certification" section later in this appendix.

## NOVELL SERVICES FOR LINUX

Novell announced a major Linux strategy at BrainShare 2003: making a commitment to deliver a complete range of Linux-related products and services to the market. A key component is the availability of Novell services to customers running Linux instead of NetWare. Novell's commitment is to make all services associated with the NetWare operating system available on Linux in an effort to become a provider of services that run on both NetWare and Linux servers. The Novell Linux strategy has the following major components:

- A comprehensive set of support services
- Products and solutions
- A commitment to the open-source community
- Training and certification

The following sections introduce these components and explain how Novell is implementing them in the Linux strategy.

## Support Services

In addition to a phone hotline, support services include finding and obtaining the latest patches and drivers and offering technical support information on problems and fixes. As described in the previous section, IT organizations are concerned about open-source software not having the level of support normally offered by proprietary software vendors, such as Microsoft and Sun. Novell has provided a high level of support services for NetWare operating systems since the early 1980s and is now committed to bringing that same level of professionalism and support services to the Linux platform. Novell has many experienced consultants around the world who are prepared to deliver a comprehensive portfolio of services that help clients make the transition to Linux and open-source systems. Table F-1 lists some of the key support services Novell has made available to the Linux and open-source community.

**Table F-1**  Key Support Services for Linux

| Service | Description |
|---------|-------------|
| Discovery | Consulting services designed to help business leaders understand the ramifications of implementing Linux. These services include a summary of business and tactical goals, a high-level technical and business justification, and recommended steps for implementing Linux in the organization's IT environment. |
| Strategy | A more in-depth assessment of the business justification for implementing Linux and its effect on the organization's IT infrastructure. |
| Implementation | Implementation options, such as training, software design and development, techniques for migrating from existing systems to Linux, integration with existing systems, testing, and deployment. |
| Application | Enables clients to work with Novell consultants to effectively implement a wide variety of applications on the Linux platform. |

## Products and Solutions

Although the Linux operating system provides a solid open-source environment that offers many advantages, it doesn't have some of the higher level services and utilities that network administrators have come to expect from an enterprise operating system. Novell has made the commitment to enable Linux environments to run many of the same Novell services that are available on the NetWare kernel. Novell Nterprise Linux Services 1.0 is a comprehensive set of products and utilities that give the Linux operating system many of NetWare 6.5's enterprise service capabilities. The Nterprise Linux Services product not only enhances the Linux platform; it also leverages a large support base of IT professionals with experience in managing NetWare networks using these same services and tools. As shown in Table F-2, Nterprise Linux Services is a bundle of Novell network services and utilities running on enterprise-class Linux distributions.

**Table F-2**  Nterprise Linux Services

| Service | Description | Comparable NetWare Product |
|---------|-------------|----------------------------|
| Identity services | Novell eDirectory service that includes connectors to NT domains, Active Directory, and Web address books | eDirectory for Linux |
| File services | Personal file management services with automatic built-in file encryption, anywhere/anytime Internet access, and automatic synchronization between server and client | iFolder and NetStorage |
| Print services | Internet Printing Protocol (IPP)-based printing for Windows, Macintosh, and Linux clients | iPrint |
| Messaging services | A message and calendaring system that supports up to 50,000 users per server | GroupWise and NetMail |

**Table F-2**    Nterprise Linux Services (continued)

| Service | Description | Comparable NetWare Product |
|---------|-------------|----------------------------|
| Web services | A Web access system based on the open-source Apache Web Server and Tomcat Java Virtual Machine (JVM) to access Nterprise Linux Services | Apache and Tomcat |
| Management services | Patch and application distribution to Linux servers in Remote Patch Management (RPM) format | Remote Manager |
| Install services | Server-based install services that support express (single server) or custom (distributed) deployments | ZENworks for Desktops |
| Administration services | Browser-based single point of administration for all Nterprise Linux Services | iManager 2.0, eGuide, Novell Modular Authentication Service (NMAS) |

As you can see in Table F-2, Nterprise Linux Services enables you to apply much of what you have learned about NetWare 6 and 6.5 to managing Linux-based network environments. A key to Novell's success in getting Linux-based IT organizations to adopt Nterprise Linux Services will be reaching the necessary threshold of market share through Linux distribution channels. Red Hat and SuSE are the major distributors of enterprise-level Linux operating systems. Red Hat is a leading distributor of Linux in the United States, and SuSE is the main European distributor. With Novell's acquisition of SuSE in the fall of 2003, Nterprise Linux Services can be packaged with SuSE Linux distributions, making it available to many European Linux-based organizations. In addition, Novell has partnered with IBM, Hewlett-Packard, and Dell, who will also be shipping Nterprise Linux Services to their customers. These combined distribution channels should help jump-start the Linux community by providing a set of standard and well-known network services. As a Certified Novell Administrator for NetWare 6, you'll be well on your way to having the skills and knowledge needed to manage a Linux-based network environment. In the following section, you learn how to install Novell's iManager utility on the Linux operating system.

## Installing iManager 2.0 on Linux

You have learned how to use iManager to perform many administrative tasks on NetWare 6 and 6.5 servers. In addition to serving as a browser-based administrative tool for NetWare, iManager 2.0 has been enhanced to provide a single point of administration for Novell eDirectory and other network resources on operating systems such as Linux, Windows, and Solaris. In this section, you learn how to install iManager 2.0 on a Linux server, but first you need to meet the prerequisites listed in Table F-3.

**Table F-3** iManager 2.0 for Linux Prerequisites

| Requirement | Prerequisite Value |
|---|---|
| Operating system | SuSE Linux Enterprise Server 8.x, Red Hat Linux 8 |
| Java Virtual Machine | Sun JVM 1.4.1 or later |
| Processor | Pentium III 800 MHz or higher |
| RAM | 360 MB |
| Rights | Root (Supervisor) rights to the Web server |
| eDirectory | eDirectory version 8.7.1 or later must be installed on Linux |
| Ports | Apache, Tomcat, and JVM are installed with iManager 2.0 and by default need to use the following ports: 80 and 443 for Apache and 8080, 8005, and 8009 for Tomcat; to avoid port conflicts that interfere with iManager operations, be sure existing applications on the Linux host are not using these ports |
| Gettext software | Use the Gettext -v command to verify that your Linux server has the latest version of the Gettext software (obtained from your Linux distributor) |

If you're installing iManager with Nterprise Linux Services, follow the prerequisites and instructions in the accompanying installation guide.

After verifying that your Linux environment meets the prerequisites in Table F-3, you can use these steps to install iManager 2.0 on your Linux server:

1. Mount the CD containing Novell iManager on your Linux file system.

2. Use the following command to extract iManager from the compressed file:

   ```
   tar -zxvf iMan_202_linux.tgz
   ```

3. Open a shell and change to the iManager_linux directory (a subdirectory of the directory where you copied or extracted the iManager files in Step 2).

4. Enter the following command to start the installation process:

   ```
   ./install.sh
   ```

5. Follow the onscreen prompts and instructions. Press Enter to accept the default text shown in brackets.

6. When prompted to enter the iManager server addresses or DNS host name, the IP address is automatically detected. Press Enter to accept it.

7. Use dot notation when entering the Admin user name (for example, cn=admin.o=RockyRidge).

F.

8. If you're installing iManager 2.0.1, use these steps to set a password for the the Portal Configuration Object (PCO):

   a. In an eDirectory tree with an existing PCO, you need to use the existing password, which is stored in the PortalServlet properties files in the TOMCAT_HOME\webapps\nps\WEB-INF directory. Search for the System Password=[password] field.

   b. When setting a new password, don't use the password for your Admin users. The default password of "novell" should be changed for increased security.

9. The default LDAP server IP address is the local machine. Be sure to use the IP address of the eDirectory LDAP server for the eDirectory tree in which you're installing iManager.

10. After finishing the installation, start a supported browser (Netscape or Internet Explorer) and enter the URL https://*ip_address*:port/nps/iManager.html (replacing *ip_address* with the IP address of the server running iManager). The port number can be left blank if you're using the default port of 443 for secure connections. Be careful when entering the URL, as it's case sensitive.

## Setting Up Role Based Services

As described in Appendix E, authorization is the security system component that assigns a set of rights or permissions to authenticated users for the purpose of accessing and managing network resources. Because both Linux and NetWare have separate systems for granting users permission to access and maintain data in the file system, NetWare administrators need to learn about Linux file system security to manage Linux environments. With Role Based Services (RBS), Novell has created a standardized system of delegating authority to users to use iManager on both Linux and NetWare servers. RBS consists of administrative tasks grouped into roles that can be assigned to users within a specific eDirectory context. RBS consists of a number of objects, described in Table F-4.

**Table F-4**    RBS eDirectory Objects

| RBS Icon | Name | Description |
|----------|------|-------------|
| | rbsCollection | A container object that holds all RBS Role and Module objects. A tree can have multiple rbsCollection objects located in any of the following containers:<br>Country<br>Domain<br>Locality<br>Organization<br>Organizational Unit<br>The main rbsCollection is normally located in the same container as the server holding the master copy of the eDirectory partition. |
| | rbsRole | Specifies the tasks that users who are members of the role are allowed to perform. rbsRole is a container object that holds rbsTasks and can be located only within a rbsCollection container. Role members can be users, groups, or Organizational Units and are associated with a specific context in the tree called a scope. rbsRole objects are automatically created and deleted as necesssary by Role Based Services. |
| | rbsTask | Represents a leaf object that holds a specific function, such as creating printers or resetting passwords. |
| | rbsBook | Represents a leaf object located in an rbsModule that consists of pages containing roles and tasks for members. |
| | rbsScope | Represents a leaf object used for access control list (ACL) assignments instead of assigning rights for each user object. rbsScope objects define the context in the tree where a role will be performed and are associated with rbsRole objects. |

RBS objects are placed in the eDirectory tree as shown in Figure F-2.

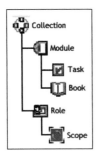

**Figure F-2** RBS tree objects

By default, RBS is not installed with iManager, so only the eDirectory administrator can use iManager to manage network objects. To give other users rights to administer eDirectory objects in a Linux or NetWare environment, first you need to use these steps to install RBS:

1. Open your Web browser and use the steps in Appendix D to start iManager. Log in as the Admin user.

2. Click the Configure button to display the RBS configuration options, expand the RBS Configuration item, and click the Configure iManager link to display the Available Options window (see Figure F-3).

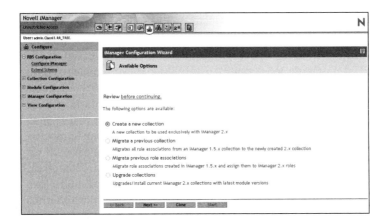

**Figure F-3** RBS installation options

3. Select the Create a new collection radio button and click Next to display the Collection Information window (similar to the one in Figure F-4). In this window, you enter the name and context where the new rbsCollection object will be located. Enter a name for the rbsCollection object in the Name text box and the context of the container where the collection will be stored in the Container text box. Click Next to display the setup window shown in Figure F-5.

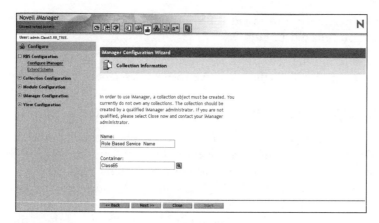

**Figure F-4**   The Collection Information window

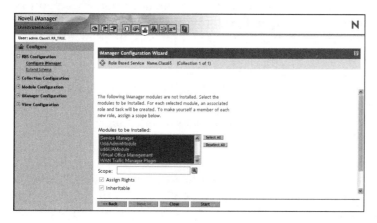

**Figure F-5**   Selecting RBS modules

4. Select the modules to be installed (all are selected by default), and enter a scope for your administrative user name in the Scope text box.

Several tasks in iManager require users to have Supervisor rights in the container to perform updates. When assigning roles to users or groups, the administrator is prompted for a scope that defines the area of the tree in which the user or group's role will be effective. To automatically assign the eDirectory rights necessary for the selected user or group to perform the tasks in the assigned role, click the Assigned Rights check box, as shown previously in Figure F-5.

5. Leave the Assign Rights and Inheritable check boxes selected to automatically assign the eDirectory rights users need to perform the tasks listed in each role. With these check boxes selected, you can simply add a user to an administrative role, and RBS will assign that user eDirectory Entry and Attribute rights.

F

6. Click the Start button to install RBS and set up the roles and tasks for the modules you selected in Step 4.

7. After completing the setup, exit iManager and close your Web browser. You can now assign users to administrative roles as described in the textbook.

## Commitment to Open Source

NetWare 6.5 has continued to enhance the commitment to open source that Novell started with NetWare 6. As described in Appendix D, NetWare 6.5 comes with a number of open-source features, such as a second copy of Apache Web Server for hosting corporate Web sites, the Tomcat Servlet engine, and several developer tools, including MySQL, PHP and Perl scripting languages, and Novell exteNd. Although these open-source tools and utilities are available to the public, Novell has made them more usable by integrating them with NetWare 6.5 and providing support services. NetWare 6 includes a copy of Apache Web Server, but it was intended only to support Novell Web services, such as iPrint, iFolder, and NetStorage. NetWare 6 also includes NetWare Enterprise Web Server so that organizations can host their own Web sites on the NetWare 6 server. A major change in NetWare 6.5 is replacing NetWare Enterprise Web Server with a second copy of Apache. Apache Web Server is the most popular Web server on the Internet. As of this writing, 62% of all Web sites are hosted by Apache Web servers. Along with the enterprise version of Apache Web Server, NetWare 6.5 includes the Apache Web Server utility for managing and maintaining Apache Web sites hosted on Linux and NetWare 6.5 servers.

Apache Web Server is configured by using directives stored in the httpd.conf file. Figure F-6 shows these directions displayed in Apache Manager. Apache Web Server reads the httpd.conf file at startup and periodically during operation to maintain the Web server's configuration. The httpd.conf file is a simple text file containing all the directives needed to configure the Web server and any other modules that might be loaded. These directives and modules are well documented on the Apache Web site, making it relatively easy to configure and manage your server.

| Configuration view: sys:/apache2/conf/http | |
|---|---|
| ServerRoot | "SYS:/APACHE2" |
| Timeout | 300 |
| KeepAlive | On |
| MaxKeepAliveRequests | 100 |
| KeepAliveTimeout | 15 |
| ThreadStackSize | 65536 |
| StartThreads | 25 |
| MinSpareThreads | 10 |
| MaxSpareThreads | 50 |
| MaxThreads | 1024 |
| MaxRequestsPerChild | 0 |
| Listen | 80 |
| SecureListen | 443 "SSL CertificateDNS" |
| ServerAdmin | you@your.address |
| ServerName | 172.20.0.65 |
| UseCanonicalName | Off |
| DocumentRoot | "SYS:/APACHE2/htdocs" |
| DirectoryIndex | index.html index.html.var |
| AccessFileName | .htaccess |
| TypesConfig | conf/mime.types |
| DefaultType | text/plain |
| HostnameLookups | Off |

**Figure F-6**  Viewing the default Apache configuration file in Apache Manager

However, changing the configuration requires knowledge of the httpd.conf file's directives and their syntax. When manually editing the httpd.conf file, it's easy to introduce errors by incorrectly typing a directive name or omitting necessary components of the syntax, which can cause interruptions in the organization's Web services that require extra troubleshooting and configuration time. In addition, if you're managing several installations of Apache, keeping all their httpd.conf files synchronized can waste time and cause additional problems.

NetWare 6.5 solves many of the problems of administering Apache Web Server running on Linux or NetWare servers with a new Web-based administration tool: Apache Manager. Apache Manager is more than a simple GUI interface for editing the httpd.conf file. With the multiple-server administration mode, you can manage several installations of Apache running on multiple servers from eDirectory (sometimes referred to as a "server farm"). Because Apache Manager is a Java application, it runs on both Linux and NetWare 6.5. This tool offers the following advantages over manually configuring the httpd.conf configuration file:

- Changes to directives are made electronically, reducing the risk of errors.
- You don't have to know all the Apache directives or modules to configure Apache.

- You can manage multiple installations of Apache Web Server from a single interface.

- You don't need to edit and maintain several configuration files, in which many of the same directives are used on each Apache Web server.

In the chapter on installing and configuring Web services, you learned how to use NetWare Enterprise Web Server to start and stop the Novell Enterprise Web server, change the path of the default Web content, and create a virtual document directory. In the following sections, you learn how to use Apache Manager to perform some of the same functions on the Apache Web server. If you have access to an administrative user name and password, you can perform these configuration changes on your Apache Web server.

## Starting and Stopping Apache Web Server

The Rocky Ridge company is using the copy of Apache Web Server that came with NetWare 6.5 to host its own Web site. After installing the server, Kathleen used the following steps to check the Apache Web server's status:

1. She started her workstation, clicked Start, Run, and entered the URL https://*ip_address*:2200 (replacing *ip_address* with the address of the NetWare 6.5 server) to open the Login window.

2. She entered her Admin user name and password and clicked the Login button to display the Welcome to NetWare 6.5 window.

3. In the navigation frame on the left, she clicked the Open Source heading and then the Apache 2.0 link (see Figure F-7).

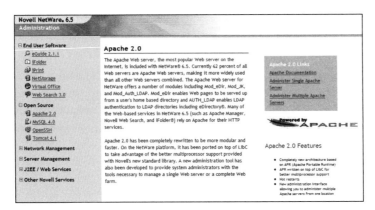

**Figure F-7** Starting Apache Manager

4. Kathleen clicked the Administer Single Apache Server link under the "Apache 2.0 Links" heading on the right to open the Apache Manager Server Status window shown in Figure F-8.

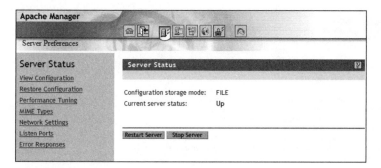

**Figure F-8**   The Server Status window

From the information in this window, Kathleen knows that the server configuration is coming from the httpd.conf file and the server is up and running. She can use the tool-bar buttons to view server logs, modify Web site content locations, view loaded mod-ules, and change administration mode. Two buttons at the bottom of the Server Status window are available for restarting or stopping the Apache Web server. If Web server configuration changes don't seem to be working, restarting the Apache Web server to reload the httpd.conf directives is a good idea.

## Changing Administration Mode

Novell Apache 2.0 Web Server can be configured via directives in the httpd.conf file or eDirectory. When you're administering only a single Apache Web server, using the default httpd.conf file to store configuration directives is often simpler. However, if you're administering a server farm consisting of several Apache Web servers running on different server platforms, working with multiple httpd.conf configuration files can be time-consuming and increase the chance of inconsistencies. Changing the administra-tion mode to eDirectory simplifies managing multiple Apache Web servers by storing configuration directives as an eDirectory object, where they can be accessed by all Apache Web servers. To change the administration mode of the Rocky Ridge Apache Web server to eDirectory, Kathleen performed the following steps:

1. She clicked the Administration Mode button on the Apache Manager toolbar to display the Administration Mode window shown in Figure F-9.

2. She clicked the eDirectory Import Wizard radio button, and then clicked the Save button to start the Administration Mode Wizard.

3. She clicked Next to display the Change from File to Directory Mode win-dow, clicked the Create a new server object radio button, and then clicked Next again.

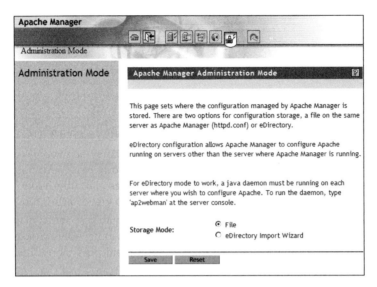

**Figure F-9**    Selecting an administration mode for Apache Manager

4. She selected a server group and entered the NetWare 6.5 server's name and IP address (see Figure F-10).

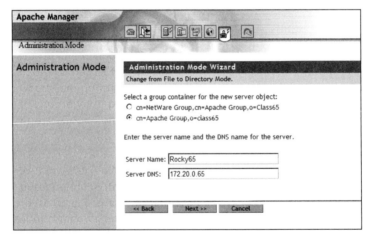

**Figure F-10**    The Administration Mode Wizard

5. She clicked Next to display a window asking whether to use the httpd.conf file or the inherited eDirectory configuration. She verified that the Import configuration from httpd.conf radio button was selected, and then clicked Next to display a summary window.

6. She clicked Finish to complete the conversion from File to eDirectory administration mode.

7. She clicked the Logout button to return to the Login window, and then closed her browser.

## Changing the Path of the Default Web Content

To prevent the SYS volume from filling up, Kathleen wants to move the Rocky Ridge Web site content to the USERDATA volume. Before starting Apache Manager, Kathleen created an Apache2 directory on the USERDATA volume and a RockyRidge subdirectory under the Apache2 directory. To configure Apache Web Server to use the new directory, Kathleen clicked the Content Management button to display the Primary Document Directory window shown in Figure F-11.

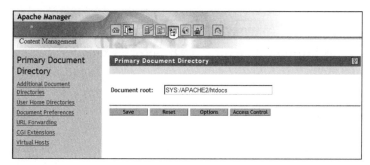

**Figure F-11**    The Primary Document Directory window in Apache Manager

She entered the path USERDATA:Apache2\RockyRidge in the Document root text box, and then clicked the Save button. Next, she clicked the Logout button on the toolbar to close the Apache Manager utility and return to the Login window. Apache Web Server will now look to the new directory for all incoming Web server requests.

## Creating a Virtual Document Site

As you learned in the chapter on installing and configuring Web services, in organizations with several departments, giving each department a separate content directory can simplify management. In the following activity, you learn how to use Apache Manager to create a virtual document directory for your Web content.

## Activity F-1: Creating a Virtual Document Site

**Time Required:** 15 minutes

**Objective:** Use Apache Manager to configure your own virtual document site

**Description:** In this activity, you use Apache Manager to set up an additional document site that points to a subdirectory in your assigned directory. To perform this activity, you need access to a user name and password that has rights to administer Apache Web Server.

1. Follow these steps to start Apache Manager:

   a. Click **Start, Run** and enter **https://*ip_address*:2200** (replacing *ip_address* with the ip address of your server). Press **Enter** or click **OK**. If necessary, click **Yes** to close the security alert message box and open the Login dialog box.

   b. Enter the password for the Admin user and click **Login** to display the Welcome to NetWare 6.5 window.

   c. Click the **Open Source** heading, and then click the **Apache 2.0** link.

   d. Click **Administer Single Apache Server** under the "Apache 2.0 Links" heading on the right to display the Server Status window.

2. Follow these steps in Content Management to create an additional document directory:

   a. Click the **Content Management** button on the toolbar.

   b. Click the **Additional Document Directories** link in the navigation frame on the left (see Figure F-12).

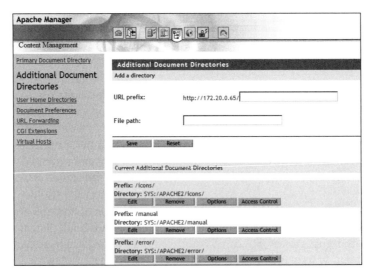

**Figure F-12**   The Additional Document Directories window

   c. In the Additional Document Directories window, enter **##RRHome** in the URL prefix text box (replacing ## with your assigned student number).

   d. Enter the path to your assigned student directory (for example, Rocky65\USERDATA\##UserData) in the File path text box.

   e. Click **Save** to open the Save and Apply Changes dialog box.

    f. Click **Save and Apply** to apply your changes to the httpd.conf file and display the Success! message box.

    g. Click **OK** to close the message box and return to Apache Manager.

3. Click the **Logout** button to close Apache Manager and return to the Login window.

4. Close the Login window, and exit your Web browser. Your Web site should now be ready for testing.

# Training and Certification

There's a growing demand for Linux in the IT industry, and Novell is fueling this growth by offering support and a host of mature network services and utilities with the Nterprise Linux Services product. IT staff need a combination of Linux and Novell skills to implement Nterprise Linux Services on enterprise networks. To help train and certify network administrators for this new Linux enterprise environment, Novell has worked with other Linux-based companies, such as Red Hat and SuSE, to create the Certified Linux Engineer (CLE) program. As a CNA, you'll already have much of the knowledge and skills you need to complete this certification. With a CLE certification, you can capitalize on the growing demand for Linux and open-source solutions. As you learned earlier in this appendix, Novell currently offers several products for Linux, and others are on their way. The CLE exam tests your abilities with the Linux operating system and with Novell services. Figure F-13 illustrates the process of getting your CLE certification.

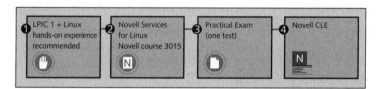

**Figure F-13**    The Novell Certified Linux Engineer certification process

Before taking the CLE exam, you should pursue the Linux Professional Institute's (LPI's) LPIC 1 certification. This certification isn't a requirement for the CLE exam, but the skills you gain in preparing for the LPIC 1 certification are important in knowing how to set up and maintain the Linux operating system kernel. With the LPI knowledge as a base, next you should become familiar with Nterprise Linux Services by taking the Novell 3015 course or comparable training or by studying self-paced material available from Novell. After becoming familiar with how to implement

Nterprise Linux Services, you should be ready to take the CLE certification, which consists of one practical exam. Following is a list of objectives for the CLE exam:

- Objective 1: Be able to install the Linux operating system
- Objective 2: Be able to install Ximian Desktop 2
- Objective 3: Demonstrate basic Linux skills necessary for using Novell Nterprise Linux Services (NNLS)
- Objective 4: Describe NNLS
- Objective 5: Perform an NNLS installation
- Objective 6: Update NNLS with Red Carpet
- Objective 7: Describe the purpose of a directory
- Objective 8: Describe how eDirectory works
- Objective 9: Perform eDirectory maintenance tasks
- Objective 10: View user information with eGuide
- Objective 11: Manage user accounts with Linux User Management (LUM)
- Objective 12: Manage user objects with iManager
- Objective 13: Describe the purpose of DirXML
- Objective 14: Identify how DirXML works
- Objective 15: Install and implement the DirXML drive for eDirectory
- Objective 16: Describe what iFolder is and how it works
- Objective 17: Synchronize files between PCs
- Objective 18: Describe Samba
- Objective 19: Secure and back up files using iFolder
- Objective 20: Describe what iPrint is and how it works
- Objective 21: Identify iPrint features
- Objective 22: Identify clients supported by iPrint
- Objective 23: Install a printer using iPrint
- Objective 24: Describe NetMail and how it works
- Objective 25: Identify standards that NetMail conforms to
- Objective 26: Identify calendaring features of NetMail
- Objective 27: Describe Virtual Office and how it works
- Objective 28: Identify security features of Virtual Office
- Objective 29: Identify benefits of Web experience unification

# Glossary

**10Base2** — A 10 Mbps linear bus implementation of CSMA/CD Ethernet using coaxial cable with T-connectors to attach networked computers. A terminator is used at each of the coaxial cable wire segments.

**10BaseT** — A 10 Mbps star implementation of CSMA/CD Ethernet using twisted-pair wires to connect all stations to a central concentrator.

**100BaseFX** — A 100 Mbps star implementation of CSMA/CD Ethernet using fiber-optic cables to connect all stations to a central concentrator.

**100BaseT** — A 100 Mbps star implementation of CSMA/CD Ethernet using twisted-pair wires to connect all stations to a central concentrator.

**1000BaseT** — A 1000 Mbps star implementation of CSMA/CD Ethernet.

**absolute directory path** — Another name for a complete directory path, which identifies the location of a file or directory by specifying the path: NetWare Server/ Volume:Directory\ Subdirectory[\Subdirectory].

**Accelerated** or **Advanced Graphics Port (AGP)** — A new type of connector on system boards for attaching high-performance screen adapter cards.

**access arm** — A device used on disk drives to position the recording heads over the disk track.

**Access Control [A] right** — A NetWare file and directory right that allows a user to assign rights to other users.

**access control list (ACL)** — A property of an eDirectory object that stores the trustee list for that object.

**access time** — The time required for a storage device to locate and transfer a block of data into RAM.

**Add/Remove Self [A] right** — An eDirectory attribute right that lets users add themselves to or remove themselves from the object's access control list.

**address** — When referring to a workstation's memory, a number used to identify the location of data in the computer system.

**address bus** — The number of bits sent from the CPU to the memory, indicating the memory byte to be accessed. The size of the address bus determines the amount of memory that can be directly accessed. The 20-bit address bus on the 8088 computer limited it to 1 MB. The 24-bit address bus on 80286 and 80386SX computers provides for up to 16 MB. The 32-bit address bus used on 80386DX and above computers can access up to 2 GB of memory.

**address restrictions** — Used to limit a user to logging in from only certain workstation addresses.

**administrative role** — A group of administrative tasks that can be assigned to Admin users so that they can perform administrative functions, such as managing eDirectory, printing, licensing, and DHCP/DNS services.

**AFP Server object** — An eDirectory informational leaf object that represents a network's AppleTalk File Protocol server in the directory tree.

**Alias object** — An eDirectory leaf object that represents an eDirectory leaf object located in another part of the directory tree.

**analog signal** — A signal carried by a broadband system, such as radio or television.

**Apple Address Resolution Protocol (AARP)** — A component of the AppleTalk protocol that works at the physical and data link layers.

**AppleTalk** — Apple's network protocol developed to enable Macintosh computers to work in peer-to-peer networks.

**application layer** — The top software layer of the OSI model that interacts with the user to perform a communication process on a network.

**Application object** — An eDirectory used to represent an application available on the network.

**application service** — A network service that runs software applications on a server for use by networked workstations.

**application-oriented structure** — A directory structure that groups directories and subdirectories according to application or use rather than by department or owner.

**Archive Needed (A)** — A NetWare file attribute set by the computer whenever the contents of a file have changed.

**assign** — The act of giving rights to a trustee. *See also* grant.

**assigned rights** — The set of rights granted or assigned to a trustee.

**asynchronous communication** — A form of communication in which each byte is encapsulated with start and stop bits and then sent separately across the transmission media.

**attribute** — A flag that NetWare uses to determine the type of processing that can be performed on files and directories.

**attribute rights** — The set of rights to the properties of an eDirectory object that can be granted to a trustee. Attribute rights include Supervisor [S], Compare [C], Read [R], Write [W], and Add/Remove Self [A].

**AutoComplete addressing** — An e-mail client feature used to search the address book for matching names when a user enters an e-mail address.

**automatic load printer** — A printer that's attached directly to the server's printer port or a port on the workstation.

**backbone network** — A network cable system used to connect network servers and host computer systems. Each network server or host can contain a separate network card that attaches it to client computers.

**back-end process** — Software such as an e-mail server that processes the data or messages received from the front-end process running on a client.

**balanced trees (B-trees)** — The NSS file system storage access method used to provide fast access to files stored on NSS volumes.

**bandwidth** — A measurement of the range of signals that can be sent across a communications system.

**baseband** — A digital signaling system that consists of only two signals, representing one and zero.

**baud rate** — A measurement of the number of signal changes per second.

**bidirectional communication** — Communication between a printer agent and the client that enable clients to locate printers based on printer type and availability.

**bindery** — The NetWare 3.1x files that contain security information, such as user names, passwords, and account restrictions. The bindery files, stored on NetWare 3.1x servers in the SYS:System directory, consist of NET$OBJ.SYS, NET$PROP.SYS, and NET$VAL.SYS.

**block** — When referring to a database, a collection of data records that can be read or written from the computer RAM to a storage device at one time. When referring to a hard disk, a storage location on the physical disk volume consisting of 4 KB, 8 KB, 16 KB, 32 KB, or 64 KB.

**block suballocation** — A method that allows data from more than one file to be placed in a single data block.

**bounded media** — A type of cable that confines the signal within eletromagnetic shielding.

**bridge** — A device used to connect two segments of a network. Operates at the data link layer.

**broadband** — A signaling system that uses analog signals to carry data across the media.

**Broker** — An NDPS component responsible for sending printer messages and notifications by using the Event Notification System (ENS), Resource Management Service (RMS), and Service Registry Services (SRS).

**Browse [B] right** — An eDirectory entry right that enables a trustee to see the object in the eDirectory tree and have the object's name appear in search results.

**bundled pair** — Fifty or more pairs of twisted wire put together in one large cable.

**bus** — An electronic pathway that connects computer components.

**bus mastering** — A technique used by certain high-speed adapter cards to transfer data directly into a computer's RAM.

**cable system** — The physical wire system used to connect computers in a local area network.

**cache memory** — The memory area used to temporarily hold data from lower-speed storage devices to provide better access time.

**caching mode** — An e-mail client feature that automatically stores all messages and attachments on the local hard disk of the user workstation.

**Can't Compress (Cc)** — A NetWare file attribute used to flag files that can't be compressed.

**Carrier Sense Multiple Access with Collision Detection (CSMA/CD)** — A media access control method used on Ethernet networks in which a computer waits for the media to have an open carrier signal before attempting to transmit. Collisions occur when two or more devices sense an open carrier and attempt to transmit at the same time.

**Category 5 cable** — A network cable specification most commonly used today with 10BaseT and 100BaseT.

**central processing unit (CPU)** — Sometimes referred to as the "brain" of the computer. It is where most calculations and processing are done.

**centralized processing** — A processing method in which program execution takes place on a central host computer rather than at a user workstation.

**Certified Novell Administrator (CNA)** — A network administrator who has taken and passed the Novell CNA exam.

**child partition** — In eDirectory, a partition that is below (farther away from the [Root]) a parent partition in the directory tree structure. The child partition is subordinate to the parent partition.

**children** — In eDirectory, container levels that are subordinate (farther away from the [Root]) to another container. The superior (closer to the [Root]) container level is called the parent.

**circuit-level gateway** — A firewall gateway that inspects packet heading information, including type of service, port number, user name, and DNS name.

**client** — When referring to Windows 2000/XP, a client is the software providing network connectivity for the workstation, which is called a network interface card (NIC) driver in NetWare.

**client-server** — A network operating system that uses a separate computer as a dedicated server, which acts as a central storage unit for client workstations.

**client-server applications** — A type of application in which part of the application runs on the network server and part of the application runs on the client workstations.

**client workstation** — A networked computer that runs user application software and is able to request data from a file server.

**clock** — A device in the system unit of a computer that sends out a fixed number of pulses or signals per second. The clock pulses are used to synchronize actions in the system unit. The clock speed is measured in billions of cycles per second, called gigahertz (GHz). The faster the clock speed, the more work a system unit can do per second.

**clustering** — A form of server duplexing, in which two or more servers can act as one. Novell's clustering supports up to 32 computers.

**coaxial cable** — A thick plastic cable containing a center conductor and shield.

**collision** — An event that occurs when two or more nodes attempt to transmit on the network at the same time. After the collision, the nodes wait a random time interval before retrying.

**command queuing** — A method of storing commands for future processing.

**command-line utility** — A NetWare utility that performs a specific function from the DOS prompt given specific command-line parameters. Examples are NDIR, NCOPY, and MAP.

**committed transaction** — A completed directory service transaction that is placed in the log file.

**common name (CN)** — The name type associated with an eDirectory leaf object.

**compact disc read-only memory (CD-ROM)** — A data storage device that uses the compact disc format and can store about 680 MB of data. The data is recorded by the manufacturer and cannot be altered by the user.

**Compare [C] right** — An eDirectory attribute right that enables a trustee to compare a value to the value of the property, but not see the value itself. (The Read [R] right is needed to see the value.)

**compiler** — A program that converts source commands to a form that the computer can run.

**complementary metal oxide semiconductor (CMOS) memory** — A type of memory capable of holding data with very little power requirements. This type of memory stores configuration data that is backed up by a battery on the system board. The battery prevents CMOS from being erased when power is turned off.

**complete directory path** — Identifies the location of a file or directory by specifying the path: NetWare Server/Volume:Directory\Subdirectory [\Subdirectory].

**complete path** — A directory path that includes the server, volume, and all necessary directories and subdirectories leading to the file or folder.

**complex instruction set computer (CISC)** — A computer with a microprocessor that uses instructions in a wide range of formats and can require more that one clock cycle to complete.

**Compressed (Co)** — A NetWare file attribute used to flag files that are compressed.

**computer network** — Two or more computers connected together so they can communicate.

**Computer object** — An eDirectory object used to represent workstations in a network.

**consistent** — The same throughout. When referring to eDirectory, all the replicas of a partition must be updated so that they are consistent. Because the updating process takes time, the directory database is said to be loosely consistent at any moment in time.

**console command** — A command function built into the NetWare kernel Server.exe program and, therefore, is always in memory.

**ConsoleOne** — Both a server and workstation Java-based NetWare utility that can be used to perform administrative tasks.

**container login script** — A login script stored in a container object and used by all users in the container unless the user is assigned a profile login script or has a user login script.

**container object** — An eDirectory object that contains other eDirectory objects. The main eDirectory container objects are [Root], Country, Organization, and Organizational Unit.

**contention access method** — A media access method in which computer nodes are allowed to talk whenever they detect that the channel is not in use. This often results in collisions between packets. In Ethernet, this becomes the Carrier Sense Multiple Access with Collision Detection (CSMA/CD) method.

**context** — The location of an eDirectory object in the directory tree.

**contextless login** — A NetWare login during which the user does not have to specify a context. Instead, NetWare is configured to understand the

User object's context or the user selects it from a list of valid users.

**controlled access printer** — An NDPS printer that exists as an object in the eDirectory tree. By default, only users in the same container as the controlled access printer can send output to it.

**controller card** — An adapter card used to control storage devices, such as disk drives.

**conventional memory** — The first 640 KB of memory used by DOS to run application programs.

**Copy Inhibit (Ci)** — A NetWare file attribute that prevents Macintosh computers from accessing certain PC file types.

**Country object** — An eDirectory container object that represents a country in the directory tree.

**Create [C] right** — An eDirectory entry right that lets a user create new objects in a container (applies to container objects only). Also a NetWare directory and file right that allows users to create new files and subdirectories.

**current context** — The user's current location in the eDirectory tree.

**cycle** — The time it takes a signal to return to its starting state.

**cyclic redundancy check (CRC)** — An error-checking system that enables a receiving computer to determine whether a block of data was received correctly; the system applies a formula to the data and checks the results against the value supplied by the sending computer.

**cylinder** — The number of disk tracks that can be accessed without moving the access arm of the hard drive mechanism.

**data bus** — The "highway" that leads from a device to the CPU. Computers based on 80286 and 80386SX have 16-bit data bus architecture compared to 32 bits on the 80386DX and 80486 computer models and 64 bits on Pentium-based computers.

**data link layer** — The OSI software layer that controls access to the network card.

**Datagram Delivery Protocol (DDP)** — A component of the AppleTalk protocol that works at the network layer.

**datagram packet** — The packet created at the network layer by wrapping the information in the segment packet with packet routing information.

**date variable** — A login script variable that contains date information, such as month, day of the week, and year.

**dedicated** — A server that only performs services for other workstations.

**default directory** — The directory from which data will be accessed when no path is supplied.

**default drive** — The drive from which data will be accessed when no path is supplied.

**default login script** — The login script that's used if no other login script exists for a user.

**Delete [D] right** — An eDirectory entry right that enables users to delete the object from the eDirectory tree.

**Delete Inhibit (Di)** — A NetWare attribute that prevents a file or directory from being removed.

**denial-of-service attack** — A form of network attack that loads the server with packets to shut down network services.

**departmental structure** — A directory structure that groups directories and sub-directories according to the workgroup or department that uses or controls them.

**differential backup** — A backup strategy in which only files that have changed since the last full backup are copied to the backup tape. When performing a differential backup, the SBACKUP utility backs up all files that have the Archive attribute enabled but does not reset the Archive attribute, thus making it easier to restore all data after a disaster.

**digital signal** — A signal that can have a value of only zero or one.

**Digital Versatile Disc (DVD)** — An upgraded version of CD-ROM, often called DVD-ROM, which holds up to 4.7 GB of data in the current versions.

**direct memory access (DMA) channel** — A device used to transfer data between RAM and an external device without taking time from the processor.

**directory** — When referring to the network file system, a logical storage unit on a volume; called a "folder" in Windows.

**directory caching** — A method of improving hard disk access time by keeping the directory entry table (DET) and file allocation table (FAT) in memory.

**directory database** — A database used to store information about network objects.

**directory entry table (DET)** — A table on a storage device that contains the names and locations of all files.

**directory hashing** — A method of improving access time by indexing entries in the directory entry table.

**Directory Information Base (DIB)** — The name of the X.500 directory database.

**Directory Information Tree (DIT)** — A tree structure for the DIB containers that represents the hierarchical relationship between entries.

**Directory Map object** — An eDirectory server-related leaf object that is used in the directory tree to reference a drive mapping.

**directory path** — A list of network file system components, such as the names of directories and subdirectories, identifying the location of data on a storage device.

**directory rights** — The set of rights to directories in the network file system that can be granted to a trustee. Directory rights include Supervisor [S], Read [R], Write [W], Create [C], Erase [E], Modify [M], File Scan [F], and Access Control [A].

**Directory Schema** — A set of rules for ensuring that the information in the DIB is not damaged or lost.

**directory service** — Software that provides discovery, security, relational management, storage, and retrieval of directory database information.

**Directory System Agent (DSA)** — Software running on a server that consists of a collection of services and protocols for managing specific portions of the DIB.

**Directory User Agent (DUA)** — Runs on the user workstation and acts as a client to send requests from the user to the directory service.

**disk duplexing** — A RAID 1 fault-tolerance methodology, in which two disks and two disk controllers are used.

**distinguished name** — The complete name when referring to an eDirectory object, consisting of the object's common name plus the object's context. A distinguished name always shows the path to the object from the [Root]. An example of a distinguished name is .EFranklin.FDR_Admin.FDR.

**distributed database** — A database split into parts, with each part residing on a different server.

**distributed processing** — A processing method in which application software is executed on the client workstations.

**distribution list** — A GroupWise object consisting of a set of users who can be addressed as a group by using a unique name.

**document management** — An e-mail client feature that enables you to share documents with a group of users.

**Domain Controller object** — An eDirectory container object used to hold DNS entities, such as name servers and zones.

**Don't Compress (Dc)** — A NetWare file attribute used to flag files that you do not want compressed.

**Don't Migrate (Dm)** — A NetWare file attribute used to flag files that you do not want migrated.

**Don't Suballocate (Ds)** — A NetWare file attribute used to flag files that you do not want suballocated.

**dot pitch** — A measurement of the spacing between color spots on video monitors. A smaller dot pitch provides sharper images.

**dotted decimal notation** — A method of writing TCP/IP addresses that separates each byte (represented by a decimal number) with a period.

**drive mapping** — The assignment of a drive pointer to a storage area on a hard disk.

**drive pointer** — A letter of the alphabet that is used to reference storage areas in the file system.

**driver software** — When referring to a network interface card (NIC), the software needed to control the NIC and interface between the data link layer and the network layer software.

**DSMERGE.NLM** — The utility used to manage eDirectory trees.

**dual in-line memory module (DIMM)** — A combination of two SIMMs that are read alternately in memory-access cycles.

**duplexing** — A method of synchronizing data on storage devices attached to different controller cards.

**dynamic execution** — A feature of the Intel Pentium Pro CPU. It consists of three processing techniques: multiple branch prediction, data flow analysis, and speculative execution.

**dynamic RAM (DRAM)** — A common form of dynamic memory chip, used in computer RAM, that requires a refresh cycle to retain data contents.

**e-mail application** — A software application that allows network users to send messages to each other.

**eDirectory** — The Novell LDAP-compatible directory service system implemented in NetWare 6.

**eDirectory Management Framework (eMFrame)** — A Web application for building modular eDirectory management services called plug-ins. eMFrame plug-ins define management roles and implement tasks associated with those roles.

**eDirectory security** — A security system that controls access and management of objects in the eDirectory database.

**eDirectory tree** — The visual and logical design used to organize data into a hierarchical structure.

**effective rights** — A subset of access rights that controls which disk processing a user can perform on a directory or file. Effective rights consist of a combination of rights the user has as a user and as a member of groups, container objects, and so on.

**electromagnetic interference (EMI)** — An undesirable electronic noise created on a wire cable when it runs close to a strong power source or magnetic field.

**elevator seeking** — A technique used in NetWare file servers to increase disk access performance by smoothly moving an access arm across a hard disk surface to read and write the requested data blocks in the sequence they are encountered rather than in the sequence received.

**Enhanced IDE (EIDE)** — A disk drive system that improves on the standard IDE system by supporting up to four disk drives with higher-drive capacities (above the 528 MB limitation of IDE), and faster performance.

**entry** — A record in the directory database that stores information on a network object.

**entry rights** — The set of rights to eDirectory objects that can be granted to a trustee. Entry rights include Supervisor [S], Browse [B], Create [C], Delete [D], Rename [R], and Inheritable [I].

**Erase [E] right** — A NetWare directory and file right that allows users to delete files and remove subdirectories when assigned to a directory.

**error-checking and correcting (ECC) memory** — A type of RAM that can automatically recognize and correct memory errors.

**Ethernet** — A network system that uses the CSMA/CD access method to connect networked computers. Originally, the term also meant only the 10Base2 system, but now refers to the entire Ethernet family, including 10BaseT, 100BaseT, and 100BaseFX.

**Execute Only (X)** — A NetWare file attribute that can be used with executable (.com and .exe) program files to prevent the files from being copied yet still allow users to run them.

**expansion bus** — The system board bus that allows expansion cards plugged into expansion slots on a computer's system board to connect the adapter cards to the rest of the computer.

**expansion card** — A circuit board that plugs into an expansion slot and extends the computer's capabilities, such as a network interface card or modem.

**expansion slot** — An electrical connection on the system board into which expansion cards are plugged.

**extended data output (EDO) RAM** — A faster version of RAM now standard in Pentium, Pentium MMX, and Pentium Pro computers.

**eXtended Graphics Array (XGA)** — A video adapter that is the latest in monitor technology for laptops and notebook computers. It offers up to 1024×768 resolution, similar to the SVGA standard, but with additional colors.

**Extended Industry Standard Architecture (EISA) bus** — A system board expansion bus that supports ISA cards and high-speed 32-bit cards for increased performance.

**extended memory** — Memory above 1 MB. This memory requires special software to access it.

**external entity** — An object type created to give users outside the organization an account in a GroupWise post office.

**extranet** — A network system that uses the Internet to connect different organizations for business transactions.

**failover** — The process used in server clustering to automatically switch an NSS volume from a failed server to an operational server.

**fault tolerance** — A measurement of how well a system can continue to operate despite the failure of certain hardware components.

**fiber-optic cable** — A cable made of light-conducting glass fibers that allows high-speed communications.

**file allocation table (FAT)** — A table stored on a disk used to link the storage blocks belonging to each file.

**file caching** — A method used by a NetWare file server to increase performance by storing the most frequently accessed file blocks in RAM.

**file compression** — A method of coding the data in a file to reduce file size.

**file rights** — The set of rights to files in the network file system that can be granted to a trustee. File rights include Supervisor [S], Read [R], Write [W], Create [C], Erase [E], Modify [M], File Scan [F], and Access Control [A].

**File Scan [F] right** — A NetWare directory and file right that allows users to view file and directory names.

**file server** — A server computer that provides file and print servers to client workstations. Also called a NetWare file server in earlier versions of NetWare.

**file service** — A network service that provides access to shared files on a server computer.

**file system security** — A security system that prevents unauthorized users from accessing or modifying file data.

**Filtered replica** — Similar to the Read/Write replica in eDirectory, except it filters the types of objects included in the replica.

**firewall** — A point of access between an organization's internal private network and the Internet, used to filter packets and reduce the risk of unauthorized access to or malicious attacks on the organization's private network system and services.

**FLexible and Adaptive Information Manager (FLAIM)** — The database system used to store eDirectory tree objects.

**folder** — When referring to the network file system or a user's workstation, the Windows term for a directory or subdirectory.

**frame** — An information packet at the data link layer.

**front-end process** — Software such as an e-mail client that runs on a user's workstation and provides an interface that allows users to communicate with services running on a server.

**full backup** — A backup strategy in which all data is copied to the backup tape daily, regardless of when it changed.

**gateway** — The NDPS component that works with the printer agent to send output from the printer agent to the network print device.

**general-purpose application** — An application package, such as a word processor or a spreadsheet, used to perform many different functions.

**global shared directory** — A directory in which all users in an organization can store and retrieve files.

**grant** — To give trustee rights to a user, a group, or another eDirectory object. *See also* assign.

**graphics accelerator** — A video adapter with a microprocessor programmed to speed up graphics operations.

**Group object** — An eDirectory user-related leaf object that is used in the Directory tree to manage groups of users.

**Hidden (H)** — A NetWare attribute used to prevent a file or directory from appearing on directory listings.

**hierarchical structure** — A logical organizational structure that starts at one point, called the [Root], and branches out from the starting point. Points in the structure are logically above or below other points on the same branch.

**home directory** — A private directory in which a user typically stores personal files and works on projects that are not shared with other users.

**host** — A computer or other device that is provided with a unique IP address on a TCP/IP network.

**host server** — The NetWare server that runs the backup program and has the attached tape or other backup media.

**hot fix** — A NetWare feature for copying data on bad and unreliable disk storage sectors to a reserved redirection area, located in a different area on the hard disk.

**hot swapping** — A fault-tolerant system that allows a disk drive to be replaced without shutting down the computer system.

**hub** — A central connection device in which each cable of a star topology network is connected together.

**identifier variable** — A login script variable used in login script commands to represent such information as the user login name, date, time, and DOS version.

**IEEE 802.3** — A standard issued by the Institute of Electrical and Electronic Engineers specifying an Ethernet protocol.

**IEEE 802.5** — Similar to 802.3, except that it specifies a token ring standard.

**iFolder** — A NetWare service that enables files to be kept on a local computer (or one that's not attached to the network) and synchronized with the network.

**iManager** — A browser-based utility for managing eDirectory and configuring iPrint, NetWare Licensing, and DNS/DHCP.

**Immediate Compress (Ic)** — A NetWare file attribute used to flag files that should be compressed immediately instead of waiting for the standard waiting period to elapse.

**Immediate Sync** — A type of replica synchronization that occurs by default within 10 seconds of adding or deleting new objects and making changes to object properties.

**iMonitor** — A Novell OneNet utility that enables a network administrator to work with the eDirectory system from a Web browser and perform such tasks as checking for eDirectory replica synchronization, tracing eDirectory activity, viewing error reports, and performing repair operations.

**incremental backup** — A backup strategy that backs up only the files that have changed (the Archive attribute is on) that day, and then resets the Archive attribute on all files that are backed up.

**Index (I)** — NetWare automatically sets this attribute when a file reaches a certain size in relation to the block size on the volume.

**Industry Standard Architecture (ISA) bus** — A system board bus structure that supports 16-bit data and 24-bit address buses at 8 MHz clock speed. This bus was developed for the IBM AT computer in 1984 and is still popular. However, used with high-speed processors, it reduces the performance of expansion cards.

**information theft** — A form of network attack that uses wire taps and sniffer software to illegally intercept data.

**infrared** — An unbounded media system that uses infrared light to transmit information. Commonly used on television remote control devices and small wireless LANs.

**Inheritable [I] right** — An eDirectory entry right that changes the way rights flow down the eDirectory tree.

**inherited rights** — Rights that flow down into a container object, directory, or file from a higher level.

**Inherited Rights Filter (IRF)** — Each container object, directory, and file contains an IRF that controls what access rights can flow down to the container object, directory, or file from a higher level.

**input/output (I/O) port** — An interface used to transfer data and commands to and from external devices.

**Institute of Electrical and Electronic Engineers (IEEE)** — A U.S. professional organization that has established network standards, including those for LAN topologies.

**instruction set** — The set of binary command codes a CPU chip can recognize and execute.

**Integrated Drive Electronics (IDE)** — A type of hard disk controller that can control up to two hard drives with capacities up to 528 MB.

**internal network number** — A network address used internally by NetWare to communicate with its software components.

**International Standards Organization (ISO)** — The group responsible for administering the OSI model.

**Internet** — An information highway that is not controlled by any single organization and is used worldwide to connect business, government, education, and private users.

**Internet Message Access Protocol (IMAP)** — A standardized protocol used to access and store messages from the post office server.

**Internet Printing Protocol (IPP)** — An industry-standard protocol that enables printers to be installed, managed, and accessed from a Web browser.

**internetwork** — One or more network cable systems connected by bridges or routers.

**Internetwork Packet Exchange (IPX)** — The NetWare protocol that manages packet routing and formatting at the network layer.

**interoperability** — The ability of computers on different networks to communicate.

**interrupt request (IRQ)** — A signal sent from an external device to notify the CPU that it needs attention.

**intranet** — A computer network based on Internet technology (TCP/IP), but designed to meet the needs of a single organization.

**intruder detection** — A part of login security that works at the container level by setting a limit on the number of incorrect login attempts that can be made on a user account in that container during a specified time period.

**intrusion** — A form of network attack that involves gaining unauthorized and illegal access to an organization's information, usually through obtaining a user's account and password.

**iPrint** — Novell's implementation of the IPP protocol that makes it possible to access and manage NDPS printers through a Web browser.

**Java applet** — An application written in the Java programming language to run on a client workstation's Web browser.

**Java servlet** — An application written in the Java programming language to run on a Web server.

**LDAP Group object** — An eDirectory object that contains configuration information and security policies for LDAP services running on one or more NetWare servers.

**LDAP proxy user** — A user account that's a member of the LDAP server group and provides the LDAP server with rights to read certain information from the eDirectory tree.

**LDAP Server object** — An eDirectory object that contains configuration information for the LDAP service running on a NetWare server.

**leaf object** — An eDirectory tree object that cannot contain other objects. Leaf objects are used to store data about network resources, such as NetWare servers, volumes, users, groups, and printers.

**License Certificate object** — An eDirectory object that represents user or server connections.

**License Container object** — An eDirectory object that houses server and user license certificates.

**Lightweight Directory Access Protocol (LDAP)** — A simplified version of the X.500 protocol that specifies a common set of directory operations and commands that can be implemented on multiple vendor platforms.

**Lightweight Directory Interchange Format (LDIF)** — An ASCII text file that use a standardized syntax to add, change, or delete objects in LDAP-compatible directory systems.

**linear bus topology** — A LAN topology that consists of a coaxial cable segment that connects computers by running from one machine to the next with a terminating resistor on each end of the cable segment.

**local area network (LAN)** — A high-speed, limited-distance communication system designed to support distributed processing.

**local bus** — The internal address, data, and instruction buses of the system board, often used to refer to a high-speed expansion bus structure that allows adapter cards to operate close to the speed of the internal system board.

**local drive pointer** — A drive pointer (normally A: through F:) that is used to reference a local device on the workstation such as a floppy or hard disk drive.

**local shared directory** — A directory in which all users of a department or workgroup can store and retrieve files.

**logging in** — The process of authenticating yourself to a Novell network by supplying a user name and password.

**logging on** — The process of authenticating yourself to a Windows network by supplying a user name and password.

**Logical Block Addressing (LBA)** — A feature of the Enhanced Integrated Drive Electronics (EIDE) interface that allows EIDE drives to provide up to 8.4 GB of storage.

**logical entity** — In eDirectory, a network resource that exists as a logical or mental creation, such as an organizational entity that models the structure of an organization.

**logical link control (LLC) layer** — A sublayer of the OSI model's data link layer, used in interfaces with the physical layer.

**login name** — The name a user enters at the login prompt or in the Novell Client Login window when logging in to the network. The login name is also the name displayed for the user's User object in the eDirectory tree.

**login script** — A set of NetWare commands performed each time a user logs in to the file server.

**login script variable** — A reserved word that can be used to substitute values into login script statements to modify processing.

**loosely consistent** — The same throughout, more or less. When referring to eDirectory, all partition replicas need to be updated so that they are consistent. Because the updating process takes time, the directory database is said to be loosely consistent at any moment in time.

**machine language** — A program consisting of binary codes that the CPU can directly interpret and execute.

**magnetic disk drive** — The component of the disk storage system in which data is stored by means of magnetic fields representing ones and zeros.

**mailbox mode switching** — A GroupWise client feature that enables users to change mailbox modes between online, caching, and remote.

**mainframe computer** — Large computers in which the processing power is in the computer and users access it via terminals.

**manual load printer** — A remote printer attached to a port on a networked workstation and controlled by the print server.

**Master replica** — In eDirectory, the main copy of a partition. There is only one Master replica for each partition. A Master replica can be read from and written to, and can be used for login purposes.

**math coprocessor** — An extension of the CPU that enables it to perform mathematical functions and floating-point arithmetic.

**media** — The device or material used to record and retrieve data.

**media access control (MAC) layer** — A sublayer of the OSI model's data link layer, used in interfaces with the network layer.

**media access method** — A method of controlling when a device can transmit data over a local area network. Common access methods include token ring and CSMA/CD.

**message packet** — A packet containing data being sent via the network from one user to another.

**message service** — A network service that transfers messages and notifications between networked computers.

**Message Transfer Agent (MTA)** — A software component that assists the core post office software in transferring messages between mailboxes.

**metropolitan area network (MAN)** — A communication system that uses fiber optics or microwave to connect computers in the same geographic location.

**Micro Channel bus** — A system board design patented by IBM that allows for 32-bit expansion cards along with automatic card configuration.

**microprocessor** — The central processing unit (CPU) of a microcomputer system.

**Migrated (M)** — A NetWare file attribute used to flag files that have been migrated.

**millions of instructions per second (MIPS)** — A measure of speed for computer CPUs.

**minicomputer** — A scaled down version of a mainframe computer in which processing power is within the centralized computer and accessed via terminals. Minicomputers can also run network operating system software that allow them to act as servers to PCs attached to the local area network.

**mirroring** — A disk fault-tolerance system that synchronizes data on two drives attached to a single controller card.

**mission-critical application** — An application that's necessary to perform the day-to-day operations of a business or an organization.

**Modify [M] right** — A NetWare directory and file right that allows users to change file and directory attributes and rename files and subdirectories.

**MONITOR utility** — A NetWare console utility that displays essential information about NetWare server performance.

**multiple NetWare server network** — A network with more than one NetWare server attached.

**multiple station access unit (MSAU)** — A central hub device used to connect IBM token ring network systems.

**multiplexing** — Placing multiple message packets into one segment.

**name type** — An eDirectory descriptor of object types. There are four name types: Country (abbreviated as C), Organization (abbreviated as O), Organizational Unit (abbreviated as OU), and common name (which refers to all leaf objects and is abbreviated as CN). There is no name type for the [Root] object.

**narrowband radio transmission** — An unbounded media system that uses radio waves to transmit information.

**Native File Access Protocol (NFAP)** — A Session-layer protocol that enables clients to use other protocols to access files stored on a NetWare server.

**NCP Server object** — Another name for the NetWare Server object. NCP is an abbreviation for NetWare Core Protocol.

**NDPS Broker object** — An eDirectory object that contains configuration information for the Service Registry Service, Event Notification Service, and Resource Management Service.

**NDPS Manager** — The NDPS component that manages the printer agent for printers that do not have one embedded.

**NDPS Manager object** — An eDirectory object that represents the NDPS Manager software used to provide a platform for running printer agents on a NetWare server.

**NDPS Printer object** — An eDirectory object that represents the printer agent for a physical printer.

**NetBEUI** — Microsoft's network protocol stack, integrated into Windows for Workgroups, Windows 95/98, and Windows NT. It consists of NetBIOS and Service Message Blocks (SMBs) at the session layer and NetBIOS frames (NBFs) at the transport layer. NBF can be replaced with NetBIOS over TCP/IP (NBT) for direct communication over TCP/IP-based networks.

**NetBIOS frames (NBF)** — One component of Microsoft's NetBEUI protocol.

**NetBIOS over TCP/IP (NBT)** — An alternate component of Microsoft's NetBEUI protocol that enables its use with TCP/IP networks.

**Net Services** — A set of hardware and software components that work together to provide access to information services across the Internet or company intranet.

**NetWare 6 Server certificate** — A license certificate installed during the NetWare 6 server installation that is necessary for the server to run.

**NetWare 6 User certificate** — A UAL license certificate that supports user connections to the network. This certificate is not installed during the NetWare 6 server installation; it's installed later by using iManager.

**NetWare Administrator (NWAdmin)** — A graphical utility that runs in Windows, used to perform administrative tasks. Novell is attempting to phase out this utility with its newer product, ConsoleOne.

**NetWare Command File (NCF)** — A file similar to a DOS batch file in that it contains console commands and program startup commands that the operating system will run. Startup.ncf and Autoexec.ncf are two examples.

**NetWare Core Protocol (NCP)** — The NetWare protocol that provides session- and presentation-layer services.

**NetWare Loadable Module (NLM)** — A program that can be loaded and run on the NetWare server. There are four types of NLMs, identified by their three-letter extension. The filename extension .NLM is used for general-purpose programs; .DSK is for disk drivers; .LAN, for network card drivers; and .NAM for name space support modules.

**NetWare server name** — The name that a NetWare server broadcasts over the network; when referring to eDirectory, the name of the NetWare Server object.

**NetWare server object** — An eDirectory object used to represent a network's NetWare server in the directory tree.

**network address** — An address used by the network layer to identify computers on the network.

**Network Address Translation (NAT)** — An Internet standard that maps internal private IP addresses to Public IP addresses.

**network administrator** — The network user in charge of the network and all its resources, who is responsible for maintaining, allocating, and protecting the network.

**Network Basic Input/Output System (NetBIOS)** — The system developed by IBM, now used in Microsoft's NetBEUI protocol.

**network drive pointer** — A network drive pointer is a letter that is assigned to a location on a NetWare server and controlled by NetWare, normally G: through Z:.

**Network Driver Interface Specifications (NDIS)** — A set of standard specifications developed by Microsoft to allow network card suppliers to interface their network cards with the Microsoft Windows operating system.

**network-centric** — A network in which a user logs in only once to the network itself, not to each network server he or she needs access to.

**network file system** — The logical organizational structure of file storage on network volumes.

**network interface card (NIC)** — An adapter card that attaches a computer system to the physical network cable system.

**network interface card driver** — The software that controls a network interface card (NIC) and access to the network.

**network layer** — An OSI software layer that is responsible for routing packets between different networks.

**network layout** — An installation-planning document that consists of the following information: the NetWare server's name and internal network number, the network topology and NICs, IP addresses of all devices connected to the network, and the frame type used on the cable system.

**network standard** — An agreement about how to operate a network.

**nickname** — A GroupWise object that assigns an account name to a role or position in the company.

**Non-NDPS Printer object** — An eDirectory object that represents a network printer using queue-based printing.

**nondedicated** — A server that can run applications for a local user while still providing network services for attached workstations.

**Normal (N)** — A NetWare file attribute used to identify files that have no attributes set.

**Novell Distributed Print Services (NDPS)** — A new printing system developed by Hewlett-Packard and Novell that makes it more convenient to configure and access network printers.

**Novell NetStorage** — A NetWare service that gives users secure access to files on the NetWare server from any Internet location.

**Novell Portal Services (NPS)** — A Net Services component running on a NetWare server that provides customized pages or portals for users based on users' rights and personal style specifications.

**Novell Storage Services (NSS)** — The file system used primarily by NetWare 6. In NSS, logical volumes are created from storage pools that consist of one or more disk partitions.

**NSS volume** — A logical division of a storage pool used to organize information in the NSS file system.

**null modem cable** — A special type of RS232 cable used to connect two DTE computers without using a modem.

**object** — In eDirectory, the representation of a network resource in the directory database; it appears as an icon in the directory tree. eDirectory objects can be associated with physical entities and logical entities.

**OneNet** — Novell's strategy of making multiple networks, consisting of diverse clients and services, work together as one network.

**Open Data Interface (ODI)** — A set of standard specifications developed by Novell to allow network card suppliers to interface their network cards with multiple protocols, including the IPX protocol used with the NetWare operating system.

**Open Systems Interconnect (OSI) model** — A model for developing network systems consisting of the following seven layers: application, presentation, session, transport, network, data link, and physical.

**Organization object** — An eDirectory container object used to organize the structure of the directory tree; it can contain Organizational Unit objects and leaf objects.

**organizational entity** — In eDirectory, a logical entity that models the structure of an organization.

**Organizational Role object** — An eDirectory user-related leaf object used in the directory tree to manage users' privileges by associating them with specific positions, such as president, vice president, and so on, in an organizational structure. The privileges are assigned to the Organizational Role object, and the users assigned to that role inherit those privileges.

**Organizational Unit object** — An eDirectory container object used to organize the structure of the directory tree; it can contain other Organizational Unit objects and leaf objects.

**overbooking** — The process in which the total space assigned to two or more NSS volumes exceeds the space available in the storage pool.

**packet** — A group of consecutive bits sent from one computer to another over a network.

**packet filtering** — A process performed by a screening router to determine whether a packet is from a trusted, untrusted, or unknown network.

**parallel port** — A communications interface that transfers 8 or more bits of information at one time.

**parent** — In eDirectory, a designated container level that has other subordinate container levels (farther away from the [Root]). The subordinate container levels are called children. In the network file system, a parent is a data set such as a directory or subdirectory.

**parent partition** — In eDirectory, a partition that is above (closest to the [Root]) a child partition in the directory tree structure.

**parity bit** — A ninth bit added to a byte for error-checking purposes.

**partition** — A logical division of the directory database based on the directory tree structure.

**partition** — A physical storage area on a disk drive that is formatted for a particular file system.

**password restrictions** — Can be used to force users to periodically change passwords, set minimum password lengths, and use a different password each time they change.

**patch cable** — A cable segment used to connect a network card to the main cable system.

**patch panel** — A panel that consists of a connector for each cable segment, used to connect the cable segments with a central hub.

**peer-to-peer** — A network system in which each computer can act as both a server and client.

**peripheral** — An external device, such as a printer, a monitor, or a disk drive.

**Peripheral Component Interconnect or Interface (PCI) bus** — The current expansion bus design by Intel used in older 80486, Pentium, Pentium MMX, and Pentium Pro computers. It is a local bus design that moves data at 60 to 66 MHz.

**physical address** — A unique hexadecimal network interface card (NIC) address coded into the NIC's electronics. This first part of the address identifies the manufacturer, and the second part is a unique number for that manufacturer.

**physical entity** — In eDirectory, a network resource that has a physical existence, such as a NetWare server.

**physical layer** — A layer of the OSI model, consisting of the cable system and connectors.

**pixel** — A picture element; the smallest point on a monitor screen that can be addressed individually for color changes and so forth.

**Policy Package object** — An eDirectory object used to manage the way users access their workstations and connect to the network. Policy Package objects can consist of Workstation policies or User policies.

**Post Office Agent (POA)** — An e-mail software component that is responsible for transferring messages from the client to the correct mailbox on the e-mail server.

**Post Office Protocol (POP)** — A standardized client-server protocol used for sending and receiving e-mail messages between the client and the e-mail server.

**presentation layer** — The OSI layer responsible for translating and encoding data to be transferred over a network system.

**print queue** — A network object representing a holding area where print jobs are kept until the printer is available. In NetWare, a print queue is a subdirectory of the Queues directory, located in the volume specified during print queue creation.

**Print Queue object** — An eDirectory object that represents a holding area in which print jobs are kept until the printer is available to print them. In NetWare, a print queue is a subdirectory on an assigned volume.

**print server** — A component of queue-based printing that manages network printers by taking jobs from print queues and sending them to the correct network printer.

**Print Server object** — An eDirectory object that stores configuration information for queue-based printing software.

**print service** — The software component of the network printing environment that makes printing happen by taking jobs from user workstations and sending them to a networked printer.

**printer agent** — The software component of NDPS that transfers output from the client workstation and controls the physical printer.

**printer-related leaf object** — In eDirectory, a group of leaf objects used to manage printers in a network.

**private key** — The digital key code used in public key cryptography that is kept solely by the owner and used to decode data and create digital signatures.

**profile login script** — A login script stored in a Profile object and used by all users assigned to that script.

**Profile object** — An eDirectory user-related leaf object used in the directory tree to manage users' login scripts. The login script is stored in the Profile object, and the users assigned to that profile use the login script.

**property** — An aspect of an eDirectory object, such as the user's last name for the User object. The actual last name—for example, Burns—is the property value.

**property value** — In eDirectory, an actual value of an eDirectory object property. For example, the user's last name is a property of the User object, and an actual user's last name—for example, Burns—is the property value.

**protected mode** — The mode used by 80286 and above processor chips that allows access to up to 16 MB of memory and the ability to run multiple programs in memory without one program conflicting with another.

**protocol** — Rules that define the formatting and transmission of data across network systems.

**protocol stack** — The software used to send and receive packets among networked computers.

**proxy service** — A high-level firewall service that works at the application level to give clients on an organization's network both incoming and outgoing access to Internet services.

**[Public]** — A special trustee, [Public] is similar to a group. When [Public] is made a trustee of an object, every object in the eDirectory tree inherits the [Public] rights. In addition, [Public] rights are available to users who are not even logged in to the eDirectory tree, as long as they have Novell Client running on their computers.

**public access printer** — An NDPS printer that's attached to the network but does not have an eDirectory object. Any user attached to the network can send output to a public access printer without having to log in to the network.

**public key** — The digital key code used in public key cryptography for clients to encrypt data being sent to a host and to verify a host's digital signature.

**public key cryptography** — An Internet security system that uses public and private keys to encrypt and decrypt data and create digital signatures for authenticating users.

**Purge (P)** — A NetWare file or directory attribute that specifies the storage space of a file that is to be made available for immediate reuse by the server.

**queue** — A space in the e-mail database where the server temporarily stores outgoing messages while waiting to contact the destination server at a predefined interval.

**queue-based printing** — A printing system implemented in NetWare 3 that's designed to support simple printers and DOS-based applications.

**RAM shadowing** — A method of increasing computer system performance by copying instructions from slower ROM to high-speed RAM.

**rambus dynamic RAM (RDRAM)** — A type of memory that has a transfer rate up to 800 MHz.

**random access memory (RAM)** — The main work memory of the computer, used to store program instructions and data currently being processed.

**RConsoleJ** — A NetWare Java-based remote console tool that enables an administrator to access a server's console screen from ConsoleOne.

**Read Only (Ro)** — A NetWare file attribute that prevents data in a file from being erased or changed.

**read-only memory (ROM)** — Memory that is set at the factory and cannot be erased. ROM stores startup and hardware control instructions for your computer.

**Read-Only replica** — In eDirectory, a copy of the Master replica that can only be read from, not written to, and cannot be used for login purposes.

**Read [R] right** — An eDirectory attribute right that enables a trustee to see the property values of an object. Also a directory and file right that allows users to open and read data from a file or run programs.

**Read/Write replica** — In eDirectory, a copy of the Master replica that can only be read from and written to, and can be used for login purposes.

**Read Write (Rw)** — A NetWare file attribute that allows data in a file to be modified or appended to.

**real mode** — The processing mode used by 8088 computers.

**reduced instruction set computer (RISC)** — A computer with a microprocessor that uses instructions in a uniform format that require only one clock cycle to complete. A RISC workstation provides high performance for CAD workstations and scientific applications by using a simplified and highly efficient set of instructions that lends itself to parallel processing.

**redundant array of independent disks (RAID)** — A method of writing data across several disks that provides fault-tolerance.

**register** — A storage location inside the microprocessor unit.

**regular drive pointer** — A network drive pointer that is normally assigned to a file storage directory on the NetWare server.

**relative directory path** — Identifies the location of a file or directory by specifying all directories and subdirectories starting from the user's current default directory location.

**relative distinguished name** — In eDirectory, this name specifies the path to the object from an object other than the [Root]. An example of a relative distinguished name is EFranklin.FDR_Admin. Note that there is no leading period because the path is not from the root of the tree.

**Remote Manager** — A Novell OneNet utility that enables a network administrator to manage a NetWare server console from a Web browser.

**Rename Inhibit (Ri)** — A NetWare file or directory attribute that prevents changing the name of a file or directory.

**Rename [R] right** — An eDirectory entry right that enables users to change an object's name.

**repeater** — A network device for connecting multiple network cable segments.

**replica** — In eDirectory, a copy of a partition. There are five types of replicas: Master, Read/Write, Read-Only, Subordinate Reference, and Filtered.

**replica synchronization** — In eDirectory, the process of updating all replicas of a partition so that they are consistent.

**resolution** — A measurement of the number of bits on a display screen. Higher resolution produces better screen images.

**resource** — A GroupWise object representing a physical asset that can be checked out or scheduled, such as a conference room or a company vehicle.

**rights** — When referring to eDirectory or the network file system, the type of access that has been granted or assigned to a user, who is called a *trustee*. In eDirectory, there are entry rights and attribute rights; the network file system has directory rights and file rights.

**ring topology** — A cable system in which the cable runs to each computer and then back to the first, forming a circle.

**Role Based Service object** — Allows the network administrator to provide specific types of administrative tasks to selected users.

**root drive pointer** — A regular drive pointer that appears to DOS and applications as though it were the beginning or "root" of a drive or volume.

**[Root]** — The starting point of a hierarchical structure, such as a tree, that starts at one point (the [Root]) and branches out from there. When referring to eDirectory, [Root] is the [Root] object.

**[Root] object** — The starting point of the eDirectory tree.

**[Root] partition** — The partition of the eDirectory tree that contains the [Root] object.

**rotational delay** — The time required for a disk sector to make a complete circle and arrive at the disk drive's read/write head.

**router** — A device used to connect complex networks consisting of different topologies. Routers operate at the network layer.

**rule** — A GroupWise object containing actions that are applied to incoming messages that meet certain conditions.

**scalability** — The capability to work with systems of different sizes.

**scheduling application** — A software application used to create and maintain personal and workgroup time schedules.

**SCSI-2** — An advanced version of the SCSI controller specification that allows for higher speed and more device types.

**SCSI-3** — Also referred to as Ultra Wide SCSI. Uses a 16-bit bus and supports data rates of 40 MBps.

**search drive pointer** — A network drive pointer that has been added to the DOS path. Search drives are usually assigned to directories containing software to make the software available to run from any other location.

**sector** — A physical recording area on a disk recording track. Each recording track is divided into multiple recording sectors to provide direct access to data blocks.

**security equivalence** — An eDirectory object assignment that grants one object the same set of rights as another object.

**Security object** — An eDirectory container object that holds global policies for login security and authentication using public key encryption.

**security service** — The service used to authenticate user logins.

**seek time** — A measurement of the amount of time required to move the recording head to the specified disk track or cylinder.

**segment** — When referring to packets on a network, the name of an information packet at the transport layer. When referring to the physical network structure, a single cable run.

**Sequential Packet eXchange (SPX)** — The NetWare protocol that operates at the transport layer.

**serial port** — A communication port that sends 1 bit of data per time interval.

**server** — A network computer used for a special purpose such as storing files, controlling printing, or running network application software.

**server-centric** — A network in which a user logs in to each network server that he or she needs access to, instead of logging in only once to the network itself.

**server clustering** — A setup in which two or more servers can share a common disk system, making the data available in case one of the servers has a hardware failure.

**Server Connection Licensing (SCL)** — The license model used by pre–NetWare 6 servers that requires each server to have a license for each connection, including connections made by printers and other non-user resources.

**server duplexing** — A fault-tolerance technique that uses two identical servers so that if one goes down, the other is still available.

**Server Management console** — The iFolder component that enables network administrators to perform administrative tasks, such as managing iFolder user accounts.

**server-related leaf object** — In eDirectory, a group of leaf objects used to manage servers in a network.

**Service Message Blocks (SMB)** — The Microsoft protocol that provides session- and presentation-layer services to client computers.

**session layer** — The OSI software layer that establishes and maintains a communication session with the host computer.

**shadowing** — The X.500 process of distributing and synchronizing the DIB among multiple locations.

**Shareable (Sh)** — A NetWare file attribute that allows multiple users to access or update data in a file at the same time.

**shielded twisted-pair (STP) cable** — A type of twisted-pair cable that has electromagnetic shielding, and is thus less susceptible to external electrical interference.

**Simple Mail Transfer Protocol (SMTP)** — A TCP/IP-based e-mail protocol used to transfer messages between mail servers.

**single in-line memory module (SIMM)** — A memory circuit that consists of multiple chips and provides the system board with memory expansion capabilities.

**Slow sync** — An eDirectory replica synchronization process that by default occurs within 22 minutes of including information, such as login time, change of network address, or updated properties.

**small computer system interface (SCSI)** — A general-purpose controller card bus that can be used to attach disk drives, CD-ROMs, tape drives, and other external devices to a computer system.

**social engineering** — Social engineering can be regarded as "people hacking." Hackers use this technique to persuade targets to volunteer information or assistance instead of breaking into systems independently.

**spoofing** — A method of illegally accessing network resources or attacking a network service by creating falsified packets that appear to come from an authorized entity.

**spooling** — Sending output from a user's workstation to a print job.

**star topology** — A cable system in which the cables radiate out from central hubs.

**static RAM (SRAM)** — Static RAM provides high-speed memory that can operate at CPU speeds without the use of wait states. SRAM chips are often used on high-speed computers in order to increase system performance by storing the most frequently used memory bytes.

**storage area network (SAN)** — A specialized network that often uses very high-speed fiber cable to connect storage devices to two or more servers.

**Storage Management System (SMS)** — The NetWare backup service that includes several NetWare Loadable Modules and workstation software that enables the host server to back up data from one or more target devices by using SBACKUP NLM.

**storage pool** — An NSS file system component used to group one or more partitions into a storage area that can be divided into one or more volumes.

**suballocation** — A method used on traditional volumes to save disk space by dividing blocks into 512-byte units as a way to store information from multiple files in the same block.

**subdirectory** — A division of a directory, when referring to the network file system.

**subordinate** — Below or under. In eDirectory, a child partition is a partition that is below (farther away from the [Root]) a parent partition in the eDirectory tree structure. The child partition is subordinate to the parent partition.

**Subordinate Reference replica** — In eDirectory, a copy of the Master replica that NetWare 6 automatically generates to make sure a child partition has a replica on the NetWare server containing a replica of the parent partition. The Subordinate Reference replica cannot be modified. Subordinate reference replicas are used to ensure that there are enough replicas of all partitions.

**SuperVGA (SVGA)** — Video systems that provide higher resolutions (800×600 pixels and higher) and additional color combinations (up to 16.7 million colors) than the VGA systems.

**Supervisor [S] right** — A NetWare access right that provides a user with all rights to an eDirectory object and its properties and the entire directory structure. Once assigned, the Supervisor right cannot be restricted on the network file system (directory and file rights), but it can be restricted for eDirectory rights (entry and attribute rights).

**support pack (SP)** — An update to software that fixes or improves on current software.

**switch** — A device operating at the data link layer that functions like a multiport bridge.

**switching power supply** — A power supply used with most computers that will cut off power in the event of an electrical problem.

**synchronous communication** — A serial communication system that sends data in blocks or packets; each packet includes necessary control and error checking bits.

**synchronous dynamic RAM (SDRAM)** — High-speed random access memory (RAM) technology that can synchronize itself with the clock speed of the CPU's data bus. Used in high-end systems.

**syntax** — The rules of a programming language and of NetWare login scripts.

**System (Sy)** — A NetWare file attribute used to flag system files.

**system board** — The main circuit board of a computer system that contains the CPU, memory, and expansion bus (also called the motherboard).

**system console** — The monitor and keyboard on a network server.

**system console security** — A security system that prevents unauthorized users from accessing the system console.

**target server** — A server whose data is backed up by a host server.

**Template object** — An eDirectory object used to define a common set of attributes that can be applied to new user accounts.

**terminal** — A user workstation that connects to a mainframe computer or minicomputer without a CPU of its own so that the mainframe computer or minicomputer must do all the processing.

**terminal service** — A network service that allows applications to be run on the server while the user workstation acts as a graphical window to the application running on the server.

**ThinNet** — An Ethernet network system that uses T-connectors to attach networked computers to the RG-58 coaxial cable system.

**thread** — A process that's currently being worked on by the CPU.

**time restrictions** — Used to limit the times that a user can be logged in to the network.

**time variable** — A login script variable that contains system time information, such as hour, minute, and A.M./P.M.

**token** — A special packet sent from one computer to the next to control which computer can transmit when using a token passing media access method.

**token passing method** — A media access method that requires a computer to obtain the token packet before transmitting data on the network cable system.

**topology** — The geometry of a network cable system.

**track** — A circular recording area on a disk surface.

**Transaction Tracking System (TTS)** — A NetWare fault-tolerance system that returns database records to their original value if a client computer system fails while processing a transaction.

**Transactional (T)** — A NetWare file attribute that enables transaction tracking on a database file.

**transfer time** — The time required to transfer a block of data to or from a disk sector.

**Transmission Control Protocol (TCP)** — A transport layer protocol that is reliable and requires acknowledgements.

**Transmission Control Protocol/Internet Protocol (TCP/IP)** — TCP/IP is the most common communication protocol used to connect heterogeneous computers over both local and wide area networks. In addition to being used on the Internet, the Unix operating system uses TCP/IP to communicate between host computers and file servers. Today, NetWare 6 uses TCP/IP as its native protocol, with IPX/SPX as an option.

**transport layer** — The OSI layer responsible for reliable delivery of a packet to the receiving computer; requires some sort of acknowledgment to ensure delivery.

**Tree object** — An eDirectory object that represents the beginning of the eDirectory database structure. This object is also referred to as a [Root] object.

**trusted network** — A network with an IP address range that's known to be safe or can be controlled and monitored by your organization.

**trustee** — A user given access to eDirectory objects or network file system directories and files. Access is given when rights are assigned or granted to the user or another eDirectory object the user is associated with.

**trustee assignment** — The set of eDirectory or file system rights granted to a user.

**trustee list** — The set of trustee assignments for an eDirectory object or a network file system directory or file.

**twisted-pair cable** — Cable consisting of pairs of wires twisted together to reduce errors.

**typeful name** — When an eDirectory object's distinguished name is written with name type abbreviations, it's referred to as a typeful name. An example of a typeful name is .CN=EFranklin.OU=FDR_Admin.O=FDR.

**typeless name** — When an eDirectory object's distinguished name is written without name type abbreviations, it's referred to as a typeless name. An example of a typeless name is .EFranklin.FDR_Admin.FDR.

**unbounded media** — A type of twisted-pair cable that has no electromagnetic shielding, and is thus susceptible to external electrical interference.

**uninterruptible power system (UPS)** — A battery backup power system that can continue to supply power to a computer for a limited time in the event of a commercial power failure.

**Universal Data Format (UDF)** — A specification for how data is stored on storage media. Originally intended for all storage devices, it is most commonly used on CD-ROM and DVD-ROM discs.

**Universal Naming Convention (UNC)** — A naming system that specifies the path to a shared directory with two backslashes, the server name, a single backslash, and the name of the shared folder.

**Universal Serial Bus (USB)** — An upgraded specification for the venerable serial port, providing for multiple devices to be attached on the same port and at higher speeds.

**unknown network** — A network that is not specified as a trusted or untrusted network in a firewall. Firewalls treat unknown networks as untrusted networks.

**Unknown object** — An eDirectory miscellaneous object used in the directory tree to identify corrupted objects that eDirectory cannot recognize.

**unshielded twisted-pair (UTP) cable** — A type of twisted-pair cable that has no electromagnetic shielding, so it is susceptible to external electrical interference.

**untrusted network** — An IP address range that might contain hackers or other malicious entities. Packets from networks listed as untrusted are inspected by the network firewall.

**upper memory** — The memory above 640 KB used by controller cards and by DOS when loading device drivers into high memory.

**User Access Licensing (UAL)** — The NetWare 6 licensing system, in which each user account is provided with a fixed license to access any server in the tree the first time the user logs in.

**User Datagram Protocol (UDP)** — A transport layer protocol that is unreliable and requires no acknowledgment.

**user-defined variable** — A login script variable that enables users to enter parameters for their personal user login scripts.

**user login script** — A login script stored in a User object; this script runs for only a single user.

**User object** — An eDirectory user-related leaf object used in the directory tree to manage network users.

**user-related leaf object** — In eDirectory, a group of leaf objects used to manage users in a network.

**user template** — A property that defines standard settings and configures restrictions for each user in a particular container.

**user variable** — A login script variable containing information about the currently logged in user, such as the user's login name, full name, or hexadecimal ID.

**vertical application** — A software application designed for a specific type of processing. Vertical applications are often unique to a certain type of business, such as a dental billing system or an auto parts inventory system.

**VESA bus** — An older fast local bus expansion bus designed by the Video Electronics Standards Association, now largely replaced by PCI.

**video graphics array (VGA)** — A standard video circuit used in many conventional PCs that provides up to 640 × 320 resolution and up to 256 different colors.

**virtual file allocation table (VFAT)** — A 32-bit extension to the standard FAT introduced in Windows 95/98 and MS-DOS 7.0.

**virtual memory** — Allows the computer system to use its disk drive as though it were RAM, by swapping between disk and memory.

**virtual private network (VPN)** — A trusted network that sends packets over an untrusted network, such as the Internet.

**virtual real mode** — An instruction mode available in 80386 and above microprocessors that allows access to 2 GB of memory and concurrent DOS programs running at the same time.

**virus** — A self-replicating program that can be embedded in software to propagate between computers and eventually can be triggered to affect computer performance or destroy data.

**volume** — The major division of the NetWare file system consisting of the physical storage space on one or more hard drives or CD-ROMs of a file server.

**Volume object** — An eDirectory server-related leaf object used in the directory tree to manage volumes on NetWare servers.

**wait state** — A clock cycle in which the CPU does no processing. This allows the slower DRAM memory chips to respond to requests from the CPU.

**Web Services** — A set of hardware and software components that provide WWW and FTP information services to clients located on the Internet or company intranet.

**wide area network (WAN)** — Two or more local area networks in geographically separated locations connected by telephone lines.

**word size** — The number of bits in the microprocessor's registers.

**workstation variable** — A login script variable containing information about the workstation's environment, such as machine type, operating system, operating system version, and station node address.

**Write [W] right** — An eDirectory attribute right that enables users to change, add, or delete the value of the property. Also a directory or file right that allows users to change or add data to a file.

**X.500** — Specifications developed by International Telecommunication Union (ITU) that define directory service functions and format.

**Zero Effort Networking (ZENworks) for Desktops (ZfD)** — A Novell product that enables network administrators to centrally manage users' desktop environments.

**zone file** — A file that contains all computer names for a specific domain.

# Index